S0-BEG-349

Contemporary Theatre, Film and Television

A Biographical Guide Featuring Performers, Directors, Writers, Producers, Designers, Managers, Choreographers, Technicians, Composers, Executives, Dancers, and Critics in the United States, Canada, Great Britain and the World

Joshua Kondek, Editor

Angela Yvonne Jones, Associate Editor

Volume 25

Includes Cumulative Index Containing References to *Who's Who in the Theatre* and *Who Was Who in the Theatre*

Detroit
San Francisco
London
Boston
Woodbridge, CT

STAFF

Joshua Kondek, *Editor*

Angela Yvonne Jones, *Associate Editor*

Christine Tomassini, *Editorial Research Consultant*

James P. Draper, *Managing Editor*

Victoria B. Cariappa, *Research Manager*

Andrew Guy Malonis, *Research Specialist*

Barbara McNeil, Gary Oudersluys, Maureen Richards, and Cheryl L. Warnock, *Research Specialists*

Corrine A. Boland, Tamara C. Nott, Tracie A. Richardson, and Robert Whaley, *Research Associates*

Phyllis Blackman, Tim Lehnerer, and Patricia Love, *Research Assistants*

Library of Congress Catalog Card Number 84-649371

ISBN 0-7876-3184-1
ISSN 0749-064X

Printed in the United States of America

10 9 8 7 6 5 4 3 2 1

Contents

Preface

Provides Broad, Single-Source Coverage in the Entertainment Field

Contemporary Theatre, Film and Television (*CTFT*) is a biographical reference series designed to provide students, educators, researchers, librarians, and general readers with information on a wide range of entertainment figures. Unlike single-volume reference works that focus on a limited number of artists or on a specific segment of the entertainment field, *CTFT* is an ongoing publication that includes entries on individuals active in the theatre, film, *and* television industries. Before the publication of *CTFT,* information-seekers had no choice but to consult several different sources in order to locate the in-depth biographical and credit data that makes *CTFT's* one-stop coverage the most comprehensive available about the lives and work of performing arts professionals.

Scope

CTFT covers not only performers, directors, writers, and producers, but also behind-the-scenes specialists such as designers, managers, choreographers, technicians, composers, executives, dancers, and critics from the United States, Canada, Great Britain, and the world. With over 300 entries in *CTFT 25,* the series now provides biographies on approximately 9,800 people involved in all aspects of theatre, film, and television.

CTFT gives primary emphasis to people who are currently active. New entries are prepared on major stars as well as those who are just beginning to win acclaim for their work. *CTFT* also includes entries on personalities who have died but whose work commands lasting interest.

Compilation Methods

CTFT editors identify candidates for inclusion in the series by consulting biographical dictionaries, industry directories, entertainment annuals, trade and general interest periodicals, newspapers, and online databases. Additionally, the editors of *CTFT* maintain regular contact with industry advisors and professionals who routinely suggest new candidates for inclusion in the series. Entries are compiled from published biographical sources and then mailed to the listees or their agents for review and verification.

Revised Entries

To ensure *CTFT's* timeliness and comprehensiveness, entries from previous volumes, as well as from Gale's *Who's Who in the Theatre,* are updated for individuals who have been active enough to require revision of their earlier biographies. Such individuals will merit revised entries as often as there is substantial new information to provide. Obituary notices for deceased entertainment personalities already listed in *CTFT* are also published.

Accessible Format Makes Data Easy to Locate

CTFT entries, modeled after those in Gale's highly regarded *Contemporary Authors* series, are written in a clear, readable style designed to help users focus quickly on specific facts. The following is a summary of the information found in *CTFT* sketches:

ENTRY HEADING: the form of the name by which the listee is best known.

- *PERSONAL:* full or original name; dates and places of birth and death; family data; colleges attended, degrees earned, and professional training; political and religious affiliations when known; avocational interests.
- *ADDRESSES:* home, office, agent, publicist and/or manager addresses.
- *CAREER:* tagline indicating principal areas of entertainment work; resume of career positions and other vocational achievements; military service.
- *MEMBER:* memberships and offices held in professional, union, civic, and social organizations.
- *AWARDS, HONORS:* theatre, film, and television awards and nominations; literary and civic awards; honorary degrees.
- *CREDITS:* comprehensive title-by-title listings of theatre, film, and television appearance and work credits, including roles and production data as well as debut and genre information.
- *RECORDINGS:* album, single song, video, and taped reading releases; recording labels and dates when available.
- *WRITINGS:* title-by-title listing of plays, screenplays, scripts, and musical compositions along with production information; books, including autobiographies, and other publications.
- *ADAPTATIONS:* a list of films, plays, and other media which have been adapted from the listee's work.
- *SIDELIGHTS:* favorite roles; portions of agent-prepared biographies or personal statements from the listee when available.
- *OTHER SOURCES:* books, periodicals, and internet sites where interviews or feature stories can be found.

Access Thousands of Entries Using *CTFT*'s Cumulative Index

Each volume of *CTFT* contains a cumulative index to the entire series. As an added feature, this index also includes references to all seventeen editions of *Who's Who in the Theatre* and to the four-volume compilation *Who Was Who in the Theatre.*

Available in Electronic Format

Online. Recent volumes of *CTFT* are available online as part of the Gale Biographies (GALBIO) database accessible through LEXIS-NEXIS. For more information, contact LEXIS-NEXIS, P.O. Box 933, Dayton, OH 45401-0933; phone (937) 865-6800, toll-free: 800-543-6862.

Suggestions Are Welcome

Contemporary Theatre, Film and Television is intended to serve as a useful reference tool for a wide audience, so comments about any aspect of this work are encouraged. Suggestions of entertainment professionals to include in future volumes are also welcome. Send comments and suggestions to: The Editor, *Contemporary Theatre, Film and Television,* Gale Group, 27500 Drake Rd., Farmington Hills, MI 48331-3535; call toll-free at 1-800-877-GALE.

Contemporary Theatre, Film and Television

** Indicates that a listing has been compiled from secondary sources believed to be reliable, but has not been personally verified for this edition by the listee.*

ABRAHAMS, Jim 1944-

PERSONAL

Born May 10, 1944, in Shorewood, WI; married Nancy; children: Joseph, Jamie, Charlie. *Education:* Attended University of Wisconsin, Madison.

Addresses: *Agent*—Jim Berkys, United Talent Agency, 9560 Wilshire Blvd., Suite 500, Beverly Hills, CA 90212.

Career: Producer, director, and screenwriter. Kentucky Fried Theatre (improvisation company), Madison, WI, co-founder, 1971; Kentucky Fried Theatre, Los Angeles, CA, co-founder, 1972. Also worked as a private investigator.

Member: Directors Guild of America.

Awards, Honors: Writers Guild of America Award, best comedy, 1980, for *Airplane!;* Emmy Award nomination, best writing in a comedy series, 1982, for *Police Squad!*

CREDITS

Film Work; Director, Except Where Indicated:

(With David Zucker and Jerry Zucker) And executive producer, *Airplane!* (also known as *Flying High*), Paramount, 1980.

(With D. Zucker and J. Zucker) And executive producer, *Top Secret!,* Paramount, 1984.

(With D. Zucker and J. Zucker) *Ruthless People,* Buena Vista, 1986.

Big Business, Buena Vista, 1988.

Executive producer, *The Naked Gun: From the Files of Police Squad!* (also known as *The Naked Gun*), Paramount, 1988.

Welcome Home, Roxy Carmichael, Paramount, 1990.

Executive producer, *Cry-Baby,* Imagine/Universal, 1990.

Hot Shots!, Twentieth Century-Fox, 1991.

Co-executive producer, *Naked Gun 2-1/2: The Smell of Fear,* Paramount, 1991.

Hot Shots! Part Deux (also known as *Hot Shots! 2*), Twentieth Century-Fox, 1993.

Executive producer, *Naked Gun 33-1/3: The Final Insult* (also known as *Naked Gun 3*), Paramount, 1994.

Jane Austen's Mafia (also known as *Mafia!*), Buena Vista, 1998.

Film Appearances:

Announcer in the courtroom and first technician, "Eyewitness News" (segment), *The Kentucky Fried Movie,* United Film, 1977.

Religious zealot, *Airplane!* (also known as *Flying High*), Paramount, 1980.

The face on the cutting room floor, *Coming to America,* 1988.

Television Work; Series:

Creator, executive producer, and director, *Police Squad!,* ABC, 1982.

Television Work; Movies:

Director, producer, and executive producer,... *First Do No Harm,* ABC, 1997.

Television Appearances; Specials:

Hearts of Hot Shots! Part Deux—A Filmmaker's Apology, HBO, 1993.

WRITINGS

Screenplays:

(With D. Zucker and J. Zucker) *The Kentucky Fried Movie,* United Film, 1977.

(With D. Zucker and J. Zucker) *Airplane!* (also known as *Flying High*), Paramount, 1980.
(With D. Zucker, J. Zucker, and Martyn Burke) And lyricist, "Spend This Night with Me," *Top Secret!,* Paramount, 1984.
(With D. Zucker, J. Zucker, and Pat Proft) *The Naked Gun: From the Files of Police Squad!,* Paramount, 1988.
(With Proft) *Hot Shots!,* Twentieth Century-Fox, 1991.
(With others) *Naked Gun 2-1/2: The Smell of Fear,* Paramount, 1991.
(With Proft) *Hot Shots! Part Deux,* Twentieth Century-Fox, 1993.
Naked Gun 33-1/3: The Final Insult (also known as *Naked Gun 3*), Paramount, 1994.
Jane Austen's Mafia (also known as *Mafia!*), Buena Vista, 1998.

Television Episodes:
(With others) *Police Squad!,* ABC, 1982.

OTHER SOURCES

Periodicals:
Chicago Tribune, December 2, 1988.
Entertainment Weekly, August 9, 1991, p. 38.
People Weekly, April 17, 1995, p. 54.
Rolling Stone, October 2, 1980.
Time, August 29, 1977; July 14, 1980; March 29, 1982; July 2, 1984; June 30, 1986; June 13, 1988.
Times (London), February 9, 1989.
Variety, August 9, 1991, p. 93.
Video Business, August 19, 1994, p. 58.
Village Voice, March 30, 1982; June 14, 1988.*

ALEA, Tomas Gutierrez 1928-1996

PERSONAL

Born December 11, 1928, in Havana, Cuba; died of cancer, April 17, 1996, in Havana, Cuba. *Education:* Attended the University of Havana.

Addresses: *Contact*—Instituto Cubano del Arte e Industria Cinemato-grafias (ICAIL), Calle 23, No. 1155, Vedado, Havana, Cuba.

Career: Director, writer, and actor.

Awards, Honors: Audienu Award, Sao Paulo International Film Festival, best feature, 1978, for *La Ultima cena;* Silver Berlin Bear, Berlin International Film Festival, Special Jury Prize, and Golden Kikito, Gramado Latin Film Festival, best Latin film, both 1994, Special Jury Award, Sundance Film Festival, special mention, 1995, all for *Fresa y chocolate;* Golden Lion, Venice Film Festival, 1994, Jury Award, Fort Lauderdale International Film Festival, best foreign film, and Golden Kikito, Gramado Latin Film Festival, best Latin film, both 1996, all for *Guantanamera.*

CREDITS

Film Appearances:
Memorias del subdesarrollo (also known as *Memories of Underdevelopment*), Instituto Cubano del Arte e Industrias Cinematograficos, 1968.

Film Work; Director:
El Faquir, 1947.
La Caperucita, 1947.
Una Confusion cotidiana, 1950.
Il Songo de Giovanni, 1953.
El Megano, 1955.
The Charcoal Worker, 1956.
Esta Tierra es Nuestra, Instituto Cubano del Arte e Industrias Cinematograficos (ICAIC), 1959.
Asamblea general, 1960.
Muerte al invasor, 1961.
Historias de la revolucion (also known as *Stories of the Revolution*), Instituto Cubano del Arte e Industrias Cinematograficos, 1961.
Las doce sillas (also known as *The Twelve Chairs*), Instituto Cubano del Arte e Industrias Cinematograficos, 1962.
Cumbite, Instituto Cubano del Arte e Industrias Cinematograficos, 1961.
La Muerte de un burocrate (also known as *Death of a Bureaucrat*), Instituto Cubano del Arte e Industrias Cinematograficos, 1966.
Paper Is Paper, 1966.
Memorias del subdesarrollo (also known as *Memories of Underdevelopment*), Instituto Cubano del Arte e Industrias Cinematograficos, 1968.
Una Pelea Cubana Contra los demonios (also known as *A Cuban Fight Against Demons*), Instituto Cubano del Arte e Industrias Cinematograficos, 1971.
El Arte del tabaco, 1974.
(Scenario) *El Otro Francisco* (also known as *The Other Francisco*), 1974.
El Camino de la mirra y el incienso, 1975.
La Ultima cena (also known as *The Last Supper*), Instituto Cubano del Arte e Industrias Cinematograficos, 1976.

La Sexta parte del mundo, 1977.

De Cierta manera (also known as *One Way or Another*), Instituto Cubano del Arte e Industrias Cinematograficos, 1977.

Los Sobrevivientes (also known as *The Survivors*), Instituto Cubano del Arte e Industrias Cinematograficos, 1978.

Hasta cierto punto (also known as *Up to a Certain Point*), Instituto Cubano del Arte e Industrias Cinematograficos, Instituto Cubano del Arte e Industrias Cinematograficos, 1984.

Se Permuta, 1985.

Cartas del Parque (also known as *Letters from the Park*), Radio Television Espanola, 1988.

Contigo en la distancia (also known as *Far Apart*), RA Associates, 1991.

Fresa y chocolate (also known as *Strawberry and Chocolate*), Miramax, 1993.

Guantanamera, Cine' 360, 1995.

WRITINGS

Screenplays:

Esta Tierra es Nuestra, Instituto Cubano del Arte e Industrias Cinematograficos, 1959.

Historias de la revolucion (also known as *Stories of the Revolution*), Instituto Cubano del Arte e Industrias Cinematograficos, 1961.

Las doce sillas (also known as *The Twelve Chairs*),Instituto Cubano del Arte e Industrias Cinematograficos, 1962.

La Muerte de un burocrate (also known as *Death of a Bureaucrat*), Instituto Cubano del Arte e Industrias Cinematograficos, 1966.

Memorias del subdesarrollo (also known as *Memories of Underdevelopment*), Instituto Cubano del Arte e Industrias Cinematograficos, 1968.

Una Pelea Cubana Contra los demonios (also known as *A Cuban Fight Against Demons*), Instituto Cubano del Arte e Industrias Cinematograficos, 1971.

La Ultima cena (also known as *The Last Supper*), Instituto Cubano del Arte e Industrias Cinematograficos, 1976.

Los Sobrevivientes (also known as *The Survivors*), Instituto Cubano del Arte e Industrias Cinematograficos, 1978.

Hasta cierto punto (also known as *Up to a Certain Point*), Instituto Cubano del Arte e Industrias Cinematograficos, 1984.

Cartas del Parque (also known as *Letters from the Park*), Radio Television Espanola, 1988.

Guantanamera, Cine' 360, 1995.

OTHER SOURCES

Books:

Burton, Julianne, editor, *Cinema and Social Change in Latin America: Conversations with Filmmakers,* Austin, Texas, 1986.

Chanan, Michael, *The Cuban Image,* London, 1985.

Fornet, Ambrosio, *Alea: Una retrospectiva critica,* Havana, 1987.

Myerson, Michael, editor, *Memories of Underdevelopment: The Revolutionary Films of Cuba,* New York, 1973.

Periodicals:

Artforum, December, 1994, p. 62.

Cineaste, winter/spring, 1995, p. 16.

New York Times, January 22, 1995.*

ALEXANDER, Jason 1959-

PERSONAL

Original name, Jay Scott Greenspan; born September 23, 1959, in Newark (some sources say Livingston), NJ; son of Alexander B. (an accounting manager) and Ruth Minnie (a nurse and health care administrator; maiden name, Simon) Greenspan; married Daena E. Title (an actress and writer), May 31, 1982; children: Gabriel, Noah. *Education:* Attended Boston University.

Addresses: *Agent*—William Morris Agency, 151 South El Camino Dr., Beverly Hills, CA 90212-2704.

Career: Actor.

Awards, Honors: Drama Desk Award nomination, best actor in a musical, 1985, Antoinette Perry Award, Drama Desk Award, and Outer Critics' Circle Award, all best actor in a musical, 1989, for *Jerome Robbins' Broadway;* Emmy Award nominations, best supporting actor in a comedy series, 1992,1993, and 1995, Golden Globe Award nominations, best actor in a series, 1992, 1993, and 1995, and Directors Guild of America Award nomination, 1993, all for *Seinfeld; Drama-Logue* Award, 1993, for *Give 'em Hell, Harry.*

CREDITS

Television Appearances; Series:

Harold Stickley, *E/R,* CBS, 1984-85.

Julian Beeby, *Everything's Relative,* CBS, 1987.
George Costanza, *Seinfeld* (also known as *The Seinfeld Chronicles*), NBC, 1989-98.
Voice of Duckman, *Duckman* (animated), USA Network, 1994.
Storytime, PBS, 1994.
Muppets Tonight, ABC, 1996.
Alan Ballinger, *Remember WENN,* AMC, 1996.
Narration, *Sex and the Silver Screen,* Showtime, 1996.
Jack, *The Nanny,* CBS, 1996.
Voice, *Disney's Hercules,* ABC/syndicated, 1998.

Television Appearances; Specials:
"Music by Richard Rodgers," *Great Performances,* PBS, 1990.
The Search for the New Ideal Man, ABC, 1992.
Comic Relief V, HBO, 1992.
The Kennedy Center Honors: A Celebration of the Performing Arts, CBS, 1993.
The 1st Annual Comedy Hall of Fame, NBC, 1993.
Frank, *Sexual Healing,* Showtime, 1993.
A Day in the Life of Melrose Place, Fox, 1994.
Comic Relief VI, HBO, 1994.
Howie, "Down at the Waterfront," *Alive TV,* PBS, 1994.
Smithsonian Fantastic Journey, CBS, 1996.
The Late Show with David Letterman Video Special 2, CBS, 1996.
Host, *The Making of Disney's The Hunchback of Notre Dame,* ABC, 1996.
Narration, *Sideshow,* TLC, 1997.
Hollywood & Vinyl: Disney's 101 Greatest Musical Moments, VH-1, 1998.
George Costanza, *Seinfeld: The Chronicle,* NBC, 1998.

Television Appearances; Awards Presentations:
The 43rd Annual Tony Awards, CBS, 1989.
The American Television Awards, ABC, 1993.
The 46th Annual Primetime Emmy Awards, ABC, 1994.
Host, *The 47th Annual Primetime Emmy Awards,* Fox, 1995.
The 9th Annual American Comedy Awards, ABC, 1995.
Presenter, *Screen Actors Guild Awards,* NBC, 1995.
Presenter, *The Screen Actors Guild Awards,* NBC, 1997.

Television Appearances; Movies:
(Television debut) Pete, *Senior Trip!,* CBS, 1981.
Lieutenant Ernest Foy, *Rockabye,* CBS, 1986.
Chris Van Allen, *Favorite Son,* NBC, 1988.
Albert Peterson, *Bye Bye Birdie,* ABC, 1995.
Lionel, *Rodgers & Hammerstein's Cinderella,* ABC, 1997.
Art Witz, *Denial,* 1998.

Television Appearances; Episodic:
Ramming, *Newhart,* CBS, 1988.
Moira's attorney, "Oral Sex, Lies, and Videotape," *Dream On,* HBO, 1990.
Himself, *The Larry Sanders Show,* HBO, 1992.
Voice of Abis Mal, *Aladdin,* CBS, 1994.
"A Tribute to Stephen Sondheim," *A & E Stage,* Arts and Entertainment, 1995.

Television Appearances; Pilots:
George Costanza, *The Seinfeld Chronicles,* NBC, 1989.

Television Work; Episodic:
Director, *Seinfeld,* NBC, 1993.
Director, *Remember WENN,* AMC, 1996.
Clip Director, *Seinfeld: The Chronicle,* ABC, 1998.

Film Appearances:
(Film debut) Dave, *The Burning,* Filmways, 1981.
Pool hustler, *Brighton Beach Memoirs,* Universal, 1986.
Hardware store clerk, *The Mosquito Coast,* Warner Bros., 1986.
Philip Stuckey, *Pretty Woman,* Buena Vista, 1990.
Neil Horowitz, *White Palace,* Universal, 1990.
Geary, *Jacob's Ladder,* TriStar, 1990.
Bernie Fishbine, *I Don't Buy Kisses Anymore,* Skouras, 1992.
Larry Farber, *Coneheads,* Paramount, 1993.
Down on the Waterfront, 1993.
Voice of Abis Mal, *The Return of Jafar* (animated), Buena Vista Home Video, 1994.
North's dad, *North,* Columbia, 1994.
Mr. Stone, *Blankman,* Columbia, 1994.
Marion Sandusky, *The Paper,* Universal, 1994.
For Better or Worse, Columbia, 1995.
Guest—The Anti-environmentalist, *The Last Supper,* Columbia, 1995.
Robert, *Dunston Checks In,* Twentieth Century-Fox, 1996.
Voice characterization, *Hunchback of Notre Dame* (animated), Buena Vista, 1996.
Buzz Hauser, *Love!Valour!Compassion!,* Fine Line Features, 1997.
Music coordinator, *Disturbing Behavior,* Columbia TriStar, 1998.
(Cameo appearance), *With Friends Like These. . .,* Mom's Roof, Inc., 1998.

Film Work:

Director, *For Better or Worse* (also known as *Stranger Things*), Columbia, 1995.

Stage Appearances:

(Broadway debut) Joe Josephson, *Merrily We Roll Along,* Alvin Theatre, 1981.

America Kicks Up Its Heels, 1982.

On Hold with Music, 1982.

Fragments, 1982.

Ensemble, *Forbidden Broadway* (revue), Palsson's Theatre, New York City, 1983.

Lino, Lenny, Punk, and Uncle Fausto, *The Rink,* Martin Beck Theatre, New York City, 1984.

Billy, *D.,* Manhattan Theatre Club, New York City, 1985.

Louis, *Personals,* Minetta Lane Theatre, New York City, 1985-86.

Stanley, *Broadway Bound,* Broadhurst Theatre, New York City, 1986.

(London debut) Lino, *The Rink,* Her Majesty's Theatre, 1988.

Emcee and various roles, *Jerome Robbins' Broadway,* Imperial Theatre, New York City, 1988-90.

Accomplice, Richard Rodgers Theatre, New York City, 1990.

Sidney Black, *Light Up the Sky,* Roundabout Theatre, New York City, 1990.

Harry S Truman, *Give 'em Hell, Harry,* produced in Los Angeles, 1993.

Appeared off-Broadway in *Stop the World . . . I Want to Get Off.*

WRITINGS

For Stage:

Narrative, *Jerome Robbins' Broadway,* Imperial Theatre, New York City, 1988.

OTHER SOURCES

Periodicals:

Cosmopolitan, July, 1994, p. 68.

Entertainment Weekly, December 1, 1995, p. 36.

New York Times, May 24, 1992, p. 21.

People Weekly, July 1, 1996, p. 38.

Playboy, August, 1997, p. 72.

TV Guide, April 23, 1994, p. 12.*

ALLEN, Steve 1921-
(William Christopher Stevens)

PERSONAL

Full name, Stephen Valentine Patrick William Allen; born December 26, 1921, in New York, NY; son of Carroll (a vaudeville performer, under stage name Billy Allen) and Isabelle (a vaudeville comedienne, under stage name Belle Montrose; maiden name, Donohue) Allen; married Dorothy Goodman (an actress), August 23, 1943 (divorced, 1952); married Jayne Meadows (an actress and comedienne), July 31, 1954; children: (first marriage) Steve, Jr., Brian, David; (second marriage) William Christopher. *Education:* Attended Drake University, 1940-41, and Arizona State Teachers College (now Arizona State University), 1941-42.

Addresses: *Contact*--15201 Burbank Blvd., Suite B, Van Nuys, CA 91411.

Career: Comedian, actor, producer, composer, and writer. KOY-Radio, Phoenix, AZ, announcer, pianist, producer, and writer, 1942-43; KFAC-Radio, Los Angeles, CA, announcer, c. 1944; KNX-Radio, Los Angeles, talk show host, 1947-50; Columbia Broadcasting System, New York City, appeared on early evening talk shows, 1950-53; KMTR-Radio, Los Angeles, announcer. Appeared as a musician at The Blue Note and Michael's Pub, both New York City; performed with symphonies and pop orchestras around the United States. Meadowlane Enterprises, Inc., producer. Radford University, guest lecturer in history and philosophy, 1986; chair, Council for Media Integrity (a watchdog group), 1994-?. *Military service:* U.S. Army, 1942 (some sources say 1943).

Awards, Honors: Award for best television documentary on organized crime, New York City Board of Trade, 1953, for *The Commandment;* Sylvania Award, words and music, 1954, for *The Bachelor;* Emmy Award nominations, best continuing performance by a male personality, best series performance by a person who essentially plays himself, both 1956, and best actor in a musical or variety series, all for *The Steve Allen Show;* SANE Education Fund/Consider the Alternatives Peace Award, Consider the Alternatives Productions, 1962; Grammy Award, best jazz composition, and Grammy Award nomination, best instrumental theme, 1963, for "Gravy Waltz"; George Foster Peabody Broadcasting Award, television, Henry W. Grady School of Journalism and Mass Communication, University of Georgia, Television Critics Circle Award, *Encyclopaedia Britannica* Award, and Film Advisory Board Award, all 1977, Emmy Award nomination, program achievement, special class, 1979, and Emmy Award nomination, best writing for a drama series, all for *A Meeting of the Minds;* Best Play Award nomination, 1978, for *The Wake;* Grammy Award nomination, best spoken word or non-musical recording, 1983, for *Everything You Wanted to Know about Home Computers;* Emmy Award nomination, best host of a talk or service show, 1984, for *Stooge Snapshots: 50 Years with the Funniest Guys in the World;* included in *Guinness Book of World Records* as the most prolific composer of modern times, 1984; Emmy Award, inducted into Television Hall of Fame, 1986; Emmy Award nomination, best guest performer in a drama series, 1986, for *St. Elsewhere;* American Comedy Award, lifetime achievement, George Schlatter Productions, 1987; American Book Award, educational materials, Before Columbus Foundation, 1988, for *Shakin' Loose with Mother Goose;* Emmy Award nomination, individual achievement in religious programming, for *Wait Till We're 65.*

CREDITS

Television Appearances; Series:

Host, *The Steve Allen Show,* CBS, 1950-52.
Master of ceremonies, *Songs for Sale,* CBS, 1951-52.
Master of ceremonies, *Talent Patrol* (also known as *Soldier Parade*), ABC, 1953.
Panelist, *What's My Line?,* CBS, 1953-54.
Host, *Tonight,* syndicated, 1953-54.
Host, *The Tonight Show,* NBC, 1954-57.
Host, *The Steve Allen Show,* NBC, 1956-59, retitled *The Steve Allen Plymouth Show,* NBC, 1959-60, then ABC, 1960-61.
Host, *The New Steve Allen Show,* ABC, 1961.
Host, *The Steve Allen Show,* syndicated, 1962.
Moderator, *I've Got a Secret,* CBS, 1964-67.
Host, *The Steve Allen Comedy Hour,* CBS, 1967, then 1967-69.
Host, *The Steve Allen Show,* syndicated, 1968.
Steve Allen, syndicated, 1968-72.
Host, *I've Got a Secret,* syndicated, 1972-73.
Vaudeville, syndicated, 1975.
Host, *Steve Allen's Laugh-Back,* syndicated, 1976-77.
Moderator, *A Meeting of the Minds,* PBS, 1977-81.
Solid Gold, syndicated, 1980.
Host, *The Steve Allen Comedy Hour,* NBC, 1980-81.
Host, *Steve Allen's Music Room,* The Disney Channel, 1984.
Host, *The Start of Something Big,* 1985.
Host, *Life's Most Embarrassing Moments,* ABC, 1985-86, and syndicated, 1988.
The Eyes of War, syndicated, 1989.
Comics Only, syndicated, 1991.

Also appeared as host, *Host-to-Host; That Was the Week That Was.*

Television Appearances; Miniseries:

Bayard Nichols, *Rich Man, Poor Man—Book I,* ABC, 1976.

Television Appearances; Movies:

Herschel Lucas, *Now You See It, Now You Don't,* NBC, 1968.
Joys, 1976.
Stone, ABC, 1979.
The Gossip Columnist, Operation Prime Time, 1980.
Himself, *The Ratings Game* (also known as *The Mogul*), The Movie Channel, 1984.
Gentleman in the paper suit, *Alice in Wonderland* (also known as *Alice Through the Looking Glass*), CBS, 1985.

Television Appearances; Pilots:

Host, *The Timex All-Star Jazz Show I,* NBC, 1957.
The Apartment House, CBS, 1964.
Solid Gold '79, Operation Prime Time, 1980.

Also appeared as Perry Knowland, *Warning Shot,* syndicated.

Television Appearances; Specials:

Tonight Preview, NBC, 1954.
Host, *Sunday in Town,* NBC, 1954.
Fanfare, NBC, 1954.
Good Times, NBC, 1955.
The Bob Hope Show, NBC, 1956.
Texaco Command Performance, NBC, 1957.
The Bob Hope Show, NBC, 1962.
Shoot-In at NBC (also known as *A Bob Hope Special*), NBC, 1967.
Romp, ABC, 1968.
The Bob Hope Show, NBC, 1969.
Plimpton! Did You Hear the One About. . .?, ABC, 1971.
Host, *The Unofficial Miss Las Vegas Showgirl Beauty Pageant,* ABC, 1974.
Mitzi and a Hundred Guys, CBS, 1975.
The Mad Mad Mad Mad World of the Super Bowl, NBC, 1977.
The Lucille Ball Special, CBS, 1977.
The Arthur Godfrey Special, syndicated, 1979.
Steve Martin: Comedy Is Not Pretty, NBC, 1980.
Host, *I've Had It Up to Here,* NBC, 1981.
Texaco Star Theatre: Opening Night, NBC, 1982.

Life's Most Embarrassing Moments II, ABC, 1983.
Life's Most Embarrassing Moments III, ABC, 1984.
Life's Most Embarrassing Moments IV, ABC, 1984.
Narrator, *Stooge Snapshots: 50 Years with the Funniest Guys in the World*, syndicated, 1984.
Steve Allen's Comedy Room, The Disney Channel, 1984.
Host, *The Start of Something Big*, syndicated, 1985.
TV's Funniest Game Show Moments, ABC, 1985.
The Television Academy Hall of Fame, NBC, 1986.
NBC . . . Tuned in to America, NBC, 1986.
NBC's 60th Anniversary Celebration, NBC, 1986.
George Burns's 90th Birthday Special (also known as *Kraft Salutes the George Burns 90th Birthday Special*), CBS, 1986.
Funny, ABC, 1986.
Mancini and Friends, PBS, 1987.
Lifetime Salutes Mom, Lifetime, 1987.
Great Confrontations at the Oxford Union: Resolved That Englishmen Are Funnier Than Americans, PBS, 1987.
Comic Relief II, HBO, 1987.
Grand marshal, *The 54th Annual King Orange Jamboree Parade*, NBC, 1987.
Happy Birthday, Bob—50 Stars Salute Your 50 Years with NBC, NBC, 1988.
The 58th Annual Hollywood Christmas Parade, syndicated, 1989.
Scott Ross: The Search for Real Heroes, syndicated, 1990.
Judge, *The 1990 Miss Universe Pageant*, CBS, 1990.
The Very Best of the Ed Sullivan Show—II, CBS, 1991.
Living in America, syndicated, 1991.
George Burns's 95th Birthday Party, CBS, 1991.
Tom Arnold: The Naked Truth 2, HBO, 1992.
Laurel and Hardy: A Tribute to the Boys, The Disney Channel, 1992.
Elvis: The Great Performances, CBS, 1992.
The Creative Spirit, PBS, 1992.
Mo' Funny: Black Comedy in America, HBO, 1993.
Addicted to Fame, 1994.
Hal Roach: Hollywood's King of Laughter, The Disney Channel, 1994.
Great American Music: A Salute to Fast Cars, syndicated, 1994.
Comic Relief VII, 1995.
Abbott and Costello Meet Biography, Arts and Entertainment, 1996.
Himself, *James Dean: A Portrait*, 1996.
Jack Benny: Now Cut That Out!, Arts and Entertainment, 1996.
Jackie Mason: An Equal Opportunity Offender, Bravo, 1996.
Nichols and May-Take Two, HBO, 1996.
50 Years of Television: A Celebration of the Academy of Television Arts & Sciences Golden Anniversary, HBO, 1997.
Love, Lust & Marriage: Why We Stray and Why We Stay, ABC, 1997.
Steve Allen's 75th Birthday Celebration, PBS, 1997.
The 67th Annual Hollywood Christmas Parade, 1998.
Donna Reed: I'll Take the Moon, Arts and Entertainment, 1998.
Jonathon Winters: Without a Net, Arts and Entertainment, 1998.
"Ernie Kovacs," *Biography*, Arts and Entertainment, 1999.
Martian Mania: The True Story of "War of the Worlds," Sci-Fi Channel, 1998.
NYTV: By the People Who Made It, PBS, 1998.
Skitch Henderson at 80, PBS, 1998.
Narrator, *The Unreal Story of Professional Wrestling*, Arts and Entertainment, 1998.
Gypsy Rose Lee: Naked Ambition, Arts and Entertainment, 1999.

Also appeared on *American Academy of Humor*, NBC.

Television Appearances; Awards Presentations:

Master of ceremonies, *The Emmy Awards*, NBC, 1980.
The 38th Annual Emmy Awards, NBC, 1986.
The Grammy Lifetime Achievement Award Show, CBS, 1987.
The 30th Annual Grammy Awards, CBS, 1988.
The 3rd Annual American Comedy Awards, ABC, 1989.
Host, *The Fifth Annual Trumpet Awards*, 1997.

Television Appearances; Episodic:

Arthur Godfrey's Talent Scouts, CBS, 1948-58.
This Is Show Business, CBS, 1950.
"Five Minutes to Die," *Danger*, 1953.
Danger, CBS, 1950-55.
What's My Line?, CBS, 1951.
Max Liebman Presents, NBC, 1955.
"The Man on Rollerskates," *Kraft Television Theatre*, NBC, 1956.
Mike Wallace Interview, ABC, 1957.
The June Allyson Show, CBS, 1959-61.
Allan Stevens, "The Cat's Meow," *Batman*, 1966.
The Andy Williams Show, 1966.
Showtime, CBS, 1968.
One Man Show, syndicated, 1969.
Guest host, *The Golddiggers*, syndicated, 1971.
Vaudeville, 1975.
Marvin Kaplan, "Have I Got a Christmas for You," *Hallmark Hall of Fame*, NBC, 1977.

Guest host, *The Big Show,* NBC, 1980.
An Evening at the Improv, syndicated, 1981.
Darkroom, ABC, 1981.
The Comedy Zone, CBS, 1984.
Lech Osoranski, "Visiting Daze," *St. Elsewhere,* NBC, 1986.
Lech Osoranski, "Russian Roulette," *St. Elsewhere,* NBC, 1987.
This Is Your Life, NBC, 1987.
Super Dave, Showtime, 1987.
Way Off Broadway, Lifetime, 1987.
"The Montreal International Comedy Festival," *HBO Comedy Hour,* HBO, 1988.
"The Abby Singer Show," *St. Elsewhere,* NBC, 1988.
"Mort Sahl: The Loyal Opposition," *American Masters,* PBS, 1989.
"Rodney Dangerfield's The Really Big Show," *HBO Comedy Hour,* HBO, 1991.
Bart's electronically altered voice, "Separate Vocations," *The Simpsons* (animated), Fox, 1992.
Himself, *The Bold and the Beautiful,* 1993.
"Addicted to Fame," *First Person with Maria Shriver,* NBC, 1994.
Himself, "Boatshow," *Space Ghost Coast to Coast,* Cartoon Network, 1994.
Voice, "Round Springfield," *The Simpsons* (animated), Fox, 1994.
Voice, *The Critic* (animated), ABC, 1994.
"Mel Torme," *Biography,* Arts and Entertainment, 1995.
Voice, *Dr. Katz: Professional Therapist* (animated), Comedy Central, 1995.
Fear, "Fear Strikes Up a Conversation," *Sabrina, the Teenage Witch,* ABC, 1996.
Mr. Cochran, "Shaggy Dog, City Goat," *Homicide: Life on the Street,* NBC, 1997.

Also appeared in *Nightline,* ABC; *The Love Boat,* ABC.

Other Television Appearances:
The Commandment, 1953.
Co-host, *The Book of Lists,* CBS, 1982.
Inside Your Schools, syndicated, 1985.

Also appeared as host, *Wait Till We're 65,* NBC.

Television Work; Series:
Executive producer, *Steve Allen's Music Room,* The Disney Channel, 1984.

Television Work; Specials:
Producer, *The Unofficial Miss Las Vegas Showgirl Beauty Pageant,* ABC, 1974.
Executive producer, *Steve Allen's 75th Birthday Celebration,* PBS, 1997.

Film Appearances:
Himself, *Down Memory Lane,* Eagle-Lion, 1949.
Peter Pepper, *I'll Get By,* Twentieth Century-Fox, 1950.
Title role, *The Benny Goodman Story,* Universal, 1956.
Guest star, *The Big Circus,* Allied Artists, 1959.
Steve Macinter, *College Confidential,* Universal, 1960.
Don't Worry, We'll Think of a Title, United Artists, 1966.
Himself, *The Universal Mind of Bill Evans,* 1966.
Perry Knowland, *Warning Shot,* Paramount, 1967.
Radio announcer, *Where Were You When the Lights Went Off?,* Metro-Goldwyn-Mayer, 1968.
Himself, *The Comic,* Columbia, 1969.
(Uncredited) *The Sunshine Boys,* United Artists, 1975.
Himself, *Lenny Bruce Without Tears,* 1975.
Himself, *Heart Beat,* Warner Bros., 1979.
Himself, *The Funny Farm,* 1983.
Himself "Roast Your Loved One," *Amazon Women on the Moon* (also known as *Cheeseburger Film Sandwich*), Universal, 1987.
Himself, *Great Balls of Fire!,* Orion, 1989.
Himself, *The Player,* Fine Line Features, 1992.
Julia's grandfather, *The St. Tammany Miracle,* 1994.
Himself, *Casino,* Universal, 1995.
Himself, *Off the Menu: The Last Days of Chasen's,* 1996.
Himself, *Lenny Bruce: Swear to Tell the Truth,* 1998.

Also appeared in the film *The Burglar.*

Radio Appearances; Series:
(With announcer Wendell Noble) *Smile Time,* Mutual Broadcasting Co., 1945-47.

Stage Appearances:
The Pink Elephant, Broadway production, 1953.
Gilbert and Sullivan: The Mikado (opera), Symphony Space, New York City, 1995.

Major Tours
Tonight at 8:30, 1975.
The Wake, eastern U.S. cities, 1978.

RECORDINGS

Albums:
Steve Allen, Columbia, 1951.
Steve Sings Steve Allen, Coral, 1955.
The James Dean Story, Coral, 1956.
Piano Tonight, Columbia, 1956.

Anthony Plays Allen, Capitol, 1958.
And All That Jazz, Dot, 1959.
Steve Allen Plays, Dot, 1959.
Steve Allen Plays Bossa Nova Jazz, Dot, 1963.
Steve Allen Presents Twelve Golden Hits, Dot, 1963.
Everything You Wanted to Know about Home Computers, Casablanca, 1983.
Steve Allen's Hip Fables, Doctor Jazz, 1983.
Steve's Songs, Dot, 1983.
Paul Smith Plays Steve Allen, Pausa, 1985.
The Best of Jose Jimenez, GNP Crescendo, 1985.
Radio Comedy Classics, 1988.
The Positive Power of Criticism, International Center for Creative Thinking, 1990.
The Jack Kerouac Collection, Rhino, 1990.

Other albums include *Venetian Serenade: A Romantic Suite, The Poetry of Love, The Jazz Story,* and *Songs Everybody Knows,* all for Coral; *Some of My Favorites,* Hamilton; *Around the World, Steve Allen Plays the PianoGreats, Great Ragtime Hits,* and *I Play for You,* all for Dot.

Videos:
Narrator (with wife, Jayne Meadows), *The Perfumed Handkerchief* (a Chinese opera), Kultur, 1985.
Steve Allen's Golden Age of Comedy, 1988.

WRITINGS

Poetry:
Windfall, privately printed, 1946.
Wry on the Rocks, Holt, 1956.
A Flash of Swallows, Droke, 1969, 2nd edition, 1972.

Fiction:
Fourteen for Tonight (stories), Holt (New York), 1955.
Not All of Your Laughter, Not All of Your Tears (novel), Bernard Geis Associates, 1962.
Murder in Manhattan (novel), Kensington Publishing, 1990.
The Murder House (novel), Zebra Books (New York City), 1993.

Autobiography:
Mark It and Strike It, Holt, 1960.

Juvenile:
Princess Snip Snip and the Puppy-Kittens, Platt & Munk (New York City), 1973.

Other Books:
Steve Allen's Bop Fables, Simon & Schuster (New York City), 1955.
The Funny Men, Simon & Schuster, 1956.
The Girls on the Tenth Floor and Other Stories, Holt, 1958.
The Question Man, Bellmeadows Press, 1959.
Contributor, *How to Write a Song,* by Henry Kane, Avon (New York City), 1962.
Letter to a Conservative, Doubleday (Garden City, NY), 1965.
The Ground Is Our Table, Doubleday, 1966.
Bigger Than a Breadbox, Doubleday, 1967.
Curses; or, How Never to Be Foiled Again, J. P. Tarcher (Los Angeles, CA), 1973.
(With William F. Buckley, Jr., Robert M. Hutchins, L. Brent Bozell, and others) *Dialogues in Americanism,* Regnery, 1974.
(With Thomas Ellis Katen) *Schmock-Schmock!,* Doubleday, 1975.
What to Say When It Rains, Price, Stern (Los Angeles), 1975.
Chopped-Up Chinese, Price, Stern, 1978.
Meeting of Minds, Volume 1, Hubris House (Los Angeles), 1978, reprinted as *Meeting of Minds: The Complete Scripts,* four volumes, Prometheus Books (Buffalo, NY), 1989.
Meeting of Minds, Volume 2, Crown (New York City), 1979.
(With Roslyn Bernstein and Donald H. Dunn) *Ripoff: A Look at Corruption in America,* Lyle Stuart (Secaucus, NJ), 1979.
Explaining China, Crown, 1980.
The Funny People, Stein & Day (New York City), 1981.
Beloved Son: A Story of the Jesus Cults, Bobbs-Merrill (Indianapolis, IN), 1982.
More Funny People, Stein & Day, 1982.
The Talk Show Murders, Delacorte (New York City), 1982.
How to Make a Speech, McGraw (New York City), 1986.
(With Jane Wollman) *How to Be Funny: Discovering the Comic You,* McGraw, 1987.
(With Jayne Meadows, David Zaslow, and others) *Shakin' Loose with Mother Goose,* Kids Matter, 1988.
Dumbth and Eighty-One Ways to Make Americans Smarter, Prometheus Books, 1989.
Murder on the Glitter Box, Kensington Publishing (New York City), 1989.
(With Rod L. Evan, Irwin M. Berent, and Isaac Asimov) *Fundamentalism: Hazards and Heartbreaks,* 1989.
(With Bill Adler) *The Passionate Nonsmoker's Bill of Rights: The First Guide to Enacting Nonsmoking Legislation,* Morrow (New York City), 1989.
Meeting of the Minds, Volume 3, 1989.

Meeting of the Minds, Volume 4, 1989.
The Public Hating: A Collection of Short Stories, Dembner (New York City), 1990.
Steve Allen on the Bible, Religion, and Morality, Prometheus Books, 1990.
Steve Allen's Funny Songs, Meadowlane Music (Van Nuys, CA), 1990.
Murder in Vegas, Kensington Publishing, 1991.
Hi-Ho, Steverino! My Adventures in the Wonderful Wacky World of TV, Thorndike (Thorndike, ME), 1992.
The Hustler's Handbook: How to Play Pool for Fun and Profit, Premier Publishers (Smyrna, GA), 1993.
Make 'em Laugh, Prometheus Books, 1993.
The Murder Game, 1993.
More Steve Allen on the Bible, Religion, and Morality, Book Two, Prometheus Books, 1993.
Reflections, Prometheus Books, 1994.
The Man Who Turned Back the Clock and Other Short Stories, 1995.
Murder on the Atlantic, 1995.
The Bug and the Slug in a Rug, 1995.
But Seriously, 1996.
Wake Up to Murder, 1996.
Die Laughing, 1998.

Television Series:
The Steve Allen Comedy Hour, NBC, 1980-81.

Television Episodes:
A Meeting of the Minds, PBS, 1977-81.
Fantasy Island, ABC, 1983.

Television Specials:
Composer, *The Bachelor,* NBC, 1954.
Songwriter, "This Could Be the Start of Something Big" (theme song), *The Start of Something Big,* syndicated, 1985.

Also wrote *I Remember Illinois* (documentary), NBC.

Television Movies:
Songwriter (nineteen songs), *Alice in Wonderland,* CBS, 1985.
Songwriter, *Run for the Dream: The Gail Devers Story,* Showtime, 1996.

Film Composer:
A Man Called Dagger, 1967.
Contributor of lyrics, *Goodfellas,* Warner Bros., 1990.
Songwriter, *I'll Be Home for Christmas,* 1998.

Stage Plays:
The Wake, Masquers Theatre, Hollywood, CA, 1971, published by Doubleday, 1972.
The Al Chemist Show, Los Angeles Actors Theatre, Los Angeles, 1980.
Book, score, and lyrics, *Seymour Glick Is Alive But Sick,* St. Regis Hotel, New York City, then The Horn, Los Angeles, 1983-84.

Wrote book, score, and lyrics for the plays *Sophie,* produced on Broadway, and *Belle Star.*

Other:
Contributor of articles, poems, and reviews to magazines, including *National Geographic Traveler, America, Look, Saturday Review, Cavalier, Progressive,* and *Playboy.* Songwriter, composer, and lyricist, including "This Could Be the Start of Something Big," 1956, and (with Ray Brown) "Gravy Waltz," 1963; also "Pretend You Don't See Her," "South Rampart Street Parade," "I Love You Today," "Impossible," and "Let's Go to Church Next Sunday Morning"; songs for films include "Picnic," "Houseboat," "On the Beach," "Sleeping Beauty," and "Bell, Book, and Candle." Composer of more than four-thousand songs and instrumental pieces, including the special compositions "The Mort Glosser March," 1985, and "Ten Feet Tall," for the Professional Football Hall of Fame, 1985.

OTHER SOURCES

Periodicals:
Discover, February, 1997, p. 82.
Emmy, September/October, 1989, p. 32.*

ALLEN, Woody 1935-

PERSONAL

Born Allen Stewart Konigsberg, December 1, 1935, in Brooklyn, NY; legal name, Heywood Allen; son of Martin (a waiter and jewelry engraver) and Nettie (maiden name, Cherry) Konigsberg; married Harlene Rosen, March 15, 1956 (divorced, 1962); married Louise Lasser (an actress), February 2, 1966 (divorced, 1969); married Soon-Yi Previn, December 22, 1997; children: Satchel O'Sullivan Farrow (with Mia Farrow); one daughter. *Education:* Attended New York University and City College (now of the City University of New York), both 1953. *Politics:* Democrat.

Addresses: *Office*—930 Fifth Avenue, New York, NY 10021.

Career: Actor, director, and screenwriter. National Broadcasting Corp., staff writer, including gag writer for such performers as Jack Paar, Garry Moore, Herb Shriner, 1953, Art Carney, 1958-59, Kaye Ballard, Buddy Hackett, and Carol Channing. As a stand-up comedian, appeared throughout the United States and Europe during the 1960s; plays jazz clarinet with New Orleans Funeral and Ragtime Orchestra, New York City, through 1997, then Eddie Davids New Orleans Jazz Band, New York City, 1997—.

Awards, Honors: Sylvania Award, 1957, for *The Sid Caesar Show;* Emmy Award nomination, 1957; Nebula Award, dramatic presentation, Science Fiction Writers of America, 1974, for *Sleeper;* Special Silver Bear Award, Berlin Film Festival, 1975; Golden Bear Award nomination, Berlin Film Festival, 1975, for *Love and Death;* Academy Awards, best director and best original screenplay, Academy Award nomination, best actor, British Academy of Film and Television Arts Awards, best film, best director, and best screenplay (with Marshall Brickman), British Academy of Film and Television Arts Award nomination, best actor, Golden Globe Award nominations, best director–motion picture, best motion picture actor–musical or comedy, and best screenplay (with Marshall Brickman), National Society of Film Critics' Award, best screenplay (with Marshall Brickman), Directors Guild of America Award, outstanding directorial achievement in motion pictures, New York Film Critics' Circle Awards, best director and best screenplay (with Marshall Brickman), Los Angeles Film Critics Association Award, best screenplay (with Marshall Brickman), all 1977, Bodil Award, Bodil Festival, best American film, 1978, all for *Annie Hall;* Academy Award nominations, best director and best original screenplay, Golden Globe Award nominations, best director–motion picture and best screenplay–motion picture, 1978, all for *Interiors;* Academy Award nomination, best original screenplay (with Marshall Brickman), British Academy of Film and Television Arts Awards, best film and best screenplay, British Academy of Film and Television Arts Award nominations, best actor and best direction, New York Film Critics' Award, best director, National Society of Film Critics Award, best director, 1979, Cesar Award, best foreign film, Bodil Award, Bodil Festival, best American film, 1980, all for *Manhattan;* Robert Honorary Award, Robert Festival, 1984; Golden Globe Award nomination, best performance by an actor in a motion picture-comedy/musical, British Academy of Film and Television Arts Award nomination, best original screenplay, Bodil Award, Bodil Festival, best American film, 1984, all for *Zelig;* Academy Award nominations, best director and best original screenplay, 1984, British Academy of Film and Television Arts Award, best original screenplay, Writers Guild of America Screen Award, best screenplay written directly for the screen, 1985, all for *Broadway Danny Rose;* Academy Award nomination, best original screenplay, British Academy of Film and Television Arts Awards, best film (with Robert Greenhut) and best original screenplay, New York Critics' Circle Award, best screenplay, all 1985, Golden Globe Award, best screenplay, Cesar Award, best foreign film, Bodil Award, Bodil Festival, best American film, 1986, all for *The Purple Rose of Cairo;* Laurel Award, lifetime achievement in the motion picture industry, Writers Guild of America, 1986; American Comedy Awards, funniest lead actor in a motion picture and Lifetime Achievement Award, George Schlatter Productions, both 1987, Academy Award, best original screenplay, Academy Award nomination, best director, British Academy of Film and Television Arts Awards, best director and best original screenplay, British Academy of Film and Television Arts Award nominations, best actor, best film (with Robert Greenhut), Directors Guild of America Award nomination, outstanding achievement in feature films, Golden Globe Award nominations, best director and best screenplay, London Film Critics' Award, best screenplay, London Film Critics' Award nomination, best director, Los Angeles Film Critics' Association Award, best screenplay, D. W. Griffith Award, best director, National Board of Review, New York Film Critics' Award, best director, National Board of Review Award, best director, Writers Guild of America Award, best screenplay written directly for the screen, 1986, Moussinac Prize, best foreign film, French Film Critics' Union, Bodil Award, Bodil Festival, best American film, 1987, all for *Hannah and Her Sisters;* Academy Award nomination, best original screenplay, and Writers Guild of America Award nomination, best screenplay written directly for the screen, 1987, British Academy Award nominations, best film (with Robert Greenhut) and best original screenplay, 1988, all for *Radio Days;* Academy Award nomination, best original screenplay, 1990, for *Alice;* Academy Award nominations, best director and best original screenplay, Writers Guild of America Award, best screenplay written directly for the screen, Edgar Allan Poe Award nomination, best movie, 1990, British Academy of Film and Television Arts Award nominations, best direction, best original screenplay, and best film (with Robert Greenhut), 1991, all for *Crimes* *and Misdemeanors;* Academy Award nomination, best original screenplay, British Academy of Film and Television Arts Award, best original screenplay, 1993, both for *Husbands and Wives;* Independent Spirit Award, best screenplay (with Doug McGrath), 1995, and Academy Award nominations, best original screenplay and best directing, British Academy of Film and Television Arts Award nomination, best original screenplay (with McGrath), 1996, all for *Bullets Over Broadway;* Golden Lion Award, Venice Film Festival, 1995; D.W. Griffith Award, Directors Guild of America, 1996; Academy Award nomination, best writing, screenplay written directly for the screen, 1996, for *Mighty Aphrodite;* Five Continents Award nomination, European Films Awards, 1997, for *Deconstructing Harry* and *Everyone Says I Love You;* Academy Fellowship, British Academy of Film and Television Arts, 1997; Academy Award nomination, best writing, screenplay written directly for the screen, and Cesar Award nomination, best foreign film, both 1998, for *Everyone Says I Love You.*

CREDITS

Film Appearances:

Victor Shakapopulis, *What's New, Pussycat?,* United Artists, 1965.

Narrator, host, and voice characterization, *What's Up, Tiger Lily?,* American International, 1966.

Jimmy Bond and Dr. Noah, *Charles K. Feldman's Casino Royale,* Columbia, 1967.

Virgil Starkwell, *Take the Money and Run,* Cinerama, 1969.

Fielding Mellish, *Bananas,* United Artists, 1971.

Allan Felix, *Play It Again, Sam* (also known as *Aspirins for Three*) Paramount, 1972.

Victor, Fabrizio, Fool, and Sperm, *Everything You Always Wanted to Know about Sex* (*but were afraid to ask),* United Artists, 1972.

Miles Monroe, *Sleeper,* United Artists, 1973.

Boris Dimitovich Grushenko, *Love and Death,* United Artists, 1975.

Howard Prince, *The Front,* Columbia, 1976.

Alvy Singer, *Annie Hall,* United Artists, 1977.

Isaac Davis, *Manhattan,* United Artists, 1979.

Sandy Bates, *Stardust Memories,* United Artists, 1980.

Andrew Hobbs, *A Midsummer Night's Sex Comedy,* Warner Bros., 1982.

Leonard Zelig, *Zelig,* Warner Bros., 1983.

Title role, *Broadway Danny Rose,* Orion, 1984.

Mickey Sachs, *Hannah and Her Sisters,* Orion, 1986.

Himself, *Fifty Years of Action!,* 1986.

Meeting Woody Allen (also known as *J.L.G. Meets W.A.*), 1986.

Narrator, *Radio Days,* Orion, 1987.

Mr. Alien, *King Lear,* Cannon, 1987.

Sheldon Mills, "Oedipus Wrecks," *New York Stories,* Buena Vista, 1989.

Cliff Stern, *Crimes and Misdemeanors,* Orion, 1989.

Nick, *Scenes from a Mall,* Buena Vista, 1991.

Kleinman, *Shadows and Fog,* Orion, 1992.

Gabe Roth, *Husbands and Wives,* TriStar, 1992.

Larry Lipton, *Manhattan Murder Mystery,* TriStar, 1993.

Lenny, *Mighty Aphrodite* (also known as *Eros*), Miramax, 1995.

Joe, *Everyone Says I Love You,* Miramax, 1996.

Harry Block, *Deconstructing Harry,* Fine Line, 1997.

(Uncredited) Theater director, *The Imposters,* Fox Searchlight Pictures,1998.

Voice of Z-4165, *Antz* (animated), DreamWorks Distribution, 1998.

Himself, *Wild Man Blues* (documentary), Fine Line, 1998.

Stuck on You, 1999.

Company Man, 1999.

Woody Allen Spring Project 1999, forthcoming.

Tex, *Picking up the Pieces,* forthcoming.

Film Director, Except Where Indicated:

Associate producer, *What's Up, Tiger Lily?,* American International, 1966.

Take the Money and Run, Cinerama, 1969.

Bananas, United Artists, 1971.

Everything You Always Wanted to Know about Sex (*but were afraid to ask),* United Artists, 1972.

Sleeper, United Artists, 1973.

Love and Death, United Artists, 1975.

Annie Hall, United Artists, 1977.

Interiors, United Artists, 1978.

Manhattan, United Artists, 1979.

Stardust Memories, United Artists, 1980.

A Midsummer Night's Sex Comedy, Warner Bros., 1982.

Zelig, Warner Bros., 1983.

Broadway Danny Rose, Orion, 1984.

The Purple Rose of Cairo, Orion, 1985.

Hannah and Her Sisters, Orion, 1986.

Radio Days, Orion, 1987.

September, Orion, 1987.

Another Woman, Orion, 1988.

"Oedipus Wrecks," *New York Stories,* Buena Vista, 1989.

Crimes and Misdemeanors, Orion, 1989.

Alice, Orion, 1990.

Husbands and Wives, TriStar, 1992.

Shadows and Fog, Orion, 1992.

Manhattan Murder Mystery, TriStar, 1993.

Bullets Over Broadway, Miramax, 1994.
Mighty Aphrodite (also known as *Eros*), Miramax, 1995.
Everyone Says I Love You, Miramax, 1996.
Deconstructing Harry, Fine Line, 1997.
Celebrity, Miramax, 1998.
Woody Allen Fall Project 1998, 1999.
Woody Allen Spring Project 1999, forthcoming.

Television Appearances; Specials:
The Best on Record, NBC, 1965.
Host, *Woody's First Special,* CBS, 1969.
The Woody Allen Special, NBC, 1969.
Plimpton! Did You Hear the One about . . .?, ABC, 1971.
The Sensational, Shocking, Wonderful, Wacky 70s, NBC, 1980.
Storytellers: The P.E.N. Celebration, PBS, 1987.
Martha Graham: The Dancer Revealed, 1994.
Cannes ... les 400 coups, 1997.
Canned Ham: Deconstructing Harry, Comedy Central, 1997.
Woody Allen: A to Z, Turner Classic Movies, 1997.
Himself, *AFI's 100 Years ... 100 Movies,* CBS, 1998.
NYTV: By the People Who Made It, PBS, 1998.
Sugar Ray Robinson: The Bright Lights and Dark Shadows of a Champion, HBO, 1998.

Also appeared in *Gene Kelly in New York.*

Television Appearances; Episodic:
Candid Camera, CBS, 1963.
The Andy Williams Show, NBC, 1965.
Guest host, *Hippodrome,* CBS, 1966.
Host, "Woody Allen Looks at 1967," *The Kraft Music Hall,* NBC, 1967.
"Martha Graham: The Dancer Revealed," *American Masters,* PBS, 1994.
Voice, "My Dinner with Woody," *Just Shoot Me,* NBC, 1997.

Also appeared on *The Dick Cavett Show,* ABC; *Hullabaloo,* NBC; and *The Tonight Show,* NBC.

Television Appearances; Movies:
Title role, *Men of Crisis: The Harvey Wallinger Story,* 1971.
Walter Hollander, *Don't Drink the Water,* ABC, 1994.
Al Lewis, *The Sunshine Boys,* CBS, 1995.

Television Appearances; Series:
Regular, *Hot Dog,* NBC, 1970-71.

Also appeared in *That Was the Week That Was.*

Television Work; Movies:
Director, *Don't Drink the Water,* ABC, 1994.

Stage Appearances:
(Broadway debut) Allan Felix, *Play It Again, Sam,* Broadhurst Theatre, 1969.

RECORDINGS

Albums:
Woody Allen, Colpix, 1964.
Woody Allen, Volume 2, Colpix, 1965.
Woody Allen, Stand-Up Comic: 1964-1968, United Artists Records, 1978.

Also recorded *Woody Allen, The Night Club Years.*

WRITINGS

Screenplays:
The Laughmaker, 1962.
What's New, Pussycat?, United Artists, 1965.
(With Frank Buxton, Len Maxwell, Louise Lasser, Mickey Rose, Julie Bennett, Kazuo Yamada, and Bryna Wilson) *What's Up, Tiger Lily?,* American International, 1966.
Charles K. Feldman's Casino Royale, 1967.
(With Rose) *Take the Money and Run,* Cinerama, 1969.
Don't Drink the Water (based on his stage play), 1969.
(With Rose) *Bananas,* United Artists, 1971, published in *Four Screenplays,* Random House, 1978.
Play It Again, Sam (based on his stage play; also known as *Aspirins for Three*), Paramount, 1972.
Everything You Always Wanted to Know about Sex (*but were afraid to ask)* (based on the book by David Ruben), United Artists, 1972.
(With Marshall Brickman; also composer) *Sleeper,* United Artists, 1973, published in *Four Screenplays,* Random House, 1978.
Love and Death, United Artists, 1975, published in *Four Screenplays,*Random House, 1978.
(With Brickman) *Annie Hall,* United Artists, 1977, published in *Four Screenplays,* Random House, 1978, and in *Four Films of Woody Allen,* Random House, 1982.
Interiors, United Artists, 1978, published in *Four Films of Woody Allen,* Random House, 1982.
(With Brickman) *Manhattan,* United Artists, 1979, published in *Four Films of Woody Allen,* Random House, 1982.
Stardust Memories, United Artists, 1980, published in *Four Films of Woody Allen,* Random House, 1982.

A Midsummer Night's Sex Comedy, Warner Bros., 1982.

Zelig, Warner Bros., 1983, published in *Three Films of Woody Allen,* Random House, 1987.

Broadway Danny Rose, Orion, 1984, published in *Three Films of Woody Allen,* Random House, 1987.

The Purple Rose of Cairo, Orion, 1985, published in *Three Films of Woody Allen,* Random House, 1987.

Hannah and Her Sisters, Orion, 1986, published by Random House, 1986.

Radio Days, Orion, 1987.

September, Orion, 1987.

Another Woman, Orion, 1988.

"Oedipus Wrecks" in *New York Stories,* Buena Vista, 1989.

Crimes and Misdemeanors, Orion, 1989.

Alice, Orion, 1990.

Husbands and Wives, TriStar, 1992.

Shadows and Fog, Orion, 1992.

Manhattan Murder Mystery, TriStar, 1993.

(With Douglas McGrath) *Bullets Over Broadway,* Miramax, 1994.

Mighty Aphrodite (also known as *Eros*), Miramax, 1995.

Everyone Says I Love You, Miramax, 1996.

Deconstructing Harry, Fine Line, 1997.

Count Mercury Goes to the Suburbs, 1997.

Celebrity, Miramax, 1998.

Woody Allen Fall Project 1998, 1999.

Woody Allen Spring Project 1999, forthcoming.

Film Composer:

Sleeper, 1973.

Television Movies:

Men of Crisis: The Harvey Wallinger Story, 1971.

Don't Drink the Water (based on his stage play), ABC, 1994.

Television Specials:

(With Larry Gelbart) *The Sid Caesar Show,* NBC, 1958.

(With Gelbart) *Hooray for Love,* CBS, 1960.

Woody's First Special, CBS, 1969.

(With Brickman and Rose) *The Woody Allen Special,* NBC, 1969.

Television Series:

The Sid Caesar Show, 1957.

Staff writer for *The Colgate Comedy Hour,* NBC; *Your Show of Shows,* NBC; *The Pat Boone-Chevy Showroom,* ABC; *The Tonight Show,* NBC; *The Garry Moore Show,* CBS.

Stage Plays:

(Contributor) *From A to Z* (revue), Plymouth Theatre, New York City,1960.

Don't Drink the Water, Morosco Theatre, New York City, 1966, published by Samuel French (New York City), 1967.

Play It Again, Sam, Broadhurst Theatre, 1969, published by Random House, 1969.

God: A Comedy in One Act, published by Samuel French, 1975.

The Floating Light Bulb, Vivian Beaumont Theatre, New York City, 1981, published by Random House, 1982.

Death Defying Acts, 1995.

Radio Plays:

Death: A Comedy in One Act (staged as *Death Knocks*), 1975, published by Samuel French, 1975.

God, performed by the National Radio Theatre of Chicago, 1978, published by Samuel French, 1975.

Other:

Getting Even, Random House, 1971.

Without Feathers (humor collection), Random House, 1975.

Non-Being and Somethingness (collections from the comic strip *Inside Woody Allen*), illustrated by Stuart Hemple, Random House, 1978.

Side Effects (humor collection), Random House, 1980.

The Lunatic's Tale, Redpath Press, 1986.

The Illustrated Woody Allen Reader, 1993.

Contributor to magazines, including *New Yorker, Saturday Review, Playboy,* and *Esquire.*

OTHER SOURCES

Books:

Adler, Bill, and Jeff Feinman, *Woody Allen: Clown Prince of American Humor,* Pinnacle Books (New York City), 1975.

Anobile, Richard, editor, *Woody Allen's "Play It Again, Sam,"* Grosset (New York City), 1977.

Brode, Douglas, *Woody Allen: His Films and Career,* Citadel (Secaucus, NJ), 1985.

Cohen, Sarah Blacher, editor, *From Hester Street to Hollywood: The Jewish-American Stage and Screen,* Indiana University Press (Bloomington, IN), 1983.

De Navacelle, Thierry, *Woody Allen on Location*, Morrow (New York City), 1987.

Dictionary of Literary Biography, Volume 44: *American Screenwriters, Second Series*, Gale (Detroit, MI), 1986.

Guthrie, Lee, *Woody Allen: A Biography*, Drake, 1978.

Hirsch, F., *Love, Sex, Death, and the Meaning of Life: Woody Allen's Comedy*, McGraw (New York City), 1981.

Kael, Pauline, *Reeling*, Little, Brown (Boston, MA), 1976.

Lahr, John, *Automatic Vaudeville: Essays on Star Turns*, Knopf (New York City), 1984.

Lax, Eric, *On Being Funny: Woody Allen and Comedy*, Charterhouse, 1975.

Lax, Eric, *Woody Allen*, Knopf, 1991.

Palmer, M., *Woody Allen*, Proteus Press, 1980.

Yacowar, Maurice, *Loser Takes All: The Comic Art of Woody Allen*, Ungar (New York City), 1979.

Periodicals:

Atlantic, August, 1971; December, 1982; May, 1985.

Comparative Drama, winter, 1980-81.

Cosmopolitan, February, 1995, p. 216.

Esquire, April, 1987; October, 1994, p. 84.

Film Comment, March/April, 1974; March/April, 1978; May/June, 1979; May/June, 1986.

Film Quarterly, winter, 1972; March/April, 1987.

Newsweek, July 20, 1998, p. 67.

New York Times Magazine, January 7, 1973; April 22, 1979; January 19, 1986.

People Weekly, August 12, 1995, p. 39; January 12, 1998, p. 63.

Psychology Today, May-June, 1993, p. 22.

Rolling Stone, April 9, 1987.

Time, October 23, 1989, p. 76; March 18, 1996, p. 89; December 9, 1996, p. 81.

Times (London), May 24, 1990; July 21, 1990.*

ANDERSON, Richard Dean 1950-

PERSONAL

Born January 23, 1950, in Minneapolis, MN; son of Stuart Anderson (a jazz musician, schoolteacher, and director); mother, an artist. *Education:* Attended St. Cloud State College and Ohio University; studied acting with Peggy Feury.

Addresses: *Agent*—International Creative Management, 8942 Wilshire Blvd., Beverly Hills, CA 90211.

Career: Actor and producer. Member of the rock band Ricky Dean and Dante; street mime, jester, and juggler with an Elizabethan-style cabaret, Los Angeles; Improvisation Theatre, stage manager; writer, director, and actor at Marineland.

CREDITS

Television Appearances; Series:

Dr. Jeff Webber, *General Hospital*, ABC, 1976-81.

Adam McFadden, *Seven Brides for Seven Brothers*, CBS, 1982-83.

Lieutenant Simon Adams, *Emerald Point, N.A.S.*, CBS, 1983-84.

Title role, *MacGyver*, ABC, 1985-92.

Ernest Pratt/Nicodemus, *Legend*, syndicated, 1995.

Firehouse, CBS, 1996.

Television Appearances; Movies:

Tony Kaiser, *Ordinary Heroes*, ABC, 1986.

Ray Bellano, *Through the Eyes of a Killer* (also known as *The Master Builder*), CBS, 1992.

Jack Rourke, *In the Eyes of a Stranger*, CBS, 1992.

Title role, *MacGyver: Trail to Doomsday*, ABC, 1994.

Title role, *MacGyver: Lost Treasure of Atlantis*, ABC, 1994.

Bradley Mathews, *Beyond Betrayal*, CBS, 1994.

Bill Parish, *Past the Bleachers*, ABC, 1995.

Television Appearances; Specials:

Battle of the Network Stars, ABC, 1984.

The American Red Cross Emergency Test, ABC, 1990.

Victory and Valor: A Special Olympics All-Star Celebration, ABC, 1991.

The 18th Annual People's Choice Awards, CBS, 1992.

Jim Thorpe Pro Sports Awards, ABC, 1994.

Host, *The World of Audubon 10th Anniversary Special*, TBS, 1994.

Television Appearances; Pilots:

Brian Parker, *The Parkers* (broadcast as an episode of *The Facts of Life*), NBC, 1981.

Television Appearances; Episodic:

Appeared in an episode of *The Love Boat*, ABC.

Television Work; Series:

Executive producer, *Legend*, syndicated, 1995.

Television Work; Movies:

Executive producer, *MacGyver: Trail to Doomsday*, ABC, 1994.

Executive producer, *MacGyver: Lost Treasure of Atlantis*, ABC, 1994.

Film Appearances:

Dr. Jeff Webber, *Young Doctors in Love,* ABC, 1982.
Spud, *Odd Jobs,* TriStar, 1986.

Stage Appearances:

Appeared in *Superman in the Bones,* Pilgrimage Theatre, Los Angeles.*

ANISTON, Jennifer 1969-

PERSONAL

Original surname, Anistonapoulos; born February 11, 1969, in Sherman Oaks, CA; daughter of John (an actor) and Nancy (an actress and photographer) Aniston. *Education:* Graduated from the High School for the Performing Arts, 1987.

Addresses: *Office*—c/o Hedrick Whitesell, Creative Artists Agency, 9830 Wilshire Blvd, Beverly Hills, CA 90212.

Career: Actress. Has worked as a waitress and in telemarketing.

CREDITS

Stage Appearances:

Emily, *For Dear Life,* Martinson Hall, New York City, 1988-89.

Film Appearances:

Tory, *Leprechaun,* Trimark, 1993.
Renee, *She's the One,* Twentieth Century-Fox, 1996.
Debbie,*'Til There Was You,* Paramount Pictures, 1997.
Kate, *Picture Perfect,* Twentieth Century-Fox, 1997.
Allison, *Dream For an Insomniac,* Columbia/TriStar Home Video, 1998.
Nina Borowski, *The Object of My Affection,* Twentieth Century-Fox, 1998.
Joanna, *Office Space,* Twentieth Century-Fox, 1999.
Voice of Annie Hughes, *The Iron Giant* (animated), Warner Bros., 1999.

Television Appearances; Episodic:

Suzie Brooks, "Twisted Sister," *Herman's Head,* Fox, 1992.
Kiki Wilson, "Nowhere to Run," *Quantum Leap,* NBC, 1992.
Suzie Brooks, "Jay Is for Jealousy," *Herman's Head,* Fox, 1993.
Linda Campbell, "Who Killed the Beauty Queen?," *Burke's Law,* ABC, 1994.
Herself, "Conflict of Interest," *The Larry Sanders Show,* HBO, 1995.
CPA Suzanne, "Follow the Clams?," *Partners,* Fox, 1995.
Herself, "Ellen: A Hollywood Tribute Part 2," *Ellen,* ABC, 1997.
Voice of Galatea, "Dream Date," *Disney's Hercules* (animated), ABC/syndicated, 1998.
"Rainforest Schmainforest," *Southpark,* Comedy Central, 1999.

Television Appearances; Series:

Jeannie Bueller, *Ferris Bueller,* NBC, 1990.
Courtney Walker, *Molloy,* Fox, 1990.
The Edge, Fox, 1992.
Madeline Cooper, *Muddling Through,* CBS, 1994.
Rachel Green, *Friends* (also known as *Friends Like Us*), NBC, 1994—.

Television Appearances; Movies:

Ava Schector, *Camp Cucamonga,* NBC, 1990.

Television Appearances; Specials:

Comic Relief VII, HBO, 1995.
47th Annual Primetime Emmy Awards, Fox, 1995.
The 22nd Annual Daytime Emmy Awards, NBC, 1995.
The 10th Annual American Comedy Awards, 1996.
Celine, Aretha, Gloria, Shania and Mariah: Divas Live, VH-1, 1998.

OTHER SOURCES

Periodicals:

Entertainment Weekly, December 15, 1995, pp. 29-30.
People Weekly, December 25, 1995, pp. 92-93; August 11, 1997, p. 98.
Rolling Stone, March 7, 1996, pp. 34-38, 60-61.
Us, February, 1996.*

ANNIS, Francesca 1944(?)-

PERSONAL

Born May 14, 1944 (some sources say 1946), in London, England; daughter of Anthony and Mariquita Annis; children: (with Patrick Wiseman) one son, two daughters.

Addresses: *Agent*—International Creative Management, 76 Oxford Street, London, England W1N 0AX.

Career: Actress. Royal Shakespeare Company, member of company, 1975-78.

Awards, Honors: British Academy of Film and Television Arts Awards, both best television actress, both 1978, for *Lillie* and *The Comedy of Errors;* British Academy of Film and Television Arts Award nomination, best actress, 1999, for *Reckless: The Movie.*

CREDITS

Television Appearances; Miniseries:
Estella, *Great Expectations,* 1967.
Title role, *Madame Bovary,* BBC, then broadcast as a segment of *Masterpiece Theatre,* PBS, 1976.
Lillie Langtry, *Edward the King,* 1979.
Lillie Langtry, *Lillie,* London Weekend Television, then broadcast as a segment of *Masterpiece Theatre,* PBS, 1979.
Tuppence Beresford, "Partners in Crime" (also known as "Agatha Christie's Partners in Crime"), *Mystery!,* PBS, 1986.
Prudence "Tuppence" Cowley, "The Secret Adversary," *Mystery!,* PBS, 1987.
Lily Amberville, *I'll Take Manhattan,* 1987.
Paula Croxley, *Inside Story,* 1988.
Jacqueline Kennedy, *The Richest Man in the World: The Story of Aristotle Onassis* (also known as *Onassis: The Richest Man in the World, Ari: The Private Life of Aristotle Onassis,* and *Onassis*), ABC, 1988.
Anna Fairley, *Reckless,* PBS, 1997.

Television Appearances; Movies:
Girls in Uniform, 1967.
The Wood Demon, 1974.
Stronger than the Sun, 1977.
Galina, *Coming Out of the Ice,* CBS, 1982.
Lily Amberville, *I'll Take Manhattan,* CBS, 1987.
Katya Princip, *The Gravy Train Goes East,* 1991.
Leila, *Weep No More, My Lady,* syndicated, 1992.
Sophie, *Doomsday Gun,* HBO, 1994.
Bonnie Fielding, *Dalziel and Pascoe: An Autumn Shroud,* Arts and Entertainment, 1996.
Celia Harcourt, *Deadly Summer,* 1997.
Anna Fairley, *Reckless: The Movie* (also known as *Reckless: The Sequel*), 1998.

Television Appearances; Specials:
Tracy Conway, *Sign It Death,* 1974.
Luciana, *The Comedy of Errors,* 1978.
Lady Frances Derwent, *Why Didn't They Ask Evans?,* syndicated, 1981.
Tuppence Beresford, *Partners in Crime* (Series II), 1986.
Luciana, *The Comedy of Errors* (also known as *Shakespeare Festival: The Comedy of Errors*), Arts and Entertainment, 1990.
Backstage at Masterpiece Theatre: A 20th Anniversary Special, PBS, 1991.
A Slight Case of Murder, HBO, 1996.

Television Appearances; Episodic:
Sheila, "That's Two of Us Sorry," *Secret Agent,* CBS, 1965.
Judy, "No Marks for Servility," *Secret Agent,* CBS, 1965.
Tracy Conway, "Sign It Death," *Thriller,* ABC, 1974.
"The Maze," *Shades of Darkness,* 1984.
Penelope St. Clair, "Deja Vu," *Magnum, P.I.,* CBS, 1985.
Katherine O'Shea, "Parnell and the Englishwoman," *Masterpiece Theatre,* PBS, 1991.

Television Appearances; Series:
Angela Berridge, *Between the Lines* (also known as *Inside the Line*), 1992.

Television Appearances; Other:
A Pin to See the Peepshow, 1973.
The Ragazza, 1978.
Absolute Hell, 1991.

Also appeared in *Penny Gold; Love Story; Danger Man; The Human Jungle.*

Film Appearances:
Sylvia, *The Cat Gang,* Realist/CFF, 1959.
Young Jacobites, 1959.
Wanda, *His and Hers,* Sabre/Eros, 1961.
Phyl, *West 11,* Associated British/Warner Bros./Pathe, 1963.
Annie Jones, *The Eyes of Annie Jones,* Twentieth Century-Fox, 1963.
Eiras, *Cleopatra,* Twentieth Century-Fox, 1963.
Jean, *Saturday Night Out,* Compton Cameo, 1964.
June, *Crooks in Cloisters,* Associated British/Warner Bros./Pathe, 1964.
Sheila Upward, *Murder Most Foul,* Metro-Goldwyn-Mayer, 1964.
Gwen, *Flipper's New Adventure* (also known as *Flipper and the Pirates*), Metro-Goldwyn-Mayer, 1964.
Jean Parker, *Run with the Wind,* GEFD, 1966.
Sally Feathers, *The Pleasure Girls,* Times Films, 1966.

Arabella Dainton, *The Walking Stick,* Metro-Goldwyn-Mayer, 1970.
Uptight girl, *The Sky Pirate,* Filmmakers Distribution Center, 1970.
Lady Macbeth, *Macbeth,* Columbia, 1971.
Kate, *Stronger Than the Sun,* BBC, 1980.
Widow of the Web, *Krull* (also known as *The Dungeons of Krull,* and *Krull: Invaders of the Black Fortress*), Columbia, 1983.
Lady Jessica, *Dune,* Dino De Laurentiis/Universal, 1984.
Dubarry, *El rio de oro* (also known as *The Golden River*), Tesauro/Incine S.A./Fedèral, 1986.
Mrs. Wellington, *Under the Cherry Moon,* Warner Bros., 1986.
Voice of Juliet, *Romeo-Juliet,* 1990.
Sally Hall, *Headhunters,* 1992.
Edward the King, 1997.
Milk, 1999.
Val Dryden, *The Debt Collector,* 1999.
Kotichka, *Onegin,* 1999.

Stage Appearances:
Ophelia, *Hamlet,* Lunt-Fontanne Theatre, New York City, 1969.
Isabella, *Measure for Measure,* Royal Shakespeare Company, Stratford-on-Avon, England, 1974.
Juliet, *Romeo and Juliet,* Royal Shakespeare Company, Stratford-on-Avon, 1976.
Cressida, *Troilus and Cressida,* Royal Shakespeare Company, Stratford-on-Avon, 1976.
Miranda, *The Tempest,* Royal Shakespeare Company, Stratford-on-Avon, 1976.
Luciana, *The Comedy of Errors* (musical), Royal Shakespeare Company, Stratford-on-Avon, 1976.
Juliet, *Romeo and Juliet,* Royal Shakespeare Company, Aldwych Theatre, London, 1977.
Cressida, *Troilus and Cressida,* Royal Shakespeare Company, Aldwych Theatre, 1977.
Natalya, *A Month in the Country,* National Theatre, London, England, 1981.
Masha, *Three Sisters,* Albery Theatre, London, England, 1987.
Melitta, *Mrs. Klein,* National Theatre, London, England, 1988.
Rebekka West, *Rosmersholm,* Young Vic Theatre, London, 1992.
Mrs. Erlynne, *Lady Windermere's Fan,* Birmingham Repertory Theatre, Albery Theatre, London, 1994.
Hamlet, Belasco Theatre, New York City, 1995.

Also appeared in *The Passion Flower Hotel; The Heretic.**

APPEL, Richard 1964-

PERSONAL

Born in 1964; married Mona Simpson, 1991; children: Gabriel. *Education:* Graduated from Harvard University, 1985, and Harvard Law School.

Career: Producer, writer, and editor. Clerk for Judge John Walker, U.S. District Court, New York, 1987-89; assistant U.S. attorney, Southern District of New York, 1990-93.

Awards, Honors: Emmy Awards, outstanding animated program, 1997 and 1998, for *The Simpsons.*

CREDITS

Television Producer; Series:
The Simpsons, Fox, 1989—.
King of the Hill, Fox, 1998—.

WRITINGS

Television Series:
The Simpsons, Fox, 1994-98.

OTHER SOURCES

Periodicals:
Chicago Tribune Magazine, 1999, p.14.*

ARAKI, Gregg 1959-

PERSONAL

Born in 1959, in Los Angeles, CA. *Education:* Attended University of California, B.A. (film studies), 1982; University of Southern California, M.F.A. (film production), 1985.

Addresses: c/o Steven Pegner, Inc., 248 West 73rd St., New York, New York 10023.

Career: Producer, director, screenwriter, editor, and cinematographer.

Awards, Honors: Ernest Artaria Award, Locarno International Film Festival, 1987, for *Three Bewildered People in the Night;* Best Film nomination, Catalonian International Film Festival, 1997, for *Nowhere.*

CREDITS

Film Work; Director, Except Where Indicated:

Three Bewildered People in the Night, Desperate Pictures, Ltd., 1987.

(And producer) *The Long Weekend (o'despair),* Desperate Pictures, Ltd., 1989.

The Living End, Strand Releasing, 1992.

(And producer) *Totally F***ed Up,* Strand Releasing, 1993.

(And producer) *The Doom Generation,* Trimark Pictures, 1995.

(And producer) *Nowhere,* Fine Line Features, 1997.

(And producer) *Splendor,* Souvlaki Space Station, 1999.

Other Film Work:

Director of photography, *Three Bewildered People in the Night,* Desperate Pictures Ltd., 1987.

Cinematography, *The Long Weekend (o'despair),* Desperate Pictures Ltd., 1989.

Director of photography, *The Living End,* Strand Releasing, 1992.

Cinematography, *Totally F***ed Up,* Strand Releasing, 1993.

Film Appearances:

Mod Fuck Explosion, 1994.

Himself, *At Sundance,* 1995.

Color of a Brisk and Leaping Day, 1996.

Television Appearances; Series:

American Cinema, PBS, 1995.

Television Work; Movies:

Assistant to co-producer, *A Flight For Jenny,* NBC, 1986.

Assistant, *Can You Feel Me Dancing?,* NBC, 1986.

Production assistant, *On Fire,* ABC, 1987.

WRITINGS

Screenplays:

Three Bewildered People in the Night, Desperate Pictures Ltd., 1987.

The Long Weekend (o'despair), Desperate Pictures Ltd., 1989.

The Living End, Strand Releasing, 1992.

*Totally F***ed Up,* Strand Releasing, 1993.

The Doom Generation, Trimark Pictures, 1995.

Nowhere, Fine Line Features, 1997.

Splendor, Souvlaki Space Station, 1999.

OTHER SOURCES

Periodicals:

Village Voice, May 13, 1997, p. 88.*

ARGENZIANO, Carmen 1943-
(Carmine Argenziano)

PERSONAL

Full name, Carmen Antimo Argenziano; surname is pronounced "Ar-jen-zi-ano" (rhymes with "piano"); born October 27, 1943, in Sharon, PA; son of Joseph Guy (a restaurateur) and Elizabeth Stella (Falvo) Argenziano. *Education:* Attended Youngstown University; trained for the stage at the American Academy of Dramatic Arts and the Actors' Studio; also studied with Lee Grant, Michael V. Gazzo, Milton Katselas, and Sanford Meisner.

Addresses: *Agent*—Gold/Marshak Associates, 3500 West Olive Ave., Suite 1400, Burbank, CA 91505.

Career: Actor.

Member: Academy of Motion Picture Arts and Sciences, Actors' Studio.

Awards, Honors: *Drama-Logue* Award, 1988, for *El Salvador; Drama-Logue* Award and *Los Angeles Weekly* Award, both for *Last Lucid Moment;* Los Angeles Drama Critics' Award and *Los Angeles Weekly* Award, both for *A Prayer for My Daughter.*

CREDITS

Stage Appearances:

(Stage debut) Coffee house poet, *The Hairy Falsetto,* Fourth Street Theatre, New York City, 1965.

A View from the Bridge, Strasberg Institute, Los Angeles, 1981.

John Fletcher, *El Salvador,* GNU Theatre, Los Angeles, 1988.

Also appeared with the Center Theatre Group, Mark Taper Forum, Los Angeles, CA, 1983; and in *Last Lucid Moment,* Los Angeles; *A Prayer for My Daughter,* Los Angeles; *Sweet Bird of Youth; Made in America.*

Film Appearances:

Student, *Cover Me Babe,* Twentieth Century-Fox, 1970.

Gang member, *The Jesus Trip,* Emco, 1971.
Jay Kaufman, *Punishment Park,* Francoise, 1971.
Flavio, *The Hot Box,* New World, 1972.
(As Carmine Argenziano) Second Hawk, *The Outside Man,* United Artists, 1973.
The Slams, Metro-Goldwyn-Mayer, 1973.
Michael's bodyguard, *The Godfather, Part II,* Paramount, 1974.
Caged Heat, New World, 1974.
Supermarket manager, *Crazy Mama,* New World, 1975.
Jack McGurn, *Capone,* Twentieth Century-Fox, 1975.
Lieutenant, *Shark's Treasure,* United Artists, 1975.
Brian, *Vigilante Force,* United Artists, 1976.
Jennings, *Two-Minute Warning,* Universal, 1976.
Death Force, Capricorn Three, 1978.
Dr. Mandrakis, *When a Stranger Calls,* Columbia, 1979.
Tony Annese, *Mystique,* Telecine International/Qui, 1981.
D'Ambrosia, *Sudden Impact,* Warner Bros., 1983.
Ron Bell, *Heartbreakers,* Orion, 1984.
Stan, *Into the Night,* Universal, 1985.
Voice of Dagg, *Starchaser: The Legend of Orin* (animated), Atlantic, 1985.
Matty, *Dangerously Close,* Cannon, 1986.
Detective Russo, *Naked Vengeance* (also known as *Satan Vengeance*), Concorde, 1986.
Lieutenant Leonard, *Under Cover,* Cannon, 1987.
Board member, *Big Business,* Buena Vista, 1988.
District Attorney Paul Rudolph, *The Accused,* Paramount, 1988.
Molina, *Stand and Deliver,* Warner Bros., 1988.
Zayas, *Red Scorpion,* Shapiro/Glickenhaus Entertainment, 1989.
Lieutenant Grimes, *The First Power,* Orion, 1990.
Transit, 1990.
Jerome Lurie, *Unlawful Entry,* Twentieth Century-Fox, 1992.
Lieutenant Stein, *Dead Connection,* Gramercy, 1994.
Abe Weinstein, *Rave Review,* 1994.
Don Alfonzo, *Don Juan DeMarco,* New Line Cinema, 1995.
Phil Hawkes, *The Tie That Binds,* Buena Vista, 1995.

Television Appearances; Series:
Dr. Nathan Solt, *HeartBeat,* ABC, 1988-89.
Charles "Chick" Sterling, *Booker,* Fox, 1989-90.
Lieutenant Anthony Bartoli, *Crime & Punishment,* NBC, 1993.

Television Appearances; Miniseries:
Adam Brand, *Once an Eagle,* NBC, 1977.
From Here to Eternity, NBC, 1979.

Television Appearances; Pilots:
Twin Detectives, ABC, 1976.
Santeen, *The 3,000 Mile Chase,* NBC, 1977.
Kingston, *The Phoenix,* ABC, 1981.
Varela, *Waco and Rhinehart* (also known as *U.S. Marshals: Waco and Rhinehart*), ABC, 1987.
Tony, *Remo Williams,* ABC, 1988.

Television Appearances; Movies:
Wheeler, *Search for the Gods,* ABC, 1975.
Lieutenant, *Kill Me If You Can,* NBC, 1977.
Cameraman, *Hot Rod* (also known as *Rebel of the Road*), ABC, 1979.
Ed Ainsworth, *Quarterback Princess,* CBS, 1983.
Rooney, *The Last Ninja,* ABC, 1983.
Lieutenant Clifford, *Best Kept Secrets,* ABC, 1984.
Colonel Pruett, *Fatal Vision,* NBC, 1984.
Robert Walker, *Between Two Women,* ABC, 1986.
The Man Who Fell to Earth, ABC, 1987.
Judge, *Too Good to Be True* (also known as *Leave Her to Heaven*), NBC, 1988.
MacDonald, *The Watch Commander* (also known as *Police Story: The Watch Commander*), ABC, 1988.
Roy Simmons, *Baja Oklahoma,* HBO, 1988.
Sam Liberace, *Liberace,* ABC, 1988.
Morelli, *A Mom for Christmas,* NBC, 1990.
Maddock, *Knight Rider 2000,* NBC, 1991.
First Officer Bill Records, *A Thousand Heroes* (also known as *Crash Landing: The Rescue of Flight 232*), ABC, 1992.
Assistant District Attorney Harvey Mellors, *Perry Mason: The Case of the Skin-Deep Scandal* (also known as *Perry Mason: The Case of the Unhappy Birthday*), NBC, 1993.
Triumph over Disaster: The Hurricane Andrew Story, NBC, 1993.
Alfredo Sezero, *The Burning Season* (also known as *The Life and Death of Chico Mendes*), HBO, 1994.
Dr. Cantore, *Moment of Truth: To Walk Again* (also known as *Moment of Truth: Fighting Back*), NBC, 1994.
Jack Guthrie, *Moment of Truth: Cradle of Conspiracy* (also known as *Moment of Truth: To Sell a Child*), NBC, 1994.
Against the Wall (also known as *Attica: Line of Fire* and *Attica! Attica!*), HBO, 1994.
Buddy Fortune, *In the Line of Duty: Kidnapped* (also known as *In the Line of Duty: Taxman*), NBC, 1995.

Television Appearances; Episodic:
Stone, ABC, 1980.
Anarumo, *Cagney and Lacey,* CBS, 1986.
Neil Robertson, *L.A. Law,* NBC, 1986.

Mel, *Designing Women*, CBS, 1987.
Dr. Schneider, *Hunter*, NBC, 1987.
Mr. Mendez, *Coming of Age*, CBS, 1988.

Also appeared in *Scarecrow and Mrs. King*, CBS; *Cheers*, NBC; *Hill Street Blues*, NBC; *T.J. Hooker*, ABC; *Lou Grant*, CBS.

Other Television Appearances:
Appeared in (television debut) *Judd, for the Defense*, ABC.*

ARGENZIANO, Carmine
See ARGENZIANO, Carmen

ARMITAGE, Frank
See CARPENTER, John

ARMSTRONG, Curtis 1953-

PERSONAL

Born November 27, 1953, in Detroit, MI; son of Robert Leroy and Norma E. (a teacher; maiden name, D'Amico) Armstrong. *Education:* Attended Oakland University, 1973-75; studied acting at the Academy of Dramatic Arts.

Addresses: *Agent*—Paradigm, 10100 Santa Monica Blvd., 25th Floor, Los Angeles, CA 90067.

Career: Actor. Co-founder, Roadside Attractions, Inc.

CREDITS

Film Appearances:
Miles, *Risky Business*, Warner Bros., 1983.
Booger, *Revenge of the Nerds*, Twentieth Century-Fox, 1984.
Dennis Gladstone, *Bad Medicine*, Twentieth Century-Fox, 1985.
Charles De Mar, *Better Off Dead*, Warner Bros., 1985.
Goov, *The Clan of the Cave Bear*, Warner Bros., 1986.
Ack Ack Raymond, *One Crazy Summer*, Warner Bros., 1986.
Booger, *Revenge of the Nerds II: Nerds in Paradise*, Twentieth Century-Fox, 1987.
Country Jake, *The Adventures of Huck Finn*, Buena Vista, 1993.

Also appeared in *How I Got into College*, Twentieth Century-Fox; and *Big Bully*, Morgan Creek.

Television Appearances; Series:
Herbert Viola, *Moonlighting*, ABC, 1986-89.

Television Appearances; Movies:
Arnold Pishkin, *Hi Honey, I'm Dead*, Fox, 1991.
Dudley "Booger" Dawson, *Revenge of the Nerds III: The Next Generation*, Fox, 1992.
Booger Dawson, *Revenge of the Nerds IV: Nerds in Love*, Fox, 1994.

Also appeared in *Country Comfort*.

Television Appearances; Specials:
Barry Delbert, *Public Enemy Number 2*, Showtime, 1991.
Tom, "The Parsley Garden," *ABC Weekend Specials*, ABC, 1992.
Alvin Gershowitz, *Sex, Shock and Censorship in the 90s*, Showtime, 1993.

Television Appearances; Episodic:
Appeared in episodes of *Grand*, NBC; *Murphy Brown*, CBS; *Parker Lewis Can't Lose*, syndicated; *Mann and Machine*, syndicated; *Sirens*, ABC; *M.A.N.T.I.S.*, Fox; *Cybill*, CBS; and *Lois and Clark*, ABC.

Stage Appearances:
The Corn Is Green, Meadow Brook Theatre, Rochester, MI, 1977.
The Caine Mutiny Court-Martial, Meadow Brook Theatre, 1978.
The boy, *The Irish Hebrew Lesson*, Colonnades Theatre Lab, New York City, 1980.
Cooney, *Guests of the Nation*, Colonnades Theatre Lab, New York City, 1980.
The Life of Galileo, Pittsburgh Public Theatre, Pittsburgh, PA, 1981.
Moliere in Spite of Himself, Hartman Theatre Company, Stamford, CT, 1981.
The reporter, *How I Got That Story*, Attic Theatre, Detroit, MI, 1983.
Present Laughter, Meadow Brook Theatre, 1985.
Lord Fancourt Babberley, *Charley's Aunt*, Totem Pole Playhouse, Fayetteville, PA, 1990.

Also appeared off-Broadway in *El Hermano;* in regional productions of *Dracula*, *Arsenic and Old Lace*, and *A Midsummer Night's Dream;* and with Meadow Brook Theatre, 1975-85; New Jersey Shakespeare Festival, Madison, NJ, 1981; and Attic Theatre.

Major Tours:
Young Charlie, *Da,* U.S. cities, 1979-80.*

ARRLEY, Richmond
See NOONAN, Tom

ATTENBOROUGH, Richard 1923-

PERSONAL

Full name, Richard Samuel Attenborough; born August 29, 1923, in Cambridge, England; son of Frederick Levi (a scholar and academic administrator) and Mary (Clegg) Attenborough; married Sheila Beryl Grant Sim (an actress), January 22, 1945; children: Michael, Jane, Charlotte. *Education:* Studied acting at the Royal Academy of Dramatic Art, 1941. *Politics:* Social Democratic party. *Avocational interests:* Listening to music, collecting paintings and sculpture, watching soccer.

Addresses: *Office*—Lambeth Productions, Beaver Lodge, Richmond Green Surrey TW9 1NQ, England. *Agent*—Martin Baum, Creative Artists Agency, 9830 Wilshire Blvd., Beverly Hills, CA 90212.

Career: Actor, producer, and director. Founder (with Bryan Forbes), Beaver Films (a production company), 1959; founder, Allied Film Makers (a production company), 1960; chair, Royal Academy of Dramatic Art, 1970; governor, National Film School, 1970-81; chair, Capital Radio, 1972—; chair, Duke of York's Theatre, 1979—; deputy chair, Channel Four Television, 1980-86, chair, 1987—; director and chair, Goldcrest Films, 1981-85, (renamed Goldcrest Films and Television) deputy chair, 1985—; president, Brighton Festival, 1984—; chair, Sussex University Arts Center Board. Combined Theatrical Charities Appeals Council, 1964—; director, Chelsea Football Club (soccer), 1969-82; pro-chancellor, Sussex University, 1970—; president, Muscular Dystrophy Group of Great Britain, 1971—; vice president, Save the Children Fund, 1971—; trustee, Tate Gallery, London, 1976—; chair, Committee of Inquiry into the Arts and Disabled People, 1983-85; president, Gandhi Foundation, 1983—. *Military service:* Royal Air Force, Film Unit, 1942-46.

Member: British Actors' Equity Association (council member, 1949-73), Cinematograph Films Council (1967-73), Arts Council of Great Britain (1970-73), British Film Institute (governor and chair, 1982—), British Academy of Film and Television Arts (vice president, 1971—), Actors' Charitable Trust (chair), Garrick Club, Beefstake Club, Green Room Club.

Awards, Honors: Leverhulme scholarship, 1940; Bancroft Medal from the Royal Academy of Dramatic Art, 1942; Best Actor Awards, Variety Club of Great Britain, 1959 and 1965; Best Actor Awards, San Sebastian Film Festival, 1961 and 1964; British Academy of Film and Television Arts Award, best British actor, 1964, for *Guns at Batasi* and *Seance on a Wet Afternoon;* San Sebastian Film Festival Award, 1964, for *Seance on a Wet Afternoon;* Golden Globe Award, best supporting actor, 1967, for *The Sand Pebbles;* decorated Commander, Order of the British Empire, 1967.

Cinematograph Exhibitors Association Award, 1967, for Distinguished Service to British Cinema; Golden Globe Award, best supporting actor, 1968, for *Doctor Doolittle;* Golden Globe Award, best English-language foreign film, 1970, for *Oh! What a Lovely War;* Golden Globe Award, best English-language foreign film, 1972, for *Young Winston;* knighted in the New Year Honours, 1976; United Nations Award, 1977; Best Drama Award, London *Evening News,* 1977, for *A Bridge Too Far;* Academy Awards, best picture and best director, British Academy of Film and Television Arts Awards, best picture and best director, Directors Guild of America Award, outstanding directorial achievement for feature films, all 1982, and Golden Globe Awards, best foreign film and best director, 1983, all for *Gandhi.*

British Academy of Film and Television Arts Award, film fellowship, 1983; Martin Luther King, Jr. Non-Violent Peace Prize, 1983; Padma Bhushan from India, 1983; Society of the Family of Man, Artist of the Year Award, 1984; named commander of French Order of Arts and Letters, 1985; Berlinale Kamera, 1987, Golden Globe Award nomination and British Academy of Film and Television Arts Award nomination, both best director, 1988, all for *Cry Freedom;* European Film Award (Felix Award), award of merit, 1988; named chevalier of French Legion of Honor, 1988; British Academy of Film and Television Arts Award, best British film, 1993, for *Shadowlands;* Cine Expo, Life Achievement Award, 1995. Recipient of honorary degrees: University of Leicester, D. Litt., 1970; University of Newcastle, D.C.L., 1974; University of Kent, D. Litt., 1981; Dickinson College, L.L.D., 1983; University of Sussex, D. Litt., 1987.

CREDITS

Film Appearances:

Young stoker, *In Which We Serve,* British Lion, 1942.

Tommy Draper, *The Hundred Pound Window,* Warner Bros./First National, 1943.

Railway worker, *Schweik's New Adventures* (also known as *It Started at Midnight*), Coronet, 1943.

English pilot, *Stairway to Heaven* (also known as *A Matter of Life and Death*), Universal, 1946.

David Wilton, *Journey Together,* English Films Inc., 1946.

Jack Arnold, *School for Secrets* (also known as *Secret Flight*), General Film Distributors, 1946.

Pinkie Brown, *Brighton Rock* (also known as *Young Scarface*), Associated British, 1947.

Ted Peters, *Dancing with Crime,* Paramount, 1947.

Percy Boon, *Dulcimer Street* (also known as *London Belongs to Me*), General Film Distributors, 1948.

Francis Andrews, *The Smugglers* (also known as *The Man Within*), Eagle-Lion, 1948.

Jackie Knowles, *Boys in Brown,* General Film Distributors, 1949.

Jack Read, *The Outsider* (also known as *The Guinea Pig*), Variety, 1949.

Jan, *The Lost People,* General Film Distributors, 1950.

Pierre Bonnet, *Hell Is Sold Out,* Eros, 1951.

Stoker Snipe, *Operation Disaster* (also known as *Morning Departure*), Universal, 1951.

Dougall, *Father's Doing Fine,* Associated British, 1952.

Dripper Daniels, *The Gift Horse* (also known as *Glory at Sea*), Independent Film Distributors, 1952.

Jack Carter, *The Magic Box,* British Lion, 1954.

Tom Manning, *Eight O'Clock Walk,* British Lion, 1954.

Private Cox, *Private's Progress,* British Lion, 1956.

George Hoskins, *The Ship that Died of Shame* (also known as *P.T. Raiders*), Continental/General Film Distributors, 1956.

Knocker White, *The Baby and the Battleship,* British Lion, 1957.

Henry Marshall, *Brothers in Law,* BC, 1957.

Holden, *Dunkirk,* Metro-Goldwyn-Mayer, 1958.

Sidney de Vere Cox, *I'm All Right, Jack,* British Lion, 1959.

Stephen Leigh, *Strange Affection,* Brenner, 1959.

Peter Watson, *The Man Upstairs,* British Lion, 1959.

Tom Curtis, *The Angry Silence,* British Lion, 1960.

Captain Bunter Phillips, *Breakout* (also known as *Danger Within*), Continental, 1960.

Whitey, *S.O.S. Pacific,* Universal, 1960.

Rod Hamilton, *All Night Long,* Rank, 1961.

Ernest Tilley, *Jet Storm,* Britannia/British Lion, 1961.

Edward Lexy, *The League of Gentlemen,* Kingsley, 1961.

Trooper Brody, *Desert Patrol,* Universal, 1962.

Gareth Probert, *Only Two Can Play,* Kingsley/Columbia, 1962.

Various roles, *Trial and Error* (also known as *The Dock Brief*), Metro-Goldwyn-Mayer, 1962.

Roger "Big X" Bartlett, *The Great Escape,* United Artists, 1963.

Narrator, *A Boy's Day,* 1964.

Regimental Sergeant Major Lauderdale, *Guns at Batasi,* Twentieth Century-Fox, 1964.

Billy Savage, *Seance on a Wet Afternoon,* Artixo, 1964.

Alfred Price-Gorham, *The Third Secret,* Twentieth Century-Fox, 1964.

Lew Moran, *The Flight of the Phoenix,* Twentieth Century-Fox, 1965.

Frenchy Burgoyne, *The Sand Pebbles,* Twentieth Century-Fox, 1966.

Albert Blossom, *Doctor Doolittle,* Twentieth Century-Fox, 1967.

Robert Blossom, *The Bliss of Mrs. Blossom,* Paramount, 1968.

Silas, *Only When I Larf,* Paramount, 1968.

Narrator, *Don't Make Me Laugh,* 1969.

Mr. Tungay, *David Copperfield,* Twentieth Century-Fox, 1970.

General Charles Whiteley, *The Last Grenade,* Cinerama, 1970.

Oxford coach, *The Magic Christian,* Commonwealth, 1970.

Inspector Truscott, *Loot,* Cinevision, 1971.

Palmer Anderson, *A Severed Head,* Columbia, 1971.

John Reginald Halliday Christie, *10 Rillington Place,* Columbia, 1971.

Narrator, *Cup Glory,* 1972.

The Village (also known as *Il viaggio*), 1974.

Death in Persepolis, 1974.

Commander Swann, *Brannigan,* United Artists, 1975.

Major Lionel Roach, *Conduct Unbecoming,* Allied Artists, 1975.

Judge Cannon, *Ten Little Indians* (also known as *And Then There Were None*), Avco Embassy, 1975.

Sloat, *Rosebud,* United Artists, 1975.

General Outram, *The Chess Players,* Creative Films, 1978.

Colonel John Daintry, *The Human Factor,* Metro-Goldwyn-Mayer/United Artists, 1979.

Narrator, *Mother Teresa,* Petrie, 1985.

Dr. John Hammond, *Jurassic Park,* Universal, 1993.

Kriss Kringle, *Miracle on 34th Street,* Twentieth Century-Fox, 1994.

The Visitor, *E=mc2,* Trident Releasing, 1995.

Film Work:

Producer (with Bryan Forbes), *The Angry Silence,* British Lion, 1960.

Producer, *Whistle down the Wind,* Pathe-America, 1961.

Producer (with James Woolf), *The L-Shaped Room,* Davis/Royal/Columbia, 1962.

Producer (with Bryan Forbes), *Seance on a Wet Afternoon,* Artixo, 1964.

Producer (with Brian Duffy) and director, *Oh! What a Lovely War,* Paramount, 1969.

Producer and director, *Young Winston,* Columbia, 1972.

Director, *A Bridge Too Far,* United Artists, 1977.

Director, *Magic,* Twentieth Century-Fox, 1978.

Producer and director, *Gandhi,* Columbia, 1982.

Director, *A Chorus Line,* Columbia, 1985.

Producer (with Norman Spencer and John Briley) and director, *Cry Freedom,* Universal, 1987.

Producer and director, *Chaplin,* TriStar, 1992.

Producer (with Brian Eastman) and director, *Shadowlands,* Savoy Pictures, 1993.

Television Appearances; Episodic:

"Killer Whales: Wolves of the Sea," *National Geographic Explorer,* TBS, 1993.

"John Barry's Moviola," *Great Performances,* PBS, 1993.

Other Television Appearances:

Mr. Tungay, *David Copperfield* (movie), NBC, 1970.

Clue: Movies, Murder, and Mystery (special), CBS, 1986.

Freedomfest: Nelson Mandela's 70th Birthday Celebration (special), syndicated, 1988.

Stage Appearances:

(Stage debut) Richard Miller, *Ah! Wilderness,* Intimate Theatre, London, 1941.

Sebastian, *Twelfth Night,* Arts Theatre, London, 1942.

Ralph Berger, *Awake and Sing,* Arts Theatre, 1942.

Ba, *The Holy Isle,* Arts Theatre, 1942.

Andrew, *London W1,* Q Theatre, London, 1942.

Leo Hubbard, *The Little Foxes,* Piccadilly Theatre, London, 1942.

Pinkie Brown, *Brighton Rock,* Garrick Theatre, London, 1943.

Coney, *The Way Back,* Westminster Theatre, London, 1949.

Valentine Crisp, *Sweet Madness,* Vaudeville Theatre, London, 1952.

Detective Trotter, *The Mousetrap,* Ambassadors' Theatre, London, 1952.

David and Julian Fanshaw, *Double Image,* Savoy Theatre, London, 1956.

Also appeared as Toni Rigi, *To Dorothy, a Son,* 1950; Theseus, *The Rape of the Belt,* 1957.

WRITINGS

Books:

In Search of Gandhi (nonfiction), Newmarket, 1982, New Century Publications, 1983.

(Compiler) *The Words of Gandhi,* Newmarket, 1982.

(Author of afterword and editor of photographic selections) Gerald Gold, *Gandhi: A Pictorial Biography,* Newmarket, 1983.

Richard Attenborough's Chorus Line, edited by Diana Carter, New American Library, 1985.

Richard Attenborough's Cry Freedom: A Pictorial Record, Knopf, 1987.

Also author of introductions to numerous publications, including *British Films, 1985;* contributor to periodicals, including *Humanist.*

OTHER SOURCES

Periodicals:

UNESCO Courier, August, 1989, pp. 4-7.

Variety, June 26, 1995, pp. 44-45.*

B

BEALE, Simon Russell 1961-

PERSONAL

Born in 1961; father, a military doctor. *Education:* Studied English at Gonville and Caius College, Cambridge, England.

Career: Actor.

Awards, Honors: Olivier Award, best supporting actor, 1995, for *Volpone;* Olivier Award nomination, best actor, 1998, for *Othello.*

CREDITS

Film Appearances:
Earl of Moray, *Orlando,* Adventure Pictures, 1993.
Charles Musgrove, *Persuasion,* Sony Pictures Classics, 1995.
Second Gravedigger, *Hamlet* (also known as *William Shakespeare's Hamlet*), Sony Pictures Entertainment, 1996.

Television Appearances:
Mark Stibbs, "Art and Illusion," *A Very Peculiar Practice* (series), 1988.
Kenneth Widmerpool, *A Dance to the Music of Time* (miniseries), Channel Four, 1997.

Stage Appearances:
Constantin, *Seagull,* Royal Shakespeare Company, Royal Shakespeare Theatre, Stratford-upon-Avon, England, 1991.
Iago, *Othello,* Royal National Theatre, London, 1997.

Also appeared as Sir Politic Wouldbe, *Volpone;* as Ariel, *The Tempest;* as title role, *Richard III;* and in *The Man of Mode* and *Troilus and Cressida.*

Radio Appearances:
Appeared in *Art,* BBC.

RECORDINGS

Taped Readings:
Narrator, *Betrayal,* 1996.
Narrator, *The Keys to the Street,* Chivers Audio Books, 1997.
Reader, *The Secret House of Death,* 1997.

OTHER SOURCES

Periodicals:
New York Times, April 5, 1998, p. AR4.*

BEGHE, Jason 1960-

PERSONAL

Born March 12, 1960, in New York, NY.

Addresses: *Contact*—c/o Progressive Artists, 400 South Beverly Dr., Suite #216, Beverly Hills, CA 90212.

Career: Actor.

CREDITS

Film Appearances:
Cupcake, *Compromising Positions,* 1985.
Bret, *Maid to Order,* 1987.
Allan Mann, *Monkey Shines: An Experiment in Fear* (also known as *Ella* and *Monkey Shines*), 1988.
State Trooper, *Thelma & Louise,* Metro-Goldwyn-Mayer/United Artists, 1991.

Detective, *Jimmy Hollywood,* Paramount, 1994.
Royce, *G.I. Jane,* Buena Vista, 1997.

Television Appearances; Movies:
Hank Beaumont, *Dress Gray,* 1986.
Billy Peale, *Easy Come, Easy Go,* ABC, 1989.
Sammy Turner, *Man against the Mob: The Chinatown Murders,* NBC, 1989.
Robert Spencer, *Perry Mason: The Case of the All-Star Assassin,* NBC, 1989.
Peter Howard, *Johnny Ryan,* NBC, 1990.
John Kopiak, *The Operation* (also known as *Bodily Harm*), CBS, 1990.
Doug Crane, *Full Eclipse,* HBO, 1993.
Thomas Crighton, *Matlock: The Heist,* ABC, 1995.
Joe Mulvey, *Suddenly,* ABC, 1996.
Mike Donahue, *Cab to Canada,* CBS, 1998.
Matt Whitten, *Baby Monitor: Sound of Fear,* USA Network, 1998.

Television Appearances; Series:
Tom Yinessa, *1st & Ten: The Championships* (also known as *Training Camp: The Bulls Are Back* and *1st & Ten: Going for Broke*), HBO, 1986-87.
Skaggs, *Quantum Leap,* NBC, 1989.
Paul, *Homefront,* ABC, 1991.
Mark Myers, *In the Heat of the Night,* NBC then CBS, 1992.
District Attorney Brian Petrovek, *Picket Fences,* CBS, 1992.
Jeffrey Lindley, *Melrose Place,* Fox, 1993-94.
Ron Nash, *Good Company,* CBS, 1996.
Ron, *George & Leo,* CBS, 1997.
Danny Blaines (recurring) and Charles Blades, *Chicago Hope,* CBS, 1997.
Sean McGrail, *To Have & To Hold,* CBS, 1998.

Television Appearances; Episodic:
Steve Chambers, "Alma Murder," *Murder, She Wrote,* CBS, 1989.
Wayne Bennett, "A Body to Die For," *Murder, She Wrote,* CBS, 1990.
Detective Riley, "Cold Shower," *L.A. Law,* NBC, 1993.
Larry Moore, "Darkness Falls," *The X-Files,* Fox, 1993.
Julian Kerbis, "One Big Happy Family," *NYPD Blue,* ABC, 1995.
Russell Snow, "Order on the Court," *Courthouse,* CBS, 1995.

Other Television Appearances:
Ray Brooks, *Intruders* (miniseries), CBS, 1992.
Tom Wallace, *Treasure Island: The Adventure Begins* (special), NBC, 1994.*

BIEHN, Michael 1956-

PERSONAL

Born Michael Connell Biehn, July 31, 1956, in Anniston, AL; father, a lawyer; married Carlene Olson (divorced); married Gina Marsh, 1988; children: Caelan Michael (second marriage), Devon, and Taylor (first marriage). *Education:* Attended the University of Arizona.

Addresses: *Agent*—International Creative Management, 8942 Wilshire Blvd., Beverly Hills, CA 90211.

Career: Actor.

CREDITS

Film Appearances:
Jack, *Coach,* Crown International, 1978.
Tim Warner, *Hog Wild,* Avco Embassy, 1980.
Douglas Breen, *The Fan,* Paramount, 1981.
Alexander, *The Lords of Discipline,* Paramount, 1983.
Kyle Reese, *The Terminator,* Orion, 1984.
Corporal Hicks, *Aliens,* Twentieth Century-Fox, 1986.
Russell Quinn, *The Seventh Sign,* TriStar, 1988.
Garnet Montrose, *In a Shallow Grave,* Skouras, 1988.
Lieutenant Coffey, *The Abyss,* Twentieth Century-Fox, 1989.
Lieutenant James Curran, *Navy Seals,* Orion, 1990.
Eddie Kay, *Time Bomb,* Metro-Goldwyn-Mayer/Pathe, 1991.
Anthony Fraser, *Rampage,* Vestron Video, 1992.
Taylor Brooks, *K2,* Paramount, 1992.
Johnny Ringo, *Tombstone,* Buena Vista, 1993.
Joe Donan, *Deadfall,* Trimark Pictures, 1993.
Joe Keyes, *Deep Red,* Columbia/TriStar, 1994.
Jackie Ryan, *In the Kingdom of the Blind, the Man with One Eye is King* (also known as *In the Kingdom of the Blind*), 1994.
Lieutenant Bob Hargrove, *Jade,* Paramount, 1995.
Boyd, *Mojave Moon,* New Moon Productions, 1996.
Charles Anderson, *The Rock,* Buena Vista, 1996.
Robert Hart, *Dead Men Can't Dance,* Imperial Entertainment, 1997.
Detective Tony Luca, *Double Edge* (also known as *American Dragons*), Orion Home Video, 1998.
Smokey Banks, *The Ride,* World Wide Pictures, 1998.
Bill, *Susan's Plan,* 1998.
John Holmes, *Wonderland,* 1999.
Sheriff Brent Marken, *Cherry Falls,* 1999.

Also appeared in *The Boarder;* and *Dead-Bang.*

Television Appearances; Series:
Mark Johnson, *Operation: Runaway,* NBC, 1978-79.
Chris Larrabee, *The Magnificent Seven,* CBS, 1998—.

Television Appearances; Mini-series:
Jack Wallach, *Asteroid,* NBC, 1997.

Television Appearances; Pilots:
Tony, *James at 15,* NBC, 1977.
Larry DeWitt, *The Paradise Connection,* CBS, 1979.
Gibby Anderson, *Steeltown,* CBS, 1979.

Television Appearances; Episodic:
(Television debut) *Logan's Run,* CBS, 1977.
Seth, "The Terrible Secret," *ABC Afterschool Specials,* ABC, 1979.
Officer Randall Buttman, "Bangladesh Slowly" and "Fowl Play," *Hill Street Blues,* NBC, 1984.
Rookie Patrolman Randall Buttman, "Rookie Nookie," *Hill Street Blues,* NBC, 1984.
Lieutenant Matt McCrae, "Strapped," *HBO Showcase,* HBO, 1993.

Also appeared in *Police Story,* NBC; and *Family,* ABC.

Television Appearances; Movies:
J.D., *Zuma Beach,* NBC, 1978.
Tom Reardon, *A Fire in the Sky,* NBC, 1978.
Daniel Allen, *China Rose,* CBS, 1983.
Charles Raynor, *Deadly Intentions,* ABC, 1985.
Bo Landry, *A Taste for Killing* (also known as *In the Company of a Killer*), USA Network, 1992.
Joe Keyes, *Deep Red,* Sci-Fi Channel, 1994.
Stash Horak, *Conundrum* (also known as *Frame by Frame*), Showtime, 1996.
Roy McLean, *Silver Wolf,* Fox Family Channel, 1999.

RECORDINGS

Video Games:
Commander Michael McNeil, *Command & Conquer: Tiberian Sun,* 1998.*

BLAKE, Yvonne

PERSONAL

Born in northern England. *Education:* Manchester Regional College of Art.

Career: Costume designer. At age 21, became the youngest member to join the Costume Designers Guild in London. Assisted the designers Cecil Beaton and Oliver Messel. Received commissions to design costumes for the London Festival Ballet.

Member: Costume Designers Guild, London.

Awards, Honors: Academy Award (with Antonio Castillo), best costume design, 1971, for *Nicholas and Alexandra;* British Academy Award nomination, best costume design, 1973, for *Jesus Christ Superstar;* Academy Award nomination (with Ron Talsky), best costume design, 1975, for *The Four Musketeers;* Emmy Award nomination, best costume design for a miniseries or special, 1986, *Casanova;* Goya Award, best costume design, 1987, *Remando al Viento;* Goya Award, best costume design, 1994, *Cancion de Cuna.*

CREDITS

Film Work; Costume Designer:
Judith (also known as *Conflict*), 1966.
The Idol, 1966.
The Spy with a Cold Nose, 1966.
Charlie Bubbles, Universal, 1967.
Assignment K, Columbia, 1968.
Duffy, 1968.
The Best House in London, Metro-Goldwyn-Mayer, 1969.
Country Dance (also known as *Brotherly Love*), 1970.
The Last Valley, 1970.
Puppet on a Chain, 1970.
Nicholas and Alexandra, 1971.
Jesus Christ Superstar, Universal, 1973.
The Four Musketeers (also known as *The Revenge of Milady*), Twentieth Century-Fox, 1974.
The Three Musketeers, 1974.
All Creatures Great and Small, 1974.
The Eagle Has Landed, 1976.
Robin and Marian, Columbia, 1976.
Superman (also known as *Superman: The Movie*), Warner Bros., 1978.
Escape to Athena, 1979.
Superman II, Warner Bros., 1980.
Green Ice, 1981.
Las Aventuras de Enrique y Ana, 1981.
Bearn, 1982.
Escarabajos Asesinos (also known as *Scarab),* 1982.
Finders Keepers, 1984.
Flesh and Blood (also known as *The Rose and the Sword*), Orion, 1985.
Remando al Viento, 1987.
Rowing with the Wind, 1988.
The Return of the Musketeers, Universal, 1989.
Company Business, Metro-Goldwyn-Mayer, 1991.
La Reina Anonima, 1992.

The Detective and Death (also known as *El Detective y la Muerte*), 1994.
Cradle Song, Nickel Odeon Dos, 1994.
Looking for Richard, 1996.
What Dreams May Come, PolyGram Filmed Entertainment, 1998.
Joan of Arc: The Virgin Warrior, 1999.

Film Appearances:
"The Jewish Question," *Fahrenheit 451,* Universal, 1966.
What Dreams May Come, 1998.

Television Work; Costume Designer; Movies:
Casanova, ABC, 1987.
Crime of the Century, HBO, 1996.
The Price of Heaven, CBS, 1997.

Television Work; Costume Designer; Miniseries:
Harem, ABC, 1986.
The Richest Man in the World: The Story of Aristotle Onassis, ABC, 1988.*

BLESSED, Brian 1937-

PERSONAL

Born October 9, 1937, in Mexborough, Yorkshire, England; son of William Blessed (a coal miner) and Hilda Wall; married Ann Bomann (divorced); married Hildegarde Neil (an actress); children: (first marriage) Catherine; (second marriage) Rosalind. *Education:* Trained for the stage at the Bristol Old Vic Theatre School. *Avocational interests:* Judo (black belt) and mountaineering.

Addresses: *Manager*—Derek Webster, Associated International Management, 5 Denmark St., London, WC2H 8LP, England.

Career: Actor. Member, Royal Shakespeare Company, Stratford-on-Avon, England, 1985. *Military service:* Royal Air Force, parachute regiment.

CREDITS

Film Appearances:
Policeman, *The Christmas Tree,* CFF, 1966.
Sergeant, *Alf 'n' Family* (also known as *Till Death Do Us Part*), Sherpix, 1968.
Jock Baird, *Brotherly Love* (also known as *Country Dance*), Metro-Goldwyn-Mayer, 1970.
Korski, *The Last Valley,* Cinerama, 1971.
Tathybius, *The Trojan Women,* Cinerama, 1971.
Suffolk, *Henry VIII and His Six Wives,* Metro-Goldwyn-Mayer/EMI, 1972.
Pedro, *Man of La Mancha,* United Artists, 1972.
Barry Lyndon, Warner Bros., 1975.
Prince Vultan, *Flash Gordon,* Universal, 1980.
Suleiman Khan, *High Road to China,* Warner Bros., 1983.
Geoffrey Lyons, *The Hound of the Baskervilles,* Weintraub, 1983.
Exeter, *Henry V,* Samuel Goldwyn, 1989.
Voice of Caous (English version), *Asterix et le coup du menhir* (also known as *Asterix and the Big Fight* and *Asterix and the Stone's Blow;* animated), Gaumont/Palace, 1989.
Galahad of Everest, 1991.
Lord Locksley, *Robin Hood: Prince of Thieves,* Warner Bros., 1991.
Pozzo, *Waiting for Godot,* 1991.
Chazov, *Back in the U.S.S.R.,* FoxVideo, 1992.
Voice of El Supremo, *Freddie as F.R.O.7* (animated), Miramax, 1992.
Antonio, *Much Ado about Nothing,* Samuel Goldwyn, 1993.
Major Elliot, *Chasing the Deer,* 1994.
Ghost, *Hamlet* (also known as *William Shakespeare's Hamlet*), Columbia, 1996.
Edward I, *The Bruce,* Cromwell Productions, 1996.
Edward the Confessor, *Macbeth,* 1997.
Teiresias, *The Bacchae,* 1999.
Boss Nass, *Star Wars: Episode I: The Phantom Menace,* 1999.
Voice of Clayton, *Tarzan* (animated feature), 1999.

Film Work:
Special director, "Witches Scene," *Macbeth,* 1997.

Television Appearances; Series:
King Richard IV, *Blackadder* (also known as *The Black Adder*), BBC, 1983, then Arts and Entertainment.

Appeared on *My Family and Other Animals,* BBC, then Arts and Entertainment; Constable Fancy Smith, *Z Cars,* BBC.

Television Appearances; Miniseries:
Cold Comfort Farm, BBC, then "Cold Comfort Farm," *Masterpiece Theatre,* PBS, 1971.
Notorious Woman, BBC, then "Notorious Woman," *Masterpiece Theatre,* PBS, 1975.
Augustus, *I, Claudius,* BBC, then "I, Claudius," *Masterpiece Theatre,* PBS, 1977.
Olinthus, *The Last Days of Pompeii,* ABC, 1984.

General Yevlenko, *War and Remembrance,* ABC, 1988.
Long John Silver, *Return to Treasure Island,* The Disney Channel, 1989.
Cluny, *Kidnapped,* The Family Channel, 1995.
Squire Western, *Henry Fielding's Tom Jones,* Arts and Entertainment, 1998.

Television Appearances; Movies:
Abner, *The Story of David,* ABC, 1976.
Captain Teach, *The Master of Ballantrae,* CBS, 1984.
The Sweeney, 1984.
General Gonse, *Prisoner of Honor,* HBO, 1991.
Atticus, *MacGyver: Lost Treasure of Atlantis,* ABC, 1994.

Television Appearances; Episodic:
George Briggs, "Appointment with a Killer" (also known as "A Midsummer Nightmare"), *Thriller,* ABC, 1975.
"Death's Other Dominion," *Space 1999,* syndicated, 1975.
"The Metamorph," *Space 1999,* syndicated, 1976.
Jackanory, BBC, 1976.
Vargas, *Blake's 7,* BBC, 1978.
"Lamb to the Slaughter," *Tales of the Unexpected,* syndicated, 1979.
Yrcanos, "Mindwarp," *Doctor Who,* syndicated, 1986.
Lambert Sampson, "Banbury Blue," *Boon,* Central-TV, 1988.
"Black Virgin of Vladimir," *Lovejoy Mysteries,* Arts and Entertainment, 1991.
Himself, *Television's Greatest Hits,* 1992.

Television Appearances; Specials:
Wine of India, BBC, 1970.
Rudolf Kammerling, *Once in a Lifetime,* BBC, then *Great Performances,* PBS, 1988.
Voice characterization, *Pyramid* (animated), PBS, 1988.
Voice of General Gaius Valerius, *City* (animated; documentary), PBS, 1994.
Hey, Mr. Producer! The Musical World of Cameron Mackintosh, PBS, 1998.

Also appeared as host, narrator, and Johann Sebastian Bach, *The Joy of Bach,* PBS; narrator, *The Natural World,* BBC.

Other Television Appearances:
Also appeared in *The Little World of Don Camillo,* 1980; *The Three Musketeers, William the Conqueror, Lorna and Ted, Arthur of the Britons, Justice, Boy Dominic, Hadleigh, Public Eye, Brahms, The Aphrodite Inheritance, Son of a Man, Churchill's People,* and *The Recruiting Officer.*

Stage Appearances:
Edmund, *The Exorcism,* Comedy Theatre, London, 1975.
Gorky, *State of Revolution,* National Theatre Company, Lyttelton Theatre, London, 1977.
Old Deuteronomy, *Cats,* New London Theatre, London, 1981.
John Freeman, *Metropolis,* Piccadilly Theatre, London, 1989.

Also appeared in *Incident at Vichy* and *Oedipus,* both in London; and in repertory at Nottingham, England, and Birmingham, England.

WRITINGS

Books:
Author of *The Turquoise Mountain, The Dynamite Kid, Nothing's Impossible,* and *Blessed Everest.**

BLOCK, Larry 1942-

PERSONAL

Born October 30, 1942, in New York, NY; son of Harold (in the garment industry) and Sonia (a travel agent; maiden name, Kutcher) Block; married Jolly King (an actress), September 25, 1981; children: Zoe Lenna, Zachary Harold. *Education:* University of Rhode Island, B.A. (English) 1964; trained for the stage with Wynn Handman. *Politics:* Liberal Democrat. *Religion:* Ethical Culture.

Addresses: *Agent*—The Gage Group, 315 West 57th St., Ste. 4H, New York, NY 10019.

Career: Actor. *Military service:* U.S. Army, Special Services, specialist fourth class, 1967-69; received Commendation Medal, 1969.

CREDITS

Stage Appearances:
(Stage debut) Mercutio's page, *Romeo and Juliet,* American Shakespeare Festival, Stratford, CT, 1965.
Coriolanus, American Shakespeare Festival, Stratford, CT, 1965.

The Taming of the Shrew, American Shakespeare Festival, Stratford, CT, 1965.

King Lear, American Shakespeare Festival, Stratford, CT, 1965.

(Broadway debut) Understudy for Malcolm Scrawdyke, *Hail, Scrawdyke,* Booth Theatre, New York City, 1966.

Boy, *La Turista,* St. Clement's Church Theatre, New York City, 1967.

Eh?, Circle in the Square Theatre, New York City, 1967.

Harry, Noon, and Night, Theatre of the Living Arts, Philadelphia, PA, 1970.

The Recruiting Officer, Theatre of the Living Arts, 1970.

Jesse, *Fingernails Blue As Flowers,* American Place Theatre, New York City, 1971-72.

Lucky, *Waiting for Godot,* St. Clement's Church Theatre, New York City, 1974.

Johann Sebastian Fabiani and Whimsey, *Where Do We Go from Here?,* New York Shakespeare Festival, Public Theatre, New York City, 1974.

Dromio of Ephesus, *The Comedy of Errors,* New York Shakespeare Festival, Delacorte Theatre, New York City, 1975.

The Last Days of British Honduras, New York Shakespeare Festival, 1976.

Manny Alter, *Coming Attractions,* Playwrights Horizons, New York City, 1980-81.

Gadshill, *Henry IV, Part One,* New York Shakespeare Festival, Delacorte Theatre, 1981.

Sir Toby Belch, *Twelfth Night,* Shakespeare and Company, Lee, MA, 1981.

Leon, *The Workroom* (also known as *L'Atelier*), Center Stage, Baltimore, MD, 1981.

Martin Bormann, *The Fuehrer Bunker,* American Place Theatre, 1981.

Manhattan Love Songs, Actors' Studio, New York City, 1982.

A Tantalizing, Actors Theatre of Louisville, Louisville, KY, 1983.

Benny Silverman, *The Value of Names,* Actors Theatre of Louisville, 1983, then Hartford Stage Company, Hartford, CT, 1984.

The Hotel Manager, *Souvenirs,* Cubiculo Theatre, New York City, 1984.

One-Eyed, *The Golem,* New York Shakespeare Festival, Delacorte Theatre, 1984.

Sir Toby Belch, *Twelfth Night,* Tyrone Guthrie Theatre, Minneapolis, MN, 1984.

Mr. Fezziwig, *A Christmas Carol,* Tyrone Guthrie Theatre, 1984.

Randolph, *Responsible Parties,* Vineyard Theatre, New York City, 1985.

Del Bates, *The Hit Parade,* Manhattan Punch Line, New York City, 1985.

Lada I, *Largo Desolato,* New York Shakespeare Festival, Public Theatre, 1986.

Yuri Brushnik, *Coup d'Etat,* Playwrights Horizons, New York City, 1986.

Censor, *Hunting Cockroaches,* Manhattan Theatre Club, New York City, 1987.

Elliot Atlas, *The Square Root of Three,* Jewish Repertory Theatre, New York City, 1987.

Antonio, *Two Gentlemen of Verona,* New York Shakespeare Festival, Delacorte Theatre, 1987.

Willis, *Moonchildren,* Second Stage Theatre, New York City, 1987.

Cecil, *The Yellow Dog Contract,* Apple Corps Theatre, New York City, 1988.

Augustin Feraillon, *A Flea in Her Ear,* Long Wharf Theatre, New Haven, CT, 1989.

Herbie, *The Loman Family Picnic,* Manhattan Theatre Club, New York City, 1989.

Temptation, New York Shakespeare Festival, Public Theatre, 1989.

Bernie Weiner, *Selling Off,* John Houseman Theatre, New York City, 1991.

Lord/Fisherman/Cerimon/Pandar, *Pericles,* New York Shakespeare Festival, Public/Newman Theatre, 1991.

Alvin, *One of the All-Time Greats,* Vineyard Theatre, New York City, 1992.

The Last Laugh, Jewish Repertory Theatre, New York City, 1992.

Angelo, *The Comedy of Errors,* New York Shakespeare Festival, Delacorte Theatre, 1992.

Director/Fyodor, *The Flying Karamazov Brothers in The Brothers Karamazov,* Seattle Repertory Theatre, Seattle, WA, 1992, then Arena Stage, Washington, DC, 1993.

Shlemiel, *Shlemiel the First,* American Repertory Theatre, Cambridge, MA, 1995, then American Music Theatre Festival, Philadelphia, PA, later Lincoln Center's Serious Fun Festival, New York City.

Mr. Appopolous, *Wonderful Town,* New York City Opera, 1995.

Him, New York Shakespeare Festival, 1995.

Leporello, *Don Juan in Chicago,* Primary Stages, New York City, 1996.

Also appeared in *Young Playwrights Festival; Festival of One Acts; The Faithful Brethren of Pitt Street.*

Film Appearances:

Springy, *Shamus* (also known as *Passion for Danger*), Columbia, 1973.

Peterboro referee, *Slap Shot,* Universal, 1977.
Ted Peters, *Heaven Can Wait,* Paramount, 1978.
Detective Burrows, *Hardcore* (also known as *The Hardcore Life*), Columbia, 1979.
Taxi driver, *After Hours,* Warner Bros., 1985.
Bar owner, *Cocktail,* Touchstone, 1988.
Routed (short film), Izar, 1989.
Barber, *Betsy's Wedding,* Buena Vista, 1990.
Defense attorney, *My Blue Heaven,* 1990.
Man in restaurant, *Big Night,* Samuel Goldwyn, 1996.
Andy, *The Electric Urn,* 1996.

Also appeared in *First Family.*

Television Appearances; Series:
Appeared as Mickey Potter, *The Secret Storm,* CBS; Tom, *Sesame Street,* PBS; Cal Jamison, *General Hospital,* ABC.

Television Appearances; Miniseries:
Lasie, "Roanoak," *American Playhouse,* PBS, 1986.

Television Appearances; Pilots:
Harry, *Rosetti and Ryan: Men Who Love Women,* NBC, 1977.
Private Arnold Fleck, *Space Force,* NBC, 1978.

Television Appearances; Episodic:
Eddie Hendrix, "Images," *M*A*S*H,* CBS, 1977.
Arlo Spinner, "Game, Set, Death," *Charlie's Angels,* ABC, 1978.
*M*A*S*H,* CBS, 1978.
Clerk, *Tattingers,* NBC, 1988.
Al Henderson, *Murphy Brown,* CBS, 1989.
Feldman, "His Hour Upon the Stage," *Law & Order,* NBC, 1991.
Stan, "Divorce," *Law & Order,* NBC, 1991.
Slater, *Law & Order,* NBC, 1994.
New York Undercover, Fox, 1995.

Also appeared on *Miami Vice,* NBC; *One Life to Live,* ABC; *Barney Miller,* ABC; *CHiPs,* NBC; *Kojak,* CBS; *Police Story,* NBC; *Baretta,* ABC; *Ellery Queen,* NBC; *Family Matters,* ABC.

Television Appearances; Movies:
Springy, *A Matter of Wife . . . and Death,* NBC, 1976.
The Lindbergh Kidnapping Case, NBC, 1976.
Leroy Keenan, *The Last Ride of the Dalton Gang,* NBC, 1979.
Kleinfeld, *Dead Man Out,* HBO, 1989.

Television Appearances; Specials:
Hardcore TV, HBO, 1993.
Voices of Yaacov Baror, Judge Moshe Landau, and Gavriel Bach, *The Trial of Adolf Eichmann,* PBS, 1997.

Radio Appearances; Series:
Appeared on *Work in Progress.*

Radio Appearances; Episodic:
Appeared on "Pilot," *National Public Radio Playhouse,* National Public Radio; "Prairie du Chien," *Earplay,* National Public Radio; *Under the Gun,* WBAI (New York).*

BLUM, Mark 1950-

PERSONAL

Born May 14, 1950, in Newark, NJ. *Education:* Studied drama at the University of Minnesota, the University of Pennsylvania, and with Andre Gregory, Aaron Frankel, and Daniel Seltzer.

Addresses: *Agent*—Jonathan Trumper, William Morris Agency, 1325 Avenue of the Americas, New York, NY 10019.

Career: Actor. National Shakespeare Company, Ulster County Community College, Stone Ridge, NY, stage manager, 1974.

Awards, Honors: Obie Award, *Village Voice,* 1989, for *Gus and Al.*

CREDITS

Stage Appearances:
Valentine, *Two Gentlemen of Verona,* National Shakespeare Company, Ulster County Community College, Stone Ridge, NY, 1974, then Rutgers University, New Brunswick, NJ, 1975.
Cleante, *The Miser,* National Shakespeare Company, Ulster County Community College, 1974, then Rutgers University, 1975.
(Off-Broadway debut) Post office clerk, *The Cherry Orchard,* Roundabout Theatre, 1976.
Villager, first angel, and man, *The World of Sholem Aleichem,* Roundabout Theatre, 1976.
Brothers, George Street Playhouse, New Brunswick, NJ, 1976.
(Broadway debut) Venetian, *The Merchant,* Plymouth Theatre, 1977.

Steve, *Say Goodnight, Gracie,* Playwrights Horizons, Manhattan Main Stage Theatre, New York City, 1978, then Actors Playhouse, New York City, 1979.
Younger son, *Table Settings,* Playwrights Horizons, then Chelsea Theatre Center, New York City, 1980.
Michael, *Key Exchange,* Orpheum Theatre, New York City, 1981.
Close Ties, Long Wharf Theatre, New Haven, CT, 1981.
The Cherry Orchard, Long Wharf Theatre, 1982.
Iago, *Othello,* Shakespeare Festival of Dallas, Dallas, TX, 1982.
Johnson, *Loving Reno,* New York Theatre Studio, AMDA Studio One, New York City, 1983.
Max Whitcomb, *An American Comedy,* Center Theatre Group, Mark Taper Forum, Los Angeles, CA, 1983-84.
Lee Baum, *The American Clock,* Center Theatre Group, Mark Taper Forum, 1983-84.
Harry, *Wild Oats,* Center Theatre Group, Mark Taper Forum, 1983-84.
Peter Austin, *It's Only a Play,* Manhattan Theatre Club, New York City, 1984.
Asher, *Messiah,* Manhattan Theatre Club, Space at City Center Theatre, 1985.
Ben, *Little Footsteps,* Playwrights Horizons, 1986.
Ben, *The Downside,* Long Wharf Theatre, 1987.
Cave of Life, Circle Repertory Theatre, 1988.
Eddie, *Lost in Yonkers,* Richard Rodgers Theatre, New York City, 1991.
Tom, *Laureen's Whereabouts,* WPA Theatre, New York City, 1993.

Also appeared in *Moby Dick Rehearsed,* Mark Taper Forum; *Gus and Al,* produced in New York City, c. 1989; and *Green Julia.*

Film Appearances:
Intern Murphy, *Lovesick,* Warner Bros., 1983.
Gary Glass, *Desperately Seeking Susan,* Orion, 1985.
George Margolin, *Just between Friends,* Orion, 1986.
Richard Mason, *Crocodile Dundee,* Paramount, 1986.
Denny Gordon, *Blind Date,* TriStar, 1987.
Arthur Peale, *The Presidio,* Paramount, 1988.
Ned Braudy, *Worth Winning,* 1989.
Ben Winchek, *Emma and Elvis,* 1991.
Peter, *Miami Rhapsody,* Buena Vista, 1995.
Matthew Greenberg, *The Low Life,* 1995.
Louis, *Sudden Manhattan,* Phaedra Cinema, 1996.
Edward Cooperberg, *You Can Thank Me Later,* 1998.
Darrell, *Getting to Know You,* 1999.

Film Work:
Executive producer, *The Low Life,* 1995.
Associate producer, *Search and Destroy* (also known as *The Four Rules*), October Films, 1995.

Television Appearances; Series:
Ken Holden, *Sweet Surrender,* NBC, 1987.
Edison King, *Capital News* (also known as *Powerhouse*), ABC, 1990.

Television Appearances; Movies:
Condition Critical (also known as *Critical Condition*), NBC, 1992.
Wayne Satz, *Indictment: The McMartin Trial* (also known as *The Naked Movie Star Games* and *Nothing But the Truth: The McMartin Story*), HBO, 1995.
Ben, *Stag,* HBO, 1996.
Jackson, *The Defenders: Payback,* Showtime, 1997.

Television Appearances; Episodic:
"Two Balls and a Strike," *St. Elsewhere,* NBC, 1984.
Miami Vice, NBC, 1987.
Mike Summers, "Aliens," *Roseanne,* ABC, 1992.
"Jurisdiction," *Law & Order,* NBC, 1993.
Dr. Sachs, "From Hare to Eternity," *NYPD Blue,* ABC,1993.
"Seed," *Law & Order,* NBC, 1995.
Dr. Vincent, *New York Undercover,* Fox, 1995.
Agent Mike Francis, *NYPD Blue,* ABC, 1995.
Larry Mohr, *Wings,* NBC, 1995.
Greg Garfield, *Ink,* CBS, 1996.
John, "The 1000th Show," *Frasier,* NBC, 1997.
"Agony," *Law & Order,* NBC,1998.
Mike Francis, "Show & Tell," *NYPD Blue,* ABC, 1999.

Other Television Appearances:
Ray Litertini, *Things Are Looking Up* (pilot), CBS, 1984.
MTV, Give Me Back My Life: A Harvard Lampoon Parody (special), Comedy Central, 1991.*

BLUTH, Don 1938-

PERSONAL

Born September 13, 1938, in El Paso, TX. *Education:* Attended Brigham Young University.

Addresses: *Office*—Fox Animation Studios, 1747 East Camelback Rd., Phoenix, AZ 85016-4322.

Career: Animator, director, producer, and writer. Disney Studios,animator, 1956; Filmation, animator, 1967; Disney Studios, animator, 1971-79; Don Bluth Productions, founder, 1979, co-director, 1979-85; Sullivan Bluth Studios, Van Nuys, CA, animator, 1985; Sullivan Bluth Studios, Dublin, Ireland, animator, 1986—. Sullivan Bluth Interactive Media, co-producer of interactive arcade games, including *Dragon's Lair* and *Dragon's Lair II: Time Warp,* both 1984, and *Space Ace.*

Awards, Honors: Time-Machine Honorary Award, Catalonian International Film Festival, Sitges, Spain, 1993; Annie Award nomination, outstanding individual achievement for directing in an animated feature (with Gary Goldman) and Golden Satellite Award nomination, best motion picture—animated or mixed media (with Goldman), both 1998, for *Anastasia.*

CREDITS

Film Work:

Animator, *Robin Hood,* Buena Vista, 1973.

Director of animation, *The Rescuers,* Buena Vista, 1977.

Director of animation, *Pete's Dragon,* Buena Vista, 1977.

Producer and director, *The Small One,* Buena Vista, 1978.

Animator, *Xanadu,* Universal, 1980.

Producer (with Gary Goldman and John Pomeroy), director, and director of animation, *The Secret of Nimh,* Metro-Goldwyn-Mayer/United Artists, 1982.

Producer (with Goldman and Pomeroy), director, and production designer, *An American Tail,* Universal, 1986.

Producer (with Goldman and Pomeroy), director, and production designer, *The Land before Time,* Universal, 1988.

Producer (with Goldman and Pomeroy), director, and production designer (with Larry Leker), *All Dogs Go to Heaven,* United Artists, 1989.

Producer (with Goldman and Pomeroy) and director, *Rock-a-Doodle,* Samuel Goldwyn, 1992.

Producer and director, *Hans Christian Andersen's Thumbelina,* Warner Bros., 1994.

Producer and director, *The Pebble and the Penguin,* 1994.

Producer and director, *A Troll in Central Park,* Warner Bros., 1994.

Producer and director, *Anastasia,* Twentieth Century-Fox, 1997.

Producer and director, *Planet Ice,* forthcoming.

Television Work; Specials:

Producer and director, *Banjo, the Woodpile Cat,* 1982.

WRITINGS

Screenplays:

Songwriter, *The Small One,* Buena Vista, 1978.

(With Goldman, Pomeroy, and Will Finn) *The Secret of Nimh* (based on the novel *Mrs. Frisby and the Rats of N.I.M.H.* by Robert C. O'Brien), Metro-Goldwyn-Mayer/United Artists, 1982.

Hans Christian Andersen's Thumbelina, Warner Bros., 1994.

Television Specials:

Story, music, and lyrics for *Banjo, the Woodpile Cat,* 1982.

Adaptations: The film *All Dogs Go to Heaven,* released by United Artists in 1989, was based on a story by Bluth, David N. Weiss, Ken Cromar, and others. The film *Rock-a-Doodle,* released by Samuel Goldwyn in 1992, was based on a story by Bluth, Weiss, John Pomeroy, and others.

OTHER SOURCES

Periodicals:

Business Wire, December 17, 1998, p. 1109.*

BORMAN, M.
See SKERRITT, Tom

BOWMAN, Rob 1960 (?)-

PERSONAL

Born c. 1960, in Texas.

Addresses: *Agent*—Patty Detroit, International Creative Management, 8942 Wilshire Blvd., Beverly Hills, CA 90211.

Career: Producer and director. Has worked as an electrician, a salesman, and a bartender.

Awards, Honors: Three Emmy Award nominations (with others), outstanding drama series, 1995, 1996, and 1998, all for *The X-Files.*

CREDITS

Film Work; Director:
Airborne, Warner Bros., 1993.
The X-Files, Twentieth Century-Fox, 1998.

Television Work; Series:
Director and producer, *The X-Files,* Fox, 1994-98.

Television Work; Director; Episodic:
"Where No One Has Gone Before," "The Battle," "Too Short a Season," "Datalore," and "Heart of Glory," *Star Trek: The Next Generation* syndicated, 1987.
21 Jump Street, Fox, 1987.
Werewolf, Fox, 1987.
The Highwayman, NBC, 1988.
"Metamorphic Anthropoidic Prototype Over You," *Probe,* ABC, 1988.
Hardball, NBC, 1989.
"Ma Dalton," *MacGyver,* ABC, 1989.
Quantum Leap, NBC, 1991.
Parker Lewis Can't Lose (also known as *Parker Lewis*), Fox, 1991-92.
The Hat Squad, CBS, 1992.
The Adventures of Brisco County, Jr., Fox, 1993.
The X-Files, Fox, 1993.
MANTIS, 1994.
Traps, CBS, 1994.
VR.5, Fox, 1995.

Also directed episodes of *Sonny Spoon,* NBC; and *Stingray,* syndicated.

Television Work; Associate Producer; Movies:
Stingray, NBC, 1985.
The Last Precinct, NBC, 1986.

Television Work; Specials:
Segment producer and director, "The Giant Beside our House" and "Miracle on Highway 5," *Miracles and Other Mysteries,* ABC, 1991.*

BRENNAN, Eileen 1935-

PERSONAL

Full name, Verla Eileen Regina Brennan; born September 3, 1935, in Los Angeles, CA; daughter of John Gerald (a doctor) and Regina "Jeanne" (a silent film actress; maiden name, Menehan) Brennan; married David John Lampson, December 28, 1968 (divorced, 1974); children: Samuel John, Patrick Oliver. *Education:* Attended Georgetown University; studied acting at the American Academy of Dramatic Arts, 1955-56.

Addresses: *Agent*—David Shapira and Associates, 15301 Ventura Blvd., Suite 345, Sherman Oaks, CA 91403.

Career: Actress.

Member: Actors' Equity Association, Screen Actors Guild, American Federation of Television and Radio Artists, American Guild of Variety Artists.

Awards, Honors: Page One Award from the Newspaper Guild, *Theatre World* Award, Obie Award, *Village Voice,* and Kit-Kat Artists and Models Award, all 1960, for *Little Mary Sunshine;* British Academy of Film and Television Arts Award nomination, best supporting actress, 1972, for *The Last Picture Show;* Academy Award nomination, best supporting actress, 1981, for *Private Benjamin;* Emmy Award, outstanding supporting actress in a comedy, variety, or music series, 1981, and Golden Globe Award, best television actress in a series—comedy or musical, 1982, both for *Private Benjamin;* Emmy Award nomination, best guest actress in a drama series, 1991, for *thirtysomething.*

CREDITS

Film Appearances:
(Film debut) Eunice, *Divorce: American Style,* Columbia, 1967.
Genevieve, *The Last Picture Show,* Columbia, 1971.
Darlene, *Scarecrow,* Warner Bros., 1973.
Billie, *The Sting,* Universal, 1973.
Mrs. Walker, *Daisy Miller,* Paramount, 1974.
Elizabeth, *At Long Last Love,* Twentieth Century-Fox, 1975.
Paula Hollinger, *Hustle,* Paramount, 1975.
Tess Skeffington, *Murder by Death,* Columbia, 1976.
Penelope, *The Great Smokey Roadblock* (also known as *The Last of the Cowboys*), Dimension, 1976.
Betty DeBoop, *The Cheap Detective,* Columbia, 1978.
Mother, *FM* (also known as *Citizen's Band*), Universal, 1978.
Captain Doreen Lewis, *Private Benjamin,* Warner Bros., 1980.
Pandemonium (also known as *Thursday the 12th*), Metro-Goldwyn-Mayer/United Artists, 1981.

Gail Corbin, *The Funny Farm,* New World/Mutual, 1982.
Mrs. Peacock, *Clue,* Paramount, 1985.
Stella, *Sticky Fingers,* Spectrafilm, 1988.
Hotel desk clerk, *Rented Lips,* Cineworld, 1988.
Miss Bannister, *The New Adventures of Pippi Longstocking,* Columbia, 1988.
Judith, *It Had to Be You,* 1989.
Mrs. Wilkerson, *Stella,* Buena Vista, 1990.
Genevieve, *Texasville,* Columbia, 1990.
Judy, *White Palace,* Universal, 1990.
Laura, *Joey Takes a Cab,* 1991.
Frieda, *I Don't Buy Kisses Anymore,* Skouras, 1992.
Mrs. Randozza, *Nunzio's Second Cousin,* 1994.
Sister Margaret, *Reckless,* 1995.
Mother Superior, *Changing Habits,* A-pix Entertainment, 1996.
Mom, *Pants on Fire,* Elevator Pictures, 1997.
Mimi, *The Last Great Ride,* 1999.

Television Appearances; Series:
Regular, *Rowan and Martin's Laugh-In,* NBC, 1968.
Verla Grubb, *All My Children,* ABC, 1970.
Ma Packer, *All That Glitters,* syndicated, 1977.
Felicia Winters, *13 Queens Boulevard,* ABC, 1979.
Kit Flanagan, *A New Kind of Family,* ABC, 1979-80.
Captain Doreen Lewis, *Private Benjamin,* CBS, 1981-83.
Kate Halloran, *Off the Rack,* ABC, 1985.

Television Appearances; Miniseries:
Annie Gray, *Black Beauty,* NBC, 1978.

Television Appearances; Pilots:
Kate Halloran, *Off the Rack,* ABC, 1984.
Siobhan Owens, *Off Duty* (broadcast as an episode of *CBS Summer Playhouse*), CBS, 1988.

Television Appearances; Episodic:
Angelique McCarthy, "The Elevator Story," *All in the Family,* CBS, 1972.
Dora, "Night of the Wizard," *McMillan and Wife,* NBC, 1972.
Ruth MacKenzie, "Thy Boss's Wife," *Taxi,* ABC, 1981.
Host, *The Shape of Things,* NBC, 1982.
Brenda Babcock, "The Love That Lies," *Magnum, P.I.,* CBS, 1987.
Marion Simpson, "Old Habits Die Hard," *Murder, She Wrote,* CBS, 1987.
Mrs. O'Brien, *The Cavanaughs,* CBS, 1988.
Corinne Denby, "Draw Partner," *Newhart,* CBS, 1988.
Corinne Denby, "The Little Match Girl," *Newhart,* CBS, 1989.
Agnes, "Pilot," *Blossom,* NBC, 1990.
"Touched with Fire," *The Ray Bradbury Theatre,* USA Network, 1990.
Rick Moranis in Gravedale High (animated), NBC, 1990.
Agnes, "Dad's Girlfriend" and "My Sister's Keeper," *Blossom,* NBC, 1991.
Wanda, "Heavy Meddle," *Home Improvement,* ABC, 1992.
"Till Death Do We Part," *Tales from the Crypt,* HBO, 1993.
Loretta Lee, "Dear Deadly," *Murder, She Wrote,* CBS, 1994.
Joelle Harper, "Mean Streets," *Walker, Texas Ranger,* CBS, 1995.
Betty, "Don't Ask, Don't Tell" and "Let the Games Begin," *ER,* NBC, 1996.
Mrs. Bink, *7th Heaven* (also known as *Seventh Heaven*), The WB, 1996 and 1997.
Inspector No. 10, "Cheating on Sheila," *Mad About You,* NBC, 1997.
Lorreta Betina Rooney, *Nash Bridges,* CBS, 1997.
Grammy Anderson, "Veronica's First Thanksgiving," *Veronica's Closet,* NBC, 1997.

Also appeared in the episode, "Sifting the Ashes," *thirtysomething,* c. 1991.

Television Appearances; Movies:
Amy, *Playmates,* ABC, 1972.
Glenda, *The Blue Knight,* NBC, 1973.
Mrs. Lindholm, *My Father's House,* ABC, 1975.
Ann Muldoon, *The Night That Panicked America,* ABC, 1975.
Carol Werner, *The Death of Richie,* NBC, 1977.
Mary Jensen, *When She Was Bad. . .,* ABC, 1979.
Marie, *My Old Man,* CBS, 1979.
Jessy, *When the Circus Came to Town,* CBS, 1981.
Sara Davis, *Incident at Crestridge,* CBS, 1981.
Judith, *The Fourth Wise Man,* ABC, 1985.
Mrs. Piper/Widow Hubbard, *Babes in Toyland,* NBC, 1986.
Sylvia Zimmerman, *Blood Vows: The Story of a Mafia Wife,* NBC, 1987.
Maude Roberti, *Going to the Chapel* (also known as *Wedding Day Blues*), NBC, 1988.
Charlotte Raynor, *Deadly Intentions . . . Again?,* ABC, 1991.
Vicki Martin, *Taking Back My Life: The Nancy Ziegenmeyer Story* (also known as *The Rape of Nancy Ziegenmeyer*), CBS, 1992.
Martha Catlin, *Poisoned by Love: The Kern County Murders* (also known as *Blind Angel* and *Murder So Sweet*), CBS, 1993.
Minnie Gray, *Precious Victims,* CBS, 1993.

Barbara Mannix, *My Name Is Kate,* ABC, 1994.
Sada, *Take Me Home Again* (also known as *The Lies Boys Tell*), NBC, 1994.
The Who-Villain, *In Search of Dr. Seuss,* TNT, 1994.
Clara Cook, *Trail of Tears,* NBC, 1995.
Principal Handel, *Freaky Friday,* ABC, 1995.
Tessie, *If These Walls Could Talk,* HBO, 1996.
Board Member No. 2, *Toothless,* ABC, 1997.

Television Appearances; Specials:
Aunt, *Kraft Salutes Walt Disney World's 10th Anniversary,* CBS, 1982.
Maggie, *Lily for President,* CBS, 1982.
Working, PBS, 1982.
The Screen Actors Guild 50th Anniversary Celebration, CBS, 1984.

Stage Appearances:
(Off-Broadway debut) Title role, *Little Mary Sunshine,* Orpheum Theatre, New York City, 1959-61.
Anna Leonowens, *The King and I,* City Center Theatre, New York City, 1963.
Merry May Glockenspiel, *The Student Gypsy, or The Prince of Liederkranz,* 54th Street Theatre, New York City, 1963.
Irene Molloy, *Hello, Dolly!,* St. James Theatre, New York City, 1964-66.
And Where She Stops Nobody Knows, Center Theatre Group, Mark Taper Forum, Los Angeles, 1976.
Gethesemane Springs, Center Theatre Group, Mark Taper Forum Laboratory Production, Los Angeles, 1977.
Triptych, Center Theatre Group, Mark Taper Forum Laboratory Production, 1978.
A Couple of White Chicks Sitting around Talking, Astor Place Theatre, New York City, 1980.
Maxine Faulk, *The Night of the Iguana,* Morris Mechanic Theatre,Baltimore, MD, 1985.
Virginia Noyes, *It's Only a Play,* Center Theatre Group, Ahmanson Theatre, Los Angeles, CA, 1992.
Mrs. Malloy, *Hello, Dolly,* New York, NY, 1996.

Also appeared in *Camelot; Guys and Dolls; Bells Are Ringing; An Evening with Eileen Brennan* (one-woman show).

Major Tours:
Annie Sullivan, *The Miracle Worker,* U.S. cities, 1961-62.
Ellen Manville, *Luv,* U.S. cities, 1967.*

BRENNEMAN, Amy 1965(?)-

PERSONAL

Born in 1965 (some sources say 1964), in Connecticut; mother, a superior court judge; married Brad Silberling (a director), c. 1996. *Education:* Attended Harvard University; studied Eastern religions in Nepal.

Addresses: *Agent*—Creative Artists Agency, 9830 Wilshire Blvd., Beverly Hills, CA 90212-1804.

Career: Actress and producer. Toured as a member of the Cornerstone Theater Company (repertory group).

Awards, Honors: Emmy Award nomination, outstanding guest actress in a drama series, 1994, for "For Whom the Skell Tolls," *NYPD Blue.*

CREDITS

Film Appearances:
Susan, *Bye, Bye Love,* Twentieth Century-Fox, 1995.
Amelia, *Casper,* Universal, 1995.
Eady, *Heat,* Warner Bros., 1995.
Madelyne Thompson, *Daylight,* Universal, 1996.
Laura Walker, *Fear* (also known as *No Fear* and *Obsession mortelle*), Universal, 1996.
Annie, *Lesser Prophets,* 1997.
Chrysty, *Nevada,* Storm Entertainment, 1997.
Mary, *Your Friends & Neighbors,* Gramercy Pictures, 1998.
Grace, *The Suburbans,* 1999.

Film Work; Producer:
Nevada, Storm Entertainment, 1997.

Television Appearances; Series:
Detective Janice Licalsi, *NYPD Blue,* ABC, 1993-94.
Judge Amy Madison Gray, *Judging Amy,* CBS, 1999—.

Television Appearances; Episodic:
Blanche, *Middle Ages,* CBS, 1992.
Amy Wainwright, "A Christmas Secret," *Murder, She Wrote,* CBS, 1992.
Detective Janice Licalsi, "For Whom the Skell Tolls," *NYPD Blue,* ABC, 1993.
Faye Moskowitz, "Merry Christmas, Mrs. Moskowitz," *Frasier,* NBC, 1998.

Television Appearances; Movies:
Pig in the Python, 1992.
A.T.F., 1998.

Stage Appearances:
Saint Joan of the Stockyards, Yale Repertory Theatre, New Haven, CT, 1992.

RECORDINGS

Taped Readings:
Reader on *The Claiming of Sleeping Beauty,* Simon & Schuster.

OTHER SOURCES

Periodicals:
Interview, August, 1998, pp. 118-119.*

BRIGGS, Joe Bob 1959(?)-

PERSONAL

Original name, John Bloom; born January 27, 1959 (some sources say 1953), in Texas; married Joyce Karns, September 2, 1978 (divorced, August 7, 1979); married Paula Leigh Bowen, July 3, 1988. *Education:* Attended Vanderbilt University, Nashville, TN.

Career: Television and radio host, comedian, and writer. Auto mechanic, Hooks, TX, 1974-76; singer, Lawton, OK, 1974-77; critic, *Dallas Times Herald,* Dallas, TX, 1976-77; *Texas Monthly,* Austin, staff writer, 1978-81; *Dallas Times Herald,* columnist, 1981-85; Creators Syndicate, columnist, 1984—; stand-up comedian performing in *An Evening with Joe Bob Briggs,* U.S. cities, beginning in 1985.

Member: Free Press Association (member of national board of directors).

Awards, Honors: Named Spot News Reporter of the Year, United Press International, 1976; Robert F. Kennedy Award, social reporting, 1977; Cable ACE Award nominations, 1989 and 1990.

CREDITS

Film Appearances:
Gonzo Mothcock, *The Texas Chainsaw Massacre, Part 2,* Cannon, 1986.
Dewey "Daddy-O" Phillips, *Great Balls of Fire,* Orion, 1989.
Himself, *Back to Hollywood Boulevard* (also known as *Hollywood Boulevard II*), Metro-Goldwyn-Mayer/United Artists Home Video, 1991.
(As John Bloom) Don Ward, *Casino,* 1995.
(As John Bloom) Shock Technician, *Face/Off* (also known as *Face Off*), 1997.

Television Appearances; Series:
Host, *Joe Bob's Drive-In Theatre,* The Movie Channel, 1986-93.
Host, *Monstervision,* TNT, 1994—.
Contributor, "God Stuff," *The Daily Show* (also know as *The Daily Show with Jon Stewart*), Comedy Central, 1996—.

Television Appearances; Other:
(As Joe-Bob Brentwood) *The Stand* (miniseries; also known as *Stephen King's The Stand*), 1994.

Also appeared on *The Tonight Show.*

Radio Appearances; Series:
Host, *Media America,* syndicated, 1988—.
Host of *Joe Bob's Drive-In Review,* 1989-91.

RECORDINGS

Videos:
The Chiller Theatre Expo Video, Vol. 1, 1992.
Himself, *After Sunset: The Life & Times of the Drive-In Theater,* 1995.

WRITINGS

Radio Series:
Writer for *Joe Bob's Drive-In Review,* 1989-91.

Books:
(With Jim Atkinson) *Evidence of Love,* 1984.
Joe Bob Goes to the Drive-In, Delacorte (New York City), 1987.
A Guide to Western Civilization; or, My Story, Delacorte, 1988.
Joe Bob Goes Back to the Drive-In, Delacorte, 1990.
The Cosmic Wisdom of Joe Bob Briggs, Random House (New York City), 1990.
Iron Joe Bob, Atlantic Monthly Press (New York City), 1992.

Other:
Syndicated columns include "Joe Bob Goes to the Drive-In," 1984—, and "Joe Bob's America," 1988—. Contributor of articles and reviews to magazines and newspapers, including *Playboy, Washingtonian, Texas Monthly,* and *The Door.* Author of the biweekly newsletter *We Are the Weird,* Briggs Museum of American Culture, 1985.

Adaptations: *Evidence of Love* was adapted for the television movie, *A Killing in a Small Town.**

BRILL, Fran 1946-

PERSONAL

Full name, Frances Joan Brill; born September 30, 1946, in Chester, PA; daughter of Joseph M. (a doctor) and Linette Brill; married Clint Ramsden, July 14, 1979 (divorced, 1983); married Francis Robert Kelly (a writer), June 17, 1988. *Education:* Boston University, B.F.A. *Religion:* Methodist.

Addresses: *Agent*—Ambrosio/Mortimer and Associates, 165 West 46 St., Suite 1214, New York, NY 10036-2501.

Career: Actress and puppeteer.

Awards, Honors: Emmy Awards, 1974, 1986, 1987, 1988, and 1995, for *Sesame Street;* Drama Desk Award nominations, 1975, for *What Every Woman Knows* and 1981, for *Knuckle.*

CREDITS

Stage Appearances:

(Broadway debut) Student leader, *Red, White, and Maddox,* Cort Theatre, New York City, 1969.

Nancy Twinkle, *Little Mary Sunshine,* Equity Library Theatre, Master Theatre, New York City, 1970.

Ruth, *The Effect of Gamma Rays on Man-in-the-Moon Marigolds,* Washington Theatre Club, Washington, DC, 1970.

Mrs. Sullen, *The Beaux' Stratagem,* Center Stage, Baltimore, MD, 1971.

Essie, *You Can't Take It with You,* Actors Theatre of Louisville, Louisville, KY, 1972.

Margaret, *A Man for All Seasons,* Actors Theatre of Louisville, 1972.

Maggie Wylie, *What Every Woman Knows,* Roundabout Theatre, New York City, 1975.

Lily Bart, *The House of Mirth,* Long Wharf Theatre, New Haven, CT, 1976.

Portia, *The Merchant of Venice,* Meadow Brook Theatre, Rochester, MI, 1977.

Mrs. June, *How He Lied to Her Husband,* Counterpoint Theatre Company, New York City, 1977.

Overruled, Counterpoint Theatre Company, New York City, 1977.

Ersilia, *To Clothe the Naked,* Roundabout Theatre, New York City, 1977.

Lorraine, *Scribes,* Phoenix Theatre Company, Marymount Manhattan Theatre, New York City, 1977.

Fish, *Dusa, Fish, Stas, and Vi,* Center Theatre Group, Mark Taper Forum, Los Angeles, 1978.

Helena Charles, *Look Back in Anger,* Roundabout Theatre, New York City, 1980.

Leona, *Jacob's Ladder,* Workshop of the Players Art Theatre, New York City, 1980.

Jenny Wilbur, *Knuckle,* Hudson Guild Theatre, New York City, 1981.

Jenny, *Chapter Two,* Meadow Brook Theatre, 1982.

Stella, *A Streetcar Named Desire,* Hartman Theatre Company, Stamford, CT, 1982.

Varya, *The Cherry Orchard,* Long Wharf Theatre, New Haven, CT, 1982.

Marathon of One-Act Plays '82, Ensemble Studio Theatre, New York City, 1982.

Jenny, *Real Estate,* Arena Stage, Washington, DC, 1983.

Rita, *Skirmishes,* Manhattan Theatre Club, New York City, 1983.

Helen, *Baby with the Bathwater,* Playwrights Horizons, New York City, 1983.

Extremities, Japan, 1983.

Dorine, *Tartuffe,* Yale Repertory Theatre, New Haven, CT, 1984.

Holding Patterns, Musical Theatre Works, New York City, 1984.

Mary Hutton, *Paris Bound,* Long Wharf Theatre, 1985.

Festival of Original One-Act Comedies, Manhattan Punch Line, New York City, 1985-86.

Lydia, *A Delicate Situation,* Young Playwright's Festival, Playwrights Horizons, New York City, 1986.

Elizabeth, *Taking Steps,* York Theatre Company, Church of the Heavenly Rest, New York City, 1986.

Sybil Swensen, *Claptrap,* Manhattan Theatre Club, 1987.

Beth, *Otherwise Engaged,* Parker Playhouse, Ft. Lauderdale, FL, 1988.

Betty Armstrong, *Hyde in Hollywood,* Playwrights Horizons, American Place Theatre, New York City, 1989.

Emilia, *Desdemona, a Play about a Handkerchief,* Circle Repertory Company, New York City, 1993.

Also appeared at (stage debut) Theatre Atlanta, 1968.

Major Tours:
Appeared in touring productions of *Lend Me a Tenor* and *Quartermaine's Terms.*

Film Appearances:
Sally Hayes, *Being There,* United Artists, 1979.
Reuben, Reuben, Twentieth Century-Fox, 1983.
Mrs. Sloan, *Old Enough,* Orion Classics, 1984.
Mother, *Seize the Day,* 1986.
Debbie, *Lip Service,* 1988.
Dana Mardukas, *Midnight Run,* Universal, 1988.
Routed (short film), Izar, 1989.
Lily, *What about Bob?,* Buena Vista, 1991.
Angie, *City Hall,* Columbia Pictures an Castle Rock, 1996.
Voice of Mrs. Perigrew, *Doug's 1st Movie* (animated), Buena Vista, 1999.

Television Appearances; Series:
Fran Bachman, *How to Survive a Marriage,* NBC, 1974-75.
The Jim Henson Hour, NBC, 1989.

Also appeared as various Muppet characters, *Sesame Street,* PBS; and provided voice characterization for *Doug* (animated), Nickelodeon and ABC.

Television Appearances; Movies:
Suze Winter, *Amber Waves,* ABC, 1980.
Lip Service, HBO, 1988.

Television Appearances; Episodic:
Mother, "Seize the Day," *American Playhouse,* PBS, 1986.
Kate and Allie, CBS, 1986.
(As Francesca Brill) Angie Fry, "We Love You, That's Why We're Here," *A Very Peculiar Practice,* 1986.
Joan Cahill, *Spenser: For Hire,* ABC, 1987.
Jill, *All My Children,* ABC, 1987.
Katherine, *A Year in the Life,* NBC, 1988.
Sondra More, "Prisoner of Love," *Law & Order,* NBC, 1990.
Eileen, *As the World Turns,* ABC, 1991.
(As Francesca Brill) Friend, "Mrs. Hat and Mrs. Red," *Murder Most Horrid,* 1991.
"Privileged," *Law & Order,* NBC, 1995.
Robbie Winston, *All My Children,* ABC, 1996.
Beverly, *The Guiding Light,* CBS, 1997.
"Carrier," *Law & Order,* NBC, 1998.

Also appeared as Leah Barllett, *Law & Order,* NBC; and in *Nurse,* CBS; *Family,* ABC; *Today's F.B.I.,* ABC; *Barnaby Jones,* CBS; *Conan O'Brien,* NBC; and *Against the Law,* Fox.

Television Appearances; Specials:
Kaye, "Oh, Boy! Babies!," *NBC Special Treat,* NBC, 1983.
Sesame Street . . . Twenty and Still Counting, NBC, 1989.
The Muppets Celebrate Jim Henson, CBS, 1990.
Betty Armstrong, "Hyde in Hollywood," *American Playhouse,* PBS, 1991.
Voice of Prairie Dawn, *Big Bird's Birthday or Let Me Eat Cake,* PBS,1991.
Renaissance, PBS, 1993.
Sesame Street Stays Up Late! A Monster New Year's Eve Party, PBS, 1993.
Mrs. DiFazio, "Same Difference," *CBS Schoolbreak Specials,* CBS, 1994.
Voices of Prairie Dawn and Zoe, *Sesame Street's All-Star 25th Birthday: Stars and Street Forever,* ABC, 1994.
Voice, *Doug's Secret Christmas,* ABC, 1996.
Elmo Saves Christmas, PBS, 1996.

Also appeared in *Look Back in Anger,* Showtime.

RECORDINGS

Albums:
Performed in the recordings *Red, White, and Maddox* (original cast recording), Metromedia Records; and *The Muppet Show,* Pye Records (U.K.).*

BROWN, Arvin 1940-

PERSONAL

Full name, Arvin Bragin Brown; born May 24, 1940, in Los Angeles, CA; son of Herman S. and Annette R. (Edelman) Brown; married Joyce Ebert (an actress), November 2, 1969. *Education:* Stanford University, B.A., 1961; University of Bristol, certificate in drama, 1962; Harvard University, M.A., 1963; postgraduate work, Yale University, 1963-65.

Addresses: *Office*—Long Wharf Theatre, 222 Sargent Dr., New Haven, CT 06511-5955.

Career: Director and producer. Long Wharf Theatre, New Haven, CT, supervisor of apprentice program, 1965, director of Children's Theatre, 1965-67, artistic director, 1967—; Williamstown Theatre Festival, Williamstown, MA, associate director, 1969; Salzburg Seminar, Salzburg, Austria, lecturer on directing, 1972; International Theatre Conference, Bulgaria,

Hungary, delegate, 1979; guest lecturer, New Play Center, Vancouver, British Columbia, Canada, 1980, and University of Illinois at Urbana, 1980 and 1982.

Member: Theatre Communications Group (co-director, 1972-1976), Theatre Advisory Panel, National Endowment for the Arts, International Theatre Institute, Society of Stage Directors and Choreographers, Directors Guild.

Awards, Honors: Fulbright Scholarship, 1962; Vernon Rice Award, best off-Broadway director, 1971, for *Long Day's Journey into Night; Variety* Poll Award, best off-Broadway director, 1971; Antoinette Perry Award nomination, best director of a play, 1975, for *The National Health;* Antoinette Perry Award nominations, best reproduction, 1983, for *A View from the Bridge,* and 1984, for *American Buffalo;* Antoinette Perry Awards, best reproduction, 1985, for *Joe Egg,* and 1987, for *All My Sons;* George Abbott Award, 1992; O'Neill's People Award, 1995; honorary degrees from University of New Haven, 1976, University of Bridgeport, 1978, Fairfield University, 1985, and Albertus Magnus, 1993.

CREDITS

Stage Work; Director:

Long Day's Journey into Night, Long Wharf Theatre, New Haven, CT, 1966.
Misalliance, Long Wharf Theatre, 1967.
The Glass Menagerie, Long Wharf Theatre, 1967.
The Rehearsal, Long Wharf Theatre, 1967.
The Indian Wants the Bronx, London, 1967.
A Whistle in the Dark, Long Wharf Theatre, 1968.
Don Juan in Hell, Long Wharf Theatre, 1968.
The Lion in Winter, Long Wharf Theatre, 1968.
A Whistle in the Dark, Mercury Theatre, New York City, 1969.
The Indian Wants the Bronx and *It's Called Sugar Plum* (double-bill), Long Wharf Theatre, 1969.
Ghosts, Long Wharf Theatre, 1969.
Tango, Long Wharf Theatre, 1969.
Hay Fever, Helen Hayes Theatre, New York City, 1970.
Country People, Long Wharf Theatre, 1970.
Spoon River Anthology, Long Wharf Theatre, 1970.
Yegor Bulichov, Long Wharf Theatre, 1970.
Long Day's Journey into Night, Promenade Theatre, New York City, 1971.
You Can't Take It with You, Long Wharf Theatre, 1971.
The Contractor, Long Wharf Theatre, 1971.
Solitaire/Double Solitaire, Long Wharf Theatre, 1971, then John Golden Theatre, New York City, 1971.
Hamlet, Long Wharf Theatre, 1972.
The Iceman Cometh, Long Wharf Theatre, 1972.
What Price Glory?, Long Wharf Theatre, 1972.
The Changing Room, Long Wharf Theatre, 1972.
"A Swan Song" in *Troika,* Long Wharf Theatre, 1972.
Juno and the Paycock, Long Wharf Theatre, 1973.
The Widowing of Mrs. Holroyd, Long Wharf Theatre, 1973.
Forget-Me-Not Lane, Long Wharf Theatre, 1973, then Center Theatre Group, Mark Taper Forum, Los Angeles, 1973.
The Seagull, Long Wharf Theatre, 1974.
The National Health, Long Wharf Theatre, 1974, then Circle in the Square, New York City, 1974.
Saint Joan, Ahmanson Theatre, Los Angeles, 1974.
Juno and the Paycock, Williamstown Theatre Festival, Williamstown, MA, 1974.
Ah, Wilderness!, Long Wharf Theatre, 1974, then Circle in the Square, 1975.
Artichoke, Long Wharf Theatre, 1975.
The Archbishop's Ceiling, Kennedy Center for the Performing Arts, Washington, DC, 1976-77.
Privates on Parade, Long Wharf Theatre, 1978.
I Sent a Letter to My Love, Long Wharf Theatre, 1978.
Mary Barnes, Long Wharf Theatre, 1979.
Who's Afraid of Virginia Woolf?, Long Wharf Theatre, 1979.
Strangers, John Golden Theatre, New York City, 1979.
Watch on the Rhine, Long Wharf Theatre, 1979, then John Golden Theatre, New York City, 1980.
American Buffalo, Long Wharf Theatre, 1980, then Circle in the Square Downtown, New York City, 1981-82, later Booth Theatre, New York City, 1983-84.
Open Admissions, Long Wharf Theatre, 1982.
The Cherry Orchard, Long Wharf Theatre, 1982.
Free and Clear, Long Wharf Theatre, 1982.
A View from the Bridge, Long Wharf Theatre, 1982, then Ambassador Theatre, New York City, 1983.
Tobacco Road, Long Wharf Theatre, 1984.
Albert Herring, Long Wharf Theatre, 1984.
Requiem for a Heavyweight, Long Wharf Theatre, 1984, then Martin Beck Theatre, New York City, 1985.
Joe Egg (also known as *A Day in the Death of Joe Egg*), Roundabout Theatre, New York City, 1984-85, then Longacre Theatre, New York City, 1985.
The Normal Heart, Long Wharf Theatre, 1985.
All My Sons, Long Wharf Theatre, 1986, then John Golden Theatre, New York City, 1987.
Self Defense, Long Wharf Theatre, 1987, then Joyce Theatre, New York City, 1987.
Our Town, Long Wharf Theatre, 1987.

Ah, Wilderness!, Yale Repertory Theatre, New Haven, CT, 1988, then Neil Simon Theatre, New York City, 1988.
The Crucible, Long Wharf Theatre, 1989.
Stage II Workshops: Established Price, Long Wharf Theatre, 1990.
The Voysey Inheritance, Long Wharf Theatre, 1990.
Picnic, Long Wharf Theatre, 1990.
Booth Is Back, Long Wharf Theatre, 1991.
A Touch of the Poet, Long Wharf Theatre, 1991.
Chinese Coffee, Circle in the Square Uptown, New York City, 1992.
Private Lives, Broadhurst Theatre, New York City, 1992.
A Month in the Country, Long Wharf Theatre, 1992.
The Twilight of the Golds, Booth Theatre, New York City, 1993.
Absurd Person Singular, Long Wharf Theatre, 1993.
Misalliance, Long Wharf Theatre, 1994.
Saturday, Sunday, Monday, Long Wharf Theatre, 1994.
The Entertainer, Long Wharf Theatre, 1995.
Denial, Long Wharf Theatre, 1995.
A Song at Twilight, Long Wharf Theatre, 1996.

Also directed *The Stronger,* University of Bristol, Bristol, U.K.

Stage Work; Director; Opera:
Albert Herring, Long Wharf Theatre, 1985.
Turandot, Connecticut Grand Opera, 1986.
The Tender Land, Long Wharf Theatre, 1987.
Don Giovanni, Virginia Opera, 1987.
Regina, Long Wharf Theatre, 1988.
Anna Bolena, Virginia Opera, 1989.
Cosi Fan Tutte, Virginia Opera, 1991.
Porgy and Bess, Metropolitan Opera, 1992.
The Crucible, Tulsa Opera, 1995.

Television Work; Director; Episodic:
Chicago Hope, CBS, 1995.
Picket Fences (three episodes), CBS, 1995.
413 Hope Street, Fox, 1997.
Nothing Sacred, ABC, 1997.
Party of Five, Fox, 1997.
The Practice, ABC, 1997 and 1998.
Ally McBeal, Fox, 1998.
Dawson's Creek, The WB, 1998.
To Have & to Hold, CBS, 1998.

Television Work; Director; Specials:
"The Widowing of Mrs. Holroyd," *Theatre in America,* PBS, 1974.
"Forget-Me-Not Lane," *Theatre in America,* PBS, 1975.
"Ah, Wilderness!," *Theatre in America,* PBS, 1976.
Close Ties, Entertainment Channel, 1983.

Television Work; Director; Movies:
Diary of the Dead, 1980.
A Change of Heart, Lifetime, 1998.*

BUELL, Bill 1952-

PERSONAL

Born September 21, 1952, in Taipai, Taiwan; son of William Ackerman Buell (a diplomat). *Education:* Attended Portland State University and East 15 Acting School; studied with Nikos Psachorapolous and Sue Seton in New York.

Career: Actor.

CREDITS

Stage Appearances:
(Off-Broadway debut) *Crazy Now,* 1972.
(Broadway debut) Derek, *Once a Catholic,* Helen Hayes Theater, 1979.
Jailer, *Promenade,* Theatre Off Park, New York City, 1983.
Nick Finchling, *The Common Pursuit,* Promenade Theatre, New York City, 1986-87.
Charlie, *The Foreigner,* Alaska Repertory Theatre, Anchorage, 1987.
Red, *Coyote Ugly,* New York Theatre Workshop, New York City, 1987.
Bowery Boy and Mr. Thompson, *Alias Jimmy Valentine,* Musical Theatre Works, New York City, 1988.
Wally Gruber, *Kiss Me Quick Before the Lava Reaches the Village,* Music Theatre Works, New York City, 1988.
Gus Bottomly, *Welcome to the Club,* The Music Box, New York City, 1989.
Maitre Simon and Officer's Assistant, *The Miser,* Circle in the Square Uptown, New York City, 1990.
Harry, *The Life,* Westbeth Theatre Center, New York City, 1990.
Leslie Bainbridge, *Taking Steps,* Circle in the Square Uptown, New York City, 1991.
Judge Alex T. Waldman, *Groundhog,* Stage II, New York City, 1992.
Stagehand, Elmo, Out of Work Man, Fisherman, Bumfork Tramp, and Spectacle Inspector, *On the*

Bum, or The Next Train Through, New York City, 1992.

Minister and Mr. Simpson, *The Who's Tommy,* St. James Theatre, New York City, 1993-95.

Edgar Beane, *Titanic,* Lunt-Fontanne Theatre, New York City, 1997-98.

Also appeared in *Lorenzaccio;* as Jimmy Johnson/Louis Howe, *Annie,* Broadway production; Patsy/Brian Waterhouse, *The First,* Broadway production; Harry, *Declasse,* Lion Theater, New York; Verges, *Much Ado About Nothing,* Yale Repertory Theatre; Perry, *The Royal Family,* Philadelphia Drama Guild; Jim, *The Glass Menagerie,* Philadelphia Drama Guild; Bernardo/Second Grave Digger, *Hamlet,* Philadelphia Drama Guild; Poulengey/D'Estivet, *St. Joan,* Philadelphia Drama Guild; Albert Proesser, *Hobson's Choice,* Philadelphia Drama Guild; Tom Snout, *A Midsummer's Night Dream,* Alaska Repertory; Slovitch, *Fools,* Alaska Repertory, Alaska Repertory; Christopher Wren, *The Mousetrap,* Birmingham Theatre; appeared as The King, *Big River,* Broadway production; *Anna Karenina,* Broadway production; Francis and Ponce, *Bad Habits,* Manhattan Theatre Club; Derek, *Quartermaine's Terms,* Playhouse 91 and Old Globe Theatre, Sand Diego, CA; Casimir, *Aristocrats,* Manhattan Theatre Club; Bert Lahr, *Lahr and Mercedes,* Denver Center Theatre; *Vandals,* Eugene O'Neill Theatre Center; Marcellus, *The Music Man,* Starlight Theatre; and as Mendy, *Lisbon Lisbon Traviata,* Seattle Repertory Theatre.

Major Tours:

Appeared as Judas/Herbie, *Godspell,* Jameson, *Passion of Dracula,* and as Thatcher, Harvey Wilkes, and Silas Phelps, *Big River,* all U.S. cities.

Film Appearances:

Danny, *Wind,* TriStar, 1992.

Band director, *Miracle on 34th Street,* Twentieth Century-Fox, 1994.

Mr. Wiener, *Welcome to the Dollhouse* (also known as *Middle Child*), Sony Pictures Classics, 1995.

Officer Dan, *The Love Letter,* DreamWorks, 1999.

Also appeared in *Wet Exit* and *Quiz Show.*

Television Appearances; Episodic:

Douglas Pomeratz, *Law & Order,* NBC, 1992.

Also appeared in *Ryan's Hope,* ABC; Homer, *All My Children,* ABC; and as Cavanaugh, *One Life to Live,* ABC.*

BUSCEMI, Steve 1957-

PERSONAL

Born December 13, 1957, in Brooklyn, NY; married Jo Andres (a filmmaker/choreographer); children: Lucian. *Education:* Studied acting at Lee Strasberg Institute, New York City.

Addresses: *Agent*—c/o William Morris Agency, 151 El Camino Dr., Beverly Hills, CA 90212.

Career: Actor, director, and writer. Began as a stand-up comedian in New York City; also worked as a fireman.

Member: Academy of Motion Picture Arts and Sciences.

Awards, Honors: Independent Spirit Award nomination, best supporting male, 1990, for *Mystery Train;* Independent Spirit Award, best supporting male, 1993, for *Reservoir Dogs;* Independent Spirit Award nomination, best first feature, 1997, for *Trees Lounge;* (With Peter Stormare) MTV Movie Award nomination, best on-screen duo, 1997, for *Fargo;* Directors Guild of America Award nomination, outstanding directorial achievement in a dramatic series, night, 1999, for episode "Finnegan's Wake," *Homicide: Life on the Street.*

CREDITS

Film Appearances:

The Way It Is, or Eurydice in the Avenue, 1984.

Dead pimp, *No Picnic,* 1986.

Nick, *Parting Glances,* Cinecom, 1986.

Worker, *Sleepwalk,* Sultan Entertainment, 1986.

Nicky, *Heart,* Starmaker, 1987.

Johnny, *Kiss Daddy Good Night* (also known as *By Any Other Name*), Academy Entertainment, 1987.

Switch Blade, *Call Me,* Vestron, 1988.

Fred, *Vibes,* Columbia/TriStar, 1988.

Eddy, *Heart of Midnight,* Samuel Goldwyn, 1989.

Whining Willie, *Bloodhounds of Broadway,* Columbia, 1989.

Young physics student, *Borders,* Mystic Fire, 1989.

Coffee and Cigarettes, 1989.

Gregory Stark—performance artist, "Life Lessons," *New York Stories,* Buena Vista, 1989.

Wilfredo, *Slaves of New York,* TriStar, 1989.

Charlie, *Mystery Train,* Orion, 1989.

Edward Bellingham, "Lot 249," *Tales from the Dark Side: The Movie,* Paramount, 1990.
Virgil the farmhand, *Force of Circumstance,* Ad Hoc, 1990.
Kaggs, *The Grifters,* Universal, 1990.
Mink, *Miller's Crossing,* Twentieth Century-Fox, 1990.
Test Tube, *King of New York,* New Line, 1990.
Opp man, *Zandalee,* Live Home Video, 1991.
Chet, *Barton Fink,* Twentieth Century-Fox, 1991.
Irving, *Billy Bathgate,* Buena Vista, 1991.
Louis, *CrissCross,* Metro-Goldwyn-Mayer, 1992.
Adolpho Rollo, *In the Soup* (also known as *In the soup: en la sopa*), Triton Pictures, 1992.
Painted Heart, 1992.
Mr. Pink, *Reservoir Dogs,* Miramax, 1992.
Conspiracy nut, *Me and the Mob,* Arrow Video, 1992.
Stranger, *What Happened to Pete?,* 1992.
Frank, *Twenty Bucks,* Triton Pictures, 1993.
Danny, *Trusting Beatrice,* Castle Hill, 1993.
Willy "The Weasel" Wilhelm, *Rising Sun,* Twentieth Century-Fox, 1993.
Ed Chilton, *Ed and His Dead Mother,* Twentieth Century-Fox, 1993.
Beatnik Barman, *The Hudsucker Proxy,* Warner Bros., 1994.
Rex, *Airheads,* Twentieth Century-Fox, 1994.
Buddy Holly waiter, *Pulp Fiction,* Miramax, 1994.
Nick Reve, *Living in Oblivion* (also known as *Scene Six, Take One*), Lemon Sky Productions, 1994.
Ned, *Floundering,* Strand, 1994.
Mickey, *Somebody to Love,* 1994.
(Uncredited) Danny McGrath, *Billy Madison,* 1995.
(Uncredited) Bartender, *Dead Man,* 1995.
Buscemi, *Desperado,* Columbia, 1995.
Mr. Shhh, *Things to Do in Denver When You're Dead,* Miramax, 1995.
Black Kites, 1996.
Carl Rolvaag, *Fargo,* Gramercy, 1996.
"Map to the Stars" Eddie, *John Carpenter's Escape from L.A.* (also known as *Escape from L.A.*), Paramount, 1996.
Johnny Flynn, *Kansas City,* Fine Line, 1996.
Ed Hoyt, *The Search For One-Eye Jimmy,* Cabin Fever Entertainment, 1996.
Tommy, *Trees Lounge,* Live Entertainment, 1996.
Garland Greene, *Con Air,* Buena Vista, 1997.
Divine Trash, Stratosphere and Divine Trash, 1997.
Nick, *The Real Blonde,* Paramount, 1997.
Rockhound, *Armageddon,* Buena Vista, 1998.
Franky Goes to Hollywood, 1998.
Drexel, *Louis and Frank,* 1998.
Donny, *The Big Lebowski,* Gramercy, 1998.
Happy Franks, *The Imposters,* Twentieth Century-Fox, 1998.
(Uncredited) David Veltri, *The Wedding Singer,* 1998.
Shanghai Noon, forthcoming.

Film Work:
Producer and director, *What Happened to Pete?,* 1993.
Director, *Tress Lounge,* Live Entertainment, 1996.

Television Appearances; Episodic:
Rickles, *Miami Vice,* 1984.
Electronics store clerk, "Re-Entry," *The Equalizer,* 1986.
Death-row schizophrenic, *L.A. Law,* NBC, 1991.
Howie Balenger, "Token Friend," *Mad About You,* NBC, 1992.
"Forever Ambergris," *Tales from the Crypt,* HBO, 1993.
Gordon Pratt, "End Game," *Homicide: Life on the Street,* NBC, 1995.
Mr. Marchetti, "Mr. Louder's Birthday Party," *The Drew Carey Show,* ABC, 1998.

Television Appearances; Miniseries:
Luke, *Lonesome Dove,* CBS, 1989.

Television Appearances; Movies:
Philo, *The Last Outlaw,* HBO, 1993.

Television Appearances; Specials:
The Adventures of Pete and Pete: Space, Geeks, and Johnny Unitas, Nickelodeon, 1992.
Mr. Hickle, *The Adventures of Pete and Pete: Apocalypse Pete,* Nickelodeon, 1994.
Forever Ambergris, 1993.
Quentin Tarantino: Hollywood's Boy Wonder, 1994.
In Bad Taste: The John Waters Story, Independent Film Channel, 1999.

Television Work; Director:
"Finnegan's Wake," *Homicide: Life on the Street,* NBC, 1997.

WRITINGS

Screenplays:
What Happened to Pete?, 1993.
Trees Lounge, Live Entertainment, 1996.

Other:
Contributor to periodicals, including *Interview.*

OTHER SOURCES

Periodicals:

Entertainment Weekly, August 19, 1994, p. 43; March 7, 1997, p. 74; November/December 1997, p. 52.

Interview, October, 1996, pp. 106-110.

People Weekly, October 21, 1996, p. 22; July 13, 1998, p. 128.*

BUSFIELD, Timothy 1957-

PERSONAL

Born June 12, 1957, in Lansing, MI; son of Roger (a drama professor) and Jean (a secretary) Busfield; married Radha Delamarter (an actress and director; divorced); married Jennifer Merwin (a fashion designer); children: (first marriage) Willy; (second marriage) Daisy, Samuel. *Education:* Graduated from East Tennessee State University; trained for the stage at the Actors Theatre of Louisville.

Addresses: *Agent*—c/o William Morris Agency, 151 South El Camino Dr., Beverly Hills, CA 90212-2704.

Career: Actor and director. Member, Circle Repertory Co., New York City, NY; founder, director and writer, Fantasy Theatre, Sacramento, CA, 1986—; founder and co-producer, The "B" Theatre, 1992.

Awards, Honors: Emmy Award, outstanding supporting actor in a drama series, 1991, for *thirtysomething.*

CREDITS

Film Appearances:

Soldier with mortar, *Stripes,* Columbia, 1981.

Arnold Poindexter, *Revenge of the Nerds,* Twentieth Century-Fox, 1984.

Arnold Poindexter, *Revenge of the Nerds II: Nerds in Paradise,* Twentieth Century-Fox, 1987.

Mark, *Field of Dreams,* Universal, 1989.

Dick Gordon, *Sneakers,* Universal, 1992.

Frank, *The Skateboard Kid,* Concorde/New Horizons Corp., 1993.

Tony Sacco, *Striking Distance,* Columbia, 1993.

Lou Collins, *Little Big League,* Columbia, 1994.

Fred, *Quiz Show,* Buena Vista, 1994.

Woods, *First Kid,* Buena Vista, 1996.

Robert Levin, *The Souler Opposite,* Curb Entertainment, 1997.

Brian, *Erasable You,* Dorian Productions, 1998.

Wanted, 1999.

Television Appearances; Series:

Mark Potter, *Reggie,* ABC, 1983.

Dr. John "J.T." McIntyre, Jr., *Trapper John, M.D.,* CBS, 1984-86.

Elliot Weston, *thirtysomething,* ABC, 1989-91.

Sam Byrd, *The Byrds of Paradise,* ABC, 1994.

Tom McManus, *Champs,* ABC, 1996.

Television Appearances; Movies:

Paul Jarrett, *Strays,* USA Network, 1991.

Elfred Schultz, *Calendar Girl, Cop Killer? The Bambi Bembenek Story* (also known as *The Heart of the Lie*), ABC, 1992.

Del Calvin, *Fade to Black,* USA Network, 1993.

Assistant District Attorney John Thorn, *Murder between Friends,* NBC, 1994.

Detective Walt Keller, *In the Shadow of Evil,* CBS, 1995.

Pete Honeycutt, *In the Line of Duty: Kidnapped* (also known as *In the Line of Duty: Taxman*), NBC, 1995.

Matthew Grissom, *Shadow of a Scream* (also known as *The Unspeakable*), 1997.

Major Robert Carr, *Buffalo Soldiers,* TNT, 1997.

Ray, *Trucks,* USA Network, 1997.

Walter Ference, *When Secrets Kill,* ABC, 1997.

Connor Thornton, *Dream House,* UPN, 1998.

The Darklings, Fox Family Channel, 1999.

Frank Shawson, *Time at the Top,* Showtime, 1999.

Television Appearances; Episodic:

Doug, *Family Ties,* 1984.

Spy Guy, *Lois & Clark: The New Adventures of Superman,* 1995.

Dr. Jon Hoffman, "Under the Bed," *The Outer Limits,* Showtime, 1995.

Tracey Takes On. . ., HBO, 1996.

Appeared in *After M*A*S*H,* CBS; *The Paper Chase,* Showtime; *Matlock,* NBC/ABC; *Love American Style,* ABC; *Hotel,* ABC.

Television Appearances; Specials:

Host, "Don't Divorce the Children," *Your Family Matters,* Lifetime, 1990.

The Search for the New Ideal Man, ABC, 1992.

"Addicted to Fame," *First Person with Maria Shriver,* NBC, 1994.

The ESPY Awards, ESPN, 1996.

Walter Gordon, *What's Right with America,* CBS, 1997.

Television Work; Episodic:
Directed episodes of *thirtysomething,* ABC.

Stage Appearances:
A Life, Long Wharf Theatre, New Haven, CT, 1981.
Hotspur, *Richard II,* Circle Repertory Company, Entermedia Theatre, New York City, 1982.
Eugene and Stanley (understudy), *Brighton Beach Memoirs,* Alvin Theatre, New York City, 1983.
(Broadway debut) Lieutenant Daniel Kaffee, *A Few Good Men,* Music Box Theatre, New York City, 1990.

Also appeared in *Young Playwrights Festival,* Circle Repertory Company; *Robin Goodfellow, Richard II, A Tale Told, Mass Appeal, The Tempest, Getting Out, A Life.* Company member of Actors Theatre of Louisville, Louisville, KY, 1980-81, and Circle Repertory Company, New York City.*

BYRNE, David 1952-

PERSONAL

Born May 14, 1952, in Dumbarton, Scotland; immigrated to the United States, 1958; British citizen; son of Thomas (an electrical engineer) and Emily Anderson (a special education teacher; maiden name, Brown) Byrne; married Adelle Ann Lutz (a costume designer and actress), July 8, 1987; children: Malu Abeni Valentine. *Education:* Attended Rhode Island School of Design, 1970-71, and Maryland Institute College of Art, 1971-72.

Addresses: *Contact*—c/o Luaka Bop, Warner Brothers Records, 75 Rockefeller Plaza, New York, NY, 10019-6908.

Career: Musician, composer, producer, director, and screenwriter. Songwriter, singer, and guitarist, Talking Heads, 1975-92; Index Video, director and producer, 1983—. Designer for the concert stage, lighting, album covers, and posters, 1977—; producer of record albums, 1980—; producer and director of music videos, with several in the permanent collection of the Museum of Modern Art, New York City; illustrator, including art for Talking Heads albums.

Member: Screen Actors Guild, Writers Guild of America East, Musicians Union.

Awards, Honors: National Society of Film Critics Award, best documentary, 1984, for *Stop Making Sense;* Video Vanguard Award, MTV, 1985, for directing Talking Heads rock videos; New York Dance and Performance (Bessie) Award, Dance Theatre Workshop, best choreographer or creator, 1987, for *The Knee Plays;* shared Academy Award and Golden Globe Award, best original score, both 1988, for *The Last Emperor.*

CREDITS

Film Appearances:
The True Story of Eskimo Nell, Filmways, 1975.
Performer, *Stop Making Sense,* Cinecom International, 1983.
Narrator and lip syncher, *True Stories,* Warner Bros., 1986.
Performer, *Dead End Kids,* Ikon, 1986.
Completely Pogued, 1988.
Heavy Petting, 1988.
Bartender, *Checking Out,* Warner Bros., 1989.
Ile Aiye, 1989.
Between the Teeth (documentary), Todo Mundo, 1994.

Film Work; Director, Except Where Indicated:
True Stories, Warner Bros., 1986.
April 16, 1989, 1988.
Ile Aiye, 1989.
Executive producer, *Umbabarauma,* 1989.
Between the Teeth (documentary), Todo Mundo, 1994.

Television Appearances; Specials:
Rolling Stone Magazine's 20 Years of Rock and Roll (also known as *Rolling Stone Magazine's 20th Anniversary Special* and *Rolling Stone Presents 20 Years of Rock 'n' Roll*), ABC, 1987.
Decade (also known as *MTV's Decade*), syndicated, 1989.
Red, Hot, and Blue, ABC, 1990.
Racism: Points of View, syndicated, 1991.
An Astronaut's View of Earth, PBS, 1992.
Lou Reed: Rock and Roll Heart, PBS, 1998.

Television Appearances; Episodic:
Byron, "A Family Tree," *Trying Times,* PBS, 1987.
Alive from Off-Center, PBS, 1987.
Survival Guides, PBS, 1987.
Rock & Roll, 1995.
Himself, "Fire Drill," *Space Ghost Coast to Coast,* 1995.
Host, *Sessions at West 54th,* PBS, 1997.

Television Work; Specials:

Segment director, *Red, Hot, and Blue,* ABC, 1990.

RECORDINGS

Albums:

(With The Talking Heads) *Talking Heads 77,* Sire, 1977.

(With The Talking Heads) *More Songs about Building and Food,* Sire, 1978.

(With The Talking Heads) *Fear of Music,* Sire, 1979.

(With The Talking Heads) *Remain in Light,* Sire, 1980.

(With Brian Eno) *My Life in the Bush of Ghosts,* Sire, 1981.

(With The Talking Heads) *The Name of This Band Is Talking Heads,* Sire, 1982.

David Byrne: Songs from the Broadway Production of "The Catherine Wheel," Sire, 1982.

(With The Talking Heads) *Speaking in Tongues,* Sire, 1983.

(With The Talking Heads) *Stop Making Sense,* Sire, 1984.

Music for the Knee Plays, Sire, 1985.

(With The Talking Heads) *Little Creatures,* Sire, 1985.

(With The Talking Heads) *True Stories,* Sire, 1986.

(With The Talking Heads) *Naked,* Sire, 1988.

The Making of The Last Emperor, Virgin, 1988.

O Samba, Luaka Bop/Sire, 1989.

Rei Momo, Luaka Bop/Sire, 1989.

Beleza Tropical: Brazil Classics I, Sire/Fly, 1989.

Canciones Urgentes, 1991.

The Forest, Sire, 1991.

Uh-Oh, Warner Bros. Records, 1992.

(With The Talking Heads) *Popular Favorites 1976-1991/Sand in the Vaseline,* 1992.

David Byrne, 1994.

Feelings, Luaka Bop/Warner Bros., 1997.

Visible Mas, Imprint, 1999.

Videos:

Producer, director, and performer, *Storytelling Giant,* 1988.

(With Toni Basil) director, *Once in a Lifetime,* 1980.

Burning Down the House, 1982.

This Must Be the Place (Naive Melody), 1982.

(With Steven Johnson) *Road to Nowhere,* 1985.

Executive producer, *Blind,* 1988.

Nothing But Flowers, 1988.

WRITINGS

Screenplays:

Stop Making Sense, Cinecom International, 1983.

Ile Aiye, 1989.

Films; Composer:

(With The Talking Heads) *Stop Making Sense,* Cinecom International, 1983.

(With The Talking Heads) *True Stories,* Warner Bros., 1986.

(With Ryuichi Sakamoto and Cong Su) *The Last Emperor,* Columbia, 1987.

Heat and Sunlight, 1987.

Married to the Mob, Orion, 1988.

A Rustling of Leaves: Inside the Philippine Revolution, 1988.

Until the End of the World, 1991.

Merci, la vie, 1991.

The Book of life, True Fiction Pictures, 1998.

Films; Songwriter:

"Life During Wartime," *Times Square,* Associated Film Distributors, 1980.

"Mind," *The Animals Film,* Blue Dolphin, 1981.

"Swamp," *The King of Comedy,* Twentieth Century-Fox, 1982.

America Is Waiting, Canyon Cinema, 1982.

"Burning Down the House," *Revenge of the Nerds,* Twentieth Century-Fox, 1983.

"Once in a Lifetime," *Down and Out in Beverly Hills,* Buena Vista, 1985.

Opening song, *Something Wild,* Orion, 1986.

"Psycho Killer," "Heaven," "Thank You for Sending Me an Angel," "Found a Job," "Life During Wartime," "Slippery People," "Burning Down the House," "Making Flippy Floppy," "Swamp," "This Must Be the Place (Naive Melody)," "Girlfriend Is Better," "What a Day That Was," "Once in a Lifetime," and "Crosseyed and Painless," *True Stories,* Warner Bros., 1986.

"Perfect World," *Cross My Heart,* 1987.

"America Is Waiting," "This Must Be the Place," and "Mea Culpa," *Wall Street,* 1987.

"Creatures of Love," *Immediate Family,* 1989.

"Road to Nowhere," *Little Monsters,* 1989.

"And She Was," *Look Who's Talking,* 1989.

"Wild Wild Life," *Cool Runnings,* 1993.

"Heaven," *Philadelphia,* 1993.

"Road to Nowhere," *Reality Bites,* 1994.

"Miss America," *Palmetto,* Columbia, 1997.

Television; Composer:

Alive from Off-Center (episode), PBS, 1987.

Magicians of the Earth: The Giant Woman and the Lightning Man (movie), 1989.

Magicians of the Earth: A Young Man's Dream and a Woman's Secret (movie), 1990.

An Astronaut's View of Earth (special), PBS, 1992.

Television; Songwriter:
"Burning Down the House," *Bonnie Raitt: Road Tested* (special), 1995.
"And She Was," *Flying Blind* (episode), 1992.

Other Television Writing:
Lyricist, *Songs from Liquid Days,* CBS, 1987.

Stage Plays:
The Tourist Way of Knowledge (performance art), Public Theatre, New York City, 1985.
(With Robert Wilson) *The Forest,* Brooklyn Academy of Music Opera House, Brooklyn, NY, then Berlin, Germany, both 1988.

Stage Plays; Composer:
The Knee Plays (interludes from Wilson's epic opera *The Civil Wars*), Walker Art Center, Minneapolis, MN, 1984, then Alice Tully Hall, New York City, 1986, published by Walker Art Center, 1984.
The Forest, Brooklyn Academy of Music Opera House, then Berlin, Germany, both 1988.
Music of the Spirits (concert), Town Hall, New York City, 1989.

Composer (with Johnny Pacheco) of the dance piece *The Catherine Wheel,* performed in New York City, 1981.

Other:
(Co-author) *What the Songs Look Like: The Illustrated Talking Heads* (lyrics), Harper (New York City), 1987.
(With David Mellor and William A. Ewing) *Occupied Territory* (edited by Lynne Cohen), Aperture Foundation (New York City), 1987.

Contributor of cover illustrations to *Time*. Contributor to magazines.

Adaptations: Byrne's song "Stay Up Late" was adapted for a children's book by Maria Kalman, published by Viking Kestrel (New York City), 1987.

OTHER SOURCES

Books:
Howell, John, *David Byrne,* Thunder's Mouth Press (New York City), 1992.

Periodicals:
Billboard, September 7, 1996, pp. 8-10; May 17, 1997, pp. 14-15.
Rolling Stone, April 21, 1988, p. 42.*

BYRNES, Jim 1948-

PERSONAL

Full name, James Thomas Byrnes; born September 22, 1948; raised in St. Louis, MO; father, a municipal accountant and mother, a homemaker; companion of Robyn Post; children: (with former companion, Annette) Serene, (with Post) Caitlin. *Education:* Attended Boston University and St. Louis University.

Addresses: *Agent*—Leonard Bonnell, Characters Talent Agency, 200-105 West 2nd Ave., Vancouver, BC, V6H 3Y4, Canada. *Contact*—8184 East Blvd., Vancouver, BC, V6P 5R6, Canada. *Publicist*—SSA Public Relations, 16027 Ventura Blvd., Suite 206, Encino, CA 91436.

Career: Actor and musician. Former Easter Seals spokesperson, c. 1990. Worked variously as blues musician, fisherman, and shepherd. *Military service:* U.S. Army, 1969.

Awards, Honors: JUNO Award, Canadian Academy of Recording Arts and Sciences, best blues/gospel album, 1996, for *That River.*

CREDITS

Television Appearances; Series:
Lifeguard, *Wiseguy,* CBS, 1987-90.
Voice, *Dragon Warrior* (animated), syndicated, 1990.
Kevin, *Neon Rider* (also known as *Tenderfoot* and *Dude*), syndicated, 1990.
Joe Dawson, *Highlander: The Series,* syndicated, 1993—.

Television Appearances; Movies:
Jack Fine, *The Red Spider,* CBS, 1988.
Kurt, *In the Best Interest of the Child* (also known as *A Mother's Plea*), CBS, 1990.
Noah, *Omen IV: The Awakening,* Fox, 1991.
Benedetti, *Christmas on Division Street,* CBS, 1991.
Stan, *Dirty Work,* USA Network, 1992.
Vet, *Serving in Silence: The Margarethe Cammermeyer Story,* NBC, 1995.
Lieutenant McMahon, *Bloodhounds II,* USA Network, 1996.
Daniel Benjamin Burroughs ("Lifeguard"), *Wiseguy,* ABC, 1996.
Duke, *Final Descent,* CBS, 1997.
Doc Humphries, *Lost Treasure of Dos Santos,* 1997.

Television Appearances; Episodic:

Jim, "Should Old Acquaintance Be Forgot?, *Out of This World,* 1987.

Carl Drake, "Dead Man Walking," *The Hat Squad,* 1993.

Brett Shrager, "The Kid," *The Commish,* 1995.

Voice of Inferno, *Beast Wars* (also known as *Beast Wars: Transformers, Beasties,* and *Beasties: Transformers;* animated), syndicated, 1996.

Nelson, *G.I. Joe Extreme* (animated), 1996.

Voice of Dr. Light, *Mega Man* (animated), syndicated, 1996.

Colonel Maxwell Foley, "The Reckoning," *Two,* 1997.

Joe Dawson, "A Matter of Time," *Highlander: The Raven,* syndicated, 1998.

Gary Latimer, "The Joining," *The Outer Limits,* 1998.

Voice of Grand Vizier, *War Planets,* syndicated, 1998.

Also appeared in episodes of *Lightening Force, Danger Bay,* and *The Hitchhiker.*

Television Appearances; Miniseries:

Hands of a Stranger (also known as *Double Standard*), NBC, 1987.

Film Appearances:

Party singer, *Out of the Blue* (also known as *No Looking Back* and *Plus rien a perdre*), 1980.

Frank Hay, *Harmony Cats,* Triboro Entertainment Group, 1994.

Whale Music, Seventh Art Releasing, 1994.

Lieutenant Jim 'The Loot' Garrity, *Dream Man,* 1995.

Lieutenant Rayburn, *Under the Gun,* 1995.

Rod, *Starlight,* Astral, 1996.

Dr. Glen Green, *Drive, She Said,* Beyond Films, 1997.

Stage Appearances:

Hans, *Principia Scriptoriae,* The Studio Theatre, Washington, DC, 1989-90.

Also appeared in stage productions with a St. Louis repertory company, c. 1964.

RECORDINGS

Albums:

That River, 1995.

Burning/I Turned My Nights Into Days, 1998.

Videos:

Voice, *Mummies Alive! The Legend Begins,* 1998.

WRITINGS

Film Scores:

"That River," *The Final Cut,* Republic, 1995.

OTHER SOURCES

Periodicals:

Maclean's, January 15, 1996, p. 53.

People Weekly, May 21, 1990, pp. 105-106.*

C

CALLOW, Simon 1949-

PERSONAL

Full name, Simon Phillip Hugh Callow; born June 15, 1949, in London, England; son of Neil Francis (in business) and Yvonne Mary (a secretary; maiden name, Guise) Callow. *Education:* Attended Queen's University, Belfast, Ireland, 1967-68; trained for the stage at the London Drama Centre.

Addresses: *Agent*—(Acting) Marina Martin Associates, 12-13 Poland St., London W1V 3DE, England; Clifford Stevens, Paradigm, 200 West 57th St., Suite 900, New York, NY 10019; (directing) Harriet Cruickshank, 97 Old South Lambeth Rd., London SW8 1XU, England; (writing) Maggie Hanbury, 27 Walcot St., London SE11 4UB, England.

Career: Actor, director, and writer. Worked as a box office attendant at a London theatre.

Awards, Honors: BAFTA Film Award nomination, British Academy Awards, best supporting actor, 1987, for *A Room with a View;* Drama Desk Award nomination, best director, 1989, for *Shirley Valentine;* BAFTA Film Award nomination, British Academy Awards, best supporting actor, 1995, for *Four Weddings and a Funeral;* (with others) SAG Award, outstanding performance by a cast, 1999, for *Shakespeare in Love.*

CREDITS

Stage Appearances:

(Stage debut)*The Three Estates,* Assembly Hall Theatre, Edinburgh, Scotland, 1973.

(London debut) Crown Prince Maximilian, *Schippel,* Open Space Theatre, London, 1974.

Crown Prince Maximilian, *Schippel,* Traverse Theatre, Edinburgh, Scotland, 1974.

Passing By, Gay Sweatshop, 1975.

Redpenny, *The Doctor's Dilemma,* Mermaid Theatre, London, 1975.

Crown Prince Maximilian, *Plumber's Progress* (previously known as *Schippel*), Prince of Wales Theatre, London, 1975.

Mrs. Grabowski's Academy, Theatre Upstairs, London, 1975.

Pieter de Groot, *Soul of the White Ant,* Bush Theatre, London, 1976.

Oliver, Jack, Putter, and Rider, *Blood Sports,* Bush Theatre, 1976.

Juvenalia (one-man show), Bush Theatre, 1976.

Kutchevski, *Devil's Island,* Joint Stock Company, Royal Court Theatre, London, 1977.

Sayers, *A Mad World, My Masters,* Joint Stock Company, Young Vic Theatre, London, 1977.

Sandy, *Epsom Downs,* Joint Stock Company, Round House Theatre, London, 1977.

Title role, *Titus Andronicus,* Bristol Old Vic Theatre, Bristol, England, 1978.

Boyd, *Flying Blind,* Royal Court Theatre, London, 1978.

Title role, *The Resistible Rise of Arturo Ui,* Half Moon Theatre, London, 1978.

Ure, the old reaper, and a drunk, *The Machine Wreckers,* Half Moon Theatre, 1978.

Eddie, *Mary Barnes,* Birmingham Repertory Studio, Birmingham, England, then Royal Court Theatre, both 1978.

Orlando, *As You Like It,* National Theatre Company, Olivier Theatre, London, 1979.

Mozart, *Amadeus,* National Theatre Company, Olivier Theatre, 1979.

Stafford, *Sisterly Feelings,* National Theatre Company, Olivier Theatre, 1979.

Beefy, *The Beastly Beatitudes of Balthazar B.,* Bristol Old Vic Theatre, 1981, then Duke of York's Theatre, London, 1982.
Verlaine, *Total Eclipse,* Lyric Theatre-Hammersmith, London, 1982.
Lord Are, *Restoration,* Royal Court Theatre, 1982.
Lord Foppington, *The Relapse,* Lyric Theatre-Hammersmith, 1983.
Perelli, *On the Spot,* Albery Theatre, 1984.
Rousseau, *Melancholy Jacques,* Bush Theatre, 1984.
Kiss of the Spider Woman, Bush Theatre, 1985.
Title role, *Faust,* Lyric Theatre-Hammersmith, 1988.
Guy Burgess, "An Englishman Abroad," *Single Spies,* National Theatre Company, Queen's Theatre, London, 1988-89.
Ned, *The Destiny of Me,* Haymarket Theatre, Leicester, 1993.

Also appeared in repertory in Lincoln, U.K., 1973-74.

Stage Work; Director:
Loving Reno, Bush Theatre, 1983.
The Passport, Offstage Downstairs Theatre, London, 1985.
Nicholson Fights Croydon, Offstage Downstairs Theatre, 1986.
The Infernal Machine, Lyric Theatre-Hammersmith, 1986.
Cosi Fan Tutte, Lucerne Theatre, 1987.
Jacques and His Master, Los Angeles Theatre Center, Los Angeles, CA, 1987.
Shirley Valentine, Vaudeville Theatre, London, 1988.
Die Fledermaus, Scottish Opera, 1988.
Facades, Lyric Theatre-Hammersmith, 1988.
"An Englishman Abroad," *Single Spies,* National Theatre Company, Queen's Theatre, 1988-89.
Shirley Valentine, Booth Theatre, New York City, 1989.
Die Fledermaus, Scottish Opera, 1989-90.
Stevie Wants to Play the Blues, Los Angeles Theatre Center, 1990.
Carmen Jones, Old Vic Theatre, London, 1991.
My Fair Lady, U.K. cities, 1992.
Shades, Albery Theatre, 1992.
The Destiny of Me, Haymarket Theatre, Leicester, 1993.
Carmen Jones, U.K. and Japanese cities, 1994.
Il Trittico, Broomhill Opera, 1995.
Les Enfants du Paradis, Royal Shakespeare Company, Barbican Theatre, London, 1996.

Film Appearances:
Gossip, Boyd's Company, 1983.
Emanuel Schikaneder, *Amadeus,* Orion, 1984.
Handel, *Honor, Profit, and Pleasure,* Spectre Productions, 1985.
Mark Varner, *The Good Father,* Skouras, 1986.
Reverend Arthur Beebe, *A Room with a View,* Cinecom, 1986.
Mr. Ducie, *Maurice,* Cinecom, 1987.
Police Chief Hunt, *Manifesto* (also known as *For a Night of Love*), Cannon, 1988.
Dr. Alexis Sauer, *Mr. and Mrs. Bridge,* Miramax, 1990.
Simon Asquith, *Postcards from the Edge,* Columbia, 1990.
Music lecturer, *Howards End,* Sony Pictures Classics, 1992.
Eddie Cherdowski, *Soft Top, Hard Shoulder,* 1992.
Gareth, *Four Weddings and a Funeral,* Gramercy, 1994.
A.N. Official, *Street Fighter,* Universal, 1994.
Victory, 1994.
Charles II, *England, My England,* 1995.
Richard Cosway, *Jefferson in Paris,* Buena Vista, 1995.
Vincent Cadby, *Ace Ventura: When Nature Calls,* Warner Bros., 1995.
Le Passager Clandestin, 1995.
England, My England, 1995.
Voice of Grasshopper, *James and the Giant Peach* (animated), Buena Vista, 1996.
Captain John Fairfax, *The Scarlet Tunic,* Marie Hoy Film & Television, 1997.
San Giacomo, *Victory,* Miramax, 1997.
Keith, *Bedrooms and Hallways,* ARP Selection, 1998.
Tilney—Master of the Revels, *Shakespeare in Love,* Miramax, 1998.

Film Work; Director:
Charles Laughton: A Difficult Actor (documentary), 1988.
The Ballad of the Sad Cafe, Angelika, 1991.

Television Appearances; Miniseries:
Tom Chance, *Chance in a Million,* Thames, 1982-84.
Mr. Micawber, *David Copperfield,* BBC, 1986, then broadcast as segments of *Masterpiece Theatre,* PBS, 1988.

Television Appearances; Episodic:
Wings of Song, Granada, 1977.
Instant Enlightenment, BBC, 1979.
The poet, *La Ronda,* BBC, 1980.
Man of Destiny, BBC, 1982.
Dr. Theodore Kemp, "The Wolvercote Tongue," *Inspector Morse, Series II,* Granada, then *Mystery!,* PBS, 1988.

Voice of the Dragon, "The Reluctant Dragon," *Long Ago and Far Away,* PBS, 1989.
Politically Incorrect, Comedy Central, 1996.
Voice of Menephtah ("Moses"), *Testament: The Bible in Animation,* HBO, 1997.

Also appeared in *All the World's a Stage* and *The Dybbuk.*

Television Appearances; Specials:
Count Fosco, *The Woman in White,* PBS, 1998.

Television Appearances; Movies:
Inspector Lestrade, *Crucifer of Blood,* TNT, 1991.

Other Television Appearances:
Hugo, *Deadhead,* BBC, 1984.
Handel, *Handel,* Channel 4 Film, 1985.
Raimondi, *Cariani and the Courtesan,* BBC Film, 1987.
Quass, *Old Flames,* BBC Film, 1989.
Patriot Witness, BBC, 1989.
John Mortimer, *Trial of Oz,* BBC, 1991.
Bye Bye Columbus, Greenpoint, 1992.
Vicar Ronnie, *Femme Fatale,* BBC Film, 1993.
Little Napoleons, BBC, 1994.

Television Work; Director:
Charles Laughton (documentary), BBC, 1987.

Radio Appearances:
Michael MacLiammoir (documentary), BBC, 1991.
Dr. Johnson, *Poonsh,* BBC, 1994.
Shakespeare's Sonnets, BBC, 1994.

Also appeared in *Charles Laughton* (documentary).

WRITINGS

Plays:
(Translator) *Jacques and His Master,* Los Angeles Theatre Center, Los Angeles, 1987, published by Faber, 1986.
(Adapter) *Les Enfants du Paradis* (based on Jacques Prevert's screenplay), Barbican Theatre, London, 1996.

Also translator of *The Infernal Machine,* 1986.

Other:
Being an Actor (autobiography), Methuen, 1984, St. Martin's, 1986.
(with Adam Godley and Mark McGlynn) *Zero Hour,* 1986.
Charles Laughton: A Difficult Actor (biography), Methuen, 1987, Grove, 1988.
(With Dusan Makavejev) *Shooting the Actor; or, The Choreography of Confusion* (nonfiction), Hern, 1990.
Acting in Restoration Comedy (nonfiction), Applause Theatre Book Publishers, 1991.
Orson Welles: The Road to Xanadu, two volumes, J. Cape, 1995, HarperCollins, in press.

Also contributor of book reviews to periodicals, including *Times* (London), *Sunday Times, Observer,* and *Evening Standard.**

CANARY, David 1938-

PERSONAL

Born August 25, 1938, in Elwood, IN; married Julie Anderson (divorced); married Marilyn; children: (first marriage) one daughter. *Education:* University of Cincinnati, B.A. (music).

Addresses: *Agent*—Marilyn Scott-Murphy, Professional Artists, 321 West 44th St., Suite 605, New York, NY 10036.

Career: Actor. Actors Theatre of Louisville, Louisville, KY, company member, 1972-73; Meadow Brook Theatre, Rochester, MI, guest artist, 1976-77; The Guthrie Theatre, Minneapolis, MN, company member, 1978-79.

Awards, Honors: Daytime Emmy Awards, outstanding actor in a daytime drama series, 1986, 1988, 1989, 1993, Daytime Emmy Award nominations, outstanding actor in a daytime drama series, 1997-98, all for *All My Children.*

CREDITS

Television Appearances; Series:
Dr. Russ Gehring, *Peyton Place,* ABC, 1965-66.
"Candy" Canaday, *Bonanza,* NBC, 1967-70, 1972-73.
Steven "Steve" Frame, *Another World* (also known as *Another World: Bay City*), NBC, 1981-83.
Adam Chandler, *All My Children,* ABC, 1983—.
Stuart Chandler, *All My Children,* ABC, 1984—.

Television Appearances; Episodic:
"Sense of Duty," *Bonanza,* NBC, 1967.

George McClaney, "Nitro: Parts 1 & 2," *Gunsmoke,* CBS, 1967.
"The Last Job," *The FBI,* ABC, 1971.
"Everything Else You Can Steal," *Alias Smith and Jones,* ABC, 1971.
"The Strange Fate of Conrad Meyer Zulick," *Alias Smith and Jones,* ABC, 1972.
Neebo, "The Elixir," *Kung Fu,* ABC, 1973.
"Kill S.W.A.T.," *S.W.A.T.,* ABC, 1975.
Narrator, "Work Song," *Reading Rainbow,* PBS, 1983.
Luke Langley, "Strange Bedfellows," *Remember WENN,* AMC, 1997.
Jeremy Orenstein, "Venom," *Law & Order,* NBC, 1998.

Also appeared as George, "3000 Crooked Miles," *Hawaii Five-O,* CBS.

Television Appearances; Movies:
Peter Gallagher, *Incident on a Dark Street,* NBC, 1972.
Eugene T. Farber, *Melvin Purvis: G-Man* (also known as *The Legend of Machine Gun Kelly*), ABC, 1974.

Television Appearances; Miniseries:
Jack Santos, *Dashiell Hammett's "The Dain Curse,"* CBS, 1978.

Television Appearances; Specials:
Bingham, *King of America,* PBS, 1982.
Guiding Light: The Primetime Special, CBS, 1992.
The All My Children 25th Anniversary Special, ABC, 1995.

Television Appearances; Awards Presentations:
The 14th Annual Daytime Emmy Awards, 1987.
Host, *Soap Opera Digest Awards,* 1988.
The 16th Annual Daytime Emmy Awards, 1989.
The 17th Annual Daytime Emmy Awards, 1990.
Soap Opera Digest Awards, 1992.
The Ninth Annual Soap Opera Awards, 1993.
The 21st Annual Daytime Emmy Awards, 1994.
Soap Opera Update Awards, 1997.

Film Appearances:
Lamar Dean, *Hombre,* Twentieth Century-Fox, 1967.
Frank Gusenberg, *The St. Valentine's Day Massacre,* Twentieth Century-Fox, 1967.
Sheriff Jesse, *Johnny Firecloud,* 1975.
Larry Hicks, *Sharks' Treasure,* United Artist, 1975.
Pensteman, *Posse,* Paramount, 1975.
Dr. Huntoon, *In a Pig's Eye,* 1989.
Santa Claus, *Secret Santa,* 1994.

Stage Appearances:
A Streetcar Named Desire, Syracuse Stage, Syracuse, NY, 1977.
Othello, Hartman Theatre Company, Stamford, CT, 1977-78.
The Sea Horse, ACT: A Contemporary Theatre, Seattle, WA, 1978-79.
Man of La Mancha, Cincinnati Playhouse, Cincinnati, OH, 1979.
Intern/Edouard, *Clothes for a Summer Hotel,* Cort Theatre, New York City, 1980.
Richard, *Summer,* Hudson Guild Theatre, New York City, 1980.
Alan, *Blood Moon,* The Production Company, New York City, 1982.
Educating Rita, Alliance Theatre Company, Atlanta, GA, 1983.
Henry Decker, *Sally's Gone, She Left Her Name,* Perry Street Theatre, New York City, 1985.
Nub McKaty, *Mortally Fine,* Actors Outlet, New York City, 1985.

Made off-Broadway debut in *Kittywake Island;* made Broadway debut in *Great Day in the Morning;* also appeared in *The Fantasticks; The Father; Hi, Paisano; Happiest Girl in the World; The Night of the Bear; Cobb; Macbeth,* Actors Theatre, Louisville, KY; *Beggar's Opera,* Guthrie Theatre, Minneapolis, MN; *The Sea Gull,* Pittsburgh Public Theatre. *

CARLIN, George 1937-

PERSONAL

Full name, George Denis Patrick Carlin; born May 12, 1937, in New York, NY; son of Patrick and Mary Carlin; married Brenda Hosbrook, 1961 (deceased, 1997); children: Kelly. *Education:* Attended Cardinal Hayes High School, New York City.

Addresses: *Office*—Carlin Productions, 11911 San Vincente Blvd., Los Angeles, CA 90049-5086.

Career: Actor and writer. Comedian in nightclubs, theatres, concert halls, and colleges throughout the United States. Worked as a disc jockey for KJOE-Radio, Shreveport, LA, WEZE-Radio, Boston, MA, KXOL-Radio, Fort Worth, TX, and KDAY-Radio, Los Angeles, CA. *Military service:* U.S. Air Force.

Member: Screen Actors Guild, American Federation of Television and Radio Artists, American Guild of Variety Artists, Writers Guild of America.

Awards, Honors: Grammy Award nomination, best comedy album, 1967, for *Take-Offs and Put-Ons;* Grammy Award, best comedy album, 1972, for *FM and AM;* Grammy Award nomination, best comedy recording, 1973, for *Occupation: Foole;* Grammy Award nomination, best comedy recording, 1975, for *An Evening with Wally Londo Featuring Bill Slaszo;* Grammy Award nomination, best comedy recording, 1977, for *On the Road;* Grammy Award nomination, best comedy recording, 1982, for *A Place for My Stuff;* Grammy Award nomination, best comedy recording, 1986, for *Playin' with Your Head;* CableACE Award, best stand-up comedy special, 1990, for "George Carlin: Doin' It Again," *HBO Comedy Hour;* CableACE Award, best stand-up comedy special, 1992, for *George Carlin: Jammin' in New York;* Grammy Award, best spoken comedy album, 1994, for *Jammin' in New York.*

CREDITS

Television Appearances; Series:

Regular, *The Kraft Summer Music Hall,* NBC, 1966.
George Lester, *That Girl,* ABC, 1966-67.
Co-host, *Away We Go,* CBS, 1967.
Regular, *Tony Orlando and Dawn,* CBS, 1976.
Mr. Conductor, *Shining Time Station,* PBS, 1991.
George O'Grady, *The George Carlin Show,* Fox, 1994.

Television Appearances; Episodic:

On Broadway Tonight, CBS, 1964.
The Tonight Show, NBC, 1967.
Talent Scouts, CBS, 1968.
The Burns and Schreiber Comedy Hour, ABC, 1973.
Saturday Night Live, NBC, 1975.
Wally, "Radio Free Freddie," *Welcome Back, Kotter,* 1976.
"University of Southern California," *On Location,* HBO, 1977.
"Phoenix," *On Location,* HBO, 1978.
Fridays, 1980.
Rotating host, *The Late Show,* Fox, 1986.
"George Carlin: Doin' It Again," *HBO Comedy Hour,* HBO, 1990.
Alan King: Inside the Comedy Mind, syndicated, 1991.
"George Carlin Live at the Paramount," *HBO Comedy Hour,* HBO, 1992.
Narration, *Mister Moose's Fun Time,* Fox, 1998.
Voice of Munchie, "D'oh-in in the Wind," *The Simpsons,* Fox, 1998.

Also appeared in episodes of *The Merv Griffin Show.*

Television Appearances; Specials:

The Perry Como Springtime Show, NBC, 1967.
The Flip Wilson Comedy Special, NBC, 1975.
Perry Como's Hawaiian Holiday, NBC, 1976.
The Mad Mad Mad Mad World of the Super Bowl, NBC, 1977.
Mac Davis . . . Sounds Like Home, NBC, 1977.
A Tribute to "Mr. Television" Milton Berle, NBC, 1978.
Make 'em Laugh, CBS, 1979.
100 Years of Golden Hits, NBC, 1981.
Host, *George Carlin at Carnegie Hall,* HBO, 1983.
Carlin on Campus, HBO, 1984.
Apartment 2-C, Starring George Carlin, HBO, 1985.
George Carlin—Playin' with Your Head, HBO, 1986.
Welcome Home, 1987.
An All-Star Celebration: The '88 Vote, 1988.
George Carlin: What Am I Doing in New Jersey?, HBO, 1988.
What's Alan Watching? (also known as *Outrageous*), CBS, 1989.
The Tonight Show Starring Johnny Carson: 28th Anniversary Special, NBC, 1990.
Comic Relief IV, HBO, 1990.
George Carlin: Jammin' in New York, 1992.
HBO's 20th Anniversary—We Hardly Believed It Ourselves, HBO, 1992.
New Year's Eve '94, Fox, 1993.
More of the Best of the Hollywood Palace, ABC, 1993.
But . . . Seriously, Showtime, 1994.
The 2nd Annual Comedy Hall of Fame, NBC, 1994.
The Human Language, PBS, 1995.
Mr. Conductor, *Shining Time Station Family Special: Once upon a Time,* PBS, 1995.
Mr. Conductor, *Shining Time Station Family Special: Queen for a Day,* PBS, 1995.
Mr. Conductor, *Shining Time Station Family Special: Second Chances,* PBS, 1995.
George Carlin: Back in Town, HBO, 1996.
George Carlin: 40 Years of Comedy, HBO, 1997.
George Carlin's Personal Favorites, HBO, 1997.
Jerry Seinfeld: I'm Telling You for the Last Time, HBO, 1998.
George Carlin: You Are All Diseased, HBO, 1999.

Television Appearances; Awards Presentations:

The 1st Annual American Comedy Awards, 1987.
The 2nd Annual American Comedy Awards, 1988.
The 7th Annual American Comedy Awards, ABC, 1993.
The 8th Annual American Comedy Awards, ABC, 1994.
12th Annual American Comedy Awards, 1998.

Television Appearances; Movies:
Title role, *Justin Case,* ABC, 1988.
Ralph Sawatski, *Working Trash* (also known as *Garbage Blues*), Fox, 1990.

Other Television Appearances:
Star Search (pilot), syndicated, 1983.
Billy Williams, *Larry McMurtry's Streets of Laredo* (miniseries), CBS, 1995.

Television Work; Series:
Creator and executive producer, *The George Carlin Show,* Fox, 1994.

Television Work; Executive Producer, Except Where Indicated:
"George Carlin Live at the Paramount," *HBO Comedy Hour* (episodic), HBO, 1992.
Producer, *George Carlin's Personal Favorites,* HBO, 1997.
George Carlin: You Are All Diseased, HBO, 1999.

Film Appearances:
Herbie Fleck, *With Six You Get Egg Roll* (also known as *A Man in Mommy's Bed*), National General, 1968.
Taxi driver, *Car Wash,* Universal, 1976.
Narrator, *Americathon,* United Artists, 1979.
Frank, *Outrageous Fortune,* Buena Vista, 1987.
Rufus, *Bill and Ted's Excellent Adventure,* Orion, 1989.
Rufus, *Bill and Ted's Bogus Journey,* Orion, 1991.
Eddie Detreville, *The Prince of Tides,* Columbia, 1991.
Cardinal Glick, *Dogma,* 1999.

RECORDINGS

Albums:
Burns and Carlin at the Playboy Club Tonight, ERA Records, 1960.
Take-Offs and Put-Ons, RCA, 1967.
FM and AM, Little David, 1972.
Class Clown, Little David, 1972.
Occupation: Foole, Little David, 1973.
Toledo Window Box, Little David, 1974.
An Evening with Wally Londo Featuring Bill Slaszo, Little David, 1975.
On the Road, Little David, 1977.
Indecent Exposure, Little David, 1978.
A Place for My Stuff, Atlantic, 1982.
The George Carlin Collection, Little David, 1984.
Carlin on Campus, Eardrum, 1984.
Playin' with Your Head, Eardrum, 1986.
What Am I Doing in New Jersey?, Eardrum, 1988.
Parental Advisory—Explicit Lyrics, 1990.
Jammin' in New York, 1992.

WRITINGS

Television Specials:
George Carlin at Carnegie Hall, HBO, 1983.
Carlin on Campus, HBO, 1984.
Apartment 2-C, Starring George Carlin, HBO, 1985.
George Carlin—Playin' with Your Head, HBO, 1986.
George Carlin: What Am I Doing in New Jersey?, HBO, 1988.
George Carlin: Back in Town, HBO, 1996.
George Carlin: 40 Years of Comedy, HBO, 1997.
George Carlin's Personal Favorites, HBO, 1997.
George Carlin: You Are All Diseased, HBO, 1999.

Television Episodes:
"University of Southern California," *On Location,* HBO, 1977.
"Phoenix," *On Location,* HBO, 1978.
"George Carlin: Doin' It Again," *HBO Comedy Hour,* HBO, 1990.
"George Carlin Live at the Paramount," *HBO Comedy Hour,* HBO, 1992.

Other Writings:
The George Carlin Show (television pilot), Fox, 1994.
Brain Droppings (a book), Hyperion, 1997.

Also author of the book *Sometimes a Little Brain Damage Can Help.*

OTHER SOURCES

Periodicals:
Mother Jones, March-April, 1997, pp. 54-58.
U.S. News & World Report, June 16, 1997.*

CARLOS, Walter
See CARLOS, Wendy

CARLOS, Wendy 1939-
(Walter Carlos)

PERSONAL

Born Walter Carlos, November 14, 1939, in Pawtucket, RI. *Education:* Brown University, A.B.

(music and physics), 1962; Columbia University, M.A. (music composition), 1965. *Avocational interests:* Solar eclipse chasing, astronomy, photography, map making, reading, gourmet food, film, and animals.

Career: Composer and musician. Worked as a recording engineer; helped develop the Moog Synthesizer, c. 1964; developed the LSI Philharmonic Orchestra, c. 1985; developed Digi-Surround Stereo Sound, c. 1992-95; consultant for Macintosh developers, designed musical fonts, and libraries and tunings for Kurzweil/Young Chang; recording artist with East Side Digital, 1998—.

Member: Audio Engineering Society, the Society for Motion Picture and Television Engineers, National Academy of Recording Arts and Sciences.

Awards, Honors: Three Grammy Awards for *Switched on Bach.*

CREDITS

Film Work:

Music performer and arranger, *Ziggy Stardust and the Spiders from Mars,* 1973.
Music synthesizer performances and processing, *Tron,* Buena Vista, 1982.

RECORDINGS

Albums:

Switched-On Bach, Columbia, 1968.
Switched-On Brandenburgs, Vol. 1, Columbia, 1969.
Switched-On Brandenburgs, Vol. 2, Columbia, 1969.
Sonic Seasonings, Columbia, 1972.
A Clockwork Orange, East Side Digital, 1972.
Digital Moonscapes, Columbia, 1984.
Beauty in the Beast, Audion, 1986.
Switched-On Bach 2000, Telarc, 1992.
Tales of Heaven & Hell, East Side Digital, 1998.
Secrets of Synthesis, CBS, 1998.

Also recorded *The Complete Carlos Score; Peter and the Wolf/Carnival of the Animals Part 2; Well-Tempered Synthesizer.*

WRITINGS

Film Scores:

(As Walter Carlos) *A Clockwork Orange,* 1971.
Stanley Kubrick's The Shining (also known as *The Shining*), Warner Bros., 1980.
Tron, Buena Vista, 1982.
Beauty in the Beast, 1986.
Woundings, 1998.

Musical Compositions:

Noah (opera), 1964-65.
Timesteps, 1970.
Pompous Circumstances, 1974-75.
Variations on Dies irae, 1980.

OTHER SOURCES

Periodicals:

Billboard, October 3, 1998, p. 69.*

CARPENTER, John 1948-
(Frank Armitage, Johnny Carpenter, James T. Chance, John T. Chance, Rip Haight, Martin Quatermass)

PERSONAL

Full name, John Howard Carpenter; born January 16, 1948, in Carthage, NY (raised in Bowling Green, KY); son of Howard Ralph (a music professor) and Milton Jean (Carter) Carpenter; married Adrienne Barbeau (an actress), January 1, 1979 (divorced, November, 1988); married Sandy King (a producer), December 1, 1990; children: (first marriage) John Cody. *Education:* Attended Western Kentucky University, c. 1968; graduate work in film at the University of Southern California, 1968-72. *Avocational interests:* Helicopter piloting, music.

Addresses: *Agent*—c/o Jim Wiatt, International Creative Management, 8942 Wilshire Blvd., Beverly Hills, CA 90211.

Career: Director, producer, actor, screenwriter, and composer. Performer in the rock group, Coup de Ville.

Member: Directors Guild of America, Writers Guild of America—West, American Society of Composers, Authors, and Publishers.

Awards, Honors: Academy Award, best short subject (live action), 1970, *The Resurrection of Bronco Billy;* London Film Festival special award, 1977; Edgar Allan Poe Award, best made-for-television mystery movie, Mystery Writers of America, 1978, for *Someone's Watching Me!;* New Generation Award, Los Angeles Film Critics Association Awards, 1979; Critics' Prize, Avoriaz Film Festival, 1980, for *The Fog;* American

Institute for Public Service Jefferson Award, outstanding public service benefiting local communities, 1980; George Pal career award, Saturn Award, Academy of Science Fiction, Fantasy and Horror Films, 1996.

CREDITS

Film Work:

Editor, *The Resurrection of Bronco Billy* (short film), Universal, 1970.

Producer, director, and music director, *Dark Star,* Jack H. Harris, 1974.

Director and (as John T. Chance) editor, *Assault on Precinct 13* (also known as *John Carpenter's Assault on Precinct 13*), Turtle Releasing Company, 1976.

Director, *Halloween* (also known as *John Carpenter's Halloween*), Compass, 1978.

Director, *The Fog,* Avco Embassy, 1980.

Director, *Escape from New York,* Avco Embassy, 1981.

(With Debra Hill) Producer, *Halloween II,* Universal, 1981.

(With Hill) Producer, *Halloween III: Season of the Witch,* Universal, 1982.

Director, *The Thing* (also known as *John Carpenter's The Thing*), Universal, 1982.

Director, *Christine* (also known as *John Carpenter's Christine*), Columbia, 1983.

Executive producer, *The Philadelphia Experiment,* New World, 1984.

Director, *Starman* (also known as *John Carpenter's Starman*), Columbia, 1984.

Director, *Big Trouble in Little China,* Twentieth Century-Fox, 1986.

(As Martin Quatermass) Director, *Prince of Darkness,* Universal, 1987.

(As Frank Armitage) Director, *They Live* (also known as *John Carpenter's They Live*), Universal, 1988.

Director, *Memoirs of an Invisible Man,* Warner Bros., 1992.

Director, *In the Mouth of Madness* (also known as *John Carpenter's In the Mouth of Madness*), New Line Cinema, 1995.

Director, *Village of the Damned,* Universal, 1995.

Director, *Escape from L.A.* (also known as *John Carpenter's Escape from L.A.;* also see below), Paramount, 1996.

Director, *John Carpenter's Vampires* (also known as *Vampires;* also see below), Sony Pictures, 1998.

Also director (as Johnny Carpenter) of such short films as *Revenge of the Colossal Beasts, Gorgo Versus Godzilla, Terror from Space, Sorcerer from Outer Space, The Warrior and the Demon,* and *Gorgon, the Space Monster.*

Film Appearances:

No Place to Land, 1958.

(Uncredited) Bennett, *The Fog,* Avco Embassy, 1980.

(Uncredited) Norwegian video footage, *The Thing* (also known as *John Carpenter's The Thing*), 1982.

(Uncredited) Man in helicopter, *Starman* (also known as *John Carpenter's Starman*), 1984.

(With the Coupe de Villes) *The Boy Who Could Fly,* 1986.

(As Rip Haight) Helicopter pilot, *Memoirs of an Invisible Man,* 1992.

Trench Coat Man, *The Silence of the Hams* (also known as *Il Silenzio dei prosciutti*), 1994.

(Uncredited) Man at phone booth, *Village of the Damned,* 1995.

Television Work; Movies:

Director, *Someone's Watching Me!,* NBC, 1978.

Director, *Elvis,* ABC, 1979.

Executive producer, *El Diablo*, 1990.

Executive producer and segment director "The Gas Station," and "Hair," *John Carpenter Presents Body Bags* (also known as *Body Bags*), Showtime, 1993.

Television Appearances:

Firstworks (episode), 1988.

Coroner, *John Carpenter Presents Bady Bags* (movie; also known as *Body Bags*), Showtime, 1993.

After Sunset: The Life and Times of the Drive-In (special), AMC, 1998.

Masters of Fantasy: John Carpenter (special), Sci-Fi Channel, 1998.

The Directors (episode), Encore, 1999.

WRITINGS

Screenplays, Unless Otherwise Noted:

(With Jim Rokos) And composer, *The Resurrection of Bronco Billy* (short film), Universal, 1970.

(With Dan O'Bannon) And composer, *Dark Star,* Jack H. Harris, 1974.

And composer, *Assault on Precinct 13* (also known as *John Carpenter's Assault on Precinct 13*), Turtle Releasing Company, 1976.

(With David Zelag Goodman) *The Eyes of Laura Mars,* Columbia, 1978.

(With Debra Hill) And composer, *Halloween* (also known as *John Carpenter's Halloween*), Compass, 1978.

(With Hill) And composer, *The Fog,* Avco Embassy, 1980.

(With Nick Castle) And composer (with Alan Howarth), *Escape from New York,* Avco Embassy, 1981.

(With Hill) And composer (with Howarth), *Halloween II,* Universal, 1981.

Composer (with Howarth), *Halloween III: Season of the Witch,* Universal, 1982.

Composer (with Howarth), *Christine* (also known as *John Carpenter's Christine*), Columbia, 1983.

Composer (with Howarth), *Big Trouble in Little China,* Twentieth Century-Fox, 1986.

(With Desmond Nakano and William Gray) *Black Moon Rising,* New World, 1986.

(As Martin Quatermass) And composer (with Howarth), *Prince of Darkness,* Universal, 1987.

(As Frank Armitage) And composer, *They Live* (also known as *John Carpenter's They Live*), Universal, 1988.

Composer (with Howarth), *Halloween 5: The Revenge of Michael Myers,* Galaxy International, 1989.

Composer (with Jim Lang), *In the Mouth of Madness* (also known as *John Carpenter's In the Mouth of Madness,* New Line Cinema, 1995.

Composer (with Dave Davies), *Village of the Damned,* Universal, 1995.

And composer (with Shirley Walker), *Escape from L.A.* (also known as *John Carpenter's Escape from L.A.*), Paramount, 1996.

Theme composer, "Halloween," *Halloween: H2O* (also known as *Halloween H2O: Twenty Years Later*), Miramax, 1998.

Composer, *John Carpenter's Vampires* (also known as *Vampires*), Sony Pictures, 1998.

Meltdown, 1999.

Television; Movies:

(With William A. Schwartz) *Zuma Beach,* NBC, 1978.

Someone's Watching Me!, NBC, 1978.

(With Greg Strangis) *Better Late Than Never,* NBC, 1979.

El Diablo, 1990.

Blood River, 1991.

And composer (with Jim Lang), *John Carpenter Presents Body Bags* (also known as *Body Bags*), Showtime, 1993.

OTHER SOURCES

Periodicals:

Entertainment Weekly, November-December, 1997, pp. 98-103.

Film Comment, September-October, 1996, pp. 50-54.

Hollywood Reporter, October 26, 1998, p. 13.*

CARPENTER, Johnny

See CARPENTER, John

CARRIERE, Jean-Claude 1931-

PERSONAL

Born September 17 (some sources say September 19), 1931, in Colombieres-sur-Orbes (some sources say Languedoc), France; son of Felix and Alice Carriere; married Nicole (a painter and interior decorator) December 27, 1952; children: Iris.

Addresses: *Agent*—c/o Writers Guild of America East, 555 West 57th St., New York, NY 10019-2925.

Career: Screenwriter, actor, and director. Head of the French film school FEMIS, 1986—; conductor of writing and directing workshops.

Awards, Honors: Academy Award (with Pierre Etaix), best short film, 1962, for *Heureux anniversaire;* Venice International Film Festival, best picture prize (with Luis Bunuel), 1967, for *Belle de jour;* Academy Award (with Bunuel), best foreign film, Academy Award nomination (with Bunuel), best screenplay based on material from another medium, and British Academy of Film and Television Arts Award (with Bunuel), best original screenplay, all 1972, for *Le Charme discret de la bourgeoisie;* Academy Award nomination (with Bunuel), best screenplay based on material from another medium, 1977, for *Cet Obscure Objet du desir;* Best Picture Prize (with Volker Schloendorff, Franz Seitz, and Gunter Grass), Cannes Film Festival, 1979, and Academy Award (with Schloendorff, Seitz, and Grass), best foreign film, 1980, both for *The Tin Drum;* Cesar Award (with Daniel Vigne), 1982, for *Le Retour de Martin Guerre;* British Academy of Film and Television Arts Award (with Philip Kaufman), best adapted screenplay, 1988, and Academy Award nomination (with Kaufman), best adapted screenplay, 1989, both for *The Unbearable Lightness of Being;* Best Screenplay Award (with Peter Fleischmann), Catalonian International Film Festival, Sitges, Spain, 1990, for *Es ist nicht leicht ein Gott zu sein;* British Academy of Film and Television

Arts Award nomination (with Jean-Paul Rappeneau), best adapted screenplay, 1992, for *Cyrano de Bergerac.*

CREDITS

Film Appearances:

Insomnie, 1963.

Cure, *Le Journal d'une femme de chambre* (also known as *Il diario di una cameriera* and *Diary of a Chambermaid*), Cocinor, 1964.

Narrator, *Les Cocardiers,* 1967.

Priscillian, *La Voie lactee* (also known as *La via lattea* and *The Milky Way*), U-M, 1969.

Hughes, *L'Alliance* (also known as *The Wedding Ring*), CAPAC, 1970.

Un Peu de soleil dans l'eau froide (also known as *A Little Sun in Cold Water*), Societe Nouvelle de Cinema, 1971.

La Chute d'un corps, 1973.

Chief, *Serieux comme le plaisir* (also known as *Serious as Pleasure*), Lugo, 1974.

Le Jardin des supplices (also known as *The Garden of Torment*), New Realm Distributors/Parafrance, 1976.

Adam, *Le Jeu du solitaire,* 1976.

Doctor, *Photo Souvenir,* FR3, 1977.

Psychiatrist, *Ils sont grands ces petits* (also known as *These Kids Are Grown- Ups*), United Artists/Exportation Francaise Cinematographique, 1979.

Le sourd-muet, *Vive les femmes!,* 1984.

The Governor, *The Night and the Moment* (also known as *La Nuit et le moment* and *La Notte e il momento*), 1994.

Professor, *Jaya Ganga,* Kismet Talkies, 1996.

Film Work; Director:

(With Pierre Etaix), *Rupture* (short film), 1961.

(With Etaix), *Heureux anniversaire* (also known as *Happy Anniversary;* short film), 1961.

La Pince a ongles (also known as *The Nail Clippers;* short film), 1968.

(With Jerome Diamant-Berger and Olivier Assayas) *L'Unique* (also known as *The One and Only*), AA Revcon/Films du Scorpion, 1985.

Film Work; Producer:

Heureux anniversaire, 1961.

Television Appearances:

Narrator, *Bouvard et Pecuchet,* 1989.

Milos Forman: Portrait (special), 1989.

Narrator, *Eugenie Grandet,* 1993.

WRITINGS

Stage:

L'Aide-Memoire, produced in Paris, 1968, then on Broadway as *The Little Black Book,* 1972, translation by Jerome Kilty published by Samuel French, c. 1973.

(With Colin Higgins) *Harold and Maude,* 1971.

Le Client (also known as *The Customer*), Paris, 1971.

(With Peter Brook and Marius Constant) *La Tragedie de Carmen* (opera; abridgement of Georges Bizet's opera *Carmen*), produced in New York City, 1983, published by Centre International de Creations Theatrales (Paris), 1981.

The Conference of the Birds, published by Dramatic Publishing (Chicago, IL), 1982.

(With Bernard Slade) *La fille sur la banquette arriere,* published by L'Avant Scene, 1983.

(Adaptor; with Peter Brook) *The Mahabharata,* produced at New Wave Festival, Brooklyn Academy of Music, New York City, 1987; published by Harper, c. 1987.

The Little Black Book, 1999.

Also adaptor of *The Cherry Orchard; Timon of Athens; Measure for Measure;* and *The Tempest.*

Screenplays:

(With Pierre Etaix) *Rupture,* 1961.

(With Etaix) *Heureux anniversaire* (also known as *Happy Anniversary;* short film), 1961.

(With Etaix) *Nous n'irons plus au bois,* 1963, re-released as *Tant qu'on a la sante,* 1965.

(With Etaix) *Insomnie,* 1963.

Le Bestiaire d'amour, 1963.

(With Etaix) *Le Soupirant* (also known as *The Suitor*), Atlantic, 1963.

La Reine verte (also known as *The Green Queen*), 1964.

(With Luis Bunuel) *Le Journal d'une femme de chambre* (also known as *Il diario di una cameriera* and *The Diary of a Chambermaid*), Cocinor, 1964.

(With Louis Malle) *Viva Maria!,* United Artists, 1965.

(With Jesus Franco) *Miss Muerte* (also known as *Dans les griffes du maniaque* and *The Diabolical Dr. Z*), U.S. Films, 1966.

(With Peter Glenville) *Hotel Paradiso,* Metro-Goldwyn-Mayer, 1966.

Cartes sur table (also known as *Attack of the Robots*), American International, 1967.

(With Malle) *Le Voleur* (also known as *The Thief of Paris*), Lopert, 1967.

(With Etaix) *Yo Yo,* Magna, 1967.

(With Bunuel) *Belle de jour,* Allied Artists, 1968.

La Pince a ongles (also known as *The Nail Clippers;* short film), 1968.

Le Grand Amour, 1968.

(With Bunuel) *La Voie lactee* (also known as *La via lattea* and *The Milky Way*), U-M, 1969.

(With John-Emmanuel Conil and Jacques Deray) *La Piscine* (also known as *La piscina* and *The Swimming Pool*), 1969, released in the United States by Avco Embassy, 1970.

(With Christian De Chalonge) *L'Alliance* (also known as *The Wedding Ring*), CAPAC, 1970.

(With Jean Cau, Claude Sautet, and Deray) *Borsalino,* Paramount, 1970.

(With Milos Forman, John Guare, and John Klein) *Taking Off,* Universal, 1971.

Un Peu de soleil dans l'eau froide (also known as *A Little Sun in Cold Water*), Societe Nouvelle de Cinema, 1971.

(With Francoise Xenakis, Jean Bolvary, and Eric Le Hung) *Le Droit d'aimer* (also known as *The Right to Love*), Twentieth Century-Fox/Lira Films, 1972.

(With Bunuel) *Le Charme discret de la bourgeoisie* (also known as *The Discreet Charm of the Bourgeoisie*), Twentieth Century-Fox/Castle Hill, 1972, published in *Avant-Scene,* April, 1973.

(With Deray and Ian McLellen Hunter) *Un Homme est mort* (also known as *A Man Is Dead* and *The Outside Man*), Valoria, 1972, released in the United States by United Artists, 1973.

(With Marco Ferreri) *La cagna,* 1972, released in the United States as *Liza,* CFDC/Pathe/Oceanic/Sirius, 1976.

(With Bunuel) *Le Moine* (also known as *The Monk*), Maya, 1973.

(With Peter Fleischmann) *Dorothea's Rache* (also known as *Dorothea's Revenge*), Planfilm, 1973.

(With Bunuel) *Le Fantome de la liberte* (also known as *The Phantom of Liberty* and *The Specter of Freedom*), Twentieth Century-Fox, 1974.

(With Robert Benayoun) *Serieux comme le plaisir* (also known as *Serious as Pleasure*), Lugo, 1974.

(With Jean-Claude Brialy) *Un Amour de pluie* (also known as *A Rainy Love*), Lira, 1974.

(With Patrice Chereau) *La Chair de l'orchidee* (also known as *The Flesh of the Orchid*), Fox-Lira, 1974.

France Societe Anonyme (also known as *France Incorporated*), Albina, 1974.

(With Martin Walser) *La Faille* (also known as *The Weak Spot*), Gaumont, 1975.

(With Jean Curtelin and Joel Santoni) *Les Oeufs brouilles* (also known as *The Scrambled Eggs*), Columbia/Warner Distributors, 1975.

(With Alphonse Boudard) *Le Gang* (also known as *The Gang*), Warner Bros., 1976.

(With Bunuel) *Cet Obscur Objet du desir* (also known as *That Obscure Object of Desire*), CCFC/Greenwich/Janus, 1976, released in the United States by First Artists, 1977.

(With others) *Leonor,* CIC/New Line Cinema, 1977.

(With Pierre Lary and Huguette Debasieux) *Le Diable dans la boite* (also known as *The Devil in the Box*), Madeleine/Societe Novelle de Cinema, 1977.

Julie pot de colle (also known as *Julie Glue Pot*), Davis/Societe Nouvelle Prodis, 1977.

(With Edmond Sechan) *Photo Souvenir,* FR3, 1977.

(With Tonino Guerra) *Un Papillon sur l'epaule* (also known as *A Butterfly on the Shoulder*), Gaumont, 1978.

(With Jean-Francois Davy) *Chaussette surprise* (also known as *Surprise Sock*), GEF/CCFC/Albatros, 1978.

(With Daniel Boulanger and Joel Santoni) *Ils sont grands ces petits* (also known as *These Kids Are Grown-Ups*), United Artists/Exportation Francaise Cinematographique, 1979.

(With Rene Gainville) *L'Associe* (also known as *The Associate*), Columbia/Warner Distributors, 1979.

(With Claude Pinoteau and Charles Israel) *L'Homme en colere* (also known as *The Angry Man*), Films Ariane/United Artists, 1979.

(With Volker Schloendorff, Franz Seitz, and Gunter Grass) *The Tin Drum,* United Artists/New World, 1979.

(With Jean-Francois Adam, Georges Perec, and Benoit Jacquot) *Retour a la bien- aimee* (also known as *Return to the Beloved*), Societe Nouvelle Prodis/World Marketing, 1979.

(With Jean-Luc Godard and Anne-Marie Mieville) *Sauve qui peut la vie* (also known as *Everyone for Himself, Every Man for Himself,* and *Slow Motion*), Artifical Eye/MK2/New Yorker, 1980.

(With Volker Schloendorff, Margarethe Von Trotta, and Kai Hermann) *Die Falschung* (also known as *Circle of Deceit* and *False Witness*), United International/United Artists Classics, 1981.

(With Carlos Saura) *Antonieta,* Gaumont/Conacina/Nuevo Cine, 1982.

(With Christian Drillaud) *Itineraire bis* (also known as *Sideroads*), Films de l'Arquebuse, 1982.

(With Andrzej Wajda, Agnieszka Holland, Boleslaw Michalek, and Jacek Gasiorowski) *Danton,* Triumph, 1983.

(With Daniel Vigne) *Le Retour de Martin Guerre* (also known as *The Return of Martin Guerre*), European International, 1983.

(With Luciano Tovoli and Michel Piccoli) *Le General de l'armee morte* (also known as *The General of the Dead Army*), World Marketing/Union Generale Cinematographique, 1983.

(With Marius Constant and Peter Brook) *La Tragedie de Carmen* (also known as *The Tragedy of Carmen*), British Film Institute/MK2, 1983.

(With Volker Schloendorff, Brook, and Marie-Helen Estienne) *Un Amour de Swann* (also known as *Swann in Love, Swann's Way,* and *Remembrance of Things Past*), Orion Classics, 1984.

La Jeune fille et l'enfer (also known as *The Young Girl and Hell*), Orphee Arts/Exportation Francaise Cinematographique, 1984.

(With Jerome Diamant-Berger, Olivier Assayas, and Jacques Dorfman) *L'Unique* (also known as *The One and Only*), AA Revcon/Films du Scorpion, 1985.

(With Nagisa Oshima) *Max mon amour* (also known as *Max, My Love*), Greenwich/AAA, 1986.

(With Peter Fleischmann and Gianfranco Mingozzi) *Les Exploits d'un jeune Don Juan* (also known as *The Exploits of a Young Don Juan*), Exportation Francaise/AAA, 1987.

(With Wajda, Holland, and Edward Zebrowsky) *Les Possedes* (also known as *The Possessed*), Gaumont International, 1987.

Hard to Be a God (also known as *Es ist nicht leicht ein Gott zu sein*), 1988.

(With Nicholas Klotz) *La Nuit Bengali* (also known as *Bengali Nights* and *The Bengali Night*), Gaumont International, 1988.

(With Philip Kaufman) *The Unbearable Lightness of Being,* Orion, 1988.

(With Jerzy Kawlerowicz) *Hostage of Europe,* La Societe Cine-Alliance, 1989.

J'ecris dans l'espace (also known as *I Write in Space* and *Vite et loin*), 1989.

(With Peter Fleischman) *Jeniec Europy,* 1989.

(With Milos Forman) *Valmont,* Orion Classics, 1989.

(With Jean-Paul Rappeneau) *Cyrano de Bergerac,* Orion Classics, 1990.

(With Malle) *Milou en mai* (also known as *May Fools*), Orion Classics, 1990.

(With Brook and Estienne) *The Mahabharata,* Reiner Moritz, 1990.

(With Hector Babenco) *At Play in the Fields of the Lord* (also known as *Brincando nos Campos do Senhor*), Universal, 1991.

Le Retour de Casanova (also known as *The Return of Casanova* and *Casanova's Return*), 1992.

L'Otage de l'Europe, 1992.

Sommersby, Warner Bros., 1993.

The Night and the Moment, 1994.

Le Hussard sur le toit (also known as *The Horseman on the Roof*), 1995, released in the United States by Miramax Zoe Films, 1995.

The Ogre (also known as *Der Unhold* and *Le Roi des aulnes*), 1996.

Chinese Box, Trimark Pictures, 1997.

The Dicing, 1998.

La Guerre dans le Haut-Pays (also known as *War in the Highlands*), Rezo Films, 1998.

For Television:

Robinson Crusoe (series), 1965.

Bouvard et Pecuchet, 1989.

(Adaptor) *The Mahabharata* (special), Channel Four, 1989.

Associations de bienfaiteurs (miniseries), 1994.

Clarissa (movie), 1998.

Books:

Le Lezard, 1957.

Monsieur Hulot's Holiday (novelization of film), 1959.

L'Alliance, 1963.

Mon Oncle (novelization of film), 1972.

(Translator) *Le Clou brulant,* 1972.

Le Pari, 1973.

(Translator) *Harold et Maude,* 1974.

Le Carnaval et la politique, 1979.

(Translator) *The Mahabharata,* Harper and Row, 1987.

With Daniel Vigne, also authored *Le Retour de Martin Guerre* (novelization of film); and contributor to journals and periodicals.

Adaptations: The film *Chinese Box* was adapted by Carriere from his original story and released in 1997. The film *The Bunuel Paradox* was adapted from an idea of Carriere's and released in 1997.*

CARSON, Kris
See KRISTOFFERSON, KRIS

CATTRALL, Kim 1956-

PERSONAL

Born August 21, 1956, in Liverpool, England; father, a construction engineer; married Andre J. Lyson, 1982 (divorced, 1989); married Mark Levinson, 1998. *Education:* Graduated from the American Academy of Dramatic Arts.

Addresses: *Agent*—c/o Jeffrey Witjas, William Morris Agency, 151 El Camino Dr., Beverly Hills, CA 90212.

Career: Actress.

CREDITS

Film Appearances:

(Film debut) Joyce, *Rosebud,* United Artists, 1975.

The Other Side of the Mountain—Part II, Universal, 1978.

Sally Haines, *Tribute,* Twentieth Century-Fox, 1980.

Ruthie, *Ticket to Heaven,* United Artists, 1981.

Honeywell, *Porky's,* Twentieth Century-Fox, 1982.

Karen Thompson, *Police Academy,* Warner Bros., 1984.

Dr. Helen Wickings, *City Limits,* Atlantic, 1985.

Lise, *Hold-Up,* AMLF, 1985.

Danny Boudreau, *Turk 182!,* Twentieth Century-Fox, 1985.

Gracie Law, *Big Trouble in Little China,* Twentieth Century-Fox, 1986.

Emmy, *Mannequin,* Twentieth Century-Fox, 1987.

Brooke Morrison, *Masquerade,* Metro-Goldwyn-Mayer/United Artists, 1988.

Lexa Shubb, *Midnight Crossing,* Vestron, 1988.

Odessa, *Palais Royale,* Spectrafilm, 1988.

Chris Nelson, *For Better or For Worse* (also known as *Honeymoon Academy*), Trans World Entertainment, 1989.

Justine DeWinter, *The Return of the Musketeers* (also known as *The Return of the Three Musketeers*), Universal, 1989.

Aunt Eva, *Brown Bread Sandwiches,* Shapiro Glickenhaus, 1989.

Judy McCoy, *The Bonfire of the Vanities,* Warner Bros., 1990.

Lieutenant Valeris, *Star Trek VI: The Undiscovered Country,* Paramount, 1991.

Lisa/Caroline, *Double Vision,* Republic, 1992.

Michelle, *Split Second,* InterStar, 1992.

Allison Meadows, *Breaking Point,* Worldvision, 1994.

Title role, *Running Delilah,* 1994.

Jamie, *Live Nude Girls,* 1995.

Kelly, *Unforgettable,* Metro-Goldwyn-Mayer, 1996.

Raquel Chambers, *Where Truth Lies,* Dove International, 1996.

Robin Bobbins, *Baby Geniuses,* Sony Pictures, 1999.

Modern Vampyres, 1999.

Television Appearances; Series:

Genna Harrison, *Angel Falls,* CBS, 1993.

Paige Katz, *Wild Palms,* ABC, 1993.

Samantha Jones, *Sex and the City,* HBO, 1998—.

Television Appearances; Miniseries:

Melanie Adams, *Scruples,* CBS, 1980.

Jane Hood, *Tom Clancy's OP Center* (also known as *OP Center*), NBC, 1995.

Dr. Sheila Moran, *Robin Cook's Invasion* (also known as *Invasion*), NBC, 1997.

Amanda Macy, *Peter Benchley's Creature* (also known as *Creature*), ABC, 1998.

Television Appearances; Movies:

Linda Isley, *Good against Evil,* ABC, 1977.

Anne Ware, *The Bastard* (also known as *The Kent Family Chronicles*), syndicated, 1978.

Anne Kent, *The Rebels,* syndicated, 1979.

Paula Bennett, *Sins of the Past,* ABC, 1984.

Dora Adams, *Miracle in the Wilderness,* TNT, 1991.

Gail, *Above Suspicion,* HBO, 1995.

Susan Johnson, *The Heidi Chronicles,* TNT, 1995.

Liz, *Every Woman's Dream,* CBS, 1996.

Carla Reiner, *Exception to the Rule,* HBO, 1997.

Kim Stone, *36 Hours to Die,* 1999.

Television Appearances; Pilots:

Regina Kenton, *The Night Rider,* ABC, 1979.

Dina Moran, *The Gossip Columnist,* syndicated, 1980.

Amanda Tucker, *The Good Witch of Laurel Canyon* (never broadcast), 1982.

Television Appearances; Episodic:

Quincy, NBC, 1976.

Rama II, "Half Life," *Logan's Run,* CBS, 1977.

Marie Claire, "Voodoll Doll: Parts 1 and 2" *The Hardy Boys/Nancy Drew Mysteries,* ABC, 1978.

Emily Harrison, "Blindfold," *Starsky and Hutch,* ABC, 1978.

Sharon, "Angels at the Altar," *Charlie's Angels,* ABC, 1979.

Dolores, "The Slavers," *How the West Was Won,* ABC, 1979.

The Incredible Hulk, CBS, 1979 and 1980.

Princess Zara, "The Visitor," *Vegas,* ABC, 1979.

Whitney Bunting, "Naka Jima Kill," *Tales of the Gold Monkey,* ABC, 1983.

Jeannie, "The Homecoming Queen," *Dream On,* HBO, 1994.

Voice of Tammy, *Duckman,* 1994.

Rebecca, "Re-Generation," *The Outer Limits,* Showtime, 1997.

Also appeared in *Columbo,* NBC; *Family,* ABC; *The Bionic Woman,* ABC.

Television Appearances; Specials:

Star Trek: 30 Years and Beyond, UPN, 1996.

Stage Appearances:

Masha, *The Three Sisters,* Los Angeles Theatre Center, Los Angeles, CA, 1985.

(Broadway debut) Sofya, *Wild Honey,* Virginia Theatre, New York City, 1986.

Celimene, *The Misanthrope,* Goodman Theatre, Chicago, IL, 1989.

Title role, *Miss Julie,* McCarter Theatre, Princeton, NJ, 1992.

Also appeared in *A View from the Bridge,* Los Angeles; *Agnes of God,* Los Angeles.

OTHER SOURCES

Periodicals:

Maclean's, October 19, 1998, p. 15.*

CHANCE, James T.
See CARPENTER, John

CHANCE, John T.
See CARPENTER, John

CHAPMAN, Michael 1935-

PERSONAL

Born November 21, 1935, in New York, NY; married Amy Holden Jones (a film editor and director).

Addresses: *Agent*—The Gersh Agency, 232 North Canon Dr., Beverly Hills, CA 90210-5302. *Contact*—c/o American Society of Cinematographers, P.O. Box 2230, Hollywood, CA 90078.

Career: Cinematographer, director, writer, and actor. Began career working on documentaries in New York.

Member: American Society of Cinematographers.

Awards, Honors: Academy Award nomination, best cinematography, 1981, and National Society of Film Critics Award, best cinematography, 1980, both for *Raging Bull;* Academy Award nomination, best cinematography, and American Society of Cinematographers Award, outstanding achievement in cinematography, both 1994, for *The Fugitive.*

CREDITS

Film Work; Cinematographer:

The Last Detail, Columbia, 1973.

The White Dawn, Paramount, 1974.

The Front, Columbia, 1976.

The Next Man (also known as *The Arab Conspiracy* and *Double Hit*), Allied Artists, 1976.

Taxi Driver, Columbia, 1976.

Invasion of the Body Snatchers, United Artists, 1978.

Fingers, United Artists, 1978.

The Last Waltz (concert film), Universal, 1978.

Hardcore (also known as *The Hardcore Life*), Columbia, 1979.

The Wanderers, Orion, 1979.

Raging Bull, United Artists, 1980.

Dead Men Don't Wear Plaid (also known as *Dead Men Wear No Plaid*), Universal, 1982.

Personal Best, Warner Bros., 1982.

The Man with Two Brains, Warner Bros., 1983.

The Lost Boys, Warner Bros., 1987.

Scrooged, Paramount, 1988.

Shoot to Kill (also known as *Deadly Pursuit*), Buena Vista, 1988.

Ghostbusters II, Columbia, 1989.

Quick Change, Warner Bros., 1990.

Kindergarten Cop, Universal, 1990.

Doc Hollywood, Warner Bros., 1991.

Whispers in the Dark, Paramount, 1992.

Rising Sun, Twentieth Century-Fox, 1993.

The Fugitive, Warner Bros., 1993.

Primal Fear, Paramount, 1996.

Space Jam, Warner Bros., 1996.

Six Days/Seven Nights (also known as *6 Days 7 Nights*), Buena Vista, 1998.

Film Work; Director:

All the Right Moves (also known as *All Right*), Twentieth Century-Fox, 1983.

The Clan of the Cave Bear, Warner Bros., 1986.

(And story) *The Viking Sagas* (also known as *The Icelandic Sagas*), 1995.

Other Film Work:

Camera operator, *End of the Road,* Allied Artists, 1970.

Camera operator, *The Landlord,* United Artists, 1970.

Camera operator, *Klute,* Warner Bros., 1971.

Camera operator, *The Godfather,* Paramount, 1972.
Camera operator, *Jaws,* 1975.
Production assistant, *American Boy* (documentary; also known as *American Boy: A Profile of Steve Prince*), Cinegate, 1977.

Film Appearances:
Taxi driver, *The Last Detail,* Columbia, 1973.
Lawyer, *Shoot to Kill* (also known as *Deadly Pursuit*), Buena Vista, 1988.
Dr. Berg, *The Abyss,* 1989.
Policeman at grocery, *Quick Change,* Warner Bros., 1990.
Firefighter, *Kindergarten Cop,* Universal, 1990.
Shooting gallery operator, *Doc Hollywood,* Warner Bros., 1991.
Visions of Light: The Art of Cinematography (documentary), American Film Institute, 1993.
Fred Hoffman, *Rising Sun,* Twentieth Century-Fox, 1993.
Handsome Mechanic, *Six Days/Seven Nights* (also known as *6 Days 7 Nights*), Buena Vista, 1998.

Television Work; Movies:
Cinematographer, *Death Be Not Proud,* ABC, 1975.
Director, *The Annihilator,* NBC, 1986.
Cinematographer, *Gotham* (also known as *The Dead Can't Lie*), Showtime, 1988.

Other Television Work:
Cinematographer, *King* (miniseries), NBC, 1978.
Cinematographer, *Steve Martin: Comedy Is Not Pretty* (special), NBC, 1980.
Cinematographer, "Kathleen Battle and Wynton Marsalis: Baroque Duet," *Great Performances,* PBS, 1992.

Television Appearances:
Landlord, *Gotham* (movie; also known as *The Dead Can't Lie*), 1988.
Dan Rourke, *Third Degree Burn,* 1989.*

CHARBONNEAU, Patricia 1958(?)-

PERSONAL

Born in 1958 (some sources say 1959), in Valley Stream, NY.

Addresses: *Agent*—Steve Dontanville, International Creative Management, 8942 Wilshire Blvd., Beverly Hills, CA 90211.

Career: Actor. Member, Actors Theatre of Louisville, Louisville, KY, 1980-81 and 1982-83.

Awards, Honors: Independent Spirit Award nomination, best female lead, 1987, for *Desert Hearts.*

CREDITS

Film Appearances:
Cay Rivvers, *Desert Hearts,* Samuel Goldwyn, 1985.
Mrs. Sherman, *Manhunter* (also known as *Red Dragon: The Pursuit of Hannibal Lecter*), De Laurentiis Entertainment Group, 1986.
Stalking Danger, Vidmark Entertainment, 1986.
Anna, *Call Me,* Vestron, 1988.
Susan Cantrell, *Shakedown* (also known as *Blue Jean Cop*), Universal, 1988.
Dana Martin, *Brain Dead* (also known as *Paranoia*), Concorde, 1990.
RoboCop 2, 1990.
Jacki Metcalfe, *K2* (also known as *K2: The Ultimate High*), Paramount, 1992.
Portraits of a Killer (also known as *Portraits of Innocence*), Live Entertainment, 1996.
Franny, *Kiss the Sky,* 1998.
Lois Siler, *She's All That,* Miramax, 1999.

Television Appearances; Series:
Inga Thorson, *Crime Story,* NBC, 1986-87.
Sheriff Lynn Roberts, *Extreme,* ABC, 1995.

Television Appearances; Pilots:
Nikki Blake, *C.A.T. Squad* (also known as *Stalking Danger*), NBC, 1986.
Officer Dakota Goldstein, *Dakota's Way,* ABC, 1988.
Danny Santerre, *The Owl,* CBS, 1991.

Television Appearances; Episodic:
"High Performance," *The Equalizer,* CBS, 1986.
Linda Shannon, "Mary Hamilton," *Spenser: For Hire,* ABC, 1987.
Sally Stevens, *The Equalizer,* CBS, 1987.
Carole Bernstein, *Wiseguy,* CBS, 1989.
Lucille Benoit, *UNSUB,* NBC, 1989.
Madeline Medford, *Matlock,* NBC, 1989.
Clara, "Who Framed Roger Thornton?," *Booker,* Fox, 1990.
Diana Snowcroft, "From the Horse's Mouth," *Murder, She Wrote,* CBS, 1990.
Catherine Belzer, "Sex, Lies, and Kerosene," *The Commish,* ABC, 1991.
"Strung Along," *Tales from the Crypt,* HBO, 1992.
Robin Henley, "Storm Warning," *Walker, Texas Ranger,* CBS, 1993.

Ella Keats, *Viper,* NBC, 1994.
Elaine Morse, *SeaQuest 2032,* NBC, 1995.
Camilla, "Bad Moon Rising," *Kindred: The Embraced,* Fox, 1996.
Jennifer Lewis, *New York Undercover,* Fox, 1996.
Wife, *Profiler,* NBC, 1996.
Monica Shattuck, *Diagnosis Murder,* CBS, 1997.

Also appeared in the episode "Vanished," *Renegade,* syndicated.

Television Appearances; Movies:
Kathy Fitzgerald, *Disaster at Silo 7,* ABC, 1988.
Emily Harris, *Desperado: Badlands Justice,* NBC, 1989.
Karen, *Captive* (also known as *Season of Fear*), ABC, 1991.
Blade Squad, Fox, 1998.

Stage Appearances:
My Sister in This House, New Dramatists Inc., New York City, 1980.
Arms and the Man, Merrimack Regional Theatre, Lowell, MA, 1983.*

CLANCY, Tom 1947-

PERSONAL

Full name, Thomas L. Clancy, Jr.; born April 12, 1947, in Baltimore, MD; son of a mail carrier and credit employee; married Wanda Thomas (an insurance agency manager and eye surgeon), August, 1969 (divorced, 1998); children: Michelle, Christine, Tom, Kathleen. *Education:* Graduated from Loyola College, Baltimore, MD, 1969. *Politics:* Conservative. *Religion:* Roman Catholic. *Avocational interests:* Technology and military history.

Addresses: *Agent*—c/o Putnam, 200 Madison Ave., New York, NY 10016.

Career: Novelist and producer. Worked as an insurance agent in Baltimore, MD, and Hartford, CT, through 1973; O.F. Bowen Agency (insurance company), Owings, MD, agent, 1973-80, owner, 1980—; owner of the Baltimore Orioles, a professional baseball team; formed Red Storm Entertainment, 1997. *Military service:* United States Army Reserve Officers Training Corps.

CREDITS

Television Appearances; Episodic:
"Flight," *Understanding,* The Learning Channel, 1994.
Himself, "Power Players Tournament," *Jeopardy!,* 1997.

Television Work; Executive Producer, Except Where Indicated; Miniseries:
Tom Clancy's OP Center, NBC, 1955.
And creator, *Tom Clancy's NetForce,* ABC, 1999.

RECORDINGS

Video Games:
Politika, Red Storm Entertainment, 1997.
Tom Clancy SSN, Simon & Schuster, 1997.
ruthless.com, Red Storm Entertainment, 1998.
Rainbow Six, Red Storm Entertainment, 1998.
Force 21, Red Storm Entertainment, 1999.
Rainbow Six: Eagle Watch, Red Storm Entertainment, 1999.
Rogue Spear, Red Storm Entertainment, 1999.

Also created the game *Dominant Species.*

WRITINGS

Novels:
The Hunt for Red October, Naval Institute Press, 1984.
Red Storm Rising, Putnam, 1986.
Patriot Games, Putnam, 1987.
Cardinal of the Kremlin, Putnam, 1988.
Clear and Present Danger, Putnam, 1989.
The Sum of All Fears, Putnam, 1991.
Red Storm Rising, The Cardinal of the Kremlin: Two Complete Novels, Putnam, 1993.
Without Remorse, Putnam, 1994.
Debt of Honor, 1994.
Three Complete Novels: Patriot Games, Clear and Present Danger, The Sum of Fears, Putnam, 1994.
(Created with Steve Pieczenik), *Tom Clancy's OP Center,* Berkley, 1995.
(Created with Pieczenik), *Tom Clancy's OP Center II: Mirror Image,* Berkley, 1995.
(Created with Pieczenik), *Tom Clancy's OP Center III: Games of State,* Berkley, 1996.
SSN: Strategies of Submarine Warfare, Berkley, 1996.
Executive Orders, Putnam, 1996.
(Created with others), *Tom Clancy's Power Plays: Politika,* Berkley, 1997.
(Created with others), *Tom Clancy's Power Plays: ruthless.com,* Berkley, 1998.
Rainbow Six, Putnam, 1998.

(Created with Pieczenik), *Tom Clancy's Net Force,* Berkley, 1999.
(Created with Pieczenik), *Tom Clancy's Net Force: The Deadliest Game,* Berkley, 1999.
(Created with Pieczenik), *Tom Clancy's Net Force: One Is the Loneliest Number,* Berkley, 1999.
(Created with Pieczenik), *Tom Clancy's Net Force: Virtual Vandals,* Berkley, 1999.

Nonfiction:
(Foreword only) Steve Kaufman, *Silent Chase: Submarines of the U.S. Navy,* Thomasson-Grant, 1989.
Submarine: A Guided Tour inside a Nuclear Warship, Berkley, 1993.
Armed Cav: A Guided Tour of an Armored Calvary Regiment, Putnam, 1994.
Fighter Wing: A Guided Tour of an Air Force Combat Wing, Berkley, 1995.
Marine: A Guided Tour of a Marine Expeditionary Unit, Berkley, 1996.
(With General Fred Franks, Jr.) *Into the Storm: A Study in Command,* Putnam, 1997.
Reality Check: What's Going on Out There?, Putnam, 1997.
Airborne: A Guided Tour of an Airborn Task Force, 1997.
Carrier: A Guided Tour of an Aircraft Carrier, Berkley, 1999.
(With General Chuck Horner) *Every Man a Tiger,* Putnam, 1999.

Contributed article to *Proceedings* (the magazine of the U.S. Naval Institute).

Adaptations: *The Hunt for Red October* was adapted for film and released by Paramount, directed by John McTiernan and starring Sean Connery and Alec Baldwin, 1990; *Patriot Games* was adapted for film and released by Paramount, directed by Phillip Noyce and starring Harrison Ford and Anne Archer, 1992; *Clear and Present Danger* was adapted for film and released by Paramount, directed by Phillip Noyce and Starring Harrison Ford and William Dafoe, 1994; *Tom Clancy's OP Center* was adapted as a television miniseries for NBC in 1995; *The Sum of All Fears* was adapted for film and will be released in 2000.

OTHER SOURCES

Books:
Contemporary Authors: New Revision Series, Volume 62, Gale (Detroit, MI), 1998.

Periodicals:
Entertainment Weekly, August 14, 1998, p. 73.
Independent, December 9, 1997, p. N6.
Newsweek, August 8, 1988, p. 60.
Publishers Weekly, July 13, 1998, p. 43; July 27, 1998, p. 55.
Washington Post, January 29, 1985, p. C1.

Electronic:
"Tom Clancy," Penguin Putnam Inc. Online, http://www.penguinputnam.com/clancy.

CLARK, Matt 1936-

PERSONAL

Born November 25, 1936, in Washington, DC; son of Frederick William (a carpenter) and Theresa (a teacher; maiden name, Castello) Clark; married Erica Lann (a poet and storyteller), 1958 (divorced, 1966); children: Matthias, Jason, Seth, Aimee.

Addresses: *Agent*—The Kohner Agency, 9169 Sunset Blvd., Los Angeles, CA 90069.

Career: Actor and director.

CREDITS

Film Appearances:
Packy Harrison, *In the Heat of the Night,* United Artists, 1967.
Romulus, *Will Penny,* Paramount, 1968.
Colonel Jellicoe, *The Bridge at Remagen,* United Artists, 1969.
Jailer, *Macho Callahan,* Avco Embassy, 1970.
Rufus Brady, *Monte Walsh,* National General, 1970.
Bailey, *The Grissom Gang,* Cinerama, 1971.
Honky, Jack H. Harris, 1971.
Smiley, *The Cowboys,* Warner Bros., 1972.
Pete, *The Culpepper Cattle Company,* Twentieth Century-Fox, 1972.
Bob Younger, *The Great Northfield, Minnesota Raid,* Universal, 1972.
Qualen, *Jeremiah Johnson,* Warner Bros., 1972.
Nick the Grub, *The Life and Times of Judge Roy Bean,* National General, 1972.
Yardlet, *Emperor of the North Pole* (also known as *Emperor of the North*), Twentieth Century-Fox, 1973.
Coroner, *The Laughing Policeman* (also known as *An Investigation of Murder*), Twentieth Century-Fox, 1973.

Deputy J. W. Bell, *Pat Garrett and Billy the Kid,* Metro-Goldwyn-Mayer, 1973.

Dude Watson, *White Lightning* (also known as *McKlusky*), United Artists, 1973.

Gerhard, *The Terminal Man,* Warner Bros., 1974.

Jackson, *Hearts of the West* (also known as *Hollywood Cowboy*), Metro-Goldwyn-Mayer/United Artists, 1975.

Billy Bob, *Outlaw Blues,* Warner Bros., 1977.

Grover, *Kid Vengeance* (also known as *Take Another Hard Ride* and *Vengeance Vendetta*), Golan-Globus/Irwin Yablans, 1977.

Red plainclothesman, *The Driver,* Twentieth Century-Fox, 1978.

Spider, *Dreamer,* Twentieth Century-Fox, 1979.

Purcell, *Brubaker,* Twentieth Century-Fox, 1980.

Tom McCoy, *An Eye for an Eye,* Avco Embassy, 1981.

Sheriff Wiatt, *The Legend of the Lone Ranger,* Associated Film Distribution, 1981.

Dwayne, *Bustin' Loose,* Universal, 1981.

Ruckus (also known as *The Loner, Big Ruckus in a Small Town* and *Ruckus in Madoc Country*), New World, 1981.

Virgil, *Honkytonk Man,* Warner Bros., 1982.

Mickey, *Some Kind of Hero,* Paramount, 1982.

Chuck Winter, *Love Letters* (also known as *My Love Letters* and *Passion Play*), New World, 1983.

Secretary of Defense, *The Adventures of Buckaroo Banzai: Across the Eighth Dimension* (also known as *Buckaroo Banzai*), Twentieth Century-Fox, 1984.

Tom McMullen, *Country,* Buena Vista, 1984.

Uncle Henry, *Return to Oz* (also known as *The Adventures of the Devil from the Sky* and *Oz*), Buena Vista, 1985.

Stuart Hiller, *Tuff Turf,* New World, 1985.

Walt Clayton, *Let's Get Harry,* TriStar, 1987.

Dr. Tower, *The Horror Show* (also known as *Horror House* and *House III*), Metro-Goldwyn-Mayer/United Artists, 1989.

Bartender, *Back to the Future Part III,* Universal, 1990.

Judge Syms, *Class Action,* Twentieth Century-Fox, 1991.

Bean, Sr., *Cadence* (also known as *Count a Lonely Cadence* and *Stockade*), New Line/Republic Pictures, 1991.

J. F. Hughes, *Frozen Assets,* RKO, 1992.

Hank, *The Harvest,* Arrow Releasing, 1993.

Honore Thibideaux, *Candyman: Farewell to the Flesh,* Gramercy Pictures, 1995.

Ben Wilson, *The Haunted Heart* (also known as *Mother*), Overseas Filmgroup, 1995.

Claude, *Sink or Swim* (also known as *Hacks*), Rigorous Productions, 1997.

A Stranger in the Kingdom, Kingdom Come Pictures, 1998.

Pelican, *Claudine's Return,* Jazz Pictures, 1998.

Sheriff, *Homegrown,* Sony/TriStar, 1998.

Film Work:

Director, *Da,* FilmDallas, 1988.

Television Appearances; Series:

Lieutenant Arthur Kipling, *Dog and Cat,* ABC, 1977.

Emmett Kelly, *Grace under Fire,* ABC, 1994-95.

Walt Bacon, *The Jeff Foxworthy Show* (also known as *Somewhere in America*), ABC, 1995.

Television Appearances; Miniseries:

Chief Clark, *The Winds of War,* ABC, 1983.

Chief Clark, *War and Remembrance,* ABC, 1988.

Television Appearances; Pilots:

Captain Kipling, *Dog and Cat,* ABC, 1977.

Reynolds, *Lacy and the Mississippi Queen,* NBC, 1978.

Dan O'Keefe, *The Big Easy,* NBC, 1982.

Wolfe Crawley, *Highway Honeys,* NBC, 1983.

Matt, *Traveling Man* (broadcast as an episode of *CBS Summer Playhouse*), CBS, 1987.

Television Appearances; Episodic:

Corporal Meekin, "The Kingdom Come Raid," *The Rat Patrol,* ABC, 1967.

Fantan, "The Witness," *Bonanza,* NBC, 1969.

"The Elixir," *Kung Fu,* ABC, 1973.

Seth Berwick, "Mortal Mission," *Little House on the Prairie,* NBC, 1975.

Eric Boulton, "Plague," *Little House on the Prairie,* NBC, 1975.

Dale Cutler, *Hardcastle and McCormick,* ABC, 1985.

Peter Holden, *Midnight Caller,* NBC, 1989.

Emmett Kelly, "With This Ring," *Grace under Fire,* ABC, 1994.

The Reverend, *Lonesome Dove,* CBS, 1995.

Hank Cotton, "The Seige," *Walker, Texas Ranger,* CBS, 1995.

The Pretender, NBC, 1997.

Markus, *Touched by an Angel,* CBS, 1997.

Monroe, "The Devil's Rainbow," *The Visitor,* Fox, 1997.

Jesse Manning, "Body Count," *The Practice,* Fox, 1998.

Television Appearances; Movies:

Dunn, *The Execution of Private Slovik,* NBC, 1974.

Georgie, *The Great Ice Rip-Off,* ABC, 1974.

Charles Parimetter, *Melvin Purvis: G-Man* (also known as *The Legend of Machine Gun Kelly* and *G-Man*), ABC, 1974.
Buffalo Bill Cody, *This Is the West That Was,* NBC, 1974.
Verne Miller, *The Kansas City Massacre,* ABC, 1975.
George Newcombe, *The Last Ride of the Dalton Gang,* NBC, 1979.
Bill Westbrook, *The Children Nobody Wanted,* CBS, 1981.
Mike Raines, *In the Custody of Strangers,* ABC, 1982.
Fennie Groda, *Love, Mary,* CBS, 1985.
John Hubbard, *Out of the Darkness,* CBS, 1985.
Doc Shabitt, *The Quick and the Dead,* HBO, 1987.
Sergeant Grinder, *Kenny Rogers as "The Gambler" III—The Legend Continues* (also known as *The Gambler III*), CBS, 1987.
Jim Warren, *Terror on Highway 91,* CBS, 1989.
Buck Dobbs, *A Seduction in Travis County* (also known as *Body of Evidence* and *Blind Evidence*), CBS, 1991.
Ed Horrigan, *Barbarians at the Gate: The Fall of RJR Nabisco,* HBO, 1993.
John DeSilva, *Dead before Dawn,* ABC, 1993.
Paul Coughlin, *She Stood Alone: The Tailhook Scandal,* ABC, 1995.
Porter, *A Season of Hope* (also known as *Lemon Grove*), CBS, 1995.
Doug Kinross, *Crazy for a Kiss,* BBC, 1995.
Ed Hudson, *Raven Hawk* (also known as *Ravenhawk*), HBO, 1996.
Ansford, "The Graveyard Rats," *Trilogy of Terror II,* USA Network, 1996.

Also appeared as Lieutenant Shapper, *Blind Witness.*

Television Appearances; Specials:
Phil Cranston, "Andrea's Story: A Hitchhiking Tragedy," *ABC Afterschool Specials,* ABC, 1983.
Pawnshop clerk, "Gambler," *CBS Schoolbreak Specials,* CBS, 1988.

Television Work; Episodic:
Director, *Midnight Caller,* NBC, 1989.

Television Work; Specials:
Director, "My Dissident Mom," *CBS Schoolbreak Specials,* CBS, 1987.

Stage Appearances:
Stephen Dedalus, *A Portrait of the Artist as a Young Man,* Martinique Theatre, New York City, 1963.
Timmy Cleary (understudy), *The Subject Was Roses,* Royale Theatre, then Winthrop Ames Theatre, later Helen Hayes Theatre, Henry Miller's Theatre, and Belasco Theatre, all New York City, 1964-66.
The Trial of the Catonsville Nine, Center Theatre Group, New Theatre for Now, Los Angeles, 1970.

Also appeared in *One Flew Over the Cuckoo's Nest,* Burt Reynold's Jupiter Dinner Theatre, Jupiter, FL; *The Connection,* Living Theatre; and *Tonight We Improvise,* Living Theatre.

Stage Work:
Stage manager, *The Subject Was Roses,* Royale Theatre, then Winthrop Ames Theatre, later Helen Hayes Theatre, Henry Miller's Theatre, and Belasco Theatre, all New York City, 1964-66.

WRITINGS

Screenplays:
(With Claude Harz) *Homer,* National General, 1970.*

CLARKSON, Paul

Career: British actor.

Awards, Honors: Laurence Olivier Award, Society of West End Theatre, actor of the year, 1985, for *The Hired Man.*

CREDITS

Stage Appearances:
Appeared in *The Hired Man,* London, c. 1984.

Television Appearances; Movies:
David Biggs, *Eleven Men Against Eleven,* Channel 4, 1995.

Television Appearances; Episodic:
Pat Pringle, "Sally's Libel," *Drop the Dead Donkey,* Channel 4, 1993.*

CLENNON, David 1943-

PERSONAL

Born in 1943, in Waukegan, IL; son of Cecil (an accountant) and Virginia (a homemaker) Clennon; married Perry, 1996. *Education:* Attended University of Notre Dame; studied drama at Yale.

Addresses: *Agent*–Susan Smith and Associates, 121 North San Vincente, Beverly Hills, CA 90211.

Career: Actor.

Awards, Honors: Emmy Award nomination, outstanding supporting actor in a drama series, 1990, for *thirtysomething;* Emmy Award, outstanding guest actor in a comedy series, 1993, for *Dream On.*

CREDITS

Film Appearances:

Toombs, *The Paper Chase,* Twentieth Century-Fox, 1973.
Tim, *Coming Home,* United Artists, 1977.
Captain, *The Greatest,* Columbia, 1977.
Gray Lady Down, Universal, 1977.
Lieutenant Finley Wattsberg, *Go Tell the Spartans,* Avco Embassy, 1978.
Social worker, *Billy in the Lowlands,* FIF Inc., 1978.
Psychiatrist, *On the Yard,* Midwest Film, 1978.
Thomas Franklin, *Being There,* United Artists, 1979.
Richard Fieldston, *Hide in Plain Sight,* Metro-Goldwyn-Mayer/United Artists, 1980.
Dave Robell, *Ladies and Gentlemen, the Fabulous Stains,* Paramount, 1981.
Consul Phil Putnam, *Missing,* Universal, 1981.
Geb, *Star 80,* Warner Bros., 1982.
Palmer, *The Thing* (also known as *John Carpenter's The Thing*), Universal, 1982.
Newspaper editor, *The Escape Artist,* Orion/Warner Bros., 1982.
Liaison man, *The Right Stuff,* Warner Bros., 1983.
Amnon, *Hannah K.,* Universal, 1983.
Brian Gilmore, *Falling in Love,* Paramount, 1984.
Randy Hughes, *Sweet Dreams,* TriStar, 1985.
Lars, *The Trouble with Dick,* Frolix, 1986.
Blanchard, *Legal Eagles,* Universal, 1986.
Mason Mogan, *He's My Girl,* Scotti Brothers, 1987.
Lawrence Baird, *The Couch Trip,* Orion, 1988.
Jack Carpenter, *Betrayed,* Metro-Goldwyn-Mayer/United Artists, 1988.
Jerome Sweet, *Downtown,* Twentieth Century-Fox, 1990.
Robert, *Light Sleeper,* Fine Line, 1992.
Lewie Duart, *Man Trouble,* Twentieth Century-Fox, 1992.
Jack, *Matinee,* Universal, 1993.
Two Crimes (also known as *Kissing Cousin* and *Dos crimenes*), 1994.
Dr. Jones "Jonesy," *Grace of My Heart,* Gramercy, 1996.
Street Preacher, *Mad City,* Warner Bros., 1997.

Also appeared in *Bound for Glory.*

Television Appearances; Series:

Jeff O'Neal, *Park Place,* CBS, 1981.
Miles Drentell, *thirtysomething,* ABC, 1989-c. 1992.
Neal Luder, *Almost Perfect* (also known as *You Can't Have It All*), CBS, 1995- 96.

Also appeared in *Rafferty.*

Television Appearances; Movies:

Tom Trimpin, *The Migrants,* CBS, 1974.
Harry Jones, *Helter Skelter,* CBS, 1976.
James Fitzpatrick, *Gideon's Trumpet,* CBS, 1980.
The Day the Bubble Burst, NBC, 1982.
Dr. Bruce Lyman, *Special Bulletin,* NBC, 1983.
Reverend Werner, *Best Kept Secrets,* ABC, 1984.
Phillip Murray, *Blood and Orchids,* CBS, 1986.
U.S. Attorney Richard Schultz, *Conspiracy: The Trial of the Chicago 8,* HBO, 1987.
The Image, HBO, 1990.
Reverend Dwight Moore, *Black Widow Murders: The Blanche Taylor Moore Story,* NBC, 1993.
Mr. Johnstone, *And the Band Played On,* HBO, 1993.
Dr. Ruland Beesley, *Nurses on the Line: The Crash of Flight 7* (also known as *Race against the Dark: The Crash of Flight 7*), CBS, 1993.
Jimbo, *Original Sins* (also known as *Acts of Contrition*), CBS, 1995.
Harrison, *Tecumseh: The Last Warrior,* TNT, 1995.
Mr. Filger, *The Staircase,* CBS, 1998.

Television Appearances; Pilots:

Peter Karpf, *Crime Club,* CBS, 1975.
Panic in Echo Park, NBC, 1977.
David, *Marriage Is Alive and Well,* NBC, 1980.
Steve Rawlin, *Reward,* ABC, 1980.
Lester Brotman, *First Time, Second Time,* CBS, 1980.

Television Appearances; Episodic:

Barney Miller, ABC, 1977-81.
John Tate, *Alfred Hitchcock Presents,* NBC, 1985.
Harold Bell, "Sledge in Toyland," *Sledge Hammer!,* ABC, 1987.
Cullen, *Beauty and the Beast,* CBS, 1988.
Wilton Tibbles, "Benedict Arnold Slipped Here," *Murder, She Wrote,* CBS, 1988.
Mitch Duprete, *Almost Grown,* CBS, 1989.
Peter Brewer, "For Peter's Sake," *Dream On,* HBO, 1992.

Judge, "Rose Bowl," *NewsRadio,* NBC, 1996.
Prosser, *Michael Hayes,* CBS, 1997.
Nathan Cahill, "Good Dog Karl," *Maximum Bob,* ABC, 1998.
EMH, "Nothing Human," *Star Trek: Voyager,* 1998.
Martin Spencer, "Maya's Nude Photos," *Just Shoot Me,* NBC, 1999.

Also appeared as Norris Breeze in the episode, "The Consultant," *WKRP in Cincinnati,* CBS.

Television Appearances; Specials:
Medvedenko, "The Seagull," *Theatre in America,* PBS, 1975.
Martian High Council Leader, *Toonces, the Cat Who Could Drive a Car* (also known as *Toonces and Friends*), NBC, 1992.

Television Appearances; Miniseries:
Lee Silver, *From the Earth to the Moon,* HBO, 1998.

Stage Appearances:
Messenger to King John, *King John,* New York Shakespeare Festival, Delacorte Theatre, New York City, 1967.
Martius, *Titus Andronicus,* New York Shakespeare Festival, Delacorte Theatre, 1967.
"The Golden Goose," *Story Theatre,* Yale Repertory Theatre, New Haven, CT, 1968.
The Blood Knot, Long Wharf Theatre, New Haven, CT, 1970.
Kid, *The Unseen Hand* and Emmett, *Forensic and the Navigators* (double-bill), Astor Place Theatre, New York City, 1970.
Loot, Hartford Stage Company, Hartford, CT, 1972.
Marat/Sade (also known as *The Persecution and Assassination of Jean-Paul Marat As Performed by the Inmates of the Asylum of Charenton under the Direction of the Marquis de Sade*), Actors' Theatre of Louisville, Louisville, KY, 1972.
Oliver, *As You Like It,* New York Shakespeare Festival, Delacorte Theatre, 1973.
Boy, *Welcome to Andromeda* and narrator, *Variety Obit* (double-bill), Cherry Lane Theatre, New York City, 1973.
Alfred Allmers, *Little Eyolf,* Manhattan Theatre Club, New York City, 1974.
The Seagull, Long Wharf Theatre, 1974.
Doctor, *Medal of Honor Rag,* Folger Theatre Group, Washington, DC, then Theatre De Lys, New York City, both 1976.
Pyotr Sergeyevich Trofimov, *The Cherry Orchard,* New York Shakespeare Festival, Vivian Beaumont Theatre, New York City, 1977.
Tales from the Vienna Woods, Yale Repertory Theatre, 1978.
Mistaken Identities, Yale Repertory Theatre, 1978.
S.S. Glencairn, Long Wharf Theatre, 1978.
Beyond Therapy, Los Angeles Public Theatre, Los Angeles, CA, 1983.
Jeremy M., *Talking Things Over with Chekov,* Victory Theatre, Hollywood, CA, 1987.

Also appeared in *Operation Sidewinder* and *Rosencrantz and Guildenstern Are Dead,* both Williamstown Theatre Festival, Williamstown, MA.

OTHER SOURCES

Periodicals:
People Weekly, October 8, 1990, pp. 51-52.*

CLOONEY, George 1961-

PERSONAL

Born May 6, 1961, in Lexington, KY; son of Nick (a television news anchor and talk-show host) and Nina Clooney; nephew of Rosemary Clooney (a singer and actress); married Talia Balsam, 1989 (divorced, 1992). *Education:* Attended Northern Kentucky University.

Addresses: *Agent*—William Morris Agency, 151 South El Camino Dr., Beverly Hills, CA 90212-2775.

Career: Actor and producer.

Awards, Honors: Two Emmy Award nominations, outstanding lead actor in a drama series, 1995 and 1996, three Golden Globe nominations, best performance by an actor in a television series–drama, 1996, 1997, and 1998, two Screen Actors Guild Award nominations, 1996 and 1997, and (with others) two Screen Actors Guild Awards, outstanding performance by an ensemble in a drama series, 1998 and 1999, all for *ER;* MTV Movie Award, best breakthrough performance, 1996, for *From Dusk Til Dawn;* Golden Apple Award nomination, 1996, male star of the year; (with Jennifer Lopez) MTV Movie Award nomination, best kiss, 1999, for *Out of Sight.*

CREDITS

Film Appearances:
(Film debut) *Grizzly II—The Predator,* 1984.
Oliver, *Return to Horror High,* New World, 1987.

Matt, *Return of the Killer Tomatoes,* New World, 1988.
Mark Remar, *Red Surf,* Arrowhead Entertainment, 1990.
Mac, *Un-Becoming Age* (also known as *The Magic Bubble*), 1992.
Lip sync-ing transvestite, *The Harvest,* 1993.
Seth Gecko, *From Dusk till Dawn,* Miramax, 1996.
Jack Taylor, *One Fine Day,* Twentieth Century-Fox, 1996.
Batman/Bruce Wayne, *Batman & Robin,* Warner Bros., 1997.
Himself, *Full Tilt Boogie,* Miramax, 1997.
Thomas Devoe, *The Peacemaker,* 1997.
Jack Foley, *Out of Sight,* Universal, 1998.
Himself, *Waiting for Woody,* 1998.
Captain Charles Bosche, *The Thin Red Line,* Twentieth Century-Fox, 1998.
Three Kings, 1999.
Designated Survivor, 1999.
Voice, *South Park: Bigger, Longer and Uncut* (animated), 1999.
Oh Brother, Where Art Thou?, forthcoming.

Film Work:
Producer, *Designated Survivor,* 1999.
Executive producer, *Time Tunnel: The Movie,* forthcoming.
Producer, *Five Past Midnight,* forthcoming.

Television Appearances; Series:
Ace, *E/R,* CBS, 1984.
George Burnett, *The Facts of Life,* NBC, 1985-86.
Booker Brooks, *Roseanne,* ABC, 1988-89.
Chic Chesbro, *Sunset Beat,* ABC, 1990.
Joe, *Baby Talk,* ABC, 1990-91.
Captain Ryan Walker, *Bodies of Evidence,* CBS, 1992.
Detective James Falconer, *Sisters,* NBC, 1993-94.
Dr. Doug Ross, *ER,* NBC, 1994-99.

Television Appearances; Pilots:
Ben Braddock, *Hot Prospects,* CBS, 1989.
Nick Biano, *Rewrite for Murder,* CBS, 1991.

Television Appearances; Movies:
Major Biff Woods, *Combat High* (also known as *Combat Academy*), NBC, 1986.
Kevin Shea, *Without Warning: Terror in the Towers,* NBC, 1993.

Television Appearances; Specials:
Tom Bennett, *Bennett Brothers,* NBC, 1987.
The Rosemary Clooney Golden Anniversary Celebration, Arts and Entertainment, 1995.
National Memorial Day Concert, PBS, 1995.
The Barbara Walters Special, ABC, 1995.
Master of Fantasy: Joel Schumacher, Sci-Fi Channel, 1997.
Larry King Meets ER, TNT, 1998.
Paparazzi, E! Entertainment Channel, 1998.
Tony Bennett: An All-Star Tribute—Live By Request, Arts and Entertainment, 1998.
Interviewee, *The Warner Bros. Story: No Guts, No Glory: 75 Years of Blockbusters,* TNT, 1998.

Television Appearances; Awards Presentations:
Breakthrough Awards, E! Entertainment Television, 1995.
The Blockbuster Entertainment Awards, CBS, 1995.
The 47th Annual Primetime Emmy Awards, Fox, 1995.
The 21st Annual People's Choice Awards, CBS, 1995.
The 1996 Emmy Awards, ABC, 1996.

Television Appearances; Episodic:
Lenny Colwell, "Where The Girls Are," *Riptide,* NBC, 1984.
"A Second Self," *Street Hawk,* ABC, 1985.
Bobby Hopkins, "To Catch a Neighbour," *The Golden Girls,* NBC, 1987.
Matthew Winfield, "Double Exposure," *Hunter,* NBC, 1987.
Kip Howard, "No Laughing Murder," *Murder, She Wrote,* CBS, 1987.
Joe, *Baby Talk,* ABC, 1991.
Bonnie's fiancee, *The Building,* CBS, 1993.
Dr. Michael Mitchell, "The One with Two Parts: Part 2," *Friends,* NBC, 1995.
Doctor No. 2, *Murphy Brown,* CBS, 1997.
Voice of Sparky, "Big Gay Al's Big Gay Boat Ride," *South Park,* Comedy Central, 1997.
The Entertainment Business, Bravo, 1998.

OTHER SOURCES

Periodicals:
Entertainment Weekly, January 26, 1996, pp. 25-29.
People Weekly, May 6, 1996, p. 127; December 30, 1996, pp. 60-62; November 17, 1997, pp. 77-87; February 22, 1999.
Premiere, December, 1995, pp. 87-92, 131.*

COEN, Ethan 1958-
(Roderick Jaynes, a joint pseudonym)

PERSONAL

Born September 21, 1958, in St. Louis Park, MN; son

of Edward (a professor of economics) and Rena (an art historian and university teacher) Coen; brother of Joel Coen (a director and screenwriter); married first wife, Hilary, December, 1985 (marriage ended); married Tricia Cooke (a film editor). *Education:* Princeton University, B.A. (philosophy), 1980.

Addresses: *Agent*—United Talent Agency, 9560 Wilshire Blvd., Beverly Hills, CA 90212.

Career: Producer and screenwriter. Macy's (department store), New York City, statistical typist, 1979-80.

Awards, Honors: Grand Jury Prize, U.S. Film Festival, 1984, and Sundance 77 Award, best dramatic feature, 1985, and Independent Spirit Award, best director, Independent Film Project/West, 1986, all for *Blood Simple;* Golden Palm, best film, Cannes International Film Festival, 1991, for *Barton Fink;* Golden Palm, best film, Cannes International Film Festival, 1994, for *The Hudsucker Proxy;* (with Joel Coen) Los Angeles Film Critics Association Award, best screenplay, (with Joel Coen) Best Foreign Film Award, Australian Film Institute, (with Joel Coen) Best Director Award, Cannes Film Festival, and (with Joel Coen) Golden Palm Award nomination, Cannes Film Festival, all 1996, (with Joel Coen) Academy Award, best writing, screenplay written directly for the screen, (with Joel Coen as Roderick Jaynes) two Academy Award nominations, best film editing and best picture, (with Joel Coen) Eddie Award nomination, best edited feature film, (with Joel Coen) three BAFTA Film Award nominations, British Academy Awards, best editing, best film, and best original screenplay, (with Joel Coen) Chicago Film Critics Association Award, best screenplay, (with Joel Coen) Cesar Award nomination, best foreign film, (with Joel Coen) Golden Globe Award nomination, best screenplay—motion picture, Golden Satellite Award, best motion picture—drama, (with Joel Coen) two Independent Spirit Awards, best feature and best screenplay, and Writers Guild of America Screen Award, best screenplay written directly for the screen, all 1997, for *Fargo.*

CREDITS

Film Producer, Except Where Indicated:

Producer, director (with brother Joel Coen, under joint pseudonym Roderick Jaynes), and editor, *Blood Simple,* Circle Releasing Corp., 1984.
Raising Arizona, Twentieth Century-Fox, 1987.
Miller's Crossing, Twentieth Century-Fox, 1990.
(As Roderick Jaynes) Editor, *Barton Fink,* Twentieth Century-Fox, 1991.
The Hudsucker Proxy, Warner Bros., 1994.
(As Roderick Jaynes) Editor, *Fargo,* Gramercy, 1996.
(As Roderick Jaynes) Editor, *The Big Lebowski,* Gramercy, 1998.
To the White Sea, forthcoming.

Television Appearances:

American Cinema (documentary series), PBS, 1995.
Inside the Academy Awards (special), TNT, 1997.

WRITINGS

Screenplays; With Joel Coen:

(Under joint pseudonym Roderick James) *Blood Simple,* Circle Releasing Corp., 1984.
(With Sam Raimi) *Crimewave* (also known as *The XYZ Murders* and *Broken Hearts and Noses*), limited release, Columbia, 1986.
Raising Arizona, Twentieth Century-Fox, 1987.
Miller's Crossing, Twentieth Century-Fox, 1990.
Barton Fink, Twentieth Century-Fox, 1991.
(With Raimi) *The Hudsucker Proxy,* Warner Bros., 1994.
Fargo, Gramercy, 1996.
The Big Lebowski, Gramercy, 1998.
The Naked Man, 1998.
Oh Brother, Where Art Thou?, forthcoming.
To the White Sea, forthcoming.

Books; With Joel Coen:

Blood Simple: An Original Screenplay, St. Martin's (New York), 1988.
Raising Arizona: An Original Screenplay, St. Martin's, 1988.
Barton Fink; Miller's Crossing, Faber (Boston, MA), 1991.

Other:

Contributor to periodicals, including *Playboy.*

OTHER SOURCES

Periodicals:

Entertainment Weekly, April 1, 1994, pp. 30-33.
Interview, March, 1996, pp. 56-58.
Los Angeles Magazine, March, 1998, pp. 112-114.
New York Times Magazine, July 8, 1990, pp. 23-26, 29-30, 45.*

COEN, Joel 1955-
(Roderick Jaynes, a joint pseudonym)

PERSONAL

Born November 29, 1955, in St. Louis Park, MN; son of Edward (a professor of economics) and Rena (an art historian and university teacher) Coen; brother of Ethan Coen (a screenwriter and producer); divorced from first wife, c. 1980; married Frances McDormand (an actress), 1984; children: (second marriage) Pedro. *Education:* Attended Simon's Rock College; New York University, degree (film); graduate study in film at University of Texas at Austin.

Addresses: *Agent*—United Talent Agency, 9560 Wilshire Blvd., Beverly Hills, CA 90212.

Career: Director and screenwriter. Worked as a production assistant on documentaries and industrial films; also worked on rock music video crews.

Awards, Honors: Grand Jury Prize, U.S. Film Festival, 1984, best dramatic feature, Sundance 77, 1985, and Independent Spirit Award, best director, Independent Film Project/West, 1986, all for *Blood Simple;* Concha de Oro, best director, San Sebastian International Film Festival, 1990, for *Miller's Crossing;* Golden Palm, best film, and award, best director, Cannes International Film Festival, 1991, both for *Barton Fink;* Golden Palm, best film, Cannes International Film Festival, 1994, for *The Hudsucker Proxy;* (With Ethan Coen) Los Angeles Film Critics Association Award, best screenplay, NBR Award, best director, (with Ethan Coen) Best Foreign Film Award, Australian Film Institute, (with Ethan Coen) Best Director Award, Cannes Film Festival, and (with Ethan Coen) Golden Palm Award nomination, Cannes Film Festival, all 1996, (with Ethan Coen) Academy Award, best writing, screenplay written directly for the screen, (with Ethan Coen) three Academy Award nominations, (with Ethan Coen as Roderick Jaynes) best film editing, best director, and best picture, (with Ethan Coen as Roderick Jaynes) Eddie Award nomination, best edited feature film, (with Ethan Coen) three BAFTA Film Award nominations, British Academy Awards, best editing, best film, and best original screenplay, (with Ethan Coen), Chicago Film Critics Association Award, best screenplay, (with Ethan Coen) Cesar Award nomination, best foreign film, (with Ethan Coen) Golden Globe Award nomination, best screenplay/motion picture, Golden Satellite Award, best director of a motion picture, two Independent Spirit Awards, best director and (with Ethan Coen) best screenplay, and Writers Guild of America Screen Award, best screenplay written directly for the screen, David Lean Award for Direction, British Academy Awards, all 1997, all for *Fargo;* Five Continents Award, European Film Awards, 1997, and Golden Berlin Bear Award nomination, 1998, both for *The Big Lebowski.*

CREDITS

Film Director, Except Where Indicated:

Assistant editor, *The Evil Dead,* New Line Cinema, 1980.

Assistant editor, *Fear No Evil,* Avco Embassy, 1981.

Producer and director (with brother Ethan Coen, under joint pseudonym Roderick Jaynes) and editor, *Blood Simple,* Circle Releasing Corp., 1984.

Raising Arizona, Twentieth Century-Fox, 1987.

Miller's Crossing, Twentieth Century-Fox, 1990.

(As Roderick Jaynes) Editor, *Barton Fink,* Twentieth Century-Fox, 1991.

The Hudsucker Proxy, Warner Bros., 1994.

(As Roderick Jaynes) Editor, *Fargo,* Gramercy, 1996.

(As Roderick Jaynes) Editor, *The Big Lebowski,* Gramercy, 1998.

Oh Brother, Where Art Thou?, forthcoming.

To The White Sea, forthcoming.

Film Appearances:

Security guard, *Spies Like Us,* Warner Bros., 1985.

Television Appearances:

American Cinema (documentary series), PBS, 1995.

Inside the Academy Awards (special), TNT, 1997.

WRITINGS

Screenplays; With Ethan Coen:

(Under joint pseudonym Roderick James) *Blood Simple,* Circle Releasing Corp., 1984.

(With Sam Raimi) *Crimewave* (also known as *The XYZ Murders* and *Broken Hearts and Noses*), limited release, Columbia, 1986.

Raising Arizona, Twentieth Century-Fox, 1987.

Miller's Crossing, Twentieth Century-Fox, 1990.

Barton Fink, Twentieth Century-Fox, 1991.

(With Raimi) *The Hudsucker Proxy,* Warner Bros., 1994.

Fargo, Gramercy, 1996.

The Big Lebowski, Gramercy, 1998.

Oh Brother, Where Art Thou?, forthcoming.

To The White Sea, forthcoming.

Books; With Ethan Coen:

Blood Simple: An Original Screenplay, St. Martin's (New York), 1988.

Raising Arizona: An Original Screenplay, St. Martin's, 1988.

Barton Fink; Miller's Crossing, Faber (Boston, MA), 1991.

OTHER SOURCES

Periodicals:

Entertainment Weekly, April 1, 1994, pp. 30-33.

Interview, March, 1996, pp. 56-58.

Los Angeles Magazine, March, 1998, pp. 112-114.

New York Times Magazine, July 8, 1990, pp. 23-26, 29-30, 45.*

COLLINS, Joan 1933 (?)-

PERSONAL

Full name, Joan Henrietta Collins; born May 23 (some sources say May 21), 1933 (some sources say 1931 or 1935), in London, England; immigrated to the United States, 1938; daughter of Joseph William (an agent) and Elsa (Bessant) Collins (a dance teacher); sister of Jackie Collins (an author); married Maxwell Reed (an actor; divorced); married Anthony Newley (an actor, singer, director, and composer), May 27, 1963 (divorced, 1971); married Ronald S. Kass (a film producer), March, 1972 (divorced, 1984); married Peter Holm, 1985 (divorced, 1987) married Maxwell Reed; children: (second marriage) Tara Cynara, Sacha; (third marriage) Katyana. *Education:* Attended Royal Academy of Dramatic Art.

Addresses: *Agent*—c/o Jeffrey Lane and Associates, 8380 Melrose Ave., Ste. 206, Los Angeles, CA 90069. *Contact*—16 Bulbeck Walk, South Woodham Ferreis, Chelmsford, GB-Essex, CM3 5ZN, United Kingdom.

Career: Actress, writer, and producer.

Member: Actors' Equity Association, American Federation of Television and Radio Artists, Screen Actors Guild.

Awards, Honors: Golden Apple Award, star of the year, Hollywood Women's Press Club, 1982; Golden Globe Award, best television actress in a drama series, 1983, five Golden Globe Award nominations, best television actress in a drama series, 1982, 1984, 1985, 1986, and 1987, Emmy Award nomination, outstanding lead actress in a drama series, 1984, People's Choice Award, outstanding actress in a drama series, 1985, all for *Dynasty;* People's Choice Award, best female performer on television, 1985; Annual Cable Excellence (ACE) Award; named Officer of the British Empire, 1997.

CREDITS

Television Appearances; Series:

Alexis Carrington Colby, *Dynasty,* ABC, 1981-89.

Panelist, *To Tell the Truth,* NBC, 1990.

Christina Hobson, *Pacific Palisades,* 1997.

Television Appearances; Miniseries:

Avril Devereaux, *Arthur Hailey's "The Moneychangers"* (also known as *The Moneychangers*), NBC, 1976.

Helene Junot, *Sins,* CBS, 1986.

Alexis, *Dynasty: The Reunion* (also known as *Dynasty: The Miniseries*), ABC, 1991.

Television Appearances; Movies:

Carole Bradley, *Drive Hard, Drive Fast,* NBC, 1973.

Kay Dillon, *The Making of a Male Model,* ABC, 1983.

Cartier Rand, *The Cartier Affair,* NBC, 1984.

Pam Dugan, *Her Life As a Man,* NBC, 1984.

Katrina Petrovna, *Monte Carlo,* CBS, 1986.

Alexis Morrell Carrington Colby Dexter Rowan, *Dyntasty: The Reunion,* 1991.

Tonight at 8:30, 1991.

Lady Edwina Hogbottom, *Annie: A Royal Adventure,* 1995.

Lady Camilla Ashley, *Two Harts in 3/4 Time,* 1995.

Arianna Stanton, *Sweet Deception* (also known as *Sweet Lies*), Fox Family Channel, 1998.

Television Appearances; Specials:

The Bob Hope Show, NBC, 1959.

The Bob Hope Show, NBC, 1962.

The Bob Hope Show, NBC, 1966.

Lorraine, "The Man Who Came to Dinner," *Hallmark Hall of Fame,* NBC, 1972.

Steve Martin—Comedy Is Not Pretty, NBC, 1980.

Battle of the Network Stars, ABC, 1982.

Bob Hope's Women I Love—Beautiful But Funny, NBC, 1982.

Blondes vs. Brunettes, ABC, 1984.

The Dean Martin Celebrity Roast: Joan Collins, NBC, 1984.

All Star Party for Lucille Ball, CBS, 1984.

ABC All-Star Spectacular, ABC, 1985.

The Night of 100 Stars II, ABC, 1985.

On Top All Over the World, syndicated, 1985.
Hollywood Christmas Parade, syndicated, 1987.
Secrets Women Never Share, NBC, 1987.
All Star Party for Joan Collins, CBS, 1987.
The 75th Anniversary of Beverly Hills, ABC, 1989.
Night of 100 Stars III, NBC, 1990.
Mama's Back, 1993.
Joan Collins: Actress, Author, Defendant, Court TV, 1996.
Roseanne: Tabloids, Trash & Truth, ABC, 1996.
Star Trek: 30 Years and Beyond, UPN, 1996.
Hidden Hollywood: Treasure From the 20th Century Fox Vaults, AMC, 1997.
Joan Collins, Arts and Entertainment, 1997.
Oscar Levant: Brilliant Shadow, Arts and Entertainment, 1997.
An All Star Party for Aaron Spelling, ABC, 1998.
Paparazzi, E! Entertainment Channel, 1998.

Also appeared in *The Human Jungle.*

Television Appearances; Awards Presentations:
The 39th Annual Emmy Awards, 1987.
Host, *The Golden Globe Awards,* 1989.
The 47th Annual Golden Globe Awards, TBS, 1990.
The 45th Annual Tony Awards, CBS, 1991.
The 17th Annual People's Choice Awards, CBS, 1991.

Television Appearances; Pilots:
Racine, *Paper Dolls,* ABC, 1982.
Annie McCulloch, *The Wild Women of Chastity Gulch,* ABC, 1982.

Television Appearances; Episodic:
Baroness Bibi de Chasseur/Rosy Shlagenheimer, "The Galatea Affair," *The Man from U.N.C.L.E.,* NBC, 1966.
Lorelei Circe/The Siren, "The Wail of the Siren," and "Ring around the Riddler," *Batman,* ABC, 1967.
Edith Keeler, "The City on the Edge of Forever," *Star Trek,* NBC, 1967.
"The Lady from Wichita," *The Virginian,* NBC, 1967.
Nicole Vedette, "Nicole," *Mission Impossible,* ABC, 1969.
Sidonie, "Five Miles to Midnight," *The Persuaders,* ABC, 1972.
Janice, "Starsky and Hutch on Playboy Island," *Starsky and Hutch,* ABC, 1975.
Kara, "Mission of the Dariens," *Space 1999,* syndicated, 1976.
Queen Halyana, *Fantastic Journey,* NBC, 1977.
The Love Boat, ABC, 1977.
Julia/Mother, "Georgy Porgy," *Tales of the Unexpected,* NBC, 1979.
"Hansel and Gretel," *Faerie Tale Theater,* Showtime, 1982.
Fame, Fortune, and Romance, syndicated, 1986.
Stella and Leonora Vail, "Collins Meets Coward" (also known as "Ways and Means," and "Still Life—A Romantic Interlude"), *A&E Stage,* Arts and Entertainment, 1992.
Ronnie, "First Cousin, Twice Removed," *Roseanne,* ABC, 1993.
Clive James, PBS, 1994.
Die Harald Schmidt Show, 1996.
Joan Sheffield, *The Nanny,* CBS, 1996.
Coronation Street, 1998.

Also appeared in episodes of *Run for Your Life,* NBC; *Baretta,* ABC; *Ellery Queen,* NBC; *Switch,* CBS; *Police Woman,* NBC; *Fantasy Island,* ABC; and *Orson Welles' Great Mysteries,* syndicated.

Television Work; Miniseries:
Executive producer, *Sins,* CBS, 1986.

Television Work; Movies:
Costume designer, *The Cartier Affair,* NBC, 1984.
Executive producer, *Monte Carlo,* CBS, 1986.

Television Work; Episodic:
Associate producer, "Collins Meets Coward," *A&E Stage,* Arts and Entertainment, 1992.

Film Appearances:
Lil Carter, *Judgment Deferred,* Associated British, 1952.
Pampinea, *Decameron Nights,* Film Locations, 1953.
Norma, *I Believe in You,* Universal, 1953.
Rene Collins, *The Slasher,* Lippert, 1953.
Mary, *The Good Die Young,* Independent Film Distributors, 1954.
Stella Jarvis, *Turn the Key Softly,* Arvis, 1954.
Marina, *The Woman's Angle,* Stratford, 1954.
Sadie Patch, *The Adventures of Sadie* (also known as *Our Girl Friday*), Twentieth Century-Fox, 1955.
Evelyn Nesbit Thaw, *The Girl in the Red Velvet Swing,* Twentieth Century-Fox, 1955.
Princess Nellifer, *Land of the Pharaohs,* Warner Bros., 1955.
Frankie, *The Square Ring,* Republic, 1955.
Beth Throgmorton, *The Virgin Queen,* Twentieth Century-Fox, 1955.
Lady Godiva Rides Again, Carroll, 1955.
Crystal Allen, *The Opposite Sex,* Metro-Goldwyn-Mayer, 1956.
Jocelyn Fleury, *Island in the Sun,* Twentieth Century-Fox, 1957.

Title role, *Sea Wife* (also known as *Sea Wyf and Biscuit*), Twentieth Century-Fox, 1957.
Tina, *Stopover Tokyo,* Twentieth Century-Fox, 1957.
Alice Chicoy, *The Wayward Bus,* Twentieth Century-Fox, 1957.
Josefa Velarde, *The Bravados,* Twentieth Century-Fox, 1958.
Angela Hoffa, *Rally 'round the Flag, Boys!,* Twentieth Century-Fox, 1958.
Esther, *Esther and the King,* Twentieth Century-Fox, 1960.
Melanie, *Seven Thieves,* Twentieth Century-Fox, 1960.
Diane, *The Road to Hong Kong,* United Artists, 1962.
Jane, *One Million Dollars,* Columbia, 1965.
Joanie Valens, *Warning Shot,* Paramount, 1967.
Polyester Poontang, *Can Heironymus Merkin Ever Forget Mercy Humppe and Find True Happiness?,* Regional, 1969.
Anne Langley, *Subterfuge,* Commonwealth United Entertainment, 1969.
If It's Tuesday, This Must Be Belgium, United Artists, 1969.
Pat Camber, *Up in the Cellar* (also known as *Three in the Cellar*), American International, 1970.
Sarah Booth, *The Executioner,* Columbia, 1970.
Tough Guy (also known as *Kung Fu: The Head Crusher* and *Tough Guys*), 1970.
Carol Radford, *Terror from under the House* (also known as *Revenge, Inn of the Frightened People,* and *After Jenny Died*), Hemisphere, 1971.
Ottilie, *Quest for Love,* Rank, 1971.
The Aquarian, 1972.
Joanne Clayton, "All Through the House," *Tales from the Crypt,* Cinerama, 1972.
Molly Carmichael, *Fear in the Night* (also known as *Dynasty of Fear* and *Honeymoon of Fear*), International, 1972.
State of Siege, Cinema V, 1973.
Bella Thompson, "Mel," *Tales That Witness Madness,* Paramount, 1973.
Fay, *Alfie Darling* (also known as *Oh Alfie*), EMI, 1974.
Sarah Mandeville, *Dark Places,* Cinerama, 1974.
The Referee (also known as *Playing the Field* and *L'Arbitro*), 1974.
Black Bess, *The Bawdy Adventures of Tom Jones,* Universal, 1976.
Lucy, *The Devil within Her* (also known as *The Baby, It's Growing Inside Her, The Monster, Sharon's Baby,* and *I Don't Want to Be Born*), American International, 1976.
The Great Adventure, Pacific International, 1976.
Marilyn Fryser, *Empire of the Ants,* American International, 1977.
Brigitte, *Poliziotto senza Paula* (also known as *Fatal Charm, Fearless,* and *Die Zuhalterin*), 1977.
Agnes Lozelle, *The Big Sleep,* United Artists, 1978.
Gloria, *Zero to Sixty* (also known as *Repo*), First Artists, 1978.
Fontaine Khaled, *The Stud,* Trans-American, 1979.
Fontaine Khaled, *The Bitch,* Brent Walker, 1979.
Nera, *Sunburn,* Paramount, 1979.
Nicolle, *A Game for Vultures,* New Line Cinema, 1980.
Diana, *Homework* (also known as *Growing Pains* and *Short People*) Jensen Farley, 1982.
Madame Carrere, *Nutcracker,* Rank, 1982.
Georgy Porgy, 1983.
Neck, 1983.
Helen/Sybil, *Decadence,* 1993.
Margaretta D'Arville, *In the Bleak Mid-Winter* (also known as *A Midwinter's Tale*), Sony Picture Classics, 1995.
Herself, *Line King: Al Hirschfeld,* 1996.
The Clandestine Marriage, 1999.
Pearl Slaghoople, *The Flintstones in Viva Rock Vegas,* 1999.

Stage Appearances:

A Doll's House, Arts Theatre, London, 1946.
The Night of 100 Stars II, Radio City Music Hall, New York City, 1985.
The Night of 100 Stars III, Radio City Music Hall, 1990.
(Broadway debut) Amanda Prynne, *Private Lives,* Aldwych Theatre, London, 1990, then Broadhurst Theatre, 1992.

Also appeared in productions of *Jassy, The Praying Mantis, The Skin of Our Teeth, Claudia and David, The Last of Mrs. Cheyney,* and *Murder in Mind.*

Major Tours:

Amanda Prynne, *Private Lives,* U.S. cities, 1991-92.

RECORDINGS

Videos:

The Joan Collins Video Special, 1981.
Joan Collins: Personal Workout, 1995.

WRITINGS

Novels:

Past Imperfect: An Autobiography, W. H. Allen, 1978, revised edition, Simon & Schuster (New York), 1984.

The Joan Collins Beauty Book, Macmillan (New York), 1980.
Katy: A Fight for Life (biography), Gollancz, 1982.
Prime Time (novel), Simon & Schuster, 1988.

Other novels include *Love and Desire and Hate,* 1991, and *My Secret,* 1994.

OTHER SOURCES

Periodicals:
Entertainment Weekly, October 25, 1996, p. 128.
New York Times, February 9, 1992.
People Weekly, January 20, 1997, p. 100; June 20, 1997, pp. 121-124.*

CORENBLITH, Michael

PERSONAL

Education: Graduated from the University of Texas at Austin; also attended University of California, Los Angeles.

Addresses: *Agent*—Spyros Skouras, 725 Arizona Ave., Suite 406, Santa Monica, CA 90401.

Career: Production designer, art director, key set designer, and set decorator. Began career as lighting designer.

Awards, Honors: Emmy Award, outstanding art direction for a variety or music program, 1983, for *The 55th Annual Academy Awards Presentation* (with Ray Klausen); Academy Award nomination, British Academy of Film and Television Arts Award, best production design, both for *Apollo 13.*

CREDITS

Film Production Designer, Except Where Indicated:
Prince Jack, Castle Hill, 1984.
Private Resort, Unity Pictures Corp., 1985.
Art direction assistant, *Tough Guys,* Buena Vista, 1986.
Key set designer, *Down and Out in Beverly Hills,* Buena Vista, 1986.
Hollywood Vice Squad, Concorde, 1986.
Art direction, *Burglar,* Warner Bros., 1987.
Art direction, *Red Heat,* 1988.
Zandalee, LIVE Home Video, 1991.
He Said, She Said, Paramount, 1991.
Cool World, Paramount, 1992.
The Gun in Betty Lou's Handbag, Buena Vista, 1992.
And art director, *Apollo 13,* Universal, 1995.
Down Periscope, Twentieth Century-Fox, 1996.
Ransom, Buena Vista, 1996.
Mighty Joe Young, Buena Vista, 1998.
Edtv, Universal, 1999.

Also worked on *Cat People; Die Hard 2: Die Harder.*

Television Production Designer, Except Where Indicated; Movies:
The Ratings Game (also known as *The Mogul*), 1984.
Little White Lies, NBC, 1989.
A Family for Joe, NBC, 1990.
Visual consultant, *The President's Child,* CBS, 1992.
With Hostile Intent (also known as *With Hostile Intent: Sisters in Black and Blue*), CBS, 1993.
Precious Victims, CBS, 1993.
It's Nothing Personal, NBC, 1993.
Search for Grace, CBS, 1994.

Television Production Designer, Except Where Indicated; Series:
Art direction, *Private Eye,* NBC, 1987-88.
TV 101, CBS, 1988.
Second Chances, CBS, 1993.

Television Production Designer, Specials:
San Berdoo, ABC, 1989.

Also designed the set for *The 55th Annual Academy Awards Presentation.**

COSTA-GAVRAS 1933-

PERSONAL

Full name, Konstantin Costa-Gavras; original name, Kostantinos Gavras; born February 12, 1933, in Athens (some sources say Loutra-Iraias), Greece; naturalized French citizen, 1956; married Michele Ray (a journalist), 1968; children: Alexandre, Helene, Romain. *Education:* Received a diploma from the Hautes Etudes Cinematographiques, Paris, France; also attended the Sorbonne, the University of Paris.

Addresses: *Agent*—John Ptak, William Morris Agency, 151 El Camino Dr., Beverly Hills, CA 90212.

Career: Director, producer, and screenwriter.

Cinematheque Francaise, president, 1982—. Worked as a ballet dancer and as an assistant to film directors Yves Allegret, Jacques Demy, Marcel Ophuls, Rene Clair, Jean Giorno, and Rene Clement. Involved with K. G. Productions.

Awards, Honors: Moscow Film Festival Award, 1966, for *Un homme de trop;* New York Film Critics Award, best director, Jury Prize, Cannes International Film Festival, Academy Award nominations, best director and best screenplay based on material from another medium (with Jorge Semprun), and Raoul-Levy Prize, all 1969, for *Z;* Louis Delluc Prize, 1973, for *Etat de siege;* Best Director Award, Cannes International Film Festival, 1975, for *Section speciale;* Academy Award (with Donald Stewart), best screenplay, Golden Palm Award, Cannes International Film Festival, Writers Guild of America Screen Award (with Donald Stewart), Writers Guild of America Award, best dramatic screenplay based on material previously produced or published, and Golden Globe Award nominations, best director of a motion picture and best screenplay (with Donald Stewart), all 1982, for *Missing;* Golden Berlin Bear, Berlin International Film Festival, 1990, for *Music Box;* French Legion of Honor, named a commander of Arts and Letters of France and named a chevalier.

CREDITS

Film Work; Director, Unless Otherwise Noted:

Assistant director, *La baie des anges* (also known as *Bay of Angels* and *Bay of the Angels*), Pathe, 1962.

Assistant director, *Le jour et l'heure* (also known as *The Day and the Hour, Today We Live,* and *Il giorno e l'ora*), Metro-Goldwyn-Mayer, 1963.

Assistant director, *Les felins* (also known as *Joy House* and *The Love Cage*), Metro-Goldwyn-Mayer, 1964.

Compartiment tueurs (also known as *The Sleeping Car Murder* and *The Sleeping Car Murders*), Twentieth Century-Fox, 1965.

Un homme de trop (also known as *Shock Troops*), United Artists, 1967.

Z, Cinema V, 1969.

L'aveu (also known as *The Confession*), Paramount, 1970.

Etat de siege (also known as *State of Siege, L'amerikano,* and *Der Unsichtbare Aufstand*), Cinema V, 1972.

Section speciale (also known as *Special Section* and *L'affare della sezione speciale*), Universal, 1975.

Clair de femme (also known as *Womanlight*), Atlantic Releasing, 1979.

Missing, Universal, 1982.

And producer, *Hanna K.,* Universal, 1983.

Family Business (also known as *Family Council* and *Le conseil de famille*), European Classics, 1986.

Betrayed, Metro-Goldwyn-Mayer/United Artists, 1988.

Summer Lightning (also known as *Sundown*), 1988.

Music Box, TriStar, 1989.

Segment of the film *Z, Splendor,* Cecchi Gori, 1989.

Contre l'oubli (also known as *Against Oblivion, Lest We Forget,* and *Ecrire contre l'oubli*), Amnesty International, 1991.

La petite apocalypse (also known as *The Little Apocalypse* and *La piccola apocalisse*), K. G. Productions, 1993.

Lumiere et compagnie (also known as *Lumiere and Company* and *Lumiere y compania*), Fox Lorber, 1995.

"Les Kankobales," *A propos de Nice, la suite,* 1995.

Mad City, Warner Bros., 1997.

Film Appearances:

Ramon, *Madame Rosa* (also known as *A Life Ahead* and *La vie devant soi*), Atlantic Releasing, 1977.

Tadzhik highway patrol officer, *Spies Like Us,* Warner Bros., 1985.

Person at gas station, *The Stupids,* New Line Cinema, 1996.

Himself, *Enredando sombras,* Instituto Mexicano de Cinematografia, 1998.

Television Appearances; Specials:

Jessica Lange: It's Only Make-Believe, Cinemax, 1991.

Stage Work; Director; Operas:

Il mondo dela luna, 1994.

WRITINGS

Screenplays, Unless Otherwise Noted:

(With Sebastien Japrisot) *Compartiment tueurs* (also known as *The Sleeping Car Murder* and *The Sleeping Car Murders*), Twentieth Century-Fox, 1965.

Un homme de trop (also known as *Shock Troops*), United Artists, 1967.

(With Jorge Semprun) *Z,* Cinema V, 1969.

(with Franco Solinas) *Etat de siege* (also known as *State of Siege, L'amerikano,* and *Der Unsichtbare Aufstand*), Cinema V, 1972.

Section speciale (also known as *Special Section* and *L'affare della sezione speciale*), Universal, 1975.

Clair de femme (also known as *Womanlight*), Atlantic Releasing, 1979.

(With Donald Stewart) *Missing,* Universal, 1982.
(With Franco Solinas) *Hanna K.,* Universal, 1983.
The au harem d'Archimede (also known as *Tea in the Harem*), M and R Films, 1985.
Family Business (also known as *Family Council* and *Le conseil de famille*), European Classics, 1986.
Summer Lightning (also known as *Sundown*), 1988.
Segment of the film *Z, Splendor,* Cecchi Gori, 1989.
La petite apocalypse (also known as *The Little Apocalypse* and *La piccola apocalisse*), K. G. Productions, 1993.
"Cliff's Theme Song," *Mad City,* Warner Bros., 1997.

Other Writings:
Contributor to periodicals, including *Cahiers de la Cinematheque, Cineaste, Film Comment, Films and Filming, Independent, Take One,* and *Time Out.*

OTHER SOURCES

Books:
International Dictionary of Films and Filmmakers, Volume 2: *Directors/Filmmakers,* St. James Press (Chicago, IL), 1991.

Periodicals:
American Film, March, 1982.
Cineaste, Volume 12, number 1, 1982.
Film Comment, March/April, 1982.
Image et Son, December, 1977.
Jeune Cinema, November, 1983.
New Perspectives Quarterly, fall, 1995, pp. 4-8.
Sight and Sound, summer, 1984.*

CRONENBERG, David 1943-

PERSONAL

Born May 15, 1943, in Toronto, Ontario, Canada; son of a journalist and a musician; married first wife (divorced); married; wife's name, Carolyn; children: (first marriage) Cassandra (an assistant director); (second marriage) three. *Education:* Graduated from the University of Toronto (with distinction).

Addresses: *Office*—David Cronenberg Productions, Ltd., 217 Avenue Rd., Toronto, Ontario M5R 2J3, Canada. *Agent*—William Morris Agency, 151 El Camino Dr., Beverly Hills, CA 90212.

Career: Director, screenwriter, and actor. Cannes International Film Festival, Cannes, France, president of feature film jury, 1999. Affiliated with Emergent Films. Also worked as a film editor and a camera operator.

Awards, Honors: Best Science Fiction Film Award, Brussels International Festival of Fantasy Film, and Genie Award, Academy of Canadian Cinema and Television, best achievement in direction, both 1983, for *Videodrome;* Los Angeles Film Critics Association Award, best director, and Genie Awards, best achievement in direction and best motion picture (with Marc Boyman), all 1988, for *Dead Ringers;* Saturn Awards, Academy of Science Fiction, Fantasy, and Horror Films, and George Pal Memorial Award, all 1989; National Society of Film Critics Awards, best director and best screenplay, New York Film Critics Circle Award, best screenplay, and Genie Award, best achievement in direction, all 1991, for *Naked Lunch;* Genie Awards, best achievement in direction and best adapted screenplay, and Special Jury Prize and Golden Palm nomination, both Cannes International Film Festival, all 1996, for *Crash.*

CREDITS

Film Work; Director, Unless Otherwise Noted:
And producer, editor, and cinematographer, *Transfer* (short film), [Canada], 1966.
And editor and cinematographer, *From the Drain* (short film), [Canada], 1967.
And producer, editor, and cinematographer, *Stereo,* Emergent Films, 1969.
And producer, editor, and cinematographer, *Crimes of the Future,* Emergent Films, 1970.
And producer, editor, and cinematographer, *Jim Ritchie, Sculptor,* [Canada], 1971.
They Came from Within (also known as *Frissons, Orgy of the Blood Parasites, The Parasite Murders,* and *Shivers*), American International Pictures, 1975.
Rabid (also known as *Rage*), New World Pictures, 1977.
Fast Company, Topar, 1978.
The Brood (also known as *La clinique de la terreur*), New World Pictures, 1979.
Scanners (also known as *Telepathy 2000*), Avco Embassy, 1981.
Videodrome, Universal, 1983.
The Dead Zone, Paramount, 1983.
The Fly, Twentieth Century-Fox, 1986.
And producer (with Marc Boyman), *Dead Ringers* (also known as *Gemini* and *Twins*), Twentieth Century-Fox, 1988.
Naked Lunch, Twentieth Century-Fox, 1991.
M. Butterfly, Warner Bros., 1993.

And producer, *Crash,* Fine Line Features, 1996.
Executive producer, *I'm Losing You,* Lions Gate Films, 1998.
And producer, *eXistenZ* (also known as *Crimes of the Future*), Miramax, 1999.

Producer of short films at the University of Toronto.

Film Appearances:
Group supervisor, *Into the Night,* Universal, 1985.
Gynecologist, *The Fly,* Twentieth Century-Fox, 1986.
Dr. Decker, *Nightbreed,* Twentieth Century-Fox, 1990.
Naked Making Lunch, 1992.
Blue, Miramax, 1993.
The director, *Trial by Jury,* Warner Bros., 1994.
Doc Fisher, *Henry and Verlin,* Original Motion Picture Company, 1994.
Man at lake, *To Die For,* Columbia, 1995.
Stephen, *Blood & Donuts,* Malofilm, 1995.
Voice of auto salesperson, *Crash,* Fine Line Features, 1996.
Postal supervisor, *The Stupids,* New Line Cinema, 1996.
Hospital attorney, *Extreme Measures,* Columbia, 1996.
Duncan, *Last Night,* Lions Gate Films, 1998.

Television Work; Director; Series:
Friday the 13th: The Series, syndicated, 1987.

Television Appearances; Movies:
Clem Clayton, *Moonshine Highway,* Showtime, 1996.

Television Appearances; Specials:
Long Live the New Flesh: The Films of David Cronenberg (documentary), CBC, 1987.

Television Appearances; Episodic:
Himself, "Idella's Breakdown," *Maniac Mansion,* The Family Channel, 1992.
Himself, "Meltdown: Part 1," *The Newsroom,* CBC, 1997.

RECORDINGS

Taped Readings:
"Sneakers," *Nightmares and Dreamscapes,* Volume 2, Penguin HighBridge Audio (St. Paul, MN), 1994.

WRITINGS

Screenplays:
Transfer (short film), [Canada], 1966.
From the Drain (short film), [Canada], 1967.
Stereo, Emergent Films, 1969.
Crimes of the Future, Emergent Films, 1970.
Jim Ritchie, Sculptor, [Canada], 1971.
They Came from Within (also known as *Frissons, Orgy of the Blood Parasites, The Parasite Murders,* and *Shivers*), American International Pictures, 1975.
Rabid (also known as *Rage*), New World Pictures, 1977.
Fast Company, Topar, 1978.
The Brood (also known as *La clinique de la terreur*), New World Pictures, 1979.
Scanners (also known as *Telepathy 2000*), Avco Embassy, 1981.
Videodrome, Universal, 1983.
(With Charles Pogue) *The Fly* (based on a story by George Langelaan), Twentieth Century-Fox, 1986.
(With Norman Snider) *Dead Ringers* (also known as *Gemini* and *Twins;* based on the book *The Twins* by Bari Wood and Jack Geasland), Twentieth Century-Fox, 1988.
Naked Lunch (based on the novel by William S. Burroughs), Twentieth Century-Fox, 1991.
Crash (based on a novel by J. G. Ballard), Fine Line Features, 1996.
eXistenZ (also known as *Crimes of the Future*), Miramax, 1999.

Nonfiction:
Cronenberg on Cronenberg, edited by Chris Rodley, Faber & Faber (London, England), 1992.

OTHER SOURCES

Books:
Dompierre, Louise, *Prent/Cronenberg: Crimes against Nature,* Power Plant (Toronto, Ontario, Canada), 1987.
Gruenberg, Serge, *David Cronenberg,* Cahiers du Cinema (Paris, France), 1992.
Handling, Piers, editor, *The Shape of Rage: The Films of David Cronenberg,* General Publishing (Toronto, Ontario, Canada), 1983.

Periodicals:
Artforum, March, 1997, p. 76.
Film Comment, March/April, 1997, p. 14.
Interview, January, 1992, p. 80; August, 1996, p. 64.
Maclean's, June 3, 1996, p. 54; November 11, 1996, p. 72.
Rolling Stone, February 6, 1992, p. 66.
Saturday Night, September, 1993, p. 42; October, 1996, p. 119.*

CRONENBERG, Denise

PERSONAL

Born in Toronto, Ontario, Canada. *Education:* Graduated from Ryerson Polytech; studied ballet at the American Ballet Theatre.

Career: Costume designer. Appeared as a ballet dancer with the Royal Winnipeg Ballet; appeared as a dancer on CBS variety shows for fifteen years, through 1983.

CREDITS

Film Costume Designer, Except Where Indicated:
The Fly, Twentieth Century-Fox, 1986.
Dead Ringers, Twentieth Century-Fox, 1986.
Costumes, *Shoot Me,* 1988.
Naked Lunch, Twentieth Century-Fox, 1991.
M. Butterfly, Warner Bros., 1993.
Moonlight and Valentino, Gramercy, 1995.
Crash, Fine Line Features, 1996.
Murder at 1600, Warner Bros., 1997.
A Cool Dry Place (also known as *Dance Real Slow*), Twentieth Century-Fox, 1998.
EXistenZ, Miramax, 1999.

Trained as a wardrobe designer on *Videodrome;* worked as a wardrobe mistress, *The Dead Zone.*

Television Costume Designer; Movies:
Child of Rage, CBS, 1992.
Sugartime, HBO, 1995.
Friends at Last, CBS, 1995.
Mistrial, HBO, 1996.
Rebound: The Legend of Earl "The Goat" Manigault, HBO, 1996.

Also worked as costume designer on *The Guardian; Scales of Justice.*

Television Costume Designer; Miniseries:
Worked as costume designer on *Murder Ordained,* CBS.*

D

DALY, Tim
See DALY, Timothy

DALY, Timothy 1956-
(Tim Daly)

PERSONAL

Born March 1, 1956, in New York, NY; son of James Daly (an actor) and Hope Newell (an actress); brother of Tyne Daly (an actress); married Amy Van Nostrand (an actress), September 18, 1982; children: Sam. *Education:* Bennington College, B.A., 1979.

Addresses: *Agent*—Gersh Agency, Inc., 232 North Canon Dr., Beverly Hills, CA 90210-5302.

Career: Actor, sometimes credited as Tim Daly. Guitarist, singer, and composer in rock bands; performed in cabaret at the Williamstown Theatre Festival, Williamstown, MA, and at benefits in New York City.

Member: Actors' Equity Association.

Awards, Honors: *Theatre World* Award, 1987, for *Coastal Disturbances.*

CREDITS

Television Appearances; Series:

Dr. Edward Gillian, *Ryan's Four,* ABC, 1983.
Norman Foley, *Almost Grown,* CBS, 1988.
Joe Hackett, *Wings,* NBC, 1990-97.
Voice of Clark Kent/Superman, *Superman* (also known as *Superman: The Animated Series*), The WB, 1996.
Voice of Clark Kent/Superman, *The New Batman/Superman Adventures* (animated), The WB, 1997.

Television Appearances; Miniseries:

Toby Amberville, *I'll Take Manhattan,* CBS, 1987.
Colonel James Jackson, Jr., *Alex Haley's "Queen"* (also known as *Queen*), CBS, 1993.
Jim Lovell, *From the Earth to the Moon,* HBO, 1998.
Mike Anderson, *Storm of the Century* (also known as *Stephen King's Storm of the Century*), ABC, 1999.

Television Appearances; Movies:

Kevin Coates, *I Married a Centerfold,* NBC, 1984.
Chris Philips, *Mirrors,* NBC, 1985.
Guy Pehrsson, *Red Earth, White Earth* (also known as *Snake Treaty*), CBS, 1989.
David Koresh, *In the Line of Duty: Ambush in Waco* (also known as *In the Line of Duty: Assault in Waco*), NBC, 1993.
Dennis Casterline, *Witness to the Execution,* NBC, 1994.
Angel Perno, *Dangerous Heart,* USA Network, 1994.

Television Appearances; Awards Presentations:

The 41st Annual Tony Awards, CBS, 1987.
The 18th Annual People's Choice Awards, CBS, 1992.
The 19th Annual People's Choice Awards, CBS, 1993.
The Golden Globe's 50th Anniversary Celebration, NBC, 1994.
The 4th Annual Environmental Media Awards, TBS, 1994.
Presenter, *The 8th Annual American Comedy Awards,* ABC, 1994.
Presenter, *The 51st Annual Golden Globe Awards,* TBS, 1994.
Co-host, *The 21st Annual People's Choice Awards,* CBS, 1995.
Presenter, *The 47th Annual Primetime Emmy Awards,* Fox, 1995.

Television Appearances; Episodic:

Richard, "The Rise and Rise of Daniel Rocket," *American Playhouse,* PBS, 1986.

Elliot Chase, *Midnight Caller,* NBC, 1989.

Thor Merrick, "Bad Pennies," *The John Larroquette Show,* 1995.

Also appeared on *Hill Street Blues,* NBC; and *Alfred Hitchcock Presents.*

Other Television Appearances:

Joe Hackett, *Wings* (pilot), NBC, 1990.

Wendy's Ski Family Challenge (special), syndicated, 1995.

Voice, *Invasion America,* 1998.

Dan White, *Execution of Justice,* 1999.

Film Appearances:

William "Billy" Howard, *Diner,* Metro-Goldwyn-Mayer/United Artists, 1982.

Frank, *Just the Way You Are,* Metro-Goldwyn-Mayer/United Artists, 1984.

Tom Donnelly, *Made in Heaven,* Lorimar, 1987.

Jeff Mills, *Spellbinder,* Metro-Goldwyn-Mayer/United Artists, 1988.

Chris Murdoch, *Love or Money,* 1989.

Oliver Plexico, *Year of the Comet,* Columbia, 1992.

(As Tim Daly) Detective Ray Dillon, *Caroline at Midnight* (also known as *Someone's Watching*), New Horizons Home Video, 1994.

(As Tim Daly) Dr. Richard Jacks, *Dr. Jekyll and Ms. Hyde,* Savoy Pictures, 1995.

(As Tim Daly) Frank Oliver, *Denise Calls Up,* Sony Pictures Classics, 1995.

Clark Kent/Kal-El/Superman, *Superman: The Last Son of Krypton,* 1996.

(As Tim Daly) Frank, *The Associate,* Buena Vista, 1996.

Voice of Clark Kent/Superman, *The Batman/Superman Movie* (animated), Warner Home Video, 1998.

(As Tim Daly) Dr. Robert Joley, *The Object of My Affection,* Twentieth Century-Fox, 1998.

Wonderland, 1999.

Jesse, *Seven Girlfriends,* 1999.

Stage Appearances:

The Fifth of July, Trinity Square Repertory Company, Providence, RI, 1981.

Buried Child, Trinity Square Repertory Company, 1981.

(Off-Broadway debut) Trevor, Chris, Nicky, Victor, and Eddie, *Fables for Friends,* Playwrights Horizons Theatre, 1984.

Title role, *Oliver Oliver,* Manhattan Theatre Club, City Center Theatre Space, New York City, 1985.

(Broadway debut) Leo Hart, *Coastal Disturbances,* Second Stage Theatre, then Circle in the Square, both New York City, 1987.

Also appeared in *Bus Stop* and *Mass Appeal,* both Trinity Square Repertory Company; *The Glass Menagerie,* Santa Fe Festival Theatre, SantaFe, NM; and *Jenny Kissed Me,* Bucks County Playhouse, New Hope, PA.

OTHER SOURCES

Periodicals:

Knight-Ridder/Tribune News Service, February 27, 1996, p. 227.

People Weekly, March 30, 1998, p. 116; January 18, 1999, p. 112.*

DANES, Claire 1979-

PERSONAL

Full name, Claire Catherine Danes; born April 12, 1979, in New York, NY; daughter of Chris (an architectural photographer and computer consultant) and Carla (a textile designer and schoolteacher) Danes. *Education:* Attended Professional Performing Arts School, New York City; attended Yale University, 1998; studied acting at Lee Strasberg Studio. *Avocational interests:* Surfing.

Addresses: *Manager*—Addis/Wechsler and Associates, 955 South Carrillo Dr., Los Angeles, CA 90048-5400. *Publicist*—Susan Geller and Associates, 335 North Maple Dr., Suite 254, Beverly Hills, CA 90210.

Career: Actress.

Awards, Honors: Emmy Award nomination, best lead actress in a drama series, and Golden Globe Award, best actress in a drama, both 1995, for *My So-Called Life;* ALFS Award, actress of the year, London Critics Circle, Blockbuster Entertainment Award, favorite actress in a romance, MTV Movie Award, best female performance, and MTV Movie Award nominations, best kiss and best onscreen duo (both with Leonardo DiCaprio), all 1996, for *William Shakespeare's Romeo and Juliet;* Blockbuster Entertainment Award nomination, favorite supporting actress in a drama, 1997, for *The Rainmaker;* ShoWest Award, female star of tomorrow, National Association of Theatre Owners, 1997; named one of the fifty most beautiful people of the year, *People Weekly,* 1997.

CREDITS

Film Appearances:

Dreams of Love, 1992.

30 (short), 1993.

Beth March, *Little Women,* Columbia, 1994.

Lou, *Dead Man's Jack,* Columbia University, 1994.

Young Glady Joe, *How to Make an American Quilt,* Universal, 1995.

Kitt, *Home for the Holidays,* PolyGram, 1995.

Daisy, *I Love You, I Love You Not,* Miramax, 1996.

Rachel Lewis, *To Gillian on Her 37th Birthday,* TriStar, 1996.

Juliet, *William Shakespeare's Romeo and Juliet* (also known as *Romeo and Juliet*), Twentieth Century-Fox, 1996.

Voice of San (English-language version), *Mononoke Hime,* 1997, released as *The Princess Mononoke,* Miramax/Dimension, 1999.

Jenny, *U Turn,* Sony Pictures Entertainment, 1997.

Kelly Riker, *The Rainmaker* (also known as *John Grisham's The Rainmaker*), Paramount, 1997.

Hala Pzoniak, *Polish Wedding,* Fox Searchlight Pictures, 1998.

Cosette, *Les Miserables,* Columbia, 1998.

Julie Barnes, *The Mod Squad,* Metro-Goldwyn-Mayer, 1999.

Alice, *Brokedown Palace,* Twentieth Century-Fox, 1999.

Flora Plum, *Flora Plum,* October Films, 2000.

Monterey Pop, 2000.

Television Appearances; Series:

Angela Chase, *My So-Called Life,* ABC, 1994-95.

Television Appearances; Specials:

More Than Friends: The Coming Out of Heidi Leiter (also known as *The Coming Out of Heidi Leiter*), HBO, 1994.

Presenter, *The 69th Annual Academy Awards,* ABC, 1997.

The ShoWest Awards, 1997.

Television Appearances; Episodic:

Tracy Brandt, "Skin Deep," *Law and Order,* NBC, 1992.

The Entertainment Business, Bravo, 1998.

RECORDINGS

Videos:

Appeared in the Soul Asylum music video "Just like Anyone."

OTHER SOURCES

Periodicals:

Interview, January, 1995, p. 68.

People Weekly, October 3, 1994, pp. 131-33; November 18, 1996, p. 70; October 12, 1998, p. 11.

Teen, August, 1997, p. 86.*

DAVIS, Don 1957-

PERSONAL

Born February 4, 1957, in Anaheim, CA; married Megan Jeanne MacDonald, 1986.

Addresses: *Agent*—Gorfaine Schwartz Agency, 3301 Barham Blvd., Suite 201, Los Angeles, CA 90068-1477.

Career: Composer, orchestrator, music director, song producer and musician.

Awards, Honors: Grammy Award, best rhythm & blues song, 1976, for "Disco Lady" (with others); Emmy Award, individual achievement in creative technical crafts, 1981, for *Astronomical Artists, Cosmos, The Shores of the Cosmic Ocean* (with others); Emmy Award nomination, best musical composition-series (dramatic underscore), 1988, Emmy Award, outstanding achievement in music composition for a series (dramatic underscore), 1990, for *Beauty and the Beast;* Emmy Award nomination, outstanding achievement in music composition for a series (dramatic underscore), 1991, for *My Life and Times;* Emmy Award nomination, outstanding achievement in music composition for a series (dramatic underscore), 1991, for *Lies Before Kisses;* Emmy Award, outstanding achievement in music composition for a series (dramatic underscore), 1991, for *SeaQuest DSV;* Emmy Award nomination, outstanding achievement in music composition for a miniseries or special (dramatic underscore), 1992, for *A Little Piece of Heaven;* Emmy Award nomination, outstanding achievement in music compositionfor a series (dramatic underscore), 1994, for *SeaQuest DSV;* Emmy

Award nomination, outstanding music composition for a miniseries or a movie (dramatic underscore), 1998, for *House of Frankenstein 1997.*

CREDITS

Film Work:

Music director, *Flowers in the Attic,* New World, 1987.

Song producer, *La Bamba,* Columbia, 1987.

WRITINGS

Film Scores:

Hyperspace, 1985.

Blackout, 1988.

Tiny Toon Adventures: How I Spent My Vacation (animated), 1992.

Session Man, 1993.

Additional music and song, *When a Man Loves a Woman* (also known as *To Have and To Hold*), Buena Vista, 1994.

Additional music, *A Goofy Movie,* Buena Vista, 1995.

The Perfect Daughter, 1996.

Bound, Gramercy, 1996.

Warriors of Virtue, 1997.

Song writer, *She's So Lovely,* Miramax, 1997.

The Lesser Evil, Orion Home Entertainment Corp, 1998.

The Matrix, Warner Bros., 1999.

The House on Haunted Hill, Warner Bros., 1999.

Film Orchestrations, Except Where Indicated:

Additional orchestrations, *Police Academy 3: Back in Training,* Warner Bros., 1986.

Additional orchestrations, *Police Academy 4: Citizens on Patrol,* Warner Bros., 1987.

Die Hard 2 (also known as *Die Hard 2: Die Harder*), Twentieth Century-Fox, 1990.

Robin Hood: Prince of Thieves, 1991.

If Looks Could Kill (also known as *Teen Agent*), 1991.

Hudson Hawk, TriStar, 1991.

Ricochet, Warner Bros., 1991.

Death Becomes Her, Universal, 1992.

We're Back! A Dinosaur's Story (animated), Universal, 1993.

Cop & 1/2, Universal, 1993.

Hocus Pocus, Buena Vista, 1993.

Last Action Hero, Columbia, 1993.

The Pelican Brief, Warner Bros., 1993.

Legends of the Fall, TriStar, 1994.

Clean Slate, United International Pictures, 1994.

I Love Trouble, Buena Vista, 1994.

Maverick, Warner Bros., 1994.

Clear and Present Danger, Paramount, 1994.

The Pagemaster (animated), Twentieth Century-Fox, 1994.

Casper, Universal, 1995.

Apollo 13, Universal, 1995.

Toy Story (animated), Buena Vista, 1995.

Balto (animated), Universal, 1995.

And song arrangements, *James and the Giant Peach,* Buena Vista, 1996.

The Phantom, Paramount, 1996.

(Uncredited) *Courage Under Fire,* Twentieth Century-Fox, 1996.

Ransom, Buena Vista, 1996.

Michael, New Line, 1996.

Additional orchestrations, *Titanic,* Paramount, 1997.

Pleasantville, New Line, 1998.

A Bug's Life (animated), Buena Vista, 1998.

Lost in Space (also known as *LS*), New Line Cinema, 1998.

Television Scores; Series:

Beauty and the Beast, CBS, 1987-88.

Star Trek: The Next Generation (also known as *Star Trek: TNG*), 1987.

Tiny Toon Adventures (animated), 1990.

My Life and Times, 1991.

Capitol Critters, 1992.

SeaQuest DSV (also known as *SeaQuest 2032*), NBC, 1993-94.

Television Scores; Movies:

A Stoning in Fulham County, NBC, 1988.

Quiet Victory: The Charlie Wedemeyer Story, CBS, 1988.

Home Fires Burning, CBS, 1989.

Running Against Time, USA Network, 1990.

Lies Before Kisses, CBS, 1991.

A Little Piece of Heaven, NBC, 1991.

Notorious, Lifetime, 1992.

Woman with a Past, NBC, 1992.

Murder of Innocence, CBS, 1993.

Leave of Absence, NBC, 1994.

Sleep, Baby, Sleep, ABC, 1995.

In the Lake of the Woods, Fox, 1996.

Ivana Trump's For Love Alone, CBS, 1996.

Not in This Town, USA Network, 1997.

The Alibi, ABC, 1997.

A Match Made in Heaven, CBS, 1997.

Weapons of Mass Destruction, HBO, 1997.

Life of the Party: The Pamela Harriman Story, Lifetime, 1998.

The Agency, 1998.

The Lake, NBC, 1998.

And synthesizer sequencing, *Route 9,* HBO, 1998.

Television Orchestrator; Movies:
Eagles: Hell Freezes Over, 1995.

Television Scores; Miniseries:
Bluegrass, CBS, 1988.
In the Best of Families: Marriage, Pride & Madness (also known as *Bitter Blood*), CBS, 1994.
Peter Benchley's The Beast, NBC, 1996.
Pandora's Clock (also known as *Doomsday Virus*), NBC, 1996.
Robin Cook's Invasion, NBC, 1997.
House of Frankenstein 1997, NBC, 1997.
Ken Follett's The Third Twin, CBS, 1997.

Television Scores; Specials:
Session Man, Showtime, 1992.
Country Estates, ABC, 1993.
Between Mother and Daughter, CBS, 1995.*

DEVLIN, Alan

Career: Actor.

Awards, Honors: Olivier Award, best actor in a supporting role, 1984, for *A Moon for the Misbegotten.*

CREDITS

Film Appearances:
Phoelix, 1979.
Edward, *The Mouse and the Woman,* Facelift, 1980.
Priest, *The Long Good Friday,* Embassy, 1980.
"Clicky," *Traveler,* 1981.
Bill, *Angel* (also known as *Danny Boy*), 1982.
Quinn, *Honor, Profit and Pleasure,* 1985.
Father Quigley, *The Lonely Passion of Judith Hearne,* Island, 1987.
Mick Barry, *Clack of the Ash,* 1987.
Lord Waterstone, *Rebecca's Daughters,* 1992.
Malone, *The Playboys,* Samuel Goldwyn, 1992.
Mr. Riley, *War of the Buttons,* Warner Bros., 1994.
Manley, *High Boot Benny,* 1994.
John Joe, *Moondance,* 1995.
Chalky White, *Resurrection Man,* PolyGram, 1997.

Television Appearances; Movies:
Sir Rex Ferriday, *Nineteen 96,* 1989.
Doctor, *Oliver Twist,* ABC, 1997.

Television Appearances; Specials:
Mick Barry, *Clash of the Ash,* PBS, 1992.

Stage Appearances:
Appeared in *A Moon for the Misbegotten,* London, England, c. 1984.*

DIAMOND, Neil 1941-

PERSONAL

Full name, Neil Leslie Diamond; born January 24, 1941, in Brooklyn, NY; married Jaye Posner (divorced, 1967); married Marcia Murphey, 1969 (divorced, March, 1995); children: (first marriage) Marjorie, Elyn; (second marriage) Jesse, Micah. *Education:* Attended New York University.

Addresses: *Office*—Columbia Records, 2100 Colorado Ave., Santa Monica, CA 90404-3504.

Career: Singer, musician, composer, and actor. Bang Records, recording artist, 1965-68, then Uni Records, 1968-73, then Columbia Records, 1973—.

Awards, Honors: Grammy Award nomination, outstanding pop vocal-male, 1971, for "I Am, I Said"; Grammy Award nomination, record of the year, 1972, for "Song Sung Blue" (with others); Grammy Award nomination, album of the year, 1972, for Moods (with others); Grammy Award, outstanding original score-motion picture or a television special, 1973, Golden Globe Award, best original film score, 1974, both for *Jonathon Livingston Seagull;* Emmy Award nomination, outstanding special-variety or music, 1977, for *The Neil Diamond Special* (with others); Emmy Award nomination, outstanding special-comedy-variety or music, 1978, for *Neil Diamond: I'm Glad You're Here with Me Tonight* (with others); Grammy Award nomination, song of the year, 1978, for "You Don't Bring Me Flowers" (with others); Grammy Award nomination, record of the year and outstanding pop vocal-duo, group, or chorus, 1979, both for "You Don't Bring Me Flowers" (with others); Grammy Award nomination, best original score-motion picture or a television special, Golden Globe Award nomination, best original song-motion picture and best motion picture actor-musical/comedy, 1981, all for *The Jazz Singer* (with others); American Music Award, special award of merit, 1990.

CREDITS

Film Appearances:
The Last Waltz, 1978.

Yussel Rabinowitz, *The Jazz Singer,* 1980.
Himself, *Neil Diamond: Under a Tennessee Moon,* 1996.

Film Song Performer:
Donnie Brasco, 1997.

Television Appearances; Specials:
The Neil Diamond Special, NBC, 1977.
The Neil Diamond Special: I'm Glad You're Here with Me Tonight, NBC, 1977.
The Barbara Walters Special, ABC, 1985.
An All-Star Celebration Honoring Martin Luther King, Jr., NBC, 1986.
Liberty Weekend, ABC, 1986.
Neil Diamond... Hello Again, CBS, 1986.
Welcome Home, HBO, 1987.
Neil Diamond's Greatest Hits-Live, HBO, 1988.
The American Music Awards, 1990.
American Bandstand 40th Anniversary Special, ABC, 1992.
Christmas in Washington, NBC, 1992.
Neil Diamond's Christmas Special, HBO, 1992.
Neil Diamond: The Christmas Story, ABC, 1993.
Opryland's Country Christmas, CBS, 1994.
Sinatra Duets, CBS, 1994.
Neil Diamond ... Under a Tennessee Moon, ABC, 1996.
The 23rd Annual American Music Awards, ABC, 1996.
Neil Diamond: The Making of "The Movie Album," AMC, 1998.

Television Appearances; Episodic:
Appeared as himself, *The Music Scene.*

Television Song Performer; Specials:
(Theme song only) *Chris and the Magical Drip,* syndicated, 1981.

Stage Appearances:
(Broadway debut) *Neil Diamond One Man Show,* Winter Garden Theatre, 1972-73.

RECORDINGS

Albums:
The Feel of Neil Diamond, Bang, 1966.
Just for You, Bang, 1967.
Neil Diamond's Greatest Hits, Bang, 1968.
Velvet Gloves and Spit, MCA, 1968.
Brother Love's Traveling Salvation Show/Sweet Caroline, MCA/UNI, 1969.
Touching You, Touching Me, MCA, 1970.
Tap Root Manuscript, MCA, 1970.
Shilo, Bang, 1970.
Neil Diamond, MFP, 1970.
Stones, MCA, 1971.
Do It!, Bang, 1971.
Neil Diamond Gold, MCA, 1971.
Moods, MCA, 1972.
Hot August Night, MCA, 1972.
Jonathon Livingston Seagull, Columbia, 1973.
Rainbow, MCA, 1973.
Double Gold, Bang, 1973.
Gold, Universal City, 1973.
His Twelve Greatest Hits, MCA, 1974.
Serenade, Columbia, 1974.
Focus on Neil Diamond, London, 1975.
And the Singer Sings His Songs, MCA, 1976.
Beautiful Noise, Columbia, 1976.
Love at The Greek, Columbia, 1976.
I'm Glad You're here with Me Tonight, Columbia, 1977.
You Don't Bring Me Flowers, Columbia, 1978.
Early Classics, Frog King, 1978.
20 Golden Greats, EMI, 1978.
Carmelita's Eyes, CBS, 1978.
September Morn, Columbia, 1980.
The Jazz Singer, Capitol, 1980.
Diamonds, MCA, 1981.
Solitary Man, Hallmark, 1981.
Love Songs, MCA, 1981.
On the Way to the Sky, Columbia, 1981.
Best of Neil Diamond, World, 1981.
Song Sung Blue, MFP, 1982.
Live Diamond, MCA, 1982.
Heartlight, Columbia, 1982.
Twelve Greatest Hits, Vol. 2, Columbia, 1982.
Very Best of Neil Diamond, Vols. 1 & 2, K-Tel, 1983.
Greatest Hits, CBS, 1983.
Stones/Moods, MCS, 1983.
Classics: The Early Years, Columbia, 1983.
Love Songs: Gold, MCA, 1984.
Primitive, Columbia, 1984.
Hot August Night II, Columbia, 1986.
Headed for the Future, Columbia, 1986.
Red Red Wine, Pickwick, 1988.
The Best Years of Our Lives, Columbia, 1988.
Lovescape, Columbia, 1991.
The Christmas Album, Columbia, 1992.
Up on the Roof-Songs from the Brill Building, Columbia, 1993.
Live in America, Columbia, 1994.
The Christmas Album, Volume II, Columbia, 1994.
I Knew Love, Ariola Express, 1996.
Tennessee Moon, Columbia, 1996.
In My Lifetime, 1996.

Live in Concert, Reader's Digest, 1997.
The Movie Album-As Times Goes By, Sony, 1998.
The Best of the Movie Album-As Time Goes By, Sony, 1999.

Recorded *Voices of Vista: Show #200,* Nola.

Videos:
Neil Diamond Open-End Interview, Uni, 1971.
Love at The Greek, Vestron, 1977.
Greatest Hits Live, CBS, 1988.

WRITINGS

Film Scores:
Jonathon Livington Seagull, Paramount, 1973.
The Jazz Singer, 1980.

Film Songs:
Every Which Way But Loose, Warner Bros., 1978.
Something Wild, Orion, 1986.
Arthur 2 on the Rocks, Warner Bros., 1988.
Theme music, *Switching Channels,* 1988.
Donnie Brasco, 1997.
Edtv, 1999.

Stage Music:
(With others) *Dancin',* Broadhurst Theatre, New York City, 1978-80, then U.S., Canadian, and European cities, 1980-84.

Television Songs; Specials:
Neil Diamond ... Hello Again, CBS, 1986.
The Temptations and Four Tops, Showtime, 1986.
Neil Diamond's Greatest Hits-Live, HBO, 1988.
Neil Diamond's Christmas Special, HBO, 1992.
Neil Diamond: The Christmas Story, ABC, 1993.
The 1994 Billboard Music Awards, 1994.
Neil Diamond ... Under a Tennessee Moon, ABC, 1996.
Neil Diamond: The Making of "The Movie Album," AMC, 1998.

Songs:
"Cherry, Cherry," 1966.
"I'm a Believer," 1966.
"I Am ... I Said," 1971.

Songbooks:
Deluxe Book of Songs, G. Hansen Publishing, 1970.
The Neil Diamond Songbook, Putnam Publishing Group, 1982.

OTHER SOURCES

Books:
Grossman, Alan, Bill Truman, and Roy Oki Yamanaka, *Diamond, A Biography,* Contemporary Books, 1987.
Harvey, Diana Karanikas and Jackson Harvey, *Neil Diamond,* MetroBooks, 1996.
Wiseman, Rich, *Neil Diamond, Solitary Star,* Dodd, Mead & Co., 1987.

Periodicals:
Entertainment Weekly, February 9, 1996, p. 26.
Interview, January 1994, p. 30.
New York Times, July 20, 1986.
People Weekly, April 29, 1996, p. 124.*

DICKSON, Barbara 1948-

PERSONAL

Born September 27,1948, in Dunfermline, Fife, Scotland; daughter of Alastair H. W. and Ruth (maiden name, Malley) Dickson; married Oliver F. Cookson, 1984; children: three sons. *Education:* Woodmill High School, Dunfermline. *Avocational interests:* Walking, theater, antiques, wine, paintings and politics.

Addresses: *Contact*—Rostrum House, Cheriton Place, Folkestone, Kent CT20 2DS United Kingdom.

Career: Actress and musician. Robert Stigwood Organization, recording artist, 1975-78, then CBS Records, beginning 1978. Previously worked in the Registrar General's Office, Edinburgh, Scotland.

Awards, Honors: Bronze Prize, 1978, for *Second Sight;* Olivier Award and Society of West End Theatres Award, best actress in a musical, 1984, both for *Blood Brothers;* Liverpool Echo Arts &Y Entertainment Award, best actress in theatre, 1997, for *The 7 Ages of Women;* Scot of the Year Award.

CREDITS

Television Appearances; Series:
Anita Braithwaite, *Band of Gold,* HBO, 1994-95.
Linda Taylor, *The Missing Postman,* 1996.

Also appeared in *The Afternoon Show.*

Television Appearances; Episodic:
Marie McDonald, *Taggart,* 1994.
Herself, "Port Talbot," *Lenny Goes to Town,* 1998.

Film Appearances:
Sgt. Pepper's Lonely Hearts Club Band, Universal, 1978.

Film Song Performer:
Caravans, IBEX, 1978.
The Chain, Rank, 1985.
Freddie as F.R.O. 7, Miramax, 1992.

Stage Appearances:
John, Paul, George, Ringo and Bert, Everyman Theatre, Liverpool, England, 1974, then London.
Mrs. Johnston, *Blood Brothers,* Liverpool Playhouse, Liverpool, England, 1983.
The 7 Ages of Women, Liverpool Playhouse, Liverpool, England, 1997, then British cities, 1997-98, then London, 1999.

Also appeared as Sveltana, *Chess,* Melbourne, Australia, 1997.

Radio Appearances:
Dinner Ladies, BBC Radio 4, 1997.

RECORDINGS

Albums:
Fate O'Charlie, Trailer, 1969.
From the Beggars Mantle, Decca, 1972.
John, Paul, George, Ringo & Bert, RSO, 1974.
Answer Me, 1976.
Morning Comes Quickly, RSO, 1977.
Sweet Oasis, CBS, 1978.
The Barbara Dickson Album, Epic, 1980.
I Will Sing, Decca, 1981.
You Know It's Me, Epic, 1981.
Here We Go, Epic, 1982.
All For a Song, Epic, 1982.
Barbara Dickson, Contour, 1982.
Blood Brothers, Columbia/Legacy, 1983.
Heartbeats, Epic, 1984.
Songbook, K-Tel, 1985.
Gold, K-Tel, 1985.
The Right Moment, K-Tel, 1986.
After Dark, Theobald, 1987.
Very Best of Barbara Dickson, Telstar, 1987.
Collection, Castle, 1987.
Coming Alive Again, Telstar, 1989.
Don't Think Twice, It's All Right, 1990.
Parcel of Rogues, Castle Communications, 1994.
The Dark End of the Street, Theobald Dicks, 1995.
Now & Then, Alex, 1995.
The Best of Barbara Dickson, Epic, 1996.

Singles:
"Answer Me," 1976.
"Another Suitcase, Another Hall," 1977.
"Carvans," 1980.
"January, February," 1980.
(With Elaine Page) "I Know Him So Well," 1985.*

DIESEL, Vin 1967(?)-

PERSONAL

Born c. 1967, in New York, NY. *Education:* Studied acting at the Theater for the New City, New York City; attended Hunter College.

Addresses: *Contact*—International Business Management, 9696 Culver Blvd., Suite 203, Culver City, CA 90232.

Career: Actor, director, producer, and screenwriter. Previously worked as a bouncer, New York City.

Awards, Honors: Screen Actors Guild Award nomination, outstanding performance by a cast, 1999, for *Saving Private Ryan.*

CREDITS

Film Appearances:
Rick, *Strays,* 1997.
Private Caparzo, *Saving Private Ryan,* DreamWorks, 1998.
Voice of the Iron Giant, *The Iron Giant* (animated), Warner Bros., 1999.
Riddick, *Pitch Black,* Intrepid Pictures, 1999.
Chris, *Boiler Room,* New Line Cinema, 1999.

Film Work:
Director and producer, *Strays,* 1997.

Also producer and director, *Multi-Facial* (short).

WRITINGS

Screenplays:
Strays, 1997.

Also wrote *Multi-Facial* (short).

OTHER SOURCES

Periodicals:

Hollywood Reporter, June 22, 1998, p. 8; March 24, 1999, p.4.

Interview, February 1999, p. 40.*

DIGGS, Taye 1971(?)-

PERSONAL

Born c. 1971, in New Jersey. *Education:* Graduated from Syracuse University with a degree in theater. *Avocational interests:* Modern dance, working out.

Career: Actor. Worked at Disneyland in Tokyo after graduating from college.

Awards, Honors: Obie Award, *Village Voice,* 1996, for *Rent.*

CREDITS

Film Appearances:

Donnell's older brother, *Full Court Press,* 1997.

Winston Shakespeare, *How Stella Got Her Groove Back,* Twentieth Century-Fox, 1998.

Mary Jane's Last Dance, Metro-Goldwyn-Mayer, 1999.

The House on Haunted Hill, Warner Bros., 1999.

Harper, *The Best Man,* Universal, 1999.

Marcus, *Go,* Columbia/TriStar, 1999.

Roland, *The Wood,* Paramount, 1999.

Way of the Gun, forthcoming.

Also appeared as Gabriel, *Blind Date;* made appearances in the films *The Greeks; Black Love Song #1;* and *Dutchman.*

Television Appearances; Series:

Adrian "Sugar" Hill, *The Guiding Light,* CBS, 1997-98.

Television Appearances; Episodic:

Stephon, *New York Undercover,* Fox, 1996.

Also appeared in *Law & Order,* NBC.

Stage Appearances:

Cyrus Hamilton and Police, *Carousel,* Vivian Beaumont Theatre, New York City, 1994-95.

Benjamin "Benny" Coffin III, *Rent,* New York Theatre Workshop, 1996, then Nederlander Theatre, New York City, 1996-97.

OTHER SOURCES

Periodicals:

Newsweek, August 24, 1998, p. 58.

People Weekly, May 10,1999, p. 125.*

DILLON, Denny 1951-

PERSONAL

Born May 18, 1951, in Cleveland, OH. *Education:* Graduated from Syracuse University.

Addresses: *Agent*—Duva Flack & Associates, 200 West 57th Street, Suite 1008, New York, NY 10019.

Career: Actress. Actors Theatre of Louisville, Louisville, KY, company member, 1977-78.

Awards, Honors: Antoinette Perry Award nomination, best featured actress in a musical, 1983, for *My One and Only;* CableACE Award, best actress in a comedy series, 1995, for *Dream On.*

CREDITS

Television Appearances; Series:

Herself, *Saturday Night Live* (also known as *NBC's Saturday Night, SNL,* and *Saturday Night*), NBC, 1980-81.

Meg Bando, *Women in Prison,* Fox, 1987.

Toby Pedalbee, *Dream On,* HBO, 1990-96, Fox, 1995.

Television Appearances; Movies:

Roseanne, *Roseanne: An Unauthorized Biography,* Fox, 1994.

Television Appearances; Specials:

Roseanne, *AFI Presents "TV or Not TV?,"* NBC, 1990.

Jim Thorpe Pro Sports Awards Presented by Footlocker, 1993.

The 16th Annual CableACE Awards, 1995.

Weinerville Chanukah Special, Nickelodeon, 1995.

Television Appearances; Episodic:

Herself and Nun, *Saturday Night Live* (also known as *NBC's Saturday Night, SNL,* and *Saturday Night*), NBC, 1975.

Hot Hero Sandwich, NBC, 1979.
Judy, *Dr. Science,* syndicated, 1987.
Rhoda, "Educating Rhoda," *Night Court,* NBC, 1989.
Big Edie, "The Wilderness Experience," *Designing Women,* CBS, 1989.
Rhoda, "Blue Suede Bull," *Night Court,* NBC, 1990.
Guest, *Women Aloud,* Comedy Central, 1992.
Miss Perkins, "The Operation," *The Crew,* Fox, 1995.

Also appeared as voice of Jessy, *Batman: The Animated Series* (animated).

Film Appearances:
Doreen, *Saturday Night Fever,* Paramount, 1977.
Young woman, *Author! Author!,* CBS/Fox Video, 1982.
Nurse, *Grace Quigley* (also known as *The Ultimate Solution of Grace Quigley*), Metro-Goldwyn-Mayer Home Video, 1984.
Elaine, *Garbo Talks,* Metro-Goldwyn-Mayer, 1984.
Aunt Gail, *Seven Minutes in Heaven,* Warner Bros., 1985.
Verna Klump, *House IV: Home Deadly Home,* New Line Home Video, 1992.
Sunray Tours travel agent, *Only You,* Live Home Video, 1992.
Shelli Summers, *Life on the Edge,* Festival Film, 1992.

Stage Appearances:
Agnes, *Gypsy,* Broadway production, New York City, 1974.
Mammoth and Monkey Man, *The Skin of Our Teeth,* Mark Hellinger Theatre, New York City, 1975.
Scapino!, Studio Arena Theatre, Buffalo, NY, 1975-76.
Sylvie Gazel, *Harold and Maude,* Martin Beck Theatre, New York City, 1980.
Servant of Two Masters, Philadelphia Drama Guild, Philadelphia, PA, 1981-82.
Mickey, *My One and Only,* St. James Theatre, New York City, 1983-84.
The Imaginary Invalid, Hartman Theatre, Stamford, CT, 1985-86.
Detective, *Clue: The Musical,* Players Theatre, New York City, 1997.

Major Tours:
Agnes, *Gypsy,* U.S. and Canadian cities, 1974-75.

OTHER SOURCES

Periodicals:
Hollywood Reporter, August 30, 1995, p. S6.
People Weekly, November 24, 1997, p. 58.*

DOE, John 1954-

PERSONAL

Real name, John N. Duchac; born 1954, in Decatur, IL; married Exene Cervenka (a musician; divorced); married Gigi Blair, 1987.

Addresses: *Agent*—Writers & Artists Agency, 924 Westwood, Suite 900, Los Angeles, CA 90024.

Career: Actor and musician. Founder and member of X (a punk rock band).

CREDITS

Film Appearances:
Urgh! A Music War, Lorimar, 1981.
The Decline of Western Civilization, 1981.
Himself, *The Unheard Music,* 1986.
Roberto, restaurant owner, *Salvador,* Hemdale Film Corporation, 1986.
Gilbert, *Slamdance,* Island, 1987.
Dean, *Border Radio,* Pacific Arts, 1987.
Pat McGurn, *Road House,* Metro-Goldwyn-Mayer/United Artists, 1989.
J.W. Brown, *Great Balls of Fire!,* Orion, 1989.
Himself, *Without You I'm Nothing,* M.C.E.G., 1990.
Peter Downs, *A Matter of Degrees,* Prism Entertainment, 1990.
Cab driver, *Liquid Dreams,* Academy Entertainment, 1992.
Joe Mosely, *Roadside Prophets,* Fine Line, 1992.
Earl Blackstock, *Pure Country,* Warner Bros., 1992.
Tommy Behind-the-Deuce, *Wyatt Earp,* Warner Bros., 1994.
Bobby, *Georgia,* Miramax, 1995.
Cop, *Scorpion Spring,* New Line Home Video, 1997.
Mouse, *The Price of Kissing,*1997.
Thomas, Amber Waves' ex-husband, *Boogie Nights,* New Line Cinema, 1997.
Bodigillo, *Black Circle Boys,* A-pix Entertainment, 1997.
Elwin Worrel, *Touch,* Metro-Goldwyn-Mayer, 1997.
Lew, *The Last Time I Committed Suicide,* New City Releasing, 1997.
The Pass, Dream Entertainment, 1998.
Carl, *Sugar Town* (also known as *Forces of Nature*), DreamWorks, 1999.
Eight #1, *The Specials,* MindFire Entertainment, 1999.
Boyd, *The Rage: Carrie 2,* Metro-Goldwyn-Mayer, 1999.

Film Song Performer, Except Where Indicated:
The Decline of Western Civilization, 1980.
The Unheard Music, 1986.
A Matter of Degrees, Prism Entertainment, 1990.
And song producer, *The Bodyguard,* Warner Bros., 1992.
Georgia, Miramax, 1995.
Touch, Metro-Goldwyn-Mayer, 1997.
Vocalist, *First Love,* Last Rites, 1997.

Television Appearances; Movies:
Lucky, *Shake, Rattle, and Rock!,* Showtime, 1994.
Sammy, *Vanishing Point,* Fox, 1997.
Joe Maphis, *Get to the Heart: The Barbara Mandrell Story,* CBS, 1997.
Harlan James, *Black Cat Run,* HBO, 1998.

Television Appearances; Episodic:
The History of Rock 'n Roll, syndicated, 1995.
Carter, *Party of Five,* Fox, 1996.

RECORDINGS

Albums (as a solo artist):
Meet John Doe, Geffen, 1990.
Kissingsohard, Forward/Rhino, 1995.
For the Rest of Us (EP), Kill Rock Stars, 1998.

Albums (with X):
Los Angeles, 1980.
Wild Gift, 1981.
Under the Big Black Sun, 1982.
More Fun in the New World, 1983.
Ain't Love Grand!, 1985.
See How We Are, 1987.
Live at the Whisky a Go-Go, 1988.
Hey Zeus, 1993.
Unclogged, 1995.
Beyond & Back: The X Anthology, 1997.

Soundtracks:
Roadside Prophets, 1992.
Georgia, 1996.

Also appeared on *Touch; The X-Files.*

Videos:
Appeared in "L.A. Woman," 1985.

WRITINGS

Film Songs:
The Decline of Western Civilization, 1980.
The Unheard Music, 1986.
A Matter of Degrees, Prism Entertainment, 1990.
Thelma & Louise, Metro-Goldwyn-Mayer/Pathe, 1991.
Roadside Prophets, Fine Line, 1992.
SubUrbia, Sony Pictures Classics, 1996.
Touch, Metro-Goldwyn-Mayer, 1997.

Television Songs; Movies:
Vanishing Points, Fox, 1997.

OTHER SOURCES

Books:
Drew, William, *The Lady in the Main Title: On the Twenties and Thirties,* Vestal Press, 1997.

Periodicals:
Entertainment Weekly, January 16, 1998, p. 14.*

DOW, Ellen Albertini 1918-

PERSONAL

Born in 1918; raised in Mount Carmel, PA; married Eugene Dow, 1950. *Education:* Graduated from Cornell University, 1935.

Addresses: *Contact*—Sutton, Barth & Vennari, Inc., 145 South Fairfax Ave., Suite 103, Los Angeles, CA 90036.

Career: Actress. Taught drama and dance for 30 years.

CREDITS

Film Appearances:
Allison, *American Drive-In,* 1985.
Old lady, *Tough Guys,* Buena Vista, 1986.
Organist, *Walk Like a Man,* Metro-Goldwyn-Mayer/United Artists, 1987.
Little old lady, *Munchies,* Metro-Goldwyn-Mayer/United Artists, 1987.
Organist, *Body Slam,* New Line Home Video, 1987.
Nun, *My Blue Heaven,* Warner Bros., 1990.
Receptionist, *Genuine Risk,* IRS Entertainment, 1990.
Old lady, *Blood and Concrete* (also known as *Blood and Concrete, a Love Story*), IRS Releasing, 1991.
Mrs. Norton, *Twogether,* 1992.
Mrs. Coulson, *Memoirs of an Invisible Man,* Warner Bros., 1992.
Choir nun, *Sister Act,* Buena Vista, 1992.
Choir nun, *Sister Act 2: Back in the Habit,* Buena Vista, 1993.

Organist (radio performer), *Radioland Murders,* Universal, 1994.
Rosie, *The Wedding Singer,* New Line Cinema, 1998.
Disco Dottie, *54* (also known as *Studio 54*), Miramax, 1998.
Aggie, *Patch Adams,* Universal, 1998.

Television Appearances; Movies:
Grandma Haldane, *Going to the Chapel* (also known as *Wedding Day* and *Wedding Day Blues*), NBC, 1988.
Nanny, *Easy Come, Easy Go,* ABC, 1989.
Lydia, *Things That Go Bump in the Night,* ABC, 1989.
Lila Duvane, *Problem Child 3* (also known as *Problem Child 3: Junior in Love*), NBC, 1995.

Television Appearances; Miniseries:
Murder One: Diary of a Serial Killer, ABC, 1997.

Television Appearances; Episodic:
Old woman, "The Storyteller," *The Twilight Zone,* CBS, 1986.
Dorothy Benson, "Utley Exposed," *Newhart,* CBS, 1989.
Miss Gilbert, "The Big Reunion," *Family Matters,* ABC, 1989.
Aunt Belle, "The Bitch's Back," *Murphy Brown,* CBS, 1989.
Tight Lips, "Miss Trial," *Designing Women,* CBS, 1990.
Mrs. Ferguson, *Family Matters,* ABC, 1990.
Sarah, "Older and Wiser," *The Golden Girls,* NBC, 1991.
The old woman, *Down the Shore,* Fox, 1992.
Second woman, *Frannie's Turn,* CBS, 1992.
Jennifer Simpson-Riley, *Jack's Place,* ABC, 1992.
Grandma, "Dr. Ruth: April 25, 1985," *Quantum Leap,* NBC, 1992.
Debbie, *Wings,* NBC, 1992.
The salesclerk, *The Building,* CBS, 1993.
Elderly lady, "Scenes from a Mall," *Family Matters,* ABC, 1993.
Mrs. Ostendorf, "That's What Friends Are For," *Family Matters,* ABC, 1993.
Emily, *Second Chances,* CBS, 1993.
Old woman, *The John Larroquette Show,* NBC, 1993.
Mildred, *Empty Nest,* NBC, 1994.
Miss Abbington, *Hearts Afire,* CBS, 1994.
First little old lady, "Baby Blues," *On Our Own,* ABC, 1994.
Betty, *Sister, Sister,* ABC, 1994.
Mrs. Gunther, *The Boys Are Back,* CBS, 1994.
Felisa, "Sub Rosa," *Star Trek: The Next Generation,* syndicated, 1994.
Elderly woman, *Cybill,* CBS, 1995.
Mrs. Riblet, "Hell and High Water," *ER,* NBC, 1995.
Miss Mae, *Hope & Gloria,* NBC, 1995.
Mrs. Porter, *Ned and Stacey,* Fox, 1995.
Momma, "The Secret Code," *Seinfeld,* NBC, 1995.
Aunt Ida Watherwax, *Sisters,* NBC, 1995.
Mrs. DiNovio, *Cosby,* CBS, 1996.
Craft Granny, *Dave's World,* CBS, 1996.
Nurse, *Clueless,* UPN, 1997.
Old lady, *Sabrina, the Teenage Witch,* ABC, 1997.
Lily, *Suddenly Susan,* NBC, 1998.
Flo, "What Ever Happened to Baby Payne?," *Payne,* CBS, 1999.
Flo, "Gossip Checks In and a Cat Checks Out," *Payne,* CBS, 1999.
Flo, "Pacific Ocean Duck," *Payne,* CBS, 1999.

Also appeared in *Vibe.*

Television Appearances; Specials:
Mrs. Pitman, *K-9,* ABC, 1991.

OTHER SOURCES

Periodicals:
Entertainment Weekly, March 6, 1998, p. 79.*

DOYLE, Chris
See DOYLE, Christopher

DOYLE, Christopher 1952-
(Chris Doyle, Kefeng Du)

PERSONAL

Born in 1952, in Sydney, Australia. *Education:* Studied Chinese art at the University of Maryland.

Career: Cinematographer and actor. Was employed by the Norwegian Merchant Marine.

Awards, Honors: Hong Kong Film Award, best cinematography, 1987, for *Lao niang gou sao;* Hong Kong Film Award nomination, best cinematography, 1990, for *Shou huang de nu ren;* Hong Kong Film Award, best cinematography, 1991, *A Fei jing juen;* Hong Kong Film Award nomination, best cinematography, 1995, for *Chongqing senlin* (with Wai Keung Lau); Hong Kong Film Award, best cinematography, 1995, for *Dung che sai duk;* Hong Kong Film Award, best cinematography, 1996, for *Duoluo tianshi;* Hong Kong Film Award nomination, best cinematography, 1997, for *Feng yue;* Golden Horse Award, Golden Horse Film Festival, best cinematography, 1997, Hong Kong Film Award nomination, best cinematography, 1998, both for *Cheun gwong tsa sit.*

CREDITS

Film Cinematographer, Except Where Indicated:

Hai-t'an-shang-te Yi T'ien (also known as *That Day, On the Beach*), 1983.
Lao niang gou sao (also known as *Soul*), 1986.
Sha shou hu die meng (also known as *My Heart is That Eternal Rose*), 1987.
Shou huang de nu ren (also known as *Her Beautiful Life Lies, I Am Sorry,* and *I'm Sorry*), 1988.
As Tears Go By, 1989.
Noir et blanc (also known as *Black and White*), Greycat Films, 1991.
A Fei jing juen (also known as *Ah Fei's Story, Days of Being Wild,* and *The True Story of Ah Fei*), In-Gear Films, 1991.
Mungsing Sifan (also known as *Awakening* and *Mary from Beijing*), 1992.
And lighting, *Anlian taohuayuan* (also known as *The Peach Blossom Landand Secret Love for the Peach Blossom Spring*), 1992.
Producer, *Beijing Zazhong,* 1993.
Hong meigui, bai meigui (also known as *Red Rose, White Rose*), 1994.
Feixia Ahda (also known as *The Red Lotus Society*), 1994.
Dung che sai duk (also known as *Ashes of Time*), 1994.
Chongqing senlin (also known as *Chungking Express* and *Hong Kong Express*), Miramax, 1994.
Wo de mei li yu ai chou (also known as *The Peony Pavilion*), 1995.
Duoluo tianshi (also known as *Fallen Angels*), Kino International, 1995.
Yang & Yin: Gender in Chinese Cinema, 1996.
Si mian xia wa (also known as *Four Faces of Eve* and *Sei min ha wa*), Margin Films, 1996.
Feng yue (also known as *Temptress Moon*), Miramax, 1996.
Second unit cinematographer, *Chinese Box,* Trimark Pictures, 1997.
Motel Seoninjang (also known as *Motel Cactus*), Fortissimo World Sales, 1997.
First Love: A Litter on the Breeze (also known as *Choh chin luen hau dik yi yan sai gaai* and *First Love: The Litter on the Breeze*), 1997.
Cheun gwong tsa sit (also known as *Happy* and *Happy Together*), Golden Harvest, 1997.
4 Mian Xiawa, 1998.
Beijing Summer, 1998.
Psycho, Universal, 1998.
Liberty Heights, 1999.

Film Appearances:

Jeremy, *Tianmimi* (also known as *Comrades: Almost a Love Story*), Gordon's Film Company, 1996.

OTHER SOURCES

Periodicals:

New York Times, November 11, 1998, pp. 13, 27.*

DU, Kefeng
See DOYLE, Christopher

DUNN, Linwood G. 1904-1998

PERSONAL

Full name, Linwood Gale Dunn; born December 27, 1904, in Brooklyn, NY; died of cancer, May 20, 1998, in Burbank, CA; married Alice; children: Nancy, Pamela, Gayle, Judy. *Education:* Attended Manual Training High School, Brooklyn, NY.

Career: Special effects technician and optical photographer. Projectionist, New York City, 1923-25; assistant camera operator, Pathe, New York then Hollywood, 1925-29; International Photographers Guild, founder, 1928; RKO Radio Pictures, cinematographer and head of photographic effects department, 1929-56; designed special-effects photographic equipment for Eastman Kodak and the U.S. armed forces during World War II; Film Effects of Hollywood, founder and president, 1946-80; also founded the Technology Council of the Motion Picture and Television Industry.

Member: Academy of Motion Pictures Arts and Sciences (board member), American Society of Cinematographers (president twice, treasurer, board member for 25 years).

Awards, Honors: Academy Award, technical achievement award, 1945 (with Cecil Love); Academy Award nomination, best visual effects, 1966, for *Hawaii;*

Emmy Award, best photographic special effects, 1967, for *Star Trek* (with Darrell Anderson and Joseph Westheimer); Academy Award, Medal of Commendation, 1979 (with Loren L. Ryder and Waldon O. Watson); Academy Award (Scientific or Technical), 1980 (with Cecil Love and Acme Tool and Manufacturing Company); Academy Award, Gordon E. Sawyer Award, 1984; American Society of Cinematographers, lifetime achievement award, 1990; National Cinephile Society, lifetime achievement award, 1992; Golden Hugo Award, Chicago Film Festival; honorary doctorate, San Francisco Art Institute.

CREDITS

Film Special Effects Technician:

Danger Lights, RKO Radio Pictures, 1930.
Cimarron, RKO Radio Pictures, 1930.
The Most Dangerous Game, RKO Radio Pictures, 1932.
Bird of Paradise, RKO Radio Pictures, 1932.
Flying Down to Rio, RKO Radio Pictures, 1933.
Optical photography, *King Kong* (also known as *Kong, The Beast, King Ape, The Eighth Wonder of the World,* and *The Eighth Wonder*), RKO Radio Pictures, 1933.
The Monkey's Paw, RKO Radio Pictures, 1933.
Down to Their Last Yacht (also known as *Hawaiian Nights*), RKO Radio Pictures, 1934.
Optical effects, *She,* RKO Radio Pictures, 1935.
The Last Days of Pompeii, RKO Radio Pictures, 1935.
Bringing Up Baby, RKO Radio Pictures, 1938.
Gunga Din, RKO Radio Pictures, 1939.
The Hunchback of Notre Dame, RKO Radio Pictures, 1939.
The Swiss Family Robinson, RKO Radio Pictures, 1940.
Optical effects, *Citizen Kane* (also known as *American* and *John Citizen, U.S.A.*), RKO Radio Pictures, 1941.
Photographic effects, *Cat People,* RKO Radio Pictures, 1942.
The Navy Comes Through, RKO Radio Pictures, 1942.
Bombardier, RKO Radio Pictures, 1943.
Days of Glory, RKO Radio Pictures, 1944.
Experiment Perilous, RKO Radio Pictures, 1944.
A Game of Death, RKO Radio Pictures, 1945.
Mighty Joe Young (also known as *Mr. Joseph Young of Africa*), RKO Radio Pictures, 1949.
The Thing from Another World (also known as *The Thing*),RKO Radio Pictures, 1951.
Androcles and the Lion, RKO Radio Pictures, 1952.
The French Line, RKO Radio Pictures, 1953.
The Conqueror, RKO Radio Pictures, 1956.
Optical effects, *Forty Guns,* Twentieth Century-Fox, 1957.
Special photographic effects, *China Gate,* Twentieth Century-Fox, 1957.
Special effects photography, *I Married a Woman,* Universal, 1958.
Photographic effects and title photography, *West Side Story,* United Artists, 1961.
Photographic effects, *It's a Mad Mad Mad Mad World,* Metro-Goldwyn-Mayer, 1963.
Special photographic effects consultant, *Circus World* (also known as *The Magnificent Showman* and *Samuel Bronston's Circus World*), Paramount, 1964.
The Great Race, Warner Bros., 1965.
The Bible-In the Beginning, Twentieth Century-Fox, 1966.
What Did You Do in the War, Daddy?, 1966.
Special photographic effects, *Hawaii,* United Artists, 1966.
Airport, Universal, 1969.
Special effects photography, *Darling Lili,* Paramount, 1970.
Special photographic effects, *The Devil's Rain,* Joseph Brenner Associates, Inc., 1975.
Consultant, *Star Wars,* Twentieth Century-Fox, 1977.
Assistance, *Spaced Invaders,* Smart Egg Releasing Corp., 1990.

Television Work; Series:

Special effects, *Star Trek,* NBC, 1966-69.

Television Appearances; Episodic:

Hollywood: The Golden Years, Arts and Entertainment, 1988.

WRITINGS

Books:

(With George E. Turner) *The ASC Treasury of Visual Effects,* Hollywood, 1983.

Periodicals:

Contributor to *American Cinematographer, Journal of the University Film Association, Wide Angle,* and *Classic Images.*

OTHER SOURCES

Books:

Brosnan, John, *Movie Magic: The Story of Special Effects in the Cinema,* St. Martin's Press (New York City), 1974.

Eyman, Scott, *Five American Cinematographers,* Scarecrow Press (Metuchen, NJ), 1987.

Periodicals:

American Cinematographer, April, 1985.

Los Angeles Times, May 22, 1998.*

E - F

ESPOSITO, Jennifer 1972-

PERSONAL

Born April 19, 1972, in Brooklyn, New York, NY; daughter of Phyllis (an interior decorator) and Bob (a music producer and computer consultant).

Addresses: *Contact*—Huvane Baume-Halles, 130 West 57th St., Suite 6A, New York, NY 10019.

Career: Actress. Appeared in advertisements for Bongo jeans.

CREDITS

Film Appearances:

Donna Delgrosso, *A Brooklyn State of Mind,* Miramax, 1997.
A Brother's Kiss, First Look Pictures Releasing, 1997.
Debbie, *Kiss Me, Guido,* Paramount, 1997.
Teresa, *No Looking Back* (also known as *Long Time, Nothing New*), Gramercy Pictures, 1997.
Nancy, *I Still Know What You Did Last Summer* (also known as *I Know What You Did Last Summer: The Sequel, I Know What You Did Last Summer . . . The Story Continues, I Know What You Did Last Summer 2, I Know What You Did Two Summers Ago* and *I Still Know*), Sony Pictures Entertainment, 1998.
Ms. Janus, *He Got Game,* Buena Vista, 1998.
Summer of Sam, Buena Vista, 1999.

Television Appearances; Series:

Connie Soleito, *The City,* ABC, 1995-97.
Stacey Paterno, *Spin City* (also known as *Spin*), ABC, 1997—.

Television Appearances; Movies:

Jeannie, *The Sunshine Boys,* CBS, 1997.

Television Appearances; Episodic:

Tanze, *All My Children,* ABC, 1970.
Gina Tucci, "Good Girl," *Law & Order,* NBC, 1996.
Gina, *New York Undercover,* Fox, 1997.

Stage Appearances:

XXX Love Act, Ohio Theatre, New York City, 1995.
Painting X's on the Moon, Crane Theatre, New York City, 1995.
Renee and waitress, *Dark Rapture,* Second Stage Theatre, New York City, 1996.

OTHER SOURCES

Periodicals:

Brandweek, January 18, 1999, p. 5.*

FERRELL, Will 1968-

PERSONAL

Born July 16, 1968, in Irvine, CA; son of Lee Ferrell (a musician). *Education:* Graduated from the University of Southern California.

Addresses: *Agent*—United Talent Agency, 9560 Wilshire Blvd., Suite 500, Beverly Hills, CA 90212.

Career: Actor and screenwriter. Appeared with The Groundlings (a comedy/improv troupe).

CREDITS

Television Appearances; Series:

Saturday Night Live (also known as *NBC's Saturday Night, SNL,* and *Saturday Night*), NBC, 1995—.

Television Appearances; Movies:

Young man, *Bucket of Blood* (also known as *Dark Secrets, The Death Artist* and *Roger Corman Presents Bucket of Blood*), Showtime, 1995.

Television Appearances; Episodic:

White guy, *The George Wendt Show,* CBS, 1995.

Voice, *Disney's Hercules* (animated), ABC and syndicated, 1998.

Also appeared in *Late Night with Conan O'Brien,* NBC; *The Rosie O'Donnell Show,* ABC; *Grace Under Fire,* ABC; and *Living Single,* Fox.

Television Appearances; Specials:

Canned Ham: A Night at the Roxbury, Comedy Central, 1998.

Host, *Saturday Night Live Goes Commercial, Volume II,* NBC, 1998.

Host, *The Bad Boys of Saturday Night,* NBC, 1998.

Film Appearances:

Mustafa, *Austin Powers: International Man of Mystery,* New Line, 1997.

Steve Butabi, *A Night at the Roxbury,* Paramount, 1998.

The Whistleblower, 1999.

Superstar, 1999.

The Suburbans, 1999.

Bob Woodward, *Dick,* 1999.

WRITINGS

Screenplays:

A Night at the Roxbury, Paramount, 1998.

OTHER SOURCES

Electronic:

http://www.nbc.com/snlplayers/Bio/Will_Ferrell_bio_nf.html.*

FIELD, Sylvia 1901(?)-1998

PERSONAL

Original name, Harriet Johnson; born February 14, 1901 (some sources say 1902), in Allston, MA; died July 31, 1998, in Fallbrook, CA; daughter of Eugene Malcolm and Ednah (Bishop) Johnson; married Robert J. Froelich (divorced); married Harold Le Roy Moffett (deceased); married Ernest Truex (died, June 26, 1973). *Education:* Attended public schools in Boston, MA.

Career: Actress.

CREDITS

Stage Appearances:

Joy Berlingot, *The Betrothal,* Shubert Theatre, New York City, 1918.

Azalea, *Thunder,* Criterion Theatre, New York City, 1919.

Annabelle West, *The Cat and the Canary,* 1922.

Connie, *Connie Goes Home,* 49th Street Theatre, New York City, 1923.

Clare Clark, *Cock o' the Roost,* Liberty Theatre, New York City, 1924.

Delight Partridge, *Mrs. Partridge Presents,* Belmont Theatre, New York City, 1925.

Millicent, *Something to Brag About,* Booth Theatre, New York City, 1925.

Jane Weston, *The Butter and Egg Man,* Longacre Theatre, New York City, 1925.

Gypsy, *The Little Spitfire,* Cort Theatre, New York City, 1926.

"Billie" Moore, *Broadway,* Broadhurst Theatre, New York City, 1926.

Melodie, *Behold This Dreamer,* Cort Theatre, 1927.

Gwen, *The Royal Family,* Selwyn Theatre, New York City, 1927.

Sulla, *R.U.R.,* Liberty Theatre, 1930.

Princess Kukachin, *Marco Millions,* Liberty Theatre, 1930.

Colomba, *Volpone,* Liberty Theatre, 1930.

Bee, *The Up and Up,* Biltmore Theatre, New York City, 1930.

Jennifer Lee, *Queen at Home,* Theatre at Times Square, New York City, 1930.

Sally, *Give Me Yesterday,* Charles Hopkins Theatre, 1931.

Doris Sabin, *Just to Remind You,* Broadhurst Theatre, 1931.

Elizabeth Betts, *Caught Wet,* John Golden Theatre, New York City, 1931.

Jennie Adams, *Adam's Wife,* Ritz Theatre, New York City, 1931.

Mamie Kimmel, *Hildy Cassidy,* Martin Beck Theatre, New York City, 1933.

Marie, *Uncle Tom's Cabin,* Alvin Theatre, New York City, 1933.

Clara, *Birthright,* 49th Street Theatre, 1933.

Sylvia Jillson, *Sing and Whistle,* Fulton Theatre, 1934.

Fanny Grey, *Autumn Focus,* Shubert Theatre, Minneapolis, MN, 1934.

Sylvia Sheldon, *The Distant Shore,* Morosco Theatre, New York City, 1935.

Leonora, *There's Always Juliet,* New Rochelle, NY, 1935.

All This While, Stockbridge, MA, 1935.

Judy Linden, *The Shining Hour,* Newport, RI, 1935.

Lou, *Achilles Had a Heel,* 44th Street Theatre, New York City, 1935.

Lucy Hough, *Stick in the Mud,* 48th Street Theatre, New York City, 1935.

Fern Davidson, *I Want a Policeman,* Lyceum Theatre, New York City, 1936.

Jean Hammond, *Pre-Honeymoon,* Lyceum Theatre, 1936.

The Bishop Misbehaves, Matunick, RI, 1936.

Crab Apple, Matunick, RI, 1936.

Two Orphans, Matunick, RI, 1936.

Liliom, Matunick, RI, 1936.

Pansy Washington, *White Man,* National Theatre, New York City, 1936.

Mrs. Robert Levy-de Coudray, *Matrimony Pfd.,* Playhouse Theatre, New York City, 1936.

Una Perkins, *Something for Nothing,* Windsor Theatre, 1937.

Berkeley Square, 1938.

Accent on Youth, 1938.

Biography, Littlewood Theatre, Skowhegan, ME, 1939.

Susan and God, Littlewood Theatre, 1939.

Fanny Grey, *Autumn Crocus,* 1939.

Florence, *Popsy,* Playhouse Theatre, 1941.

Jennifer Griggs,*. . . But Not Goodbye,* 48th Street Theatre, 1944.

The Magnificent Yankee, Chicago, IL, 1946.

Sophie MacDonald, *Oh, Mr. Meadow-Brook,* John Golden Theatre, 1948.

George Washington Slept Here, 1949.

"Billie" Moore, "Scene from *Broadway,*" *ANTA Album,* Ziegfeld Theatre, New York City, 1951.

Carrie McColl, *The Fig Leaf,* 1952.

Understudy for the role of Mrs. Lord, *A Very Rich Woman,* Belasco Theatre, New York City, 1965.

Major Tours:

The Front Page, U.S. cities, 1938.

Adam Ate the Apple, U.S. cities, 1945.

Film Appearances:

Stewed, Fried, and Boiled, Fox Film Corporation, 1929.

Beebe, *Voice of the City,* Metro-Goldwyn-Mayer, 1929.

Marjorie, *The Exalted Flapper,* Fox Film Corporation, 1929.

Teacher, *Tillie the Toiler,* Columbia, 1941.

Mrs. Williams, *Blondie for Victory* (also known as *Troubles through Billets*), Columbia, 1942.

Nobody's Darling, Republic, 1943.

Aunt Martha, *Her Primitive Man,* Universal, 1944.

Maid, *Salome, Where She Danced,* Universal, 1945.

Mrs. Graves, *Junior Miss,* Twentieth Century-Fox, 1945.

Leila Delbert, *All Mine to Give* (also known as *The Day They Gave Babies Away*), Universal, 1957.

Aunt Lila McCloud, *Annette,* 1958.

Television Appearances; Series:

Martha Wilson, *Dennis the Menace,* 1959-62.

Television Appearances; Episodic:

"The Visitors," *Philco Television Playhouse,* NBC, 1951.

"Her Prince Charming," *Goodyear Playhouse,* NBC, 1953.

Belle Adrian, "The Case of the Angry Mourner," *Perry Mason,* CBS, 1957.

Laura Bentley, "Young Love," *Petticoat Junction,* CBS, 1966.*

FINERMAN, Wendy

PERSONAL

Married Mark Canton (a studio executive and producer), 1985 (divorced); children: three. *Education:* University of Pennsylvania, B.S. (economics).

Addresses: *Office*—Wendy Finerman Productions, 224 TriStar Bldg., 10202 Washington Blvd., Culver City, CA 90232-3195.

Career: Producer. Wendy Finerman Productions, Culver City, CA, founder, 1988. The Movie Channel, financial analyst in film acquisitions; Universal Television, business affairs executive; Tisch/Avnet Productions, vice president for development and production; University of Pennsylvania, member of the undergraduate executive board committee for the Wharton School.

Awards, Honors: Independent Spirit Award nomination, best first feature, 1994, for *I Like It Like That;* Academy Award and National Board of Review Award (both with Steve Starkey and Steve Tisch), both best picture,PGA Golden Laurel Award (with Steve Tisch, Steve Starkey, and Charles Newirth), motion picture producer of the year, and British Academy of Film and Television Arts Award nomination (with Steve Tisch, Steve Starkey, and Robert Zemeckis), best film, all 1995, for *Forrest Gump.*

CREDITS

Film Work; Producer, Unless Otherwise Noted:

(With others) *Hot to Trot,* Warner Bros., 1988.

Executive producer, *I Like It Like That* (also known as *Black Out*), Columbia, 1994.

Executive producer, *Holy Matrimony,* Buena Vista, 1994.

(With Steve Starkey and Steve Tisch) *Forrest Gump,* Paramount, 1994.

The Fan, TriStar, 1996.

Fairy Tale: A True Story (also known as *Fairy Tale* and *Illumination*), Paramount, 1997.

Stepmom (also known as *Class Divided* and *Good Night Moon*), Columbia, 1998.

The Betty Schimmel Story, 1999.

Sugar and Spice and Semiautomatics, New Line Cinema, forthcoming.*

FOSTER, Jodie 1962-

PERSONAL

Original name, Alicia Christian Foster; born November 19, 1962, in Los Angeles, CA; daughter of Lucius III (an Air Force officer) and Evelyn "Brandy" (a personal manager; maiden name, Almond) Foster; children: Charles. *Education:* Yale University, B.A. (literature; magna cum laude), 1985.

Addresses: *Office*—Egg Pictures, 7920 West Sunset Blvd., Suite 200, Los Angeles, CA 90046-3300. *Agent*—International Creative Management, 8942 Wilshire Blvd., Beverly Hills, CA 90211.

Career: Actress. Egg Pictures, Los Angeles, CA, owner and chairperson. Appeared in television commercials beginning at the age of three; original "Coppertone Girl" character in advertisements for suntan lotion.

Awards, Honors: Emmy Award, outstanding actress in a special, 1973, for "Rookie of the Year," *ABC Afterschool Special;* National Society of Film Critics Award, Los Angeles Film Critics Award, David Di Donatello Award, British Academy Award, British Academy of Film and Television Arts, Academy Award nomination, and New York Film Critics Award nomination, all best supporting actress, 1976, for *Taxi Driver;* British Academy Award, most promising newcomer to leading film roles, and Italian Situation Comedy Award, both 1976, for *Bugsy Malone;* New Generation Award, Los Angeles Film Critics Association, 1976; Golden Globe Award nomination, best motion picture actress in a musical or comedy, 1977, for *Freaky Friday;* Independent Spirit Award, best female lead, 1987, for *Five Corners;* Academy Award, best actress, Golden Globe Award, best actress in a motion picture drama, National Board of Review Award, best actress, and David Award, all 1988, for *The Accused;* Academy Award, best actress, Golden Globe Award, best performance by an actress in a motion picture drama, and New York Film Critics Circle Award, best actress, all 1991, for *The Silence of the Lambs;* ShoWest Award, female star of the year, National Association of Theatre Owners, 1992; named woman of the year, Hasty Pudding Theatricals, 1992; Academy Award nomination, best actress, Golden Globe Award nomination, best performance by an actress in a motion picture drama, and Screen Actors Guild Award, outstanding performance by a female actor in a leading role, all 1995, for *Nell;* Germany's Golden Camera Award, 1995; Board of Governors Award, American Society of Cinematographers, 1996; Berlinale Camera Award, Berlin International Film Festival, 1996; Golden Globe Award nomination, best performance by an actress in a motion picture drama, Saturn Award, best actress, Academy of Science Fiction, Horror, and Fantasy Films, Audience Award, best actress, Rembrandt Awards, and Blockbuster Entertainment Award nomination, favorite actress in a drama, all 1997, for *Contact;* Audience Award, best actress, European Film Awards, 1997; honorary doctorate, Yale University, 1997.

CREDITS

Film Appearances:

(Film debut) Samantha, *Napoleon and Samantha,* Buena Vista, 1972.

Rita, *Kansas City Bomber,* Metro-Goldwyn-Mayer, 1972.

Martha McIver, *One Little Indian,* Buena Vista, 1973.

Becky Thatcher, *Tom Sawyer,* United Artists, 1973.

Menace on the Mountain, Buena Vista, 1973.

Audrey, *Alice Doesn't Live Here Anymore,* Warner Bros., 1975.

Tallulah, *Bugsy Malone,* Paramount, 1976.

Deirdre Striden, *Echoes of a Summer* (also known as *The Last Castle*), Cine Artists, 1976.

Iris Steensman, *Taxi Driver,* Columbia, 1976.

Annabel Andrews, *Freaky Friday,* Buena Vista, 1977.
Rynn Jacobs, *The Little Girl Who Lives down the Lane* (also known as *La Petite Fille au Bout du Chemin*), American International Pictures, 1977.
Teresina, *Il Casotto* (also known as *The Beach House, The Beach Hut,* and *In the Beach House*), Medusa Distribuzione, 1977.
Rosebud, the title role, *Moi, Fleur Bleue* (also known as *Stop Calling Me Baby!*), Megalo/CIC, 1978.
Casey Brown, *Candleshoe,* Buena Vista, 1978.
Donna, *Carny,* United Artists, 1980.
Jeanie, *Foxes,* United Artists, 1980.
Barbara O'Hara, *O'Hara's Wife,* Davis-Panzer, 1983.
Helene, *Le Sang des Autres* (also known as *The Blood of Others*), Parafrance/Prism, 1984.
Franny Berry, *The Hotel New Hampshire,* Orion, 1984.
Victoria, *Mesmerized* (also known as *Shocked*), Thorn-EMI, 1984.
Nancy, *Siesta,* Lonmar, 1987.
Linda, *Five Corners,* Cineplex Odeon, 1987.
Sarah Tobias, *The Accused,* Paramount, 1988.
Katie Chandler, *Stealing Home,* Warner Bros., 1988.
Clarice Starling, *The Silence of the Lambs,* Orion, 1991.
Dede Tate, *Little Man Tate,* Orion, 1991.
Prostitute, *Shadows and Fog,* Orion, 1992.
Anne Benton, *Backtrack* (also known as *Catchfire* and *Do It the Hard Way*), Vestron Video, 1992.
Laurel, *Sommersby,* Warner Bros., 1993.
Narrator, *It Was a Wonderful Life,* 1993.
Title role, *Nell,* Twentieth Century-Fox, 1994.
Annabelle Bransford, *Maverick,* Warner Bros., 1994.
A Personal Journey with Martin Scorsese through American Movies, 1995.
Dr. Eleanor "Ellie" Arroway, *Contact,* Warner Bros., 1997.
Anna Leonowens, *Anna,* 1998.
Flora Plum, forthcoming.

Film Work:
Co-producer, *Mesmerized* (also known as *Shocked*), Thorn-EMI, 1984.
Director, *Little Man Tate,* Orion, 1991.
Co-producer, *Nell,* Twentieth Century-Fox, 1994.
Co-producer and director, *Home for the Holidays,* Paramount, 1995.
Producer, *Waking the Dead,* 1999.

Also director of "Hands on Time," *Americans* (documentary), Time-Life/BBC.

Television Appearances; Series:
(Television debut) *Mayberry, R.F.D.,* CBS, 1969.
Voice of Anne Chan, *The Amazing Chan and the Chan Clan* (animated), CBS, 1972.
Elizabeth Henderson, *Bob and Carol and Ted and Alice,* ABC, 1973.
Voice of Pugsley Addams, *The Addams Family* (animated), NBC, 1973-75.
Addie Pray, *Paper Moon,* ABC, 1974-75.

Television Appearances; Pilots:
Henrietta "Hank" Bennett, *My Sister Hank,* CBS, 1972.
Liberty Cole, *Smile Jenny, You're Dead* (also known as *Don't Call the Police* and *Harry-O*), ABC, 1974.

Television Appearances; Episodic:
Cindy, "Romeo and Julia," *Julia,* NBC, 1969.
Susan Sadler, "Roots of Fear," *Gunsmoke,* CBS, 1969.
Joey Kelley, *The Courtship of Eddie's Father,* ABC, 1969-72.
Rachel, "Bringing Up Josh," *Daniel Boone,* NBC, 1970.
Priscilla, "The Love God," *My Three Sons,* CBS, 1971.
Patricia, "P.S. Merry Christmas," *Gunsmoke,* CBS, 1971.
Ghost Story, NBC, 1972.
Marienne, "The Predators," *Gunsmoke,* CBS, 1972.
Pip Barker, "Bubble, Bubble, Toil, and Murder," *Ironside,* NBC, 1972.
My Three Sons, CBS, 1972.
Bluebird, "A Place to Hide," *Bonanza,* NBC, 1972.
Love Story, NBC, 1973.
Julie Lawrence, "The Eleven Year Itch," *The Partridge Family,* ABC, 1973.
Alethea Ingram, "Alethea," *Kung Fu,* ABC, 1973.
Hildy Haynes, "The Case of the Deadly Deeds," *The New Perry Mason,* 1973.
Host, *Saturday Night Live* (also known as *NBC's Saturday Night, Saturday Night,* and *SNL*), NBC, 1976.
Who's Who, CBS, 1977.
Sam, CBS, 1978.
Narrator, "The Fisherman and His Wife," *Storybook Classics,* Showtime, 1989.
Guest caller Marlene, "Moon Dance," *Frasier,* NBC, 1996.
Voice of Betty, "Never Again," *The X Files,* Fox, 1997.

Also appeared in *Adam-12,* NBC; and *The Wonderful World of Disney,* NBC.

Television Appearances; Movies:
Suellen McIver, *Menace on the Mountain,* 1970.

Zoe Alexander, *Svengali,* CBS, 1983.
Helene Bertrand, *The Blood of Others,* HBO, 1984.

Television Appearances; Specials:
Sharon Lee, "Rookie of the Year," *ABC Afterschool Special,* ABC, 1973.
Sue, "Alexander," *ABC Afterschool Special,* ABC, 1973.
Title role, "The Secret Life of T. K. Dearing," *ABC Weekend Special,* ABC, 1975.
Entertainers '91: The Top 20 of the Year, ABC, 1991.
Oprah: Behind the Scenes, ABC, 1992.
Behind Closed Doors with Joan Lunden, ABC, 1994.
Voice of Alice Paul, *A Century of Women,* TBS, 1994.
Host, *All about Bette,* TNT, 1994.
Hollywood's Most Powerful Women, 1995.
Voice, *A Century of Women,* CNN, 1998.
Robert Downey, Jr.: The E! True Hollywood Story, E! Entertainment Television, 1998.
Host, *AFI's 100 Years . . . 100 Movies,* TNT, 1998.

Television Appearances; Awards Presentations:
The 3rd Annual Hollywood Insider Academy Awards Special, USA Network, 1989.
The 62nd Annual Academy Awards Presentation, ABC, 1990.
The 63rd Annual Academy Awards Presentation, ABC, 1991.
The 49th Annual Golden Globe Awards, ABC, 1992.
The 65th Annual Academy Awards Presentation, ABC, 1993.
Presenter, *The 2nd Annual Screen Actors Guild Awards,* 1996.
Presenter, *The 53rd Annual Golden Globe Awards,* 1996.
A Salute to Martin Scorsese (also known as *The American Film Institute Salute to Martin Scorsese* and *The 25th American Film Institute Life Achievement Award: A Salute to Martin Scorsese*), CBS, 1997.
Presenter, *The 69th Annual Academy Awards,* ABC, 1997.
Presenter, *The 55th Golden Globe Awards,* 1998.

Television Work; Movies:
Executive producer, *The Baby Dance,* 1998.

WRITINGS

Author of "Hands on Time," *Americans* (documentary), Time-Life/BBC. Also contributor of article "Why Me?" to *Esquire.*

OTHER SOURCES

Periodicals:
American Film, October, 1988.
Cosmopolitan, April, 1996, p. 176.
Entertainment Weekly, fall, 1996, p. 97.
People Weekly, July 28, 1997, p. 114; August 3, 1998, p. 9.
Shoot, January 5, 1996, p. 7.*

FRYE, Soleil Moon 1976-

PERSONAL

Born August 6, 1976, in Glendora, CA (some sources say Glendale, CA); daughter of Virgil Frye (an actor) and Sondra Peluce (a talent manager and caterer); sister of Meeno Peluce (an actor and director) and Sean Frye (an actor); married Jason Goldberg, October 25, 1998.

Addresses: *Contact*—P.O. Box 3743, Glendale, CA 91201.

Career: Actress, director, and screenwriter. Began acting at the age of two.

CREDITS

Television Appearances; Series:
Penelope "Punky" Brewster, *Punky Brewster,* NBC, then syndicated, 1984-87.
Voice of Punky Brewster, *It's Punky Brewster* (also known as *Punky Brewster;* animated), NBC, then syndicated, 1985-89.
Herself, *Girl Talk,* 1989.

Television Appearances; Movies:
Mary Elizabeth, *Missing Children: A Mother's Story,* CBS, 1982.
Linda Fray, *Who Will Love My Children?,* ABC, 1983.
Chrissie Winslow, *Invitation to Hell,* ABC, 1984.
Elizabeth number two, *Ernie Kovacs: Between the Laughter,* ABC, 1984.
Minerva, *You Ruined My Life,* ABC, 1987.
Peggy-head cheerleader, *Summertime Switch,* ABC, 1994.
Laura, *Roger Corman Presents Piranha,* 1995.
Emily DeCapprio, *The Secret* (also known as *The Killing Secret*), NBC, 1997.
Kyra, *I've Been Waiting for You,* NBC, 1998.

Television Appearances; Episodic:

Guest, *Teen Win, Lose or Draw,* The Disney Channel, 1989.

Mimi Detweiler, "Growing Up," *The Wonder Years,* ABC, 1990.

Voice of Amanda Duff, "Take Elmyra Please," *Tiny Toon Adventures* (animated), 1992.

Robin, "Screech's Spaghetti Sauce," *Saved by the Bell* (also known as *Good Morning, Miss Bliss*), NBC, 1992.

Voice of Amanda Duff, "Grandma's Dead," *Tiny Toon Adventures* (animated), 1992.

Voice, *Johnny Bravo* (animated), Cartoon Network, 1997.

Jen Miller, *Working,* NBC, 1999.

Katie, "The One with Girl Who Hits," *Friends,* NBC, 1999.

Television Appearances; Specials:

Samantha, *Little Shots,* NBC, 1983.

Andy Williams and the NBC Kids Search for Santa, NBC, 1985.

The 37th Annual Prime Time Emmy Awards, 1985.

The NBC All-Star Hour, NBC, 1985.

The Night of 100 Stars II, ABC, 1985.

Punky Brewster, *Alvin Goes Back to School,* NBC, 1986.

NBC's 60th Anniversary Celebration, NBC, 1986.

Disney's Golden Anniversary of Snow White and the Seven Dwarfs, NBC, 1987.

Tyler McKay, *Cadets,* ABC, 1988.

Host, *Here's to You, Mickey Mouse,* The Disney Channel, 1988.

The Hollywood Christmas Parade, syndicated, 1988-89.

Sonia, *Where's Rodney,* NBC, 1990.

Tina, *Choose Your Own Adventure: The Case of the Silk King,* ABC, 1992.

Film Appearances:

Gigi, *The Liars Club,* New Horizon Picture Corp., 1993.

Julia, *The St. Tammany Miracle,* 1994.

Marcie, *Pumpkinhead II: Blood Wings,* 1994.

Sharon, *Twisted Love,* 1995.

Becky Hanson, *Mind Games,* Brimstone Productions, 1996.

Agent Kyle Rivers, *Motel Blue,* 1997.

Wild Horses (also known as *Lunch Time Special*), 1998.

Running with Scissors, 1998.

Casey, *The Girls' Room,* 1999.

Film Work:

Director (with brother Meeno Peluce), *Wild Horses* (also known as *Lunch Time Special*), 1998.

Stage Appearances:

Appeared in *Orestes/I Murdered My Mother,* Los Angeles.

RECORDINGS

Video Games:

Marcie, *Bloodwings: Pumpkinhead's Revenge,* 1995.

WRITINGS

Screenplays:

Wild Horses (also known as *Lunch Time Special*), 1998.

OTHER SOURCES

Periodicals:

People Weekly, April 26, 1993, pp. 82-84.*

G

GAINSBOURG, Charlotte 1971-

PERSONAL

Born July 22, 1971, in London, England; daughter of Serge Gainsbourg (an actor, composer, director, and screenwriter) and Jane Birkin (an actress, director, and screenwriter); children: (with Yvan Attal, an actor and director) Ben.

Addresses: *Agent*—VMA, 10 avenue George-V, 75008 Paris, France.

Career: Actress.

Awards, Honors: Cesar Award, Academie des Arts et Techniques du Cinema, most promising young actress, 1985, for *L'effrontee;* Cesar Award nomination, best actress, 1996, for *Love, etc.*

CREDITS

Film Appearances:

Charlotte, *Paroles et musique* (also known as *Love Songs* and *Words and Music*), 7 Films Cinema, 1984.

The child, *La tentation d'Isabelle,* Strada Films, 1985.

Charlotte Castang, *L'effrontee* (also known as *Charlotte and Lulu* and *An Impudent Girl*), Oliane Productions, 1985.

Charlotte, *Charlotte Forever,* GPFI, 1986.

Lucy, *Kung Fu Master* (also known as *Le petit amour*), Heritage Entertainment/Prism Entertainment, 1987.

Herself, *Jane B. par Agnes V.* (also known as *Jane B. by Agnes V., Agnes V. sur Jane B.,* and *Jane B. sur Agnes V.;* documentary), [France], 1987.

Janine Castang, *La petite voleuse* (also known as *The Little Thief*), Orly Films, 1989.

Juliette Mangin, *Aux yeux du monde* (also known as *Autobus* and *In the Eyes of the World*), France 3 Cinema, 1990.

Matilda, *Il sole anche di notte* (also known as *Night Sun* and *Sunshine, Even by Night*), Sara Film, 1990.

Contre l'oubli (also known as *Against Oblivion, Lest We Forget,* and *Ecrire contre l'oubli*), Amnesty International, 1991.

Camille, *Merci la vie* (also known as *Thank You, Life* and *Thanks for Life*), Orly Films, 1991.

Marie, *L'amoureuse,* Films A2, 1992.

Julie, *The Cement Garden* (also known as *Der Zementgarden*), October Films, 1993.

Herself, *Grosse fatigue* (also known as *Dead Tired*), Miramax, 1994.

Title role, *Jane Eyre* (also known as *Charlotte Bronte's Jane Eyre*), Miramax, 1996.

Title role, *Anna Oz,* Athena Films, 1996.

Marie and performer of title song, *Love, etc.,* Aliceleo, 1996.

The Intruder, 1999.

RECORDINGS

Singles:

Recorded the single "Lemon Zest."*

GASSMAN, Alessandro 1965-

PERSONAL

Born February 24 (one source says February 27), 1965, in Rome, Italy; son of Vittorio Gassman (an actor) and Juliette Mayniel (an actress).

Addresses: *Contact*—Cecchi Gori, Via Valadier 42, Rome 00193, Italy.

Career: Actor. Appeared in commercials for Max Factor cosmetics. Owner and operator of a theatre company in Modena, Italy.

CREDITS

Film Appearances:

Di padre in figlio, [Italy], 1983.

La monaca di Monza (also known as *Devils of Monza, Sacrilege,* and *Eccessi, misfatti, delitti*), Clemi Cinematografica, 1986.

Federico the sexologist, *Quando eravamo repressi* (also known as *When We Were Repressed*), [Italy], 1992.

Ostinato destino, [Italy], 1992.

Jester, *Schneewittchen und das Geheimnis der Zwerge* (also known as *Snow White*), Omnia Films, 1992.

Miguel, *Huevos de oro* (also known as *Golden Balls, Macho,* and *Uova d'oro*), Lola Films, 1993.

Vittorio Balsari, *A Month by the Lake* (also known as *Un mese sul lago*), Miramax, 1994.

Alex, *Uomini senza donne* (also known as *Men without Women*), [Italy], 1996.

Mi fai un favore, Medusa Films, 1996.

Lovest, [Italy], 1997.

Francesco, *Hamam* (also known as *Hamam: The Turkish Bath, Steam: The Turkish Bath, Turkish Bath: The Hamam, The Turkish Baths, Il bagno turco,* and *Hamam: El bano turco*), Strand Releasing, 1997.

Sandro, *Facciamo fiesta* (also known as *Let's Fiesta*), Cecchi Gori, 1997.

Title role, *Toni,* Ariane Distribution, 1998.

Rossano, *I miei piu cari amici,* Cecchi Gori, 1998.

L'Bomba, [Italy], 1999.

Television Appearances; Miniseries:

Jesus Christ as an adult, *Un bambino di nome Gesu* (also known as *A Child Called Jesus*), syndicated, 1987.

Francesco Granacci, *A Season of Giants,* TNT, 1991.

Nessuno escluso, [Italy], 1997.

Game Over, [Italy], 1999.

Television Appearances; Movies:

Fabrizio, *Comprarsi la vita,* RAI, 1989.

Spareggio con l'assassino, [Italy], 1992.

Deux fois vingt ans, RAI Due, 1993.

Amrok, *Samson and Delilah* (also known as *Sansone e Dalila*), TNT, 1996.

Nuda proprieta vendesi, Lux Vide, 1997.

Also appeared in *Casa Ricordi.*

Stage Appearances:

K2: Teatro in verticale, Teatro Astra di Bassano del Grappa, Modena, Italy, 1999.

Also appeared in *Affabulazione, Camper, Dialoghi delle carmelitane*(also known as *Dialogue of the Carmelites*), *Testimoni,* and *Ulisse e la balena blanca.*

WRITINGS

Screenplays:

(With Vittorio Gassman) *Di padre in figlio,* [Italy], 1983.

OTHER SOURCES

Electronic:

Salon, http://www.salonmagazine.com/ent/movies/int/1999/03/04int.html, March 4, 1999.*

GERSON, Betty Lou 1914-1999

PERSONAL

Born April 20, 1914, in Chattanooga, TN; died after a stroke, January 12, 1999, in Los Angeles, CA; married Joe Ainley (a radio producer; deceased); married Lew Lauria (an owner of a telephone answering service), 1966; stepchildren: (second marriage) Lynne, Don, Lou. *Education:* Studied at the Goodman Theatre School, Chicago, IL.

Career: Actress.

CREDITS

Film Appearances:

Greta Bloch/Yvonne Kraus, *The Red Menace,* Republic, 1949.

Pat the nurse, *Undercover Girl,* Universal, 1950.

Narrator, *Cinderella* (animated), RKO, 1950.

Mrs. Lord, *The Annapolis Story* (also known as *The Blue and the Gold*), Allied Artists, 1955.

Mrs. Ferguson, *The Green-Eyed Blonde,* Warner Bros., 1957.

Nurse Andersone, *The Fly,* Twentieth Century-Fox, 1958.

Kate Peacock, *The Miracle of the Hills,* Twentieth Century-Fox, 1959.

Voice of Cruella De Vil/Miss Birdwell, *One Hundred and One Dalmatians* (animated), Buena Vista, 1961.

Mary Poppins, Buena Vista, 1964.
Voice of Francis the fish, *Cats Don't Dance* (animated), Warner Bros., 1997.

Television Appearances; Episodic:
Agnes Sims, "The Case of the Lonely Heiress," *Perry Mason,* CBS, 1958.
Marjory Davis, "The Case of the Footloose Doll," *Perry Mason,* CBS, 1959.
"One Mother Too Many," *Wanted: Dead or Alive,* CBS, 1960.
Trudie Braun, "The Case of the Cowardly Lion," *Perry Mason,* CBS, 1961.
Mrs. Fellows, "I'm No Henry Walden," *The Dick Van Dyke Show,* CBS, 1963.
Hostess, "Who and Where Was Antonio Stradivarius," *The Dick Van Dyke Show,* CBS, 1963.
Cici, "Ring-a-Ding Girl," *The Twilight Zone,* CBS, 1963.

Appeared in episodes of *77 Sunset Strip* and *The Untouchables,* both ABC.

Radio Appearances; Series:
First Nighter, NBC, 1935-36.
Grand Hotel, NBC Blue, 1937-40.
Mary Marlin, *The Story of Mary Marlin,* NBC, 1938-41.
Box 13, Mutual, 1948-49.

Appeared as Constance, *Arnold Grimm's Daughter,* CBS; in *Aunt Mary;* as Mercedes Colby, *Don Winslow of the Navy,* NBC Blue; as Sue, *Flying Time;* as Helen Adams, *Girl Alone,* NBC; as Charlotte Brandon, *The Guiding Light,* NBC; as Marilyn Larimore, *Lonely Women,* NBC; as Laura, *Ma Perkins,* NBC; in *One Man's Family,* NBC; as Helen Gowan Stephenson, *The Road of Life,* CBS; as Marilyn, *Today's Children,* NBC; as the title role (Karen Adams Harding), *Woman in White,* NBC; and in *The Chicago Theatre of the Air,* Mutual.

Radio Appearances; Episodic:
Appeared in *Cavalcade of America,* CBS; *Knickerbocker Playhouse,* NBC; *Lux Radio Theatre,* NBC Blue and CBS; and *The Railroad Hour,* ABC and NBC.

OTHER SOURCES

Books:
Buxton, Frank, and Bill Owen, *The Big Broadcast,* introduction by Henry Morgan, Viking (New York City), 1972.

Periodicals:
Business Wire, January 14, 1999, p. 203.
Variety, January 18, 1999, p. 147.

Electronic:
Excite.com, http://www.nt.excite.com/news/r/990115/00/entertainment-gerson, January 15, 1999.*

GIAMATTI, Paul 1967-

PERSONAL

Full name, Paul Edward Valentine Giamatti; born June 6, 1967; son of Angelo Bartlett (a teacher, university president, and major league baseball commissioner) and Toni (an actress and teacher; maiden name, Smith) Giamatti; married Elizabeth "Liz" Cohen (a screenwriter). *Education:* Yale University, A.B. (English), M.F.A. (drama).

Addresses: *Agent*—Endeavor Talent Agency, 380 Lafayette St., Suite 304A, New York, NY 10003.

Career: Actor.

Awards, Honors: Drama Desk Award nomination, best featured actor in a play, 1999, for *The Iceman Cometh.*

CREDITS

Film Appearances:
Kissing man, *Singles,* Warner Bros., 1992.
Extras Guild researcher, *Mighty Aphrodite,* Miramax, 1995.
Scott, *Sabrina,* Paramount, 1995.
George, *Breathing Room* (also known as *'Til Christmas*), Arrow Releasing, 1996.
F.B.I. technician, *Donnie Brasco,* TriStar, 1997.
Kenny "Pig Vomit" Rushton, *Private Parts* (also known as *Howard Stern's Private Parts*), Paramount, 1997.
Richard the bellboy, *My Best Friend's Wedding,* TriStar, 1997.
Hotel clerk, *The Break,* Trimark, 1997.
Professor Abbot, *Deconstructing Harry,* Fine Line Features, 1997.
Psychiatrist, *Dr. Dolittle,* Twentieth Century-Fox, 1998.
Control room director Simeon, *The Truman Show,* Paramount, 1998.

Sergeant Hill, *Saving Private Ryan,* DreamWorks SKG, 1998.
Rudy, *The Negotiator,* Warner Bros., 1998.
Veal Chop, *Safe Men,* October Films, 1998.
Todd, *Duets,* Buena Vista, 1999.
Bob Zmuda, *Man on the Moon* (also known as *Andy Kaufman*), Universal, 1999.

Television Appearances; Movies:
Second heckler, *She'll Take Romance,* ABC, 1990.
Larry Canipe, *Past Midnight,* USA Network, 1992.
Herman Klurfeld, *Winchell,* HBO, 1998.
Jeremiah Piper, *Tourist Trap,* ABC, 1998.

Television Appearances; Episodic:
Man in sleeping bag, "You Bet Your Life," *NYPD Blue,* ABC, 1994.
Jeffrey Rothman, *The Show,* Fox, 1996.
Harry Tjarks, *Homicide: Life on the Street* (also known as *H: LOTS* and *Homicide*), NBC, 1997.

Stage Appearances:
St. Joan of the Stockyards, Yale Repertory Theatre, New Haven, CT, 1992-93.
As You Like It, Yale Repertory Theatre, 1993-94.
Baby Anger, Studio, Playwrights' Horizons Theatre, New York City, 1994.
Harlequin, *The Triumph of Love,* La Jolla Playhouse, San Diego, CA, 1994-95.
Ezra Chater, *Arcadia,* Vivian Beaumont Theatre, New York City, 1995.
Reverend Donald "Streaky" Bacon, *Racing Demon,* Vivian Beaumont Theatre, 1995.
Jimmy Tomorrow, *The Iceman Cometh,* Almeida Theatre, London, England, 1988-99, then Brooks Atkinson Theatre, New York City, 1999—.

Also appeared in *Three Sisters,* Broadway production; *The Blues Are Running,* Manhattan Theatre Club, New York City; also performed at La MaMa Etc. Theatre, New York City.

RECORDINGS

Video Games:
Dr. Bud Cable, *Ripper,* Take 2 Interactive, 1996.

OTHER SOURCES

Periodicals:
Entertainment Weekly, July 31, 1998, p. 18.*

GLEN, Iain 1961-

PERSONAL

Born June 24, 1961, in Edinburgh, Scotland; married Susannah Harker (an actress); children. *Education:* Attended the University of Aberdeen; trained for the stage at the Royal Academy of Dramatic Arts.

Addresses: *Contact*—Actors' Equity Association, 165 West 46th St., New York, NY 10036.

Career: Actor.

Member: Actors' Equity Association.

Awards, Honors: Silver Berlin Bear, Berlin International Film Festival, best acting performance, Scottish Academy Award, British Academy of Film and Television Arts Award, and Michael Powell Award, all 1990, for *Silent Scream; Evening Standard* Award, best actor, 1990, for *Mountains of the Moon;* Laurence Olivier Award nomination, best actor, 1999, for *The Blue Room;* British Academy of Film and Television Arts Award nomination, for *Death of a Salesman;* Laurence Olivier Award nomination, best actor in a musical, for *Martin Guerre;* Mayfest Award, best actor, for *Macbeth;* Ian Charles Award, for *Hamlet.*

CREDITS

Film Appearances:
Wallace Sharp, *Paris by Night,* [Great Britain], 1988.
Brendan, *Gorillas in the Mist,* Universal, 1988.
Larry Winters, *Silent Scream,* [Great Britain], 1990.
Willie Quinton, *Fools of Fortune,* Laurenfilm, 1990.
John Hanning Speke, *Mountains of the Moon,* Carolco Pictures, 1990.
Hamlet, *Rosencrantz and Guildernstern Are Dead,* Cinecom International, 1991.
Joey, *Ferdydurke* (also known as *30 Door Key*), [Poland], 1992.
Edward Foster, *The Young Americans,* PolyGram Filmed Entertainment, 1993.
Paranoia, Sky Pictures, forthcoming.

Also appeared in *Mararia,* Aiete Films.

Stage Appearances:
Title role, *Henry V,* Royal Shakespeare Theatre, Stratford-upon-Avon, England, 1994.
Arnaud Du Thil, *Martin Guerre,* Prince Edward Theatre, London, England, 1996-97.

Cab driver and other characters, *The Blue Room,* Donmar Warehouse, London, England, 1998, then Cort Theatre, New York City, 1998-99.

Appeared in the title role, *Macbeth,* Dundee Repertory Theatre, Dundee, Scotland; and as the title role in *Hamlet,* Bristol Old Vic Theatre, Bristol, England. Appeared in *Accidental Death of an Anarchist* and *The Recruiting Officer,* both Birmingham Repertory Theatre, Birmingham, England; *Coriolanus* and *She Stoops to Conquer,* both Chichester Festival Theatre, Chichester, England; *Edward II,* Royal Exchange Theatre, Manchester, England; *Hapgood,* Aldwych Theatre, London, England; *Here,* Donmar Warehouse; *King Lear* and *Road,* both Royal Court Theatre, London, England; *The Man Who Had All the Luck,* Young Vic Theatre, London, England, then Bristol Old Vic Theatre; and in *The Broken Heart,* with the Royal Shakespeare Company.

Television Appearances; Series:
Carl Galton, *The Fear,* Euston Films, 1988.

Television Appearances; Miniseries:
Tim Page, *Frankie's House,* Arts and Entertainment, 1992.
Sebastian Stafford, *Painted Lady,* PBS, 1997.

Television Appearances; Specials:
Title role, "Adam Bede," *Masterpiece Theatre,* PBS, 1991.

Also appeared in *Death of a Salesman.*

Other Television Appearances:
Commander Powell, *Black and Blue,* [Great Britain], 1992.

Also appeared in *Blood Hunt, The Picnic, Will You Love Me Tomorrow?,* and *Trial and Retribution II.*

OTHER SOURCES

Periodicals:
People Weekly, January 18, 1999, p. 11.*

GOLDWYN, Samuel 1882(?)-1974

PERSONAL

Original name, Shmuel (some sources spell name Schmuel) Gelbfisz; name changed to Samuel Goldfish, then to Samuel Goldwyn; born in 1882 (some sources say in 1879), in Warsaw, Poland; immigrated to the United States, 1896 (some sources say 1898); became naturalized citizen, 1902; died January 31, 1974, in Los Angeles, CA; son of Abraham and Hannah Gelbfisz, surname changed to Goldfish; married Blanche Lasky, May 8, 1910 (divorced, September 23, 1915); married Frances Howard, April 23, 1925; children: Samuel, Jr. *Education:* Attended night school.

Career: Producer, film presenter, and studio founder and executive. Jesse Lasky Feature Photoplay Company, organizer, 1913; Goldwyn Pictures Corporation, organizer, 1916; Eminent Authors Pictures, Inc., organizer, 1919; United Artists Corporation, director, ending in 1940; Goldwyn Distributing Company, founder; Samuel Goldwyn Productions, Inc., chair of the board of directors; Samuel Goldwyn, Inc., organizer; Famous Players-Lasky Corporation, organizer; Metro-Goldwyn-Mayer, founder (with Louis B. Mayer and others).

Awards, Honors: Academy Award, best picture, 1946, for *The Best Years of Our Lives;* Irving Thalberg Memorial Award, Academy of Motion Picture Arts and Sciences, 1946; Jean Hersholt Humanitarian Award, Academy of Motion Picture Arts and Sciences, 1957; Presidential Medal of Freedom, 1971; Cecil B. DeMille Award, Hollywood Foreign Press Association, 1973; elected posthumously to the Junior Achievement National Business Hall of Fame. Academy Award nominations, best picture, 1931 (with Merritt Hulburd), for *Arrowsmith,* 1936 (with Merritt Hulburd), for *Dodsworth,* 1937, for *Dead End,* 1939, for *Wuthering Heights,* 1941, for *The Little Foxes,* 1942, for *The Pride of the Yankees,* and 1947, for *The Bishop's Wife.*

CREDITS

Film Work; Producer, Unless Otherwise Noted:
The Fighting Odds, Goldwyn Distributing Corporation, 1917.
Executive producer, *Water, Water Everywhere,* 1920.
Executive producer, *The Paliser Case,* Goldwyn Distributing Corporation, 1920.
Partners of the Night, Goldwyn Distributing Corporation, 1920.
Jes' Call Me Jim, Goldwyn Distributing Corporation, 1920.
The Penalty, Goldwyn Distributing Corporation, 1920.
Executive producer, *Sherlock Holmes,* Goldwyn Distributing Corporation, 1922.

Potash and Perlmutter, Associated First National Pictures, 1923.
The Day of Faith, Goldwyn-Cosmopolitan Distributing Corporation, 1923.
In Hollywood with Potash and Perlmutter, Associated First National Pictures, 1924.
Cytherea (also known as *The Forbidden Way*), Associated First National Pictures, 1924.
Stella Dallas, United Artists, 1925.
The Winning of Barbara Worth, United Artists, 1926.
Partners Again (also known as *Partners Again, with Potash and Perlmutter*), United Artists, 1926.
Ben-Hur (also known as *Ben-Hur: A Tale of Christ*), Metro-Goldwyn-Mayer, 1926.
The Magic Flame, United Artists, 1927.
The Night of Love (also known as *Innocent*), United Artists, 1927.
Two Lovers, United Artists, 1928.
This Is Heaven, United Artists, 1929.
Bulldog Drummond, United Artists, 1929.
Condemned (also known as *Condemned to Devil's Island*), United Artists, 1929.
Whoopee, United Artists, 1930.
The Devil to Pay, United Artists, 1930.
Raffles, United Artists, 1930.
The Unholy Garden, United Artists, 1931.
Tonight or Never, United Artists, 1931.
Palmy Days, United Artists, 1931.
One Heavenly Night, United Artists, 1931.
Street Scene, United Artists, 1931.
(With Merritt Hulburd) *Arrowsmith,* United Artists, 1931.
The Kid from Spain, United Artists, 1932.
Greeks Had a Word for Them (also known as *Three Broadway Girls*), United Artists, 1932.
Cynara (also known as *I Was Faithless*), United Artists, 1932.
(Uncredited) *Arsene Lupin,* Metro-Goldwyn-Mayer, 1932.
Roman Scandals, United Artists, 1933.
The Masquerader, United Artists, 1933.
Nana (also known as *Lady of the Boulevards*), United Artists, 1934.
Kid Millions, United Artists, 1934.
We Live Again, United Artists, 1934.
The Wedding Night, United Artists, 1935.
Splendor, United Artists, 1935.
Barbary Coast, United Artists, 1935.
These Three, United Artists, 1936.
(With Merritt Hulburd) *Dodsworth,* United Artists, 1936.
Come and Get It (also known as *Roaring Timbers*), United Artists, 1936.
Beloved Enemy, United Artists, 1936.
Strike Me Pink, United Artists, 1936.
Stella Dallas, United Artists, 1937.
Woman Chases Man, United Artists, 1937.
Dead End (also known as *Cradle of Crime*), United Artists, 1937.
The Hurricane, United Artists, 1937.
The Goldwyn Follies, United Artists, 1938.
The Cowboy and the Lady, United Artists, 1938.
The Adventures of Marco Polo, United Artists, 1938.
Wuthering Heights, United Artists, 1939.
The Real Glory, United Artists, 1939.
They Shall Have Music (also known as *Melody of Youth* and *Ragged Angels*), United Artists, 1939.
Raffles, United Artists, 1939.
The Westerner, United Artists, 1940.
Ball of Fire (also known as *The Professor and the Burlesque Queen*), RKO, 1941.
The Little Foxes, RKO, 1941.
The Pride of the Yankees, RKO, 1942.
The North Star (also known as *Armored Attack*), RKO, 1943.
They Got Me Covered, RKO, 1943.
Up in Arms, RKO, 1944.
Wonder Man, RKO, 1945.
The Kid from Brooklyn, RKO, 1946.
The Best Years of Our Lives, RKO, 1946.
The Bishop's Wife, RKO, 1947.
The Secret Life of Walter Mitty, RKO, 1947.
A Song Is Born, RKO, 1948.
Enchantment, RKO, 1948.
My Foolish Heart, RKO, 1949.
Roseanna McCoy, RKO, 1949.
Edge of Doom, RKO, 1950.
Our Very Own, RKO, 1950.
I Want You, RKO, 1951.
Hans Christian Andersen, RKO, 1952.
Guys and Dolls, Metro-Goldwyn-Mayer, 1955.
Porgy and Bess, Columbia, 1959.

Film Work; Presenter:
Day Dreams, Goldwyn Distributing Company, 1919.
The Bondage of Barbara, Goldwyn Pictures Corporation, 1919.
Daughter of Mine, Goldwyn Distributing Company, 1919.
Spotlight Sadie (also known as *The Saintly Show Girl*), Goldwyn Distributing Company, 1919.
A Man and His Money, Goldwyn Distributing Company, 1919.
The Pest, Goldwyn Distributing Company, 1919.
The Eternal Magdalene, Goldwyn Distributing Company, 1919.
When Doctors Disagree, Goldwyn Pictures Corporation, 1919.

The Fear Woman, Goldwyn Distributing Company, 1919.
The City of Comrades, Goldwyn Distributing Company, 1919.
The Loves of Letty, Goldwyn Distributing Company, 1919.
Jinx, Goldwyn Pictures Corporation, 1919.
Out of the Storm, Goldwyn Distributing Company, 1920.
Going Some, Goldwyn Distributing Company, 1920.
A Double-Dyed Deceiver, Goldwyn Distributing Company, 1920.
A Cup of Fury, Goldwyn Distributing Company, 1920.
The Branding Iron, Goldwyn Distributing Company, 1920.
Dangerous Days, Goldwyn Distributing Company, 1920.
The Silver Horde, Goldwyn Distributing Company, 1920.
Milestones, Goldwyn Distributing Company, 1920.
The North Wind's Malice, Goldwyn Distributing Company, 1920.
The Highest Bidder, Goldwyn Pictures Corporation, 1921.
Potash and Perlmutter, Associated First National Pictures, 1923.
The Eternal City, Associated First National Pictures, 1923.
Tarnish, Associated First National Pictures, 1924.
In Hollywood with Potash and Perlmutter, Associated First National Pictures, 1924.
Cytherea (also known as *The Forbidden Way*), Associated First National Pictures, 1924.
His Supreme Moment, First National Pictures, 1925.
The Dark Angel, First National Pictures, 1925.
Stella Dallas, United Artists, 1925.
Partners Again (also known as *Partners Again, with Potash and Perlmutter*), United Artists, 1926.
The Rescue, United Artists, 1929.

OTHER SOURCES

Books:
Berg, A. Scott, *Goldwyn,* Knopf (New York City), 1989.*

GOMEZ, Ian

PERSONAL

Born December 27, in New York, NY; father was an artist and mother was a dancer; married Nia Vardalos (an actress).

Addresses: *Agent*—Stone Manners Agency, 8436 West 3rd St., Los Angeles, CA, 90048.

Career: Actor and comedian. Member of the Second City comedy troupe, Chicago; worked in the Second City box office before joining the group.

CREDITS

Film Appearances:
Lucas, *Excessive Force,* New Line Cinema, 1992.
Odd bellman, *Rookie of the Year,* Twentieth Century-Fox, 1993.
'Til There Was You, Paramount, 1997.
McIlvaine, *Edtv,* Universal, 1999.
The Big Tease, forthcoming.
Meet Prince Charming, forthcoming.

Appeared in *Courting Courtney.*

Television Appearances; Episodic:
First car wash employee, "Get the Dodge Outta Hell," *Married ...With Children,* Fox, 1995.
Mimicking secretary, *Murphy Brown,* CBS, 1996.
"Divorce Dominican Style," *Melrose Place,* Fox, 1998.
"Long Way to Tip-A-Rory," *Melrose Place,* Fox, 1998.
Smart Guy, The WB, 1998.

Television Appearances; Series:
Larry Almada, *The Drew Carey Show* (recurring), ABC, 1995-99.
Danny, *The Norm Show,* ABC, 1998-99.
Himself, *Whose Line Is It Anyway?,* ABC, 1998-99.
Javier, *Felicity,* The WB, 1998-99.

OTHER SOURCES

Electronic:
ABC.com, http://abc.go.com/primetime/norm_show/cast/bios/gomez.html.*

GRAHAM, Lauren 1967(?)-

PERSONAL

Born c. 1967, in Honolulu, HA. *Education:* Attended Barnard College/Columbia University, B.A. (English); SMU, master's degree (acting).

Addresses: *Agent*—Writers and Artists Agency, 924 Westwood Blvd., Suite 900, Los Angeles, CA 90024.

Career: Actress.

CREDITS

Film Appearances:

Tracy, *Confessions of a Sexist Pig,* Pizza Productions, 1998.

Marie, *Nightwatch,* Miramax, 1998.

Jules, *One True Thing,* Universal, 1998.

Kristie Sue, *Dill Scallion,* Conspiracy Entertainment, 1999.

Television Appearances; Episodic:

Shelly, "Caroline and the Younger Man," *Caroline in the City,* NBC, 1995.

Laurie, *3rd Rock From the Sun,* NBC, 1996.

Lisa Lundquist, "D-Girl," "Turnaround," and "Showtime," *Law & Order,* NBC, 1996.

Valerie, "The Millennium," *Seinfeld,* NBC, 1996.

Andrea, "Planbee," "The Public Domain," "Super Karate Monkey Death Car," and "French Diplomacy," *NewsRadio,* NBC, 1997.

Television Appearances; Series:

Liz Gibson, *Good Company,* ABC, 1995-96.

Denise Garibaldi Callahan, *Townies,* ABC, 1996-97.

Molly, *Conrad Bloom,* NBC, 1998-99.

OTHER SOURCES

Periodicals:

Entertainment Weekly, October 16, 1998, p. 66.*

GRAMMER, Kelsey 1955-

PERSONAL

Full name, Allen Kelsey Grammer; born February 21 (some sources cite February 20), 1955, in St. Thomas, Virgin Islands; son of Allen (a coffee shop and bar and grill owner) and Sally (Cranmer) Grammer; married Doreen Alderman (a dancer), May 30, 1982 (divorced, 1990); married Leigh-Anne Csuhany, September 11, 1992 (divorced, 1993); married Camille Donatacci (a model), August 2, 1997; children: (first marriage) Spencer; (with Barrie Buckner) Kandace Greer. *Education:* Trained for the stage at the Juilliard School for two years. *Avocational interests:* Gardening.

Addresses: *Office*—Grammnet, Inc., 207 Lucy Bungalow, 555 Melrose Ave., Los Angeles, CA 90038-3112. *Agent*—Artists Agency, 10000 Santa Monica Blvd., Suite 305, Los Angeles, CA 90067-7007.

Career: Actor and producer. Old Globe Theatre, San Diego, CA, member of ensemble, c. 1976-78; Grammnet, Inc., Los Angeles, CA, founder and principal. Appeared in television commercials for Honey Nut Cheerios, Lexus automobiles, MCI, and General Foods International Coffees.

Awards, Honors: Emmy Award nomination, best supporting actor in a comedy series, 1987, for *Cheers;* Emmy Awards, outstanding lead actor in a comedy series, 1994, 1995, and 1998, Emmy Award nominations, outstanding lead actor in a comedy series, 1996 and 1997, American Comedy Awardnomination, funniest male performer in a leading role in a television series, 1999, People's Choice Award, favorite male in a new television series, and Golden Globe Award nomination, best actor in a comedy series, all for *Frasier;* Directors Guild of America Award nomination, outstanding directorial achievement in a comedy series, 1999, for the episode, "Merry Christmas, Mrs. Moskowitz," *Frasier.*

CREDITS

Television Appearances; Series:

Dr. Canard, *Another World,* NBC, 1984-85.

Dr. Frasier Crane, *Cheers,* NBC, 1984-93.

Dr. Frasier Crane, *Frasier,* NBC, 1993—.

Tom Whitman, *Fired Up,* NBC, 1997.

Television Appearances; Miniseries:

Stephen Smith, *Kennedy,* NBC, 1983.

Lieutenant Stewart, *George Washington,* CBS, 1984.

Craig Lawson, *Crossings,* ABC, 1986.

Television Appearances; Movies:

Ed Strull, *Dance 'til Dawn,* NBC, 1988.

Ron McNally, *Beyond Suspicion* (also known as *Appointment for a Killing*), NBC, 1993.

Detective Frank Barlow, *The Innocent* (also known as *Silent Witness*), NBC, 1994.

Sidney Nichols, *London Suite* (also known as *Neil Simon's "London Suite"*), NBC, 1996.

General Partridge, *The Pentagon Wars,* HBO, 1998.

Voice of Snowball, *Animal Farm,* TNT, 1999.

Television Appearances; Specials:

Stuart Cooper, *You Are the Jury,* NBC, 1987.

Paul Reiser: Out on a Whim, HBO, 1987.

Mickey's 60th Birthday Special, 1988.
Cheers: Special 200th Episode Celebration, NBC, 1990.
Super Bloopers and New Practical Jokes, NBC, 1990.
Disneyland's 35th Anniversary Celebration, NBC, 1990.
Macy's Thanksgiving Day Parade, NBC, 1991.
The Return of TV's Censored Bloopers 2, NBC, 1993.
Last Call! A Cheers Celebration, NBC, 1993.
The Barbara Walters Special, ABC, 1994.
Host, *Montreal International Comedy Festival '94,* Showtime, 1994.
Voice, *The American Revolution,* 1994.
Host, *An Affectionate Look at Fatherhood,* 1995.
Kelsey Grammer Salutes Jack Benny, 1995.
Comedy Central Spotlight: Kelsey Grammer, Comedy Central, 1996.
Celebrity Weddings InStyle, Lifetime, 1998.
The 1998 Live Emmy Award Post-Show, E! Entertainment Television, 1998.

Television Appearances; Episodic:
Narrator, *Sex and the Silver Screen,* Showtime, 1996.
The Rodman World Tour, MTV, 1996.

Appeared as Frasier Crane in an episode of *Wings;* appeared in the initial episode of *Kate and Allie,* CBS; also has performed voice characterizations on an episode of *The Simpsons* (animated), Fox; and has appeared on *The Tracy Ullman Show.*

Television Appearances; Awards Presentations:
The 4th Annual Desi Awards, syndicated, 1992.
Soap Opera Digest Awards, NBC, 1992.
The 2nd Annual Comedy Hall of Fame, NBC, 1994.
The 4th Annual Environmental Media Awards, TBS, 1994.
The 46th Annual Primetime Emmy Awards, ABC, 1994.
1994 Billboard Music Awards, Fox, 1994.
Host, *10th Annual Soap Opera Digest Awards,* NBC, 1994.
Host, *1994 Clio Awards,* Fox, 1994.
The 10th Annual American Comedy Awards, 1996.
Host, *The Blockbuster Entertainment Awards,* 1996.
Presenter, *The 54th Annual Golden Globe Awards,* 1997.
Presenter, *The 11th Annual American Comedy Awards,* 1997.
American Comedy Honors, Fox, 1997.
Presenter, *The 50th Emmy Awards,* 1998.
Host, *The 40th Annual Grammy Awards,* 1998.

Other Television Appearances:
Top of the Hill, 1989.
Peter, *Galaxies Are Colliding* (also known as *Planet of Love*), 1992.

Appeared in the pilot *Lame Duck.*

Television Work; Series:
Performer of theme song "Tossed Salad and Scrambled Eggs," *Frasier,* NBC, 1993—.
Executive producer, *Fired Up,* NBC, 1997.
Executive producer, *Frasier,* NBC, 1998.

Television Work; Director; Episodic:
Frasier, NBC, 1996 and 1997.
"Merry Christmas, Mrs. Moskowitz," *Frasier,* NBC, 1999.

Other Television Work:
Executive producer, *The Innocent* (miniseries; also known as *Silent Witness*), NBC, 1994.
Producer, *Kelsey Grammer Salutes Jack Benny* (special), 1995.

Stage Appearances:
Laertes, *Hamlet,* North Shore Music Festival, MA, 1979.
Aleksei Belyayev, *A Month in the Country,* Roundabout Stage One Theatre, New York City, 1980.
The Mousetrap, Studio Arena Theatre, Buffalo, NY, 1980.
Lennox, *Macbeth,* Vivian Beaumont Theatre, New York City, 1981.
Gloucester, *Henry V,* American Shakespeare Theatre, Stratford, CT, 1981.
Cassio, *Othello,* American Shakespeare Theatre, 1981, then Winter Garden Theatre, New York City, 1982.
Codename Lazar, *Plenty,* New York Shakespeare Festival, Public Theatre, New York City, 1982.
Mark Sackling, *Quartermaine's Terms,* Long Wharf Theatre, New Haven, CT, then Playhouse 91, New York City, both 1983.
Young man, soldier, and Alex Savage, *Sunday in the Park with George,* Playwrights Horizons, New York City, 1983.
Arms and the Man, Studio Arena Theatre, 1984.
Demeter Stanzides and Lucio, *Measure for Measure,* Center Theatre Group, Mark Taper Forum, Los Angeles, CA, 1985.

Also appeared in *As You Like It,* Globe Theatre, San Diego, CA.

Film Appearances:

Voice of Dr. Frankenollie, *Runaway Brain,* 1995.

Lieutenant Commander Thomas Dodge, *Down Periscope,* Twentieth Century-Fox, 1996.

Voice of Captain Morgan Bateson, *Star Trek: First Contact,* Paramount, 1996.

Voice of Vladimir, *Anastasia* (animated), Twentieth Century-Fox, 1997.

Title role, *The Real Howard Spitz,* Artisan Entertainment, 1998.

Verk, *Standing on Fishes,* 1999.

New Jersey Turnpikes, 1999.

15 Minutes, New Line Cinema, 1999.

Voice of the Prospector, *Toy Story 2,* Buena Vista, 1999.

Narrator, *First Dogs* (documentary), 1999.

RECORDINGS

Taped Readings:

So Far (based on his autobiography), Dove, 1996.

WRITINGS

Autobiography:

So Far. . ., Dutton (New York City), 1995.

OTHER SOURCES

Books:

1996 Current Biography Yearbook, Gale (Detroit, MI), 1996.

Periodicals:

Entertainment Weekly, October 11, 1996, p. 8.

People Weekly, August 18, 1997, p. 71.

Electronic:

Kelsey and Camille Grammer Website, http://kelseylive.com.*

GREENBERG, Richard 1958(?)-

PERSONAL

Born February 22, 1958 (some sources say 1959), in East Meadow, NY; son of Leon (an executive) and Shirley (a homemaker) Greenberg. *Education:* Princeton University, A.B. (English), 1980; graduate study at Harvard University, 1980-81; Yale University, M.F.A. (drama), 1985.

Addresses: *Agent*—George Lane, William Morris Agency, 1325 Avenue of the Americas, New York, NY 10019.

Career: Writer. Ensemble Studio Theatre, New York City, member of the company.

Awards, Honors: Oppenheimer Award, best new playwright, 1985, for *The Bloodletters;* DramaLogue Award, 1991.

WRITINGS

Stage Plays, Unless Otherwise Noted:

The Bloodletters, Ensemble Studio Theatre, New York City, 1984.

Life under Water (one-act), *Marathon '85* Series A, Ensemble Studio Theatre, 1985, published by Dramatists Play Service (New York City), 1985.

Vanishing Act (one-act), *Marathon '86* Series B, Ensemble Studio Theatre, 1986, published by Dramatists Play Service, 1987.

The Maderati, off-Broadway production, 1987, published by Dramatists Play Service, 1987.

The Author's Voice (one-act), off-Broadway production, 1987, published by Dramatists Play Service, 1987.

Neptune's Hips (one-act), *Marathon '88* Series A, Ensemble Studio Theatre, 1988.

Eastern Standard, Manhattan Theatre Club, New York City, 1988, then John Golden Theatre, New York City, 1989, published by Grove (New York City), 1989.

The American Plan, Manhattan Theatre Club, 1990-91, published by Dramatists Play Service, 1991.

The Extra Man, Stage I, Manhattan Theatre Club, 1992.

Adaptor, *Pal Joey* (based on the musical by John O'Hara), Huntington Theatre Company, Boston, MA, 1992-93.

Jenny Keeps Talking, Stage II, Manhattan Theatre Club, 1993, published by Dramatists Play Service, 1993.

Night and Her Stars, American Place Theatre, Manhattan Theatre Club, 1995.

Mixed Media Productions:

The Hunger Artist (based on stories and letters by Franz Kafka), 1987.

Teleplays; Series:

Sisters, NBC, 1991-92.

Teleplays; Specials:

"Ask Me Again," *American Playhouse*, PBS, 1989.

Life under Water (based on his one-act stage play), PBS, 1989.

Teleplays; Episodic:

"The Sad Professor," *Trying Times*, PBS, 1989.

OTHER SOURCES

Books:

Contemporary Literary Criticism, Volume 57, Gale 1990.

Periodicals:

American Theatre, January, 1993, p. 29.*

HAIGHT, Rip
See CARPENTER, John

HALL, Arsenio 1955-

PERSONAL

Born February 12, 1955, in Cleveland, OH; son of Fred (a Baptist minister) and Anne Hall. *Education:* Attended Ohio University; Kent State University, B.A. (communications).

Addresses: *Office*—Arsenio Hall Communications, 5555 Melrose Ave., Los Angeles, CA 90038-3197. *Agent*—International Creative Management, 8560 Wilshire Blvd., Beverly Hills, CA 90212.

Career: Talk show host, actor, and comedian. Performed stand-up comedy act throughout the United States, 1979; also appeared as a magician and a drummer with a pop music band.

Awards, Honors: NAACP Image Award, best supporting actor in a motion picture, 1988, and American Comedy Award, funniest supporting male in a motion picture, 1989, both for *Coming to America;* Soul Train Music Award, Entertainer of the Year, 1990.

CREDITS

Film Appearances:

(Film debut) Apartment victim, *Amazon Women on the Moon,* Universal, 1987.
Semmi, Morris, extremely ugly girl, and Reverend Brown, *Coming to America,* Paramount, 1988.
Crying man, *Harlem Nights,* Paramount, 1989.
Bopha!, Paramount, 1993.
Blankman, Columbia, 1994.

Film Work; Executive Producer:

Bopha!, Paramount, 1993.
Blankman, Columbia, 1994.

Television Appearances; Talk Shows:

Co-host, *Thicke of the Night,* syndicated, 1984.
Host, *The Late Show,* Fox, 1987.
Host, *The Arsenio Hall Show,* syndicated, 1989-94.

Television Appearances; Series:

Co-host, *The Half Hour Comedy Hour,* ABC, 1983.
The New Love, American Style, ABC, 1985.
Motown Revue, NBC, 1985.
Voice of Winston Zeddmore, *The Real Ghostbusters* (also known as *Slimer and the Real Ghostbusters;* animated), ABC, 1986.
Co-host, *Solid Gold,* syndicated, 1987.
Michael Atwood, *Arsenio,* ABC, 1996-97.
Terrell Parker, *Martial Law,* CBS, 1998—.

Television Appearances; Episodic:

Cleavon, *Alfred Hitchcock Presents,* NBC, 1986.
"Uptown Comedy Express," *On Location,* HBO, 1987.
Face to Face with Connie Chung, CBS, 1990.
First Person with Maria Shriver, NBC, 1991.
Guest, *The Magic Hour,* syndicated, 1998.

Television Appearances; Specials:

The R.A.C.E., NBC, 1989.
Mike Tyson—A Portrait of the People's Champion, syndicated, 1989.
Comic Relief III, HBO, 1989.
A Laugh, A Tear, syndicated, 1990.
Racism: Points of View, MTV, 1991.
A Party for Richard Pryor, CBS, 1991.
In a New Light, ABC, 1992.

The Comedy Store's 20th Birthday, NBC, 1992.
Kathie Lee Gifford's Celebration of Motherhood, ABC, 1993.
Apollo Theatre Hall of Fame, NBC, 1993.
Host, *In a New Light '93,* ABC, 1993.
Host, *The Soul Train 25th Anniversary Hall of Fame Special,* 1995.
Celebrate the Dream: 50 Years of Ebony, ABC, 1996.
Comic Relief American Comedy Festival, ABC, 1996.
Happy Birthday Elizabeth—A Celebration of Life, ABC, 1997.
Intimate Portrait: Patti LaBelle, Lifetime, 1998.

Also host, *The Magic of Christmas,* broadcast on a local station in Cleveland, OH.

Television Appearances; Awards Presentations:
Host, *MTV's 1988 Video Music Awards Show,* MTV, 1988.
The Comedy Store 15th Year Class Reunion, NBC, 1989.
The Twenty-First Annual NAACP Image Awards, NBC, 1989.
The 41st Annual Emmy Awards, Fox, 1989.
The 3rd Annual American Comedy Awards, ABC, 1989.
The 15th Annual People's Choice Awards, CBS, 1989.
Host, *MTV's 1989 Video Music Awards,* MTV, 1989.
The 4th Annual Soul Train Music Awards, syndicated, 1990.
Host, *MTV's 1990 Video Music Awards,* MTV, 1990.
Host, *MTV's 1991 Video Music Awards,* MTV, 1991.
The 24th Annual NAACP Image Awards, NBC, 1992.
Soul Train Comedy Awards, syndicated, 1993.
The American Television Awards, ABC, 1993.
The 51st Annual Golden Globe Awards, TBS, 1994.
Tribute segment host, *The 23rd Annual American Music Awards,* 1996.
The 27th Annual NAACP Image Awards, 1996.
Host, *The 28th Annual NAACP Image Awards,* 1997.
Presenter, *The 11th annual American Comedy Awards,* 1997.
Presenter, *The 24th Annual American Music Awards,* 1997.

Television Work; Executive Producer:
The Arsenio Hall Show (talk show), syndicated, 1989-94.
The Party Machine with Nia Peeples (series), syndicated, 1991.
One on One with Magic Johnson (special), Fox, 1994.
Arsenio (series), ABC, 1996-97.

WRITINGS

Television Series:
Motown Revue, NBC, 1985.
The Arsenio Hall Show, syndicated, 1989-94.

OTHER SOURCES

Periodicals:
Newsweek, March 10, 1997, p. 78.
New York Times Magazine, October 1, 1989, pp. 29-31, 65-66, 92-93.
Time, March 10, 1997, pp. 82-83.
TV Guide, September 30, 1989, pp. 16-19.
US, September 18, 1989, pp. 24-28, 30, 32-33.
Village Voice, May 23, 1989, pp. 27-31.*

HALL, Philip Baker 1931-

PERSONAL

Born September 10, 1931, in Toledo, OH; children: two daughters. *Education:* Graduated from University of Toledo.

Addresses: *Agent*—Writers and Artists Agency, 924 Westwood Blvd., Suite 900, Los Angeles, CA 90024.

Career: Actor. South Coast Repertory Theatre, Costa Mesa, CA, guest artist, 1979-80.

Awards, Honors: Independent Spirit Award nomination, best male lead, 1996, for *Hard Eight;* Screen Actor's Guild Award nomination, outstanding performance by a cast, 1998, for *Boogie Nights.*

CREDITS

Film Appearances:
Father Reis, *Cowards,* Jaylo, 1970.
Dr. Inman, *The Man with Bogart's Face* (also known as *Sam Marlowe, Private Eye*), Twentieth Century-Fox, 1980.
The Last Reunion (also known as *Revenge of the Bushido Blade*), 1980.
Dream On, Magic Cinema, 1981.
Richard Nixon, *Secret Honor* (also known as *Lords of Treason, Secret Honor: The Last Testament of Richard M. Nixon,* and *Secret Honor: A Political Myth*), Vestron Video, 1984.
Detective Mulvahill, *Three O'Clock High,* Universal, 1987.

Sidney, *Midnight Run,* Universal, 1988.
Judge Lavet, *An Innocent Man* (also known as *Hard Rain*), Buena Vista, 1989.
Dean Patterson, *How I Got into College,* Twentieth Century-Fox, 1989.
Police commissioner, *Ghostbusters II,* Columbia, 1989.
IRS boss, *Say Anything,* Twentieth Century-Fox, 1989.
Joe, *Blue Desert* (also known as *Silent Victim*), Academy Entertainment, 1991.
Senator Thyme, *Live Wire,* New Line Cinema, 1992.
Cigarettes and Coffee, 1993.
The Last Laugh, 1994.
Detective Snyder, *The Little Death,* PolyGram, 1995.
Big Junior Brown, *Kiss of Death,* Twentieth Century-Fox, 1995.
(Uncredited) Chief justice, *The Rock,* Buena Vista, 1996.
Lenny Ish, *Hit Me,* Castle Hill Productions, 1996.
Sydney, *Hard Eight* (also known as *Sydney*), Columbia/TriStar, 1996.
Sidney Hughes, *Eye for an Eye,* Paramount, 1996.
Floyd Gondolli, *Boogie Nights,* New Line Cinema, 1997.
Minister, *Buddy,* Columbia, 1997.
U.S. Attorney General Ward, *Air Force One* (also known as *AFO*), Columbia, 1997.
Kathie's Dad, *Implicated* (also known as *Wishful Thinking*), Columbia/TriStar, 1998.
Dean's boss, *Enemy of the State,* Buena Vista, 1998.
Mr. Bell, *Sour Grapes,* Columbia, 1998.
Christof's World: Network Executive, *The Truman Show,* Paramount, 1998.
Captain Diel, *Rush Hour,* New Line Cinema, 1998.
Sheriff Chambers, *Psycho,* Universal, 1998.
Magnolia, New Line Cinema, 1999.
Lost Souls, New Line Cinema, 1999.
Let the Devil Wear Black, Trimark Pictures, 1999.
MacCarron, *The Talented Mr. Ripley,* Paramount, 1999.
Gray Mathers, *The Cradle Will Rock,* Buena Vista, 1999.

Also appeared in *Love-In '72.*

Film Work:
Costume designer, *Secret Honor* (also known as *Lords of Treason, Secret Honor: The Last Testament of Richard M. Nixon,* and *Secret Honor: A Political Myth*), Vestron Video, 1984.

Television Appearances; Series:
Superintendent James Malone, *Mariah,* ABC, 1987.
Ed Meyers, *Falcon Crest,* CBS, 1989-90.
William Vaughn, *Michael Hayes,* CBS, 1997.

Television Appearances; Movies:
First reporter, *Mayday at 40,000 Feet!,* CBS, 1976.
George, *Man from Atlantis,* NBC, 1977.
Phillips, *Kill Me If You Can,* NBC, 1977.
Starrett, *Terror out of the Sky,* CBS, 1979.
Professor Gordon Owens, *Samurai,* ABC, 1979.
Clerk, *This House Possessed,* ABC, 1981.
Lester Greene, *Games Mother Never Taught You,* CBS, 1982.
Warren Meech, *The Night the Bridge Fell Down,* NBC, 1983.
Dean May, *Who Is Julia?,* CBS, 1986.
Cabbie, *The Spirit,* ABC, 1987.
Detective Charles, *The Goddess of Love,* NBC, 1988.
Judge Blumenfeld, *A Cry for Help: The Tracey Thurman Story,* NBC, 1989.
Dr. Leo Manus, *Incident at Dark River* (also known as *Dark River—A Father's Revenge*), TNT, 1989.
Sam Gochenour, *Crash Landing: The Rescue of Flight 232* (also known as *A Thousand Heroes*), ABC, 1992.
Ernie Horshack (some sources cite Dr. Comden), *Stormy Weathers,* ABC, 1992.
Roswell general, *Roswell* (also known as *Roswell: The U.F.O. Cover-Up*), Showtime, 1994.
Jake Sawyer, *Implicated,* Cinemax, 1999.
Poppy Malavero, *The Judas Kiss,* Cinemax, 1999.

Television Appearances; Miniseries:
The Bastard, syndicated, 1978.
Toddo Aurello, *Witness to the Mob,* NBC, 1998.

Television Appearances; Specials:
Mr. Durfee, *Riding for the Pony Express,* CBS, 1980.
Campus Culture Wars: Five Stories about P.C., PBS, 1993.

Television Appearances; Episodic:
"The Light that Failed," *M*A*S*H,* CBS, 1977.
Judge Wallace, "A Cry for Help," *T. J. Hooker,* ABC, 1982.
Judge, "The Mother," *Matlock,* NBC, 1990.
Baker, *L.A. Law,* NBC, 1990.
Ed Costner, *Murder, She Wrote,* CBS, 1990.
Judge Bianchi, *Civil Wars,* ABC, 1991.
Lieutenant Bookman, "The Library," *Seinfeld,* NBC, 1991.
Mr. Todd, *Nurses,* NBC, 1992.
Kevin Fogerty, "Woody Gets an Election," *Cheers,* NBC, 1993.
Jerod, *Empty Nest,* NBC, 1993.

Mr. Wellington, "You Gotta Have Heart," *Chicago Hope,* CBS, 1994.
Beanball McGee, *Hardball,* Fox, 1994.
Oscar Kern, *Madman of the People,* NBC, 1994.
Mr. Humphreys, "Melissa the Thief," *The Good Life,* NBC, 1994.
Judge Conklin, "Contempt," *Life's Work,* ABC, 1996.
President Dewey, "Proud Dick," *Third Rock from the Sun,* 1997.
Judge Joseph Vinocour, "Part I," *The Practice,* ABC, 1997.
Judge Joseph Vinocour, "Part V," *The Practice,* ABC, 1997.
Judge Joseph Vinocour, "Part VI," *The Practice,* ABC, 1997.
Judge Canker, "Betrayal," *The Practice,* ABC, 1997.
The Group Elder, "Owls," *Millennium,* Fox, 1998.
The Group Elder, "Roosters," *Millennium,* Fox, 1998.
Lieutenant Bookman, "The Finale," *Seinfeld,* NBC, 1998.

Other Television Appearances:
The Last Survivors, 1975.
M.A.N.T.I.S., 1994.
Dr. Kurt Lowden, *Without Warning,* 1994.
Dr. Bardwell, *Tempting Fate* (also known as *Parallels*), 1998.

Stage Appearances:
Leader, *Donogoo,* Greenwich Mews Theatre, 1961.
In White America, Players Theatre, New York City, 1965.
Prinz, *The World of Gunter Grass,* Pocket Theatre, 1966.
The Ecstasy of Rita, Washington Theatre Club, Washington, DC, 1972-73.
Ralph, *An Absence of Light,* Equity Library Theatre, New York Public Library at Lincoln Center, New York City, 1973.
Title role, *Gorky,* American Place Theatre, New York City, 1975.
Conjuring an Event, Center Theatre Group, Mark Taper Forum, Los Angeles, 1976-77.
Photographer, Pete Costas, *Hoagy, Bix, and Wolfgang Beethoven Bunkhaus,* Center Theatre Group, Mark Taper Forum, 1980-81.
Mr. Nixon, *Secret Honor: The Last Testament of Richard M. Nixon* (solo show), Provincetown Playhouse, New York City, 1983, then Los Angeles Actors' Theatre, Los Angeles, 1983-84.
Duke Mantee, *The Petrified Forest,* Los Angeles Theatre Center, Los Angeles, 1985-86.
All My Sons, Los Angeles Theatre Center, 1986-87.
The Crucible, Los Angeles Theatre Center, 1990-91.
A Map of the World, Odyssey Theatre Ensemble, Los Angeles, 1991-92.

Appeared as the boy's father, *The Fantasticks,* Sullivan Street Playhouse, New York City; also appeared in *The Skin of Our Teeth.*

Major Tours:
In White America, U.S. cities, 1965.

Stage Work:
Director (with Andrew Frye), *The Far Other Side of a Very Thin Line,* Center Theatre Group, Mark Taper Forum, 1978-79.

WRITINGS

Plays:
(With James Shepard) *The Far Other Side of a Very Thin Line,* Center Theatre Group, Mark Taper Forum, 1978-79.

OTHER SOURCES

Periodicals:
Los Angeles Times, "Calendar," November 29, 1998, pp. 25-26.*

HALLAHAN, Charles 1943-1997

PERSONAL

Born July 29, 1943, in Philadelphia, PA; died of heart attack after a car crash, November 25, 1997, in Los Angeles, CA; married Barbara Gryboski, 1983; children: two sons. *Education:* Temple University, M.A. (fine arts), 1972.

Addresses: *Agent*—The Gersh Agency, 232 North Canon Dr., Beverly Hills, CA 90210.

Career: Actor. Appeared in numerous productions with the American Conservatory Theatre Company, San Franscico, CA 1972-77.

CREDITS

Stage Appearances:
Doc, *Come Back, Little Sheba,* Los Angeles Theatre Center, Los Angeles, 1986.
Kentucky Cycle, Center Theatre Group, Mark Taper Forum, Los Angeles, 1991.

Film Appearances:

Pete, *Going in Style,* Warner Bros., 1979.
Henry, *Nightwing,* Columbia, 1979.
Dixon—bartender, *Hide in Plain Sight,* Metro-Goldwyn-Mayer, 1980.
Bazooka, *P.K. and the Kid,* Lorimar, 1982.
Norris, *The Thing,* Universal, 1982.
Earl Lapin, *Silkwood,* Twentieth Century-Fox, 1983.
Ray, *Twilight Zone—The Movie,* Warner Bros., 1983.
Richard Cessna, *Kidco,* Twentieth Century-Fox, 1984.
McGill, *Pale Rider,* Warner Bros., 1985.
Coach, *Vision Quest,* Warner Bros., 1985.
Deputy Getz, *Fatal Beauty,* Metro-Goldwyn-Mayer, 1987.
Vincent Dennehy, *True Believer,* Columbia, 1989.
Dr. McCurdy, *Body of Evidence,* Union Films, 1993.
Policeman, *Dave,* Warner Bros., 1993.
Ethan Larson, *Warlock: The Armageddon,* Vidmark Entertainment, 1993.
Mind Lies, 1995.
General Sarlow, *Executive Decision,* Warner Bros., 1996.
Coop, *The Fan,* Sony Pictures Entertainment, 1996.
Dan Fredricks, *The Rich Man's Wife,* Buena Vista, 1996.
Paul Dryfus, *Dante's Peak,* Universal, 1997.
Angus, *The Pest,* TriStar, 1997.

Television Appearances; Episodic:

Larry Kent, "Deadly Doubles," *Hawaii Five-O,* CBS, 1977.
Warren Sanford, "A Question of Innocence," *Hart to Hart,* ABC, 1980.
Charlie Weeks, "Rites of Spring, Parts I and II," and "Jungle Madness: Parts I and II," *Hill Street Blues,* NBC, 1981.
Colonel Turnbull, "Taking the Fifth," *M*A*S*H,* CBS, 1981.
Terrible Fred McShane, "Anything For a Friend," *Bret Maverick,* NBC, 1981.
George Cook, "Back Home," *The Equalizer,* CBS, 1985.
Ted Cobb, *Wings,* NBC, 1990.
Ralph Negroponte, *Civil Wars,* ABC, 1992.
Stone, "Frank, the Potato Man," *Picket Fences,* CBS, 1992.
Bob Pinkney, *In the Heat of the Night,* CBS, 1992.
Law & Order, NBC, 1992.
Bob Witkow, "Umper," *Sirens,* ABC, 1993.
Frankie, *Jack's Place,* ABC, 1993.
Gavin Whitehope, *Wild Palms,* ABC, 1993.
Sloopy Dunbar, "Legacy," *Mad About You,* NBC, 1994.
Barry Noble, *Murder, She Wrote,* CBS, 1994.
Frank Kellogg, *Sweet Justice,* NBC, 1994.
University President Charles W. Kisley, *Coach,* ABC, 1994-95.
Billy's father, *Sisters,* NBC, 1995.
General Thomas Williams, "Desert Son," *JAG,* NBC, 1995.
Tom Ryan, "Movin In, Parts I and II," *Almost Perfect,* CBS, 1995.
Earl Dawkins, "What a Dump!," *NYPD Blue,* ABC, 1996.
Jack Clancy, "Three of a Con," *Players,* NBC, 1997.
The Visitor, Fox, 1997.

Television Appearances; Series:

Ernie (recurring), *The Paper Chase,* CBS, 1978-79.
Captain Charles Devane, *Hunter,* NBC, 1984-91.
Bill Davis (recurring), *Grace Under Fire,* ABC, 1992-93.
Voice of Travis Marshall (recurring), *Gargoyles* (animated), syndicated, 1994-97.

Television Appearances; Miniseries:

Detective Whalen, *When Love Kills: The Seduction of John Hearn,* CBS, 1993.

Television Appearances; Movies:

Corporal Sebastian, *A Death in Canaan,* CBS, 1978.
Tibbles, *Terror Out of the Sky,* CBS, 1978.
Fisher, *Skag,* NBC, 1980.
John Ryan, *Chicago Story,* NBC, 1981.
Pat Chambers, *Mickey Spillane's Margin For Murder* (also known as *Margin For Murder*), CBS, 1981.
Sergeant Beatty, *Allison Sidney Harrison,* NBC, 1981.
Nelson Gary, Sr., *A Winner Never Quits,* ABC, 1986.
Joseph McCarthy, *J. Edgar Hoover,* Showtime, 1987.
Muldowney, *The Revenge of Al Capone,* NBC, 1989.
Detective Lieutenant Bradbury, *Cast a Deadly Spell,* HBO, 1991.
Bud Taylor, *Nails,* Showtime, 1992.
Roy Galvin, *Jack Reed: A Search For Justice,* NBC, 1994.
Older pilot MacIntire, *Roswell,* Showtime, 1994.
Captain Charles Devane, *The Return of Hunter,* NBC, 1995.
Sheriff Carter, *Ambushed,* HBO, 1998.

Television Appearances; Specials:

Sergeant Beatty, *Allison Sidney Harrison,* NBC, 1983.
Sergeant, *The Old Reliable,* PBS, 1988.
The Hollywood Christmas Parade, syndicated, 1989.
Wrecker, *Perfect Date,* ABC, 1990.
Chief Garrett, *Things That Go Bump,* NBC, 1997.*

HAMILTON, Linda 1956-

PERSONAL

Born September 26, 1956, in Salisbury, MD; married Bruce Abbott (an actor), December 19, 1982 (divorced, 1989); married James Cameron (a director and writer), March 24, 1997 (divorced); children: (first marriage) Dalton, (second marriage) Josephine Archer. *Education:* Attended Washington College, Chesterton, MD; studied acting under Lee Strasberg.

Addresses: *Agent*—c/o International Creative Management, 8942 Wilshire Blvd., Beverly Hills, CA 90211. *Manager*—Bobbie Edrick, Artist Circle Entertainment, 8957 Norma Place, Los Angeles, CA 90069.

Career: Actress.

Awards, Honors: Golden Globe Award nominations, best actress in a dramatic television series, 1988 and 1989, both for *Beauty and the Beast;* MTV Movie Awards, best female performance and most desirable female, both 1992, for *Terminator 2: Judgement Day;* Golden Globe Award nomination, best performance by an actress in a miniseries or motion picture made for television, 1996, for *A Mother's Prayer;* Blockbuster Entertainment Award, favorite actress—action/adventure, 1998, for *Dante's Peak.*

CREDITS

Stage Appearances:

Reporter, *Looice,* New York Shakespeare Festival, Public Theatre, New York City, 1975.

Young Elizabeth, *Richard III,* Actors' Studio Theatre, New York City, 1977.

Film Appearances:

(Film debut) Susan, *T.A.G.: The Assassination Game,* New World, 1982.

Eva the Crescent Moon Lady, *The Stone Boy,* Twentieth Century-Fox, 1983.

Vicky Baxter, *Children of the Corn,* New World, 1984.

Sarah Connor, *The Terminator,* Orion, 1984.

Nina, *Black Moon Rising,* New World, 1986.

Amy Franklin, *King Kong Lives,* De Laurentiis Entertainment Group, 1986.

Sticky Fingers, 1988.

Ellen Burrows, *Mr. Destiny,* Buena Vista, 1990.

Sarah Connor, *Terminator 2: Judgment Day,* TriStar, 1991.

Karen Rainer, *Silent Fall,* Warner Bros., 1994.

Lauren Porter, *Separate Lives,* 1995.

Rachel Wando, *Dante's Peak,* Universal Pictures, 1997.

Amanda Givens, *Shadow Conspiracy,* Buena Vista Pictures, 1997.

Television Appearances; Episodic:

Sandy Valpariso, "Fuchs Me? Fuchs You!," "Grace Under Pressure," and "Parting Is Such Sweet Sorrow," *Hill Street Blues,* NBC, 1984.

Carol McDermott, "Menace, Anyone?," *Murder, She Wrote,* CBS, 1986.

Guest Caller Claire, "The Good Son," *Frasier,* NBC, 1993.

Laura, "Odd Man Out," *Frasier,* NBC, 1996.

Voice of Nemesis, "Hercules and the King for a Day," *Disney's Hercules* (animated), ABC/syndicated, 1998.

Susan Maguire Wayne, "Chemistry," *Batman: Gotham Knights,* Fox, 1998.

Dr. Stephanie Lake, "Meltdown," *Batman Beyond,* 1999.

Also hosted *Saturday Night Live,* NBC.

Television Appearances; Series:

Lisa Rogers, *Secrets of Midland Heights,* CBS, 1980-81.

Lauren Hollister, *King's Crossing,* ABC, 1982.

Catherine Chandler, *Beauty and the Beast,* CBS, 1987-89.

Television Appearances; Specials:

Toonces, the Cat Who Could Drive a Car, NBC, 1992.

Narrator, *Robots Rising,* Discovery Channel, 1998.

Television Appearances; Movies:

Greta Rideout, *Rape and Marriage—The Rideout Case,* CBS, 1980.

Anne Samoorian, *Reunion,* CBS, 1980.

Josie Greenwood, *Country Gold,* CBS, 1982.

Susan Decker, *Secrets of a Mother and Daughter,* CBS, 1983.

Elena Koslov, *Secret Weapons,* NBC, 1985.

Kate, *Club Med,* ABC, 1986.

Claire Madison, *Go toward the Light,* CBS, 1988.

Rosemary Holmstrom, *A Mother's Prayer,* USA Network, 1995.

Beth MacAlpine, *The Way to Dusty Death,* 1995.

Detective Jean Martin, *On the Line,* ABC, 1998.

Rachel, *Point Last Seen,* CBS, 1998.
Marie Taquet, *Rescuers: Stories of Courage: Two Couples,* Showtime, 1998.
Anna Sipes, *The Color of Courage,* USA Network, 1999.
Ruby Sanford, *Unglued* (also known as *The Secret Life of Girls*), 1999.

Television Appearances; Awards Presentations:
MTV's 1991 Video Music Awards, MTV and syndicated, 1991.
MTV Movie Awards, MTV, 1992.
Presenter, *The 17th Annual CableACE Awards,* 1995.
Presenter, *The Screen Actor's Guild Awards,* 1997.
Blockbuster Entertainment Awards, 1998.

Other Television Appearances:
Mattie MacGregor, *Wishman* (pilot), ABC, 1983.*

HAMMOND, Darrell

PERSONAL

Born in Melbourne, FL. *Education:* Attended University of Florida at Gainesville.

Addresses: *Agent*—International Creative Management, 8942 Wilshire Blvd., Beverly Hills, CA 90211.

Career: Actor and comedian.

CREDITS

Film Appearances:
Greenkeeper, *Greenkeeping,* Central Park Films, 1992.
Chris McCarthy, *Celtic Pride,* Buena Vista, 1996.
Mr. Robertson, *Blues Brothers 2000,* Universal, 1998.
Voice of Master Little, *The King and I* (animated), Warner Bros., 1999.

Television Appearances; Series:
Saturday Night Live, NBC, 1995—.

Television Appearances; Episodic:
Premium Blend, Comedy Central, 1998.

Television Appearances; Specials:
William & Ree Comedy Central, The Nashville Network, 1991.
71st Annual Macy's Thanksgiving Day Parade, 1997.*

HAMORI, Andras

PERSONAL

Born in Hungary. *Education:* Attended Budapest University of Law, doctorate degree and diploma in film and theatre journalism.

Addresses: *Office*—c/o Accent Entertainment Corporation, 207 Adelaide Street East, Suite 300, Toronto, Ontario M5A 1M8.

Career: Producer. Founding partner and senior vice president, Alliance Entertainment (1985-89); co-founder, Accent Entertainment Corporation (1989); president, Alliance Pictures (1995-).

CREDITS

Film Work:
Assistant producer, *Bedroom Eyes,* Pan-Canadian Film Distributors, 1985.
Associate producer, *Heavenly Bodies,* Metro-Goldwyn-Mayer, 1985.
Executive in charge of production, *La Nuit Magique,* 1985.
Associate, producer, *Separate Vacations,* Alliance, 1986.
Producer, *The Wraith,* New Century, 1986.
Producer, *Nowhere to Hide,* Alliance Entertainment, 1987.
Co-producer, *The Gate,* Vestron Video, 1987.
Executive producer, *Iron Eagle II: The Battle Beyond the Flag,* Alliance Entertainment, 1988.
Executive producer, *Gnaw: Food of the Gods Part II,* Carolco, 1989.
Producer, *The Big Deal,* 1989.
Producer, *Gate II,* Triumph Releasing, 1990.
Executive producer, *South of Wawa,* Accent Entertainment Corporation, 1992.
Producer, *Magic Hunter,* Shadow Distribution, 1994.
Co-producer, *Mesmer,* Mayfair Entertainment, 1994.
Producer, *Never Talk to Strangers,* Imperial Entertainment, 1995.
Co-executive producer, *Crash,* Fine Line Features, 1996.
Executive producer, *The Sweet Hereafter,* Fine Line Features, 1997.
Executive producer, *Strike!,* Miramax, 1998.
Producer, *eXistenZ,* Miramax, 1999.
Producer, *The Taste of Sunshine,* Alliance Pictures, 1999.

Executive producer, *A Room for Romeo Brass,* forthcoming.

Television Work; Series:

Producer, *Hot Shots,* PBS, 1986-87.

Producer (executive producer, 1991-92), *Sweating Bullets,* CBS/syndicated, 1990-95.

Television Work; Movies:

Producer, *God Bless the Child,* ABC, 1988.

Producer, *Daughter of Darkness,* CBS, 1990.

Producer, *Storm and Sorrow,* Lifetime, 1990.

Producer, *Mrs. 'Arris Goes to Paris,* CBS, 1992.

Executive producer, *City Boy,* PBS, 1994.

Television Work; Specials:

Assistant to the producer, *Overdrawn at the Memory Bank,* PBS, 1985.*

HARRIS, Ed 1950-

PERSONAL

Full name, Edward Allen Harris; born November 28, 1950, in Tenafly, NJ; son of Bob L. and Margaret Harris; married Amy Madigan (an actress), 1983; children: one daughter. *Education:* California Institute of the Arts, Los Angeles, CA, B.F.A., 1975; attended Columbia University, 1969-71, and Oklahoma State University, 1972-73.

Addresses: *Agent*—Creative Artists Agency, 9830 Wilshire Blvd., Beverly Hills, CA 90212.

Career: Actor. Trustee, California Institute of the Arts, 1985—.

Member: Screen Actors Guild, Actors' Equity Association.

Awards, Honors: Los Angeles Drama Critics Circle Award, 1981, for *Prairie Avenue;* Obie Award, *Village Voice,* 1983, for *Fool for Love;* San Francisco Critics Award, 1985, for *Scar; Theatre World* Award, Drama Desk Award, best actor in a play, and Antoinette Perry Award nomination, best dramatic actor, all 1986, for *Precious Sons;* Golden Globe Award nomination, best performance by an actor in a supporting role in a motion picture, 1990, for *Jacknife;* Academy Award nomination, best supporting actor, Screen Actors Guild Award, outstanding performance by a male actor in a supporting role, and Golden Globe Award nomination, best performance by an actor in a supporting role in a motion picture, all 1996, for *Apollo 13;* Screen Actors Guild Award nomination, outstanding performance by a male actor in a television movie or miniseries, 1997, for *Riders of the Purple Sage;* Academy Award nomination, best supporting actor, Blockbuster Entertainment Award, favorite supporting actor—drama, British Academy of Film and Television Arts Award nomination, best performance by an actor in a supporting role, Golden Globe Award, best performance by an actor in a supporting role in a motion picture, and National Board of Review Award, best supporting actor, all 1999, for *The Truman Show.*

CREDITS

Stage Appearances:

Lee, *True West,* South Coast Repertory, Costa Mesa, CA, 1981.

(Off-Broadway debut) Eddie, *Fool for Love,* Circle Repertory Theatre, 1983.

Eddie, *Fool for Love,* Douglas Fairbanks Theatre, New York City, 1983.

Scar, Magic Theatre, San Francisco, CA, 1985.

(Broadway debut) Fred Small, *Precious Sons,* Longacre Theatre, 1986.

Scar, Met Theater, Los Angeles, CA, 1992.

Simpatico, Joseph Papp Public Theater, New York City, 1994.

Also appeared in *Prairie Avenue,* c. 1981; and in *A Streetcar Named Desire, Sweet Bird of Youth, Julius Caesar, Hamlet, Camelot, Are You Lookin'?, The Time of Your Life, Cowboy Mouth, Learned Ladies, Kingdom of Earth, The Grapes of Wrath, Present Laughter, Balaam,* and *Killers' Head.*

Film Appearances:

(Film debut) Pathology resident, *Coma,* United Artists, 1978.

Hotchkiss, *Borderline,* ITC, 1980.

Billy, *Knightriders,* United Film, 1981.

Dream On, Magic Cinema, 1981.

Hank Blaine, "Father's Day," *Creepshow,* Warner Bros., 1982.

Oates, *Under Fire,* Orion, 1983.

John Glenn, *The Right Stuff,* Warner Bros., 1983.

Wayne Lomax, *Places in the Heart,* TriStar, 1984.

Jimmy Wing, *A Flash of Green,* Spectrafilm, 1984.

Jack Walsh, *Swing Shift,* Warner Bros., 1984.

Shang Pierce, *Alamo Bay,* TriStar, 1985.

Gus Lang, *Code Name: Emerald,* Metro-Goldwyn-Mayer/United Artists, 1985.

Charlie Dick, *Sweet Dreams,* TriStar, 1985.
William Walker, *Walker,* Universal, 1987.
Stefan, *To Kill a Priest,* Columbia, 1989.
Dave, *Jacknife,* Cineplex Odeon, 1989.
Virgil "Bud" Brigman, *The Abyss,* Twentieth Century-Fox, 1989.
Tommy Flannery, *State of Grace,* Orion, 1990.
Dave Moss, *Glengarry Glen Ross,* New Line Cinema, 1992.
Sheriff Alan Pangborn, *Needful Things,* Columbia, 1993.
Wayne Tarrance, *The Firm,* Paramount, 1993.
Tom Wheeler, *Milk Money,* Paramount, 1994.
Kyle Bodine, *China Moon,* Orion, 1994.
Blair Sullivan, *Just Cause,* Warner Bros., 1995.
Gene Kranz, *Apollo 13,* Universal, 1995.
E. Howard Hunt, *Nixon,* 1995.
Mack McCann, *Eye for an Eye,* Paramount, 1996.
General Francis X Hummel, *The Rock,* Buena Vista, 1996.
Seth Frank, *Absolute Power,* Columbia, 1997.
Luke Harrison, *Stepmon,* Columbia/TriStar, 1998.
Christof, *The Truman Show,* Paramount, 1998.
The Third Miracle, Sony Pictures Classics, 1999.
Pollock, forthcoming.

Also appeared in *Portalana* and *Suspect.*

Film Work:
Script consultant, *A Flash of Green,* Spectrafilm, 1984.
Trainee model maker, *Lost in Space,* New Line Cinema, 1998.

Also received appreciation credit in *Boxing Helena,* 1993.

Television Appearances; Movies:
Chuck Polcheck, *The Aliens Are Coming,* NBC, 1980.
Harry Nash, *The Last Innocent Man,* HBO, 1987.
Harry Seagraves, *Paris Trout* (also known as *Rage*), Showtime, 1991.
Hugh Hathaway, *Running Mates,* HBO, 1992.
Lassiter, *Riders of the Purple Sage,* TNT, 1996.

Television Appearances; Episodic:
"Kill the Messenger," *The Rockford Files,* NBC, 1978.
Mechanic, *Lou Grant,* CBS, 1979.
Lonny, "Vagabounds," *CHiPs,* NBC, 1977.
Guest Caller Rob, "Leapin' Lizards," *Frasier,* NBC, 1995.

Television Appearances; Specials:
Premiere: Inside the Summer Blockbusters, Fox, 1989.
Narrator, *Moon Man from Massachusetts: The Robert Goddard Story,* The Disney Channel, 1994.
Voice, *Baseball* (also known as *The History of Baseball,* series), PBS, 1994.
Interviewee, *Big Guns Talk: The Story of the Western,* TNT, 1997.
Presenter, *The Screen Actors Guild Awards,* 1997.
Sam Shepard: Stalking Himself, PBS, 1998.

Television Appearances; Miniseries:
Russ, *The Amazing Howard Hughes,* CBS, 1977.
Lieutenant William Clark, *The Seekers,* HBO, 1979.
General William Starkey, *Stephen King's "The Stand,"* ABC, 1994.

Television Work; Executive Producer:
Riders of the Purple Sage (movie), TNT, 1996.

RECORDINGS

Videos:
Virgil "Bud" Brigman, *The Abyss—Special Edition,* Twentieth Century-Fox, 1993.

OTHER SOURCES

Periodicals:
Entertainment Weekly, March 1, 1999, p. 64.
Interview, September, 1992, pp. 112-115.
Premiere, November, 1990, p. 76.*

HARRIS, Jared 1961-

PERSONAL

Born 1961, in London, England; son of Richard (an actor) and Elizabeth Harris; brother of Damien (a director best known for *The Rachel Papers*) and Jamie (an actor) Harris. *Education:* Graduated from Duke University, 1984; Central University, London.

Addresses: *Agent*—William Morris Agency, 151 El Camino Dr., Beverly Hills, CA 90212.

Career: Actor. Member of the Royal Shakespeare Company.

Awards, Honors: Obie Award, *Village Voice,* for *Ecstasy.*

CREDITS

Stage Appearances:

Hotspur, *Henry IV,* New York Shakespeare Festival, Public Theatre, New York City, 1991.

Soranzo,*'Tis Pity She's A Whore,* New York Shakespeare Festival, Public Theatre, 1992.

Val, *Ecstasy,* New Group, John Houseman Studio, 1995.

Edmund, *King Lear,* Public Theatre, 1996.

Film Appearances:

Geof, *The Rachel Papers,* Virgin, 1989.

Paddy, *Far and Away,* Universal, 1992.

British Lieutenant, *The Last of the Mohicans,* Twentieth Century-Fox, 1992.

Danny the Doorman, *The Public Eye,* Universal, 1992.

Edgar, *Nadja,* October Films, 1994.

London boy, *Natural Born Killers,* Warner Bros., 1994.

Jimmy Rose, *Blue in the Face,* Miramax, 1994.

Benmont Tench, *Dead Man,* Miramax, 1995.

Jimmy Rose, *Smoke,* Miramax, 1995.

Head Thug Pug, *Tall Tale: The Unbelievable Adventures of Pecos Bill,* Walt Disney Productions, 1995.

Andy Warhol, *I Shot Andy Warhol,* Samuel Goldwyn, 1996.

Chinese Box, Trimark Pictures, 1997.

Lee, *Father's Day,* Warner Bros., 1997.

Owen, *Gold in the Streets,* Carlton, 1997.

Ray, *Sunday,* Prime Films, 1997.

Vlad, *Happiness,* Prime Films, 1998.

Older Will, *Lost in Space,* New Line Cinema, 1998.

John Kerr, *The Weekend,* 1999.

Jones, *Bullfighter,* ScanBox Entertainment, 1999.

Film Work:

Production associate, *Hurricane Streets,* Metro-Goldwyn-Mayer, 1997.

Television Appearances; Episodic:

Seth Baines, *New York Undercover,* Fox, 1995.

OTHER SOURCES

Periodicals:

Entertainment Weekly, May 17, 1996, p. 41.

People Weekly, November 6, 1995, p. 88.*

HARRIS, Thomas 1940-

PERSONAL

Born in 1940, in Jackson, MS; son of William Thomas (an electrical engineer and farmer) and Polly (a high school teacher) Harris; married Harriet (divorced, mid-1960s); children: Anne. *Education:* Baylor University, B.A. (English), 1964. *Avocational interests:* Cooking, painting.

Addresses: *Office*—c/o Dell Publishing, 1540 Broadway, New York, NY 10036.

Career: Novelist. *Waco News-Tribune,* night police reporter, 1963-66; *Associated Press,* New York City, general assignment reporter and night editor, 1968-74; *True* and *Argosy* magazines, contributed stories, 1960s; novelist, 1968—; full-time writer, 1975—.

WRITINGS

Novels:

Black Sunday, Putnam, 1975.

Red Dragon, Putnam, 1981.

Silence of the Lambs, St. Martin's Press, 1988.

Hannibal, Delacorte, 1999.

Adaptations: *Black Sunday* was adapted and filmed by John Frankenheimer and released by Paramount, 1977; *Red Dragon* was adapted for film as *Manhunter* (also known as *Red Dragon: The Pursuit of Hannibal Lecter*) by Michael Mann and released by De Laurentiis Entertainment Group, 1986; *Silence of the Lambs* was adapted and filmed by Jonathon Demme and released by Orion, 1991.

OTHER SOURCES

Books:

A Dark Night's Dreaming: Contemporary American Horror Fiction, University of South Carolina Press (Columbia, SC), 1996.

It's a Print!: Detective Fiction from Page to Screen, Popular Press (Bowling Green, OH), 1994.

Periodicals:

Entertainment Weekly, May 7, 1999, p. 22.

Journal of American Culture, spring, 1995.

Los Angeles Times Book Review, July 17, 1988.

New York Times, August 15, 1988; March 25, 1990; June 13, 1999.

Notes on Contemporary Literature, January, 1995.

Times (London), May 25, 1991.

Tribune Books (Chicago), August 14, 1988.

Washington Post Book World, August 21, 1988; May 21, 1989.

Electronic:

http://www.randomhouse.com/features/thomasharris/.*

HASSELHOFF, David 1952-

PERSONAL

Born July 17, 1952, in Baltimore, MD; son of Joe (a business executive) and Dolores (a homemaker); married Catherine Hickland (an actress; divorced); married Pamela Bach (an actress), 1989; children: Taylor Ann, Hayley Amber. *Education:* Attended Academy of Dramatic Arts, Pontiac, MI; and California Institute of the Arts, Valencia, CA. *Avocational interests:* scuba diving.

Addresses: *Office*—c/o Jan McCormack, 11342 Dona Lisa Dr., Studio City, CA 91604-4315. *Agent*—c/o William Morris Agency, 151 El Camino Dr., Beverly Hills, CA 90212. *Publicist*—Jonni Hartman, Slade, Grant, Hartman, and Hartman, 9145 Sunset Blvd., Suite 218, Los Angeles, CA 90069.

Career: Actor and producer for television and film, and recording artist.

Member: Screen Actors Guild, American Federation of Television and Radio Artists.

Awards, Honors: People's Choice Award, best male performer in a new television program, 1983.

CREDITS

Television Appearances; Series:

Dr. Greg "Snapper" Foster, *The Young and the Restless,* CBS, 1975-82.
Marvin "Shake" Tiller, *Semi-Tough,* ABC, 1980.
Michael Knight, *Knight Rider,* NBC, 1982-86.
Fame, Fortune, and Romance, syndicated, 1986.
Mitch Buchannon, *Baywatch,* NBC, 1989, then syndicated, 1991—.
Mitch Buchannon, *Baywatch Nights,* syndicated, 1995—.
Mr. B, *NightMan,* syndicated, 1997.

Television Appearances; Pilots:

Scott, *Pleasure Cove,* NBC, 1979.
Guest, *Star Search,* syndicated, 1983.
Michael Knight, *All That Glitters,* NBC, 1984.
Detective, *Scene of the Crime,* NBC, 1984.

Television Appearances; Episodic:

"September Song," *The Love Boat,* ABC, 1980.
"Humpty Dumpty," *The Love Boat,* ABC, 1981.
"Hooray for Hollywood," *Diff'rent Strokes,* NBC, 1984.
Man using phone, *Santa Barbara,* NBC, 1984.
"Don't Drink and Drive," *One to Grow On,* NBC, 1988.

Also appeared in *Police Story,* CBS.

Television Appearances; Movies:

Griffin and Phoenix: A Love Story, ABC, 1976.
Curt Taylor, *The Cartier Affair,* NBC, 1984.
Don Gregory, *Bridge across Time* (also known as *Arizona Ripper*), NBC, 1985.
Billy Travis, *Perry Mason: The Case of the Lady in the Lake,* NBC, 1988.
Knight Rider the Movie, 1988.
Mitch Buchannon, *Baywatch: Panic at Malibu Pier* (also known as *Inferno at Malibu Beach*), NBC, 1989.
Dr. Dan Meyer, *Fire and Rain,* USA Network, 1989.
Michael Knight, *Knight Rider 2000,* NBC, 1991.
Duncan Snyder, *Avalanche* (also known as *Snowbound*), Fox and CTV Television Network, 1994.
Jake Gorski, *Gridlock,* NBC, 1996.
Mitch Buchannon, *Baywatch: White Thunder at Glacier Bay,* 1997
Nick Fury, *Nick Fury: Agent of SHIELD,* Fox, 1998.
Shaka Zulu: The Citadel, 1998.

Television Appearances; Specials:

After Hours: Getting to Know Us, CBS, 1977.
Disneyland's Thirtieth Anniversary Celebration, NBC, 1985.
The NBC All-Star Hour, NBC, 1985.
On Top All Over the World, syndicated, 1985.
The Night of 100 Stars II, 1985.
NBC's Sixtieth Anniversary Celebration, NBC, 1986.
The Noel Edmonds Show, ABC, 1986.
A Crystal Christmas (also known as *A Crystal Christmas in Sweden*), syndicated, 1987.
AIDS: The Global Explosion, syndicated, 1988.
Super Bloopers and New Practical Jokes, NBC, 1990.
Star-athon '92: A Weekend with the Stars, syndicated, 1992.
The 61st Annual Hollywood Christmas Parade, syndicated, 1992.
Michael Bulkin, *The Bulkin Trail,* Family Channel, 1993.
All-New All Star TV Censored Bloopers—Unplugged!, 1995.
Sea World/Busch Gardens Party for the Planet, 1995.
Team "Baywatch" USA, syndicated, 1996.
Grand Marshall, *Hollywood Christmas Parade,* 1996.
All-Star Moms, CBS, 1997.

Television Appearances; Awards Presentations:
The 37th Annual Prime Time Emmy Awards, 1985.
The American Music Awards, ABC, 1994.
The 27th Annual NAACP Image Awards, 1996.
The 23rd Annual American Music Awards, 1996.
Presenter, *The 53rd Annual Golden Globe Awards,* 1996.
Presenter, *The 25th Annual People's Choice Awards,* 1999.

Television Work; Executive Producer, Except as Noted; Series:
Baywatch, syndicated, 1991—.
And creator, *Baywatch Nights,* syndicated, 1995—.

Film Appearances:
Revenge of the Cheerleaders, 1976.
Simon, *Starcrash* (also known as *Stella Star* and *Star Crash*), New World, 1979.
Starke Zeiten, 1988.
W.B. Blue and the Bean, 1989.
Gary, *Witchcraft,* 1989.
Will Colton, *The Final Alliance,* RCA, 1989.
White Bread, *Bail Out,* 1990.
John D'Artagnan Smith, *Ring of the Musketeers,* Columbia/TriStar, 1994.
Legacy, Quantum Entertainment, 1998.

Also appeared in *Neon City.*

Film Work:
(With Max Kleven) Co-producer, *W.B. Blue and the Bean,* 1989.
Producer, *Bail Out,* 1990.

Stage Appearances:
Appeared as Dr. Frank-n-Furter, *The Rocky Horror Picture Show,* Los Angeles, 1995.

Videos:
Baywatch: Forbidden Paradise, 1995.

RECORDINGS

Albums:
Looking for Freedom, White, 1989.
Crazy for You, White, 1991.
David, 1991.
Everybody's Sunshine, 1992.
You Are Everything, Ariola, 1993.
Du, 1994.
Best of David Hasselhoff, 1995.
David Hasselhoff, 1995.
Hooked on a Feeling, 1997.

Recorded five albums that were released in Austria and Germany.

WRITINGS

Television Series Music:
Maint title song, "After the Sun Goes Down," and end title song, "Into the Night," both for *Baywatch Nights,* syndicated, 1995—.

OTHER SOURCES

Periodicals:
Entertainment Weekly, October 8, 1993, p. 14.
People Weekly, October 3, 1994, pp. 65-66, 68.
Playboy, May, 1995, p. 136.
Skin Diver, November, 1998, p. 100.*

HAUER, Rutger 1944-

PERSONAL

Born January 23, 1944, in Breukelen, Netherlands; married.

Addresses: *Agent*—c/o William Morris Agency, 151 El Camino Dr., Beverly Hills, CA 90212.

Career: Actor. *Military service:* Served in the Dutch Army and Navy.

Member: Screen Actors Guild.

Awards, Honors: Golden Globe Award, best performance by an actor in a supporting role in a television miniseries or motion picture, 1987, for *Escape from Sobibor.*

CREDITS

Film Appearances:
Turkish Delight (also known as *Turks Fruit*), Nederland, 1973.
Rik Van de Loo, *Pusteblume* (also known as *Hard to Remember*), Cinecenta, 1974.
Keetje Tippl'e, Tuschinski Film Distribution, 1975.
Blaine Van Nierkirk, *The Wilby Conspiracy,* United Artists, 1975.
Duclari, *Max Havelaar,* Netherlands Fox Film Corporation, 1976.
Johan Nagel, *Mysteries,* Cine-Vog, 1978.

Driann, *A Woman between Dog and Wolf* (also known as *Een Vrouw Tussen Hond en Wolf*), Gaumont International, 1979.
Erik, *Soldier of Orange,* International Picture Show, 1979.
Gerrit Witkamp, *Spetters,* Embassy, 1980.
Etienne De Balsan, *Chanel Solitaire,* United Film Distribution, 1981.
Wulfgar, *Nighthawks,* Universal, 1981.
Roy Batty, *Blade Runner,* Warner Bros., 1982.
Claude Maillot Van Horn, *Eureka,* United Artists, 1983.
John Tanner, *The Osterman Weekend,* Twentieth Century-Fox, 1983.
Brigadier Rinus de Gier, *Outsider in Amsterdam* (also known as *Fatal Error* and *The Outsider*), Verenigade Nederland, 1983.
Jim Malden, *A Breed Apart,* Orion, 1984.
Martin, *Flesh and Blood,* Riverside, 1985.
Navarre, *Ladyhawke,* Warner Bros., 1985.
John Ryder, *The Hitcher,* TriStar, 1986.
Nick Randall, *Wanted: Dead or Alive,* New World, 1986.
The Brain, *Bloodhounds of Broadway,* Columbia, 1989.
Nick Parker, *Blind Fury,* TriStar, 1989.
Sallow, *The Blood of Heroes* (also known as *The Salute of the Jugger*), Filmpac, 1990.
Harley Stone, *Split Second,* InterStar, 1992.
Lothos, *Buffy the Vampire Slayer,* Twentieth Century-Fox, 1992.
Tom Burton, *Beyond Justice,* Vidmark, 1992.
Ben Jordan, *Past Midnight,* Columbia, 1992.
Mystic Monk, *Nostradamus,* Orion Classics, 1994.
Burns, *Surviving the Game,* New Line Cinema, 1994.
Reuben Bean, *The Beans of Egypt, Maine* (also known as *Forbidden Choices*), LIVE, 1994.
Crossworlds, Trimark, 1996.

Made film debut in *Repelsteeltje,* 1973; appeared as Andreas Kartak, *La Legenda del Santo Bevitore,* 1988; as John Knot, *In una notte di chiaro di luna,* 1989; and in *Dandelions,* 1974, *Het Jaar van de Kreeft, Griechische Feigen, Pastorale 1943, Legend of the Holy Drinker, Ocean Point,* and *On a Moonlit Night.*

Film Work:
Coproducer, *Mysteries,* Cine-Vog, 1978.

Also dialogue collaboration, *In una notte di chiaro di luna,* 1989.

Television Appearances; Movies:
Albert Speer, *Inside the Third Reich,* ABC, 1982.
Lieutenant Alexander "Sasha" Pechersky, *Escape from Sobibor,* CBS, 1987.
Frank, *Deadlock* (also known as *Wedlock*), HBO, 1991.
Jake Shell, *Blind Side,* HBO and NBC, 1993.
Morgan Norvell, *Voyage,* USA Network, 1993.
Xavier March, *Fatherland,* HBO, 1994.
Fred Noonan, *Amelia Earhart: The Final Flight,* TNT, 1994.
Doctor Lem, *Angel of Death* (also known as *Blood of the Innocent*), Showtime, 1994.

Other Television Appearances:
Emil, "Indian Poker," *The Edge,* HBO, 1989.
The 49th Annual Golden Globe Awards, TBS, 1992.

Appeared in the series *Floris,* made for Dutch television; also appeared in the miniseries *Maketub: The Law of the Desert,* made for Italian television.

Stage Appearances:
Performed onstage in Amsterdam for six years before starting film career.*

HEALY, David 1932-1995

PERSONAL

Born May 15, 1932; died of a heart ailment, October 25, 1995, in London, England.

Career: Actor.

Awards, Honors: Laurence Olivier Award, best actor in a supporting role, 1983, for *Guys and Dolls.*

CREDITS

Film Appearances:
Hilton Bass, *Be My Guest,* 1965.
Halstead, *The Double Man,* Warner Bros., 1967.
David, *Assignment K,* Columbia, 1968.
Jones, *Only When I Larf,* 1968.
Chicago theatre manager, *Isadora,* Universal, 1968.
Clergyman, *Patton* (also known as *Patton: A Salute to a Rebel* and *Patton: Lust for Glory*), Twentieth Century-Fox, 1970.
Phelan, Embassy, 1971.
Jason, *Agatha Christie's Endless Night* (also known as *Endless Night*), British Lion, 1971.
Raymond Pelley, *Lust for a Vampire* (also known as *To Love a Vampire*), 1971.

(Uncredited) Vandenburg Lanuch director, *Diamonds Are Forever,* 1971.
Sam Bundler, *Scott Joplin,* Universal, 1977.
Major Winters, *Twilight's Last Gleaming,* Allied Artists, 1977.
First general, *The Ninth Configuration* (also known as *Twinkle, Twinkle, Killer Kane*), Lorimar, 1980.
Mr. Danvers, *Supergirl: The Movie,* TriStar, 1984.
P.R. man, *Haunted Honeymoon,* Orion, 1986.
Voice of Right Door Knocker, *Labyrinth,* TriStar, 1986.
Deadly Illusion, 1989.
Todd Whitbread, *The Unbelievable Truth,* Miramax, 1990.
Businessman, *Puerto Rican Mambo (Not a Musical),* 1993.
Movie producer, *All Men Are Mortal,* Warner Bros., 1995.

Television Appearances; Series:
Supporting voices, *Captain Scarlet and the Mysterons* (also known as *Revenge of the Mysterons from Mars* and *Revenge of the Mysterons*), syndicated, 1966.

Television Appearances; Movies:
Braden, *Madame Sin,* ABC, 1972.
Doc Baugh, *Cat on a Hot Tin Roof,* NBC, 1976.
Donat, *Panache,* ABC, 1976.
Theodore Roosevelt, *Eleanor and Franklin: The White House Years,* ABC, 1977.
Dr. John Watson, *Sherlock Holmes' The Sign of Four* (also known as *The Sign of Four*), 1983.
Dr. George Hyatt, *The Ted Kennedy Jr. Story,* NBC, 1986.
Newscaster, *Yuri Nosenko, KGB,* HBO, 1986.
Father Kerry, *Three Wishes for Jamie,* syndicated, 1987.
Calvin Bailey, *The Price of the Bride,* 1990.
Judge, *Doomsday Gun,* HBO, 1994.
Unnatural Pursuits, Arts and Entertainment, 1994.
Hobbs, *Little Lord Fauntleroy,* The Disney Channel, 1994.
Main gate guard, *The Colony,* ABC, 1995.

Television Appearances; Miniseries:
Diamond Jim Brady, *Lillie,* 1978.
The First Olympics: Athens 1986 (also known as *Dream One* and *The First Modern Olympics*), NBC, 1984.
Mayor, *Lace II,* ABC, 1985.

Television Appearances; Episodic:
Greg Powell, "The Prophet," *Out of the Unknown,* BBC, 1967.
Colonel Adler, "Element of Risk," *The Persuaders,* ABC, 1971.
Cavendish, "Target: Angels," *Charlie's Angels,* ABC, 1976.
Voice of Sphere, "Terminal," *Blake's 7,* 1980.
Dave, *Wish You Were Here,* CBS, 1990.
"Leftover Man," *In the Heat of the Night,* CBS, 1992.
Waterbury, "Honoria Glossop Turns Up," *Jeeves and Wooster,* 1993.
Jacob, "Faith," *Frank Stubbs Promotes,* 1994.

Also appeared in "Alien Friends," *Keep It in the Family.*

Stage Appearances:
Marcellus, Bernardo, Ghost, Gravedigger, Osirc, Fortinbras, *Fifteen Minute Hamlet,* and Birdboot, *Real Inspector Hound* (double-bill), Criterion Center Stage Right Theatre, New York City, 1992.

Also appeared in *Guys and Dolls,* London production, c. 1982.*

HENNER, Marilu 1952-

PERSONAL

Born April 6, 1952, in Chicago, IL; married Frederic Forrest (an actor), September 28, 1980 (divorced, 1982); married Rob Lieberman (a producer), 1990; children: (second marriage) Nicholas Morgan, Joseph Marlin, two stepchildren. *Education:* Attended University of Chicago.

Addresses: *Agent*—William Morris Agency, 151 El Camino Dr., Beverly Hills, CA 90212-2704. *Contact*—2101 Castilian, Los Angeles, CA 90068.

Career: Actress and producer.

Awards, Honors: Golden Globe Award nominations, best television actress in a supporting role, 1979-83, for *Taxi.*

CREDITS

Television Appearances; Series:
Elaine Nardo, *Taxi,* ABC, 1978-82, then NBC, 1982-83.
Ava Evans Newton, *Evening Shade* (also known as *Arkansas*), CBS, 1990-94.

The Legend of Prince Valiant (animated), The Family Channel, 1991.
Host, *Marilu* (talk show), syndicated, 1994-95.

Television Appearances; Movies:
Laura Griffith, *Dream House,* CBS, 1981.
Victoria Ducane, *Love with a Perfect Stranger,* Showtime, 1986.
Freddy Grand, *Grand Larceny,* Lifetime, 1988.
Samantha Flannery, *Ladykillers,* ABC, 1988.
Jackie, *Chains of Gold,* 1991.
Nancy Conn, *Fight for Justice: The Nancy Conn Story,* 1995.
Mrs. Debbie Challender, *For the Children: The Irvine Fertility Scandal* (also known as *For the Future: The Irvine Fertility Scandal*), Lifetime, 1996.
Margaret Sutter, *My Son is Innocent,* ABC, 1996.
Voice of Veronica Vreeland, *Batman & Mr. Freeze: SubZero* (animated), The WB, 1998.

Television Appearances; Miniseries:
Molly Brown, *Titanic,* CBS, 1996.

Television Appearances; Pilots:
Janet, *Off Campus,* CBS, 1977.
Ashley Walters, *Stark,* CBS, 1985.
Susan McDowell, *Channel 99,* NBC, 1988.

Television Appearances; Specials:
Celebrity interviewer, *The Celebrity Football Classic,* NBC, 1979.
Nurse Girard, "Mr. Roberts," *NBC Live Theater,* NBC, 1984.
Louise, *Grown Ups,* Showtime, 1985.
Voices That Care, Fox, 1991.
Host, *CBS All-American Thanksgiving Parade,* CBS, 1993.
Host, *Best of Taxi* (also known as *Hey Taxi*), CBS, 1994.
Disney's Most Unlikely Heroes, ABC, 1996.
Host, *We're Having a Baby!,* ABC, 1996.
Broadway '97: Launching the Tonys, PBS, 1997.
Andy Kaufman: The E! True Hollywood Story, E! Entertainment Channel, 1998.
Broadway '98: Launching the Tony Awards, PBS, 1998.
Bob Fosse: The E! True Hollywood Story, E! Entertainment Channel, 1999.

Television Appearances; Episodic:
Susu, "Great Expectations," *The Paper Chase,* CBS, 1978.
"Method Actor," *Alfred Hitchcock Presents,* NBC, 1985.
"Seductive Neighbor," *Who's the Boss?,* ABC, 1986.
Diane Wilmington, "Angela's New Best Friend," *Who's the Boss?,* ABC, 1986.
The Tonight Show, NBC, 1991.
"The Cameo Episode," *George & Leo,* CBS, 1997.
Voice of Veronica Vreeland, "Chemistry," *Batman: The Animated Series* (animated), 1998.

Television Appearances; Awards Presentations:
The 43rd Annual Primetime Emmy Awards Presentation, Fox, 1991.
The 17th Annual People's Choice Awards, CBS, 1991.
The 44th Annual Primetime Emmy Awards, Fox, 1992.
The 50th Annual Golden Globe Awards, TBS, 1993.
The 52nd Annual Golden Globe Awards, TBS, 1995.
The 1998 Creative Arts Emmy Awards, 1998.
The 52nd Annual Tony Awards, 1998.
The 25th International Emmy Awards, 1998.

Television Work; Series:
Executive producer, *Marilu* syndicated, 1994-95.
Executive producer, *Medicine Ball,* Fox, 1995.

Film Appearances:
(Film debut) Danielle, *Between the Lines,* Midwest Film, 1977.
Annette, *Blood Brothers* (also known as *A Father's Love*), Warner Bros., 1978.
Kit Conger and Sue Alabama, *Hammett,* Orion/Warner Bros., 1982.
Agnes, *The Man Who Loved Women,* Columbia, 1983.
Sister Betty, *Cannonball Run II,* Warner Bros., 1983.
Kit Conger and Sue Alabama, Hammett, 1983.
Lil, *Johnny Dangerously,* Twentieth Century-Fox, 1984.
Sally, *Perfect,* Columbia, 1984.
Miss Tracy, *Rustler's Rhapsody,* Paramount, 1985.
Trudi, *L.A. Story,* TriStar, 1991.
Belinda Blair/Flavia Brent, *Noises Off,* Buena Vista, 1992.
Jackie, *Chains of Gold,* Academy Entertainment, 1992.
Voice of angry woman at party, *Batman: Mask of the Phantasm* (animated), 1993.
Katie, *Chasers,* Warner Bros., 1994.
Mrs. Stuart While, *The Titanic Chronicles,* 1999.
Herself, *Man on the Moon,* 1999.

Stage Appearances:
Marty, *Grease,* Royale Theatre, New York City, 1972.
(Broadway debut) Donna, *Over Here!,* Shubert Theatre, New York City, 1974.

Marilu, *Pal Joey,* Circle in the Square, New York City, 1976.

Sonia Walsk, *They're Playing Our Song,* Burt Reynolds' Dinner Theatre, Jupiter, FL, 1984.

Barbara Kahn, *Social Security,* Ethel Barrymore Theatre, New York City, 1987.

Also appeared as Roxie Hart, *Chicago,* Broadway production; in *Carnal Knowledge,* Los Angeles, CA; *Super Sunday; Grown-Ups; Once upon a Mattress; The Roar of the Greasepaint, the Smell of the Crowd.*

Major Tours:

Grease, U.S. cities, 1971.

WRITINGS

Books:

By All Means Keep on Moving (autobiography), Pocket Books, 1994.

Marilu Henner's Total Health Makeover, 1998.

OTHER SOURCES

Periodicals:

Redbook, April 1993, p. 32.

WWD, October 9, 1997, p. 19.*

HERZOG, Werner 1942-

PERSONAL

Real name, Werner H. Stipetic; born September 5, 1942, in Munich (some sources say Sachrang), Germany; married Martje Grohmann (a journalistand actress), 1966 (some sources say c. 1960); children: Rudolph Amos Achmed. *Education:* Attended University of Munich, University of Pittsburgh, and Duquesne University.

Addresses: *Office*—c/o New Yorker Films, 16 West 61st St., New York, NY 10023-7606.

Career: Director, producer, writer, and actor. Werner Herzog Filmproduktion, founder, 1963; Werner Herzog Foundation, founder; staged several operas. Worked for National Aeronautics and Space Administration (NASA), 1966; also dockworker in Manchester, England; steel factory worker, parking lot attendant, and rodeo hand, Pittsburgh, PA.

Awards, Honors: Oberhausen Film Festival Prize, 1968, for *Letzte Worte;* Bundesfilmpreis Award and Silver Bear Award, best first film, both from Berlin Film Festival, Filmstrip in Silver, German Film Awards, outstanding feature film, 1968, all for *Lebenszeichen;* Bundesfilmpreis and Special Jury Prize, Cannes International Film Festival, Film Strip in Silver, German Film Awards, best shaping of a feature film, 1975, all for *Jeder fur sich und Gott gegen alle;* shared German Film Critics Prize, 1977, for *Stroszek;* Rauriser Literaturpreis, 1978, for *Vom Gehen im Eis;* Film Strip in Silver, German Film Awards, outstanding short film, 1978, for *La Soufriere;* Best Director Award, Cannes International Film Festival, 1982, British Academy of Film and Television Award nomination, best foreign language film, both for *Fitzcarraldo;* Golden Osella Award, Venice Film Festival, 1991, for *Cerro Torre: Schrei aus Stein;* International Documentary Association Award, best feature documentary, 1998, for *Little Dieter Needs to Fly* (with others).

CREDITS

Film Producer and Director, Except Where Indicated:

Herakles (short film) 1962.

Spiel im Sand (also known as *Playing in the Sand* and *Game in the Sand;* uncompleted), 1964.

Die beispiellose Verteidigung der Festung Deutschkreuz (also known as *The Unparalleled Defense of the Fortress of Deutschkreuz*), Werner Herzog Filmproduktion, 1966.

Letzte Worte (short film; also known as *Last Words*), Werner Herzog Filmproduktion, 1968.

Lebenszeichen, Werner Herzog Filmproduktion, 1968, released in the United States as *Signs of Life,* New Yorker, 1981.

Massnahmen gegen Fanatiker (also known as *Measures against Fanatics* and *Precautions Against Fanatics*), Werner Herzog Filmproduktion, 1969.

Die fliegenden Arzte von Ostafrika (documentary short film; also known as *The Flying Doctors of East Africa*), Werner Herzog Filmproduktion, 1970.

Auch Zwerge haben klein angefangen (also known as *Even Dwarfs Started Small*), New Line Cinema, 1970.

Behinderte Zukunft (documentary; also known as *Frustrated Future* and *Impeded Future*), Werner Herzog Filmproduktion, 1970.

Fata Morgana, Werner Herzog Filmproduktion, 1970.

Land des Schweigens und der Dunkelheit (documentary; also known as *Land of Silence and Darkness*), New Yorker, 1971.

Aguirre, der Zorn Gottes (also known as *Aguirre, the Wrath of God*), New Yorker, 1972.

Die grosse Ekstase des Bildschnitzers Steiner (documentary short film; also known as *The Great Ecstasy of the Sculptor Steiner* and *The Strange Ecstasy of Woodcarver Steiner*), New Yorker, 1974.

Jeder fur sich und Gott gegen alle (also known as *Every Man for Himself and God against All, The Enigma of Kaspar Hauser,* and *The Mystery of Kaspar Hauser*), Cine International/Cinema V, 1974.

How Much Wood Would a Woodchuck Chuck? (documentary short film), Werner Herzog Filmproduktion, 1976.

Mit mir will keiner spielen (short film; also known as *No One Will Play with Me*), Werner Herzog Filmproduktion, 1976.

Herz aus Glas (also known as *Heart of Glass*), Cine International Filmvertrieb, 1976.

Director, *La Soufriere* (documentary short film), New Yorker, 1977.

Stroszek, Werner Herzog Filmproduktion, 1977.

Nosferatu—Phantom der Nacht (also known as *Nosferatu, the Vampire* and *Nosferatu, Phantom of the Night*), Twentieth Century-Fox, 1979.

Werner Herzog's Woyzeck, Werner Herzog Filmproduktion, 1979.

Huie's Predigt (documentary short film; also known as *Huie's Sermon*), New Yorker, 1980.

Director, *Glaube und Wahrung* (also known as *God's Angry Man*), New Yorker, 1980.

Fitzcarraldo, New World, 1982.

Ballade vom kleinen Soldaten (also known as *Ballad of the Little Soldier*), New Yorker, 1984.

Gasherbrum—Der leuchtende Berg (documentary; also known as *The Dark Glow of the Mountains*), New Yorker, 1984.

Director, *Wo die grunen Ameisen traumen* (also known as *Where the Green Ants Dream*), Orion, 1985.

Director, *Cobra Verde,* De Laurentiis Entertainment Group, 1988.

Director, *Les Gauloises,* 1988.

Director, *Cobra Verde* (also known as *Slave Coast*), 1988.

Echos aus einem Dusteren Reich, 1990.

Director, *Schrei aus Stein* (also known as *Cerro Torre: Schrei aus Stein, Cerro Torre-Scream of Stone,* and *Scream of Stone*), 1991.

Director, *Herdsmen of the Sun* (documentary; also known as *Wodaabe-Die Hirten der Sonne.Nomaden am Sudrand der Shara*), Interama, 1991.

Lektionen in Finsternis (also known as *Lessons in Darkness*), 1992.

Echoes from a Somber Empire, 1992.

Director (with others), *Les Francais Vus Par,* 1993.

Bells from the Deep: Faith and Superstition in Russia, 1993.

Director, *Little Dieter Needs to Fly,* 1997.

Director, *Mexico,* 1999.

Film Appearances:

Geschichten vom Kubelkind, 1970.

Glass carrier, *Herz aus Glas* (also known as *Heart of Glass*), Cine International Filmvertrieb, 1976.

Narrator, *La Soufriere* (documentary short film), New Yorker, 1977.

Himself, *Was Ich Bin, Sind Meine Filme* (documentary; also known as *I Am My Films: A Portrait of Werner Herzog, I Am My Films,* and *I Am What My Films Are*), Filmwelt verleib/New Yorker, 1978.

Monk, *Nosferatu—Phantom der Nacht* (also known as *Nosferatu, the Vampire* and *Nosferatu, Phantom of the Night*), Twentieth Century-Fox, 1979.

Garlic Is As Good As Ten Mothers, Les Blank, 1980.

Himself, *Werner Herzog Eats His Shoe* (short film), Les Blank, 1980.

Burden of Dreams (documentary about the making of *Fitzcarraldo;* also known as *Die Last der Traume*), Contemporary Films Ltd., 1982.

Werner Herzog in Peru (short film), Les Blank, 1982.

Chambre 666 (documentary; also known as *Chambre 666 n'importe quand. . .* and *Room 666*), Gray City, 1982.

Narrator, *Ballade vom kleinen Soldaten* (also known as *Ballad of theLittle Soldier*), New Yorker, 1983.

The father, *Man of Flowers,* International Spectrafilm, 1984.

Himself, *Tokyo-Ga* (documentary), Filmverlag der Autoren, 1984.

Himself, *Lightning over Braddock: A Rustbowl Fantasy,* 1988.

Gemeindeschreiber Businger, *Gekauftes Gluck* (also known as *Bride of the Orien*), 1988.

Mita, *Hard to Be a God* (also known as *Es ist nicht leicht ein Gott zu sein*), 1989.

Gekauftes Gluck, 1989.

Himself, *Schneeweißrosenrot* (also known as *SnowwhiteRosered*), 1991.

Brennendes Herz (also known as *Burning Heart*), 1995.

The Night of the Film-makers, 1995.

Narrator, *Little Dieter Needs to Fly,* 1997.

Face, *What Dreams May Come,* PolyGram Filmed Entertainment, 1998.

Television Work; Specials:

Producer and director, *Lessons of Darkness* (documentary), syndicated, 1992.

Television Work; Director; Movies:

Jag Mandir: Das excentrische Privattheater des Maharadscha von Udaipur, 1991.

The Transformation of the World into Music, 1994.

Tod fuf funf Stimmen (also known as *Death for Five Voices*), 1995.

Television Appearances; Specials:

Narrator, *Lessons of Darkness* (documentary), syndicated, 1992.

Stage Work:

Directed operas in Bayreuth, Germany, Milan Scala, Italy, and Washington, DC.

WRITINGS

Screenplays:

Herakles (short) 1962.

Spiel im Sand (also known as *Playing in the Sand* and *Game in the Sand;* uncompleted), 1964.

Die beispiellose Verteidigung der Festung Deutschkreuz (also known as *The Unparalleled Defense of the Fortress of Deutschkreuz*), Werner Herzog Filmproduktion, 1966.

Lebenszeichen (based on the story "Der tolle Invalide auf dem Fort Ratonneau" by Achim von Armin; also known as *Signs of Life*), Werner Herzog Filmproduktion, 1968.

Letzte Worte (short film; also known as *Last Words*), Werner Herzog Filmproduktion, 1968.

Massnahmen gegen Fanatiker (also known as *Measures against Fanatics*), Werner Herzog Filmproduktion, 1969.

Die fliegenden Arzte von Ostafrika (documentary short film; also known as *The Flying Doctors of East Africa*), Werner Herzog Filmproduktion, 1970.

Auch Zwerge haben klein angefangen (also known as *Even Dwarfs Started Small*), New Line Cinema, 1970.

Behinderte Zukunft (documentary; also known as *Frustrated Future* and *Impeded Future*), Werner Herzog Filmproduktion, 1970.

Fata Morgana, Werner Herzog Filmproduktion, 1970.

Land des Schweigens und der Dunkelheit (documentary; also known as *Land of Silence and Darkness*), New Yorker, 1971.

Aguirre, der Zorn Gottes (also known as *Aguirre, the Wrath of God*), NewYorker, 1972 (dialogue and cutting continuity published as "Aguirre, la colere de Dieu" in *Avant-Scene du Cinema,* June 15, 1978).

Die grosse Ekstase des Bildschnitzers Steiner (documentary short film; also known as *The Great Ecstasy of the Sculptor Steiner*), New Yorker, 1974.

Jeder fur sich und Gott gegen alle (also known as *Every Man for Himself and God against All* and *The Mystery of Kaspar Hauser*), Cine International/Cinema V, 1974 (dialogue and cutting continuity published as "L'enigme de Kaspar Hauser" in *Avant-Scene du cinema,* June, 1976).

How Much Wood Would a Woodchuck Chuck? (documentary short film), Werner Herzog Filmproduktion, 1976.

(With Herbert Achternbusch) *Mit mir will keiner spielen* (short film; also known as *No One Will Play with Me*), Werner Herzog Filmproduktion, 1976.

Coauthor, *Herz aus Glas* (also known as *Heart of Glass;* based in part on Achternbusch's novel *Die Stunde des Todes*), Cine International Filmvertrieb, 1976.

La Soufriere (documentary short film), New Yorker, 1977.

Stroszek, Werner Herzog Filmproduktion, 1977 (published in *2 Filmerzahlungen,* 1979).

Nosferatu—Phantom der Nacht (also known as *Nosferatu, the Vampire* and *Nosferatu, Phantom of the Night*), Twentieth Century-Fox, 1979 (published in *2 Filmerzahlungen*), 1979.

Werner Herzog's Woyzeck, Werner Herzog Filmproduktion, 1979.

Huie's Predigt (documentary short film; also known as *Huie's Sermon*), New Yorker, 1980.

Glaube und Wahrung (also known as *God's Angry Man*), New Yorker, 1980.

Werner Herzog Eats His Shoe (short film), Les Blank, 1980.

Fitzcarraldo, New World, 1982 (published as *Fitzcarraldo: The Original Story,* translated by Martje Herzog and Alan Greenberg, Fjord Press, 1982).

Ballade vom kleinen Soldaten (also known as *Ballad of the Little Soldier*), New Yorker, 1984.

Gasherbrum—Der leuchtende Berg (documentary; also known as *The Dark Glow of the Mountains*), New Yorker, 1984.

(With Bob Ellis) *Wo die grunen Ameisen traumen* (also known as *Where the Green Ants Dream*), Orion, 1985.

Cobra Verde (also known as *Slave Coast*), De Laurentiis Entertainment Group, 1988.

Little Dieter Needs to Fly, 1997.

Television Writing:

Lektionen in Finsternis (special; also known as *Lessons in Darkness*), 1992.

Tod fur funf Stimmen (movie; also known as *Death for Five Voices*), 1995.

Film Composer:

Auch Zwerge haben klein angefangen (also known as *Even Dwarfs Started Small*), 1971.

Other:

Werner Herzog: Drehbucher I, 1977.

Werner Herzog: Drehbucher II, 1977.

Vom Gehen im Eis, 1978, translation by Alan Greenberg published as *Walking on Ice,* Tanan Press, 1980.

Sur la chemin des glaces: Munich-Paris 23.11 au 14.12 1974, 1979.

Screenplays (collection) translation by Greenberg, Tanan Press, 1980.

Also contributed of articles to film magazines.

OTHER SOURCES

Periodicals:

Interview, November, 1997, p. 88.

Journal of European Studies, September, 1996, p. 239.*

HICKS, Scott 1953-

PERSONAL

Born March 4, 1953, in Australia; raised in eastern Africa; son of a civil engineer and a homemaker; married Kerry Heyson (a creative consultant); children: two sons.

Addresses: *Agent*—Beth Swofford, Creative Artists Agency, 9830 Wilshire Blvd., Beverly Hills, CA 90212.

Career: Producer, director, and writer.

Awards, Honors: Emmy Award, outstanding individual directorial achievement, 1993, for *Submarines, Sharks of Steel: The Hidden Threat;* Jury Award for best film, Fort Lauderdale International Film Festival, Toronto Film Festival Award, best picture, Citroen Audience Award, Rotterdam International Film Festival, Directors' Week Award, Fantasporto, best director, Academy Award nominations, best director and best original screenplay (with Jan Sardi), Golden Globe Award nomination, best director of a motion picture, Writers Guild of America Screen Award nomination (with Jan Sardi), Writers Guild of America, best original screenplay written directly for the screen, and Directors' Week Award nomination, best film, Fantasporto, all 1996, British Academy of Film and Television Arts Award nomination (with Jane Scott), best film, 1997, and David Lean Award for Direction nomination, British Academy of Film and Television Arts, 1997, all for *Shine;* George Foster Peabody Broadcasting Award, for Discovery Channel documentaries.

CREDITS

Film Work:

Director and producer, *Down the Wind,* Chrysalis Films, 1975.

Assistant director, *Dawn!,* Aquataurus Film Corporation, 1978.

Assistant director, *Money Movers,* [Australia], 1978.

Production assistant, *The Irishman,* Australian Film Commission, 1978.

Assistant director, *Final Cut,* Wilgar Productions, 1980.

Assistant director, *The Club* (also known as *Players*), South Australian Film Corporation, 1980.

Director, *Freedom,* [Australia], 1982.

Director, *Call Me Mr. Brown,* Kino Film, 1986.

Director and producer, *Sebastian and the Sparrow,* Kino Film, 1989.

Director, *Shine,* Fine Line Features, 1996.

Director, *Arkansas,* 1998.

Director, *Snow Falling on Cedars,* Universal, 1998.

Television Work; Documentary Specials:

Director, *Submarines, Sharks of Steel: The Hidden Threat,* The Discovery Channel, 1993.

Director, *The Space Shuttle,* The Discovery Channel, 1994.

Producer and director, *The Ultimate Athlete: Pushing the Limit,* TheDiscovery Channel, 1996.

Television Appearances; Specials:

Inside the Academy Awards, TNT, 1997.

Television Work; Director; Music Videos:

"Don't Change," INXS, [Australia], 1982.

"Spy of Love," INXS, [Australia], 1982.

WRITINGS

Screenplays:

(With Terry Jennings) *Call Me Mr. Brown,* Kino Film, 1986.

Sebastian and the Sparrow, Kino Film, 1989.
(With Jan Sardi) *Shine,* Fine Line Features, 1996.

Teleplays; Specials:
The Space Shuttle, The Discovery Channel, 1994.

OTHER SOURCES

Periodicals:
New York Times, November 20, 1996, pp. C17, C21.
USA Today, March 24, 1997, p. 2D.*

HOBLIT, Gregory

PERSONAL

Born in Abilene, TX; son of an agent of the Federal Bureau of Investigation; married Debrah Farentino (an actress). *Education:* Studied political science at University of California, Berkeley; studied film and television at University of California, Los Angeles.

Addresses: *Agent*—Nancy Josephson, International Creative Management, 8942 Wilshire Blvd., Beverly Hills, CA 90211.

Career: Producer and director. Creative Film Management, New York City, director of television commercials, beginning in 1994. Worked as a production assistant for *The Joey Bishop Show,* 1970s; producer of talk shows for a television station in Chicago, IL; also worked as a television scriptwriter.

Member: Directors Guild of America.

Awards, Honors: Emmy Awards, best drama series, 1980, 1981, 1982, and 1983, Emmy Award nomination, best drama series, 1984, and Peabody Award, all for *Hill Street Blues;* Emmy Awards, outstanding directing in a drama series and best drama series, both 1986, Emmy Award nomination, best drama series, 1987, and Peabody Award, all for *L.A. Law;* Emmy Award, outstanding directing in a comedy series, 1988, for *Hooperman;* Directors Guild of America Award, outstanding directorial achievement in nighttime dramatic shows, 1993, for the pilot of *NYPB Blue;* Emmy Award, 1994, for *Roe vs. Wade;* shared Emmy Award, outstanding drama series, 1995, for *NYPD Blue;* other awards include Peabody Award and Annual Cable Excellence (ACE) Award, both for *The Los Altos Story,* Humanitas Award, Human Family Institute, Golden Globe Award, and People's Choice Award.

CREDITS

Television Work; Series:
Supervising producer, *Paris,* CBS, 1979.
Executive producer, *Hill Street Blues,* NBC, 1981-87.
Executive producer, *Bay City Blues,* NBC, 1983.
Co-executive producer, *L.A. Law,* NBC, 1986-94.
Producer, *Hooperman,* ABC, 1987-89.
Co-executive producer, *Cop Rock,* ABC, 1990.
Producer, *Civil Wars,* ABC, 1991-93.
Executive producer, *NYPD Blue,* ABC, 1993—.

Television Work; Pilots; Director, Unless Otherwise Noted:
Associate producer, *Dr. Strange,* CBS, 1978.
Hill Street Blues, NBC, 1981.
Bay City Blues, NBC, 1983.
L.A. Law, NBC, 1986.
Hooperman, ABC, 1987.
Cop Rock, ABC, 1990.
Civil Wars, ABC, 1991.
NYPD Blue, ABC, 1993.

Television Work; Movies:
Producer, *Vampire,* 1979.
Producer and director, *Roe vs. Wade,* NBC, 1989.
Director, *Class of '61,* ABC, 1993.

Television Work; Episodic:
Director, *NYPD Blue,* ABC, 1993 and 1994.

Other Television Work:
Associate producer, *Loose Change* (miniseries; also known as *Those Restless Years*), NBC, 1978.
Supervising producer, *Every Stray Dog and Kid* (special), NBC, 1981.

Also worked on the documentary *The Los Altos Story,* 1990.

Film Director:
Dawn Horse (documentary), 1972.
Primal Fear, Paramount, 1996.
Fallen, Warner Bros., 1998.
Frequency, New Line Cinema, 1999.

OTHER SOURCES

Periodicals:
Shoot, April 1, 1994, p. 7; March 29, 1996, p. S104.*

HOCH, Danny 1970-

PERSONAL

Born in 1970, in New York, NY. *Education:* Graduated from the High School of Performing Arts, New York City; trained for the stage at the North Carolina School of the Arts and in London, England. *Religion:* Judaism.

Addresses: *Agent*—The Gersh Agency, 130 West 42nd St., Suite 2400, New York, NY 10036.

Career: Actor and writer. New York University, New York City, performed with the Creative Arts Team for adolescents in alternative high schools and correctional institutions.

Awards, Honors: Obie Award, *Village Voice,* and Fringe First Award, Edinburgh Festival, both 1994, for *Some People;* CableACE Award nomination, 1996, for *Danny Hoch: Some People;* Sundance Writers fellow, 1996; CalArts/Alpert Award in theatre, 1998; Tennessee Williams fellow, 1999; solo theatre fellowship, National Endowment for the Arts.

CREDITS

Stage Appearances:

Pot Melting (solo show), Under One Roof Theatre Company, One Dream Theatre, New York City, 1992.

Various characters, including Tono, Kazmierczack, Floe, Doris, Cesar, Caribbean Tiger, Bill, and Madman, *Some People* (solo show), Theatre at Performance Space 122, New York City, 1993, then New York Shakespeare Festival, Public Theatre, New York City, 1994; later Stage II, Long Wharf Theatre, New Haven, CT, 1994-95.

Evolution of a Homeboy: Jails, Hospitals, and Hip-Hop (solo show), Julia Morgan Theatre, Berkeley, CA, 1997, then Public Theatre, 1998.

Sonny, *The Flattered Fifth,* New Group, 1998.

Major Tours:

Toured in the solo show *Some People,* U.S., Austrian, Cuban, and Scottish cities.

Television Appearances; Specials:

Various characters, including Tono, Kazmierczack, Floe, Doris, Cesar, Caribbean Tiger, and Bill, *Danny Hoch: Some People* (solo show), HBO, 1995.

Television Appearances; Episodic:

Edward, "Honey-Getter," *Subway Stories: Tales from the Underground,* HBO, 1997.

Film Appearances:

First robber, *His and Hers,* Alliance Independent Films, 1997.

Private Carni, *The Thin Red Line,* Twentieth Century-Fox, 1998.

WRITINGS

Solo Shows for the Stage:

Pot Melting, Under One Roof Theatre Company, One Dream Theatre, 1992.

Some People, Theatre at Performance Space 122, 1993, then New York Shakespeare Festival, Public Theatre, 1994, later Stage II, Long Wharf Theatre, 1994-95, also toured U.S., Austrian, Cuban, and Scottish cities.

Evolution of a Homeboy: Jails, Hospitals, and Hip-Hop, Julia Morgan Theatre, 1997, then Public Theatre, 1998.

Teleplays; Episodic:

"Honey-Getter," *Subway Stories: Tales from the Underground,* HBO, 1997.

Contributor to periodicals, including *Harper's Bazaar, New Theatre Review,* and *Out of Character.*

OTHER SOURCES

Periodicals:

American Theatre, July/August, 1998, p. 30.

Back Stage, November 11, 1994, p. 31.

Variety, November 3, 1997, p. 110.*

HOFFMAN, Phil
See HOFFMAN, Philip Seymour

HOFFMAN, Philip
See HOFFMAN, Philip Seymour

HOFFMAN, Philip S.
See HOFFMAN, Philip Seymour

HOFFMAN, Philip Seymour 1968-
(Phil Hoffman, Philip Hoffman, Philip S. Hoffman)

PERSONAL

Born in 1968. *Education:* Graduated from the Tisch School of the Arts, New York University.

Addresses: *Contact*—Screen Actors Guild, 5757 Wilshire Blvd., Hollywood, CA 90036.

Career: Actor. Also worked as a waiter, a lifeguard, and with children.

Member: Screen Actors Guild.

CREDITS

Film Appearances:
(As Phil Hoffman) Klutch, *Triple Bogey on a Par Five Hole,* Poe Productions, 1991.
(As Phil Hoffman) *Szuler* (also known as *Cheat*), [Poland], 1992.
(As Philip S. Hoffman) George Willis, Jr., *Scent of a Woman,* Universal, 1992.
Chris, *My New Gun,* I.R.S. Media, 1992.
(As Philip S. Hoffman) Matt, *Leap of Faith,* Paramount, 1992.
(As Philip Hoffman) Chuck, *My Boyfriend's Back* (also known as *Johnny Zombie*), Buena Vista, 1993.
(As Philip S. Hoffman) Cochran, *Money for Nothing,* Hollywood Pictures, 1993.
Wiley McCall, *Joey Breaker,* Skouras Pictures, 1993.
(As Philip S. Hoffman) Reporter, *Sliver* (also known as *Sliver—Gier der Augen*), Paramount, 1993.
Officer Raymer, *Nobody's Fool,* Paramount, 1994.
(As Philip Hoffman) Frank Hansen, *The Getaway,* Twentieth Century-Fox/Universal, 1994.
Gary, *When a Man Loves a Woman* (also known as *Significant Other* and *To Have and to Hold*), Buena Vista, 1994.
(As Philip S. Hoffman) Bernardo, Horatio, and Laertes, *The Fifteen Minute Hamlet,* Cin-Cine 19, 1995.
Young craps player, *Hard Eight* (also known as *Sydney*), Samuel Goldwyn, 1996.
Dusty, *Twister* (also known as *Catch the Wind* and *Wind Devils*), Universal/Warner Bros., 1996.
Scotty J., *Boogie Nights,* New Line Cinema, 1997.
Mitch, *Patch Adams,* Universal, 1998.
(As Phil Hoffman) Sean, *Next Stop Wonderland* (also known as *Last Train to Wonderland*), Miramax, 1998.
Brandt, *The Big Lebowski,* Gramercy Pictures, 1998.
Allen, *Happiness,* Good Machine, 1998.
Freddie Miles, *The Talented Mr. Ripley* (also known as *The Strange Mr. Ripley*), Miramax/Paramount, 1999.
Magnolia, New Line Cinema, 1999.
Flawless, Metro-Goldwyn-Mayer, 1999.

Television Appearances; Miniseries:
Joseph Plumb Martin, *Liberty! The American Revolution,* PBS, 1997.

Television Appearances; Movies:
Buck Forrester, *The Yearling,* CBS, 1994.
Duncan, *Montana,* HBO, 1998.

Television Appearances as Philip Hoffman; Episodic:
Hypnotherapist, *Law and Order,* NBC, 1990.
Hanauer, *Law and Order,* NBC, 1990.
Eddie Feldman, *Law and Order,* NBC, 1992.

Television Appearances as Philip Hoffman; Specials:
Steward and performer of songs "Into the Woods," "First Midnight," "Second Midnight," and "Ever After," *Into the Woods,* PBS, 1991.

Stage Appearances:
Earl, *Food and Shelter,* Vineyard 15th Street Theatre, New York City, 1991.
Launcelot, *The Merchant of Venice,* Goodman Theatre, Chicago, IL, 1994-95.
Greensboro (A Requiem), McCarter Theatre, Princeton, NJ, 1995-96.
RawHeadAndBloodyBones, *The Skriker,* New York Shakespeare Festival, Public/Newman Theatre, New York City, 1996.
*Shopping and F***ing,* New York Theatre Workshop, New York City, 1998.

Also appeared in *King Lear.*

Major Tours:
Appeared in touring productions, European cities.

OTHER SOURCES

Periodicals:
Back Stage West, March 12, 1998, p. 4.
Entertainment Weekly, June 26, 1998, p. 24.
Interview, February, 1999, pp. 98-101.
Los Angeles Times, April 5, 1998, pp. 28-32.*

HOGAN, Paul 1939(?)-

PERSONAL

Born October 8, 1939 (some sources say 1940), in Lightning Ridge, New South Wales, Australia; married first wife, Noelene (marriage ended); married Linda Kozlowski (an actress), May 5, 1990; children: (first marriage) Loren, Scott, Clay, Todd, Brett; (second marriage) one child.

Addresses: *Office*—c/o Australian Broadcasting Commission, 145-153 Elizabeth St., P.O. Box 9994, Sydney, Australia. *Contact*—Level 29, 133 Castlereagh Street, Sydney, N.S.W. 2000, Australia.

Career: Actor, producer, and screenwriter. JP Productions, co-founder, 1972, partner, 1972—. Appeared in television commercials for the Australian Tourist Commission, Foster's beer, and Winfield cigarettes; also worked as bridge rigger, prizefighter, construction worker, and in sales.

Awards, Honors: Named Star Presenter of the Year, *Advertising Age* Awards, 1986; Golden Globe Award, best actor in a comedy or musical, Hollywood Foreign Press Association, and Academy Award nomination, best screenplay, both 1987, for *"Crocodile" Dundee.*

CREDITS

Film Appearances:

Fatty Finn, 1980.

Michael J. "Crocodile" Dundee, *"Crocodile" Dundee,* Paramount, 1986.

Michael J. "Crocodile" Dundee, *"Crocodile" Dundee II,* Paramount, 1988.

Terry Dean, *Almost an Angel,* Paramount, 1990.

Jack, *Maniac Warriors,* AIP Home Video, 1992.

Lightning Jack Kane, *Lightning Jack* (also known as *To Be an Outlaw*), Savoy Pictures, 1994.

Porter, *Flipper,* Universal, 1996.

Film Work:

Executive producer, *"Crocodile" Dundee II,* Paramount, 1988.

Director, *The Humpty Dumpty Man,* 1989.

Executive producer, *Almost an Angel,* Paramount, 1990.

Producer, *Lightning Jack* (also known as *To Be an Outlaw*), Savoy Pictures, 1994.

Television Appearances; Specials:

Co-host, *The 59th Annual Academy Awards Presentation,* ABC, 1987.

Australia Live: Celebration of a Nation, Nine Network (Australia), 1988.

The Barbara Walters Special, ABC, 1988.

Planet Hollywood Salutes the Top 10 Comedy Movies of All-Time, 1995.

Other Television Appearances:

Host, *The Paul Hogan Show* (series), syndicated, 1981.

Pat Cleary, *ANZACS: The War Down Under* (movie), syndicated, 1987.

Shane, *Floating Away,* Showtime, 1998.

Contestant on the Australian program *New Faces;* commentator on the Australian series *A Current Affair.*

Television Work; Series:

Producer, *The Paul Hogan Show,* syndicated, 1981.

Stage Appearances:

Performed the live solo show *Paul Hogan's America,* 1991.

WRITINGS

Screenplays:

(With Ken Shade and John Cornell) *"Crocodile" Dundee,* Paramount, 1986.

(With Bret Hogan) *"Crocodile" Dundee II,* Paramount, 1988.

Vicious, SVS Films, 1988.

The Humpty Dumpty Man, 1989.

Almost an Angel, Paramount, 1990.

Lightning Jack (also known as *To Be an Outlaw*), Savoy Pictures, 1994.

Television Series:

The Paul Hogan Show, syndicated, 1981.

OTHER SOURCES

Periodicals:

People Weekly, June 13, 1988, p. 102.

Playboy, July, 1988, p. 59.*

HOLMES, Katie 1978-

PERSONAL

Original name, Kate Noelle Holmes; born December 18, 1978, in Toledo, OH; daughter of an attorney and a homemaker. *Education:* Attended Notre Dame Academy, near Toledo, OH.

Addresses: *Agent*—Creative Artists Agency, 9830 Wilshire Blvd., Beverly Hills, CA 90212.

Career: Actress.

Awards, Honors: MTV Movie Award, best breakthrough female performance, 1999, for *Disturbing Behavior;* named of one of "twenty-one hottest stars under twenty-one," *Teen People,* 1999.

CREDITS

Television Appearances; Series:
Josephine "Joey" Potter, *Dawson's Creek,* The WB, 1998—.

Television Appearances; Specials:
Dawson's Creek: Behind the Scenes, The WB, 1998.
MTV's New Year's Eve Live, MTV, 1998.
Seventeen: The Faces for Fall, The WB, 1998.

Television Appearances; Awards Presentations:
Presenter, *The 50th Emmy Awards,* 1998.
Presenter, *The 11th Annual Kids' Choice Awards,* Nickelodeon, 1998.
1998 MTV Movie Awards, MTV, 1998.
1999 MTV Movie Awards, MTV, 1999.

Television Appearances; Episodic:
The Tonight Show with Jay Leno, NBC, 1998.

Television Appearances; Music Videos:
"Got You (Where I Want You)," the Flys, 1998.
"Kiss Me," Sixpence None the Richer, 1999.

Film Appearances:
Libbets Casey, *The Ice Storm,* Twentieth Century-Fox, 1997.
Rachel Wagner, *Disturbing Behavior,* Metro-Goldwyn-Mayer, 1998.
Hannah Green, *Wonder Boys,* Paramount, 1999.
Claire Montgomery, *Go,* TriStar, 1999.
Leigh Ann Prescott, *Teaching Mrs. Tingle* (also known as *Killing Mrs. Tingle*), Dimension Films, 1999.

RECORDINGS

Albums:
(With others) *Holiday Man,* Trauma Records, 1998.

OTHER SOURCES

Periodicals:
Entertainment Weekly, June 26, 1998, p. 72.
Teen, August, 1998, p. 58.*

HUGGINS, Erica

PERSONAL

Raised in Ann Arbor, MI, and Southern California. *Education:* Hampshire College, B.A.

Addresses: *Office*—Interscope Communications, Inc., 10900 Wilshire Blvd., Suite 1400, Los Angeles, CA 90024.

Career: Producer and film editor. Interscope Communications, Los Angeles, CA, producer, 1994—.

CREDITS

Film Work:
First assistant editor, *The Sicilian,* Twentieth Century-Fox, 1987.
Assistant editor, *Hairspray,* New Line Cinema, 1988.
Assistant editor, *Cry Baby,* Universal, 1990.
Assistant editor, *Desperate Hours,* Metro-Goldwyn-Mayer, 1990.
Additional editor, *Big Girls Don't Cry . . . They Get Even* (also known as *Stepkids*), New Line Cinema, 1991.
Additional editor, *Freddy's Dead: The Final Nightmare,* New Line Cinema, 1991.
Editor, *The Gun in Betty Lou's Handbag,* Buena Vista, 1992.
Editor, *Ghost in the Machine* (also known as *Deadly Terror*), Twentieth Century-Fox, 1993.
Editor, *Serial Mom,* Savoy Pictures, 1994.
Producer, *Boys,* Buena Vista, 1996.
Producer, *Gridlock'd* (also known as *Gridlock* and *Gridlocked*), Gramercy Pictures, 1997.
Executive producer, *What Dreams May Come,* PolyGram Filmed Entertainment, 1998.
Producer (with others), *Earl Watt,* PolyGram Filmed Entertainment, 1998.
Producer (with others), *The 59-Story Crisis,* Interscope Communications, 1998.
Producer, *Democracy,* forthcoming.
Producer, *West of the Rising Sun,* forthcoming.*

HUGH-KELLY, Daniel
See KELLY, Daniel Hugh

HURLEY, Elizabeth 1965-

PERSONAL

Born June 10,1965, in Basingstoke, England; father, an army officer and mother, an elementary schoolteacher; companion of Hugh Grant (an actor). *Education:* Attended London Studio Centre.

Addresses: *Agent*—Creative Artists Agency, 9830 Wilshire Blvd., Beverly Hills, CA 90212.

Career: Actress, model, and producer; spokesperson for Estee Lauder; head developer, Simian Films, London and Los Angeles, 1994—.

Awards, Honors: Special Award, ShoWest Convention, supporting actress of the year, 1997; Blockbuster Entertainment Award, favorite actress in a comedy, 1998, for *Austin Powers: International Man of Mystery.*

CREDITS

Film Appearances:

Marietta, "Die Tote Stadt," *Aria,* Virgin Vision, 1987.
Claire Clairmont, *Rowing with the Wind* (also known as *Remando al Viento*), Viking, 1988.
Lou, *Der Skipper* (also known as *Kill Cruise* and *The Storm*), 1990.
Natalie, *The Orchid House,* 1991.
Emma Stapleton, *El Largo Invierno* (also known as *The Long Winter*), 1992.
Sabrina Ritchie, *Passenger 57,* Warner Bros., 1992.
Stephanie Lyell, *Beyond Bedlam,* 1993.
Antonio Dyer, *Mad Dogs and Englishmen* (also known as *Shameless*), 1993.
Vanessa Kensington, *Austin Powers: International Man of Mystery,* New Line Cinema, 1997.
Karen, *Dangerous Ground,* New Line Cinema, 1997.
Sandra, *Permanent Midnight,* Artisan Entertainment, 1998.
Jill, *Edtv,* Universal, 1999.
Brace Channing, *My Favorite Martian,* Buena Vista, 1999.
Vanessa Kensington, *Austin Powers: The Spy Who Shagged Me,* New Line Cinema, 1999.
The House on the Haunted Hill, Warner Bros., forthcoming.

Film Work:

Producer, *Extreme Measures,* Columbia, 1996.
Producer, *Mickey Blue Eyes,* Warner Bros., 1999.

Television Appearances; Episodic:

Julia, "Last Seen Wearing," *Inspector Morse,* Central-TV, 1988.
Vicky, "London May 1916," *The Young Indiana Jones Chronicles,* ABC, 1992.

Television Appearances; Movies:

Christina, *An Act of Will,* 1989.
Julia Latham, *Death Has a Bad Reputation,* 1990.
Cecila Harrison, *The Shamrock Conspiracy,* UPN, 1995.
Cecila Harrison, *Harrison: Cry of the City,* UPN, 1996.

Television Appearances; Specials:

Christabel Bielenberg, "Christabel," *Masterpiece Theatre,* PBS, 1989.
Rosie Japhet, "Rumpole and the Barrow Boy," *Mystery!,* PBS, 1989.
Lady Isabella Farthingdale, "Sharpe II," *Masterpiece Theatre,* PBS, 1995.
Host, *World of James Bond,* Fox, 1995.
Delilah, *Samson and Delilah* (miniseries), TNT, 1996.
Happy Birthday Elizabeth—A Celebration of Life, ABC, 1997.

Television Appearances; Awards Presentations:

Presenter, *The VH-1 Fashion Awards,* VH-1, 1996.
Presenter, *The VH-1 Fashion Awards,* VH-1, 1997.
The ShoWest Awards, 1997.

OTHER SOURCES

Periodicals:

Esquire, July, 1997, p. 60.
Harper's Bazaar, September, 1996, pp. 412-416; March, 1999, p. 366.
Interview, May, 1997, p. 42-46.
Los Angeles Magazine, September, 1998, pp. 98-103.*

I

IRONS, Jeremy 1948-

PERSONAL

Full name, Jeremy John Irons; born September 19, 1948, in Cowes, Isle of Wight, England; son of Paul Dugan and Barbara Anne (Sharpe) Irons; married first wife (marriage ended); married Sinead Moira Cusack (an actress; professional name, Sinead Cusack), March 28, 1978; children: Samuel James Brefni, Maximilian Paul Diarmiud. *Education:* Attended Sherborne School, Dorset, and Bristol Old Vic Theatre School.

Addresses: *Manager*—c/o Hutton Management, 4 Old Manor Close, Askett Bucks, HP27 9NA, England.

Career: Actor.

Member: British Actors' Equity Association, Screen Actors Guild, Actors' Equity Association.

Awards, Honors: Clarence Derwent Award, British Actors' Equity Association, best actor, 1978, for *The Rear Column;* Variety Artists of Great Britain Award and British Academy of Film and Television Arts Award nomination, both best actor, both 1981, for *The French Lieutenant's Woman;* British Academy of Film and Television Arts Award nomination, Golden Globe Award nomination, and Emmy Award nomination, best actor, limited series or special, all 1982, for *Brideshead Revisited;* Antoinette Perry Award, best actor, and Drama League Distinguished Performance Award, both 1984, for *The Real Thing;* Grammy Award nomination, spoken word or non-musical recording, 1984, for *The Real Thing;* New York Film Critics Circle Award, best actor, 1988, and Genie Award, best actor, 1989, both for *Dead Ringers;* Academy Award, best actor, 1990, and Golden Globe Award, best actor, 1991, for *Reversal of Fortune.*

CREDITS

Stage Appearances:

Simon, *Hay Fever,* Bristol Old Vic Theatre, Bristol, England, 1971.

Nick, *What the Butler Saw,* Bristol Old Vic Theatre, 1971.

Florizel, *The Winter's Tale,* Bristol Old Vic Theatre, 1971.

John the Baptist, *Godspell,* Round House Theatre, London, then Wyndham's Theatre, London, 1971.

Diary of a Madman, Act Inn Lunchtime Theatre, London, 1973.

Don Pedro, *Much Ado about Nothing,* Young Vic Theatre, London, 1974.

Mick, *The Caretaker,* Young Vic Theatre, 1974.

Petruchio, *The Taming of the Shrew,* New Shakespeare Company, Round House Theatre, 1975.

An Inspector Calls, Key Theatre, Peterborough, England, 1975.

Harry Thunder, *Wild Oats,* Royal Shakespeare Company, Aldwych Theatre, London, 1976, then Piccadilly Theatre, London, 1977.

James Jameson, *The Rear Column,* Globe Theatre, London, 1978.

Gustav Manet, *An Audience Called Edouard,* Greenwich Theatre, London, 1978.

(Broadway debut) Henry Boot, *The Real Thing,* Plymouth Theatre, 1984.

The Rover, Mermaid Theatre, London, 1986.

Leontes, *The Winter's Tale,* Royal Shakespeare Company, Royal Shakespeare Theatre, Stratford-on-Avon, England, 1986.

Richard II, Royal Shakespeare Company, Royal Shakespeare Theatre, 1986.

Film Appearances:

(Film debut) Mikhail Fokine, *Nijinsky,* Paramount, 1980.

Charles Smithson/Mike, *The French Lieutenant's Woman,* United Artists, 1981.
The Masterbuilders, 1982.
Nowak, *Moonlighting,* Universal, 1982.
Jerry, *Betrayal,* Twentieth Century-Fox, 1983.
Harold Ackland, *The Wild Duck,* Orion, 1983.
Charles Swann, *Swann in Love,* Orion, 1984.
Father Gabriel, *The Mission,* Warner Bros., 1986.
Beverly and Elliot Mantle, *Dead Ringers,* Twentieth Century-Fox, 1988.
Guy Jones, *A Chorus of Disapproval,* J&M, 1988.
Edouard Pierson, *Australia,* 1989.
Claus von Bulow, *Reversal of Fortune,* Warner Bros., 1990.
Prisoner, *Opera Zebracka,* 1991.
Title role, *Kafka,* Miramax, 1991.
Tom Crick, *Waterland,* Fine Line, 1992.
Dr. Stephen Fleming, *Damage,* New Line, 1993.
Rene Gallimard, *M. Butterfly,* Warner Bros., 1993.
Esteban Trueba, *The House of the Spirits,* Miramax, 1993.
Voice of Scar, *The Lion King* (animated), Buena Vista, 1994.
Simon, *Die Hard with a Vengeance* (also known as *Die Hard 3*), Twentieth Century-Fox, 1995.
Beyond the Clouds, 1995.
Alex Parrish, *Stealing Beauty,* Twentieth Century-Fox, 1996.
Chinese Box, Trimark Pictures, 1997.
Humbert, *Lolita,* Samuel Goldwyn Company, 1997.
Father Aramis, *The Man in the Iron Mask,* Metro-Goldwyn-Mayer, 1998.
Rupert Gould, *Longitude,* Granada Films, forthcoming.
Dungeons & Dragons, Silver Pictures, forthcoming.

Television Appearances; Miniseries:
Franz Liszt, "Notorious Woman," *Masterpiece Theatre,* PBS, 1975.
Frank Tregear, *The Pallisers,* PBS, 1977.
Charles Ryder, "Brideshead Revisited," *Great Performances,* PBS, 1982.
Voice, *The Civil War,* PBS, 1990.

Also appeared as Alex Sanderson, "Love for Lydia," *Masterpiece Theatre,* PBS.

Television Appearances; Movies:
William Smith, *Danny, the Champion of the World,* The Disney Channel, 1989.

Television Appearances; Specials:
Alex Hepburn, *The Captain's Doll,* BBC, 1982.
Voice, *Statue of Liberty,* PBS, 1985.
The Talk Show, HBO, 1986.
The Bugs Bunny/Looney Tunes All-Star Fiftieth Anniversary, CBS, 1986.
Sesame Street Special, PBS, 1988.
Larry King TNT Extra, TNT, 1991.
The Barbara Walters Special, ABC, 1991.
Odon von Horvath, "Tales from Hollywood," *American Playhouse,* PBS, 1992.
"Living Shakespeare: A Year with the RSC," *A&E Stage,* Arts and Entertainment, 1992.
Narration, "Carnival of the Animals," *A&E Stage,* Arts and Entertainment, 1992.
Host, "Placido Domingo: The Concert for Planet Earth," *Great Performances,* PBS, 1992.
Voice, *Earth and the American Dream,* HBO, 1993.
The Man, "The Dream," *Texaco Performing Acts Showcase,* Bravo, 1993.
Movie News Hot Summer Sneak Preview, CBS, 1994.
The First 100 Years: A Celebration of American Movies, HBO, 1995.
Narration, *Russia's Last Tsar,* NBC, 1996.
Hollywood & Vinyl: Disney's 101 Greatest Musical Moments, VH-1, 1998.
The Making of the Lion King, The Disney Channel, 1994.
D-Day Remembered—A Musical Tribute from the QE2, PBS, 1994.
Seekers of the Lost Treasure, 1995.

Also appeared as Otto Beck, *Langrishe Go Down,* BBC; Edward Voysey, *The Voysey Inheritance,* BBC; *Autogeddon;* and *The Dream of a Ridiculous Man.*

Television Appearances; Awards Presentations:
The 45th Annual Tony Awards, CBS, 1991.
The 49th Annual Golden Globe Awards, TBS, 1992.
The 66th Annual Academy Awards Presentation, ABC, 1994.
Presenter, *The 67th Annual Academy Awards,* 1995.
The 70th Annual Academy Awards, 1998.
Presenter, *The 56th Annual Golden Globe Awards,* 1999.

RECORDINGS

Albums:
The Real Thing (original cast recording), Nonesuch, 1984.
Henry Higgins, *My Fair Lady,* Telarc, 1989.

OTHER SOURCES

Periodicals:
Film Comment, September-October, 1988, p. 26.

Interview, June, 1990, p. 102.
Maclean's, April 11, 1994, p. 68.
Vogue, January, 1993, p. 134.*

ISAAK, Chris 1956-

PERSONAL

Born June 26, 1956, in Stockton, CA; son of Joe (a forklift driver) and Dorothy (a factory worker) Isaak. *Education:* University of Pacific, Stockton, CA, B.A. (English and communications), 1980.

Addresses: *Contact*—c/o Reprise Records, 3300 Warner Blvd., Burbank, CA 91510-4632.

Career: Musician and actor. Amateur boxer, 1976-80. With James Calvin Wilsey, Jenney Dale Johnson, and Rowland Salley, formed band Silvertone, 1981.

CREDITS

Film Appearances:
Let's Get Lost (documentary), 1988.
Arrowhead, "The Clown," *Married to the Mob,* Orion, 1988.
SWAT commander, *The Silence of the Lambs,* Orion, 1991.
Special Agent Chester Desmond, *Twin Peaks: Fire Walk With Me,* New Line Cinema, 1992.
Dean Conrad, *Little Buddha,* 1993.
Matthew Lewis, *Grace of My Heart,* Gramercy, 1996.
Uncle Bob, *That Thing You Do,* Twentieth Century-Fox, 1996.
Emerson, *Shepherd* (also known as *The End of Innocence*), New Horizons, 1999.

Television Appearances; Episodic:
Himself, "The P.A.," *The Larry Sanders Show,* HBO, 1995.
Rob Donnen, "The One After the Super Bowl," *Friends,* NBC, 1996.
Himself, "Ryan's Choice," *Melrose Place,* Fox, 1999.

Television Appearances; Specials:
Roy Orbison Tribute to Benefit the Homeless, Showtime, 1990.
Coca-Cola Pop Music "Backstage Pass to Summer," Fox, 1991.
Independence Day Concert, ABC, 1993.
"Addicted to Fame," *First Person with Maria Shriver,* NBC, 1994.
ABC's Independence Day Concert, ABC, 1995.
LIFEbeat Benefit Concert—The Beat Goes on 2, VH-1, 1995.
Ed White, *From the Earth to the Moon,* HBO, 1998.

Television Appearances; Awards Presentations:
The 38th Annual Grammy Awards, CBS, 1996.
Presenter, *Blockbuster Entertainment Awards,* 1997.
Presenter, *The 1998 VH-1 Fashion Awards,* VH-1, 1998.

RECORDINGS

Albums:
Silvertone, Warner Bros., 1985.
Chris Isaak, Warner Bros., 1987.
Heart Shaped World, Warner Bros., 1991.
San Francisco Days, Reprise, 1993.
Forever Blue, 1996.
Baja Sessions, 1996.
Speak of the Devil, Reprise, 1998.

Also recorded the soundtracks *Blue Velvet, Modern Girls, North Shore, Shag: The Movie, Married to the Mob, Wild at Heart, The Cutting Edge, Leaving Normal, A Perfect World, Tin Cup,* and *Fools Rush In;* also featured in the television movie soundtrack of *The Preppie Murder.*

OTHER SOURCES

Periodicals:
Cosmopolitan, January, 1994, pp. 64-66.
Esquire, January, 1996, pp. 112-115.
Interview, March, 1993, p. 126.
People Weekly, May 13, 1991, p. 111.
Rolling Stone, May 21, 1987; April 18, 1991.*

IZZARD, Eddie 1962-

PERSONAL

Born February 7, 1962, in Aden, Yemen; raised in England; son of an accountant. *Education:* Attended Sheffield University.

Addresses: *Agent*—William Morris Agency, 151 El Camino Dr., Beverly Hills, CA 90212-2775.

Career: Actor, comedian, screenwriter. Worked as a street performer in London.

Awards, Honors: Voted Best Live Comic, 1993.

CREDITS

Film Appearances:

Himself, *Live at the Ambassadors,* 1993.
Himself, *Unrepeatable,* 1994.
Vladimir, *The Secret Agent* (also known as *Joseph Conrad's The Secret Agent*), Fox Searchlight, 1996.
Bailey, *The Avengers,* Warner Bros., 1996.
Himself, *Definite Article,* 1996.
Jerry Divin, *Velvet Goldmine,* Miramax, 1998.
Himself, *Dress to Kill,* 1998.
Tony Pompadour, *Mystery Men,* Universal, 1999.
Troy Cabrara, *Circus,* 1999.
Gustav von Wangenheim, *Burned to Light,* Lions Gate Films, forthcoming.

Television Appearances; Movies:

Rich, *Open Fire,* 1994.
Himself, *It's Just a Ride,* 1994.
Himself, *Lust for Glorious,* 1997.
Voice, *Inspector Derrick,* 1997.

Television Appearances; Episodic:

Have I Got News for You?, BBC, 1994-96.
The End of the Year Show, 1996.
Narrator, "David Bowie," *Legends TV,* VH-1, 1996.
Himself, *Shooting Stars,* 1997.

Also appeared as himself, *Who's Line Is It Anyway?* and in *Channel Izzard,* Channel 4.

Television Appearances; Specials:

Confession, HBO, 1996.
Comic Relief VIII, HBO, 1998.

Stage Appearances:

The Cryptogram, London, 1994.
Dress to Kill, Tiffany Theater, San Francisco, CA, 1996, then Westbeth Theatre, New York City, 1998.
Glorious, Performance Space 122, New York City, 1997.
Lenny, Queens Theatre, London, 1999.

Appeared in *Edward II,* London; *One Word Improv,* 1997.

WRITINGS

One Man Shows:

Dress to Kill, 1996.
Glorious, 1997.
One Word Improv, 1997.

Screenplays:

Live at the Ambassadors, 1993.
Unrepeatable, 1994.
Definite Article, 1996.
Dress to Kill, 1998.

Television Pilots:

Cows, Channel 4, 1996.

OTHER SOURCES

Periodicals:

Artforum, September, 1998, p. 150.
Entertainment Weekly, June 26, 1998, p. 24.
Los Angeles Times, September 6, 1998, pp. 6, 65 (calendar section).
Variety, March 30, 1998, p. 171.*

J

JACKSON, Joshua 1978-

PERSONAL

Full name, Joshua Carter Jackson; born June 11, 1978, in Vancouver, British Columbia, Canada; son of Fiona (a casting director).

Addresses: *Agent*—Teresa Peters, William Morris Agency, 151 El Camino Dr., Beverly Hills, CA 90212.

Career: Actor.

CREDITS

Film Appearances:

Tom (age 11), *Crooked Hearts,* Metro-Goldwyn-Mayer, 1991.
Charlie Conway, *The Mighty Ducks* (also known as *Champions*), Buena Vista, 1992.
Charlie Conway, *D2: The Mighty Ducks* (also known as *The Mighty Ducks 2*), Buena Vista, 1994.
Mark Baker, *Andre* (also known as *Andre the Seal*), Paramount, 1994.
Billy, *Digger,* Paramount Home Video, 1995.
Joshua Black, *Magic in the Water* (also known as *Glenorky*), TriStar, 1995.
Charlie Conway, *D3: The Mighty Ducks,* Buena Vista, 1996.
Film class guy #1, *Scream 2* (also known as *Scream Again, Scream Louder,* and *Scream: The Sequel*), Dimension, 1997.
Joey, *Apt Pupil,* Paramount, 1998.
Damon Brooks, *Urban Legend* (also known as *Mixed Culture* and *Urban Legends*), Sony Pictures Entertainment, 1998.
Blaine Tuttle, *Cruel Intentions* (also known as *Cruel Inventions*), Sony Pictures Entertainment, 1998.
Gossip, Warner Bros., 1999.
(Uncredited) Pacey, *Muppets from Space,* Columbia, 1999.
Luke McNamara, *Skulls,* Universal, forthcoming.

Television Appearances; Series:

Pacey Witter, *Dawson's Creek,* The WB, 1998—.

Television Appearances; Movies:

John Prince, Jr., *Robin of Locksley,* Showtime, 1996.
Ronnie Monroe, *Ronnie & Julie,* Showtime, 1997.
Sammy, *On the Edge of Innocence,* NBC, 1997.

Television Appearances; Episodic:

Devon Taylor, "Music of the Streets," *The Outer Limits,* Showtime, 1995.
Matt Mazzilli, *Champs,* ABC, 1996.
Himself, *Vibe,* 1998.

Television Appearances; Specials:

Dawson's Creek: Behind the Scenes, The WB, 1998.
Host, *Seventeen: Faces for Fall,* The WB, 1998.

OTHER SOURCES

Periodicals:

Maclean's, April 20, 1998, p. 49.
Teen Magazine, February, 1999, p. 44.*

JACOBI, Derek 1938-

PERSONAL

Full name, Derek George Jacobi; born October 22, 1938, in Leystone, London, England; son of Alfred George (a store manager) and Daisy Gertrude (a secretary; maiden name, Masters) Jacobi. *Education:* St. John's College (M.A.; with honors), Cambridge. *Avocational interests:* Music, gardening, and reading.

Addresses: *Agent*—c/o International Creative Management, Oxford House, 76 Oxford St., London W1N 0AX, England.

Career: Actor and director. Appeared with Birmingham Repertory Theatre, 1960-63; National Repertory Theatre, 1963-71; Prospect Theatre Company, 1972, 1974, 1976-78; artistic associate, Prospect Theatre Company (later Old Vic Company), 1976-81; associate actor, Royal Shakespeare Company; vice president, National Youth Theatre, 1982—; artistic director, Chichester Festival Theatre, 1995-96.

Awards, Honors: Variety Club of Great Britain Award, Television Personality of the Year, Royal Television Society Award, and Press Guild Award, all 1976, and British Academy of Film and Television Arts Award, best actor, 1977, all for *I, Claudius;* Antoinette Perry Award nomination, best actor in a play, 1980, for *The Suicide;* Emmy Award nomination, outstanding supporting actor in a limited series or special, 1982, for *Inside the Third Reich;* Plays and Players Award, and Laurence Olivier Award, Society of West End Theatre, actor of the year, 1983, both for *Cyrano de Bergerac; Evening Standard* Award, best actor, 1983, for *Much Ado about Nothing;* Antoinette Perry Award, best actor in a play, 1985, for *Much Ado about Nothing;* Drama League of New York Distinguished Performance Award, 1985; Commander of the British Empire, 1985.

Honorary fellow, Cambridge University, 1987; Antoinette Perry Award nomination and Drama Desk Award nomination, both best actor in a play, both 1988, for *Breaking the Code;* Golden Globe Award nomination, best performance by an actor in a supporting role in a series, miniseries, or motion picture made for television, 1988, Emmy Award nomination, outstanding supporting actor in a miniseries or special, 1989, both for *The Tenth Man;* British Academy of Film and Television Arts Award nomination, best actor in a supporting role, 1992, for *Dead Again;* knighted, 1994; Edinburgh International Film Festival Award, best British performance, 1998, Golden Satellite Award nomination, best actor in a motion picture-drama, 1999, both for *Love Is the Devil; Evening Standard* Award, best actor, for *Little Dorrit.*

CREDITS

Stage Appearances:

Title role, *Hamlet,* English National Youth Theatre, Edinburgh Festival, Edinburgh, Scotland, 1955.

Title role, *Edward II,* Marlowe Society, Cambridge, England, 1959.

Henry VIII, Birmingham Repertory Theatre, Birmingham, England, 1960.

Stanley Honeybone, *One Way Pendulum,* Birmingham Repertory Theatre, 1961.

Brother Martin, *Saint Joan,* Chichester Festival Theatre, Chichester, England, 1963.

P.C. Liversedge, *The Workinghouse Donkey,* Chichester Festival Theatre, 1963.

(London debut) Laertes, *Hamlet,* National Theatre Company, Old VicTheatre, London, England, 1963.

Fellipillo, *The Royal Hunt of the Sun,* National Theatre Company, Old Vic Theatre, 1964.

Cassio, *Othello,* National Theatre Company, Old Vic Theatre, 1964.

Simon Bliss, *Hay Fever,* National Theatre Company, Old Vic Theatre, 1964.

Don John, *Much Ado about Nothing,* Chichester Festival Theatre, 1965.

Brindsley Miller, *Black Comedy,* Chichester Festival Theatre, then Old Vic Theatre, then Queen's Theatre, London, 1966.

Tusenbach, *The Three Sisters,* National Theatre Company, Old Vic Theatre, 1967.

Touchstone, *As You Like It,* National Theatre Company, Old Vic Theatre, 1967.

King of Navarre, *Love's Labour's Lost,* National Theatre Company, Old Vic Theatre, 1968.

Edward Hotel, *Macrune's Guevara,* National Theatre Company, Old Vic Theatre, 1969.

Adam, *Back to Methuselah,* National Theatre Company, Old Vic Theatre, 1969.

Myshkin, *The Idiot,* National Theatre Company, Old Vic Theatre, 1970.

Lodovico, *The White Devil,* National Theatre Company, Old Vic Theatre, 1970.

Sir Charles Mountford, *A Woman Killed with Kindness,* National Theatre Company, Old Vic Theatre, 1971.

Orestes, *Electra,* Greenwich Theatre, London, 1971.

Title role, *Oedipus Rex,* Birmingham Repertory Company, 1972.

Mr. Puff, *The Critic,* Birmingham Repertory Company, 1972.

Buckingham, *Richard III,* 1972.

Title Role, *Ivanov,* Prospect Theatre Company, London, 1972.

The Grand Tour, Goldsmith's Hall, London, 1973.

Sir Andrew Aguecheek, *Twelfth Night,* Prospect Theatre Company, Round House Theatre, London, then Prospect Theatre Company, European and Middle Eastern cities, all 1973.

Title role, *Pericles,* Prospect Theatre company, Round House Theatre, 1973, then Prospect Theatre Company, European and Middle Eastern cities, 1973, later Her Majesty's Theatre, London, 1974.
Rakitin, *A Month in the Country,* Chichester Festival Theatre, 1974.
Will Mossop, *Hobson's Choice,* Yvonne Arnaud Theatre, Guildford, England, 1975.
Rakitin, *A Month in the Country,* Prospect Theatre Company, Albery Theatre, London, 1975.
Cecil Vyse, *A Room with a View,* Prospect Theatre Company, Albery Theatre, 1975.
Pleasure and Repentance, 1975.
The Hollow Crown, 1975.
Title role, *Hamlet,* Prospect Theatre Company, Old Vic Theatre, 1977.
Octavius Caesar, *Antony and Cleopatra,* Prospect Theatre Company, Old Vic Theatre, 1977.
The Lunatic, the Lover, and the Poet, Old Vic Theatre, 1978.
The Grand Tour, Old Vic Theatre, 1978.
Thomas Mendip, *The Lady's Not for Burning,* Prospect Theatre Company, Old Vic Theatre, 1978.
Title role, *Ivanov,* Prospect Theatre Company, Old Vic Theatre, 1978.
Title role, *Hamlet,* Prospect Theatre Company, Old Vic Theatre, then Elsinore, 1979.
(Broadway debut) Semyon Semyonovich Podsekalnikov (Senya), *The Suicide,* American National Theatre and Academy, New York City, 1980.
Title role, *Peer Gynt,* 1982.
Benedick, *Much Ado about Nothing,* Royal Shakespeare Company, AldwychTheatre, London, 1982, then Gershwin Theatre, New York City, 1984.
Prospero, *The Tempest,* Royal Shakespeare Company, Aldwych Theatre, 1983.
Title role, *Cyrano de Bergerac,* Royal Shakespeare Company, Aldwych Theatre, 1983, then Gershwin Theatre, 1984.
Alan Turing, *Breaking the Code,* Haymarket Theatre, London, 1986, then Eisenhower Theatre, Kennedy Center for the Performing Arts, Washington, DC, 1986, later Neil Simon Theatre, New York City, 1987.
Title role, *Richard II,* Phoenix Theatre, London, 1988.
Title role, *Richard III,* Phoenix Theatre, 1989.
Lord Byron, *Mad, Bad, and Dangerous to Know,* Center Theatre Group, Ahmanson Theatre, Los Angeles, CA, 1989-90.
Title role, *Kean; or, Disorder and Genius,* Old Vic Theatre, 1990.
Title role, *Becket,* Haymarket Theatre, London, 1991.
Lord Byron, *Mad, Bad, and Dangerous to Know,* Ambassadors' Theatre, London, 1992.
Macbeth, Royal Shakespeare Company, Barbican Theater, London, 1993.
Title role, *Hadrian VII,* Chichester Festival Theatre, 1995.
Playing the Wife, Chichester Festival Theatre, 1995.
Uncle Vanya, Chichester Festival Theatre, 1996.

Also appeared in *Little Dorrit.*

Major Tours:
Also toured in *The Grand Tour* and *Hamlet,* Scandinavian, Australian, Japanese, and Chinese cities.

Stage Work:
Director, *Hamlet,* Phoenix Theatre, 1988.

Film Appearances:
(Film debut) Cassio, *Othello,* Warner Bros., 1965.
Paul, *Interlude,* Columbia, 1968.
Caron-Lebel's Assistant, *The Day of the Jackal,* Universal, 1973.
Gregory, *Blue Blood,* Mallard/Impact Quadrant, 1973.
Andrei, *Three Sisters,* British Lion, 1974.
Klaus Wenzer, *The Odessa File,* Columbia, 1974.
Andrei, *The Three Sisters,* American Film Theatre, 1974.
Townley, *The Medusa Touch,* Warner Bros., 1978.
Arthur Davis, *The Human Factor,* Metro-Goldwyn-Mayer/United Artists, 1979.
Martin Beck, *Mannen som gick upp i rok* (also known as *The Man Who Went Up in Smoke*), Svenska Filminstiet/Europafilm, 1980.
Daberlohn, *Charlotte,* 1981.
Voice of Nicodemus, *The Secret of NIMH* (animated), Metro-Goldwyn-Mayer/United Artists, 1982.
Kurt Limmer, *Enigma,* Embassy, 1982.
Arthur Clennam (The Clenman House), *Little Dorrit* (also known as *Little Dorrit's Story* and *Nobody's Fault*), Sands Films/Cannon, 1987.
Chorus, *Henry V,* Samuel Goldwyn, 1989.
Director, *Discovering Hamlet,* PBS Home Video, 1990.
Sir John/Mr. Frederick, *The Fool,* Barcino Barcino Films, 1990.
Franklyn Madson, *Dead Again,* Paramount, 1991.
Leper of St. Giles, 1994.
Himself, *Looking for Richard,* Twentieth Century-Fox, 1996.
Claudius, *William Shakespeare's Hamlet,* Columbia, 1996.

Francis Bacon, *Love Is the Devil,* Strand Releasing, 1998.
Father Frederick, *Basil,* Kushner-Locke, 1998.
Up at the Villa, October Films, 1999.
Joan of Arc: The Virgin Warrior, 1999.
Gracchus, *Gladiator,* DreamWorks, 1999.
Father Leonor Fouesnel, *Father Damien,* Vine International Pictures, 1999.

Television Appearances; Miniseries:
Josef Lanner, *The Strauss Family,* ABC, 1973.
Title role, *I, Claudius,* BBC, 1976, then PBS, 1977.
Lord Fawn, *The Pallisers,* PBS, 1977.
Adolf Hitler, *Inside The Third Reich,* ABC, 1982.
The Civil War (also known as *The American Civil War;* documentary), PBS, 1990.
Daedalus, "Daedalus & Icarus," *The Storyteller: Greek Myths* (also known as *Jim Henson's The Storyteller: Greek Myths*), HBO, 1990.
Voice, *Baseball* (also known as *The History of Baseball;* documentary), PBS, 1994.

Television Appearances; Movies:
Guy Burgess, *Philby, Burgess, and MacLean,* Granada TV, 1977.
Dom Claude Frollo, *The Hunchback of Notre Dame* (also known as *Hunchback*), CBS, 1982.
Title role, *Cyrano de Bergerac,* 1985.
Randal, *Circle of Deceit,* 1993.
Voice of Archibald Craven, *The Secret Garden* (animated), ABC, 1994.
General, *Witness Against Hitler,* 1996.
Basil, Romance Classics, 1998.

Television Appearances; Specials:
Don Pedro, *Much Ado About Nothing,* 1967.
Narrator, *Statue of Liberty* (documentary), PBS, 1985.
Narrator of animated sequences, *Cathedral* (documentary), PBS, 1986.
Host, *Jessye Norman's Christmas Symphony,* PBS, 1987.
Narrator, *Pyramid* (documentary), PBS, 1988.
Voice, *The Congress* (documentary), PBS, 1989.
Backstage at Masterpiece Theatre: A 20th Anniversary Special, PBS, 1991.
Narration, *Carnivore!,* Arts and Entertainment, 1992.
Narration, *Three Tenors: The Impossible Dream,* PBS, 1993.
Title role, *Cyrano de Bergerac,* Bravo, 1994.
Voice of Marcus Fabricius, *City,* 1994.
Brother Cadfael, "Cadfael," *Mystery!,* PBS, 1995.
Sister Wendy: Pains of Glass, 1995.
Narrator, *The Crown Jewels,* 1995.
Alan Turning, *Breaking the Code,* PBS, 1997.
Master of ceremonies, "San Francisco Opera Gala Celebration," *Great Performances,* PBS, 1997.
Brother Cadfael, *Cadfael 2,* PBS, 1997.
Daedalus, *Daedalus & Icarus,* HBO, 1997.
Voice, *Thomas Jefferson,* PBS, 1997.
Brother Cadfael, *Cadfael 3,* PBS, 1998.
Voiceover, *Margaret Sanger,* PBS, 1998.
Brother Cadfael, *Cadfael 4,* PBS, 1999.

Television Appearances; Episodic:
Herbert Fletcher, "Do Me a Favour," *Budgie,* LWT, 1972.
Title role, "Richard II," *The BBC Television Shakespeare,* BBC, 1978, then PBS, 1979.
"Angela's Skin," *Tales of the Unexpected,* syndicated, 1979.
Title role, "Hamlet" (also known as "Hamlet, Prince of Denmark"), *TheShakespeare Plays* (also known as *BBC Television Shakespeare*), PBS, 1980.
Archibald Craven, "The Secret Garden," *Hallmark Hall of Fame,* CBS, 1987.
Imposter, "Graham Greene's The Tenth Man," *Hallmark Hall of Fame,* CBS, 1988.
Voice, *The West,* PBS, 1996.

Also appeared as himself, *Morecambe & Wise.*

Television Appearances; Other:
Man of Straw, 1971-72.
Markheim, [Scotland], 1973.
Affairs of the Heart, 1973.
Paths of the Future, 1979.
Skin, 1979.
Burgess, *Philby, Burgess, and MacLean,* 1979-80.
A Stranger in Town, 1982.
Saint John the Divine, *The Revelation,* 1990.

Also appeared in *She Stoops to Conquer; Mr. Pye.*

Radio Appearances:
Appeared as King of France, *King Lear,* BBC.

RECORDINGS

Taped Readings:
Appeared as King of France, *King Lear,* Random House Audiobooks; recorded taped readings of *1984* for Listen for Pleasure, and *A Severed Head* for G.K. Hall.

OTHER SOURCES

Periodicals:
Advocate, October 13, 1998, p. 82.
Artforum, September, 1998, p. 136.
Interview, October, 1998, p. 80.*

JAMES, Brion 1945-

PERSONAL

Born February 20, 1945, in Beaumont, CA; married; wife's name, Maxine. *Education:* Graduated from San Diego State University, 1968.

Addresses: *Agent*—Agency for the Performing Arts, 888 Seventh Ave., Suite 602, New York, NY 10106.

Career: Actor and producer.

CREDITS

Film Appearances:

Johnny Banco, Chrysaor Film, 1967.
Hard Times (also known as *The Streetfighter*), Columbia, 1975.
Roustabout, *Treasure of Matecumbe,* Buena Vista, 1976.
Hayseed, *Harry and Walter Go to New York,* Columbia, 1976.
Tony, *Blue Sunshine,* Walt Disney Pictures, 1976.
Marathon Man, Paramount, 1976.
Bailiff, *Nickelodeon,* Columbia, 1976.
Jeff, *Corvette Summer* (also known as *The Hot One* and *Stingray*), Metro-Goldwyn-Mayer, 1978.
The Driver, Twentieth Century-Fox, 1978.
Man in bar, *The Jazz Singer,* EMI Films, 1980.
Guard at banquet, *Wholly Moses!,* Columbia, 1980.
Trapper, *Southern Comfort,* EMI Films, 1981.
Crapshooter, *The Postman Always Rings Twice,* Lorimar, 1981.
Captain Rogers, *The Ballad of Gregorio Cortez,* Embassy Pictures, 1982.
Ben Kehoe, *48 Hrs.* (also known as *48 Hours*), Paramount, 1982.
Leon, *Blade Runner,* Warner Bros., 1982.
Mr. Aitkens, *Moving Out,* Pattison Ballantyne Production, 1983.
Huey Miller, *A Breed Apart,* Orion, 1984.
Arthur Coddish, *Crimewave* (also known as *Broken Hearts and Noses* and *The XYZ Murders*), Columbia, 1985.
Karsthans, *Flesh and Blood* (also known as *Flesh+Blood* and *The Rose and the Sword*), Orion, 1985.
Stubbs, *Enemy Mine,* Twentieth Century-Fox, 1985.
Anthony Lazarus, *Armed and Dangerous,* Columbia, 1986.
Tark, *Steel Dawn,* Vestron/Silver Lion, 1987.
Stacy, *Cherry 2000,* Orion, 1987.
Glen Grunski, *The Wrong Guys,* New World Pictures, 1988.
Detective Ulner, *D.O.A.,* Buena Vista, 1988.
Streak, *Red Heat* (also known as *Dimitri*), TriStar, 1988.
The albino, *Nightmare at Noon,* Republic Pictures, 1988.
Dekker, *Dead Man Out* (also known as *Dead Man Walking*), Republic Pictures, 1989.
Krasnov, *Red Scorpion,* Shapiro Glickenhaus, 1989.
Max Jenke, *The Horror Show* (also known as *Horror House* and *House III*), United Artists, 1989.
David Allen, *Mutator* (also known as *Time of the Beast*), Prism Entertainment, 1989.
Courier and Requin, *Tango and Cash,* Warner Bros., 1989.
Reverend Munny, *Street Asylum,* Manson International, 1990.
Trucker, *Enid Is Sleeping* (also known as *Over Her Dead Body*), Vestron Pictures, 1990.
Ben Kehoe, *Another 48 Hrs.,* Paramount, 1990.
Nestor Duvalier, *Mom,* Trans World Entertainment, 1991.
Statton Jack Rose, *Wishman,* Monarch Home Video, 1991.
Wolfgang "Wolf" Friedman, *Ultimate Desires* (also known as *Beyond the Silhouette*), North American Releasing, 1992.
Joel Levison, *The Player,* Fine Line Features, 1992.
Neila, *Time Runner* (also known as *In Exile*), Excalibur Pictures, 1993.
Detective Eddie Eiler, *Striking Distance,* Columbia, 1993.
Martiz, *Nemesis,* Imperial Entertainment, 1993.
Jack Porter, *Future Shock,* Hemdale Home Video, 1993.
Professor Tanzer, *Frogtown II* (also known as *Return to Frogtown*), York Home Video, 1993.
Brown, *Brain Smasher . . . a Love Story* (also known as *The Bouncer and the Lady* and *Brainsmasher: A Love Story*), Vidmark Entertainment, 1993.
Uncredited role, *Spitfire,* Trimark Pictures, 1994.
Ben McCarthy, *The Soft Kill,* Dream Entertainment, 1994.
Assistant principal, *Showdown,* 1994.
Dr. Hampton, *Scanner Cop,* Republic Films, 1994.
Cyrus, *Savage Land,* Motion Picture Village, 1994.
Salvador Dali and Sam, *Pterodactyl Woman from Beverly Hills,* Experimental Pictures/Troma Team Video, 1994.
Simon Alexander, *Hong Kong '97,* Trimark Pictures, 1994.
Sheriff Rudy Morgan, *F.T.W.* (also known as *The Last Ride*), Nu Image Films, 1994.

Buckner, *The Dark,* Imperial Entertainment, 1994.
Big Teddy, *Cabin Boy,* Buena Vista, 1994.
Jim Wexler, *Art Deco Detective,* Trident Releasing, 1994.
Bernie King, *Radioland Murders,* Universal, 1994.
General J. W. Quantrell, *Steel Frontier,* P. M. Entertainment Group, 1995.
Sheriff Gordon, *The Nature of the Beast* (also known as *The Hatchet Man*), New Line Cinema, 1995.
Warden Walker, *Malevolence,* Ajv Productions, 1995.
Stavinski, *Evil Obsession,* Century Film Partners, 1995.
Lynwood, *Dominion,* Prism Pictures, 1995.
Sam Horton, *Precious Find,* Republic Pictures, 1996.
Marco Polo: Haperek Ha'aharon (also known as *Marco Polo* and *Marco Polo: The Missing Chapter*), Canamedia, 1996.
Dr. Vincent Garret, *The Killing Jar,* Curb Entertainment, 1996.
Billy Lone Bear, 1996.
Oris, *American Strays,* A-pix Entertainment, 1996.
Captain Hilton, *The Underground,* P. M. Entertainment Group, 1997.
General Munro, *The Fifth Element* (also known as *The 5th Element* and *Le cinquieme element*), Columbia/TriStar, 1997.
Deadly Ransom, Deadly Ransom Productions, 1997.
Shoe, *The Thief and the Stripper,* 1998.
Goering, *Snide and Prejudice,* Bombastic Pictures, 1998.
Haywood Cathcart, *Brown's Requiem,* Artist View Entertainment, 1998.
Card shark, *Border to Border,* Stage 15 Productions, 1998.
Black Sea 213, Playboy Entertainment Group, 1998.
Captain, *In God's Hands,* TriStar, 1998.
Moench, *Kai Rabe gegen die Vatikankiller* (also known as *Kai Rabe vs. the Vatican Killers*), 1998.
The Operator, Operator Films, 1999.
Renault, *Farewell, My Love,* Win's Entertainment, 1999.
Trent, *Arthur's Quest,* 1999.
Sheriff Foulkes, *Hunter's Moon,* Monarch Home Video, 1999.

Film Work:
Associate producer, *Pterodactyl Woman from Beverly Hills,* Experimental Pictures/Troma Team Video, 1994.

Television Appearances; Series:
Ollie Mathers, *The Marshal,* ABC, 1995.

Television Appearances; Miniseries:
Reece, *Kenny Rogers as the Gambler: The Adventure Continues* (also known as *The Gambler II*), CBS, 1983.

Television Appearances; Movies:
Mrs. Sundance, ABC, 1974.
The Kansas City Massacre, ABC, 1975.
Ben Jones, *The Invasion of Johnson County,* NBC, 1976.
Guard, *KISS Meets the Phantom of the Park* (also known as *Attack of the Phantoms* and *KISS in Attack of the Phantoms*), NBC, 1978.
Clyde Boyer, *Flying High,* CBS, 1978.
Willy, *Conquest of the Earth,* 1980.
Eddie Rhodes, *Trouble in High Timber Country,* ABC, 1980.
Turkey Jones, *Killing at Hell's Gate* (also known as *Hell and HighWater*), CBS, 1981.
Bobby Boy Burns, *Hear No Evil,* CBS, 1982.
Alien leader, *The Annihilator,* NBC, 1986.
Andre, *Love among Thieves* (also known as *Here a Thief, There a Thief* and *King of a Lady*), ABC, 1987.
Grimes, *Desperado: The Outlaw Wars,* NBC, 1989.
Tom McKay, *Black Magic,* Showtime, 1992.
Bruce Munster, *Overkill: The Aileen Wuornos Story,* CBS, 1992.
Jake Walker, *Rio Diablo* (also known as *Devil's River*), CBS, 1993.
Agent Jimmy Bivens, *Precious Victims,* CBS, 1993.
Jared, "Knight Rider 2010," *Action Pack,* syndicated, 1994.
Ron Cochran, *The Companion,* USA Network, 1994.
Terminal Virus, Showtime, 1995.
Larry Walker, *Sketch Artist II: Hands That See* (also known as *A Feel for Murder* and *Sketch Artist II*), Showtime, 1995.
Nassim, *Cyberjack* (also known as *Virtual Assassin*), The Sci-Fi Channel, 1995.
Chairman, *Assault on Dome 4* (also known as *Chase Morran*), The Sci-Fi Channel, 1996.
Emery Ryker, *Back in Business* (also known as *Heart of Stone*), HBO, 1997.
Donald, *Bombshell,* The Sci-Fi Channel, 1997.
General, *Men in White* (also known as *National Lampoon's Men in White*), 1998.

Television Appearances; Specials:
The McLean Stevenson Show, NBC, 1975.

Television Appearances; Episodic:
Henry Ferris, Jr., "The Birthday," *The Waltons,* CBS, 1974.

Ackerman, "Drive, Lady, Drive" (two parts), *CHiPs,* NBC, 1979.
Monk, "Bomb Run," *CHiPs,* NBC, 1981.
Amos, "A Faraway Cry," *Little House on the Prairie,* NBC, 1982.
Jenkins, "Big Daddy," *The Dukes of Hazzard,* CBS, 1982.
"The Taxicab Wars," *The A Team,* NBC, 1983.
Captain Slater, "Cool Hands, Luke and Bo," *The Dukes of Hazzard,* CBS, 1984.
Plout, "A Lease with an Option to Die," *The A Team,* NBC, 1985.
Lynch, *Downtown,* CBS, 1986.
Felix, "If I Had a Little Hammer," *Sledge Hammer!,* ABC, 1986.
Glock, "The Author," *Matlock,* NBC, 1987.
"Renegade," *Hunter,* NBC, 1988.
Edward Reese, "Borrasca," *Miami Vice,* NBC, 1988.
"Fall from Grace," *The Young Riders,* ABC, 1990.
Dixon (lumberjack's boss), "Split Second," *Tales from the Crypt,* HBO, 1991.
Thomas Duffy, "Under Suspicion," *Hunter,* NBC, 1991.
Tommy Testeroni, *Johnny Bago,* CBS, 1993.
Solomon Box, *M.A.N.T.I.S.* (also known as *MANTIS*), Fox, 1994.
Rupert Tarlow, "T.K.O.," *Silk Stalkings,* USA Network, 1994.
Armand Thorne/John Durgan, "The Cross of St. Antoine," *Highlander,* syndicated, 1994.
Voice characterizations of Rudy Jones/the parasite, "Feeding Time," *Superman* (animated), The WB, 1996.
Warren Chapel, *The Sentinel,* UPN, 1997.
Rafer Cobb, *Walker, Texas Ranger,* CBS, 1997.
Stuart James, "One Day Out West," *The Magnificent Seven* (also known as *The Magnificent Seven: The Series*), CBS, 1998.
Sheriff Bowman, "Luminary," *Millennium,* Fox, 1998.
"Justice," *Vengeance Unlimited* (also known as *Mr. Chapel*), ABC, 1998.
Stuart James, "The New Law," *The Magnificent Seven* (also known as *The Magnificent Seven: The Series*), CBS, 1999.

Appeared as Eli Starke in "Moody River," *Renegade,* syndicated; and as Don Merrill in "Model Dearest," *Sledge Hammer!,* ABC; also appeared in episodes of *Benson,* ABC; *Cagney and Lacey,* CBS; *Dynasty,* ABC; *Quincy, M.E.* (also known as *Quincy*), NBC; and *The Rockford Files,* NBC.

Television Appearances; Pilots:
T-Bone, *Goober and the Truckers' Paradise,* CBS, 1978.
Shug, *Joshua's World,* CBS, 1980.
Breyer, *Lone Star,* NBC, 1983.

Stage Appearances:
Appeared in *The Basic Training of Pavlo Hummell, George Washington Slept Here, Lady Windermere's Fan, Long Day's Journey into Night, Mother Courage, Picnic, Spec,* and *West Side Story.*

RECORDINGS

Video Games:
Voice of Leon, *Blade Runner,* Virgin Interactive Entertainment, 1997.*

JAMES, Sid 1913-1976
(Sidney James, Sydney James)

PERSONAL

Real name, Solly Cohen; born May 8, 1913, in Johannesburg, South Africa; died of a heart attack, April 26, 1976, in Sunderlan, England. *Avocational interests:* Gambling.

Career: Actor. Made stage debut at 10. Before becoming an actor, James worked as a diamond cutter and polisher, coal heaver, stevedore, amateur boxer, ladies hairdresser, singer, and dancer. *Military service:* British Army, anti-tank corps, World War II; lieutenant.

CREDITS

Film Appearances:
Eddie Clinton, *Black Memory,* Ambassador, 1947.
Nixon, *Night Beat,* British Lion, 1948.
Ted/Barman, *No Orchids for Miss Blandish,* Alliance, 1948.
Freddy Evans, *Paper Orchid,* Columbia, 1949.
Murdin, *Give Us This Day* (also known as *Salt and the Devil* and *Salt to the Devil*), Eagle-Lion/Rank, 1949.
Knucksie, *The Small Back Room* (also known as *Hour of Glory*), British Lion, 1949.
Rowton, *Once a Jolly Swagman* (also known as *Maniacs on Wheels*), International Releasing, 1950.
Joe Clarence, *Last Holiday,* Stratford/Watergate, 1950.
Henry Clavering/Hodson, *The Man in Black,* Exclusive, 1950.
Carlo, *The Lady Craved Excitement,* Exclusive, 1950.

Sergeant in storeroom, *The Magic Box,* British Lion, 1951.

Bookmaker, *The Galloping Major,* IFD, 1951.

John C. Moody, *Talk of a Million* (also known as *You Can't Beat the Irish*), Stratford, 1951.

Eric Hace, *Time Gentleman Please!* (also known as *Nothing to Lose*), Mayer/Kingsley, 1952.

Sidney, *Miss Robin Hood,* Union, 1952.

(As Sidney James) Lackery, *The Lavender Hill Mob,* Universal, 1952.

Sergeant Brodie, *I Believe in You,* Universal, 1952.

Danny Marks, *Emergency Call* (also known as *The Hundred Hour Hunt* and *Emergency!*), Nettleford, 1952.

Bernardo, *The Assassin* (also known as *El Alamein* and *Venetian Bird*), United Artists, 1952.

Taxi Driver, *Father's Doing Fine,* ABP, 1952.

Ned Hardy, *The Gift Horse* (also known as *Glory at Sea*), Independent, 1952.

Barrow Boy, *The Yellow Balloon,* Allied Artists, 1953.

(As Sidney James) Sid Baden, *The Weak and the Wicked,* Allied Artists, 1953.

(As Sidney James) Hawkins, *The Titfield Thunderbolt,* Universal, 1953.

Mr. Spencer, *The Frightened Bride* (also known as *The Tall Headlines*), Grand National, 1953.

Sharkey, *The Flanagan Boy* (also known as *Bad Blonde*), Lippert, 1953.

Superintendent Williams, *Park Plaza 605* (also known as *Norman Conquest*), Lippert, 1953.

Sergeant, *Coshy Boy* (also known as *The Slasher*), Lippert, 1953.

Fennimore Hunt, *The Wedding of Lilli Marlene,* Monarch, 1953.

Hank Hanlon, *Is Your Honeymoon Really Necessary?,* Adelphi, 1953.

Malta Story, United Artists, 1954.

Harry, *The Rainbow Jacket,* General Films, 1954.

Beverly Forrest, *Heat Wave* (also known as *The House Across the Lake*), Lippert, 1954.

The Foreman, *For Better, For Worse* (also known as *Cocktails in the Kitchen*), Stratford, 1954.

Charlie Badger, *Crest of the Wave* (also known as *Seagulls Over Sorrento*), Metro-Goldwyn-Mayer, 1954.

Parkinson, *Father Brown* (also known as *The Detective*), Columbia, 1954.

Benny, *The Belles of St. Trinians,* London Film, 1954.

Gino Rossi, *Escape by Night,* Eros, 1954.

Watchman, *The Crowded Day,* Adelphi, 1954.

Honest Sid, *Aunt Clara,* British Lion, 1954.

Mr. Hobson, *Will Any Gentleman?,* Stratford, 1955.

Lew Beeson, *Lady Godiva Rides Again,* Carroll, 1955.

Banky, *Joe MacBeth,* Columbia, 1955.

Tony Lewis, *The Glass Cage* (also known as *The Glass Tomb*), Lippert, 1955.

Ice Berg, *A Kid for Two Farthings,* Lopert, 1955.

Adams, *The Square Ring,* Republic, 1955.

Man in Street, *The Deep Blue Sea,* Twentieth Century-Fox, 1955.

Manager, *A Yank in Ermine,* Monarch, 1955.

Paul, *The Iron Petticoat* (also known as *Not for Money*), Metro-Goldwyn-Mayer, 1956.

Barney West, *The Extra Day,* British Lion, 1956.

Flash Harry, *Dry Rot,* British Lion, 1956.

(As Sidney James) Snake charmer, *Trapeze,* United Artists, 1956.

Harry Mason, *It's a Great Day,* Grove/Butchers, 1956.

Frank Allen, *Wicked as They Come* (also known as *Portrait in Smoke*), Columbia, 1956.

Black Jake, *Ramsbottom Rides Again,* British Lion, 1956.

Mr. Pritchett, *John and Julie,* British Lion, 1957.

Gambler, *Out of the Clouds,* Rank, 1957.

Ryan, *The Story of Esther Costello* (also known as *The Golden Virgin*), Columbia, 1957.

Mr. Hogg, *The Smallest Show on Earth* (also known as *Big Time Operators*), Times, 1957.

Jimmy Hall, *Quatermass II* (also known as *Enemy from Space*), United Artists, 1957.

Mr. Johnson, *A King in New York,* Archway, 1957.

Timid Driver, *Campbell's Kingdom,* Rank, 1957.

Joe, *Interpol* (also known as *Pickup Alley*), Columbia, 1957.

Luke, *The Shiralee,* Metro-Goldwyn-Mayer, 1957.

The Drunk, *The Sheriff of Fractured Jaw,* Twentieth Century-Fox, 1958.

Porter, YMCA, *I Was Monty's Double* (also known as *Hell, Heaven or Hoboken*), National, 1958.

Dusty, *Hell Drivers* (also known as *Hard Drivers*), Rank, 1958.

Jake Klein, *Another Time, Another Place,* Paramount, 1958.

Franklin, *The Man Inside,* Columbia, 1958.

Chief Petty Officer Thorpe, *The Silent Enemy,* Universal, 1958.

Next to No Time, Show, 1958.

Bert Bennett, *Desert Mice,* Rank, 1959.

(As Sidney James) Perce, *The Thirty-Nine Steps* (also known as *The 39 Steps*), Twentieth Century-Fox, 1959.

Ed Waggermeyer, *Orders Are Orders,* British Lion, 1959.

Sid, *Too Many Crooks,* Lopert, 1959.

Herbie, *Idol on Parade,* Columbia, 1959.

Chief Petty Officer Mundy, *Watch Your Stern,* Magna, 1960.

Cadena, *Tommy the Toreador,* Warner Bros., 1960.

Sergeant Frank Wilkins, *Carry on Constable,* Anglo-Amalgamated, 1960.
Sammy Gatt, *And the Same to You,* Monarch, 1960.
Police Constable Edwards, *Upstairs and Downstairs,* Twentieth Century-Fox, 1961.
Harry, *What a Whopper!,* Regal, 1961.
Sid, *Raising the Wind* (also known as *Roommates*), Harts-Lion, 1961.
Alphonse O'Reilly, *The Pure Hell of St. Trinians,* British Lion, 1961.
Sid Randall, *Double Bunk,* British Lion, 1961.
Bert Handy, *Carry on Regardless,* Anglo-Amalgamated, 1961.
Richie Launder, *The Green Helmet,* Metro-Goldwyn-Mayer, 1961.
Cafe Patron, *A Weekend with Lulu,* Columbia, 1962.
Syd Butler, *No Place Like Homicide!* (also known as *What a Carve Up!*), Embassy, 1962.
Captain Crowther, *Carry on Cruising,* Anglo-Amalgamated, 1962.
We Joined the Navy, Warner Bros., 1962.
Charlie, *Carry on Cabby* (also known as *Carry on Taxi* and *Call Me a Cab*), Warner Bros., 1963.
Mark Anthony, *Carry on Cleo,* Warner Bros., 1964.
(As Sydney James) "Butlin" Judge, *The Beauty Jungle* (also known as *Contest Girl*), Rank, 1964.
The Rumpo Kid, *Carry on Cowboy* (also known as *The Rumpo Kid*), Warner Bros., 1965.
Sid Gibson, *Make Mine a Million,* Schoenfeld, 1965.
George the Brain, *The Big Job,* Warner Pathe, 1965.
Mortuary Attendant, *Where the Bullets Fly,* Embassy, 1966.
Sir Rodney Ffing, *Don't Lose Your Head* (also known as *Carry On: Don't Lose Your Head* and *Carry on Pimpernel*), Rank, 1966.
Arabesque, Universal, 1966.
Sid Marks, *Three Hats for Lisa,* Warner Bros., 1966.
Charlie Roper, *Carry on Doctor,* Rank, 1967.
Sir Sidney Ruff-Diamond, *Carry On Up the Khyber* (also known as *Carry on Gunga Din*), Rank, 1968.
(As Sidney James) Sid Boggle, *Carry on Camping,* Rank, 1969.
Gladstone Screwer, *Carry On Again, Doctor,* Rank, 1969.
Billy Boosey, *Carry On Up the Jungle* (also known as *Carry On Up the Congo* and *Carry On Jungleboy*), Rank, 1970.
Sidney Bliss, *Carry on Loving,* Rank, 1970.
Blind Man, *Tokoloshe,* 1971.
King Henry VIII, *Carry on Henry* (also known as *Carry On Henry VIII*), Rank/American International Pictures, 1971.
Sid Pummer, *Carry on at Your Convenience* (also known as *Carry on Round the Bend*), Rank, 1971.
Sid Carter, *Carry on Matron,* Rank, 1972.
Sid Abbot, *Bless This House,* Rank, 1972.
Sidney Fiddler, *Carry On Girls,* Rank, 1973.
Vic Flange, *Carry on Abroad* (also known as *A Mad Holiday!*), Rank, 1973.
Dick Turpin/Reverend Flasher, *Carry on Dick,* Rank, 1974.

Television Appearances; Series:
Hildy Johnson, *The Front Page,* BBC, 1948.
Sharkey Morrison, *Kid Flanagan,* BBC, 1948.
Sidney, *Hancock's Half Hour,* BBC, 1956-60.
Citizen James, BBC, 1960-62.
Sid Stone, *Taxi!,* BBC, 1963-64.
George Russell, *George and the Dragon,* ATV, 1966-68.
Sid Turner, *Two in Clover,* Thames TV, 1969-70.
Sid Abbot, *Bless This House,* Thames TV, 1971-76.
Carry on Laughing, ATV, 1975.

Television Appearances; Specials:
Carry On Christmas, Thames TV, 1969.
Carry On Again Christmas, Thames TV, 1970.

Radio Appearances:
Hancock's Half Hour, 1954-59.

OTHER SOURCES

Books:
Goodwin, Cliff, *Sid James,* Century Publishing, 1995.*

JAMES, Sidney
See JAMES, Sid

JAMES, Sydney
See JAMES, Sid

JARRE, Maurice 1924-

PERSONAL

Full name, Maurice Alexis Jarre; born September 13, 1924, in Lyon, France; son of Andre and Gabrielle (Boullou) Jarre; married France Pejot, 1946 (marriage ended); married Dany Saval (an actress), January 30, 1965 (divorced); married Laura Devon, December

30, 1967 (divorced); married Khong Fui Fong, December 6, 1984; children: (first marriage) Jean-Michel (a composer); (second marriage) Stephanie. *Education:* Studied at Conservatoire National Superieur de Musique, Sorbonne, University of Paris.

Addresses: *Contact*—c/o Paul Kohner, Inc., 9169 West Sunset Blvd., Hollywood, CA 90069-3129.

Career: Composer and conductor. Radiodiffusion Francaise, musician, 1946-50; Theatre National Populaire, director of music, 1950-63. Conducted several orchestras, including London Philharmonic Orchestra, Japan Philharmonic, Osaka Symphonic Orchestra, Quebec Symphonic Orchestra, Central Symphony Orchestra of the Chinese People's Republic, Symphony Orchestra of Madrid, Los Angeles Philharmonic, and Pacifico Symphony of Chile. Composer for stage productions by Jean Louis Barrault's theatre company, Paris, France, for four years. *Military service:* Served in the French Army, World War II.

Awards, Honors: Prix Italia, 1955 and 1962; Academy Award, best original score, 1962, for *Lawrence of Arabia;* Grand Prix de Disque, Academie Charles Cros, 1962; Academy Award nomination, best music, scoring of music, adaptation or treatment, 1964, for *Les Dimanches de ville d'Avray;* Academy Award, best original score, Grammy Award, best original motion picture or television show score, National Academy of Recording Arts and Sciences, and Golden Globe Award, best original score, all 1965, for *Dr. Zhivago;* Golden Globe Award nomination, best original score, 1967, for *Paris Brule-t-Il?;* Academy Award nomination (with others), best music—song, and Golden Globe Award nomination, best original song, both 1973, for "Marmalade, Molasses & Honey," from *The Life and Times of Judge Roy Bean;* Golden Globe Award nomination, best original score, 1976, for *The Man Who Would Be King;* Academy Award nomination, best original score, 1978, for *The Message;* Academy Award, best original score, and Golden Globe Award, both 1984, and British Academy of Film and Television Arts Award nomination, 1986, all for *A Passage to India;* British Academy of Film and Television Arts Award, best score, 1985, Golden Globe Award nomination, best original score, and Academy Award nomination, best original score, both 1986, for *Witness;* American Cinema Editors Award, 1986, for *Apology;* Golden Globe Award nomination, best original score, 1987, for *The Mosquito Coast;* Golden Globe Award, best original motion picture score, 1988, and Academy Award nomination, best original score, 1989, both for *Gorillas in the Mist;* British Academy of Film and Television Arts Award, best original film score, 1990, for *Dead Poet's Society;* Academy Award nomination, best original score, 1991, for *Ghost;* Golden Globe Award, best original score, 1996, for *A Walk in the Clouds;* Sydney Film Critics Circle Award, for *The Year of Living Dangerously;* Japanese Film Awards, for *Ryan's Daughter* and *Ghost;* award from American Society of Composers, Authors, and Publishers, for *Fatal Attraction;* People's Choice Award, for *The Tin Drum;* Cesar Award pour l'ensemble de sa carriere; Sept d'Or pour l'ensemble de sa carriere; Harriet Cohen Medal of London; officer, French Legion of Honor; commander, French Order of Arts and Letters.

CREDITS

Film Work; Music Director:

The Damned, Warner Bros., 1969.
The Extraordinary Seaman, Metro-Goldwyn-Mayer, 1969.
Topaz, Universal, 1969.
El Condor, National General, 1970.
The Man Who Would Be King, Allied Artists, 1975.
Shout at the Devil, American International, 1976.
March or Die, Columbia, 1977.
The Magician of Lublin (also known as *Der Magier* and *Ha-Kosem Mi'Lublin*), Cannon, 1979.
Lion of the Desert (also known as *Omar Mukhtar: Lion of the Desert*), United Film Distributors, 1980.
Resurrection, Universal, 1980.
The Last Flight of Noah's Ark, Buena Vista, 1980.
Young Doctors in Love, Twentieth Century-Fox, 1982.
Top Secret!, Paramount, 1984.

Film Work; Musical Conductor:

The Big Gamble, Twentieth Century-Fox, 1961.
Behold a Pale Horse, Columbia, 1964.
The Train (also known as *Le Train* and *Il Treno*), United Artists, 1964.
Dr. Zhivago, Metro-Goldwyn-Mayer, 1965.
Is Paris Burning? (also known as *Paris Brule-t-Il?*), Paramount, 1966.
Gambit, Universal, 1966.
Five Card Stud, Paramount, 1968.
The Fixer, Metro-Goldwyn-Mayer, 1968.
The Only Game in Town, Twentieth Century-Fox, 1970.
Ryan's Daughter, Metro-Goldwyn-Mayer, 1970.
Pope Joan (also known as *The Devil's Imposter*), Columbia, 1972.

The Last Tycoon, Paramount, 1976.
Firefox, Warner Bros., 1982.
A Passage to India, Columbia, 1984.
Mad Max, Beyond Thunderdome (also known as *Mad Max 3*), Warner Bros., 1985.
Enemy Mine, Twentieth Century-Fox, 1985.
Tai-Pan, De Laurentiis Entertainment Group, 1986.
Moon over Parador, Universal, 1988.
Chances Are, TriStar, 1989.
Prancer, Orion, 1989.
Only the Lonely, Twentieth Century-Fox, 1991.
A Walk in the Clouds, Twentieth Century-Fox, 1995.

Film Work; Music Supervisor:
The Mosquito Coast, Warner Bros., 1986.
Gaby—A True Story, TriStar, 1987.

Film Work; Orchestrator:
Fatal Attraction (also known as *Diversion*), Paramount, 1987.
Ghost, Paramount, 1990.

Television Work:
Music conductor, *Jesus of Nazareth* (miniseries; also known as *Gesu di Nazareth*), NBC, 1977.
Music director, *Shogun* (miniseries; also known as *James Clavell's Shogun*), NBC, 1980.
Producer and music conductor, *Lean by Jarre* (special), PBS, 1993.

Television Appearances:
Lean by Jarre (special), PBS, 1993.
Doctor Zhivago: The Making of a Russian Epic, PBS, 1995.

WRITINGS

Film Scores:
Hotel des Invalides, 1952.
Tout la Memoire du Monde, 1956.
La Theatre National Populaire, 1956.
Sur la Pont d'Avignon, 1956.
Le Feu aux Poudres (also known as *X3, Operazione Dinamite*), 1957.
La Tete contre les Murs (also known as *The Keepers*), 1958.
Le Bel Indifferent, 1958.
Crack in the Mirror, Twentieth Century-Fox, 1959.
Eyes without a Face (also known as *The Horror Chamber of Dr. Faustus, House of Dr. Rasanoff,* and *Les Yeux sans Visage*), 1959.
Les Dragеurs (also known as *The Chasers* and *The Dredgers*), 1959.
Vous N'avez Rien a Declarer?, 1959.
The Big Gamble, Twentieth Century-Fox, 1960.
La Main Chaude (also known as *La Mano Calda*), 1960.
Les Etoiles de Midi, 1960.
La Corde Raide, 1960.
Recours en Grace (also known as *Tra Due Donne*), 1960.
The Witnesses, 1961.
Le Temps du Ghetto, 1961.
Spotlight on Murder, 1961.
Sun in Your Eyes (also known as *Le Soleil dans l'Oeil*), 1961.
Pleins Feux sur l'Assassin, 1961.
Le President (also known as *Il Presidente*), 1961.
Sundays and Cybele (also known as *Cybele, Cybele ou les Dimanches de Ville d'Avray,* and *Les Dimanches de Ville d'Avray*), Davis-Royal/Columbia, 1962.
The Longest Day, Twentieth Century-Fox, 1962.
Lawrence of Arabia, Columbia, 1962.
(And song "I'm Gonna Spread My Wings"), *Gambit,* Universal, 1962.
Therese Desqueyroux (also known as *Therese*), Pathe Contemporary, 1962.
L'Oiseau de Paradis (also known as *Dragon Sky*), Speva/Alliance/F5, 1962.
The Animals, 1963.
To Die in Madrid (also known as *Mourir a Madrid*), 1963.
Judex (also known as *L'Uomo in Nero*), Continental, 1964.
Behold A Pale Horse, Columbia, 1964.
Weekend at Dunkirk (also known as *Week-End a Zuydcoote*), Twentieth Century-Fox, 1964.
The Train (also known as *Le Train* and *Il Treno*), United Artists, 1964.
The Collector, Columbia, 1965.
Dr. Zhivago, Metro-Goldwyn-Mayer, 1965.
Is Paris Burning? (also known as *Paris Brule-t-Il?*), Paramount, 1966.
The Professionals, American International, 1966.
Grand Prix, Metro-Goldwyn-Mayer, 1966.
The Night of the Generals (also known as *La Nuit des Generaux*), Columbia, 1967.
(And title song) *Five Card Stud,* Paramount, 1968.
Villa Rides!, Paramount, 1968.
The Fixer, Metro-Goldwyn-Mayer, 1968.
Isadora (also known as *The Loves of Isadora*), Universal, 1968.
Barbarella, Paramount, 1968.
The Extraordinary Seaman, Metro-Goldwyn-Mayer, 1969.
Topaz, Universal, 1969.

The Damned (also known as *La Caduta degli Dei* and *Goetterdaemmerung*), Warner Bros., 1969.
The Only Game in Town, Twentieth Century-Fox, 1970.
Ryan's Daughter, Metro-Goldwyn-Mayer, 1970.
El Condor, National General, 1970.
Airborne, 1970.
Plaza Suite, Paramount, 1971.
Red Sun (also known as *Soleil Rouge*), National General, 1971.
A Season in Hell (also known as *Una Stagione all'Inferno*), 1971.
Pope Joan (also known as *The Devil's Imposter*), Columbia, 1972.
The Effect of Gamma Rays on Man-in-the-Moon Marigolds, Twentieth Century-Fox, 1972.
The Life and Times of Judge Roy Bean, National General, 1972.
Ash Wednesday, Paramount, 1973.
The Mackintosh Man, Warner Bros., 1973.
Mrs. Uschyck, 1973.
Grandeur Nature (also known as *Life Size, Love Doll,* and *Tamano Natural*), 1973.
Island at the Top of the World, Buena Vista, 1974.
Mr. Sycamore, Film Venture, 1974.
Great Expectations, Transcontinental Film Productions, 1975.
Mandingo, Paramount, 1975.
The Man Who Would Be King, Allied Artists, 1975.
Posse, Paramount, 1975.
Shout at the Devil, American International Pictures, 1976.
The Last Tycoon, Paramount, 1976.
Mohammed, Messenger of God (also known as *The Message*), Tarik, 1976.
Al-Risalah, 1976.
Two Solitudes, New World-Mutual, 1977.
March or Die, Columbia, 1977.
The Spy Who Loved Me, United Artists, 1977.
Mon Royaume pour un Cheval, 1978.
Crossed Swords (also known as *The Prince and the Pauper*), Warner Bros., 1978.
(And song "The Magician") *The Magician of Lublin* (also known as *Der Magier* and *Ha-Kosem Mi'Lublin*), Cannon, 1979.
Winter Kills, Avco Embassy, 1979.
The Tin Drum (also known as *Die Blechtrommel* and *Le Tambour*), Argos Films, 1979.
The American Success Company (also known as *American Success, The Ringer,* and *Success*), Columbia, 1979.
Black Marble, Avco Embassy, 1980.
Don't Cry It's Only Thunder, Sanrio, 1980.
Resurrection, Universal, 1980.
Lion of the Desert (also known as *Mukhtar: Lion of the Desert*), United Film Distributors, 1980.
(And song "Half of Me") *The Last Flight of Noah's Ark,* Buena Vista, 1980.
Taps, Twentieth Century-Fox, 1981.
Circle of Deceit (also known as *False Witness, Die Faelschung,* and *Le Faussaire*), United Artists Classics, 1981.
Firefox, Warner Bros., 1982.
Young Doctors in Love, Twentieth Century-Fox, 1982.
Wrong Is Right, Columbia, 1982.
Au Nom de Tous les Miens (also known as *For Those I Loved*), Twentieth Century-Fox, 1983.
The Year of Living Dangerously, Metro-Goldwyn-Mayer/United Artists, 1983.
The Life of Martin Gray, 1983.
Top Secret!, Paramount, 1984.
Dreamscape, Twentieth Century-Fox, 1984.
A Passage to India, Columbia, 1984.
Witness, Paramount, 1985.
The Bride, Columbia, 1985.
Mad Max, Beyond Thunderdome (also known as *Mad Max 3*), Warner Bros.,1985.
Enemy Mine, Twentieth Century-Fox, 1985.
Solarbabies (also known as *Solar Warriors*), Metro-Goldwyn-Mayer/United Artists, 1986.
Tai-Pan, De Laurentiis Entertainment Group, 1986.
The Mosquito Coast, Warner Bros., 1986.
Gaby—A True Story, TriStar, 1987.
Julia and Julia (also known as *Giulia e Giulia*), Cinecom, 1987.
No Way Out, Orion, 1987.
Fatal Attraction (also known as *Diversion*), Paramount, 1987.
Shuto Shoshitsu, 1987.
Tokyo Blackout, 1987.
Wildfire, Vestron, 1988.
Gorillas in the Mist, Universal, 1988.
Distant Thunder, Paramount, 1988.
Moon over Parador, Universal, 1988.
"Theme from Lawrence of Arabia," *Buster,* Hemdale, 1988.
Chances Are, TriStar, 1989.
Dead Poets Society, Buena Vista, 1989.
Prancer, Orion, 1989.
Enemies, a Love Story, Twentieth Century-Fox, 1989.
Le Palanquin des Larmes (also known as *The Palanquin of Tears*), 1989.
Solar Crisis (also known as *Crisis 2050, Starfire,* and *Kuraishisu Niju-Goju Nen*), Vidmark Entertainment, 1990.
Ghost, Paramount, 1990.
After Dark, My Sweet, Avenue Pictures, 1990.

Jacob's Ladder (also known as *Dante's Inferno*), TriStar, 1990.
Almost an Angel, Paramount, 1990.
Fires Within, Metro-Goldwyn-Mayer/United Artists, 1991.
Only the Lonely, Twentieth Century-Fox, 1991.
Setting Sun, 1991.
The Shadow of the Wolf (also known as *Agaguk*), Triumph Releasing, 1992.
School Ties, Paramount, 1992.
Rakuyo, 1992.
Mr. Jones, TriStar, 1993.
Fearless (also known as *Joyride*), Warner Bros., 1993.
Song "Somewhere My Love," *Super Mario Bros.,* Buena Vista, 1993.
Music excerpts, *A Hundred and One Nights,* 1995.
A Walk in the Clouds, Twentieth Century-Fox, 1995.
Sunchaser, Warner Bros., 1996.
Song "Lawrence of Arabia End Credits," *The Mirror Has Two Faces,* Sony Pictures Entertainment, 1996.
Le Jour et la Nuit (also known as *Day and Night*), President Films, 1997.
The Taste of Sunshine, Ascot Elite, 1999.

Also musical composer for numerous French films including *Puccini.*

Television Music; Movies:
The Silence, NBC, 1975.
The Users, ABC, 1978.
Theme music, *Verna: USO Girl,* PBS, 1978.
Ishi: The Last of His Tribe, HBO, 1978.
Enola Gay, NBC, 1980.
Coming out of the Ice, CBS, 1982.
The Sky's No Limit (also known as *The Sky's the Limit*), CBS, 1984.
Samson and Delilah, ABC, 1984.
(And song "Alone in the Night") *Apology,* HBO, 1986.

Television Music; Miniseries:
Jesus of Nazareth (also known as *Gesu di Nazareth*), NBC, 1977.
Shogun (also known as *James Clavell's Shogun*), NBC, 1980.
Vendredi ou la vie Sauvage (also known as *Robinson Crusoe and Man Friday*), 1981.
The Murder of Mary Phagan, NBC, 1988.

Television Music; Specials:
One of a Kind, CBS, 1964.
Theme music, *Guys and Dolls off the Record,* 1992.
Lean by Jarre, PBS, 1993.
Theme music, *In the Wings: Angels in America on Broadway,* 1993.

Television Music; Series:
Les Amours Celebres, 1961.

Stage Compositions:
Notre Dame de Paris, Paris Opera, Paris, 1966.

Composed orchestral works, including *Armide, Mobiles, Mouvements en Relief, Passacaille a la Memoire d'Honegger,* and *Polyphonies Conertantes.*

Ballets:
Author of ballets, including *Facheuse Rencontre, The Hunchback of Notre Dame, Maldroror, Masques de Femmes,* and *The Murdered Poet.**

JAY, Tony 1933(?)-

PERSONAL

Born c. 1933, in Great Britain; became U.S. citizen; married third wife, Kathy Rogers Jay (a makeup artist); children: Adam.

Addresses: *Agent*—Jeff Davis, International Creative Management, 8942 Wilshire Blvd., Beverly Hills, CA 90211; Bryan Drew Ltd., Quadrant House, 80/82 Regent St., London W1R 6AU, England.

Career: Actor.

CREDITS

Film Appearances:
Natie Kaplan, *My Way* (also known as *The Winner*), Joseph Brenner, 1974.
Vladimir Maximovitch, *Love and Death,* United Artists, 1975.
Doctor, *The Greek Tycoon,* Universal, 1978.
Voice of the Supreme Being, *Time Bandits,* Avco Embassy, 1980.
Council Chief, *My Stepmother Is an Alien,* Columbia, 1988.
Doctor, *Little Dorrit* (also known as *Little Dorrit's Story* and *Nobody's Fault*), Cannon, 1988.
Werner, *Twins,* Universal, 1988.
Voice of Monsieur D'Arque, *Beauty and the Beast* (animated), Buena Vista, 1991.
Voice of Lickboot, *Tom and Jerry: The Movie* (animated), Miramax, 1992.
Voice of Reginald, *All Dogs Go to Heaven 2* (animated), Metro-Goldwyn-Mayer, 1996.

Voice of Frollo, *The Hunchback of Notre Dame* (animated), Buena Vista, 1996.

Might Ducks: The First Face Off, Buena Vista Home Video, 1997.

Voice of Jarlsburg, *Bruno the Kid: The Animated Movie,* Live Entertainment, 1997.

Voice of Dr. Lipshitz, *The Rugrats Movie* (animated), Paramount, 1998.

Television Appearances; Movies:

Merchant, *Timon of Athens* (also known as *BBC Television Shakespeare: Timon of Athens*), PBS, 1981.

Habib, *Riviera,* ABC, 1987.

Max Hollister, *Rainbow Drive,* Showtime, 1990.

In Vino Veritas, ABC, 1990.

Weisfeld, *Absolute Strangers,* CBS, 1991.

Wilfred Plimsoll, *Fugitive Nights: Danger in the Desert* (also known as *Fugitive Nights*), NBC, 1993.

Voice of Sul-Van, *Superman: The Last Son of Krypton* (animated), 1996.

Television Appearances; Miniseries:

Dr. Jobinet, *Dynasty: The Reunion,* ABC, 1991.

Television Appearances; Series:

Voice of Lord Dregg, *Teenage Mutant Ninja Turtles* (animated), syndicated, 1987.

Voice of Shere Khan, *Tale Spin,* syndicated, 1990-94.

Voice of Virgil, *Mighty Max,* 1991.

Nigel St. John, *Lois & Clark: The New Adventures of Superman* (also known as *Lois & Clark* and *The New Adventures of Superman*), ABC, 1993-95.

Voice of Galactus, *The Fantastic Four* (animated), 1994.

Voice of Skull, *Skeleton Warriors* (animated), CBS, 1994.

Voice of Megabyte, *ReBoot* (animated), ABC, 1994—.

Voice of the Overlord, *Savage Dragon* (animated), USA Network, 1995.

Voice of Chairface Chippendale, *The Tick* (animated), Fox, 1995-97.

Voice of Jarlesburg, *Bruno the Kid* (animated), syndicated, 1996.

Voice of Wraith, *Mighty Ducks* (animated), ABC/syndicated, 1996.

Voice of Dragit, *Invasion America* (animated), The WB, 1998.

Television Appearances; Episodic:

Lambourne, "Golden Boy," *The Sweeney,* Thames TV, 1975.

Foreign Observer 1, "Blind Run," *The Professionals,* LWT, 1978.

Bagatu, "How to Get Rid of It," *Whoops Apocalypse,* LWT, 1982.

Paracelsus, *Beauty and the Beast,* CBS, 1987.

"Allegra," *Hunter,* NBC, 1987.

Voice, *The Adventures of Don Coyote and Sancho Panda* (animated), syndicated, 1990.

John Bosley Hackett, "The Critic," *Matlock,* NBC, 1991.

Charles Dickens, *Sisters,* NBC, 1991.

Dr. Wade Benolt, "Q & A on FYI," *Murphy Brown,* CBS, 1991.

Joseph Schiavelli, "Guess Who's Listening to Dinner?," *Night Court,* NBC, 1992.

Campio, "Cost of Living," *Star Trek: The Next Generation,* syndicated, 1992.

Albert, *Lois & Clark: The New Adventures of Superman* (also known as *Lois & Clark* and *The New Adventures of Superman*), ABC, 1993.

Rabbi Fishman, *Picket Fences,* CBS, 1993.

Judge Silot Gatt, "Brisco for the Defense," *The Adventures of Brisco County, Jr.,* Fox, 1993.

"Ridge the High School," *Duckman* (animated), USA Network, 1994.

Voice of Anubis, "Grief," *Gargoyles,* 1995.

Voice of Peeking Duck, *The Twisted Tales of Felix the Cat* (animated),CBS, 1995.

Baron Mordo, "Dr. Strange," *Spider-Man* (animated), 1996.

Voice of Sul-Van, "The Last Son of Krypton, Part 1," *Superman* (animated), The WB, 1996.

The Chairman, "The Silent Tower," *The Burning Zone,* UPN, 1996.

Appeared as Marcel Du Beret, *Supercarrier;* voice of Yeti, *Captain Planet and the Planeteers* (animated); voice of Dr. Lipschitz, *Rugrats* (animated), Nickelodeon; and Voice of Macrobe, *Extreme Ghostbusters* (animated).

Television Appearances; Specials:

Conrad, *Circus,* ABC, 1987.

Voice of Lord of the Amulet, *Arabian Nights,* syndicated, 1994.

Voice, *Siegfried & Roy: Masters of the Impossible,* Fox, 1996.

Narrator, *Doomsday: What Can You Do?,* Fox, 1997.

Stage Appearances:

Vincent Crummles, *The Life and Adventures of Nicholas Nickelby,* Broadhurst Theatre, New York City, 1986.

Also appeared as Shylock, *Merchant of Venice,* London; *Great Expectations,* Old Vic Theatre, London; *The Unknown Soldier and His Wife,* London; *The Doctor's Dilemma,* London; *Three Sisters,* London; *The Deep Blue Sea,* London; and *A View from the Bridge,* London.

RECORDINGS

Video Games:

Voice of Maritanius and William the Just, *Blood Omen: The Legacy of Kain,* Activision, 1996.

Voice of the Lieutenant, *Fallout,* Interplay, 1997.

OTHER SOURCES

Periodicals:

USA Today, June 26, 1996.*

JAYNES, Roderick

See COEN, Ethan and COEN, Joel

JENKINS, Tamara 1963(?)-

PERSONAL

Born c. 1963; raised in Southern California; daughter of a strip club owner and car salesperson and a hat check person. *Education:* New York University, M.F.A., 1993. *Religion:* Judaism.

Addresses: *Contact*—Directors Guild of America, 7920 Sunset Blvd., Los Angeles, CA 90046.

Career: Director, screenwriter, and actress. Also worked as a solo performance artist.

Member: Directors Guild of America.

Awards, Honors: Student Academy Awards, regional winner and finalist, and Fellowship Prize, RiminiCinema Film Festival, all 1992, and First Place Mobil Award, graduate division, all for *Fugitive Love;* Sundance Film Festival Award, special recognition for excellence in short filmmaking, Locarno Film Festival Award, special recognition award for excellence, and selection as part of the New Directors/New Films Festival at the Museum of Modern Art, all 1994, for *Family Remains;* Guggenheim fellow for filmmaking, 1995; Sundance Institute Screenwriting and Filmmakers' Lab fellow, 1995; Independent Spirit Award nominations, best first feature (with Michael Nozik and Stan Wlodkowski) and best first screenplay, 1999, both for *The Slums of Beverly Hills.*

CREDITS

Film Work; Director, Unless Otherwise Noted:

And editor, *Fugitive Love* (short film), Boyfriend Productions, 1991.

Family Remains (short film), Boyfriend Productions, 1993.

The Slums of Beverly Hills, Fox Searchlight Pictures, 1998.

Stage Appearances:

Suzy, "Terry Won't Talk," *Terry by Terry,* Manhattan Punch Line, New York City, 1988.

Eleanor, Pittsburgh Public Theatre, Pittsburgh, PA, 1990-91.

Appeared as a performing artist at various venues, including the American Repertory Theatre, Performance Stage 122, Brattle Theatre, Home for Contemporary Theatre and Art, Creative Time, and the Kentucky Center for the Arts.

Major Tours:

Cosette, *Les Miserables,* U.S. cities, beginning in 1987.

WRITINGS

Screenplays:

Family Remains (short film), Boyfriend Productions, 1993.

The Slums of Beverly Hills, Fox Searchlight Pictures, 1998.

Writings for the Stage:

Wrote performance pieces produced at various venues, including the American Repertory Theatre, Performance Stage 122, Brattle Theatre, Home for Contemporary Theatre and Art, Creative Time, and the Kentucky Center for the Arts.

OTHER SOURCES

Periodicals:

Entertainment Weekly, August 21, 1998, p. 96.

Independent, November 26, 1998, p. S13.

Los Angeles Magazine, August, 1998, pp. 136-137.

Newsweek, August 17, 1998, p. 61.

People Weekly, August 31, 1998, p. 31.*

JENNINGS, Alex 1957(?)-

PERSONAL

Born c. 1957, in Essex, England; children: Ralph, Georgia.

Addresses: *Contact*—c/o Dava Flack, 200 West 57th St., Suite 1407, New York, NY 10019.

Career: Actor.

Awards, Honors: Laurence Olivier Award, Society of West End Theatre, comedy performance of the year, and Critic's Circle Theatre Award (England), best actor, both 1988, for *Too Clever by Half;* Laurence Olivier Award, best actor, 1996, for *Peer Gynt;* Helen Hayes Award, best lead actor, non-resident production, 1999, for *Hamlet*.

CREDITS

Stage Appearances:

Gloumov, *Too Clever by Half,* Old Vic Theatre, London, England, 1988.

The Wild Duck, 1990.

Dorante, *The Liar,* 1990.

Richard II, 1990.

Captain Plume, *Recruiting Officer,* National Theatre, London, 1992.

Jack, *The Importance of Being Earnest,* Aldwych Theatre, London, 1993.

Peer Gynt, Royal Shakespeare Company, Swan Theatre, Stratford-upon-Avon, England, 1994.

Angelo, *Measure for Measure,* Royal Shakespeare Company, Main House Theatre, 1994.

Easter Bonnet Competition, Palace Theatre, New York City, 1996.

Theseus/Oberon, *A Midsummer Night's Dream,* Royal Shakespeare Company, Lunt-Fontanne Theatre, New York City, 1996.

Title role, *Hamlet,* Royal Shakespeare Company, Kennedy Center for the Performing Arts, Washington, DC, 1998.

Also appeared as Kittel, *Ghetto,* Royal National Theatre.

Film Appearances:

Blind soldier, *War Requiem,* Anglo International, 1988.

Lord Mark, *The Wings of the Dove,* Miramax, 1997.

Television Appearances; Specials:

Victor Preece, *The Sins of the Fathers* (also known as *Inspector Morse: The Sins of the Fathers*), PBS, 1992.

Sebastian Parish, "Death at the Bar," *The Inspector Alleyn Mysteries* (also known as *Mystery!*), PBS, 1995.

Bitzer, *Hard Times,* 1995.

King George III, *Liberty! The American Revolution,* PBS, 1997-1998.

Reader (voiceover), *The Noel Coward Story,* PBS, 1999.

Television Appearances; Movies:

King Ferdinand, *Bye Bye Columbus,* BBC, 1991.

Alexander, *The Hunley,* TNT, 1999.

Television Appearances; Miniseries:

Smiley's People, syndicated, 1982.

John Ashenden, *Ashenden,* Arts and Entertainment, 1992.

OTHER SOURCES

Periodicals:

Interview, May, 1990, pp. 44.*

JENNINGS, Peter 1938-

PERSONAL

Full name, Peter Charles Jennings; born July 29, 1938, in Toronto, Ontario, Canada; immigrated to the United States, 1964; son of Charles (a broadcast journalist and television executive) and Elizabeth (maiden name, Osborne) Jennings; married Annie Malouf (divorced); married Valerie Godsoe (divorced); married Kati Marton (a writer and former news bureau chief in Bonn, West Germany), 1979 (divorced, 1993); married Kayce Freed (a television producer), December 6, 1997; children: (third marriage) Elizabeth, Christopher. *Education:* Attended the University of Ottawa and Carleton University.

Addresses: *Contact*—c/o ABC Press Relations, 1330 Avenue of the Americas, New York, NY 10019.

Career: Television journalist. Worked with CBC in Montreal, Quebec; CJOH-TV, Ottawa, Ontario; parliamentary correspondent and network anchorman with Canadian TV, Ottawa. Royal Bank of Canada, teller, 1957.

Member: American Federation of Television and Radio Artists, International Radio and Television Society, Overseas Press Club.

Awards, Honors: Overseas Press Club Award, 1972; George Foster Peabody Award, 1974; Emmy Award, best coverage of a single breaking news story, 1982, for *Personal Note: Beirut;* George Polk Award, Long Island University Journalism Department, best television reporting—network, and Robert F. Kennedy Journalism Award, 1990 (with Tom Yellin and Leslie Cockburn); Edward Weintal Prize for Diplomatic Reporting, Georgetown University Institute for the Study of Diplomacy, 1991; another Overseas Press Club Award; National Headliner Award; Alfred I. DuPont-Columbia University Award; named America's Best National Television Anchor, *Washington Journalism Review* for several years in a row; LL.D. (honorary degree), Rider College.

CREDITS

Television Appearances; Series:

Co-anchor, *CTV National News,* CTV (Ottawa, Ontario, Canada), 1962-64.
Correspondent, *ABC News,* ABC, 1964.
Co-anchor, *ABC Evening News,* ABC, 1965-68.
Host, *A.M. America,* ABC, 1975.
Chief foreign correspondent, *ABC News,* ABC, 1975-78.
London anchor, *World News Tonight,* ABC, 1978-1983.
Anchor, *World News Tonight,* ABC, 1983—.
We the People, ABC, 1987.
Host and narrator, *The AIDS Quality,* PBS, 1989.
Anchor, *Peter Jennings Reporting,* ABC, 1990—.
Anchor, *Turning Point,* ABC, 1994.
Anchor, *ABC News Saturday Night,* ABC, 1998.

Also appeared as anchor, *Capital to Capital;* host, *Let's Face It,* CBC; host, *Time Out,* CBC.

Television Appearances; Specials:

Violence in a Tube, ABC, 1988.
Co-host, "Opening Ceremonies," *The 1998 Winter Olympic Games,* ABC, 1988.
Anchor, *Drugs: Why This Plague?,* ABC, 1988.
Anchor, *Drugs: A Plague Upon the Land,* ABC, 1988.
Anchor, *The '88 Vote: Election Night,* ABC, 1988.
The Television Academy Hall of Fame, ABC, 1989.
Host, *Christmas at Starcross,* ABC, 1989.
Host and commentator, *Images of the '80s,* ABC, 1989.
Anchor, *Worlds in Turmoil,* ABC, 1989.
Anchor, *Presidential Inauguration,* ABC, 1989.
Anchor, *Capital to Capital: The Environment,* ABC, 1989.
Anchor, *Beyond the Cold War: The Risk and the Opportunity,* ABC, 1989.
The Television Academy Hall of Fame, ABC, 1990.
Fifteen Years of MacNeil/Lehrer, 1990.
Edward R. Murrow: This Reporter, ABC, 1990.
Host and moderator, *Future Forum: A World of Competition,* ABC, 1990.
Anchor, *Peter Jennings Reporting: Guns,* ABC, 1990.
Anchor, *Peter Jennings Reporting: From the Killing Fields,* ABC, 1990.
Anchor (Washington, DC) *Capital to Capital: Leadership in the '90s,* ABC, 1990.
Dangerous Assignments, ABC, 1991.
Host, *Carnegie Hall: Live at 100! The Gala Celebration,* ABC, 1991.
Anchor, *War in the Gulf: Answering Children's Questions,* ABC, 1991.
Anchor, *Peter Jennings Reporting: From the Heart of Harlem,* ABC, 1991.
Anchor, *A Line in the Sand: What Did America Win?,* ABC, 1991.
Anchor, *A Line in the Sand: War or Peace?,* ABC, 1991.
Anchor, *The Health Quarterly,* ABC, 1991.
The Class of the 20th Century, ABC, 1992.
Moderator, *Prejudice: Answering Children's Questions,* ABC, 1992.
Moderator, *The '92 Vote: The Democratic Candidates Debate,* ABC, 1992.
Host, *Peter Jennings Reporting: The Cocaine War, Lost in Bolivia,* ABC, 1992.
Host, *A National Town Meeting: Who Is Ross Perot?,* ABC, 1992.
Host, *Growing Up in the Age of AIDS: An ABC News Town Meeting for the Family-with Peter Jennings,* ABC, 1992.
Host, *Alfred I. DuPont/Columbia University Awards in Broadcast Journalism,* ABC, 1992.
Anchor, *Peter Jennings Reporting: Who Is Ross Perot?,* ABC, 1992.
Anchor, *Peter Jennings Reporting: Men, Sex, and Rape,* ABC, 1992.
Anchor, *The Missiles of October: What the World Didn't Know,* ABC, 1992.
Anchor, *'92 Vote: The Democratic Convention,* ABC, 1992.
Peter Jennings Reporting: The Land of the Demons, ABC, 1993.
Host, *Cover-Up at Ground Zero,* ABC, 1993.
Anchor, *Kids in the Crossfire: Violence in America,* ABC, 1993.

House on Fire: America's Haitian Crisis, ABC, 1994.
Moderator, *President Clinton: Answering Children's Questions,* ABC, 1994.
Host, *While America Watched: The Bosnia Tragedy,* ABC, 1994.
Host, *Peter Jennings Reporting: In the Name of God,* ABC,1995.
Host and reporter, *Hiroshima: Why the Bomb Was Dropped,* ABC, 1995.
Host and interviewer, *The Peacekeepers: How the UN Failed in Bosnia,* ABC, 1995.
Anchor, *Into the Jury's Hands,* ABC, 1995.
Anchor, *Children First: Real Kids, Real Solutions,* ABC, 1995.
Host, *Rage and Betrayal: The Lives of Tim McVeigh and Terry Nichols,* ABC, 1996.
Himself, *The People and the Power Game,* ABC, 1996.
Anchor, *Peter Jennings Reporting: Never Say Die-How the CigaretteCompanies Keep On Winning,* ABC, 1996.
Anchor, *Peter Jennings Reporting: Jerusalem Stories,* ABC, 1996.
Anchor, *The '96 Vote: The Republican National Convention,* ABC, 1996.
Anchor, *The '96 Vote: The Democratic National Convention,* ABC, 1996.
Anchor, *The '96 Vote: Election Night,* ABC, 1996.
The Daily Show Year-End Spectacular '97, Comedy Central, 1997.
The ESPY Awards, ESPN, 1997.
Anchor, *Peter Jennings Reporting: Who Is Tim McVeigh?,* ABC, 1997.
Anchor, *Dangerous World: The Kennedy Years,* ABC, 1997.
ABC News Town Meeting: Kids . . . Parents . . . Straight Talk on Drugs, ABC, 1997.
Correspondent, *Peter Jennings Reporting: Unfinished Business: The C.I.A. and Saddam Hussein,* ABC, 1997.
Anchor, *Peter Jennings Reporting: The American Game,* ABC, 1998.
Anchor, *Crisis in the White House: The President Testifies,* ABC, 1998.
Anchor, *Cancer: Race for a Cure,* ABC, 1998.

Television Appearances; Episodic:
Ethics in America, 1989.

Television Work; Series:
Middle East bureau chief, *ABC News,* ABC, 1968-75.
Senior editor, *World News Tonight,* ABC, 1983—.

Radio Appearances:
Host, *Peter's People,* Canadian Broadcasting Corporation, c. 1947.

Also appeared as news reporter, CFJR, Canada.

Film Appearances:
Himself, *The Last Party,* 1993.

WRITINGS

Television Specials:
Worlds in Turmoil, ABC, 1989.
Peter Jennings Reporting: Guns, ABC, 1990.
Peter Jennings Reporting: From the Killing Fields, ABC, 1990.
Peter Jennings Reporting: From the Heart of Harlem, ABC, 1991.
The Health Quarterly, ABC, 1991.
The Missiles of October: What the World Didn't Know, ABC, 1992.
Cover-Up at Ground Zero, ABC, 1993.
Common Miracles: The New American Revolution in Learning, ABC, 1993.
Hiroshima: Why the Bomb Was Dropped, ABC, 1995.
Children First: Real Kids, Real Solutions, ABC, 1995.
Rage and Betrayal: The Lives of Tim McVeigh and Terry Nichols, ABC, 1996.

Books:
Co-author, *The Pope in Britain: Pope John Paul II British Visit,* Bodley Head (London), 1982.
"Introduction," *The '84 Vote,* 1985.
Co-interviewer, *Children of the Troubles: Growing Up in Northern Ireland,* Stranmillis College, 1986.
(With Todd Brewster) *The Century,* Doubleday, 1998.

OTHER SOURCES

Periodicals:
America, April 30, 1994, p. 18.
Broadcasting & Cable, September 27, 1993, p. 36.
Economist, October 23, 1993, p. A38.
People Weekly, August 30, 1993, p. 48.*

JIAWEI, Wang
See WONG, Kar-Wai

JILLETTE, Penn 1955-

PERSONAL

Born March 5, 1955, in Greenfield, MA.

Addresses: *Agent*—William Morris Agency, 151 El Camino Dr., Beverly Hills, CA 90212.

Career: Actor, screenwriter, producer, creator, and composer. Half of comedy/magic team, Penn & Teller.

CREDITS

Film Appearances:
Security guard (US version), *Savage Island,* 1985.
Norman, *Off Beat,* Buena Vista, 1986.
Bone, *My Chauffeur,* Crown, 1986.
Penn & Teller's Cruel Tricks for Dear Friends, 1987.
Big Stoop, *Tough Guys Don't Dance,* Cannon, 1987.
Voice of the Chief of the Deformed, *Light Years* (also known as *Gandahar*), Miramax, 1988.
Penn, *Penn & Teller Get Killed* (also known as *Dead Funny*), Warner Bros., 1989.
Himself, *Half Japanese: The Band Who Would Be King,* Tara Releasing, 1993.
Luthers, *Car 54, Where Are You?,* 1994.
Hal, *Hackers,* Metro-Goldwyn-Mayer, 1995.
Voice of TV announcer, *Toy Story* (animated), Buena Vista, 1995.
Nothing Sacred, 1997.
Fred, *Life Sold Separately,* 1997.
Himself, *Lou Reed: Rock and Roll Heart,* Fox Lorber, 1997.
Barker at Bazooko Circus, *Fear and Loathing in Las Vegas,* Universal, 1998.
Ked Nerd, 1998.

Television Appearances; Series:
Himself, *The Unpleasant World of Penn & Teller,* 1994.
Voice of Flea, *The Moxy Show* (animated), Cartoon Network, 1994-95.
Drell, *Sabrina, The Teenage Witch,* ABC, 1996-97.
Host, *Penn & Teller's Sin City Spectacular,* FX, 1998—.

Television Appearances; Specials:
Penn & Teller Go Public, PBS, 1985.
Penn & Teller's Invisible Thread, Showtime, 1987.
Ron Reagan Is the President's Son, Cinemax, 1988.
Host, *Showtime Comedy Club All-Stars III,* Showtime, 1989.
Woodstock: Return to the Planet of the '60s, CBS, 1989.
Penn & Teller: Don't Try This At Home!, NBC, 1990.
Host, *This is MST3K,* Comedy Central, 1992.
Harley-Davidson's 90th Birthday Blast, Showtime, 1993.
Host, *Discover Magazine's 5th Annual Technology Awards,* 1994.
Narrator, *Hal Roach: Hollywood's King of Laughter,* The Disney Channel, 1994.
The World' Greatest Magic, NBC, 1995.
Penn & Teller's Home Invasion Magic, 1997.

Television Appearances; Episodic:
Jimmy Borges, "Prodigal Son," *Miami Vice,* NBC, 1985.
The Original Max Talking Headroom Show, Cinemax, 1987.
Darrin Romick, "Illusions of Grandeur," *Lois & Clark: The New Adventures of Superman,* ABC, 1994.
Mr. Orwell Katz, "Series Premiere," *VR.5,* Fox, 1995.
Archibald Fenn, "Drew Meets Lawyers," *The Drew Carey Show,* ABC, 1995.
Himself, "$20.01," *Space Ghost Coast to Coast,* Cartoon Network, 1996.
Archibald Fenn, "See Drew Run," *The Drew Carey Show,* ABC, 1997.
Encyclopedia salesman, "The One with the 'Cuffs," *Friends,* NBC, 1997.
Rebo, "Day of the Dead," *Babylon 5,* syndicated, 1998.
(Uncredited) Pimp, "The Cat's Out of the Bag," *Dharma & Greg,* ABC, 1998.
Himself, "Knee Deep," *Home Improvement,* ABC, 1999.

Also appeared in *Saturday Night Live,* NBC; *Late Night with David Letterman,* CBS.

Television Work:
Creator, *Penn & Teller Go Public* (special), PBS, 1985.
Co-executive producer and concept originator, *Penn & Teller's Home Invasion Magic* (special), ABC, 1997.
Co-executive producer, *Penn & Teller's Sin City Spectacular* (series), FX, 1998—.

Stage Appearances:
Penn & Teller, Ritz Theatre, New York City, 1987-88.
Penn & Teller: The Refrigerator Tour, Eugene O'Neill Theatre, New York City, 1991.
Penn & Teller Rot in Hell, John Houseman Theatre, New York City, 1991-92.

Made Off-Broadway debut in 1985.

RECORDINGS

Video Games:

Leroy Paine, *Steven Spielberg's Director's Chair,* 1996.

Voice of Drell, *Sabrina, the Teenage Witch: Spellbound,* 1998.

WRITINGS

Screenplays:

Penn & Teller's Cruel Tricks for Dear Friends, 1987.

Penn & Teller Get Killed (also known as *Dead Funny*), Warner Bros., 1989.

Film Scores:

Penn & Teller's Cruel Tricks for Dear Friends, 1987.

Television Specials:

Penn & Teller Go Public?, 1985.

Penn & Teller's Invisible Thread, Showtime, 1987.

Ron Reagan Is the President's Son, Cinemax, 1988.

Penn & Teller: Don't Try This at Home!, NBC, 1990.

Penn & Teller's Home Invasion Magic, ABC, 1997.

Television Episodes:

The Moxy Show, Cartoon Network, 1994-95.

Nonfiction:

(With Teller) *Penn & Teller's Cruel Tricks for Dear Friends,* Villard Books, 1989.

(With Teller) *Penn & Teller's How to Play with Your Food,* Villard Books, 1992.

(With Teller) *Penn & Teller's How to Play in Traffic,* Boulevard Books, 1997.

Other:

Wrote a monthly column for *PC/Computing*. Contributor to other magazines, including *Playboy.*

OTHER SOURCES

Periodicals:

Entertainment Weekly, November 21, 1997, p. 122.

Newsbytes, June 14, 1994, p. 1994.

Reason, April, 1994, p. 35.*

JOHNSON, Anne-Marie 1960-

PERSONAL

Born July 18, 1960, in Los Angeles, CA; married Martin Grey, 1996. *Education:* University of California, Los Angeles, B.A. (theater arts).

Addresses: *Contact*—c/o Light Company, 901 Bringham Ave., Los Angeles, CA 90049.

Career: Actress.

CREDITS

Television Appearances; Series:

Aileen Lewis, *Double Trouble,* NBC, 1984-85.

Nadine Thomas, *What's Happening Now,* syndicated, 1985-88.

Althea Tibbs, *In the Heat of the Night,* NBC, 1988-93.

In Living Color, Fox, 1993-94.

Arlene (recurring), *Melrose Place,* Fox, 1995-96.

Denise Williams, *Smart Guy,* The WB, 1996-97.

Television Appearances; Episodic:

Lynn Williams, "Blues for Mr. Green," *Hill Street Blues,* NBC, 1984.

"Undercover Cover," *Diff'rent Strokes,* NBC, 1984.

Lynn Williams, "You're in Alice's," *Hill Street Blues,* NBC, 1985.

Isabel/Nella Watkins, "Saturday Night Special," *Hunter,* NBC, 1986.

"Vigilante," *Houston Knights,* CBS, 1988.

Body by Jake, syndicated, 1988.

The Liar's Club, syndicated, 1988.

Win, Lose, or Draw (two segments), syndicated, 1988.

Win, Lose, or Draw (one segment), NBC, 1989.

"Guest Host," *The Larry Sanders Show,* HBO, 1992.

Sheila Kelly, *Living Single,* Fox, 1993.

Mariah Cirrus, "The Long Dark," *Babylon 5,* syndicated, 1994.

Priscilla Dauphin, "Big Easy Murder," *Murder, She Wrote,* CBS, 1995.

Arlene, *Minor Adjustments,* NBC, 1995.

Patient, "Ask Me No Questions, I'll Tell You No Lies," *E/R,* NBC, 1996.

Congresswoman Bobbi Latham, "The Court Martial of Sandra Gilbert," *JAG,* NBC, 1997.

Pre-school principal, *Mad About You,* NBC, 1997.

Congresswoman Bobbi Latham, "Clipped Wings," *JAG,* CBS, 1998.

Congresswoman Bobbi Latham, "Chains of Command," *JAG,* CBS, 1998.

Lieutenant Alison Fawkes, "Once in a Blue Moon," *The Pretender,* NBC, 1998.

Janice, *Damon,* Fox, 1998.

Happy Hour, USA Network, 1999.

Mrs. Jamison, "Vanishing Acts," *Chicago Hope,* CBS, 1999.

Cabil, *It's Like You Know. . .,* ABC, 1999.

District Attorney Foster, "Love's Illusions," *Ally McBeal,* Fox, 1999.

Television Appearances; Specials:

Super Bloopers and New Practical Jokes, NBC, 1992.

Host, *The CBS All-American Thanksgiving Parade,* CBS, 1992.

La Creasia, *Why Colors?,* Showtime, 1995.

Television Appearances; Movies:

Dawn, *His Mistress,* NBC, 1984.

Dream Date, 1989.

Also appeared in *The Atlanta Child Murders.*

Television Appearances; Pilots:

Beth Franklin, *High School, U.S.A.,* NBC, 1984.

Television Appearances; Miniseries:

Carrie, *Jackie Collins' "Lucky/Chances"* (also known as *Jackie Collins' Lucky, Chances* and *Lucky, Lucky* and *Chances*), NBC, 1990.

Karen Dodd, *Asteroid,* NBC, 1997.

Film Appearances:

Lydia, Willie Mae, and 5th Hooker, *Hollywood Shuffle,* Samuel Goldwyn, 1987.

Cherry, *I'm Gonna Git You Sucka,* Metro-Goldwyn-Mayer/United Artists, 1988.

Athena, *Robot Jox,* Triumph, 1990.

Kristi Reeves, *True Identity,* Buena Vista, 1991.

Diedre, *Strictly Business,* Warner Bros., 1991.

Sydney Todd, *The Five Heartbeats,* Twentieth Century-Fox, 1991.

Monica, *Down in the Delta,* Miramax, 1998.*

JONES, Gemma 1942-

PERSONAL

Born Jennifer Jones, December 4, 1942, in London, England; daughter of Griffith (an actor) and Irene (Isaac) Jones; children: (with Sebastian Graham-Jones, a theatre director) Luke. *Education:* Attended Francis Holland School, London; trained for the stage at Royal Academy of Dramatic Arts, 1960-62.

Addresses: *Agent*— c/o Larry Dalzell Associates Ltd., 126 Kennington Park Rd., London SE11 4DJ, England.

Career: Actress.

Awards, Honors: Bancroft Gold Medal, Royal Academy of Dramatic Arts, 1962; Clarence Derwent Award, 1965, for *The Cavern;* Society of West End Theater Management Award, best actress in a new London play, 1979, for *And a Nightingale Sang.*

CREDITS

Stage Appearances:

(Stage debut) Cherry, *The Beaux Stratagem,* Ashcroft Theatre, Croydon, England, 1963.

(London debut) Johanna, *Baal,* Phoenix Theatre, 1963.

Gilda, *Alfie,* Mermaid Theatre, then Duchess Theatre, both London, 1963.

Portia, *The Merchant of Venice,* Playhouse Theatre, Nottingham, England, 1964-65.

Adele, *The Cavern,* Playhouse Theatre, Nottingham, 1964-65, then Strand Theatre, London, 1965.

Eugenie, *The Pastime of M Robert,* Hampstead Theatre, London, 1966.

Victoria, *Portrait of a Queen,* Thorndike Theatre, Leatherhead, England, 1966.

Title role, *Saint Joan,* Wimbledon Theatre, London, 1966.

Helen Schlegel, *Howard's End,* New Theatre, London, 1967.

Julia, *Two Gentleman of Verona,* Regent's Park, London, 1968.

Ophelia, *Hamlet,* Repertory Theatre, Birmingham, 1969.

Valerie Jordan, *There'll Be Some Changes Made,* Fortune Theatre, London, 1969.

Nina, *The Seagull,* Thorndike Theatre, London, 1969.

Christina of Sweden, *The Abdication,* Theatre Royal, Bath, England, 1971.

Polly Oliver, *Getting On,* Queen's Theatre, London, 1971.

Susan Lloyd, *Next of Kin,* National Theatre Company, Old Vic Theatre, London, 1974.

Countess, *The Marriage of Figaro,* National Theatre Company, Old Vic Theatre, 1974.

Blanche DuBois, *A Street Car Named Desire,* Nottingham Playhouse, 1975.

Ruth, *The Homecoming,* Garrick Theatre, London, 1978.

Helen, *And a Nightingale Sang,* Queen's Theatre, London, 1979.

Sally Bowles, *Cabaret,* Crucible Theatre, Sheffield, England, 1979.

Henry IV, Barbican Center for Arts and Conferences, London, 1982.

Clay, 1982.

Twelfth Night, 1983.

Henry VIII, Stratford-upon-Avon, England, 1983.
Goneril, *King Lear,* Old Vic Theatre, 1989.
Purcell: The Fairy Queen, Theatre de l'Archeveche, Aix-en-Provence, France, 1989.
The Ride Down Mt. Morgan, London, 1991.
Paulina, *The Winter's Tale,* Barbican Theatre, London, 1993, then Kennedy Center, Washington, DC, 1994.
Alice, *The Dance of Death,* Almeida Theatre, London, 1995.
Tolstoy, Aldwych Theatre, London, 1996.

Also appeared in *Breaking the Silence.*

Major Tours:
Hippolyta/Titania *A Midsummer Night's Dream,* Royal Shakespeare Company, world tour, 1972-73.

Film Appearances:
Madeleine, *The Devils,* Warner Bros., 1971.
Mary Jones, *On the Black Hill,* 1987.
Dr. Sarah Nichols, *Paperhouse,* Vestron, 1990.
Mrs. Wainwright, *Feast of July,* Buena Vista, 1995.
Mrs. Dashwood, *Sense and Sensibility,* Columbia, 1995.
Mrs. Wiggins, *O.K. Garage,* 1997.
Lady Queensberry, *Wilde,* PolyGram Filmed Entertainment, 1997.
Eunice, *Captain Jack,* 1998.
Anne, *The Theory of Flight,* Fine Line Features, 1998.
Grace Winslow, *The Winslow Boy,* Sony Pictures Classics, 1999.
Elizabeth Harrison, *Longitude,* forthcoming.

Television Appearances; Series:
Louisa Trotter, *The Duchess of Duke Street,* British Broadcasting Company, 1976-77, then broadcast in U.S., *Masterpiece Theatre,* PBS, 1978-79.

Television Appearances; Episodic:
Queen, "The Heartless Giant," *The Jim Henson Hour,* NBC, 1989.

Television Appearances; Movies:
Mrs. Fairfax, *Charlotte Bronte's Jane Eyre* (also known as *Jane Eyre*), Arts and Entertainment, 1997.

Television Appearances; Specials:
Fleda Vetch, *The Spoils of Poynton,* 1971.
Helen Curry, "Dial a Deadly Number," *Thriller,* ABC, 1975.
Anne Staveley, "Dead of Jericho," *Inspector Morse,* Central-TV, 1988, then broadcast in U.S., *Mystery!,* PBS, 1988.
Alice Mair, "Devices and Desires," *Mystery!,* PBS, 1991.
Julia Hampson, *A Last Embrace,* PBS, 1998.

Also appeared in *The Seagull,* PBS; *The Fall of Eagles,* PBS; *Devices and Desires, The Lie, The Way of the World, The Merchant of Venice,* and *Something Like a Whale.**

JONES, Jeffrey 1947-

PERSONAL

Full name, Jeffrey Duncan Jones; born September 28, 1947, in Buffalo, NY; son of Douglas Bennett and Ruth (an art historian; maiden name, Schooley) Jones. *Education:* Lawrence University, B.A., 1968; trained for the stage at London Academy of Music and Dramatic Arts.

Addresses: *Agent*—J. Michael Bloom, 9255 Sunset Blvd., Suite 710, Los Angeles, CA 90069.

Career: Actor. Playhouse Holiday (touring children's theatre company), Vancouver, member of company, 1973-74.

Member: Actors' Equity Association, Screen Actors Guild, American Federation of Television and Radio Artists.

Awards, Honors: Tyrone Guthrie Award, 1971; Golden Globe Award nomination, best supporting actor in a motion picture, 1985, for *Amadeus.*

CREDITS

Stage Appearances:
(Stage debut) Chorus, *The House of Atreus,* Tyrone Guthrie Theatre, Minneapolis, MN, 1967.
(London debut) Joseph Surface, *A School for Scandal,* Logan Place Theatre, 1970.
Watch, *Much Ado about Nothing,* Stratford Shakespeare Festival, Festival Stage, Stratford, Ontario, 1971.
Third murderer and messenger, *Macbeth,* Stratford Shakespeare Festival, Festival Stage, 1971.
Officer, *The Duchess of Malfi,* Stratford Shakespeare Festival, Festival Stage, 1971.
Guide, *Volpone,* Stratford Shakespeare Festival, Festival Stage, 1971.

Crookfinger Jake, *The Threepenny Opera,* Stratford Shakespeare Festival, Avon Stage, 1972.

Limester, *Lotta,* New York Shakespeare Festival, Public Theatre, New York City, 1973.

Francisco, *The Tempest,* New York Shakespeare Festival, Mitzi E. Newhouse Theatre, New York City, 1974.

Ivan, *Carmilla,* Actors Theatre of Louisville, 1974-75.

Kerry, *Noon,* Actors Theatre of Louisville, 1974-75.

Baron Frank, *Frankenstein,* Actors Theatre of Louisville, 1974-75.

Matt, *The Threepenny Opera,* Actors Theatre of Louisville, 1974-75.

Title role, *The Real Inspector Hound,* Actors Theatre of Louisville, 1974-75.

Feraillon, *A Flea in Her Ear,* Actors Theatre of Louisville, 1974-75.

Merlie, *The Ballad of the Sad Cafe,* Actors Theatre of Louisville, 1974-75.

Sarge, *Female Transport,* Actors Theatre of Louisville, 1974-75.

Captain DeFoenix, *Trelawney of the Wells,* Vivian Beaumont Theatre, New York City, 1975.

Dr. Pinch, *The Comedy of Errors,* Delacorte Theatre, New York City, 1975.

Randall Underwood, *Heartbreak House,* Arena Stage, Washington, DC, 1975.

Roy, *Scribes,* Phoenix Theatre, then Marymount Manhattan Theatre, New York City, 1976.

Sergeant Wilson, *Secret Service,* Phoenix Theatre, then Playhouse Theatre, New York City, 1976.

Major Thompson, *Boy Meets Girl,* Phoenix Theatre, then Playhouse Theatre, 1976.

Giles Ralston, *The Mousetrap,* Seattle Repertory Theatre, Seattle, WA, 1976.

Heartbreak House, Philadelphia Drama Guild, Philadelphia, PA, 1976.

Chadebise and Poche, *A Flea in Her Ear,* Hartford Stage Company, Hartford, CT, 1977.

Carver (Leo), *Design for Living,* McCarter Theatre, Princeton, NJ, 1977.

Tom, *The Utter Glory of Morrisey Hall,* McCarter Theatre, 1978.

Harold, *They Are Dying Out,* Yale Repertory Theatre, New Haven, CT, 1979.

Understudy for Sherlock Holmes, *The Crucifer of Blood,* Booth Theatre, New York City, 1979.

Pinhead manager, policeman, Will, and Lord John, *The Elephant Man,* Booth Theatre, 1980.

Clive and Edward, *Cloud 9,* Theatre de Lys, New York City, 1981.

Karl Bodenschatz, *The Death of Von Richtofen, as Witnessed from Earth,* New York Shakespeare Festival, Public Theatre, 1982.

Montjoy, *Henry V,* New York Shakespeare Festival, Delacorte Theatre, 1984.

Maurice Stapleton, *Love Letters on Blue Paper,* Hudson Guild Theatre, New York City, 1984.

Hans Christian Anderson, *Rainsnakes,* Long Wharf Theatre, New Haven, CT, 1984.

Gregor, *Between East and West,* McCarter Theatre, 1992-93.

London Suite, Seattle Repertory Theatre, 1994, then Union Square Theatre, New York City, 1995.

Also appeared as Donald, *Porcelain Time,* Berkshire Theatre Festival, Stockbridge, MA; as Antipholus of Syracuse, *The Comedy of Errors,* Manitoba Theatre Centre, Winnipeg, Manitoba; as Tony Cavendish, *The Royal Family,* American Stage Festival, Milford, NH; as Jim, *The Glass Menagerie,* American Stage Festival; as Raymond de Chelles, *Custom of the Country,* Shakespeare and Company, Lee, MA; as Sarge, *Female Transport,* New York Shakespeare Festival, Public Theatre; and as Sergius, *Arms and the Man,* Vancouver Playhouse, Vancouver, British Columbia; appeared at Tyrone Guthrie Theatre in *The Shoemakers Holiday, The Visit, Harper's Ferry;* and *The Merchant of Venice,* Stratford Shakespeare Festival.

Major Tours:

Pinhead manager, policeman, Will, and Lord John, *The Elephant Man,* U.S. cities, 1979-80.

Film Appearances:

(Film debut) Fred, *The Revolutionary,* United Artists, 1970.

Ruteledge child, *A Wedding,* Twentieth Century-Fox, 1978.

U.S. Assistant Secretary of Defense, *The Soldier* (also known as *Codename: The Soldier*), Embassy, 1982.

Clive Barlow, *Easy Money,* Orion, 1983.

Emperor Joseph II, *Amadeus,* Orion, 1984.

Mayor Lepescu, *Transylvania 6-5000,* New World, 1985.

Ed Rooney, *Ferris Bueller's Day Off,* Paramount, 1986.

Dr. Jenning, *Howard the Duck,* Universal, 1986.

Major Fischer, *The Hanoi Hilton,* Cannon, 1987.

Charles Deitz, *Bettlejuice,* Warner Bros., 1988.

Inspector Lestrade, *Without a Clue,* Orion, 1988.

Eliot Draisen, *Who Is Harry Crumb?,* TriStar, 1989.

Monsieur DeGercourt, *Valmont,* Orion, 1989.

Skip Tyler, *The Hunt for Red October,* Paramount, 1990.

Floyd, *Enid Is Sleeping* (also known as *Over Her Dead Body*), Vestron, 1990.

Angel Square, 1991.

Spike, *Stay Tuned,* TriPictures, 1992.
Matt Skearns/Mayor Peter Van der Haven, *Out on a Limb,* Universal, 1992.
Dick Nelson, *Mom and Dad Save the World,* 1992.
Criswell, *Ed Wood,* Buena Vista, 1994.
Ron Timmerman, *Houseguest,* Buena Vista, 1995.
Thomas Putnam, *The Crucible,* Twentieth Century-Fox, 1996.
Gustav, *The Pest,* TriStar, 1997.
Dr. Raskins, *Santa Fe,* 1997.
Roger, *Flypaper,* 1997.
Eddie Barzoon, *The Devil's Advocate,* Warner Bros., 1997.
Minister Pete, *There's No Fish Food in Heaven,* Storm Entertainment, 1998.
Hart, *Ravenous,* Twentieth Century-Fox, 1999.
Steenwyck, *Sleepy Hollow,* Paramount, 1999.

Also appeared in and *Heaven and Earth.*

Television Appearances; Miniseries:
The Adams Chronicles, PBS, 1976.
Mr. Acme, *Fresno,* CBS, 1986.

Television Appearances; Movies:
Budge Hollander, *If Tomorrow Comes,* CBS, 1986.
Thomas Jefferson, *George Washington II: The Forging of a Nation,* CBS, 1986.
Buffalo Bill, *Kenny Rogers as "The Gambler" III—The Legend Continues,* CBS, 1987.

Television Appearances; Episodic:
(Television debut) *Kojak,* CBS, 1971.
Sergeant Jones, "Secret Service," *Theatre in America,* PBS, 1977.
Clifford Connant, "A Steele at Any Price," *Remington Steele,* NBC, 1983.
Carl Wilkerson, "Opening Day," *The Twilight Zone,* CBS, 1985.
John Baldwin, *Amazing Stories,* NBC, 1986.
Professor Finley, "Creep Course," *Tales From the Crypt,* HBO, 1993.
Voice, "I, Duckman," *Duckman* (animated), USA Network, 1994.
Voice of Sloth, "The Race," *Eek! the Cat* (animated), Fox, 1996.
Dr. Scott Perkins, "The Joining," *The Outer Limits,* Showtime, 1998.

Also appeared in *Ryan's Hope,* and *One Life to Live,* both ABC.

Television Appearances; Series:
Walter Kellogg, *The People Next Door,* CBS, 1989.

Television Appearances; Pilots:
Harry, *A Fine Romance,* CBS, 1983.

Television Appearances; Specials:
Voice of the man in the magic mirror, *Disney's DTV Monster Hits* (animated), NBC, 1987.
Milos Forman: Portrait, 1989.
The CBS Premiere Preview Spectacular, CBS, 1989.
The Avenging Angel, 1995.

RECORDINGS

Video Games:
Voice of the President, *Fallout 2,* Interplay, 1998.*

JONES, Quincy 1933-

PERSONAL

Full name, Quincy Delight Jones, Jr.; born March 14, 1933, in Chicago, IL; son of Quincy Delight (a carpenter and semi-professional baseball player) and Sarah Jones; married Jeri Caldwell (divorced); married Ulla Anderson (a model; divorced, 1974); married Peggy Lipton (an actress), 1974 (divorced, 1986); children: Jolie, Martina-Lisa, Quincy III, Kidada, Rashida, Rachelle, Kenya (daughter with Nastassja Kinski). *Education:* Attended Seattle University, Berklee College of Music, and Boston Conservatory; studied music with Nadia Boulanger and Messiaen, Paris.

Addresses: *Publicist*—Arnold Robinson, Rogers and Cowan, 1888 Century Park East, 5th Floor, Los Angeles, CA 90067.

Career: Composer, arranger, producer, and musician. Lionel Hampton Orchestra, trumpeter and music arranger, 1950-53; Dizzy Gillespie's Orchestra, music director and trumpeter, 1956; Mercury Records, music director, 1961, vice president in charge of artists and repertory, 1964; Qwest Records, founder, 1981; QDE (a multi-media entertainment company), founder (with David Salzman and Time-Warner), 1993, co-CEO and chair, 1993—; executive producer of the outdoor concert *A Call for Reunion,* Lincoln Memorial, Washington, DC, 1993. QD7 (an interactive multi-media publishing company), founder (with Salzman and 7th Level, Inc.), 1996; Qwest Broadcasting, founder (with others), c. 1996, CEO and chair 1996—; QJ Entertainment Co., television producer; Disques Barclay, Paris, France, music arranger. *Vibe* (magazine), founder. Music arranger for performers, including Ray Anthony, Tony Bennett, Count Basie, Ray Charles, Peggy Lee, Johnny Mathis, Frank Sinatra, Sara Vaughn, Dinah Washington, and Andy Williams; record producer for Patti Austin, George Benson, Brook Benton, Billy Eckstein, Aretha Franklin, Lesley Gore, Lena Horne, James Ingram, Michael Jackson, Al Jarreau, The Brothers Johnson, Little Richard, Rufus, Rod Temperton, U.S.A. for Africa, and others. Assembled the choir for "We Are the World" benefit record, 1985.

Awards, Honors: Grammy Award nomination, best jazz from a large group, 1960, for *The Great Wild World of Quincy Jones;* Grammy Award nomination, best arrangement, 1960, for "Let the Good Times Roll"; Grammy Award nomination, best orchestra for dancing, 1961, for "I Dig Dancer"; Grammy Award nominations, best original jazz composition and best instrumental arrangement, both 1962, for "Quintessence"; Grammy Award nomination, best orchestra for dancing, 1962, for *Big Band Bossa Nova;* Grammy Award, best instrumental arrangement, 1963, for "I Can't Stop Loving You," recorded by Count Basie; Grammy Award nominations, best jazz from a large group and best orchestra for dancing, both 1963, for *Quincy Jones Plays the Hip Hits;* Grammy Award nomination, best jazz from a large group or soloist with a large group, 1964, for *Quincy Jones Explores the Music of Henry Mancini;* Grammy Award nomination, best original jazz composition, 1964, for "The Witching Hour"; Grammy Award nominations, best non-jazz instrumental and best instrumental arrangement, both 1964, for "Golden Boy"; Academy Award nomination, best song, 1967, for "The Eyes of Love" from *Banning;* Academy Award nomination, best original music score, 1967, for *In Cold Blood;* Grammy Award nomination, best original score for a motion picture or television show, 1967, for *In the Heat of the Night;* Academy Award nomination, best music, song category, 1968, for the title song from *Love of Ivy;* Emmy Award nomination, best music composition for a series, 1969, for *The Bill Cosby Show;* Grammy Award, best instrumental jazz performance from a large group or soloist with a large group, and Grammy Award nomination, best instrumental arrangement, both 1969, for *Walking Space;* Grammy Award nominations, best original score for a motion picture or television show, both 1969, for *The Lost Man* and *McKenna's Gold.*

Grammy Award nominations, best instrumental composition, best instrumental arrangement, and best jazz from a large group or soloist with a large group, all 1970, for *Gula Materi;* Grammy Award nomination, bestcontemporary instrumental, 1970, for "Soul Flower"; Golden Globe Award nomination (shared with Cynthia Weil), best original song, 1970, for "The Time for Love Is Anytime," from *Cactus Flower;* Grammy Award, best pop instrumental performance, 1971, for *Smackwater Jack;* Grammy Award nominations, best instrumental arrangement and best pop instrumental performance, both 1972, for "Money Runner"; Grammy Award nomination, best score for a motion picture or television show, 1972, for *$;* Grammy Award, best instrumental arrangement, 1973, for *Summer in the City;* Grammy Award nomination, best pop instrumental, 1973, for "You've Got It Bad Girl"; Golden Globe Award nomination, best original score, 1973, for *The Getaway;* Gold Record Award, Recording Industry Association of America, and Grammy Award nomination, best pop vocal for duo, group, or chorus, both 1974, for *Body Heat;* Grammy Award nomination, best pop instrumental, 1974, for "Along Came Betty"; Image Award, National Association for the Advancement of Colored People (NAACP), 1974; Grammy Award nomination, best instrumental composition, 1976, for "Midnight Soul Patrol"; Emmy Award, best music composition, and Grammy Award nomination, best instrumental composition, both 1977, for *Roots;* Grammy Award nominations, best arrangement for voices and best inspirational performance, both 1977, for "Oh, Lord, Come By Here"; Academy Award nomination, best score for an adaptation, and Grammy Award, best instrumental arrangement, for the main title song, both 1978, for *The Wiz;* Grammy Award nomination, best instrumental composition, 1978, for "End of the Yellow Brick Road," from *The Wiz;* Grammy Award nomination, producer of the year, 1978; Grammy Award nomination, best arrangement for voices, 1978, for "Stuff Like That"; Grammy Award nomination, best disco recording, 1979, for "Don't Stop 'til You Get Enough."

Grammy Award, best instrumental arrangement, 1980, for "Dinorah, Dinorah"; Grammy Award nomination, producer of the year, 1980; Hollywood Walk of Fame Star, 1980; Image Awards, NAACP, 1980, 1981; Grammy Awards, album of the year and best rhythm and blues performance by a duo or group with vocal, both 1981, for *The Dude;* Grammy Award, best arrangement, on an instrumental recording, Grammy Award nomination, best pop instrumental, both 1981, for "Velas" from *The Dude;* shared Grammy Award, best instrumental arrangement accompanying vocal(s), 1981, for "Ai no corrida" from *The Dude;* Grammy Award, best cast show album,

1981, for *Lena Horne: The Lady and Her Music Live on Broadway;* Grammy Award, producer of the year, 1981; Golden Note Award, American Society of Composers, Authors, and Publishers, 1982; Man of the Year Award, City of Hope, 1982; Grammy Award nominations, nonclassical producer of the year, 1982 and 1983; shared Grammy Award, record of the year, 1983, for *Beat It* and Grammy Award, album of the year, 1983, for *Thriller* (both by Michael Jackson).

Grammy Award, best recording for children, 1983, for *E.T. the Extra-Terrestrial;* shared Grammy Award, producer of the year, 1983; Readers' Poll Award, *Rolling Stone,* producer of the year, 1983; Trendsetters Award, *Billboard,* 1983; Image Award, NAACP, 1983; Grammy Award nomination, best rhythm and blues instrumental, 1983, for "Billy Jean"; Grammy Award nomination, best rhythm and blues song, 1983, for "P.Y.T. (Pretty Young Thing)"; shared Grammy Award, best arrangement on an instrumental, 1984, for "Grace," the gymnastics theme from *Official Music of the XXIII Olympiad In Los Angeles;* Grammy Award nomination, best rhythm and blues song, 1984, for "Ya Mo Be There"; Academy Award nominations, best picture (with others) and best original music score, both 1985, Golden Globe Award nomination, best original score for a motion picture, 1986, for *The Color Purple;* Academy Award nomination, best song, 1985, for "Miss Celie's Blues (Sister)" from *The Color Purple;* Grammy Award, record of the year, 1985, for "We Are the World" by U.S.A. for Africa; Grammy Award, best music video (short form), 1985, for *We Are the World—The Video Event;* Humanitarian Award nomination, T.J. Martell Foundation, 1986; Whitney Young, Jr. Award, Urban League,1986; Grammy Award nomination, nonclassical producer of the year, 1987; Grammy Award nomination, album of the year, 1987, for *Bad* by Michael Jackson; Trustee Award, nonperforming contributions, National Academy of Recording Arts and Sciences, 1989; Lifetime Achievement Award, National Academy of Songwriters, 1989.

Grammy Awards, album of the year and best rap performance, both 1990, for *Back on the Block;* Grammy Award, nonclassical producer of the year, 1990; Grammy Awards, best arrangement on an instrumental and best fusion jazz performance, both 1990, for "Birdland;" Grammy Award, best instrumental arrangement accompanying vocals, 1990, for *The Places You Find Love;* French Legion of Honor, 1990; Image Awards, NAACP, 1990, 1991; Scopus Award, Hebrew University of Jerusalem, 1991; named Entrepreneur of the Year, *U.S.A. Today,* and *Financial News Network,* 1991; Sons of Liberty Award, People for the American Way, 1992; Grammy Award, best jazz instrumental, individual or group, 1994, for *Miles and Quincy: Live at Montreux;* Emmy Award nomination, outstanding informational series, 1995, for *The History of Rock 'n' Roll;* Jean Hersholt Humanitarian Award, National Academy of Motion Picture Arts and Sciences, 1995; Critics' Poll Award and Readers' Poll Award, both from *Downbeat;* Antonio Carlos Jobim Award; award from German Jazz Federation; Edison International Award of Sweeden. *Honorary degrees:* Berklee College of Music, 1983; Howard University, 1985; Seattle University, 1990; Wesleyan University, Loyola University, and Brandeis University, all 1991; Clark University, 1993.

CREDITS

Film Appearances:

Save the Children (documentary), Paramount, 1973.
Himself, *Listen Up: The Lives of Quincy Jones,* Warner Bros., 1990.
Boys N the Hood, Columbia, 1991.
Narrator, *A Great Day in Harlem,* Castle Hill, 1994.

Also appeared in *Blues for Trumpet, Koto,* and *Life Goes On.*

Film Work:

Music director, *A Dandy in Aspic,* Columbia, 1968.
Music supervisor, *Man and Boy,* Levitt-Pickman, 1971.
Music supervisor, *Come Back Charleston Blue,* Warner Bros., 1972.
Music supervisor, *The Wiz,* Universal, 1978.
Producer (with Steven Spielberg, Kathleen Kennedy, and Frank Marshall), *The Color Purple,* Warner Bros., 1985.
Executive music producer, *Fast Forward,* Columbia, 1985.
Executive music producer, *The Slugger's Wife,* Columbia, 1985.
Executive music producer, *Fever Pitch,* Metro-Goldwyn-Mayer/United Artists, 1985.
Executive producer, *Brooms,* QDE Entertainment, 1995.
Producer, *Steel,* Warner Bros., 1997.
Song producer, "9-5," *Office Space,* Twentieth Century-Fox, 1999.

Also executive producer of *Stalingrad.*

Television Appearances; Series:

The History of Rock 'n' Roll, syndicated, 1995.

Television Appearances; Specials:

Duke Ellington. . .We Love You Madly, CBS, 1973.

Diana, CBS, 1981.

Bugs Bunny/Looney Tunes All-Star 50th Anniversary, CBS, 1986.

Whatta Year. . .1986, ABC, 1986.

An All-Star Celebration Honoring Martin Luther King, Jr., NBC, 1986.

Mancini and Friends, PBS, 1987.

All-Star Tribute to Kareem Abdul-Jabbar, NBC, 1989.

"Bernstein at Seventy," *Great Performances,* PBS, 1989.

The Songwriters Hall of Fame 20th Anniversary. . .The Magic of Music, CBS, 1989.

The Unforgettable Nat "King" Cole, The Disney Channel, 1989.

Sammy Davis Jr.'s 60th Anniversary Celebration, ABC, 1990.

Time Warner Presents the Earth Day Special, ABC, 1990.

Sinatra 75: The Best Is Yet to Come (also known as *Frank Sinatra: 75th Birthday Celebration*), CBS, 1990.

Save the Planet: A CBS/Hard Rock Cafe Special (also known as *The Hard Rock Cafe Presents Save the Planet*), CBS, 1990.

The MDA Jerry Lewis Telethon (also known as *The 25th Anniversary MDA Jerry Lewis Labor Day Telethon*), syndicated, 1990.

The Meaning of Life, CBS, 1991.

A Party for Richard Pryor, CBS, 1991.

Host, *Ray Charles: 50 Years in Music, Uh-Huh!,* Fox, 1991.

A Very Special Christmas II, syndicated, 1992.

"Ray Charles: The Genius of Soul," *American Masters,* PBS, 1992.

Michael Jackson. . .The Legend Continues, CBS, 1992.

Malcom X: The Real Story, CBS, 1992.

The 25th Montreux Music Festival, The Disney Channel, 1992.

An American Reunion: New Beginnings, Renewed Hope (also known as *An American Reunion: The People's Inaugural Celebration*), HBO, 1993.

"Miles Davis: A Tribute" (also known as "Miles at Montreux"), *Great Performances,* PBS, 1993.

Shirly Horn: Here's to Life, PBS, 1993.

People's 20th Birthday, ABC, 1994.

The Jackson Family Honors, NBC, 1994.

"We Are the World:" A 10th Anniversary Tribute, The Disney Channel, 1995.

The American Film Institute Salute to Steven Spielberg (also known as *The American Film Institute Life Achievement Award*), NBC, 1995.

Interviewee, *Television's Greatest Performances,* ABC, 1995.

Celebrate the Dream: 50 Years of Ebony, ABC, 1996.

Interviewee, *Intimate Portrait: Gloria Estefan,* Lifetime, 1996.

Star Trek: 30 Years and Beyond, UPN, 1996.

An Evening of Stars: A Celebration of Educational Excellence Benefiting the United Negro College Fund, syndicated, 1998.

Frame After Frame: The Images of Herman Leonard, PBS, 1998.

Interviewee, *Monica Mancini. . .On Record,* PBS, 1998.

Quincy Jones—The First 50 Years, ABC, 1998.

I'll Make Me a World: A Century of African-American Arts, PBS, 1999.

Television Appearances; Awards Presentations:

The Kennedy Center Honors: A Celebration of the Performing Arts, CBS, 1986.

The 31st Annual Grammy Awards, 1989.

Grammy Legends Show (also known as *Grammy Living Legends Awards*), CBS, 1990.

The 4th Annual Soul Train Music Awards, syndicated, 1990.

The 33rd Annual Grammy Awards, CBS, 1991.

The 23rd NAACP Image Awards, NBC, 1991.

Presenter, *Celebrate the Soul of American Music,* syndicated, 1991.

The 24th NAACP Image Awards, NBC, 1992.

The 1993 Billboard Music Awards, Fox, 1993.

Presenter, *The 65th Annual Academy Awards Presentations,* ABC, 1993.

The Essence Awards, Fox, 1994.

The 10th Annual Television Academy Hall of Fame, The Disney Channel, 1994.

Presenter, *The 4th Annual Environmental Media Awards,* TBS, 1994.

The American Music Awards, ABC, 1995.

The Horatio Alger Awards, CBS, 1995.

Honoree, *The 67th Annual Academy Awards,* ABC, 1995.

The 68th Annual Academy Awards, ABC, 1996.

The 27th Annual NAACP Image Awards, 1996.

Presenter, *The 10th Annual Essence Awards,* 1997.

Presenter, *The 23rd Annual People's Choice Awards,* 1997.

The 39th Annual Grammy Awards, 1997.

The 11th Annual Soul Train Music Awards, 1997.

The 12th Annual Soul Train Music Awards, 1998.

The 24th Annual People's Choice Awards, 1998.

Television Appearances; Episodic:

Host, *Saturday Night Live,* NBC, 1990.

Himself, "Someday Your Prince Will Be in Effect," *The Fresh Prince of Bel-Air,* NBC, 1990.
Himself, *New York Undercover,* Fox, 1996.

Television Work; Series:

Music director, *The New Bill Cosby Show,* CBS, 1972-73.
Creator and executive producer, *The Jesse Jackson Show* (also known as *Voices of America with Jesse Jackson*), syndicated, 1990.
Executive producer, *The Fresh Prince of Bel-Air* (also known as *The Fresh Prince Show*), NBC, 1990.
Executive producer, *Mad TV,* Fox, 1995.
Executive producer, *In the House,* NBC, 1995-97.
Co-executive producer, *The History of Rock 'n' Roll,* syndicated, 1995.
Executive producer, *Vibe,* syndicated, 1997-98.

Television Work; Specials:

Producer and music director, *Duke Ellington. . .We Love You Madly,* CBS, 1973.
Music director, *A Show Business Salute to Milton Berle,* NBC, 1973.
Music director, *An All-Star Celebration Honoring Martin Luther King, Jr.,* NBC, 1986.
Executive producer, *The Meaning of Life,* CBS, 1991.
Conductor, "Great Performances' 20th Anniversary Special," *Great Performances,* PBS, 1992.
Executive producer, *A Cool Like That Christmas,* Fox, 1993.
Executive producer, *An American Reunion: New Beginnings, Renewed Hope* (also known as *An American Reunion: The People's Inaugural Celebration*), HBO, 1993.
Executive producer, "Miles Davis: A Tribute" (also known as "Miles at Montreux"), *Great Performances,* PBS, 1993.
Executive producer, *The Roots of Country: Nashville Celebrates the Ryman,* CBS, 1994.
Executive producer, *On Trial,* NBC, 1994.
Executive Producer, *Concert of the Americas* (also known as *The Kennedy Center Presents*), PBS, 1994.
Music conductor, *Frank, Dean and Sammy: An Evening With the Rat Pack,* TV Land, 1998.
Music conductor, *Phil Collins—The Big Band,* PBS, 1998.

Television Work; Awards Presentations:

Producer, *The 68th Annual Academy Awards,* ABC, 1996.

Television Work; Pilots:

Co-executive producer, *Heart and Soul,* NBC, 1988.
Executive producer, *Livin' Large,* ABC, 1989.

Television Work; Movies:

Executive producer, *Passing Glory,* Fox, 1999.

RECORDINGS

Albums:

The Birth of the Band, Mercury, 1959.
The Great Wild World of Quincy Jones, Mercury, 1960.
Newport, Mercury, 1961.
I Dig Dancers, Mercury, 1961.
Quintessence, Impulse, 1961.
Brand New Bag, Mercury, 1963.
Quincy Jones Plays the Hip Hits, Mercury, 1963.
Quincy Jones Explores the Music of Henry Mancini, Mercury, 1964.
Golden Boy, Mercury, 1964.
Quincy Plays for Pussycats, Mercury, 1965.
Sinatra at the Sands, 1966.
Walking in Space, A&M, 1969.
Gula Matari, A&M, 1970.
Smackwater Jack, A&M, 1971.
Summer in the City, A&M, 1973.
You've Got It Bad Girl, A&M, 1973.
(With others) *This Is How I Feel About Jazz,* Impulse, 1974.
Mode (re-issue), Impulse, 1974.
Body Heat, A&M, 1974.
Mellow Madness, A&M, 1975.
I Heard That, A&M, 1976.
Roots, A&M, 1978.
Go West, Man, Impulse, 1978.
Sounds. . .and Stuff Like That, A&M, 1978.
The Great Wide World of Quincy Jones, Mercury, 1981.
The Dude, A&M, 1981.
Lena Horne: The Lady and Her Music Live on Broadway, Qwest/Warner Bros., 1981.
The Best of Quincy Jones, A&M, 1982.
Back on the Block, Qwest Records/Warner Bros., 1989.
Boys N the Hood (original soundtrack), 1991.
Miles and Quincy: Live at Montreux, Reprise Records, 1993.
Q's Jook Joint, Qwest Records, 1995.

WRITINGS

Film Scores:

Pojken i tradet (also known as *The Boy in the Tree*), 1964.

The Pawnbroker, Landau/Allied Artists/American International, 1965.
The Slender Thread, Paramount, 1965.
Walk Don't Run, Columbia, 1966.
Made in Paris, Metro-Goldwyn-Mayer, 1966.
Banning, Universal, 1967.
The Deadly Affair, Columbia, 1967.
Enter Laughing, Columbia, 1967.
In Cold Blood, Columbia, 1967.
In the Heat of the Night, United Artists, 1967.
Mirage, Universal, 1968.
The Counterfeit Killer, Universal, 1968.
A Dandy in Aspic, Columbia, 1968.
For Love of Ivy, Cinerama, 1968.
The Hell With Heroes, Universal, 1968.
Jigsaw, Universal, 1968.
The Split, Metro-Goldwyn-Mayer, 1968.
Bob and Carol and Ted and Alice, Columbia, 1969.
Cactus Flower, Columbia, 1969.
The Italian Job, Paramount, 1969.
John and Mary, Twentieth Century-Fox, 1969.
The Lost Man, Universal, 1969.
Mackena's Gold, Columbia, 1969.
The Out-of-Towners, Columbia, 1970.
They Call Me Mister Tibbs!, United Artists, 1970.
Up Your Teddy Bear (also known as *The Toy Grabbers* and *Mother*), Geneni/Richard, 1970.
The Last of the Mobile Hotshots (also known as *Blood Kin*), Warner Bros., 1970.
Eggs (short film), 1970.
Of Men and Demons (short film), 1970.
The Anderson Tapes, Columbia, 1971.
Brother John, Columbia, 1971.
Honky, Jack H. Harris, 1971.
$ (also known as *Dollars* and *The Heist*), Columbia, 1971.
(With Donny Hathaway) *Some Back Charleston Blue,* Warner Bros., 1972.
The Getaway, National General, 1972.
The Hot Rock (also known as *How to Steel a Diamond in Four Easy Lessons*), Twentieth Century-Fox, 1972.
The New Centurions (also known as *Precinct 45: Los Angeles Police*), Columbia, 1972.
Mother, Jugs and Speed, Twentieth Century-Fox, 1976.
The Wiz, Universal, 1978.
The Color Purple, Warner Bros., 1985.
(With Thomas Dolby) *Fever Pitch,* Metro-Goldwyn-Mayer/United Artists, 1985.
Listen Up: The Lives of Quincy Jones, Warner Bros., 1990.

Also composer of the scores for *Blues for Trumpet, Koto,* and *Life Goes On.*

Television Music; Series:
Hey Landlord, NBC, 1966-67.
The Bill Cosby Show, NBC, 1969-71.
Sanford and Son, NBC, 1972-77.
Sanford Arms, NBC, 1977.
Theme music, *The Oprah Winfrey Show,* syndicated, 1989.
The Fresh Prince of Bel-Air (also known as *The Fresh Prince Show*), NBC, 1990.
Out All Night (also known as *Up All Night* and *The Neighborhood*), NBC, 1992.

Television Music; Pilots:
Ironside, NBC, 1967.
Split Second to an Epitaph, NBC, 1968.
Killer by Night, CBS, 1972.

Other Television Music:
(With Gerald Fried) *Roots* (miniseries), ABC, 1977.
The Meaning of Life (special), CBS, 1991.
The Return of Ironside (movie), NBC, 1993.

Autobiography:
Listen Up: The Lives of Quincy Jones, Warner Books, 1990.

Adaptations: *Listen Up: The Lives of Quincy Jones* was adapted for film and produced by Courtney Sale Ross, 1990, released by Warner Bros.

OTHER SOURCES

Periodicals:
Billboard, December 16, 1995, pp. 22-30.
Black Enterprise, June, 1996, pp. 244-251.
Interview, November, 1995, pp. 28-30.
New York Times, November 18, 1990.
People Weekly, October 15, 1990, p. 105; May 6, 1996, p. 172.*

JONES, Tommy Lee 1946-

PERSONAL

Born September 15, 1946, in San Saba, TX; son of Clyde C. (an oil field worker) and Lucille Marie (police officer, schoolteacher, and beauty shop owner; maiden name, Scott) Jones; married Kate Lardner, 1971 (divorced, 1978); married Kimberlea Gayle Cloughley (a photojournalist), May 30, 1981 (divorced, 1996); children: Austin Leonard, Victoria

Kafka. *Education:* Harvard University, B.A. (English; cum laude), 1969. *Avocational Interests:* Polo.

Addresses: *Agent*—Michael Black, International Creative Management, 8942 Wilshire Blvd., Beverly Hills, CA 90211.

Career: Actor, director and screenwriter. Worked in the Texas oil fields prior to his acting career; voice of Red Dog in commercials for Red Dog beer.

Member: Actors' Equity Association, Screen Actors Guild, American Federation of Television and Radio Artists, Academy of Television Arts and Sciences, Academy of Motion Picture Arts and Sciences, Writers Guild of America, Directors Guild of America.

Awards, Honors: Golden Globe Award nomination, best actor in a motion picture—comedy or musical, 1981, for *The Coal Miner's Daughter;* Emmy Award, outstanding lead actor in a miniseries or special, 1983, for *The Executioner's Song;* Emmy Award nomination, outstanding lead actor in a miniseries or special, 1989, Golden Globe Award nomination, best performance by an actor in a supporting role in a series, miniseries or motion picture made for television, 1990, for *Lonesome Dove;* Academy Award nomination, and Golden Globe Award nomination, both best supporting actor, both 1991, for *JFK;* named Hasty Pudding Man of the Year, Hasty Pudding Theatricals, c. 1992; Los Angeles Film Critics Award, Chicago Film Critics Award, British Academy of Film and Television Arts Award, and Academy Award, best supporting actor, 1993, Golden Globe Award, best performance by an actor in a supporting role in a motion picture, MTV Movie Award, best on-screen duo (with Harrison Ford), 1994, all for *The Fugitive;* MTV Movie Award nomination, best villain, 1996, for *Batman Forever;* Screen Actors Guild Award nomination, outstanding performance by a male actor in a television movie or miniseries, 1996, for *The Good Old Boys;* MTV Award nomination, best on-screen duo (with Will Smith), Golden Satellite Award nomination, best actor in a motion picture—comedy or musical, Blockbuster Entertainment Award nomination, favorite science-fiction actor, all 1998, for *Men in Black.*

CREDITS

Film Appearances:

(Film debut; as Tom Lee Jones) Hank, *Love Story,* Paramount, 1970.
Tommy, *Eliza's Horoscope,* O-Zali Films, 1970.
Gus, *Life Study,* Nebbco, 1972.
Coley Blake, *Jackson County Jail* (also known as *Outside Chance*), New World, 1976.
Johnny Vohden, *Rolling Thunder,* American International, 1977.
Angelo Perino, *The Betsy* (also known as *Harold Robbins' The Betsey*), Allied Artists, 1978.
John Neville, *Eyes of Laura Mars,* Columbia, 1978.
Doolittle "Mooney" Lynn, *The Coal Miner's Daughter,* Universal, 1980.
Elmore Pratt, *Back Roads,* Warner Bros., 1981.
Captain Bully Hayes, *Nate and Hayes* (also known as *Savage Islands*), Paramount, 1983.
Billy, *The River Rat,* Paramount, 1984.
Quint, *Black Moon Rising,* New World, 1986.
George Cole, *The Big Town,* Columbia, 1987.
Cosmo, *Stormy Monday,* Atlantic Releasing, 1988.
Thomas Boyette, *The Package,* Orion, 1989.
Brad Little, *Fire Birds* (also known as *Wings of the Apache*), Buena Vista, 1990.
Clay Shaw, *JFK,* Warner Bros., 1991.
William Strannix, *Under Siege,* Warner Bros., 1992.
U.S. Marshal Samuel Gerard, *The Fugitive,* Warner Bros., 1993.
Steve Butler, *Heaven & Earth,* Warner Bros., 1993.
Dr. Jake Beerlander, *House of Cards,* Miramax, 1993.
Colonel Hank Marshall, *Blue Sky,* Orion, 1994.
Ryan Gaerity, *Blown Away,* Metro-Goldwyn-Mayer/United Artists, 1994.
Dwight McClusky, *Natural Born Killers,* Warner Bros., 1994.
"Reverend" Roy Foltrigg, *The Client,* Warner Bros., 1994.
Tyrus Raymond Cobb, *Cobb,* Warner Bros., 1994.
Harvey "Two-face" Dent, *Batman Forever* (also known as *Forever*), Warner Bros., 1995.
Mike Roark, *Volcano,* Twentieth Century-Fox, 1997.
Agent K, *Men in Black* (also known as *MIB*), Columbia, 1997.
Chief Deputy Marshal Samuel Gerard, *U.S. Marshals,* Warner Bros., 1998.
Voice of Major Chip Hazard, *Small Soldiers* (also known as *The Commando Elite*), DreamWorks, 1998.
Mike Hodges, *Rules of Engagement,* 1999.
Parole officer, *Double Jeopardy,* Paramount, 1999.

Television Appearances; Movies:

Officer Hutton, *Smash-up on Interstate 5,* ABC, 1976.
Title role, *The Amazing Howard Hughes,* CBS, 1977.
Bill Starbuck, *The Rainmaker,* HBO, 1982.
Mitch Harris, *The Park Is Mine,* HBO, 1985.
Steve Daley, *Yuri Nosenko, KGB,* HBO, 1986.

Father Joseph McMahon, *Broken Vows* (also known as *Where the Dark Streets Go* and *Hennessey*), CBS, 1987.
Buddy, *Stranger on My Land,* ABC, 1988.
Moses Cooper, "April Morning," *Hallmark Hall of Fame,* CBS, 1988.
Eddie Martel Mallard, *Gotham* (also known as *The Dead Can't Lie*), Showtime 1988.
Hewey Collaway, *The Good Old Boys,* TNT, 1995.

Television Appearances; Miniseries:
Gary Gilmore, *The Executioner's Song,* NBC, 1982.
Woodrow F. Call, *Lonesome Dove,* CBS, 1989.

Television Appearances; Specials:
Brick, *Cat on a Hot Tin Roof,* Showtime, 1984, rebroadcast on *American Playhouse,* PBS, 1985.
Texas 150: A Celebration, ABC, 1986.
Lonesome Dove: The Making of an Epic, TNN, 1992.
Riddle Me This: Why is Batman Forever?, ABC, 1995.
The 67th Annual Academy Awards, 1995.
Presenter, *The 69th Annual Academy Awards,* 1997.

Also appeared as Abner Snopes, "Barn Burning," *American Short Stories.*

Television Appearances; Episodic:
"Fatal Witness," *Barnaby Jones,* CBS, 1975.
"Al Gore: A Burning Ambition," *Biography,* Arts and Entertainment, 1997.

Also appeared in *Inside the Actors Studio;* as Prisoner, *Baretta.*

Television Appearances; Series:
Dr. Mark Toland, *One Life to Live* (also known as *Between Heaven and Hell*), ABC, 1971-75.

Television Appearances; Pilots:
Aram Kolegian, *Charlie's Angels,* ABC, 1976.

Television Work; Movies:
Director, *The Good Old Boys,* TNT, 1995.

Stage Appearances:
(Broadway debut) *A Patriot for Me,* Imperial Theatre, New York City, 1969.
Fortune and Men's Eyes, Stage 73, New York City, 1969.
Delivery Man, *House of Dunkelmayer,* Broadhurst Theatre, New York City, 1971.
Joel, *Toreador,* Broadhurst Theatre, New York City, 1971.
Four on a Garden, Broadhurst Theatre, New York City, 1971.
Simpson and Papa, *Blue Boys,* Martinique Theatre, New York City, 1972.
Stephen Dedalus, *Ulysses in Nighttown,* Winter Garden Theatre, New York City, 1974.
Austin, *True West,* New York Shakespeare Festival, Public Theatre, New York City, 1981.

Also appeared in *The Time Trial* and *Fishing,* both New York Shakespeare Festival.

Stage Work; Director:
The Authentic Life of Billy the Kid, Josephine Street Theatre, San Antonio, TX, 1990.

WRITINGS

Television Writing:
The Good Old Boys, TNT, 1995.

OTHER SOURCES

Periodicals:
Elle, August, 1993.
Entertainment Weekly, December 23, 1994, pp. 28-33.
Film Comment, January-February, 1994, pp. 30-36.
GQ, March, 1994, pp. 210-215.
Interview, June, 1995, p. 80.
Jet, June 23, 1997, p. 62.
Los Angeles Times, August 1, 1993, sec. F, pp. 6, 28-30.
New Yorker, April 4, 1994, pp. 57-63.
New York Times, March 5, 1995, sec. 2.
People Weekly, September 6, 1993, pp. 83-85; December 27, 1993-January 3, 1994, pp. 106-107; August 28, 1995, p. 42.
Texas Monthly, October, 1993, p. 106.
Time, September 6, 1993, p. 65.
USA Weekend, January 6-8, 1995, pp. 4-5.*

JORDAN, Neil 1950-

PERSONAL

Full name, Neil Patrick Jordan; born February 25, 1950, in County Sligo, Ireland; son of Michael (a teacher) and Angela (a painter; maiden name, O'Brien) Jordan; married Vivienne (divorced); children: (with Vivienne) Sarah, Anna, Ben; (with Brenda

Rawn) Daniel. *Education:* National University of Ireland, University College, Dublin, B.A., 1972.

Addresses: *Office*—c/o Jenne Casarotto/Casarotto Co. Ltd., National House 60/66 Wardour St., London WIV 3HP, England.

Career: Director and writer. Irish Writers Cooperative, co-founder, administrator, and chairperson of board of directors, beginning 1974; worked as a laborer, teacher, and saxophonist.

Awards, Honors: Grant from British Arts Council, 1976; fiction prize, *Guardian,* 1979, for "Night in Tunisia"; named "most promising newcomer" by *Evening Standard,* 1982, and Best First Feature Film Award, Durban International Film Festival, 1983, for *Angel;* Arts Award, *Sunday Independent,* 1984; London Critics Circle Award, best film, Fantasy Film Festival Award, best film, Critics Prize, best film, all 1985, for *The Company of Wolves;* Golden Scroll, Academy of Science Fiction, Fantasy, and Horror Films, outstanding achievement, 1985; Golden Globe Award, Hollywood Foreign Press Association, New York Film Critics Award, Balladolid Award, Los Angeles Critics Circle Award, London Critics Circle Award, all 1986, for *Mona Lisa;* Ireland's People of the Year Award, 1986; Academy Award nominations, best picture and best director, Academy Award, best original screenplay, Alexander Korda Award (shared with Stephen Woolley), British Academy Awards, best British film, BAFTA Film Award nominations, British Academy Awards, best direction, best film, and best original screenplay, all 1993, for *The Crying Game;* Silver Berlin Bear Award, Berlin International Film Festival, best director, Golden Berlin Bear Award nomination, Berlin International Film Festival, both 1998, for *The Butcher Boy.*

CREDITS

Film Work; Director, Except Where Indicated:

Angel, Motion Picture Co., 1982, released as *Danny Boy,* Triumph Films, 1984.
The Company of Wolves, Cannon, 1984.
Mona Lisa, Island Pictures, 1986.
Executive producer (with others), *The Courier,* Vestron Pictures, 1987.
High Spirits, TriStar, 1988.
We're No Angels, Paramount, 1989.
The Miracle, Miramax, 1991.
The Crying Game, Miramax, 1992.
Interview with the Vampire, Warner Bros., 1994.
Michael Collins, Warner Bros., 1996.
And executive producer, *The Butcher,* Warner Bros., 1997.
In Dreams, DreamWorks, 1999.
And producer, *The End of the Affair,* Columbia, forthcoming.

Also director of a documentary on the making of *Excalibur.*

Television Work; Director; Specials:

"Miss Otis Regrets/Just One of Those Things," a segment of *Red, Hot, and Blue,* ABC, 1990.

Television Appearances; Specials:

Independent Spirit: Close Up, Bravo, 1993.

WRITINGS

Screenplays:

Traveller, 1981.
Script consultant, *Excalibur,* Warner Bros., 1981.
Angel, Motion Picture Co., 1982, released as *Danny Boy,* Triumph Films, 1984.
(With Angela Carter) *The Company of Wolves* (based on a story by Carter), Cannon, 1984.
(With David Leland) *Mona Lisa,* Island Pictures, 1986, published by Faber, 1986.
High Spirits, TriStar, 1988.
The Miracle (based on his story "Night in Tunisia"), Miramax, 1991.
The Crying Game, Miramax, 1992.
Michael Collins, Warner Bros., 1996.
The Butcher Boy, Warner Bros., 1997.
In Dreams, DreamWorks, 1999.
The End of the Affair, Columbia, forthcoming.

Television Movies:

Mr. Solomon Wept, BBC, 1978.
Seduction, RTE (Ireland), 1978.
Tree, RTE, 1978.
Miracles and Miss Langan, RTE, 1979.
Night in Tunisia (also known as *Channel Crossing;* based on his story "Night in Tunisia"), RTE, 1980.

Radio Plays:

Miracles and Miss Langan, RTE, 1977.

Other:

Night in Tunisia and Other Stories, Co-Op Books (Dublin), 1976, Braziller, 1980.
The Past (novel), J. Cape/Braziller, 1979.
The Dream of a Beast (novel), Chatto & Windus, 1983, Random House, 1988.
A Neil Jordan Reader (stories), Vintage, 1993.

Sunrise with Sea Monster, Chatto & Windus (London), 1994, published in the U.S. as *Nightlines,* Random (New York City), 1995.

Works are also represented in anthologies including *Paddy No More,* Longship Press, 1978; and *New Writing and Writers 16,* Humanities, 1979; contributor of poems to magazines.

OTHER SOURCES

Periodicals:

American Film, January, 1990, p. 36.
Chicago Tribune, April 22, 1985; November 21, 1988.
Cineaste, fall, 1996, p. 20.
Film Comment, January-February, 1990, p. 9.
Interview, December, 1989, p. 75.
Los Angeles Times, November 19, 1980; April 19, 1985; June 20, 1985; November 18, 1988.
Newsweek, May 6, 1985; June 16, 1986.
New Yorker, June 16, 1986.
New York Times, May 18, 1984; April 19, 1985; June 13, 1986; November 18, 1988.
New York Times Magazine, January 9, 1994, p. 22.
People Weekly, June 16, 1986.
Time International, February, 23, 1998, p. 52.
Village Voice, May 29, 1984; April 30, 1985; June 17, 1986.
Washington Post, November 9, 1988.*

K

KAGAN, Jeremy 1945-
(Jeremy Paul Kagan)

PERSONAL

Full name, Jeremy Paul Kagan; born December 14, 1945, in Mt. Vernon, NY; son of Henry Enoch and Esther (Miller) Kagan; married Elaine Goren, March 17, 1974; children: Eve Laura. *Education:* Harvard University, B.A. (magna cum laude), 1967; New York University, M.F.A., 1969; American Film Institute, 1971. *Avocational interests:* Playing the clarinet, painting.

Addresses: *Agent*—Larry Becsey, Becsey, Wisdom, and Kalajian, 9229 Sunset Blvd., Suite 710, Los Angeles, CA 90069. *Office*—c/o Our Own Co./Brentwood Management, 11812 San Vicente Blvd., Los Angeles, CA 90049-5022.

Career: Director and writer. Worked as animator, 1968; multimedia show designer, White House Conference on Youth and Education.

Member: Writers Guild of America, Directors Guild of America, Phi Beta Kappa.

Awards, Honors: American Animators, first prize, 1968, for *Once Upon a Line;* Golden Eagle Award, and Silver Knight Award, Malta Festival, both 1973, for *The Love Song of Charles Faberman;* Emmy Award nomination, 1973, for *My Dad Lives in a Downtown Hotel;* Grand Prize, Montreal Film Festival, and Christopher Award, 1982, for *The Chosen;* Gold Prize, Moscow Film Festival, 1987, for *The Journey of Natty Gann;* CableACE Award, 1987, for *Conspiracy: The Trial of the Chicago Eight.*

CREDITS

Film Work; Director:

Once Upon a Line (animated), 1968.
The Love Song of Charles Faberman, American Film Institute, 1973.
Scott Joplin, Universal, 1977.
Heroes, Universal, 1977.
The Big Fix, Universal, 1977.
The Chosen, Contemporary, 1982.
The Sting II, Universal, 1983.
The Journey of Natty Gann, Buena Vista, 1985.
Big Man on Campus, Vestron Video/Live Home Video, 1991.
By the Sword, Hansen Entertainment, 1991.

Film Appearances:

Someone to Love, Castle Hill, 1988.

Television Work; Director; Episodic:

Nichols (also known as *James Garner as Nichols*), NBC, 1971-72.
Columbo, NBC, 1972.
"The Doctors," *The Bold Ones,* NBC, 1972.
Faerie Tale Theater, Showtime, 1982.
Dr. Quinn: Medicine Woman, ABC, 1993.
Chicago Hope, CBS, 1994-95.
Picket Fences, CBS, 1995.
Ally McBeal, Fox, 1997.

Television Work; Director; Movies, Except Where Indicated:

Unwed Father, ABC, 1974.
Katherine, ABC, 1975.
Sleeping Beauty, 1983.
Courage, CBS, 1986.
The Trial of the Chicago Eight, HBO, 1987.
Descending Angel, HBO, 1990.
And co-producer, *Roswell* (also known as *Roswell: The U.F.O. Cover-Up*), Showtime, 1994.

The Hired Heart, Lifetime, 1997.
Color of Justice, Showtime, 1997.

Television Work; Director; Specials:
"My Dad Lives in a Downtown Hotel," *ABC After-School Special,* ABC, 1973.

Television Work; Director; Pilots:
Judge Dee in the Monastery Murders, ABC, 1974.

Television Appearances; Specials:
Moderator, *The Director's Vision: Hollywood's Best Discuss Their Craft,* Sundance Channel, 1998.

WRITINGS

Screenplays:
The Love Song of Charles Faberman, American Film Intstitute, 1973.

Television Movies:
Katherine, ABC, 1975.
Conspiracy: The Trial of the Chicago Eight, HBO, 1987.
Roswell, 1994.*

KAGAN, Jeremy Paul
See KAGAN, Jeremy

KAHN, Madeline 1942-

PERSONAL

Born September 29, 1942, in Boston, MA; daughter of Bernard B. Wolfson and Paula Kahn. *Education:* Hofstra University, B.A., 1964; studied acting at Warren Robertson Actors' Workshop; trained as an opera singer.

Addresses: *Agent*—c/o Marc Schwartz, William Morris Agency, 151 El Camino Dr., Beverly Hills, CA 90212.

Career: Actress and singer. Upstairs at the Downstairs, New York City, 1966-67.

Awards, Honors: Academy Award nomination, best supporting actress and Golden Globe Award nomination, both 1973, for *Paper Moon;* Antoinette Perry Award nomination, best actress in a drama, and Drama Desk Award, both 1974, for *The Boom Boom Room;* Academy Award nomination, best actress, 1974, and First Annual Academy of Humor Award, 1975, for *Blazing Saddles;* Distinguished Service Award, Hofstra University Alumni Association, 1975; Golden Globe Award nomination, best actress, 1975, for *Young Frankenstein;*Antoinette Perry Award nomination, best actress in a musical, 1978, for *On the Twentieth Century;* People's Choice Award, best female performer in a new television program, 1984, for *Oh Madeline;* Emmy Award, 1986, for Ellie Coleman, "Wanted: The Perfect Guy," *ABC After School Specials;* Antoinette Perry Award nomination, best leading actress in a play, 1989, for *Born Yesterday;* Antoinette Perry Award, best leading actress in a play, 1993, Drama Desk Award, and Outer Critics Cirlce Award, all for *The Sisters Rosensweig;* honorary arts doctorate degree, Boston Conservatory.

CREDITS

Stage Appearances:
Kiss Me Kate, City Center Theatre, New York City, 1965.
(Broadway debut) Ensemble, *New Faces of 1968* (revue), Booth Theatre, New York City, 1968.
Cunegonde, *Candide in Concert* (opera), Philharmonic Hall, New York City, 1968.
Servant, *Promenade,* Promenade Theatre, New York City, 1969.
Goldie, *Two by Two,* Imperial Theatre, New York City, 1970.
Chrissy, *The Boom Boom Room,* New York Shakespeare Festival, Vivian Beaumont Theatre, New York City, 1973.
Amalia Balash, *She Loves Me,* Town Hall, New York City, 1977.
Diane McBride, *Marco Polo Sings a Solo,* New York Shakespeare Festival, Public Theatre, New York City, 1977.
Mildred Plotka and Lily Garland, *On the Twentieth Century,* St. James Theatre, New York City, 1978.
Madame Arcati, *Blithe Spirit,* Santa Fe Festival Theatre, Santa Fe, NM, 1983.
Shirley, *What's Wrong with This Picture?,* Manhattan Theatre Club, New York City, 1985.
Billie Dawn, *Born Yesterday,* 46th Street Theatre, New York City, 1989.
Sondheim: A Celebration at Carnegie Hall, Carnegie Hall, New York City, 1992.
Gorgeous Teitelbaum, *The Sisters Rosensweig,* Mitzi E. Newhouse Theatre, New York City, 1992-93, then Ethel Barrymore Theatre, New York City, 1993.

Co-host, *Broadway Canteen 7th Annual Easter Bonnet Competition,* Broadway Theatre, New York City, 1993.

Also appeared off-Broadway in *A Christmas Memory;* appeared in *America,* Santa Fe Festival Theatre; also appeared in the operas *La Boheme,* Washington Opera Society, Washington, DC, and *La Perichole,* Carnegie Hall, New York City.

Film Appearances:

(Film debut) *The Dove* (short film), Coe/Davis/Love, 1968.

Eunice Burns, *What's Up Doc?,* Warner Bros., 1972.

Schoolteacher, *From the Mixed-Up Files of Mrs. Basil E. Frankweiler* (also known as *The Hideaways*), Cinema V, 1973.

Trixie Delight, *Paper Moon,* Paramount, 1973.

Lili Schtupp, *Blazing Saddles,* Warner Bros., 1974.

Elizabeth, *Young Frankenstein,* Twentieth Century-Fox, 1974.

Jenny Hill, *The Adventures of Sherlock Holmes' Smarter Brother,* Twentieth Century-Fox, 1975.

Kitty O'Kelly, *At Long Last Love,* Twentieth Century-Fox, 1975.

Estie Del Ruth, *Won Ton Ton, the Dog Who Saved Hollywood,* Paramount, 1976.

Victoria Brisbane, *High Anxiety,* Twentieth Century-Fox, 1977.

Mrs. Montenegro, *The Cheap Detective,* Columbia, 1978.

El Sleezo patron, *The Muppet Movie,* Associated Film Distribution, 1979.

Mrs. Constance Link, *First Family,* Warner Bros., 1980.

Bunny Weinberger, *Happy Birthday, Gemini,* United Artists, 1980.

Cynthia, *Simon,* Warner Bros., 1980.

Sorceress, *Wholly Moses!,* Columbia, 1980.

Empress Nympho, *History of the World Part I,* Twentieth Century-Fox, 1981.

Betty, *Yellowbeard,* Orion, 1983.

Caroline Howley, *City Heat,* Warner Bros., 1984.

Eliza Swain and Letitia Swain, *Slapstick of Another Kind,* Entertainment Releasing/International Film Marketing, 1984.

Mrs. White, *Clue,* Paramount, 1985.

Voice of Draggle, *My Little Pony* (animated), De Laurentiis Entertainment Group, 1986.

Voice of Gussie Mausheimer, *An American Tale* (animated), Universal, 1986.

Lola Hopper, *Betsy's Wedding,* Buena Vista, 1990.

Mrs. Munchnik, *Mixed Nuts* (also known as *Lifesavers* and *The Night Before Christmas*), TriStar, 1994.

Martha Mitchell, *Nixon,* Buena Vista, 1995.

Voice of Gypsy Moth, *A Bug's Life* (animated), Buena Vista, 1998.

Alice Gold, *Judy Berlin,* Caruso/Mendelsohn Productions, 1999.

Television Appearances; Series:

Madeline Wayne, *Oh Madeline,* ABC, 1983-84.

Lois Gullickson, *Mr. President,* Fox, 1987-88.

Pidgeon Plumtree, *Avonlea,* The Disney Channel, 1990.

Nan Chase, *New York News,* CBS, 1995.

Pauline, *Cosby,* CBS, 1996—.

Television Appearances; Movies:

Miss Kelly, "Harvey," *Hallmark Hall of Fame,* NBC, 1972.

Violet Kingsley, *Chameleon,* ABC, 1986.

For Richer, For Poorer (also known as *Getting There*), HBO, 1992.

Sabrina, *Ivana Trump's "For Love Alone"* (also known as *Ivana—For Love Alone*), CBS, 1996.

Sharon Semple, *Neil Simon's "London Suite,"* (also known as *London Suite*), NBC, 1996.

Television Appearances; Specials:

Comedy Night, CBS, 1970.

The George Burns Special, CBS, 1976.

Comic Relief, HBO, 1986.

Ellie Coleman, "Wanted: The Perfect Guy," *ABC Afterschool Specials,* ABC, 1986.

Irving Berlin's 100th Birthday Celebration, CBS, 1988.

Sesame Street Special, PBS, 1988.

Lovelaughs, Lifetime, 1991.

Carnegie Hall at 100: A Place of Dreams, PBS, 1991.

Host and Pat Nixon, *Saturday Night Live's Presidential Bash* (also known as *Saturday Night Live's Election Special*), NBC, 1992.

Night of About 14 CBS Stars, Comedy Central, 1996.

Narrator, *Intimate Portrait: Phylicia Rashad,* Lifetime, 1998.

Television Appearances; Awards Presentations:

The 2nd Annual American Comedy Awards, 1988.

The 3rd Annual American Comedy Awards, 1989.

The 47th Annual Tony Awards, CBS, 1993.

The 48th Annual Tony Awards, CBS, 1994.

Television Appearances; Episodic:

Evening at the Improv, syndicated, 1981.

The ABC Comedy Special, ABC, 1986.

"Celebrating Gershwin," *Great Performances,* PBS, 1987.

Grace Anderson, "More Stately Mansions," *Kurt Vonnegut's Monkey House,* Showtime, 1991.

"Sondheim: A Celebration at Carnegie Hall," *Great Performances,* PBS, 1993.

Also appeared on *The Carol Burnett Show,* CBS; *The Muppet Show,* syndicated; and *Saturday Night Live,* NBC.

RECORDINGS

Albums:

New Faces of 1968 (original cast recording), Warner Bros., 1968.
Two by Two (original cast recording), Columbia, 1970.
Blazing Saddles (original soundtrack), Elektra, 1974.
Young Frankenstein (original soundtrack), ABC, 1975.
At Long Last Love (original soundtrack), RCA-Victor, 1975.
Frank Loesser Revisited, Painted Smiles, 1975.
On the Twentieth Century (original cast recording), Columbia, 1978.

Also performed on the original cast recording *Two Revues.*

Videos:

Scrambled Feet, RKO, 1983.

OTHER SOURCES

Periodicals:

Entertainment Weekly, December 13, 1996, p. 26.
New York Times, April 8, 1993.*

KANAKAREDES, Melina 1967-

PERSONAL

Surname is pronounced "ka-na-KA-ree-deez"; born April 23, 1967, in Akron, OH; daughter of an insurance salesperson and homemaker; married Peter Constantinades (a chef), 1992. *Education:* Point Park College, B.F.A. (theatre; magna cum laude); also attended Ohio State University. *Avocational interests:* Visiting family, swimming, reading, exercising, traveling, listening to music, watching sports.

Addresses: *Agent*—Bill Butler, The Gersh Agency, 130 West 42nd St., Suite 2400, New York, NY 10036.

Career: Actress. Appeared in advertisements, including television commercials for Clairol, Diet Rite, Hyundai, Kmart, Rave, Semicid, and Sony.

Awards, Honors: Two Daytime Emmy Award nominations, 1994 and 1995, for *Guiding Light;* first runner up, Miss Ohio Pageant, 1986; Miss Columbus.

CREDITS

Television Appearances; Series:

The first Eleni Andros Spaulding Cooper, *Guiding Light,* CBS, 1991-94.
Benita Alden, *NYPD Blue,* ABC, 1994-95.
Angela Villanova, *New York News,* CBS, 1995.
Libby Gallante, *Leaving L.A.,* ABC, 1997.
Dr. Sydney Hansen, *Providence,* NBC, 1999—.

Television Appearances; Movies:

Rita, *Saint Maybe* (also known as *Anne Tyler's Saint Maybe*), CBS, 1998.

Television Appearance; Specials:

Presenter, *20th Annual Daytime Emmy Awards,* 1993.
50 Years of Soaps: An All-Star Celebration, CBS, 1994.

Television Appearances; Episodic:

Victoria Metcalfe, "Letting Go," *Due South,* CBS, 1995.
Victoria Metcalfe, "Victoria's Secret" (two parts), *Due South,* CBS, 1995.
Andrea Wexler, "First Degree" and "Sex, Lies, and Murder," *The Practice,* ABC, 1997.
"Great Men," *Oz,* HBO, 1998.
Herself, *The View,* ABC, 1999.

Film Appearances:

Daphne, *White Man's Burden* (also known as *Bleeding Hearts*), Savoy Pictures, 1994.
Trin, *The Long Kiss Goodnight,* New Line Cinema, 1996.
Barbara, *Rounders,* Miramax, 1998.
Livia, *Dangerous Beauty* (also known as *Courtesan, The Honest Courtesan,* and *Venice*), Warner Bros., 1998.
Nicolette, *15 Minutes,* New Line Cinema, 1999.

Stage Appearances:

Isabelle, *Down by the Ocean,* York Theatre Company, New York City, 1994.

Appeared in off-Broadway productions; appeared in plays at the Pittsburgh Playhouse and the Pittsburgh Public Theatre, both Pittsburgh, PA; also appeared in community theatre productions in Ohio; worked in productions on a dinner boat, New York City.

OTHER SOURCES

Periodicals:

Entertainment Weekly, April 29, 1994, p. 64; January 8, 1999, p. 52.*

KANE, Carol 1952-

PERSONAL

Born June 18, 1952, in Cleveland, OH.

Addresses: *Office*—Krost/Chapin Artists Talent Agency, 9911 West Pico Blvd., Ph I, Los Angeles, CA 90035-2715.

Career: Actress.

Member: Screen Actors Guild.

Awards, Honors: Academy Award nomination, best actress, 1975, for *Hester Street;* Emmy Award, outstanding lead actress in a comedy series, 1982, and Emmy Award, outstanding supporting actress in a comedy, variety, or music series, 1983, both for *Taxi.*

CREDITS

Film Appearances:

Jennifer, *Carnal Knowledge,* Avco Embassy, 1971.
Young girl, *Desperate Characters,* Paramount, 1971.
Jeannie, *Wedding in White,* Avco Embassy, 1972.
Young whore, *The Last Detail,* Columbia, 1973.
Jenny, *Dog Day Afternoon,* Warner Bros., 1975.
Gitl, *Hester Street,* Midwest, 1975.
Florence, *Harry and Walter Go to New York,* Columbia, 1976.
Allison, *Annie Hall,* United Artists, 1977.
Fatty's girl, *Valentino,* United Artists, 1977.
Annie Hickman, *The World's Greatest Lover,* Twentieth Century-Fox, 1977.
Cissy Carpenter, *The Mafu Cage* (also known as *My Sister, My Love*), Cloud 5, 1978.
Daisy, *The Sabiana* (also known as *La Babina*), El Iman-Svenska Film Institute, 1979.
Jill Johnson, *When a Stranger Calls,* Columbia, 1979.
"Myth," *The Muppet Movie,* Associated Film Distribution, 1979.
Louise, *Les Jeux de la Comtesse Donlingen de Gratz,* 1981.
Candy Jefferson, *Pandemonium* (also known as *Thursday the Twelfth*), Metro-Goldwyn-Mayer/United Artists, 1982.
Rose, *Norman Loves Rose,* Atlantic, 1982.
Cafe customer, *Can She Bake a Cherry Pie?,* World Wide Classics, 1983.
Cheryl Goodman, *Over the Brooklyn Bridge,* Metro-Goldwyn-Mayer/United Artists, 1984.
Annie, *Racing with the Moon,* Paramount, 1984.
Martha Bernays, *The Secret Diary of Sigmund Freud,* Twentieth Century-Fox, 1984.
Lupi, *Transylvania 6-5000,* New World, 1985.
Cynthia Sparks, *Jumpin' Jack Flash,* Twentieth Century-Fox, 1986.
Carol, *Ishtar,* Columbia, 1987.
Valerie, *The Princess Bride,* Twentieth Century-Fox, 1987.
Kitty, *Sticky Fingers,* Spectra Film, 1988.
Mom, *License to Drive,* Twentieth Century-Fox, 1988.
Ghost of Christmas Present, *Scrooged,* Paramount, 1988.
Franki D'Angelo, *The Lemon Sisters,* Miramax, 1990.
Shaldeen, *My Blue Heaven,* Warner Bros., 1990.
Maggie, *Flashback,* Paramount, 1990.
Hairdresser, *Joe versus the Volcano,* Warner Bros., 1990.
Colette and Colette's twin sister, *Ted and Venus,* Double Helix Films, 1991.
Barbara, *In the Soup,* Triton Pictures, 1992.
Maria, *Baby on Board,* Prism Entertainment, 1993.
Granny Addams, *Addams Family Values,* Paramount, 1993.
Cowgirl Carla, *Even Cowgirls Get the Blues,* New Line, 1994.
Crazysitter, Concorde/New Horizons, 1995.
Helen, *American Strays,* A-pix Entertainment, 1996.
Faith, *Big Bully,* Warner Bros., 1996.
Mona, *Sunset Park,* TriStar, 1996.
Tom's Mom, *The Pallbearer,* Miramax, 1996.
Connie, *Trees Lounge,* Live Entertainment, 1996.
Donna Waters, *Gone Fishin',* Buena Vista, 1997.
Voice of Spider, *Napoleon,* Samuel Goldwyn, 1997.
Dorine Douglas, *Office Killer,* Miramax, 1997.
The Tic Code, Jazz Films, 1998.
Miss Sherman, *Jawbreaker,* TriStar, 1999.
Herself, *Man on the Moon,* Universal, 1999.

Television Appearances; Series:

Simka Gravas, *Taxi,* ABC, 1981-82, then NBC, 1982-83.
Nicolette Bingham, *All Is Forgiven,* NBC, 1986.
Lillian Abernathy, *American Dreamer,* NBC, 1990-91.
Aunt Sylvia, *Brooklyn Bridge,* CBS, 1990-91.

Annie Caraldo, *Pearl,* 1996-97.
Lydia (L.L.) Luddin, *Beggars and Choosers,* Showtime, 1999.

Television Appearances; Pilots:
Let's Get Mom (unaired), Fox, 1989.

Television Appearances; Movies:
Ilene Cohen, *An Invasion of Privacy,* CBS, 1983.
Mary Harwood, *Burning Rage,* CBS, 1984.
Maxine, *Drop out Mother,* CBS, 1988.
Jill Johnson, *When a Stranger Calls Back,* Showtime, 1993.
Gloria, the angel, *Dad, the Angel, and Me,* Family Channel, 1995.
Miss Futterman, "Freaky Friday," *The Disney Family Film,* ABC, 1995.

Also appeared in *Many Mansions.*

Television Appearances; Miniseries:
Sarah, *Noah's Ark,* NBC, 1999.

Television Appearances; Episodic:
Mrs. Carny, "Shadow of the Swan," *The Fugitive,* ABC, 1966.
"Outcast," *The Virginian,* NBC, 1966.
"Epitaph for a Cop," *The Felony Squad,* ABC, 1968.
Susannah White, "We the Women," *American Parade,* CBS, 1974.
"Fans of the Kosko Show," *Visions,* PBS, 1978.
"The Greatest Man in the World," *American Short Story,* PBS, 1980.
"Jinxed," *Laverne and Shirley,* ABC, 1982.
"Keeping on," *American Playhouse,* PBS, 1983.
"Sleeping Beauty," *Faerie Tale Theater,* Showtime, 1983.
Amanda Boyer, "A Ditch in Time," *Cheers,* NBC, 1984.
"Snip, Snip," *Tales from the Darkside,* syndicated, 1985.
"Bum Tip," *Crazy Like a Fox,* CBS, 1985.
"Tomorrow's Child," *The Ray Bradbury Theater,* USA Network, 1987.
Judy, "You're Not Yourself Today," *Tales from the Crypt,* HBO, 1990.
Voice of Ollie, "A Quack in the Quarks," *Tiny Toon Adventures,* 1990.
"Tomorrow's Child," *The Ray Bradbury Theatre,* USA Network, 1992.
Voice of Brawnhilda, *Aladdin* (animated), CBS, 1994.
Corinne, "The Marine Biologist," *Seinfeld,* NBC, 1994.
Emily Roebling, *A. J.'s Time Travelers,* Fox, 1994.
Shelby, *Empty Nest,* NBC, 1994.
Marguerite Birch, "Stand," *Chicago Hope,* CBS, 1995.
Lily Penney, "A Penney Saved ...," *Ellen,* ABC, 1996.
"Blue's Big Treasure Hunt", *Blue's Clues,* Nickelodeon, 1996.
Voiceover, *Hey Arnold!,* Nickelodeon, 1996-99.
Munch's Ex-Wife, *Homicide: Life on the Street,* NBC, 1997.
Simka Gravaas, "The Milk Run," *The Tony Danza Show,* NBC, 1997.
Tooth Fairy, *The Noddy Shop,* PBS, 1998-99.

Television Appearances; Specials:
Eliza Southgate, *Out of Our Fathers' House,* 1978.
"Bob Goldthwait—Don't Watch This Show," *Cinemax Comedy Experiment,* Cinemax, 1986.
Barbara, "Casey at the Bat" (also known as "Shelley Duvall's Tall Tales and Legends"), *On Location,* HBO, 1986.
"Paul Reiser: Out on a Whim," *On Location,* HBO, 1987.
"Rap Master Ronnie—A Report Card," *Cinemax Comedy Experiment,* Cinemax, 1988.
The 3rd Annual American Comedy Awards, ABC, 1989.
Voices That Care, Fox, 1991.
The 43rd Annual Primetime Emmy Awards Presentation, Fox, 1991.
Why Bother Voting?, PBS, 1992.
Best of Taxi (also known as *Hey Taxi*), CBS, 1994.
A Comedy Salute to Andy Kaufman, NBC, 1995.

Stage Appearances:
The Prime of Miss Jean Brodie, Public Theatre, New York City, 1966.
Esme Train, *Ring 'round the Bath Tub,* Martin Beck Theatre, New York City, 1972.
Miranda, *The Tempest,* Mitzi E. Newhouse Theatre, New York City, 1974.
Tillie, *The Effect of Gamma Rays on Man-in-the-Moon Marigolds,* Biltmore Theatre, New York City, 1978.
Benefit of a Doubt, Folger Theatre Group, Washington, DC, 1978.
Lillian Hellman, *Are You Now or Have You Ever Been?,* Promenade Theatre, New York City, 1978.
Tales from the Vienna Woods, 1979.
Sunday Runners in the Rain, 1980.
The Tempest, Lincoln Center, New York City, 1980.
Macbeth, Lincoln Center, 1980.
Fairy, *The Fairy Garden,* Walter McGinn/John Cazale Theatre, New York City, 1984.
The Debutante Ball, Manhattan Theatre Club, New York City, 1988.

Frankie and Johnny in the Clair de Lune, Westside Arts Theatre, New York City, 1988.
Demon Wine, Los Angeles Theatre Center, Los Angeles, CA, 1988-89.

Also appeared in *The Prime of Miss Jean Brodie,* Charles Playhouse, Boston, MA; and *Wasp.**

KAPOOR, Shekar
See KAPUR, Shekhar

KAPUR, Shekhar 1954(?)-
(Shekar Kapoor)

PERSONAL

Born c. 1954, in Bombay, India; immigrated to England, 1970; married Suchitra Krishnamurti (a singer), 1996. *Education:* Studied economics in New Delhi, India, and film in London, England.

Addresses: *Contact*—Amanda Conroy, Corporate Communications, PolyGram International, 8 St. James's Sq., London SW1Y 4JU, England.

Career: Producer, director, and actor. Worked as a model, an accountant, and a management consultant planner. Also billed as Shekar Kapoor.

Awards, Honors: National Board of Review Award, best director, 1998, Golden Globe Award nomination and Golden Satellite Award nomination, both best director of a motion picture, and David Lean Award for Direction nomination, British Academy of Film and Television Arts, all 1999, for *Elizabeth.*

CREDITS

Film Work; Director, Unless Otherwise Noted:
Masoom (also known as *Innocent*), Krsna Film Unit, 1983.
Uncredited director of scenes, *Joshilay,* [India], 1985.
Mr. India, [India], 1987.
Time Machine, [India], 1992.
Bandit Queen (also known as *Phoolan Devi*), Arrow Films, 1994.
Uncredited director of some scenes, *Dushmani,* [India], 1996.
Elizabeth (also known as *Elizabeth: The Virgin Queen*), PolyGram Filmed Entertainment, 1998.
Producer, *Dil Se* (also known as *From the Heart* and *Uyire*), Madras Talkies, 1998.
Long Way to Freedom (also known as *Long Walk to Freedom*), PolyGram Filmed Entertainment, 1999.

Also made commercial films.

Film Appearances:
Pal Do Pal ka Saath, [India], 1978.
Jeena Yahan, [India], 1981.
Nikhil, *Drishti* (also known as *Vision*), Udbhav, 1990.
Nazar (also known as *Eye* and *The Gaze*), [India], 1991.

Television Appearances:
Appeared in television productions.

OTHER SOURCES

Periodicals:
New Republic, July 10, 1995, p. 24.
New York Times, November 13, 1998, p. E14.
Time, August 14, 1995, p. 67.
Time International, November 2, 1998, p. 71.
Village Voice, November 10, 1998, p. 126.*

KAR WEI WONG
See WONG, Kar-Wai

KEACH, Stacy 1941-

PERSONAL

Full name, Walter Stacy Keach, Jr.; born June 2, 1941, in Savannah, GA; son of Stacy (an actor) and Mary Cain (an actress; maiden name, Peckham) Keach; brother of James Keach (an actor and director known for *The Stars Fell on Henrietta*); married Marily Aiken, 1975 (marriage ended); married Jill Donahue, 1981 (marriage ended); married Malgosia Tomassi, 1986; children: (with Tomassi) Shannon, Karolina. *Education:* University of California at Berkeley, A.B. (English and drama), 1963; trained for the stage at Yale School of Drama, 1963-64, and London Academy of Dramatic Art, 1964-65. *Avocational interests:* Tennis, bicycle riding, and skiing.

Addresses: *Manager*—James R. Palmer & Associates, 1901 Avenue of the Stars, Los Angeles, CA 90067-

6001. *Agent*—William Morris Agency, 151 El Camino Dr., Beverly Hills, CA 90212.

Career: Actor, director, writer, and producer. Founder and president, Positron Productions Ltd.; associate professor of drama, Yale University School of Drama, 1967-68. Entertainment Industry Council before the House select committee on drug abuse, member, 1985; American Cleft Palate Foundation, honorary chair, 1995—, and master of ceremonies, Capitol Mall, 1995; member, National Play Award committee, National Repertory Foundation; and artists committee, Kennedy Center Honors committee.

Member: Actors' Equity Association, Screen Actors Guild, Directors Guild of America, American Federation of Television and Radio Artists, Academy of Motion Picture Arts and Sciences, Academy of Television Arts and Sciences (panelist, Substance Abuse Conference), Artists and Athletes Against Apartheid, National Humane Education Society, United Indian Development Association, National Citizens Communication Lobby, America Cleft Palate Association (spokesperson), Yale Theatre Circle (charter member).

Awards, Honors: Best Actor Award, University of California, 1963; Best Actor Award, Oregon Shakespeare Festival, 1963; Oliver Thorndike Acting Award, Yale University School of Drama, 1963-64; Fulbright scholarship, 1964-65; Obie Awards and Vernon Rice Drama Desk Awards, 1967, for *Macbird!* and 1972, for *Long Day's Journey into Night;* Antoinette Perry Award nomination, and Drama Desk Award, both 1970, both for *Indians;* Grammy Award nomination, 1971, for *Long Day's Journey into Night;* Cine Golden Eagle Award, 1971, and Outstanding Film designation, London Film Festival, 1972, both for *The Repeater;* Obie Award and Vernon Rice Award, both 1972, for *Hamlet;* David Award, 1983; voted one of Ten Most Watchable Men of 1984 by Man Watchers of America; Golden Globe Award nomination, best actor in a television series, 1985, for *Mike Hammer;* Veterans Appreciation Award, 1986, for *Mike Hammer;* Emmy Award nomination, best actor in a miniseries or special, 1988, and Golden Globe Award, best actor in a miniseries or motion picture made for television, 1989, both for *Hemingway;* Cable Ace Award nomination, best actor, for *Bags;* Helen Hayes Award, best actor, Drama League Award, outstanding performance, 1993, both for *The Kentucky Cycle;* American Cleft Palate Foundation, celebrity outreach honoree, 1995.

CREDITS

Film Appearances:

(Film debut; as Stacy Keach, Jr.) Blount, *The Heart Is a Lonely Hunter,* Warner Brothers/Seven Arts, 1968.

Jonas Candide, *The Traveling Executioner,* Metro-Goldwyn-Mayer, 1968.

Jacob Horner, *The End of the Road,* Allied Artists, 1970.

Abraham Wright, *Brewster McCloud,* Metro-Goldwyn-Mayer, 1970.

Doc Holiday, *Doc,* United Artists, 1971.

Bad Bob, *The Life and Times of Judge Roy Bean,* National General, 1971.

Roy Fehler, *The New Centurions* (also known as *Precinct 45: Los Angeles Police*), Columbia, 1972.

Tully, *Fat City,* Columbia, 1972.

Mike Mandell and Sonny, *Watched!,* Palmyra Films, 1973.

Oklahoma Crude, Columbia, 1973.

Calvin, *The Gravy Train* (also known as *The Dion Brothers*), Columbia, 1974.

Martin Luther, *Luther,* American Film Theatre, 1974.

Narrator, *One by One,* 1974.

Narrator, *James Dean, the First American Teenager,* 1975.

Adjutant, *Conduct Unbecoming,* Allied Artists, 1975.

Charlie Hanson and Phil, *Street People* (also known as *The Executioner, The Executors, The Sicilian Cross,* and *Gli esecutori*), American International Pictures, 1976.

Lou Ford, *The Killer Inside Me,* Warner Bros., 1976.

Jim Naboth, *The Squeeze,* Warner Bros., 1976.

Manfred Roland, *The Greatest Battle* (also known as *Battle Force, The Battle of the Mareth Line, The Great Battle,* and *Il grande attacco*), 1977.

Narrator, *The Duelists,* Paramount Home Video, 1977.

Huntley McQueen, *Two Solitudes,* Compass, 1977.

Dr. Edward Foster, *La Montagna del dio Cannibale* (also known as *Mountain of Cannibal Gods, Prisoner of the Cannibal God,* and *Slave of the Cannibal God*), Vestron, 1978.

Captain Bennett, *Gray Lady Down,* Universal, 1978.

Sergeant Stedenko, *Up in Smoke* (also known as *Cheech and Chong's Up in Smoke*), Paramount, 1978.

Colonel Hudson Kane, *The Ninth Configuration* (also known as *Twinkle, Twinkle, Killer Kane*), New World, 1979.

Narrator, *The Search for Solutions,* 1979.

Frank James, *The Long Riders,* United Artists, 1980.

Patrick Quid, *Road Games,* Avco Embassy, 1981.

Sergeant Stedenko, *Cheech & Chong's Nice Dreams,* Columbia, 1981.
Jess Tyler, *Butterfly,* LIVE, 1982.
James Daley, *That Championship Season,* Cannon Films, 1982.
Harlan Errickson, *False Identity,* Pavillion Pictures, 1990.
Dr. Bob Forrest, *Class of 1999,* Taurus Entertainment, 1990.
Jesenski, *Milena* (also known as *The Lover*), 1990.
Harrison Shelgrove, *Sunset Grill,* New Line, 1993.
Voice of Phantasm/Carl Beaumont, *Batman: Mask of the Phantasm* (also known as *Batman: The Animated Movie;* animated), Warner Bros., 1993.
Warren Oates: Across the Border, 1993.
Jenkins, *Raw Justice* (also known as *Good Cop, Bad Cop* and *Skip-Tracer*), Republic Pictures Home Video, 1994.
Wynorski, *New Crime City* (also known as *Los Angeles 2020*), Concorde-New Horizons, 1994.
Pembrooke, *Young Ivanhoe,* Cabin Fever Entertainment, 1995.
The commander, *Prey of the Jaguar,* JFW Productions, 1996.
Malloy, *John Carpenter's Escape from L.A.,* Paramount, 1996.
Wolf Larsen, *Jack London's The Sea Wolf,* Concorde Pictures, 1997.
General Wallace, *Future Fear,* Cinequanon Pictures, 1997.
Captain John Savienko, *Birds of Passage,* First Preferred Communications, 1998.
Cameron Alexander, *American History X,* New Line Cinema, 1998.
Icebreaker, 1999.
Dr. Michaels, *Children of the Corn 666: Isaac's Return,* Buena Vista Home Video, 1999.
Narrator, *Olympic Glory,* MegaSystems, 1999.

Film Work:
Executive producer (with others), *The Long Riders,* United Artists, 1980.

Television Appearances; Series:
How to Marry a Millionaire, syndicated, 1957.
Professor Carlson, *Get Smart,* NBC, 1966-67.
Dr. Grey, *Johnny Belinda,* ABC, 1967.
Lieutenant Ben Logan, *Caribe,* ABC, 1975.
Title role, *Mickey Spillane's Mike Hammer,* CBS, 1984-85.
Title role, *The New Mike Hammer,* CBS, 1986-87.
Host, *Missing/Reward,* syndicated, 1989.
Nitecap, ABC, 1992.
Host, *Case Closed,* USA Network, 1993.
Bosco, *Gang, Die,* 1997.
Title role, *Mike Hammer, Private Eye,* syndicated, 1997-98.

Television Appearances; Episodic:
"Last Chance," *Colt .45,* ABC, 1957.
"The Lass with the Poisonous Air," *Maverick,* ABC, 1959.
"Lost Gold," *Shotgun Slade,* syndicated, 1960.
"The Traitor," *Wagon Train,* NBC, 1961.
Lieutenant Gibson, "The Case of the Frightened Fisherman," *Perry Mason,* CBS, 1964.
Judge, "The Case of the Cheating Chancellor," *Perry Mason,* CBS, 1965.
He and She, CBS, 1968.
Feste, "Twelfth Night," *Actors Company,* Shakespeare Repertory Theatre, PBS, 1968.
Banquo, "Macbeth," *Actors Company,* Shakespeare Repertory Theatre, PBS, 1968.
Farmer, "The Weary Willies," *Bonanza,* NBC, 1970.
"The Repeater," *The Great American Dream Machine,* PBS, 1971.
"Biography," *N.E.T. Playhouse,* PBS, 1971.
"Particular Men," *Playhouse New York,* PBS, 1972.
"Antigone," *Playhouse New York,* PBS, 1972.
"The 26th Grave," *Bonanza,* NBC, 1972.
"The Man of Destiny," *Hollywood Television Theater,* PBS, 1975.
"Good Cop," *Delvecchio,* CBS, 1976.
"Sighting 4007: The Forest City Incident," *Project U.F.O.,* NBC, 1978.
"Edwin Drake," *An American Portrait,* CBS, 1984.
George Teller, "Heartbreak Hotel," *Freddy's Nightmares,* syndicated, 1989.
Narrator, "Russian Right Stuff," *Nova,* PBS, 1990.
Narrator, "Making a Dishonest Buck," *Nova,* PBS, 1992.
Narrator, "The Kennedys," *American Experience,* PBS, 1992.
Narrator, "In the White Man's Image," *American Experience,* PBS, 1992.
Narrator, "The Lost Fleet of Guadalcanal," *National Geographic Explorer,* TBS, 1993.
Narrator, "Secret of the Wild Child," *Nova,* PBS, 1994.
Narrator, "Killer Quake!" *Nova,* PBS, 1994.
Narrator, "The Universe Within," *Nova,* PBS, 1994.
Ty Duncan, "Sympathy for the Devil," *Touched by an Angel,* CBS, 1995.
Narrator, "Aircraft Carrier," *True Stories,* 1995.
Narrator, "Terror in the Mine Fields," *Nova,* PBS, 1995.
Ned Bernhart, *Promised Land,* CBS, 1996.

Also appeared in *The Sheriff of Cochise,* syndicated; as Autolycus, *The Winter's Tale,* Shakespeare Repertory Theatre, PBS; voice of Marvin Finster, "The Family Tree, Parts I & II," *The Rugrats* (animated).

Television Appearances; Pilots:

Dr. Eberly, *Kingston: The Power Play,* NBC, 1976.

New Year (also known as *New Year's* and *New Year's 1999*), ABC, 1993.

Television Appearances; Movies:

Orville and Wilbur, PBS, 1971.

Classics for Today, PBS, 1972.

Jimmy Wheeler, *All the Kind Strangers* (also known as *Evil in the Swamp*), ABC, 1974.

Matt Blackwood, *James A. Michener's "Dynasty,"* NBC, 1975.

Diary of a Young Comic, NBC, 1977.

Judge Murdock, *Portrait of a Rebel: The Remarkable Mrs. Sanger* (also known as *Portrait of a Rebel: Margaret Sanger*), CBS, 1980.

Harry Roat, *Wait until Dark,* HBO, 1982.

Title role, *Mickey Spillane's Mike Hammer: Murder Me, Murder You,* CBS, 1983.

Mike Hammer, *Mickey Spillane's Mike Hammer: More than Murder,* CBS, 1984.

Dr. Jeffrey Bierston, *Intimate Strangers,* CBS, 1986.

Title role, *The Return of Mickey Spillane's Mike Hammer,* CBS, 1986.

Title role, *Mickey Spillane's Mike Hammer: Murder Takes All* (also known as *Murder Takes All* and *Mike Hammer in Las Vegas*), CBS, 1989.

Adam Roth, *The Forgotten,* USA Network, 1989.

Captain Charles McVay, *Mission of the Shark: The Saga of the U.S.S. Indianapolis,* CBS, 1991.

Claude Sams, *Revenge on the Highway* (also known as *Overdrive* and *Silent Thunder*), NBC, 1992.

Harris Stone, *Irresistible Force,* 1993.

Richard, "Hair," *John Carpenter Presents Body Bags* (also known as *Body Bags*), Showtime, 1993.

Kansas, *Rio Diablo* (also known as *Devil's River*), CBS, 1993.

Jack Devlin, *Against Their Will: Women in Prison,* ABC, 1994.

Emmitt Mallory, *Amanda and the Alien,* Showtime, 1995.

Compte de Leon, *The Pathfinder,* Showtime, 1996.

Narrator, *Plague Fighters* (also known as *Ebola: Inside an Outbreak*), 1996.

Agent Cargill, *Murder in My Mind,* CBS, 1997.

Dr. Bent, *Legend of the Lost Tomb,* Showtime, 1997.

Television Appearances; Miniseries:

Barabbas, *Jesus of Nazareth,* NBC, 1977.

Major Ball, *A Rumor of War,* CBS, 1980.

Jonas Steele, *The Blue and the Gray,* CBS, 1982.

Prince Stash Valensky, *Princess Daisy,* NBC, 1983.

Julien Mistral, *Mistral's Daughter,* CBS, 1985.

Ernest Hemingway, *Hemingway,* syndicated, 1988.

I misteri della giungla nera (also known as *The Mysteries of the Dark Jungle*), 1990.

Sam Houston, *James A. Michener's Texas,* 1994.

Television Appearances; Specials:

Hamlet, CBS, 1964.

Voice of Merchant, *Beauty and the Beast,* CBS, 1983.

38th Annual Emmy Awards, NBC, 1986.

Host, *CBS All-American Thanksgiving Day Parade,* CBS, 1986.

Sex Symbols: Past, Present, and Future, syndicated, 1987.

44th Annual Golden Globe Awards, syndicated, 1987.

Host, *Missing/Reward,* syndicated, 1988.

Ringmaster, *14th Annual Circus of the Stars,* CBS, 1989.

Host, *La Boheme,* Arts and Entertainment, 1989.

Night of 100 Stars III, NBC, 1990.

Voice of General George McClellan, *Lincoln,* ABC, 1992.

20th International Emmy Awards, PBS, 1992.

Narrator, *Haunted Lives: True Ghost Stories,* CBS, 1992.

Narrator, *The Secret World of Bats,* CBS, 1992.

Narrator, "Reflections on Elephants," *National Geographic Special,* PBS, 1994.

Host, *A Capitol Fourth,* 1995.

Flight Over the Equator, 1995.

Narrator, *Real Ghosts,* 1995.

Narrator, *The Orphan Trains,* 1995.

Narrator, *In Search of the Oregon Trail,* PBS, 1996.

Narrator, *Mary Lincoln's Insanity File,* Discovery Channel, 1996.

Narrator, *Real Ghosts III,* UPN, 1996.

Narrator, *The World's Most Dangerous Animals,* CBS, 1996.

Narrator, *The World's Most Dangerous Animals II,* CBS, 1996.

Narrator, *The World's Most Dangerous ...,* CBS, 1996.

Narrator, *Avalanche!,* PBS, 1997.

Narrator, *Faster than Sound,* PBS, 1997.

Narrator, *Mysteries of Deep Space,* PBS, 1997.

Narrator, *Secrets of Lost Empires,* PBS, 1997.

Narrator, *The Proof,* PBS, 1997.

Narrator, *The World's Most Dangerous Animals III,* CBS, 1997.

Narrator, *Ice Mummies,* PBS, 1998.

Narrator, *Mysterious Mummies of China,* PBS, 1998.

Narrator, *Planet of Life,* Discovery Channel, 1998.

Narrator, *Savage Earth,* PBS, 1998.

Narrator, *Sea Monsters: Search for the Giant Squid,* NBC, 1998.

Narrator, *Search for the Lost Cave People,* PBS, 1998.
Narrator, *The Brain Eater,* PBS, 1998.
Narrator, *Dolphins: The Wild Side,* NBC, 1999.

Television Work; Director, Except Where Indicated:

And producer, "The Repeater," *The Great American Dream Machine,* PBS, 1971.

"A Blinding Fear," *The New Mike Hammer,* CBS, 1987.

Executive producer (with others) *Mike Hammer: Private Eye,* syndicated, 1997-98.

Also director, *Six Characters in Search of an Author,* PBS.

Stage Appearances:

Armand, *Camille,* Tufts Arena, CA, 1961.

Antiopholus, *The Comedy of Errors,* Ashland, Oregon Shakespeare Festival, 1962.

Westmoreland, *Henry IV, Part II,* Ashland, Oregon Shakespeare Festival, 1962.

Mercutio, *Romeo and Juliet,* Ashland, Oregon Shakespeare Festival, 1963.

Berowne, *Love's Labour's Lost,* Ashland, Oregon Shakespeare Festival, 1963.

Title role, *Henry V,* Ashland, Oregon Shakespeare Festival, 1963.

The Voyage, Yale School of Drama, New Haven, CT, 1963.

(Off-Broadway debut) Marcellus and First Player, *Hamlet,* New York Shakespeare Festival, Delacorte Theatre, 1964.

Cutler and Turnkey, *Danton's Death,* Repertory Theatre of Lincoln Center, Vivian Beaumont Theatre, New York City, 1965.

Mr. Horner, *The Country Wife,* Repertory Theatre of Lincoln Center, Vivian Beaumont Theatre, 1965.

The Caucasian Chalk Circle, Repertory Theatre of Lincoln Center, Vivian Beaumont Theatre, 1966.

Annie Get Your Gun, Williamstown Summer Theatre Festival, MA, 1966.

You Can't Take It with You, Williamstown Summer Theatre Festival, 1966.

The Lion in Winter, Williamstown Summer Theatre Festival, 1966.

Marat/Sade (also known as *The Persecution and Assassination of Jean-Paul Marat as Performed by the Inmates of the Asylum of Charenton under the Direction of the Marquis de Sade*), Williamstown Summer Theatre Festival, 1966.

Baron Tusenbach, *The Three Sisters,* Long Wharf Theatre, New Haven, CT, 1966.

Oh, What a Lovely War, Long Wharf Theatre, 1966.

Title role, *MacBird!,* Village Gate Theatre, New York City, 1967.

Captain Starkey, *We Bombed in New Haven,* Yale Repertory Theatre, 1967.

August, "The Demonstration" [and] The man, "Man and Dog," *The Niggerlovers,* Orpheum Theatre, New York City, 1967.

Henry IV, Yale Repertory Theatre, 1968.

Coriolanus, Yale Repertory Theatre, 1968.

The Three Sisters, Yale Repertory Theatre, 1968.

Sir John Falstaff, *Henry IV, Parts I and II,* New York Shakespeare Festival, Delacorte Theatre, 1968.

Edmund, *King Lear,* Vivian Beaumont Theatre, 1968.

Buffalo Bill, *Indians,* Arena Stage, Washington, DC, then Brooks Atkinson Theatre, New York City, 1969.

Title role, *Peer Gynt,* New York Shakespeare Festival, Delacorte Theatre, 1969.

Benedict, *Beatrice and Benedict,* Los Angeles Music Center, 1970.

James Tyrone, Jr., *Long Day's Journey into Night,* Promenade Theatre, New York City, 1971.

Title role, *Hamlet,* Long Wharf Theatre, 1971, then New York Shakespeare Festival, Delacorte Theatre, 1972; repeated role for Center Theatre Group, Mark Taper Forum, Los Angeles, 1974.

Title role, *Cyrano de Bergerac,* Long Beach Theatre Festival, CA, 1978.

Sydney Bruhl, *Deathtrap,* Music Box Theatre, New York City, 1979.

Eric Smith, *Hughie,* National Theatre Company, Cottesloe Theatre, London, 1980.

Harry Van, *Idiot's Delight,* Kennedy Center, Washington, DC, 1986.

Title role, *Richard III,* Folger Shakespeare Festival, Washington, DC, 1990-91.

Title role, *Macbeth,* Folger Shakespeare Festival, Washington, DC, 1995.

An Inspector Calls, Center Theatre Group, Ahmanson Theatre, Los Angeles, CA, 1995-96.

Appeared in *The Antifarce of John and Leporello, To Learn to Love, Galileo, Purple Dust, The Changeling, Bartholomew Fair, Escurrial, A Touch of the Poet,* and *Don Juan,* all at the University of California, Berkeley, 1959-63; *The King & I,* 1989; *Love Letters,* 1990-93; *Confinement,* Broadway production, 1992; *The Kentucky Cycle,* Broadway production, 1993; *Stieglitz Loves O'Keefe,* Off-Broadway production, 1995.

Major Tours:

Playing with Fire, U.K. cities, 1965.

Phineas Taylor Barnum, *Barnum,* U.S. cities, 1981.
Sleuth, U.S. cities, 1988.

Stage Work; Director:
The American Dream, University of California at Berkeley, 1959-63.
C'est la vie, University of California at Berkeley, 1959-63.
Pullman Car Hiawatha, London Academy of Music and Dramatic Art, 1964-65.
The Stronger, London Academy of Music and Dramatic Art, 1964-65.
The Maids, London Academy of Music and Dramatic Art, 1964-65.

RECORDINGS

Books on Tape:
Mickey Spillane's Works, 1990.
Impulse, by Michael Weaver, Time Warner Audio Books, 1993.
There Was a Little Girl, by Ed McBain, Time Warner Audio Books, 1994.
Hardboiled, 1994.
Black Alley, by Mickey Spillane, Penguin Audio Books, 1996.
High Stakes, by John Lutz, 1997.
Skeleton Rattle Your Mouldy Leg, by Bill Pronzini, Durkin Hayes, 1997.

CDROMs:
Ten Lost Tribes of Israel, 1994.

Videos:
Earth Day, Caedmon, 1974.
Host, *High on the Job,* Time Life Video, 1986.

Albums:
Long Day's Journey into Night, c. 1971.

WRITINGS

Plays:
The 1960 Axe Revue, University of California at Berkeley, 1960.

Screenplays:
(With Bill Bryden and Steven Phillip Smith) *The Long Riders,* United Artists, 1980.

Teleplays:
"The Repeater," *The Great American Dream Machine,* PBS, 1971.

Articles for Periodicals:
"The Take: A Screen Actor in Search of His Character," *New York Times Magazine,* August 24, 1970.*

KELLY, Andrew
See WALKER, Andrew Kevin

KELLY, Daniel Hugh 1954-
(Daniel Hugh-Kelly)

PERSONAL

Born August 10, 1954, in Elizabeth, NJ; married; wife's name, Kathryn; children: Joseph. *Avocational interests:* Fishing, farming.

Addresses: *Contact*—Screen Actors Guild, 5757 Wilshire Blvd.,Hollywood, CA 90036.

Career: Actor. Also billed as Daniel Hugh-Kelly.

Member: Screen Actors Guild.

CREDITS

Film Appearances:
Vic Trenton, *Cujo,* Warner Bros., 1983.
Scotty, *Someone to Watch over Me,* Columbia, 1987.
Rob Cutter, *Nowhere to Hide* (also known as *Fatal Chase*), Alliance Entertainment, 1987.
Wallace, *The Good Son,* Twentieth Century-Fox, 1993.
Les Goodwin, *Bad Company,* Buena Vista, 1995.
Sojef, *Star Trek: Insurrection* (also known as *Star Trek IX, Star Trek: Millennium, Star Trek: Nemesis, Star Trek: Past and Future, Star Trek: Pathfinder, Star Trek: Prime Directive, Star Trek: Rebellion, Star Trek: Stardust,* and *Star Trek: Transcendence*), Paramount, 1998.

Television Appearances; Series:
Frank Ryan, *Ryan's Hope,* ABC, 1975.
Detective Frank Wajorski, *Chicago Story,* NBC, 1982.
"Skid" Mark McCormick, *Hardcastle and McCormick,* 1983-86.
Peter Farrell, *I Married Dora,* ABC, 1987-88.
Barry Tarberry, *Disney Presents the 100 Lives of Black Jack Savage,* NBC, 1991.
The second Travis Montgomery, *All My Children,* ABC, 1993-94.

Noah Beckett, *Second Noah,* ABC, 1995-96.
Grant, *Oh Baby,* Lifetime, 1998—.

Television Appearances; Miniseries:
Mike George, *Nutcracker: Money, Madness and Murder,* NBC, 1987.
Eugene Cernan, *From the Earth to the Moon,* HBO, 1998.

Television Appearances; Movies:
Jack McCormick, *Thin Ice,* CBS, 1981.
Paul Forrest, *Night of Courage,* ABC, 1987.
Congressional Representative Neil Gallagher, *Citizen Cohn,* HBO, 1992.
Franklin Carter, *MacShayne: Final Roll of the Dice,* NBC, 1994.
Dr. Brian Allen, *Moment of Truth: A Mother's Deception* (also known as *Moment of Truth: Cult Rescue*), NBC, 1994.
Donald Prescott, *A Child's Cry for Help,* NBC, 1994.
Colonel Noel Rogers, *The Tuskegee Airmen,* HBO, 1995.
Steve Sohmer, *Never Say Never: The Deidre Hall Story,* ABC, 1995.
Ben Jones, *No Greater Love* (also known as *Danielle Steel's No Greater Love*), NBC, 1996.
Doug Martin, *Stranger in My Home,* CBS, 1997.
Jim Ballard, *Five Desperate Hours,* NBC, 1997.
Lonn Reisman, *Bad As I Wanna Be: The Dennis Rodman Story,* ABC, 1998.
Mr. Yates, *Atomic Dog,* USA Network, 1998.
Gordon O'Connell, *Labor of Love,* Lifetime, 1998.
Mike Malone, Sr., *Passing Glory,* TNT, 1999.

Television Appearances; Specials:
ABC team member, *Battle of the Network Stars XV,* ABC, 1983.
Sergeant Lou Ireland, *Murder Ink,* CBS, 1983.
Michael McGann, *Dark Eyes,* ABC, 1995.

Television Appearances; Episodic:
Council member Kevin Crossley, "Pride," *Law and Order,* NBC, 1995.
Julian Spector, "Empire," *Law and Order,* NBC, 1999.

Television Appearances; Pilots:
Barry Tarberry, *Disney Presents the 100 Lives of Black Jack Savage,* NBC, 1991.

Stage Appearances:
Paul Verrall, *Born Yesterday,* 46th Street Theatre, New York City, 1989.*

KEYMAH, T'Keyah Crystal 1962-

PERSONAL

Name pronounced, Ta-*Kee*-ah Kristle Kee-*Mah;* born Crystal Walker, October 13, 1962, in Chicago, IL. *Education:* Florida A & M University, B.S. (theater), 1984. *Avocational interests:* Travel, gardening, writing, physical fitness, meditation.

Addresses: *Office*—c/o In Black World, P.O. Box 93425, Los Angeles, CA 90093.

Career: Actress, writer, and producer. Teacher of theatre, dance, and pantomime; Chicago Public Schools, substitute teacher, 1984-89; Call to Action Touring Company, member, 1989; former member of Wavelength, Chocolate Chips, Light Opera Works, and the Najwa (West African) Dance Corps. Established T'Keyah Keymah Theatre Scholarship, Florida A & M University (FAMU) 1990; Women in the Arts, panelist (with Rosalind Cash and Trazana Beverly), 1991.

Member: National Association for the Advancement of Colored People (NAACP), My Good Friend, National Council of Negro Women, FAMU Alumni Association, Institute for Black Parenting, Citizens Committee for Juvenile Court, Illinois Visually Handicapped Institute, Delta Sigma Theta.

Awards, Honors: Miss Black Illinois, 1985; Miss Black America Pageant, first runner-up, 1985; Emmy Award, 1990, Soul Train Comedy Award nomination, and Image Award nomination, all for *In Living Color;* Amazing Love Award, Institute for Black Parenting, 1993; NAACP Theatre Awards, best actress and best play, 1994, both for *Some of My Best Friends: A Collection of Characters Speaking in Verse and Prose;* Silver Star award, Houston Worldfest International Film Festival, 1995, for *One Last Time;* Image Award nominations, outstanding supporting actress in a comedy series, 1998 and 1999, for *Cosby;* NAACP Theatre Award nomination, best actress, for *The Five Heartbeats Live.*

CREDITS

Television Appearances; Series:
In Living Color, Fox, 1989-93.

Sara Jones, *The John Larroquette Show,* NBC, 1994-95.
Scotti Decker, *On Our Own,* ABC, 1995.
Denise Everett, *The Show,* Fox, 1996.
Voice of Roz and Aki, *Waynehead* (animated), The WB, 1996-97.
Erica Lucas, *Cosby,* CBS, 1996—.

Television Appearances; Episodic:
Paula, "A Song for the Soul: April 7, 1963," *Quantum Leap,* NBC, 1992.
Darnelle, *Roc,* Fox, 1992.
ROC—Live, HBO, 1993.
Grace Caldwell, "Born in the USA," *The Commish,* ABC, 1994.

Television Appearances; Specials:
Voice, *Cool Like That* (animated), 1993.
Voice of Charlene and Jaquita, *A Cool Like That Christmas,* 1993.
Host (Hawaii), *The All-American Thanksgiving Parade,* 1998.
Host, *The Orange Bowl Parade,* 1998.

Stage Appearances:
A Christmas Carol, Goodman Theatre, Chicago, IL, 1987-89.
Playboy of the West Indies, International Theater Festival, 1988.
Love Letters, 1991.
The Five Heartbeats Live (also known as *5 Heartbeats: The Musical*), 1994.

Also appeared in *Moon on a Rainbow Shawl* and *An Evening with Ntozake Shange;* also performed in *The Old Settler* in Shelykova and Moscow, Russia.

Major Tours:
Some of My Best Friends: A Collection of Characters Speaking in Verse and Prose, Call to Action Touring Company, U.S. cities, 1991—.

Film Appearances:
One Last Time, 1995.
Raynelle-Ordell's junkie friend, *Jackie Brown,* Buena Vista, 1997.

Film Work:
Executive producer, *One Last Time,* 1995.

Also produced *Circle of Pain* (short).

WRITINGS

Plays:
Some of My Best Friends: A Collection of Characters Speaking in Verse and Prose, Call to Action Touring Company, 1991.

Screenplays:
One Last Time, 1995.

Also wrote *Circle of Pain* (short).

OTHER SOURCES

Books:
George, Nelson, *In Living Color: The Authorized Companion to the Fox TV Series,* Warner Books, 1991.
Hill, George, and Spencer Moon, *Blacks in Hollywood: Five Favorable Years in Film and Television,* Daystar Publishing, 1992.

Periodicals:
Chicago Defender, September, 1991, p. 22.
Ebony Man, October, 1991, p. 41.
Washington Post, May, 1991, p. G1.*

KOEPP, David 1963-

PERSONAL

Born in 1963, in Pewaukee, WI. *Education:* Attended college in Madison, WI, and at University of California, Los Angeles, Film School.

Addresses: *Agent*—United Talent Agency, 9560 Wilshire Blvd., Suite 500, Beverly Hills, CA 90212. *Office*—100 Universal City Plaza, Universal City, CA 91608.

Career: Screenwriter, director, producer, and actor.

CREDITS

Film Work:
Producer (with Martin Donovan), *Apartment Zero,* Skouras, 1989.

Assistant to executive producers, *Hawks,* Paramount Home Video, 1989.
Director, *Suspicious* (short), 1994.
Co-producer, *The Paper,* Universal, 1994.
Director, *The Trigger Effect,* Universal, 1995.
Second unit director, *The Lost World: Jurassic Park,* Universal, 1997.
Director, *A Stir of Echoes,* Artisan Entertainment, 1999.

Film Appearances:
Unlucky bastard, *The Lost World: Jurassic Park,* Universal, 1997.

WRITINGS

Screenplays:
(With Martin Donovan) *Apartment Zero,* Skouras, 1989.
Bad Influence, Triumph, 1990.
(With Daniel Petrie Jr.) *Toy Soldiers,* TriStar, 1991.
(With Donovan) *Death Becomes Her,* Universal, 1992.
(With Michael Crichton) *Jurassic Park,* Universal, 1993.
Carlito's Way, Universal, 1993.
The Shadow, Universal, 1994.
(With brother, Stephen Koepp) *The Paper,* Universal, 1994.
Suspicious (short), 1994.
The Trigger Effect, Universal, 1995.
Mission: Impossible, Paramount, 1996.
The Lost World: Jurassic Park, Universal, 1997.
(Uncredited) *Men in Black* (also known as *MIB*), Columbia/TriStar, 1997.
Story writer, *Snake Eyes,* Paramount, 1998.
A Stir of Echoes, Artisan Entertainment, 1999.
Mr. Hughes, forthcoming.
Spider-Man, Sony Pictures Entertainment, forthcoming.

OTHER SOURCES

Periodicals:
New Yorker, March 21, 1994, pp. 57-58.*

KRISTOFFERSON, Kris 1936-
(Kris Carson)

PERSONAL

Born June 22, 1936, in Brownsville, TX; son of a U.S. Air Force major general; married Fran Beir, 1960 (divorced, 1969); married Rita Coolidge (a singer and composer), August 19, 1973 (divorced, 1980); married Lisa Meyers (an attorney), February 18, 1983; children: (first marriage) Tracy, Kris; (second marriage) Casey; (third marriage) Jesse, Jody, Johnny, Kelly, Blake. *Education:* Pomona College, B.A., 1958; studied literature and poetry at Oxford University as a Rhodes scholar.

Addresses: *Contact*—One Way, 1 Prospect Ave., P.O. Box 6429, Albany, NY 12206.

Career: Actor, composer, and singer. Formerly an English teacher at West Point; also a former bartender, janitor, oil helicopter pilot, and boxer. *Military service:* U.S. Army, captain, 1960-65.

Awards, Honors: Song of the Year Award, Country Music Association, 1970, for "Sunday Mornin' Comin' Down"; Grammy Award, best song, and Best Song Award, TNN/*Music City News,* both 1971, for "Help Me Make It through the Night"; Grammy Award nomination, best song, 1971, for "Me and Bobby McGee"; Grammy Award nomination, country song of the year, 1971, for "For the Good Times"; Best Songwriter Awards, TNN/*Music City News,* 1971 and 1972; Best Song Award, TNN/*Music City News,* 1972, and Grammy Award nominations, country song of the year and best country vocal—male, both 1973, all for "Why Me?"

Grammy Awards, best vocal performance by a duo (with Rita Coolidge), 1973, for "From the Bottle to the Bottom," and 1975, for "Lover Please"; Grammy Award nomination, best vocal performance by a duo (with Coolidge), 1974, for "Loving Arms"; British Academy of Film and Television Arts Award nomination, best newcomer, 1974, for *Pat Garrett and Billy the Kid;* Golden Globe Award, best actor in a film musical/comedy, 1977, for *A Star Is Born;* Academy Award nomination, best original song score, 1984, for *Songwriter.*

Grammy Award nomination, best country group with vocal (with Willie Nelson, Waylon Jennings, and Johnny Cash), 1985, and American Music Awards, favorite country video single (with Nelson, Jennings, and Cash), 1986, both for *Highwayman; Music City News* Country Songwriters Awards, Roger Miller Memorial Award, 1995; Blockbuster Entertainment Award, favorite supporting actor--horror, 1999, for *Blade.* Honorary doctorate, Pomona College, 1974; received Rhodes scholarship.

CREDITS

Film Appearances:

(Film debut) Minstral Wagner, *The Last Movie* (also known as *Chinchero*), Universal, 1971.
Title role, *Cisco Pike,* Columbia, 1971.
Billy the Kid, *Pat Garrett and Billy the Kid,* Metro-Goldwyn-Mayer, 1973.
Elmo Cole, *Blume in Love,* Warner Bros., 1973.
Vocalist, *The Gospel Road,* Twentieth Century-Fox, 1973.
Paco, *Bring Me the Head of Alfredo Garcia,* United Artists, 1974.
David, *Alice Doesn't Live Here Anymore,* Warner Bros., 1975.
John Norman Howard, *A Star Is Born,* Warner Bros., 1976.
Aaron Arnold, *Vigilante Force,* United Artists, 1976.
Jim Cameron, *The Sailor Who Fell from Grace with the Sea,* Avco Embassy, 1976.
Marvin "Shake" Tiller, *Semi-Tough,* United Artists, 1977.
Rubber Duck, *Convoy,* United Artists, 1978.
James Averill, *Heaven's Gate* (also known as *Johnson County Wars*), UnitedArtists, 1980.
Hub Smith, *Rollover,* Warner Bros., 1981.
Blackie Buck, *Songwriter,* TriStar, 1984.
Bob Logan, *Flashpoint,* TriStar, 1984.
Hawk, *Trouble in Mind,* Island Alive, 1986.
Mace Montana, *Big Top Pee-Wee,* Paramount, 1988.
Lieutenant Jack Robbins, *Welcome Home,* Columbia, 1989.
Bill Smith, *Millennium,* Twentieth Century-Fox, 1989.
Tom Holte, *Sandino,* 1990.
Stan Wozniak, *Perfume of the Cyclone* (also known as *Night of the Cyclone*), Republic Home Video, 1990.
Jack Saunders, *Original Intent,* Paramount, 1992.
Gabriel, *Knights,* Paramount, 1993.
Joe Garvey, *No Place to Hide,* Cannon, 1993.
Tom, *Cheatin' Hearts* (also known as *Paper Hearts*), Trimark, 1993.
Preacher, *Pharaoh's Army,* Orion Home Entertainment, 1995.
Sheriff Charlie Wade, *Lone Star,* Sony Pictures Classics, 1996.
Himself, *Message to Love: The Isle of Wight Festival,* Castle Music Pictures, 1997.
Orin Hanner, Sr., *Fire Down Below,* Warner Bros., 1997.
Ghost of Hank Williams, *Forever Is a Long Time,* 1997.
Bill Willis, *A Soldier's Daughter Never Cries,* October Films, 1998.
Voice of Doc, *The Land Before Time VI: The Secret of Saurus Rock* (animated), Universal Home Video, 1998.
Cody, *Girls' Night,* Granada Films, 1998.
Abraham Whistler, *Blade,* New Line Cinema, 1998.
John Burnett, *Dance with Me,* Columbia, 1998.
Eddie, *The Joyriders,* Trident Releasing, 1999.
Detox, Universal, 1999.
Bronson, *Payback,* Paramount, 1999.
Rudolph Meyer, *Father Damien,* Vine International Pictures, 1999.
Smilin' Jack, *Limbo,* Sony Pictures Entertainment, 1999.

Film Work:

(With wife, Rita Coolidge) Singer, *The Last Movie,* Universal, 1971.

Television Appearances; Movies:

Ben Cole, *The Lost Honor of Kathryn Beck* (also known as *Act of Passion*), CBS, 1984.
Jesse James, *The Last Days of Frank and Jesse James,* NBC, 1986.
Ringo, *Stagecoach,* CBS, 1986.
Noble Adams, *The Tracker* (also known as *Dead or Alive*), HBO, 1988.
Captain Rip Metcalf, *Pair of Aces,* CBS, 1990.
Captain Rip Metcalf, *Another Pair of Aces: Three of a Kind,* CBS, 1991.
Jericho Adams, *Miracle in the Wilderness,* TNT, 1991.
Jefferson Jones, *Christmas in Connecticut,* TNT, 1992.
Stan Mather, *Trouble Shooters: Trapped beneath the Earth* (also known as *Trapped*), NBC, 1993.
Destiny, *Sodbusters,* Showtime, 1994.
Big Dreams and Broken Hearts: The Dottie West Story (also known as *Paper Mansions: The Dottie West Story*), CBS, 1995.
Abraham Lincoln, *Tad,* Family Channel, 1995.
Guthrie, *Inflammable,* CBS, 1995.
Himself, *Big Dreams & Broken Hearts: The Dottie West Story,* CBS, 1995.
Davis, *Brother's Destiny* (also known as *The Road Home* and *Long Road Home*), 1996.
Owen Whistler, *Blue Rodeo,* CBS, 1996.
Narrator, *Dead Man's Gun,* Showtime, 1997.
Torrance, *Outlaw Justice,* CBS, 1998.
Hugh Allison, *Two for Texas,* TNT, 1998.

Television Appearances; Miniseries:

Abner Lait, *Freedom Road,* NBC, 1979.
Curt Maddox, *Blood and Orchids,* CBS, 1986.
Devin Milford, *Amerika,* ABC, 1987.
Steve Day, *Tom Clancy's Netforce,* ABC, 1999.

Television Appearances; Specials:
I Believe in Music, NBC, 1973.
Marlo Thomas and Friends in Free to Be . . . You and Me, ABC, 1974.
Johnny Cash: The First 25 Years, CBS, 1980.
Country Comes Home, CBS, 1981.
A Special Anne Murray Christmas, CBS, 1981.
Glen Campbell and Friends: The Silver Anniversary, HBO, 1984.
Johnny Cash: Christmas on the Road, CBS, 1984.
The 10th Anniversary Johnny Cash Christmas Special, CBS, 1985.
The Door Is Always Open, syndicated, 1985.
Texas 150: A Celebration Special, ABC, 1986.
The Best of Farm Aid: An American Event, HBO, 1986.
The Academy of Country Music's 20th Anniversary Reunion, NBC, 1986.
A Tribute to Ricky Nelson, syndicated, 1987.
Welcome Home, HBO, 1987.
Kenny Rogers Classic Weekend, ABC, 1988.
A Country Music Celebration: The 30th Anniversary of the Country Music Association, CBS, 1988.
An All-Star Celebration: The '88 Vote, ABC, 1988.
Host, *Buddy Holly and the Crickets—A Tribute,* PBS, 1988.
Judy Collins: Going Home, The Disney Channel, 1989.
Texas and Tennessee . . . A Musical Affair, TNN, 1990.
In the Hank Williams Tradition, PBS, 1990.
Farm Aid IV, TNN, 1990.
Martin Luther King, Jr. National Holiday Parade, TBS, 1991 and 1992.
Highwaymen Live!, The Disney Channel, 1991.
The Highwaymen, TNN, 1992.
Farm Aid V, TNN, 1992.
Host, *In Country: Songs of the Vietnam War,* PBS, 1992.
Willie Nelson, the Big Six-O: An All-Star Birthday Celebration, CBS, 1993.
Sam Peckinpah: Man of Iron, Arts & Entertainment, 1993.
Farm Aid VI, TNN, 1993.
Host, *The Bob Dylan 30th Anniversary Celebration* (also known as *In the Spotlight*), PBS, 1993.
Willie Nelson: My Life, Arts & Entertainment, 1994.
Elvis Aron Presley: The Tribute, syndicated, 1994.
Coming and Going, PBS, 1994.
American Music Shop, TNN, 1994.
Host and narrator, *The Songs of Six Families,* 1994.
Kris Kristofferson: Songwriter, 1995.
Dolly Parton: Treasures, CBS, 1996.
The 25th American Film Institute Life Achievement Award: A Salute to Martin Scorsese, CBS, 1997.
Big Guns Talk: The Story of the Western, TNT, 1997.
The Life and Times of Willie Nelson, TNN, 1997.
CMA 40th: A Celebration, CBS, 1998.

Television Appearances; Series:
Super Dave, Showtime, 1987.
The Texas Connection, TNN, 1990.
Country Music Spotlight, Family Channel, 1994.
Host and narrator, *Adventures of the Old West,* The Disney Channel, 1994.

Television Appearances; Episodic:
Dean Martin Presents Music Country, U.S.A., NBC, 1973.
The Muppet Show, 1978.
The Larry Sanders Show, HBO, 1992.
Host and narrator, "The Songs of Six Families," *Great Performances,* PBS, 1994.
"Arthur's Crises (aka Artie's Crisis)," *The Larry Sanders Show,* HBO, 1994.
Country Music Spotlight, 1994.
Narrator, *Legends,* VH-1, 1996.
Narrator, *Dead Man's Gun,* Showtime, 1997.

Also appeared as a guest on segments of the *Johnny Cash Show,* ABC; *Rollin' on the River,* syndicated; *The Tonight Show,* NBC; and *Late Night with David Letterman,* NBC.

Television Appearances; Awards Presentations:
The 19th Annual Country Music Association Awards, CBS, 1985.
The American Music Awards, ABC, 1986.
The 29th Annual Grammy Awards, CBS, 1987.
The 23rd Annual Academy of Country Music Awards, NBC, 1988.
Grammy Living Legends, CBS, 1989.
The 21st Annual NAACP Image Awards, NBC, 1989.
Presenter, *The 32nd Annual Grammy Awards,* CBS, 1990.
The 26th Annual Academy of Country Music Awards, NBC, 1991.
The 27th Annual Academy of Country Music Awards, NBC, 1992.
The 27th Annual Country Music Association Awards, CBS, 1993.
Music City News Country Songwriters Awards, TNN, 1995.
The 30th Annual CMA Awards, 1996.
The Kennedy Center Honors: A Celebration of the Performing Arts, CBS, 1996.

The 32nd Annual CMA Awards, 1998.
The Kennedy Center Honors, CBS, 1998.
The Kennedy Center Mark Twain Prize Celebrating the Humor of Richard Pryor, Comedy Central, 1999.

Stage Appearances:

Concert tours and appearances include Newport Folk Festival, Newport, RI, 1969, and *Welcome Home,* Washington, DC, 1987. Numerous tours, with Johnny Cash, Waylon Jennings, and Willie Nelson, as part of country band, The Highwaymen. Appeared in England as folk singer under the name Kris Carson.

RECORDINGS

Videos:

A Celebration, DID Productions, 1981.

Albums:

Kristofferson, Monument, 1970.
Me & Bobby McGee, Monument, 1971.
The Silver-Tongued Devil and I, Monument, 1971.
Jesus Was a Capricorn, Monument, 1972.
Border Lord, One Way, 1972.
Full Moon, A&M, 1973.
(With Rita Coolidge) *Breakaway,* Monument/Sony, 1974.
Spooky Lady's Sideshow, One Way, 1974.
Who's to Bless and Who's to Blame, One Way, 1975.
Third World Warrior, Mercury, 1976.
Surreal Thing, One Way, 1976.
The Songs of Kristofferson, Monument, 1977.
A Star Is Born, Monument, 1977.
(With Coolidge) *Natural Act,* A&M, 1978.
Easter Island, Columbia, 1978.
Big Sur Festival, 1978.
Shake Hands with the Devil, Columbia, 1979.
(With Willie Nelson) *A Tribute to Willie and Kris,* Columbia, 1981.
To the Bone, Columbia, 1981.
Winning Hand, Monument, 1983.
(With Nelson) *Music from Songwriter,* Columbia, 1984.
My Songs, CBS, 1984.
(With The Highwaymen [with Nelson, Cash, and Jennings]) *Highwaymen,* Columbia, 1985.
Repossessed, Mercury, 1987.
(Contributor) Randy Travis, *Heroes & Friends,* Warner, 1990.
(With The Highwaymen) *Highwayman 2,* Columbia, 1990.
(With The Borderlords) *Third World Warrior,* Mercury, 1990.
The Best of Kris Kristofferson, Sony, 1991.
Singer, Songwriter, Monument, 1991.
(With others) *Live at the Philharmonic,* Monument, 1992.
The Best of Kris Kristofferson, Sony, 1995.
(With The Highwaymen) *The Road Goes on Forever,* Liberty, 1995.

Also recorded (with Rita Coolidge) *Full Moon.*

WRITINGS

Film Songwriter:

The Last Movie, Universal, 1971.
Cisco Pike, Columbia, 1971.
Two-Lane Blacktop, Universal, 1971.
Fat City, Columbia, 1973.
The Gospel Road, Twentieth Century-Fox, 1973.
Blume in Love, Warner Bros., 1973.
Janis, Universal Studios Home Video, 1974.
The Sailor Who Fell from Grace with the Sea, Avco Embassy, 1976.
Saint Jack, New World, 1979.
Honeysuckle Rose, Warner Bros., 1980.
One-Trick Pony, Warner Bros., 1980.
Beyond Reasonable Doubt, Endeavour, 1980.
Traveler, 1981.
Maeve, 1981.
Songwriter, TriStar, 1984.
Trouble in Mind, Island Alive, 1985.
Something Wild, Orion, 1986.
Mascara, Cannon, 1987.
Walking after Midnight, 1988.
Cheatin' Hearts, Trimark, 1993.
The War at Home, Buena Vista, 1996.
U-Turn, Sony, 1997.

Television Songwriter:

The Fear Inside (movie), Showtime, 1992.
Kris Kristofferson: Songwriter (special), 1995.
Outlaw Justice (movie), CBS, 1999.

Television Writing:

Just Friends (special), 1970.

Songwriter:

"Vietnam Blues," Buckhorn Music, 1965.
"For the Good Times," Buckhorn Music, 1968.
(With Fred L. Foster) "Me and Bobby McGee," Combine Music, 1969.

"Sunday Mornin' Comin' Down," Combine Music, 1969.
"Help Me Make It through the Night," Combine Music, 1970.
"Loving Her Was Easier (Than Anything I'll Ever Do Again)," Combine Music, 1970.
"Once More with Feeling," Combine Music, 1970.
(With Shel Silverstein) "The Taker," Evil Eye Music, 1970.
"Please Don't Tell Me How the Story Ends," Combine Music, 1971.
"I'd Rather Be Sorry," Buckhorn Music, 1971.
"Why Me?," Resaca Music, 1972.

Also wrote numerous other songs, including "Jody and the Kid" and "When I Loved Her"; and with wife, Rita Coolidge, "From the Bottle to the Bottom," "Lover Please," and "Loving Arms."

OTHER SOURCES

Books:

Kalet, Beth, *Kris Kristofferson,* Quick Fox, 1979.

Periodicals:

Billboard, April 20, 1996, p. 50.
Entertainment Weekly, September 25, 1998, p. 68.
Interview, September, 1998, p. 124.
People Weekly, September 21, 1998, p. 103.
Texas Monthly, March, 1997, p. 126.*

L

LANDAU, Martin 1934(?)-

PERSONAL

Born June 20, 1934 (some sources say 1931), in Brooklyn, NY; son of Morris (a machinist) and Selma (maiden name, Buchanan) Landau; married Barbara Bain (an actress), January 31, 1957 (divorced, 1993); children: Susan Meredith, Juliet Rose. *Education:* Studied art at the Pratt Institute and Art Students League; trained for the stage with Lee Strasberg, Harold Clurman, and Elia Kazan at Actors Studio.

Addresses: *Office*—23717 Long Valley Rd., Calabasas, CA 91302-2409.

Career: Actor and director. Actors Studio, member of board of directors, 1985—; Actors Studio West, executive director and teacher. *Daily News,* New York City, worked as an editorial artist and staff cartoonist; illustrator for Billy Rose's newspaper column "Pitching Horseshoes"; cartoonist for the comic strip "The Gumps."

Member: Actors' Equity Association, Screen Actors Guild, American Federation of Television and Radio Artists, Academy of Motion Picture Arts and Sciences, Academy of Television Arts and Sciences.

Awards, Honors: Emmy Award nominations, outstanding supporting actor in a dramatic series, 1967, 1968, 1969, and Golden Globe Award, best male television star, 1968, all for *Mission: Impossible;* Academy Award nomination, best supporting actor, and Golden Globe Award, best supporting actor in a motion picture, 1989, both for *Tucker: The Man and His Dream;* Academy Award nomination, best supporting actor, 1989, for *Crimes and Misdemeanors;* CableACE Award nominations, 1990, for *Max and Helen* and *By Dawn's Early Light;* Berlinale Camera Award, Berlin International Film Festival, 1990; CableACE Award nominations, 1992, for *Legacy of Lies;* Lifetime Achievement Award, Charleston Film Festival, 1994; Lifetime Achievement Award, Houston Film Festival, 1994; American Comedy Award, Chicago Film Critics Award, Boston Film Critics Award, Texas Film Critics Award, National Society of Film Critics Award, New York Film Critics Circle Award, Los Angeles Film Critics Association Award, best supporting actor, 1994, Academy Award, best supporting actor, Screen Actors Guild Award, outstanding performance by a male actor in a supporting role, Golden Globe Award, best performance by an actor in a supporting role in a motion picture, 1995, British Academy of Film and Television Arts Award nomination, best performance by an actor in a supporting role, all for *Ed Wood;* Lifetime Achievement Award, San Diego Film Festival, 1998; also awarded Germany's Bravo Award, Belgium's Viewers Award, and Brazil's SACI Award.

CREDITS

Film Appearances:

Leonard, *North by Northwest,* Metro-Goldwyn-Mayer, 1959.

The duke, *The Gazebo,* Metro-Goldwyn-Mayer, 1959.

Marshall, *Pork Chop Hill,* United Artists, 1959.

Dade Coleman, *Stagecoach to Dancer's Park,* Universal, 1962.

Rufio, *Cleopatra,* Twentieth Century-Fox, 1963.

Caiaphas, *The Greatest Story Ever Told,* United Artists, 1965.

Chief Walks-Stooped-Over, *The Hallelujah Trail,* United Artists, 1965.

Jesse Coe, *Nevada Smith,* Paramount, 1966.

Rollin Hand, *Mission Impossible Versus the Mob,* 1968.

Reverend Logan Sharpe, *They Call Me Mister Tibbs,* United Artists, 1970.

Operation SNAFU (also known as *Rosolino Paterno: Soldato, Situation Normal, All Fouled Up,* and *Situation Normal: A.F.U.*), American International Pictures, 1970.

Under the Sign of Capricorn, 1971.

The colonel, *A Town Called Hell* (also known as *A Town Called Bastard*), Scotia International, 1971.

Capelli, *Black Gunn,* Columbia, 1972.

Dr. George Tracer, *Strange Shadows in an Empty Room* (also known as *Shadows in an Empty Room, A Special Magnum for Tony Saitta,* and *Blazing Magnum*), American International Pictures, 1977.

Captain Garrity, *The Last Word* (also known as *Danny Travis*), International, 1979.

General Barry Adlon, *Meteor,* American International Pictures, 1979.

Roderick Usher, *The Fall of the House of Usher,* Sunn Classic, 1980.

Marshal, *The Return* (also known as *The Alien's Return* and *Earthright*), Greydon Clark, 1980.

Fred "Sarge" Dobbs, *Without Warning* (also known as *It Came . . . Without Warning, Alien Warning,* and *The Warning),* Filmways, 1980.

Operation Moonbase Alpha, 1980.

Beauty and the Beast, 1981.

Byron "Preacher" Sutcliff, *Alone in the Dark,* New Line Cinema, 1982.

Garson Jones, *The Being* (also known as *Easter Sunday, Freak,* and *The Pottsville Horror*), BFV, 1983.

Trial by Terror, 1983.

Access Code, Prism Entertainment, 1984.

The old captain, *L'Ile au Tresor* (also known as *Treasure Island*), Films du Passage/Cannon, 1985.

Bosarian, *Cyclone,* Cinetel, 1987.

Chuck, *Empire State,* Virgin/Miracle, 1987.

W.A.R. Women Against Rape (also known as *Death Blow*), 1987.

Cicero, *Sweet Revenge,* Concorde, 1987.

Run If You Can, Allied Artists, 1987.

Abe Karatz, *Tucker: The Man and His Dream,* Paramount, 1988.

Bud, *Delta Fever,* New World Video/Image Organization, 1988.

Judah Rosenthal, *Crimes and Misdemeanors,* Orion, 1989.

Real Bullets, Vidmark, 1990.

Daniel Lambert, *Paint It Black,* Vestron, 1990.

Admiral Pendleton, *Firehead,* AIP Home Video, 1991.

L'Oeil de la Veuve, 1991.

Jack Roth, *Mistress,* Rainbow Releasing/Tribeca Productions, 1992.

Mayor Howard Baines, *Eye of the Stranger,* Silver Lake International Pictures, 1993.

Frank McCay, *No Place to Hide,* Cannon, 1993.

Alex, *Silver,* Paramount, 1993.

Neal, *Intersection* (also known as *The Things of Life*), Paramount, 1994.

Bela Lugosi, *Ed Wood,* Buena Vista, 1994.

Max Loeb, *The Color of Evening,* York Home Video, 1994.

Mac, *Time Is Money,* 1994.

The Elevator, 1996.

Judge Walker Stern, *City Hall,* Columbia, 1996.

Merisairas (also known as *Seasick*), S. Andrews, 1996.

Geppeto, *The Adventures of Pinocchio* (also known as *Carlo Collodi's Pinocchio* and *Pinocchio*), New Line Cinema, 1996.

Voice of Storyteller, *Legend of the Spirit Dog,* Republic, 1997.

Mr. Blakemore, *B*A*P*S,* New Line Cinema, 1997.

Voice, *The Long Way Home,* Seventh Art Releasing, 1997.

Winter, 1998.

Off the Menu: The Last Days of Chasen's, Northern Arts Entertainment, 1998.

Professor Petrovsky, *Rounders,* Miramax, 1998.

Dr. Alvin Kurtzweil, *The X-Files,* Twentieth Century-Fox, 1998.

Gordon Trout, *The Joyriders,* Trident Releasing, 1999.

Al, *Edtv,* Universal, 1999.

Carlo Torello, *Carlo's Wake,* 1999.

Also appeared in *Decision at Midnight* and *Tipperary.*

Film Work:

Director, *Meteor,* American International Pictures, 1979.

Television Appearances; Series:

Rollin Hand, *Mission: Impossible,* CBS, 1966-69.

Commander John Koenig, *Space 1999,* syndicated, 1975-77.

Voice of MacDonald "Mac" Gargan/Scorpion, *Spider-Man* (animated), Fox, 1995.

Television Appearances; Episodic:

"Salome," *Omnibus,* CBS, 1955.

"House Divided," *The Big Story,* NBC, 1957.

"Sanctuary," *Harbourmaster,* CBS, 1957.

Henrique Fllipe, "The Jeweled Gun," *Maverick,* ABC, 1957.

Thorp, "The Patsy," *Gunsmoke,* CBS, 1958.

"Flight to Freedom: File Number 36," *The Walter Winchell File,* ABC, 1958.

"High Card Hangs," *Maverick,* ABC, 1958.

"The Ghost," *Sugarfoot,* ABC, 1958.
"The Outcast," *Lawman,* ABC, 1958.
"The Sounds of Eden," *Playhouse 90,* CBS, 1959.
Hotaling, "Mr. Denton on Doomsday," *The Twilight Zone,* CBS, 1959.
"Survival," *General Electric Theatre,* CBS, 1959.
"Doc Holliday," *Tales of Wells Fargo,* NBC, 1959.
"Incident Below the Brazos," *Rawhide,* CBS, 1959.
"Lucky Silva," *The Lawless Years,* NBC, 1959.
Jerry Fanning, "Mexican Stake-Out," *The Untouchables,* ABC, 1959.
Jerry Fanning, "The Monsters," *Wanted: Dead or Alive,* CBS, 1960.
"Nightmare in Napuka," *Adventures in Paradise,* ABC, 1960.
"The Derelict," *Johnny Ringo,* CBS, 1960.
"Tiger," *Tate,* NBC, 1960.
"The Cathy Eckhardt Story," *Wagon Train,* NBC, 1960.
"Moment of Truth," *Checkmate,* CBS, 1960.
"The House of Seven Gables," *Shirley Temple Theatre,* NBC, 1960.
"Duel of Strangers," *The Islanders,* ABC, 1960.
"Mr. Flotsam," *Adventures in Paradise,* ABC, 1961.
"Dark Moment," *The Tall Man,* NBC, 1961.
"The Gentleman from Brazil," *Acapulco,* NBC, 1961.
"The Avengers," *Outlaws,* NBC, 1961.
"Hot Wind in a Cold Town," *Checkmate,* CBS, 1961.
"The Vasqueros," *The Rifleman,* ABC, 1961.
"Shadow of His Brother," *The Detectives,* ABC, 1961.
"The Lonely House," *Bonanza,* NBC, 1961.
Larry Coombs, "Loophole," *The Untouchables,* ABC, 1961.
"The Gift," *Bonanza,* NBC, 1961.
"The Black Robe," *The Tall Man,* NBC, 1962.
"Pay the Two Dollars," *Mr. Novak,* NBC, 1963.
Andro, "The Man Who Was Never Born," *The Outer Limits,* ABC, 1963.
Richard Bellero, Jr., "The Bellero Shield," *The Outer Limits,* ABC, 1964.
Major Ivan Kuchenko, "The Jeopardy Room," *The Twilight Zone,* CBS, 1964.
"The Secret," *The Defenders,* CBS, 1964.
"The Night the Monkey Died," *The Greatest Show on Earth,* ABC, 1964.
"The Second Verdict," *The Alfred Hitchcock Hour,* CBS, 1964.
"Child in Danger," *The Purex Special for Women,* ABC, 1964.
"Danny Was a Million Laughs," *I Spy,* NBC, 1965.
"The Night of the Red-Eyed Madman," *The Wild Wild West,* CBS, 1965.
"Enter a Strange Animal," *Mr. Novak,* NBC, 1965.
"The Way to Kill a Killer," *The Big Valley,* ABC, 1965.
"The Locket," *A Man Called Shenandoah,* ABC, 1965.
"This Stage of Fools," *Branded,* NBC, 1966.
Count Zark, "The Bat Cave Affair," *The Man from U.N.C.L.E.,* NBC, 1966.
Britton, "The Goldtakers," *Gunsmoke,* CBS, 1966.
Maxwell Smart, "Pheasant Under Glass," *Get Smart,* NBC, 1969.
The Andy Williams Show, NBC, 1970.
"Double Shock," *Columbo,* NBC, 1973.
"The Hunted," *Matt Houston,* ABC, 1983.
Slocum, "Confrontations," *Hotel,* ABC, 1983.
Al Drake, "Birds of a Feather," *Murder, She Wrote,* CBS, 1984.
Hayden Stone, "Company, Ink," *Buffalo Bill,* NBC, 1984.
William Cooper-James, "The Beacon," *The Twilight Zone,* CBS, 1985.
Miles Broderick, "Last Flight from Moscow," *Blacke's Magic,* NBC, 1986.
Wallace Garrison, "The Final Twist," *Alfred Hitchcock Presents,* USA Network, 1987.
Inside the Actors Studio, 1995.
Voice of Woodrow Wilson, *The Great War* (also known as *The Great War and the Shaping of the 20th Century*), PBS, 1996.

Also appeared in episodes of *Studio One,* CBS; *Philco Playhouse,* NBC; *Goodyear Playhouse,* NBC; and *Kraft Television Theatre.*

Television Appearances; Movies:
Captain Johnny Bristol, *Welcome Home, Johnny Bristol,* CBS, 1972.
Paul Savage, *Savage,* 1973.
Commander John Koenig, *Journey Through the Black Sun,* 1976.
Commander John Koenig, *Destination Moonbase Alpha* (also known as *Space: 2100*), 1976.
Commander John Koenig, *Cosmic Princess,* 1976.
Commander John Koenig, *Alien Attack,* 1976.
Tom Flood, *The Death of Ocean View Park,* ABC, 1979.
J. J. Pierson, *The Harlem Globetrotters on Gilligan's Island,* NBC, 1981.
Roderick Usher, *The Fall of the House of Usher,* NBC, 1982.
John Martin Perkins III, *Kung Fu: The Movie,* CBS, 1986.
Simon Wiesenthal, *Max and Helen,* TNT, 1990.
The U.S. president, *By Dawn's Early Light* (also known as *The Grand Tour*), HBO, 1990.
Jerry Gertz, *Something to Live For: The Alison Gertz Story* (also known as *The Ali Gertz Story*), ABC, 1992.
Abraham Zelnick, *Legacy of Lies,* USA Network, 1992.

Dr. Thadius Moxley, *12:01,* Fox, 1993.
Joseph Bonanno, *Bonanno: A Godfather's Story,* Showtime, 1999.

Television Appearances; Miniseries:
Max, *The Neon Empire,* Showtime, 1989.
Jacob, *Joseph* (also known as *The Bible: Joseph*), TNT, 1995.

Television Appearances; Pilots:
The Ghost of Sierra de Cobra, CBS, 1966.
Paul Savage, *Savage* (also known as *Watch Dog*), NBC, 1973.
Lyle Stenning, *The Return of the Six Million Dollar Man and the Bionic Woman,* NBC, 1987.

Television Appearances; Specials:
The Screen Actors Guild 50th Anniversary Celebration, CBS, 1984.
Starathon '90: Weekend with the Stars for Cerebral Palsy, syndicated, 1990.
The Golden Globe Awards, TBS, 1990.
Narrator, *Secrets of the Unknown,* CBS, 1991.
Narrator, *Visitors from the Unknown,* CBS, 1992.
The Golden Globe's 50th Anniversary Celebration, NBC, 1994.
The 21st Annual People's Choice Awards, 1995.
Family Film Awards, 1996.
The 22nd Annual People's Choice Awards, 1996.
The 53rd Annual Golden Globe Awards, 1996.
The 68th Annual Academy Awards, 1996.
Mr. Potter, *Merry Christmas, George Bailey,* PBS, 1997.
Peter Graves: Mission Accomplished, Arts and Entertainment, 1997.
Elizabeth Taylor: The E! True Hollywood Story, E! Entertainment Television, 1998.
Intimate Portrait: Halle Berry, Lifetime, 1998.
Lee Strasberg: The Method Man, Arts and Entertainment, 1998.
Steve McQueen: The King of Cool, AMC, 1998.
The 70th Annual Academy Awards, 1998.
Host, *The X-Files Movie Special,* Fox, 1998.

Stage Appearances:
Charley Gemini, *Detective Story,* Peaks Island Playhouse, Peaks Island, ME, 1951.
Nick, *First Love,* Provincetown Playhouse, New York City, 1951.
Lally, *The Penguin,* Current Stages Theatre, New York City, 1952.
Juvan, *Goat Song,* Equity Library Theatre, New York City, 1953.
(Broadway debut) The husband, *Middle of the Night,* American National Theatre and Academy, New York City, 1957.

Appeared in *Uncle Vanya; Wedding Breakfast;* and *Stalag 17.*

Stage Work:
Director, *The Warm-Up,* American Jewish Theatre, New York City, 1995.

Major Tours:
Stalag 17, U.S. cities, 1952.
The husband, *Middle of the Night,* U.S. and Canadian cities, 1957-58.
Dracula, U.S. cities, 1984-85.*

LANDIS, John 1950-

PERSONAL

Full name, John David Landis; born August 3, 1950, in Chicago, IL; son of Marshall David and Shirley (maiden name, Magaziner) Landis; married Deborah Nadoolman (a costume designer), July 27, 1980; children: Rachel, Max.

Addresses: *Agent*—William Morris Agency, 151 El Camino Dr., BeverlyHills, CA 90212-2704.

Career: Producer, director, screenwriter, stuntman, and actor. American Lung Association of Los Angeles County, member of board of directors.

Member: Writers Guild of America, Directors Guild of America, Screen Actors Guild, Academy of Motion Picture Arts and Sciences.

Awards, Honors: Chevalier, French Order of Arts and Letters, 1985; CableACE Awards for *Dream On;* Image Awards, W.C. Handy Award, People's Choice Awards, and other awards.

CREDITS

Film Work; Director, Except Where Indicated:
And stuntman, *Schlock* (also known as *The Banana Monster*), Jack Harris, 1973.
Kentucky Fried Movie, United Film, 1977.
National Lampoon's Animal House, Universal, 1977.
The Blues Brothers, Universal, 1980.

And stuntman, *An American Werewolf in London,* Universal, 1981.

Coming Soon, 1982.

Producer (with Steven Spielberg) and director of the segments "Prologue" and "Back There," *Twilight Zone—The Movie,* Warner Bros., 1983.

And producer, *Making Michael Jackson's "Thriller"* (documentary), Palace/Virgin Vision/Gold, 1983.

Trading Places, Paramount, 1983.

Into the Night, Universal, 1985.

Spies Like Us, Warner Bros., 1985.

Executive producer, *Clue,* Paramount, 1985.

Three Amigos!, Orion, 1986.

Executive producer and director (with Joe Dante, Carl Gottlieb, Peter Horton, and Robert K. Weiss), *Amazon Women on the Moon* (also known as *Cheeseburger Film Sandwich*), Universal, 1987.

Coming to America, Paramount, 1988.

Oscar, Buena Vista, 1991.

Innocent Blood (also known as *A French Vampire in America*), Warner Bros., 1992.

Beverly Hills Cop III, Paramount, 1994.

The Stupids, New Line Cinema, 1996.

Character creator, *An American Werewolf in Paris* (also known as *American Werewolf 2*), Buena Vista, 1997.

And producer, *Susan's Plan,* Kushner-Locke, 1998.

And producer and music executive producer, *Blues Brothers 2000,* Universal, 1998.

Film Appearances:

Schlockthropus, *Schlock* (also known as *The Banana Monster*), Jack Harris, 1973.

Jake's friend, *Battle for the Planet of the Apes* (also known as *Colonization of the Planet of the Apes*), Twentieth Century-Fox, 1973.

Mechanic, *Death Race 2000,* New World, 1975.

(Uncredited) Studio crew member, *Kentucky Fried Movie,* United Film, 1977.

Mizerany, *1941,* Universal, 1979.

Trooper La Fong, *The Blues Brothers,* Universal, 1980.

(Uncredited) Man hit by a car, *An American Werewolf in London* (alsoknown as *American Werewolf*), Universal, 1981.

(Uncredited) Man in bank, *Eating Raoul,* Twentieth Century-Fox, 1982.

Making Michael Jackson's "Thriller" (documentary), Palace/Virgin Vision/Gold, 1983.

The Muppets Take Manhattan, TriStar, 1984.

Savak, *Into the Night,* Universal, 1985.

Physician, *Darkman,* Universal, 1990.

Radio technician, *Spontaneous Combustion,* Taurus Entertainment, 1990.

Lab technician, *Stephen King's Sleepwalkers,* Columbia, 1992.

Himself, *Venice/Venice,* International Rainbow Pictures, 1992.

Dr. Edwards, *Body Chemistry II: Voice of a Stranger,* Columbia TriStar Home Video, 1992.

FBI Agent, *Silence of the Hams* (also known as *Il silenzio dei prosciutti*), October Films, 1994.

Himself, *Who Is Henry Jaglom?,* 1995.

Astronaut 1, *Vampirella,* Concorde, 1996.

Mad City, Warner Bros., 1997.

Narrator, *Hollywood Rated "R,"* 1997.

Television Work; Series:

Executive producer, *Dream On,* HBO, 1990-96.

Executive producer, *Weird Science,* USA Network, 1994.

Executive consultant, *Sliders,* Fox, 1995-96.

Executive producer, *Campus Cops,* USA Network, 1996.

Executive producer and development, *Disney's Honey, I Shrunk the Kids: The TV Show,* syndicated, 1997-99.

Also executive produced and directed *Topper.*

Television Work; Episodic:

Director, *George Burns Comedy Week,* CBS, 1985.

Executive producer, "Fuzzbucket," *The Disney Sunday Movie,* ABC, 1986.

Director, *Dream On,* HBO, 1990-96.

Director, "Black or White," *Dangerous,* Fox, 1991.

Director, *Campus Cops,* USA Network, 1996.

Television Work; Executive Producer; Movies:

Here Come the Munsters, 1995.

The Munsters' Scary Little Christmas, Fox, 1996.

Sir Arthur Conan Doyle's The Lost World, DirecTV, 1999.

Television Work; Specials:

Executive producer, *Fuzzbucket,* 1986.

Director, "Disneyland's 35th Anniversary Celebration," *The Magical World of Disney,* NBC, 1990.

Dangerous, 1991.

Associated with the special *B. B. King: Into the Night.*

Television Appearances; Episodic:

Herb, "Futile Attraction," *Dream On,* HBO, 1991.

Herb, "Where There's Smoke, You're Fired," *Dream On,* HBO, 1994.

Himself, "Caroline and the Movie," *Caroline and the City,* NBC, 1995.
The Big Scary Movie Show, Sci-Fi Channel, 1996.

Also appeared as Voice, *Eek! The Cat* (animated).

Television Appearances; Specials:
Stand-Up Comics Take a Stand!, syndicated, 1989.
Jerry Lewis, Total Filmmaker (also known as *Martin and Lewis: Their Golden Age of Comedy*), The Disney Channel, 1994.

Television Appearances; Movies:
Mike Calvecchio, *Psycho IV: The Beginning,* Showtime, 1990.
Surgical assistant, *Quicksilver Highway,* Fox, 1997.

Television Appearances; Miniseries:
Russ Dorr, *Stephen King's "The Stand"* (also known as *The Stand*), ABC, 1994.

RECORDINGS

Music Videos:
Co-producer, director, and co-writer, "Thriller," Michael Jackson, 1983.
Director, "Black or White," Michael Jackson, 1991.

WRITINGS

Screenplays:
Schlock (also known as *The Banana Monster*), Jack Harris, 1973.
(With Dan Aykroyd) *The Blues Brothers,* Universal, 1980.
An American Werewolf in London (also known as *American Werewolf*), Universal, 1981.
(Prologue and segment one only) *Twilight Zone—The Movie,* Warner Bros., 1983.
Contributing writer, *Making Michael Jackson's "Thriller"* (documentary), Palace/Virgin Vision/Gold, 1983.
Into the Night, Universal, 1985.
Story writer (with Jonathon Lynn), *Clue,* Paramount, 1985.
Susan's Plan, Kushner-Locke, 1998.
Blues Brothers 2000, Universal, 1998.

OTHER SOURCES

Periodicals:
American Film, May, 1982.
Entertainment Weekly, July 25, 1997, p. 86.
People Weekly, August 4, 1980; July 18, 1983; February 26, 1985.
Rolling Stone, August 7, 1980; July 7, 1983.*

LANSBURY, Angela 1925-

PERSONAL

Full name, Angela Brigid Lansbury; born October 16, 1925, in London, England; immigrated to the United States in 1940; naturalized citizen, 1951; daughter of Edgar Isaac (a lumber merchant) and Moyna (an actress; maiden name, Macgill) Lansbury; married Richard Cromwell (an actor), 1945 (divorced, 1946); married Peter Pullen Shaw (an agent), August 12, 1949; children: (second marriage) Anthony Peter, Deirdre Angela; David (stepson). *Education:* Attended Academy of Music, London, Webber-Douglas School for Dramatic Arts, 1939-40, and Feagin School of Dramatic Arts, New York, 1940-42.

Addresses: *Agent*—William Morris Agency, 151 El Camino Drive, Beverly Hills, CA 90212. *Contact*—c/o Universal TV, 100 Universal City Plaza, Universal City, CA 91508.

Career: Actress and singer.

Member: Actors' Equity Association, Screen Actors Guild, American Federation of Television and Radio Artists, Players Club.

Awards, Honors: Hollywood Foreign Correspondents' Association Award, and Academy Award nomination, best supporting actress, all 1945, for *Gaslight;* Golden Globe Award and Academy Award nomination, both best supporting actress, both 1946, for *The Picture of Dorian Gray;* National Board of Review Awards, both best supporting actress, both 1962, for *All Fall Down* and *The Manchurian Candidate;* Golden Globe Award and Academy Award nomination, both best supporting actress, both 1963, for *The Manchurian Candidate;* Antoinette Perry Award, best actress in a musical, 1966, for *Mame;* Hasty Pudding Woman of the Year, Harvard Hasty Pudding Theatricals, 1968; Antoinette Perry Award, best actress in a musical, 1969, for *Dear World;* Golden Globe Award nomination, best motion picture actress--comedy/musical, 1971, for *Something for Everyone;* Golden Globe Award nomination, best motion picture actress--musical/comedy, 1972, for *Bedknobs and Broomsticks;* Antoinette Perry Award, best actress in a musical, and

Sarah Siddons Award, both 1975, for *Gypsy;* National Board of Review Award, best supporting actress, 1978, and British Academy of Film and Television Arts Film Award nomination, best supporting actress, 1979, for *Death on the Nile;* Antoinette Perry Award, best actress in a musical, Drama Desk Award, outstanding actress in a musical, and Ruby Award (*After Dark* magazine), Performer of the Year, all 1979, for *Sweeney Todd;* Sarah Siddons Award, 1980, for *Mame;* inducted into the Theatre Hall of Fame, 1982; Emmy Award nomination, best actress in a limited series or special, 1983, for *Little Gloria . . . Happy At Last;* Golden Globe Award nomination, best performance by an actress in a supporting role in a series, miniseries, or motion picture made for television, 1984, for *The Gift of Love: A Christmas Story.*

Golden Globe Awards, best performance by an actress in a television series—drama, 1985, 1987, 1990, and 1992, Golden Globe Award nominations, best performance by an actress in a television series-drama, 1986, 1988, 1989, 1991, 1992, 1993, and 1995, Emmy Award nominations, outstanding lead actress in a drama series, 1985, 1986, 1987, 1988, 1989, 1990, 1991, 1992, 1993, 1994, 1995, and 1996, People's Choice Award, female performer in a new television program, 1985, and Screen Actors Guild Award nomination, outstanding performance by a female in a drama series, 1995, all for *Murder, She Wrote;* Emmy Award nomination, outstanding individual performance in a variety or musical program, 1985, for *Sweeney Todd;* Emmy Award nomination, individual performance in a variety or music program, 1987, for *The 1987 Antoinette Perry Awards;* Louella Parsons Award, Hollywood Women's Press Club, 1989; Commander of British Empire by Queen Elizabeth II, 1994; TV Hall of Fame, 1996; Luce Award, Women in Film, 1996; Lifetime Achievement Award, Screen Actors Guild, 1997; National Medal of Arts, 1997; Annie Award nomination, outstanding individual achievement for voice acting by a female performer in an animated feature production, 1998, for *Anastasia.*

CREDITS

Stage Appearances:

(Broadway debut) Marcelle, *Hotel Paradiso,* Henry Miller's Theatre, 1957.

Helen, *A Taste of Honey,* Lyceum Theatre, New York City, 1960.

Cora Hoover Hooper, *Anyone Can Whistle,* Majestic Theatre, New York City, 1964.

Title role, *Mame,* Winter Garden Theatre, New York City, 1966.

Countess Aurelia, *Dear World,* Mark Hellinger Theatre, New York City, 1969.

Prettybelle Sweet, *Prettybelle,* Shubert Theatre, Boston, MA, 1971.

Title role, *Mame,* Westbury Music Fair, Long Island, NY, 1972.

(London debut) Mistress, *All Over,* Royal Shakespeare Company, Aldwych Theatre, 1972.

Ensemble, *Sondheim: A Musical Tribute* (revue), Shubert Theatre, New York City, 1973.

Mama Rose, *Gypsy,* Piccadilly Theatre, London, 1973, then Shubert Theatre, Los Angeles, CA, then Winter Garden Theatre, New York City, both 1974.

Gertrude, *Hamlet,* National Theatre Company, Old Vic Theatre, London, 1975, then Lyttleton Theatre, London, 1976.

Counting the Ways, Hartford Stage Company, Hartford, CT, 1976-77.

Listening, Hartford Stage Company, 1976-77.

Anna, *The King and I,* Uris Theatre, New York City, 1978.

Mrs. Lovett, *Sweeney Todd,* Uris Theatre, 1979, then U.S. cities, 1980.

A Little Family Business, Center Theatre Group, Ahmanson Theatre, Los Angeles, then Martin Beck Theatre, New York City, both 1982.

Title role, *Mame,* Gershwin Theatre, New York City, 1983.

The Players Club Centennial Salute, Shubert Theatre, 1989.

Film Appearances:

(Film debut) Nancy Oliver, *Gaslight* (also known as *The Murder in Thornton Square*), Metro-Goldwyn-Mayer, 1944.

Edwina Brown, *National Velvet,* Metro-Goldwyn-Mayer, 1944.

Sybil Vane, *The Picture of Dorian Gray,* Metro-Goldwyn-Mayer, 1945.

Dusty Millard, *The Hoodlum Saint,* Metro-Goldwyn-Mayer, 1946.

Guest performer, *Till the Clouds Roll By,* Metro-Goldwyn-Mayer, 1946.

Em, *The Harvey Girls,* Metro-Goldwyn-Mayer, 1946.

Mabel Sabre, *If Winter Comes,* Metro-Goldwyn-Mayer, 1947.

Clottide de Marelle, *The Private Affairs of Bel Ami,* United Artists, 1947.

Kay Thorndyke, *State of the Union* (also known as *The World and His Wife*), Metro-Goldwyn-Mayer, 1948.

Susan Bratten, *Tenth Avenue Angel,* Metro-Goldwyn-Mayer, 1948.

Queen Anne, *The Three Musketeers,* Metro-Goldwyn-Mayer, 1948.

Audrey Quail, *The Red Danube,* Metro-Goldwyn-Mayer, 1949.

Semador, *Samson and Delilah,* Paramount, 1949.

Mrs. Edwards, *Kind Lady,* Metro-Goldwyn-Mayer, 1951.

Leslie, *Mutiny,* United Artists, 1952.

Valeska Chauvel, *Remains to Be Seen,* Metro-Goldwyn-Mayer, 1953.

Doris Hillman, *Key Man* (also known as *A Life at Stake*), Anglo-Amalgamated, 1954.

Tally Dickinson, *A Lawless Street,* Columbia, 1955.

Madame Valentine, *The Purple Mask,* Universal, 1955.

Princess Gwendolyn, *The Court Jester,* Paramount, 1956.

Myra Leeds, *Please Murder Me,* Distributors Corporation of America, 1956.

Minnie Littlejohn, *The Long, Hot Summer,* Twentieth Century-Fox, 1958.

Mabel Claremont, *The Reluctant Debutante,* Metro-Goldwyn-Mayer, 1958.

Countess Lina, *A Breath of Scandal,* Paramount, 1960.

Mavis Pruitt, *The Dark at the Top of the Stairs,* Warner Bros., 1960.

Sarah Lee Gates, *Blue Hawaii,* Paramount, 1961.

Pearl, *Season of Passion* (also known as *Summer of the Seventeenth Doll*), United Artists, 1961.

Annabel Willart, *All Fall Down,* Metro-Goldwyn-Mayer, 1962.

Voice of Marguerite Laurier, *The Four Horsemen of the Apocalypse,* Metro-Goldwyn-Mayer, 1962.

Mrs. Iselin, *The Manchurian Candidate,* United Artists, 1962.

Sibyl Logan, *In the Cool of the Day,* Metro-Goldwyn-Mayer, 1963.

Phyllis, *Dear Heart,* Warner Bros., 1964.

Isabel Boyd, *The World of Henry Orient,* United Artists, 1964.

Lady Blystone, *The Amorous Adventures of Moll Flanders,* Paramount, 1965.

Claudia, *The Greatest Story Ever Told,* United Artists, 1965.

Mama Jean Bello, *Harlow,* Paramount, 1965.

Gloria, *Mister Buddwing* (also known as *Woman without a Face*), Metro-Goldwyn-Mayer, 1966.

Countess Herthe von Ornstein, *Something for Everyone* (also known as *The Rook* and *Black Flowers for the Bride*), National General, 1970.

Eglantine Price, *Bedknobs and Broomsticks,* Buena Vista, 1971.

Mrs. Salome Otterbourne, *Death on the Nile,* Paramount, 1978.

Miss Froy, *The Lady Vanishes,* Rank/Group 1, 1979.

Miss Jane Marple, *The Mirror Crack'd,* Associated Film Distribution, 1980.

Voice of Mommy Fortuna, *The Last Unicorn* (animated), ITC, 1982.

Ruth, *The Pirates of Penzance,* Universal, 1982.

Granny, *The Company of Wolves,* Cannon, 1985.

Ingrid (documentary), Wombat Productions, 1985.

Voice of Mrs. Potts, *Beauty and the Beast* (animated), Buena Vista, 1991.

Stephen Verona: Self Portrait, 1995.

Frank Capra's American Dream, Columbia, 1997.

Voice of Dowager Empress Marie, *Anastasia* (animated), Twentieth Century-Fox, 1997.

Television Appearances; Series:

Jessica Beatrice Fletcher, *Murder, She Wrote,* CBS, 1984-96.

Television Appearances; Miniseries:

Gertrude Vanderbilt Whitney, *Little Gloria . . . Happy at Last,* NBC, 1982.

Aunt Hortense Boutin, *Lace,* ABC, 1984.

Alice Garrett, *The First Olympics—Athens, 1896,* NBC, 1984.

Marchesa Allabrandi, *Rage of Angels: The Story Continues,* NBC, 1986.

Television Appearances; Movies:

Amanda Fenwick, *The Gift of Love: A Christmas Story,* CBS, 1983.

A Talent for Murder, Showtime, 1984.

Nan Moore, *Shootdown,* NBC, 1988.

Agatha McGee, *The Love She Sought* (also known as *Last Chance for Romance* and *A Green Journey*), NBC, 1990.

Title role, *Mrs. 'arris Goes to Paris,* CBS, 1992.

Title role, *Mrs. Santa Claus,* CBS, 1996.

Jessica Fletcher, *Murder, She Wrote: South by Southwest,* CBS, 1997.

Voice of Mrs. Potts, *Beauty and the Beast: The Enchanted Christmas* (animated), Walt Disney, 1997.

Emily Pollifax, *The Unexpected Mrs. Pollifax,* CBS, 1999.

Television Appearances; Specials:

The Perry Como Christmas Show, NBC, 1964.

The Perry Como Thanksgiving Show, NBC, 1966.

Voice of Sister Theresa, *The Story of the First Christmas Snow* (animated), NBC, 1975.

Ringmaster, *Circus of the Stars,* CBS, 1980.
Mrs. Lovett, *Sweeney Todd,* E! Entertainment Channel, 1982.
The Barbara Walters Special, ABC, 1985.
Clue: Movies, Murder, and Mystery, CBS, 1986.
The Spencer Tracy Legacy: A Tribute by Katharine Hepburn, PBS, 1986.
Liberty Weekend, ABC, 1986.
People Magazine on TV, CBS, 1988.
Grammy Living Legends, CBS, 1989.
CBS Premiere Preview Spectacular, CBS, 1989.
MDA Jerry Lewis Telethon, syndicated, 1990.
Host, *The Wonderful Wizard of Oz: 50 Years of Magic,* CBS, 1990.
The Dream Is Alive: The 20th Anniversary Celebration of Walt Disney World, CBS, 1991.
Bob Hope and Friends: Making New Memories, NBC, 1991.
Be Our Guest: The Making of Disney's Beauty and the Beast, The Disney Channel, 1991.
The Grand Opening of Euro Disney, CBS, 1992.
The Defense Rests: A Tribute to Raymond Burr, NBC, 1993.
Coming Up Roses, CBS, 1993.
The American Film Institute Salute to Elizabeth Taylor, ABC, 1993.
Host, *Bob Hope: The First Ninety Years,* NBC, 1993.
Host, *The Best of Disney Music: A Legacy in Song,* CBS, 1993.
Grand Marshal, *The 104th Tournament of Roses Parade,* CBS, 1993.
Sinatra: 80 Years My Way, 1995.
Inside the Dream Factory, 1995.
Host, *The Wizard of Oz: 40 Years on Television,* CBS, 1996.
Voices of Hope. . . Finding the Cures for Breast and Ovarian Cancer, Lifetime, 1997.
Guest Host, *CBS: The First 50 Years,* CBS, 1998.
Interviewee, *Angela Lansbury: A Balancing Act,* Arts and Entertainment, 1998.
AFI's 100 Years. . . 100 Movies, CBS, 1998.
Narrator, *Glorious Technicolor,* Turner Classic Movies, 1998.
Hollywood & Vinyl: Disney's 101 Greatest Musical Moments, VH-1, 1998.

Television Appearances; Episodic:
"The Citadel," *Robert Montgomery Presents Your Lucky Strike Theatre,* NBC, 1950.
"The Wonderful Night," *The Lux Video Theater,* CBS, 1950.
"Operation Weekend," *The Lux Video Theater,* CBS, 1952.
"Stone's Throw," *The Lux Video Theater,* CBS, 1952.
"Cakes and Ale," *Robert Montgomery Presents Your Lucky Strike Theatre,* NBC, 1953.
"Dreams Never Lie," *Revlon Mirror Theater,* CBS, 1953.
"The Ming Lama," *Ford Television Theatre,* NBC, 1953.
"Storm Swept," *Schlitz Playhouse of Stars,* CBS, 1953.
"A String of Beads," *Four Star Playhouse,* CBS, 1954.
"The Crime of Daphne Rutledge," *General Electric Theatre,* CBS, 1954.
"The Indiscreet Mrs. Jarvis," *Fireside Theater,* NBC, 1955.
Henry Fonda Presents the Star and the Story, syndicated, 1955.
"Madeira, Madeira," *Four Star Playhouse,* CBS, 1955.
"Billy and the Bride," *Stage 7,* CBS, 1955.
"The Treasure," *Rheingold Theatre,* NBC, 1955.
Star Time Playhouse, CBS, 1955.
"The Rarest Stamp," *Studio '57,* syndicated, 1956.
"The Force of Circumstance," *Rheingold Theatre,* NBC, 1956.
"Instant of Truth," *Front Row Center,* CBS, 1956.
"Claire," *Screen Directors Playhouse,* NBC, 1956.
"The Brown Leather Case," *Studio '57,* syndicated, 1956.
"The Devil's Brook," *Climax!,* CBS, 1957.
"Verdict of Three," *Playhouse 90,* CBS, 1958.
"The Grey Nurse Said Nothing," *Playhouse 90,* CBS, 1959.
"Something Crazy's Going on in the Back Room," *The Eleventh Hour,* NBC, 1963.
"The Deadly Toys Affair," *Man from U.N.C.L.E.,* NBC, 1965.
"Leave It to Me," *The Trials of O'Brien,* CBS, 1965.
"Novel Connection," *Magnum, P.I.,* CBS, 1986.
Penelope Keeling, "The Shell Seekers," *Hallmark Hall of Fame,* ABC, 1989.
"Helen Hayes: First Lady of the American Theatre," *American Masters,* PBS, 1991.
Narration, "The Christmas Witch," *Shelley Duvall's Bedtime Stories,* Showtime, 1992.
"Jerry Herman's Broadway at the Bowl," *Great Performances,* PBS, 1994.
"A Tribute to Stephen Sondheim," *A&E Stage,* Arts and Entertainment, 1995.

Also appeared on *The Danny Kaye Show,* CBS; *Alcoa Preview,* ABC; *The Merv Griffin Show,* syndicated; *The Today Show,* NBC; *Suspense Theatre,* syndicated; *The Art of Film,* NET; *Studio One,* CBS; and in *Kraft Theatre* and *Pantomime Quiz.*

Television Appearances; Awards Presentations:
The 37th Annual Prime Time Emmy Awards, 1985.

The 39th Annual Emmy Awards, 1987.
The 1987 Antoinette Perry Awards, 1987.
The Kennedy Center Honors: A Celebration of the Performing Arts, CBS, 1987.
Host, *The 41st Annual Tony Awards,* CBS, 1987.
Host, *The 42nd Annual Tony Awards,* CBS, 1988.
Host, *The 43rd Annual Tony Awards,* CBS, 1989.
The 41st Annual Emmy Awards, Fox, 1989.
The 42nd Annual Primetime Emmy Awards Presentation, Fox, 1990.
The Kennedy Center Honors: A Celebration of the Performing Arts, CBS, 1990.
The 43rd Annual Primetime Emmy Awards Presentation, Fox, 1991.
The 64th Annual Academy Awards Presentation, ABC, 1992.
The 44th Annual Primetime Emmy Awards, Fox, 1992.
The 18th Annual People's Choice Awards, CBS, 1992.
The 65th Annual Academy Awards Presentation, ABC, 1993.
The 19th Annual People's Choice Awards, CBS, 1993.
Host, *The 45th Annual Primetime Emmy Awards,* ABC, 1993.
The Kennedy Center Honors: A Celebration of the Performing Arts, CBS, 1993.
The 46th Annual Primetime Emmy Awards, ABC, 1994.
The 20th Annual People's Choice Awards, CBS, 1994.
Honoree, *The Screen Actors Guild Awards,* 1997.
Presenter, *The 52nd Annual Tony Awards,* 1998.

Television Appearances; Pilots:
Detective, *Scene of the Crime,* NBC, 1984.

Television Work:
Executive producer, *Murder, She Wrote,* CBS, 1992-96.

RECORDINGS

Videos:
Angela Lansbury's Positive Moves: A Personal Plan for Fitness and Well-Being at Any Age, 1988.

Albums:
Anyone Can Whistle (original cast recording), CBS Special Products, 1964.
Mame (original cast recording), Columbia, 1966.
Dear World (original cast recording), CBS Special Products, 1969.
Sweeney Todd (original cast recording), RCA, 1979.

Also recorded *The Beggar's Opera,* 1982.

WRITINGS

Books:
Author of (with Mimi Avins) *Angela Lansbury's Positive Moves: My Personal Plan for Fitness and Well-Being* and *Wedding Speeches and Toasts.**

LARROQUETTE, John 1947-

PERSONAL

Full name, John Bernard Larroquette; born November 25, 1947, in New Orleans, LA; son of John Edgar and Berthalla Oramous (maiden name, Helmstetter) Larroquette; married Elizabeth Ann Cookson, July 4, 1975; children: Lisa Katherina, Jonathan Preston, Benjamin Lawrence. *Avocational interests:* Collecting first edition books.

Addresses: *Agent*—Creative Artists Agency, 9830 Wilshire Blvd., Beverly Hills, CA 90212-1825.

Career: Actor, producer, and director. Worked as a disc jockey, New Orleans, LA.

Awards, Honors: Emmy Awards, outstanding supporting actor in a comedy series, 1985, 1986, 1987, and 1988, and Golden Globe Award nomination, best performance by an actor in a supporting role in a series, miniseries, or motion picture made for television, 1988, all for *Night Court;* Emmy Award nomination, best actor, 1994, for *The John Larroquette Show;* Emmy Award, outstanding guest actor in a drama series, Q Award, Viewers for Quality Television, best recurring player, 1998, both for *The Practice;* Drama League Award, for *Endgame.*

CREDITS

Television Appearances; Series:
Dr. Paul Herman, *Doctors' Hospital,* NBC, 1975-76.
Lieutenant Bob Anderson, *Baa Baa Black Sheep* (also known as *The Black Sheep Squadron*), NBC, 1976-78.
Assistant District Attorney Dan Fielding, *Night Court,* NBC, 1984-92.
John Hemingway, *The John Larroquette Show,* NBC, 1993-97.
Royal Payne, *Payne,* CBS, 1999—.

Television Appearances; Movies:
Leading man, *Stunts Unlimited,* 1980.

Arthur Williams, *Bare Essence,* CBS, 1982.
Army officer, *The Last Ninja,* ABC, 1983.
Douglas Forbes, *Convicted,* ABC, 1986.
Gus, *Hot Paint,* CBS, 1988.
Brock (Bo) Arner, *One Special Victory* (also known as *Good Enough to Win*and *Another Side of Winning*), NBC, 1991.
Michael Lane, *The Defenders: Payback,* ABC, 1997.

Television Appearances; Specials:
Hello Sucker!, Showtime, 1985.
Secrets Men Never Share, NBC, 1988.
Host, *Jackie Gleason: The Great One* (also known as *How Sweet It Is: A Wake for Jackie Gleason*), CBS, 1988.
Host, *Fifty Years of Television: A Golden Celebration,* CBS, 1989.
Night of 100 Stars III, NBC, 1990.
Comic Relief VI, 1994.
The Tony Bennett Special: Here's to the Ladies: A Concert of Hope, 1995.
Star Trek: 30 Years and Beyond, UPN, 1996.

Also appeared in *Comic Relief III* and *Comic Relief IV.*

Television Appearances; Awards Presentations:
Host, *The 9th Annual ACE Awards* (also known as *The Golden ACE Awards*), HBO, 1988.
The 47th Annual Golden Globe Awards, TBS, 1990.
Presenter, *The 8th Annual American Comedy Awards,* ABC, 1994.
Presenter, *The 46th Annual Primetime Emmy Awards,* ABC, 1994.
Host, *The 11th Annual Soap Opera Awards,* NBC, 1995.
Host, *The 52nd Annual Golden Globe Awards,* TBS, 1995.
Presenter, *The Second Annual Screen Actors Guild Awards,* 1996.
Presenter, *The 50th Emmy Awards,* 1998.

Television Appearances; Episodic:
Sailor, "Winner Takes Nothing," *Kojak,* CBS, 1975.
A cop, *Three's Company,* ABC, 1979.
"Dick Doesn't Live Here Anymore," *9 to 5,* ABC, 1982.
"Breath of Steele," *Remington Steele,* NBC, 1984.
Guest, *The Barbour Report,* ABC, 1986.
Skip, "The Rec Room," *NBC Presents the AFI Comedy Special,* NBC, 1987.
Host, "The 11th Annual Young Comedians Show," *On Location,* HBO, 1987.
Himself, *Madman of the People,* NBC, 1994.
Grayson Delamorte, *Dave's World,* CBS, 1995.
Joey Heric, "Betrayal," *The Practice,* ABC, 1997.
Joey Heric, "Another Day" and "Checkmate," *The Practice,* ABC, 1998.

Appeared as drunken man, *The Sonny and Cher Show.*

Television Appearances; Pilots:
Lieutenant Jackson MacCalvey, *The 416th,* CBS, 1979.

Television Work; Executive Producer; Series:
The John Larroquette Show, NBC, 1993-97.
Payne, CBS, 1999—.

Television Work; Episodic:
Directed episodes of *Night Court,* NBC.

Television Work; Movies:
Executive producer, *One Special Victory* (also known as *Good Enough to Win*), NBC, 1991.

Film Appearances:
Narrator, *The Texas Chainsaw Massacre,* Bryanston, 1974.
Television talk show host, *Heart Beat,* Warner Bros., 1979.
X-ray technician, *Altered States,* Warner Bros., 1980.
Captain Stillman, *Stripes,* Columbia, 1981.
Claude, *Green Ice,* ITC, 1981.
Bronte Judson, *Cat People,* Universal, 1982.
Klansman, *Twilight Zone: The Movie,* Warner Bros., 1983.
Bob X Cursion, *Hysterical,* Embassy, 1983.
Maltz, *Star Trek III: The Search for Spock,* Paramount, 1984.
Foxglove, *Meatballs Part II,* TriStar, 1984.
Billy Ace, *Choose Me,* Island Alive, 1984.
Don Moore, *Summer Rental,* Paramount, 1985.
David Bedford, *Blind Date,* TriStar, 1987.
Willis, *Second Sight,* Warner Bros., 1989.
Mark Bannister, *Madhouse,* Orion, 1990.
Dr. Albert Quince, *Tune In Tomorrow* (also known as *Aunt Julia and the Scriptwriter*), Cinecom, 1990.
Jerry Johnson, *JFK: The Director's Cut,* Warner Bros., 1991.
Lawrence Van Dough, *Richie Rich,* Warner Bros., 1995.
Slasher, *Tales from the Crypt: Demon Knight* (also known as *Demon Keeper*), Universal, 1995.
Maury Manning, *Isn't She Great,* Universal, 1999.

Stage Appearances:
Casimir, *Aristocrats,* Center Theatre Group, Mark Taper Forum, Los Angeles, 1989-90.

Night of 100 Stars III, Radio City Music Hall, New York City, 1990.

Also appeared as Reverend Hale, *The Crucible,* and in *Enter Laughing* and *Endgame.**

LASSETER, John 1957-

PERSONAL

Born in 1957, in Hollywood, CA; mother was an art teacher. *Education:* Attended California Institute of the Arts.

Addresses: *Office*— Pixar Animation Studios, 1001 West Cutting Blvd., Point Richmond, CA 94804.

Career: Animator, producer, screenwriter, and director. Disney, animator, 1979-83, then Pixar, 1984—.

Awards, Honors: Academy Award nomination, best animated short film, 1986, Silver Berlin Bear, Berlin International Film Festival, Best Short Film, 1987, both for *Luxo, Jr.* (with others); Golden Nica Award, Prix Ars Electronica, Austrian Broadcasting Corporation, 1988; Academy Award, Best Short Animated Film, 1989, for *Tin Toy;* Special Award, ShoWest Convention, Outstanding Achievement, 1996; Special Achievement Award, Academy of Motion Picture Arts & Sciences, Academy Award nomination, best writing, screenplay written directly for the screen, Annie Award, best individual achievement: directing, 1996, all for *Toy Story;* Humanitarian Award, ShoWest Convention, 1997.

CREDITS

Film Work:

Creative collaborator, *Mickey's Christmas Carol* (animated), Buena Vista, 1983.

Director, character designer and animator, *The Adventures of Andre and Wally B.,* 1984.

Computer animator, *Young Sherlock Holmes,* Paramount, 1985.

Producer, director, model designer, and animator, *Luxo Jr.* (animated short), 1986.

Director, model designer, and animator, *Red's Dream,* 1987.

Director, model designer, and animator, *Tin Toy* (animated), 1988.

Director, *Knickknack,* Twentieth Century-Fox, 1989.

Animator, *Luxo, Jr., in "Surprise" and "Light & Heavy"* (also known as *Light & Heavy* and *Surprise*), 1991.

Director, model designer, and animation system developer, *Toy Story* (animated), Buena Vista, 1995.

Executive producer, *Geri's Game,* 1997.

Director, *A Bug's Life* (also known as *Bugs;* animated), Buena Vista, 1998.

Executive producer, *Toy Story 2* (animated), Buena Vista, 1999.

Film Appearances:

Computer Illusions (animated), 1997.

Voice of director, grasshopper in bar, and bug attracted to light, *A Bug's Life* (also known as *Bugs;* animated), Buena Vista, 1998.

WRITINGS

Screenplays:

Luxo Jr. (animated short), 1986.

Red's Dream, 1987.

Tin Toy (animated), 1988.

Knickknack, Twentieth Century-Fox, 1989.

Story writer, *Toy Story* (animated), Buena Vista, 1995.

Story writer, *A Bug's Life* (also known as *Bugs;* animated), Buena Vista, 1998.

OTHER SOURCES

Periodicals:

Entertainment Weekly, December 8, 1995, p. 26.

Forbes, December 1, 1997, p. S130.

Time, December 14, 1998, p. 100.*

LEIGH, Mike 1943-

PERSONAL

Born February 20, 1943, in Salford, Lancashire, England; son of Alfred Abraham (a doctor) and Phyllis Pauline (maiden name, Cousin) Leigh; married Alison Steadman (an actress), September 15, 1973 (divorced); children: Toby, Leo. *Education:* Attended Royal Academy of Dramatic Art, 1960-62, Camberwell School of Arts and Crafts, 1963-64, London School of Film Technique, 1963-64, and Central School of Art and Design, 1964-65.

Addresses: *Agent*—Peters Fraser & Dunlop, The Chambers, Chelsea Harbour, Lots Rd., London SW10 0XF, England.

Career: Director, writer, and set designer. Dramagraph (production company), London, England, co-founder, 1965; Midlands Art Centre for Young People, Birmingham, England, associate director, 1965-66; Victoria Theatre, Stoke-on-Trent, England, actor, 1966; Royal Shakespeare Company, assistant director, 1967-68; De La Salle College, lecturer, 1968-69; Sedgely Park College, Manchester, England, lecturer, 1968-69; London Film School, London, lecturer, 1970-73. Arts Council of Great Britain, member of Drama Panel, 1975-77, member of Director's Working Party and Specialist Allocation Board, 1976-87; National Council for Drama Training, member of Accreditation Panel, 1978—; Independent Broadcasting Authority (IBA), member of general advisory council, 1980-82.

Awards, Honors: Golden Leopard Award, best film, Locarno International Film Festival, and Golden Hugo Award, Chicago Film Festival, both 1972, for *Bleak Moments;* George Devine Award, 1973; *Evening Standard* Award, and London Critics Choice Award, best comedy, 1981, both for *Goose-Pimples; Evening Standard* Award, 1982; People's Prize, Berlin Film Festival, 1984, for *Meantime;* British Academy of Film and Television Arts Award nomination, best short film, 1988, for *The Short and Curlies;* Critics Award, Venice Film Festival, 1988, Stars de Demain Coup de Coeur, and Peter Sellers Comedy Award, *Evening Standard,* 1989, all for *High Hopes;* honorary M.A. degree, University of Salford, 1991; Independent Spirit Award nomination and Bodil Festival Award, best foreign film, 1992, both for *Life Is Sweet;* decorated Officer, Order of the British Empire, 1993; British Academy of Film and Television Arts Award nomination, best short film, 1993, for *A Sense of History* (with Simon Channing-Williams); Cannes Film Festival Award, best director, 1993, Alexander Korda Award nomination for Best British Film, British Academy of Film and Television Arts, Independent Spirit Award nomination, best foreign film, 1994, all for *Naked;* Michael Balcon Award, British Academy of Film and Television Arts, 1996; Golden Palm Award, Cannes Film Festival, European Film Award nomination, best film, Los Angeles Film Critics Association Award, best director, 1996, Academy Award nominations, best director and best writing-screenplay written directly for the screen, Alexander Korda Award for Best British Film (with Simon Channing-Williams), British Academy of Film and Television Arts and British Academy of Film and Television Arts Award, best screenplay-original, British Academy Film and Television Arts Awards nominations, best film (with Simon Channing-Williams) and David Lean Award for Direction, Cesar Award nomination, best foreign film, Independent Spirit Award, best foreign film, Humanitas Prize, feature film category, Writers Guild of American Screen Award nomination, best screenplay written directly for the screen, 1997, all for *Secrets & Lies;* Golden Spike Award nomination, Valladolid International Film Festival, 1997, for *Career Girls;* Golden Lion nomination, Venice Film Festival, 1999, for *Topsy-Turvy.*

CREDITS

Film Director:

Bleak Moments (also known as *Loving Moments*), Contemporary, 1972.
Four Days in July, BBC, 1984.
High Hopes, Skouras, 1989.
Life Is Sweet, October Films, 1991.
Mike Leigh's Naked (also known as *Naked*), Fine Line Features, 1993.
Secrets & Lies, October Films, 1996.
Career Girls, October Films, 1997.
Topsy-Turvy, October Films, 1999.

Film Appearances:

Himself, *Welcome to Hollywood,* 1998.

Stage Director, Except Where Indicated:

And set designer, *Little Malcolm and His Struggle against the Eunuchs,* Unity Theatre, London, 1965.
The Box Play, Midlands Art Centre Theatre, Birmingham, England, 1965.
My Parents Have Gone to Carlisle, Midlands Art Centre Theatre, 1966.
The Last Crusade of the Five Little Nuns, Midlands Art Centre Theatre, 1966.
NENAA, Royal Shakespeare Company, Studio Theatre, Stratford-on-Avon, England, 1967.
The Knack, Royal Shakespeare Company, Theatregoround, 1967.
Individual Fruit Pies, East-15 Acting School, London, 1968.
Down Here and Up There, Royal Court Theatre Upstairs, London, 1968.
Big Basil, Manchester Youth Theatre, Manchester, England, 1968.
Epilogue, Sedgely Park and De La Salle Colleges, Manchester, 1969.
Glum Victoria and the Lad with Specs, Manchester Youth Theatre, 1969.
Bleak Moments, Open Space Theatre, London, 1970.
The Life of Galileo, Bermuda Arts Festival, 1970.
A Rancid Pong, Basement Theatre, London, 1971.

Wholesome Glory, Royal Court Theatre Upstairs, 1973.

Dick Whittington and His Cat, Royal Court Theatre Upstairs, 1973.

The Jaws of Death, Traverse Theatre, Edinburgh, Scotland, 1973.

The Silent Majority, Bush Theatre, London, 1974.

Babies Grow Old, Royal Shakespeare Company, The Other Place, London, 1974.

Abigail's Party, Hampstead Theatre Club, London, 1977.

Ecstasy, Hampstead Theatre Club, 1979.

Goose-Pimples, Hampstead Theatre Club, then Garrick Theatre, London, both 1981.

Smelling a Rat, Hampstead Theatre Club, London, 1988.

Greek Tragedy, Edinburgh Festival, Edinburgh, Scotland, then Theatre Royal, Stratford-on-Avon, later Sydney, Australia, all 1990.

Television Director; Movies:

Hard Labour, BBC, 1973.

Nuts in May, BBC, 1976.

The Kiss of Death, BBC, 1977.

Who's Who, BBC, 1978.

Grown Ups, BBC, 1980.

Home Sweet Home, BBC, 1981.

Meantime, BBC, 1983.

The Short and Curlies, BBC, 1987.

High Hopes, BBC, 1988.

A Sense of History, Channel 4, 1992.

Television Director; Specials:

A Mug's Game, 1973.

The Permissive Society, BBC, 1975.

Knock for Knock, BBC, 1976.

Abigail's Party, BBC, 1977.

Television Director; Episodic:

"The Birth of the 2001 F.A. Cup Final Goalie," *Five Minute Plays,* 1982.

"Old Chums," *Five Minute Plays,* 1982.

"Probation," *Five Minute Plays,* 1982.

"A Light Snack," *Five Minute Plays,* 1982.

"Afternoon," *Five Minute Plays,* 1982.

Television Appearances; Specials:

Inside the Academy Awards, TNT, 1997.

Radio Director:

Director of the radio play *Too Much of a Good Thing,* banned from release, 1979.

WRITINGS

Screenplays:

Bleak Moments (also known as *Loving Moments;* from the play by Leigh), Contemporary, 1972.

Four Days in July, BBC, 1984.

High Hopes, Skouras, 1989.

Life Is Sweet, October Films, 1991.

Mike Leigh's Naked (also known as *Naked*), Fine Line Features, 1993.

Secrets & Lies, October Films, 1996.

Career Girls, October Films, 1997.

Stage Plays:

The Box Play, Midlands Art Centre Theatre, 1965.

My Parents Have Gone to Carlisle, Midlands Art Centre Theatre, 1966.

The Last Crusade of the Five Little Nuns, Midlands Art Centre Theatre, 1966.

NENAA, Royal Shakespeare Company, Studio Theatre, 1967.

Individual Fruit Pies, East-15 Acting School, 1968.

Down Here and Up There, Royal Court Theatre Upstairs, 1968.

Big Basil, Manchester Youth Theatre, 1968.

Epilogue, Sedgely Park and De La Salle Colleges, 1969.

Glum Victoria and the Lad with Specs, Manchester Youth Theatre, 1969.

Bleak Moments, Open Space Theatre, 1970.

A Rancid Pong, Basement Theatre, 1971.

Wholesome Glory, Royal Court Theatre Upstairs, 1973.

Dick Whittington and His Cat, Royal Court Theatre Upstairs, 1973.

The Jaws of Death, Traverse Theatre, 1973.

The Silent Majority, Bush Theatre, 1974.

Babies Grow Old, Royal Shakespeare Company, The Other Place, 1974.

Abigail's Party, Hampstead Theatre Club, 1977, published by Samuel French, 1979.

Ecstasy, Hampstead Theatre Club, 1979.

Goose-Pimples, Hampstead Theatre Club, then Garrick Theatre, London, both 1981.

Greek Tragedy, Edinburgh Festival, then Theatre Royal, later Sydney, Australia, all 1990.

Television Movies:

Hard Labour, BBC, 1973.

Nuts in May, BBC, 1976.

The Kiss of Death, BBC, 1977.

Who's Who, BBC, 1978.

Grown Ups, BBC, 1980.

Home Sweet Home, BBC, 1981.

Meantime, BBC, 1983.
The Short and Curlies, BBC, 1987.
High Hopes, BBC, 1988.

Television Specials:
A Mug's Game, 1973.
The Permissive Society, BBC, 1975.
Knock for Knock, BBC, 1976.
Abigail's Party, BBC, 1977.

Television Episodes:
"The Birth of the 2001 F.A. Cup Final Goalie," *Five Minute Plays,* 1982.
"Old Chums," *Five Minute Plays,* 1982.
"Probation," *Five Minute Plays,* 1982.
"A Light Snack," *Five Minute Plays,* 1982.
"Afternoon," *Five Minute Plays,* 1982.

Play Collections:
Abigail's Party and Goose-Pimples, Penguin, 1983.

Radio Plays:
Too Much of a Good Thing, banned from release, 1979.

OTHER SOURCES

Books:
Clements, Paul, *The Improvised Play: The Work of Mike Leigh,* Methuen, 1983.
Coveney, Michael, *The World According to Mike Leigh,* HarperCollins, 1996.

Periodicals:
Cineaste, fall, 1996, p. 53.
Los Angeles Times, March 9, 1989.
New Statesman and Society, April 23, 1993, p. 26.
New York Times, February 19, 1989.
Time, September 30, 1996, p. 66.
Washington Post, April 7, 1989.*

LETSCHER, Matt
See LETSCHER, Matthew

LETSCHER, Matthew 1970-
(Matt Letscher)

PERSONAL

Born June 26, 1970, in Michigan. *Education:* Graduated from the University of Michigan, 1992.

Addresses: *Agent*—J. Michael Bloom & Associates, 9255 Sunset Blvd., Suite 710, Los Angeles, CA 90069.

Career: Actor. Appeared with the Purple Rose Theatre Company, Chelsea, MI.

CREDITS

Film Appearances:
Young second Maine man, *Gettysburg,* New Line Cinema, 1993.
Needlemeyer, *Prehysteria 3!,* Moonbeam Entertainment, 1995.
Voice of Eddie, *Power 98,* Warner Home Video, 1995.
Not This Part of the World, 1995.
Danny, *Lovelife,* Trimark Home Video, 1997.
Captain Harrison Love, *The Mask of Zorro,* Columbia/TriStar, 1998.

Also appeared in *Friends of Friends.*

Television Appearances; Movies:
Nathan, "Long Shadows," *American Playhouse,* PBS, 1994.
Eddie, *Stolen Innocence,* CBS, 1995.

Television Appearances; Series:
Rob Paley, *Almost Perfect,* CBS, 1995.
Will Marek, *Living in Captivity,* Fox, 1998.

Television Appearances; Episodic:
Rick, "Rush Week," *Saved by the Bell: The College Years,* NBC, 1993.
"Life and Death," *Dr. Quinn, Medicine Woman,* CBS, 1994.
Harley Eastlake, "Head 'N' Tail," *Silk Stalkings,* USA Network, 1994.
Daniel Pryor, "The Fourteenth Floor," *The Larry Sanders Show,* HBO, 1994.
Steven, "The Toast," *Ellen,* ABC, 1994.
Roger Barrows, "I Know What Scares You," *Silk Stalkings,* USA Network, 1995.

Stage Appearances:
Appeared as Ray Dolenz, *Proposals,* Broadway production, New York City.*

LEWIS, Clea

PERSONAL

Born on July 19, in Cleveland Heights, OH; father, a lawyer and mother, a writer. *Education:* Brown University, B.A.; also attended University of California; studied acting at the Cleveland Playhouse, London Royal Academy of Dramatic Arts, the London Academy of Music and Drama, and Second City, Chicago.

Addresses: *Contact*—Innovative Artists, 1999 Avenue of the Stars, #2850, Los Angeles, CA 90067.

Career: Actress. Appeared in productions at Wisdom Bridge and Body Politic, both in Chicago.

CREDITS

Film Appearances:

Sylvia, *Hero* (also known as *Accidental Hero*), Columbia, 1992.
Lisa Campos, *Diabolique,* Warner Bros., 1996.
Nora Golden, *Rich Man's Wife,* Buena Vista, 1996.
Ilsa, *Scotch and Milk,* 1998.

Television Appearances; Series:

Megan Traynor, *Flying Blind,* Fox, 1992.
Audrey Penney, *Ellen* (also known as *These Friends of Mine*), ABC, 1994-98.
Voice of Nicky, *Pepper Ann* (also known as *Disney's Pepper Ann;* animated), ABC, 1997—.
Rachel Tomlinson, *Maggie Winters,* CBS, 1998.

Television Appearances; Episodic:

Lyla, *Doogie Howser, M.D.,* ABC, 1991.
Krista, "Hilary Gets a Life," *The Fresh Prince of Bel-Air,* NBC, 1991.
Franny, "The One Where Monica Gets a Roommate," *Friends,* NBC, 1994.
Glove salesman, *Mad About You,* NBC, 1995.
Danielle, "Love Letters," *Double Rush,* CBS, 1995.

Stage Appearances:

Emma, *Pterodactyls,* South Coast Repertory, Costa Mesa, CA, 1994-95.
All in the Timing, Geffen Playhouse, Hartford, CT, 1998.*

LONDON, Jeremy 1972-

PERSONAL

Full name, Jeremy Michael London; born November 7, 1972, in San Diego, CA; son of Frank (a sheet metal worker) and Debbie (a waitress) London; twin brother of Jason London (an actor).

Addresses: *Agent*—The Gersh Agency, 232 North Canon Dr., Beverly Hills, CA 90210-5302.

Career: Actor, producer, and stuntman.

CREDITS

Film Appearances:

T. S. Quint, *Mallrats,* Gramercy Pictures, 1995.
Jack, *The Babysitter,* Spelling Films, 1995.
The Red Lion, Recycle Pictures, 1997.
Bob, *Levitation,* Tenth Muse Productions, 1997.
Jeff, *Happenstance,* Dayjob Films, 1998.

Film Work:

Stuntman, *The Man in the Moon,* Metro-Goldwyn-Mayer/Pathe, 1991.
Producer, *Dreamers,* Dark Lantern Pictures, 1998.

Television Appearances; Series:

Nathaniel Bedford, *I'll Fly Away,* NBC, 1991-93.
Sonny Snow, *Angel Falls,* CBS, 1993-94.
Griffin Holbrook, *Party of Five,* Fox, 1995—.

Television Appearances; Episodic:

Billy Rabe, "Anatomy Lesson," *Perversions of Science,* HBO, 1997.

Television Appearances; Movies:

First teenager, *In Broad Daylight,* NBC, 1991.
Delivery boy, *A Seduction in Travis County* (also known as *Blind Judgement*), CBS, 1991.
Rick Chilton, *Breaking Free,* The Disney Channel, 1995.
Mickey Hackett, *A Season of Hope* (also known as *Lemon Grove*), CBS, 1995.
Adult John Deal, "A Mother's Gift" (also known as "A Lantern in Her Hand"), *Kraft Premier Movie,* CBS, 1995.
Mason, *White Wolves II: Legend of the Wild,* The Disney Channel, 1996.
Danny Wells, *Bad to the Bone,* ABC, 1997.
Wyman James, *The Defenders: Taking the First,* Showtime, 1998.
Journey to the Center of the Earth, 1999.

OTHER SOURCES

Periodicals:

People Weekly, October 11, 1993, p. 71; May 6, 1996, p. 156.*

M

MADSEN, Virginia 1961(?)-

PERSONAL

Born September 11, 1961 (some sources say 1963), in Chicago, IL; daughter of Cal (a firefighter) and Elaine (a writer of documentaries); sister of Michael (an actor); children: (with Antonio Sabato, Jr.) one. *Education:* Attended Northwestern University; studied acting with Ted Liss for three years.

Addresses: *Agent*—c/o Creative Artists Agency, 9830 Wilshire Blvd., Beverly Hills, CA 90212.

Career: Actress. Has appeared in commercials.

Awards, Honors: Avoriaz Award, and Saturn Award, both for best actress, 1992, for *Candyman*.

CREDITS

Film Appearances:

(Film debut) Lisa, *Class,* Orion, 1983.
Madeline, *Electric Dreams,* Metro-Goldwyn-Mayer/United Artists, 1984.
Princess Irulan, *Dune,* De Laurentiis Entertainment Group/Universal, 1984.
Barbara Spencer, *Creator,* Universal, 1985.
Lisa Taylor, *Fire with Fire,* Paramount, 1986.
Kelly, *Modern Girls,* Atlantic, 1986.
Yolanda Caldwell, *Slam Dance,* Island, 1987.
Andrea Miller, *Zombie High,* Cinema Group, 1987.
Sally Boffin, *Mr. North,* Samuel Goldwyn, 1988.
Allison Rowe, *Hot to Trot,* Warner Bros., 1988.
Delia June Curry, *Heart of Dixie,* Orion, 1989.
Dolly Harshaw, *The Hot Spot,* Orion, 1990.
Louise Marcus, *Highlander 2: The Quickening,* Interstar Releasing, 1991.
Helen Lyle, *Candyman,* TriStar, 1992.
Polaire Sorel, *Becoming Colette,* Castle Hill, 1992.
Caroline at Midnight, 1993.
The Prophecy, 1995.
Just Your Luck, Polygram, 1996.
Dixie DeLaughter, *Ghosts of Mississippi,* Sony, 1996.
Jackie Lemanczyk, *John Grisham's The Rainmaker* (also known as *The Rainmaker*), Paramount, 1997.
Ballad of the Nightingale, August Entertainment, 1998.
McClintock's Peach, West Wind Entertainment, 1999.
Carrie Fredericks, *The Haunting,* DreamWorks, 1999.
Molly, *The Florentine,* Bcb Productions, 1999.
After Sex, 1999.

Also appeared in *The Dead Can't Lie.*

Television Appearances; Movies:

Marion Davies, *The Hearst and Davies Affair,* ABC, 1985.
Dixie Lee Boxx, *Long Gone,* HBO, 1987.
Rachel Carlyle, *Gotham,* Showtime, 1988.
Anne Scholes, *Third Degree Burn,* HBO, 1989.
Rebecca Bishop, *Love Kills,* USA Network, 1991.
Carla Simmons, *Victim of Love,* CBS, 1991.
Betty Stuart, *Ironclads,* TNT, 1991.
Carolyn Warmus, *A Murderous Affair: The Carolyn Warmus Story* (also known as *Lovers of Deceit*), ABC, 1992.
Linda Cowley, *Linda,* USA Network , 1993.
Gena Hayes, *Blue Tiger,* HBO, 1994.
Annie Culver Westford, *Bitter Vengeance,* USA Network , 1994.
Lucy Monroe, *Ambushed,* HBO, 1998.

Televison Appearances; Series:

Co-host, *Unsolved Mysteries,* NBC, 1998.

Television Appearances; Episodic:

"Perfect Order," *The Hitchhiker,* HBO, 1987.

Annie Charnock, "Eine Kleine Nacht Murder," *Moonlighting,* ABC, 1989.
Kellin, "Unforgettable," *Star Trek: Voyager,* UPN, 1997.
Cassandra Stone, "Three Valentines," "When a Man Loves a Woman," and "Shutout In Seattle Parts 1 and 2," *Frasier,* NBC, 1999.

Also appeared in an episode of *The Hitchhiker,* HBO.

Television Appearances; Miniseries:
Claretta Petacci, *Mussolini: The Untold Story,* NBC, 1985.
Karin de Vries, *Robert Ludlum's The Apocalypse Watch,* ABC, 1997.

Television Appearances; Specials:
(Television debut) Lou Ellen Purdy, *A Matter of Principle,* PBS, 1984.*

MAIN, Marjorie 1890-1975

PERSONAL

Real name, Mary Tomlinson; born February 24, 1890, in Acton, IN; died April 10, 1975, in Los Angeles, CA; buried in Forest Lawn Memorial Park; daughter of Samuel Joseph (a minister) and Jennie (McGaughey) Tomlinson; married Stanley LeFevre Krebs (a doctor), December 2, 1921 (died, 1935). *Education:* Graduated from Hamilton College; attended Franklin College; studied dramatic art at Carnegie Hall, New York City.

Career: Actress. Appeared with Shakespearean companies in Chautauqua, NY. Appeared in radio programs, including *The Goldbergs,* NBC, and *Grits and Gravy.*

Member: Daughters of the American Revolution, Friday Morning Club (Los Angeles, CA), Delta Delta Delta.

Awards, Honors: Academy Award nomination, best supporting actress, 1947, for *The Egg and I.*

CREDITS

Film Appearances:
Woman, *A House Divided,* Universal, 1931.
A gossip, *Hot Saturday,* Paramount, 1932.
Woman, *Take a Chance,* Paramount, 1933.
Woman, *Crime without Passion,* Paramount, 1934.
(Uncredited) Woman sitting on painting, *Art Trouble,* Vitaphone Corporation, 1934.
Anna, *Music in the Air,* Fox Film Corporation, 1934.
Mrs. Martin, *Stella Dallas,* United Artists, 1937.
Hannah Gillespie, *The Shadow,* Columbia, 1937.
Amelia Bradley, *The Man Who Cried Wolf,* Universal, 1937.
Mrs. Ward, *City Girl,* Twentieth Century-Fox, 1937.
Miss Emma Bisbee, *Love in a Bungalow,* Universal, 1937.
Mrs. Martin, *Dead End* (also known as *Cradle of Crime*), United Artists/Goldwyn Pictures, 1937.
Martha Foster, *The Wrong Road,* Republic Pictures, 1937.
Sara, *Under the Big Top,* Monogram Pictures, 1938.
Miss Wayne, *Too Hot to Handle,* Metro-Goldwyn-Mayer, 1938.
Irate customer, *There Goes My Heart,* United Artists, 1938.
Nora, *Romance of the Limberlost,* Monogram Pictures, 1938.
Matron Brand, *Prison Farm,* Paramount, 1938.
Katie, *Penitentiary,* Columbia, 1938.
Miss Armstrong, *Girls' School,* Columbia, 1938.
Mrs. Brennan, *Boy of the Streets,* Monogram Pictures, 1938.
Mrs. Stephens, *King of the Newsboys,* Republic Pictures, 1938.
Landlady, *Test Pilot,* Metro-Goldwyn-Mayer, 1938.
Old woman, *Three Comrades,* Metro-Goldwyn-Mayer, 1938.
Mrs. Boylan, *Little Tough Guy,* Universal, 1938.
Lucy (a dude ranch owner), *The Women,* Metro-Goldwyn-Mayer, 1939.
Hildegarde Carey, *Two Thoroughbreds,* RKO Radio Pictures, 1939.
Mrs. Briggs, *Lucky Night,* Metro-Goldwyn-Mayer, 1939.
Mrs. Arkelian, *The Angels Wash Their Faces,* Warner Bros., 1939.
Gertie, *I Take This Woman,* Metro-Goldwyn-Mayer, 1939.
Mrs. Miller, *They Shall Have Music* (also known as *Melody of Youth* and *Ragged Angels*), United Artists, 1939.
Mrs. Dolley, *Another Thin Man* (also known as *Return of the Thin Man*), Metro-Goldwyn-Mayer, 1939.
Mrs. Lowery, *Women without Names,* Paramount, 1940.
Nora, *Turnabout,* United Artists, 1940.
Mary, *Susan and God* (also known as *The Gay Mrs. Trexel*), Metro-Goldwyn-Mayer, 1940.

Sarah May Willett, *The Captain is a Lady,* Metro-Goldwyn-Mayer, 1940.
Elizabeth Adams (Mrs. Cantrell), *The Dark Command,* Republic Pictures, 1940.
Mehitabel, *Wyoming* (also known as *Bad Man of Wyoming*), Metro-Goldwyn-Mayer, 1940.
Emma Kristiansdotter, *A Woman's Face,* Metro-Goldwyn-Mayer, 1941.
Mrs. Collins, *The Trial of Mary Dugan,* Metro-Goldwyn-Mayer, 1941.
Mrs. Varner, *Honky Tonk,* Metro-Goldwyn-Mayer, 1941.
Susie, *The Bugle Sounds* (also known as *Steel Cavalry*), Metro-Goldwyn-Mayer, 1941.
Marge Cavendish, *Barnacle Bill,* Metro-Goldwyn-Mayer, 1941.
Irma, *The Wild Man of Borneo,* Metro-Goldwyn-Mayer, 1941.
Granny Becky, *The Shepherd of the Hills,* Paramount, 1941.
Judge Sidney Hawkes, *We Were Dancing,* Metro-Goldwyn-Mayer, 1942.
Letitia Carberry, *Tish,* Metro-Goldwyn-Mayer, 1942.
Mrs. Fisher, *Tennessee Johnson* (also known as *The Man on America's Conscience*), Metro-Goldwyn-Mayer, 1942.
Clementine Tucker, *Jackass Mail,* Metro-Goldwyn-Mayer, 1942.
Mrs. McKessick, *The Affairs of Martha* (also known as *Once Upon a Thursday*), Metro-Goldwyn-Mayer, 1942.
Gashouse Mary, *Johnny Come Lately* (also known as *Johnny Vagabond*), Republic Pictures, 1943.
Mrs. Strabel, *Heaven Can Wait,* Twentieth Century-Fox, 1943.
Iris Tuttle, *Rationing,* Metro-Goldwyn-Mayer, 1944.
Katie, *Meet Me in St. Louis,* Metro-Goldwyn-Mayer, 1944.
Annie Goss, *Gentle Annie,* Metro-Goldwyn-Mayer, 1944.
Mamie Johnson, *Murder, He Says,* Paramount, 1945.
Mrs. Fisher, *The Show-Off,* Metro-Goldwyn-Mayer, 1946.
Abbey Hanks, *Bad Bascomb,* Metro-Goldwyn-Mayer, 1946.
Sonora Cassidy, *The Harvey Girls,* Metro-Goldwyn-Mayer, 1946.
Lucy, *Undercurrent,* Metro-Goldwyn-Mayer, 1946.
Widow Hawkins, *The Wistful Widow of Wagon Gap* (also known as *The Wistful Widow*), Universal, 1947.
Ma Kettle, *The Egg and I,* Universal, 1947.
Maribel Mathews, *Feudin', Fussin' and A-Fightin',* Universal, 1948.
Ma Kettle, *Ma and Pa Kettle* (also known as *The Further Adventures of Ma and Pa Kettle*), Universal, 1949.
Flap Jack Kate, *Big Jack,* Metro-Goldwyn-Mayer, 1949.
Esme, *Summer Stock* (also known as *If You Feel Like Singing*), Metro-Goldwyn-Mayer, 1950.
Hattie O'Malley, *Mrs. O'Malley and Mr. Malone,* Metro-Goldwyn-Mayer, 1950.
Ma Kettle, *Ma and Pa Kettle Go to Town,* Universal, 1950.
Mrs. Cabot, *Mr. Imperium* (also known as *You Belong to My Heart*), Metro-Goldwyn-Mayer, 1951.
Ma Kettle, *Ma and Pa Kettle Back on the Farm,* Universal, 1951.
Mrs. Wortin, *The Law and the Lady,* Metro-Goldwyn-Mayer, 1951.
Mrs. Wrenley, *It's a Big Country,* Metro-Goldwyn-Mayer, 1951.
Ma Kettle, *Ma and Pa Kettle at the Fair,* Universal, 1952.
Mrs. Phineas Hill, *The Belle of New York,* Metro-Goldwyn-Mayer, 1952.
Ma Kettle, *Ma and Pa Kettle on Vacation* (also known as *Ma and Pa Kettle Go to Paris* and *Ma and Pa Kettle Hit the Road*), Universal, 1953.
Ma Parkson, *Fast Company,* Metro-Goldwyn-Mayer, 1953.
Pansy Jones, *Ricochet Romance,* Universal, 1954.
Ma Kettle, *Ma and Pa Kettle at Home,* Universal, 1954.
Lady Jane Dunstock, *Rose Marie,* Metro-Goldwyn-Mayer, 1954.
Mrs. Hittaway, *The Long, Long Trailer,* Metro-Goldwyn-Mayer, 1954.
Ma Kettle, *Ma and Pa Kettle at Waikiki,* Universal, 1955.
Ma Kettle, *The Kettles in the Ozarks,* Universal, 1956.
Widow Hudspeth, *Friendly Persuasion,* Allied Artists, 1956.
Ma Kettle, *The Kettles on Old MacDonald's Farm,* Universal, 1957.
Song performer in archival footage, *That's Entertainment III,* Metro-Goldwyn-Mayer, 1994.

Television Appearances; Episodic:

Herself, *December Bride,* CBS, 1956.
Cassie Tanner, "The Cassie Tanner Story," *Wagon Train,* NBC, 1958.
"The Sacramento Story," *Wagon Train,* NBC, 1958.

Stage Appearances:

Appeared in the plays *Burlesque, Cheating Cheaters, Dead End, Salvation, The Wicked Age, The Women,* and *Yes or No.**

MAJORINO, Tina 1985-

PERSONAL

Born February 7, 1985; daughter of Bob (a real estate agent) and Sarah Majorino. *Avocational interests:* Tang Soo Do, singing, playing the piano.

Addresses: *Agent*—Barbara Gale, Envoy Entertainment, 1640 South Sepulveda, Suite 530, Los Angeles, CA 90025.

Career: Actress.

Awards, Honors: YoungStar Award nomination, best performance by a young actress in a miniseries/made for television movie, 1998, for *Before Women Had Wings.*

CREDITS

Film Appearances:

Toni Whitney, *Andre,* Paramount, 1994.

Molly Singer, *Corrina, Corrina,* New Line Cinema, 1994.

Jess Green, *When a Man Loves a Woman* (also known as *To Have and to Hold*), Buena Vista, 1994.

Enola, *Waterworld,* Universal, 1995.

New York Crossing, 1996.

Crystal Thomas, *Sante Fe,* NuImage, 1997.

Television Appearances; Series:

Sophie Wilder, *Camp Wilder* (also known as *Camp Bicknell*), ABC, 1992-93.

Television Appearances; Miniseries:

Euphemia Ashby as a child, *True Women,* CBS, 1997.

Television Appearances; Movies:

Avocet Abigail "Bird" Jackson, *Oprah Winfrey Presents: Before Women Had Wings* (also known as *Before Women Had Wings*), ABC, 1997.

Janie Bailey, *Merry Christmas, George Bailey,* PBS, 1997.

Alice, *Alice in Wonderland,* NBC, 1999.

Television Appearances; Episodic:

Storytime, PBS, 1994.

Television Appearances; Specials:

The 53rd Annual Golden Globe Awards, NBC, 1996.

Family Film Awards, CBS, 1996.

OTHER SOURCES

Periodicals:

Entertainment Weekly, August 19, 1994, p. 39.

New York Times, August 7, 1994, p. H12.

People, August 21, 1995, p. 73.*

MAJORS, Lee 1940(?)-

PERSONAL

Real name, Harvey Lee Yeary II; born April 23, 1940 (some sources say 1939, 1941, and 1942), in Wyandotte, MI; married Kathy Robinson, 1961 (divorced, 1964); married Farrah Fawcett (an actress), July 28, 1973 (divorced, 1980); married Karen Valez (a model; divorced); children: (first marriage) Lee II; (third marriage) Nikki, Dane and Trey (twins). *Education:* Graduated from Eastern Kentucky State College; also attended University of Indiana; studied acting with Estelle Harmon at Metro-Goldwyn-Mayer Studios.

Addresses: *Agent*—David Shapira and Associates, Inc., 15301 Ventura Blvd., Suite 345, Sherman Oaks, CA 91403-3129. *Office*—3000 Holiday Dr., Ph 1, Fort Lauderdale, FL 33316-2439.

Career: Actor, producer, and director. Founded Fawcett-Majors Productions in 1977 with then-wife, Farrah Fawcett. Turned down an offer from the St. Louis Cardinals baseball team in his final year at college to pursue an acting career.

Member: American Federation of Television and Radio Artists, Academy of Motion Picture Arts and Sciences.

Awards, Honors: Golden Globe Award nomination, best television actor-drama, 1977, for *The Six Million Dollar Man.*

CREDITS

Television Appearances; Series:

Heath Barkley, *The Big Valley,* ABC, 1965-69.

Roy Tate, *The Men from Shiloh* (also known as *The Virginian*), NBC, 1970-71.

Jess Brandon, *Owen Marshall, Counselor at Law,* ABC, 1971-74.

Colonel Steve Austin, *The Six Million Dollar Man,* ABC, 1973-78.

Colonel Steve Austin, *The Bionic Woman,* ABC, 1976-77, NBC, 1977-78.

Colt Seavers, *The Fall Guy,* ABC, 1981-85.
Herman "Ski" Jablonski, *Raven,* CBS, 1992-93.

Television Appearances; Movies:
Title role, *The Ballad of Andy Crocker,* ABC, 1969.
Larry, *Weekend of Terror,* ABC, 1970.
Colonel Steve Austin, *The Secret of Bigfoot,* 1975.
Title role, *Francis Gary Powers: The True Story of the U-2 Spy Incident,* NBC, 1976.
Frank Logan, *Just a Little Convenience,* NBC, 1977.
Will Kane, *High Noon Part II—The Return of Will Kane,* CBS, 1980.
Captain Cody Briggs, *Starflight: The Plane That Couldn't Land* (also known as *Starflight One*), ABC, 1983.
Bob Clayton, *The Cowboy and the Ballerina,* CBS, 1984.
Mountain Dan, *A Smoky Mountain Christmas,* ABC, 1986.
Steve Austin, *The Return of the Six Million Dollar Man and the Bionic Woman,* NBC, 1987.
Reed Harris, *Danger Down Under* (also known as *Harris Down Under* and *Austral Downs*), NBC, 1988.
Steve Austin, *The Bionic Showdown: The Six Million Dollar Man and the Bionic Woman* (also known as *The Return of the Six Million Dollar Man and the Bionic Woman II*), NBC, 1989.
Jesse Pruitt, *Road Show* (also known as *Travellin'* and *O'Malley*), CBS, 1989.
Captain Sterling, *Fire! Trapped on the 37th Floor,* ABC, 1991.
Rex Kingman, *The Cover Girl Murders,* USA Network, 1993.
Steve Austin, *Bionic Ever After?* (also known as *Bionic Breakdown*), CBS, 1994.
Stark, *Lost Treasure of Dos Stantos,* The Family Channel, 1997.

Television Appearances; Episodic:
"Song for Dying," *Gunsmoke,* CBS, 1965.
"The Monkey's Paw—A Retelling," *Alfred Hitchcock Hour,* NBC, 1965.
"Super Star," *Bracken's World,* NBC, 1970.
"Men Who Love," *Marcus Welby, M.D.,* ABC, 1971.
Joe Briggs, "The McCreedy Bust-Going, Going, Gone," *Alias Smith and Jones,* ABC, 1972.
"With This Ring, I Thee Kill," *The Sixth Sense,* ABC, 1972.
"Notes about Courage," *Trauma Center,* ABC, 1983.
Thomas "Pop" Scarlet, *Tour of Duty,* CBS, 1990.
Jim Walker, "The Secret," *Promised Land,* CBS, 1996.
Sheriff Bell, "On the Border," *Walker, Texas Ranger,* CBS, 1998.

Television Appearances; Pilots:
Steve Austin, *The Six Million Dollar Man* (also known as *Cyborg: Six Million Dollar Man*), ABC, 1973.
Colt Seavers, *How Do I Kill a Thief—Let Me Count the Ways* (broadcast as a segment of *The Fall Guy*), ABC, 1982.
Ski, *Raven: Return of the Black Dragons,* 1992.

Television Appearances; Specials:
Funshine Saturday Sneakpeak, ABC, 1974.
The Wayne Newton Special, NBC, 1974.
The Donny and Marie Osmond Show, ABC, 1975.
A Special Olivia Newton-John, ABC, 1976.
The Olivia Newton-John Show, ABC, 1976.
Host, *Battle of the Network Stars XI,* ABC, 1981.
Host, *The Stuntman Awards,* syndicated, 1986.

Television Work; Series:
(With others) Producer, *The Fall Guy,* ABC, 1981-85.

Television Work; Episodic:
Director, *The Six Million Dollar Man,* ABC, 1973-78.

Television Work; Movies:
Executive producer, *Just a Little Convenience,* NBC, 1977.
(With Jerry Weintraub) Executive producer, *The Cowboy and the Ballerina,* CBS, 1984.
Executive producer, *Danger Down Under* (also known as *Harris Down Under* and *Austral Downs*), NBC, 1988.
Co-producer, *The Bionic Showdown: The Six Million Dollar Man and the Bionic Woman* (also known as *The Return of the Six Million Dollar Man and the Bionic Woman II*), NBC, 1989.
Executive producer, *Road Show* (also known as *Travellin'* and *O'Malley*), CBS, 1989.

Television Work; Specials:
Executive producer, *The Stuntman Awards,* syndicated, 1986.

Film Appearances:
(Uncredited) Frank Harbin, *Strait-Jacket,* Columbia, 1964.
Blue, *Will Penny,* Paramount, 1968.
Steve Mundine, *The Liberation of L. B. Jones,* Columbia, 1970.
Thorvald Helge, *The Norseman,* American International Pictures, 1978.
Steve Austin, *Sharks!,* 1978.
Robert Lasky, *Killer Fish* (also known as *Treasure of the Piranha*), Associated Film, 1979.

Mike Catton, *Steel* (also known as *Look Down and Die* and *Men of Steel*), Vestron Video, 1980.
Philip Morgan, *Agency* (also known as *Mind Games*), Vestron Video, 1980.
Franklyn Hart, *The Last Chase,* Crown International, 1981.
Himself, *Scrooged,* Paramount, 1988.
Mike Gable, *Keaton's Cop,* 1990.
Officer Austin, *Trojan War* (also known as *No Night Stand* and *Rescue Me*), Warner Bros., 1997.
Austin, *The Protector,* New Horizons, 1999.
Manatee Man, *Chapter Zero,* Dilonra Films, 1999.

Film Work:
Executive producer, *Steel,* Vestron Video, 1980.

OTHER SOURCES

Books:
Zanderbergen, George, *Stay Tuned: Henry Winkler, Lee Majors, Valerie Harper,* Crestwood House, 1976.

Periodicals:
Entertainment Weekly, January 24, 1997, p. 68; July 24, 1998, p. 84.*

MAKO 1932(?)-
(Jimmy Sakuyama)

PERSONAL

Full name, Makoto Iwamatsu; born December 10, 1932 (some sources say 1933), in Kobe, Japan; naturalized citizen (United States), 1956; married Shizuko Hoshi (a dancer, choreographer, dance teacher, and actress); children: two daughters. *Education:* Attended Pratt Institute; studied for the theatre at the Pasadena Playhouse and with Nola Chilton.

Addresses: *Agent*—Amsel, Eisenstadt & Frazier, Inc., 6310 San Vicente Blvd., Los Angeles, CA 90048-5426.

Career: Actor, director, and playwright. East/West Players, Los Angeles, CA, founder and artistic director, 1966—; Children's Workshop, Los Angeles, founder and artistic director, 1966—; Inner City Repertory Theatre, Los Angeles, member of company, 1967-68. *Military service:* Served in U.S. armed forces during Korean War.

Member: Actors' Equity Association, Screen Actors Guild, American Federation of Television and Radio Artists.

Awards, Honors: Academy Award nomination, Golden Globe Award nomination, best supporting actor, 1967, both for *The Sand Pebbles;* Antoinette Perry Award nomination, best actor in a musical, 1976, for *Pacific Overtures;* Margaret Harford Award, Los Angeles Drama Critics, 1986.

CREDITS

Film Appearances:
Po-Han, *The Sand Pebbles,* Twentieth Century-Fox, 1966.
Kenji, *The Ugly Dachshund,* Buena Vista, 1966.
Calvin Coolidge Ishimura, *The Private Navy of Sergeant O'Farrell,* United Artists, 1968.
Secret Service Agent Eliot Fong, *The Great Bank Robbery,* Warner Bros.,1969.
Psychiatrist, *Fools,* Cinerama, 1970.
Mun Ki, *The Hawaiians* (also known as *Master of the Islands*), United Artists, 1970.
Tora! Tora! Tora!, Twentieth Century-Fox, 1970.
Chinmoku, 1972.
Oomiak, *The Island at the Top of the World,* Buena Vista, 1974.
Yuen Chung, *The Killer Elite,* United Artists, 1975.
Sergeant Nguyen, *Prisoners,* 1975.
Herbert, *The Big Brawl* (also known as *Battle Creek, Battle Creek Brawl,* and *Sha shou hao*), Warner Bros., 1980.
James Chan, *An Eye for an Eye,* Avco Embassy, 1981.
Nakamura, *Under the Rainbow,* Orion/Warner Bros., 1981.
Friend, *The Bushido Blade* (also known as *The Bloody Bushido Blade*), Trident, 1982.
Akiro the Wizard, *Conan the Barbarian,* Universal, 1982.
Mike, *Testament,* Paramount, 1983.
Akiro the Wizard, *Conan the Destroyer,* Universal, 1984.
Akira Tanaka, *Armed Response* (also known as *Jade Jungle*), CineTel, 1986.
Captain Vinh, *P.O.W.: The Escape* (also known as *Behind Enemy Lines*), Cannon, 1986.
Nobu, *The Wash,* Skouras, 1988.
Dyama, *Silent Assassins,* Action Brothers, 1988.
Jimmy Sakuyama, *Tucker: The Man and His Dream,* Paramount, 1988.
Max Chin, *An Unremarkable Life,* CFG, 1989.
Sakamoto, *Taking Care of Business* (also known as *Filofax*), Buena Vista, 1990.

Toshio Watanabe, *Pacific Heights,* Twentieth Century-Fox, 1990.
Trang, *Fatal Mission* (also known as *Enemy*), Media Home Entertainment, 1990.
Kim, *The Perfect Weapon,* Paramount, 1991.
Strawberry Road, 1991.
Mr. Lee, *Sidekicks,* Triumph Releasing, 1993.
Kanemitsu, *Robocop 3,* Orion, 1993.
Mr. Tszing, *My Samurai,* Imperial Entertainment, 1993.
Katsu, *Cultivating Charlie,* 1993.
Yoshida-San, *Rising Sun,* Twentieth Century-Fox, 1993.
Nakano, *Highlander: The Final Dimension* (also known as *Highlander III: The Sorcerer* and *Highlander III: The Magician*), Dimension Films, 1994.
Buun Som, *Midnight Man* (also known as *Blood for Blood*), 1994.
Sensei, *A Dangerous Place,* PM Home Video, 1995.
Shudo Shmizaki, *Crying Freeman,* Warner Bros., 1995.
Mr. Young, *Sworn to Justice* (also known as *Blonde Justice*), Maslak/Friedenn Films, 1996.
Matsumoto, *Balance of Power,* Live Entertainment, 1996.
Kungo Tsarong, *Seven Years in Tibet,* Sony Pictures Entertainment, 1997.
The Sea Wolf, Concorde Pictures, 1997.
Shen, *Chugoku no chojin* (also known as *The Bird People in China*), 1998.

Television Appearances; Series:
Major Taro Oshira, *Hawaiian Heat,* ABC, 1984.
Main title narrator, *Dexter's Laboratory* (also known as *Dexter's Lab;* animated), Cartoon Network, 1996—.

Television Appearances; Movies:
Yuro, *The Challenge,* ABC, 1970.
Tadashi, *If Tomorrow Comes* (also known as *The Glass Hammer*), ABC, 1971.
Fukimoto, *Farewell to Manzanar,* NBC, 1976.
Kanji Ousu, *Columbo: Murder Under Glass,* 1977.
Bai, *When Hell Was in Session,* NBC, 1979.
Mori, *Girls of the White Orchid* (also known as *Death Ride to Osaka*), NBC, 1983.
The Manchu, *Kung Fu: The Movie,* CBS, 1986.
Captain Kilalo, *Murder in Paradise,* NBC, 1990.
Sergeant Moritaki, *Hiroshima: Out of the Ashes,* NBC, 1990.
Buntoro Iga, *Red Sun Rising,* HBO, 1994.
Mr. Lee, "Gold Mountain," *Riot* (also known as *Riot in the Streets*), Showtime, 1997.

Television Appearances; Episodic:
Kato, "Jeannie and the Marriage Caper," *I Dream of Jeannie,* NBC, 1965.
"No Exchange on Damaged Merchandise," *I Spy,* NBC, 1965.
"From Karate with Love," *F Troop,* ABC, 1967.
Lieutenant Nakamura, "Kill Two by Two," *The Time Tunnel,* ABC, 1967.
Wong Lo, "Rimfire," *The Big Valley,* ABC, 1968.
"Southwind," *The F.B.I.,* ABC, 1968.
"The Tide," *Kung Fu,* ABC, 1973.
Dr. Lin Tam, "Rainbow Bridge," *M*A*S*H,* CBS, 1974.
Kazuo Tahashi, "Legacy of Terror," *Hawaiian Eye,* ABC, 1976.
ROK Surgeon, "Hawkeye Get Your Gun," *M*A*S*H,* CBS, 1976.
The Incredible Hulk, CBS, 1978.
The Incredible Hulk, CBS, 1979.
"Going, Going, Gone," *Wonder Woman,* CBS, 1979.
Lieutenant Hung Lee Park, "Guerilla My Dreams," *M*A*S*H,* CBS, 1979.
North Korean soldier, "The Best of Enemies," *M*A*S*H,* CBS, 1980.
"The Arrow that is not Aimed," *Magnum, P.I.,* CBS, 1982.
"The Pied Piper," *Bring 'Em Back Alive,* CBS, 1982.
Master of Flowers, "Thirty Seconds over Little Tokyo," *The Greatest American Hero,* ABC, 1983.
Lin, "Recipe for Heavy Bread," *The A-Team,* NBC, 1983.
Inspector Toshi, *Ohara,* ABC, 1987.
Tommy Nguyen, "My Brother's Keeper," *Spenser: For Hire,* ABC, 1987.
Trahn, *Tour of Duty,* CBS, 1987.
Thanarat, "Riding the Elephant," *The Equalizer,* CBS, 1988.
Yo Tin, *Supercarrier,* ABC, 1988.
Kao, *Paradise,* CBS, 1990.
"The Wash," *American Playhouse,* PBS, 1990.
Makumura, *Shaky Ground,* Fox, 1992.
Li Sung, "Tournament," *Kung Fu: The Legend Continues,* syndicated, 1994.
Sam Tanaka, "Author, Author," *Frasier,* NBC, 1994.
Mr. Loo, *Platypus Man,* UPN, 1995.
Dr. Henry Lee, "Heart of the Dragon," *Walker, Texas Ranger,* CBS, 1997.
Ichiro Higashimori, *JAG,* CBS, 1998.
Master Reng, "Requiem" and "Red Storm," *Martial Law,* CBS, 1999.

Also appeared in *Ironside,* NBC; *Hawaii Five-0,* CBS; *Mannix,* CBS; *McHale's Navy; Ensign O'Toole;* and *77 Sunset Strip.*

Television Appearances; Pilots:
Simba, *Alfred of the Amazon,* CBS, 1967.
Kenji, *Streets of San Francisco,* ABC, 1972.
Tao Gan, *Judge Dee in the Monastery Murders* (also known as *The Haunted Monastery*), ABC, 1974.
Mataro Sakura, *The Last Ninja,* ABC, 1983.
Major Taro Oshira, *Hawaiian Heat,* ABC, 1984.

Television Appearances; Specials:
Ben Chang, *The Last Ferry Home,* syndicated, 1992.

Stage Appearances:
Taki, *A Banquet for the Moon,* Theatre Marquee, New York City, 1961.
Pacific Overtures, East/West Players, Los Angeles, 1967-68.
Hokusai Sketchbooks, East/West Players, 1967-68.
Gold Watch, Inner City Repertory Theatre, Los Angeles, 1972.
(Broadway debut) The Reciter, Shogun, and Jonathan Goble, *Pacific Overtures,* Winter Garden Theatre, New York City, 1976.
Station J, East/West Players, 1981.
Sam Shikaze, *Yellow Fever,* Pan Asian Repertory Theatre, 47th Street Theatre, New York City, 1983.
Nobu, *The Wash,* Center Theatre Group, Mark Taper Forum, Los Angeles, 1985.
Shimada/Toshio Uchiyama, *Shimada,* Broadhurst Theatre, New York City, 1992.

Stage Director:
(With Shizuko Hoshi) *The Fisher King,* Center Theatre Group, Mark Taper Forum, Los Angeles Music Center, Los Angeles, 1976.
The Music Lessons, New York Shakespeare Festival, Public Theatre, New York City, 1980.
F.O.B. (Fresh Off the Boat), New York Shakespeare Festival, Public Theatre, 1980.

WRITINGS

Plays:
There's No Place Like a Tired Ghost, Inner City Repertory Theatre, Los Angeles, 1972.
(With Dom Magwili) *Christmas in Camp,* East/West Players, LosAngeles, 1981.*

MALICK, Wendie 1950-

PERSONAL

Born December 13, 1950, in Buffalo, NY; daughter of Ken (in sales) and Gigi (a former model) Malick; married Mitch Glazer (a screenwriter), 1982 (divorced, 1989); married Richard Erickson (a carpenter), 1995. Education: Graduated from Ohio Wesleyan University (theatre), 1972.

Addresses: *Agent*—c/o Innovative Artists, 1999 Avenue of the Stars, Suite 2850, Los Angeles, CA 90067.

Career: Actress. Worked for New York Congressman Jack Kemp in Washington, DC; spent five years as a model in Paris, France, and New York City. Worked with Adopt-a-Family and has appeared in commercials for Cadillac.

Awards, Honors: Artistic Directors Award, best lead actress in a play, 1995, for *Round Trip;* Golden Globe Award nomination, best performance by an actress in supporting role in a series, miniseries, or motion picture, and Emmy Award nomination, outstanding supporting actress in a comedy series, both 1999, for *Just Shoot Me;* four CableACE Awards, all best actress in a comedy series, all for *Dream On.*

CREDITS

Television Appearances; Series:
Dr. Brigitte Blaine, *Trauma Center* (also known as *Medstar*), ABC, 1983.
Dr. Susan Layden, *Supercarrier,* ABC, 1988.
Gayle Bucannon, *Baywatch,* NBC, 1989-92.
Judith Tupper Stone, *Dream On,* HBO, 1990-96.
Zoe Hellstrom, *Good Company,* CBS, 1996.
Barb, *Champs,* ABC, 1996.
Nina Van Horn, *Just Shoot Me,* NBC, 1997—.

Television Appearances; Movies:
Stephie, *How to Pick Up Girls!,* 1978.
Tippi, *Private Sessions,* NBC, 1985.
Trudence Barron, *Easy Come, Easy Go,* ABC, 1989.
The Keys, NBC, 1992.
Camille Barbone, *Madonna: Innocence Lost* (also known as *Madonna: Unauthorized*), Fox, 1994.
Lafferty, *The Return of Hunter* (also known as *The Return of Hunter: Everyone Walks in L.A.*), NBC, 1995.
Sarah Powell, *Hart to Hart: Secrets of the Hart* (also known as *Hart to Hart: The Locket*), NBC, 1995.
Pat Collins, *Apollo 11: The Movie,* The Family Channel, 1996.
Janet Bradley, *Perfect Body,* NBC, 1997.
Shimma, *North Shore Fish,* Showtime, 1997.
Dead Husbands (also known as *Last Man on the List*), USA Network, 1998.

Ann Landers/Abigail Van Buren, *Take My Advice: The Ann and Abby Storey,* Lifetime, 1999.

Television Appearances; Miniseries:
Carol Marshall, *Dynasty: The Reunion,* ABC, 1991.

Television Appearances; Episodic:
"Boomerang," *Hunter,* NBC, 1988.
Gayle Bucannon, "Panic at Malibu Pier," *Baywatch,* NBC, 1989.
Alie, "Burning the Toad," *Anything But Love,* ABC, 1989.
"This Is Not a Date," *Anything But Love,* ABC, 1989.
Cindy Finnegan, "Obsessed," *MacGyver,* ABC, 1991.
Civil Wars, ABC, 1993.
Susan Wagner, "Brown Appetite," *NYPD Blue,* ABC, 1993.
Susan Wagner, "True Confessions," *NYPD Blue,* ABC, 1993.
Denise, "Absence Makes the Nurse Grow Weirder," *Empty Nest,* NBC, 1994.
"Finish Line," *L.A. Law,* NBC, 1994.
Carol, "The Ride Home," *Mad about You,* NBC, 1994.
Nancy Lambert, "Nanny with the Laughing Face," *The Commish,* ABC, 1994.
Gary's sister, "In the Groove," *Tales from the Crypt,* HBO, 1994.
Iris Nevelson, *Viper,* NBC, 1994.
Judy, "Cybill with an 'S'," *Cybill,* CBS, 1995.
Wendy, "The Kiss Hello," *Seinfeld,* NBC, 1995.
Nina Van Horn, "To Bare is Human," *Boston Common,* NBC, 1996.
Zoey Green's mom (Femme Fatale), "Looking for Mr. Goodbar," *Mr. Rhodes,* NBC, 1996.
Dr. Cornick-therapist, "New Year," *The Single Guy,* NBC, 1997.
Olivia McClure, "Dates," *Life's Work,* ABC, 1997.
A.D. Maslin, "The Beginning," *The X-Files,* Fox, 1998.

Also appeared as Louis Jordan, "Too Young to Die," *Mickey Spillane's Mike Hammer,* CBS; Taylor, *Paper Dolls;* Claire, "Bringing Up Charles," *Kate & Allie;* and Trudy Barron, "Easy Come, Easy Go," *Christine Cromwell.*

Television Appearances; Pilots:
(As Wendy Malick) *Supercarrier* (also known as *Deadly Enemies*), ABC, 1988.
Carol Hobart, *The Ed Begley, Jr., Show,* CBS, 1989.
Lindsay, *Faith,* CBS, 1994.
Nina Horn, *Just Shoot Me,* NBC, 1996.

Film Appearances:
Mr. Mike's Mondo Video, New Line Cinema, 1980.
Philomena, *A Little Sex,* Universal, 1982.
Wendie Cross, *Scrooged,* Paramount, 1988.
Nurse Nancy, *Funny about Love,* Paramount, 1990.
Woman on train, *Bugsy,* TriStar, 1991.
Susan Sloan, *The American President,* Columbia, 1995.
Beverly Kimble, *Trojan War* (also known as *No Night Stand* and *Rescue Me*), Warner Bros., 1997.
Terry, *Divorce: A Contemporary Western,* 1998.
Jane, *Jerome,* Jet Film, 1998.
Mildred Tilman, *On the Edge,* forthcoming.

Stage Appearances:
Appeared in *North Shore Fish; Round Trip; Guys and Dolls; Bah! Humbug;* and *Mame.*

OTHER SOURCES

Periodicals:
Entertainment Weekly, March 4, 1994, p. 52.
People, March 16, 1998, p. 107.*

MANDYLOR, Costas 1965-

PERSONAL

Born Costas Theodosopoulos, in 1965, in Melbourne, Australia; son of John (a taxi driver) and Louise (maiden name, Mandylaris) Theodosopoulos; married Talisa Soto (an actress), May, 1997.

Addresses: *Agent*—Innovative Artists Talent, 1999 Avenue of the Stars, Los Angeles, CA 90067-6022.

Career: Actor. Played soccer with the Melbourne team, Green Gully, and trained with Panathinaikos.

CREDITS

Film Appearances:
Avram Arouch, *Triumph of the Spirit,* Triumph, 1989.
Italian Count, *The Doors,* TriStar, 1991.
Frank Costello, *Mobsters,* Universal, 1991.
Mark, *Soapdish,* Paramount, 1991.
Costello, *Fatal Past,* Skouras, 1994.
John Donovan, *Virtuosity,* Paramount, 1995.
Martin Niconi, *Crosscut,* Pavlic-Raimondi Pictures, 1995.
Vegas, *Venus Rising,* IRS Releasing, 1995.
George G. Kendall, *Portraits of a Killer* (also known as *Portraits of Innocence*), Live Entertainment, 1996.

Martin Niconi, *Crosscut,* A-pix Entertainment, 1996.
Jack, *Stand-Ins,* Overseas Filmgroup, 1997.
Rich Adams, *Just Write,* Curb Entertainment, 1997.
Hector Stroessner and Ray Soldado, *Double Take,* Twice Removed Productions, Inc., 1997.
McCarthy, *Shame, Shame, Shame,* Playboy Entertainment, 1998.
Conversations in Limbo, 1998.
Alan Decker, *Intrepid,* 1999.

Television Appearances; Series:
Kenny Lacos, *Picket Fences,* CBS, 1992-96.
Alphonse Royo, *Players,* NBC, 1997-98.

Television Appearances; Movies:
Lawrence, *Delta of Venus,* Showtime, 1995.
Paul Blankenship/Eric, *Falling for You,* CBS, 1995.
Lord Shin, *Fist of the North Star,* HBO, 1996.
Dominic Delaserra, *Almost Dead,* HBO, 1996.
Captain Jaid, *Roger Corman Presents Last Exit to Earth,* Showtime, 1996.
Adult Cupid on Earth, *Love-Struck,* The Family Channel, 1997.
Mike Hanlon, *The Fury Within,* USA Network, 1998.
Gianni Uzielli, *Exiled: A Law and Order Movie,* NBC, 1998.
Nikos, *Shelter,* HBO, 1998.
Salvatore Bonanno, *Bonanno: A Godfather's Story,* Showtime, 1999.

Television Appearances; Episodic:
"Half Way Horrible," *Tales from the Crypt,* HBO, 1993.
Jerry Tamblin, "Get Fast," *F/X: The Series,* 1996.
Lee, "The Heist," *The Outer Limits,* Showtime, 1996.
Colombian drug lord, *Players,* NBC, 1997.

Television Appearances; Specials:
The 17th Annual People's Choice Awards, CBS, 1991.
Half Way Horrible, 1993.*

MANTELLO, Joe 1962-
(Joseph Mantello)

PERSONAL

Full name, Joseph Mantello; born December 27, 1962, in Rockford, IL. *Education:* Attended the North Carolina School of the Arts; studied directing at the Circle Repertory Company.

Addresses: *Agent*—Writers & Artists Agency, 19 West 44th St., Suite 1000, New York, NY 10036-6095.

Career: Actor and director.

Awards, Honors: Drama Desk Award, best featured actor in a play, 1994, for *Angels in America;* Grand Special Prize nomination, Deauville Film Festival, 1997, for *Love! Valour! Compassion!;* also received an Antoinette Perry Award, Obie Award, Outer Critics Circle Award, Helen Hayes Award, Clarence Derwent Award, and the Joe A. Callaway Award.

CREDITS

Stage Appearances:
Crackwalker, off-Broadway production, 1987.
(As Joseph Mantello) Ticket inspector, gymnast, and second reporter, *The Visit,* Courtyard Playhouse, New York City, 1989.
Stan, *Walking the Dead,* Circle Repertory Theatre, New York City, 1991.
Third man, *The Baltimore Waltz,* Circle Repertory Theatre, 1992.
Louis Ironson, *Angels in America: Millennium Approaches,* Center Theatre Group, Mark Taper Forum, Los Angeles Music Center, Los Angeles, CA, 1992-93, then Walter Kerr Theatre, New York City, 1993-94.
Louis Ironson and Sarah Ironson, *Angels in America: Perestroika,* Center Theatre Group, Mark Taper Forum, Los Angeles Music Center, 1992-93, then Walter Kerr Theatre, 1993-94.
Easter Bonnet Competition: Back to Basics, Palace Theatre, New York City, 1995.

Also appeared in *Progress.*

Stage Work; Director:
Nebraska, Naked Angels Theatre, New York City, 1991.
Coq au Vin, Naked Angels Theatre, 1991.
Babylon Gardens, Circle Repertory Theatre, 1991.
The Innocents' Crusade, Long Wharf Theatre, New Haven, CT, 1991-92.
Three Hotels, Circle Repertory Theatre, 1993.
Fat Men in Skirts, Naked Angels Theatre, 1994.
What's Wrong with the Picture?, Brooks Atkinson Theatre, New York City, 1994.
Three Hotels, Centre Theatre Group, Mark Taper Forum, Los Angeles Music Center, Los Angeles, 1994-95.
Love! Valour! Compassion!, Manhattan Theatre Club, Stage I, New York City, 1994-95, then the Walter Kerr Theatre, New York City, 1995, then at the Geffen Playhouse, Los Angeles, CA, 1996-97.
Blue Window, Manhattan Theatre Club, Stage I, 1996.

The Santaland Diaries, Atlantic Theatre, New York City, 1996.
God's Heart, Lincoln Center, New York City, 1997.
Proposals, Broadhurst Theatre, New York City, 1997.
Mizlansky/Zilinsky or "Schmucks," Manhattan Theatre Club, 1998.
Lillian, New Theatre Wing, New York City, 1998.
House, Bay Street Theatre, Sag Harbor, NY, 1998.
Corpus Christi, Manhattan Theatre Club, 1998.

Also directed *Snakebit,* New York Stage and Film; *Three Hotels,* Bay Street Theatre Festival, Sag Harbor, NY; and *Imagining Brad.*

Film Appearances:
Dominick, *Cookie,* Warner Bros., 1989.

Film Work; Director:
Love! Valour! Compassion!, Fine Line Features, 1997.

Television Appearances; Specials:
In the Wings: Angels in America on Broadway, PBS, 1993.

Television Appearances; Episodic:
Public defender, "Confession," *Law & Order,* NBC, 1991.
Adam Oldenberg, *Sisters,* NBC, 1992.
Ian Walker, *CPW* (also known as *Central Park West*), CBS, 1995.
Philip Marco, "Tabloid," *Law & Order,* NBC, 1998.

OTHER SOURCES

Periodicals:
Advocate, November 24, 1998, p. 77.
Back Stage, June 21, 1996, pp. 3-5; November 29, 1996, p. 28; February 20, 1998, pp. 3-4.
Entertainment Weekly, October 23, 1998, p. 65.
Variety, April 14, 1997, pp. 100-101; November 10, 1997, p. 51; February 23, 1998, p. 185; June 22, 1998, p. 63; August 31, 1998, p. 102.*

MANTELLO, Joseph
See MANTELLO, Joe

MARCEAU, Sophie 1966-

PERSONAL

Real name, Sophie Daniele Sylvie Maupu; born November 17, 1966, in Paris, France; daughter of Benoit Maupu (a truck driver) and Simone Morisset; children (with Andrzej Zulawski, a director) Vincent. *Avocational interests:* Animals, environmental issues, spending time in the country, reading, listening to music, traveling.

Addresses: *Agent*—Artmedia, 10 avenue George-V, 75008 Paris, France. *Contact*—13 rue Madeleine Michelle, F-92200 Neuilly-sur-Seine, France.

Career: Actress, director, and writer. Also worked as a model.

Awards, Honors: Cesar Award, most promising young actress, 1983, for *La Boum 2;* Festival International du Film Romantique Award, best romantic actress, 1988, for *Chouans!;* Moliere Award, best theatrical revelation, 1991; named an "ambassador of charm" to represent France in East Asia.

CREDITS

Film Appearances:
Vic, *La Boum,* Gaumont, 1981.
Vic, *La Boum 2,* Gaumont, 1982.
Madeleine de Saint-Ilette, *Fort Saganne,* Connoisseur Video, 1984.
Juile, *Joyeuses Paques* (also known as *Happy Easter*), Cerito Films/Sara Film, 1984.
Mary, *L'amour braque,* Sara Film, 1985.
Noria (the dealer's girlfriend), *Police,* Gaumont, 1985.
Lola Kobler, *Descente aux enfers* (also known as *Descent into Hell*), La Cinq/Partner's Production, 1986.
Celine, *Chouans!,* Antenne-2/Partner's Production, 1988.
Valentine, *L'etudiante* (also known as *The Student*), Gaumont, 1988.
Blanche, *Mes nuits sont plus belles que vos jours* (also known as *My Nights Are More Beautiful Than Your Days*), Saris, 1989.
Bernadette, *Pacific Palisades,* 1990.
Laura, *Pour Sacha* (also known as *For Sacha*), Alexandre Films, 1991.
Solange at the age of twenty, *La note bleue* (also known as *Blue Note*), Erato Films, 1991.
Title role, *Fanfan* (also known as *Fanfan and Alexandre*), Gaumont, 1993.
Eloise (D'Artagnan's daughter), *La fille de d'Artagnan* (also known as *D'Artagnan's Daughter* and *The Daughter of D'Artgnan*), Little Bear Films, 1994.
Faire un film pour moi c'est vivre (also known as *Making a Film for Me Is to Live;* documentary), 1995.

Princess Isabelle, *Braveheart,* Paramount/Twentieth Century-Fox, 1995.
The girl, "The Girl, the Crime," *Beyond the Clouds* (also known as *Ai di la delle nuvole, Jenseits der Wolken* and *Par-dela les nuages*), Cecchi Gori/ Sunshine, 1995.
Elisabeth Laurier, *Firelight* (also known as *Firelight—Le lien secret*), Miramax, 1997.
Title role, *Anna Karenina* (also known as *Leo Tolstoy's Anna Karenina* and *Anna Karenine*), Warner Bros., 1997.
Marquise Du Parc (title role), *Marquise,* Columbia/ TriStar, 1997.
Lila Dubois, *Lost and Found,* Warner Bros., 1999.
Hippolyta, *A Midsummer's Night Dream* (also known as *William Shakespeare's A Midsummer Night's Dream*), Fox Searchlight Pictures, 1999.
Franck Spadone, 1999.
Elektra King, *The World Is Not Enough* (also known as *Bond 19, Bond 2000, Death Waits for No Man, Fire and Ice, Pressure Point,* and *T.W.I.N.E.*), United Artists, 1999.

Film Work; Director:
L'aube a l'envers (short film), Sepia Productions, 1995.

Stage Appearances:
Eurydice, 1991.
Pygmalion, 1993.

WRITINGS

Screenplays:
L'aube a l'envers (short film), Sepia Productions, 1995.

Novels:
Menteuse, Editions Stock (Paris, France), 1995.

OTHER SOURCES

Periodicals:
Los Angeles Times, April 10, 1997, p. 14.*

MARCIL, Vanessa 1969-

PERSONAL

Real name, Vanessa Ortiz; born October 15, 1969; raised in Palm Desert, CA; daughter of Peter (a contractor) and Patricia (an herbalist) Ortiz; married Corey Feldman (an actor), 1989 (divorced); married Tyler Christopher (an actor). *Education:* Attended the College of the Desert. *Avocational interests:* Volunteering at rehabilitation centers.

Addresses: *Contact*—9000 Sunset Blvd., Suite 1200, Los Angeles, CA 90069.

Career: Actress. Also appeared in television commercials.

Awards, Honors: *Soap Opera Digest* Awards, hottest female star, 1997, and outstanding lead actress, 1998, Daytime Emmy Award nominations, outstanding supporting actress in a daytime drama series, 1997 and 1998, all for *General Hospital.*

CREDITS

Television Appearances; Series:
Brenda Barrett, *General Hospital,* ABC, 1992-98.
Host, *ABC in Concert* (also known as *In Concert*), ABC, 1995-98.
Gina Kincaid, *Beverly Hills, 90210,* Fox, 1998—.
Sara Pezzini, *Witchblade,* TNT, 1999—.

Television Appearances; Movies:
Sydnee Carpenter, *To Love, Honor and Deceive* (also known as *The Protected Wife*), ABC, 1996.

Television Appearances; Specials:
Brenda Barrett, *General Hospital: Twist of Fate,* ABC, 1996.
ABC Soaps' Most Unforgettable Love Stories, ABC, 1998.
Sex with Cindy Crawford, ABC, 1998.
The General Hospital 35th Anniversary Show, ABC, 1998.

Television Appearances; Awards Presentations:
Presenter, *The Ninth Annual Soap Opera Awards,* 1993.
Presenter, *The 21st Annual Daytime Emmy Awards,* 1994.
Presenter, *The 14th Annual Soap Opera Awards,* 1998.
Presenter, *The 25th Annual Daytime Emmy Awards,* 1998.

Television Appearances; Episodic:
Live with Regis and Kathie Lee, syndicated, 1994.
Kerry Andrews, "Hot Wire," *High Incident,* ABC, 1996.
Kerry Andrews, "Remote Control," *High Incident,* ABC, 1996.

Television Appearances; Pilots:
Sara Pezzini, *Witchblade,* TNT, 1999.

Other Television Appearances; Music Videos:
"The Most Beautiful Girl in the World," by the Artist Formerly Known As Prince, 1994.

Film Appearances:
Carla Pestalozzi, *The Rock,* Buena Vista, 1996.
Danielle, *976-WISH,* David Bertman Productions, 1997.
Maggie Harty, *This Space between Us,* Fault Line Pictures, 1998.
Erin, *Nice Guys Sleep Alone,* Lunacy Unlimited Productions, 1999.

Stage Appearances:
Cat on a Hot Tin Roof, Los Angeles, CA, 1992.

Appeared in productions of the Circle Theatre Acting Company.

OTHER SOURCES

Periodicals:
Entertainment Weekly, February 17, 1995, p. 50.
People Weekly, May 8, 1995, p. 144; June 17, 1996, pp. 178-179.*

MARGOLYES, Miriam 1941-

PERSONAL

Surname is pronounced "Margoleez"; born May 18, 1941, in Oxford, England; daughter of Joseph (a physician) and Ruth (a real estate investor; maiden name, Walters) Margoyles. *Education:* Attended the Oxford High School for Girls and Newnham College, Cambridge University, where she joined the Footlights Club theatre group; Guildhall School of Music and Drama, 1959. *Religion:* Jewish. *Avocational interests:* reading, talking, eating, Italy.

Addresses: *Agent*—c/o Kate Feast Management, 43-A Princess Road, London NW1, England.

Career: Actress. Known in Britain as the "Voice-Over Queen"; has appeared in television commercials for Cadbury and Brooke Bond Tea.

Member: British Actors' Equity Association (council member, 1979-82).

Awards, Honors: Best supporting acress, LA Critics Circle, 1989; British Academy of Film and Television Artists Award, best supporting actress, 1993.

CREDITS

Film Appearances:
(Film debut) *A Nice Girl Like Me,* Avco Embassy, 1969.
The Battle of Billy's Pond, Children's Film Foundation, 1976.
Elephant Ethel, *Stand Up Virgin Soldiers,* Warner Bros., 1977.
On a Paving Stone Mounted, 1978.
Dr. Kadira, *The Awakening,* Warner Bros., 1980.
Landlady, *The Apple,* Cannon, 1980.
Political activist, *Reds,* Paramount, 1981.
Officer Jones, *Scrubbers,* Orion, 1982.
Newsreader, *Crystal Gazing,* 1982.
Sarah, *Yentl,* Metro-Goldwyn-Mayer/United Artists, 1984.
Ticket girl, *Electric Dreams,* Metro-Goldwyn-Mayer/United Artists, 1984.
Lady scientist, *Morons from Outer Space,* 1985.
Dental receptionist, *Little Shop of Horrors,* Warner Bros., 1986.
Jane Powell, *The Good Father,* Skouras, 1987.
Flora Finching, *Little Dorritt,* Cannon, 1987.
Nellie, *Old Flames,* 1989.
Mrs. Browning, *The Fool,* 1990.
Realtor, *Pacific Heights,* Twentieth Century-Fox, 1990.
Joey's Mother, *I Love You to Death,* TriStar, 1990.
Gina, *The Butcher's Wife,* Paramount, 1991.
Audrey, *As You Like It,* 1992.
Mrs. Mingott, *The Age of Innocence,* Columbia, 1993.
Mother, *Ed and His Dead Mother,* Twentieth Century-Fox, 1993.
Nanette Streicher, *Immortal Beloved,* Columbia/TriStar, 1994.
Narration, *Liberation* (documentary), Samuel Goldwyn, 1994.
Different for Girls, 1995.
Babe, 1995.
Balto (animated), 1995.
Nurse, *William Shakespeare's Romeo and Juliet,* Twentieth Century-Fox, 1996.
Voice, *The Long Way Home,* Seventh Art Releasing, 1996.
Aunt Sponge and Voice of Glowworm, *James and the Giant Peach* (portions animated), Buena Vista, 1996.
Mrs. Goldman, *Left Luggage,* Greystone Films, 1997.
Voice of Fly, *Babe: Pig in the City,* Universal, 1998.

Also appeared in *Handel—Honour, Profit, and Pleasure.*

Television Appearances; Movies:

Oliver Twist, BBC, 1985.
Nurse Hopkins, *The Life and Loves of a She-Devil,* Arts and Entertainment, 1987.
Murderers among Us: The Simon Wiesenthal Story, HBO, 1989.
Vee Talbot, *Orpheus Descending,* TNT, 1990.
Krupskaya, *Stalin,* HBO, 1992.
Mrs. Beetle, *Cold Comfort Farm,* BBC, 1995.

Television Appearances; Series:

The Living Body, Films for the Humanities, 1985.
Frannie Escobar, *Frannie's Turn,* CBS, 1992.

Television Appearances; Episodic:

Infanta Maria Escalosa of Spain, "The Queen of Spain's Beard," *The Black Adder,* BBC, rebroadcast on Arts and Entertainment and PBS, 1983.
Miss Amelia, "The Little Princess," *WonderWorks,* PBS, 1987.
Poll, "The Finding," *WonderWorks,* PBS, 1990.
"Collins Meets Coward," *A&E Stage,* Arts and Entertainment, 1992.

Also appeared in *The Stanley Baxter Christmas Show,* London Weekly Television; as Wife, "Fat Chance," *Tales of the Unexpected,* Anglia; and in *The Ken Dodd Show,* BBC.

Other Television Appearances:

Elsa Maxwell, *Poor Little Rich Girl: The Barbara Hutton Story* (miniseries), NBC, 1987.
Queen Victoria, *Blackadder's Christmas Carol* (special), BBC, 1988.

Also appeared in *Enter Solly Gold*; as Melissa Todoroff, *The History Man,* BBC; as Queenie, *The Lost Tribe,* BBC; as Maria, *Take a Letter, Mr. Jones,* Southern TV; as Mrs. King, *Crown Court,* Granada; as Baroness, *Freud,* BBC; as Alice, *Strange But True: Flights of Fancy,* TVS; as Hoffman, *A Rough Stage: The Mexican Rebels,* Channel Four; as Mrs. Bumble and Mrs. Goko, *Rates of Exchange,* BBC; *You Tell Such Dreadful Lies,* Granada; *Fall of Eagles,* BBC; *Girls of Slender Means,* BBC; *Kizzy,* BBC; *The Eleventh Hour,* BBC; *The Widowing of Mrs. Holroyd,* BBC; *Glittering Prizes,* BBC, then PBS; *Angels,* BBC; *Scotch and Wry,* BBC-Scotland; *The First Schlemiel,* Channel Four; *Secret Diaries of Film Censors; The Chip Show,* BBC; and *The Johnny Carson Show.*

Stage Appearances:

(London debut) Nelly, *The Threepenny Opera,* Prince of Wales Theatre, then Piccadilly Theatre, London, 1972.
Rona, *Kennedy's Children,* Arts Theatre, London, 1975.
Zanche, *The White Devil,* Old Vic Theatre, London, 1976.
Mercedes Mordecai, *Flaming Bodies,* Institute of Contemporary Arts Theatre, London, 1979.
Wooman, Lovely Wooman, Tiffany Theatre, West Hollywood, CA, 1990.
Title roles, *Dickens' Women* (one-woman show), Duke of York's Theatre, London, 1991.
Mrs. Hardcastle, *She Stoops to Conquer,* Queen's Theatre, London, 1993.
June Buckridge/Sister George, *The Killing of Sister George,* Ambassador's Theatre, London, 1995.

Also appeared as Wife of Bath, *The Canterbury Tales,* Bristol Old Vic Theatre, Bristol, U.K.; as Gertrude Stein, *Gertrude Stein and a Companion,* Edinburgh Festival, Edinburgh, Scotland, then Tron Theatre, Glasgow, Scotland, later Bush Theatre; as Helen Hanff, *84 Charing Cross Road,* Mercury Theatre; and as Widow Begbick, *Man Equals Man,* Almeida Theatre.

Radio Appearances:

Appeared in *The Queen and I,* 1993.

Major Tours:

Toured as the Matchmaker, *Fiddler on the Roof,* U.K. cities; *Cloud Nine,* U.K. cities.

RECORDINGS

Taped Readings:

Miriam Margoyles Reads a Bad Spell for the Worst Witch, Cover to Cover, 1984.

Videos:

Echoes that Remain, Simon Weisenthal Center, 1991.

OTHER SOURCES

Periodicals:

New York Times, October 17, 1993, pp. 2, 21.*
People Weekly, November 8, 1993, p. 77.

MARSHALL, Paula 1964-

PERSONAL

Born June 12, 1964, in Rockville, MD; married Thomas Lee Ardavany, October 14, 1989 (divorced, 1998).

Addresses: *Agent*—Innovative Artists, 1999 Avenue of the Stars, Los Angeles, CA 90067.

Career: Actress.

CREDITS

Television Appearances; Series:
Bonnie Douglas, *The Wonder Years,* ABC, 1992-93.
Shelly Thomas, *Wild Oats,* Fox, 1994-95.
Lindsay Sutton, *Chicago Sons,* NBC, 1997.
Laurie Parres, *Spin City,* ABC, 1997-98.
Dr. Claire Allen, *Cupid,* ABC, 1998-99.
Dana Plant, *Snoops,* Fox, 1999—.

Television Appearances; Movies:
Jill Houston, *Nurses on the Line: The Crash of Flight 7,* CBS, 1993.
Liza Block, *Full Eclipse,* HBO, 1993.
Margo Rentell and Debra Walters, *A Perry Mason Mystery: The Case of the Wicked Wives* (also known as *Case of the Wicked Wives*), NBC, 1993.
Abby, *W.E.I.R.D. World,* Fox, 1995.

Television Appearances; Episodic:
Iris West, *The Flash,* CBS, 1990.
"Hickory, Dickory, Dock," *True Blue,* NBC, 1990.
Caveperson, *Dinosaurs,* ABC, 1991.
Jill Gordon, *Life Goes On,* ABC, 1992.
Fran, "The Fran and Joey Story," *Grapevine,* CBS, 1992.
Sharon Leonard, "The Outing," *Seinfeld,* NBC, 1993.
Cindy Marsh, "Flashdance with Death," *Diagnosis Murder,* CBS, 1993.
Eve Adamson, "Night Train," *Nash Bridges,* CBS, 1996.
Eve Adamson, *Nash Bridges,* CBS, 1996.
Isabella, "Grandfather Clause," *The Single Guy,* NBC, 1997.

Film Appearances:
Terri, *Hellraiser III: Hell on Earth,* Dimension Films/Paramount, 1992.
Samantha Ellison, *Warlock: The Armageddon* (also known as *Warlock II*), Trimark Pictures, 1993.
Alison Gale, *The New Age,* Wechsler Productions, 1994.
Karen, *A Family Thing,* Metro-Goldwyn-Mayer/United Artists, 1996.
Molly De Mora, *That Old Feeling,* Universal, 1997.
Christine Wells, *Thursday,* Volcanic Films, 1998.
Deborah and the girl in the photograph, *A Gun, a Car, a Blonde,* Showcase Entertainment, 1998.*

MASTERSON, Mary Stuart 1966-

PERSONAL

Born June 28, 1966, in New York, NY; daughter of Peter Masterson (an actor, director, and writer) and Carlin Glynn (an actress). *Education:* Attended Goddard College; studied acting with Estelle Parsons and Gary Swanson.

Addresses: *Agent*—Creative Artists Agency, 9830 Wilshire Blvd., Beverly Hills, CA 90212.

Career: Actress. Member, Actors Studio; attended Sundance Institute and Stage Door Manor.

Member: SANE/FREEZE.

Awards, Honors: National Board of Review Award, 1989.

CREDITS

Film Appearances:
Kim, *The Stepford Wives,* Columbia, 1975.
Danni, *Heaven Help Us* (also known as *Catholic Boys*), TriStar, 1984.
Terry, *At Close Range,* Orion, 1985.
Franny Bettinger, *My Little Girl,* Hemdale, 1986.
Rachel Feld, *Gardens of Stone,* TriStar, 1987.
Watts "drummer girl," *Some Kind of Wonderful,* Paramount, 1987.
Elspeth Skeel, *Mr. North,* Samuel Goldwyn, 1988.
Miranda Jeffries, *Chances Are,* TriStar, 1989.
Lucy Moore, *Immediate Family,* Columbia, 1989.
Daphne Delillo, *Funny about Love,* Paramount, 1990.
Idgie Threadgoode, *Fried Green Tomatoes,* Universal, 1991.
Nina Bishop, *Married to It,* Orion, 1993.
Jenny, *Mad at the Moon,* Republic, 1993.
The Last Party, Triton, 1993.
Joon, *Benny and Joon,* Metro-Goldwyn-Mayer, 1993.
Penny Henderson, *Radioland Murders,* Universal, 1994.

Anita Crown, *Bad Girls,* Twentieth Century-Fox, 1994.
Robin Gaddis, *Heaven's Prisoners,* New Line Cinema, 1996.
Lisa, *Bed of Roses,* New Line Cinema, 1996.
Gwen Frankovitz, *Digging to China,* The Ministry of Film, 1997.
Dorothy Sternen, *Dogtown,* 1997.

Television Appearances; Movies:
City in Fear (also known as *Panic on Page One*), ABC, 1980.
Susan Wallace, *Love Lives On,* ABC, 1985.
Title role, *Lily Dale,* Showtime, 1996.
Trish, *On the 2nd Day of Christmas,* Lifetime, 1997.

Television Appearances; Episodic:
Cynthia, "Go to the Head of the Class," *Amazing Stories,* NBC, 1986.
Interviewee, *Inside the Actors Studio,* Bravo, 1995.

Other Television Appearances:
Presenter, *MTV Movie Awards* (special), MTV, 1993.
Voice, *The West* (series), PBS, 1996.

Stage Appearances:
Small white rabbit and Four of Hearts, *Alice in Wonderland,* Virginia Theatre, New York City, 1982.
Margaret, *Been Taken,* Ensemble Studio Theatre, New York City, 1985.
Cassidy Smith, *The Lucky Spot,* Manhattan Theatre Club, New York City, 1987.
Lily Dale, Samuel Beckett Theatre, New York City, 1987.

Also appeared in regional theatre productions of *Three Sisters* and *Moonlight and Valentines.**

MASTROIANNI, Chiara 1972-

PERSONAL

Born May 28, 1972; daughter of Marcello Mastroianni (an actor) and Catherine Deneuve (an actress); half-sister of Christian Vadim (an actor).

Addresses: *Agent*—Artmedia, 10 avenue Georges-V, 75008 Paris, France.

Career: Actress.

CREDITS

Film Appearances:
Claire, *A la belle etoile,* Bac Films, 1993.
Anne, *Ma saison preferee* (also known as *My Favorite Season*), Vertigo Films, 1993.
Sophie Choiset (Kitty Potter's assistant), *Pret-a-Porter* (also known as *Ready to Wear*), Miramax, 1994.
3000 scenarios contre un virus (also known as *3,000 Scenarios to Combat a Virus*), [France], 1994.
Claudia, *N'oublie pas que tu vas mourir* (also known as *Don't Forget You're Going to Die*), La Sept Cinema, 1995.
Claire Conti, *Le journal du seducteur* (also known as *Diary of a Seducer*), Gemini Films, 1995.
Francoise, *All Men Are Mortal,* Warner Bros., 1995.
Cecile, *Trois vies et une seule mort* (also known as *Three Lives and Only One Death* and *Tres vidas e uma so morte*), Laurenfilm, 1996.
Graduate student, *Les voleurs* (also known as *The Child of the Night* and *Thieves*), Sony Pictures Classics, 1996.
Lea, *Cameleone,* Rezo Films, 1996.
Patricia, *Comment je me suis dispute . . . (ma vie sexuelle)* (also known as *My Sex Life . . . or How I Got into an Argument*), Zeitgeist Films, 1997.
On a tres peu d'amis, Gemini Films, 1997.
Kriss, *Nowhere,* Fine Line Features, 1997.
Mireille, *A vendre* (also known as *For Sale*), Le Studio Canal/Le Sept Cinema, 1998.
Albertine, *Le temps retrouve,* Gemini Films, 1999.
Mme. de Cleves, *A carta* (also known as *A princesa de Cleves*), Gemini Films, 1999.

OTHER SOURCES

Periodicals:
People Weekly, May 8, 1995, p. 156.
Time, February 23, 1993, p. 75.*

McCLOSKEY, Leigh 1955-
(Leigh J. McCloskey)

PERSONAL

Born June 21, 1955, in Los Angeles, CA; married Carla, 1978.

Addresses: *Contact*—Global Business Management, 15250 Ventura Blvd., Suite 710, Sherman Oaks, CA 91403.

Career: Actor.

CREDITS

Television Appearances; Series:

Brian Walling, *Executive Suite,* CBS, 1976-77.
Billy Baker, *Married: The First Year,* CBS, 1979.
Doctors' Private Lives, ABC, 1979.
Mitch Cooper, *Dallas,* CBS, 1979-82, 1985.
Dr. Zach Kelton, *Santa Barbara,* NBC, 1988-89.
Ethan Asher, *Santa Barbara,* NBC, 1989-90.
Dr. Michael Baranski, *General Hospital,* ABC, 1992.
Damien Smith, *General Hospital,* ABC, 1993-95.
Dr. Kurt Costner, *The Young and the Restless,* CBS, 1997.

Television Appearances; Pilots:

Kenny Wise, *Doctors' Private Lives,* ABC, 1978.
James Barstow (guest), *Velvet,* ABC, 1984.

Television Appearances; Episodic:

Gil, "Most Likely to Succeed," *The Streets of San Francisco,* ABC, 1976.
"Tounai," *Hawaii Five-0,* CBS, 1977.
"Man in the Chair," *The Paper Chase,* CBS, 1979.
Jay, "Cruise Ship to the Stars," *Buck Rogers in the 25th Century,* NBC, 1979.
Webb Convington, Jr., "Nashville Pirates," *The Fall Guy,* ABC, 1983.
"Vicki's Song," *Mickey Spillane's Mike Hammer,* CBS, 1984.
"Murder in the Museum," *Partners in Crime,* NBC, 1984.
"White Lies," *Finder of Lost Loves,* ABC, 1984.
Todd Amberson, *Murder, She Wrote,* CBS, 1985.
"Passports," *Hotel,* ABC, 1986.
"Revenge of Esperanza," *Blacke's Magic,* NBC, 1986.
"Much Too Personal," *New Love American Style,* ABC, 1986.
"The Man I Love," *Jake and the Fatman,* CBS, 1987.
"Wizard of Odds," *Sonny Spoon,* NBC, 1988.
"On the Land, on the Sea, and in the Hills," *The Bronx Zoo,* NBC, 1988.
Phillip Jorgens, *Life Goes On,* ABC, 1992.
Pirate, "Bloody Beach," *Raven,* CBS, 1993.
Randall, "Rip Off," *Raven,* CBS, 1993.
Soap doctor, "Death Be Proud," *Chicago Hope,* CBS, 1994.
Tieran, "Warlord," *Star Trek: Voyager,* UPN, 1996.
(As Leigh J. McCloskey) Matthew-yoga instructor, "Tricky Dick," *3rd Rock from the Sun,* NBC, 1997.
(As Leigh J. McCloskey) Tommy, "The Laws," *Almost Perfect,* CBS, 1997.
Thomas, "A Tragedy of Telepaths," *Babylon 5,* syndicated, 1998.
Thomas, "Phoenix Rising," *Babylon 5,* syndicated, 1998.
Dan Lander, *JAG,* CBS, 1998.
Joran Belar, "Field of Fire," *Star Trek: Deep Space Nine,* syndicated, 1999.
Bigelow, "Fortune Cookie," *Beverly Hills, 90210,* Fox, 1999.

Also appeared as Donald Ralston, "Bess, Is You a Woman Now?," *Phyllis,* CBS.

Television Appearances; Movies:

Alexander, *Dawn: Portrait of a Teenage Runaway,* NBC, 1976.
Alexander Duncan, *Alexander: The Other Side of Dawn,* NBC, 1977.
Magnus, *The Bermuda Depths* (also known as *It Came Up from the Depths*), ABC, 1978.
Frank Mather, *Trouble Shooters: Trapped Beneath the Earth,* NBC, 1993.
Richard, *Accidental Meeting,* 1994.
Alex Williams, *Terror in the Shadows,* 1995.

Television Appearances; Miniseries:

Billy Abbott, *Rich Man, Poor Man* (also known as *Rich Man, Poor Man—Book I;* miniseries), ABC, 1976.

Television Appearances; Specials:

Jeff, "Blind Sunday," *ABC Afterschool Special,* ABC, 1976.
CBS team member, *Battle of the Network Stars,* ABC, 1981.

Film Appearances:

Mark Elliot, *Dario Argento's Inferno,* Twentieth Century-Fox, 1980.
Rinaldo, *I Paladini Storia d'Armi e d'Amori* (also known as *Hearts and Armor*), Warner Home Video, 1983.
Charles "Chas" Lawlor III, *Fraternity Vacation,* New World, 1985.
Kevin, *Just One of the Guys,* Columbia, 1985.
Mark Elliot, *Dario Argento's World of Horror,* 1985.
Russell, *Hamburger . . . The Motion Picture* (also known as *Hamburger* and *Hamburger U.*), FM, 1986.
Jay, *Dirty Laundry,* Skouras, 1987.
Detective Pete Groom, *Cameron's Closet,* SVS, 1989.
Eric West, *Lucky Stiff* (also known as *That Shamrock Touch*), Columbia TriStar Home Video, 1989.
Mick Taylor, *Double Revenge,* Republic Home Video, 1990.*

MCCLOSKEY, Leigh J.
See McCLOSKEY, Leigh

MCEACHIN, James 1930-

PERSONAL

Born May 20, 1930, in Rennert, NC; married Lois Davis; children: Alainia, Lyle.

Addresses: *Contact*—P.O. Box 5166, Sherman Oaks, CA 91403.

Career: Actor. *Military service:* U.S. Army, 1947-1953.

Member: Screen Actors Guild; American Federation of Television and Radio Artists.

Awards, Honors: Purple Heart.

CREDITS

Film Appearances:

Jimmy Collins, *The Undefeated,* Twentieth Century-Fox, 1969.
Al Monte, *Play Misty For Me,* Universal, 1971.
Kingston, *Buck and the Preacher,* Columbia, 1972.
Detective Brown, *Fuzz,* United Artists, 1972.
Donovan, *Christina,* International Amusement Corp., 1974.
Herb, *Every Which Way But Loose,* Warner Bros., 1978.
Detective Barnes, *Sudden Impact,* Warner Bros., 1983.

Television Appearances; Movies:

The Brotherhood of the Bell, CBS, 1970.
O'Hara, *United States Treasury: Operation Cobra,* CBS, 1971.
Don Cope, *The Cable Car Murder,* CBS, 1971.
Eddie Jewell, *The D.A.: Conspiracy to Kill,* NBC, 1971.
Highway Patrolman, *The Neon Ceiling,* NBC, 1971.
Ed Mullins, *Short Walk to Daylight,* ABC, 1972.
Mr. Early-Conductor, *That Certain Summer,* ABC, 1972.
Quint, *The Judge and Jake Wyler,* NBC, 1972.
Harry Tenafly, *Tenafly,* NBC, 1973.
Scat, *The Alpha Caper,* ABC, 1973.
Frankie Specht, *The Dead Don't Die,* NBC, 1975.
Richardson, *Samurai,* ABC, 1979.
Harris McIntyre, *This Man Stands Alone,* NBC, 1979.
Speed-O, *The Great American Traffic Jam,* NBC, 1980.
Nate Walker, *Honeyboy,* NBC, 1982.
Lieutenant Jesse Herman, SFPD, *Allison Sidney Harrison,* NBC, 1983.
Lieutenant Daniels, *Diary of a Perfect Murder,* NBC, 1986.
Detective Brock, *Perry Mason: The Case of the Notorious Nun,* NBC, 1986.
Perry Mason: The Case of the Scandalous Scoundrel, NBC, 1987.
Perry Mason: The Case of the Avenging Ace, NBC, 1988.
Lieutenant Ed Brock, *Perry Mason: The Case of the All-Star Assassin,* NBC, 1989.
Lieutenant Ed Brock, *Perry Mason: The Case of the Musical Murder,* NBC, 1989.
Frank, *Guess Who's Coming For Christmas?,* NBC, 1990.
Lieutenant Ed Brock, *Perry Mason: The Case of the Poisoned Pen,* NBC, 1990.
Lieutenant Ed Brock, *Perry Mason: The Case of the Silenced Singer,* NBC, 1990.
Lieutenant Ed Brock, *Perry Mason: The Case of the Glass Coffin,* NBC, 1991.
Lieutenant Ed Brock, *Perry Mason: The Case of the Maligned Mobster,* NBC, 1991.
Lieutenant Ed Brock, *Perry Mason: The Case of the Ruthless Reporter,* NBC, 1991.
Lieutenant Ed Brock, *Perry Mason: The Case of the Fatal Framing,* NBC, 1992.
Lieutenant Ed Brock, *Perry Mason: The Case of the Heartbroken Bride,* NBC, 1992.
Lieutenant Ed Brock, *Perry Mason: The Case of the Reckless Romeo,* NBC, 1992.
Lieutenant Ed Brock, *Perry Mason: The Case of the Wicked Wives,* NBC, 1993.
Lieutenant Ed Brock, *Perry Mason: The Case of the Killer Kiss,* NBC, 1993.
Lieutenant Ed Brock, *Perry Mason: The Case of the Skin-Deep Scandal,* NBC, 1993.
Lieutenant Ed Brock, *Perry Mason: The Case of the Telltale Talk Show Host,* NBC, 1993.
Willie, *Sworn To Vengeance,* CBS, 1993.
Lieutenant Ed Brock, *Perry Mason: The Case of the Lethal Lifestyle,* NBC, 1994.
Lieutenant Ed Brock, *Perry Mason: The Case of the Jealous Jokester,* NBC, 1995.

Television Appearances, Series:

Performer, *Escape,* NBC, 1972-1973.
Harry Tenafly, *Tenafly,* NBC, 1973-1974.

Grover Dillon, *Murder, She Wrote,* 1984-1985.
Reverend James, *I'll Fly Away,* NBC, 1991-1992.
Leon Lomax, *Diagnosis Murder,* CBS, 1993-1994.

WRITINGS

Books:
Tell Me A Tale Of The South, Presidio/Lyford, 1996.*

MCELHONE, Natascha 1971-

PERSONAL

Born Natasha Taylor, March 23, 1971, in Hampstead, England; married Martin Hirigoyen (a plastic surgeon). *Education:* Trained at London Academy of Music and Drama.

Addresses: *Agent*—Creative Artists Agency, 1888 Century Park East, Suite 1400, Los Angeles, CA 90069.

Career: Actress.

CREDITS

Film Appearances:
Francoise Gilot, *Surviving Picasso,* Warner Bros., 1996.
Young Clarissa Dalloway, *Mrs. Dalloway* (also known as *Virginia Woolf's Mrs. Dalloway*), First Look Pictures, 1997.
Megan Doherty, *The Devil's Own,* Columbia Pictures, 1997.
Deirdre, *Ronin,* United Artists, 1998.
Lauren Garland/Sylvia, *The Truman Show,* Paramount, 1998.
Love's Labour Lost, 1999.

Television Appearances; Series:
Cast, *Absolutely Fabulous,* Comedy Central, 1993-1996.

Television Appearances; Specials:
Angie, *Cold Lazarus,* Bravo, 1996.
Angie, *Karaoke,* Bravo, 1996.

RECORDINGS

Taped Readings:
Picasso - Creator and Destroyer, by Arianna Huffington, Ten Speed Press Audio, 1996.*

MCGLONE, Mike 1972(?)-

PERSONAL

Born in 1972 (some sources say 1973); raised in Fairfield, CT. *Education:* Attended New York University's Tisch School of the Arts.

Addresses: *Agent*—Innovative Artists Talent, 1999 Avenue of the Stars, Los Angeles, CA, 90067-6011.

Career: Actor.

CREDITS

Film Appearances:
Patrick McMullen, *The Brothers McMullen,* Fox Searchlight, 1995.
Oliver Barnett, *Ed,* Universal, 1996.
Francis Fitzpatrick, *She's the One,* Twentieth Century-Fox, 1996.
Rickie La Cassa, *One Tough Cop,* Stratosphere Entertainment, 1998.

OTHER SOURCES

Periodicals:
Movieline, August, 1996, p. 12.*

MCGRATH, Douglas

PERSONAL

Married Jane Martin. *Education:* Graduated from Princeton University, 1980.

Addresses: *Agent*—ICM, 3921 Wilshire Blvd., Suite 303, Los Angeles, CA 90010-3324.

Career: Writer and director.

Awards, Honors: Academy Award nomination, best screenplay, for *Bullets Over Broadway,* 1994.

CREDITS

Film Appearances:
Snodgrass, *Quiz Show,* Buena Vista, 1994.
Chap - Louis' Boss, *The Daytrippers,* Columbia/TriStar, 1996.
Tom, *Happiness,* Good Machine, 1998.
Bill Gaines, *Celebrity,* 1998.

Film Work:
Writer, *Born Yesterday,* Buena Vista, 1993.
Writer and director, *Emma,* Miramax, 1996.

Television Appearances; Series:
Plainclothesman, *Helter Skelter,* CBS, 1976.

Television Work; Series:
Writer, *L.A. Law,* NBC, 1989-90.
Writer, *Saturday Night Live,* NBC, 1975-99.

Television Work; Specials:
Writer, *The Stephen Banks Show,* Showtime, 1991.

WRITINGS

Screenplays:
Emma (adapted from Jane Austen's book of the same title), Miramax, 1996.
(With Woody Allen) *Bullets Over Broadway,* Miramax, 1994.
Born Yesterday, Buena Vista, 1993.

OTHER SOURCES

Periodicals:
New York Times, August 25, 1996, pp. H-11, H-16.*

MCKINNEY, Mark 1963-

PERSONAL

Born in 1963, in Ottawa, Ontario, Canada; married Marina Gharabegian, September, 1995; children: Christopher Thomas Russell. *Education:* Attended Memorial University in Newfoundland.

Career: Comedy writer and actor.

Awards, Honors: Gemini Award, best writing in a comedy or variety program or series, 1989, and Emmy Award nomination, outstanding individual achievement in writing for a variety or music program, 1995, both for *The Kids in the Hall;* Gemini Award, best writing in a comedy or variety program or series, 1990, for *The Kids in the Hall: Show No. 1.*

CREDITS

Film Appearances:
Father Williams, *A Night at the Roxbury,* Paramount, 1998.
Graydon, *Spice World,* Sony Pictures, 1998.

Television Appearances; Series:
Various characters, *Kids in the Hall: Brain Candy,* CBC, 1989-94, CBS, 1992-95.
Cast, *Saturday Night Live,* NBC, 1994-97.
Mr. Why, *Yo-Yo Ma: Inspired by Bach,* PBS, 1997-98.

Television Work; Series:
Writer, *The Kids in the Hall,* CBC, 1989-94.
Writer, *Saturday Night Live,* NBC, 1994-97.*

McMURRAY, Sam

PERSONAL

Born April 15, in New York, NY; son of Richard (an actor) and Jane (an actress; maiden name, Hoffman) McMurray; married Elizabeth Collins (an actress); children: two daughters. *Education:* Studied English literature and acting at Washington University, St. Louis, MO.

Addresses: *Agent*—Bresler, Kelly, and Associates, 11500 West Olympic Blvd., Suite 510, Los Angeles, CA 90064.

Career: Actor and producer. O'Neill Playwrights Conference, New London, CT, member for seven years.

Awards, Honors: Two Drama-Logue Awards.

CREDITS

Film Appearances:
(Film debut) Young man at party, *The Front,* Columbia, 1976.
Young vagrant, *Union City,* Kinesis, 1980.
Mr. McManus, *Baby, It's You,* Paramount, 1983.
Crespi, *C.H.U.D.,* New World, 1984.
Clem Friedkin, *Fast Forward,* Columbia, 1985.
Glen, *Raising Arizona,* Twentieth Century-Fox, 1987.
Peter Harriman, *Ray's Male Heterosexual Dance Hall* (short), Discovery Program/Chanticleer, 1988.
Bateman, *The Wizard,* Universal, 1989.
Bill, *National Lampoon's Christmas Vacation,* Warner Bros., 1989.
Kreimach, *Little Vegas,* IRS Releasing, 1990.
Lance, *Stone Cold,* Columbia, 1991.
Morris Frost, *L.A. Story,* TriStar, 1991.
Skip Wankman, *Class Act,* Warner Bros., 1992.
Don Buckman, *Addams Family Values,* Paramount, 1993.
Alex, *Getting Even with Dad,* Metro-Goldwyn-Mayer/United Artists, 1994.

Federal prosecutor, *Dear God,* Paramount, 1996.
Edgar Wallace, *Savage,* Conquistador Entertainment, 1997.
Boccoli, *Slappy and the Stinkers,* TriStar, 1998.
Tricky, *The Mod Squad,* Metro-Goldwyn-Mayer/ United Artists, 1999.
Goon Bob, *Baby Geniuses,* Sony Pictures Entertainment, 1999.
Lester Leeman, *Drop Dead Gorgeous,* New Line Cinema, 1999.
Jerry Brock, *Carlo's Wake,* 1999.

Film Work:
Co-producer, *Slappy and the Stinkers,* TriStar, 1998.

Television Appearances; Series:
Wes Leonard, *Ryan's Hope,* ABC, 1975.
Officer Harvey Schoendorf, *Baker's Dozen,* CBS, 1982.
Regular, *The Tracey Ullman Show,* Fox, 1987-90.
Voice of Roy Hess, *Dinosaurs,* ABC, 1991-93.
Roger Dumphy, *Stand by Your Man,* Fox, 1992.
Detective Marshak, *Likely Suspects,* Fox, 1992.
Coach Jimmy Dugan, *A League of Their Own,* CBS, 1993.
Dr. Douglas McGill, *Medicine Ball,* Fox, 1995.
Charlie Sweet, *Matt Waters,* CBS, 1995-96.

Television Appearances; Movies:
The trendy liberal, *Mom's On Strike,* 1984.
Morrison, *Out of the Darkness,* CBS, 1985.
Police lieutenant, *Adam: His Song Continues,* NBC, 1986.
David Thomas, *Take My Daughters, Please* (also known as *All My Darling Daughters*), NBC, 1988.
Dick Langley, "He Never Game Me Orgasm," in *National Lampoon's Attack of the 5 Ft. 2 In. Woman,* Showtime, 1994.
Herman Munster, *The Munsters' Scary Little Christmas,* Fox, 1996.
Soccer Dog: The Movie, HBO, 1999.

Television Appearances; Miniseries:
Pearson, *Hands of a Stranger,* CBS, 1987.

Television Appearances; Episodic:
Ned, "The Devil's Work," *Ourstory,* PBS, 1976.
Gann, "More Skinned Against than Skinning," *Hill Street Blues,* NBC, 1986.
Stu Angry, *You Again?,* NBC, 1986.
Michael Saxon, *O'Hara,* ABC, 1987.
Mike, *Dear John,* NBC, 1988.
Lieutenant Tony Brandt, "Raising Marijuana," *21 Jump Street,* Fox, 1988.
Coach Finelli, *Head of the Class,* ABC, 1988.
Brent, *Empty Nest,* NBC, 1988.
Mark Howard Haper, "Heather Can Wait," *Who's the Boss?,* NBC, 1989.
Bart Hess, "The Model," *Matlock,* NBC, 1989.
Dear John, NBC, 1989.
Mr. Kane, "Cheaters," *The Golden Girls,* NBC, 1990.
Voice of Gulliver Dark, "Homer's Night Out," *The Simpsons* (animated), Fox, 1990.
Andy, "Dance Show," *Married ... With Children,* Fox, 1990.
Rondall Kittleman, "Satellite on a Hot Tim's Roof," *Home Improvement,* ABC, 1991.
Mr. Rips, "Goodbye Mr. Rips," *Parker Lewis Can't Lose,* Fox, 1992.
Detective Dorn, "Camp Counselor: Part 2," *Deadly Games,* UPN, 1995.
Thomas, "Change Partners ... and Dance," *Party of Five,* Fox, 1995.
Detective Dorn, "Car Mechanic," *Deadly Games,* UPN, 1995.
Voice of Shawn, *Steven Spielberg Presents Pinky and the Brain* (animated), The WB, 1995.
Dr. David Stockton, *Chicago Hope,* CBS, 1996.
Freddy Rizzo, *Pearl,* CBS, 1996.
Dennis Lundy, *Wings,* NBC, 1996.
Ken, *Cosby,* CBS, 1997.
Bob Ware, *Diagnosis: Murder,* CBS, 1997.
Voice of Ernie, "Joker's Millions," *Batman: Gotham Knights* (animated), 1997.
Marco, "To Catch a Thief," *Living Single,* 1997.
Oliver Marley, *Soul Man,* ABC, 1997.
Lieutenant Griswalk, "The New Kid," *Recess* (animated), 1997.
Morris Clancy, "Prison Story," *The Pretender,* NBC, 1997.
Dr. David Stockton, "Take My Wife, Please," *Chicago Hope,* CBS, 1997.
Dr. David Stockton, "Missed Conception (1)," *Chicago Hope,* CBS, 1997.
Chandler's boss Doug, "The One with the Ultimate Fighting Champion," *Friends,* NBC, 1997.
Voice of Lieutenant Griswald, "Gus' Last Stand," *Recess* (animated), 1998.
Voice of Harry Tully, "Rebirth: Part 1," *Batman Beyond* (animated), The WB, 1999.
Voice of Chelsea's Dad, "Spellbound," *Batman Beyond* (animated), The WB, 1999.
Doug, "The One with Chandler's Work Laugh," *Friends,* NBC, 1999.

Also appeared as voice of Wesayso interviewer, *Dinosaurs;* voice of Buddy Glimmer, *Dinosaurs;* voice of Andre, *Dinosaurs;* voice of Dolf, *Dinosaurs;* voice of John, *Dinosaurs;* voice of video teacher, *Steven Spielberg Presents Pinky and the Brain* (animated), The WB; Detective Dorn, "Camp Counselor, Part I," *Deadly Games;* in *Moonlighting,* ABC; *Miami Vice,* NBC; *Easy Street,* CBS; and *Kojak,* CBS.

Television Appearances; Pilots:
Not Necessarily the News, HBO, 1982.
Frank McGee, *Hope Division,* ABC, 1987.
Glen Mattson, *Teenage Confidential,* ABC, 1996.

Also appeared in *Dads,* ABC.

Television Appearances; Specials:
Tracey Ullman Backstage, 1988.

Stage Appearances:
(Off-Broadway debut) Lonnie, *The Taking of Miss Janie,* New York Shakespeare Festival, Mitzi E. Newhouse Theatre, New York City, 1975.
Otis Fitzhugh, *Ballymurphy,* Manhattan Theatre Club, New York City, 1976.
Bobby Wheeler, *Clarence,* Roundabout Theatre, New York City, 1976.
Doalty, *Translations,* Manhattan Theatre Club, 1981.
The Great Magoo, Hartford Stage Company, Hartford, CT, 1982.
Mick Connor, *Comedians,* Manhattan Punch Line Theatre, New York City, 1983.
Man Overboard, Sargent Theatre, New York City, 1983.
Benjamin "Kid Purple" Schwartz, *Kid Purple,* Manhattan Punch Line Theatre, 1984.
Homesteaders, Long Wharf Theatre, New Haven, CT, 1984.
Phil, "Desperadoes," in *Marathon '85,* Ensemble Studio Theatre, New York City, 1985.
Mike Connor, *The Philadelphia Story,* Hartman Theatre, Stamford, CT, 1985.
Union Boys, Yale Repertory Theatre, New Haven, CT, 1985.
L.A. Freewheeling, Hartley House Theatre, New York City, 1986.
Savage in Limbo, O'Neill Theatre Center, New London, CT, 1987, then Cast Theatre, Los Angeles.

Also appeared as Phil, *The Dumping Ground,* Ensemble Studio Theatre; and in *Welfare, The Store,* and *Lucky Star,* all Ensemble Studio Theatre; also appeared in New York City productions of *A Soldier's Play, The Merry Wives of Windsor,* and *The Connection.**

MEANEY, Colm 1953-

PERSONAL

Born May 30, 1953, in Dublin, Ireland; married Baibre (divorced); children: one daughter. *Education:* Studied acting at the Abbey Theatre School of Acting.

Addresses: *Agent*—The Gage Group, 9229 Sunset Blvd., Suite 515, Los Angeles, CA 90069.

Career: Actor.

Awards, Honors: *Drama-Logue* Award, 1986, for *Diary of a Hunger Strike;* Golden Globe Award nomination, best actor in a musical or comedy, 1994, for *The Snapper.*

CREDITS

Film Appearances:
Mr. Bergin, *The Dead,* Vestron/Zenith, 1987.
Omega Syndrome (also known as *Omega Seven*), New World, 1987.
A cop at Tess', *Dick Tracy,* Buena Vista, 1990.
A pilot (Windsor plane), *Die Hard 2: Die Harder,* Twentieth Century-Fox, 1990.
Gerry McGurn, *Come See the Paradise,* Twentieth Century-Fox, 1990.
Mr. Rabbitte, *The Commitments,* Twentieth Century-Fox, 1991.
Major Ambrose, *The Last of the Mohicans,* Twentieth Century-Fox, 1992.
Kelly, *Far and Away,* Universal, 1992.
Daumer, *Under Siege,* Warner Bros., 1992.
Barreller, *Into the West,* Miramax, 1992.
Dessie, *The Snapper,* Miramax, 1993.
Dr. Lionel Badger, *The Road to Wellville,* Columbia, 1994.
Geronimo's dad, *The War of the Buttons* (also known as *Ca Guerre des boutons* and *La recommence*), Warner Bros., 1994.
Morgan the Goat, *The Englishman Who Went up a Hill But Came down a Mountain,* Miramax, 1995.
Ripple (short), 1995.
Larry, *The Van,* Fox Searchlight, 1996.
Owd Bob, 1997.
Duncan Malloy, *Con Air,* Buena Vista, 1997.
Jim Davern, *The Last of the High Kings* (also known as *Summer Fling*), Miramax, 1998.
Seamus Kearney-owner of the bed and breakfast (present day), *This Is My Father,* Sony Pictures Classics, 1998.

Chief Miles O'Brien, *Star Trek: IMAX,* 1998.
Jackie O'Hara, *Snitch,* Lions Gate Films, 1998.
Patron, *October 22,* 1998.
Roland Cain, *Claire Dolan,* Serene Films, 1998.
Fury, *Four Days,* 1999.
Frank Lazarus, *Chapters Zero,* Dilonra Films, 1999.
Mystery, Alaska, Buena Vista, 1999.

Television Appearances; Series:
Patrick London (#1), *One Life to Live,* ABC, 1986-87.
Engineer Miles O'Brien, *Star Trek: The Next Generation,* syndicated, 1987-93.
Chief Operations Officer Miles O'Brien, *Star Trek: Deep Space Nine,* syndicated, 1993-99.

Television Appearances; Movies:
Chief Miles O'Brien, *Star Trek: The Next Generation-Encounter at Farpoint,* 1987.
Meagher, *Perfect Witness,* HBO, 1989.
Chief Miles O'Brien, *Star Trek: Deep Space Nine-Emissary,* 1993.
Al Sheehan, *VIG,* Cinemax, 1998.
Seamus Muldoon, *Leprechauns,* NBC, 1999.

Also appeared in *The Hidden Curriculum,* BBC; *Strangers,* Granada; and *Nailed,* Granada.

Television Appearances; Miniseries:
Tinker, *Kenny Rogers as The Gambler, Part III-The Legend Continues,* 1987.
Father Colum O'Hara, *Scarlett,* CBS, 1994.

Television Appearances; Episodic:
Smollett, "Charlie's Brother's Birthday," *Strangers,* 1982.
Kevin Murphy, "Easter 2016," *Play for Tomorrow,* 1982.
"Steel Hanging in There: Part 2," *Remington Steele,* NBC, 1986.
"Atomic Shakespeare," *Moonlighting,* ABC, 1986.
Battle Bridge Conn, "Encounter at Farpoint," *Star Trek: The Next Generation,* syndicated, 1987.
"Lonely Among Us," *Star Trek: The Next Generation,* syndicated, 1987.
"Good Knight MacGyver: Part 1," *MacGyver,* ABC, 1991.
Mr. Cramer, *Brooklyn Bridge,* CBS, 1992.
Mickey Ford, *Jack's Place,* ABC, 1992.
Falcon, "Our Man Bashir," *Star Trek: Deep Space Nine,* syndicated, 1995.
Voice of Mr. Dugahn, "The Hound of Ulster," *Gargoyles,* 1996.
Albert, "Far Beyond the Stars," *Star Trek: Deep Space Nine,* syndicated, 1998.

Also appeared in "Beetles," *Tales from the Darkside,* syndicated; *Father Dowling Mysteries,* NBC/ABC; and *Adam 12,* NBC.

Television Appearances; Pilots:
Jake Slicker, *Dr. Quinn, Medicine Woman,* CBS, 1993.

Television Appearances; Specials:
The Science of Star Trek, 1995.

Stage Appearances:
Derek and Vince, *Fish in the Sea,* Half Moon Theatre, London, 1975.
Yobbo Nowt, 7:84 Theatre Company, Shaw Theatre, London, 1975.
Lin Piao, *History of the Tenth Struggle,* Scarab Theatre, ICA Theatre, London, 1976.
Kevin, *The Poker Session,* Theatre-Off-Park, New York City, 1984.
Patrick O'Connor, *Diary of a Hunger Strike,* Los Angeles Theatre Center, Los Angeles, 1985.
Mick Ross, *Breaking the Code,* Kennedy Center for the Performing Arts, Washington, DC, 1987, then Neil Simon Theatre, New York City, 1987-88.

Appeared in stage debut at Abbey Theatre, Dublin, Ireland. Also appeared with the Great Lakes Shakespeare Festival, Cleveland, OH, 1982-83; appeared in *Alpha,* Los Angeles Theatre Center; and *The Birthday Party,* Los Angeles Theatre Center.*

MEYER, Breckin 1974-

PERSONAL

Born May 7, 1974, in Minneapolis, MN.

Addresses: *Agent*—Gersh Agency, Inc., 232 North Canon Drive, Beverly Hills, CA, 90210-5302.

Career: Actor.

CREDITS

Film Appearances:
Spencer, *Freddy's Dead: The Final Nightmare,* New Line Cinema, 1991.
Boy, *Payback,* 1994.
Travis, *Clueless,* Paramount, 1995.
Surfer, *John Carpenter's Escape from L.A.,* Paramount, 1996.
Mitt, *The Craft,* Columbia, 1996.
Pat Tyson, *Prefontaine,* Buena Vista, 1997.

Greg Czarnicki, *Touch,* Metro-Goldwyn-Mayer, 1997.
Greg Randazzo, *54* (also known as *Studio 54*), Miramax, 1998.
Keller Coleman, *Dancer, Texas,* Sony, 1998.
Lead singer in the band, *Can't Hardly Wait,* 1998.
Tail Lights Fade, 1999.
Tiny, *Go,* TriStar, 1999.

Television Appearances; Movies:
Cast, *Camp Cucamonga,* NBC, 1990.
Eric Nelson, *Betrayed: A Story of Three Women,* ABC, 1995.

Television Appearances; Series:
L.A. Law, NBC, 1989-90.
Thomas, *Drexell's Class,* Fox, 1991-92.
Chas Walker, *The Jackie Thomas Show,* ABC, 1992-93.
Mike Solomon, *The Home Court,* NBC, 1995-96.
Harrison, *Clueless,* UPN, 1996-97.
Alec, *Party of Five,* Fox, 1996-97.

Television Appearances; Specials:
Nick, *Where's Rodney?,* NBC.
Eddie Sturio, *Crosses on the Lawn,* CBS, 1993.
Cast, *Tom Arnold: The Naked Truth 3,* HBO, 1993.*

MINTER, Kristin 1967(?)-

PERSONAL

Born c. 1967, in Miami, FL; daughter of Charlie (a financial executive) and Dottie (a horse trainer).

Addresses: *Agent*—Innovative Artists Talent, 1999 Avenue of the Stars, Los Angeles, CA, 90067-6002.

Career: Actress.

CREDITS

Film Appearances:
Heather, *Home Alone,* 1990.
Kathy, *Cool As Ice,* Universal, 1991.
Cousin Karen, *Passed Away,* 1992.
Tracy, *There Goes My Baby,* Orion, 1994.
Cheryl, *Lover's Knot,* Astra Cinema, 1995.
Marie Belot, *Savage,* Sogepaq, 1995.
Stella, *Tyrone,* 1999.

Television Appearances; Movies:
Valerie Thayer, *Danielle Steele's Family Album,* NBC, 1994.
Lisa Cates, *Flashfire,* HBO, 1994.
Rita, *Dad, the Angel, and Me,* The Family Channel, 1995.

Television Appearances; Episodic:
Rachel MacLeod, "Homeland," *Highlander,* 1995.
Rachel MacLeod, "Promises," *Highlander,* 1996.
Rachel MacLeod, "Deliverance," *Highlander,* 1996.
Emma, "Black Widow," *Kung Fu: The Legend Continues,* 1996.

Television Appearances; Series:
Rebecca, *Moon Over Miami,* ABC, 1993-94.
Christine, *Pig Sty,* UPN, 1994-95.
Sue Hambleton ("Fly Paper"), *Fallen Angels,* Showtime, 1995-96.
Randi, *ER,* NBC, 1995-99.
Gianna, *Nash Bridges,* NBC, 1996-97.
Jenny Nowack, *Brimstone,* Fox, 1998-99.*

MOORE, Brian 1921-1999

PERSONAL

Born August 25, 1921, in Belfast, Northern Ireland; died of pulmonary fibrosis, January 11, 1999, in Malibu, CA; immigrated to Canada, 1948; son of James Brian (a surgeon) and Eileen (McFadden) Moore; married Jacqueline Scully, 1951, (divorced); married Jean Denney, October, 1967; children: (first marriage) Michael. *Education:* Graduated from St. Malachy's College, 1939. *Religion:* Reared in a strict Catholic environment, Moore became agnostic, although his writings frequently involve Catholicism and moral dilemmas.

Career: Writer. *Military service:* Served with British Ministry of War Transport in North Africa, Italy, and France during World War II.

Member: Royal Society of Literature, fellow.

Awards, Honors: Author's Club First Novel Award, 1956; Quebec Literary Prize, 1958; Guggenheim Fellowship, 1959; Governor General's Award for Fiction, 1960, for *The Luck of Ginger Coffey;* U.S. National Institute of Arts and Letters fiction grant, 1961; Canada Council Fellowship for Travel in Europe, 1962 and 1976; W.H. Smith Prize, 1972, for *Catholics;* Governor General's Award for Fiction and James Tait Black Memorial Award, both 1975, for *The Great*

Victorian Collection; Booker shortlist for *The Doctor's Wife,* 1976; Neill Gunn International Fellowship, Scottish Arts Council, 1983; "ten best books of 1983" citation, *Newsweek* magazine, 1983, for *Cold Heaven;* Heinemann Award, Royal Society of Literature, 1986, and Australian Film Institute Award nomination, best screenplay, original or adapted, 1992, both for *Black Robe;* Booker Prize shortlist citation, 1987, and Sunday Express Book of the Year Prize, 1988, both for *The Color of Blood;* Honorary Literature Degree, Queens University, Belfast, Ireland, 1989; Booker shortlist for *Lies of Silence,* 1990; Honorary Literature Degree, National University of Ireland, Dublin, Ireland, 1991; Lifetime Achievement Award, *Los Angeles Times,* 1994.

RECORDINGS

Taped Readings:
The Lonely Passion of Judith Hearne, Lies of Silence, and *The Color of Blood* have been recorded on audiocassette.

WRITINGS

Screenplays:
The Luck of Ginger Coffey (based on his novel of the same title), Continental, 1964.
Torn Curtain, Universal, 1966.
The Slave (based on his novel *An Answer from Limbo*), 1967.
The Blood of Others, 1984.
Brainwash, 1985.
Black Robe (based on his novel of the same title), Alliance Communications, 1987.
Gabrielle Chanel, 1988.

Novels:
Judith Hearne, A. Deutsch, 1955, published as *The Lonely Passion of Judith Hearne,* Little, Brown, 1956.
The Feast of Lupercal, Little, Brown, 1957.
The Luck of Ginger Coffy, Little, Brown, 1960.
An Answer from Limbo, Little, Brown, 1962.
The Emperor of Ice-Cream, Viking, 1965.
I Am Mary Dunne, Viking, 1968.
Fergus, Holt, 1970.
The Revolution Script, Holt, 1971.
Catholics, J. Cape, 1972, Harcourt, 1973.
The Great Victorian Collection, Farrar, Straus, 1975.
The Doctor's Wife, Farrar, Straus, 1976.
The Mangan Inheritance, Farrar, Straus, 1979.
Two Stories, Santa Susana Press, 1979.
The Temptation of Eileen Hughes, Farrar, Straus, 1981.
Cold Heaven, Holt, 1983.
Black Robe, Dutton, 1985.
The Color of Blood, Dutton, 1987.
Lies of Silence, Doubleday, 1990.
No Other Life, Doubleday, 1993.
The Statement, Dutton, 1996.
The Magician's Wife, Dutton, 1998.

Also contributed articles and short stories to *Spectator, Holiday, Atlantic,* and other periodicals.

Adaptations: Moore's novel, *Cold Heaven,* was broadcast as a television movie, 1981; *Temptation of Eileen Hughes* was broadcast as a television movie, BBC, 1988; and the novel, *The Lonely Passion of Judith Hearne* was shown as a feature film, Island Pictures, 1998.*

MORRIS, Greg 1933-1996

PERSONAL

Born September 27, 1933, in Cleveland, OH; died of cancer (some reports say natural causes), August 27, 1996, in Las Vegas, NV; father, a trumpet player, and mother's name, Iona; married Lee Keys, 1957; children: Iona (an actress), Phil (an actor), and Linda (a film production executive). *Education:* Attended Ohio State University and the University of Iowa.

Career: Actor. *Military service:* Served in U.S. Army, 1952-1955.

Awards, Honors: Fashion, Television, and Costume Designers Guild, most promising newcomer, 1968-69; Los Angeles Father of the Year, 1969; honorary degree, Miles College, 1969; Emmy Award nominations, best supporting actor—drama, *Mission Impossible,* 1969, 1970, and 1972; Image Award, National Association for the Advancement of Colored People (NAACP), 1971; Star of the Year, Hollywood Women's Press Club, 1971; Television Father of the Year, National Father's Day Committee, 1971; VIVA citation, 1971; Ethics Award, Sisterhood Temple Emanuel, 1971; Unity Award, 1973.

CREDITS

Film Appearances:
Policeman, *The Lively Set,* Universal, 1964.
Clark, *The New Interns,* Columbia, 1964.
Yusef, *The Sword of Ali Baba,* Universal, 1965.

Barney Collier, *Mission Impossible Versus the Mob* (also known as *Mission: Impossible vs. the Mob*), Paramount, 1968.
Richard Hill, *S.T.A.B.*, 1976.
Red Salter, *Countdown at Kusini*, 1976.
Monsieur Laurent, *Tropical Gamble* (also known as *Jogo Tropical*), Yorkshire, 1990.

Television Appearances; Movies:
The Doomsday Flight, 1966.
Captain George Benson, *Killer by Night*, CBS, 1972.
Dr. Jeff Evans, *Flight to Holocaust*, NBC, 1977.
George Nelson, *Vega$*, ABC, 1978.
Brian Haley, *Crisis in Mid-Air*, CBS, 1979.
Mel Walker, *The Jesse Owens Story*, syndicated, 1984.
Private Jacob Dorn, *The Firing Squad* (also known as *Le Peloton d'execution*), CTV Television Network, 1991.

Television Appearances; Miniseries:
Beeman Jones, *Roots: The Next Generations*, ABC, 1979.

Television Appearances; Series:
Barney Collier, *Mission: Impossible*, CBS, 1966-73.
Narrator, *Go*, NBC, 1973.
Larry Clemens (Dwayne's father), *What's Happening!*, ABC, 1976-79, syndicated, 1985-88.
Lieutenant Dave Nelson, *Vega$*, ABC, 1979-81.
Lieutenant Cal Andrews, *Murder, She Wrote*, CBS, 1984-85.
Barney Collier (recurring), *Mission Impossible* (remake of the 1966-73 series), ABC, 1988-89.

Television Appearances; Episodic:
Dr. Felix Martin, "Allie," *Ben Casey*, ABC, 1963.
Mr. Peters, "That's My Boy," *The Dick Van Dyke Show*, CBS, 1963.
Lieutenant, "The 7th Is Made up of Phantoms," *The Twilight Zone*, CBS, 1963.
Branded, CBS, 1965.
Frank Mandalay, "Bupkis," *The Dick Van Dyke Show*, CBS, 1965.
Mickey Deming, "Wings of an Angel," *The Fugitive*, ABC, 1965.
"Lori," *I Spy*, NBC, 1966.
Injured pilot, *The Six Million Dollar Man*, ABC, 1974.
Eddie Griffin, "Merchants of Death," *The Streets of San Francisco*, ABC, 1975.
Cliff Collier, "A Night to Raise the Dead," *Quincy, M.E.*, NBC, 1978.
Lieutenant Dave Reemer, "Exercise in Murder," *T.J. Hooker*, ABC, 1984.
General Masters, "The Second Seal," *War of the Worlds*, syndicated, 1988.
Hacker, "Killer Instinct," *TekWar*, 1995.

Television Appearances; Specials:
Cast, *Mitzi and a Hundred Guys*, CBS, 1975.
Cast, *Swing Out, Sweet Land*, NBC, 1976.
Ben Price, *Valentine's Second Chance*, ABC, 1977.

OTHER SOURCES

Periodicals:
Newsweek, September 9, 1996, p. 81.
People Weekly, September 9, 1996, p. 106.*

MULL, Martin 1943-

PERSONAL

Born August 18, 1943, in Chicago, IL; married Kristin Johnson (an artist), 1972 (divorced, 1978); married Sandra Baker, 1978 (marriage ended); married Wendy (a musician and composer for film and television); children: (third marriage) Maggie Rose. *Education:* Rhode Island School of Design, B.F.A., 1965, M.F.A., (painting), 1967.

Addresses: *Agent*—Agency for the Performing Arts, 9000 Sunset Blvd., Suite 315, Los Angeles, CA 90069.

Career: Actor, comedian, singer, producer, and screenwriter. Songwriter for Warner Bros. Artist; has exhibited his paintings at galleries, such as the Boston Museum of Fine Art, the Cincinnati Institute of Contemporary Art, the Boston Institute of Contemporary Art, Gallery Henoch (New York City), Molly Barnes Gallery (Los Angeles), the Los Angeles Institute of Contemporary Art, Red Piano Gallery (Hilton Head, SC), and the Greenville County Museum of Art (South Carolina). Instructor in painting at the Rhode Island School of Design.

Awards, Honors: Grammy Award nomination, best comedy recording, 1978, for *Sex and Violins;* Grammy Award nomination, best comedy recording, c. 1979, for *Near Perfect, Perfect;* Writers Guild Award and CableACE Award, both 1986, AFI Billboard Award and CableACE Award nomination, both 1987, all for *The History of White People in America;* One Club Award, consistent excellence in the area of television commercials, 1987.

CREDITS

Film Appearances:

Eric Swan, *FM* (also known as *Citzens' Band*), Universal, 1978.

Mr. Peache, *My Bodyguard,* Twentieth Century-Fox, 1980.

Harvey, *Serial,* Paramount, 1980.

Dick Ebersol, *Take This Job and Shove It,* Avco Embassy, 1981.

Ron Richardson, *Mr. Mom* (also known as *Mr. Mum*), 1983.

(Uncredited) Drug store clerk, *Private School* (also known as *Private School for Girls*), 1983.

Warren Fitzpatrick, *Growing Pains* (also known as *Bad Manners*), 1984.

Colonel Mustard, *Clue,* Paramount, 1985.

Tony Dugdale, *The Boss' Wife,* TriStar, 1986.

Big City Comedy, 1986.

Arthur/Tang, *Flicks* (also known as *Hollyweird* and *Loose Joints*), United, 1987.

Carson Boundy, *Home Is Where the Hart Is,* Atlantic, 1987.

Pat Coletti, *O.C. and Stiggs,* Metro-Goldwyn-Mayer/United Artists, 1987.

Host, *The History of White People in America: Volume II,* 1987.

Archie Powell, *Rented Lips,* Cineworld, 1988.

William Carson III, *Cutting Class,* Gower Street, 1989.

Psychiatrist, *Far Out Man* (also known as *Soul Man II*), CineTel, 1990.

Maris, *Ski Patrol,* Triumph Releasing, 1990.

Dr. Bruckner, *Think Big,* 1990.

Ted's attorney, *Ted and Venus,* Double Helix, 1991.

Art, *Dance with Death,* HBO Video, 1992.

Donald Burbank, *Miracle Beach,* Columbia TriStar, 1992.

Himself, *The Player,* Fine Line, 1992.

Justin Gregory, *Mrs. Doubtfire,* Twentieth Century-Fox, 1993.

Norman Roberts, *The Day My Parents Ran Away* (also known as *Missing Parents*), New Line Cinema, 1994.

Dan, *Mr. Write,* Shapiro Glickenhaus, 1994.

DJ, *Jingle All the Way,* Twentieth Century-Fox, 1996.

Mr. Rich, *Richie Rich's Christmas Wish* (also known as *Richie Rich: A Christmas Story*), Warner Bros. Home Video, 1998.

Zack and Reba, 1998.

Also appeared in *Love in Venice.*

Film Work:

Executive producer, *Rented Lips,* Cineworld, 1988.

Television Appearances; Series:

Garth and Barth Gimble (twins), *Mary Hartman, Mary Hartman,* syndicated, 1976-77.

Barth Gimble, *Fernwood 2-Night,* syndicated, 1977.

Barth Gimble, *America 2-Night,* syndicated, 1978.

Martin Crane, *Domestic Life,* CBS, 1984.

The History of White People in America, Cinemax, 1986-87.

Doug Lambert, *His and Hers,* CBS, 1990.

Doug Talbot, *The Jackie Thomas Show,* ABC, 1992.

Leon, *Roseanne,* ABC, 1991-97.

Voice of Skip Binford, *Family Dog* (animated), CBS, 1993.

Vice Principal Kraft, *Sabrina, The Teenaged Witch,* ABC, 1997—.

Television Appearances; Movies:

Kingston: The Power Play, NBC, 1976.

Mel Shaver, *Sunset Limousine,* CBS, 1983.

Elliot, *California Girls,* ABC, 1985.

Frank Maris, *Lots of Luck,* The Disney Channel, 1985.

Martin Mull in "Portrait of a White Marriage," Cinemax, 1988.

Norman Roberts, *The Day My Parents Ran Away,* 1993.

Bart, *How the West Was Fun,* ABC, 1994.

Johnnie Sparkle, *Edie & Pen,* HBO, 1996.

Doug Robinson, *Beverly Hills Family Robinson,* ABC, 1997.

Also appeared in *Here Comes Summer,* HBO.

Television Appearances; Episodic:

Hamlin Rule, "The Pied Piper," *Wonder Woman,* ABC, 1977.

Roger Chapman, "Hollywood Calling," *Taxi,* ABC, 1979.

Guest host, *Evening at the Improv,* syndicated, 1981.

Don Vermillion, "It's Academical," *Square Pegs,* CBS, 1983.

Himself, "The Smiths," *George Burns Comedy Week,* CBS, 1985.

Governor Peasley, "Pecos Bill, King of the Cowboys," *Shelley Duvall's Tall Tales and Legends,* Showtime, 1986.

"What Is Life?," *Fast Times,* CBS, 1986.

D.C. Follies, syndicated, 1988.

Smothers Brothers Comedy Hour, CBS, 1988.

Jimmy, "Snap Out of It," *The Golden Girls,* NBC, 1990.

Therapist, "Futile Attraction," *Dream On,* HBO, 1991.

Himself, "Party," *The Larry Sanders Show,* HBO, 1992.

Himself, "The Grand Opening," *The Larry Sanders Show,* HBO, 1993.

Foreign correspondent, *L.A. Law,* NBC, 1993.
"Who Killed Good Time Charlie?," *Burke's Law,* CBS, 1994.
Thurston Howell III, *Roseanne,* ABC, 1994.
Storytime, PBS, 1994.
Marlin Pfinch-Lupus, "Whine, Whine, Whine," *Lois & Clark: The New Adventures of Superman,* ABC, 1995.
Narrator, "Busby Berkeley," "Memo to Joe Breen," "Hollis Alpert," "Hugh Hefner," and "Lou Perry," *Sex and the Silver Screen,* Showtime, 1996.
(Uncredited) Himself, "Drewstock," *The Drew Carey Show,* ABC, 1997.
In the Prime, PBS, 1997.
Dr. Sharpstein, *Life ... and Stuff,* CBS, 1997.
Himself, *The Nanny,* CBS, 1998.
Voice of Paul Prickly, "The Challenge," *Recess,* 1998.
Voice of Seth, "D'oh-in' in the Wind," *The Simpsons* (animated), Fox, 1998.
Hollywood Squares, CBS, 1998.
Himself, "Connor Family Reunion," *The Roseanne Show,* ABC, 1998.

Also appeared as guest host, *The Tonight Show,* NBC; also appeared on episodes of *Soundstage,* PBS and *Family,* ABC.

Television Appearances; Pilots:
The TV Show, ABC, 1979.
Guest, *Twilight Theatre II,* NBC, 1982.
Guest, *Prime Times,* NBC, 1983.
Guest/Gambler, *The Jerk, Too,* NBC, 1984.
Panelist, *Wanna Bet?,* CBS, 1993.

Television Appearances; Specials:
The Chevy Chase National Humor Test, NBC, 1979.
The Johnny Cash Spring Special, CBS, 1979.
Magic with the Stars, NBC, 1982.
Grandpa, Will You Run with Me?, 1983.
The Funniest Joke I Ever Heard, ABC, 1984.
Michael Nesmith in Television Parts, NBC, 1985.
The History of White People in America (also known as *The History of White People in America: Volume 1*), 1985.
Host, *Clue: Movies, Murder and Mystery,* CBS, 1986.
Comic Relief, HBO, 1986.
Candid Camera Christmas Special, CBS, 1987.
Comic Relief II, HBO, 1987.
Jonathan Winters: On the Ledge, Showtime, 1987.
Martin Mull Live from North Ridgeville, HBO, 1987.
Memories Then and Now, CBS, 1988.
Ringmaster, *The 13th Annual Circus of the Stars,* CBS, 1988.
An All-Star Celebration: The '88 Vote, ABC, 1988.
An All-Star Toast to the Improv, HBO, 1988.
Merrill Markoe's Guide to Glamorous Living, Cinemax, 1988.
Sally Field & Tom Hanks' Punchline Party, HBO, 1988.
The Smothers Brothers Thanksgiving Special, CBS, 1988.
All-Star Tribute to Kareem Abdul-Jabbar, NBC, 1989.
Montreal International Comedy Festival, HBO, 1989.
Woodstock: Return to the Planet of the '60s, CBS, 1989.
Happy Birthday, Bugs: 50 Looney Years (also known as *Hollywood Celebrates Bugs Bunny's 50th Birthday*), CBS, 1990.
Just for Laughs: The Montreal International Comedy Festival, Showtime,1990.
The 25th Anniversary MDA Jerry Lewis Labor Day Telethon, syndicated, 1990.
Retaining Laughter, Lifetime, 1991.
Tom Arnold: The Naked Truth, HBO, 1991.
Martin Mull: Talent Takes a Holiday, Showtime, 1992.
Roseanne and Tom: Getting Away with It, HBO, 1992.
Super Bowl Saturday Night, TNT, 1992.
"Neighborhood" Host, *Sex, Shock and Censorship in the 90's,* Showtime, 1993.
Harvey Doe, "The Whole Shebang," *General Motors Playwrights Theater,* Arts and Entertainment, 1993.
Segment host, *A 70's Celebration: The Beat Is Back,* NBC, 1993.
Comedy Central's Documentary of the Making of the Remake of "Attack of the 50 Ft. Woman," Comedy Central, 1993.
Tom Arnold: The Naked Truth 3, HBO, 1993.
Host, *Little Rascals: Mischief Loves Company,* NBC, 1994.
People's 20th Birthday, ABC, 1994.
Subaru Presents Fair Enough: Martin Mull at the Iowa State Fair, Comedy Central, 1994.
American Comedy Honors, Fox, 1997.

Also appeared in *Martin Mull's White America,* Cinemax; *Sixty Minutes to Kill,* HBO; *Martin Mull in Concert,* HBO; *Orson Welles' Magic Show;* and *The Susan Anton Special.*

Television Appearances; Awards Presentations:
The 5th Annual American Comedy Awards, ABC, 1991.
The 19th Annual People's Choice Awards, CBS, 1993.
The 21st Annual People's Choice Awards, CBS, 1995.

Television Work; Series:
Producer, *The History of White People in America,* Cinemax, 1986-87.

Television Work; Movies:

Executive producer, *Martin Mull in "Portrait of a White Marriage,"* Cinemax, 1988.

Television Work; Specials:

Producer, *Candid Camera Christmas Special,* CBS, 1987.

Executive producer, *Martin Mull Live from North Ridgeville,* HBO, 1987.

Executive producer, *Martin Mull: Talent Takes a Holiday,* Showtime, 1992.

Executive producer, *Subaru Presents Fair Enough: Martin Mull at the Iowa State Fair,* Comedy Central, 1994.

RECORDINGS

Albums:

Martin Mull, Capricorn, 1972.

Martin Mull and His Fabulous Furniture in Your Living Room, Capricorn, 1973.

Normal, Capricorn, 1974.

Days of Wine and Neuroses, Capricorn, 1975.

No Hits, Four Errors, Capricorn, 1977.

Sex and Violins, ABC, 1978.

Near Perfect, Perfect, Elektra, 1979.

A Paler Shade of White: The History of White People in America, Simon and Schuster, 1987.

Also recorded *I'm Everyone I've Ever Loved,* MCA; also composed many other songs.

WRITINGS

Books:

(With Allen Rucker) *The History of White People in America,* Putnam, 1985.

Also wrote (with Rucker) *A Paler Shade of White.*

Screenplays:

(With others) *The History of White People in America: Volume II,* 1987.

Rented Lips, Cineworld, 1988.

Television Movies:

Martin Mull in "Portrait of a White Marriage," Cinemax, 1988.

Television Series:

The History of White People in America, Cinemax, 1986-87.

Also wrote episodes of *Roseanne,* ABC.

Television Specials:

Martin Mull Live from North Ridgeville, HBO, 1987.

Candid Camera Christmas Special, CBS, 1987.

Martin Mull: Talent Takes a Holiday, Showtime, 1992.

Television Writing; Other:

Wrote *The Great American Dream Machine* and *The Fifty-first State.**

MUNRO, Lochlyn
(Locklyn Munro)

PERSONAL

Born in Lac la Hache, British Columbia, Canada. *Avocational interests:* Water skiing.

Career: Actor.

CREDITS

Film Appearances:

(As Locklyn Munro) College buddy, *Run,* Buena Vista, 1991.

Bartender, *Cadence,* New Line Cinema, 1991.

Texas Slim, *Unforgiven,* Warner Bros., 1992.

John LaPointe, *Needful Things,* Columbia, 1993.

Sebastian, *Trancers 4: Jack of Swords,* Paramount Home Video, 1994.

Trancers 5: Sudden Deth, Paramount Home Video, 1994.

Billy, *Wagons East!,* TriStar, 1994.

Mark, *Digger,* Paramount Home Video, 1995.

Spider Bolton, *Downhill Willie* (also known as *Ski Hard* and *Ski Nuts*), BMG Home Video, 1996.

Craig, *A Night at the Roxbury,* Paramount, 1998.

Cliff, *Dead Man on Campus,* Paramount, 1998.

Marty Mackenzie, *Camouflage,* Hope Street, 1999.

Television Appearances; Movies:

Sam, *Posing: Inspired By Three Real Stories,* CBS, 1991.

Earl West, *The Girl from Mars,* Family Channel, 1991.

Trooper Mike Fox, *Dead Ahead: The Exxon Valdez Disaster,* HBO, 1992.

Shame, Lifetime, 1992.

Alan Preston, *A Stranger in the Mirror* (also known as *Sidney Sheldon's A Stranger in the Mirror*), ABC, 1993.

Jeff Laneer, *Moment of Truth: Broken Pledges,* NBC, 1994.

Nick, *A Secret Between Friends: A Moment of Truth Movie,* NBC, 1996.

Eddie Spencer, *Abduction of Innocence: A Moment of Truth Movie,* NBC, 1996.
Mickey Holloway, *Justice for Annie: A Moment of Truth Movie,* NBC, 1996.
Kevin Shane, *Mother, May I Sleep with Danger?,* NBC, 1996.
Josh Kelly, *Stand Against Fear: A Moment of Truth Movie,* NBC, 1996.
Sheriff Cole Harper, *Them,* UPN, 1996.
Steve, *A Champion's Fight: A Moment of Truth Movie,* NBC, 1998.
Larry, *High Voltage,* HBO, 1998.
Juston Decker, *I Know What You Did,* ABC, 1998.
Eddie Baltran, *One Hot Summer Night: A Crimes of Passion Movie,* ABC, 1998.
Billy, *Silencing Mary,* NBC, 1998.
Norwood, *A Murder of Crows,* Cinemax, 1999.
Officer Salke, *Our Guys: Outrage in Glen Ridge,* ABC, 1999.

Television Appearances; Episodic:
"The Girl Next Door," *21 Jump Street,* Fox, 1987.
Bobby, "A One Horse Town," *Wiseguy,* CBS, 1990.
Ralston, "The Heart of the Mystery," *Nightmare Cafe,* NBC, 1992.
Evan Henderson, *Blossom,* NBC, 1993.
Tim, "Under Color of Authority," *Highlander,* syndicated, 1994.
Walters, "The Voice of Reason," *The Outer Limits,* Showtime, 1995.
Dirk Moody, "She Was," *Strange Luck,* Fox, 1995.
Billy "The Kid" Gates, "The Good, the Bad, the Wealthy," *Sliders,* Fox, 1996.
Viper, 1997.
Todd Barnard, "The Light," *Poltergeist: The Legacy,* 1998.

Television Appearances; Series:
Jason, *Northwood,* SRC Television, [Canada], 1991.
McKinney, *Hawkeye,* syndicated, 1994.
FBI Agent Andrew Forbes, *Two,* syndicated, 1996-97.*

MUNRO, Locklyn
See MUNRO, Lochlyn

MURPHY, Audie 1924-1971

PERSONAL

Full name, Audie Leon Murphy; born June 20, 1924, in Kingston, TX; died in a plane crash, May 21 (some sources cite May 28), 1971, near Roanoke, VA; buried in Arlington National Cemetery, Arlington, VA; father, a sharecropper; married Wanda Hendrix, 1949 (divorced, 1950); married Pamela Archer, 1951; children: two sons.

Career: Actor and producer. Owner and breeder of race horses. *Military service:* U.S. Army, Infantry, 1942-45; served in European theater; became second lieutenant; received more than two dozen U.S. decorations, including Congressional Medal of Honor and five decorations from France and Belgium.

Awards, Honors: Inducted into National Cowboy Hall of Fame, 1996.

CREDITS

Film Appearances:
Copy boy, *Texas, Brooklyn, and Heaven* (also known as *The Girl from Texas*), United Artists, 1948.
Thomas, *Beyond Glory,* Paramount, 1948.
Danny Lester, *Bad Boy* (also known as *The Story of Danny Lester*), Allied Artists, 1949.
Ring Hassard, *Sierra,* Universal, 1950.
Billy the Kid, *The Kid from Texas* (also known as *Texas Kid, Outlaw*), Universal, 1950.
Jesse James, *Kansas Raiders,* Universal, 1950.
Henry Fleming, *The Red Badge of Courage,* Metro-Goldwyn-Mayer, 1951.
Bill Doolin, *The Cimarron Kid,* Universal, 1951.
The Silver Kid, *The Duel at Silver Creek,* Universal, 1952.
Jim Harvey, *Tumbleweed,* Universal, 1953.
Reb Kittridge, *Gunsmoke,* Universal, 1953.
Lieutenant Jed Sayre, *Column South,* Universal, 1953.
Clay O'Mara, *Ride Clear of Diablo,* Universal, 1954.
Gary Brannon, *Drums across the River,* Universal, 1954.
Tom Destry, *Destry,* Universal, 1954.
Himself, *To Hell and Back,* Universal, 1955.
John P. Clum, *Walk the Proud Land* (also known as *Apache Agent*), Universal, 1956.
Tommy Shea, *World in My Corner,* Universal, 1956.
Private John Woodley, *Joe Butterfly,* Universal, 1957.
The Guns of Fort Petticoat, Columbia, 1957.
The Utica Kid, *Night Passage,* Universal, 1957.
Joe Maybe, *Ride a Crooked Trail,* Universal, 1958.
John Gant, *No Name on the Bullet,* Universal, 1958.
Sam Martin, *The Gun Runners* (also known as *Gunrunners*), 1958.
Alden Pyle, *The Quiet American,* Figaro Films, 1958.
Yancey, *The Wild and the Innocent,* Universal, 1959.

Matt Brown, *Cast a Long Shadow,* United Artists, 1959.
Seven Jones, *Seven Ways from Sundown,* Universal, 1960.
Cash Zachary, *The Unforgiven,* United Artists, 1960.
Clay Santell, *Hell Bent for Leather,* Universal/International, 1960.
Banner Cole, *Posse from Hell,* Universal/International, 1961.
Craig Benson, *Battle at Bloody Beach* (also known as *Battle on the Beach*), Twentieth Century-Fox, 1961.
Ben Lane, *Six Black Horses,* Universal, 1962.
Showdown, Universal, 1963.
Narrator, *War Is Hell,* 1964.
Clint Cooper, *The Quick Gun,* Columbia, 1964.
Bob "Gif" Gifford, *Gunfight at Comanche Creek,* Allied Artists, 1964.
Jeff Stanton, *Apache Rifles,* Twentieth Century-Fox, 1964.
Logan Keliher, *Bullet for a Badman,* Universal, 1964.
Chad Lucas, *Gunpoint,* Universal, 1965.
Clint, *Arizona Raiders,* Columbia, 1965.
Mike Merrick, *Trunk to Cairo,* 1966.
Jess Carlin, *The Texican* (also known as *Texas Kid*), MCR Productions, 1966.
Captain Coburn, *40 Guns to Apache Pass,* Paramount, 1966.
Jesse James, *A Time for Dying,* 1971.

Film Work:
Producer, *The Guns of Fort Petticoat,* Columbia, 1957.
Song performer, "Touch of Pink," *The Wild and the Innocent,* Universal, 1959.
Producer, *A Time for Dying,* 1971.

Television Appearances; Series:
Detective Tom "Whispering" Smith, *Whispering Smith,* NBC, 1961.

Television Appearances; Episodic:
"The Flight," *Suspicion,* NBC, 1959.
"The Man," *Star Time,* Dumont, 1960.

WRITINGS

Other:
Author of the autobiography *To Hell and Back.* Also country music songwriter.

Adaptations: The screenplay *To Hell and Back* was adapted from Murphy's autobiography of the same title. Biographical material and archival footage were used to produce "Audie Murphy—Great American Hero," an episode of *Biography,* Arts and Entertainment, 1996.*

MURPHY, Donna 1958-

PERSONAL

Born March 7, 1958, in Corona, Queens, NY; married Shawn Elliot (an actor) in 1990; children: (stepdaughter) Justine (an actress). *Education:* Attended New York University's Tisch School of the Arts.

Addresses: *Agent*—William Morris Agency, 1325 Avenue of the Americas, New York, NY 10019-6026.

Career: Actress.

Awards, Honors: Antoinette Perry Award and Drama Desk Award, both 1994, for *Passion;* Antoinette Perry Award nomination, Drama Desk Award nomination, and Outer Critics Circle nomination, all 1996, for *The King and I;* CableAce Award, best actress in a dramatic special/series, 1998, for *Someone Had to Be Benny.*

CREDITS

Stage Appearances:
(Broadway debut) Voice of Sonia Walsk, *They're Playing Our Song,* Imperial Theatre, New York City, 1979.
Clare de Favorone, *Francis,* The Praxis Group, Theatre at St. Peter's Church, New York City, 1981-82.
Bess/Mary Arena (understudy), *The Human Comedy,* Royale Theatre, New York City, 1984.
Beatrice/Florence Gill, *The Mystery of Edwin Drood,* New York Shakespeare Festival, Public/Delacorte/Circle in the Square Downtown, 1985, then Imperial Theatre, all New York City, 1985-87.
Hope, *Birds of Paradise,* Promenade Theatre, New York City, 1987-88.
Celia, *Where She Went, What She Did,* Manhattan Punch Line Festival of One Act Plays, Judith Anderson Theatre, New York City, 1988.
Showing Off, Steve McGraw's Theatre, New York City, 1989.
Rose, *Song of Singapore,* 17 Irving Place Theatre, New York City, 1991.
Tatum O'Neal, *A Terrible Beauty,* Triangle Theatre, New York City, 1991-92.

Vera, *Pal Joey,* Huntington Theatre Company, Boston, MA, 1992.
Kristin, *Miss Julie,* McCarter Theatre, Princeton, NJ, 1992-93.
The Whore, *Hello Again,* Lincoln Center Theatre, New York City, 1994.
Cast, *Gypsy of the Year,* St. James Theatre, New York City, 1994.
Fosca, *Passion,* Plymouth Theatre, New York City, 1994-95.
Dorothy Trowbridge, *Twelve Dreams,* Lincoln Center Theatre, 1995.

Also appeared in *Hey Love: The Song of Mary Rodgers, Privates on Parade, Showing Off, Birds of Paradise, A My Name Is Alice,* and *Little Shop of Horrors.*

Film Appearances:
Karen Heller, *Jade,* Paramount, 1995.
October 22, 1998.
Anij, *Star Trek: Insurrection,* Paramount, 1998.
Natalie Streck, *The Astronaut's Wife,* New Line Cinema, 1999.

Television Appearances; Movies:
Vocalist, *Power, Passion and Murder,* 1987.
Mary Todd Lincoln, *The Day Lincoln Was Shot,* TNT, 1998.

Television Appearances; Miniseries:
Abigail Adams, *LIBERTY! The American Revolution,* PBS, 1997.

Television Appearances; Specials:
Vocalist, *A Table at Ciro's,* PBS, 1987.
Someone Had to Be Benny, HBO, 1986.
Fosca, *Passion,* PBS, 1996.
Leonard Bernstein's New York, PBS, 1997.
2 Chicks, 2 Bikes, 1 Cause, Lifetime, 1998.

Television Appearances; Series:
Karen Unger, *Law & Order,* NBC, 1992-93.
Francesca Cross, *Murder One,* ABC, 1995-96.

Television Appearances; Episodic:
Ruth Geddy, "Behind Every Great Woman," *Remember WENN,* 1996.
"Spirit and Substance," *Nothing Sacred,* 1997.
Carla Tyrell, "Thrill," *Law & Order,* NBC, 1997.
Marie Hanson, *Ally McBeal,* Fox, 1997.
Linda Penny, *Michael Hayes,* CBS, 1998.
Marie Hanson, *The Practice,* ABC, 1998.

OTHER SOURCES

Periodicals:
Parade Magazine, April 12, 1998, p. 12.

Electronic:
The Official Donna Murphy HomePage, http://www.inch.com/-maleman/donna.htm.*

MURRAY, Joel 1963-

PERSONAL

Born April 17, 1963, in Evanston, IL; brother of Bill Murray (an actor and comedian) and Brian Doyle-Murray (an actor); married Eliza Coyle; children: one.

Addresses: *Agent*—Special Artist, 345 North Maple Dr., Suite 302, Beverly Hills, CA 90210-3869.

Career: Actor.

CREDITS

Television Appearances; Series:
Norris Weldon, *Grand,* NBC, 1990.
Ken Epstein, *Pacific Station,* NBC, 1991.
Ray Litvak, *Love and War,* CBS, 1992-95.
Voice of Beethoven, *Beethoven,* CBS, 1994.
Pete Cavanaugh, *Dharma & Greg,* ABC, 1997—.

Television Appearances; Movies:
Bart Polonski, *Long Gone,* HBO, 1987.
Mr. Jones, *Encino Woman,* ABC, 1996.

Television Appearances; Episodic:
Doug LeMuere, *Blossom,* NBC, 1991.
Voice of Beethoven, *Beethoven,* CBS, 1994.
Ron Wolfe, "Who's Afraid of Ron and Cindy Wolfe?," *Partners,* Fox, 1995.
Vince, *The Nanny,* CBS, 1996.
Voice, *Disney's Hercules* (animated), ABC, 1998.

Film Appearances:
George Calamari, *One Crazy Summer,* Warner Bros., 1986.
Guest, *Scrooged,* Paramount, 1988.
Shopping Elvis and Paul, *Elvis Stories,* 1989.
Bert, *Only You,* 1992.
Milkman, *Shakes the Clown,* IRS Releasing, 1992.
Basketball player, *The Cable Guy,* Columbia, 1996.

Also appeared in *Men Will Be Boys.**

N

NEMES, Scott 1974-

PERSONAL

Born in 1974. *Education:* Attended University of Southern California.

Career: Actor. Spiral West (no-alcohol nightclub), founder, 1993.

CREDITS

Television Appearances; Series:
Grant Schumacher, *It's Garry Shandling's Show* (also known as *The Garry Shandling Show*), Showtime and Fox, 1986.
Ricky Halsenbach, *The Wonder Years,* ABC, 1991-93.

Television Appearances; Movies:
Greg Harper, *This Wife for Hire,* ABC, 1985.
First boy, "The Thanksgiving Promise" (also known as "Chester, I Love You"), *The Disney Sunday Movie,* ABC, 1986.
Wendell, "Little Spies," *The Disney Sunday Movie,* ABC, 1986.

Television Appearances; Pilots:
Spike Travalian, *Full House,* CBS, 1983.
Rodney Sherman, *The Invisible Woman,* NBC, 1983.

Television Appearances; Episodic:
Young MacDonald, "Flower Power," *The Super Mario Bros. Super Show!,* syndicated, 1989.

Other Television Appearances:
Top Kids, 1987.
Robbie, *Straight Up* (special), PBS, 1988.

Film Appearances:
Ambassador's son, *D.C. Cab* (also known as *Street Fleet*), Universal, 1983.
Young Mr. Weinstein, *Twilight Zone: The Movie,* Warner Bros., 1983.
Butterball, *Meatballs Part II* (also known as *Space Kid*), TriStar, 1984.
Frank, *Konrad,* 1985.
Nephew, *St. Elmo's Fire,* Columbia, 1985.
Yogurt boy, *Tough Guys,* Buena Vista, 1986.
Bobby Lollar, *Last Resort* (also known as *She Knew No Other Way*), Concorde, 1986.*

NEWELL, Mike 1942-

PERSONAL

Born March 28, 1942, in St. Albans, England. *Education:* Graduated with an English degree from Cambridge University; took a three-year directorial training course at Granada Television.

Addresses: *Office*—Dogstar Films, 5 Carlisle St., London W1V 5RG, England.

Career: Director and producer.

Awards, Honors: Cleveland International Film Festival Award, best film, 1992, for *Enchanted April;* Cleveland International Film Festival Award, best film, 1993, for *Into the West;* British Academy of Film and Television Arts Awards, David Lean Award, for direction and best film (with Duncan Kenworthy), Cesar Award, best foreign film, 1995, all for *Four Weddings and a Funeral;* Boston Society of Film Critics Third Place Award, best director, Five Continents Award nomination, European Film Awards, 1997, both for *Donnie Brasco.*

CREDITS

Film Work; Director:
The Awakening, Warner Bros., 1980.
Bad Blood, Southern Pictures/New Zealand Film Commission, 1983.
Dance with a Stranger, Twentieth Century-Fox, 1985.
The Good Father, Skouras, 1986.
Amazing Grace and Chuck (also known as *Silent Voice*), TriStar, 1987.
Soursweet, British Screen/Film Four/Zenith, 1988.
Enchanted April, Miramax, 1992.
Into the West, Miramax/Family Films, 1993.
Four Weddings and a Funeral, Gramercy Pictures, 1994.
An Awfully Big Adventure, Fine Line, 1995.
Donnie Brasco, Sony Pictures Entertainment, 1997.
Pushing Tin, Twentieth Century-Fox, 1999.

Film Work; Executive Producer:
Photographing Fairies (also known as *Apparition*), PolyGram Video, 1997.
Best Laid Plans, Fox Searchlight, 1999.
200 Cigarettes, Paramount, 1999.

Film Appearances:
Himself, *At Sundance,* 1995.

Television Work; Director; Movies:
69 Murder-The Blood Relation, 1968.
Arthur Wants You for a Sunbeam, 1970.
Mrs. Mouse, Are You Within?, 1971.
Not Counting the Savages, 1972.
Just Your Luck, 1972.
£12 Look, 1973.
The New Word, 1973.
The Melancholy Hussar, 1973.
Barbara's Wedding, 1973.
Silver Wedding, 1973.
Ms. or Jill and Jack, 1974.
The Gift of Friendship, 1974.
The Childhood Friend, 1974.
Of the Fields Lately, 1975.
Mrs. Ackland's Ghosts, 1975.
The Midas Connection, 1975.
Lost Yer Tongue?, 1975.
Jack Flea's Birthday Celebration, 1975.
Brassneck, 1975.
The Boundary, 1975.
Ready When You Are, Mr. McGill, 1976.
Buffet, 1976.
The Man in the Iron Mask, NBC, 1977.
The Mayor's Charity, 1977.
Honey, 1977.
The Fosdyke Saga, 1977.
Charm, 1977.
Mr. & Mrs. Bureaucrat, 1978.
Little Girls Don't, 1978.
Destiny, 1978.
The Awakening, 1980.
Birth of a Nation, 1982.

Also directed the television movies *Eleventh Hour; Chan; First for Luck; Tales out of School; Big Soft Nelly; Mrs. Mouse;* and *The Gift of Friendship.*

Television Work; Director; Miniseries:
Blood Feud, syndicated, 1983.
Common Ground, CBS, 1990.

Television Work; Director; Episodic:
Directed episodes of *Spindoe; Big Breadwinner Hog; Budgie; The Guardians; The Man from Haven;* and *Smith and Jones in Small Doses.*

Television Work; Director; Specials:
"Baa Baa Blacksheep," *Childhood,* 1977.*

NEWIRTH, Charles

PERSONAL

Born in New York, NY. *Education:* Ohio State University, degree in film; graduate study at New York University.

Career: Producer. Sometimes credited as Charles J. Newirth.

CREDITS

Film Work:
Location manager, *The Seduction,* Embassy, 1982.
Location manager and production assistant, *Cat People,* Universal, 1982.
Unit production manager, *Parasite,* 1982.
Location manager, *Flashdance,* Paramount, 1983.
Location manager, *Thief of Hearts,* Paramount, 1984.
Unit manager, *Fear City* (also known as *Border* and *Ripper*), Zuprik-Curtis Enterprises, 1984.
Location manager, *Perfect,* Columbia, 1985.
Location manager, *Pretty in Pink,* Paramount, 1986.
Location manager, *Ferris Bueller's Day Off,* Paramount, 1986.
Production manager, *Throw Momma from the Train,* Orion, 1987.

Production manager, *RoboCop,* Orion, 1987.
Location manager, *Blind Date,* TriStar, 1987.
Unit production manager, *The Great Outdoors,* Universal, 1988.
Associate producer and production manager, *The Package,* Orion, 1989.
Associate producer and unit production manager, *Avalon,* 1990.
Producer (with Mark Johnson and Barry Levinson) and production manager, *Bugsy,* TriStar, 1991.
Producer (with Johnson and Levinson) and unit production manager, *Toys,* Twentieth Century-Fox, 1992.
Co-producer and unit production manager, *Forrest Gump,* Paramount, 1994.
Executive producer and unit production manager, *The American President,* Columbia, 1995.
Executive producer and unit production manager, *Phenomenon,* Buena Vista, 1996.
Executive producer, *Ghosts of Mississippi* (also known as *Ghosts from the Past*), Columbia, 1996.
Producer, *Patch Adams,* Universal, 1998.
Producer, *Home Fries,* Warner Bros., 1998.
Executive producer, *City of Angels,* Warner Bros., 1998.*

NIVOLA, Alessandro 1973-

PERSONAL

Born in 1973, in Boston, MA; father, a university professor; mother, an artist; grandson of Constantino Nivola (a sculptor). *Education:* Studied English literature at Yale University.

Career: Actor.

Awards, Honors: Blockbuster Entertainment Award nomination, favorite supporting actor in an action or adventure film, 1997, for *Face/Off.*

CREDITS

Stage Appearances:
Saint Joan of the Stockyards, Yale Repertory Theatre, New Haven, CT, 1992-93.
Paddywhack, Long Wharf Theatre, New Haven, 1994-95.
Aleksei Nikolaevich Belyaev, *A Month in the Country,* Center Stage Right, Criterion Theatre, New York City, 1995.

Film Appearances:
Robin, *Reach the Rock,* Gramercy Pictures, 1997.
Peter Vanlaningham, *Inventing the Abbotts,* Twentieth Century-Fox, 1997.
Pollux Troy, *Face/Off,* Paramount, 1997.
Martin, *I Want You* (also known as *Beloved*), Gramercy Pictures/PolyGram Filmed Entertainment, 1998.
Nick, *Best Laid Plans,* Fox Searchlight, 1999.
King, *Love's Labour's Lost,* Miramax, 1999.
Henry Crawford, *Mansfield Park,* Miramax, 1999.

Television Appearances; Episodic:
Paul Rice, "Valentino Speaks," *Remember WENN,* 1996.

Other Television Appearances:
The Almost Perfect Bank Robbery (movie), 1996.
Danielle Steel's "The Ring" (miniseries), NBC, 1996.

OTHER SOURCES

Periodicals:
New York Times, September 13, 1998, p. 70.*

NOIRET, Philippe 1930-

PERSONAL

Born October 1, 1930, in Lille, France; son of Pierre (a clothing store worker) and Lucy (maiden name, Heirman) Noiret; married Monique Chaumette (an actress), 1962; children: Frederique. *Education:* Trained for the stage with Roger Blin and at the Centre Dramatique de l'Ouest (Dramatic Center of the West).

Addresses: *Office*—c/o Artmedia, 10 avenue George V, 75008 Paris, France.

Career: Actor. Appeared with Theatre National Populaire, 1951-63. Also worked as a nightclub entertainer.

Member: Screen Actors Guild.

Awards, Honors: Best Actor Award, Venice Film Festival, 1963, for *Therese Desqueryoux;* National Board of Review Award, best supporting actor, 1969, for *Topaz;* Etoile de cristal, best actor, 1974, for *L'Horloger de Saint-Paul;* Cesar Award, best actor, 1976, for *Le Vieux Fusil;* Rio de Janeiro Film Festival

Award, best actor, 1984, for *Les Ripoux;* European Film Award, actor of the year, 1989, and British Academy of Film and Television Arts Award, best actor, 1990, for *Cinema Paradiso;* European Film Award, actor of the year, 1989, Cesar Award, best actor, 1990, and David Award, best foreign actor, 1990, all for *Life and Nothing But.*

CREDITS

Film Appearances:

(Film debut; uncredited) *Gigi,* 1948.
Olivia (also known as *The Pit of Loneliness*), 1950.
Un passant, *Agence matrimoniale,* 1951.
Lui, *La Pointe courte,* 1955.
Maurice, *Ravissante,* 1960.
Louis XIV, "Lauzun," *Les Amours celebres,* 1960.
Uncle Gabriel, *Zazie dans le metro* (also known as *Zazie in the Underground* and *Zazie in the Subway*), Astor, 1960.
Herode, *Le Capitaine Fracasse,* 1961.
Inspector Maillard, *Le Rendez-vous,* 1961.
Victor Hardy, *Tout l'or du monde* (also known as *All the Gold in the World*), 1961.
Clovis Hugues, "L'Affaire Hugues," in *Le Crime ne paie pas* (also known as *Crime Does Not Pay* and *The Gentle Art of Murder*), Embassy, 1962.
Bellini, *Le Massaggiatrici,* 1962.
Comme un poisson dans l'eau, 1962.
Inspector Mathieu, *Ballade pour un voyou,* 1963.
Director General, *Clementine Cherie,* 1963.
Jacques Garaud and Paul Harmant, *La Porteuse de pain,* 1963.
Bernard Desqueyroux, *Therese Desqueyroux,* Pathe Contemporary, 1963.
Jean, *Frenesia dell'estate* (also known as *Shivers in the Summer*), 1963.
Ballade pour un voyou, 1963.
Edmond Bernadac, *Monsieur,* Comacico, 1964.
Ambrose Gerome, *Lady L,* Metro-Goldwyn-Mayer, 1964.
Louis XIII, *Cyrano et d'Artagnan,* 1964.
Brassy, *Mort, ou est ta victoire?,* 1964.
Benin, *Les Copains,* 1964.
Jean-Jacques Georges, *Qui etes-vous, Polly Magoo?* (also known as *Who Are You, Polly Magoo?*), 1966.
Gynecologist (Michou), *Les Sultans,* 1966.
Bibi Dumonceux, *Tendre Voyou* (also known as *Tender Scoundrel*), 1966.
Traveler, *Le Voyage du pere,* 1966.
Jerome, *La Vie de chateau* (also known as *A Matter of Resistance* and *Gracious Resistance*), Royal Films International, 1966.
Victor, *Woman Times Seven,* Embassy, 1967.
Inspector Morand, *The Night of the Generals,* Columbia, 1967.
Andre, *L'Une et l'autre,* 1967.
Title role, *Alexandre le bienheureux* (also known as *Very Happy Alexander*), 1968.
De Pourtalain, *Adolphe, ou l'age tendre* (also known as *Adolphe* and *The Tender Age*), 1968.
Moujik Man, *Mister Freedom,* 1969.
Title role, *Clerambard,* 1969.
Lucoville, *The Assassination Bureau,* Paramount, 1969.
Pombal, *Justine,* Twentieth Century-Fox, 1969.
Henri Jarve, *Topaz,* Universal, 1970.
Gabriel, *Les Caprices de Marie* (also known as *Give Her the Moon*), United Artists, 1970.
Louis Brezan, *Murphy's War,* Paramount, 1971.
Chief Inspector, *Most Gentle Confessions,* Metro-Goldwyn-Mayer, 1971.
Marcel, *A Time for Loving* (also known as *Paris Was Made for Lovers*), 1971.
Inspector Muller, *Les Aveux les plus doux,* 1971.
Judge Jannacone, *Siamo tutti in liberta provisoria,* 1972.
Gabriel Marcassus, *La Vieille Fille* (also known as *Old Maid*), Valoria, 1972.
Alfred, *Le Trefle a cinq feuilles* (also known as *Five-Leaf Clover*), 1972.
Georges, *La Mandarine* (also known as *Sweet Deception*), Societe Nouvelle Prodis, 1972.
Garcin, *L'Attentat* (also known as *The Assassination* and *The French Conspiracy*), Cine Globe, 1972.
Monsieur Lepic, *Poil de carotte,* United Artists, 1973.
Phillippe, *La Grande Bouffe* (also known as *Blow-Out, The Big Feast* and *The Big Feed*), 1973.
Lucien Berthon, *Le Serpent* (also known as *The Serpent* and *Night Flight from Moscow*), Avco Embassy, 1973.
General Terry, *Touche pas a la femme blanche* (also known as *Don't Touch White Women* and *Don't Touch the White Woman!*), 1974.
Gaspard de Montfermeil, *Les Gaspards* (also known as *The Holes* and *The Down-in-the-Hole Gang*), 1974.
Thomas Barthlot, *Le Secret* (also known as *The Secret*), Valoria, 1974.
Malisard, *Un Nuage entre les dents* (also known as *Cloud in the Teeth*), United Artists, 1974.
Michel Descombe, *L'Horloger de Saint-Paul* (also known as *The Clockmaker* and *The Watchmaker of St. Paul's*), Pathe, 1974.
Georges de Saxe, *Le Jeu avec le feu* (also known as *Playing with Fire*), 1974.
Julien Dandieu, *Le Vieux Fusil* (also known as *The Old Gun*), United Artists, 1975.

Philippe D'Orleans, "Les Nobles," *Que la fete commence!* (also known as *Let Joy Reign Supreme*), Specialty Films/CIC, 1975.

Title role, *Monsieur Albert,* Gaumont, 1976.

Giorgio Perozzi, *Amici Miei* (also known as *My Friends*), Gaumont, 1976.

General, *Desert of the Tartars,* Gaumont, 1976.

Judge Emil Rousseau, *Le Juge et l'assassin* (also known as *The Judge and the Assassin*), Libra, 1976.

Constanzo, *Il commune senso del pudore* (also known as *A Common Sense of Modesty*), 1976.

Ladislas, *Coup de foudre,* 1976.

Raoul Malfosse, *Une Femme a sa fenetre* (also known as *A Woman at Her Window*), 1976.

The General, *Il deserto dei tartari,* 1977.

Antoine Lemercier, *Tendre Poulet* (also known as *Dear Detective, Dear Inspector,* and *Tender Cop*), Cinema V, 1978.

Jean-Claude Moulineau, *Who Is Killing the Great Chefs of Europe?* (also known as *Too Many Chefs* and *Someone Is Killing the Great Chefs of Europe*), Warner Bros., 1978.

Phillippe Marchal, *Un Taxi mauve* (also known as *The Purple Taxi*), Quartet, 1978.

Robert Maurisson, *Le Temoin* (also known as *The Witness*), Europex, 1978.

Eugene Pottier, *La Barricade du point du jour* (also known as *The Barricade at Point Du Jour*), World Marketing, 1978.

Father, *Street of the Crane's Foot,* World Marketing/ CIC, 1979.

Pepper, *Two Pieces of Bread* (also known as *Due pezzi di pane* and *Happy Hobos*), United Artists, 1979.

Salto nel vuoto (also known as *A Leap into the Void*), 1979.

La Mort en direct (also known as *Deathwatch*), 1979.

Antoine Lermercier, *On a vole la cuisse de Jupiter* (also known as *Jupiter's Thigh*), Films Ariane, 1980.

Baroni, *Pile ou face* (also known as *Heads or Tails*), 1980.

Michel Descombe, *Une Semaine de vacances* (also known as *A Week's Vacation*), ParaFrance, 1980.

Athanase, *Il faut tuer Birgitt Haas* (also known as *Birgit Haas Must Be Killed*), 1981.

Raffaele Giuranna, *Tre fratelli* (also known as *Three Brothers*), New World, 1981.

Lucien Cordier, *Coup de torchon* (also known as *Clean Slate*), ParaFrance, 1982.

Edouard Binet, *L'etoile du nord* (also known as *The North Star*), ParaFrance, 1982.

Giorgio Perozzi, *Amicimiei, atto due* (also known as *My Friends II*), Gaumont, 1983.

Etienne Lebrouche, *La Grande Carnaval,* Gaumont, 1983.

Victor, *L'Africain* (also known as *The African*), AMLF, 1983.

Un Ami de Vincent (also known as *A Friend of Vincent's*), World Marketing, 1983.

Dubreuilh, *Fort Saganne,* Roissy-AAA, 1984.

Principal, *Souvenirs, Souvenirs* (also known as *Memories, Memories*), Metro-Goldwyn-Mayer/United Artists, 1984.

Rene, *Les Ripoux* (also known as *My New Partner*), Orion, 1984.

Edouard, *L'Ete prochain* (also known as *Next Summer*), European Classics, 1985.

Count Leonardo, *Speriamo che sia femmina* (also known as *Pourvu que ce soit une fille* and *Let's Hope It's a Girl*), President Films, 1985.

Yves Dorget, *Le Quatrieme Pouvoir* (also known as *The Fourth Power*), President Films, 1985.

Cop, 1985.

Qualcosa di biondo, 1985.

Redon,*'Round Midnight* (also known as *Autour de minuit*), Warner Bros., 1986.

Pierre Franchin, *La Femme secrete* (also known as *The Secret Wife*), AAA,1986.

Igor Tatiatev, *Twist Again in Moscow* (also known as *Twist again a Moscou*), Gaumont, 1986.

Christian Legagneur, *Masques* (also known as *Masks*), Cannon, 1986.

Doctor Fadigati, *The Gold-Rimmed Glasses* (also known as *Gli occhiala d'oro*), Ofer/OmniFilms, 1987.

Inspector Molinat, *Noyade interdite* (also known as *No Drowning Allowed* and *Widow's Walk*), Bac Films, 1987.

Narrator (French version), *L'Homme qui plantait des arbres* (animated short; also known as *The Man Who Planted Trees*), Societe Radio, 1987.

Jean-Luc, *La famiglia* (also known as *The Family*), 1987.

Savinien de Kerfardec, *Chouans!,* 1988.

Dom Pedro II, *Il Giovane Toscanini,* 1988.

Major Dellaplanne, *La Vie et rien d'autre* (also known as *Life and Nothing But*), Union Generale Cinematographique, 1989.

Gabriele Battistini, *Il frullo del passero,* Medusa, 1989.

La femme de mes amours, 1989.

Cardinal Mazarin, *The Return of the Musketeers,* 1989.

Rene Lesbuch, *Ripoux contre ripoux* (also known as *Le Cop 2* and *My New Partner II*), 1990.

Anatole Hirsch, *Faux et usage de Faux* (also known as *Forgery and the Use of Forgeries*), 1990.

Alfredo, *Cinema Paradiso* (also known as *Nuovo Cinema Paradiso*), Miramax, 1990.

Hotel Manager, *The Palermo Connection* (also known as *Dimenticare Palermo* and *To Forget Palermo*), Gaumont, 1991.
Watrin, *Uranus,* Miramax, 1991.
Romain, *J'embrasse pas* (also known as *I Don't Kiss*), 1991.
Gioacchino Rossini, *Rossini, Rossini,* 1991.
Contre l'oubli (also known as *Against Oblivion* and *Lest We Forget*), 1992.
Toussaint, *Nous deux* (also known as *The Two of Us*), 1992.
Robert "Max" Maxendre, *Max et Jeremie* (also known as *Max and Jeremy*), 1992.
Alberto, *Zuppa di pesce* (also known as *Fish Soup*), 1992.
The Elegant Man, *Tango,* 1993.
Antonio, "The Blue Dog," in *Especially on Sunday* (also known as *La Domenica Specialmente*), Miramax, 1993.
Himself, *Grosse Fatigue* (also known as *Dead Tired* and *High Stress*), Gaumont, 1994.
Pablo Neruda, *Il Postino* (also known as *The Postman*), Miramax, 1994.
Himself, *Veilles d'armes: Le Journalisme en temps de guerre* (also known as *Troubles We've Seen: A History of Journalism in Wartime* and *1st and 2nd Journeys*), 1994.
Le General, *Les Milles* (also known as *Les Milles: Le train de la liberte*), 1994.
D'Artagnan, *La Fille de de'Artagnan* (also known as *D'Artagnan's Daughter* and *The Daughter of D'Artagnan*), 1994.
Bertelli-Claudia's father, *Facciamo paradiso,* 1995.
Victor Derval, *Le roi de Paris* (also known as *The King of Paris*), 1995.
Duke Signoretto, *Marianna Ucria* (also known as *La vie silencieuse de Marianna Ucria*), 1997.
Victor Vialat, *Les grand ducs* (also known as *The Grand Dukes*), 1996.
Philippe Bruneau-Tessier, *Fantome avec chauffeur,* 1996.
Joseph Levy, *Soleil,* 1997.
Monsieur Schultz, *Les palmes de M. Schutz,* 1997.
Philippe d'Orleans, *Le bossu* (also known as *On Guard*), 1997.
In and Out of Fashion, 1998.

Also appeared in *The Billionaire* and *Moments of Love.*

Television Appearances; Movies:
Dr. Andre Feretti, *Aurora* (also known as *Qualcosa di biondo* and *Aurora By Night*), NBC, 1984.
Le veilleur de nuit, 1996.

Also appeared in *The Thrill of Genius,* RAI-TV; and as the announcer, *Discorama.*

Television Appearances; Series:
Les amours celebres, 1961.

Stage Appearances:
(Broadway debut) Duke Alexandre, *Lorenzaccio,* Theatre National Populaire, Broadway Theatre, New York City, 1958.
Simon Renard, *Marie Tudor,* Theatre National Populaire, Broadway Theatre, 1958.
Count Don Gormas, *Le Cid,* Theatre National Populaire, Broadway Theatre, 1958.

Also appeared in *Richard II, Oedipus,* and *Don Juan,* all Theatre National Populaire, Paris, France; *The Night of the Kings,* Theatre de l'Oeuvre, Paris; *Dona Rosita,* Noctabules Theatre, Paris; *Castle in Sweden,* 1960; *Photo Finish;* and *The Odd Couple.*

OTHER SOURCES

Books:
Maillet, Dominique, *Philippe Noiret,* [Paris], 1978, revised edition, 1989.

Periodicals:
Cinema, April, 1983.
Cine Revue, February 10, 1983.
Ecran, March, 1978.
Films, August, 1982.
Films in Review, March-April, 1983.
Revue de Cinema, April, 1987.
Sequences, April, 1984; June, 1989.*

NOONAN, Tom 1951-
(Richmond Arrley, Tommy Noonan, Lodovico Sorret, Ludovico Sorret)

PERSONAL

Born April 12, 1951, in Greenwich, CT; son of a dentist; married Karen Young (an actress); children: Wanda. *Education:* Graduated from Yale University.

Addresses: *Agent*—Innovative Artists Talent Agency, 1999 Avenue of the Stars, Los Angeles, CA 90067-6022.

Career: Actor, director, screenwriter, music composer, and editor.

Awards, Honors: Sundance Film Festival, Grand Jury Prize, and WaldoSalt Screenwriting Award, both 1994, and Independent Spirit Award nomination, best first screenplay, 1995, all for *What Happened Was . . .*; Obie Award, *Village Voice,* 1994, for *The Wife.*

CREDITS

Film Appearances:

Man in park, *Willie and Phil,* Twentieth Century-Fox, 1980.

Gangster and second man, *Gloria,* Columbia, 1980.

Jake, *Heaven's Gate* (also known as *Johnson County Wars*), United Artists, 1980.

Ferguson, *Wolfen,* Warner Bros., 1981.

Paddy, *Easy Money,* Orion, 1983.

Daryl Potts, *Eddie Macon's Run,* Universal, 1983.

Holtzman, *Best Defense,* Paramount, 1984.

Reese, *The Man with One Red Shoe,* Twentieth Century-Fox, 1985.

Varrick, *F/X* (also known as *F/X-Murder by Illusion* and *Murder by Illusion*), Orion, 1986.

Francis Dollarhyde, *Manhunter* (also known as *Red Dragon: The Pursuit of Hannibal Lecter*), De Laurentiis Entertainment Group, 1986.

Tom Goes to the Bar (short film), Cinecom International, 1986.

Frankenstein, *The Monster Squad,* TriStar, 1987.

Man in diner, "A Ghost," *Mystery Train,* Orion Classics, 1989.

Scully, *Collision Course* (also known as *East/West Cop*), Recorded Releasing/Rich International, 1989.

Cain, *Robocop 2,* Orion, 1990.

Ripper, *Last Action Hero,* Columbia, 1992.

Michael, *What Happened Was . . .,* Samuel Goldwyn, 1994.

Kelson, *Heat,* Warner Bros., 1995.

Jack, *The Wife,* Artistic License, 1996.

Mickey Hounsell, *Wang Dang,* 1999.

The Opportunists, 1999.

Jackson McLaren, *The Astronaut's Wife,* New Line Cinema, 1999.

Film Work; Director, Except Where Indicated:

BoneDaddy, 1991.

And film editor (as Richmond Arrley), *What Happened Was . . .,* Samuel Goldwyn, 1994.

And sound designer and film editor (as Richmond Arrley), *The Wife,* Artistic License, 1996.

Wang Dang, 1999.

Television Appearances; Movies:

Bo, *Rage!,* NBC, 1980.

Mr. Y., *The 10 Million Dollar Getaway,* USA Network, 1991.

Chicago, *Phoenix,* HBO, 1998.

Television Appearances; Miniseries:

Willard Fenway, *John Jakes' Heaven and Hell: North and South, Part III,* ABC, 1994.

Television Appearances; Episodic:

Brandon Thornton, *The Equalizer,* CBS, 1989.

"The Moving Finger," *Monsters,* 1990.

John Lee Roche, "Paper Hearts," *The X-Files,* Fox, 1996.

Frank Price, *Early Edition,* CBS, 1996.

Television Work; Producer; Movies:

Red Wind, USA Network, 1991.

Television Work; Director; Episodic:

Directed episodes of *Monsters.*

Stage Appearances:

(Off-Broadway debut) Tilden, *Buried Child,* Theatre De Lys, 1978.

Sepp, *Farmyard,* Theater for the New City, New York City, 1981.

Rube Janik, *Spookhouse,* Playhouse 91, New York City, 1984.

Also appeared in *The Invitational,* New York City; *The Breakers,* New York City; *Five of Us,* New York City; and *Marathon '88,* New York City.

WRITINGS

Screenplays:

What Happened Was . . . (film; based on Noonan's play of the same name), Samuel Goldwyn, 1994.

The Wife (based on Noonan's play of the same name), Artistic License, 1996.

Wang Dang, 1999.

Film Scores:

(As Ludovico Sorret) *What Happened Was ...,* Samuel Goldwyn, 1994.

(As Ludovico Sorret) *The Wife,* Artistic License, 1996.

Also wrote the score for *Romance.*

Television Movies:

Red Wind, USA Network, 1991.

Television Scores; Miniseries:

John Jakes' Heaven & Hell: North & South, Book III, ABC, 1994.

Television Scores; Episodic:

Wrote scores for episodes "The Bargain," *Monsters;* "Malcolm," *Monsters;* and "The Odds," *Monsters.*

Stage Plays:

What Happened Was. . ., Paradise Theater, New York City, 1992.

The Wife (also known as *Wifey*), Paradise Theater, New York City, 1994.*

NOONAN, Tommy

See NOONAN, Tom

O

O'BRIEN, Richard 1942-

PERSONAL

Real name, Richard Smith; born March 25, 1942, in Cheltenham, Gloucestershire, England; married Kimi Wong (marriage ended); married Jane Moss; children: (first marriage) Linus.

Career: Playwright, screenwriter, composer, actor, and novelist.

Awards, Honors: Grammy Award nomination, best score from the original cast show album, 1974, for *The Rocky Horror Picture Show.*

CREDITS

Film Appearances:

A Tiger Walks, Buena Vista, 1964.
(Uncredited) Indian Rider, *Carry on Cowboy* (also known as *The Rumpo Kid*), 1965.
Dr. Cobb, *Chamber of Horrors,* Warner Bros., 1966.
Ryan, *Rough Night in Jericho,* Universal, 1967.
Monsignor Francis Hurley, *Pieces of Dreams,* United Artists, 1970.
Matt Weber, *The Honkers,* United Artists, 1972.
Driver, *The Loners,* Fanfare, 1972.
Sergeant Del Conte, *The Thief Who Came to Dinner,* Warner Bros., 1973.
Riff Raff, *The Rocky Horror Picture Show,* Twentieth Century-Fox, 1975.
Desk Sergeant, *The Shaggy D.A.,* Buena Vista, 1976.
Dodge, *The Pack* (also known as *The Long Dark Night*), Warner Bros., 1977.
Former Owner's Adviser, *Heaven Can Wait,* Paramount, 1978.
John Dee, *Jubilee,* Cinegate, 1978.
Batch, *The Odd Job,* 1978.
Fico, *Flash Gordon,* Universal, 1980.
Cosmo McKinley, *Shock Treatment,* Twentieth Century-Fox, 1981.
Digital Dreams, 1983.
Lord Hampton, *Revolution,* Warner Bros., 1985.
The Contraption, 1985.
James, *The Wolves of Willoughby Chase,* 1988.
Damien, *Spice World,* Sony Pictures Entertainment, 1997.
Pierre Le Pieu, *Ever After,* Twentieth Century-Fox, 1998.
Mr. Hand, *Dark City,* New Line Cinema, 1998.

Film Work:

Continuity, *Tunes a Plenty,* 1989.

Television Appearances; Series:

Host, *The Crystal Maze,* Channel 4, 1990-94.

Television Appearances; Movies:

Priest, *Ransom for a Dead Man,* NBC, 1971.
Mr. Riley, *Dead Men Tell No Tales,* CBS, 1971.
Jasper Mahoney, *Incident in San Francisco,* ABC, 1971.
Construction Boss, *In Tandem,* NBC, 1974.
Chief of Detectives, *The Art of Crime,* NBC, 1975.
Mr. Cameron, *Returning Home,* ABC, 1975.
Chief, *The Two-Five,* ABC, 1978.
Bridge Foreman, *The Golden Gate Murders,* CBS, 1979.
Holman, *The Ordeal of Patty Hearst,* ABC, 1979.
Commissioner Avery, *The Kids Who Knew Too Much,* 1980.

Television Appearances; Miniseries:

Cowboy, *The Racing Game,* 1979.
Judge, *Centennial,* NBC, 1979.
Herb Ellsworth, *The Top of the Hill,* syndicated, 1980.

Television Appearances; Pilots:
Ulysses Barnes, *Landon, Landon, and Landon,* CBS, 1980.

Television Appearances; Specials:
The Sheriff, *Arthur the Kid,* 1981.

Television Appearances; Episodic:
Appeared in "Cromm Cruac," *Robin of Sherwood;* and as Dr. Phibes, *The Detectives.*

RECORDINGS

Video Games:
Game devil, *The Interactive Rocky Horror Show,* 1999.

WRITINGS

Stage Plays:
(With Richard Hartley) *The Rocky Horror Show* (adapted from O'Brien's novel *They Came from Denton High*), first produced in 1973, Belasco Theatre, New York City, 1975, published by Samuel French, 1983.
T. Zee (based on characters by Edgar Rice Burroughs), 1976.
Disaster, 1978.
Top People, 1984.

Screenplays:
(With Jim Sharman) *The Rocky Horror Picture Show* (adapted from O'Brien's play *The Rocky Horror Show*), Twentieth Century-Fox, 1975.
Digital Dreams, 1983.

Film Music:
The Rocky Horror Picture Show (adapted from O'Brien's play *The Rocky Horror Show*), Twentieth Century-Fox, 1975.
Shock Treatment (based on O'Brien's novel), Twentieth Century-Fox, 1981.
(Lyrics only) *The Return of Captain Invincible* (also known as *Legend in Leotards*), 1983.

Television Movies:
A Hymn from Jim, 1977.

Novels:
They Came from Denton High, 1977.

Also wrote *Shock Treatment.*

Adaptations: *The Rocky Horror Picture Show* was adapted by Richard J. Anobile as *The Official Rocky Horror Picture Show Movie Novel,* for A and W Visual Library, 1980.*

ORBACH, Jerry 1935-

PERSONAL

Full name, Jerome Orbach; born October 20, 1935, in Bronx, NY; son of Leon (a restaurant manager) and Emily (a greeting card manufacturer; maiden name, Olexy) Orbach; married Marta Curro (an actress and writer), June 21, 1958 (divorced, 1975); married Elaine Cancilla, October 7, 1979; children: (first marriage) Anthony Nicholas, Christopher Ben. *Education:* Attended University of Illinois at Urbana-Champaign, 1952-53, and Northwestern University, 1953-55; trained for the stage with Herbert Berghof, Mira Rostova, and Lee Strasberg; studied singing with Hazel Schweppe.

Addresses: *Agent*—Paradigm, 10100 Santa Monica Blvd., 25th Floor, Los Angeles, CA 90067.

Career: Actor. Show Case Theatre, Evanston, IL, member of company, 1953-54.

Member: Actors' Equity Association, Screen Actors Guild, American Federation of Television and Radio Artists, Lone Star Boat Club.

Awards, Honors: New March of Dimes Horizon Award, 1961; Actors Fund Award of Merit, 1961; Antoinette Perry Award nomination, best supporting or featured actor in a musical, 1965, for *Guys and Dolls;* Antoinette Perry Award, best actor in a musical, and Drama Desk Award, outstanding performance, both 1969, for *Promises, Promises;* Antoinette Perry Award nomination, best actor in a musical, 1976, for *Chicago;* Emmy Award nomination, outstanding guest actor in a comedy series, 1990, for *The Golden Girls;* Emmy Award nomination, outstanding supporting actor in a miniseries or special, 1992, for *Neil Simon's Broadway Bound;* Annie Award nomination, outstanding individual achievement for voice acting by a male performer in an animated feature production, 1998, for *Beauty and the Beast: The Enchanted Christmas;* Q Award nomination, Viewers for Quality Television, best supporting actor in a quality dramatic series, 1998, Screen Actors Guild Award nomination, outstanding performance by an ensemble in a drama series (with others), 1998-99, all for *Law & Order.*

CREDITS

Stage Appearances:

(Stage debut) Typewriter man, *Room Service,* Chevy Chase Tent Theatre, Wheeling, IL, 1952.

Picnic, Gristmill Playhouse, Andover, NJ, 1955.

The Caine Mutiny Court-Martial, Gristmill Playhouse, 1955.

(Off-Broadway debut) Streetsinger and other roles, *The Threepenny Opera,* Theatre de Lys, 1955.

Mannion, *Mister Roberts,* Dayton Municipal Auditorium, Dayton, OH, then Shubert Theatre, Cincinnati, OH, both 1959.

Kralohome, *The King and I,* Dayton Municipal Auditorium, then Shubert Theatre, both 1959.

Dr. Sanderson, *Harvey,* Dayton Municipal Auditorium, then Shubert Theatre, both 1959.

Benny, *Guys and Dolls,* Dayton Municipal Auditorium, then Shubert Theatre, both 1959.

The Student Prince, Dayton Municipal Auditorium, then Shubert Theatre, both 1959.

El Gallo, the narrator, *The Fantasticks,* Sullivan Street Playhouse, New York City, 1960.

Paul Berthalet, *Carnival!,* Imperial Theatre, New York City, 1961, then Shubert Theatre, Chicago, IL, 1963.

Larry Foreman, *The Cradle Will Rock,* Theatre Four, New York City, 1964.

Sky Masterson, *Guys and Dolls,* City Center Theatre, New York City, 1965.

Jigger Craigin, *Carousel,* State Theatre, New York City, 1965.

Charlie Davenport, *Annie Get Your Gun,* State Theatre, 1966.

Malcolm, *The Natural Look,* Longacre Theatre, New York City, 1967.

Harold Wonder, *Scuba Duba,* New Theatre, New York City, 1967.

Chuck Baxter, *Promises, Promises,* Shubert Theatre, New York City, 1968.

Paul Friedman, *6 Rms Riv Vu,* Helen Hayes Theatre, New York City, 1972.

The Rose Tattoo, Philadelphia Drama Guild, Walnut Street Theatre, Philadelphia, PA, 1973.

The Trouble with People . . . And Other Things, Coconut Grove Theatre, Miami, FL, 1974.

Billy Flynn, *Chicago,* 46th Street Theatre, New York City, 1975.

Julian Marsh, *42nd Street,* Winter Garden Theatre, New York City, 1980, then Majestic Theatre, New York City, 1981.

Major Tours:

Paul Friedman, *6 Rms Riv Vu,* U.S. cities, 1973.

Billy Flynn, *Chicago,* U.S. cities, 1977-78.

George Schneider, *Chapter Two,* U.S. cities, 1978-79.

Film Appearances:

Gang leader-Mumzer, *Cop Hater,* United Artists, 1958.

Joe, *Mad Dog Coll,* Columbia, 1961.

Pinkerton, *John Goldfarb, Please Come Home,* Twentieth Century-Fox, 1964.

Kid Sally Palumbo, *The Gang That Couldn't Shoot Straight,* Metro-Goldwyn-Mayer, 1971.

Fred, *A Fan's Notes,* Warner Bros., 1972.

Lorsey, *Foreplay* (also known as *The President's Women* and *Foreplay*), Cinema National, 1975.

Michael Dayton, film director, *The Sentinel,* Universal, 1977.

Gus Levy, *Prince of the City,* Warner Bros., 1981.

Underground Aces, 1981.

Charley Pegler, *Brewster's Millions,* Universal, 1985.

Nicholas DeFranco, *F/X* (also known as *F/X: Murder by Illusion*), Orion, 1986.

Byron Caine, *The Imagemaker,* Castle Hill/Manson, 1986.

Dr. Jake Houseman, *Dirty Dancing,* Vestron, 1987.

Leo, *I Love N.Y.,* Manley, 1987.

Lieutenant Garber, *Someone to Watch Over Me,* Columbia, 1987.

Jack Rosenthal, *Crimes and Misdemeanors,* Orion, 1989.

Boyce, *Last Exit to Brooklyn,* Cinecom, 1989.

Bartoli, *Dead Women in Lingerie,* Monarch Home Video, 1990.

Voice of Lumiere, *Beauty and the Beast* (animated), Buena Vista, 1991.

Lou Sherwood, *Delirious,* Metro-Goldwyn-Mayer/Pathe, 1991.

Larry, *Delusion,* IRS Releasing, 1991.

Detective Ronnie Donziger, *Out for Justice,* Warner Bros., 1991.

Constantin, *California Casanova,* Academy Home Entertainment, 1991.

(Uncredited) Albert Trotta, *Toy Soldiers,* 1991.

Phil Gussman, *Mr. Saturday Night,* Columbia, 1992.

Milo Jacoby, *Straight Talk,* Buena Vista, 1992.

Dr. Gregor, *Universal Soldier,* TriStar, 1992.

Stan Walton, *The Adventures of a Gnome Called Gnorm* (also known as *Upworld*), 1993.

Voice of Sa'luk, *Aladdin and the King of Thieves* (animated), Walt Disney Home Video, 1996.

Belle's Magical World (animated), 1997.

Voice of Lumiere, *Beauty and the Beast: The Enchanted Christmas* (animated), Walt Disney Home Video, 1997.

Prince of Central Park, 1999.
Jake, *Chinese Coffee,* 1999.

Also appeared in *The Cemetery Club.*

Television Appearances; Series:

Voice of Zachary Foxx, *Adventures of the Galaxy Rangers* (animated), syndicated, 1986.
Harry McGraw, *The Law and Harry McGraw,* CBS, 1987-88.
Detective Leonard "Lennie" Briscoe, *Law & Order,* NBC, 1992—.

Television Appearances; Movies:

Sam Bianchi, *An Invasion of Privacy,* CBS, 1983.
Spicer, *Love Among Thieves,* ABC, 1987.
Blaine Counter, *Perry Mason: The Case of the Musical Murder* (also known as *Perry Mason: The Case of the Final Curtain* and *The Case of the Musical Murder*), NBC, 1989.
Alan Michelson, *In Defense of a Married Man,* ABC, 1990.
Tony Salducci, "None So Blind" (also known as "Kojak"), *The ABC Saturday Mystery,* ABC, 1990.
Vic St. John, *Perry Mason: The Case of the Ruthless Reporter* (also known as *Perry Mason: The Case of the Late Newsman*), NBC, 1991.
Vincent Callafato, *Quiet Killer* (also known as *Panic in the City* and *Black Death*), CBS, 1992.
Jack Jerome, *Neil Simon's Broadway Bound,* ABC, 1992.
Congressman Byers, *Mastergate,* Showtime, 1992.
Detective Lennie Briscoe, *Exiled: A Law & Order Movie,* NBC, 1998.

Television Appearances; Miniseries:

John Sutter, *Dream West,* CBS, 1986.
Mort Viner, *Out on a Limb,* ABC, 1987.

Television Appearances; Episodic:

"Field of Battle," *The Nurses,* CBS, 1963.
Bob Hope Presents the Chrysler Theatre, NBC, 1964.
"The Sworn Twelve," *The Defenders,* CBS, 1965.
"Never, Never, Ever Again . . . Maybe," *Diana,* NBC, 1973.
Love, American Style, ABC, 1973.
Brubaker, "A Question of Answers," *Kojak,* CBS, 1975.
"Captives," *Medical Center,* CBS, 1975.
Lars Mangros, "Space Rockers," *Buck Rogers in the 25th Century,* NBC, 1980.
"Hot Line," *Trapper John, M.D.,* CBS, 1980.
Brian Merrick, *Our Family Honor,* ABC, 1985.
Harry McGraw, "Tough Guys Don't Die," *Murder, She Wrote,* CBS, 1985.
Harry McGraw, "One Good Bid Deserves Murder," *Murder, She Wrote,* CBS, 1986.
Harry McGraw, "Death Takes a Dive," *Murder, She Wrote,* CBS, 1987.
"Cabin Fever," *The Hitchhiker,* HBO, 1987.
Malcolm Shanley III, *Simon & Simon,* CBS, 1988.
Harry McGraw, "Double Exposure," *Murder, She Wrote,* CBS, 1989.
Sal Scarlatti, "Son and Heir," *Hunter,* NBC, 1990.
Glen, "Cheaters," *The Golden Girls,* NBC, 1990.
Voice, "Coney Island," *The American Experience,* PBS, 1991.
Harry McGraw, "From the Horse's Mouth," *Murder, She Wrote,* CBS, 1991.
Harry McGraw, "The Skinny According to Nick Culhane," *Murder, She Wrote,* CBS, 1991.
Frank Lehrman, "The Wages of Love," *Law & Order,* NBC, 1991.
Detective Lennie Briscoe, "For God and Country," *Homicide: Life on the Street,* NBC, 1996.
Voice of Mitch, "High Crane Drifter," *Frasier,* NBC, 1996.
Gourmet Getaways with Robin Leach, Food Network, 1996.
Detective Lennie Briscoe, "Baby, It's You: Part 2," *Homicide: Life on the Street,* NBC, 1997.

Also appeared on *The Shari Lewis Show,* NBC; and *The Jack Paar Show,* NBC.

Television Appearances; Specials:

Cristol, *Twenty-Four Hours in a Woman's Life,* CBS, 1961.
Charles Davenport, *Annie Get Your Gun,* NBC, 1967.
Mitzi: A Tribute to the American Housewife, CBS, 1974.
The Way They Were, syndicated, 1981.
Sam Nash, "Visitor from Mamaroneck," Jesse Kiplinger, "Visitor from Hollywood," and Rob Hubley, "Visitor from Forest Hills," in *Plaza Suite,* HBO, 1982.
Sergeant Max Grozzo, *The Streets* (also known as *Street Heat*), NBC, 1984.
Irving Berlin's 100th Birthday Celebration, CBS, 1988.
"A Salute to Broadway: The Shows," in *Performance at the White House,* PBS, 1988.
Phil Brody, *The Flamingo Kid,* ABC, 1989.
Be Our Guest: The Making of Disney's "Beauty and the Beast," The Disney Channel, 1991.
The 64th Annual Academy Awards Presentation, ABC, 1992.
Judge, *The 1995 Miss America Pageant,* 1995.

Host, *You Be The Judge,* NBC, 1998.
Bob Fosse: The E! True Hollywood Story, E! Entertainment Television, 1999.

RECORDINGS

Albums:
The Fantasticks (original cast recording), Metro-Goldwyn-Mayer, 1960, reissued by Polydor.
Carnival! (original cast recording), Metro-Goldwyn-Mayer, 1961.
Jerry Orbach Off-Broadway, Metro-Goldwyn-Mayer, 1961.
The Cradle Will Rock (cast recording), Metro-Goldwyn-Mayer, 1965.
Carousel (cast recording), RCA Victor, 1965.
Annie Get Your Gun (cast recording), RCA Victor, 1966.
Alan Jay Lerner Revisited, Crewe, 1966, reissued by Painted Smiles.
Promises, Promises (original cast recording), United Artists Records, 1969, reissued by Liberty.
Chicago (original cast recording), Arista, 1975.
42nd Street (original cast recording), RCA Red Seal, 1980.

Singles:
"Love Stolen," Take Home Tunes, 1976.

OTHER SOURCES

Periodicals:
Entertainment Weekly, December 5, 1997, pp. 61-62.
People Weekly, October 14, 1996, p. 49; August 17, 1998, p. 23.*

ORMOND, Julia 1965-

PERSONAL

Full name, Julia Karin Ormond; born January 4, 1965, in Epsom, Surrey, England; married Rory Edwards (an actor; divorced). *Education:* Webber Douglas Academy of Dramatic Art, graduated in 1988.

Addresses: *Agent*—Kevin Huvane, Creative Artists Agency, 9830 Wilshire Blvd., Beverly Hills, CA 90212.

Career: Actress and producer. Fox Searchlight Pictures, two-year contract to produce, direct, and write films, 1997-99.

Awards, Honors: London Critics' Award, best newcomer, 1989, for *Faith, Hope and Charity;* ShoWest Award, Female Star of Tomorrow, 1995.

CREDITS

Film Appearances:
(Film debut) The daughter, *The Baby of Macon,* 1992.
Susannah Finncannon, *Legends of the Fall,* TriStar, 1994.
Marie, *Nostradamus,* Orion Classics, 1994.
Rachel Clifford, *Captives,* Miramax, 1994.
Guinevere, *First Knight,* Columbia, 1995.
Sabrina Fairchild, *Sabrina,* Paramount, 1995.
Smilla Jaspersen, *Smilla's Sense of Snow* (also known as *Smilla's Feeling for Snow*), Twentieth Century-Fox, 1997.
Jane Callahan, *The Barber of Siberia* (also known as *Sibirskij tsiryulnik*), Intermedia Film Distribution, 1998.

Film Work:
Executive producer, *Calling the Ghosts: A Story About Rape, Women and War,* 1996.

Television Appearances; Miniseries:
Caroline Lithgow, "Traffik," *Masterpiece Theatre,* PBS, 1990.
Catherine, *Young Catherine,* TNT, 1991.

Television Appearances; Movies:
Nadya Alliluyeva, *Stalin,* HBO, 1992.

Television Appearances; Episodic:
Capital City, 1989.

Television Appearances; Specials:
The 67th Annual Academy Awards, ABC, 1995.
The 54th Annual Golden Globe Awards, 1997.

Stage Appearances:
Worked in regional theaters in London, 1988-94, including an appearance in the stage production of *Faith, Hope and Charity,* 1989; and also made an appearance as Cathy in *Wuthering Heights.*

OTHER SOURCES

Periodicals:
Entertainment Weekly, April 21, 1995, pp. 6-7.
New York Times Magazine, April 9, 1995, pp. 49-53, 70, 78, 86-87.
Premiere, September, 1994, p. 87.*

O'TOOLE, Peter 1932-

PERSONAL

Born Seamus O'Toole, August 2, 1932, in Connemara, County Galway, Ireland; son of Patrick Joseph (a bookie) and Constance Jane (maiden name, Ferguson) O'Toole; married Sian Phillips, 1959 (divorced, 1979); married Karen Brown (a model), 1983 (divorced, 1988); children: (first marriage) Kate, Pat, (second marriage) Lorcan. *Education:* Trained for the stage at the Royal Academy of Dramatic Art, 1952-54. *Avocational Interests:* Coaching cricket.

Addresses: *Agent*—William Morris Agency, 31-32 Soho Square, London W1V 5DG, England.

Career: Actor. Artistic director, Royal Alexandra Theatre, U.S. tour, 1978; partner, Keep Films, Ltd. Worked as a newspaper copy boy and reporter before becoming an actor. *Military service:* Royal Navy.

Member: The Garrick Club.

Awards, Honors: Actor of the Year, London, 1959; British Academy of Film and Television Arts Award, best British actor in a film, and Academy Award nomination, best actor, both 1962, for *Lawrence of Arabia;* Grammy Award nomination, documentary, spoken word or drama recording, 1964, for *Dialogue Highlights from "Becket";* Academy Award nomination, best actor, 1964, Golden Globe Award, best motion picture actor—drama, and British Academy of Film and Television Arts Award nomination, best British actor, both 1965, all for *Becket;* Academy Award nomination, best actor, 1968, and Golden Globe Award, best actor in a dramatic film, 1969, both for *The Lion in Winter;* National Board of Review Award, best actor, 1969, Academy Award nomination, best actor, and Golden Globe Award, best actor in a musical/comedy film, both 1970, all for *Goodbye, Mr. Chips;* National Board of Review Award, best actor, 1972, for *Man of La Mancha;* National Board of Review Award, best actor, 1972, and Academy Award nomination, best actor, 1973, both for *The Ruling Class;* Golden Globe Award nomination, best motion picture actor-musical/comedy, 1973, for *Man of La Mancha;* Academy Award nomination, best actor, National Society of Film Critics Award, best actor 1980, and Golden Globe Award nomination, best motion picture actor—drama, 1981, all for *The Stunt Man;* Emmy Award nomination, best actor in a limited series or special, 1981, and Golden Globe Award nomination, best performance by an actor in a miniseries or motion picture made for television, 1982, both for *Masada;* Academy Award nomination, best actor, 1982, and Golden Globe Award nomination, best actor in a motion picture—comedy/musical, 1983, both for *My Favorite Year;* Decorated Commander des Arts et des Lettres, 1988; British Academy of Film and Television Arts Award nomination, best actor in a supporting role, 1989, for *The Last Emperor.*

CREDITS

Film Appearances:

Robin MacGregor, *Kidnapped,* Buena Vista, 1960.
Captain Fitch, *The Day They Robbed the Bank of England,* Metro-Goldwyn-Mayer, 1960.
First trooper, *The Savage Innocents,* Paramount, 1961.
Title role, *Lawrence of Arabia,* Columbia, 1962.
King Henry II, *Becket,* Paramount, 1964.
Title role, *Lord Jim,* Columbia, 1965.
Michael James, *What's New Pussycat,* United Artists, 1965.
(Uncredited) Voice, *The Sandpiper,* Metro-Goldwyn-Mayer, 1965.
The Three Angels, *The Bible . . . in the Beginning* (also known as *La Bibbia*), Twentieth Century-Fox, 1966.
Simon Dermott, *How to Steal a Million* (also known as *How to Steal a Million Dollars* and *Live Happily Ever After*), Twentieth Century-Fox, 1966.
General Tanz, *The Night of the Generals,* Columbia, 1967.
(Uncredited) Piper, *Charles K. Feldman's Casino Royale,* Columbia, 1967.
King Henry II, *The Lion in Winter,* Avco Embassy, 1968.
Captain Charles Edstaston, *Great Catherine,* Warner Bros., 1968.
Arthur Chipping, *Goodbye Mr. Chips,* Metro-Goldwyn-Mayer, 1969.
Sir Charles Henry Arbuthot Pinkerton Ferguson, *Brotherly Love* (also known as *Country Dance*), Metro-Goldwyn-Mayer, 1970.
Murphy, *Murphy's War,* Paramount, 1971.
Miguel de Cervantes, Don Quixote-Quijana, *Man of La Mancha,* United Artists, 1972.
Jack Arnold Alexander Tancred Gurney, 14th Earl of Gurney, *The Ruling Class,* Avco Embassy, 1972.
Captain Cat, *Under Milk Wood,* Altura, 1973.
Liviu, *Foxtrot* (also known as *The Far Side of Paradise* and *The Other Side of Paradise*), New World, 1975.
Robinson Crusoe, *Man Friday,* Avco Embassy, 1975.

Larry Martin, *Rosebud,* United Artists, 1975.
Coup d'Etat, 1977.
Colonel Zeller, *Power Play* (also known as *Operation Overthrow* and *State of Shock*), Robert Cooper, 1978.
Tiberius, *Caligula,* PAC, 1979.
Lord Chelmsford, *Zulu Dawn,* Warner Bros., 1979.
The Antagonists, 1981.
Eli Cross, *The Stunt Man,* Twentieth Century-Fox, 1981.
Alan Swann, *My Favorite Year,* Metro-Goldwyn-Mayer, 1982.
Zaltar, *Supergirl* (also known as *Supergirl: The Movie*), TriStar, 1984.
Buried Alive, Aquarius, 1984.
Dr. Harry Wolper, *Creator,* Universal, 1985.
Governor Anthony Cloyden Hayes, *Club Paradise,* Warner Bros., 1986.
Reginald "R.J." Johnston, *The Last Emperor,* Columbia, 1987.
Peter Plunkett, *High Spirits,* TriStar, 1989.
Professor McShoul, *On a Moonlit Night* (also known as *In una notte di chiaro di luna, As Long As It's Love,* and *Crystal or Ash, Fire or Wind, as Long as It's Love*), 1989.
Cesar Valentin, *Wings of Fame,* 1990.
Prince Meleagre, *The Rainbow Thief,* 1990.
Voice of Pantaloon, *The Nutcracker Prince* (animated), Warner Bros., 1990.
Willingham, *King Ralph,* Universal, 1991.
Major Lyautey, *Isabelle Eberhardt,* 1991.
Lord Sarn, *Rebecca's Daughters,* 1992.
Emil Saber, *The Seventh Coin* (also known as *Worlds Apart*), Hemdale Releasing, 1993.
Sir Arthur Conan Doyle, *FairyTale: A True Story* (also known as *Fairy Tale* and *Illumination*), Paramount, 1997.
Timothy Flyte, *Dean Koontz' Phantoms,* Dimension/Miramax, 1998.
Mr. Ravenscroft, *The Manor,* 1999.
William Williamson, *Father Damien,* Vine International Pictures, 1999.

Also appeared in *Hidden Talent; Helena; Wings of Fame;* and *The Pit and the Pendulum.*

Television Appearances; Miniseries:
Strumpet City, RTE, 1979.
Cornelius Flavius Silva, *Masada,* ABC, 1981.
Sam Trump, *John Jakes' Heaven and Hell: North and South, Part III* (also known as *Heaven and Hell: North and South, Part III*), ABC, 1994.
Emperor of Lilliput, *Gulliver's Travels,* NBC, 1996.
Heim Kehr, 1998.
Bishop Cauchon, *Joan of Arc,* CBS, 1999.

Television Appearances; Movies:
Captain Robert Thorndyke, *Rogue Male,* BBC, 1976.
Anton Bosnyak, *Svengali,* CBS, 1983.
Henry Higgins, *Pygmalion,* Showtime, 1983.
Lama, *Kim,* CBS, 1984.
John Sidney Howard, *Crossing to Freedom* (also known as *Pied Piper*), CBS, 1990.
Barry Newman, *Civvies,* 1992.
Colonel Carey-Lewis, *Coming Home,* 1998.

Television Appearances; Specials:
Present Laughter, ABC, 1968.
Supergirl: The Making of the Movie, ABC, 1985.
John Hampton, "Banshee," *Ray Bradbury Theater,* HBO, 1986.
Silas Ruthyn, "The Dark Angel," BBC, 1988, then *Mystery!,* PBS, 1991.
The 18th Annual American Film Institute Life Achievement Award: A Salute to Sir David Lean, ABC, 1990.
"Peter O'Toole," *South Bank Show,* Bravo, 1993.
Clarence Earl of Emsworth, "Heavy Weather," *Mobil Masterpiece Theatre,* PBS, 1996.

Television Appearances; Episodic:
Monitor, NBC, 1983.
The Ray Bradbury Theater, USA Network, 1987.
Champlin on Film, Bravo, 1989.
TFI Friday, 1996.

Also appeared as first soldier, "A Tale of two Pigtales," *The Scarlet Pimpernel.*

Stage Appearances:
Cabman, *The Matchmaker,* Bristol Old Vic Company, Old Vic Theatre, London, 1955.
Corvino, *Volpone,* Bristol Old Vic Company, Old Vic Theatre, 1955.
Peter Shirley, *Major Barbara,* Bristol Old Vic Company, Old Vic Theatre, 1956.
Duke of Cornwall, *King Lear,* Bristol Old Vic Company, Old Vic Theatre, 1956.
Hebert, *The Empty Chair,* Bristol Old Vic Company, Old Vic Theatre, 1956.
Bullock, *The Recruiting Officer,* Bristol Old Vic Company, Old Vic Theatre, 1956.
Maupa, *The Queen and the Rebels,* Bristol Old Vic Company, Old Vic Theatre, 1956.
Cardinal Malko Barberini, *Lamp at Midnight,* Bristol Old Vic Company, Old Vic Theatre, 1956.
Lodovico, *Othello,* Bristol Old Vic Company, Old Vic Theatre, 1956.
Baron Parsnip, *The Sleeping Beauty,* Bristol Old Vic Company, Old Vic Theatre, 1956.

Mr. Jaggers, *Great Expectations,* Bristol Old Vic Company, Old Vic Theatre, 1957.
Alfred Doolittle, *Pygmalion,* Bristol Old Vic Company, Old Vic Theatre, 1957.
Lysander, *A Midsummer Night's Dream,* Bristol Old Vic Company, Old Vic Theatre, 1957.
Jimmy Porter, *Look Back in Anger,* Bristol Old Vic Company, Old Vic Theatre, 1957.
Uncle Gustave, *Oh, My Papa!,* Bristol Old Vic Company, Old Vic Theatre, 1957, then Garrick Theatre, London, 1957.
The Angel, *Sodom and Gomorrah,* Bristol Old Vic Company, Old Vic Theatre, 1957.
The General, *Romanoff and Juliet,* Bristol Old Vic Company, Old Vic Theatre, 1957.
Mrs. Millie Baba, *Ali Baba and the Forty Thieves,* Bristol Old Vic Company, Old Vic Theatre, London, 1957.
John Tanner, *Man and Superman,* Bristol Old Vic Company, Old Vic Theatre, 1958.
Title role, *Hamlet,* Bristol Old Vic Company, Old Vic Theatre, 1958.
Paddy, *The Pier,* Bristol Old Vic Company, Old Vic Theatre, 1958.
Jupiter, *Amphitryon 38,* Bristol Old Vic Company, Old Vic Theatre, 1958.
Private Banforth, *The Long and the Short and the Tall,* Royal Court Theatre, then New Theatre, London, 1959.
Shylock, *The Merchant of Venice,* Shakespeare Memorial Theatre Company, Statford-upon-Avon, England, 1960.
Petruchio, *The Taming of the Shrew,* Shakespeare Memorial Theatre Company, Statford-upon-Avon, 1960.
Thersites, *Troilus and Cressida,* Shakespeare Memorial Theatre Company, Statford-upon-Avon, 1960.
Title role, *Baal,* Phoenix Theatre, London, 1963.
Title role, *Hamlet,* with the National Theatre Company, Old Vic Theatre, London, 1963.
Peter, *Ride a Cock Horse,* Piccadilly Theatre, London, 1965.
Captain Jack Boyle, *Juno and the Paycock,* Gaiety Theatre, Dublin, Ireland, 1966.
John Tanner, *Man and Superman,* Gaiety Theatre, Dublin, Ireland, 1969.
Vladimir, *Waiting for Godot;* Abbey Theatre, Dublin, Ireland, 1969.
Title role, *Uncle Vanya,* Bristol Old Vic Company, Old Vic Theatre, 1973.
D'Arcy Tuck, *Plunder,* Bristol Old Vic Company, Old Vic Theatre, 1973.
King Magnus, *The Apple Cart,* Bristol Old Vic Company, Old Vic Theatre, 1974.
Solo reader, *Justice,* Bristol Old Vic Company, Old Vic Theatre, 1974.
Dead-Eyed Dicks, Dublin Festival Theatre, Dublin, Ireland, 1976.
Macbeth, Old Vic Theatre, London, 1978.
Man and Superman, London, 1982-83.
Professor Henry Higgins, *Pygmalion,* 1984.
Professor Henry Higgins, *Pygmalion,* Plymouth Theatre, New York City, 1987.
Jeffrey Bernard, *Jeffrey Bernard Is Unwell,* The Apollo Theatre, London, 1989, then Shaftesbury Theatre, London, 1991.
Roger Piper, *Our Song,* The Apollo Theatre, London, 1992.

Made stage debut at Civic Theatre, Leeds, England, 1949.

Major Tours:
Roger Muir, *The Holiday,* U.K. cities, 1958.
Present Laughter, Royal Alexandra Theatre, U.S. cities, 1978.
Uncle Vanya, Royal Alexandra Theatre, U.S. cities, 1978.

WRITINGS

Autobiography:
Loitering with Intent (also known as *The Child*), Hyperion (New York City), 1993.*

OZ, Frank 1944-

PERSONAL

Born Frank Richard Oznowicz, May 25, 1944, in Hereford, England; son of Isidore and Frances Oznowicz. *Education:* Attended Oakland City College, 1962.

Addresses: *Office*—Jim Henson Productions, 117 East 69th St., New York, NY 10021-5404.

Career: Puppeteer, actor, producer, director, and screenwriter. Puppeteer with the Muppets, 1963—; vice president and producer, Jim Henson Productions, New York City; directed commercials.

Member: American Federation of Television and Radio Artists, Directors Guild of America, Writers Guild of America, Screen Actors Guild, Academy of Television Arts and Sciences.

Awards, Honors: Emmy Awards, individual achievement in children's programming, 1974 and 1976, both for *Sesame Street;* Emmy Award nomination, best comedy—variety or music series, 1977, for *The Muppet Show;* Emmy Award, best comedy—variety or music series, 1978, for *The Muppet Show;* Emmy Award nominations, best variety, music, or comedy program, 1979 and 1981, for *The Muppet Show;* Creative Achievement Award, American Comedy Award, 1998.

CREDITS

Film Appearances:

Puppeteer and voice of Miss Piggy, Fozzie Bear, Animal, and Sam the Eagle, *The Muppet Movie,* Associated Film Distributors, 1979.

Corrections officer, *The Blues Brothers,* Universal, 1980.

Voice of Yoda, *The Empire Strikes Back* (also known as *Star Wars: Episode V: The Empire Strikes Back*), Twentieth Century-Fox, 1980.

Mr. Collins and voice of Miss Piggy, *An American Werewolf in London* (also known as *American Werewolf*), Universal, 1981.

Puppeteer and voice of Miss Piggy, Fozzie Bear, Animal, and Sam the Eagle, *The Great Muppet Caper,* Universal, 1981.

Puppet operator for Aughra and Skeksis Chamberlain, *The Dark Crystal,* Universal/Associated Film Distributors/ITC Entertainment, 1982.

Voice of Yoda, *Return of the Jedi* (also known as *Star Wars: Episode VI: Return of Jedi*), Twentieth Century-Fox, 1983.

Corrupt cop, *Trading Places,* Paramount, 1983.

Puppeteer and voice of Miss Piggy, Fozzie Bear, and Animal, *The Muppets Take Manhattan,* TriStar, 1984.

Puppeteer and voice of Cookie Monster, Bert, and Grover, *Sesame Street Presents: Follow That Bird!* (also known as *Follow That Bird*), Warner Bros.,1985.

Test monitor, *Spies Like Us,* Warner Bros., 1985.

Wiseman, *Labyrinth,* TriStar, 1986.

Puppeteer and voice of Fozzie Bear and Miss Piggy, *Muppet*vision 3-D* (also known as *Jim Henson's Muppet*vision 3-D, Kermit the Frog Presents Muppet*vision 3-D,* and *Muppet*vision 4-D*), 1991.

Pathologist, *Innocent Blood,* Warner Bros., 1992.

Puppeteer and voice of Miss Piggy, Fozzie Bear, Sam the Eagle, and Animal, *The Muppet Christmas Carol,* Buena Vista, 1992.

Puppeteer and voice of Miss Piggy (Benjamina Gunn), Fozzie Bear (Squire Trelawney), Sam the Eagle (Mr. Erroll), and Animal, *Muppet Treasure Island,* Buena Vista, 1996.

Warden, *Blues Brothers 2000,* Universal, 1998.

Voice of Yoda, *Star Wars: Episode 1: The Phantom Menace,* Twentieth Century-Fox, 1999.

Voice of Miss Piggy and Fozzie Bear, *Muppets from Space,* Columbia, 1999.

Voice of Bert, *The Adventures of Elmo in Grouchland,* Columbia, 1999.

Film Work:

(With David Lazer) Producer and creative consultant, *The Great Muppet Caper,* Universal, 1981.

(With Jim Henson) Director, *The Dark Crystal,* Universal/Associated Film Distributors/ITC Entertainment, 1982.

Director, *The Muppets Take Manhattan,* TriStar, 1984.

Director, *Little Shop of Horrors,* Warner Bros., 1986.

Director, *Dirty Rotten Scoundrels,* Orion, 1988.

Director, *What about Bob?,* Buena Vista, 1991.

Director, *Housesitter,* Universal, 1992.

Executive producer, *The Muppet Christmas Carol,* Buena Vista, 1992.

Director, *The Indian in the Cupboard,* Paramount, 1995.

Executive producer, *Muppet Treasure Island,* Buena Vista, 1996.

Director, *In & Out,* Paramount, 1997.

Director, *Bowfinger,* Universal, 1999.

Television Appearances; Series:

Puppeteer and voice characterizations with the Muppets, *Sesame Street,* PBS, 1969—.

Puppeteer and voice of Fozzie Bear, Animal, Miss Piggy, Sam the Eagle, Swedish Chef, and others, *The Muppet Show,* syndicated, 1976-81.

Puppeteer and voice characterizations with the Muppets, *Muppets Tonight!,* ABC, 1996.

Television Appearances; Episodic:

Puppeteer and voice of the Mighty Favag, *Saturday Night Live,* NBC, 1975-76.

Also appeared as puppeteer and voice of Miss Piggy, *Dolly.*

Television Appearances; Specials:

Puppeteer and voice characterizations with the Muppets, *Julie Andrews: One Step into Spring,* CBS, 1978.

Puppeteer and voice characterizations with the Muppets, *The Muppets Go Hollywood,* 1981.

Puppeteer and voice of Miss Piggy, *The Fantastic Miss Piggy Show,* ABC, 1982.

Puppeteer and voice of Miss Piggy, *San Francisco Ballet in Cinderella,* PBS, 1985.

Puppeteer and voice characterizations with the Muppets, *The Muppets—ACelebration of 30 Years,* CBS, 1986.

Puppeteer and voice characterizations with the Muppets, *The Television Academy Hall of Fame,* 1986.

Puppeteer and voice characterizations with the Muppets, *A Muppet Family Christmas* (also known as *Christmas at Home with the Muppets*), ABC, 1987.

Puppeteer and voice characterizations with the Muppets, *Sesame Street Special,* PBS, 1988.

Puppeteer and voice characterizations with the Muppets, *Free to Be . . . a Family,* 1988.

Puppeteer and voice characterizations with the Muppets, *Sesame Street . . . 20 and Still Counting,* PBS, 1989.

Puppeteer and voice of Miss Piggy, *The 41st Annual Emmy Awards,* Fox, 1989.

Puppeteer and voice characterizations with the Muppets, *The Muppets at Walt Disney World,* NBC, 1990.

Disneyland's 35th Anniversary Special, CBS, 1990.

The Muppets Celebrate Jim Henson, CBS, 1990.

Puppeteer and voice of Grover and Cookie Monster, *Big Bird's Birthday or Let Me Eat Cake,* PBS, 1991.

Puppeteer and voice characterizations with the Muppets, *Holiday Greetings from the Ed Sullivan Show,* CBS, 1992.

"George Lucas: Heroes, Myths and Magic," *American Masters,* PBS, 1993.

Sesame Street Stays Up Late! A Monster New Year's Eve Party, PBS, 1993.

"The World of Jim Henson," *Great Performances,* PBS, 1994.

Puppeteer and voice of Cookie Monster and Grover, *Elmo Saves Christmas,* 1996.

The 12th Annual American Comedy Awards, 1998.

Television Work:

Muppet creative consultant, *Emmet Otter's Jug-Band Christmas* (movie), 1977.

Creative consultant, *The Muppets Go Hollywood* (special), 1981.

Creator, *Frankenstein Follies* (series), 1993.

Executive consultant, *Muppets Tonight,* ABC, 1996.

WRITINGS

Screenplays:

(With Tom Patchett) *The Muppets Take Manhattan,* TriStar, 1984.*

P

PANKIN, Stuart 1946-

PERSONAL

Born April 8, 1946, in Philadelphia, PA; children: one son. *Education:* Dickinson College, B.A., 1968; Columbia University, M.F.A., 1971.

Addresses: *Agent*—Abrams Artist and Associates, 9200 Sunset Blvd., Suite 625, Los Angeles, CA 90069. *Contact*—B/G/E Management, 9150 Wilshire Blvd., Beverly Hills, CA 90212.

Career: Actor and producer.

Awards, Honors: Annual Cable Excellence (ACE) Award, best actor, for *Not Necessarily the News.*

CREDITS

Television Appearances; Series:

Anthony "Stuff" Danelli, *The San Pedro Beach Bums,* ABC, 1977.

Benny Appleman, *Knots Landing,* CBS, 1979, 1991.

Al Tuttle, *No Soap, Radio,* ABC, 1982.

Bob Charles and other roles, *Not Necessarily the News,* HBO, 1983-88.

Jace Simpson, *Falcon Crest,* CBS, 1989-90.

Mike Dooley, *Nearly Departed* (also known as *Ghost Story*), NBC, 1989.

Voice of Earl Sinclair, *Dinosaurs,* ABC, 1991-94.

Vice Principal Kurt Fust, *Nick Freno: Licensed Teacher,* The WB, 1996-97.

Television Appearances; Specials:

Earthbound, NBC, 1982.

Not Necessarily Politics, HBO, 1984.

Not Necessarily Television, HBO, 1985.

Not Necessarily the Year in Review, HBO, 1986.

Not Necessarily the News: Inside Politics, HBO, 1987.

Not Necessarily the News: Inside Entertainment, HBO, 1987.

Bob Charles, *Not Necessarily the Media,* HBO, 1987.

Comic Relief II, HBO, 1987.

Not Necessarily the Year in Review, HBO, 1988.

Not Necessarily the News: Reagan's Legacy, HBO, 1988.

Not Necessarily the News of the World, HBO, 1988.

More Best of Not Necessarily the News, HBO, 1988.

Bob Charles, *Not Necessarily the Year in Review,* HBO, 1989.

Not Necessarily the News Reunion, HBO, 1990.

HBO's 20th Anniversary—We Hardly Believe It Ourselves (also known as *HBO's 20th Anniversary Special—We Don't Believe It Ourselves*), HBO and CBS, 1992.

Baseball Relief, HBO, 1993.

The Show Formerly Known as The Martin Short Show, NBC, 1995.

Television Appearances; Awards Presentations:

The 2nd Annual American Comedy Awards, ABC, 1988.

The 9th Annual ACE Awards (also known as *The Golden ACE Awards*), HBO, 1988.

Television Appearances; Movies:

Anthony "Stuff" Danelli, *The San Pedro Beach Bums,* ABC, 1977.

Harvey, *Valentine Magic on Love Island* (also known as *Magic on Love Island*), NBC, 1980.

Robert, *A Different Affair,* CBS, 1987.

Aaron, *Father and Scout,* ABC, 1994.

Calvin Burrows, *Down, Out & Dangerous,* 1995.

James Riley, *Babylon 5: The River of Souls,* TNT, 1998.

Snipes, *Like Father, Like Santa,* Fox Family Channel, 1998.

Commander Plank, *Zenon: Girl of the 21st Century,* The Disney Channel, 1999.

Television Appearances; Episodic:

"The Radical," *Barney Miller,* ABC, 1978.
"Wheels of Fortune," *B. J. and the Bear,* NBC, 1979.
"Uniform Day," *Barney Miller,* ABC, 1980.
House Calls, CBS, 1981.
Louis, "Ponch's Angels: Parts I & II," *CHiPs,* NBC, 1981.
"Boomer and the Musket Cove Treasure," *Here's Boomer,* NBC, 1981.
"Stress," *Benson,* ABC, 1981.
"You Pays Your Money," *Trapper John, M.D.,* CBS, 1982.
"Pandora Vector," *Strike Force,* ABC, 1982.
"Accused," *The Powers of Matthew Star,* NBC, 1982.
"Killing Isn't Everything," *Matt Houston,* ABC, 1982.
"Hello, I Must Be Going," *It Takes Two,* ABC, 1982.
"The Spy Who Bugged Me," *Trapper John, M.D.,* CBS, 1983.
"Shots in the Dark," *Mickey Spillane's Mike Hammer,* CBS, 1984.
"Cash and Carry," *Matt Houston,* CBS, 1984.
Trapper John, M.D., CBS, 1985.
"Sonny's Big Chance," *It's a Living,* syndicated, 1985.
Mr. Melnick, "Up on the Roof," *Night Court,* NBC, 1985.
Plato, *Scarecrow and Mrs. King,* CBS, 1985.
Comedy Break with Mack and Jamie, syndicated, 1985.
Harry Burke, "Wishes," *Fame,* NBC, 1985.
Alex Cummings "A Star Is Born," *Three's a Crowd,* ABC, 1985.
Gary Weed, "Dead on Arrival," *Crazy Like a Fox,* CBS, 1986.
Jacques, *Golden Girls,* NBC, 1986.
Morgan, "That Terrible Swift Sword," *Stingray,* NBC, 1986.
Adelman, "Here's to You, Mrs. Robinson," *Night Court,* NBC, 1987.
Claude Jenkins, "Green Blizzard," *The New Mike Hammer,* CBS, 1987.
Marv, "The Visit," *Family Ties,* NBC, 1987.
Host, "Stuart Pankin," *Cinemax Comedy Experiment,* Cinemax, 1987.
"Mid-Term Blues," *Second Chance,* Fox, 1987.
"The Front," *Boys Will Be Boys,* Fox, 1988.
The Devil, "Trudy and Clyde," *Hooperman,* ABC, 1989.
Gary's brain, *It's Gary Shandling's Show,* Showtime, then Fox, both 1989.
Shoope, "Presumed Insolvent," *Night Court,* NBC, 1991.
Larry Keller, *Me and the Boys,* ABC, 1994.
Sisters, NBC, 1994.
Jerry, *Deadly Games,* UPN, 1995.
Mr. Handy, "They Eat Horses, Don't They?," *Ally McBeal,* Fox, 1998.
Rabbi, "Turn, Turn, Turn," *Dharma & Greg,* ABC, 1998.
Voice, *Disney's Hercules* (animated), ABC and syndicated, 1998.
Mr. Gerard, *For Your Love,* The WB, 1998.
Mad About You, NBC, 1999.

Also appeared as voices of Buddy Standler/Condiment King, *Batman: The Animated Series* (animated).

Television Appearances; Pilots:

Last Change, *Carwash,* NBC, 1979.
Harvey Kreppler, *The Eyes of Texas II,* NBC, 1980.
Lyle Floon, *The Wonderful World of Philip Malley,* CBS, 1981.

Television Work; Episodic:

Co-executive producer, "Stuart Pankin," *Cinemax Comedy Experiment,* Cinemax, 1987.

Film Appearances:

Duane, *Scavenger Hunt,* Twentieth Century-Fox, 1979.
Sam Tate, *Hangar 18* (also known as *Invasion Force*), Sunn Classic, 1980.
Dudley Laywicker, *The Hollywood Knights,* Columbia, 1980.
Nicky LaBelle, *An Eye for an Eye,* Avco Embassy, 1981.
Sweeny, *Earthbound,* Taft International, 1984.
Ronnie, *Irreconcilable Differences,* Warner Bros., 1984.
Mr. Hodgkins, *The Dirt Bike Kid* (also known as *Crazy Wheels*), Concorde/Cinema Group, 1986.
Jimmy, *Fatal Attraction,* Paramount, 1987.
Judge Samuel John, *Love at Stake* (also known as *Burnin' Love*), TriStar, 1987.
Broadcast News, Twentieth Century-Fox, 1987.
Preston Picket, Ph.D., *Second Sight,* Lorimar, 1989.
Sigmund Freud, *That's Adequate,* 1989.
Sheriff Parsons, *Arachnophobia,* Buena Vista, 1990.
Pritchard, *Life Stinks,* Metro-Goldwyn-Mayer/Pathe, 1991.
Mr. James, *Mannequin II: On the Move,* Twentieth Century-Fox, 1991.
Mr. Feemster, *The Vagrant,* Metro-Goldwyn-Mayer/United Artists Home Video, 1992.
Gabe, *Betrayal of the Dove,* Prism Pictures, 1993.
Brother Timothy, *Squanto: A Warrior's Tale* (also known as *Indian Warrior* and *The Lone Brave*), Buena Vista, 1994.

Society photographer, *I Love Trouble,* Buena Vista, 1994.
Silence of the Hams (also known as *Il Silenzio dei Prosciutti*), October Films, 1994.
The giant, *Beanstalk,* 1994.
Boyd, *Congo,* Paramount, 1995.
Voice of Father Penguin, *Napoleon,* Samuel Goldwyn, 1995.
Gerry, *Big Bully,* Warner Bros., 1996.
Alan Mordecai, *Striptease,* Columbia, 1996.
Gordon, *Honey, We Shrunk Ourselves,* Walt Disney Home Video, 1997.
The Professor/Voice of Max, *Encounter in the Third Dimension,* Iwerks Entertainment, 1999.

Stage Appearances:
Jeweler, *Timon of Athens,* New York Shakespeare Festival, Delacorte Theatre, New York City, 1971.
Beast, *The Tale of Cymbeline,* New York Shakespeare Festival, Delacorte Theatre, 1971.
Sheriff of Northampton, *Mary Stuart,* Vivian Beaumont Theatre, New York City, 1971.
Hopkins, *The Crucible,* Vivian Beaumont Theatre, 1972.
Peasant, soldier, and tribesman, *Narrow Road to the Deep North,* Vivian Beaumont Theatre, 1972.
Priest, *Twelfth Night,* Vivian Beaumont Theatre, 1972.
Blacksmith and Bear, *The Glorious Age,* Theatre Four, New York City, 1975.
Zeus, *Wings,* Eastside Playhouse, New York City, 1975.
Gavrillo and offstage speaking patient, *Gorky,* American Place Theatre,New York City, 1975.
Reuben, *Joseph and the Amazing Technicolor Dreamcoat,* Opera House, Brooklyn Academy of Music, Brooklyn, NY, 1976.
Second Lieutenant Fedotik, *The Three Sisters,* Helen Carey Playhouse, Brooklyn Academy of Music, 1977.
Dying for Laughs, Santa Monica Playhouse, Santa Monica, CA, 1994.

Made off-Broadway debut in *The Wars of the Roses* and *Richard III,* 1968; appeared in Folger Theatre productions of *The Inspector General* and *The Winter's Tale.*

WRITINGS

Television Writings; Episodic:
(With others) And songwriter, "Stuart Pankin," *Cinemax Comedy Experiment,* Cinemax, 1987.*

PANKOW, John 1955-

PERSONAL

Born in 1955, in St. Louis, MO; son of Wayne (in magazine advertising sales) and Marion (a homemaker) Pankow; married Kristine Sutherland (an actress), 1985 (some sources say 1990); children: Eleanore. *Education:* Studied acting at the St. Nicholas Theatre, Chicago.

Addresses: *Agent*—The Gersh Agency, 232 North Canon Dr., Beverly Hills, CA 90212-5302.

Career: Actor.

Awards, Honors: Screen Actors Guild Award nomination, outstanding performance by an ensemble in a comedy series, 1998, for *Mad About You* (with others).

CREDITS

Television Appearances; Series:
Danny Martin, *The Doctors,* NBC, 1981-82.
Ron Luchesse, *The Days and Nights of Molly Dodd,* NBC, 1987.
Cousin Ira Buchman, *Mad About You* (also known as *Loved By You*), NBC, 1993-99.

Television Appearances; Episodic:
Floyd, "Glades," *Miami Vice,* NBC, 1984.
Billy Hanratty, "Song of Orpheus," *Spenser: For Hire,* ABC, 1987.
Chuck Savin, *Leg Work,* CBS, 1987.
Charles Meadow, "Wedded Bliss," *Law & Order,* NBC, 1992.
Voice, "Research and Destroy," *Duckman* (animated), USA Network, 1995.

Television Appearances; Movies:
Fred, *First Steps,* 1985.

Television Appearances; Specials:
George Ritchie, *Life on the Mississippi,* 1980.

Film Appearances:
Bullie, *The Chosen,* Contemporary, 1982.
Youth in phone booth, *The Hunger,* United Artists, 1983.
John Vukovich, *To Live and Die in L.A.,* Metro-Goldwyn-Mayer, 1985.
Kovacs, **batteries not included,* Universal, 1987.

Fred Melrose, *The Secret of My Success,* Universal, 1987.

Geoffrey Fisher, *Monkey Shines: An Experiment in Fear* (also known as *Ella* and *Monkey Shines*), Orion, 1988.

Chuck Dietz, *Talk Radio,* Universal, 1988.

Italo Bianchi, *Year of the Gun,* Triumph Releasing, 1991.

Arthur Kellogg, *Mortal Thoughts,* Columbia, 1991.

Levine, *A Stranger among Us* (also known as *Closer to Eden*), Buena Vista, 1992.

Vince McBride, *The Object of My Affection,* Twentieth Century-Fox, 1998.

Stage Appearances:

Speed, *Two Gentlemen of Verona,* New York City, 1978.

Wishy Burke, *Curse of an Aching Heart,* St. Nicholas Theatre, Chicago, IL, 1979.

Lucentio, *The Taming of the Shrew,* Oak Park Festival Theatre Company, Oak Park, IL, 1979.

Cameraman, *Merton of the Movies,* Master Theatre, New York City, 1980.

Hector McKenzie, *The Slab Boys,* Hudson Guild Theatre, New York City, 1980.

Wolfgang Amadeus Mozart, *Amadeus,* Broadhurst Theatre, New York City, 1980-83.

Blow, *Forty-Deuce,* Perry Street Theatre, New York City, 1981.

Abram, *Hunting Scenes from Lower Bavaria,* Manhattan Theatre Club, New York City, 1981.

Betty and Gerry, *Cloud 9,* Theatre De Lys (renamed Lucille Lortel Theatre), New York City, 1982.

Gregory Corso, *Jazz Poets at the Grotto,* The Production Company, Theatre Guinevere, New York City, 1983.

Harry, *The Time of Your Life,* Goodman Theatre, Chicago, IL, 1983-84.

Williams, *Henry V,* New York Shakespeare Festival, Delacorte Theatre, New York City, 1984.

Rocky Pioggi, *The Iceman Cometh,* Lunt-Fontanne Theatre, New York City, 1985.

Alfred Martino, *North Shore Fish,* WPA Theatre, New York City, 1987.

Zackerman, *Serious Money,* Royale Theatre, New York City, 1988.

Huey, *Italian-American Reconciliation,* Manhattan Theatre Club, New York City, 1988.

Aristocrats, Manhattan Theatre Club, Theatre Four, New York City, 1989.

Ice Cream/Hot Fudge, Public Theatre, New York City, 1990.

Stephano, *The Tempest,* Central Park, New York City, 1995.

Larry Paterson, *Baby Anger,* Anne G. Wilder Theater, New York City, 1997.*

PARE, Michael 1959-

PERSONAL

Full name, Michael Kevin Pare; born October 9, 1959, in Brooklyn, NY; son of Francis (an owner of print shops) and Joan (a homemaker) Pare. *Education:* Graduated from the Culinary Institute of America. *Avocational interests:* Yoga.

Addresses: *Agent*—William Morris Agency, 151 El Camino Dr., BeverlyHills, CA 90212.

Career: Actor and singer. Tavern on the Green restaurant, New York City, sous-chef and other positions. Also appeared in television and print advertisements, worked as a model, and worked in fast food restaurants.

CREDITS

Film Appearances:

Eddie Wilson, *Eddie and the Cruisers,* Embassy, 1983.

Max Wylde, *Undercover,* [Australia], 1983.

David Herdeg, *The Philadelphia Experiment,* New World Pictures, 1984.

Tom Cody, *Streets of Fire,* Universal, 1984.

Grange, *Space Rage* (also known as *A Dollar a Day, Space Rage: Breakout on Prison Planet,* and *Trackers*), Vestron, 1985.

Patrick Ryan, *The Women's Club,* Lightning Pictures, 1986.

Deja View, [video], 1986.

Scott Youngblood, *Instant Justice* (also known as *Marine Issue*), Warner Bros., 1987.

George Landon, *World Gone Wild,* Lorimar Pictures, 1988.

Felix Stone, *Moon 44* (also known as *Intruder*), Centropolis Film Productions, 1989.

Eddie Wilson/Joe West, *Eddie and the Cruisers II: Eddie Lives!,* Scotti Brothers, 1989.

Ruggero Brickman, *Il sole buio* (also known as *The Dark Sun*), Laurenfilm, 1990.

Moorpark, *Dragonfight,* Warner Home Video, 1990.

Jeff, *The Last Hour* (also known as *Concrete War*), Academy, 1991.

Chris/Craig Brandt, *The Killing Streets,* Vestron, 1991.

Joey Andre, *Empire City,* Warner Bros., 1991.

Larry Freed, *The Closer,* ION Pictures, 1991.

Captain Paul Watkins, *Into the Sun,* Trimark Pictures, 1992.

Sam Browning, *Blink of an Eye* (also known as *First Light*), Vidmark Entertainment, 1992.

Jack David, *Point of Impact* (also known as *Spanish Rose*), 1993.

Brad Cartowski, *Deadly Heroes,* Columbia/TriStar Home Video, 1993.

Colin Neal, *Warriors,* Republic Pictures, 1994.

Joe Brody, *Lunarcop* (also known as *Solar Force*), Astrocop Productions, 1994.

Frank McGowan, *Village of the Damned* (also known as *John Carpenter's Village of the Damned*), Universal, 1995.

Colin, *Raging Angels,* Vidmark Entertainment, 1995.

Pershing Quinn, *Coyote Run* (also known as *Sworn Enemies*), Moonstone Entertainment, 1996.

Uncle Ted Harrison, *Bad Moon,* Warner Bros., 1996.

Hydrosphere, 1996.

Robby Durell, *Strip Search,* A-pix Entertainment/ Quadra Entertainment, 1997.

Jim Randell, *Merchant of Death,* Nu World, 1997.

Tarkis, *2103 the Deadly Wake,* Cineplex Odeon Video, 1997.

Gary, *October 22* (also known as *Bang*), C. C. Bang Productions, 1998.

Rico "Bullet" Burke, *Men of Means,* Saban Entertainment, 1998.

Bill Pruitt, *Hope Floats,* Twentieth Century-Fox, 1998.

Space Fury, 1999.

Jim Randall, *Mission of Death,* [video], 1999.

The Virgin Suicides, American Zoetrope/Muse Productions, 1999.

Also appeared in *Back to Even,* released on video.

Television Appearances; Series:

Tony Villicana, *The Greatest American Hero,* ABC, 1981-83.

Sergeant Joey LaFiamma, *Houston Knights,* CBS, 1987.

Television Appearances; Movies:

Crazy Times, ABC, 1981.

Eric Wright, *Sunset Heat* (also known as *Midnight Heat*), HBO, 1991.

Random, *The Dangerous,* HBO, 1995.

Teddy, *Triplecross,* Showtime, 1995.

Carver, *Carver's Gate* (also known as *Dream Breaker*), [Australia], 1995.

First officer Daryl Boden, "Falling Fire" (also known as "Asteroid," "The Cusp," and "Three Minutes to Impact"), *Roger Corman Presents,* The Movie Channel, 1997.

Television Appearances; Pilots:

Sergeant Joey LaFiamma, *Houston Knights,* CBS, 1987.

Alec Harken, *The Colony* (also known as *Malibu Branch*), ABC, 1996.

Stage Appearances:

The Black Marble Shoe Shine Stand, ATA Chernuchin Theatre, New York City, 1998.

Also appeared in other stage productions.

RECORDINGS

As a Member of the Fictitious Band Eddie and the Cruisers:

Eddie and the Cruisers Soundtrack, BMG/Scotti Brothers, 1990.

Eddie and the Cruisers Soundtrack Part II—Eddie Lives!, BMG/Scotti Brothers, 1990.

Unreleased Tapes (also known as *Eddie and the Cruisers: The Unreleased Tapes*), BMG/Scotti Brothers, 1991.*

PARISOT, Dean

PERSONAL

Education: New York University, graduate of Tisch School of the Arts; also attended Sundance Institute.

Addresses: *Agent*—Lou Pitt, International Creative Management, 8942 Wilshire Blvd., Beverly Hills, CA 90211.

Career: Director, writer, and producer.

Member: Directors Guild of America.

Awards, Honors: Academy Award, best live action short film, and Annual Cable Excellence (ACE) Award, best direction, both 1988, for *Steven Wright in the Appointments of Dennis Jennings;* ACE Award, 1995, for *Kathy and Mo: The Dark Side.*

CREDITS

Film Work; Director:

Tom Goes to the Bar (short film), 1985.

The Last Seat, 1994.

Home Fries, Warner Bros., 1998.

The Crew, 1999.

Television Work; Director; Movies:
Framed, HBO, 1990.
ATF, 1998.

Television Work; Pilots:
Producer and director, *Bakersfield P.D.,* Fox, 1993.
Director, *The Marshal,* ABC, 1995.

Director of the pilot, *The Conversation,* NBC.

Television Work; Director; Specials:
Steven Wright in the Appointments of Dennis Jennings, HBO, 1989.
Steven Wright: Wicker Chairs and Gravity, HBO, 1990.
Kathy and Mo: The Dark Side, HBO, 1995.

Television Work; Director; Episodic:
Northern Exposure, CBS, 1990.
Going to Extremes, ABC, 1992.
Likely Suspects, Fox, 1992.
Under Suspicion, CBS, 1994.
"What Life?," *ER* (also known as *Emergency Room*), NBC, 1995.
The Marshal, ABC, 1995.

WRITINGS

Screenplays:
Still Life (also known as *Art Killer Framed* and *Still Life: The Fine Art of Murder*), 1988.

Television Specials:
Steven Wright: Wicker Chairs and Gravity, HBO, 1990.*

PARKER, Alan 1944-

PERSONAL

Full name, Alan William Parker; born February 14, 1944, in London, England; son of William Leslie (a house painter) and Elsie Ellen (a dressmaker) Parker; married Annie Inglis, July 30, 1966 (divorced, 1992); children: Lucy Kate, Alexander James, Jake William, Nathan Charles. *Avocational interests:* Cartooning.

Addresses: *Agent*—Judy Scott-Fox, William Morris Agency, 151 El Camino Dr., Beverly Hills, CA 90212.

Career: Director, writer, and actor. Worked as an advertising copywriter, 1966-69; Collett, Dickensen & Pearce Advertising, Ltd., director of television commercials, 1969-75; Alan Parker Film Company, Buckinghamshire, England, partner, 1970—; British Screen Advisory Council, member, 1985—; lecturer at film schools.

Member: British Academy of Film and Television Arts (member of council), Directors Guild of Great Britain (founding member and vice chairperson), Directors Guild of America.

Awards, Honors: British Academy of Film and Television Arts Film Award, best screenplay, 1976, for *Bugsy Malone;* British Academy of Film and Television Arts Television Award, International Emmy Award, and British Press Guild Award, all 1976, for *The Evacuees;* British Academy of Film and Television Arts Film Award, Academy Award nomination, and Golden Globe Award nomination, all best director, 1978, for *Midnight Express;* Michael Balcon Award for Outstanding Contributions to British Film, British Academy of Film and Television Arts, 1984; Grand Prix Special du Jury, Cannes International Film Festival, 1985, for *Birdy;* British Press Guild Award, best documentary, 1985, for *The Turnip Head's Guide to British Cinema;* National Board of Review Award, Academy Award nomination, and Golden Globe Award nomination, all best director, 1988, for *Mississippi Burning;* Lifetime Achievement Award, Chicago Film Festival, 1988; Best Director Award, Tokyo International Film Festival, 1991, for *The Commitments;* Golden Satellite Award, best comedy or musical motion picture, and Golden Globe Award nomination, best director of a motion picture, both 1996, and British Academy of Film and Television Arts Film Award nomination (with Oliver Stone), best screenplay—adapted, 1997, all for *Evita.*

CREDITS

Film Work; Director, Unless Otherwise Noted:
Our Cissy (short film), 1973.
Footsteps (short film), 1973.
No Hard Feelings, 1976.
Bugsy Malone, Paramount, 1976.
Midnight Express, Columbia, 1978.
Fame, United Artists, 1980.
Shoot the Moon, Metro-Goldwyn-Mayer/United Artists, 1982.
Pink Floyd: The Wall (also known as *The Wall*), Metro-Goldwyn-Mayer, 1982.
Music conductor, *Jaws 3-D,* Universal, 1983.
Birdy, TriStar, 1984.

Angel Heart, TriStar, 1987.
Mississippi Burning, Orion, 1988.
Come See the Paradise, Twentieth Century-Fox, 1990.
And producer, *The Commitments,* Twentieth Century-Fox, 1991.
And producer (with Armyan Bernstein and Robert F. Colesberry), *The Road to Wellville,* Columbia, 1994.
And producer and music conductor (with others), *Evita,* Buena Vista, 1996.
And producer, *Angela's Ashes,* Paramount, 1999.

Film Appearances:
Fortunata y Jacinta, Brepi Films, 1969.
Consigna: matar al comandante en jefe (also known as *Commando di spie*), Italica Film, 1970.
Eejit record producer, *The Commitments,* Twentieth Century-Fox, 1991.
Tormented film director, *Evita,* Buena Vista, 1996.

Television Work; Director; Movies:
The Evacuees, BBC, 1976.

Television Work; Director; Specials:
The Turnip Head's Guide to British Cinema, Thames Television, 1986.

Television Appearances; Specials:
A Personal History of British Cinema by Stephen Frears (documentary), [Great Britain], 1994.

Television Appearances; Episodic:
"The Entertainment Business," *Bravo Profiles,* Bravo, 1998.

WRITINGS

Screenplays:
Melody (also known as *S.W.A.L.K.*), Levitt-Pickman, 1971.
Our Cissy (short film), 1973.
Footsteps (short film), 1973.
No Hard Feelings, 1976.
Bugsy Malone, Paramount, 1976, published by Bantam Books (New York City), 1976.
Angel Heart, TriStar, 1987.
Come See the Paradise, Twentieth Century-Fox, 1990.
The Road to Wellville (based on the novel by T. Coraghessan Boyle), Columbia, 1994.
(With Oliver Stone) *Evita* (based on the stage musical by Andrew Lloyd Webber and Tim Rice), Buena Vista, 1996.

Music for Films:
Score, *Jaws 3-D,* Universal, 1983.
"Jack's Theatre Song," *Come See the Paradise,* Twentieth Century-Fox, 1990.

Music for Television; Miniseries:
Rhodes, BBC, then PBS, 1997.

Fiction:
Puddles in the Lane, G. Whizzard Publications (London, England), 1977.

Cartoons:
Hares in the Gate, 1983.

Nonfiction:
A Filmmaker's Diary, 1984.
The Making of Evita, introduction by Madonna, photographs from the film by David Appleby, CollinsPublishers (New York City), 1996.

Contributor of articles and cartoons to periodicals, including *American Cinematographer, American Film, Cineaste, Films and Filming, Literature/Film Quarterly,* and *Sight and Sound.*

OTHER SOURCES

Periodicals:
American Film, September, 1990.
Campaign, September 18, 1998, p. S25.
Premiere, September, 1991.*

PARKER, Sarah Jessica 1965-

PERSONAL

Born March 25, 1965, in Nelsonville, OH; father a journalist and entrepreneur; mother's name, Barbara Forste; married Matthew Broderick (an actor), May 19, 1997.

Addresses: *Agent*—Kevin Huvane, Creative Artists Agency, 9830 Wilshire Blvd., Beverly Hills, CA 90212.

Career: Actress. Ballet dancer with Cincinnati Ballet and American Ballet Theatre.

Awards, Honors: Golden Globe Award nomination, best performance by an actress in a television series-comedy/musical, and Emmy Award nomination, best actress in a comedy series, both 1999, for *Sex and the City.*

CREDITS

Film Appearances:

(Film debut) *Rich Kids,* United Artists, 1979.
Lisa, *Firstborn,* Paramount, 1984.
Rusty, *Footloose,* Paramount, 1984.
Lori Anderson, *Somewhere Tomorrow,* Media Home Entertainment, 1984.
Janey Glenn, *Girls Just Want to Have Fun,* New World, 1985.
Carolyn McAdams, *Flight of the Navigator,* Buena Vista, 1986.
SanDeE*, *L.A. Story,* TriStar, 1991.
Betsy/Donna, *Honeymoon in Vegas,* Columbia, 1992.
Sarah Sanderson, *Hocus Pocus,* Buena Vista, 1993.
Jo Christman, *Striking Distance,* Columbia, 1993.
Dolores Fuller, *Ed Wood,* Buena Vista, 1994.
Gwyn Marcus, *Miami Rhapsody,* Buena Vista, 1995.
Lucy Ackerman, *If Lucy Fell,* TriStar, 1996.
Sarah Geldhart, *The Substance of Fire,* Miramax, 1996.
Shelly Stewart, *The First Wives Club,* Paramount, 1996.
Jodie Trammel, *Extreme Measures,* Columbia, 1996.
Natalie Lake, *Mars Attacks!,* Warner Bros., 1996.
Voice, *A Life Apart: Hasidism in America,* First Run Features, 1997.
Francesca Lanfield,*'Til There Was You,* Paramount, 1997.
Tira Gropman, *Isn't She Great,* 1999.
Nell Fenwick, *Dudley Do-Right,* Universal, 1999.

Film Work:

Song performer, *The Substance of Fire,* Miramax, 1996.

Television Appearances; Series:

Patty Greene, *Square Pegs,* CBS, 1982-83.
Kay Erickson Gardner, *A Year in the Life,* NBC, 1987-88.
JoAnn Harris, *Equal Justice,* ABC, 1990.
Carrie Bradshaw, *Sex and the City,* HBO, 1998—.

Television Appearances; Miniseries:

Kay Erickson, *A Year in the Life,* NBC, 1986.

Television Appearances; Episodic:

Evening at Pops, 1970.
Rachel Sutton, *Hotel,* ABC, 1986.
Amy-Beth, "Life under Water," *American Playhouse,* PBS, 1989.
Herself, "Episode with Sarah Jessica Parker," *The Ben Stiller Show,* Fox, 1992.
"Next Stop Bottom," *The Larry Sanders Show,* HBO, 1992.
Narrator, "Cinderella," *Stories from My Childhood,* PBS, 1997.

Also appeared on episodes of *3-2-1 Contact,* PBS; and *Another World,* NBC.

Television Appearances; Movies:

Katy, *My Body, My Child,* ABC, 1982.
Maggie, *Going for the Gold: The Bill Johnson Story,* CBS, 1985.
Mandy, *The Room Upstairs,* CBS, 1987.
Rachel Goldman, *Dadah Is Death* (also known as *A Long Way Home, A Long Way from Home, Barlow and Chambers: A Long Way from Home,* and *Deadly Decision*), CBS, 1988.
Laura, *The Ryan White Story,* ABC, 1989.
Miriam Kleiman, *Twist of Fate* (also known as *Pursuit*), NBC, 1989.
Callie Cain, *In the Best Interest of the Children,* NBC, 1992.
Nancy Clark, *The Sunshine Boys,* CBS, 1995.

Television Appearances; Specials:

Suzanne Henderson, "The Almost Royal Family," *ABC Afterschool Special,* ABC, 1984.
Mandy, "The Room Upstairs," *Hallmark Hall of Fame,* CBS, 1987.
Count on Me, PBS, 1993.
Macy's Thanksgiving Day Parade, 1996.
A Gift of Song, TNT, 1997.
Celine, Aretha, Gloria, Shania, and Mariah: Divas Live, VH-1, 1998.
Comic Relief VIII, HBO, 1998.

Also appeared in the specials, *The Little Match Girl,* NBC; *Do Me a Favor . . . Don't Vote for My Mom, Kennedy Center Tonight,* and *Meanwhile, Back at the Castle.*

Television Appearances; Pilots:

Samantha Cooper, *The Alan King Show,* CBS, 1986.
Jo Ann Harris, *Equal Justice,* ABC, 1990.

Television Appearances; Awards Presentations:

The 50th Annual Golden Globe Awards, TBS, 1993.
The 65th Annual Academy Awards Presentation, ABC, 1993.
MTV Movie Awards, MTV, 1993.
Fourth Annual Environmental Media Awards, TBS, 1994.

The 49th Annual Tony Awards, CBS, 1995.
The 67th Annual Academy Awards, ABC, 1995.
The 50th Annual Tony Awards, CBS, 1996.
The 1997 MTV Video Music Awards, MTV, 1997.
The 51st Annual Tony Awards, 1997.
VH-1 97 Fashion Awards, VH-1, 1997.
The 1999 ESPY Awards, EPSN, 1999.

Stage Appearances:

Flora, *The Innocents,* Morosco Theatre, New York City, 1976.

(Broadway debut) July, then title role, *Annie,* Alvin Theatre, New York City, 1978.

The War Brides, New Dramatists, New York City, 1981.

The Death of a Miner, Portland Stage Company, Portland, ME, 1982.

Rachel, *To Gillian on Her 37th Birthday,* Ensemble Studio Theatre, New York City, 1983, then Circle in the Square Downtown, New York City, 1984.

Darlene Magnum, "Terry Neal's Future" in *Marathon '86,* Ensemble Studio Theatre, 1986.

Becky/Clara/Denise, *The Heidi Chronicles,* Playwrights Horizons, then Plymouth Theatre, both New York City, 1989.

Sarah Geldhart, *Substance of Fire,* Playwrights Horizons, New York City, 1991, then Newhouse Theatre, Lincoln Center, New York City, 1992.

Rosemary Pilkington, *How to Succeed in Business Without Really Trying,*Richard Rogers Theatre, New York City, 1996.

Winnifred, *Once Upon a Mattress,* Broadhurst Theatre, New York City, 1996.

Also appeared in *By Strouse,* off-Broadway production; *One-Act Festival; Broadway Scandals of 1928;* and *Sylvia.*

RECORDINGS

Taped Readings:

Gilly, *The Great Gilly Hopkins* (audio adaptation of the book), Newberry Award Records, 1979.

OTHER SOURCES

Periodicals:

Cosmopolitan, July, 1998, p. 146; February, 1999, p. 138.

Entertainment Weekly, October 1, 1993, pp. 26-31.

New York Times, April 25, 1996.

People Weekly, October 14, 1996, p. 156; June 2, 1997, p. 62.

Premiere, July, 1992, p. 66.

Redbook, July, 1996, p. 54; September, 1997, p. 114.*

PATTON, Will 1954-

PERSONAL

Born June 14, 1954, in Charleston, SC. *Education:* Graduated from North Carolina School of the Arts, 1975.

Addresses: *Agent*—William Morris Agency, 151 El Camino Dr., Beverly Hills, CA 90212. *Manager*—Edwards-Curtan Management, 11664 National Blvd., Suite 108, Los Angeles, CA 90064.

Career: Actor and playwright.

Awards, Honors: Obie Award, *Village Voice,* best actor, 1984, for *Fool for Love;* Obie Award, *Village Voice,* best actor, 1989, for *What Did He See?;* Obie Award, for *Tourists and Refugees, 2;* Villager Awards for *Dark Ride* and *Goose and Tomtom.*

CREDITS

Stage Appearances:

Chicken, *Kingdom of Earth,* Staircase Theatre Company, Impossible Ragtime Theatre, New York City, 1976.

Goldie, *Heaven and Earth,* Off-Center Theatre, New York City, 1977.

Billy Cavanaugh, *Scenes from Country Life,* Perry Street Theatre, New York City, 1978.

Rearrangements (mime/puppet show), Winter Project, Other Theatre Company, La Mama Experimental Theatre Club, New York City, 1979.

Officer Gruber, *Salt Lake City Skyline,* New York Shakespeare Festival, Public Theatre, New York City, 1980.

After the Revolution, American Place Theatre, New York City, 1980.

Thief, *Dark Ride,* Soho Repertory Theatre, New York City, 1981.

Bingo, *Goose and Tomtom,* New York Shakespeare Festival, Public Theatre, New York City, 1982.

Ward and Dauphin, *Joan of Lorraine,* Mirror Theatre, New York City, 1983.

Eddie, *Fool for Love,* Circle Repertory Theatre, then Douglas Fairbanks Theatre, both New York City, 1983.

Mike, *A Lie of the Mind,* Promenade Theatre, New York City, 1985.

What Did He See?, New York Shakespeare Festival, Public Theatre, New York City, 1989.

Michael Majeski, *Valaparaiso,* American Repertory Theater at the Loeb Drama Center, Cambridge, MA, 1999.

Also appeared in *Tourists and Refugees, 1 [and] 2,* both Winter Project, La Mama Experimental Theatre Club, New York City; *The Red Snake,* Public Theatre; *The Seven Descents of Myrtle,* Impossible Ragtime Theatre; *Cops,* New York City; *Pedro Paramo,* New York City; *Limbo Tales,* New York City; performs as a member of the Winter Project (an experimental theatre group), New York City.

Film Appearances:

Bar customer, priest in diner, man in dream, and radio preacher, *King Blank,* Metafilms, 1983.

Joe, *Silkwood,* Twentieth Century-Fox, 1983.

Lang Marsh, *Chinese Boxes,* Palace, 1984.

Mark, *Variety,* Horizon, 1984.

Horst, *After Hours,* Warner Bros., 1985.

Forest ranger, *The Beniker Gang* (also known as *Dear Lola, or How to Start Your Own Family*), 1985.

Wayne Nolan, *Desperately Seeking Susan,* Orion, 1986.

Matthew Perry, *Belizaire the Cajun,* Skouras/Norstar, 1986.

Scott Pritchard, *No Way Out,* Orion, 1987.

Duane, *Stars and Bars,* Columbia, 1988.

Mr. Coughlin, Sr., *Signs of Life* (also known as *One for Sorrow, Two for Joy*), Avenue, 1989.

Jerry, *Everybody Wins,* Orion, 1990.

Lieutenant Laker, *A Shock to the System,* Corsair Pictures, 1990.

Sheriff Foster, *The Rapture,* Fine Line, 1991.

(Uncredited) Woody, *Bright Angel,* 1991.

Woody, *The Paint Job* (also known as *Painted Heart*), 1992.

Mike, *Wildfire,* MCA/Universal Home Video, 1992.

Father Niles, *Cold Heaven,* Hemdale Releasing, 1992.

Skippy, *In the Soup,* Triton Pictures, 1992.

Michael Murphy, *Natural Causes,* Columbia/TriStar Home Video, 1993.

Sergeant Hardy, *The Client,* Warner Bros., 1994.

Jack Travers, *Midnight Edition,* Shapiro Glickenhaus, 1994.

Dr. Lawrence Riggs, *Robert A. Heinlein's The Puppet Masters,* Buena Vista, 1994.

Martie Cuchinski, *Romeo Is Bleeding,* Gramercy Pictures, 1994.

Dash Pepper, *Tollbooth,* New Line Home Video, 1994.

Alan Warwick, *Judicial Consent* (also known as *My Love, Your Honor*), Warner Vision, 1994.

Nicoletti, *Copycat* (also known as *Copykill*), Warner Bros., 1995.

Nahum Goddard, *The Spitfire Grill* (also known as *Care of the Spitfire Grill*), Columbia, 1996.

Plain Pleasures, 1996.

Matthew Gibson, *Fled,* Metro-Goldwyn-Mayer, 1996.

Lloyd Abbot, *Inventing the Abbotts,* Twentieth Century-Fox, 1997.

Police Lieutenant Morgan, *This World, Then Fireworks,* Orion, 1997.

Bethlehem, *The Postman,* Warner Bros., 1997.

Sean, *O.K. Garage,* Talana Productions, 1998.

Preacher, *Ed Wood's I Woke Up Early The Day I Died,* 1998.

Charles Chick Chapple, *Armageddon,* Buena Vista, 1998.

Moe, *Breakfast of Champions,* Buena Vista, 1999.

Hector Cruz, *Entrapment,* Twentieth Century-Fox, 1999.

John Smith, *Jesus's Son,* Lions Gate Films, 1999.

Red Rafferty, *Trixie,* Sony Pictures Classics, 1999.

Also appeared in *Johns.*

Television Appearances; Series:

Ox Knowles, *Ryan's Hope,* ABC, 1975.

Dr. Frank Morgan, *VR.5* (also known as *Avenging Angel, VR* and *Virtual Reality*), Fox, 1995.

Also appeared in *Search for Tomorrow,* CBS/NBC.

Television Appearances; Movies:

Peter, *Kent State,* NBC, 1981.

Lou Dimes, *A Gathering of Old Men* (also known as *Murder on the Bayou*), CBS, 1987.

Giles Menteer, *Deadly Desire,* USA Network, 1991.

Melvin Purvis, *Dillinger* (also known as *The Last Days of John Dillinger*), ABC, 1991.

Frank Maxwell, *A Child Lost Forever* (also known as *The Jerry Sherwood Story*), NBC, 1992.

Eric Gaines, *In the Deep Woods,* NBC, 1992.

Attorney Roberts, *Taking the Heat,* Showtime, 1993.

Alan Warwick, *Judicial Consent* (also known as *My Love, My Honor*), HBO, 1995.

Also appeared in *The Book.*

Television Appearances; Episodic:

Ben Moody, "Robbers, Rooftops, and Witches," *CBS Library,* CBS, 1982.

Officer Nick Braxton, "Lady Cop," *The Equalizer,* CBS, 1985.

RECORDINGS

Taped Readings:
Recorded *Dead Man's Walk* (by Larry McMurtry). Has also recorded other audio books for Random House, Bantam Doubleday Dell Audio, and Simon & Schuster.

WRITINGS

For Stage:
(With Winter Project) *Rearrangements* (mime/puppet show), Winter Project, Other Theatre Company, La Mama Experimental Theatre Club, New York City, 1979.

Also wrote *Tourists and Refugees, 1 [and] 2,* both Winter Project, La Mama Experimental Theatre Club, New York City.*

PEEPLES, Nia 1967(?)-

PERSONAL

Born Verinia Peeples, December 10, 1967 (some sources say 1961), inHollywood, CA.

Addresses: *Agent*—Innovative Artists Talent, 1999 Avenue of the Stars, Los Angeles, CA 90067-6022.

Career: Actress and singer.

CREDITS

Film Appearances:
Herself, *All You Can Dream,* 1986.
Kiani, *North Shore,* Universal, 1987.
Scarpelli, *DeepStar Six,* TriStar, 1989.
Theresa Garabaldi, *I Don't Buy Kisses Anymore,* Skouras Pictures, 1992.
Bernadette, *Improper Conduct,* Everest Pictures, 1994.
Lieutenant Elizondo, *Blues Brothers 2000,* Universal, 1998.
Dead Simple, 1999.

Film Work; Song Performer:
Sing, 1989.
The Cutting Edge, 1992.

Television Appearances; Series:
Carla Escobar, *General Hospital,* ABC, 1983-84.
Nicole Chapman, *Fame,* syndicated, 1984-87.
Host (Los Angeles), *Top of the Pops,* CBS, 1987-88.
Serena Cruz, *Nasty Boys,* NBC, 1990.
Host, *The Party Machine with Nia Peeples,* syndicated, 1991.
Veronica Gilbert, *Courthouse* (also known as *Courtroom*), CBS, 1995.
Lisa, *Marker,* UPN, 1995.
Lily Gannon, *Crisis Center,* NBC, 1997.
Host, *It's a Miracle,* PAX-TV, 1998—.

Television Appearances; Miniseries:
Agostina Vega, *Return to Lonesome Dove,* CBS, 1993.

Television Appearances; Movies:
Serena Cruz, *Nasty Boys,* NBC, 1989.
Maria Detney, *Swimsuit,* NBC, 1989.
Cathy Redding, *Perry Mason: The Case of the Silenced Singer,* NBC, 1990.
Annie, *My Name Is Kate,* ABC, 1994.
Sasha Townes, *XXX's and OOO's,* CBS, 1994.
Allie Thompson, *Deadlocked: Escape from Zone 14* (also known as *Deadlock 2*), Fox, 1995.
Dr. Elizabeth English, *Mr. Stitch,* Sci-Fi Channel, 1995.
Janet Reardon, *Robin Cook's Terminal,* NBC, 1996.
Nikki Cruise, *Bloodhounds II,* USA Network, 1996.
Jill Whitman, *Tower of Terror,* ABC, 1997.
Angel, *Poodle Springs,* HBO, 1998.

Television Appearances; Episodic:
Zita Henriquess, "The Sultan of Swat," *Tales of the Gold Monkey,* ABC, 1983.
Maria Dominguez, "Gang War," *T.J. Hooker,* ABC, 1983.
Morgan Girard, "The Starlet," *Matlock,* NBC, 1989.
Nefertiri, "Pharoh's Daughter," *Highlander,* syndicated, 1994.
Angela Evans, "Fallen Angela," *Touched by an Angel,* CBS, 1994.
The Puzzle Place, PBS, 1995.
Sister Mary, "Angels and Devils," *Early Edition,* CBS, 1997.

Television Appearances; Specials:
The 42nd Annual Golden Globe Awards, 1985.
Grammy's Salute to Leonard Bernstein, 1986.
Happy Birthday Hollywood, ABC, 1987.
Host, *The World's Greatest Stunts, Part II,* Fox, 1990.
"I Hate the Way I Look," *ABC Afterschool Specials,* ABC, 1993.

Television Appearances; Other:
Also appeared in *MTV Street Party,* MTV; and *Teen Scene,* Fox.

RECORDINGS

Albums:
Nothin' But Trouble, Mercury, 1988.
Sing (movie soundtrack), 1989.
Nia Peeples, Charisma Records, 1991.*

PENDLETON, Austin 1940-

PERSONAL

Born March 27, 1940, in Warren, OH; married Katina Commings; children: one daughter. *Education:* Yale University, B.A., 1961; trained for the stage at the Williamstown Theatre Festival, Williamstown, MA, 1957-58; studied acting with Uta Hagen.

Addresses: *Office*—Herbert Berghof Studio, 120 Bank St., New York, NY 10014.

Career: Actor, director, and writer. Studio Arena Theatre Company, Buffalo, NY, member of the company, 1968-69; Long Wharf Theatre, New Haven, CT, member of the company, 1971-72; Mirror Repertory Company, New York City, director, 1984; Riverside Shakespeare Company, New York City, associate director, 1988-89; Circle Repertory Theatre, New York City, artistic director, 1995-96; acting teacher at the Circle in the Square Theatre School and the Herbert Berghof Studio, both New York City.

Member: Actors' Equity Association, Screen Actors Guild, American Federation of Television and Radio Artists, Society of Stage Directors and Choreographers.

Awards, Honors: Clarence Derwent Award, 1966, for *Hail Scrawdyke!;* Obie Award, Drama Desk Award, Outer Critics Circle Award, and New York Drama Critics Poll Award, all 1970, for *The Last Sweet Days of Isaac;* Antoinette Perry Award nomination, best director of a drama, 1981, for *The Little Foxes.*

CREDITS

Stage Appearances:
Jonathan Rosepettle, *Oh Dad, Poor Dad, Mama's Hung You in the Closet and I'm Feelin' So Sad,* Phoenix Theatre, New York City, 1962.
Motel, *Fiddler on the Roof,* Imperial Theatre, New York City, 1964.
Irwin Ingham, *Hail Scrawdyke!,* Booth Theatre, New York City, 1966.
Leo Hubbard, *The Little Foxes,* Vivian Beaumont Theatre, Lincoln Center,New York City, then Ethel Barrymore Theatre, New York City, 1967.
Isaac, *The Last Sweet Days of Isaac,* Eastside Playhouse, New York City, 1970, then Cincinnati Playhouse in the Park, Cincinnati, OH, 1971.
Charles, *American Glands,* New Dramatists, New York City, 1973.
Professor Bobby Rudetsky, *An American Millionaire,* Joseph E. Levine Theatre, Circle in the Square, New York City, 1974.
Title role, *Tartuffe,* Cincinnati Playhouse in the Park, 1974.
The Government Inspector, Hartman Theatre, Stamford, CT, 1975.
Frederick the Great, *The Sorrows of Frederick the Great,* American Repertory Theatre, New York City, 1976.
Title role, *Tartuffe,* Hartman Theatre, 1977.
Tusenbach, *Three Sisters,* Brooklyn Academy of Music Theatre, Brooklyn, New York City, 1977.
Mark Antony, *Julius Caesar,* Brooklyn Academy of Music Theatre, 1977.
Estragon, *Waiting for Godot,* Brooklyn Academy of Music Theatre, 1978.
Jack, *The Office Murders,* Quaigh Theatre, New York City, 1979.
Bashmachkin, *The Overcoat,* Westside Mainstage Theatre, New York City, 1982.
Uncle Vanya, The Whole Theatre, Montclair, NJ, 1982.
Adam, *Up from Paradise,* Jewish Repertory Theatre, New York City, 1983.
After the Fall, Williamstown Theatre Festival, Williamstown, MA, 1984.
The Sorrows of Frederick, The Whole Theatre, 1985.
Arnie, *Doubles,* Ritz Theatre, New York City, 1985.
Voitski, *Uncle Vanya,* Classic Stage Company, New York City, 1987-88.
Title role, *Philoctetes,* INTAR Theatre, New York City, 1989.
Erie Smith, "Hughie," *Serious Company: An Evening of One-Act Plays,* Apple Corps Theatre, New York City, 1989.
Title role, *Hamlet,* Riverside Shakespeare Company, 165 West 86th Street Theatre, New York City, 1989.
Otto Kringelein, *Grand Hotel,* Martin Beck Theatre, New York City, between 1989 and 1992.
Ivanov, Yale Repertory Theatre, New Haven, CT, 1990-91.

Frederick the Great, *The Sorrows of Frederick,* Kampo Cultural Center, New York City, 1991.
Harry Berlin, *What about Luv?,* York Theatre, New York City, 1991-92.
Il Signor Barranco, *A Joke,* Sanford Meisner Theatre, New York City, 1992.
Priest, "Show," *The Best American Short Play Series,* Evening Two, Westbeth Theatre Center, New York City, 1993.
Jeremy, *Jeremy Rudge,* Mint Theatre, New York City, 1993.
Whitey McCoy, *Sophistry,* Playwrights' Horizons Theatre, New York City, 1993.
Eric, *The Imposter,* Workhouse Theatre, New York City, 1995-96.
Title role, *Richard III,* New Perspectives Theatre Company, New York City, 1997.
Mr. Dussel, *The Diary of Anne Frank,* Music Box Theatre, New York City, 1997-98.

Appeared in productions at the Williamstown Theatre Festival, Williamstown, MA, 1957-58; the Studio Arena Theatre Company, Buffalo, NY, 1968-69; and the Long Wharf Theatre, New Haven, CT, 1971-72; appeared on Broadway in *The Runner Stumbles;* appeared off-Broadway in *Educating Rita, Master Class, Say Goodnight, Gracie, The Show-Off,* and *Two Character Play.*

Major Tours:
Toured with American Conservatory Theatre Company, San Francisco, CA, 1966-67.

Stage Work; Director:
Shelter, John Golden Theatre, New York City, 1973.
The Master Builder, Long Wharf Theatre, New Haven, CT, 1973.
The Runner Stumbles, Manhattan Theatre Club, New York City, 1974.
The Scarecrow, Eisenhower Theatre, John F. Kennedy Center for the Performing Arts, Washington, DC, 1975.
The Runner Stumbles, Hartman Theatre, then John Golden Theatre, 1976.
Benito Cereno, American Place Theatre, New York City, 1976.
Misalliance, Academy Festival Theatre, Lake Forest, IL, 1976.
The Gathering, Manhattan Theatre Club, 1977.
Say Goodnight, Gracie, 78th Street Theatre Lab, New York City, 1979.
The Little Foxes, Martin Beck Theatre, 1981.
Mass Appeal, York Theatre Company, Chancel of the Church of Heavenly Rest, New York City, 1984.
After the Fall, Williamstown Theatre Festival, Williamstown, MA, 1984.
Alterations, Chelsea Playhouse, WPA Theatre, New York City, 1986.
Fathers and Sons, Long Wharf Theatre, 1987-88.
Spoils of War, Second Stage Theatre, New York City, then Music Box Theatre, both 1988.
Who's Afraid of Virginia Woolf?, Arizona Theatre Company, Tucson, AZ, 1991-92.
Admissions, New Perspectives Theatre, New York City, 1995.
The Size of the World, Circle Repertory Theatre, New York City, 1996.
The Sea Gull, Blue Light Theatre Company, Theatre Four, New York City, 1998.

Director of *John Gabriel Borkman.*

Film Appearances:
Fred (the professor), *Skidoo,* Paramount, 1968.
Moodus, *Catch-22,* Paramount, 1970.
Oven 350, 1970.
Frederick Larrabee, *What's Up, Doc?,* Warner Bros., 1972.
Luther, *Every Little Crook and Nanny,* Metro-Goldwyn-Mayer, 1972.
Zukovsky, *The Thief Who Came to Dinner,* Warner Bros., 1972.
Earl Williams, *The Front Page,* Universal, 1974.
Lovesick, Warner Bros., 1974.
Guido, *The Great Smokey Roadblock* (also known as *The Last of the Cowboys*), Cinema Arts Associated, 1976.
Max, *The Muppet Movie,* Associated Film Distributors, 1979.
Paul, *Starting Over,* Paramount, 1979.
Dr. Becker, *Simon,* Warner Bros., 1980.
Alexander Grade, *First Family,* Warner Bros., 1980.
Dr. Klein, *Diary of the Dead,* 1980.
Talk to Me, 1982.
Mr. Greenhut, *My Man Adam,* TriStar, 1985.
Gun shop salesperson, *Off Beat,* Buena Vista, 1986.
Howard Marner, *Short Circuit,* TriStar, 1986.
Junior Lacey, *Hello Again,* Buena Vista, 1987.
Mr. Gadbury, *Mr. and Mrs. Bridge,* Miramax, 1990.
Lawyer Taylor, *The Ballad of the Sad Cafe,* Channel Four Films, 1991.
Catholic priest, *Rain without Thunder,* Taz Pictures, 1992.
Charlie's Ear, 1992.
John Gibbons, *My Cousin Vinny,* Twentieth Century-Fox, 1992.
Asa Hoffman, *Searching for Bobby Fischer* (also known as *Innocent Moves*), Paramount, 1993.

Dr. Bronson, *My Boyfriend's Back* (also known as *Johnny Zombie*), Buena Vista, 1993.
Alex Mason, Sr., *Mr. Nanny,* New Line Cinema, 1993.
Hotel clerk, *Greedy,* Universal, 1994.
Earl Fowler, *Guarding Tess,* TriStar, 1994.
Hamlet, *The Fifteen Minute Hamlet,* Cin-cine 19, 1995.
Peter Arnold, *Home for the Holidays,* Paramount, 1995.
Dr. Huffeyer, *Two Much* (also known as *Loco de amor*), Buena Vista, 1996.
Major Ebersole, *Sergeant Bilko* (also known as *Sgt. Bilko*), Universal, 1996.
Ralph Crupi, *Two Days in the Valley,* Metro-Goldwyn-Mayer, 1996.
Willy Kunst, *The Proprietor,* Warner Bros., 1996.
Aesop, *The Associate,* Buena Vista, 1996.
Barry, *The Mirror Has Two Faces,* Sony Pictures Entertainment, 1996.
Bob, *Sue,* AMKO Productions, 1997.
Professor Gibbs, *Amistad,* DreamWorks SKG, 1997.
Judge Paul Z. Graff, *Trial and Error,* New Line Cinema, 1997.
River Made to Drown In, 1997.
Jerry Trask, *Men of Means,* Saban Entertainment, 1998.
Harry Cedars, *Charlie Hoboken,* Northern Arts Entertainment, 1998.
Joe the King (also known as *Pleasant View Avenue*), Trimark Pictures, 1998.
Lucky, *Brokendown Love Story,* 1999.

Television Appearances; Series:
Dr. George Griscom, *Homicide: Life on the Street* (also known as *H: LOTS* and *Homicide*), NBC, 1998-99.

Television Appearances; Miniseries:
Benjamin Rush, *Liberty! The American Revolution,* PBS, 1997.

Television Appearances; Movies:
Passenger with a moustache, *Four Eyes and Six-Guns,* TNT, 1992.
Chef Oscar, *Don't Drink the Water,* ABC, 1994.
Dr. Motts, *Long Island Fever,* 1995.

Television Appearances; Specials:
The White Rabbit, *Alice in Wonderland,* PBS, 1983.
Dr. Arthur Ruskin, *Love, Long Distance,* 1985.
Paul Kent, "Lethal Innocence" (also known as "The Vermont/Cambodia Story"), *American Playhouse,* PBS, 1991.

Television Work; Specials:
Director (with Patterson Denny), *Say Goodnight, Gracie,* PBS, 1983.

Television Appearances; Episodic:
"Vanity," *St. Elsewhere,* NBC, 1983.
"Under Pressure," *St. Elsewhere,* NBC, 1983.
Max Rogo, "Yankee Dollar," *Miami Vice,* NBC, 1986.
The professor, "The Big Fight," *Spenser: For Hire,* ABC, 1988.
Danny, "Blind Chess," *B. L. Stryker,* ABC, 1989.
"Mr. Mom," *Anything but Love,* ABC, 1990.
Barney Gunderson, *Murder, She Wrote,* CBS, 1991.
"Doctor of Horror," *Tales from the Crypt,* HBO, 1995.
Tracey Takes On . . . , HBO, 1996.
Dr. Dorfman, "Three Days of the Condo," *Frasier,* NBC, 1997.
Sam Feldberg, "Part VI," *The Practice,* ABC, 1997.
Bobby H./wiseguy, "The Next Day," *Fired Up,* NBC, 1997.
Giles, "Losing Your Appeal," *Oz,* HBO, 1998.

Also appeared as Jonah, *The Equalizer,* CBS.

WRITINGS

Writings for the Stage:
Booth Is Back, Long Wharf Theatre, 1991-92.
Booth, York Theatre, 1994.
Uncle Bob, Mint Theatre, 1995.

OTHER SOURCES

Periodicals:
Back Stage, June 12, 1998, p. 33.*

PERKINS, Elizabeth 1960(?)-

PERSONAL

Born Elizabeth Pisperikos, November 18, 1960 (some sources say 1961), in Queens, NY; daughter of Jo Williams (a drug treatment counselor and concert pianist); father, a farmer, writer, and in business; married Terry Kinney (an actor and director). *Education:* Trained for the stage at the Goodman School of Drama, Chicago, IL, for three years. *Avocational interests:* Writing poetry and reading.

Addresses: *Agent*—Creative Artists Agency, 9830 Wilshire Blvd., Beverly Hills, CA 90212.

Career: Actress.

CREDITS

Film Appearances:

(Film debut) Joan Gunther, *About Last Night,* TriStar, 1986.
Jo Ann, *From the Hip,* De Laurentiis Entertainment Group, 1987.
Susan Lawrence, *Big,* Twentieth Century-Fox, 1988.
Adie Nims, *Sweet Hearts Dance,* TriStar, 1988.
Stella Wynkowski, *Love at Large,* Orion, 1990.
Ann Kaye, *Avalon,* TriStar, 1990.
Lorie Bryer, *He Said, She Said,* Paramount, 1991.
June, *The Doctor,* Buena Vista, 1991.
Queen's Logic, Seven Arts, 1991.
June, *Over Her Dead Body* (also known as *Enid Is Sleeping*), Vestron Video, 1992.
Jennifer Morton, *Indian Summer,* Buena Vista, 1993.
Wilma Flintstone, *The Flintstones,* Universal, 1994.
Dorey Walker, *Miracle on 34th Street,* Twentieth Century-Fox, 1994.
Rebecca Tager Lott, *Moonlight and Valentino,* Gramercy, 1995.
Sue, *Lesser Prophets,* 1997.
Aubrey, *I'm Losing You,* Strand Releasing, 1998.
Joan Blake, *Crazy in Alabama,* Columbia, 1999.
Lilly, *28 Days,* Columbia, 2000.

Television Appearances; Movies:

Sally Thompson, *For Their Own Good,* ABC, 1993.
Gertruda Babilinska, *Rescuers: Stories of Courage: Two Women,* Showtime, 1997.
Skye Weston, *Cloned,* NBC, 1997.

Television Appearances; Miniseries:

Marilyn Lovell, *From the Earth to the Moon,* HBO, 1998.

Television Appearances; Specials:

Robin, *Between Cars,* HA! TV Comedy Network, 1990.
Dr. Gerrett, "Teach 109," *American Playhouse,* PBS, 1990.
Living in America, VH-1, 1991.

Stage Appearances:

A Christmas Carol, Goodman Theatre, Chicago, IL, 1981-82.
Gardenia, Goodman Theatre, 1982.
Les Belles Soeurs, North Light Repertory Theatre, Evanston, IL, 1982.
Ann Green, neighbor, nurse, and Maureen, *The Arbor,* La Mama Experimental Theatre Club, New York City, 1983.
(Broadway debut) Nora, *Brighton Beach Memoirs,* Alvin Theatre, New York City, 1984.
Juliet, *Measure for Measure,* New York Shakespeare Festival, Delacorte Theatre, New York City, 1985.
Robin, "Between Cars," *Marathon '85,* Ensemble Studio Theatre, New York City, 1985.
Effie, *Life and Limb,* Playwrights Horizons, New York City, 1985.

Has also appeared with the Steppenwolf Theatre Company.

Major Tours:

Nora, *Brighton Beach Memoirs,* U.S. cities, 1983.

OTHER SOURCES

Periodicals:

Entertainment Weekly, May 8, 1998, p. 82.
People Weekly, October 9, 1995, p. 26.*

PHILLIPS, Lou Diamond 1962-

PERSONAL

Born Lou Diamond Upchurch, February 17, 1962, at the Subic Bay U.S. Naval Station in the Philippines; son of Gerald and Lucy Upchurch; took his stepfather's name when his mother married George Phillips (a U.S. Naval officer); married Julie Cypher (an assistant director), June 27, 1987 (divorced, 1990); married Kelly Preston (a model), April 24, 1994. *Education:* University of Texas, Arlington, B.F.A., 1984; studied acting at Adam Rourke's Film Actors Lab.

Addresses: *Contact*—Innovative Artists, 1999 Avenue of the Stars, Suite 2850, Los Angeles, CA 90067.

Career: Actor, director, producer, and writer. Adam Rourke's Film Actors Lab, assistant director/instructor, 1983-86; also appeared with band, The Pipefitters.

Awards, Honors: Independent Spirit Award, best supporting male, Golden Globe Award nomination, best performance by an actor in a supporting role in a motion picture, both 1989, for *Stand and Deliver; Theatre World* Award, and Antoinette Perry Award nomination, both 1996, for *The King and I;* Blockbuster Entertainment Award, favorite supporting actor—adventure/drama, 1997, for *Courage Under Fire.*

CREDITS

Film Appearances:

Drifter, *Trespasses,* Shapiro, 1987.
Ritchie Valens, *La Bamba,* Columbia, 1987.
Angel, *Stand and Deliver,* Warner Bros., 1988.
Jose Chavez y Chavez, *Young Guns,* Twentieth Century-Fox, 1988.
Title role, *Dakota,* Miramax, 1988.
Hank Storm, *Renegades,* Universal, 1989.
Ray Forgy, *Disorganized Crime,* Buena Vista, 1989.
Jose Chavez y Chavez, *Young Guns II,* Twentieth Century-Fox, 1990.
Jesus Fuentes, *A Show of Force,* Paramount, 1990.
Russell Logan, *The First Power* (also known as *Pentagram* and *Transit*), Orion, 1990.
Title role, *Harley,* Trimark Home Video, 1990.
Demon Wind, 1990.
Mitchell Osgood, *Ambition,* Miramax, 1991.
The Panama Deception (documentary), Empowerment Project, 1992.
Agaguk, *Shadow of the Wolf* (also known as *Agaguk*), Triumph Releasing, 1993.
Officer Jim Chee, *The Dark Wind,* LIVE Home Video, 1993.
Jesse Rainfeather Goldman, *Sioux City,* IRS Releasing, 1994.
Mick Burrows, *Dangerous Touch,* Trimark Pictures, 1994.
Wheeler, *Teresa's Tattoo,* Trimark Pictures, 1994.
Hassan, *Boulevard,* Norstar Entertainment, 1994.
Ultimate Revenge, 1995.
Monfriez, *Courage Under Fire,* Twentieth Century-Fox, 1996.
(Uncredited) Jules, *Another Day in Paradise,* Trimark Pictures, 1998.
Cisco, *The Big Hit,* TriStar, 1998.
Yerzy Penalosa, *Supernova,* Metro-Goldwyn-Mayer/United Artists, 1999.
Roy Knox, *Brokedown Palace,* Twentieth Century-Fox, 1999.
Officer Alonso, *Picking Up the Pieces,* Kushner-Locke, 1999.

Also appeared in *Walking on Water; Angel Alley;* and *Interface.*

Film Work:

Associate producer, *Dakota,* Miramax, 1988.
Director, *Dangerous Touch,* Trimark Pictures, 1994.
Director, *Sioux City,* IRS Releasing, 1994.

Television Appearances; Movies:

Tag, *The Three Kings,* ABC, 1987.
Jeff Powers, *Extreme Justice* (also known as *SIS* and *Special Investigation Section*), HBO, 1993.
Petey Martin, *The Wharf Rat,* Showtime, 1995.
Jack Ketchum, *Undertow,* Showtime, 1996.

Also appeared in *Time Bomb; Guilty or Innocent; This Property Is Condemned;* and *The Zero Hour Comedy Hour.*

Television Appearances; Episodic:

Detective Bobby Diaz, "Red Tape," *Miami Vice,* NBC, 1987.
"Oil's Well That Ends Well," *Tales from the Crypt,* HBO, 1993.
Voice of Caotl, "The Shoemaker and the Elves," *Happily Ever After: Fairy Tales for Every Child* (animated), 1995.
Voice, *Adventures from the Book of Virtues,* PBS, 1996.
Nate, "That's Entertainment," *Spin City,* ABC, 1999.

Also appeared on *Dallas,* CBS.

Television Appearances; Specials:

Host, *Teen Times,* syndicated, 1988.
An All-Star Celebration: The '88 Vote, ABC, 1988.
Big Bird's Birthday or Let Me Eat Cake, PBS, 1991.
What About Me? I'm Only 3!, CBS, 1992.
Rock the Vote, Fox, 1992.
In a New Light, ABC, 1992.
Clash, "Avenue Z Afternoon," *General Motors Playwrights Theatre,* Arts & Entertainment, 1992.
Wind in the Wire, ABC, 1993.
Narrator, "Outlaws, Rebels, and Rogues," *The Untold West* (documentary), TBS, 1993.
Host, *Farm Aid VI,* TNN, 1993.
Cal, *Override,* 1994.
Latin Nights: An All-Star Celebration, 1995.
Macy's Thanksgiving Day Parade, 1996.
Voice of Cigarette, *Smoke Alarm: The Unfiltered Truth About Cigarettes,* HBO, 1996.
Big Guns Talk: The Story of the Western, TNT, 1997.
The Christmas Concert of Hope Starring Natalie Cole, CBS, 1997.
Voice of Eliahu Rosenberg and Abba Kovner, *The Trial of Adolf Eichmann,* PBS, 1997.
The 67th Annual Hollywood Christmas Parade, 1998.
The Day the Music Died, VH-1, 1999.
Narrator, *The Surf Ballroom,* PBS, 1999.

Television Appearances; Awards Presentations:

The 45th Annual Golden Globe Awards, syndicated, 1988.

The 52nd Annual Golden Globe Awards, 1995.
Blockbuster Entertainment Awards, 1997.

Stage Appearances:
(Broadway debut) The King of Siam, *The King and I,* Neil Simon Theatre, New York City, 1996-99.

Has appeared in regional theatre productions of *A Hatful of Rain; Whose Life Is It Anyway?; P.S. Your Cat Is Dead; The Lady's Nor for Burning; Doctor Faustus;* and *Hamlet.*

RECORDINGS

Music Videos:
Appeared in video for Los Lobos' "La Bamba."

Albums:
The King and I, 1997.

WRITINGS

Screenplays:
(With Loren Bivens and Jo Carol Pierce) *Trespasses,* Shapiro, 1987.
Ambition, Miramax, 1991.
Dangerous Touch, Trimark Pictures, 1994.

OTHER SOURCES

Periodicals:
Entertainment Weekly, July 26, 1996, p. 33.
People Weekly, June 3, 1996, p. 100.
Texas Monthly, September, 1996, p. 130.*

PLANER, Nigel 1955-

PERSONAL

Born February 22, 1955.

Career: Actor.

CREDITS

Film Appearances:
Mansell, *Yellowbeard,* Orion, 1983.
Charlie—Department of Works, *Brazil,* Universal, 1985.
Gunter, *The Supergrass,* New Line Home Video, 1985.
DHSS Manager, *Eat the Rich,* Columbia/TriStar Home Video, 1987.
Den, *More Bad News,* 1987.
Bernard/old man/1st camp actor, *The Strike,* 1987.
Jeff, *Blackeyes,* British Broadcasting Company (BBC), 1989.
Grand Wazir, *Carry on Columbus,* Lauren Films, 1992.
Parkey, *Clockwork Mice,* 1995.
Car salesman, *The Wind in the Willows,* Columbia, 1997.
Gerald, *Land Girls,* Gramercy Pictures, 1998.

Television Appearances; Movies:
Andrew Veitch, *Number 27,* BBC, 1988.
Paul Hockings, *Frankenstein's Baby,* BBC, 1990.

Television Appearances; Series:
Team member in various roles, *The Comic Strip Presents,* Channel 4, 1982-88.
Neil Pye, *The Young Ones,* MTV, 1985.
Nigel Cochrane, *Roll Over Beethoven,* 1985-86.
David Castle, *King & Castle,* BBC, 1986.
Ralph Filthy, *Filthy, Rich and Catflap,* BBC, 1987.
Title role, *Nicholas Craig, the Naked Actor,* 1990.
Narrator, *The Magic Roundabout,* 1990—.
Team Member in various roles, *The Comic Strip,* BBC-2, 1990-98.
Baz Grimley, *The Grimley's,* 1997.
Voice characterization, *Romuald the Reindeer,* Fox Family Channel, 1998-99.

Television Appearances; Episodic:
Barman, *Happy Families,* 1985.
Lord Smedley, "Nob and Nobility," *Blackadder the Third,* BBC-1, 1987.
Inspector Hopkins, "The Golden Pince-Nez," *The Memoirs of Sherlock Holmes,* Grenada TV, 1994.
Shelford, "The Reconstituted Corpse," *Jonathan Creek,* 1997.
Gavin, "I Tell You It's Burt Reynolds," *Paul Merton in Galton and Simpson's. . .,* 1997.*

PLOTNICK, Jack

PERSONAL

Education: Studied drama at Carnegie-Mellon University; also studied with Mel Shapiro and Marshall Mason.

Career: Actor.

CREDITS

Television Appearances; Series:
Barrett, a recurring role, *Ellen,* ABC, 1995-97.
Uncle Ralphie, *The Weird Al Show,* 1997.

Appeared as deputy mayor of Sunnydale, *Buffy the Vampire Slayer,* The WB.

Television Appearances; Episodic:
Mitch, *Madman of the People,* NBC, 1994.
Penn, *Murphy Brown,* CBS, 1994.
Seth, *Hope and Gloria,* NBC, 1995.
Harris, "Caroline and the Younger Man," *Caroline in the City,* NBC, 1996.
Ted, *The Wayans Bros.,* The WB, 1996.
The Jenny McCarthy Show, NBC, 1997.

Also appeared in episodes of *Late Night with Conan O'Brien* and *Seinfeld.*

Television Appearances; Awards Presentations:
The 1998 VH-1 Fashion Awards, VH-1, 1998.

Film Appearances:
Edmund Kay, *Gods and Monsters* (also known as *The Father of Frankenstein*), Lions Gate Films, 1998.
Zak, *Chairman of the Board,* Trimark, 1998.

Appeared in the films *Ground Control* and *Tiara Tango.*

Stage Appearances:
Miss Industrial Northeast, *Pageant,* Blue Angel Theatre, New York City, 1991-92.
Kevin Bailey, *The Sheik of Avenue B,* Town Hall Theatre, New York City, 1992.
The News in Revue, Theatre at Del's Down Under, New York City, 1992.

Appeared in *Plotnick and Rudetsky* at Caroline's Comedy Club, New York City; appeared off-Broadway in *Class Clown.**

POITIER, Sidney 1927-

PERSONAL

Born February 20, 1927, in Miami, FL; son of Reginald James (a tomato farmer) and Evelyn (a tomato farmer; maiden name, Outten) Poitier; married Juanita Hardy (a dancer), April 29, 1950 (divorced, 1965); married Joanna Shimkus (an actress), January 23, 1976; children: (first marriage) Beverly Poitier Henderson, Pamela, Sherri, Gina; (second marriage) Anika, Sydney (an actress). *Education:* Trained for the stage with Paul Mann and Lloyd Richards. *Avocational interests:* Reading, music, golf, football, tennis, gardening, travel.

Addresses: *Office*—Ambassador to Japan, Bahamas Foreign Ministry, East Hill St., P.O. Box N-3746, Nassau, Bahamas.

Career: Actor, director, and producer. Founder (with Paul Newman, Barbra Streisand, Steve McQueen, and Dustin Hoffman), First Artists Film Production Company, 1969; Ambassador to Japan from the Bahamas, April 1997—; member of board of directors, Walt Disney Company. Has worked as a janitor, dishwasher, construction worker, messenger, and longshoreman. *Military service:* U.S. Army, physiotherapist, 1941-45.

Member: American Federation of Television and Radio Artists, Actors' Equity Association, Screen Actors Guild, Directors Guild of America, Writers Guild of America, Center Theatre Group, American Film Institute, Martin Luther King, Jr., Center for Nonviolent Social Change, National Association for the Advancement of Colored People (NAACP; lifetime member), Charles Drew Medical Group, Los Angeles Olympic Committee.

Awards, Honors: Georgio Cini Award, Venice Film Festival, 1958, for *Something of Value;* British Academy of Film and Television Arts (BAFTA) Award nomination, best foreign actor, 1958, for *Edge of the City;* Academy Award nomination, best actor, Silver Bear Award, Berlin Film Festival, best actor, New York Film Critics Award, best actor, and BAFTA Award, best foreign actor, all 1958, for *The Defiant Ones;* Antoinette Perry Award nomination, best actor in a drama, 1960, for *A Raisin in the Sun;* BAFTA Award nominations, best foreign actor, 1962 and 1965, Academy Award, best actor, 1963, Golden Globe Award, best actor in a drama, 1964, all for *Lilies of the Field;* William J. German Human Relations Award, American Jewish Congress, 1966; Golden Globe Award nomination, best motion picture actor—drama, 1966, BAFTA Award nomination, best foreign actor, 1967, both for *A Patch of Blue;* Golden Apple Star of the Year Award, Hollywood Women's Press Club, 1967; Golden Globe Award nomination, best motion picture actor—drama, and BAFTA Award, best foreign actor, 1968, both for *In the Heat of the Night;* San Sebastian

Film Festival Award, best actor, 1968, for *For Love of Ivy;* Golden Globe Award, male world film favorite, 1969; Knight Commander of the British Empire, 1974; Coretta Scott King Book Award, American Library Association Social Responsibilities Round Table, 1981, for *This Life;* Cecil B. De Mille Award, Hollywood Foreign Press Association, 1982; Emmy Award nomination, best actor in a miniseries or special, 1990, and Golden Globe Award nomination, best actor in a miniseries or telefilm, 1991, both for *Separate But Equal;* American Film Institute Life Achievement Award, 1992; National Board of Review, Career Achievement Award, 1994; Kennedy Center Honor, 1995; Image Award nomination, NAACP, outstanding actor in a television movie, miniseries, or drama special, 1996, for *A Good Day to Die;* Emmy Award nomination, outstanding lead actor in a miniseries or special, 1997, Screen Actors Guild Award nomination, outstanding performance by a male actor in a television movie or miniseries, Image Award, outstanding lead actor in a television movie, miniseries or drama special, 1998, all for *Mandela and de Klerk;* Blockbuster Entertainment Award nomination, favorite supporting actor—suspense, 1998, for *The Jackal.*

CREDITS

Film Appearances:

From Whom Cometh My Help (documentary), U.S. Army Signal Corps, 1949.
Dr. Luther Brooks, *No Way Out,* Twentieth Century-Fox, 1950.
Reverend Maimangu, *Cry, the Beloved Country* (also known as *African Fury*), Lopert, 1952.
Corporal Andrew Robertson, *Red Ball Express,* Universal, 1952.
Inman Jackson, *Go, Man, Go!,* United Artists, 1954.
Gregory W. Miller, *The Blackboard Jungle,* Metro-Goldwyn-Mayer, 1955.
Gates, *Goodbye, My Lady,* Warner Bros., 1956.
Tommy Tyler, *Edge of the City* (also known as *A Man Is Ten Feet Tall*), Metro-Goldwyn-Mayer, 1957.
Kimani, *Something of Value,* Metro-Goldwyn-Mayer, 1957.
Rau-Ru, *Band of Angels,* Warner Bros., 1957.
Noah Cullen, *The Defiant Ones,* United Artists, 1958.
Oban, *The Mark of the Hawk* (also known as *Accused*), Universal, 1958.
Porgy, *Porgy and Bess,* Columbia, 1959.
Towler, *All the Young Men,* Columbia, 1960.
Marcus, *Virgin Island* (also known as *Our Virgin Island*), Films-Around-the-World, 1960.
Eddie Cook, *Paris Blues,* United Artists, 1961.
Walter Lee Younger, *A Raisin in the Sun,* Columbia, 1961.
Doctor, *Pressure Point,* United Artists, 1962.
Homer Smith, *Lilies of the Field,* United Artists, 1963.
El Mansuh, *The Long Ships* (also known as *Dugi Brodovi*), Columbia, 1964.
Ben Munceford, *The Bedford Incident,* Columbia, 1965.
Simon of Cyrene, *The Greatest Story Ever Told,* United Artists, 1965.
Gordon Ralfe, *A Patch of Blue,* Metro-Goldwyn-Mayer, 1965.
Alan Newell, *The Slender Thread,* Paramount, 1965.
Toller, *Ralph Nelson's Duel at Diablo,* United Artists, 1966.
John Prentice, *Guess Who's Coming to Dinner,* Columbia, 1967.
Virgil Tibbs, *In the Heat of the Night,* United Artists, 1967.
Mark Thackeray, *To Sir, with Love,* Columbia, 1967.
Jack Parks, *For Love of Ivy,* Cinerama, 1968.
Jason Higgs, *The Lost Man,* Universal, 1969.
Virgil Tibbs, *They Call Me Mister Tibbs,* United Artists, 1970.
King: A Filmed Record . . . Montgomery to Memphis, Marion, 1970.
John Kane, *Brother John,* Columbia, 1971.
Lieutenant Virgil Tibbs, *The Organization,* United Artists, 1971.
Buck, *Buck and the Preacher,* Columbia, 1972.
Dr. Matt Younger, *A Warm December,* National General, 1973.
Steve Jackson, *Uptown Saturday Night,* Warner Bros., 1974.
Clyde Williams, *Let's Do It Again,* Warner Bros., 1975.
Shack Twala, *The Wilby Conspiracy,* United Artists, 1975.
Manny Durrell, *A Piece of the Action,* Warner Bros., 1977.
Warren Stantin, *Shoot to Kill* (also known as *Deadly Pursuit*), Buena Vista, 1988.
Roy Parmenter, *Little Nikita* (also known as *The Sleepers*), Columbia, 1988.
Crease, *Sneakers,* Universal, 1992.
Himself, *A Century of Cinema,* 1994.
Wild Bill: Hollywood Maverick, 1996.
Carter Preston-FBI Deputy Director, *The Jackal,* Universal, 1997.

Film Work; Director:

Buck and the Preacher, Columbia, 1972.
A Warm December, National General, 1973.
Uptown Saturday Night, Warner Bros., 1974.
Let's Do It Again, Warner Bros., 1975.

A Piece of the Action, Warner Bros., 1977.
Stir Crazy, Columbia, 1980.
Hanky Panky, Columbia, 1982.
Fast Forward, Columbia, 1985.
Ghost Dad, Universal, 1990.

Television Appearances; Miniseries:
Thurgood Marshall, *Separate But Equal,* ABC, 1991.
Gypsy Smith, *Children of the Dust* (also known as *A Good Day to Die*), CBS, 1995.

Television Appearances; Movies:
Mark Thackeray, *To Sir with Love 2,* CBS, 1996.
Nelson Mandela, *Mandela and de Klerk,* Showtime, 1997.
Dr. Jack Miller, *Oprah Winfrey Presents: David and Lisa,* ABC, 1998.
Will Cleamons, *Free of Eden,* Showtime, 1999.
Noah Dearborn, *The Simple Life of Noah Dearborn,* CBS, 1999.

Television Appearances; Specials:
The American Film Institute Tenth Anniversary Special, CBS, 1977.
The Night of 100 Stars II, ABC, 1985.
The Spencer Tracy Legacy: A Tribute by Katherine Hepburn, PBS, 1986.
Narrator, *Bopha!,* PBS, 1987.
The Kennedy Center Honors: A Celebration of the Performing Arts, CBS, 1989.
Host, *Voyager: Rendezvous with Neptune,* TBS, 1989.
Sinatra 75: The Best Is Yet to Come (also known as *Frank Sinatra: 75th Birthday Celebration*), CBS, 1990.
Celebrate the Soul of American Music, syndicated, 1991.
Back to School '92 (also known as *Education First!*), CBS, 1992.
AFI Salute to Sidney Poitier (also known as *The 20th Annual American Film Institute Life Achievement Award*), NBC, 1992.
The 19th Annual Black Filmmakers Hall of Fame, syndicated, 1992.
The American Film Institute Salute to Elizabeth Taylor, ABC, 1993.
An American Reunion: New Beginnings, Renewed Hope (also known as *An American Reunion: The People's Inaugural Celebration*), HBO, 1993.
Hollywood Stars: A Century of Cinema, 1995.
James Earl Jones, 1995.
The Kennedy Center Honors: A Celebration of the Performing Arts, 1995.
The Kennedy Center Honors, CBS, 1997.
An Evening of Stars: A Celebration of the Educational Excellence Benefitting the Negro College Fund, syndicated, 1999.

Television Appearances; Awards Presentations:
The 22nd Annual NAACP Image Awards, NBC, 1990.
The Great Ones: The National Sports Awards, NBC, 1993.
The 1997 ESPY Awards, ESPN, 1997.
The 70th Annual Academy Awards, 1998.

Television Appearances; Episodic:
"Parole Chief," *Philco Television Playhouse,* NBC, 1952.
Tommy Tyler, "A Man Is Ten Feet Tall," *Philco Television Playhouse,* NBC, 1955.
"Fascinating Stranger," *Ponds Theatre,* ABC, 1955.
"A Tribute to Eleanor Roosevelt on Her Diamond Jubilee," *Sunday Showcase,* NBC, 1959.
The Strolling '20s, CBS, 1966.
"A Time for Laughter," *ABC Stage '67,* ABC, 1967.
The New Bill Cosby Show, CBS, 1972.

Television Work; Movies:
Executive producer, *Free of Eden,* Showtime, 1999.

Stage Appearances:
(Stage debut) *Days of Our Youth,* American Negro Theatre Playhouse, New York City, 1945.
(Broadway debut) Polydorus, *Lysistrata,* Belasco Theatre, New York City, 1946.
On Striver's Row, American National Theatre Playhouse, New York City, 1946.
Lester, *Anna Lucasta,* National Theatre, New York City, 1947.
Walter Lee Younger, *A Raisin in the Sun,* Ethel Barrymore Theatre, New York City, 1959.

Appeared in *You Can't Take It with You, Rain, Freight, The Fisherman, Hidden Horizon, Sepia Cinderella,* and *Riders to the Sea,* all with American Negro Theatre.

Major Tours:
Lester, *Anna Lucasta,* U.S. cities, 1948.

Stage Work:
Director, *Carry Me Back to Morningside Heights,* John Golden Theatre, New York City, 1968.

WRITINGS

Screenplays:
(Author of original story) *For Love of Ivy,* Cinerama, 1968.

Books:

This Life (autobiography), Knopf, 1980.

(With Carol Bergman) *The Films of Sidney Poitier,* Chelsea House, 1988.

OTHER SOURCES

Books:

Marill, Alvin H., *The Films of Sidney Poitier,* Citadel, 1978.

Paige, David, *Sidney Poitier,* Creative Education, 1976.

Periodicals:

American Film, September/October, 1991, p. 18.

Entertainment Weekly, fall, 1996, p. 70.

Jet, December 18, 1995, p. 61; March 3, 1997; April 14, 1997, p 19; May 5, 1997, p. 6.

Time, September 22, 1997, p. 103.*

PORTMAN, Natalie 1981-

PERSONAL

Born June 9, 1981, in Jerusalem, Israel; father, a doctor; mother, an artist. *Education:* Attended Stagedoor Manor Performing Arts Camp, 1994-95. *Avocational interests:* Writing, dancing.

Addresses: *Agent*—International Creative Management, 8942 Wilshire Blvd., Beverly Hills, CA 90211.

Career: Actress.

Awards, Honors: YoungStar Award, best actress in a drama, *Hollywood Reporter,* 1994, for *Leon.*

CREDITS

Film Appearances:

Mathilda, *Leon* (also known as *The Cleaner* and *The Professional*), Gaumont International, 1994.

Lauren, *Heat,* Warner Bros., 1995.

Laura, *Everyone Says I Love You,* Miramax, 1996.

Marty, *Beautiful Girls,* Miramax, 1996.

Taffy Dale, *Mars Attacks!,* Warner Bros., 1996.

South Beach, 1998.

Gwyneth, *The Little Black Book,* 1998.

Ann August, *Anywhere But Here,* Twentieth Century-Fox, 1999.

Queen Amidala/Padme, *Star Wars: Episode I—The Phantom Menace,* Twentieth Century-Fox, 1999.

Novalee Nation, *Where the Heart Is,* Twentieth Century-Fox, 2000.

Queen Amidala, *Star Wars Episode II,* forthcoming.

Stage Appearances:

Anne Frank, *The Diary of Anne Frank,* Music Box Theatre, New York City, 1997-98.

OTHER SOURCES

Periodicals:

Entertainment Weekly, June 28, 1996, p. 38.

Harper's Bazaar, November, 1997, p. 222.

Interview, March, 1996, p. 116.

New York, September 8, 1997, p. 69.

People Weekly, November 18, 1996, p. 109.*

PORTMAN, Rachel 1960-

PERSONAL

Full name, Rachel Mary Berkeley Portman; born December 11, 1960, in Haslemere, England; married Uberto Pasolini, 1995. *Education:* Oxford University, B.A.

Addresses: *Agent*—Kraft-Benjamin Agency, 345 North Maple Dr., Suite 385, Beverly Hills, CA 90210.

Career: Composer and orchestrator.

Awards, Honors: Named composer of the year, British Film Institute, 1988; British Academy Award nominations, British Academy of Film and Television Arts, 1990, for *Oranges Are Not the Only Fruit,* and 1991, for *The Woman in Black;* Academy Award, best score, 1996, for *Emma;* Annie Award nomination (shared with Don Black), outstanding individual achievement for music in an animated feature production, 1997, for the song "As Long as There's Christmas."

CREDITS

Film Work; Orchestrator, Unless Otherwise Noted:

Music director, *Privileged,* New Yorker, 1982.

Music arranger, "Tannhauser," *Meeting Venus,* Warner Bros., 1991.

The Joy Luck Club, Buena Vista, 1993.

Benny & Joon, Metro-Goldwyn-Mayer, 1993.

The Road to Wellville, Columbia, 1994.

To Wong Foo, Thanks for Everything, Julie Newmar, Universal, 1995.

A Pyromaniac's Love Story (also known as *Burning Love*), Buena Vista, 1995.

Smoke, Miramax, 1995.

Score producer, *The Adventures of Pinocchio* (also known as *Carlo Collodi's Pinocchio, Pinocchio,* and *Die Legende von Pinocchio*), New Line Cinema, 1996.

Emma, Miramax, 1996.

Marvin's Room, Miramax, 1996.

Addicted to Love (also known as *Forlorn*), Miramax, 1997.

(And song performer, "Uhuru") *Beloved,* Buena Vista, 1998.

WRITINGS

Film Music; Scores, Unless Otherwise Noted:

Privileged, New Yorker, 1982.

Experience Preferred . . . But Not Essential (also known as *First Love*), Samuel Goldwyn Company, 1982.

Last Day of Summer, 1984.

Sharma and Beyond, Cinecom International, 1986.

90 Degrees South, 1987.

High Hopes, Skouras, 1988.

Life Is Sweet, October Films, 1990.

Antonia and Jane, 1991.

Where Angels Fear to Tread, Fine Line Features, 1991.

(And song, "Where Are the Words?") *Used People,* Twentieth Century-Fox, 1992.

Rebecca's Daughters, 1992.

The Joy Luck Club, Buena Vista, 1993.

Friends, First Run Features, 1993.

Ethan Frome, Miramax, 1993.

Benny & Joon, Metro-Goldwyn-Mayer, 1993.

The War of the Buttons, Warner Bros., 1994.

Only You (also known as *Him* and *Just in Time*), TriStar, 1994.

Sirens, Miramax, 1994.

The Road to Wellville, Columbia, 1994.

To Wong Foo, Thanks for Everything, Julie Newmar, Universal, 1995.

A Pyromaniac's Love Story (also known as *Burning Love*), Buena Vista, 1995.

Smoke, Miramax, 1995.

The Adventures of Pinocchio (also known as *Carlo Collodi's Pinocchio, Pinocchio,* and *Die Legende von Pinocchio*), New Line Cinema, 1996.

Emma, Miramax, 1996.

Palookaville, Samuel Goldwyn Company, 1996.

Marvin's Room, Miramax, 1996.

(And songs, including "As Long as There's Christmas," with Don Black) *Beauty and the Beast: The Enchanted Christmas,* Walt Disney Home Video, 1997.

Addicted to Love (also known as *Forlorn*), Miramax, 1997.

Home Fries, Warner Bros., 1998.

(And songs "Little Rice, Little Bean" and "Sethe's Lullaby") *Beloved,* Buena Vista, 1998.

The Other Sister, Buena Vista, 1999.

Television Music; Miniseries:

The Storyteller (also known as *Jim Henson's The Storyteller*), 1987.

The Storyteller: Greek Myths (also known as *Jim Henson's The Storyteller: Greek Myths*), HBO, 1990.

Television Music; Movies:

Reflections, 1984.

Four Days in July, 1984.

Good as Gold, 1986.

The Short and Curlies, 1987.

1914 All Out, 1987.

Sometime in August, 1988.

Loving Hazel, 1988.

Monster Maker, 1989.

Living with Dinosaurs, 1989.

The Widowmaker, 1990.

Shoot to Kill, 1990.

Oranges Are Not the Only Fruit, Arts and Entertainment, 1990.

The Woman in Black, Arts and Entertainment, 1991.

Flea Bites, 1991.

The Cloning of Joanna May, Arts and Entertainment, 1991.

Great Moments in Aviation (also known as *Shades of Fear*), 1993.

Television Music; Specials:

A Little Princess, PBS, 1987.

Fearnot, NBC, 1987.

Hans My Hedgehog, NBC, 1987.

A Story Short, NBC, 1988.

The Luck Child, NBC, 1988.

Young Charlie Chaplin, PBS, 1989.

Precious Bane, PBS, 1989.

Elizabeth R: A Year in the Life of the Queen, PBS, 1992.

The Hollywood Soundtrack Story, American Movie Classics, 1995.

Other:

Composer, *Fantasy for Cello and Piano,* 1985.*

POTTER, Monica 1971-

PERSONAL

Born June 30, 1971, in Cleveland, OH; father, an inventor; mother, a secretary; married a construction contractor; children: two sons. *Religion:* Catholic.

Career: Actress. Worked as a child model in Chicago, IL, and Miami, FL; appeared in commercials.

CREDITS

Film Appearances:

Biker's woman, *Bulletproof,* Universal, 1996.
Lilli, *Heaven or Vegas,* Storm Entertainment, 1997.
Tricia Poe, *Con Air,* Buena Vista, 1997.
Carin, *Patch Adams,* Universal, 1998.
Kate Nash, *A Cool Dry Place* (also known as *Dance Real Slow*), Twentieth Century-Fox, 1998.
Martha, *Martha, Meet Frank, Daniel, and Laurence* (also known as *The Very Thought of You*), Miramax, 1998.
March Marckx, *Without Limits* (also known as *Pre*), Warner Bros., 1998.
Amanda Pierce, *Head Over Heels,* Universal, 2000.

Television Appearances; Series:

Sharon, *The Young and the Restless,* CBS, 1994.

OTHER SOURCES

Periodicals:

Interview, May, 1998, p. 84.
New York Times, September 13, 1998, p. 71.*

PROBST, Nicholas
See PRYOR, Nicholas

PRYOR, Nicholas 1935-
(Nicholas Probst)

PERSONAL

Original name, Nicholas David Probst; born January 28, 1935, in Baltimore, MD; son of J. Stanley (a pharmaceutical manufacturer) and Dorothy (Driskill) Probst; married Joan Epstein (an actress), December 21, 1958 (divorced, 1968); married Melinda Plank (an actress and dancer), February 27, 1968 (divorced); married; wife's name, Pamela; children: (third marriage) Stacey. *Education:* Yale University, B.A. (drama), 1956.

Addresses: *Contact*—Actors' Equity Association, 165 West 46th St., 15th Floor, New York, NY 10036.

Career: Actor. Worked as a cabinet maker and inventor; developed and patented an accessory that improves the usefulness and storage capacity of household closets.

Member: Actors' Equity Association, American Federation of Television and Radio Artists, Screen Actors Guild, Writers Guild of America (East).

Awards, Honors: National scholar, Oregon Shakespeare Festival, 1953; RCA-NBC acting scholar, Yale University, 1955-56.

CREDITS

Television Appearances; Series:

The second Ernie Cooper, *Young Dr. Malone,* NBC, 1959.
Rex Stern, *The Brighter Day,* CBS, 1960-61.
Johnny Ellis, *The Secret Storm,* CBS, 1963.
Tom Baxter, *Another World* (also known as *Another World: Bay City*), NBC, 1964.
Ken Cora, *The Nurses,* ABC, 1965-67.
Paul Bradley, *Love Is a Many Splendored Thing,* CBS, 1968.
Lincoln "Linc" Tyler III, *All My Children,* ABC, 1971-72.
Joel Gentry, *The Edge of Night,* CBS, 1973 and 1981-82.
Jack Felspar, *The Bronx Zoo,* NBC, 1986.
Chancellor Milton Arnold, *Beverly Hills, 90210,* Fox, 1993-97.
Gene Bennett, *Party of Five,* Fox, 1994.
Victor Collins, *Port Charles,* ABC, 1997—.

Television Appearances; Miniseries:

Hank Ferris, *Washington: Behind Closed Doors,* ABC, 1977.
Bert Yeager, *Ruby Ridge: An American Tragedy* (also known as *Every Knee Shall Bow: The Siege at Ruby Ridge*), CBS, 1996.

Television Appearances; Movies:

Art Beresford, *Fear on Trial,* CBS, 1975.
James T. O'Neil, *Force Five,* CBS, 1975.
Mack, *Widow,* NBC, 1976.

Manners, *The Life and Assassination of the Kingfish,* NBC, 1977.
Man in a sports car, *Night Terror,* NBC, 1977.
Jeff Kramer, *Having Babies II,* ABC, 1977.
Will Gilmore, *Rainbow,* NBC, 1978.
Dick Owens, *Reunion,* CBS, 1980.
Dave Gildea, *The Plutonium Incident,* CBS, 1980.
Larry Wax, *Marriage Is Alive and Well,* NBC, 1980.
Ryan, *The Last Song,* CBS, 1980.
Jacob, *Gideon's Trumpet,* CBS, 1980.
Ed Lissik, *The $5.20 an Hour Dream,* CBS, 1980.
Ralph Dortlund, *Desperate Voyage,* CBS, 1980.
Elwin Potter, *A Few Days in Weasel Creek,* CBS, 1981.
Scott Thomas, *Homeroom,* 1981.
James Grew, *East of Eden* (also known as *John Steinbeck's East of Eden*), ABC, 1981.
Dr. Judd, *Splendor in the Grass,* NBC, 1981.
Greg Baker, Sr., *The Kid from Nowhere,* NBC, 1982.
John Cye Cheasty, *Blood Feud,* syndicated, 1983.
Dr. Thompson, *Amazons,* ABC, 1984.
Mitchell McKay, *Second Sight: A Love Story,* CBS, 1984.
Larry Walker, *Into Thin Air,* CBS, 1985.
Freddie Dayton, *Murder in Three Acts* (also known as *Agatha Christie's Murder in Three Acts*), CBS, 1986.
Richard Baxter, *A Stoning in Fulham County* (also known as *The Amish Story, Incident at Tile Mill Road,* and *The Stoning*), NBC, 1988.
Mr. Exeter, *The Diamond Trap* (also known as *The Great Diamond Robbery*), CBS, 1988.
Colonel William Devereau, *Nightbreaker* (also known as *Advance to Ground Zero*), TNT, 1989.
Majority Rule, Lifetime, 1992.
Philip Carlyle, *Love Can Be Murder* (also known as *Kindred Spirits*), NBC, 1992.
Judge Lamartine, *Murder between Friends,* NBC, 1994.
Don Barnett, *Trial by Fire,* ABC, 1995.
Paul Coster, *Cagney and Lacey: Together Again,* CBS, 1995.
Paul Cleary, *Broken Trust* (also known as *Court of Honor*), TNT, 1995.
Perry Davies, *Betrayed: A Story of Three Women,* ABC, 1995.
Ralph Gilchrist, *A Walton Wedding,* CBS, 1995.
Frank Sanborn, *Carriers,* CBS, 1998.

Television Appearances; Specials:
Hallmark Hall of Fame, NBC, 1959.

Television Appearances; Episodic:
Kraft Television Theatre, NBC, 1955.
The U.S. Steel Hour, CBS, 1958.
Omnibus, ABC, 1958.
The DuPont Show of the Month, NBC, 1960.
Ford Startime, NBC, 1960.
Dane Ross, "The Changing Heart," *Alfred Hitchcock Presents,* NBC, 1961.
Reilly, "Passport to Murder," *Hart to Hart,* ABC, 1979.
Major Burnham, "Rumor at the Top," *M*A*S*H,* CBS, 1981.
Horace Simmons, "The Late Sarah White," *Tales of the Gold Monkey,* ABC, 1982.
Royal Wilder, "Times Are Changing" (parts one and two), *Little House on the Prairie* (also known as *Little House: A New Beginning*), NBC, 1982.
Harry Parmel, "Capitol Offense," *Murder, She Wrote,* CBS, 1985.
Mr. Ardrey, "The Life and Time of Dominic Florio, Jr.," *Hill Street Blues,* NBC, 1985.
Vince, "Many Happy Returns," *Knight Rider,* NBC, 1985.
Nathan Billings, *Dallas,* CBS, 1985.
Ryan, "Four O'Clock," *Alfred Hitchcock Presents,* NBC, 1986.
"Cheek to Cheek," *St. Elsewhere,* NBC, 1986.
The Tonight Show Starring Johnny Carson, NBC, 1987.
"Plastic Fantastic Lovers," *Moonlighting,* ABC, 1989.
David Kingston, "O'Malley's Luck," *Murder, She Wrote,* CBS, 1990.
L.A. Law, NBC, 1990.
Theo Cayle, "The Committee," *Murder, She Wrote,* CBS, 1991.
Sisters, NBC, 1991.
L.A. Law, NBC, 1991.
Mr. Simpson, *Jack's Place,* ABC, 1992.
Moriarty, *Picket Fences,* CBS, 1993.
Doctor, *The Mommies,* NBC, 1993.
George Lazlo, *Jack's Place,* ABC, 1993.
Dr. Paul Dodge, "The Obsession," *Matlock,* ABC, 1993.
Senator George Stewart, "The Washington Affair," *Dr. Quinn, Medicine Woman,* CBS, 1994.
Dr. Harold Halpern, *Chicago Hope,* CBS, 1994.
Board member, "Growth Pains," *Chicago Hope,* CBS, 1995.
Phil, "The Spider Webb," *Nowhere Man,* UPN, 1995.
Felton, *Live Shot,* UPN, 1995.
Dr. Raymond Huxley, *Diagnosis Murder,* CBS, 1996.
Dr. Kloves, *The Practice,* ABC, 1997.

Also appeared in *Falcon Crest,* CBS.

Television Appearances; Pilots:
Nelson Surgess, *Starting Now,* CBS, 1989.
Captain Barrisford, *Angie, the Lieutenant* (also known as *Angie*), ABC, 1992.

Romeo in Rhythm, Metro-Goldwyn-Mayer, 1940.
Papa Gets the Bird, Metro-Goldwyn-Mayer, 1940.
The Homeless Flea, Metro-Goldwyn-Mayer, 1940.
Gallopin' Gals, Metro-Goldwyn-Mayer, 1940.
Lonesome Stranger, Metro-Goldwyn-Mayer, 1940.
Mrs. Ladybug, Metro-Goldwyn-Mayer, 1940.
Abdul the Bulbul Ameer, Metro-Goldwyn-Mayer, 1941.
The Prospecting Bear, Metro-Goldwyn-Mayer, 1941.
The Little Mole, Metro-Goldwyn-Mayer, 1941.
The Goose Goes South, Metro-Goldwyn-Mayer, 1941.
Dance of the Weed, Metro-Goldwyn-Mayer, 1941.
The Alley Cat, Metro-Goldwyn-Mayer, 1941.
Little Cesario, Metro-Goldwyn-Mayer, 1941.
Officer Pooch, Metro-Goldwyn-Mayer, 1941.
The Rookie Bear, Metro-Goldwyn-Mayer, 1941.
The Flying Bear, Metro-Goldwyn-Mayer, 1941.
The Field Mouse, Metro-Goldwyn-Mayer, 1941.
The Hungry Wolf, Metro-Goldwyn-Mayer, 1942.
The First Swallow, Metro-Goldwyn-Mayer, 1942.
The Bears and the Beavers, Metro-Goldwyn-Mayer, 1942.
Little Gravel Voice, Metro-Goldwyn-Mayer, 1942.
Bats in the Belfry, Metro-Goldwyn-Mayer, 1942.
Blitz Wolf, Metro-Goldwyn-Mayer, 1942.
The Early Bird Dood It, Metro-Goldwyn-Mayer, 1942.
Chips Off the Old Block, Metro-Goldwyn-Mayer, 1942.
Wild Honey (also known as *How to Get Along Without a Ration Book*), Metro-Goldwyn-Mayer, 1942.
Barney Bear's Victory Garden, Metro-Goldwyn-Mayer, 1942.
Bah Wilderness, Metro-Goldwyn-Mayer, 1943.
Dumb-Hounded, Metro-Goldwyn-Mayer, 1943.
The Boy and the Wolf, Metro-Goldwyn-Mayer, 1943.
Red Hot Riding Hood, Metro-Goldwyn-Mayer, 1943.
Who Killed Who?, Metro-Goldwyn-Mayer, 1943.
The Uninvited Pest, Metro-Goldwyn-Mayer, 1943.
One Ham's Family, Metro-Goldwyn-Mayer, 1943.
War Dogs, Metro-Goldwyn-Mayer, 1943.
Stork's Holiday, Metro-Goldwyn-Mayer, 1943.
What's Buzzin' Buzzard?, Metro-Goldwyn-Mayer, 1943.
Innertube Antics (also known as *Innertube Interlude* and *Strange Innertube*), Metro-Goldwyn-Mayer, 1944.
Screwball Squirrel, Metro-Goldwyn-Mayer, 1944.
Batty Baseball, Metro-Goldwyn-Mayer, 1944.
The Tree Surgeon, Metro-Goldwyn-Mayer, 1944.
Happy-Go-Nutty, Metro-Goldwyn-Mayer, 1944.
Bear Raid Warden, Metro-Goldwyn-Mayer, 1944.
Big Heel-Watha (also known as *Buck of the Month*), Metro-Goldwyn-Mayer, 1944.
Barney Bear's Polar Pest (also known as *Bedtime for Barney*), Metro-Goldwyn-Mayer, 1944.
The Screwy Truant, Metro-Goldwyn-Mayer, 1945.
Unwelcome Guest, Metro-Goldwyn-Mayer, 1945.
Jerky Turkey, Metro-Goldwyn-Mayer, 1945.
The Shooting of Dan McGoo (also known as *The Shooting of Dan McScrew*), Metro-Goldwyn-Mayer, 1945.
Swing Shift Cinderella, Metro-Goldwyn-Mayer, 1945.
Wild and Woolfy, Metro-Goldwyn-Mayer, 1945.
Lonesome Lenny, Metro-Goldwyn-Mayer, 1946.
Northwest Hounded Police (also known as *The Man Hunt*), Metro-Goldwyn-Mayer, 1946.
Henpecked Hoboes, Metro-Goldwyn-Mayer, 1946.
Hound Hunters, Metro-Goldwyn-Mayer, 1947.
Red Hot Rangers, Metro-Goldwyn-Mayer, 1947.
Uncle Tom's Cabana, Metro-Goldwyn-Mayer, 1947.
Slap Happy Lion, Metro-Goldwyn-Mayer, 1947.
King-Size Canary, Metro-Goldwyn-Mayer, 1947.
The Bear and the Bean, Metro-Goldwyn-Mayer, 1947.
What Price Fleadom, Metro-Goldwyn-Mayer, 1947.
Little 'Tinker, Metro-Goldwyn-Mayer, 1947.
The Bear and the Hare, Metro-Goldwyn-Mayer, 1948.
Half-Pint Pygmy, Metro-Goldwyn-Mayer, 1948.
Lucky Ducky, Metro-Goldwyn-Mayer, 1948.
The Cat That Hated People, Metro-Goldwyn-Mayer, 1948.
Goggle Fishing Bear (also known as *Goggle Fishing*), Metro-Goldwyn-Mayer, 1949.
Bad Luck Blackie, Metro-Goldwyn-Mayer, 1949.
Senor Droopy, Metro-Goldwyn-Mayer, 1949.
The House of Tomorrow, Metro-Goldwyn-Mayer, 1949.
Doggone Tired, Metro-Goldwyn-Mayer, 1949.
Wags to Riches (also known as *From Wags to Riches*), Metro-Goldwyn-Mayer, 1949.
Little Rural Riding Hood, Metro-Goldwyn-Mayer, 1949.
Out-Foxed, Metro-Goldwyn-Mayer, 1949.
The Counterfeit Cat, Metro-Goldwyn-Mayer, 1949.
Ventriloquist Cat, Metro-Goldwyn-Mayer, 1949.
The Cuckoo Clock, Metro-Goldwyn-Mayer, 1950.
Garden Gopher, Metro-Goldwyn-Mayer, 1950.
The Chump Champ, Metro-Goldwyn-Mayer, 1950.
The Peachy Cobbler, Metro-Goldwyn-Mayer, 1950.
Cock-a-Doodle Dog, Metro-Goldwyn-Mayer, 1951.
Daredevil Droopy, Metro-Goldwyn-Mayer, 1951.
Droopy's Good Deed, Metro-Goldwyn-Mayer, 1951.
Symphony in Slang, Metro-Goldwyn-Mayer, 1951.
Car of Tomorrow, Metro-Goldwyn-Mayer, 1951.
Droopy's Double Trouble, Metro-Goldwyn-Mayer, 1951.
Caballero Droopy, Metro-Goldwyn-Mayer, 1952.
Magical Maestro, Metro-Goldwyn-Mayer, 1952.

One Cab's Family, Metro-Goldwyn-Mayer, 1952.
Rock-a-Bye Bear, Metro-Goldwyn-Mayer, 1952.
Little Wise Quacker, Metro-Goldwyn-Mayer, 1952.
Busybody Bear, Metro-Goldwyn-Mayer, 1952.
Barney's Hungry Cousin, Metro-Goldwyn-Mayer, 1953.
Cobs and Robbers, Metro-Goldwyn-Mayer, 1953.
Little Johnny Jet, Metro-Goldwyn-Mayer, 1953.
Heir Bear, Metro-Goldwyn-Mayer, 1953.
T.V. of Tomorrow, Metro-Goldwyn-Mayer, 1953.
Wee Willie Wildcat, Metro-Goldwyn-Mayer, 1953.
Half-Pint Palomino, Metro-Goldwyn-Mayer, 1953.
The Three Little Pups, Metro-Goldwyn-Mayer, 1953.
Drag-A-Long Droopy, Metro-Goldwyn-Mayer, 1954.
Impossible Possum, Metro-Goldwyn-Mayer, 1954.
Billy Boy, Metro-Goldwyn-Mayer, 1954.
Sleepy-Time Squirrel, Metro-Goldwyn-Mayer, 1954.
Homesteader Droopy, Metro-Goldwyn-Mayer, 1954.
Bird-Brain Bird Dog, Metro-Goldwyn-Mayer, 1954.
Farm of Tomorrow, Metro-Goldwyn-Mayer, 1954.
The Flea Circus, Metro-Goldwyn-Mayer, 1954.
Dixieland Droopy, Metro-Goldwyn-Mayer, 1954.
Field and Scream, Metro-Goldwyn-Mayer, 1955.
The First Bad Man, Metro-Goldwyn-Mayer, 1955.
Deputy Droopy, Metro-Goldwyn-Mayer, 1955.
Cellbound, Metro-Goldwyn-Mayer, 1955.
Good Will to Men, Metro-Goldwyn-Mayer, 1955.

Short Film Work; All *Tom and Jerry;* Producer:
The Midnight Snack, Metro-Goldwyn-Mayer, 1941.
The Night Before Christmas, Metro-Goldwyn-Mayer, 1941.
Fraidy Cat, Metro-Goldwyn-Mayer, 1942.
Dog Trouble, Metro-Goldwyn-Mayer, 1942.
Puss n' Toots, Metro-Goldwyn-Mayer, 1942.
The Bowling Alley Cat, Metro-Goldwyn-Mayer, 1942.
Fine Feathered Friend, Metro-Goldwyn-Mayer, 1942.
Surferin' Cats, Metro-Goldwyn-Mayer, 1943.
The Lonesome Mouse, Metro-Goldwyn-Mayer, 1943.
The Yankee Doodle Mouse, Metro-Goldwyn-Mayer, 1943.
Baby Puss, Metro-Goldwyn-Mayer, 1943.
The Zoot Cat, Metro-Goldwyn-Mayer, 1944.
The Million Dollar Cat, Metro-Goldwyn-Mayer, 1944.
The Bodyguard, Metro-Goldwyn-Mayer, 1944.
Puttin' on the Dog, Metro-Goldwyn-Mayer, 1944.
Mouse Troubles (also known as *Cat Nipped* and *Kitty Foiled*), Metro-Goldwyn-Mayer, 1944.
The Mouse Comes to Dinner, Metro-Goldwyn-Mayer, 1944.
Mouse in Manhattan, Metro-Goldwyn-Mayer, 1944.
Tee for Two, Metro-Goldwyn-Mayer, 1945.
Flirty Birdy (also known as *Love Boids*), Metro-Goldwyn-Mayer, 1945.
Quiet Please, Metro-Goldwyn-Mayer, 1945.
Springtime for Thomas, Metro-Goldwyn-Mayer, 1946.
The Milky Waif, Metro-Goldwyn-Mayer, 1946.
The Hick Chick, Metro-Goldwyn-Mayer, 1946.
Trap Happy, Metro-Goldwyn-Mayer, 1946.
Solid Serenade, Metro-Goldwyn-Mayer, 1946.
Cat Fishin', Metro-Goldwyn-Mayer, 1947.
Part Time Pal (also known as *Fair Weathered Friend*), Metro-Goldwyn-Mayer, 1947.
The Cat Concerto, Metro-Goldwyn-Mayer, 1947.
Dr. Jekyll and Mr. Mouse, Metro-Goldwyn-Mayer. 1947.
Salt Water Tabby, Metro-Goldwyn-Mayer, 1947.
A Mouse in the House, Metro-Goldwyn-Mayer, 1947.
The Invisible Mouse, Metro-Goldwyn-Mayer, 1947.
Kitty Foiled, Metro-Goldwyn-Mayer, 1948.
The Truce Hurts, Metro-Goldwyn-Mayer, 1948.
Old Rockin' Chair Tom, Metro-Goldwyn-Mayer, 1948.
Professor Tom, Metro-Goldwyn-Mayer, 1948.
Mouse Cleaning, Metro-Goldwyn-Mayer, 1948.
Polka Dot Puss, Metro-Goldwyn-Mayer, 1948.
The Little Orphan, Metro-Goldwyn-Mayer, 1949.
Hatch Up Your Troubles, Metro-Goldwyn-Mayer, 1949.
Heavenly Puss, Metro-Goldwyn-Mayer, 1949.
The Cat and the Mermouse, Metro-Goldwyn-Mayer, 1949.
Love That Pup, Metro-Goldwyn-Mayer, 1949.
Jerry's Diary, Metro-Goldwyn-Mayer, 1949.
Tennis Chumps, Metro-Goldwyn-Mayer, 1949.
Little Quacker, Metro-Goldwyn-Mayer, 1950.
Saturday Evening Puss (also known as *Party Cat*), Metro-Goldwyn-Mayer, 1950.
Texas Tom, Metro-Goldwyn-Mayer, 1950.
Jerry and the Lion (also known as *Hold That Lion*), Metro-Goldwyn-Mayer, 1950.
Safety Second (also known as *F'r Safety Sake*), Metro-Goldwyn-Mayer, 1950.
The Hollywood Bowl (also known as *Tom and Jerry in the Hollywood Bowl*), Metro-Goldwyn-Mayer, 1950.
The Framed Cat, Metro-Goldwyn-Mayer, 1950.
Cue Ball Cat, Metro-Goldwyn-Mayer, 1950.
Casanova Cat, Metro-Goldwyn-Mayer, 1951.
Jerry and the Goldfish, Metro-Goldwyn-Mayer, 1951.
Jerry's Cousin (also known as *City Mouse* and *Muscles Mouse*), Metro-Goldwyn-Mayer, 1951.
Sleepy Time Tom, Metro-Goldwyn-Mayer, 1951.
His Mouse Friday, Metro-Goldwyn-Mayer, 1951.
Slicked-Up Pup, Metro-Goldwyn-Mayer, 1951.
Nit-Witty Kitty, Metro-Goldwyn-Mayer, 1951.
Cat Napping, Metro-Goldwyn-Mayer, 1951.
The Flying Cat, Metro-Goldwyn-Mayer, 1952.
Duck Doctor, Metro-Goldwyn-Mayer, 1952.

The Two Mouseketeers, Metro-Goldwyn-Mayer, 1952.
Smitten Kitten, Metro-Goldwyn-Mayer, 1952.
Triplet Trouble, Metro-Goldwyn-Mayer, 1952.
Little Runaway, Metro-Goldwyn-Mayer, 1952.
Fit to Be Tied, Metro-Goldwyn-Mayer, 1952.
Push-Button Kitty, Metro-Goldwyn-Mayer, 1952.
Cruise Cat, Metro-Goldwyn-Mayer, 1952.
The Dog House, Metro-Goldwyn-Mayer, 1952.
The Missing Mouse, Metro-Goldwyn-Mayer, 1953.
Jerry and Jumbo, Metro-Goldwyn-Mayer, 1953.
Johann Mouse, Metro-Goldwyn-Mayer, 1953.
That's My Pup, Metro-Goldwyn-Mayer, 1953.
Just Ducky, Metro-Goldwyn-Mayer, 1953.
Life With Tom, Metro-Goldwyn-Mayer, 1953.
Puppy Tale, Metro-Goldwyn-Mayer, 1954.
Posse Cat, Metro-Goldwyn-Mayer, 1954.
Hic-Up Pup (also known as *Tyke Takes a Nap*), Metro-Goldwyn-Mayer, 1954.
Little School Mouse, Metro-Goldwyn-Mayer, 1954.
Baby Butch, Metro-Goldwyn-Mayer, 1954.
Mice Follies, Metro-Goldwyn-Mayer, 1954.
Neopolitan Mouse, Metro-Goldwyn-Mayer, 1954.
Downhearted Duckling, Metro-Goldwyn-Mayer, 1954.
Pet Peeve, Metro-Goldwyn-Mayer, 1954.
Touche, Pussy Cat, Metro-Goldwyn-Mayer, 1954.
Southbound Duckling, Metro-Goldwyn-Mayer, 1955.
Pup on a Picnic, Metro-Goldwyn-Mayer, 1955.
Mouse for Sale, Metro-Goldwyn-Mayer, 1955.
Designs on Jerry, Metro-Goldwyn-Mayer, 1955.
Tom and Cherie, Metro-Goldwyn-Mayer, 1955.
Smarty Cat, Metro-Goldwyn-Mayer, 1955.
Pecos Pest, Metro-Goldwyn-Mayer, 1955.

Other Film Work:
Cartoon sequence director, *Dangerous When Wet,* Wet.*

QUINN, Declan 1957-

PERSONAL

Born in 1957; brother of Aidan (an actor) and Paul (an actor) Quinn.

Addresses: *Agent*—Dattner & Associates, 10635 Santa Monica Blvd., Suite 165, Los Angeles, CA 90025.

Career: Cinematographer and producer.

Awards, Honors: Independent Spirit Award, best cinematographer, 1996, for *Leaving Las Vegas;* Cinematography Award, Sundance Film Festival, dramatic, 1998, for *2 by 4;* Independent Spirit Award, best cinematographer, 1998, for *Kama Sutra: A Tale of Love.*

CREDITS

Film Work; Director of Photography:
Clash of the Ash, 1987.
The Kill Off, Cabriolet, 1989.
Blood and Concrete—A Love Story, IRS Releasing, 1991.
Freddy's Dead: The Final Nightmare (also known as *A Nightmare on Elm Street 6*), New Line Cinema, 1991.
Cinematographer, *Cousin Bobby,* Cinevista, 1992.
The Ballad of Little Joe, Fine Line, 1993.
All Things Bright and Beautiful, 1994.
Vanya on 42nd Street, Sony Pictures Classics, 1994.
Leaving Las Vegas, Metro-Goldwyn-Mayer, 1995.
Carried Away, Fine Line, 1996.
Kama Sutra: A Tale of Love, Trimark Pictures, 1997.
2 by 4, 1997.
One Night Stand, New Line Cinema, 1997.
One True Thing, Universal, 1998.
(And co-executive producer) *This Is My Father,* Sony Pictures Classic, 1998.

Television Work; Episodic; Director of Photography:
"Dead-End for Delia" and "The Quiet Room," *Fallen Angels,* Showtime, 1993.

Television Work; Movies: Director of Photography:
Lies of the Twins, USA Network, 1991.
The Heart of Justice, TNT, 1993.

Television Work; Specials; Director of Photography:
Over the Limit, ABC, 1990.
The Hollow Boy, PBS, 1991.
Lighting cameraman, *Clash of the Ash,* PBS, 1992.
Out of Order: Rock the Vote Targets Health Care, MTV, 1995.*

QUINN, Elizabeth

Career: Actress.

Awards, Honors: Olivier Award, Society of London Theatre, best actress in a new play, 1982, for *Children of a Lesser God.*

CREDITS

Stage Appearances:

The Trojan Women, Los Angeles Actors Theatre, Los Angeles, CA, 1980.

Sarah, *Children of a Lesser God,* 1981.

Kathy, *Fighting Chance,* Long Wharf Theatre, New Haven, CT, 1988.

Film Appearances:

The Gifted, 1989.

Lilac, *Killer Nerd,* Hollywood Home Video, 1991.

Mrs. Reed, *Love and Death on Long Island,* Cinepix Film Properties, 1997.

Television Appearances:

Mabel Hubbard—as an adult, *The Sound and the Silence* (miniseries; also known as *Alexander Bell: The Sound and the Silence* and *The Sound and the Silence: The Alexander Graham Bell Story*), TNT, 1993.

Property master, *The Redemption* (movie), HBO, 1995.*

R

RAPP, Anthony 1971-

PERSONAL

Born October 26, 1971, in Jolliet, IL.

Addresses: *Agent*—Paradigm, 299 West 57th St., Suite 900, New York, NY 10019.

Career: Actor.

CREDITS

Stage Appearances:

(Broadway debut) *The Little Prince and the Avaitor,* Alvin Theatre, New York City, 1981-82.

Louis Leonowens, *The King and I,* Warner Theatre, Washington, D.C., 1981, then Fox Theatre, San Diego, CA, 1983.

Ben, *Six Degrees of Separation,* Lincoln Center, New York City, 1990.

Alexander Weeks, *The Destiny of Me,* Circle Repertory Theatre, then Lucille Lortel Theatre, both New York City, 1992-93.

Jack Kahn, *Sophistry,* Playwrights Horizon Theatre, New York City, 1993.

Edward III, *The Making of Edward III,* Madison Avenue Theatre, New York City, 1993.

J.K. Abbot, *The Family Animal,* Circle Repertory Lab Theatre, New York City, 1994.

Andy/Man two, *Reproducing Georgia,* American Place Theatre, New York City, 1994.

Mark Cohen, *Rent,* New York Theatre Workshop, New York City, 1994.

Prosthetics and the Twenty-five Thousand Dollar, Pyramid, Workhouse Theatre, 1995.

Bobby, *Trafficking in Broken Hearts,* Atlantic Theatre Company, 1995.

Dylan Taylor Sinclair/Roger, *Raised in Captivity,* 1995.

Mark Cohen, *Rent,* Nederlander Theatre, New York City, 1996.

Charlie Brown, *You're a Good Man, Charlie Brown,* Ambassador Theatre, New York City, 1999.

Also appeared on Broadway in *Precious Sons;* appeared Off-Broadway in Scott Goodman's *Bright Lights, Big City;* and in Dan Rybicky's *Youth Is Wasted.*

Stage Work:

(With Adam Rapp) Director, *Ursula's Permanent,* Kraine Theatre, 1993.

Film Appearances:

Daryl, *Adventures in Babysitting,* Buena Vista, 1987.

Pinky Sears, *Far From Home,* Vestron, 1989.

Richard "McGoo" Collins, *School Ties,* Paramount, 1992.

Tony, *Dazed and Confused,* Gramercy Pictures, 1993.

Ben, *Six Degrees of Separation,* Metro-Goldwyn-Mayer, 1993.

David, *David Searching,* 1996.

Tony, *Twister,* United International Pictures, 1996.

Man of the Century, 1998.

Television Appearances; Episodic:

Jeff Glaser, "Detour," *The X-Files,* Fox, 1997.

Himself, "An Affair to Remember," *Spin City,* ABC, 1997.

Verity, "Panorama," *The Lazarus Man,* syndicated/TNT, 1997.

Television Appearances; Movies:

Wes, *Sky High,* NBC, 1990.

Cadet Frederick Hodgson, *Assault at West Point: The Court-Martial of Johnson Whittaker* (also known as *Assault at West Point*), Showtime, 1994.

When Trumpets Fade, HBO, 1998.

RECORDINGS

Taped Readings:
The Ultimate Rush, Reed Publishing, 1998.

WRITINGS

Plays:
(With Adam Rapp) *Ursula's Permenant,* Kraine Theatre, 1993.

OTHER SOURCES

Periodicals:
Interview, June, 1996, pp. 105-106.*

REESE, Della 1931-

PERSONAL

Full name, Delloreese Patricia Early; born July 6, 1931, in Detroit, MI; daughter of Richard (a steelworker) and Nellie (a cook); married Leroy Gray (divorced); married Vermont Taliaferro (divorced); married Franklin Lett, Jr., 1982; children: Deloreese Daniels, James Barger (adopted; a psychiatrist), Franklin, Dominique. *Education:* Attended Wayne State University, 1949; Johnnie Colemon Institute.

Addresses: *Agent*—Lett Entertainment, 1910 Bel Air Rd., Los Angeles, CA 90077.

Career: Singer, actress, and ordained minister (Universal Foundation for Better Living). Toured with the Mahalia Jackson Troupe, summers, 1945-49; formed the Meditation Singers, a gospel group, 1949; worked as a receptionist, a taxi driver, and a barber; sang with the Clara Ward Singers, the Roberta Martin Singers, Beatrice Brown's Inspirational Singers, and the Erskine Hawkins Orchestra; signed with Jubilee records, 1954; signed with RCA, 1959; performed in nightclubs across the U.S.; and has made over 300 television guest appearances on popular talk and entertainment shows.

Awards, Honors: Named most promising female singer, 1957; Grammy Award nomination, vocal—female album, 1960, for *Della;* Emmy Award nomination, best supporting actress, 1977; Grammy Award nomination, best female soloist—gospel, 1987, for "You Gave Me Love"; Hollywood Walk of Fame Star, 1993; Image Awards, NAACP, outstanding lead actress—drama series, 1996, 1998, 1999, Image Award nomination, NAACP, outstanding lead actress—drama series, 1997, Emmy Award nominations, outstanding supporting actress—drama series, 1997 and 1998, Screen Actors Guild Award nominations, outstanding performance by a female actor—drama series, 1997 and 1998, Golden Globe Award nomination, best supporting actress—series, miniseries, or motion picture, 1998, all for *Touched by an Angel.*

CREDITS

Stage Appearances:
Black Sally, *The Last Minstrel Show,* Wilbur Theatre, Boston, MA, then New Locust Theatre, Philadelphia, PA, 1978.

Film Appearances:
Mrs. Gibson, *Psychic Killer,* Avco Embassy, 1975.
Vera, *Harlem Nights,* Paramount, 1989.
Song performer, "Don't You Know," *A Bronx Tale,* Savoy Pictures, 1993.
Ma Wright, *A Thin Line Between Love & Hate,* New Line Cinema, 1996.

Television Appearances; Episodic:
Jean Tremaine, "The Gang Show," *Welcome Back, Kotter,* ABC, 1975.
Mrs. Baracus, "A Lease With an Option to Die," *The A-Team,* NBC, 1985.
Auntie Maim, *Night Court,* NBC, 1990.
Ma Colton, "Squeeze Play," *MacGyver,* ABC, 1990.
Ma Colton, "The Coltons," *MacGyver,* ABC, 1991.
Nurse, "No Deposit, No Return," *Dream On,* HBO, 1992.
Mrs. Toussant, "Wedding Redux," *Designing Women,* CBS, 1992.
Lake, "Vindaloo in the Villows," *L.A. Law,* NBC, 1992.
Naomi Grand, "The Lullaby League," *Picket Fences,* CBS, 1992.
Voice of The Blues Fairy, "Pinocchio," *Happily Ever After: Fairy Tales For Every Child* (animated), HBO, 1995.
Tess, "Homecoming," *Promise Land,* CBS, 1996.
Herself, *Entertainment Tonight,* syndicated, 1998.

Television Appearances; Series:
Della Rogers; *Chico and the Man,* NBC, 1973-78.
Judge Caroline Phillips, *It Takes Two,* NBC, 1982-83.
Victoria Royal, *The Royal Family,* CBS, 1991-92.
Tess, *Touched by and Angel,* CBS, 1994—.
Tess (recurring), *The Promise Land,* CBS, 1996—.

Television Appearances; Miniseries:

Mrs. Lydia Branch, *Roots: The Next Generation,* ABC, 1979.

Nana Fleming, *Mama Flora's Family,* CBS, 1998.

Television Appearances; Movies:

Opal Parker, *The Voyage of the Yes,* CBS, 1973.

Flo, *Twice in a Lifetime,* NBC, 1974.

Claudine, *The Return of Joe Forrester,* NBC, 1975.

Sarah, *Nightmare in Badham County,* ABC, 1976.

Voice of Ella DuChammps, *You Must Remember This,* PBS, 1992.

Katie, *A Match Made in Heaven,* CBS, 1997.

Ms. Cooper, *Miracle in the Woods,* CBS, 1997.

Martha Logan, *Having Our Say: The Delany Sisters' First 100 Years,* CBS, 1999.

Honey, *The Secret Path,* CBS, 1999.

Television Appearances; Specials:

Burt and the Girls, NBC, 1973.

Diane, *Daddy's Girl,* CBS, 1973.

Flo, *Flo's Place,* NBC, 1976.

Aunt Faith, *The Gift of Amazing Grace,* ABC, 1986.

Tennessee Ernie Ford: 50 Golden Years, TNN, 1990.

Celebrate the Soul of American Music, syndicated, 1991.

Song performer, "Come Rain or Come Shine," *Holiday Greetings From the EdSullivan Show,* CBS, 1992.

The 61st Annual Hollywood Christmas Parade, syndicated, 1992.

Mo's Funny: Black Comedy in America, HBO, 1993.

Addicted to Fame, NBC, 1993.

An All-American Thanksgiving Day Parade, 1996.

Interviewee, *The Life and Times of Tennessee Ernie Ford,* TNN, 1996.

Guest host, *CBS: The First 50 Years,* CBS, 1998.

Host, *True Stories From Touched by an Angel,* CBS, 1998.

Intimate Portrait: Della Reese, Lifetime, 1999.

Interviewee, *Intimate Portrait: Olympia Dukakis,* Lifetime, 1999.

Host, *More True Stories From Touched by an Angel,* CBS, 1999.

Interviewee, *Redd Foxx: The E! True Hollywood Story,* E! Entertainment Channel, 1999.

Television Appearances; Awards Presentations:

The 27th Annual NAACP Image Awards, 1996.

The 28th Annual NAACP Image Awards, 1997.

Presenter, *The 49th Annual Primetime Emmy Awards,* 1997.

Presenter, *The 29th Annual NAACP Image Awards,* 1998.

RECORDINGS

Albums:

Melancholy Baby, Jubilee, 1957.

Date with Della Reese, Jubilee, 1958.

Amen, Jubilee, 1958.

The Story of the Blues, Jubilee, 1958.

What Do You Know About Love?, Jubilee, 1959.

And That Reminds Me, Jubilee, 1959.

Della, RCA, 1959.

Della by Starlight, RCA Victor, 1960.

Della Della Cha-Cha-Cha, RCA Victor, 1961.

Special Delivery, RCA, 1961.

Classic Della, RCA Victor, 1961.

Della Reese on Stage, RCA Victor, 1962.

1962 Live Guard Session & At Basin St. East, Jazz Band, 1962.

Waltz with Me, RCA Victor, 1963.

Della Reese at Basin Street East, RCA Victor, 1964.

C'Mon and Hear, Paramount, 1964.

I Like It Like Dat!, Paramount, 1965.

Della Reese Live, Paramount, 1966.

One More Time, Paramount, 1967.

And Brilliance, Atlanta Intern, 1990.

Della [Import], RCA Camden, 1996.

And That Reminds Me: The Jubilee Years, Rhino/Collecto, 1996.

Best Thing for You, Jasmine, 1997.

Angel Singers, Amherst, 1997.

The Collection, Varese, 1998.

My Soul Feels Better Right Now, Homeland, 1998.

Something Cool/Bad Bobby, Allegiance, 1998.

The Jubilee Years: The Singles 1954-59, West Side, 1998.

Story of the Blues/Delta at Mr. Kelly's, West Side, 1998.

WRITINGS

Nonfiction:

Along The Way: My Life with Help from Above (autobiography), Putnam, 1997.

OTHER SOURCES

Books:

Contemporary Black Biography, Volume 20, Gale (Detroit, MI), 1999.

Periodicals:

Ebony, May, 1989, p. 96.

Jet, November 24, 1997, p. 38.

People Weekly, February 24, 1997, p. 113.

Saturday Evening Post, May-June, 1997, p. 36-40.*

REEVES, Matt 1966-

PERSONAL

Born April 27, 1966, in Rockville Center, NY; raised in Los Angeles, CA. *Education:* Graduated from the film school of the University of Southern California.

Addresses: *Agent*—c/o Endeavor Agency, 9701 Wilshire Blvd., 10th floor, Beverly Hills, CA 90212.

Career: Director, producer, and writer.

CREDITS

Film Work; Director:
"Mr. Petrified Forest," *Future Shock,* Hemdale Home Video, 1994.
The Pallbearer, Miramax, 1996.

Television Work; Series:
Director, *Relativity,* ABC, 1996.
Creator, director, and executive producer, *Felicity,* The WB, 1998—.

Television Work; Producer; Series:
Felicity, The WB, 1998.

Television Work; Director; Episodic:
"All is Bright", *Homicide: Life on the Street* (also known as *H:LOTS*), NBC, 1997.

WRITINGS

Screenplays:
Under Siege 2: Dark Territory (also known as *Under Siege 2*), Warner Bros., 1995.
The Pallbearer, Miramax, 1996.
The Yards, Miramax, 1999.*

REID, Tara 1975-

PERSONAL

Born 1975, in Wyckoff, New Jersey; daughter of Tom and Donna Reid.

Addresses: *Agent*—Endeavor, 9701 Wilshire Blvd., 10th Floor, BeverlyHills, CA 90212.

Career: Actress.

CREDITS

Film Appearances:
Amanda, *A Return to Salem's Lot,* Warner Bros., 1987.
Bunny Lebowski, *The Big Lebowski,* Gramercy, 1998.
Sasha, *Urban Legend,* TriStar/Sony Pictures, 1998.
Jennifer, *Around the Fire,* 1998.
Marci Greenbaum, *Cruel Intentions,* Columbia, 1999.
Vicky, *American Pie,* Universal, 1999.
Body Shots, New Line Cinema, 1999.
Cybil, *Girl,* Kushner-Locke, 1999.
The Visitors, forthcoming.

Television Appearances; Series:
Ashley, *Days of Our Lives,* NBC, 1995.

Television Appearances; Movies:
The girl, *What We Did That Night,* ABC, 1999.*

REMINI, Leah 1970-

PERSONAL

Born June 15, 1970, in Brooklyn, NY; daughter of George Remini (owner of an asbestos removal company) and Vicki Marshall (a Hollywood private school teacher).

Addresses: *Agent*—Gold Marchak & Liedtke, 3500 West Olive St., Suite 1400, Burbank, CA 91505.

Career: Actress.

CREDITS

Film Appearances:
Theresa, *Glory Daze,* Seventh Art Releasing, 1995.
Follow Your Heart, DMG Entertainment, 1997.

Television Appearances; Episodic:
Charlie Brisco, "Life's a Ditch," *Who's the Boss?,* ABC, 1989.
Charle Brisco "Living Dolls," *Who's the Boss?,* ABC, 1989.
Serafina Tortelli, "Unplanned Parenthood," *Cheers,* NBC, 1991.
Ellen "ET" Travis, "You Must Remember This," *Blossom,* NBC, 1991.
Serafina Tortelli, "Loathe and Marriage," *Cheers,* NBC, 1992.
Daisy, *Evening Shade,* CBS, 1992.
Gail Ross, *The Commish,* ABC, 1993.

Agnes Benedetto, "How to Murder Your Lawyer," *Diagnosis Murder,* CBS, 1995.
Lydia, "The One with the Birth," *Friends,* NBC, 1995.
Angela Bohi, "Closing Time," *NYPD Blue,* ABC, 1996.

Television Appearances; Series:
Charlie Brisco, *Living Dolls,* ABC, 1989-90.
Tina Bavasso, *The Man in the Family,* ABC, 1991.
Voice of Carbine, *Biker Mice From Mars* (animated), syndicated, 1993.
Voice of Sagan Cruz, *Phantom 2040* (animated), syndicated, 1994.
Dominique, *First Time Out,* The WB, 1995-96.
Terry, *Fired Up,* NBC, 1996-98.
Carrie Heffernan, *The King of Queens,* CBS, 1998—.

Television Appearances; Movies:
Stephanie O'Neil, *Getting Up and Going Home,* Lifetime, 1992.

Television Appearances; Specials:
ABC's Comdey Sneak Peek, ABC, 1989.
Frankie, *Harlan & Merleen,* CBS, 1993.
Woman-on-the-Street (New York), *The All-American Thanksgiving Parade,* 1998.
Funny Flubs & Screw-Ups III, CBS, 1999.

OTHER SOURCES

Periodicals:
People, March 29, 1999, p. 133.*

RENNAHAN, Ray 1896-1980

PERSONAL

Born May 1, 1896, in Las Vegas, NV; died May 19, 1980, in Tarzana, CA; son of John and Mary (McPhee); married Lilian Hunt, May 11, 1916; children: Rae (Mrs. Robert Forrest Moore). *Education:* Attended San Bernardino schools.

Career: Cinematographer. Worked as director of photography at Technicolor, Hollywood, CA; photographer of motion pictures for television, Universal Studios.

Member: American Society of Cinematographers (president 1950-51, 1965-66).

Awards, Honors: Academy Award nomination (shared with Bert Glennon), best cinematography, color, 1940, for *Drums Along the Mohawk;* Academy Award (shared with Ernest Haller), best cinematography, color, 1940, for *Gone with the Wind;* Academy Award nomination (shared with Leon Shamroy), best cinematography, color, 1941, for *Down Argentine Way;* Academy Award nomination (shared with Arthur C. Miller), best cinematography, color, 1941, for *The Blue Bird;* Academy Award nomination (shared with Harry Hallenberger), best cinematography, color, 1942, for *Louisiana Purchase;* Academy Award (shared with Ernest Palmer), best cinematography, color, 1942, for *Blood and Sand;* Academy Award nomination, best cinematography, color, 1944, for *For Whom the Bell Tolls;* Academy Award nomination, best cinematography, color, 1945, for *Lady in the Dark.*

CREDITS

Film Work; Cinematographer, Except Where Indicated:
And color photographer, *The Ten Commandments,* 1923.
Blood Test, Adventure Productions, 1923.
And technicolor photography, *The Merry Widow,* Metro-Goldwyn-Mayer, 1925.
Redskin, Paramount, 1929.
Gold Diggers of Broadway, Warner Bros., 1929.
The Vagabond King, Paramount, 1930.
The King of Jazz, Universal, 1930.
Whoopee!, United Artists, 1930.
Doctor X, Warner Bros., 1932.
Mystery of the Wax Museum (also known as *Wax Museum*), Warner Bros., 1933.
And technicolor photography, *My Grandfather's Clock,* 1934.
La Cucaracha, RKO Radio Pictures, 1934.
Kid Millions, 1934.
And technicolor photography, *The Cat and the Fiddle,* Metro-Goldwyn-Mayer, 1934.
Pirate Party on Catalina Isle, Metro-Goldwyn-Mayer, 1935.
Memories and Melodies, Metro-Goldwyn-Mayer, 1935.
Gypsy Night, Metro-Goldwyn-Mayer, 1935.
Becky Sharp (also known as *Lady of Fortune,* 1943), RKO Radio Pictures, 1935.
La Fiesta de Santa Barbara, Metro-Goldwyn-Mayer, 1935.
Wings of the Morning, Twentieth Century-Fox, 1937.
Vogues (also known as *All This and Glamour Too, Vogues of 1938,* and *Walter Wanger's Vogues of 1938*), United Artists, 1937.
Ebb Tide, Paramount, 1937.

Kentucky, Twentieth Century-Fox, 1938.
Her Jungle Love, Paramount, 1938.
And associate photographer, *Dodge City,* 1939.
Sons of Liberty, Warner Bros., 1939.
Drums Along the Mohawk, Metro-Goldwyn-Mayer, 1939.
Gone With the Wind, Metro-Goldwyn-Mayer, 1939.
Teddy the Rough Rider, Warner Bros., 1940.
The Blue Bird, Twentieth Century-Fox, 1940.
Down Argentine Way, Twentieth Century-Fox, 1940.
Chad Hanna, Twentieth Century-Fox, 1940.
Blood and Sand, Twentieth Century-Fox, 1941.
Belle Starr, Twentieth Century-Fox, 1941.
That Night in Rio, Twentieth Century-Fox, 1941.
Louisiana Purchase, Paramount, 1941.
For Whom the Bell Tolls, Paramount, 1943.
Up in Arms, RKO Radio Pictures,1944.
Belle of the Yukon, RKO Radio Pictures, 1944.
Lady in the Dark, Paramount, 1944.
It's a Pleasure, RKO Radio Pictures, 1945.
Incendiary Blonde, Paramount, 1945.
A Thousand and One Nights (also known as *1001 Nights*), Columbia, 1945.
Duel in the Sun, Vanguard Film Production, 1946.
California, Paramount, 1946.
The Perils of Pauline, Paramount, 1947.
Unconquered, Paramount, 1947.
Whispering Smith, Paramount, 1948.
The Paleface, 1948.
Streets of Laredo, 1949.
A Connecticut Yankee in King Arthur's Court, (also known as *A Yankee in King Arthur's Court*), Paramount, 1949.
The White Tower, RKO Radio Pictures, 1950.
Warpath, Paramount, 1951.
Silver City (also known as *High Vermilion*), Paramount, 1951.
The Great Missouri Raid, Paramount, 1951.
Flaming Feather, Paramount, 1951.
The Denver and Rio Grande, Paramount, 1952.
At Sword's Point (also known as *Sons of the Musketeers*), RKO Radio Pictures, 1952.
Hurricane Smith, Paramount, 1952.
Pony Express, Paramount, 1953.
Flight to Tangier, Paramount, 1953.
Arrowhead, Paramount, 1953.
La Gazza Ladra Overture (also known as *The Thieving Magpie Overture*), Metro-Goldwyn-Mayer, 1954.
Texas Lady, RKO Radio Pictures, 1955.
A Lawless Street, Columbia, 1955.
Rage at Dawn (also known as *Seven Bad Men*), RKO Radio Pictures, 1955.
Stranger on Horseback, United Artists, 1955.
Seventh Cavalry, Columbia, 1956.
The Guns of Fort Petticoat, Columbia, 1957.
The Halliday Brand, United Artists, 1957.
Terror in a Texas Town, United Artists, 1958.

Television Work; Movies:
Cinematographer, *Columbo: Prescription Murder* (also known as *Prescription: Murder*), 1968.
Cinematographer, *I Love a Mystery,* NBC, 1973.*

RENNIE, Callum Keith 1960-

PERSONAL

Born September 14, 1960, in Sunderland, England; immigrated to Edmonton, Alberta, Canada, 1964. *Education:* Graduated from Strathcona High School; studied acting at the Bruhanski Theatre Studio, Vancouver.

Addresses: *Contact*—c/o *Due South,* Alliance Communication Corp., 14th Floor, 121 Bloor St. East, Toronto, Ontario, M4W WM5, Canada.

Career: Actor. Has also worked as a tree planter, paper baler, and bartender.

Awards, Honors: Genie Award, best supporting actor, 1994, for *Double Happiness;* Gemini Award nomination, best actor in a guest role—dramatic series, 1994, for "Snap, Crackle, Pop!," *Side Effects;* Gemini Award, best actor in a children's or youth program or series, 1997, for "The Puck Stops Here," *My Life as a Dog;* Gemini Award nomination, best actor in a lead role—dramatic program or miniseries, 1998, for *For Those Who Hunt the Wounded Down;* Genie Award, best supporting actor, 1999, for *Last Night.*

CREDITS

Stage Appearances:
Bobby, *American Buffalo,* Edmonton Fringe Festival, Edmonton Theatre, Edmonton, Alberta, Canada, 1985.
Turner and man three, *Lost Souls and Missing Persons,* Firehall Arts Centre, Vancouver, British Columbia, Canada, 1989.

Film Appearances:
Mark, *Double Happiness,* Fine Line Features, 1994.
Stranger, *Timecop,* Universal, 1994.

Jim, *Curtis's Charm,* 1995.
Billy Tallent, *Hard Core Logo,* Miramax, 1996.
Drug dealer, *Unforgettable,* Metro-Goldwyn-Mayer, 1996.
Motel manager, *Excess Baggage,* Columbia/Sony Pictures Entertainment, 1997.
Ollie, *Masterminds,* Sony Pictures Entertainment, 1997.
Mamet, *Men With Guns,* Norstar Entertainment, 1997.
Craig, *Last Night,* Lions Gate Films Inc., 1998.
Carlaw, *eXistenZ,* Miramax, 1999.
The Five Senses, Alliance Atlantis Communications, 1999.
The Last Stop, 1999.
The Highwayman, Lions Gate Entertainment, forthcoming.

Television Appearances; Episodic:
Harry Piper, "Long Shot," *Lonesome Dove: The Series,* 1992.
Neal, "An Eye for an Eye," *Highlander,* syndicated, 1993.
Tommy, "Lazarus," *The X-Files,* Fox, 1994.
Michael Konichek, "Security," *The Commish,* ABC, 1994.
Cal Quill, "Protection," *The Marshall,* ABC, 1995.
Bruce Spencer, "Outside the Lines," *Forever Knight,* syndicated, 1995.
The Groundskeeper, "Fresh Bones," *The X-Files,* Fox, 1995.
Carlito, "Corner of the Eye," *The Outer Limits,* Showtime, 1995.
William T. Lenox, "Wheelman," *Viper,* UPN, 1996.
Armando, "Snap, Crackle, Pop!," *Side Effects,* CBC, 1997.
Gray Wellman, "Gray," *La Femme Nikita,* USA Network, 1997.
Gray Wellman, "Choice," *La Femme Nikita,* USA Network, 1997.
Vince, "Lullaby," *Strange World,* ABC, 1999.
Himself, *Open Mike,* 1999.
Ross, "Breathless," *Foolish Heart,* CBC, 1999.

Television Appearances; Series:
Stanley Kowalski, *Due South,* CBS, 1997-99.
Uncle Johnny Johansson, *My Life as a Dog,* Showtime, 1997.
Newbie, *Twitch City,* CBC, 1998.

Television Appearances; Movies:
Falling From the Sky! Flight 174, ABC, 1995.
Bob Levesh, *When the Dark Man Calls,* USA Network, 1995.
Big Hat, *The Ranger, The Cook, and a Hole in the Sky* (also known as *Hole in the Sky*), ABC, 1995.
Jerry Bine, *For Those Who Hunt the Wounded Down,* CBC, 1996.
Adam, *Tricks,* Showtime, 1997.

OTHER SOURCES

Periodicals:
Maclean's, October 13, 1997, p. 62.
Saturday Night, March, 1998, pp. 67-71.

Electronic:
The Original Callum Keith Rennie Bio Page, http://home.hiwaay.net/~warydbom/duesouth/callum.htm.*

REYNOLDS, Ryan 1976-

PERSONAL

Born October 23, 1976, in Vancouver, British Columbia, Canada.

Addresses: *Agency*—c/o Scott Wilson, Paul Kohner Agency, 9300 Wilshire Blvd., Suite 555, Beverly Hills, CA 90212.

Career: Actor.

Awards, Honors: Youth in Film Awards nomination, best young actor, for *Fifteen.*

CREDITS

Film Appearances:
Ganesh/Jeffrey, *Ordinary Magic* (also known as *Ganesh*), Triboro Entertainment, 1993.
Howard Ancona, *Life During Wartime* (also known as *The Alarmist*), Columbia TriStar Home Video, 1997.
Karl, *Big Monster on Campus* (also known as *Teen Monster*), Regent Entertainment, 1998.
Chip, *Dick,* TriStar, 1999.
Coming Soon, Twentieth Century-Fox, 1999.

Television Appearances; Movies:
Kevin, *My Name Is Kate,* ABC, 1994.
Andy, *Serving in Silence: The Margarethe Cammermeyer Story,* ABC, 1995.
Ben Colson, *A Secret Between Friends: A Moment of Truth Movie,* NBC, 1996.

Seth, *Sabrina the Teenage Witch,* ABC, 1996.
Wade Early, *Tourist Trap,* ABC, 1998.

Television Appearances; Series:
Billy Simpson, *Fifteen,* Nickelodeon, 1991.
Michael Leslie "Berg" Bergen, *Two Guys, a Girl and a Pizza Place,* ABC, 1998—.

Television Appearances; Miniseries:
Bobby Rupp, *In Cold Blood,* CBS, 1996.

Television Appearances; Episodic:
Rick, *The Marshal,* ABC, 1995.
Derek Tillman, "If These Walls Could Talk," *The Outer Limits,* Showtime, 1995.
Jay "Boom" DeBoom, "Syzygy," *The X-Files,* Fox, 1996.
Macro, "Welcome to the Tower," *The Odyssey,* Sci-Fi Channel, 1996.
Macro, "The One Called Brad," *The Odyssey,* Sci-Fi Channel, 1996.
Paul Nodel, "Double Helix," *The Outer Limits,* Showtime, 1997.

Also appeared on *The John Larroquette Show.**

RHAMES, Ving 1961-

PERSONAL

Real name, Irving Rhames; born, May 12, 1961, in New York City, NY; son of Ernest (a retired auto mechanic) and Reather (a homemaker) Rhames; married Valerie Scott, 1994. *Education:* Attended High School of Performing Arts, New York, NY; Juilliard, B.F.A., 1983.

Addresses: *Agent*—William Morris Agency, 151 El Camino Dr., Beverly Hills, CA 90212-2775.

Career: Actor.

Awards, Honors: Emmy Award nomination, outstanding lead actor—miniseries or movie, Golden Globe Award, best actor—miniseries or television movie, Image Award nomination, NAACP, outstanding lead actor—television movie, miniseries or drama special, Screen Actors Guild Award nomination, outstanding male actor—television movie or miniseries, all 1998, for *Don King: Only in America;* Image Award nomination, NAACP, outstanding lead actor—motion picture, 1998, for *Rosewood.*

CREDITS

Stage Appearances:
Hastings/Herbert, *Richard III,* New York Shakespeare Festival, Delacorte Theatre, New York City, 1983.
Wait Until Dark, Studio Arena Theatre, Buffalo, NY, 1984.
The Road, Goodman Theatre, Chicago, IL, 1984.
Omar, *Short Eyes,* The Second Stage Theatre, New York City, 1984.
M'Bengue, *A Map of the World,* New York Shakespeare Festival, Public Theatre, New York City, 1985.
Doc, *The Boys of Winter,* Biltmore Theatre, New York City, 1985.
Carlyle, *Streamers,* Kennedy Center for the Performing Arts, Washington, DC, 1986.
Hark/Executioner, *Ascension Day,* Huson Guild Theatre, New York City, 1992.

Film Appearances:
Young Gabriel, *Go Tell It on the Mountain,* 1984.
Cinque, *Patty Hurst,* Atlantic, 1988.
Lieutenant Reilly, *Casualties of War,* Columbia, 1989.
George, *Jacob's Ladder,* TriStar, 1990.
Herbert Cotter, *The Long Walk Home,* Miramax, 1990.
Chief Petty Officer Frank McRae, *Flight of the Intruder,* Paramount, 1991.
Randolph, *Homicide,* Triumph Releasing, 1991.
LeRoy, *The People Under the Stairs,* Universal, 1991.
Mr. Stereo, *Stop! or My Mom Will Shoot,* Universal, 1992.
Ivan, *Bound By Honor,* Buena Vista, 1993.
Duane Stevenson, *Dave,* Warner Bros., 1993.
Little Leroy, *The Saint of Fort Washington,* Warner Bros., 1993.
Garvey, *DROP Squad,* Gramercy, 1994.
Marsellus Wallace, *Pulp Fiction,* Miramax, 1994.
Omar, *Kiss of Death,* Twentieth Century-Fox, 1995.
Luther Stickell, *Mission: Impossible,* Paramount, 1996.
Shad, *Striptease,* Columbia, 1996.
Nathan "Diamond Dog" Jones, *Con Air,* Buena Vista, 1997.
Muki, *Dangerous Ground,* New Line Cinema, 1997.
Mann, *Rosewood,* Warner Bros., 1997.
Buddy Bragg, *Out of Sight,* Universal, 1998.
Thibadeaux, *Entrapment,* Twentieth Century-Fox, 1999.
Marcus, *Bringing Out the Dead,* Paramount, 1999.
Sony Liston, *Night Train* (also known as *Sony Liston*), Paramount, forthcoming.
Luther Stickell, *Mission Impossible 2,* Paramount, forthcoming.

Television Appearances; Episodic:

Georges, "The Maze," *Miami Vice,* NBC, 1985.

Hector Lincoln, "Abrams For the Defense," *Crime Story,* NBC, 1986.

Private Tucker, "Burn Baby, Burn," *Tour of Duty,* CBS, 1987.

Henry Brown, "McAllister," *Spencer: For Hire,* ABC, 1988.

Millionaire, "Suicide Squad," *The Equalizer,* CBS, 1988.

Max Villareal, "Old Thyme Religion," *New York Undercover,* Fox, 1995.

Television Appearances; Series:

Czaja Carnek, *Another World,* NBC, 1986.

Charlie Hazard, *Men,* ABC, 1988-89.

Walter (recurring), *ER,* NBC, 1994-97.

Television Appearances; Miniseries:

Charles Jones, *Iran: Days of Crisis,* TNT, 1991.

Television Appearances; Movies:

Ed, *Rising Son,* TNT, 1990.

Leon, *When You Remember Me,* ABC, 1990.

Jellyroll, *Terror on Track 9,* CBS, 1992.

Detective Jackson, *Deadly Whispers,* CBS, 1995.

Detective Artie Brown, *Ed McBains's 87th Precinct: Lightening* (also known as *87th Precinct: Lightening*), NBC, 1995.

Title role, *Don King: Only in America,* HBO, 1997.

Pike, *Body Count,* The Movie Channel, 1998.

Television Appearances; Specials:

DeWitt Wardlaw, *Philly Heat,* ABC, 1995.

Voiceover, *The Way West,* PBS, 1995.

Narrator (episode 3), *Robert F. Kennedy: A Memoir,* Discovery Channel, 1998.

OTHER SOURCES

Books:

Contemporary Black Biography, Volume 14, Gale (Detroit, MI), 1997.

Periodicals:

Entertainment Weekly, December 10, 1993, p. 52; June 14, 1996, pp. 32-25.

Esquire, August, 1998, pp. 119-24.

Jet, February 9, 1998, p. 36.

Parade Magizine, April 4, 1999, pp. 4-6.

People Weekly, June 24, 1996, pp. 77-78.*

RIFKIN, Ron 1939-

PERSONAL

Born October 31, 1939, in New York, NY; wife's name, Iva. *Education:* Graduated from New York University.

Addresses: *Agent*—William Morris Agency, 151 El Camino Drive, Beverly Hills, CA 90212.

Career: Actor.

Member: Actors Studio, Naked Angels.

Awards, Honors: Drama Desk Award, best actor in a play, Obie Award, Lucille Lortel Award, and L.A. Drama-Logue Award, all 1991, for *The Substance of Fire;* Drama Desk Award nomination, Helen Hayes Award nomination, and Lucille Lortel Award, all 1993, for *Three Hotels;* CableACE Award nomination, 1995, for work in episodes of *Outer Limits;* Antoinette Perry Award, best featured actor in a musical, 1998, for *Cabaret.*

CREDITS

Film Appearances:

Martin, *The Devil's 8,* American International Pictures, 1969.

Sailor, *Flareup,* Metro-Goldwyn-Mayer, 1969.

Barker, *Silent Running,* Universal, 1971.

Television floor manager, *The Sunshine Boys,* United Artists, 1975.

Randy, *The Big Fix,* Universal, 1978.

Baseball coach, *The Chosen,* Contemporary, 1981.

Eddie, *The Sting II,* Universal, 1983.

Mr. Goldberg, *JFK* (director's cut), Warner Bros., 1991.

Rain's analyst, *Husband's and Wives,* TriStar, 1992.

Sy, *Manhattan Murder Mystery,* TriStar, 1993.

Doctor, *Wolf,* Columbia, 1994.

Eli, *Last Summer in the Hamptons,* Rainbow Releasing, 1995.

Feigenbaum, *I'm Not Rappaport,* Gramercy Pictures, 1996.

Isaac Geldhart, *The Substance of Fire,* Miramax, 1996.

D.A. Ellis Loew, *L.A. Confidential,* Warner Bros., 1997.

Commander Grant Frost, *The Negotiator,* Warner Bros., 1998.

Marty, *The Boiler Room,* New Line Cinema, 1999.

Television Appearances; Movies:

Normand, *Get Christie Love!,* ABC, 1974.

Herb, *The Dream Makers,* NBC, 1975.

First radio actor, *The Night Than Panicked America,* ABC, 1975.

Roger, *In the Glitter Palace,* NBC, 1977.

Assistant District Attorney Verrel, *A Question of Guilt,* CBS, 1978.

Deputy District Attorney Joseph Baron, *Mrs. R's Daughter,* NBC, 1979.

The Day the Bubble Burst, NBC, 1982.

Barry Stein, *Another Woman's Child,* 1983.

Television director, *The Ratings Game,* The Movie Channel, 1984.

Gerry Kaplan, *Do You Remember Love?,* CBS, 1985.

Eppy Lucido, *Courage,* CBS, 1986.

Allen Ginsberg, *Conspiracy: The Trial of the Chicago 8,* HBO, 1987.

Johnny Hyde, *Norma Jean & Marilyn,* HBO, 1996.

Television Appearances; Series:

Roy Mendelsohn, *Adam's Rib,* ABC, 1973.

Prince John, *When Things Were Rotten,* ABC, 1975.

Nick Handris, *One Day at a Time,* CBS, 1980-81.

Dr. Lantry, *Falcon Crest,* CBS, 1983-84.

Ben Meyer, *The Trials of Rosie O'Neill,* CBS, 1990-92.

Dr. Vucelich, *ER,* NBC, 1994.

Dr. Neil Bernstein, *Leaving L.A.,* ABC, 1997.

Television Appearances; Miniseries:

Mark Hartly, *The Winds of War,* ABC, 1983.

Solly, *Evergreen,* NBC, 1985.

Major Consor, *Dress Gray,* NBC, 1986.

Television Appearances; Specials:

Assistant district attorney, *Bachelor at Law,* CBS, 1973.

Ron Cutler, *Husbands and Wives,* CBS, 1977.

Samuel Roth, *Concealed Enemies,* PBS, 1984.

Television Appearances; Episodic:

Jeff Boggs, "Mind Your Own Business," *The Bob Newhart Show,* CBS, 1973.

Ed Schroeder, "A New Sue Ann," *The Mary Tyler Moore Show,* CBS, 1974.

Warren Weeks, "The Trouble with Warren," *The Rockford Files,* NBC, 1974.

Tom Robertson, "Roundabout," *The Rockford Files,* NBC, 1974.

Ron Willis, *Husbands, Wives and Lovers,* CBS, 1978.

Monty DiMair, "Ratman and Bobbin," *Hill Street Blues,* NBC, 1984.

Phillip Nevins, "Prescription for Death," *Law & Order,* NBC, 1990.

Alex Dracos, "Self Defense," *Law & Order,* NBC, 1992.

Dr. Martin Nodell (recurring), *The Outer Limits,* Showtime, 1997.

Stage Appearances:

Come Blow Your Horn, Broadway production, 1960.

Mark, *Rosebloom,* Center Theatre Group, Mark Taper Forum, Los Angeles Music Center, Los Angeles, 1970-71, then Eastside Playhouse, New York City, 1972.

Harvey Perr's Scandalous Memories, Forum Laboratory, Los Angeles, 1972-73.

Afternoon Tea, Mark Taper Forum, 1973-74.

Three Sisters, Mark Taper Forum, 1975-76.

Gethsemane Springs, Mark Taper Forum, 1976-77.

Ice, Mark Taper Forum, 1977.

Arthur Korman, *The Goodbye People,* Belasco Theatre, New York City, 1979.

Cal, *The Art of Dining,* Public/Newman Theatre, New York City, 1979.

Talley's Folly, Alley Theater, Houston, TX, 1982.

Feinson, *Detective Story,* Ahmanson Theatre, Los Angeles, 1984.

Ghetto, Mark Taper Forum, 1986.

Morty, *Temple,* American Jewish Theatre, New York City, 1988.

Isaac Geldhart, *The Substance of Fire,* Playwrights Horizon Theatre, New York City, 1991, then Lincoln Center, New York City, 1992, then Center Theatre Group, Mark Taper Forum, 1992-93.

Kenneth Hoyle, *Three Hotels,* Circle Repertory Company, Lucille Lortel Theatre, New York City, 1993.

Phillip Gellburg, *Broken Glass,* Booth Theater, New York City, then Long Wharf Theatre, New Haven, CT, both 1994.

Mikhailo Aleksandrovich Rakitin, *A Month in the Country,* Criterion Center Stage Right Theatre, New York City, 1995.

Herr Schultz, *Cabaret,* Kit Kat Klub, New York City, 1998.

Appeared in *The Tenth Man,* Broadway production; also appeared in *Cross Country, The American Clock, Nothing Sacred,* and *Proposals.**

RIPSTEIN, Arturo 1943-
(Arturo Ripstein Rosen)

PERSONAL

Full name, Arturo Ripstein Rosen; born December 13, 1943, in Mexico City, Mexico; son of Alfredo

Ripstein, Jr. (movie producer); married Paz Alicia Garciadiego (a screenwriter and composer).

Career: Director, producer, and writer.

Awards, Honors: Golden Ariel Award, 1973, for *El Castillo de la Pureza;* Golden Ariel Award, and Special Prize of the Jury, San sebastian International Film Festival, both 1978, for *El Lugar Sin Limites;* Golden Ariel Award, 1979, for *Cadena Perpetua;* Golden Ariel Award, 1987, for *El Imperio de la Fortuna;* Golden Seashell, San Sebastian International Film Festival, 1993, for *Principio y Fin;* Golden Ariel Award, 1994, for *Principio y Fin;* Golden Lion Award nomination, Venice Film Festival, 1996, for *Profundo Carmesi;* Latin American Cinema Award-Honorable mention, Sundance Film Festival, 1997, for *Profundo Carmesi;* Special Achievement Award, San Diego International Film Festival, 1997, for *Principio y Fin;* Golden Palm, Cannes Film Festival, 1999, for *El Coronel no tiene quien le escriba;* retrospectives of Ripstein's work have appeared at the Art Institute of Chicago and the Museum of Modern Art, New York City.

CREDITS

Film Work; Director, Except Where Indicated:

Tiempo de morir (also known as *Time to Die*), Alameda Films, 1965.

Segment "HO," *Juego peligroso* (also known as *Jogo Perigoso*), Alameda Films, 1966.

Los Recuerdos del porvenir (also known as *Memories of the Future*), Alameda Films, 1968.

And producer, *La Hora de los ninos,* Cine Independiente de Mexico, 1969.

And producer, *Crimen,* 1970.

And producer, *Exorcismo,* 1970.

And producer, *La Belleza,* 1970.

El Naufrago de la Calle Providencia (documentary), 1970.

Producer, *Autobiografia,* 1971.

El Castillo de la pureza (also known as *Castle of Purity*), Estudios Churub busco Azteca, 1973.

El Santo oficio (also known as *The Holy Office*), 1975.

Foxtrot (also known as *The Far Side of Paradise,* and *The Other Side of Paradise*), New World, 1975.

Lecumberri, 1976.

La Viuda negra (also known as *The Black Widow*), 1977.

El Lugar sin limites (also known as *The Place Without Limits*), 1978.

Cadena perpetua, 1978.

La Tia Alejandra, 1979.

La Ilegal, 1979.

La Seduccion (also known as *Seduction*), 1980.

Rastro de muerte, 1981.

El Otro, Conacine, 1984.

El Imperio de la fortuna (also known as *The Realm of Fortune*), Azteca, 1986.

Mentiras piadosas (also known as *Love Lies*), 1987.

White Lies, 1988.

La Mujer del puerto (also known as *Woman of the Port*), Alta Films, 1992.

And producer, *Principio y fin* (also known as *The Beginning and the End*), Prime Films, 1993.

La Reina de la noche (also known as *The Queen of the Night,* and *La Reine de la nuit*), JMM Invest, S.L., 1994.

Profundo carmesi (also known as *Carmin profond,* and *Deep Crimson*), NewYorker Films, 1996.

El Evangelio de las Maravillas (also known as *Divine*), Wanda Films, 1998.

El Coronel no tiene quien le escriba, Alta Films, 1999.

WRITINGS

Screenplays:

La Hora de los ninos, Cine Independiente de Mexico, 1969.

Crimen, 1970.

Exorcismo, 1970.

La Belleza, 1970.

Autobiografia, 1971.

El Castillo de la Pureza (also known as *Castle of Purity*), Estudios Churub busco Azteca, 1973.

El Santo oficio, 1974.

Foxtrot, New World, 1975.

Lecumberri, 1976.

Gardena Perpetua, 1978.

El Lugar sin limites (also known as *The Place Without Limits*), 1978.

OTHER SOURCES

Electronic:

http://www.worldartists.com/world/ripstein.htm.*

ROGERS, Buddy

See ROGERS, Charles "Buddy"

ROGERS, Charles

See ROGERS, Charles "Buddy"

ROGERS, Charles "Buddy" 1904-1999
(Buddy Rogers, Charles Rogers)

PERSONAL

Born Charles Rogers, August 13, 1904, in Olathe, KS; died April 21, 1999, in Rancho Mirage, CA; son of Maude and Bert Henry Rogers; married Mary Pickford (an actress), June 26, 1937 (died, 1979); married Beverly Ricono, 1980; children: (first marriage) Roxanne, Ronald. *Education:* Attended University of Kansas; trained at Paramount School of Acting, New York City. *Avocational interests:* Music, gymnastics.

Career: Actor, producer, and bandleader. Also philanthropist active in the Motion Picture & Television Fund, the Jewish Fund for the Aged, the National Conference of Christians and Jews, the Veteran's Assistance League, the University of Southern California School of Cinema, the Los Angeles Philharmonic, and the USO.

Awards, Honors: Jean Hersholt Humanitarian Award, Academy of Motion Picture Arts and Sciences, 1986.

CREDITS

Film Appearances:

Kenneth Murchison, *So's Your Old Man,* Famous Players, 1926.
Teddy Ward, *Fascinating Youth,* Paramount, 1926.
Willia Hinchfield, *More Pay—Less Work,* Twentieth Century-Fox, 1926.
John "Jack" Powell, *Wings,* Paramount, 1927.
Joe Grant, *My Best Girl,* United Artists, 1927.
Robert de Bellecontre, *Get Your Man,* Paramount, 1927.
Abie Levy, *Abie's Irish Rose,* Paramount, 1928.
Jimmy Duffy, *Varsity,* Paramount, 1928.
William Shelby, *Someone to Love,* Paramount, 1928.
Hugh Carver/Buddy, *Red Lips* (also known as *Cream of the Earth*), Universal, 1928.
Al West, *Close Harmony,* Paramount, 1929.
Tom Rumford/Colonel Blake, *River of Romance,* Paramount, 1929.
Parson, *Perfect Day,* Metro-Goldwyn-Mayer, 1929.
Carlee Thorpe, *Illusion,* Paramount, 1929.
Ned Lee, *Halfway to Heaven,* Paramount, 1929.
Cigar clerk, *Outside the Law,* Universal, 1930.
Jack Mason, *Heads Up,* Paramount, 1930.
Lieutenant Robert Banks, *Young Eagles,* Paramount, 1930.
Guest Star, *Paramount on Parade,* Paramount, 1930.
William Butler Reynolds, *Safety in Numbers,* Paramount, 1930.
Jerry Downes, *Follow Thru,* Paramount, 1930.
Larry Brooks, *Along Came Youth,* Paramount, 1930.
Himself, *The Slippery Pearls* (also known as *The Stolen Jools*), Warner Bros., 1931.
Working Girls, Paramount, 1931.
Tom Wood, *The Road to Reno,* Paramount, 1931.
Insurgent Convict, *Pardon Us* (also known as *Jail Birds*), Metro-Goldwyn-Mayer, 1931.
Laurie Roberts, *The Lawyer's Secret,* Paramount, 1931.
Bradley Ingals, *This Reckless Age,* Paramount, 1932.
Rogers the Butler, *Pack Up Your Troubles,* Metro-Goldwyn-Mayer, 1932.
Jimmie Hartman, *The Best of Enemies,* Twentieth Century-Fox, 1933.
Kenneth Raleigh, *Take a Chance,* Paramount, 1933.
Johnny Roberts, *Old Man Rhythm,* RKO Radio Pictures, 1935.
Buddy Morgan, *Dance Band,* British Inter., 1935.
Pierre, *Weekend Millionaire,* British Inter., 1937.
Brad Morgan, *This Way Please,* Paramount, 1937.
Jack Kent, *Let's Make a Night of It,* Universal, 1937.
Larry Hays, *Sing for Your Supper,* Columbia, 1941.
Dennis Lindsay, *Mexican Spitfire's Baby,* RKO Radio Pictures, 1941.
Dean MacArdle, *Golden Hoofs,* Twentieth Century-Fox, 1941.
Double Trouble, Monogram, 1941.
Harry, *They Raid By Night,* Producers Releasing, 1942.
Dennis Lindsay, *Mexican Spitfire Sees a Ghost,* RKO Radio Pictures, 1942.
Dennis Lindsay, *Mexican Spitfire at Sea,* RKO Radio Pictures, 1942.
House of Errors, Producers Releasing, 1942.
Goebbels, *That Nazty Nuisance,* United Artists, 1943.
Butler, *The Dancing Masters,* Twentieth Century-Fox, 1943.
Claude Kimball, *Don't Trust Your Husband,* United Artists, 1948.
Reverend Jericho Jones, *The Parson and the Outlaw,* Columbia, 1957.

Film Work; Producer, Except Where Indicated:

Susie Steps Out, United Artists, 1946.
Little Iodine, United Artists, 1946.
The Adventures of Don Coyote, United Artists, 1947.
Stork Bites Man, United Artists, 1947.
The Parson and the Outlaw, Columbia, 1957.
High School Hellcats (also known as *School for Violence*), American International Pictures, 1958.
Executive producer, *Hot Rod Gang,* American International Pictures, 1958.

Television Appearances; Series:
Host, *Cavalcade of Bands,* Dumont, 1951.

Television Appearances; Episodic:
Himself, "Wings," *Petticoat Junction,* CBS, 1968.

Television Appearances; Specials:
Honoree, *The 58th Annual Academy Awards Presentation,* 1986.

OBITUARIES AND OTHER SOURCES

Periodicals:
People, May 10, 1999, p. 213.
Variety, April 26, 1999, p. 59.*

ROOS, Don 1955-
(Donald Paul Roos)

PERSONAL

Born in 1955, in New York. *Education:* Attended University of Notre Dame, and completed a course in screenwriting.

Addresses: *Agency*—c/o Endeaver Agency, 9701 Wilshire Blvd., 10th Floor, Beverly Hills, CA 90212.

Career: Director, producer, and writer.

Awards, Honors: Grand Special Prize nomination, Deauville Film Festival, 1998, Independent Spirit Award nomination (shared with David Kirkpatrick and Michael Besman), best first feature, 1999, Independent Spirit Award, best screenplay, 1999, all for *The Opposite of Sex.*

CREDITS

Film Work:
Co-producer, *Love Field,* Orion, 1992.
Executive producer, *Boys on the Side,* Warner Bros., 1995.
Director, *The Opposite of Sex,* Sony Pictures Classics, 1998.

Television Work; Producer; Series:
(With others), *Nightingales,* NBC, 1989.

WRITINGS

Screenplays:
Casebusters, 1986.
Love Field, Orion, 1992.
Single White Female, Columbia, 1992.
Boys on the Side, Warner Bros., 1995.
Diabolique (a remake of the French classic), Lider Films, S.A., 1996.
The Opposite of Sex, Sony Pictures Classics, 1998.*

ROOS, Donald Paul
See ROOS, Don

ROSEN, Arturo Ripstein
See RIPSTEIN, Arturo

ROSENBAUM, Michael

PERSONAL

Born July 11, in Oceanside, Long Island, NY; raised in Newburgh, IN. *Education:* Western Kentucky University, B.A. (theater and communications). *Avocational Interests:* Ice hockey, music.

Addresses: *Contact*—International Creative Management, 8942 Wilshire Blvd., Beverly Hills, CA 90211.

Career: Actor.

CREDITS

Film Appearances:
Bart, *The Day I Ran Into All My Ex-Boyfriends,* 1997.
George Tucker, *Midnight in the Garden of Good and Evil,* Warner Bros., 1997.
Parker, *Urban Legend,* Columbia, 1998.
Skelly, *Eyeball Eddie,* 1999.

Television Appearances; Series:
Jonathan, *The Tom Show,* The WB, 1997.
Jack Cooper, *Zoe, Duncan, Jack & Jane,* The WB, 1998—.

Also appeared on *Late Night with Conan O'Brien,* NBC.

Stage Appearances:
Performed as Scoop Rosenbaum, *The Heidi Chronicles;* performed on stage off-Broadway; and worked summer stock in North Carolina.*

ROSS, Gary 1956-

PERSONAL

Born in 1956; son of Arthur A. Ross (a screenwriter). *Education:* Attended the University of Pennsylvania; studied acting under Stella Adler.

Career: Screenwriter, producer, and actor. Author of political speeches, including speeches for President Bill Clinton. Also Chairman of Los Angeles Public Library Commission, 1993—; served as delegate for the Democratic National Convention.

Awards, Honors: Academy Award nomination, best original screenplay, and Writers Guild Award nomination, both 1998, for *Big;* Academy Award nomination, best original screenplay, 1994, for *Dave;* Golden Satellite Awards, best original motion picture screenplay and best motion picture, comedy or musical, both 1998, Writers Guild Award nomination, and Paul Selvin Award, Writers Guild of America, all for *Pleasantville.*

CREDITS

Film Work; Producer:
Big, Twentieth Century-Fox, 1988.
Trial and Error, New Line Cinema, 1997.
Pleasantville, New Line Cinema, 1998.

Film Work; Director:
Pleasantville, New Line Cinema, 1998.

Film Appearances:
Immigration officer, *Crackers,* Universal, 1984.
Policeman #2, *Dave,* Warner Bros., 1993.

Television Work; Specials:
Producer, *The High Life,* ABC, 1990.

WRITINGS

Screenplays:
Big, Twentieth Century-Fox, 1988.
Mr. Baseball, Universal, 1992.
Dave, Warner Bros., 1993.
(Uncredited) *The Flintstones,* Universal, 1994.
Lassie, Paramount, 1994.
Pleasantville, New Line Cinema, 1998.

Television Series:
The Hitchhiker, HBO, 1983.

Adaptations: The screenplay *Big* was adapted as a stage musical by David Shire, Richard Maltby Jr., and John Weidman, produced at the Shubert Theatre, New York City, 1996.*

ROSSINGTON, Norman 1928-1999

PERSONAL

Born December 24, 1928, in England, UK; died of cancer, May 21, 1999, in Manchester, England, UK.

Career: Actor.

Member: Shakespeare Recording Company.

CREDITS

Film Appearances:
Boy Lover, *Three Men in a Boat,* 1956.
Arthur, *Keep It Clean,* 1956.
Barrow Boy, *Stranger's Meeting,* 1957.
Herbert Brown, *Carry On Sergeant,* 1958.
Norm, *Carry On Nurse,* 1958.
Steerage Steward, *A Night to Remember,* 1958.
Bert, *Saturday Night and Sunday Morning,* Continental Distributing, 1960.
Referee, *Carry On Regardless,* 1961.
Private Clough, *The Longest Day,* 1962.
Corporal Jenkins, *Lawrence of Arabia,* Columbia, 1962.
Alfie, *Go to Blazes,* 1962.
Bert, *Crooks Anonymous,* 1962.
Nurse on Wheels (also known as *Carry On, Nurse On Wheels,* and *What a Carry On: Nurse On Wheels* [released in UK in 1994]), 1963.
Theodore, *The Comedy Man,* 1963.
Daylight Robbery, 1964.
Norm, *A Hard Day's Night,* United Artists, 1964.
Royal Army Corporal, *Joey Boy,* 1965.
Driver, *Cup Fever,* 1965.
Asst. Fire Chief, *Those Magnificent Men in Their Flying Machines, or How I Flew from London to Paris in 25 Hours 11 Minutes,* Twentieth Century-Fox, 1965.
First Rough, *The Wrong Box,* Columbia, 1966.
Alfie, *Tobruk,* 1967.
Arthur Babcock, *Double Trouble,* Metro-Goldwyn-Mayer, 1967.
Auctioneer, *Negatives,* Continental Distributing, 1968.

Corbett, *The Charge of the Light Brigade,* United Artists, 1968.
Phil, *Two Gentlemen Sharing,* American International Pictures, 1969.
Albert, *The Engagement,* 1970.
Guide, *The Rise and Rise of Michael Rimmer,* Warner Bros., 1970.
Fireman, *Simon Simon,* 1970.
Papilette, *The Adventures of Gerard* (also known as *Adventures of Brigadier Gerard*), United Artists, 1970.
Ferris, *Man in the Wilderness,* 1971.
Jack Foster, *Go for a Take* (also known as *Double Take*), 1972.
Detective Sergeant Rogers, *Deathline* (also known as *Raw Meat*), 1972.
Dewsnap, *Young Winston,* Columbia, 1972.
Tom, *Digby, the Biggest Dog in the World,* Prism Entertainment, 1973.
Bruno, *The Prisoner of Zenda,* Universal, 1979.
Rhubarb Rhubarb, 1980.
Station master, *House of the Long Shadows* (also known as *House of Long Shadows*), 1983.
Shopkeeper, *The Krays,* Miramax, 1990.
Postman, *Let Him Have It,* 1991.
Himself, *The Making of "A Hard Day's Night,"* 1995.

Television Appearances; Movies:
Carry On Christmas: Carry On Stuffing, 1972.
Master-at-Arms: T. King, *S.O.S. Titanic,* ABC, 1979.
Horatio Havercamp, *Sharpe's Regiment,* 1996.

Television Appearances; Miniseries:
Lorenzo, *Casanova,* syndicated, 1971.
Sergeant, *I, Claudius,* 1976.
Maro, *Masada,* ABC, 1981.

Television Appearances; Specials:
Collins Meets Coward, Arts & Entertainment, 1992.

Television Appearances; Episodic:
Private "Cupcake" Cook, *The Army Game,* Grenada-TV, 1957.
Cupcake Cook, *I Only Arsked,* 1958.
The Big Noise, 1964.
Norman, *Curry & Chips,* LWT, 1969.
Roads to Freedom, BBC-2, 1970.
His and Hers, 1970.
Samuel Baker, *Search For the Nile,* NBC, 1972.
Jack Foster, "Lost Dog", *Hunter's Walk,* ATV, 1973.
Detective Chief Constable Goddard, "Set Up", *Target,* BBC-1, 1977.
PC Goatman, *Spooner's Patch,* 1979.
Pop, *And the Beat Goes On,* 1996.

Television Appearances; Series:
Big Jim, *Big Jim and the Figaro Club,* BBC-2, 1979.

Stage Appearances:
Appeared as Feste, in *Twelfth Night;* and as Touchstone, in *As You Like It;* also appeared in the London West End stage hit *Beauty and the Beast.**

ROSSON, Hal
See ROSSON, Harold

ROSSON, Harold 1895-1988
(Hal Rosson)

PERSONAL

Born in 1895, in New York, NY; died on September 6, 1988, in Palm Beach, FL; married Jean Harlow (an actress), in 1933, (divorced, 1935).

Career: Cinematographer.

Awards, Honors: Honorary Award (shared with W. Howard Greene), best color cinematography, 1937, for *The Garden of Allah;* Academy Award nomination, best cinematography, color, 1940, for *The Wizard of Oz;* Academy Award nomination, best cinematography, black and white, 1941, for *Boom Town;* Academy Award nomination (shared with Robert Surtees), best cinematography, black and white, 1945, for *Thirty Seconds Over Tokyo;* Academy Award nomination, best cinematography, black and white, 1951, for *The Asphalt Jungle;* Academy Award nomination, best cinematography, black and white, 1957, for *The Bad Seed.*

CREDITS

Film Work; Cinematographer, Except Where Indicated:
David Harum, Paramount, 1915.
Oliver Twist, Paramount, 1916.
The Honorable Friend, Paramount, 1916.
Panthea, Lewis J. Selzick Enterprises, 1917.
The American Consul, Paramount, 1917.
Cinema Murder, Paramount, 1919.
Polly of the Storm Country, First National Pictures, 1920.
A Virginia Courtship, Paramount, 1921.
Buried Treasure, Paramount, 1921

Everything for Sale, Paramount, 1921.
Dark Secrets, Paramount, 1922.
A Homespun Vamp, Paramount, 1922.
The Cradle, Paramount, 1922.
Through a Glass Window, 1922.
For the Defense, Paramount, 1922.
Zaza, Paramount, 1923.
Quicksands, Paramount, 1923.
Garrison's Finish, Allied Producers & Distributers, 1923.
The Glimpses of the Moon, Paramount, 1923.
Lawful Larceny, Paramount, 1923.
Manhattan, 1924.
A Society Scandal, Paramount, 1924.
Manhandled, Paramount, 1924.
The Story Without a Name (also known as *Without Warning*), Paramount, 1924.
The Little French Girl, Paramount, 1925.
Too Many Kisses, Paramount, 1925.
A Man Must Live, Paramount, 1925.
The Street of Forgotten Men, Paramount, 1925.
Classified, First National Pictures, 1925.
Infatuation, First National Pictures, 1925.
Man Bait, Producers Distributing Corp., 1926.
Up in Mabel's Room, Producers Distributing Corp., 1926.
Almost a Lady, Producers Distributing Corp., 1926.
For Wives Only, Producers Distributing Corp., 1926.
Jim, the Conqueror, Producers Distributing Corp., 1927.
Getting Gertie's Garter, Producers Distributing Corp., 1927.
Evening Clothes, Paramount, 1927.
Rough House Rosie, Paramount, 1927.
Service for Ladies, Paramount, 1927.
A Gentleman of Paris, Paramount, 1927.
Open Range, Paramount, 1927.
The Dragnet, Paramount, 1928.
The Docks of New York, Paramount, 1928.
Abie's Irish Rose, Paramount, 1928.
Gentlemen Prefer Blondes, Paramount, 1928.
Sawdust Paradise, Paramount, 1928.
Three Weekends (also known as *Three Week Ends*), Paramount, 1928.
The Case of Lena Smith, Paramount, 1929.
Trent's Last Case, Fox Film Corporation, 1929.
The Far Call, Fox Film Corporation, 1929.
Frozen Justice, Fox Film Corporation, 1929.
South Sea Rose, Fox Film Corporation, 1929.
Passion Flower, Metro-Goldwyn-Mayer, 1930.
Hello Sister, Sono-Art World Wide Pictures, 1930.
This Mad World, Metro-Goldwyn-Mayer, 1930.
Madam Satan (also known as *Madame Satan*), Metro-Goldwyn-Mayer, 1930.
Son of India, Metro-Goldwyn-Mayer, 1931.
The Prodigal (also known as *The Southerner*), Metro-Goldwyn-Mayer, 1931.
Men Call It Love, Metro-Goldwyn-Mayer, 1931.
The Cuban Love Song, Metro-Goldwyn-Mayer, 1931.
En cada puerto un amor, Culver Export Corporation, 1931.
Sporting Blood, Metro-Goldwyn-Mayer, 1931.
The Squaw Man (also known as *The White Man*), Metro-Goldwyn-Mayer, 1931.
Tarzan the Ape Man, Metro-Goldwyn-Mayer, 1932.
Kongo, Metro-Goldwyn-Mayer, 1932.
Are You Listening?, Metro-Goldwyn-Mayer, 1932.
When a Fellow Needs a Friend (also known as *When a Feller Needs a Friend*), Metro-Goldwyn-Mayer, 1932.
Red-Headed Woman, Metro-Goldwyn-Mayer, 1932.
Downstairs, Metro-Goldwyn-Mayer, 1932.
Red Dust, Metro-Goldwyn-Mayer, 1932.
Turn Back the Clock, Metro-Goldwyn-Mayer, 1933.
Penthouse (also known as *Crooks in Clover*), Metro-Goldwyn-Mayer, 1933.
Hell Below, Loew's, Inc., 1933.
The Barbarian (also known as *The Arab, Man of the Nile,* and *A Night in Cairo*), Metro-Goldwyn-Mayer, 1933.
Hold Your Man, Metro-Goldwyn-Mayer, 1933.
Bombshell (also known as *Blonde Bombshell*), Metro-Goldwyn-Mayer, 1933.
This Side of Heaven, Metro-Goldwyn-Mayer, 1934.
The Cat and the Fiddle, Metro-Goldwyn-Mayer, 1934.
Treasure Island, Metro-Goldwyn-Mayer, 1934.
The Scarlet Pimpernel, London Film Productions, 1934.
The Ghost Goes West, Metro-Goldwyn-Mayer, 1935.
As You Like It, Metro-Goldwyn-Mayer, 1936.
The Devil Is a Sissy (also known as *The Devil Takes the Count*), Metro-Goldwyn-Mayer, 1936.
The Emperor's Candlesticks, Loew's, Inc., 1937.
The Man Who Could Work Miracles, United Artists, 1937.
They Gave Him a Gun, 1937.
Captains Courageous, Metro-Goldwyn-Mayer, 1937.
A Yank at Oxford, Metro-Goldwyn-Mayer, 1938.
Too Hot to Handle, Metro-Goldwyn-Mayer, 1938.
That Mothers Might Live, Metro-Goldwyn-Mayer, 1938.
The Wizard of Oz, Metro-Goldwyn-Mayer, 1939.
I Take This Woman, Metro-Goldwyn-Mayer, 1939.
Flight Command, Metro-Goldwyn-Mayer, 1940.
Dr. Kildare Goes Home, Metro-Goldwyn-Mayer, 1940.
Edison, the Man, Metro-Goldwyn-Mayer, 1940.
Boom Town, Metro-Goldwyn-Mayer, 1940.

Washington Melodrama, Metro-Goldwyn-Mayer, 1941.
Johnny Eager, Metro-Goldwyn-Mayer, 1941.
Honky Tonk, Metro-Goldwyn-Mayer, 1941.
The Penalty, Metro-Goldwyn-Mayer, 1941.
Men of Boys Town, Metro-Goldwyn-Mayer, 1941.
Tennessee Johnson (also known as *The Man on America's Conscience*), Metro-Goldwyn-Mayer, 1942.
Somewhere I'll Find You, Metro-Goldwyn-Mayer, 1942.
Slightly Dangerous, Metro-Goldwyn-Mayer, 1943.
Thirty Seconds Over Tokyo, Metro-Goldwyn-Mayer, 1944.
Between Two Women, Metro-Goldwyn-Mayer, 1944.
An American Romance, Metro-Goldwyn-Mayer, 1944.
Three Wise Fools, Metro-Goldwyn-Mayer, 1946.
No Leave, No Love, Metro-Goldwyn-Mayer, 1946.
My Brother Talks to Horses, Metro-Goldwyn-Mayer, 1946.
Duel in the Sun, Metro-Goldwyn-Mayer, 1946.
Living in a Big Way, Metro-Goldwyn-Mayer, 1947.
The Hucksters, Metro-Goldwyn-Mayer, 1947.
Homecoming, Metro-Goldwyn-Mayer, 1948.
Command Decision, Metro-Goldwyn-Mayer, 1948.
The Stratton Story, Metro-Goldwyn-Mayer, 1949.
On the Town, Metro-Goldwyn-Mayer, 1949.
Any Number Can Play, Metro-Goldwyn-Mayer, 1949.
To Please a Lady (also known as *Red Hot Wheels*), Metro-Goldwyn-Mayer, 1950.
Key to the City, Metro-Goldwyn-Mayer, 1950.
The Asphalt Jungle, Metro-Goldwyn-Mayer, 1950.
The Red Badge of Courage, Metro-Goldwyn-Mayer, 1951.
Lone Star, Metro-Goldwyn-Mayer, 1951.
Singin' in the Rain, Metro-Goldwyn-Mayer, 1952.
Love Is Better Than Ever (also known as *The Light Fantastic*), Metro-Goldwyn-Mayer, 1952.
I Love Melvin, Metro-Goldwyn-Mayer, 1953.
The Actress, Metro-Goldwyn-Mayer, 1953.
Dangerous When Wet, Metro-Goldwyn-Mayer, 1953.
Ulisse (also known as *Ulysses*), Paramount, 1954.
Mambo, Paramount, 1954.
Strange Lady in Town, Warner Bros., 1955.
Pete Kelly's Blues, 1955.
Toward the Unknown (also known as *Brink of Hell*), 1956.
The Bad Seed, Warner Bros., 1956.
The Enemy Below, Twentieth Century-Fox, 1957.
Onionhead, Warner Bros., 1958.
No Time for Sergeants, Warner Bros., 1958.
El Dorado, Paramount, 1967.

OTHER SOURCES

Periodicals:
New York Times, September 9, 1988.*

RUSSELL, Clive

PERSONAL

Raised in Fife, Scotland. *Nationality:* Scottish. *Education:* Trained as a teacher.

Career: Actor. Theatre teacher, 1969-77.

CREDITS

Television Appearances; Movies:
Terry Knapp, *Tumbledown,* BBC, 1989.
Chief Inspector Ross, *Advocates I,* ITV, 1991.
Krebs, *Fatherland,* HBO, 1994.
Arthur, *Lord of Misrule,* 1996.
Mick Boyd, *Crossing the Floor,* BBC, 1996.
Joe Gargery, *Great Expectations,* BBC, 1999.

Television Appearances; Miniseries:
Adrian Fell, *Tell Tale Hearts,* 1992.
Mr. Vandemaar, *NeverWhere,* BBC, 1996.

Television Appearances; Series:
The Shari Lewis Show, NBC, 1960-63.
Caleb Garth, *Middlemarch,* BBC, 1994.
Tucker, *Finney,* ITV, 1994.
Roughnecks, 1994.
Kevin Mott, *The Peter Principle,* BBC, 1995.
Voice, *Testament: The Bible in Animation,* Channel 4, 1996.
Duggie Strachen, *Heartburn Hotel,* BBC, 1998.
Phil Jakes, *Hope and Glory,* BBC, 1999.

Television Appearances; Episodic:
Detective Sergeant, "Joy," *Drop the Dead Donkey,* Channel 4, 1993.
Baxter, "Wheels," *Frank Stubbs Promotes,* Carlton TV, 1993.
Mark, "Fair Exchange," *Lovejoy,* BBC, 1994.
DCS Barratt, "Confess," *Murder Most Horrid,* BBC, 1996.
Saddam the thug, *Sunnyside Farm,* 1997.

Television Appearances; Specials:

The Creature, *Frankenstein: The True Story,* NBC, 1994.

Film Appearances:

Corporal Reade, *The Naked Brigade,* Universal, 1965.
Redskirts on Cyldeside, 1984.
Sergeant Bormann, *The Power of One,* Warner Bros., 1992.
Clegg, *Soft Top, Hard Shoulder,* Gruber Bros., 1992.
Chief Inspector Daybury, *The Hawk,* Castle Hill, 1993.
Seconds Out, 1993.
Neil Currie, *Margaret's Museum,* Astra Cinema, 1995.
Grazetti, *Ruffian Hearts,* BBC, 1995.
For My Baby, 1997.
Theophilus Hopkins, *Oscar and Lucinda,* Fox Searchlight, 1997.
Billy Hunch, *Bodyworks,* Wolfmoon Films, 1999.
The Tramp, *My Life So Far,* Miramax, 1999.
Viking, *The Thirteenth Warrior,* Buena Vista, 1999.

Stage Appearances:

Macluby, *The Bite of the Night,* Royal Shakespeare Company, The Pit, London, 1988.*

RUSSO, James 1953-

PERSONAL

Born April 23, 1953, in New York, NY. *Educated:* Attended New York University.

Addresses: *Agent*—Gabrielle Allabashi and Darryl Marshak, Gold/Marshak/Liedtke Talent & Literary Agency, 3500 West Olive Avenue, Suite 1400, Burbank, CA 91505.

Career: Actor.

Awards, Honors: *Theatre World* Award, 1982-83, for *Extremities.*

CREDITS

Film Appearances:

Robber, *Fast Times at Ridgemont High,* Universal, 1982.
Ronald Thompson, *A Stranger Is Watching,* United Artists, 1982.
Nick, *Exposed,* United Artists, 1983.
Anthony Demmer, *Vortex,* B Movies, 1983.
Bugsy, *Once Upon a Time in America* (also known as *Ciera una volta in America*), Warner Bros., 1984.
Mikey Tandino, *Beverley Hills Cop,* Paramount, 1984.
Vince Hood, *The Cotton Club,* Orion, 1984.
Joe, *Extremities,* Atlantic, 1986.
Alberto "Alby" Monte, *China Girl,* Vestron, 1987.
Reno, *The Blue Iguana,* Paramount, 1988.
Frank Quinn, *Freeway,* New World Entertainment, 1988.
Vittorio, *La Cintura* (also known as *Criminal Intent*), 1989.
Bobby, *We're No Angels,* Paramount, 1989.
(Uncredited) Demarco, *State of Grace,* Orion, 1990.
Richard Waters, *My Own Private Idaho,* Fine Line Features, 1991.
Dan Corelli, *A Kiss Before Dying,* Universal, 1991.
Daniel Corvin, *Cold Heaven,* Hemdale Releasing, 1992.
Bill Tanner, *Illicit Behavior* (also known as *Criminal Intent*), Prism Entertainment, 1992.
Captain Travis, *Trauma* (also known as *Dario Argento's Trauma*), Worldvision Home Video, 1992.
Francis Burns, *Dangerous Game,* Metro-Goldwyn-Mayer, 1993.
Mintz, *Da Vinci's War,* Triboro Entertainment, 1993.
Kid Jarrett, *Bad Girls,* Twentieth Century-Fox, 1994.
Rodgers, *Panther,* Gramercy Pictures, 1995.
Dan Cappelli, *Condition Red,* Arrow, 1995.
Jerry, *Small Time* (also known as *Waiting for the Man*), 1995.
Eddie, *American Strays,* A-pix Entertainment, 1996.
Rupert, *Livers Ain't Cheap* (also known as *The Real Thing*), Windy City International, 1997.
Idaho, *The Postman,* Warner Bros., 1997.
Paulie, *Donnie Brasco,* TriStar, 1997.
Tommy, *No Way Home,* Back Alley Productions, 1997.
Heist, Trident Releasing, 1997.
Gino Carlucci, *Laws of Deception,* Peachtree Entertainment, 1997.
Urban Justice (also known as *Blood Money* and *Under Oath*), Concorde/New Horizons, 1997.
Joe Massa, *Bittersweet,* Dog Ate My Script Inc., 1998.
Ziggy Rotella, *Detour,* October Films, 1998.
Targenville, *Felons,* 1998.
Otis, *Jimmy Zip,* Image Network, 1999.
Bernie, *The Ninth Gate,* Live Entertainment, 1999.
Nick Halton, *Sonic Impact,* 1999.

Also starred in prize-winning short film *Candy Store* at New York University.

Television Appearances; Movies:

Charlie Van, *In the Shadow of a Killer,* NBC, 1992.

Nick Ciccini, *Intimate Stranger,* Showtime, 1992.
Don Feeney, *Desperate Rescue: The Cathy Mahone Story,* NBC, 1992.
Joshua Kane, *Double Deception,* NBC, 1993.
Ted Burke, *The Secretary,* CBS, 1995.
Kliff, *The Set Up,* Showtime, 1995.
Sal Bianculli, *My Husband's Secret Life,* USA Network, 1998.
Brannagin, *The Girl Gets Moe,* HBO, 1998.
Gino Carlucci, *Laws of Deception,* Cinemax, 1999.

Television Appearances; Episodic:
Sacco, "Prodigal Son," *Miami Vice,* NBC, 1985.
Janos Korda, "Symphony in B#," *Friday the 13th,* syndicated, 1988.
Tommy Bats, *Dellaventura,* CBS, 1997.
Frank Saretti, *C-16,* ABC, 1997.

Stage Appearances:
Welcome to Andromeda, 1975.
Raul, *Extremities,* Westside Arts Center/Cheryl Crawford Theatre, 1982-83.

Also appeared in *Deathwatch* and *Marat/Sade.*

WRITINGS

Screenplays:
Wrote prize-winning short entitled *Candy Store.**

RYAN, Jeri
See RYAN, Jeri Lynn

RYAN, Jeri Lynn 1968-
(Jeri Ryan)

PERSONAL

Real name, Jeri Lynn Zimmermann; born February 22, 1968, in Munich, Germany; son of Jerry (an Army master sergeant) and Sharon (a social worker) Zimmerman; married Jack Ryan (an investment banker), 1991 (separated, 1998); children: Alex (son). *Education:* Northwestern University, B.A. (theater), 1990; National Merit Scholar.

Addresses: *Agent*—SDB, 1801 Avenue of the Stars, Suite 902, Los Angeles, CA 90067.

Career: Actress and model. Named Miss Illinois, 1989.

CREDITS

Television Appearances; Series:
Seven of Nine, *Star Trek: Voyager,* UPN, 1995—.
Juliet Stuart, *Dark Skies,* NBC, 1997.

Television Appearances; Movies:
Dawn Elizabeth Smith, *Nightmare in Columbia County* (also known as *Victim of Beauty*), CBS, 1991.
Holly Evans, *Overexposed,* ABC, 1992.
In the Line of Duty: Ambush in Waco, NBC, 1993.
Kimberly, *Co-ed Call Girl,* CBS, 1996.

Television Appearances: Episodic:
Lisa, "Mother, Jugs, and Zach," *Nurses,* NBC, 1991.
Tyler, "The Marrying Guy," *Top of the Heap,* Fox, 1991.
Felicia Kane, "Deadly Nightshade," *The Flash,* CBS, 1991.
Pam, "The Unsinkable Tony Micelli," *Who's the Boss?,* ABC, 1991.
Rachel, *Reasonable Doubts,* NBC, 1991.
Carrie, "Fatal Seduction: Part 1," *Matlock,* ABC, 1993.
Carrie, "Fatal Seduction: Part 2," *Matlock,* ABC, 1993.
Melissa, *Diagnosis Murder,* CBS, 1993.
Pauline Yardley, "Jackie and the Model," *The Jackie Thomas Show,* ABC, 1993.
Lauren Sanders, "Out for Blood," *Time Trax,* syndicated, 1994.
Claire, "Designer Knock-Off," *Charlie Grace,* 1995.
Maura, "Death 'N Denial," *Murder, She Wrote,* CBS, 1995.
Jennifer, *John Grisham's The Client,* CBS, 1995.
Valerie Madison, "Devil in a Wet Dress," *Melrose Place,* Fox, 1996.
Valerie Madison, "Ruthless People," *Melrose Place,* Fox, 1996.
Alexis Barnes, "Sentinel, Too" *The Sentinel,* UPN, 1998.

Television Appearances; Specials:
Nicole, *Just Deserts,* ABC, 1992.
Beth Madison, *Pier 66,* ABC, 1996.
Host, "Year of Hell," *Star Trek Voyager,* UPN, 1997.
Host, *American's Greatest Pets: Amazing But True,* UPN, 1998.
Presenter, *TV Guide Awards,* 1999.

Film Appearances:
Lydia, *Men Cry Bullets,* 1997.

Also appeared in *The Last Man.*

OTHER SOURCES

Periodicals:

Entertainment Weekly, September 19, 1997, p. 42.
Newsweek, January 19, 1998, p. 46.
People, October 13, 1997, p. 134.*

S

SAKUYAMA, Jimmy
See MAKO

SALMI, Albert 1928-1990

PERSONAL

Born March 11, 1928, in Brooklyn, NY; committed suicide, April 23, 1990, in Spokane, WA; married Peggy Ann Garner (an actress), May 10, 1956 (divorced, 1963); married Roberta Pollock (died, April 23, 1990); children: (first marriage) Katherine. *Education:* Trained for the stage at American Theatre Wing's Dramatic Workshop and at Actors Studio, both in New York City. *Avocational interests:* Painting.

Career: Actor. Also worked as a Pinkerton detective. *Military service:* Served in World War II.

Member: Screen Actors Guild, American Federation of Television and Radio Artists.

Awards, Honors: Acting award, c. 1955, for *Bus Stop;* National Board of Review Award, best supporting actor, 1958, for *The Bravados* and *The Brothers Karamazov;* Western Heritage Award, National Cowboy Hall of Fame, 1967, for portrayal of Holly in "Death Watch," an episode of *Gunsmoke; Variety* Poll of London Critics Award (with others), best male supporting performance in a play, 1969, for *The Price.*

CREDITS

Film Appearances:

Smerdjakov, *The Brothers Karamazov* (also known as *Karamazov* and *The Murderer Dmitri Karamazov*), Metro-Goldwyn-Mayer, 1958.
Ed Taylor, *The Bravados,* Twentieth Century-Fox, 1958.
Charlie Rawlins, *The Unforgiven,* United Artists, 1960.
Hank Bailey, *Wild River,* Twentieth Century-Fox, 1960.
Sheriff, *The Outrage,* Metro-Goldwyn-Mayer, 1964.
Deputy Meshaw, *The Flim Flam Man* (also known as *One Born Every Minute*), Twentieth Century-Fox, 1967.
Octavius Roy, *Hour of the Gun,* United Artists, 1967.
Jose Ortega, *The Ambushers,* Columbia, 1968.
Cletus Grogan, *Three Guns for Texas,* Universal, 1968.
Rafe Augustine, *The Man Hunter,* Universal, 1969.
Harvey Stenbaugh, *The Lawman,* United Artists, 1971.
Cobb, *Something Big,* National General, 1971.
Schmidt, *The Deserter* (also known as *Ride to Glory, Djavolja kicma,* and *La spina dorsale del diavolo*), Paramount, 1971.
"E-1," *Escape from the Planet of the Apes,* Twentieth Century-Fox, 1971.
Splint, *The Crazy World of Julius Vrooder,* Twentieth Century-Fox, 1974.
Dolek, *The Take,* Columbia, 1974.
Jack McQueen, *The Legend of Earl Durand,* 1974.
Sheriff Art Kincade, *Empire of the Ants,* American International Pictures, 1977.
Cortland, *Viva Knievel!* (also known as *Seconds to Live*), Warner Bros., 1977.
Sheriff Larkin, *Moonshine County Express,* New World Pictures, 1977.
Sheriff, *Black Oak Conspiracy,* New World Pictures, 1977.
George, *The Sweet Creek County War,* Key, 1978.
Andy, *Love and Bullets,* Metro-Goldwyn-Mayer, 1979.
Mr. Noonan, *Caddyshack,* Warner Bros., 1980.
Tank, *Steel* (also known as *Look Down and Die* and *Men of Steel*), World/Northal, 1980.
Rory Poke, *Brubaker,* Twentieth Century-Fox, 1980.
Delgato, *Cuba Crossing* (also known as *Assignment: Kill Castro, Key West Crossing, Kill Castro, The Mercenaries, Sweet Dirty Tony,* and *Sweet Violent Tony*), Key West, 1980.

Ozzie Randolph, *Cloud Dancer,* Prism Pictures, 1980.

Inspector Sturgess, *The Witch* (also known as *Superstition*), Lightning/Future Film, 1981.

Colonel Liakhov, *The Guns and the Fury,* Bordeaux, 1981.

St. Helens, Killer Volcano, Vestron Entertainment, 1981.

Greil, *Dragonslayer,* United Artists, 1981.

Captain Billingham, *Burned at the Stake* (also known as *The Coming*), 1981.

Captain Ellis, *Love Child,* Warner Bros., 1982.

Ben Martin, *I'm Dancing As Fast As I Can,* Paramount, 1982.

Johnny Lawson, *Hard to Hold,* Universal, 1984.

United States Emissary Drane, *Born American* (also known as *Arctic Heat* and *Jaeaetaevae Polte*), Concorde, 1986.

Johnny Scot, *Breaking In,* Samuel Goldwyn Company, 1989.

Television Appearances; Series:

Yadkin, *Daniel Boone,* NBC, 1964-65.

Peter "Pete" Ritter, *Petrocelli,* NBC, 1974-76.

Television Appearances; Miniseries:

Senator Bert McConnadin, *Once an Eagle,* NBC, 1976.

Peter Markevich, *Harold Robbins' 79 Park Avenue* (also known as *79 Park Avenue*), NBC, 1977.

Television Appearances; Movies:

Quinn, *The Meanest Men in the West,* 1967.

Poss Timmerlake, *Menace on the Mountain,* 1970.

Frank Taggert, *Female Artillery,* ABC, 1973.

Night Games, NBC, 1974.

Lester Mitchell, *Undercover with the KKK* (also known as *The Freedom Riders* and *My Undercover Years with the KKK*), 1979.

Portrait of a Rebel: The Remarkable Mrs. Sanger (also known as *Portrait of a Rebel: Margaret Sanger*), CBS, 1980.

The Great Cash Giveaway, NBC, 1980.

Hugh Glover, *Thou Shalt Not Kill,* 1982.

Ed Dietz, *Best Kept Secrets,* ABC, 1984.

Judge Dupree, *Fatal Vision,* NBC, 1984.

Sergeant Oliphant, *Dress Gray,* NBC, 1986.

Sheriff Bill Sommers, *Jesse* (also known as *Desert Nurse*), CBS, 1988.

Mr. Maxwell, *Billy the Kid* (also known as *Gore Vidal's Billy the Kid* and *The Kid*), TNT, 1989.

Till We Meet Again (also known as *Judith Krantz's Till We Meet Again*), CBS, 1989.

Television Appearances; Specials:

J. B. Salter, "B-Men," *CBS Summer Playhouse,* CBS, 1989.

Television Appearances; Episodic:

"Bang the Drum Slowly," *The U.S. Steel Hour,* CBS, 1956.

Holmes, "Survival," *The U.S. Steel Hour,* CBS, 1956.

"Noon on Doomsday," *The U.S. Steel Hour,* CBS, 1956.

"The Hill Wife," *The U.S. Steel Hour,* CBS, 1957.

Putnam Cox, "Most Blessed Woman," *Kraft Television Theatre,* NBC, 1957.

Jones, "The Dangerous People," *Alfred Hitchcock Presents,* CBS, 1957.

Man under Glass, CBS, 1958.

"Somewhere South of Suva," *Adventures in Paradise,* ABC, 1959.

Joe Caswell, "Execution," *The Twilight Zone,* CBS, 1960.

"Silent Thunder," *Bonanza,* NBC, 1960.

Peter Sheeran, "The Old Foolishness," *Play of the Week,* syndicated, 1961.

"Button in the Haystack," *Naked City,* syndicated, 1961.

"Wagon to Fort Anderson," *Wagon Train,* NBC, 1961.

Steve "Country Boy" Parrish, "Power Play," *The Untouchables,* ABC, 1961.

"Panic Wagon," *The Investigators,* CBS, 1961.

Causarano, "A Quality of Mercy," *The Twilight Zone,* CBS, 1961.

"The Frank Carter Story," *Wagon Train,* NBC and ABC, 1962.

"It Tolls for Thee," *The Virginian,* NBC, 1962.

Sergeant Jenkins, "Cat and Mouse," *Combat,* ABC, 1962.

William J. Feathersmith, "Of Late, I Think of Cliffordville," *The Twilight Zone,* CBS, 1963.

"Man in a Blackout," *Redigo,* NBC, 1963.

"Brother Thaddeus," *The Virginian,* NBC, 1963.

Chuck, "Angels Travel on Lonely Roads" (parts one and two), *The Fugitive,* ABC, 1964.

"The Nicest Girl in Gomorrah," *Destry,* ABC, 1964.

"The Mary S. McDowall Story," *Profiles in Courage,* NBC, 1964.

"A Little Learning," *The Virginian,* NBC, 1965.

"Weight of the World," *I Spy,* NBC, 1965.

"Jinx," *Laredo,* NBC, 1965.

Holly, "Death Watch," *Gunsmoke,* CBS, 1966.

Tucker, "The Sky Pirate," *Lost in Space,* CBS, 1966.

Keeno Nash, "Under a Dark Star," *The Big Valley,* ABC, 1966.

Captain Alfred Brent, "Dead Men's Doubloons," *Voyage to the Bottom of the Sea,* ABC, 1966.

"The Plunderers," *The F.B.I.*, ABC, 1966.
"Brotherhood," *T.H.E. Cat*, NBC, 1966.
Marcus Alley, "The Thirteenth Man," *Bonanza*, NBC, 1967.
Tucker, "Treasure of the Lost Planet," *Lost in Space*, CBS, 1967.
Ed Carstairs, "Mistaken Identity," *Gunsmoke*, CBS, 1967.
Birch, "The Buffalo Man," *The Big Valley*, ABC, 1967.
"Dangerous Prey," *Custer* (also known as *The Legend of Custer*), ABC, 1967.
"The Death Wagon," *The Virginian*, NBC, 1968.
"A Girl Named George," *Bonanza*, NBC, 1968.
Melzac/Bryk, "Graveyard of Fools," *Land of the Giants*, ABC, 1970.
Vince Ryan, "The Payoff," *Hawaii Five-0*, CBS, 1970.
Sheriff, "Search in Limbo," *Bonanza*, NBC, 1971.
White Horse/Pal Morrison, "A Man to Match the Land," *The High Chaparral*, NBC, 1971.
"Three-Way Split," *The F.B.I.*, ABC, 1971.
"Ambush at Rio Lobo," *Bonanza*, NBC, 1972.
Joe Bristol, "The Waiting Room," *Night Gallery*, NBC, 1972.
"Canyon of No Return," *The F.B.I.*, ABC, 1972.
"Nine Lives," *Kung Fu*, ABC, 1973.
Joe Rudolph, "The House on Hyde Street," *The Streets of San Francisco*, ABC, 1973.
"Cry of the Night Beast," *Kung Fu*, ABC, 1974.
Sheriff Baker, "Guess Who's Coming to Town?," *The Fall Guy*, ABC, 1982.
"Legionnaires: Part 1," *St. Elsewhere*, NBC, 1982.
Jonathan Fletcher, "Diamonds 'n Dust," *The A Team*, NBC, 1983.
Buck Rayburn, "Custom K.I.T.T.," *Knight Rider*, NBC, 1983.
Johnathan J. Rush, "Love to Take You Home," *Knots Landing*, CBS, 1984.
Johnathan J. Rush, "To Sing His Praise," *Knots Landing*, CBS, 1985.
"Home of the Brave," *The Young Riders*, ABC, 1989.

Also appeared in "Noon on Doomsday," *Theatre Guild*, CBS; appeared in episodes of *Barnaby Jones*, CBS; *The Defenders*, CBS; *Destry*, ABC; *The Eleventh Hour*, syndicated; *Have Gun Will Travel*, CBS; *Jesse James*, ABC; *Rawhide*, CBS; *Route 66*, syndicated; *Shenandoah*, ABC; *Stoney Burke*, syndicated; *Trailmaster*, ABC; and *Twelve O'Clock High*, ABC.

Television Appearances; Pilots:
Raif, *Kung Fu*, ABC, 1972.

Stage Appearances:
The Scarecrow, Theatre de Lys, New York City, 1952.
Roger Gatt, *End As a Man*, Theatre de Lys, then Vanderbilt Theatre, New York City, both 1953.
Jim Curry, *The Rainmaker*, Cort Theatre, New York City, 1954.
Bo Decker, *Bus Stop*, Music Box Theatre, New York City, 1955.
Yank Sun, *The Good Woman of Setzuan*, Phoenix Theatre, New York City, 1956.
Title role, *Howie*, 46th Street Theatre, New York City, 1958.
He, *The Failures*, Fourth Street Theatre, New York City, 1959.
John Paul Jones, *Once There Was a Russian*, Music Box Theatre, 1961.
Matt Burke, *Anna Christie*, Huntington Hartford Theatre, Hollywood, CA, 1966.
Victor Franz, *The Price*, Morosco Theatre, New York City, 1968, then Duke of York's Theatre, London, England, 1969.

Major Tours:
Bo Decker, *Bus Stop*, U.S. cities, 1955.

OTHER SOURCES

Periodicals:
New York Times, April 25, 1990.*

SANCHEZ, Marco 1970-

PERSONAL

Born January 9, 1970, in Los Angeles, CA; son of Cuban immigrants. *Education:* University of California at Los Angeles School of Theatre, Film and Television, degree (theater history), 1992. *Avocational interests:* Rollerblading and baseball.

Addresses: *Agent*—Mark Scroggs, c/o Paul Kohner Inc., 9300 Wilshire Blvd., Suite 555, Beverly Hills, CA 90212. *Contact*—*Walker, Texas Ranger*, CBS Entertainment, Farmers Branch, TX 75234.

Career: Actor.

CREDITS

Television Appearances; Series:
Sensor Chief Ortiz, *SeaQuest DSV* (also known as *SeaQuest 2032*), NBC, 1993-94.
Detective Carlos Sandoval, *Walker, Texas Ranger*, CBS, 1997-99.
Carlos Sandoval, *Sons of Thunder*, CBS, 1999.

Television Appearances; Episodic:
Emelio Suarez, *In the Heat of the Night,* NBC, 1991.
Julian, "Crazy for You. . .and You," *Flying Blind,* Fox, 1992.
Sensor Chief Miguel Ortiz, *Hearts Afire,* CBS, 1993.
Sensor Chief Miguel Ortiz, *My So-Called Life,* ABC, 1994.
Cigar Boy, *First Time Out,* The WB, 1995.
Ramon, "Shoe Room with a View," *Married. . . With Children,* Fox, 1995.
Luiz Decalde, "Death Goes Double Platinum," *Murder, She Wrote,* CBS, 1996.

Television Appearances; Movies:
Collie, *Gusmoke: The Long Ride,* CBS, 1993.
Nico Vellos, *Fall Into Darkness,* NBC, 1996.
Carlos Sandoval, *Walker, Texas Ranger,* CBS, 1997.

Television Appearances; Specials:
Ben, *But He Loves Me,* CBS, 1991.
Circus of the Stars Gives Kids the World, CBS, 1993.

Other Television Appearances:
Party of Five (series), Fox, 1994.
In the Heat of the Night (series), NBC/CBS, 1998.*

SAVANT, Doug 1964-

PERSONAL

Born June 21, 1964, in Burbank, CA; married Laura Leighton (an actress). *Education:* Attended the University of California, Los Angeles.

Addresses: *Contact*—Screen Actors Guild, 5757 Wilshire Blvd., Hollywood, CA 90036.

Career: Actor.

Member: Screen Actors Guild.

CREDITS

Film Appearances:
Uncredited role, *Swing Shift,* Warner Bros., 1984.
Boy, *Secret Admirer,* Orion, 1985.
Brad, *Teen Wolf,* Atlantic Releasing, 1985.
Tim Hainey, *Trick or Treat,* De Laurentiis Entertainment Group, 1986.
Ashby, *The Hanoi Hilton,* Cannon, 1987.
Mike McGill, *Masquerade,* Metro-Goldwyn-Mayer/United Artists, 1988.
Eric Kinsley, *Paint It Black,* Vestron, 1989.
Attila, *Red Surf,* Arrowhead, 1990.
Michael, *Shaking the Tree,* Magnificent Mile Productions, 1990.
Sergeant O'Neal, *Godzilla,* Sony Pictures Entertainment, 1998.
Brooklyn Sunset, Avenue R Films, 2000.

Television Appearances; Series:
Best Times, NBC, 1985.
Mack Mackenzie, *Knots Landing,* CBS, 1986-87.
Scott LaPierre, *In the Heat of the Night,* NBC, 1988.
Matt Fielding, *Melrose Place,* Fox, 1992-97.

Television Appearances; Movies:
The Knife and Gun Club, ABC, 1990.
Jeff Colburn, *Aftermath: A Test of Love,* CBS, 1991.
Detective Dennis Mulrooney, *Columbo: No Time to Die,* ABC, 1992.
Deputy Sheriff Ted Hinton, *Bonnie and Clyde: The True Story,* Fox, 1992.
Dr. Peter Myerson, *Maniac Cop 3: Badge of Silence* (also known as *Maniac Cop 3*), HBO, 1992.
Richard Mark Ellard, *Fight for Justice: The Nancy Conn Story* (also known as *Fighting Back: The Nancy Conn Story*), NBC, 1995.
Sean O'Grady, *Terminal* (also known as *Robin Cook's Terminal*), NBC, 1996.
A Face to Kill For (also known as *Makeover*), 1999.
Grant Carlson, *First Daughter,* TNT, 1999.

Television Appearances; Specials:
A Day in the Lives of Melrose Place, Fox, 1994.
The Road to Fame on Melrose Place and 90210, Fox, 1995.

Television Appearances; Episodic:
The Best Times, NBC, 1985.
"Violation," *Cagney and Lacey,* CBS, 1985.
Joey Medwick, "Road Hog," *Alfred Hitchcock Presents,* NBC, 1986.
O'Connor, "Night Maneuvers," *Stingray,* syndicated, 1987.
"The Thanks of a Grateful Nation," *China Beach,* ABC, 1990.
Chase Cobb, "Who Killed the World's Greatest Chef?," *Burke's Law,* CBS, 1995.
Josh Walter, "Smooth Sailing," *The Love Boat: The Next Wave,* UPN, 1998.
"Inheritance," *Profiler,* NBC, 1999.

Appeared in an episode of *Hotel,* ABC.

Television Appearances; Pilots:
Scott LaPierre, *In the Heat of the Night,* NBC, 1988.

Stage Appearances:
Appeared in a community theatre production of *Hello Dolly!*

OTHER SOURCES

Periodicals:
Entertainment Weekly, May 20, 1994, p. 12.
People Weekly, October 2, 1995, p. 142.*

SAVOCA, Nancy 1959-

PERSONAL

Born in 1959, in New York, NY; married Richard Guay (a screenwriter and film producer), 1980; children: three. *Education:* Attended Queen's College, City University of New York, and New York University Film School.

Addresses: *Agent*—United Talent Agency, 9560 Wilshire Blvd., Suite 500, Beverly Hills, CA 90212.

Career: Director and screenwriter.

Awards, Honors: Haig P. Manoogian Award for overall excellence, New York University Student Film Festival, 1984; Grand Jury Prize for Drama, Sundance Film Festival, and Prize San Sebastian, San Sebastian International Film Festival, 1989, and Independent Spirit Award nomination, best director, 1990, all for *True Love;* Independent Spirit Award nomination (shared with Richard Guay), best feature, 1993, for *Household Saints.*

CREDITS

Film Work; Director:
Renata, 1982.
Bad Timing, World Northal, 1982.
True Love, Metro-Goldwyn-Mayer/United Artists, 1989.
Dogfight, Warner Bros., 1991.
Household Saints, Fine Line Features, 1993.
The 24-Hour Woman, Artisan Entertainment, 1999.
Janis, Redeemable Features, 1999.

Other Film Work:
Production assistant, *The Brother from Another Planet,* Cinecom, 1984.
Assistant auditor, *Something Wild,* Orion, 1986.
Production auditor assistant, *Married to the Mob,* Orion, 1988.

Television Work; Director:
Dark Eyes (special), ABC, 1995.
Murder One (series), ABC, 1995-1996.
Segments "1952" and "1974," *If These Walls Could Talk* (movie), HBO, 1996.

WRITINGS

Screenplays:
Renata, 1982.
Bad Timing, World Northal, 1982.
True Love, Metro-Goldwyn-Mayer/United Artists, 1989.
Household Saints, Fine Line Features, 1993.
The 24-Hour Woman, Artisan Entertainment, 1999.
Janis, Redeemable Features, 1999.

Television Movies:
"1952," "1974," and "1996," *If These Walls Could Talk,* HBO, 1996.

OTHER SOURCES

Books:
Women Filmmakers and Their Films, St. James Press (Detroit, MI), 1998.

Periodicals:
Filmmaker, volume 2, number 1, 1993.
Interview, September, 1993.
Movieline, April, 1993.
New York Times, December 28, 1997.
Popular Literature and Film, summer, 1997.
Rolling Stone, September 21, 1989.*

SCHREIBER, Liev 1967-

PERSONAL

Born October 4, 1967, in San Francisco, CA; son of Tell Schreiber (actor) and Heather. *Education:* Graduated from Yale School of Drama, 1992; trained at the Royal Academy of Dramatic Arts.

Addresses: *Contact*—International Creative Management, 8942 Wilshire Blvd., Beverly Hills, CA 90211.

Career: Actor.

Awards, Honors: Obie Award, 1999, for *Cymbeline*.

CREDITS

Film Appearances:

Chris, *Mixed Nuts* (also known as *Lifesavers*), TriStar, 1994.
Jerry Heckerman, *Denise Calls Up,* Sony Pictures Classics, 1995.
Salesman, *Mad Love,* Buena Vista, 1995.
Nigel, *Party Girl,* First Look Pictures, 1995.
Carl, *The Daytrippers,* Columbia/TriStar, 1996.
Leo, *Big Night,* Samuel Goldwyn, 1996.
Baggage (short), 1996.
Andrew, *Walking and Talking,* Miramax, 1996.
Clark Barnes, *Ransom,* Buena Vista, 1996.
Cotton Weary, *Scream,* Miramax, 1997.
Glenn, *His and Hers,* Alliance Independent, 1997.
Cotton Weary, *Scream 2,* Miramax, 1997.
Deputy Stu Wargle, *Phantoms,* Dimension Films, 1998.
Dr. Ted Fielding, *Sphere,* Warner Bros., 1998.
Jeff Willis, *Twilight,* Paramount, 1998.
Marty Kantrowitz, *A Walk on the Moon,* Miramax, 1999.
Spring Forward, 1999.
Orson Welles, *RKO 281,* HBO Pictures, 1999.
Mischa, *Jakob the Liar,* TriStar, 1999.
Laertes, *Hamlet,* Miramax, 1999.
Sam, *Lazarus and the Hurricane,* Universal, 1999.

Television Appearances; Movies:

Owens, *Janek: The Silent Betrayal* (also known as *A Silent Betrayal*), CBS, 1994.
The Sunshine Boys, CBS, 1995.
Fred Lindorhoff, *Since You've Been Gone,* ABC, 1998.

Television Appearances; Miniseries:

Ogden, *Buffalo Girls,* CBS, 1995.

Television Appearances; Specials:

Narrator, *Rock & Roll,* PBS, 1995-96.
Narrator, *Spirit of the Games,* HBO, 1996.
Narrator, *Big Dream, Small Screen,* PBS, 1997.
Narrator, *Long Shots: The Life and Times of the American Basketball Association,* HBO, 1997.
Narrator, *Sports on the Silver Screen,* HBO, 1997.
Narrator, *Surviving the Dust Bowl,* PBS, 1998.
Narrator, *Babe Ruth,* NBC, 1998.
Narrator, *City Dump: The Story of the 1951 CCNY Basketball Scandal,* HBO, 1998.
Narrator, *Meltdown at Three Mile Island,* PBS, 1999.
Narrator, *John Steinbeck: An American Writer,* Arts and Entertainment, 1999.

Also appeared in NBC pilot *People V.*

Stage Appearances:

Ivanov, Yale Repertory Theatre, New Haven, CT, 1990-91.
The Size of the World, Yale Repertory Theatre, 1990-91.
Underground, Yale Repertory Theatre, 1990-91.
Edward the Second, Yale Repertory Theatre, 1991-92.
Iago, Romeo, Ghost, *Good Night Desdemona (Good Morning Juliet),* Classic Stage Company, 1992-93.
Escape from Happiness, Center Stage, Baltimore, MD, 1992-93, then Yale Repertory Theatre, 1992-93.
Lionel, *In the Summer House,* Vivian Beaumont Theatre, Lincoln Center, New York City, 1993.
Jake, *Moonlight,* Criterion Center/Laura Pels Theatre, New York City, 1995.
Sebastian, *The Tempest,* Shakespeare in the Park Festival, New York City, 1995.
Iachimo, *Cymbeline,* Shakespeare in the Park Festival, New York City, 1998.
Banquo, *Macbeth,* Joseph Papp Public Theater, New York City, 1998.

Also appeared in off-Broadway production of *All for One;* and also in *Richard III* and *Real Thing.**

SCHWARTZMAN, John

PERSONAL

Born in Los Angeles, CA. *Education:* Completed graduate studies at the University of Southern California Film School; apprenticed with Vittorio Storarro (a cinematographer).

Career: Cinematographer. Also performed camera work for Pepsi, Coca-Cola, Cover Girl, Nike, and American Express, and for music videos by various artists, including Madonna and Paula Abdul.

CREDITS

Film Work; Cinematographer, Except Where Indicated:

Title design sequence, *RAD,* TriStar, 1986.

Camera operator (anthology segments), *Moonwalker,* 1988.

Additional special effects photography, *The Unholy,* Vestron, 1988.

You Can't Hurry Love (also known as *Greetings from L.A.* and *Lovestruck*), Lightning, 1988.

2nd camera operator, *Limit Up,* MCEG, 1989.

Additional camera operator, *Heathers* (also known as *Fatal Game, LethalAttraction,* and *Westerberg High*), New World, 1989.

Rockula, Metro-Goldwyn-Mayer Home Entertainment, 1990.

Red Surf, Arrowhead Entertainment, 1990.

Benny & Joon, Metro-Goldwyn-Mayer, 1993.

Airheads, Twentieth Century-Fox, 1994.

A Pyromaniac's Love Story (also known as *Burning Love*), Buena Vista, 1995.

The Rock, Buena Vista, 1996.

Mr. Wrong, Buena Vista, 1996.

Conspiracy Theory, Warner Bros., 1997.

Armageddon, Buena Vista, 1998.

EDtv, Universal, 1999.

Superman Lives, Warner Bros., 2000.

The Devil's Pale Moonlit Kiss, Twentieth Century-Fox, 2000.

Television Work:

Director and cinematographer, *To Save a Child,* ABC, 1991.*

SEITZ, John F. 1892-1979

PERSONAL

Born June 23, 1892, in Chicago, IL; died, February 27, 1979, in Woodland, CA; brother of George B. Seitz (a director); married Marie Boyle, 1934.

Career: Cinematographer. Worked for St. Louis Motion Picture Company as laboratory technician, 1909; joined Metro Pictures, 1916; President, American Society of Cinematographers, 1929-30. Credited with many technical innovations: invented the matte shot (pre-photographed backgrounds with action foregrounds); held eighteen patents on photographic inventions; retired, 1960.

Awards, Honors: Academy Award nomination, best cinematography, 1930, for *The Divine Lady;* Academy Award nomination, best cinematography—black-and-white, 1943, for *Five Graves to Cairo;* Academy Award nomination, best cinematography—black-and-white, 1945, for *Double Indemnity;* Academy Award nomination, best cinematography—black-and-white, 1946, for *The Lost Weekend;* Academy Award nomination, best cinematography—black-and-white, 1950, for *Sunset Boulevard;* Academy Award nomination (shared with W. Howard Greene), best cinematography—color, 1951, for *When Worlds Collide;* Academy Award nomination, best cinematography—black-and-white, 1954, for *Rogue Cop.*

CREDITS

Film Work; Director of Photography:

Ranger of Lonesome Gulf, 1913.

The Quagmire, 1913.

Edged Tools, 1915.

Souls in Pawns, 1917.

Whose Wife?, 1917.

Beauty and the Rogue, Mutual Film Corporation, 1918.

Powers That Prey, Mutual Film Corporation, 1919.

Hearts Are Trumps, Metro Pictures Corporation, 1920.

Shores Acres, Metro Pictures Corporation, 1920.

The Four Horsemen of the Apocalypse, Stokey Video, 1921.

Uncharted Seas, Metro Pictures Corporation, 1921.

The Conquering Power, Metro Pictures Corporation, 1921.

Trifling Women, Metro Pictures Corporation, 1922.

The Prisoner of Zenda, Metro Pictures Corporation, 1922.

Turn to the Right, Metro Pictures Corporation, 1922.

Where the Pavement Ends, Metro Pictures Corporation, 1923.

Scaramouche, Metro Pictures Corporation, 1923.

The Arab, Metro Pictures Corporation, 1924.

The Price of a Party, Associated Exhibitors, 1924.

Classmates, First National Pictures, 1924.

Mare Nostrum, Metro-Goldwyn-Mayer, 1926.

The Magician, Metro-Goldwyn-Mayer, 1926.

The Fair Co-Ed, Metro-Goldwyn-Mayer, 1927.

The Patsy (also known as *The Politic Flapper*), Metro-Goldwyn-Mayer, 1928.

Across to Singapore, Metro-Goldwyn-Mayer, 1928.

Outcast, First National Pictures, 1928.

Adoration, First National Pictures, 1928.

Saturday's Children, First National Pictures, 1929.

Her Private Life, First National Pictures, 1929.

The Divine Lady, First National Pictures, 1929.

The Trail of '98, Metro-Goldwyn-Mayer, 1929.
The Squall, First National Pictures, 1929.
Careers, First National Pictures, 1929.
Hard to Get, First National Pictures, 1929.
A Most Immoral Lady, First National Pictures, 1929.
The Painted Angel (also known as *The Broadway Hostess*), Warner Bros., 1929.
Back Pay, Warner Bros., 1930.
In the Next Room, First National Pictures, 1930.
Murder Will Out, First National Pictures, 1930.
Sweethearts and Wives, First National Pictures, 1930.
Road to Paradise, Warner Bros./First National Pictures, 1930.
The Bad Man, First National Pictures, 1930.
Kismet, First National Pictures, 1930.
Young Sinners, Fox Film Corporation, 1931.
Over the Hill, Fox Film Corporation, 1931.
Misbehaving Ladies, Warner Bros., 1931.
Merely Mary Ann, Fox Film Corporation, 1931.
Men of the Sky, Warner Bros., 1931.
Hush Money, Fox Film Corporation, 1931.
East Lynne, Fox Film Corporation, 1931.
The Right of Way, Warner Bros./First National Pictures, 1931.
The Age for Love, United Artists, 1931.
The Woman in Room 13, Fox Film Corporation, 1932.
Six Hours to Live, Fox Film Corporation, 1932.
A Passport to Hell, Fox Film Corporation, 1932.
Careless Lady, Fox Film Corporation, 1932.
She Wanted a Millionaire, Fox Film Corporation, 1932.
Paddy the Next Best Thing, Fox Film Corporation, 1933.
Mr. Skitch, Fox Film Corporation, 1933.
Ladies They Talked About (also known as *Women in Prison*), Warner Bros., 1933.
Dangerously Yours, Fox Film Corporation, 1933.
Adorable, Fox Film Corporation, 1933.
Springtime for Henry, Fox Film Corporation, 1934.
Coming-Out Party, Fox Film Corporation, 1934.
Carnival in Paris, Metro-Goldwyn-Mayer, 1934.
All Men Are Enemies, Fox Film Corporation, 1934.
Marie Galante, Fox Film Corporation, 1934.
Our Little Girl, Twentieth Century-Fox, 1935.
One More Spring, Fox Film Corporation, 1935.
Navy Wife (also known as *Beauty's Daughter*), Twentieth Century-Fox, 1935.
The Littlest Rebel, Twentieth Century-Fox 1935.
Helldorado, Fox Film Corporation, 1935.
The Farmer Takes a Wife, Fox Film Corporation, 1935.
Curly Top, Twentieth Century-Fox, 1935.
Poor Little Rich Girl, Twentieth Century-Fox, 1936.
Fifteen Maiden Lane (also known as *15 Maiden Lane*), Twentieth Century-Fox, 1936.
The Country Doctor, Twentieth Century-Fox, 1936.
Captain January, Twentieth Century-Fox, 1936.
Navy Blue and Gold, Metro-Goldwyn-Mayer, 1937.
Between Two Women (also known as *Surrounded by Women*), Metro-Goldwyn-Mayer, 1937.
Madame X, Metro-Goldwyn-Mayer, 1937.
Young Dr. Kildare, Metro-Goldwyn-Mayer, 1938.
Stablemates, Metro-Goldwyn-Mayer, 1938.
Love is a Headache, Metro-Goldwyn-Mayer, 1938.
Lord Jeff (also known as *The Boy from Barnardo's*), Loew's, Inc., 1938.
The Crowd Roars, Metro-Goldwyn-Mayer, 1938.
Thunder Afloat, Metro-Goldwyn-Mayer, 1939.
Sergeant Madden, Metro-Goldwyn-Mayer, 1939.
Prophet Without Honor, Metro-Goldwyn-Mayer, 1939.
The Hardy's Ride High, Metro-Goldwyn-Mayer, 1939.
Bad Little Angel, Metro-Goldwyn-Mayer, 1939.
6000 Enemies (also known as *Six Thousand Enemies*), Metro-Goldwyn-Mayer, 1939.
Adventures of Huckleberry Finn (also known as *Huckleberry Finn*), Metro-Goldwyn-Mayer, 1939.
A Little Bit of Heaven, Universal, 1940.
Dr. Kildare's A Strange Case, Metro-Goldwyn-Mayer, 1940.
Dr. Kildare's Crisis, Metro-Goldwyn-Mayer, 1940.
Sullivan's Travels, Paramount, 1941.
The Moon and Sixpence, Favorite Films Corporation, 1942.
Lucky Jordan, Paramount, 1942.
Fly by Night (also known as *Secrets of G32*), Paramount, 1942.
This Gun for Hire, Paramount, 1942.
Five Graves to Cairo, Paramount, 1942.
The Miracle of Morgan's Creek, Paramount, 1944.
The Hour Before Dawn, Paramount, 1944.
Casanova Brown, Independent Releasing Corporation, 1944.
Hail to Conquering Hero, Paramount, 1944.
Double Indemnity, Paramount, 1944.
The Unseen, Paramount, 1945.
The Lost Weekend, Paramount, 1945.
The Well-Groomed Bride, Paramount, 1946.
Home, Sweet Homicide, Twentieth Century-Fox, 1946.
Wild Harvest, Paramount, 1947.
The Imperfect Lady (also known as *Mrs. Loring's Secrets*), Paramount, 1947.
Calcutta, Paramount, 1947.
Night Has a Thousand Eyes, Paramount, 1948.
Beyond Glory, Paramount, 1948.
On Our Merry Way (also known as *A Miracle Can Happen*), United Artists, 1948.
Saigon, Paramount, 1948.

The Great Gatsby, Paramount, 1949.
Chicago Deadline, Paramount, 1949.
The Goldbergs (also known as *Molly*), Paramount, 1950.
Captain Carey, U.S.A. (also known as *After Midnight*), Paramount, 1950.
Sunset Boulevard, Paramount, 1950.
When Worlds Collide, Paramount, 1951.
Dear Brat, Paramount, 1951.
Appointment With Danger, Paramount, 1951.
The Savage, Paramount, 1952.
The San Francisco Story, Warner Bros., 1952.
The Iron Mistress, Warner Bros., 1952.
Botany Bay, Paramount, 1953.
Desert Legion, Universal, 1953.
Invaders from Mars, Fox, 1953.
Many Rivers to Cross, Metro-Goldwyn-Mayer, 1954.
Rogue Cop, Metro-Goldwyn-Mayer, 1954.
Saskatchewan (also known as *O'Rourke of the Royal Mounted*), Universal, 1954.
The McConnell Story (also known as *The Tiger in the Sky*), Warner Bros., 1955.
A Cry in the Night, Warner Bro., 1956.
Hell on Frisco Bay, Warner Bros., 1956.
Santiago (also known as *The Gun Runner*), Warner Bros., 1956.
The Big Land (also known as *Stampeded*), Warner Bros., 1957.
The Deep Six, Warner Bros., 1957.
The Badlanders, Metro-Goldwyn-Mayer, 1958.
Island of Lost Women, Warner Bros., 1959.
The Man in the Net, United Artists, 1959.
Guns of the Timberland, Warner Bros., 1960.

OTHER SOURCES

Books:

International Dictionary of Film and Filmmakers-4, Writers and Production Artists, St. James Press (Detroit, MI), 1993.

Periodicals:

Film Comment, summer, 1972.
Films in Review, October, 1967.
Focus on Film, no. 13, 1973.*

SENNETT, Mack 1880-1960

PERSONAL

Real name, Mikall Sinnott; born, January 17, 1880, in Richmond, Eastern Townships, Quebec, Canada; immigrated to United States, 1897; died November 5, 1960, in Woodland Hills, CA; son of Irish immigrants.

Career: Actor, director, producer, and writer. Worked as a laborer at American Iron Works; acted in Biograph films, 1908-11; founded Keystone Studios, 1912; formed Triangle Films (with Thomas Ince and D.W. Griffith), 1915; founded Mack Sennett Comedies, 1917; directed stars such as Mary Pickford, Mabel Normand, "Fatty" Arbuckle, Chester Conklin, Slim Summervile, Minta Duffe, Charles Chaplin, Bobby Vernon, Gloria Swanson, and Harry Langdon.

Awards, Honors: Academy Award, best short subjects, novelty, 1933, for *Wrestling Swordfish;* Academy Award nomination, best short subjects, comedy, 1933, for *The Loud Mouth;* Honorary Academy Award, 1937, for a lasting contribution to the comedy technique of the screen.

CREDITS

Film Appearances:

Bartender, *Over the Hill to the Poorhouse,* Biograph, 1908.
Charity worker, *Old Isaacs, the Pawnbroker,* Biograph, 1908.
Soldier, *The Kings Messenger,* Biograph, 1908.
Theatre bouncer, *Thompson's Night Out,* Biograph, 1908.
Mover, *The Invisible Fluid,* Biograph, 1908.
Gang member, *The Man in the Box,* Biograph, 1908.
The Kentuckian, Biograph, 1908.
Man in bar, *The Stage Rustler,* Biograph, 1908.
Rescuer, *The Black Viper,* Biograph, 1908.
Balked at the Alter, Biograph, 1908.
Monday Morning in a Coney Island Police Court, Biograph, 1908.
The Red Girl, Biograph, 1908.
Where the Breakers Roar, Biograph, 1908.
A Smoked Husband, Biograph, 1908.
The Zula's Heart, Biograph, 1908.
Father Gets in the Game, Biograph, 1908.
The Vaquero's Crow, Biograph, 1908.
Romance of a Jewess, Biograph, 1908.
The Call of the Wild, Biograph, 1908.
Concealing a Burglar, Biograph, 1908.
The Guerilla, Biograph, 1908.
The Song of the Shirt, Biograph, 1908.
The Clubman and the Tramp, Biograph, 1908.
Money Mad, Biograph, 1908.
The Valet's Wife, Biograph, 1908.
Mrs. Jones Entertains, Biograph, 1908.

The Feud and the Turkey, Biograph, 1908.
The Reckoning, Biograph, 1908.
The Test of Friendship, Biograph, 1908.
An Awful Moment, Biograph, 1908.
The Christmas Burglars, Biograph, 1908.
Mr. Jones at the Ball, Biograph, 1908.
The Helping Hand, Biograph, 1908.
The Maniac Cook, Biograph, 1909.
Love Finds a Way, Biograph, 1909.
The Honor of Thieves, Biograph, 1909.
The Sacrifice, Biograph, 1909.
A Rural Elopement, Biograph, 1909.
The Criminal Hypnotist, Biograph, 1909.
Mr. Jones Has a Card Party, Biograph, 1909.
The Fascinating Mrs. Francis, Biograph, 1909.
The Welcome Burglar, Biograph, 1909.
Those Awful Hats, Biograph, 1909.
The Cord of Life, Biograph, 1909.
The Girls and Daddy, Biograph, 1909.
A Wreath in Time, Biograph, 1909.
Tragic Love, Biograph, 1909.
The Curtain Pole, Biograph, 1909.
The Joneses Have Amateur Theatricals, Biograph, 1909.
The Politician's Love Story, Biograph, 1909.
The Golden Louis, Biograph, 1909.
At the Alter, Biograph, 1909.
The Prussian Spy, Biograph, 1909.
His Wife's Mother, Biograph, 1909.
A Fool's Revenge, Biograph, 1909.
The Salvation Army Lass, Biograph, 1909.
The Lure of the Gown, Biograph, 1909.
The Voice of the Violin, Biograph, 1909.
The Deception, Biograph, 1909.
A Burglar's Mistake, Biograph, 1909.
Jones and His New Neighbors, Biograph, 1909.
A Drunkard's Reformation, Biograph, 1909.
Trying to Get Arrested, Biograph, 1909.
The Road to the Heart, Biograph, 1909.
Schneider's Anti-Noise Crusade, Biograph, 1909.
A Rude Hostess, Biograph, 1909.
A Sound Sleeper, Biograph, 1909.
A Trouble-Some Satchel, Biograph, 1909.
Lady Helen's Escapade, Biograph, 1909.
Twin Brothers, Biograph, 1909.
Lucky Jim, Biograph, 1909.
Tis an Ill Wind That Blows No Good, Biograph, 1909.
The Suicide Club, Biograph, 1909.
One Busy Hour, Biograph, 1909.
The Note in The Shoe, Biograph, 1909.
The French Duel, Biograph, 1909.
A Baby's Shoe, Biograph, 1909.
The Jilt, Biograph, 1909.
Resurrection, Biograph, 1909.
Jones and the Lady Book Agent, Biograph, 1909.
Two Memories, Biograph, 1909.
Eloping with Auntie, Biograph, 1909.
The Cricket on the Hearth, Biograph, 1909.
What Drink Did, Biograph, 1909.
The Violin Maker of Cremona, Biograph, 1909.
A New Trick, Biograph, 1909.
The Lonely Villa, Biograph, 1909.
The Son's Return, Biograph, 1909.
Her First Biscuits, Biograph, 1909.
Was Justice Served?, Biograph, 1909.
The Way of Men, Biograph, 1909.
The Necklace, Biograph, 1909.
The Cardinal's Conspiracy, Biograph, 1909.
A Convict's Sacrifice, Biograph, 1909.
The Slave, Biograph, 1909.
A Strange Meeting, Biograph, 1909.
The Mending Lute, Biograph, 1909.
They Would Elope, Biograph, 1909.
Mr. Jones' Burglar, Biograph, 1909.
The Better Way, Biograph, 1909.
With Her Card, Biograph, 1909.
Mrs. Jones' Lover, Biograph, 1909.
His Wife's Visitor, Biograph, 1909.
The Seventh Day, Biograph, 1909.
Oh, Uncle!, Biograph, 1909.
The Mills of the Gods, Biograph, 1909.
The Little Darling, Biograph, 1909.
Leather Stockings, Biograph, 1909.
The Hessian Renegades (also known as *1776*), Biograph, 1909.
Getting Even, Biograph, 1909.
The Broken Locket, Biograph, 1909.
In Old Kentucky, Biograph, 1909.
A Fair Exchange, Biograph, 1909.
The Awakening, Biograph, 1909.
Pippa Passes (also known as *The Song of Conscience*), Biograph, 1909.
The Little Teacher, Biograph, 1909.
His Lost Love, Biograph, 1909.
The Expiation, Biograph, 1909.
What's Your Hurry?, Biograph, 1909.
The Gibson Goddess, Biograph, 1909.
Nursing a Viper, Biograph, 1909.
The Light That Came, Biograph, 1909.
Two Women and a Man, Biograph, 1909.
A Midnight Adventure, Biograph, 1909.
The Mountaineer's Honor, Biograph, 1909.
In the Watches of the Night, Biograph, 1909.
The Trick That Failed, Biograph, 1909.
In the Window Recess, Biograph, 1909.
The Death Disc, Biograph, 1909.
A Corner in Wheat, Biograph, 1909.
In a Hempen Bag, Biograph, 1909.

A Trap for Santa Clause, Biograph, 1909.
To Save Her Soul, Biograph, 1909.
Choosing a Husband, Biograph, 1909.
The Dancing Girl of Butte, Biograph, 1910.
The Call, Biograph, 1910.
The Cloister's Touch, Biograph, 1910.
The Woman From Mellon's, Biograph, 1910.
One Night and Then, Biograph, 1910.
The Englishman and the Girl, Biograph, 1910.
Taming a Husband, Biograph, 1910.
The Newlyweds, Biograph, 1910.
In Old California, Biograph, 1910.
The Converts, Biograph, 1910.
Faithful, Biograph, 1910.
The Twisted Tale, Biograph, 1910.
Gold Is Not All, Biograph, 1910.
As It Is in Life, Biograph, 1910.
A Rich Revenge, Biograph, 1910.
The Way of the World, Biograph, 1910.
The Two Brothers, Biograph, 1910.
Love Among Roses, Biograph, 1910.
Over Silent Paths, Biograph, 1910.
An Affair of Hearts, Biograph, 1910.
A Knot in the Plot, Biograph, 1910.
A Victim of Jealousy, Biograph, 1910.
The Marked Time-Table, Biograph, 1910.
Never Again, Biograph, 1910.
The Purgation, Biograph, 1910.
A Midnight Cupid, Biograph, 1910.
What the Daisy Said, Biograph, 1910.
A Child's Faith, Biograph, 1910.
A Flash of Light, Biograph, 1910.
Serious Sixteen, Biograph, 1910.
As the Bells Rang Out!, Biograph, 1910.
The Call to Arms, Biograph, 1910.
An Arcadian Maid, Biograph, 1910.
A Salutary Lesson, Biograph, 1910.
The Usher, Biograph, 1910.
When We Were in Our Teens, Biograph, 1910.
The Modern Prodigal, Biograph, 1910.
Muggsy Becomes a Hero, Biograph, 1910.
Little Angels of Luck, Biograph, 1910.
A Mohawk's Way, Biograph, 1910.
A Summer Tragedy, Biograph, 1910.
Examination Day at School, Biograph, 1910.
The Iconoclast, Biograph, 1910.
A Gold Necklace, Biograph, 1910.
The Broken Doll, Biograph, 1910.
The Song of the Wildwood Flute, Biograph, 1910.
Not So Bad as It Seemed, Biograph, 1910.
The Manicure Lady, Biograph, 1911.
Dutch Gold Mine, Biograph, 1911.
Comrades, Biograph, 1911.
Caught with the Goods, Biograph, 1911.
After the Bell, Biograph, 1911.
The Italian Barber, Biograph, 1911.
His Trust, Biograph, 1911.
His Trust Fulfilled, Biograph, 1911.
Three Sisters, Biograph, 1911.
His Daughters, Biograph, 1911.
A Decree of Destiny, Biograph, 1911.
Lost Paradise, 1911.
The New Dress, Biograph, 1911.
The White Rose of the Wilds, Biograph, 1911.
Through His Wife's Picture, Biograph, 1911.
Mack, *The Water Nymph,* Keystone, 1912.
The Fatal Chocolate, Biograph, 1912.
A Spanish Dilemma, Biograph, 1912.
Hot Stuff, Biograph, 1912.
The Brave Hunter, Biograph, 1912.
The Furs, Biograph, 1912.
Helen's Marriage, Biograph, 1912.
Tomboy Bessie, Biograph, 1912.
Man's Genesis, Biograph, 1912.
What the Doctor Ordered, Biograph, 1912.
Stolen Glory, Keystone, 1912.
Pedro's Dilemma, Keystone, 1912.
Ambitious Butler, Keystone, 1912.
At Coney Island (also known as *Cohen at Coney Island*), Keystone, 1912.
At It Again, Keystone, 1912.
The Rivals, Keystone, 1912.
Mr. Fix-It (also known as *Mr. Fixer*), Keystone, 1912.
A Bear Escapes, Keystone, 1912.
Pat's Day Off, Keystone, 1912.
The New York Hat, Biograph, 1912.
A Family Mixup, Keystone, 1912.
The Duel, Keystone, 1912.
His Crooked Career, Keystone, 1912.
Mabel's Awful Mistakes (also known as *Her Deceitful Lover*), Keystone, 1913.
The Mistaken Masher, Keystone, 1913.
The Battle of Who Run, Keystone, 1913.
Mabel's Heroes, Keystone, 1913.
The Sleuths at the Floral Parade, Keystone, 1913.
A Strong Revenge, Keystone, 1913.
The Rube and the Baron, Keystone, 1913.
At Twelve O'Clock, Keystone, 1913.
Her New Beau, Keystone, 1913.
Barney Oldfield's Race for a Life, Keystone, 1913.
The Hansom Driver, Keystone, 1913.
Peeping Pete, Mutual Film Corporation, 1913.
Mabel's Dramatic Career (also known as *Her Dramatic Debut*), Mutual Film Corporation, 1913.
Love Sickness at Sea, Keystone, 1913.
Man in Audience/Spectator, *The Property Man* (also known as *Getting His Goat, The Roustabout,* and *Vamping Venus*), Keystone, 1914.

Mabel's Busy Day (also known as *Charlie and the Sausages, Hot Dogs,* and *Love and Lunch*), Keystone, 1914.

Reporter, *Mabel at the Wheel* (also known as *His Daredevil Queen* and *Hot Finish*), Keystone, 1914.

His Talented Wife, Keystone, 1914.

Rival suitor, *The Fatal Mallet* (also known as *Hit Him Again, The Pile Driver,* and *The Rival Suitor*), Keystone, 1914.

Back at It Again, Keystone, 1914.

Himself, *A Film Johnnie* (also known as *Charlie at the Studio, Million Dollar Job, Movie Nut*), Mutual Film Corporation, 1914.

Spectator, *The Knockout* (also known as *Counted Out* and *The Pugilist*), Mutual Film Corporation, 1914.

The Little Teacher (also known as *A Small Town Bully*), Keystone, 1915.

Hearts and Planets, Keystone, 1915.

Fatty and the Broadway Stars, Triangle Film Productions, 1915.

His valet, *My Valet,* Triangle Film Corporation, 1915.

The Judge, Keystone, 1916.

Blaa Blaa, *Oh, Mabel Behave,* Photocraft Productions, 1922.

The Hollywood Kid, Pathe, 1924.

Flickering Youth, Pathe, 1924.

Himself, *Movie Town,* Twentieth Century-Fox, 1931.

Himself, *Hollywood Cavalcade,* Twentieth Century-Fox, 1939.

Himself, *Hedda Hopper's Hollywood No. 6,* Paramount, 1942.

Himself, *Abbot and Costello Meet the Keystone Kops,* Universal, 1955.

Film Work; Producer:

The Water Nymph, Keystone, 1912.

Ambitious Butler, Keystone, 1912.

At Coney Island (also known as *Cohen at Coney Island*), Keystone, 1912.

At It Again, Keystone, 1912.

Mr. Fix-It (also known as *Mr. Fixer*), Keystone, 1912.

A Bear Escape, Keystone, 1912.

Hoffmeyer's Legacy, 1912.

Mabel's Awful Mistakes (also known as *Her Deceitful Lover*), Keystone, 1913.

His Crooked Career, Keystone, 1913.

Cohen's Outing, Keystone, 1913.

The Mistaken Masher, Keystone, 1913.

The Battle of Who Run, Keystone, 1913.

Mabel's Heroes, Keystone, 1913.

Her New Beau, Keystone, 1913.

Barney Oldfield's Race for a Life, Keystone, 1913.

Mabel's Dramatic Career (also known as *Her Dramatic Debut*), Mutual Film Corporation, 1913.

Love Sickness at Sea, Keystone, 1913.

Cohen Saves the Flag, Keystone, 1913.

Twenty Minutes of Love (also known as *Cops and Watchers, He Loves Her So,* and *Love-Friend*), Keystone, 1914.

Those Love Pangs (also known as *Busted Hearts, Oh, You Girls,* and *The Rival Mashers*), Keystone, 1914.

The Star Boarder (also known as *The Fatal Lantern, The Hash-House Hero, In Love With His Landlady,* and *The Landlady's Pet*), Keystone, 1914.

The Rounders (also known as *Going Down, The Love Thief, Oh, What a Night, Revelry, Tip, Tap, Toe,* and *Two of a Kind*), Keystone, 1914.

Recreation (also known as *Spring Fever*), Keystone, 1914.

The Property Man (also known as *Charlie on the Boards, Getting His Goat, Props, The Rustabout,* and *Vamping Venus*), Keystone, 1914.

The Noise of Bombs, Keystone, 1914.

The Masquerader (*The Female Impersonator, The Female, The Perfume Lady, The Picnic,* and *Putting One Over*), Keystone, 1914.

Mabel's Strange Predicament (also known as *Hotel Mixup*), Keystone, 1914.

Mabel's Married Life (also known as *The Squarehead* and *When You're Married*), Keystone, 1914.

Mabel's Busy Day (also known as *Charlie and the Sausages, Hot Dog Charlie, Hot Dogs,* and *Love and Lunch*), Keystone, 1914.

Mabel at the Wheel (also known as *His Daredevil Queen* and *A Hot Finish*), Keystone, 1914.

Laughing Gas (also known as *Busy Little Dentist, The Dentist, Down and Out, Laffing Gas,* and *Tuning His Ivories*), Keystone, 1914.

Kid Auto Races at Venice (also known as *The Children's Automobile Race, Kid's Auto Race,* and *The Pest*), Keystone, 1914.

His Trysting Place (also known as *Family Home, Family House, The Henpecked Spouse, The Ladies' Man,* and *Very Much Married*), Keystone, 1914.

His Talented Wife, Keystone, 1914.

His New Profession (also known as *The Good for Nothing* and *Helping Himself*), Keystone, 1914.

His Musical Career (also known as *Charlie as a Piano Mover, Musical Tramps,* and *The Piano Movers*), Keystone, 1914.

Her Friend the Bandit (also known as *Mabel's Flirtation* and *A Thief Catcher*), Keystone, 1914.

Getting Acquainted (also known as *Exchange Is No Robbery, A Fair Exchange,* and *Hello Everybody*), Keystone, 1914.

Gentlemen of Nerve (also known as *Charlie at the Races* and *Some Nerve*), Keystone, 1914.
The Fatal Mallet (also known as *Hit Him Again, The Pile Driver,* and *The Rival Suitors*), Keystone, 1914.
The Face on the Bar Room Floor (also known as *The Ham Actor* and *The Ham Artist*), Keystone, 1914.
Cruel, Cruel Love (also known as *Lord Helpus*), Keystone, 1914.
Caught in the Rain (also known as *At It Again* and *Who Got Stung?*), Keystone, 1914.
Caught in a Cabaret (also known as *Charlie the Waiter, Faking with Society, Jazz Waiter, Prime Minister Charlie,* and *The Waiter*), Keystone, 1914.
A Busy Day (also known as *Busy as Can Be, Lady Charlie,* and *Militant Suffragette*), Keystone, 1914.
Between Showers (also known as *Charlie and the Umbrella, The Flirts,* and *In Wrong Thunder and Lightening*), Keystone, 1914.
Back At It Again, Keystone, 1914.
Making a Living (also known as *A Busted Johnny, Doing His Best,* and *Troubles*), Keystone, 1914.
A Film Johnny (also known as *Charlie at the Studio, Million Dollar Job, Take My Picture,* and *Movie Nut*), Mutual Film Corporation, 1914.
Tango Tangles (also known as *Charlie's Recreation* and *Music Hall*), Mutual Film Corporation, 1914.
His Favorite Pastime (also known as *The Bonehead, Charlie's Reckless Fling,* and *The Reckless Fling*), Mutual Film Corporation, 1914.
The Knockout (also known as *Counted Out* and *The Pugilist*), Mutual Film Corporation, 1914.
The New Janitor (also known as *The Blundering Boob, The New Porter,* and *The Porter*), Keystone, 1914.
Dough and Dynamite (also known as *The Cook, The Doughnut Designer,* and *The New Cook*), Keystone, 1914.
An Incompetent Hero, Mutual Film Corporation, 1914.
Fatty's Jonah Day, Mutual Film Corporation, 1914.
Fatty's Wine Party, Mutual Film Corporation, 1914.
His Prehistoric Past (also known as *The Caveman, A Dream, The Hula-Hula Dance,* and *King Charlie*), Keystone, 1914.
Fatty's Magic Pants (also known as *Fatty's Suitless Day*), Mutual Film Corporation, 1914.
Tillie's Punctured Romance (also known as *For the Love of Tillie, Marie's Millions, Tillie's Big Romance,* and *Tillie's Nightmare*), Keystone, 1914.
Fatty and Minnie He-Haw, Mutual Film Corporation, 1914.
Mabel and Fatty's Wash Day, Mutual Film Corporation, 1915.
Mabel and Fatty's Simple Life, Keystone, 1915.
Mabel and Fatty Viewing the World's Fair at San Francisco, Keystone, 1915.
Love, Speed and Thrills, Keystone, 1915.
The Little Teacher, Keystone, 1915.
Hearts and Planets, Keystone, 1915.
A Game Old Knight, Keystone, 1915.
Fatty's Tintype Tangle (also known as *Frido's Tintype Tangle*), Keystone, 1915.
Fatty's Reckless Fling, Keystone, 1915.
Fatty's Plucky Pup (also known as *Foiled by Fido*), Keystone, 1915.
Fatty's New Role, Keystone, 1915.
Fatty's Faithful Fido, Keystone, 1915.
Fatty's Chance Acquaintance, Keystone, 1915.
Fatty and Mabel's Married Life, Keystone, 1915.
Colored Villainy, Keystone, 1915.
Ambrose's Sour Grapes, Mutual Film Corporation, 1915.
Miss Fatty's Seaside Lovers, Keystone, 1915.
Her Painted Hero, Triangle-Keystone/Sennett, 1915.
My Valet, Triangle, 1915.
The Waiters' Ball, 1916.
His Bread and Butter, Triangle, 1916.
Her First Beau, Triangle, 1916.
Fatty and Mabel Adrift, Triangle, 1916.
Ambrose's Rapid Rise, Triangle-Keystone, 1916.
The Judge, Keystone, 1916.
Her Nature Dance, Triangle-Keystone, 1917.
A Dog Catcher's Love, Triangle, 1917.
A Clever Dummy, 1917.
A Bedroom Blunder (also known as *Room 23*), Keystone, 1917.
Secrets of a Beauty Parlor, Hamilton Film Corporation, 1917.
She Loved Him Plenty, Paramount, 1918.
Mickey, States Rights/W.H. Production Comp., 1918.
His Smothered Love, Paramount, 1918.
Saucy Love, Paramount, 1918.
The Little Widow, 1919.
East Lynne with Variations, Paramount, 1919.
Cupid's Day Off, 1919.
Foxy Ambrose, Paramount, 1919.
Uncle Tom Without a Cabin (also known as *Uncle Tom's Cabin*), Mack Sennett Studios, 1919.
Married Life, First National Pictures, 1920.
Don't Weaken, 1920.
Down on the Farm, United Artists, 1920.
Molly O', Associated First National Pictures, 1921.
Call a Cop, 1921.
Bungalow Troubles, Paramount, 1921.
Bright Eyes, Associated First National Pictures, 1921.
She Sighed by the Seaside, Mack Sennett Studios, 1921.

Home Talent, Mack Sennett Studios, 1921.
Made in the Kitchen, Paramount, 1921.
Astray From the Steerage, Paramount, 1921.
Hard Knocks and Love Taps, First National Pictures, 1921.
When Summer Comes, 1922.
On Patrol, 1922.
Ma and Pa, 1922.
Gymnasium Jim, 1922.
The Duck Hunter, 1922.
The Crossroads of New York, Associated First National Pictures, 1922.
Skylarking, Mack Sennett Comedies, 1923.
Pitfalls of a Big City, Pathe, 1923.
Nip and Tuck, 1923.
The Shriek of Araby, United Artists, 1923.
Yukon Jake, Pathe, 1924.
Wandering Waistlines, 1924.
Wall Street Blues, RKO Radio Pictures, 1924.
Three Foolish Weeks, 1924.
Should Husbands Marry?, Pathe, 1924.
One Spooky Night, 1924.
The Luck of the Foolish, Pathe, 1924.
Lizzies of the Field, 1924.
The Hollywood Kid, Pathe, 1924.
His New Mama, Pathe, 1924.
The Hansom Cabman (also known as *Be Careful*), Pathe, 1924.
Galloping Bungalows, Pathe, 1924.
Flickering Youth, Pathe, 1924.
The First 100 Years, Pathe, 1924.
The Cat's Meow, Pathe, 1924.
The Cannon Ball Express, 1924.
Black Oxfords, Pathe, 1924.
Butter Fingers, 1925.
Cold Turkey, 1925.
From Rags to Britches, 1925.
Giddap, 1925.
His Marriage Wow, Pathe, 1925.
Hotsy-Totsy, Pathe, 1925.
The Iron Nag, 1925.
The Lion's Whiskers, 1925.
Lucky Stars, Pathe, 1925.
Over There-Abouts, 1925.
The Plumber's Daughter, Pathe, 1925.
Sneezers Breezers, 1925.
Trimmed in Gold, 1925.
Whispering Whiskers, 1925.
Wild Goose Chaser, Pathe, 1925.
The Divorce Dodger, 1926.
Gooseland, Pathe, 1926.
A Harem Knight, Pathe, 1926.
Hoboken to Hollywood, 1926.
Hubby's Quiet Little Game, 1926.
Kitty from Killarney, Pathe, 1926.
Masked Mamas, 1926.
Muscle Bound Music, 1926.
Wandering Willies, 1926.
The Girl from Everywhere (also known as *Hold That Pose*), Pathe, 1927.
His First Flame, Pathe, 1927.
The Bull Fighter, Pathe, 1927.
Cured in the Excitement, 1927.
Gold Digger of Weepah, 1927.
The Golf Nut, 1927.
Peaches and Plumbers, 1927.
Should Sleepwalkers Marry?, 1927.
A Small Town Princess, 1927.
His New Steno (also known as *His New Stenographer*), 1928.
Hubby's Latest Alibi, 1928.
Hubby's Weekend Trip, 1928.
The Lion's Roar, 1928.
Love at First Sight, Pathe, 1928.
Motorboat Mamas, 1928.
Motoring Mamas, 1928.
The Campus Carmen, Pathe, 1928.
The Campus Vamp, Pathe, 1928.
Run, Girl, Run, Pathe, 1928.
Pink Pajamas, 1929.
Foolish Husbands, 1929.
The Big Palooka, Educational Pictures, 1929.
The Bee's Buzz, Educational Pictures, 1929.
Button My Back, 1929.
Calling Hubby's Bluff, 1929.
Don't Get Jealous, 1929.
Sugar Plum Papa, Educational Pictures, 1930.
Bulls and Bears, Educational Pictures, 1930.
Midnight Daddies (also known as *The New Bankroll*), Sono Art-World Pictures, 1930.
I Surrender Dear, Atlantic Pictures, 1931.
The Dog Doctor, Educational Pictures, 1931.
Cow-Catcher's Daughter, Educational Pictures, 1931.
The Cannonball, Educational Pictures, 1931.
Taxi Troubles, Educational Pictures, 1931.
Wrestling Swordfish, 1931.
The Loud Mouth, Paramount, 1932.
Billboard Girl, Atlantic Pictures, 1932.
The Dentist, Paramount, 1932.
Sing, Bing, Sing, Atlantic Pictures, 1933.
Blue of Night, Paramount, 1933.
Singing Boxer, Paramount, 1933.
The Fatal Glass of Beer, Paramount, 1933.
The Pharmacist (also known as *The Druggist*), 1933.
The Barber Shop, Paramount, 1933.

Film Work; Director:
Effecting a Cure, 1910.

The Manicure Lady, Biograph, 1911.
Dutch Gold Mine, Biograph, 1911.
Comrades, Biograph, 1911.
Caught with the Goods, Biograph, 1911.
The Diving Girl, Biograph, 1911.
The Baron, Biograph, 1911.
Through His Wife's Picture, Biograph, 1911.
A Victim of Circumstance, Biograph, 1911.
Why He Gave Up, Biograph, 1911.
The Water Nymph, Keystone, 1912.
When the Fire Bell Rang, Biograph, 1912.
The Fatal Chocolate, Biograph, 1912.
A Spanish Dilemma, Biograph, 1912.
The Engagement Ring, Biograph, 1912.
Oh, Those Eyes, Biograph, 1912.
Help! Help!, Biograph, 1912.
Fickle Spanish, Biograph, 1912.
Hot Stuff, Biograph, 1912.
The Brave Hunter, Biograph, 1912.
The Furs, Biograph, 1912.
Helen's Marriage, Biograph, 1912.
Tomboy Bessie, Biograph, 1912.
Neighbors, Biograph, 1912.
Katchem Kate, Biograph, 1912.
A Dash Through the Clouds, 1912.
What the Doctor Ordered, Biograph, 1912.
The Tourist, Biograph, 1912.
Tragedy of a Dress Suit, Biograph, 1912.
The Interrupted Elopement, Biograph, 1912.
He Must Have a Wife, Biograph, 1912.
Cohen Collects, Biograph, 1912.
Riley and Schultz, Keystone, 1912.
The New Neighbor, Keystone, 1912.
Stolen Glory, Keystone, 1912.
Pedro's Dilemma, Keystone, 1912.
The Beating He Needed, Keystone, 1912.
The Flirting Husband, Keystone, 1912.
Ambitious Butler, Keystone, 1912.
The Grocery Clerk's Romance, Keystone Pictures, 1912.
At Coney Island (also known as *Cohen at Coney Island*), Keystone, 1912.
Mabel's Lovers, Keystone, 1912.
At It Again, Keystone, 1912.
A Temperamental Husband, Keystone, 1912.
The Rivals, Keystone, 1912.
Mr. Fix-It (also known as *Mr. Fixer*), Keystone, 1912.
A Bear Escapes, Keystone, 1912.
Brown's Seance, Keystone, 1912.
A Family Mixup, Keystone, 1912.
Mabel's Adventures, Keystone, 1912.
The Duel, Keystone, 1912.
The Drummer's Vacation, Keystone, 1912.
Hoffmeyer's Legacy, 1912.
Mabel's Awful Mistakes (also known as *Her Deceitful Lover*), Keystone, 1913.
Love and Pain, Keystone, 1913.
His Crooked Career, Keystone, 1913.
For Lizzie's Sake, Keystone, 1913.
Saving Mabel's Dad, Keystone, 1913.
A Double Wedding, Keystone, 1913.
How Hiram Won Out, Keystone, 1913.
The Mistaken Masher, Keystone, 1913.
Just Brown's Luck, Keystone, 1913.
The Battle of Who Run, Keystone, 1913.
Heize's Resurrection, Keystone, 1913.
The Professor's Daughter, Keystone, 1913.
A Red Hot Romance, Keystone, 1913.
The Sleuths at the Floral Parade, Keystone, 1913.
A Strong Revenge, Keystone, 1913.
The Rube and the Baron, Keystone, 1913.
At Twelve O'clock, Keystone, 1913.
Her New Beau, Keystone, 1913.
Those Good Old Days, Keystone, 1913.
The Ragtime Band (also known as *The Jazz Band*), Keystone, 1913.
Hubby's Job, Keystone, 1913.
The Foreman of the Jury, Keystone, 1913.
Barney Oldfield's Race for a Life, Keystone, 1913.
The Speed Queen, Keystone, 1913.
The Hansom Driver, Keystone, 1913.
The Waiters' Picnic, Mutual Film Corporation, 1913.
Peeping Pete, Mutual Film Corporation, 1913.
A Bandit, Mutual Film Corporation, 1913.
The Telltale Light, Mutual Film Corporation, 1913.
A Noise From the Deep, Mutual Film Corporation, 1913.
The Riot, Mutual Film Corporation, 1913.
Mabel's New Hero, Mutual Film Corporation, 1913.
Mabel's Dramatic Career (also known as *Her Dramatic Debut*), Mutual Film Corporation, 1913.
The Gypsy Queen, Mutual Film Corporation, 1913.
The Faithful Taxicab (also known as *The Fatal Taxicab*), Mutual Film Corporation, 1913.
When Dreams Come True, Mutual Film Corporation, 1913.
The Bowling Match, Keystone, 1913.
A Quiet Little Wedding, Mutual Film Corp., 1913.
Love Sickness at Sea, Keystone, 1913.
A Muddy Romance (also known as *Muddled in Mud*), Keystone, 1913.
Cohen Saves the Flag, Keystone, 1913.
The Gusher, Keystone, 1913.
Zazu, the Band Leader, Keystone, 1913.
The Noise of the Bombs, 1914.
Mabel's Strange Predicament, Keystone, 1914.
Mabel at the Wheel (also known as *His Daredevil Queen,* and *Hot Finish*), Keystone, 1914.

His Talented Wife, Keystone, 1914.
The Fatal Mallet (also known as *Hit Him Again, The Pile Driver,* and *The Rival Suitor*), Keystone, 1914.
Back at It Again, Keystone, 1914.
In the Clutches of a Gang, Mutual Film Corporation, 1914.
Tango Tangles (also known as *Charlie's Recreation* and *Music Hall*), Mutual Film Corporation, 1914.
A Rural Demon, Mutual Film Corporation, 1914.
Tillie's Punctured Romance (also known as *For the Love of Tillie, Marie's Millions, Tillie's Big Romance,* and *Tillie's Nightmare*), Keystone, 1914.
Those College Girls, 1915.
Love, Loot and Cash, Keystone, 1915.
The Little Teacher, Keystone, 1915.
Hushing Scandal (also known as *Friendly Enemies*), Keystone, 1915.
The Cannonball, 1915.
Hearts and Planets, Keystone, 1915.
Ambrose's Sour Grapes, Mutual Film Corporation, 1915.
My Valet, Triangle, 1915.
Wife and Auto Trouble, Keystone, 1916.
The Other Man, Triangle-Keystone, 1916.
An Oily Scoundrel, Triangle-Keystone, 1916.
A Clever Dummy, 1917.
Home Talent, Mack Sennett Studios, 1921.
Oh, Mabel Behave, Photocraft Productions, 1922.
Three Foolish Weeks, 1924.
The Lion's Roar, 1928.
The Goodbye Kiss, First National Pictures, 1928.
The Brides Relations, Educational Pictures, 1928.
The Old Barn, Educational Pictures, 1929.
Whirls and Swirls, Educational Pictures, 1929.
The Big Palooka, Educational Pictures, 1929.
The Bee's Buzz, Educational Pictures, 1929.
Girl Crazy, Educational Pictures, 1929.
The Barber's Daughter, Educational Pictures, 1929.
The Constable, Educational Pictures, 1929.
The Lunkhead, Educational Pictures, 1929.
The Golfers, Educational Pictures, 1929.
A Hollywood Star, Educational Pictures, 1929.
Scotch, Educational Pictures, 1929.
Sugar Plum Papa, Educational Pictures, 1930.
Bulls and Bears, Educational Pictures, 1930.
Match Play, Educational Pictures, 1930.
Fat Wives for Thin, Educational Pictures, 1930.
Campus Crushes, Educational Pictures, 1930.
The Chumps, Educational Pictures, 1930.
Average Husbands, Educational Pictures, 1930.
Vacation Loves, Educational Pictures, 1930.
Midnight Daddies (also known as *The New Bankroll*), Sono Art-World Pictures, 1930.
Grandma's Girl, Educational Pictures, 1930.
Racket Cheers, Educational Pictures, 1930.
One More Chance, 1931.
I Surrender Dear, Atlantic Pictures, 1931.
The Cannonball, Educational Pictures, 1931.
Movie Town, Twentieth Century-Fox, 1931.
Hypnotized, Son-Art World Wide Pictures, 1932.
Way Up Thar, Republic Pictures, 1935.
Road to Hollywood, Astor Pictures, 1946.

WRITINGS

Screenplays:
Monday Morning in a Coney Island Police Court, Biograph, 1908.
Trying to Get Arrested, Biograph, 1909.
The Lonely Villa, Biograph, 1909.
The Lonedale Operator, Biograph, 1911.
The Fatal Mallet (also known as *Hit Him Again, The Pile Driver,* and *The Rival Suitor*), Keystone, 1914.
Tango Tangles (also known as *Charlie's Recreation* and *Music Hall*), Mutual Film Corporation, 1914.
Dough and Dynamite (also known as *The Cook, The Doughnut Designer,* and*The New Cook*), Keystone, 1914.
A Submarine Pirate, Triangle, 1915.
The Kitchen Lady, 1918.
Hide and Seek Detectives, Paramount, 1918.
The Little Widow, 1919.
Hearts and Flowers, 1919.
East Lynne With Variations, Paramount, 1919.
Cupid's Day Off, 1919.
No Mother to Guide Him, Mack Sennett Studios, 1919.
Molly O', Associated First National Pictures, 1921.
Call a Cop, 1921.
Bright Eyes, Associated First National Pictures, 1921.
A Small Town Idol, Mack Sennett Studios, 1921.
Suzanna, Mack Sennett Studios, 1923.
The Extra Girl, Pathe, 1923.
The Shriek of Araby, 1923.
Love and Kisses, 1925.
Cold Turkey, 1925.
The Beloved Bozo, 1925.
Bashful Jim, 1925.
A Love Sundae, 1926.
The Ghost of Folly, 1926.
Flirty Four-Flushers, 1926.
The Jolly Jilter, 1927.
The Goodbye Kisses, First National Pictures, 1928.

Books:
(Autobiography) *King of Comedy,* Doubleday (Garden City, NJ), 1954, reprinted by Mercury House (San Francisco, CA), 1990.*

SERGEI, Ivan 1972-

PERSONAL

Born in 1972.

Addresses: *Contact*—Burstein Company, 15304 Sunset Blvd., Suite 208, Pacific Palisades, CA 90272.

Career: Actor.

CREDITS

Film Appearances:

Huero, *Dangerous Minds* (also known as *My Posse Don't Do Homework*), Buena Vista, 1995.

Matt Mateo, *The Opposite of Sex,* Sony Pictures Classics, 1998.

Television Appearances; Movies:

Rashid, *Bionic Ever After?,* CBS, 1994.

Jimmy Pettit, *If Someone Had Known,* NBC, 1995.

Mac Ramsey, *John Woo's Once a Thief* (also known as *Once a Thief*), Fox, 1996.

Billy Owens, *Mother, May I Sleep with Danger?,* NBC, 1996.

Phillip Jackson, *Star Command,* CBS, 1996.

Cory, *The Rockford Files: Friends and Foul Play,* NBC, 1996.

Mac Ramsey, *John Woo's Once a Thief: Brother Against Brother* (also known as *Brother Against Brother*), The Movie Channel, 1998.

Mac Ramsey, *John Woo's Once a Thief: Family Business* (also known as *Family Business*), The Movie Channel, 1998.

Television Appearances; Series:

Mac Ramsey, *Once a Thief,* Fox, 1997-98.

Television Appearances; Episodic:

Peter Enloe, "Show Me the Way Home," *Touched by an Angel,* CBS, 1994.

Kelly, *Cybill,* CBS, 1995.

Sean, *Part of Five,* Fox, 1995.

Zane, "Live Hard, Die Young, And Leave A Good Looking Corpse," *Kindred: The Embraced,* Fox, 1996.

OTHER SOURCES

Electronic:

http://www.spe.sony.com/classics/oppositeofsex/cast/is.html, February 5, 1999.*

SEVERANCE, Joan 1958-

PERSONAL

Born December 23, 1958, in Houston, TX; father, an IBM systems engineer; married Eric Milan (a model), 1977 (divorced, 1984). *Avocational interests:* Target practice, cooking, writing, playing the saxophone and listening to slow jazz and blues.

Addresses: *Agent*—Agency for the Performing Arts, 9200 Sunset Blvd., Suite 900, Los Angeles, CA, 90069.

Career: Actress and producer. Model for Elite Modeling Agency.

CREDITS

Film Appearances:

Samantha Moore, *No Holds Barred,* New Line Cinema, 1989.

Eve, *See No Evil, Hear No Evil,* TriStar, 1989.

Lizabette, *Worth Winning,* Twentieth Century-Fox, 1989.

Rachel Varney, *Bird on a Wire,* Universal, 1990.

Belle, *Write to Kill,* RCA/Columbia Pictures Home Video, 1991.

Maureen Mallory, *Almost Pregnant,* Columbia TriStar Home Video, 1992.

Melissa Yarnell, *Illicit Behavior,* Prism Pictures, 1992.

Marla Stewart, *The Runstone,* LIVE Home Video, 1992.

Detective Melanie Hudson, *Criminal Passion,* Vidmark, 1994.

Rose Gullerman, *Payback,* Trimark, 1995.

Caroline Everett, *Dangerous Indiscretion,* Paramount Home Video, 1995.

Madilyn Turner, *Hard Evidence,* Libra Home Entertainment, 1995.

Theresa, *Matter of Trust,* Two Sticks Productions, 1997.

Chapelle, *In Dark Places,* 1997.

Wendy Crow, *The Last Seduction II,* PolyGram Video, 1999.

Film Work:

Co-producer, *In Dark Places,* 1997.

Co-producer, *Matter of Trust,* Two Sticks Productions, 1997.

Television Appearances; Episodic:

Pauline, "Lady Killer," *Mickey Spillane's Mike Hammer,* CBS, 1984.

Zik-Zak hallucination girl, *Max Headroom,* ABC, 1987.
"My Enemy," *The Hitchhiker,* HBO, 1988.
"Safe Sex," *Zalman King's Red Shoe Diaries,* Showtime, 1992.
Lauren Chase, "How Much is that Bentley in the Window," *L.A. Law,* NBC, 1993.
Lauren Chase, "Foreign Co-respondent," *L.A. Law,* NBC, 1993.
Reno, *Johnny Bago,* CBS, 1993.
Private Investigator Christine Logan, "Venom," *Profiler,* NBC, 1996.

Television Appearances; Series:
Susan Profitt, *Wiseguys,* CBS, 1987-88.
Camille Hunter, *Love Boat: The Next Wave,* The WB, 1998.

Television Appearances; Movies:
Susan Davis, *Another Pair of Aces: Three of a Kind,* CBS, 1991.
Irene, *Lake Consequences,* Showtime, 1993.
Darcy Walker/title role, *Black Scorpion,* Showtime, 1995.
Darcy Walker/title role, *Black Scorpion II: Aftershock,* Showtime, 1996.
Alison Rawlings, *Frequent Flyer,* ABC, 1996.
Hanna Carras, *Profile for Murder,* HBO, 1997.
Barbara "Babe" Paley, *Life of the Party: The Pamela Harriman Story,* Lifetime, 1998.

Television Appearances; Specials:
Libby Sinclair, *Just Deserts,* ABC, 1992.
The New Arrival, HBO, 1992.
Host, *Virtual World International,* Sci-Fi Channel, 1995.
Host, *Contestants Tell All. . .Secrets of Beauty Pageants Exposed,* UPN, 1998.

Television Work:
Co-producer, *Black Scorpion II: Aftershock,* Showtime, 1996.*

SHADIX, Glenn 1952-

PERSONAL

Born William Glenn Shadix, April 15, 1952, in Bessemer, AL.

Addresses: *Agent*—Innovative Artists Agency, 1999 Avenue of the Stars, Suite 2850, Los Angeles, CA 90067; 141 Fifth Ave., 3rd Floor South, New York, NY 10010. *Contact*—Voice-Over and Commercial Special Artists, 345 North Maple Dr., Beverly Hills, CA 90210.

Career: Actor.

CREDITS

Film Appearances:
Twin Oaks Customer, *The Postman Always Rings Twice,* Paramount, 1981.
Otho, *Beetlejuice,* Warner Bros., 1988.
Roscoe Arbuckle, *Sunset,* TriStar, 1988.
Father Ripper, *Heathers* (also known as *Fatal Game, Lethal Attraction,* and *Westerberg High*), New World, 1989.
Greg Samson, *Meet the Applegates,* Triton Pictures, 1991.
Duke, *Bingo,* TriStar, 1991.
Mr. Fallows, *Stephen King's Sleepwalkers* (also known as *Sleepwalkers*), Columbia, 1992.
Associate Bob, *Demolition Man,* Warner Bros., 1993.
Voice of Mayor, *Tim Burton's The Nightmare Before Christmas* (also known as *Nightmare Before Christmas*), Buena Vista, 1993.
Leopold Doppler, *It Runs in the Family* (also known as *My Summer Story*), Metro-Goldwyn-Mayer, 1994.
Anthony Rotundo, *Love Affair,* Warner Bros., 1994.
Leon Bennini, *Dark Side of Genius,* Paramount Home Video, 1995.
Lionel Spalding, *Dunston Checks In,* Twentieth Century Fox, 1996.
Building Inspector, *Multiplicity,* Columbia/TriStar, 1996.
Hermann Goering, *The Empty Mirror,* Lions Gate Films, 1997.
Neil, *Men,* A-pix Entertainment, 1997.
Mr. Sweepstakes, *Sparkler,* Columbia/TriStar Home Video, 1998.
Larry, *Chairman of the Board,* Trimark Pictures, 1998.
Nate, *Storm,* 1998.
Virgil, *Red Dirt,* 1999.
Geoff, *More Dogs Than Bones,* 1999.

Television Appearances; Episodic:
Jay, "Chicken Hearts-Chicken Hearts," *Roseanne,* ABC, 1989.
Bud Larkin, *Empty Nest,* NBC, 1991.
Harold, "The Apartment," *Seinfeld,* NBC, 1991.
Voice of Monster, "Episode # 55," *Dinosaurs,* ABC, 1991.

Bernard, "The Beer Is Always Greener," *Cheers,* NBC, 1992.
Dermot Drake, "The 1992 Boat Show," *Nightcourt,* NBC, 1992.
Leslie Loret, *Dave's World,* CBS, 1993.
Skorpius, *The Fresh Prince of Bel-Air,* NBC, 1993.
Walker, "Amends," *The John Larroquette Show,* NBC, 1993.
Voice of Nimbar, *Tattooed Teenage Alien Fighters From Beverly Hills,* USA Network, 1994.
Typhon, *Hercules: The Legendary Journeys,* syndicated, 1995.
Voice, *Zorro,* syndicated, 1997.
Voice, *Extreme Ghosbusters,* 1997.
Voice, "Duckman and Cornfed in 'Haunted Society Plumbers'," *Duckman* (animated), USA Network, 1997.
Caligula, *Sabrina, the Teenage Witch,* ABC, 1998.

Television Appearances; Movies:
Mr. Barton, *Student Exchange,* ABC, 1987.
Chuck, *Parent Trap Hawaiian Honeymoon* (also known as *Parent Trap IV: Hawaiian Honeymoon*), NBC, 1989.

Other Television Appearances:
Great Scott! (series), Fox, 1992.
Royce Pruitt, *Locals* (special), 1994.

OTHER SOURCES

Electronic:
http://www.glennshadix.com, June 1, 1999.*

SHADYAC, Tom 1958-

PERSONAL

Born in 1958. *Education:* University of California at Los Angeles, M.A. (film), 1989.

Addresses: *Agent*—United Talent Agency, 9560 Wilshire Blvd., Beverly Hills, CA 90212.

Career: Director, writer, and producer. Joke writer for comedian Bob Hope, 1983; rewrote, directed and worked on movies-of-the-week for Fox; stand-up comedian at the Improv in Los Angeles; formed Shady Acres Productions.

CREDITS

Film Appearances:
Chris, *Jocks,* Crown, 1987.

Film Work; Director:
Ace Ventura: Pet Detective, Warner Bros., 1994.
The Nutty Professor, Universal, 1996.
Liar Liar, Universal, 1997.
Patch Adams, Universal, 1998.

Film Work; Executive Producer:
Patch Adams, Universal, 1998.
The Nutty Professor II, Universal, 2000.

Television Work; Movies:
Production consultant, *Working Trash,* syndicated, 1990.
Director, *Frankenstein: The College Years,* Fox, 1991.

WRITINGS

Screenplays:
Ace Ventura: Pet Detective, Warner Bros., 1994.
The Nutty Professor, Universal, 1996.*

SHAMROY, Leon 1901-1974

PERSONAL

Born July 16, 1901, in New York, NY; died July 6, 1974, in Los Angeles, CA; son of Elisha and Miriam (Soujon) Shamroy; married Mary Anderson, May 13, 1953. *Education:* Attended City College of the City University of New York, 1919-20; studied mechanical engineering at Columbia University.

Career: Cinematographer and director.

Member: Award Winners School of Photography Inc. (president from 1946), American Society of Cinematographers (past president), Motion Picture Association of America (chairman of photographic communication research division, 1946-50), Society of Motion Picture Engravers Club: Los Angeles Press.

Awards, Honors: Honorable Film of 1928, The National Board of Review, for *The Last Moment;* Academy Award nomination, best cinematography, 1938, for *The Young in Heart;* Academy Award nomination (with Ray Rennahan), best cinematography (color), 1940, for *Down Argentine Way;* Academy Award nomination, best cinematography (black-and-white), 1942, for *Ten Gentlemen from West Point;* Academy Award, best cinematography (color), 1942, for *The Black Swan;* Academy Award, best cinematography (color), 1944, for *Wilson;* Academy Award, best cinematography (color), 1945, for *Leave Her to Heaven;* Film Achievement Award, *Look Magazine,* for creating new technique of color-photography and lighting, 1945; Academy Award nomination, best cinematography (black-and-white), 1949, for *Prince of Foxes;* Look Award, 1949, for *Twelve O'Clock High;* Film Daily Critics Awards, 1949, 1953-55, and 1963; Academy Award nomination, best cinematography (color), 1951, for *David and Bathsheba;* Academy Award nomination, best cinematography (color), 1952, for *The Snows of Kilimanjaro;* Academy Award nomination, best cinematography (color), 1953, for *The Robe;* Academy Award nomination, best cinematography (color), 1954, for *The Egyptian;* Academy Award nomination, best cinematography (color), 1955, for *Love Is a Many-Splendored Thing;* Academy Award nomination, best cinematography (color), 1956, for *The King and I;* Academy Award nomination, best cinematography (color), 1958, for *South Pacific;* Academy Award nomination, best cinematography (color), 1959, for *Porgy and Bess;* Academy Award nomination, best cinematography (color), 1963, for *The Cardinal;* Academy Award, best cinematography (color), 1963, for *Cleopatra;* Academy Award nomination, best cinematography (color), 1965, for *The Agony and the Ecstasy;* Laurel Award, International Motion Picture Exhibitors, 1969, for *Justine.*

CREDITS

Film Work; Cinematographer, Except Where Indicated:

Tongues of Scandal, 1927.
Pirates of the Sky, 1927.
The Trunk Mystery, 1927.
Hidden Aces, 1927.
Land of the Lawless, 1927.
Out with the Tide, 1928.
And co-producer, *The Last Moment,* 1928.
Bitter Sweets, 1928.
Alma de Gaucho, 1930.
Women Men Marry, Headline, 1931.
A Strange Adventure (also known as *The Wayne Murder Case*), Monogram, 1932.
Stowaway, Universal, 1932.
Three-Cornered Moon, Paramount, 1933.
Jeannie Gerhardt, Paramount, 1933.
Her Bodyguard, Paramount, 1933.
Thirty Day Princess, Paramount, 1934.
Ready for Love, Paramount, 1934.
The Mystic Hour, States' Rights, 1934.
Good Dame (also known as *Good Girl*), Paramount, 1934.
Kiss and Make Up, Paramount, 1934.
She Couldn't Take It (also known as *Woman Tamer*), Columbia, 1935.
Private Worlds, Paramount, 1935.
Mary Burns, Fugitive, Paramount, 1935.
Accent on Youth, Paramount, 1935.
Behold My Wife, Paramount, 1935.
She Married Her Boss, Columbia, 1935.
Spendthrift, Paramount, 1936.
Soak the Rich, Paramount, 1936.
Fatal Lady, Paramount, 1936.
Wedding Present, Paramount, 1936.
You Only Live Once, United Artists, 1937.
She Asked for It, Paramount, 1937.
Her Husband Lies, Paramount, 1937.
The Great Gambini, Paramount, 1937.
Blossoms on Broadway, Paramount, 1937.
And director, *Man's Paradise,* 1938.
The Young in Heart, United Artists, 1938.
The Story of Alexander Graham Bell (also known as *The Modern Miracle*), Twentieth Century-Fox, 1939.
Second Fiddle (also known as *Irving Berlin's Second Fiddle*), Twentieth Century-Fox, 1939.
Made for Each Other, United Artists, 1939.
The Adventures of Sherlock Holmes (also known as *Sherlock Holmes*), Twentieth Century-Fox, 1939.
Little Old New York, Twentieth Century-Fox, 1940.
Lillian Russell, Twentieth Century-Fox, 1940.
Four Sons, Twentieth Century-Fox, 1940.
I Was an Adventuress, Twentieth Century-Fox, 1940.
Down Argentine Way, Twentieth Century-Fox, 1940.
Tin Pan Alley, Twentieth Century-Fox, 1940.
A Yank in the RAF, Twentieth Century-Fox, 1941.
Confirm or Deny, Twentieth Century-Fox, 1941.
The Great American Broadcast, Twentieth Century-Fox, 1941.
Moon Over Miami, Twentieth Century-Fox, 1941.
That Night in Rio, Twentieth Century-Fox, 1941.
Ten Gentlemen from West Point, Twentieth Century-Fox, 1942.
Roxie Hart, Twentieth Century-Fox, 1942.
The Black Swan, Twentieth Century-Fox, 1942.
Stormy Weather, Twentieth Century-Fox, 1943.
Claudia, Twentieth Century-Fox, 1943.
Crash Dive, Twentieth Century-Fox, 1943.
Wilson, Twentieth Century-Fox, 1944.
Greenwich Village, Twentieth Century-Fox, 1944.
Buffalo Bill, Twentieth Century-Fox, 1944.

Where Do We Go from Here?, Twentieth Century-Fox, 1945.
A Tree Grows in Brooklyn, Twentieth Century-Fox, 1945.
State Fair (also known as *It Happened One Summer*), Twentieth Century-
Fox, 1945.
Leave Her to Heaven, Twentieth Century-Fox, 1945.
The Shocking Miss Pilgrim, Twentieth Century-Fox, 1947.
Forever Amber, Twentieth Century-Fox, 1947.
Daisy Kenyon, Twentieth Century-Fox, 1947.
That Lady in Ermine, Twentieth Century-Fox, 1948.
Twelve O'Clock High, Twentieth Century-Fox, 1949.
Prince of Foxes, Twentieth Century-Fox, 1949.
Two Flags West, Twentieth Century-Fox, 1950.
Cheaper by the Dozen, Twentieth Century-Fox, 1950.
On the Riviera, Twentieth Century-Fox, 1951.
David and Bathsheba, Twentieth Century-Fox, 1951.
Wait 'Til the Sun Shines, Nellie, Twentieth Century-Fox, 1952.
The Snows of Kilimanjaro, Twentieth Century-Fox, 1952.
With a Song in My Heart, Twentieth Century-Fox, 1952.
White Witch Doctor, Twentieth Century-Fox, 1953.
Tonight We Sing, Twentieth Century-Fox, 1953.
The Robe, Twentieth Century-Fox, 1953.
King of the Khyber Rifles, Twentieth Century-Fox, 1953.
The Girl Next Door, Twentieth Century-Fox, 1953.
Down Among the Sheltering Palms, Twentieth Century-Fox, 1953.
Call Me Madam, Twentieth Century-Fox, 1953.
There's No Business Like Show Business, Twentieth Century-Fox, 1954.
The Eqyptian, Twentieth Century-Fox, 1954.
Love Is a Many-Splendored Thing, Twentieth Century-Fox, 1955.
Good Morning, Miss Dove, Twentieth Century-Fox, 1955.
Daddy Long Legs, Twentieth Century-Fox, 1955.
The Girl Can't Help It, Twentieth Century-Fox, 1956.
The Best Things in Life Are Free, Twentieth Century-Fox, 1956.
The King and I, Twentieth Century-Fox, 1956.
Desk Set (also known as *His Other Woman*), Twentieth Century-Fox, 1957.
South Pacific, Twentieth Century-Fox, 1958.
Rally 'Round the Flag, Boys, Twentieth Century-Fox, 1958.
The Bravados, Twentieth Century-Fox, 1958.
Porgy and Bess, Columbia, 1959.
Beloved Infidel, Twentieth Century-Fox, 1959.
The Blue Angel, Twentieth Century-Fox, 1959.
Wake Me When It's Over, Twentieth Century-Fox, 1960.
North to Alaska, (also known as *Go North*), Twentieth Century-Fox, 1960.
Snow White and the Three Stooges (also known as *Snow White and the Three Clowns*), Twentieth Century-Fox, 1961.
Tender Is the Night, Twentieth Century-Fox, 1962.
The Cardinal, Columbia, 1963.
Cleopatra, Twentieth Century-Fox, 1963.
What a Way to Go!, Twentieth Century-Fox, 1964.
John Goldfarb, Please Come Home, Twentieth Century-Fox, 1964.
The Agony and the Ecstasy (also known as *Irving Stone's The Agony and the Ecstasy*), Twentieth Century-Fox, 1965.
Do Not Disturb, Twentieth Century-Fox, 1965.
The Glass Bottom Boat (also known as *The Spy in Lace Panties*), Metro-Goldwyn-Mayer, 1966.
Caprice, Twentieth Century-Fox, 1967.
Skidoo, Paramount, 1968.
The Secret Life of an American Wife, Twentieth Century-Fox, 1968.
Planet of the Apes (also known as *Monkey Planet*), Twentieth Century-Fox, 1968.
Justine, Twentieth Century-Fox, 1969.*

SHANNON, Molly 1964-

PERSONAL

Born September 16, 1964, in Shaker Heights, OH. *Education:* Attended New York University, Tisch School of the Arts (drama).

Addresses: *Contact*—International Creative Management, 40 West 57th St., New York, NY 10019.

Career: Actress.

CREDITS

Film Appearances:
Meg, New York, *The Phantom of the Opera* (also known as *Gaston Leroux's The Phantom of the Opera*), 21st Century, 1989.
Traci, *Return to Two Moon Junction,* Trimark, 1994.
Homeless lady, *Lawnmower Man 2: Beyond Cyberspace* (also known as *Lawnmower Man 2: Jobe's War*), New Line Cinema, 1996.
Dinner and Driving, Argonaut Pictures, 1997.

Emily Sanderson, *A Night at the Roxbury,* Paramount, 1998.
Nancy, *Happiness,* Trimark Pictures, 1998.
Caroline, *Analyze This,* Warner Bros., 1999.
Anita, *Never Been Kissed,* Twentieth Century-Fox, 1999.
Mary Katherine Gallagher, *Superstar,* Paramount, 1999.
Betty Lou Who, *How the Grinch Stole Christmas* (also known as *Dr. Seuss's How the Grinch Stole Christmas*), Universal, 2000.

Television Appearances; Series:
Cast, *Saturday Night Live,* NBC, 1994—.

Television Appearances; Episodic:
Twin Peaks, ABC.
Assistant talent coordinator, *In Living Color,* Fox, 1992.
Vivian, *The John Larroquette Show,* NBC, 1993.
Checker, *Sister, Sister,* The WB, 1994.
Woman, *These Friends of Mine,* ABC,1994.
Woman, "The Houseguest," *Ellen,* ABC, 1994.
Melody Pugh, *The Single Guy,* NBC, 1996.
Sam, "Summer of George," *Seinfeld,* NBC, 1997.
Val Bassett, "Grace, Replaced," *Will & Grace,* NBC, 1999.

Television Appearances; Specials:
American Comedy Honors, Fox, 1998.
Interviewee, *Canned Ham: A Night at the Roxbury,* Comedy Central, 1998.
VH-1 Divas Live '99, VH-1, 1999.

Television Appearances; Music Videos:
A Change Would Do You Good, Sheryl Crow, 1997.

Stage Appearances:
Co-wrote and starred in *The Rob and Molly Show* (improvisation), Upfront Comedy Theatre, Los Angeles.

OTHER SOURCES

Periodicals:
Entertainment Weekly, May 2, 1997, p. 16.
People Weekly, June 16, 1997, p. 77; April 19, 1999, p. 33.*

SHAVER, Helen 1951-

PERSONAL

Born February 24, 1951, in St. Thomas, Ontario, Canada. *Education:* Studied acting at Banff School of Fine Arts, Banff, Alberta, Canada.

Career: Actress and director.

Awards, Honors: Genie Award, Academy of Canadian Cinema and Television, 1979, for *In Praise of Older Women;* Genie Award nomination, best supporting actress, c. 1980, for *Who Has Seen the Wind?;* Bronze Leopard Award, Locarno Film Festival, 1985, for *Desert Hearts; Theatre World* Award, for *Jake's Women.*

CREDITS

Film Appearances:
Paula Lissitzen, *Shoot,* Avco Embassy, 1976.
Girl hitchhiker, *The Supreme Kid,* Cinepix, 1976.
Jo, *Outrageous!,* Cinema V, 1977.
Pickup, *High-Ballin',* American International Pictures, 1978.
Ann MacDonald, *In Praise of Older Women,* Avco-Embassy, 1978.
Betty Duncan, *Starship Invasions* (also known as *Alien Encounter* and *Winged Serpent*), Warner Bros., 1978.
Carolyn, *The Amityville Horror,* American International Pictures, 1979.
Ruth Thompson, *Who Has Seen the Wind?,* Cinema World, 1980.
Rhonda, *Gas,* Paramount, 1981.
Catherine Tuttle, *Harry Tracy—Desperado* (also known as *Harry Tracy*), Quartet, 1982.
Virginia Tremayne, *The Osterman Weekend,* Twentieth Century-Fox, 1983.
Claire Lewis, *Best Defense,* Paramount, 1984.
Coming Out Alive, TransWorld Entertainment, 1984.
Vivian Bell, *Desert Hearts,* Samuel Goldwyn Company, 1985.
Maria, *The War Boy,* Hollywood Home Entertainment, 1985.
Janelle, *The Color of Money,* Buena Vista, 1986.
Linda, *Lost!,* Simcom-Norstar, 1986.
Jessica Halliday, *The Believers,* Orion, 1987.
Walking after Midnight, Kay Film, 1988.
Voice of Littlefoot's mother, *The Land before Time* (animated), Universal, 1988.
Benet Archdale, *Innocent Victim* (also known as *The Tree of Hands*), Castle Hill/Academy Home, 1990.
A Smile in the Dark (also known as *A Day in L.A.* and *Destination Unknown*), 1991.
Diane, *Zebrahead,* Triumph Releasing, 1992.
Ms. Dowd, *Dr. Bethune* (also known as *Bethune: The Making of a Hero*), Tara Releasing, 1993.
Lula Peaks, *Morning Glory,* Academy Entertainment, 1993.

Ann O'Connor, *That Night* (also known as *One Hot Summer*), Warner Bros., 1993.
Margaret Heller, *Born to Be Wild* (also known as *Katie*), Warner Bros., 1995.
Kate White Reilly, *Tremors 2: Aftershocks,* Universal, 1995.
Slim, *Rowing Through,* 1996.
Rachel Rowen, *Open Season,* Republic Home Video, 1996.
Grace, *The Craft,* Columbia/TriStar, 1996.
Egg Salad, 1996.

Also appeared in *Christina* and *The Naked Man.*

Television Appearances; Series:
Dr. Liz Warren, *Search and Rescue: The Alpha Team,* NBC, 1977-78.
Libby Chapin, *United States,* NBC, then Arts and Entertainment, 1980.
Title role, *Jessica Novak,* CBS, 1981.
Kelby Robinson, *WIOU,* CBS, 1990-91.
Rachel Corrigan, *Poltergeist: The Legacy,* syndicated, 1996—.

Television Appearances; Movies:
Patty, *Lovey: A Circle of Children, Part II,* CBS, 1978.
Miss Beecher, *Off Your Rocker,* 1980.
Susan Frazer, *Between Two Brothers,* CBS, 1982.
Dorian Waldorf, *Countdown to Looking Glass,* HBO, 1984.
Valery Weaver, *The Park Is Mine,* HBO, 1985.
Sally Robinson, *Many Happy Returns,* CBS, 1986.
Amy Donaldson, *No Blame,* 1988.
Claire Nichols, *Mothers, Daughters, and Lovers* (also known as *American River*), NBC, 1989.
Rose, *Pair of Aces* (also known as *RIP*), CBS, 1990.
Elaine Tipton, *Fatal Memories* (also known as *The Eileen Franklin Story* and *Memory of a Murder*), NBC, 1992.
Edie Ballew, *Poisoned by Love: The Kern County Murders* (also known as *Blind Angel* and *Murder So Sweet*), CBS, 1993.
Katherine Woodfield, *Trial and Error,* USA Network, 1993.
Stacy Larkin, *Survive the Night* (also known as *Endless Fear* and *Night Hunt*), USA Network, 1993.
Katherine Barnes, *Ride with the Wind,* ABC, 1994.
Nora Fields, *Without Consent* (also known as *Tell Laura I Love Her* and *Trapped and Deceived*), ABC, 1994.
Dr. Monique Dessier, *The Forget-Me-Not Murders* (also known as *Janek: The Wallflower Murders*), CBS, 1994.
Dr. Monique Dessier, *A Silent Betrayal* (also known as *Janek: The Brownstone Murders*), CBS, 1994.
Ellen, *Falling for You,* CBS, 1995.
Mom Martin, *The Sweetest Gift,* Showtime, 1998.

Television Appearances; Episodic:
Police Surgeon, syndicated, 1975.
"Detroit Story," *King of Kensington,* syndicated, 1976.
Teresa, "Officer of the Year," *Hill Street Blues,* NBC, 1982.
Teresa, "A Hair of the Dog," *Hill Street Blues,* NBC, 1982.
Teresa, "The Phantom of the Hill," *Hill Street Blues,* NBC, 1982.
Teresa, "No Body's Perfect," *Hill Street Blues,* NBC, 1982.
Lisa Jericho, "Shadow of Truth," *T. J. Hooker,* ABC, 1983.
Karen, "Mirror, Mirror," *Steven Spielberg's Amazing Stories* (also known as *Amazing Stories*), NBC, 1986.
"Spanish Blood," *Philip Marlowe, Private Eye,* HBO, 1986.
"Who Has Seen the Wind," *WonderWorks,* PBS, 1987.
Miss Haight, "The Emissary," *Ray Bradbury Theatre,* First Choice (Canada), then USA Network, both 1988.
Dr. Diane Decker, "The Dancer's Touch," *B. L. Stryker* (broadcast as a segment of *ABC Mystery Movie*), ABC, 1989.
Vivian Dimitri, "Rest in Peace, Mrs. Columbo," *Columbo* (broadcast as a segment of *ABC Saturday Mystery*), ABC, 1990.
Cathy Kress, "Sandkings," *The Outer Limits,* Showtime, 1995.
"Next of Kin," *Dead Man's Gun,* Showtime, 1997.

Television Appearances; Specials:
President Marjorie Litchfield, *The First Gentleman,* CBS, 1994.
*M*A*S*H, Tootsie, and God: A Tribute to Larry Gelbart,* PBS, 1998.

Television Director; Movies:
Summer's End, Showtime, 1999.

Television Director; Episodic:
"Lithia," *The Outer Limits,* Showtime, 1995.
"The Bones of St. Anthony," *Poltergeist: The Legacy,* syndicated, 1996.
"Stagecoach Marty," *Dead Man's Gun,* Showtime, 1997.

Stage Appearances:

Tamara, Los Angeles, 1984.

Julia, *Ghost on Fire,* La Jolla Playhouse, La Jolla, CA, 1985.

Appeared in a Broadway production of *Jake's Women;* also appeared in *Are You Lookin'?, A Doll's House, The Hostage,* and *The Master Builder.**

SHAWN, Wallace 1943-
(Wally Shawn)

PERSONAL

Born November 12, 1943, in New York, NY; son of William (an editor) and Cecille (a journalist; maiden name, Lyon) Shawn; companion of Deborah Eisenberg (a playwright and fiction writer). *Education:* Harvard University, B.A. (history), 1965; Magdalen College, Oxford, B.A. (philosophy, politics, and economics), 1968, M.A., 1975; studied acting with Katharine Sergava at H.B. Studio, 1971.

Addresses: *Agent*—William Morris Agency, 1350 Avenue of the Americas, New York, NY 10019-4702. *Contact*—c/o Rosenstone/Wender, 3 East 48th St., New York, NY 10017-1027.

Career: Playwright, screenwriter, and actor. Indore Christian College, Indore, India, English teacher, 1965-66; Church of Heavenly Rest Day School, New York City, teacher of English, Latin, and drama, 1968-70; Laurie Love Ltd., New York City, shipping clerk, 1974-75; Hamilton Copy Center, New York City, copying machine operator, 1975-76.

Member: Writers Guild East, Dramatists Guild, Screen Actors Guild, Actors' Equity Association.

Awards, Honors: Fulbright scholar in India, 1965-66; Obie Awards, distinguished playwriting, *Village Voice,* 1975, for *Our Late Night,* and 1986, for *Aunt Dan and Lemon;* Obie Award, best play, 1991, for *The Fever.*

CREDITS

Film Appearances:

Jeremiah, *Manhattan,* United Artists, 1979.

Workshop member, *Starting Over,* Paramount, 1979.

Assistant insurance man, *All That Jazz,* Twentieth Century-Fox, 1979.

Strong Medicine, 1979.

Mugger, *Cheaper to Keep Her,* American Cinema, 1980.

Van Dongen, *Simon,* Warner Bros., 1980.

(As Wally Shawn) Waiter, *Atlantic City* (also known as *Atlantic City, U.S.A.*), Paramount, 1981.

Wallace, *My Dinner with Andre,* New Yorker, 1981.

Oliver, *A Little Sex,* Universal, 1982.

Harold De Voto, *Deal of the Century,* Warner Bros., 1983.

Professor Jules Goldfarb, *The First Time* (also known as *Doin' It*), New Line Cinema, 1983.

Otto Jaffe, *Lovesick,* Warner Bros., 1983.

Earl, *Strange Invaders,* Orion, 1983.

Frank Judd, *Saigon—Year of the Cat,* Warner Bros., 1983.

Mr. Pardon, *The Bostonians,* Almi, 1984.

Turtle, *Crackers,* Universal, 1984.

Freud, *The Hotel New Hampshire,* Orion, 1984.

Dr. Elliot Fibel, *Micki and Maude,* Columbia, 1984.

Father Abruzzi, *Heaven Help Us* (also known as *Catholic Boys*), TriStar, 1985.

Hoover, *Head Office,* TriStar, 1986.

Defense attorney, *The Bedroom Window,* De Laurentiis Entertainment Group, 1987.

Ellen, *Nice Girls Don't Explode,* New World, 1987.

John Lahr, *Prick Up Your Ears,* Samuel Goldwyn Company, 1987.

Vizzini, *The Princess Bride,* Twentieth Century-Fox, 1987.

Masked Avenger, *Radio Days,* Orion, 1987.

Oiseau, *The Moderns,* Island Alive, 1988.

Howard Saravian, *Scenes from the Class Struggle in Beverly Hills,* Cinecom, 1989.

Dr. Fishbinder, *She's Out of Control,* Columbia, 1989.

Translator, *We're No Angels,* Paramount, 1989.

Sibor, *Mom and Dad Save the World,* Warner Bros., 1992.

Everett Willis, *Nickel and Dime,* Columbia TriStar Home Video, 1992.

Simon Carr, *Shadows and Fog,* Orion, 1992.

Dr. Block, *Un-Becoming Age* (also known as *The Magic Bubble*), 1992.

Larry, *The Cemetery Club,* Buena Vista, 1993.

Cashpot, *The Double O Kid,* Prism Pictures, 1993.

Mr. Little, *The Meteor Man,* Metro-Goldwyn-Mayer, 1993.

Horatio Byrd, *Mrs. Parker and the Vicious Circle* (also known as *Mrs. Parker and the Round Table*), Miramax, 1994.

Title role, *Vanya on 42nd Street,* Mayfair, 1994.

Kalamazoo, No. 9 Films, 1994.

Canadian Prime Minister Clark MacDonald, *Canadian Bacon,* Gramercy Pictures, 1994.

Voice of Principal Mazur, *A Goofy Movie* (animated), Buena Vista, 1995.

Cosmo, *The Wife,* Artistic License Films, 1995.

Mr. Wendell Hall, *Clueless* (also known as *I Was a Teenage Teenager* and *No Worries*), Paramount, 1995.

Voice of Rex, *Toy Story* (animated), Buena Vista, 1995.

Voice of Labrador, M.C., *All Dogs Go to Heaven 2* (animated), Metro-Goldwyn-Mayer, 1996.

Vic Finley, *House Arrest,* Metro-Goldwyn-Mayer, 1996.

Arthur Blake, *Just Write,* Curb Entertainment/Heartland Film Releasing, 1997.

Marty, *Vegas Vacation* (also known as *National Lampoon's Vegas Vacation*), Warner Bros., 1997.

Furnace man, *Critical Care,* Live Entertainment, 1997.

Die Wholesale, 1998.

Voice of Tarzan, the chimp, *The Jungle Book: Mowgli's Story,* Walt Disney Home Video, 1998.

Dr. Edward Coleye, *My Favorite Martian,* Buena Vista, 1999.

Voice of Rex, *Toy Story 2* (animated), Buena Vista, 1999.

Television Appearances; Series:

Mr. Hall, *Clueless,* UPN, 1996-97.

Voice of Freddy, *The Lionhearts,* syndicated, 1998.

Television Appearances; Movies:

Stan Spiegel, *Just like Dad,* The Disney Channel, 1995.

Zack, *Noah,* ABC, 1998.

Television Appearances; Episodic:

Arnie Ross, "The Schloogel Show," *Taxi,* ABC, 1982.

Arnie Ross, "Arnie Meets the Kids," *Taxi,* ABC, 1983.

Neighbor, *The Cosby Show,* NBC, 1984.

Howard Buckley, *Davis Rules,* ABC, 1991.

Riley Baker, *Civil Wars,* ABC, 1992.

Matrix, USA Network, 1993.

Grand Nagus Zek, "The Nagus (aka Friends and Foes)," *Star Trek: Deep Space Nine* (also known as *DS9*), syndicated, 1993.

Grand Nagus Zek, "Rules of Acquisition," *Star Trek: Deep Space Nine* (also known as *DS9*), syndicated, 1993.

Charles Haste, "Pinske Business," *The Nanny,* CBS, 1994.

Marvin, *Something Wilder,* NBC, 1994.

Stuart Best, *Murphy Brown,* CBS, 1994, 1995.

Grand Nagus Zek, "Prophet Motive," *Star Trek: Deep Space Nine* (also known as *DS9*), syndicated, 1995.

Stuart Best, *Murphy Brown,* CBS, 1996, 1997.

Grand Nagus Zek, "Ferengi Love Songs (aka Of Love and Profit)," *Star Trek: Deep Space Nine* (also known as *DS9*), syndicated, 1997.

Voice of rifle shooting instructor, "How to Fire a Rifle without Even Trying," *King of the Hill* (animated), Fox, 1997.

Jeffrey Haven, *Reunited,* 1998.

Grand Nagus Zek, "Profit and Lace," *Star Trek: Deep Space Nine* (also known as *DS9*), syndicated, 1998.

Television Appearances; Specials:

How to Be a Perfect Person in Just Three Days, 1984.

Voice, *The Third Pig,* HBO, 1996.

Stage Appearances:

Prologue and Siro, *The Mandrake,* New York Shakespeare Festival, Public Theatre, New York City, 1977.

Behemoth the Cat, *The Master and Margarita,* New York Shakespeare Festival, Public Theatre, 1978.

Ilya, *Chinchilla,* Phoenix Theatre Company, Marymount Manhattan Theatre, New York City, 1979.

Julius Goldfarb, *The First Time,* New York City, 1983.

Speaker, *Schoenberg's Ode to Napoleon,* Symphony Space Theatre, New York City, 1984.

Father, Freddie, and Jasper, *Aunt Dan and Lemon,* New York Shakespeare Festival, Public Theatre, 1985.

The Fever (monologue), Public Theatre, 1990, then Second Stage Theatre, New York City, 1991, later La Mama Experimental Theatre Club, New York City, 1991, then Lincoln Center Theatre, New York City, 1991.

Stage Work:

Director, *In the Dark* (opera), Lenox Arts Center, Lenox, MA, 1976.

WRITINGS

For Stage:

Our Late Night, produced by New York Shakespeare Festival, Public Theatre, New York City, 1975, published by Targ Editions, 1984.

(Libretto) *In the Dark* (opera), produced at Lenox Arts Center, Lenox, MA, 1976.

Three Short Plays (also known as *A Thought in Three Parts;* contains *Summer Evening, The Youth Hostel,* and *Mr. Frivolous*), produced by New York Shakespeare Festival Public Theatre, 1976, published in *Wordplays,* Volume 2, Performing Arts Journal Publications, 1982.

The Mandrake (translation of *La Mandragola* by Niccolo Machiavelli), produced by New York Shakespeare Festival, Public Theatre, 1977, published by Dramatists Play Service (New York City).
Marie and Bruce, produced by New York Shakespeare Festival, PublicTheatre, 1980, published by Grove (New York City), 1980.
The Hotel Play, produced at La MaMa Experimental Theatre Club, New York City, 1981, published by Dramatists Play Service.
Aunt Dan and Lemon, produced by New York Shakespeare Festival, Public Theatre, 1985, published by Grove, 1985.
The Fever (monologue), produced at Public Theatre, 1990, published by Noonday, 1991.
The Designated Mourner, produced at Royal National Theatre, London, c. 1996.

Also author of *Four Meals in May, The Hospital Play,* and *The Old Man,* and the libretto, *The Music Teacher.*

Screenplays:
(With Andre Gregory) *My Dinner with Andre,* New Yorker, 1981, published by Grove, 1981.
The Designated Mourner (based on his play), First Look Pictures, 1997.

Other:
Contributor of articles to periodicals.

OTHER SOURCES

Periodicals:
American Theatre, September, 1997, p. 12.
Interview, March, 1989, pp. 72-75, 124, 126.
National Review, June 16, 1997, p. 56.*

SHAWN, Wally
See SHAWN, Wallace

SHEA, Katt
(Katt Shea Reuben)

PERSONAL

Born in Detroit, MI; married Andy Ruben (a writer and director).

Career: Actress, director, and writer.

Awards: Silver Award, Houston Film Festival, screenwriting, 1996.

CREDITS

Film Appearances:
Margot, *Preppies,* Playboy, 1982.
Woman at Babylon Club, *Scarface,* Universal, 1983.
Rhonda Rivers, *R.S.V.P.,* Vestron, 1984.
Dee Dee, *Hollywood Hot Tubs,* Manson, 1984.
Estrild, *Barbarian Queen* (also known as *Queen of Naked Steel*), Concorde, 1985.
Patsy Boyle, *Psycho III,* Universal, 1986.
Audrey King, *The Devastator* (also known as *The Destroyers* and *Kings Ransom*), 1986.
Deputy District Attorney, *The Rage: Carrie 2,* Metro-Goldwyn-Mayer, 1999.

Film Work; Director:
Stripped to Kill, Concorde, 1987.
Dance of the Damned, Concorde, 1989.
Stripped to Kill II (also known as *Live Girls*), Concorde, 1989.
Streets, Concorde, 1990.
(And producer) *Poison Ivy,* New Line Cinema, 1992.
The Book of Love, 1999.
Rage: Carrie 2, Metro-Goldwyn-Mayer, 1999.

Television Appearances; Movies:
Surgeon Athena, *Last Exit to Earth* (also known as *Roger Corman Presents Last Exit to Earth*), Showtime, 1996.

Television Work; Director:
Last Exit to Earth (also known as *Roger Corman Presents Last Exit to Earth*), Showtime, 1996.

WRITINGS

Screenplays:
The Patriot, Crown, 1986.
Stripped to Kill, Concorde, 1987.
Dance of the Damned, Concorde, 1989.
Stripped to Kill II (also known as *Live Girls*), Concorde, 1989.
Streets, Concorde, 1990.
Poison Ivy, New Line Cinema, 1992.
Rumble in the Streets, Concorde, 1997.

Television Movies:
Last Exit to Earth (also known as *Roger Corman Presents Last Exit to Earth*), Showtime, 1996.*

SHEFFER, Craig 1960-

PERSONAL

Born April 23, 1960, in York, PA; father, a prison guard and scriptwriter; mother, a worker in a nursing home. *Education:* Studied drama at East Stroudsburg State College. *Avocational interests:* Motorcycle riding, rodeos, boxing, writing, and playing guitar and harmonica.

Career: Actor and producer. Desert Wind Films, cofounder. Appeared in television commercials; also worked as a waiter and busboy, and as a valet to Count Basie.

Member: Screen Actors Guild, SANE (formerly National Committee for a Sane Nuclear Policy).

CREDITS

Film Appearances:

Byron Douglas, *That Was Then . . . This Is Now,* Paramount, 1985.
Frankie, *Voyage of the Rock Aliens,* Prism Entertainment, 1985.
Joe Fisk, *Fire with Fire* (also known as *Captive Hearts*), Paramount, 1986.
Hardy Jenns, *Some Kind of Wonderful,* Paramount, 1987.
Eddie McGuinn, *Split Decisions,* New Century, 1988.
Boone, *Nightbreed,* Twentieth Century-Fox, 1990.
Randall Atkins, *Blue Desert,* Academy Home Entertainment, 1991.
Zane, *Instant Karma,* Metro-Goldwyn-Mayer/United Artists, 1991.
Rau, *Eye of the Storm* (also known as *Jack Higgins: Die Krieger*), New Line Home Video, 1992.
Norman Maclean, *A River Runs through It,* Columbia, 1992.
Allan Dallis, *Fire in the Sky,* Paramount, 1993.
Joe Kane, *The Program,* Buena Vista, 1993.
Fire on the Amazon (also known as *Lost Paradise*), 1993.
Jack Cooper, *The Desperate Trail,* Turner Home Entertainment, 1994.
Frank, *Sleep with Me,* Metro-Goldwyn-Mayer/United Artists, 1994.
Cliff, *The Road Killers* (also known as *Roadflower*), Miramax, 1994.
Henri Guillaumet, *Wings of Courage* (also known as *Guillaumet, les Ailes du Courage*), Sony Pictures Classics, 1995.
Bobby Ray, *Flypaper,* 1997.
Connor Mcewen, *Double Take,* Twice Removed Productions, 1997.
Joseph, *Bliss,* Sony Pictures Entertainment, 1997.
Nick Seger, *Executive Power,* Naegele-Derrick Productions, 1997.
Adam Ellis, *The Fall,* Movie Screen Entertainment, 1998.
Quest for Atlantis, 1999.
The Pavilion, Quantum Entertainment, 1999.
Woody Miller, *Net Worth,* 1999.
Fear of Flying, Trimark, 1999.

Film Work:

Executive producer, *Instant Karma,* Metro-Goldwyn-Mayer/United Artists, 1991.
Executive producer, *Demolition Man,* Warner Bros., 1993.

Television Appearances; Series:

Brian Chadway, *The Hamptons,* ABC, 1983.

Also appeared as Ian Hayden, *One Life to Live,* ABC.

Television Appearances; Miniseries:

Constant Bradley, *A Season in Purgatory,* CBS, 1996.

Television Appearances; Movies:

Rob Harrison, *Babycakes* (also known as *Big Girls Don't Cry* and *Sugarbaby*), CBS, 1989.
First Lieutenant Marshal Buxton, *In Pursuit of Honor,* HBO, 1995.
Mike, *Bloodknot,* 1995.
King, *The Grave,* HBO, 1996.
Henry, *Head above Water,* HBO, 1996.
Dr. Douglas, *Miss Evers' Boys,* HBO, 1997.
Laird Atkins, *Shadow of Doubt* (also known as *Reasonable Doubt*), Cinemax, 1998.
Jack Safrenek, *Rhapsody in Bloom,* Starz!, 1998.

Television Appearances; Specials:

Voice, *500 Nations,* CBS, 1995.
Ernie Bishop, Ed, and the bridge keeper, *Merry Christmas, George Bailey,* PBS, 1997.

Stage Appearances:

Alan, *Torch Song Trilogy,* Little Theatre, New York City, 1983.
Billy Dukes, *Punchy,* Westside Mainstage Theatre, New York City, 1983.
Larkin, *Fresh Horses,* Workshop for the Performing Arts (WPA) Theatre,New York City, 1986.

Also appeared in productions of *The American Dream, Death of a Salesman, The Glass Menagerie, G. R. Point,* and *The Tempest.**

SHEPARD, Sam 1942(?)-

PERSONAL

Original name, Samuel Shepard Rogers VII; born November 5, 1942 (some sources cite 1943), in Fort Sheridan, IL; son of Samuel Shepard (a U.S. Army officer, teacher, and farmer) and Jane Elaine (Schook) Rogers; married O-Lan Johnson Dark (an actress), November 9, 1969 (divorced, 1984); children: (first marriage) Jesse Mojo; (with actress Jessica Lange) Hannah Jane, Samuel Walker. *Education:* Attended Mount San Antonio College, 1960-61.

Addresses: *Agent*—International Creative Management, 8942 Wilshire Blvd., Beverly Hills, CA 90211-1934. *Contact*—c/o Loris Berman, 21 West 26th St., New York, NY 10010.

Career: Playwright, composer, actor, and director. Bishop's Company Repertory Players (touring theatre group), Burbank, CA, actor, 1962, 1963; Magic Theatre, San Francisco, CA, playwright in residence, 1974-84; Padua Hills Playwrights Workshop and Festival, Los Angeles, co-founder. Holy Modal Rounders (rock group), drummer and guitarist, 1968-71; toured with Bob Dylan's Rolling Thunder Revue, 1976. Santa Anita Race Track, "hot walker"; car wrecker in Charlemont, MA; Connolly Arabian Horse Ranch, stable hand, 1958-60; Village Gate Restaurant, busboy, 1963-64; Maria's Crisis Cafe, waiter, 1965; Huff Sheep Ranch, herder; orange picker in Duarte, CA; sheep shearer in Pomona, CA.

Member: Actors' Equity Association, Screen Actors Guild, Dramatists Guild, Writers Guild of America, American Academy and Institute of Arts and Letters.

Awards, Honors: University of Minnesota, grant, 1966, fellowship, 1969; Obie Award, best play, *Village Voice,* 1966, for *Chicago, Icarus's Mother,* and *Red Cross;* Obie Award, best play, 1967, for *La Turista;* Rockefeller Foundation grant, 1967; Obie Award, best play, 1968, for *Forensic and the Navigators* and *Melodrama Play;* fellowship from Yale University, 1968; Guggenheim fellowships, 1968, 1971; Obie Award, best play, 1973, for *The Tooth of Crime;* Academy-Institute Award for Literature, American Academy and Institute of Arts and Letters, 1974; Obie Award, best playwriting, 1975, for *Action;* award from National Institute of Arts and Letters, 1976; Creative Arts Medal, Brandeis University, 1976; Obie Award, best new play, 1977, for *Curse of the Starving Class;* Pulitzer Prize, drama, and Obie Award, both 1979, for *Buried Child;* Obie Award, sustained achievement, 1979-80; Obie Awards, best direction and best new American play, both 1984, for *Fool for Love;* Academy Award nomination, best supporting actor, 1984, for *The Right Stuff;* Golden Palm Award, Cannes Film Festival, 1984, for *Paris, Texas;* Creative Arts Award, theatre arts, Brandeis University, 1984; Obie Award, 1985, for *True West;* New York Drama Critics Circle Award, best new play, and Drama Desk Award, outstanding new play, both 1986, for *A Lie of the Mind;* Outer Critics Circle Award, 1986; inducted into Theatre Hall of Fame, 1994; grant from Office for Advanced Drama Research.

CREDITS

Film Appearances:

Jo Saville/Bronco Bullfrog, *Bronco Bullfrog,* British Lion, 1970.
Brand X, 1970.
Renaldo and Clara, Circuit, 1977.
Farmer, *Days of Heaven,* Paramount, 1978.
Cal Carpenter, *Resurrection,* Universal, 1980.
Bailey/Raggedy Man, *Raggedy Man,* Universal, 1981.
Harry York, *Frances,* Universal, 1982.
Chuck Yeager, *The Right Stuff,* Warner Bros., 1983.
Gil Ivy, *Country,* Buena Vista, 1984.
Paris, Texas, Twentieth Century-Fox, 1984.
Eddie, *Fool for Love,* Cannon, 1985.
Doc Porter, *Crimes of the Heart,* De Laurentiis Entertainment Group, 1986.
Dr. Jeff Cooper, *Baby Boom,* United Artists, 1987.
Spud Jones, *Steel Magnolias,* TriStar, 1989.
The Hot Spot, Orion, 1990.
George Beutel, *Defenseless,* Seven Arts, 1991.
Jack Russell, *Bright Angel,* Hemdale, 1991.
Walter Faber, *Voyager* (also known as *Homo Faber*), Castle Hill, 1992.
Frank Coutelle, *Thunderheart,* TriStar, 1992.
Thomas Callahan, *The Pelican Brief,* Warner Bros., 1993.
Patrick Singer, *Safe Passage,* New Line Cinema, 1994.
Reece McHenry, *The Only Thrill,* Moonstone, 1997.
Just to Be Together (also known as *Tanto per Stare Insieme*), 1999.
Ghost, *Hamlet,* Miramax, 1999.
Will Dodge, *Curtain Call,* Longfellow Pictures, 1999.

Snow Falling on Cedars, Universal, 1999.
Texas, 2000.

Film Director:
Tongues, 1982.
Far North, Alive, 1988.
Silent Tongue, Trimark, 1993.

Television Appearances; Movies:
Snort Yarnell, *The Good Old Boys,* TNT, 1995.
Pete Davenport, *Lily Dale,* Showtime, 1996.
Curtain Call, Starz!, 1998.
Sheriff Forrest and Wild Bill Hickok, *Purgatory,* TNT, 1999.
Dashiell Hammett, *Dash and Lilly,* Arts and Entertainment, 1999.

Television Appearances; Miniseries:
Pea Eye Parker, *Streets of Laredo* (also known as *Larry McMurtry's Streets of Laredo*), CBS, 1995.

Television Appearances; Specials:
"Sam Shepard: Stalking Himself," *Great Performances,* PBS, 1998.
Intimate Portrait: Jessica Lange, Lifetime, 1998.

Television Appearances; Episodic:
"Jessica Lange: It's Only Make-Believe," *Crazy about the Movies,* Cinemax, 1991.

Stage Appearances:
Cowboy Mouth, American Place Theatre, New York City, 1971.

Stage Director:
Geography of a Horse Dreamer, Royal Court Theatre Upstairs, London, 1974.
Fool for Love, Magic Theatre, San Francisco, CA, then Circle Repertory Theatre, New York City, both 1983.
A Lie of the Mind, Promenade Theatre, New York City, 1985.
Simpatico, Joseph Papp Public Theatre, New York City, 1994.

WRITINGS

Stage Plays:
Cowboys (one-act), Theatre Genesis, New York City, 1964.
The Rock Garden (one-act), Theatre Genesis, 1964, first published in *The Unseen Hand and Other Plays,* Bobbs-Merrill (Indianapolis, IN), 1971.
Up to Thursday (one-act), Cherry Lane Theatre, New York City, 1965.
4-H Club (one-act), Cherry Lane Theatre, 1965, published in *The Unseen Hand and Other Plays,* Bobbs-Merrill, 1971.
Dog (one-act), La Mama Experimental Theatre Club, New York City, 1965.
Rocking Chair, La Mama Experimental Theatre Club, 1965.
Chicago (one-act), Theatre Genesis, 1965, then in London, 1976, revived by Signature Theatre Company, Susan Stein Shiva, Joseph Papp Public Theatre, New York City, 1997, published in *Five Plays by Sam Shepard,* Bobbs-Merrill, 1967.
Icarus's Mother (one-act), Caffe Cino, New York City, 1965, then Open Space Theatre, London, 1971, published in *Five Plays by Sam Shepard,* Bobbs-Merrill, 1967.
Fourteen Hundred Thousand (one-act), Firehouse Theatre, Minneapolis, MN, 1966, published in *Five Plays by Sam Shepard,* Bobbs-Merrill, 1967.
Red Cross (one-act), Judson Poet's Theatre, New York City, 1966, then Provincetown Playhouse, New York City, 1969, produced in Glasgow, Scotland, 1969, later at King's Head Theatre, London, 1972, published in *Five Plays by Sam Shepard,* Bobbs-Merrill, 1967.
"Melodrama Play," in *Six from La Mama,* Martinique Theatre, New York City, 1966, then La Mama Experimental Theatre Club, later Mercury Theatre, London, both 1967, published in *Five Plays by Sam Shepard,* Bobbs-Merrill, 1967.
La Turista (two-act), American Place Theatre, 1967, then Royal Court Theatre Upstairs, 1969, first published by Bobbs-Merrill, 1968.
Cowboys No. 2 (one-act), Old Reliable Theatre, New York City, then Mark Taper Forum, Los Angeles, both 1967, later London, 1980, published in *Mad Dog Blues and Other Plays,* Winter House, 1972.
Forensic and the Navigators (one-act), Theatre Genesis, 1967, then Astor Place Theatre, New York City, 1970, published in *The Unseen Hand and Other Plays,* Bobbs-Merrill, 1971.
The Holy Ghostly (one-act), La Mama Experimental Theatre Club, 1969, then King's Head Theatre, 1973, published in *The Unseen Hand and Other Plays,* Bobbs-Merrill, 1971.
The Unseen Hand (one-act), La Mama Experimental Theatre Club, 1969, then Astor Place Theatre, 1970, later Royal Court Theatre Upstairs, 1973, published in *The Unseen Hand and Other Plays,* Bobbs-Merrill, 1971, published with *Action,* Faber (London), 1975.

(Contributor) *Oh! Calcutta!,* Eden Theatre, New York City, 1969-75, then Edison Theatre, New York City, 1976-89.

Operation Sidewinder (two-act), Vivian Beaumont Theatre, New York City, 1970, first published by Bobbs-Merrill, 1970.

Shaved Splits, La Mama Experimental Theatre Club, 1970, published in *The Unseen Hand and Other Plays,* Bobbs-Merrill, 1971.

Mad Dog Blues (one-act), Theatre Genesis, 1971, then in Edinburgh,Scotland, 1978, published in *Mad Dog Blues and Other Plays,* Winter House, 1972.

(Contributor) *Terminal,* Open Theatre, New York City, 1971.

(With Patti Smith) *Cowboy Mouth,* Transverse Theatre, Edinburgh, then American Place Theatre, both 1971, later in London, 1972, published in *Mad Dog Blues and Other Plays,* Winter House, 1972.

Black Bog Beast Bait (one-act), American Place Theatre, 1971, published in *The Unseen Hand and Other Plays,* Bobbs-Merrill, 1971.

The Tooth of Crime (two-act), Open Space Theatre, 1972, then Performing Garage Theatre, New York City, 1973, later Royal Court Theatre, 1974, revised version produced as *Tooth of Crime (Second Dance),* music and lyrics by T-Bone Burnett, Signature Theatre Company, Lucille Lortel Theatre, New York City, 1997, first published in *The Tooth of Crime* [and] *Geography of a Horse Dreamer,* Grove (New York City), 1974.

(With Megan Terry and Jean-Claude van Itallie) *Nightwalk,* Open Theatre, then in London, both 1973, first published in *Mad Dog Blues and Other Plays,* Winter House, 1972.

Blue Bitch, Theatre Genesis, 1973, then London, 1975.

Little Ocean, Hampstead Theatre Club, London, 1974.

Geography of a Horse Dreamer (two-act), Royal Court Theatre Upstairs, 1974, then in New Haven, CT, 1974, and New York City, 1975, first published in *The Tooth of Crime* [and] *Geography of a Horse Dreamer,* Grove, 1974.

Action (one-act), American Place Theatre, 1974, then Magic Theatre, and Royal Court Theatre, both 1975, revived by Signature Theatre Company at Susan Stein Shiva, Joseph Papp Public Theatre, 1997, published in *Angel City and Other Plays,* Urizen Books (New York City), 1976.

Killer's Head (one-act monologue), American Place Theatre, 1974, then Magic Theatre and Royal Court Theatre Upstairs, both 1975, revived by Signature Theatre Company, Susan Stein Shiva, Joseph Papp Public Theatre, 1997, published in *Angel City and Other Plays,* Urizen Books, 1976.

Angel City, Magic Theatre, 1976, then in London, 1983, later at American Repertory Theatre, Cambridge, MA, 1984, published in *Angel City and Other Plays,* Urizen Books, 1976.

The Sad Lament of Pecos Bill on the Eve of Killing His Wife (one-act), in San Francisco, 1976, then at La Mama Experimental Theatre Club, 1983, revived by Signature Theatre Company, Susan Stein Shiva, Joseph Papp Public Theatre, 1997, published with *Fool for Love,* City Lights (San Francisco, CA), 1983.

Suicide in B-Flat, in New Haven, CT, 1976, then at Impossible Ragtime Theatre, New York City, 1979, later Denver Center Theatre Company, Denver, CO, 1982, published in *Buried Child and Other Plays,* Urizen Books, 1979.

Inacoma, in San Francisco, 1977.

Curse of the Starving Class (two-act), New York Shakespeare Festival, Newman/Public Theatre, New York City, 1978, then in London, revived by Signature Theatre Company, Susan Stein Shiva, Joseph Papp Public Theatre, 1997, published by Dramatists Play Service (New York City), 1991.

(With Joseph Chaikin) *Buried Child* (two-act), Theatre De Lys, New York City, then San Francisco, both 1978, revised version, Steppenwolf Theatre Company, Chicago, IL, 1995-96, then Brooks Atkinson Theatre, New York City, 1996, published in *Buried Child and Other Plays,* Urizen Books, 1979.

Seduced, in Providence, RI, 1978, then at American Place Theatre, 1979, published in *Buried Child and Other Plays,* Urizen Books, 1979.

(With Chaikin; and composer, with Skip LaPlante and Harry Mann) *Tongues,* New York Shakespeare Festival, Other Stage Theatre, New York City, then Eureka Theatre Festival, Eureka, CA, both 1979, later Mark Taper Forum, 1981, published in *Seven Plays by Sam Shepard,* Bantam (New York City), 1981.

(With Chaikin; and composer, with LaPlante and Mann) *Savage/Love,* NewYork Shakespeare Festival, Other Stage Theatre, then Eureka Theatre Festival, both 1979, later Mark Taper Forum, 1981, published in *Seven Plays by Sam Shepard,* Bantam, 1981.

True West (two-act), in San Francisco, 1980, then New York Shakespeare Festival, Public Theatre, 1981, later Cherry Lane Theatre, 1982, published in *Seven Plays by Sam Shepard,* Bantam, 1981.

(With Jacques Levy) *Jackson's Dance,* in New Haven, 1980.

Fool for Love, Magic Theatre, 1983, then Circle Repertory Theatre, later Douglas Fairbanks Theatre, both New York City, 1983, published with *The Sad Lament of Pecos Bill on the Eve of Killing His Wife,* City Lights, 1983.

(And composer, with Catherine Stone) *Superstitions* (one-act), La Mama Experimental Theatre Club, 1983.

A Lie of the Mind, Promenade Theatre, 1985, then London, 1987, published with *The War in Heaven,* New American Library (New York City), 1987.

Hawk Moon, in London, 1989.

States of Shock, American Place Theatre, 1991, published by Vintage (New York City), 1993.

Simpatico, Joseph Papp Public Theatre, New York City, 1994.

(With Chaikin) *The War in Heaven,* Signature Theatre Company, Public Theatre, 1997, published with *A Lie of the Mind,* New American Library, 1987.

(With Chaikin) *When the World Was Green,* Signature Theatre Company, Public Theatre, 1997.

Eyes for Consuela (based on "The Blue Bouquet," a short story by Octavia Paz), City Center Stage II, Manhattan Theatre Club, New York City, 1998.

Screenplays:

(With Robert Frank) *Me and My Brother,* New Yorker, 1967.

(With others) *Zabriski Point,* Metro-Goldwyn-Mayer, 1970, published with *Anton's Red Desert,* Simon & Schuster (New York City), 1970.

(With Murray Mednick) *Ringaleevio,* 1971.

(Contributor) *Oh! Calcutta!,* Cinemation, 1972.

(With Bob Dylan) *Renaldo and Clara,* Circuit, 1977.

Fool for Love (based on his stage play), Cannon, 1985.

Far North, Alive, 1988.

Silent Tongue, Trimark, 1993.

For Television:

Fourteen Hundred Thousand (play), National Educational Television, 1969.

Blue Bitch (play), BBC, 1973, published in *Mad Dog Blues and Other Plays,* Winter House, 1972.

True West (special; based on his stage play), 1984.

Radio Plays:

(With Chaikin) *The War in Heaven,* broadcast in 1985, produced on stage in London, 1987, produced with *Struck Dumb* (double-bill), American Place Theatre, 1991, published with *A Lie of the Mind,* New American Library, 1986.

Play Collections:

Five Plays by Sam Shepard (includes *Chicago, Fourteen Hundred Thousand, Icarus's Mother, Melodrama Play,* and *Red Cross*), Bobbs-Merrill, 1967, published as *Chicago and Other Plays,* Urizen Books, 1981.

The Unseen Hand and Other Plays (includes *Black Bog Beast Bait, Forensic and the Navigators, 4-H Club, Holy Ghostly, The Rock Garden, Shaved Splits,* and *The Unseen Hand*), Bobbs-Merrill, 1971.

Mad Dog Blues and Other Plays (includes *Blue Bitch, Cowboy Mouth, Cowboys No. 2, Mad Dog Blues, Nightwalk,* and *The Rock Garden*), WinterHouse, 1972.

The Tooth of Crime [and] *Geography of a Horse Dreamer,* Grove, 1974.

Angel City and Other Plays (includes *Action, Angel City, Cowboy Mouth, Cowboys No. 2, Curse of the Starving Class, Killer's Head, Mad Dog Blues,* and *The Rock Garden*), Urizen Books (New York City), 1976.

Buried Child and Other Plays, Urizen Books, 1979 (published in England as *Buried Child, Seduced,* [and] *Suicide in B-Flat,* Faber, 1980).

Four Two-Act Plays by Sam Shepard (includes *Geography of a Horse Dreamer, La Turista, Operation Sidewinder,* and *The Tooth of Crime*), Urizen Books, 1980.

Seven Plays by Sam Shepard (includes *Buried Child, Curse of the Starving Class, La Turista, Savage/Love, Tongues, The Tooth of Crime,* and *True West*), Bantam, 1981.

The Unseen Hand and Other Plays, Urizen Books, 1981.

Fool for Love [and] *The Sad Lament of Pecos Bill on the Eve of Killing His Wife,* City Lights, 1983.

Fool for Love and Other Plays (includes *Angel City, Cowboy Mouth, Geography of a Horse Dreamer, Melodrama Play, Seduced,* and *Suicide in B-Flat*), Bantam, 1984.

The Unseen Hand and Other Plays, Bantam, 1986.

(With Joseph Chaikin) *The War in Heaven* [and] *A Lie of the Mind,* New American Library, 1987.

Other:

Hawk Moon: A Book of Short Stories, Poems, and Monologues, Black Sparrow Press (Santa Barbara, CA), 1973.

Rolling Thunder Logbook, Viking (New York City), 1977.

Motel Chronicles (includes *Hawk Moon*), City Lights, 1982 (published in England as *Motel Chronicles and Hawk Moon*), Faber, 1985.

Joseph Chaikin and Sam Shepard: Letters and Texts, 1972-1984, edited by Barry V. Daniels, New American Library, 1989.

Cruising Paradise (stories), Knopf (New York City), 1996.

Adaptations: The screenplay *Paris, Texas* was adapted by L. M. Kit Carson from Shepard's stage play *Motel Chronicles* and released by Twentieth Century-Fox in 1984. The television movie *Curse of the Starving Class* was adapted from Shepard's play of the same title and broadcast by Showtime in 1995.

OTHER SOURCES

Books:

Auerbach, Doris, *Sam Shepard, Arthur Kopit, and the Off-Broadway Theatre,* Twayne (Boston, MA), 1982.

Benet, Carol, *Sam Shepard on the German Stage: Critics, Politics, Myths,* Peter Lang (New York City), 1993.

Daniels, Barry V., editor, *Joseph Chaikin and Sam Shepard: Letters and Texts, 1972-1984,* New American Library, 1989.

De Rose, David J., *Sam Shepard,* Twayne, 1992.

Dictionary of Literary Biography, Volume 7: *Twentieth-Century American Dramatists,* Gale (Detroit, MI), 1981.

Graham, Laura J., *Sam Shepard: Theme, Image, and the Director,* Peter Lang, 1993.

Hall, Ann C.,*"A Kind of Alaska": Women in the Plays of O'Neill, Pinter, and Shepard,* Southern Illinois University Press (Carbondale, IL), 1993.

Hart, Lynda, *Sam Shepard's Metaphorical Stages,* Greenwood Press (Westport, CT), 1987.

King, Kimball, *Ten Modern American Playwrights,* Garland Publishing (NewYork City), 1982.

King, *Sam Shepard: A Casebook,* Garland Publishing, 1988.

Marranca, Bonnie, editor, *American Dreams: The Imagination of Sam Shepard,* Performing Arts Journal Publications, 1981.

McGhee, Jim, *True Lies: The Architecture of the Fantastic in the Plays of Sam Shepard,* Peter Lang, 1993.

Mottram, Ron, *Inner Landscapes: The Theatre of Sam Shepard,* University of Missouri Press (Columbia, MO), 1984.

Orr, John, *Tragicomedy and Contemporary Culture: Play and Performance from Beckett to Shepard,* University of Michigan Press (Ann Arbor, MI), 1991.

Oumano, Ellen, *Sam Shepard: The Life and Work of an American Dreamer,* St. Martin's (New York City), 1986.

Patraka, Vivian M., and Mark Siegel, *Sam Shepard,* Boise State University (Boise, ID), 1985.

Perry, Frederick J., *A Reconstruction-Analysis of Buried Child by Playwright Sam Shepard,* Mellen Research University Press (San Francisco), 1992.

Shewey, Don, *Sam Shepard,* Dell (New York City), 1985.

Trussler, Simon, *File on Shepard,* Methuen (London), 1989.

Tucker, Martin, *Sam Shepard,* Continuum (New York City), 1992.

Weales, Gerald, *The Jumping-Off Place: American Drama in the 1960's,* Macmillan, 1969.

Wilcox, Leonard, editor, *Rereading Shepard: Contemporary Critical Essays on the Plays of Sam Shepard,* St. Martin's, 1993.

Periodicals:

American Theatre, September, 1996, p. 28; July-August, 1997, p. 12.

Back Stage, May 16, 1997, p. 64.

New Republic, July 15, 1996, p. 27.

New York Times, November 13, 1994, sec. 2, pp. 1, 2.*

SHERIDAN, Jim 1949-

PERSONAL

Born in 1949, in Dublin, Ireland; son of a railroad worker and actor; wife's name, Fran. *Education:* Attended the National University of Ireland, University College, Dublin, Ireland, and New York University's Institute of Film and Television.

Addresses: *Office*—Hell's Kitchen, Inc., All Hallows College, Grace Park Rd., Dublin, Ireland. *Agent*—Creative Artists Agency, 9830 Wilshire Blvd., Beverly Hills, CA 90212.

Career: Director, producer, writer, and actor. Project Arts Theatre, Dublin, Ireland, director, 1976-80; New York Irish Arts Center, New York City, artistic director, 1982-87; Children's Theatre Company, Dublin, Ireland, founder. Worked at the Lyric Theatre, Belfast, Northern Ireland, the Abbey Theatre, Dublin, Ireland, and the English 7:84 Company.

Awards, Honors: Fringe Award, Edinburgh Festival, best play, 1983, for *Spike in the First World War;* Independent Spirit Award, best foreign film, and Academy Award nominations, best adapted screenplay (with Shane Connaughton) and best director, all 1989, for *My Left Foot;* Golden Berlin Bear, Berlin International Film Festival, and Academy Award nominations, best director, best picture, and best adapted screenplay (with TerryGeorge), all 1993, for *In the Name of the Father;* Reader Jury Award, *Berlin Morgenpost,* Golden Globe Award nomination, best director of a motion picture, and Golden Berlin Bear nomination, all 1997, for *The Boxer.*

CREDITS

Film Work:

Director, *My Left Foot* (also known as *My Left Foot: The Story of Christy Brown*), Miramax, 1989.

Producer (with Noel Pearson) and director, *The Field,* Avenue Pictures, 1990.

Producer and director, *In the Name of the Father,* Universal, 1993.

Producer, *Some Mother's Son,* Columbia, 1996.

Producer and director, *The Boxer,* Universal, 1997.

Producer, *Agnes Browne* (also known as *The Mammy*), October Films, 1999.

Film Appearances:

Jonathan Swift, *Words upon the Window Pane,* Pembridge Films, 1994.

Exasperated director, *Cannes Man,* Rocket Pictures, 1996.

Priest, *Moll Flanders,* Metro-Goldwyn-Mayer, 1996.

Stationmaster, *This Is the Sea,* First Look Pictures Releasing, 1997.

C.P.A.D. leader, *The General* (also known as *I Once Had a Life*), Sony Pictures Classics, 1998.

Stage Work:

Director, *Shadow of a Gunman,* Abbey Theatre, Dublin, Ireland, 1981, then Actors Playhouse, New York Irish Arts Center, New York City, 1984.

Television Appearances; Awards Presentations:

Presenter, *The 66th Annual Academy Awards Presentation,* ABC, 1994.

WRITINGS

Screenplays:

(With Shane Connaughton) *My Left Foot* (also known as *My Left Foot: The Story of Christy Brown;* based on the writings of Christy Brown), Miramax, 1989.

(With Noel Pearson) *The Field* (based on a play by J. B. Keane), Avenue Pictures, 1990.

Into the West, Miramax, 1992.

(With Terry George) *In the Name of the Father,* Universal, 1993.

Some Mother's Son, Columbia, 1996.

The Boxer, Universal, 1997.

Writings for the Stage:

Mobile Homes, Project Arts Center, Dublin, Ireland, published by Co-Op Books, 1978.

Spike in the First World War, 1983.

Also author of other plays.

OTHER SOURCES

Periodicals:

Entertainment Weekly, March, 1994, p. 100.

New Yorker, March 21, 1994, p. 218.*

SHIMERMAN, Armin 1949-

PERSONAL

Born November 5, 1949 in Lakewood, NJ; married Kitty Swink (an actress), May, 1981. *Education:* University of California at Los Angeles, B.A. (Renaissance studies), 1972.

Addresses: *Contact—c/o Star Trek: Deep Space Nine,* 5555 Melrose Ave., Los Angeles, CA 90038; or c/o *Buffy the Vampire Slayer,* Time Warner Bros. Television Network, 4000 Warner Blvd., Burbank, CA 91522.

Career: Actor. Member, San Diego's Old Globe Theatre Company.

CREDITS

Stage Appearances:

Filch and Ned (understudy), *Threepenny Opera,* New York Shakespeare Festival, Vivian Beaumont Theater, New York City, 1976.

Brankov, *Silk Stockings,* Equity Liberty Theatre, New York City, 1977.

Threepenny Opera, New York Shakespeare Festival, Delacorte Theater, New York City, 1977.

Steward/Warwick's page, *Saint John,* Circle in the Square Theatre, 1977.

Dolph, *Broadway,* Wilbur Theatre, Boston, MA, 1978.

Mr. Thorkelson, *I Remember Mama,* Majestic Theatre, New York City, 1979.
Makassar Reef, Act: A Contemporary Theatre, Seattle, WA, 1979.
Stepan, *When the War Was Over,* Impossible Ragtime Theatre, 1980.
Principally Pinter/Slightly Satie, The Colonnades, 1981.
Bix, *Hoagy, Bix, and Wolfgang Beethoven Bunkhaus,* Indiana Repertory Theatre, Indianapolis, IN, 1981.
Duke of York, *Richard II,* Center Theatre Group, Mark Taper Forum, Los Angeles, 1991.

Film Appearances:
Eulogy audience member, *Stardust Memories,* United Artists, 1980.
Stoogemania, Atlantic, 1986.
Interrogation sergeant, *The Hitcher,* TriStar, 1986.
French waiter, *Blind Date,* TriStar, 1987.
Mortician, *Gangland* (also known as *Verne Miller*), Alive, 1987.
Trigger's dad, *Like Father, Like Son,* TriStar, 1987.
Boggs, *Dangerous Curves,* Paramount, 1988.
Dr. Oberlander, *Big Man on Campus* (also known as *The Hunchback Hairball of L.A.*), Vestron Video, 1989.
Dr. Gottesman, *Death Warrant,* Metro-Goldwyn-Mayer/United Artists, 1990.
Weezil, *Arena,* Columbia TriStar Home Video, 1991.
Contest judge, *And You Thought Your Parents Were Weird* (also known as *Robodad*), Vidmark Entertainment, 1991.
D.A. Van Horn, *Dream Man,* Republic Pictures, 1995.
Judge Younger, *Eye for an Eye,* Paramount, 1996.
Donuts, 1998.

Television Appearances; Episodic:
Phone man, "Heat Rash," *Hill Street Blues,* NBC, 1982.
Nestor Bartholomew, "Lofty Steele," *Remington Steele,* NBC, 1984.
Murder She Wrote, CBS, 1984.
Herb, *I Had Three Wives,* CBS, 1985.
Letek, "The Last Outpost," *Star Trek: The Next Generation,* syndicated, 1987.
Malcolm Dench, "Hammeroid," *Sledge Hammer!,* ABC, 1987.
Mr. Lovejoy, "Buck the Stud," *Married. . .With Children,* Fox, 1987.
Wedding gift box, " Haven," *Star Trek: The Next Generation,* syndicated, 1989.
Daimon Bractor, "Peak Performance," *Star Trek: The Next Generation,* syndicated, 1989.
Dr. Wexler, "Nightmare in Apartment One," *Hooperman,* ABC, 1989.
Bernard, *Brooklyn Bridge,* CBS, 1991.
Victor Sofransky, *Civil Wars,* ABC, 1991.
Mr. Johnson, *Drexell's Class,* Fox, 1991.
Great Scott!, Fox, 1992.
Ernie, *L.A. Law,* NBC, 1993.
Quark, "Firstborn," *Star Trek: The Next Generation,* syndicated, 1994.
Quark, "Caretaker," *Star Trek: Voyager,* UPN, 1995.
Legend, 1995.
Stan the caddy, "The Caddy," *Seinfeld,* NBC, 1995.
Henry Munroe, "Jehovah and Son, Inc.," *The Lazarus Man,* 1996.
Himself, *Space Cadets,* 1997.
Anteaus, "The Nox," *Stargate SG-1,* Showtime, 1997.
Judge Walworth, "Boy to the World," *Ally McBeal,* Fox, 1997.
Judge Garth Moskin, "Pursuit of Dignity," *The Practice,* ABC, 1997.
Herb Rossov, "Far Beyond the Stars," *Star Trek: Deep Space Nine,* syndicated, 1998.
Shape-shifting guard, "Genesis," *Sliders,* 1998.

Television Appearances; Series:
Pascal (recurring), *Beauty and the Beast,* NBC, 1987-90.
Quark, *Star Trek: Deep Space Nine,* syndicated, 1992-99.
Principle Snyder (recurring), *Buffy the Vampire Slayer,* The WB, 1996-99.

Television Appearances; Movies:
Mr. Traverner, *Baby Girl Scott,* CBS, 1987.
Tricks of the Trade, CBS, 1988.
Plahte, *She Knows Too Much,* NBC, 1989.
Eric Weston, *Miracle Landing,* CBS, 1990.
Dr. Mort Seger, *Slaughter of the Innocents,* HBO, 1994.

Television Appearances; Specials:
The Science of Star Trek, PBS, 1995.
The Lost World, Sci-Fi Channel, 1998.

OTHER SOURCES

Periodicals:
People Weekly, April 10, 1995, pp. 109-110.

Electronic:
The Official Armin Shimerman Website, www.walrus.com/~quark/armin/index.html.*

SIDNEY, George (II) 1916-

PERSONAL

Born October 4, 1916, on Long Island, NY; son of L.K. Sidney (a veteran showman and vice president of Metro-Goldwyn-Mayer) and Hazel (an actress) Mooney; married Lillian Burns. *Education:* Attended HannemanMedical University and Hospital (Doctorate of Science).

Career: Director, actor, and producer.

Member: Director's Guild of America (president), Special Presidential Assignment to Atomic Energy Commission and U.S. Air Force, Hanna-Barbera Productions (president 1961-66), American Society of Composers, Authors, and Publishers, Directors Inc. (president since 1969), Directors Foundation (vice president), D.W. Griffith Foundation (vice president), ACTT (England), Directors Guild of America.

Awards, Honors: Golden Globe Award, best world entertainment through musical films, 1958; Gold Medal for Service, Directors Guild of America, 1959; doctorate, Collegio Barcelona, 1989; Louella Parsons Award, 1995; President's Award, 1998.

CREDITS

Film Work; Director, Unless Otherwise Indicated:
Hollywood Hobbies, 1934.
Sunday Night at the Trocadero, 1938.
Men in Fright, 1938.
Billy Rose's Casa Manana Revue, 1938.
Practical Jokers, 1938.
Love on Tap, 1939.
Clown Princes, 1939.
Alfalfa's Aunt, 1939.
Tiny Troubles, 1939.
Quicker 'n a Wink, 1940.
'What's Your I.Q.?' Number Two, 1940.
Free and Easy, Metro-Goldwyn-Mayer, 1941.
Third Dimension Murder, 1941.
Willie and the Mouse, 1941.
Of Pups and Puzzles, 1941.
Pacific Rendezvous, Metro-Goldwyn-Mayer, 1942.
Thousands Cheer, Metro-Goldwyn-Mayer, 1943.
Pilot #5 (also known as *Pilot No. 5*), Metro-Goldwyn-Mayer, 1943.
Bathing Beauty, Metro-Goldwyn-Mayer, 1944.
Anchors Aweigh, Metro-Goldwyn-Mayer, 1945.
Holiday in Mexico, Metro-Goldwyn-Mayer, 1946.
Ziegfeld Follies, Metro-Goldwyn-Mayer, 1946.
The Harvey Girls, Metro-Goldwyn-Mayer, 1946.
Cass Timberlane, Metro-Goldwyn-Mayer, 1947.
The Three Musketeers, Metro-Goldwyn-Mayer, 1948.
The Red Danube, Metro-Goldwyn-Mayer, 1949.
Key to the City, Metro-Goldwyn-Mayer, 1950.
Annie Get Your Gun, Metro-Goldwyn-Mayer, 1950.
Show Boat, Metro-Goldwyn-Mayer, 1951.
Scaramouche, Metro-Goldwyn-Mayer, 1952.
Young Bess, Metro-Goldwyn-Mayer, 1953.
Kiss Me Kate, Metro-Goldwyn-Mayer, 1953.
Jupiter's Darling, Metro-Goldwyn-Mayer, 1955.
The Eddy Duchin Story, Columbia, 1956.
And producer, *Jeanne Eagels,* Columbia, 1957.
Pal Joey, Columbia, 1957.
And producer, *Pepe,* Columbia, 1960.
And producer, *Who Was That Lady?,* Columbia, 1960.
A Ticklish Affair (also known as *Moon Walk*), Metro-Goldwyn-Mayer, 1963.
Bye Bye Birdie, Columbia, 1963.
And producer, *Viva Las Vegas* (also known as *Love in Las Vegas*), Metro-Goldwyn-Mayer, 1964.
And producer, *The Swinger,* Paramount, 1966.
And producer, *Half a Sixpence,* Paramount, 1967.
(Film extract *Viva Las Vegas*) *This is Elvis* (documentary), Warner Bros., 1981.

Film Appearances:
West Point of the South, 1936.
Himself, *50 Years of Action!,* 1986.

Television Appearances; Specials:
Interviewee, *The Republic Pictures Story,* 1991.
Unscripted Hollywood, 1995.

OTHER SOURCES

Periodicals:
Film Comment, July-August, 1994, p. 50.*

SIEGEL, Joel 1943-

PERSONAL

Born July 7, 1943, in Los Angeles, CA; son of Robert and Libby (Kantor) Siegel; married Jane Kessler, November 21, 1976 (died, December, 1982); married Melissa Nina De Mayo, August 27, 1985 (divorced); married Ena Swansea, June 21, 1996. *Education:* University of California at Los Angeles, B.A., 1965; postgraduate work, 1966-67. *Politics:* Democrat. *Religion:* Jewish.

Addresses: *Office—Good Morning America,* 147 Columbus Ave., New York, NY 10023.

Career: Writer, actor, film and book reviewer. Director, voter registration drive for Dr. Martin Luther King, Jr., Macon, GA, 1965; joke writer for Robert F. Kennedy, 1968; Carson & Roberts Advertising, Los Angeles, copywriter and producer, 1967-72; *KMET-FM,* Los Angeles, news anchorman, 1972; *WCBS-TV,* New York City, correspondent, 1972-76; *WABC-TV,* New York City, correspondent, film critic, 1976—; *Rolling Stone* magazine, *Los Angeles Times, Sports Illustrated,* freelance writer; *Good Morning America,* correspondent, film critic, 1980—. Also worked as a radio newscaster and news anchorman. *Military Service:* U.S. Army Reserves, 1967-73.

Member: American Federation of Television and Radio Artists, Dramatists Guild, Drama Desk, Gilda's Club (president, co-founder with Gene Wilder).

Awards, Honors: Antoinette Perry Award nomination, 1981, for *The First;* Public Service Award, Anti-Defamation League of B'nai B'rith, 1976, for distinguished news reporting and commitment to freedom of the press; New York State Associated Press Broadcasters Association Award, for general excellence in individual reporting; recipient of six Emmy Awards and numerous nominations from the National Academy of Television Arts and Sciences (New York chapter).

CREDITS

Television Appearances; Series:

Entertainment editor, *Good Morning America,* ABC, 1975—.

Television Appearances; Specials:

Whatta Year. . .1986, ABC, 1986.

Our Kids and the Best of Everything, ABC, 1987.

Diamond on the Silver Screen, AMC, 1992.

Interviewee, *Sports on the Silver Screen,* HBO, 1997.

Anchor, *Inside Hollywood: The Pictures, the People, the Academy Awards,* ABC, 1999.

Film Appearances:

Himself, *Deathtrap,* Warner Bros., 1982.

WRITINGS

Musicals:

The First (Broadway), New York City, 1981-82.*

SIKKING, James
See SIKKING, James B.

SIKKING, James B. 1934-
(James Sikking, Jim Sikking)

PERSONAL

Born March 5, 1934, in Los Angeles, CA. *Education:* University of California, Los Angeles, B.A.

Addresses: *Agent*—Metropolitan Talent Agency, 4526 Wilshire Blvd., Beverly Hills, CA 90210.

Career: Actor. Also billed as James Sikking and Jim Sikking.

CREDITS

Television Appearances; Series:

Dr. James Hobart, *General Hospital,* ABC, 1973-76.

Geoffrey St. James, *Turnabout,* NBC, 1979.

Lieutenant Howard Hunter, *Hill Street Blues,* NBC, 1981-87.

Dr. David Howser, *Doogie Howser, M.D.,* ABC, 1989-92.

Stan Jonas, *Brooklyn South,* CBS, 1997.

Voice of Colonel Gorden, *Invasion America* (animated), The WB, 1998.

Television Appearances; Miniseries:

Major Bassett, *Dress Gray,* NBC, 1986.

Engineer Jenks, *Around the World in 80 Days,* NBC, 1989.

Television Appearances; Movies:

Astronaut Higgins, *The Astronaut,* ABC, 1972.

Second controller, *Family Flight,* ABC, 1972.

Pipe smoker, *Man on a String,* CBS, 1972.

Henry Kellner, *The Alpha Caper* (also known as *Inside Job*), ABC, 1973.

Businessman, *Coffee, Tea, or Me?,* CBS, 1973.

Officer Geary, *Outrage* (also known as *One Angry Man*), ABC, 1973.

Dunbar's aide, *The President's Plane Is Missing,* ABC, 1973.

New Orleans S.A.C., *The F.B.I. Story: The F.B.I. versus Alvin Karpis, Public Enemy Number One* (also known as *The FBI Story: Alvin Karpis*), CBS, 1974.

Monsignor Killian, *The Last Hurrah,* NBC, 1977.

Commander Devril, *Young Joe, the Forgotten Kennedy,* ABC, 1977.
Mr. Lea, *Kill Me If You Can,* NBC, 1977.
Bricklaw, *Never Con a Killer* (also known as *The Feather and Father Gang*), ABC, 1977.
McCracken, *A Woman Called Moses,* NBC, 1978.
Avery Brundage, *The Jesse Owens Story,* syndicated, 1984.
Jim Davis, *First Steps,* CBS, 1985.
Nicholas Kline, *Bay Coven* (also known as *The Devils of Bay Cove, Eye of the Demon,* and *Strangers in Town*), NBC, 1987.
Mayor Cameron, *Police Story: The Freeway Killings,* NBC, 1987.
Russell Quinton, *Too Good to Be True,* NBC, 1988.
Ollie Hopnoodle's Haven of Bliss, PBS, 1988.
Felix, *Brotherhood of the Rose,* NBC, 1989.
Clarke, *Desperado: Badlands Justice,* NBC, 1989.
Phil Carter, *Doing Time on Maple Drive* (also known as *Faces in the Mirror*), Fox, 1992.
Mick Linsday, *Seduced by Evil,* USA Network, 1994.
Bill Cayton, *Tyson,* HBO, 1995.
General Douglas MacArthur, *In Pursuit of Honor* (also known as *Fiddler's Green*), HBO, 1995.
Ron Wells, *Dare to Love* (also known as *I Dare to Die*), ABC, 1995.
Dr. Roger Salisbury, *Jake Lassiter: Justice on the Bayou,* NBC, 1995.
Sam Liebman, *The Ring* (also known as *Danielle Steel's The Ring*), NBC, 1996.
Lieutenant Commander Tynan, *Mutiny,* NBC, 1999.

Television Appearances; Specials:
Battle of the Network Stars, ABC, 1984.
Ben Lindsay, *Mad Avenue,* 1988.
Elliot Richardson, "The Final Days," *AT&T Presents,* ABC, 1989.
The Hollywood Christmas Parade, 1989.

Appeared in "Golden Land," *Tales from the Hollywood Hills.*

Television Appearances; Episodic:
"The Big Broadcast," *Hogan's Heroes,* CBS, 1960.
Civilian engineer, "The Case of the Misguided Miracle," *Perry Mason,* CBS, 1961.
Lyles, "The Long Way Home" (part one and two), *Combat,* ABC, 1963.
"Incident of the Travellin' Man," *Rawhide,* CBS, 1963.
Bert, "Last Second of a Big Dream," *The Fugitive,* ABC, 1965.
Deputy Marsh, "Ten Thousand Pieces of Silver," *The Fugitive,* ABC, 1966.
"Wind It Up and It Betrays You," *The F.B.I.,* ABC, 1968.
Private Berger, "No Names Please," *Hogan's Heroes,* CBS, 1968.
Gestapo officer, "My Favorite Prisoner," *Hogan's Heroes,* CBS, 1969.
Corrigan, "Homecoming," *Mission: Impossible,* CBS, 1970.
Reporter, "The Nature of the Enemy," *Night Gallery,* NBC, 1970.
Police lieutenant, "Beware of the Watch Dog," *The Name of the Game,* NBC, 1971.
Trooper, "A Death in the Family," *Night Gallery,* NBC, 1971.
"Safe Deposit," *Cade's County,* CBS, 1971.
Dick, "Good Night, Nancy," *The Bob Newhart Show,* CBS, 1972.
Wilson, "Committed," *Mission: Impossible,* CBS, 1972.
Major Frank Kramer (U.S. Army doctor), "Act of Duty," *The Streets of San Francisco,* ABC, 1973.
Finance officer, "Tuttle," *M*A*S*H,* CBS, 1973.
Franklin, "To Live with Fear" (part 2), *Little House on the Prairie,* NBC, 1977.
John Hicklin, "The Becker Connection," *The Rockford Files,* NBC, 1977.
"Angels on Horseback," *Charlie's Angels,* ABC, 1977.
Ted McDermott, "The Action," *Starsky and Hutch,* ABC, 1978.
"Which One Is Jaime?," *The Bionic Woman,* NBC, 1978.
"Angels in Waiting," *Charlie's Angels,* ABC, 1979.
Cornelius, "Mona Spin Off," *Who's the Boss?,* ABC, 1987.
Jack Small, "City under Siege" (part one), *Hunter,* NBC, 1989.
Voice characterization, "The Once and Future Duck," *Duckman* (animated), USA Network, 1996.

Television Appearances; Pilots:
Bart Burton, *Calling Dr. Storm, M.D.,* NBC, 1977.
Roger Lomax, *Trouble in High Timber Country* (also known as *The Yeagers*), ABC, 1980.
Patrolman, *Inside O.U.T.,* NBC, 1984.

Film Appearances:
The Magnificent Seven, United Artists, 1960.
Artist, *The Strangler* (also known as *The Boston Strangler*), Allied Artists, 1964.
American soldier, *Von Ryan's Express,* Twentieth Century-Fox, 1965.
Hired gun, *Point Blank,* Metro-Goldwyn-Mayer, 1967.
Gunner, *Charro!,* National General Pictures, 1969.
Joe Menchell, *Daddy's Gone a-Hunting,* Warner Bros., 1969.

Bogardy, *Chandler,* Metro-Goldwyn-Mayer, 1971.
Sergeant Anders, *The New Centurions* (also known as *Precinct 45: Los Angeles Police*), Columbia, 1972.
Andy Hayes, *The Magnificent Seven Ride,* United Artists, 1972.
Harris, *Scorpio,* United Artists, 1973.
Brother on the Run (also known as *Black Force 2* and *Boots Turner*), Southern Star, 1973.
Ralph Friedman, *The Terminal Man,* Warner Bros., 1974.
(As Jim Sikking) Control room man, *Capricorn One,* Warner Bros., 1978.
Dietrich, *The Electric Horseman,* Universal, 1979.
Brudnell, *The Competition,* Columbia, 1980.
Ray, *Ordinary People,* Paramount, 1980.
Deputy Montone, *Outland,* Warner Bros., 1981.
Dr. Harold Lewin, *The Star Chamber,* Twentieth Century-Fox, 1983.
Captain Styles, *Star Trek III: The Search for Spock,* Paramount, 1984.
Tozer, *Up the Creek,* Orion, 1984.
Colonel Laribee, *Morons from Outer Space,* Universal, 1985.
Bill Watson, *Soul Man,* New World Pictures, 1986.
Nelson, *Narrow Margin,* 1990.
Colonel Jason J. Halsey, *Final Approach,* Filmquest Pictures, 1991.
F. Denton Voyles, *The Pelican Brief,* Warner Bros., 1993.
Wheeler/Aaron Feld, *Dead Badge,* 1995.

Stage Appearances:
Walter, *The Price,* Arena Stage, Washington, DC, 1993-94.

Also appeared in productions of *The Big Knife, Damn Yankees, Plaza Suite,* and *The Waltz of the Toreadors.**

SIKKING, Jim
See SIKKING, James B.

SILBERMAN, Jerry
See WILDER, Gene

SILVERMAN, Jonathan 1966-

PERSONAL

Born August 5, 1966, in Los Angeles, CA; son of Hillel Emanuel (a rabbi) and Devora (Halaban) Silverman. *Education:* Attended the University of Southern California and studied English at New York University. *Avocational interests:* Charity work.

Addresses: *Agent*—Creative Artists Agency, 9830 Wilshire Blvd., Beverly Hills, CA 90212.

Career: Actor. Appeared in public service announcements; also worked as an activist for educational and AIDS-related causes.

Member: Artists for a Free South Africa (cofounder, 1989), Young Artists United (honorary New York City and Los Angeles chairperson, 1990-91), West Coast Friends of Bar-Ilan University, Anti-Defamation League, Holocaust survivor and historical societies, Hollywood All-Stars (a celebrity baseball team for charities).

Awards, Honors: Helen Hayes Award, 1988, for *Broadway Bound;* DramaLogue Award, 1990, for *The Illusion;* Drama League Award, for *Pay or Play.*

CREDITS

Television Appearances; Series:
David Sheinfeld, *E/R,* CBS, 1984.
Jonathan Maxwell, *Gimme a Break!,* NBC, 1984-86.
Jonathan Eliot, *The Single Guy,* NBC, 1995-97.

Television Appearances; Movies:
Stephen Schoonover, *Challenge of a Lifetime,* ABC, 1985.
Billy Fox, *Traveling Man,* HBO, 1989.
Michael Katourian, *For Richer, for Poorer* (also known as *Father, Son, and the Mistress* and *Getting There*), HBO, 1992.
Stanley Jerome, *Neil Simon's Broadway Bound* (also known as *Broadway Bound*), ABC, 1992.
Barry Thomas, *12:01,* Fox, 1993.
Glenn O'Connor, *Sketch Artist II: Hands That See* (also known as *A Feel for Murder* and *Sketch Artist II*), Showtime, 1995.
Paul Dolby, *London Suite* (also known as *Neil Simon's London Suite*), NBC, 1996.
Joel, *Denial,* 1998.
Inspector Alex Urbina, *The Inspectors,* Showtime, 1998.
Lenny, *Freak City,* Showtime, 1999.

Television Appearances; Specials:
Jamie, *Couples,* ABC, 1994.
People Yearbook '95, CBS, 1995.
Comic Relief American Comedy Festival, ABC, 1996.

Television Appearances; Episodic:

Dr. Franzblau, "The One with the Birth," *Friends,* NBC, 1995.

Jonathan Eliot, "Caroline and the Folks," *Caroline in the City,* NBC, 1995.

Himself, *The Rodman World Tour,* MTV, 1996.

Himself, *The Daily Show,* Comedy Central, 1998.

Television Appearances; Awards Presentations:

The 41st Annual Tony Awards, CBS, 1987.

Presenter, *The VH-1 Fashion Awards,* VH-1, 1996.

Presenter, *The 53rd Annual Golden Globe Awards,* 1996.

Presenter, *The 24th Annual American Music Awards,* 1997.

Film Appearances:

Drew, *Girls Just Want to Have Fun,* New World Pictures, 1985.

Eugene Morris Jerome, *Brighton Beach Memoirs* (also known as *Neil Simon's Brighton Beach Memoirs*), Universal, 1986.

Alan Appleby as a teen, *Stealing Home,* Warner Bros., 1988.

Harry, *Caddyshack II,* Warner Bros., 1988.

Richard Parker, *Weekend at Bernie's* (also known as *Hot and Cold*), Twentieth Century-Fox, 1989.

Seymour, *Life in the Food Chain: Age Isn't Everything,* LIVE Home Video, 1991.

Brian, *Class Action,* Twentieth Century-Fox, 1991.

Bobby/Roberta, *Little Sister,* LIVE Home Video, 1992.

Jay Norman, *Death Becomes Her,* Universal, 1992.

Rob Konigsberg, *Breaking the Rules* (also known as *Sketches*), Miramax, 1992.

Richard Parker, *Weekend at Bernie's II,* TriStar, 1993.

Rick, *Teresa's Tattoo,* Trimark Pictures, 1994.

Jim Bowers, *Little Big League,* Columbia, 1994.

Lenny Kaminski, *Two Guys Talkin' about Girls* (also known as *At First Sight*), Trimark Pictures, 1995.

Davis, *French Exit,* Columbia/TriStar Home Video, 1995.

Hyper, *12 Bucks,* Kindred Spirits Productions, 1998.

Brucey Madison, *The Odd Couple II* (also known as *Neil Simon's The Odd Couple II* and *Odd Couple II: Travelin' Light*), Paramount, 1998.

Just a Little Harmless Sex, Phaedra Cinema, 1999.

Dirk and Betty, AMCO Entertainment Group, 1999.

Stage Appearances:

Eugene Morris Jerome, *Brighton Beach Memoirs,* Alvin Theatre (now Neil Simon Theatre), New York City, 1983.

Eugene Morris Jerome, *Biloxi Blues,* Neil Simon Theatre, 1985.

Eugene Morris Jerome, *Broadway Bound,* Broadhurst Theatre, New York City, 1986.

The Illusion, Los Angeles Theatre Center, Los Angeles, CA, 1990.

Sticks and Stones, 1994.

Also appeared in *Pay or Play.*

OTHER SOURCES

Books:

Newsmakers 1997, Gale (Detroit, MI), 1997.

Periodicals:

Entertainment Weekly, October 6, 1995, pp. 48-49; May 17, 1996, p. 14.

People Weekly, October 2, 1995, p. 18.*

SIMONDS, Robert 1964-

PERSONAL

Born in 1964, in Phoenix, AZ. *Education:* Yale University, B.A. (philosophy; summa cum laude).

Career: Producer.

CREDITS

Film Work; Producer, Unless Otherwise Indicated:

Problem Child, Universal, 1990.

Problem Child 2, Universal, 1991.

Shout, Universal, 1991.

Airheads, Twentieth Century-Fox, 1994.

Billy Madison, Universal, 1995.

Bulletproof, Universal, 1996.

Happy Gilmore, Universal, 1996.

Leave It to Beaver, Universal, 1997.

That Darn Cat, Buena Vista, 1997.

Dirty Work, Metro-Goldwyn-Mayer, 1998.

Executive producer, *Half-Baked,* Universal, 1998.

The Waterboy, Buena Vista, 1998.

The Wedding Singer, New Line Cinema, 1998.

Executive producer, *Big Daddy,* Columbia/Sony Pictures Entertainment, 1999.

Double O-Soul (also known as *OO-Soul*), Universal, forthcoming.

Television Work:

Executive producer, *Problem Child 3: Junior in Love,* NBC, 1995.

OTHER SOURCES

Periodicals:
Forbes, March 22, 1999, p. 246.*

SIRTIS, Marina 1959(?)-

PERSONAL

Born March 29, 1959 (other sources say 1961 or 1964), in London, England; daughter of John and Despina (a tailor's assistant) Sirtis; married Michael Lamper (a guitarist), June 21, 1992. *Education:* Attended the Guildhall School of Music and Drama.

Addresses: *Contact*—c/o 2436 Creston Way, Los Angeles, CA 90068.

Career: Actress.

CREDITS

Television Appearances; Series:
Counselor Deanna Troi, *Star Trek: The Next Generation* (also known as *Star Trek: TNG*), syndicated, 1987-94.
Voice of Demona, *Gargoyles* (animated), syndicated, 1994-96.
Voice of Demona, *Gargoyles: The Goliath Chronicles* (animated), ABC, 1996-97.

Television Appearances; Movies:
Harem girl, *The Thief of Baghdad,* NBC, 1978.
Counselor Deanna Troi, *Star Trek: The Next Generation—Encounter at Farpoint* (also known as *Encounter at Farpoint*), syndicated, 1987.
Maria, *One Last Chance,* BBC, 1990.
Counselor Deanna Troi, *Star Trek: The Next Generation—All Good Things . . .* (also known as *All Good Things . . .*), syndicated, 1994.
Detective Inspector Walker, *Gadgetman,* 1996.

Television Appearances; Specials:
Judge, *Miss Teen USA,* CBS, 1988.
The 57th Annual Hollywood Christmas Parade, syndicated, 1988.
The 58th Annual Hollywood Christmas Parade, syndicated, 1989.

Television Appearances; Episodic:
Melina, "Hazell Goes to the Dogs," *Hazell,* Thames Television, 1978.
Lucrezia, "The Six Napoleons," *The Return of Sherlock Holmes, Series I,* Granada Television, 1986.
Kate, "Down and Under," *Hunter,* NBC, 1987.
"Gene Roddenberry: Star Trek and Beyond," *Biography,* Arts and Entertainment, 1994.
Voice of Margot Yale, "Awakening: Part 3," *Gargoyles* (animated), syndicated, 1994.
Aurora Abromovitz, "Where No Duckman Has Gone Before," *Duckman* (animated), USA Network, 1997.
Mary Ann Eagin, "Murder at the Finish Line," *Diagnosis Murder,* CBS, 1998.
Entertainment Tonight, syndicated, 1998.

Film Appearances:
Jackson's girlfriend, *The Wicked Lady,* Metro-Goldwyn-Mayer, 1983.
Space Raiders (also known as *Star Child*), 1983.
Prostitute, *Blind Date* (also known as *Deadly Seduction*), New Line Cinema, 1984.
Maria, *Death Wish 3,* Cannon, 1985.
Gloria, *Waxwork II: Lost in Time* (also known as *Lost in Time* and *Space Shift: Waxwork II*), LIVE Home Video, 1992.
Counselor Deanna Troi, *Star Trek: Generations* (also known as *Star Trek: The Next Generation: The Movie*), Paramount, 1994.
Voice of Demona, *Gargoyles: The Heroes Awaken* (animated), Buena Vista Home Video, 1994.
Counselor Deanna Troi, *Star Trek: First Contact* (also known as *Star Trek: Borg, Star Trek: Destinies, Star Trek: Future Generations, Star Trek:Generations II,* and *Star Trek: Resurrection*), Paramount, 1996.
Counselor Deanna Troi, *Star Trek: Insurrection* (also known as *Star Trek IX* and *Star Trek: Stardust*), Paramount, 1998.

Stage Appearances:
Appeared in *Hamlet* and *Jane Eyre,* both with the Worthing Repertory Company; also appeared in *Godspell* and *The Rocky Horror Picture Show.*

RECORDINGS

Video Games:
Voice of Counselor Deanna Troi, *Star Trek: The Next Generation—A Final Unity,* Microprose/Spectrum Holobyte, 1995.
Voice of Counselor Deanna Troi, *Star Trek: Generations,* Microprose/Spectrum Holobyte, 1997.*

SISTO, Jeremy 1974-

PERSONAL

Born October 6, 1974, in Grass Valley (some sources say Nevada City), CA; mother's name, Reedy Gibbs. *Education:* Attended University of California at Los Angeles. *Avocational interests:* Bocce ball, playing the guitar.

Addresses: *Contact*—c/o Jill Littman, Bymel O'Neil, 8912 Burton Way, Beverly Hills, CA 90211.

Career: Actor.

CREDITS

Film Appearances:

Roberto, *Grand Canyon,* Twentieth Century-Fox, 1991.
Tim, *The Crew,* Live Entertainment, 1994.
Elton, *Clueless* (also known as *I Was a Teenage Teenager; No Worries*), Paramount, 1995.
Vassago, *Hideaway,* TriStar/Columbia, 1995.
Steven, *Moonlight and Valentino,* Gramercy Pictures, 1995.
Frank Beaumont, *White Squall,* Buena Vista, 1996.
T.K., *Suicide Kings,* Artisan Entertainment, 1997.
Chad, *Men* (also known as *Girl Talk* and *Some Girls*), Millenium Films, 1998.
Malcolm, *Playing by Heart* (also known as *Dancing about Architecture*), Miramax, 1998.
Frank Shorter, *Without Limits,* Warner Bros., 1998.
Don's Plum, 1998.
Robert, *Bongwater,* Alliance Independent, 1998.
Alex Harty, *This Space Between Us,* Fault Line, 1999.
Justin Peterson, *Takedown,* 1999.
Sonny James, *Trash,* 1999.

Television Appearances; Miniseries:

Kenny Klein, *The 60's,* NBC, 1999.

Television Appearances; Movies:

Josh, *Desperate Choices: To Save My Child* (also known as *The Final Choice* and *Solomon's Choice*), NBC, 1992.
Trey Miller, *The Shaggy Dog,* ABC, 1994.
Frederick Seward, *The Day Lincoln was Shot,* TNT, 1998.

Television Appearances; Specials:

Familiar Bonds-cast, *Out of Order: Rock the Vote Targets Health Care,* MTV, 1995.

Television Appearances; Episodic:

Voice of Bobby, *Duckman,* 1994.

OTHER SOURCES

Periodicals:

Teen Magazine, October, 1997, p. 56.*

SKERRITT, Tom 1933-
(M. Borman)

PERSONAL

Born August 25, 1933, in Detroit, MI; son of Roy (in business) and Helen (a homemaker) Skerritt; married; wife's name, Charlotte (divorced); married Sue Aran (an operator of a bed and breakfast establishment; divorced, 1992); children: (first marriage) Andy (a screenwriter), Erin, Matt; (second marriage) Collin. *Education:* Attended Wayne State University and the University of California, Los Angeles.

Addresses: *Agent*—Guttman Associates, 118 South Beverly Dr., Beverly Hills, CA 90212-3003.

Career: Actor, director, producer, and writer. Also appeared in television commercials. *Military service:* Served in the U.S. Air Force.

Awards, Honors: National Board of Review Award, best supporting actor, 1977, for *The Turning Point;* Emmy Award, outstanding lead actor in a drama series, 1993, Golden Globe Award nominations, best actor in a television drama, 1994 and 1995, and Screen Actors Guild Award nomination, outstanding performance by a male actor in a drama series, 1995, all for *Picket Fences;* Blockbuster Entertainment Award nomination, favorite supporting actor in a drama, 1997, for *Contact.*

CREDITS

Film Appearances:

Corporal Showalter, *War Hunt,* United Artists, 1962.
Whit Turner, *Those Callaways,* Buena Vista, 1964.
One Man's Way, 1964.
Duke Forrest, *M*A*S*H,* Twentieth Century-Fox, 1970.
(As M. Borman) Police officer on motorcycle, *Harold and Maude,* Paramount, 1971.
John Buckman, *Wild Rovers,* Metro-Goldwyn-Mayer, 1972.

Detective Bert Kling, *Fuzz,* United Artists, 1972.
Fred Diller, *Big Bad Mama,* New World Pictures, 1974.
Dee Mobley, *Thieves Like Us,* United Artists, 1974.
Margherito, *Arrivano Joe e Margherito* (also known as *Run, Run, Joe!* and *Joe y Margherito*), 1974.
Tom Preston, *The Devil's Rain,* Bryanston, 1975.
La madama, Filmes, 1975.
Chief inspector, *E tanta paura* (also known as *Too Much Fear*), C. P. C. Cinematografica/G. P. E. Enterprises, 1976.
Wayne Rodger, *The Turning Point,* Twentieth Century-Fox, 1977.
Strawberry, *Up in Smoke* (also known as *Cheech and Chong: Up in Smoke* and *Cheech and Chong's Up in Smoke*), Paramount, 1978.
Captain Dallas, *Alien,* Twentieth Century-Fox, 1979.
Marcus Winston, *Ice Castles,* Columbia, 1979.
Walter Reamer, *Silence of the North,* Universal, 1981.
Howard Anderson, *A Dangerous Summer* (also known as *A Burning Man*), Virgin Vision, 1981.
Casey, *Savage Harvest,* Twentieth Century-Fox, 1981.
John D'Angelo, *Fighting Back* (also known as *Death Vengeance*), EMI, 1982.
Sheriff George Bannerman, *The Dead Zone,* Paramount, 1983.
Commander Mike "Viper" Metcalfe, *Top Gun,* Paramount, 1986.
Zach, *Space Camp* (also known as *SpaceCamp*), Twentieth Century-Fox, 1987.
Phil Carpenter, *The Big Town,* Columbia, 1987.
Lloyd Wisdom, *Wisdom,* Twentieth Century-Fox, 1987.
Major Logan, *Opposing Force* (also known as *Hellcamp*), Orion, 1987.
Charles Montgomery, *Maid to Order,* New Century/Vista, 1987.
Bruce Gardner, *Poltergeist III,* Metro-Goldwyn-Mayer/United Artists, 1988.
Drum Eatenton, *Steel Magnolias,* TriStar, 1989.
Eugene Ackerman, *The Rookie,* Warner Bros., 1990.
Sam Cahill, *Honor Bound,* 1990.
Dr. Webster, *Big Man on Campus* (also known as *The Hunchback Hairball of L.A.* and *The Hunchback of UCLA*), Vestron, 1991.
Darryl Cooper, *Poison Ivy,* New Line Cinema, 1992.
Reverend Maclean, *A River Runs through It,* Columbia, 1992.
Mayor Weber, *Singles,* Warner Bros., 1992.
Ham, *Wild Orchid II: Two Shades of Blue* (also known as *Wild Orchid 2: Blue Movie Blue*), Triumph Releasing, 1992.
Frank Sedman, *Knight Moves* (also known as *Face to Face* and *Knight Moves—Ein moerderisches Spiel*), Columbia/TriStar, 1992.
Narrator, *The Art of Nature* (documentary), [video], 1995.
Dr. David Drumlin, *Contact,* Warner Bros., 1997.
Police chief, *Smoke Signals* (also known as *This Is What It Means to Say Phoenix, Arizona*), Miramax, 1997.
Chief Aheran, *Aftershock,* 1999.
Radley Tate, *The Other Sister,* Buena Vista, 1999.
Texas Rangers, Dimension Films, 2000.

Television Appearances; Series:
Dr. Thomas Ryan, *Ryan's Four,* ABC, 1983.
Evan Drake, *Cheers,* NBC, 1987-88.
Sheriff Jimmy Brock, *Picket Fences,* CBS, 1992-96.

Television Appearances; Miniseries:
Fred Maddux, *The Hunt for the Unicorn Killer,* NBC, 1999.

Television Appearances; Movies:
Orville "Fitz" Fitzgerald, *The Birdmen* (also known as *Escape of the Birdmen*), ABC, 1971.
Bill Powers, *The Last Day,* NBC, 1975.
John Gosford, *Maneaters Are Loose!,* CBS, 1978.
A Question of Honor, CBS, 1982.
Dan Stoner, *Calendar Girl Murders* (also known as *Insatiable* and *Victimized*), ABC, 1984.
Father Dwelle, *A Touch of Scandal* (also known as *Somebody Knows*), CBS, 1984.
Stuart Browning, *Miles to Go* (also known as *Leaving Home*), CBS, 1986.
Bill Grant, *Parent Trap II,* The Disney Channel, 1986.
Jeremy Collins, *Poker Alice,* CBS, 1987.
Ding Harris, *Nightmare at Bitter Creek,* CBS, 1988.
John Kellogg, *Moving Target,* NBC, 1988.
Ebet Berens, *The Heist,* HBO, 1989.
Bill Stoner, *Red King, White Knight,* HBO, 1989.
Thurston "T" Bass, *Child in the Night* (also known as *Murder in the Family* and *Testimone oculare*), CBS, 1990.
Sam Brodie, *The China Lake Murders,* USA Network, 1990.
Judge Warren T. Danvers, *I'll Take Romance* (also known as *She'll Take Romance*), ABC, 1990.
Jarrett Mattison, *In Sickness and in Health* (also known as *Hearts on Fire*), CBS, 1992.
Jack Montgomery, *Getting Up and Going Home,* Lifetime, 1992.
Steve Riordan, *Divided by Hate* (also known as *Bitter Markings*), USA Network, 1997.
Sam Houston, *Two for Texas,* TNT, 1998.

Television Work; Director; Movies:

Divided by Hate (also known as *Bitter Markings*), USA Network, 1997.

Producer and director of the movie *Last of the Grape Jelly Glasses.*

Television Appearances; Specials:

"Inherit the Wind," *Hallmark Hall of Fame,* NBC, 1967.
Trapani, *A Bell for Adano,* NBC, 1967.
Narrator, *Over America,* PBS, 1995.
Norm Jenkins, "What the Deaf Man Heard," *Hallmark Hall of Fame,* CBS, 1997.

Television Work; Director; Specials:

"A Question about Sex" (also known as "Kelly vs. Kelly"), *ABC Afterschool Specials,* ABC, 1990.

Television Appearances; Awards Presentations:

The Golden Globe Awards, TBS, 1990.
Host, *Wyatt Earp: Walk with a Legend,* CBS, 1994.
Presenter, *The 2nd Annual Screen Actors Guild Awards,* 1996.

Television Appearances; Episodic:

"Impasse," *The Virginian,* NBC, 1962.
"A Day in June," *Combat!,* ABC, 1962.
Glinski, "The Prisoner," *Combat!,* ABC, 1962.
"Run for Doom," *The Alfred Hitchcock Hour,* NBC, 1963.
"Thunder Gap," *Temple Houston,* NBC, 1963.
"Honor the Name Dennis Driscoll," *Death Valley Days,* syndicated, 1964.
"The Secret of Brynmar Hall," *The Virginian,* NBC, 1964.
"The Last Circle Up," *Wagon Train,* ABC, 1964.
"Those Who Are About to Die," *Twelve O'Clock High,* ABC, 1965.
Hicks, "Losers Cry Deal," *Combat!,* ABC, 1965.
Richardson, "The Enemies," *Voyage to the Bottom of the Sea,* ABC, 1965.
Sergeant Ben Rodale, "Then Came the Mighty Hunter," *Twelve O'Clock High,* ABC, 1965.
Edmund Dano, "The Pretender," *Gunsmoke,* CBS, 1965.
Corky Mardis, "Gallagher," *Walt Disney's Wonderful World of Color,* NBC, 1965.
Corky Mardis, "The Further Adventures of Gallagher," *Walt Disney's Wonderful World of Color,* NBC, 1965.
Heely Hollister, "Nicest Fella You'd Ever Want to Meet," *The Fugitive,* ABC, 1965.
"The Showdown," *The Virginian,* NBC, 1965.
Burke, "Nothing to Lose," *Combat!,* ABC, 1966.
"The 25th Mission," *Twelve O'Clock High,* ABC, 1966.
Ben Stone, "The Jailer," *Gunsmoke,* CBS, 1966.
"The Assassin," *The F.B.I.,* ABC, 1966.
Pete, "Joshua's Kingdom," *The Fugitive,* ABC, 1966.
Matthew, "The Deadly Trap," *Time Tunnel,* ABC, 1966.
Rov Timpson, "The Moonstone," *Gunsmoke,* CBS, 1966.
"A Long Way Down," *Twelve O'Clock High,* ABC, 1967.
Sergeant Decker, "The Gauntlet," *Combat!,* ABC, 1967.
"Warning: Live Blueberries," *Mannix,* CBS, 1967.
"The Legend of John Rim," *The F.B.I.,* ABC, 1967.
Corky Mardis, "Gallagher Goes West," *Walt Disney's Wonderful World of Color,* NBC, 1967.
"Knife in the Darkness," *Cimarron Strip,* CBS, 1968.
"The Killing Scene," *Run for Your Life,* NBC, 1968.
"The Crooked Path," *The Virginian,* NBC, 1968.
"The Saddle Warmer," *The Virginian,* NBC, 1968.
"Matched for Murder," *Felony Squad,* ABC, 1968.
"The Knot," *Lancer,* CBS, 1969.
"Most Likely to Murder," *Hawaii Five-O,* CBS, 1970.
"Between Dark and Daylight," *Medical Center,* CBS, 1970.
"The Noose," *Gunsmoke,* CBS, 1970.
"Cynthia Is Alive and Well and Living in Avalon," *The Name of the Game,* NBC, 1970.
"A Team of One-Legged Acrobats," *Bracken's World,* NBC, 1970.
"The Unknown Victim," *The F.B.I.,* ABC, 1971.
"Nan Allen," *The Virginian,* NBC, 1971.
"This Money Kills Dreams," *Men at Law,* CBS, 1971.
Dude, "Salinas Jackpot," *Cannon,* CBS, 1971.
"The Marrying Fool," *Nichols,* NBC, 1971.
"The Deadly Species," *The F.B.I.,* ABC, 1972.
"Jubilee," *Gunsmoke,* CBS, 1972.
Toby Hauser, "Nobody Beats the House," *Cannon,* CBS, 1972.
Corporal Bill Tanner, "The Hunter," *Bonanza,* NBC, 1973.
"Deadly Betrayal," *Get Christie Love!,* ABC, 1974.
"Flight to Nowhere," *Manhunter,* CBS, 1974.
Senator Robert W. Palmer, "The Devil's Platform," *Kolchak: The Night Stalker* (also known as *The Night Stalker*), ABC, 1974.
Sheriff Andrews, "The Conspirators," *Cannon,* CBS, 1975.
"Image of Evil," *Barnaby Jones,* CBS, 1975.
Maynard Hill, "Dragons and Owls," *S.W.A.T.,* ABC, 1976.
"The Appointment," *Baretta,* ABC, 1978.

"Sam in the Gray Flannel Suit," *Cheers,* NBC, 1983.
Detective Sheen, "True Believer," *The Hitchhiker* (also known as *Le voyageur*), HBO, 1985.
"Aqua Vita," *The Twilight Zone,* CBS, 1986.
Alex Mattingly, "What Are Friends For?," *The Twilight Zone,* CBS, 1986.
Jim Kellner, "Guns 'n' Roses," *Chicago Hope,* CBS, 1997.

Television Work; Director; Episodic:
Directed episodes of *Picket Fences,* CBS.

Television Appearances; Pilots:
Dr. Thomas Ryan, *Ryan's Four,* ABC, 1983.
Jack Shake, *On the Edge* (also known as *Dirty Work*), NBC, 1987.

Stage Appearances:
Appeared as Andrew Makepeace Ladd III in *Love Letters.*

WRITINGS

Teleplays; Movies:
Divided by Hate (also known as *Bitter Markings*), USA Network, 1997.

Wrote *The Last of the Grape Jelly Glasses.*

OTHER SOURCES

Periodicals:
People Weekly, April 17, 1995, p. 71.*

SLATER, Helen 1963-

PERSONAL

Full name, Helen Rachel Slater; born December 15, 1963, in New York (some sources cite Massapequa), NY; daughter of Gerald (a television executive) and Alice Joan (a lawyer; maiden name, Chrin) Slater; married Robert Watzke (a commercial film editor), 1990; children: Hannah Nika. *Education:* Attended High School for Performing Arts; trained for the stage with Gary Austin, Bill Esper, Sandra Seacat, Merry Conway, and at Shakespeare and Company. *Politics:* Democrat. *Religion:* Jewish.

Addresses: *Agent*—Innovative Artists, 1999 Avenue of the Stars, Suite 2850, Los Angeles, CA 90211.

Career: Actress. Naked Angels (theatre company), New York City, co-founder; composer of piano music. Appeared in television commercials for L'Oreal hair products, 1995-96.

CREDITS

Film Appearances:
Title role/Linda Lee, *Supergirl* (also known as *Supergirl: The Movie*), TriStar, 1984.
Billie Jean Davy, the title role, *The Legend of Billie Jean,* TriStar, 1985.
Sandy Kessler, *Ruthless People,* Buena Vista, 1986.
Christy Wills, *The Secret of My Success,* Universal, 1987.
Hattie, *Sticky Fingers,* Spectrafilm, 1988.
Alexandra "Alex" Paige, *Happy Together,* Apollo Pictures, 1990.
Bonnie Rayburn, *City Slickers,* Columbia, 1991.
Ellie, *Betrayal of the Dove,* Prism Pictures, 1993.
Alex Weaver, *A House in the Hills,* LIVE Home Video, 1993.
Laura Turner, *Lassie,* Paramount, 1994.
Kim, *The Steal,* 1994.
Voice, *The Long Way Home,* Seventh Art Releasing, 1997.
Lisa Torello, *Carlo's Wake,* 1999.

Also appeared in *In Deep.*

Television Appearances; Series:
Anne McKenna, *Capital News* (also known as *Powerhouse*), ABC, 1990.

Television Appearances; Movies:
Hannah, *Chantilly Lace,* Showtime, 1993.
Lisa Fredericks, *12:01,* Fox, 1993.
Elsa Freedman, *Parallel Lives,* Showtime, 1994.
Mary, *No Way Back,* HBO, 1996.
Mrs. Lewis, *Toothless,* ABC, 1997.
Pammy, *Best Friends for Life,* CBS, 1998.

Television Appearances; Episodic:
Lauren, "Wasting Away," *The Hidden Room,* Lifetime, 1991.
The Arsenio Hall Show, syndicated, 1991.
Voice of Talia, "Off Balance," *Batman: The Animated Series* (also known as *The Adventures of Batman and Robin*), Fox, 1992.
Becky Gelke, "The Good Samaritan," *Seinfeld,* NBC, 1992.
Sarah, "The Theory of Relativity," *Dream On,* HBO, 1992.
The Arsenio Hall Show, syndicated, 1993.

Voice of Talia, "Demon's Quest," Parts 1-2, *Batman: The Animated Series* (also known as *The Adventures of Batman and Robin*), Fox, 1993.
Voice of Talia, "Avatar," *Batman: The Animated Series* (also known as *The Adventures of Batman and Robin*), Fox, 1994.
Cassandra Thompson, "Caroline and the Monkeys," *Caroline in the City,* NBC, 1997.
Julie Siegel, "Retribution," *Michael Hayes,* CBS, 1997.
Julie Siegel, "Mob Mentality," *Michael Hayes,* CBS, 1998.
Julie Siegel, "Arise and Fall," *Michael Hayes,* CBS, 1998.

Television Appearances; Specials:
Amy Watson, "Amy and the Angel," *ABC Afterschool Special,* ABC, 1982.
Supergirl—The Making of the Movie, ABC, 1985.
Nina, *Couples,* ABC, 1994.

Other Television Appearances:
Anne McKenna, *Capital News* (pilot; also known as *Powerhouse*), ABC, 1990.
Jacqui Cochrane, *The Great Air Race* (also known as *Half a World Away*), 1990.

Stage Appearances:
Tina, *Responsible Parties,* Vineyard Theatre, New York City, 1985.
Nicole, "Almost Romance," in *Festival of One-Act Comedies,* Manhattan Punch Line Theatre, New York City, 1987.

Also appeared in *The Big Day,* Pasadena Playhouse, Pasadena, CA.*

SMITH, Anna Deavere 1950-

PERSONAL

Middle name is pronounced "duh-*veer*"; born September 18, 1950, in Baltimore, MD; daughter of Deavere Young (a coffee merchant) and Anna (an elementary school principal; maiden name, Young) Smith. *Education:* Beaver College, B.A., 1971; American Conservatory Theatre, M.F.A., 1976.

Addresses: *Agent*—David Williams, International Creative Management, 40 West 57th St., New York, NY 10019.

Career: Actress and writer. American Conservatory Theatre, San Francisco, CA, member of company, 1974-76; Carnegie-Mellon University, Pittsburgh, PA, assistant professor of theatre, 1978-79; Yale University, New Haven, CT, visiting artist, 1982; New York University, New York City, teacher of acting, 1983-84; National Theatre Institute, visiting teacher, 1984-85; American Conservatory Theatre, master teacher of acting, 1986, member of company, 1988-89; Stanford University, Stanford, CA, professor of theatre, 1990—, currently Ann O'Day Maples Professor of the Arts. University of Southern California, assistant professor; Lincoln Center Institute, teaching artist; Harvard University, director of Institute on the Arts and Civic Dialogue, 1998. KLM Airlines, customer service representative, 1976.

Member: Directors Guild of America, Dramatists Guild, American Federation of Television and Radio Artists, Screen Actors Guild, Actors' Equity Association.

Awards, Honors: *Drama-Logue* Award, Obie Award, *Village Voice,* Drama Desk Award, Lucille Lortel Award, George and Elisabeth Marton Award, Kesselring Prize, and Pulitzer Prize nomination, drama, all 1992, for *Fires in the Mirror: Crown Heights, Brooklyn, and Other Identities;* Antoinette Perry Award, best play, Antoinette Perry Award nomination, best actress, Obie Award, Drama Desk Award, and Special Achievement Award, Outer Critics Circle, all 1993, for *Twilight: Los Angeles, 1992; Theatre World* Award, outstanding new talent, 1993-94; Special Award, New York Drama Critics Circle, 1994, for *Three Tall Women;* grant from John D. and Catherine T. MacArthur Foundation, 1996; Ford Foundation grant, 1997; grants from National Theatre Artist Residency Program; honorary degree from Beaver College; fellow of Bunting Institute, Radcliffe College.

CREDITS

Stage Appearances:
(Stage debut) The savage, *Horatio,* American Conservatory Theatre, San Francisco, CA, 1974.
(New York debut) Marie Laveau, *Alma, the Ghost of Spring Street,* La Mama Experimental Theatre Club, 1976.
Mother Courage, New York Shakespeare Festival, New York City, 1980.
On the Road, Clear Space Theatre, New York City, 1982, then Berkeley Repertory Company, Berkeley, CA, 1983.

A Birthday Party and *Aunt Julia's Shoes* (original poems), Ward Nasse Gallery, New York City, 1983.
Doreen, *Tartuffe,* GeVa Theatre, Rochester, NY, 1983.
Charlayne Hunter Gault, Ward Nasse Gallery, 1984.
Aye, Aye, Aye, I'm Integrated, American Place Theatre, New York City, 1984.
Building Bridges, Not Walls, National Conference of Women and the Law, New York City, 1985.
On the Road: ACT, American Conservatory Theatre, 1986.
Voices of Bay Area Women, Phoenix Theatre, San Francisco, CA, 1988.
Chlorophyll Post-Modernism and the Mother Goddess: A Convers/Ation, Hahn Cosmopolitan Theatre, San Diego, CA, 1988.
Gender Bending: On the Road Princeton University, Princeton University, Princeton, NJ, 1989.
Piano, Los Angeles Theatre Center, Los Angeles, CA, 1989-90.
Gender Bending: On the Road University of Pennsylvania, University of Pennsylvania, Philadelphia, 1990.
On Black Identity and Black Theatre, Crossroads Theatre Company, New Brunswick, NJ, 1990.
From the Outside Looking In, Eureka Theatre, San Francisco, 1990.
Fragments, Conference on Intercultural Performance, Bellagio, Italy, 1991.
Identities, Mirrors, and Distortions I, Calistoga Arts Festival, Calistoga, CA, 1991.
Identities, Mirrors, and Distortions II, Bay Area Playwrights Festival, San Francisco, CA, 1991.
Identities, Mirrors, and Distortions III, Global Communities Conference, Stanford University, Stanford, CA, 1991.
Identities, Mirrors, and Distortions IV, Festival of New Voices, Joseph Papp Public Theatre, New York City, 1991.
Dream (workshop), Crossroads Theatre Company, 1992.
Fires in the Mirror: Crown Heights, Brooklyn, and Other Identities (solo show), Joseph Papp Public Theatre, 1992, then Royal Court Theatre, London, 1993.
Hymn (ballet), Alvin Ailey American Dance Theatre, City Center Theatre, New York City, 1993.
Twilight: Los Angeles, 1992 (solo show), Mark Taper Forum, Los Angeles, 1993, then Joseph Papp Public Theatre, later Cort Theatre, New York City, both 1994.
Three Tall Women, New York City production, 1994.
House Arrest: First Edition (two-act), Kreeger Theatre, Washington, DC, 1997.

Film Appearances:
(Film debut) Deborah, *Soup for One,* Warner Bros., 1982.
Anna, *Unfinished Business,* American Film Institute, 1987.
Mrs. Travis, *Dave,* Warner Bros., 1993.
Anthea Burton, *Philadelphia,* TriStar, 1993.
Robin McCall, *The American President,* Columbia, 1995.

Television Appearances: Specials:
The Issue Is Race, PBS, 1992.
"Fires in the Mirror," *American Playhouse,* PBS, 1993.
Narrator, *Hawaii's Last Queen,* PBS, 1997.
A Hymn for Alvin Ailey, PBS, 1999.

Television Appearances; Series:
(Television debut) Hazel, *All My Children,* ABC, 1983.

WRITINGS

Plays:
On the Road, produced at Clear Space, New York City, 1982, then by Berkeley Repertory Co., Berkeley, CA, 1983.
A Birthday Party (original poems), performed at Ward Nasse Gallery, New York City, 1983.
Aunt Julia's Shoes (original poems), performed at Ward Nasse Gallery, 1983.
Charlayne Hunter Gault, performed at Ward Nasse Gallery, 1984.
Aye, Aye, Aye, I'm Integrated, produced at American Place Theatre, New York City, 1984.
Building Bridges, Not Walls, performed at National Conference of Women and the Law, New York City, 1985.
On the Road: ACT, produced by American Conservatory Theatre, 1986.
Voices of Bay Area Women, produced at Phoenix Theatre, 1988.
Chlorophyll Post-Modernism and the Mother Goddess: A Convers/Ation, Hahn Cosmopolitan Theatre, 1988.
Gender Bending: On the Road Princeton University, produced at Princeton University, Princeton, NJ, 1989.
Piano, produced at Los Angeles Theatre Center, Los Angeles, 1989-90.
Gender Bending: On the Road University of Pennsylvania, produced at University of Pennsylvania, Philadelphia, 1990.
On Black Identity and Black Theatre, produced by Crossroads Theatre Company, New Brunswick, NJ, 1990.

From the Outside Looking In, produced at Eureka Theatre, San Francisco, 1990.
Fragments, performed at Conference on Intercultural Performance, Bellagio, Italy, 1991.
Identities, Mirrors, and Distortions I, produced at Calistoga Arts Festival, Calistoga, CA, 1991.
Identities, Mirrors, and Distortions II, produced at Bay Area Playwrights Festival, San Francisco, 1991.
Identities, Mirrors, and Distortions III, produced at Global Communities Conference, Stanford University, Stanford, 1991.
Identities, Mirrors, and Distortions IV, produced at Festival of New Voices, Joseph Papp Public Theatre, New York City, 1991.
Dream (workshop), produced by Crossroads Theatre Company, 1992.
Fires in the Mirror: Crown Heights, Brooklyn, and Other Identities (solo show), produced at Joseph Papp Public Theatre, 1992, then Royal Court Theatre, London, 1993, published by Anchor Books (New York), 1993.
(With Judith Jamison) *Hymn* (ballet), produced by Alvin Ailey American Dance Theatre, City Center Theatre, New York City, 1993.
Twilight: Los Angeles, 1992 (solo show), produced at Mark Taper Forum, Los Angeles, 1993, then Joseph Papp Public Theatre, later Cort Theatre, both 1994, published as *Twilight—Los Angeles, 1992 on the Road: A Search for American Character,* Anchor Books, 1994.
Three Tall Women, New York City production, 1994.
House Arrest: First Edition (two-act), Kreeger Theatre, Washington, DC, 1997.

Television Specials:
"Fires in the Mirror" (based on her stage play), *American Playhouse,* PBS, 1993.

OTHER SOURCES

Books:
Contemporary Authors, Volume 133, Gale (Detroit, MI), 1991.

Periodicals:
American Theatre, October, 1996, p. 18; December, 1998, p. 68.
Interview, September, 1996, p. 46.
New York Times, June 10, 1992, pp. C1, C6; April 23, 1993, pp. B7, C2; January 29, 1997.
Variety, February 3, 1997, p. 56.*

SMITH, Jaclyn 1947-

PERSONAL

Full name, Ellen Jaclyn Smith; born October 26, 1947, in Houston, TX; daughter of Jack and Margaret Ellen Smith; married Dennis Cole (divorced,1981); married Roger Davis (an actor), 1972 (marriage ended, 1975); married Dennis Cole (an actor), 1978 (divorced, 1981); married Anthony Richmond (a filmmaker), August 4, 1981 (some sources cite 1982; divorced, 1989); married Bradley Allen (a heart surgeon), October 11, 1997; children: (third marriage) Gaston Anthony, Spencer Margaret. *Education:* Attended Trinity University.

Addresses: *Agent*—Fred Westheimer, William Morris Agency, 151 South El Camino Dr., Beverly Hills, CA 90212-2704.

Career: Actress. Professional model; creator of a line of women's clothing and spokeswoman for K-Mart, beginning in 1985; appeared in television commercials for Breck shampoo, 1973.

Member: American Federation of Television and Radio Artists, Screen Actors Guild.

Awards, Honors: Golden Globe Award nomination, best actress in a miniseries or television movie, 1981, for *Jacqueline Bouvier Kennedy;* cited as one of the fifty most beautiful people in the world, *People Weekly,* 1990.

CREDITS

Television Appearances; Series:
Kelly Garrett, *Charlie's Angels,* ABC, 1976-81.

Television Appearances; Pilots:
Probe (pilot for the series *Search*), NBC, 1972.
Susan Cole, *Fools, Females, and Fun: Is There a Doctor in the House?,* NBC, 1974.
Alice, *Switch* (also known as *Las Vegas Roundabout*), CBS, 1975.
Kelly Garrett, *Toni's Boys* (broadcast as an episode of *Charlie's Angels*), ABC, 1980.

Television Appearances; Episodic:
Tina, "When Mother Gets Married," *The Partridge Family,* ABC, 1970.
Catherine Hart, "Showdown at the End of the World," *McCloud,* NBC, 1973.

Margaret Hart, "The Man with the Golden Hat," *McCloud,* NBC, 1975.
"A High Fashion Heist," *Get Christie Love,* ABC, 1975.
"The Old Diamond Game," *Switch,* CBS, 1975.
"The Late Show Murders," *Switch,* CBS, 1975.
"Death Heist," *Switch,* CBS, 1975.
"Go Ahead and Cry," *The Rookies,* ABC, 1975.
"The Whiz Kid and the Carnival Caper," *World of Disney,* NBC, 1976.
"The Angels and the Bums," *San Pedro Beach Bums,* ABC, 1977.
"A Tasteful Affair," *The Love Boat,* ABC, 1977.
Kelly Garrett, "Mystery of the Hollywood Phantom (Part 2)," *Hardy Boys/Nancy Drew Mysteries,* ABC, 1977.
Christine Cromwell, "Things That Go Bump in the Night," *Christine Cromwell* (broadcast as a segment of *ABC Saturday Mystery*), ABC, 1989.
Christine Cromwell, "Easy Come, Easy Go," *Christine Cromwell* (broadcast as a segment of *ABC Saturday Mystery*), ABC, 1989.
Christine Cromwell, "Plates," *B.L. Stryker* (broadcast as a segment of *ABC Saturday Mystery*), ABC, 1990.
Christine Cromwell, "Only the Good Die Young," *Christine Cromwell* (broadcast as a segment of *ABC Saturday Mystery*), ABC, 1990.
Christine Cromwell, "In Vino Veritas," *Christine Cromwell* (broadcast as a segment of *ABC Saturday Mystery*), ABC, 1990.

Also appeared on *The Rookies,* ABC.

Television Appearances; Movies:
Maggie Bowman, *Escape from Bogen County,* CBS, 1977.
Elena Schneider, *The Users,* ABC, 1978.
Katherine Atwell, *Night Kill,* NBC, 1980.
Title role, *Jacqueline Bouvier Kennedy,* ABC, 1981.
Jennifer Parker, *Rage of Angels* (also known as *Sidney Sheldon's Rage of Angels*), NBC, 1983.
Claudia Baldwin, *The Night They Saved Christmas,* ABC, 1984.
Julie Ross-Gardner, *Sentimental Journey,* CBS, 1984.
Title role, *Florence Nightingale,* NBC, 1985.
Jennifer Parker, *Rage of Angels: The Story Continues,* NBC, 1986.
Katherine "Kate" Whately, *Settle the Score* (also known as *Hidden Rage* and *Blood Knot*), NBC, 1989.
Hilary, *Danielle Steele's "Kaleidoscope"* (also known as *Kaleidoscope*), NBC, 1990.
Elaine Sanders, *Lies before Kisses,* CBS, 1991.
Dr. Kate Willis, *The Rape of Dr. Willis,* CBS, 1991.
Megan Lambert, *Nightmare in the Daylight,* CBS, 1992.
Maria Quinn, *In the Arms of a Killer* (also known as *Kiss of Death* and *The Tangled Web*), NBC, 1992.
Elizabeth Bentley, *Love Can Be Murder* (also known as *Kindred Spirits*), NBC, 1992.
Donna Yaklich, *Cries Unheard: The Donna Yaklich Story* (also known as *Victim of Rage*), CBS, 1994.
Dana Griffin, *My Very Best Friend,* CBS, 1996.
Megan Potter, *Married to a Stranger,* The Family Channel, 1997.
Bridgette Smith Michaels, *Before He Wakes,* CBS, 1998.
Renee Brennan, *Freefall,* Fox Family Channel, 1999.

Also appeared in *My Angry Son,* CBS.

Television Appearances; Miniseries:
Sally Fairfax, *George Washington,* CBS, 1984.
Mary Ashley, *Sidney Sheldon's "Windmills of the Gods"* (also known as *Windmills of the Gods*), CBS, 1988.
Marie St. Jacques, *The Bourne Identity,* ABC, 1988.
Faye Price Thayer, *Danielle Steele's "Family Album"* (also known as *Family Album*), NBC, 1994.

Television Appearances; Specials:
Battle of the Network Stars II, ABC, 1977.
Hostess, *The Mad Mad Mad Mad World of the Super Bowl,* NBC, 1977.
ABC's Silver Anniversary Celebration—25 and Still the One, ABC, 1978.
Host, *Magic with the Stars,* NBC, 1982.
The Night of 100 Stars II, ABC, 1985.
Texas 150: A Celebration Special, ABC, 1986.
Host, *The Kraft All-Star Salute to Ford's Theatre,* Lifetime, 1986.
Lifetime Salutes Mom, Lifetime, 1987.
Happy Birthday, Hollywood!, ABC, 1987.
Sea World's All-Star, Lone Star Celebration (also known as *New Friends . . . Sea World Comes to Texas*), CBS, 1988.
Host, *Voices of Hope . . . Finding the Cures for Breast and Ovarian Cancer,* Lifetime, 1997.
An All Star Party for Aaron Spelling, ABC, 1998.
Intimate Portrait: Jaclyn Smith, Lifetime, 1998.

Television Appearances; Awards Presentations:
The 39th Annual Emmy Awards, Fox, 1987.
The 13th Annual People's Choice Awards, CBS, 1987.
The 18th Annual People's Choice Awards, CBS, 1992.
Presenter, *The 1998 Creative Arts Emmy Awards,* 1998.

Film Appearances:

Model, *Goodbye Columbus,* Paramount, 1969.
Belinda, *The Adventurers,* Paramount, 1970.
Sally Fannie Tatum, *Bootleggers* (also known as *Bootlegger's Angel*), Howco International, 1974.
Maggie Rogers and Brooke Ashley, *Deja Vu,* Cannon, 1985.

Stage Appearances:

The Night of 100 Stars II, Radio City Music Hall, New York City, 1985.

Appeared in productions of *Bye Bye Birdie, Gentlemen Prefer Blondes, Peg,* and *West Side Story.*

WRITINGS

Nonfiction:

The American Look, Simon & Schuster (New York City), 1984.
The Jaclyn Smith Beauty Book, Simon & Schuster, 1985.

OTHER SOURCES

Periodicals:

People Weekly, October 27, 1997, p. 56.*

SMITH, Lane 1936-

PERSONAL

Born April 29, 1936, in Memphis, TN. *Education:* Attended Carnegie Institute of Technology (now Carnegie-Mellon University); trained for the stage with Lee Strasberg at Actors Studio, 1965.

Addresses: *Agent*—c/o 10000 Santa Monica Blvd., Suite 305, Los Angeles, CA 90067.

Career: Actor. *Military service:* U.S. Army.

Awards, Honors: Drama Desk Award, c. 1984, for *Glengarry Glen Ross;* Golden Globe Award nomination, best actor in a miniseries or television movie, 1989, for "The Final Days," *AT&T Presents.*

CREDITS

Television Appearances; Series:

Nathan Bates, *V: The Series,* NBC, 1984-85.
Dr. Robert Moffitt, *Kay O'Brien,* CBS, 1986.
Mr. R. J. Rappaport, *Good Sports,* CBS, 1991.
Harlan Shell, *Good and Evil,* ABC, 1991.
Perry White, *Lois and Clark: The New Adventures of Superman* (also known as *Lois and Clark* and *The New Adventures of Superman*), ABC, 1993-96.

Television Appearances; Movies:

Crash (also known as *Crash of Flight 401*), ABC, 1978.
Bob Hartman, *A Death in Canaan,* CBS, 1978.
John Carlson, *Disaster on the Coastliner,* ABC, 1979.
Jack Collins, *The Solitary Man,* CBS, 1979.
Brian, *City in Fear,* ABC, 1980.
Fred Turner, *Gideon's Trumpet,* CBS, 1980.
Don Payer, *Mark, I Love You,* CBS, 1980.
Sergeant William Holgren, *A Rumor of War,* CBS, 1980.
Harless Hocker, *Dark Night of the Scarecrow,* CBS, 1981.
Clarence Blake, *Thou Shalt Not Kill,* NBC, 1982.
Tom Keating, *Prime Suspect,* CBS, 1982.
Morton Sanders, *Special Bulletin,* NBC, 1983.
Officer Dealy, *Something about Amelia,* ABC, 1984.
Anson Whitfield, *Bridge across Time* (also known as *Arizona Ripper* and *Terror at London Bridge*), NBC, 1985.
Captain Max Rosenberg, *Beverly Hills Cowgirl Blues,* CBS, 1985.
Colonel King, *Dress Gray,* NBC, 1986.
Sam Gavin, *A Place to Call Home,* CBS, 1987.
Dr. Butler, *Killer Instinct* (also known as *Over the Edge*), NBC, 1988.
Colonel Blanchard, *Blind Vengeance,* USA Network, 1990.
Fryman, *Duplicates,* USA Network, 1992.
Senator Silverthorne, *Alien Nation: The Udara Legacy,* Fox, 1997.

Television Appearances; Miniseries:

Hoss Spence, *Chiefs,* CBS, 1983.
Warden Brannigan, *If Tomorrow Comes,* CBS, 1986.
Martin Busey, *False Arrest* (also known as *The Joyce Lukezic Story* and *Reasonable Doubt*), ABC, 1991.
Emmett Seaborn, *From the Earth to the Moon,* HBO, 1998.

Television Appearances; Pilots:

Randolph Dukane, *The Georgia Peaches* (also known as *Follow That Car*), CBS, 1980.
Lieutenant Frank Medley, *The Big Easy,* NBC, 1982.

Television Appearances; Episodic:

"Queen of the Gypsies," *Kojak,* CBS, 1975.
Willet, "Claire," *The Rockford Files,* NBC, 1975.

Mr. Shortley, "The Displaced Person," *The American Short Story,* PBS, 1978.
"The Battle Ax and the Exploded Cigar," *The Rockford Files,* NBC, 1979.
Prosecutor, "Gone But Not Forgotten," *Dallas,* CBS, 1981.
"Unthinkable," *Lou Grant,* CBS, 1982.
Chicago Story, NBC, 1982.
"Science for Sale," *Quincy, M.E.,* NBC, 1982.
Captain Milton Treadwell, *Hollywood Beat,* ABC, 1985.
Mike, "El Capitan," *Hill Street Blues,* NBC, 1985.
Dr. Joseph K. Fitzgerald, "Profile in Silver," *The Twilight Zone,* CBS, 1986.
Robert Warren, "Happy Birthday," *Alfred Hitchcock Presents,* NBC, 1986.
Dr. Caruso, "Dorothy and Ben," *Amazing Stories,* NBC, 1986.
Sonny Mims, "Road Kill," *In the Heat of the Night,* NBC, 1988.
Police Chief Underwood, "The Search for Peter Kerry," *Murder, She Wrote,* CBS, 1989.
Colonel Whitmore, *Dweebs,* 1995.
"Glyphic," *The Outer Limits,* Showtime, 1995.

Television Appearances; Specials:
Mr. Addams, *The Member of the Wedding,* NBC, 1982.
Richard M. Nixon, "The Final Days," *AT&T Presents,* ABC, 1989.
Larry Mulloy, "Challenger," *ABC Theater,* ABC, 1990.

Film Appearances:
Maidstone, Supreme Mix, 1970.
Rick Penny, *The Last American Hero* (also known as *Hard Driver*), Twentieth Century-Fox, 1973.
Ted Ronan, *Man on a Swing,* Paramount, 1974.
Leroy, *Rooster Cogburn* (also known as *Rooster Cogburn and the Lady*), Universal, 1975.
Robert McDonough, *Network,* United Artists, 1976.
Officer Mackie, *The Bad News Bears in Breaking Training,* Paramount, 1977.
Roy Walsh, *Between the Lines,* Midwest, 1977.
Clarence Hill, *Blue Collar,* Universal, 1978.
Captain Blake, *On the Yard,* Midwest, 1978.
Sloan, *Over the Edge,* Orion/Warner Bros., 1979.
Brag, *Honeysuckle Rose* (also known as *On the Road Again*), Warner Bros., 1980.
Preacher, *On the Nickel,* Rose's Park, 1980.
Don, *Resurrection,* Universal, 1980.
Tug Barnes, *Prince of the City,* Warner Bros., 1981.
Dr. Symington, *Frances,* Brooksfilm/Universal, 1982.
Smilin' Jack, *Soggy Bottom, U.S.A.* (also known as *Swamp Rats*), Gaylord, 1982.
Albert Denby, *Places in the Heart,* TriStar, 1984.
Commander Markel, *Purple Hearts,* Warner Bros., 1984.
Mayor Bates, *Red Dawn,* United Artists, 1984.
Britton, *Native Son,* Cinecom, 1986.
Claude, *Weeds,* De Laurentiis Entertainment Group, 1987.
Ethan Sharpe, *Prison,* Empire, 1988.
Witty, *Night Game,* Trans World, 1989.
Joe Gifford, *Race for Glory,* New Century/Vista, 1989.
Senator Davenport, *Air America,* TriStar, 1990.
Dick Dodge, *The Distinguished Gentleman,* Buena Vista, 1992.
Coach Reilly, *The Mighty Ducks* (also known as *Champions*), Buena Vista, 1992.
Jim Trotter, III, *My Cousin Vinny,* Twentieth Century-Fox, 1992.
Walter Warner, *Son-in-Law,* Buena Vista, 1993.
Ron Wilson, *The Scout,* Twentieth Century-Fox, 1994.
Stephen Hahn, *The Flight of the Dove* (also known as *The Spy Within*), New Horizons Home Video, 1994.
Ezra Grahme, *Why Do Fools Fall in Love,* Warner Bros., 1998.
Steve Shaw, *The Hi-Lo Country,* Gramercy Pictures, 1998.
Dr. Maddie, *Lost and Found,* ML Productions, 1998.

Also appeared in *American Built.*

Film Work:
Director, *Water Ride,* 1994.

Stage Appearances:
(Off-Broadway debut) *Leave It to Jane,* Sheridan Square Playhouse, New York City, 1959.
Lieutenant Addy, *Borak,* Martinique Theatre, New York City, 1960.
Max, *Children in the Rain,* Cherry Lane Theatre, New York City, 1970.
Stephen, *The Nest,* Mercury Theatre, New York City, 1970.
The Captain, *Pinkville,* Theatre at St. Clement's Church, New York City, 1971.
Randle Patrick McMurphy, *One Flew over the Cuckoo's Nest,* Mercer-Hansbury Theatre, New York City, 1971.
Mr. Hum, *A Break in the Skin,* Actors Studio Theatre, New York City, 1973.
Lon Tanner, *The Emperor of Late Night Radio,* New York Shakespeare Festival, Public Theatre, New York City, 1974.
Leroy Hollingsworth, *Barbary Shore,* New York Shakespeare Festival, Public Theatre, 1974.

P. Sigmund Furth, *The Leaf People,* Booth Theatre, New York City, 1975.

Joe, "Dialogue for Two Men," Harley Ffaulkes, "Midwestern Music," and Byron, "The Love Death," all in *Love Death Plays of William Inge (Part One),* Billy Rose Theatre, New York City, 1975.

Scott, *Jack Gelber's New Play: Rehearsal,* American Place Theatre, New York City, 1976.

Jack Kerouac, *Visions of Kerouac,* New Dramatists Theatre, then Lion Theatre, both New York City, 1976.

Billy Irish, Manhattan Theatre Club, New York City, 1977.

Harold, *Orphans,* Matrix Theatre, Los Angeles, CA, 1984.

James Lingk, *Glengarry Glen Ross,* John Golden Theatre, New York City, 1984.

Also appeared at the Center Stage Theatre, Baltimore, MD, 1972; and as Adolph Hitler, *Brechtesgarten,* New York City.*

SMITH, Shawnee 1970-

PERSONAL

Born July 3, 1970, in Orangeburg, SC. *Education:* Studied acting at the Playhouse West, run by actors Bob Carnegie and Jeff Goldblum. *Avocational interests:* Writer and singer for the rock-n-roll band Miram Fay.

Addresses: *Contact*—Innovative Artists, 1999 Avenue of the Stars, Suite 2850, Los Angeles, CA 90069.

Career: Actress.

Awards, Honors: Youth in Film Award, best actress in a television film, 1985, for *Crime of Innocence.*

CREDITS

Film Appearances:

Dancer, *Annie,* Columbia, 1982.

Joanie, *Iron Eagle,* TriStar, 1986.

Rhonda Altobello, *Summer School,* Paramount, 1987.

Meg Penny, *The Blob,* TriStar, 1988.

Nikki Downing, *Who's Harry Crumb?,* TriStar/NBC Productions, 1989.

May Cornell, *Desperate Hours,* Metro-Goldwyn-Mayer/United Artists, 1990.

Biker Girl, *Leaving Las Vegas,* Metro-Goldwyn-Mayer/United Artists, 1995.

Little Tramp Woman, *The Low Life,* CFP, 1995.

Makeup salesgirl, *Female Perversions,* October Films, 1996.

Sergeant 1st Class Addie Cooper, *Dead Men Can't Dance* (also known as *DMZ*and *Rangers*), Live Entertainment, 1997.

Tammy Hayes, *Dogtown* (also known as *Howling at the Moon*), 1997.

Redhead, *Every Dog Has Its Day,* 1997.

Clara, *Men,* A-pix Entertainment, 1997.

Carolyn, *The Party Crashers,* 1997.

Redhead, *Armageddon,* Buena Vista, 1998.

Sandra Grant, *Carnival of Souls* (also known as *Wes Craven Presents Carnival of Souls*), Trimark Pictures, 1998.

Faye-Jean Lindsay, *A Slipping Down Life,* 1999.

Bonnie McMahon, *Breakfast of Champions,* Buena Vista, 1999.

Television Appearances; Movies:

Jodi Hayward, *Crime of Innocence,* NBC, 1985.

Not My Kid, 1985.

Tina Marie Risico, *Easy Prey,* ABC, 1986.

Kim Fielding, *I Saw What You Did* (also known as *I Saw What You Did. . .and I Know Who You Are!*), CBS, 1988.

Amanda, *Brand New Life: The Honeymooners,* NBC, 1989.

Jeanelle Polk, *Face of Evil,* CBS, 1996.

Shelly, *Bombshell,* Sci-Fi Channel, 1996.

Teri Mathews, *Something Borrowed, Something Blue,* CBS, 1997.

Martie Fowler, *Twice Upon a Time,* The WB, 1998.

Also appeared in *Two Cups of Joe.*

Television Appearances; Series:

Laura Lauman, *Arsenio,* ABC, 1997.

Florence Madison, *The Tom Show,* The WB, 1997.

Linda, *Becker,* CBS, 1998.

Television Appearances; Episodic:

Sonia Russell, *All Is Forgiven,* NBC, 1986.

Amanda, *Brand New Life,* NBC, 1989.

Jill Cleveland, *Murder, She Wrote,* CBS, 1993.

Jesse O'Neil, "Firewalker," *The X Files,* Fox, 1994.

Lila, "Confidence Man," *Players,* NBC, 1998.

Television Appearances; Miniseries:

Alice Gibbs, *Bluegrass,* CBS, 1988.

Olympia Stanislopolous, *Jackie Collins' Lucky Chances* (also known as *Lucky Chances*), NBC, 1990.

Julie Lawry, *Stephen King's "The Stand"* (also known as *The Stand*), ABC, 1994.
Waitress, *Stephen King's "The Shining"* (also known as *The Shining*), ABC, 1997.

Television Appearances; Specials:
Gretchen, *On the Edge*, NBC, 1987.
Familiar Bonds/cast, *Out of Order: Rock the Vote Targets Health Care*, MTV, 1995.*

SMITH-CAMERON, J.

PERSONAL

Born in Louisville, KY; married Ken Lonergan. *Education:* Attended Florida State University.

Career: Actress. Drama Department (theatre company), founding member.

Awards, Honors: Outer Critics Circle Award, 1989, for *Lend Me a Tenor;* Antoinette Perry Award nomination, best featured actress, 1991, for *Our Country's Good;* Obie Award, *Village Voice*, nominations for Outer Critics Circle Award and Drama Desk Award, all 1997, for *As Bees in Honey Drown;* Drama Desk Award nomination, best featured actress, for *The Naked Truth*.

CREDITS

Stage Appearances:
She Stoops to Conquer, GeVa Theatre, Rochester, NY, 1981-82.
Crimes of the Heart, Broadway production, 1982.
Kaylene, *Asian Shade*, WPA Theatre, New York City, 1983.
Mary Alice, *Second Prize: Two Months in Leningrad*, Perry Street Theatre, New York City, 1983.
Nancy, *The Knack*, Stage One, Roundabout Theatre, New York City, 1983.
The Importance of Being Earnest, Guthrie Theatre, Minneapolis, MN, 1983-84.
Ruth, *The Great Divide*, Cubiculo Theatre, New York City, 1984.
Sally Middleton, *The Voice of the Turtle*, Roundabout Theatre, 1985.
Alice Mitchell, *Alice and Fred*, Cherry Lane Theatre, New York City, 1985.
Juliet, *Romeo and Juliet*, Syracuse Stage, Syracuse, NY, 1985-86.
Rhonda Louise, *Women of Manhattan*, Manhattan Theatre Club, New York City, 1986.
Marya Yerfimovna Grekova, *Wild Honey*, Virginia Theatre, New York City, 1986-87.
"Neddy," in *Winterfest 8: Four New Plays in Repertory*, Yale Repertory Theatre, New Haven, CT, 1987-88.
Diane, *The Downside*, Long Wharf Theatre, New Haven, 1987-88.
Wendy, "Splitsville," in *Four New Comedies*, 45th Street Theatre, New York City, 1988.
Maggie, *Lend Me a Tenor*, Royale Theatre, New York City, 1989.
Second Lieutenant William Faddy/Dabby Bryant, *Our Country's Good*, Nederlander Theatre, New York City, 1991.
Bernadette Waltz, *Little Egypt*, Playwrights Horizons, New York City, 1992.
Ophelia, *Fifteen Minute Hamlet*, and Felicity, *The Real Inspector Hound* (double-bill), Center Stage Right, Criterion Theatre, New York City, 1992.
Norma, *On the Bum; or, The Next Train Through*, 1992.
Marion, *Owners*, New York Theatre Workshop, Truck and Warehouse Theatre, New York City, 1993.
Christie, *Traps*, New York Theatre Workshop, Truck and Warehouse Theatre, 1993.
Title role, *Desdemona* (also known as *Desdemona: A Play about a Handkerchief*), Circle Repertory Company, Lucille Lortel Theatre, New York City, 1993.
Silence, Cunning, Exile, Seattle Repertory Theatre, Seattle, WA, 1993-94.
Dona Elvira, *Don Juan in Chicago*, Primary Stages, New York City, 1995.
Ilona Szabo, *The Play's the Thing*, Center Stage Right, Criterion Theatre, 1995.
The Naked Eye, American Repertory Theatre, Cambridge, MA, 1995-96.
Libby, *Blue Window*, Manhattan Theatre Club, New York City, 1996.
Alexa Vere de Vere, *As Bees in Honey Drown*, Lucille Lortel Theatre, 1997.
Mary, *The Memory of Water*, Stage II, City Center Theatre, New York City, 1998.

Appeared in *Mi Vida Loca*, Manhattan Theatre Club; and in *The Naked Truth*, WPA Theatre.

Film Appearances:
Elly, *Gal Young 'Un*, Nunez, 1979.
Ginny, *84 Charing Cross Road*, Columbia, 1986.
Carol Bloom, *That Night* (also known as *One Hot Summer*), Warner Bros., 1992.

Diane, *A Modern Affair* (also known as *Mr. Number 247*), Tara Releasing, 1995.
Bud's wife, *Mighty Aphrodite,* Miramax, 1995.
Sharon, *Jeffrey,* Orion Classics, 1995.
Carol, *Sabrina,* Paramount, 1995.
Ms. Sullivan, *The First Wives Club,* Paramount, 1996.
Mrs. Welsch, *Harriet the Spy,* Paramount, 1996.
Lady Texan, *The Proprietor,* Warner Bros., 1996.
Trina Paxton, *In and Out,* Paramount, 1997.
Caroline Lee, *Arresting Gena,* Fuel Films, 1997.
Barbara Lang, *The Rage: Carrie 2,* Metro-Goldwyn-Mayer, 1999.

Television Appearances; Series:
Ramona Luchesse, *The Days and Nights of Molly Dodd,* NBC and Lifetime, 1987.

Television Appearances; Movies:
Angela Anderson, *She Led Two Lives,* NBC, 1994.
Clarice, *Let It Be Me,* Starz!, 1998.

Television Appearances; Specials:
Dr. Nina Farrell, *The Recovery Room,* CBS, 1985.
Louise Bryant, *Journey into Genius,* PBS, 1988.
Mrs. Howard, *A Midwife's Tale,* PBS, 1998.

Television Appearances; Episodic:
Susan Foxworth, "Regrets Only," *The Equalizer,* CBS, 1988.
"The Sins of Our Fathers," *The Equalizer,* CBS, 1989.
Ms. Moskovitz, "Severance," *Law & Order,* NBC, 1992.
Homicide: Life on the Street (also known as *H:LOTS* and *Homicide*), NBC, 1995.
Lisa Lowell, *Spin City,* ABC, 1996.
Paula Dowling, *Law & Order,* NBC, 1998.*

SOLOMON, Ed
(Edward Solomon)

PERSONAL

Married Cynthia Cleese (an actress).

Career: Writer, producer, and actor.

CREDITS

Film Appearances:
Stupid waiter, *Bill and Ted's Excellent Adventure,* Orion, 1989.
Stupid seance member, *Bill and Ted's Bogus Journey,* Orion, 1991.
Jerk in bar, *Leaving Normal,* Universal, 1992.
Thirteenth destroyer, *Mom and Dad Save the World,* Warner Bros., 1992.

Film Work:
Co-producer, *Bill and Ted's Bogus Journey,* Orion, 1991.
(As Edward Solomon) Associate producer, *Leaving Normal,* Universal, 1992.

WRITINGS

Screenplays, Unless Otherwise Noted:
Song, "No on Fifteen," *Revenge of the Nerds II* (also known as *Revenge of the Nerds II: Nerds in Paradise*), Twentieth Century-Fox, 1987.
Bill and Ted's Excellent Adventure, Orion, 1989.
Bill and Ted's Bogus Journey, Orion, 1991.
Leaving Normal, Universal, 1992.
(With Chris Matheson) *Mom and Dad Save the World,* Warner Bros., 1992.
Super Mario Bros. (also known as *Super Mario Brothers: The Movie*), Buena Vista, 1993.
(With Terry Runte and Parker Bennett) *Men in Black* (also known as *MIB*), Columbia, 1997.

Adaptations: The characters for the 1992 television series *Bill and Ted's Excellent Adventures,* broadcast by CBS and Fox, were created by Solomon.*

SOLOMON, Edward
See SOLOMON, Ed

SOLONDZ, Todd 1960-

PERSONAL

Born in 1960, in Newark, NJ. *Education:* Studied film at New York University.

Career: Director, writer, and actor.

Awards, Honors: Grand Jury Prize, dramatic category, Sundance Film Festival, Independent Spirit Award nominations, best director and best feature, CICAE Award, Berlin International Film Festival, and Grand Special Prize nomination, Deauville Film Festival, all 1995, for *Welcome to the Dollhouse;* Golden Globe

Award nomination, best screenplay, Independent Spirit Award nomination, best director, Chicago Film Critics Association Award nomination, best screenplay, Critic's Choice Award, best film, Ford Lauderdale International Film Festival, Audience Award nomination, San Sebastian International Film Festival, International Jury Award, best feature, Sao Paulo International Film Festival, and Metro Media Award, Toronto International Film Festival, all 1998, for *Happiness.*

CREDITS

Film Work; Director, Unless Otherwise Noted:

Babysitter (short film), 1984.
Feelings (short film), 1984.
Schatt's Last Shot (short film), 1985.
Fear, Anxiety, and Depression, Samuel Goldwyn, 1989.
(And producer) *Welcome to the Dollhouse* (also known as *Middle Child*), Sony Pictures Classics, 1995.
Happiness, Good Machine, 1998.

Also directed *How I Became a Leading Artistic Figure in New York City's East Village Cultural Landscape* (short film), broadcast on *Saturday Night Live* (also known as *NBC's Saturday Night, Saturday Night,* and *SNL*), NBC.

Film Appearances:

Zany reporter, *Married to the Mob,* Orion, 1988.
Ira Ellis, *Fear, Anxiety, and Depression,* Samuel Goldwyn, 1989.
Man on bus, *As Good as It Gets,* TriStar, 1997.

Television Appearances; Specials:

SST: Screen, Stage, Television, ABC, 1989.

WRITINGS

Screenplays:

Babysitter (short film), 1984.
Feelings (short film), 1984.
Schatt's Last Shot (short film), 1985.
Fear, Anxiety, and Depression, Samuel Goldwyn, 1989.
Welcome to the Dollhouse (also known as *Middle Child*), Sony Pictures Classics, 1995.
Happiness, Good Machine, 1998.

Also wrote *How I Became a Leading Artistic Figure in New York City's East Village Cultural Landscape* (short film), broadcast on *Saturday Night Live* (also known as *NBC's Saturday Night, Saturday Night,* and *SNL*), NBC.

OTHER SOURCES

Periodicals:

Cineaste, summer, 1996, p. 24.
Film Comment, September-October, 1998, p. 72; January, 1999, p. 70.
Interview, November, 1998, p. 34.
Time, June 3, 1996, p. 77.*

SOMMERS, Stephen

PERSONAL

Wife's name, Jana; children: Samantha. *Education:* Attended St. John's University and University of Seville; University of Southern California, M.A. (cinema and television).

Career: Writer and director. Performed with theatre groups in Europe; also worked as manager of European rock and roll bands.

CREDITS

Film Work; Director, Unless Otherwise Noted:

Catch Me If You Can, 1989.
The Adventures of Huck Finn (also known as *The Adventures of Huckleberry Finn*), Buena Vista, 1993.
Rudyard Kipling's The Jungle Book (also known as *The Jungle Book*), Buena Vista, 1994.
Executive producer, *Tom and Huck* (also known as *The Adventures of Tom and Huck* and *Tom Sawyer*), Buena Vista, 1995.
Deep Rising, Buena Vista, 1998.
The Mummy, Universal, 1999.

Also directed the short film *Perfect Alibi.*

Television Work; Movies:

Co-executive producer, *Oliver Twist,* ABC, 1997.

WRITINGS

Screenplays:

Catch Me If You Can, 1989.
The Adventures of Huck Finn (also known as *The Adventures of Huckleberry Finn*), Buena Vista, 1993.

Gunmen, Dimension, 1994.
(With Ronald Yanover and Mark D. Geldman) *Rudyard Kipling's The Jungle Book* (also known as *The Jungle Book*), Buena Vista, 1994.
Tom and Huck (also known as *The Adventures of Tom and Huck* and *Tom Sawyer*), Buena Vista, 1995.
Deep Rising, Buena Vista, 1998.
The Mummy, Universal, 1999.

Also wrote the short film *Perfect Alibi.*

OTHER SOURCES

Periodicals:
Entertainment Weekly, May 14, 1999, p. 28.*

SOREL, Louise 1940-

PERSONAL

Born August 6, 1940, in Los Angeles, CA. *Education:* Attended Institut de Francais, Ville Franche sur-Mer, France. *Avocational interests:* Travel.

Career: Actress. Philadelphia Drama Guild, Philadelphia, PA, guest artist, 1971-72.

Awards, Honors: *Soap Opera Digest* Award, female showstopper, 1997, for *Days of Our Lives.*

CREDITS

Television Appearances; Series:
Jean Vale, *The Survivors* (also known as *Harold Robbins' The Survivors*), 1969-70.
Barbara Robinson, *The Don Rickles Show,* CBS, 1972.
Amanda Gibbons, *The Curse of Dracula* (also known as *The World ofDracula*), NBC, 1979.
Elaine Holstein, *Ladies' Man,* CBS, 1980.
Augusta Lockridge, *Santa Barbara,* NBC, 1984-86 and 1988-91.
Judith Russell Sanders, *One Life to Live,* 1986-87.
Vivian Alamain Kiriakis Jones DiMera, *Days of Our Lives,* NBC, 1992—.

Television Appearances; Movies:
Elena, *River of Mystery,* NBC, 1971.
Louise Lathrop, *Every Man Needs One,* ABC, 1972.
Ariane Hadrachi, *The Return of Charlie Chan* (also known as *Happiness Is a Warm Clue*), NBC, 1973.
The President's Plane Is Missing, ABC, 1973.
The Healers, 1974.
Sylvia, *The Girl Who Came Gift-Wrapped,* ABC, 1974.
Helena Varga, *Get Christie Love!,* ABC, 1974.
Inez Quintero, *The Mark of Zorro,* ABC, 1974.
Carole Simon, *One of Our Own,* NBC, 1975.
Vivian, *Widow,* NBC, 1976.
Alicia Salazar, *Perilous Voyage,* NBC, 1976.
Millie Cooper, *When Every Day Was the Fourth of July,* NBC, 1978.
Julia, *Mazes and Monsters* (also known as *Dungeons and Dragons* and *Rona Jaffe's Mazes and Monsters*), CBS, 1982.
Dolores (some sources cite Barbara) Chase, *Sunset Limousine,* CBS, 1983.
Louise, *A Masterpiece of Murder,* NBC, 1986.

Television Appearances; Episodic:
Terry Waverly, "The Survivors," *The Fugitive,* ABC, 1965.
"The Dream of Stavros Karas," *The Virginian,* NBC, 1965.
Pilon, "Hide the Children," *The Big Valley,* ABC, 1966.
"Red Sash of Courage," *I Spy,* NBC, 1967.
Rayna, "Requiem for Methuselah," *Star Trek,* NBC, 1969.
Velia Redford, "The Dead Man," *Night Gallery,* NBC, 1970.
Mavis Goldsmith, "Pickman's Model," *Night Gallery,* NBC, 1971.
Alicia Danato, "No Sign of the Cross," *Banacek,* NBC, 1972.
"Canyon of No Return," *The F.B.I.,* ABC, 1972.
Ghost Story, NBC, 1972.
Diane, "Try to Die on Time," *Hawaii Five-0,* CBS, 1974.
"An Iron-Clad Plan," *Barbary Coast,* ABC, 1975.
Bess Riker, "New Beginnings," *Knots Landing,* CBS, 1979.
Jackie, "Doubtful Target," *Vega$,* ABC, 1979.
Lily, "Caged Angel," *Charlie's Angels,* ABC, 1979.
Grace Cushing, *Once in a Million,* ABC, 1980.
"Babalao," *The Incredible Hulk,* CBS, 1980.
"One More Summer," *Magnum P.I.,* CBS, 1981.
Bess Riker, "Svengali," *Knots Landing,* CBS, 1982.
Bess Riker, "Encounters," *Knots Landing,* CBS, 1982.
Marcy Fletcher Wrightman, "Causa Mortis," *Law & Order,* NBC, 1996.
Mrs. Saberhagen, "Mom v. Magic," *Sabrina, the Teenage Witch,* ABC, 1998.

Also appeared in episodes of *Hart to Hart,* ABC; and *Kojak,* CBS.

Television Appearances; Specials:
Fifty Years of Soaps: An All-Star Celebration, CBS, 1994.
Co-host, *The 11th Annual Soap Opera Awards,* NBC, 1995.

Film Appearances:
Ruth, *B.S. I Love You,* Twentieth Century-Fox, 1971.
Miss McCormack, *Plaza Suite,* Paramount, 1971.
Marie, *Every Little Crook and Nanny,* Metro-Goldwyn-Mayer, 1972.
Stella, *Airplane II: The Sequel* (also known as *Flying High II*), Paramount, 1982.
Claudia, *Crimes of Passion* (also known as *China Blue*), New World, 1984.
Barbara Roxbury, *Where the Boys Are '84* (also known as *Where the Boys Are*), TriStar, 1984.

Stage Appearances:
Aubrey Beardsley, the Neophyte, Center Theatre Group, New Theatre for Now, 1971-72.
Susan Michaels, *The Dream,* Forrest Theatre, Philadelphia, PA, 1977.
Kate, *Later,* Marymount Manhattan Theatre, New York City, 1979.
Hamlet, Globe Playhouse, Los Angeles, 1986-87.

Appeared in Broadway productions of *The Dragon, Lorenzo, Man and Boy, Philadelphia, Here I Come, The Sign in Sidney Brustein's Window,* and *Take Her, She's Mine.**

SORRET, Lodovico
See NOONAN, Tom

SORRET, Ludovico
See NOONAN, Tom

SOTO, Talisa 1967-

PERSONAL

Original name, Miriam Soto; born March 27, 1967, in Brooklyn, NY; married Costas Mandylor, May, 1997.

Addresses: *Agent*—Flick Agency, 9057 Nemo St., West Hollywood, CA 90069-5511.

Career: Actress. Model, c. 1983—.

Awards, Honors: ShoWest Award, female star of tomorrow, ShoWest Convention, National Association of Theatre Owners, 1989; named one of the fifty most beautiful people in the world, *People Weekly,* 1990.

CREDITS

Film Appearances:
India, *Spike of Bensonhurst,* Film Dallas, 1988.
Lupe Lamora, *License to Kill,* Metro-Goldwyn-Mayer/United Artists, 1989.
Maria Rivera, *The Mambo Kings,* Warner Bros., 1992.
Joanna, *Hostage,* Skouras, 1993.
Dona Julia, *Don Juan DeMarco,* New Line Cinema, 1995.
Kitana, *Mortal Kombat,* New Line Cinema, 1995.
Susan Taylor, *The Corporate Ladder,* 1996.
Seductress in hotel room, *Spy Hard,* Buena Vista, 1996.
Navajo woman, *The Sunchaser,* Warner Bros., 1996.
Amanda, *Flypaper,* 1997.
Princess Kitana, *Mortal Kombat: Annihilation* (also known as *Mortal Kombat 2*), New Line Cinema, 1997.

Television Appearances; Series:
Cassie Valasquez, *Harts of the West,* CBS, 1993-94.

Television Appearances; Movies:
Marianna Herrera, *Silhouette,* USA Network, 1990.
Title role, *Vampirella,* Showtime, 1996.

Television Appearances; Specials:
Rosina, "Prison Stories: Women on the Inside" (also known as "Doing Time: Women in Prison"), *HBO Showcase,* HBO, 1991.
Sports Illustrated Swimsuit Special: Class of '95, NBC, 1995.

Television Appearances; Episodic:
Rosemary Vargas, *C-16: FBI,* ABC, 1998.

Television Appearances; Awards Presentations:
The 4th Annual Desi Awards, syndicated, 1992.*

SPADE, David 1964-

PERSONAL

Born July 22, 1964, in Birmingham, MI. *Education:* Graduated from Saguaro High School, Scottsdale, AZ; Arizona State University, 1988.

Addresses: *Contact*—9150 Wilshire Blvd., #350, Beverly Hills, CA 90212.

Career: Actor and comedian. Writer, *Saturday Night Live,* 1991-96.

Awards, Honors: MTV Movie Award (shared with Chris Farley), best on-screen duo, 1996, for *Tommy Boy;* Golden Globe Award nomination, best supporting actor in a series, miniseries, or motion picture, Emmy Award nomination, outstanding supporting actor in a comedy series, and American Comedy Award nomination, funniest supporting male performer in a television series, all 1999, for *Just Shoot Me.*

CREDITS

Film Appearances:

Kyle, *Police Academy 4: Citizens on Patrol,* Warner Bros., 1987.
Theological Cokehead, *Light Sleeper,* Fine Line, 1992.
Turnbull, *Coneheads,* Paramount, 1993.
Rand McPherson, *PCU,* Fox, 1994.
Richard, *Tommy Boy,* Paramount, 1995.
Steve Dodds, *Black Sheep,* Paramount, 1996.
Voice, *Beavis and Butt-head Do America* (animated), Paramount, 1996.
Ernie, *8 Heads in a Duffel Bag,* Orion Pictures, 1997.
Scott Thorpe, *Senseless,* Miramax, 1998.
Voice of Ranger Frank, *The Rugrats Movie* (animated), Paramount, 1998.
Dylan Ramsey, *Lost and Found,* Warner Bros., 1999.
Voice of Manco Capac, *Kingdom of the Sun* (animated), Walt Disney Pictures, 2000.

Television Appearances; Episodic:

Scott, *The Facts of Life,* NBC, 1988.
B.J., "Second Wave," *Baywatch,* NBC, 1989.
Comics Only, Comedy Central, 1991.
Himself, "The Promise," *The Larry Sanders Show,* HBO, 1992.
Voice of Mr. Manners, "Candy Sale," and "Manners Suck," *Beavis and Butt-head* (animated), MTV, 1993.
Voice of ticket attendant, "Babes R Us," *Beavis and Butt-head* (animated), MTV, 1993.
Himself, "The Interview," *The Larry Sanders Show,* HBO, 1998.

Television Appearances; Series:

Saturday Night Live (also known as *SNL*), NBC, 1991-96.
Dennis Finch, *Just Shoot Me,* NBC, 1996—.

Television Appearances; Movies:

Usher, *The HitMan,* ABC, 1991.

Television Appearances; Specials:

The 13th Annual Young Comedians Show Hosted By Dennis Miller, HBO, 1989.
The 2nd Annual Saturday Night Live Mother's Day Special, NBC, 1993.
Freaks, Nerds & Weirdos: An MTV News Special Report, MTV, 1994.
Hollywood Minute Guy, *Saturday Night Live Presents Bill Clinton's All-Time Favorites,* NBC, 1994.
Sea World/Busch Gardens Party For the Planet, CBS, 1996.
Interviewee, *Canned Ham: 8 Heads in a Duffel Bag,* Comedy Central, 1997.
Barbara Walters Presents 6 to Watch, ABC, 1998.
Panelist, *Canned Ham: Senseless,* Comedy Central, 1998.
David Spade: Take The Hit, HBO, 1998.

Television Appearances; Awards Presentations:

Presenter, *Blockbuster Entertainment Awards,* CBS, 1996.
Presenter, *Blockbuster Entertainment Awards,* CBS, 1997.
Presenter, *4th Annual VH-1 Honors,* VH-1, 1997.
Host, *The 1997 Billboard Music Awards,* 1997.
Presenter, *The 69th Annual Academy Awards,* ABC, 1997.
Presenter, *1998 MTV Video Music Awards,* MTV, 1998.
Presenter, *Nickelodeon's 12th Annual Kid's Choice Awards,* Nickelodeon, 1999.

Television Work:

Creative consultant, *1992 MTV Video Music Awards* (special), MTV, 1992.
Executive producer, *David Spade: Take The Hit* (special), HBO, 1998.

Screenplays:

(With others) *Lost and Found,* Warner Bros., 1999.

OTHER SOURCES

Periodicals:

Entertainment Weekly, February 16, 1996, pp. 6-7; March 14, 1997, p. 64; April 17, 1998, p. 22-25.
Newsweek, February 16, 1998, p. 73.
Playboy, February 1995, pp. 118-22.*

SPINOTTI, Dante 1943-

PERSONAL

Born August 22, 1943, in Tolmezzo, Italy; married.

Addresses: *Office*—Smith/Gosnell/Nicholson & Associates, P.O. Box 1166, 1515 Palisades Dr., Pacific Palisades, CA 90272.

Career: Cinematographer.

Awards, Honors: British Academy Award, best cinematography, American Society of Cinematographers Award nomination, outstanding achievement in cinematography in theatrical releases, both 1992, for *The Last of the Mohicans;* Los Angeles Film Critics Association Award, best cinematography, Golden Satellite Award nomination, best motion picture cinematography, British Academy Award nomination, best cinematography, American Society of Cinematographers Award nomination, outstanding achievement in cinematography in theatrical releases, Academy Award nomination, best cinematography, all 1997, for *L.A. Confidential.*

CREDITS

Film Work; Cinematographer:

Cenerentola '80 (also known as *Cinderella '80*), 1980.

Il Minestrone, 1980.

La Disubbidienza (also known as *La Desobeissance*), 1981.

Basileus Quartet, Libra, Cinema 5, Almi, 1982.

Le Armi e Gli Amori, 1983.

I Paladini—Storia d'Armi e d'Amori (also known as *Hearts and Armour*), Warner Bros., 1983.

Sogno di Una Notte d'Estate (also known as *Sogno di una notte di mezza estate*), 1983.

Cosi' Parlo' Bellavista (also known as *Il Mistero di Bellavista*), 1984.

Fotografando Patrizia (also known as *The Dark Side of Love*), 1984.

Sotto, Sotto (also known as *Softly, Softly*), Triumph Releasing, 1984.

Interno Berlinese (also known as *The Berlin Affair*), Cannon Tuschinski Film Distribution, 1985.

Voyage of the Rock Aliens, (also known as *Voyage of the Rich Aliens* and *When the Rain Begins to Fall*), Prism Pictures, 1985.

Choke Canyon (also known as *On Dangerous Ground*), UFDC, 1986.

Crimes of the Heart, DD Entertainment, 1986.

Manhunter (also known as *Red Dragon: The Pursuit of Hannibal Lecter*), DEG, 1986.

Aria (episode, *Die Tote Stadt*), Miramax/Warner Bros., 1987.

From the Hip, DEG, 1987.

Beaches (also known as *Forever Friends*), Buena Vista, 1988.

Illegally Yours, Metro-Goldwyn-Mayer/United Artists, 1988.

La Leggenda del Santo Bevitore (also known as *The Legend of the Holy Drinker*), 1988.

Mamba (also known as *Fair Game*), Vidmark Entertainment, 1988.

Acque di Primavera (also known as *Torrents of Spring*), Millimeter, 1990.

Una Vita Scellerata (also known as *Cellini, Una Vita Violenta* and *A Violent Life*), 1990.

The Comfort of Strangers (also known as *Cortesie Per Gli Ospiti*), Skouras, 1990.

True Colors, Paramount, 1991.

Hudson Hawk, TriStar, 1991.

Frankie & Johnny, Paramount, 1991.

The Last of the Mohicans, Twentieth Century-Fox, 1992.

Il Segreto del Boscho Vecchio (also known as *The Secret of the Old Woods*), 1993.

La Fine e Nota (also known as *The End Is Known*), 1993.

Blink, New Line, 1994.

Nell, Twentieth Century-Fox, 1994.

The Quick and the Dead, TriStar, 1995.

With Andrey Barkowyak, *L' Uomo Delle Stelle* (also known as *The Star Maker, The Star Man* and *Starmaker*), Miramax, 1995.

Heat, Warner Bros., 1995.

The Mirror has Two Faces, TriStar, 1996.

L.A. Confidential, Warner Bros., 1997.

Goodbye Lover, Warner Bros., 1998.

The Other Sister, Buena Vista, 1999.

Man of the People, 1999.*

SPOTTISWOODE, Roger 1943-

PERSONAL

Born in 1943, in England (some sources cite Ottawa, Ontario, Canada); married Holly Palance (divorced, 1997).

Addresses: *Agent*—International Creative Management, 8942 Wilshire Blvd., Beverly Hills, CA 90211-1934.

Career: Director, producer, and writer. Worked as a film editor of television commercials and documentaries.

Awards, Honors: Gemini Award, best direction in a dramatic program or miniseries, Academy of Canadian Cinema and Television, 1998, for *Hiroshima.*

CREDITS

Film Work; Director:

Terror Train (also known as *Train of Terror*), Twentieth Century-Fox, 1980.
The Pursuit of D. B. Cooper (also known as *Pursuit*), Universal, 1981.
Under Fire, Orion, 1983.
The Best of Times, Universal, 1986.
Shoot to Kill (also known as *Deadly Pursuit*), Buena Vista, 1988.
Turner and Hooch, Buena Vista, 1989.
Air America, TriStar, 1990.
Stop! Or My Mom Will Shoot, Universal, 1992.
Mesmer, 1994.
Tomorrow Never Dies, Metro-Goldwyn-Mayer/United Artists, 1997.

Other Film Work:

Editor (with others), *Straw Dogs,* Cinerama, 1971.
Editor, *The Getaway,* Facets Multimedia, 1972.
Editor (with others), *Pat Garrett and Billy the Kid,* Metro-Goldwyn-Mayer, 1973.
Editor, *The Gambler,* Paramount, 1974.
Editor, *Hard Times* (also known as *The Streetfighter*), Columbia, 1975.
Associate producer, *Who'll Stop the Rain?* (also known as *Dog Soldiers*), Metro-Goldwyn-Mayer, 1978.
Executive producer, *Baby: The Secret of the Lost Legend* (also known as*Dinosaur . . . Secret of the Lost Legend*), Touchstone, 1985.

Television Work; Director; Movies:

The Last Innocent Man, HBO, 1987.
Third Degree Burn, HBO, 1989.
And the Band Played On, HBO, 1993.
Murder Live!, NBC, 1997.

Television Work; Director; Miniseries:

Hiroshima, 1996.

Television Work; Director; Pilots:

The Renegades, ABC, 1982.
Turner and Hooch (also known as *The Kid*), NBC, 1990.

Other Television Work; Director:

"Time Flies When You're Alive" (special), *HBO Showcase,* HBO, 1989.
Prince Street (series), NBC, 1997.

Television Appearances; Specials:

The Secrets of 007: The James Bond Files, CBS, 1997.

WRITINGS

Screenplays:

(With Walter Hill, Larry Gross, and Steven E. de Souza) *48 Hours,* Paramount, 1982.*

STAMP, Terence 1938-

PERSONAL

Full name, Terence Henry Stamp; born July 22, 1938, in London, England; son of Thomas and Ethel Ester (Perrott) Stamp.

Addresses: *Agent*—IFA, 8730 Sunset Blvd., Suite 490, Los Angeles, CA 90069. *Contact*—Markham & Froggatt, 4 Windmill St., London W.1, England.

Career: Actor and writer.

Member: Brooks's Club.

Awards, Honors: Academy Award nomination, best supporting actor, and British Academy Award nomination, most promising newcomer to leading film roles, British Academy of Film and Television Arts, both 1962, for *Billy Budd;* Golden Globe Award, new star of the year in films, 1963; Cannes International Film Festival award, best actor in a full-length film, 1965, for *The Collector;* Doctor of Arts, University of East London, 1993; Golden Globe Award nomination, best actor in a comedy or music motion picture, British Academy Award nomination, best leading actor, Golden Space Needle Award, best actor, Seattle International Film Festival, and Australian Film Institute Award nomination, best actor, all 1994, for *The Adventures of Priscilla, Queen of the Desert.*

CREDITS

Stage Appearances:

Title role, *Dracula,* Shaftesbury Theatre, London, 1978.

Stranger, *The Lady from the Sea,* Round House Theatre, London, 1979.

Also appeared in *Alfie,* New York City, and in *Airborne Symphony.*

Film Appearances:

(Film debut) Title role, *Billy Budd,* United Artists, 1962.
Mitchell, *Term of Trial,* Warner Bros., 1962.
Alfie, 1964.
Freddy Clegg, *The Collector,* Columbia, 1965.
Willy Garvin, *Modesty Blaise,* Twentieth Century-Fox, 1966.
Sergeant Troy, *Far from the Madding Crowd,* Metro-Goldwyn-Mayer, 1967.
Dave, *Poor Cow,* National General, 1967.
Blue/Azul, *Blue,* Paramount, 1968.
Visitor, *Teorema* (also known as *Theorem*), Continental, 1968.
Tales of Mystery, 1968.
Toby Dammit, "Never Let the Devil Take Your Head, or Toby Dammit," *Spirits of the Dead* (also known as *Tales of Mystery, Tales of Mystery and Imagination, Histoires Extraordinaires, Tre Passi nel Delirio,* and *Trois Histoires Extraordinaires d'Edgar Poe*), American International Pictures, 1969.
John Soames, *The Mind of Mr. Soames,* Columbia, 1969.
A Season in Hell, 1971.
Hu-Man, Romantique-ORTF, 1975.
Daniele di Bagnasco, *The Divine Nymph* (also known as *Divine Creature*), Analysis Film Releasing, 1976.
Edgar Poe, *Black-Out,* Avia, 1977.
Striptease, 1977.
General Dru-Zod, *Superman* (also known as *Superman: The Movie*), Warner Bros., 1978.
Prince Lubovedsky, *Meetings with Remarkable Men,* Libra, 1978.
General Dru-Zod, *Superman II,* Warner Bros., 1979.
Henry, *Amo Non Amo* (also known as *I Love You, I Love You Not* and *Together?*), Titanus, 1979.
Pope Andreani, *Morte in Vaticano* (also known as *Death in the Vatican, Vatican Conspiracy,* and *Muerte en el Vaticano*), Film International, 1980.
Taskinar, *Monster Island* (also known as *The Mystery of Monster Island* and *Misterio en la Isla de los Monstruos*), Fort-Almeda, 1981.
Directed by William Wyler (documentary), Tatge Productions, 1981.
The Bloody Chamber, 1982.
Insanity, 1982.
Willie Parker, *The Hit,* Island Alive, 1984.
Prince of Darkness, *The Company of Wolves,* Cannon, 1985.
Brazil, Universal, 1985.
Dr. Steven Phillip, *Link,* Cannon, 1985.
Victor Taft, *Legal Eagles,* Universal, 1986.
Edward, *Hud* (also known as *Skin*), Synchron, 1986.
Prince Borsa, *The Sicilian,* Twentieth Century-Fox, 1986.
Sir Larry Wildman, *Wall Street,* Twentieth Century-Fox, 1987.
La Barbare, Canadian Television/TFI Films Production, 1988.
William Harcourt, *Alien Nation,* Twentieth Century-Fox, 1988.
John Tunstall, *Young Guns,* Twentieth Century-Fox, 1988.
Paul Hellwart, *Genuine Risk,* RCA/Columbia Pictures Home Video, 1991.
Darman, *Prince of Shadows* (also known as *Beltenbros*), 1991.
Jack Schmidt, *The Real McCoy,* Universal, 1992.
Bernadette, *The Adventures of Priscilla, Queen of the Desert,* Gramercy Pictures, 1993.
Joe Hartman, *Mindbender* (also known as *Uri Geller*), 1995.
Edward Lamb, *Tire a Part* (also known as *Limited Edition*), CTV International, 1997.
Baltazar Vincenza, *Bliss,* Triumph, 1997.
The Bitter End, 1997.
Kozen, *Kiss the Sky,* Metro-Goldwyn-Mayer, 1998.
Fred Moore, *Love Walked In,* Columbia/TriStar, 1998.
Chancellor Valorum, *Star Wars: Episode I—The Phantom Menace,* Twentieth Century-Fox, 1999.
Wilson, *The Limey,* Artisan Entertainment, 1999.
Terry Stricter, *Bowfinger,* Universal, 1999.

Also appeared in *Stranger in the House.*

Film Work:

Director and co-screenwriter, *Stranger in the House.*

Television Appearances; Series:

David Audley, *Chessgame,* PBS, 1987.

Television Appearances; Movies:

Wazir Jandur, *The Thief of Bagdad,* NBC, 1978.

Television Appearances; Specials:

Host, *The Prince's Trust Gala,* TBS, 1989.
The 52nd Annual Golden Globe Awards, TBS, 1995.

Television Appearances; Episodic:

Host, "The Prince of Darkness," *The Hunger,* Showtime, 1997.

WRITINGS

Stamp Album (autobiography), Bloomsbury, 1987.
Coming Attractions (autobiography), 1988.
Double Feature (autobiography), Bloomsbury, 1989.
The Night (novel), Phoenix House (London), 1992.

OTHER SOURCES

Periodicals:

Interview, August, 1994, p. 36.
Premiere, October, 1994, pp. 100-105.*

STAPLETON, Jean 1923-

PERSONAL

Real name, Jeanne Murray; born January 19, 1923, in New York, NY; daughter of Joseph E. (a billboard advertising sales representative) and Marie (a singer; maiden name, Stapleton) Murray; married William H. Putch (a theatre producer and director), October 26, 1957 (died, 1983); children: John (an actor), Pamela (an actress). *Education:* Attended Hunter College (now of the City University of New York); trained for the stage with Carli Laklan at American Apprentice Theatre, with Jane Rose and William Hansen at American Actors Company, with Joseph Anthony and Peter Frye at American Theatre Wing, and with Harold Clurman. *Avocational interests:* Swimming, singing, reading. *Religion:* Christian Scientist.

Addresses: *Agent*—Bauman Hiller and Associates, 5757 Wilshire Blvd., Suite PH5, Los Angeles, CA 90036-3635.

Career: Actress. Robert Shaw Chorale, New York City, singer, first appeared in the sketch production *Double Dozen Double Damask Dinner Napkins* on a tour of women's clubs, 1940. Actors' Fund of America, member of board of trustees. U.S. Commissioner to the International Women's Year Commission and National Conference of Women, 1977; Emerson College, honorary board member of Center for Women in the Performing Arts; Women's Research and Education Institute, Washington, DC, chairperson of advisory board; Eleanor Roosevelt's Val-Kill, Hyde Park, NY, member of board of directors; Wonder Woman Foundation, New York City, member of board of directors. Also worked as a secretary.

Member: Actors' Equity Association (council member, 1958-63), Screen Actors Guild, American Federation of Television and Radio Artists, American Federation of Musicians (honorary member).

Awards, Honors: Emmy Awards, best actress in a comedy series, 1971, 1972, and 1978, Emmy Award nominations, best actress in a comedy series, 1973, 1974, 1975, 1977, and 1979, Golden Globe Awards, best actress in a musical or comedy series, 1973 and 1974, and Golden Globe Award nominations, best actress in a musical or comedy series, 1972, 1975, 1978, 1979, and 1980, all for *All in the Family;* Grammy Award nomination, best comedy recording, National Academy of Recording Arts and Sciences, 1972, for *All in the Family;* honored by the National Commission of Working Women, 1981, for *Isabel's Choice;* Emmy Award nomination, best actress in a limited series or special, and Golden Globe Award nomination, best performance by an actress in a miniseries or television movie, both 1982, for *Eleanor, First Lady of the World;* Annual Cable Excellence (ACE) Award nomination, for "Grown Ups," *Broadway on Showtime;* Obie Award, best performance, *Village Voice,* 1990, for *Mountain Language* and *The Birthday Party;* Golden Globe Award nomination, best supporting actress in a series, miniseries, or telefilm, 1991, for *Fire in the Dark;* ACE Award nomination, 1994, for *Mrs. Piggle Wiggle;* Emmy Award nomination, outstanding guest actress in a comedy series, 1995, for *Grace under Fire.* Also nominee and winner of numerous People's Choice awards; L.H.D., Emerson College; also received honorary degrees from Hood College and Monmouth College.

CREDITS

Stage Appearances:

Mrs. Watty, *The Corn Is Green,* Equity Library Theatre, New York City, 1948.
(Broadway debut) Inez, *In the Summer House,* Playhouse Theatre, New York City, 1953.
Mother, *American Gothic,* Circle in the Square Theatre, New York City, 1953.
Sister, *Damn Yankees,* 46th Street Theatre, New York City, 1955.
Sue, *Bells Are Ringing,* Shubert Theatre, New York City, 1956.
A Soft Touch, Coconut Grove Playhouse, Miami, FL, 1957.

Swart Petry, *A Swim in the Sea,* Walnut Street Theatre, Philadelphia, PA, 1958.
Woody, *Goodbye, My Fancy,* Totem Pole Playhouse, Fayetteville, PA, 1958.
Miss Cooper, *Separate Tables,* Totem Pole Playhouse, 1958.
Mother, *Charm,* Totem Pole Playhouse, 1958.
Grace, *Bus Stop,* Totem Pole Playhouse, 1958.
Madame St. Pe, *The Waltz of the Toreadors,* Totem Pole Playhouse, 1958.
Sally Adams, *Call Me Madam,* Totem Pole Playhouse, 1959.
Maisie Madigan, *Juno,* Winter Garden Theatre, New York City, 1959.
Laura Partridge, *The Solid Gold Cadillac,* Totem Pole Playhouse, 1960.
Mrs. Ochs, *Rhinoceros,* Longacre Theatre, New York City, 1961.
Mrs. Keller, *The Miracle Worker,* Totem Pole Playhouse, 1962.
Emma, *Apple in the Attic,* Totem Pole Playhouse, 1962.
A Thurber Carnival (revue), Totem Pole Playhouse, 1962.
Title role, *Everybody Loves Opal,* Totem Pole Playhouse, 1962.
Aunt Eller, *Oklahoma!,* Totem Pole Playhouse, 1962.
Mrs. Baker, *Come Blow Your Horn,* Totem Pole Playhouse, 1963.
Mrs. Spofford, *Gentlemen Prefer Blondes,* Totem Pole Playhouse, 1963.
Nannie, *All for Mary,* Totem Pole Playhouse, 1963.
Mrs. Strakosh, *Funny Girl,* Winter Garden Theatre, 1964.
Brewster, *A Rainy Day in Newark,* Totem Pole Playhouse, 1964.
Rosemary, *Picnic,* Totem Pole Playhouse, 1964.
Annabelle, *George Washington Slept Here,* Totem Pole Playhouse, 1964.
Mrs. Walworth, *Speaking of Murder,* Totem Pole Playhouse, 1964.
Mrs. Pearce, *My Fair Lady,* Totem Pole Playhouse, 1964.
Mrs. Yoder, *Papa Is All,* Totem Pole Playhouse, 1964.
Mother Abbess, *The Sound of Music,* Totem Pole Playhouse, 1964.
Anna Leonowens, *The King and I,* Totem Pole Playhouse, 1965.
Bloody Mary, *South Pacific,* Totem Pole Playhouse, 1965.
Lottie, *The Dark at the Top of the Stairs,* Totem Pole Playhouse, 1965.
Miss Skillon, *See How They Run,* Totem Pole Playhouse, 1965.
Veta Louise, *Harvey,* Totem Pole Playhouse, 1965.
Abby Brewster, *Arsenic and Old Lace,* Totem Pole Playhouse, 1965.
Grace Kimbrough, *Never Too Late,* Totem Pole Playhouse, 1965.
Mother, *Enter Laughing,* Totem Pole Playhouse, 1965.
Anne Michaelson, *Take Her, She's Mine,* Totem Pole Playhouse, 1965.
Miss Holroyd, *Bell, Book, and Candle,* Totem Pole Playhouse, 1966.
Mrs. Deazy, *Jenny Kissed Me,* Totem Pole Playhouse, 1966.
Aunt Kate Barnaby, *How Far Is the Barn?,* Totem Pole Playhouse, 1966.
Nettie Fowler, *Carousel,* Totem Pole Playhouse, 1966.
Dorothy, *Any Wednesday,* Totem Pole Playhouse, 1966.
Dolly Gallagher Levi, *Hello Dolly!,* Totem Pole Playhouse, 1971.
Southwest Corner, 1971.
Mrs. Baer, *Butterflies Are Free,* Totem Pole Playhouse, 1972.
Lola, *Come Back, Little Sheba,* Totem Pole Playhouse, 1972.
Title role, *Everybody Loves Opal,* Totem Pole Playhouse, 1972.
The Time of the Cuckoo, 1973.
Lullaby, 1974.
The Vinegar Tree, 1974.
The Time of the Cuckoo, Center Theatre Group, Ahmanson Theatre, Los Angeles, CA, 1974.
Title role, *The Secret Affairs of Mildred Wild,* Totem Pole Playhouse, 1975.
Hay Fever, 1976.
The Late Christopher Bean, 1976.
The Reluctant Debutante, 1977.
The Show-Off, 1977.
Title role, *Daisy Mayme,* Totem Pole Playhouse, 1978.
The Great Sebastian's, 1978.
Little Mary Sunshine, 1978.
Papa Is All, 1979.
Miss Marple, *A Murder Is Announced,* Totem Pole Playhouse, 1979.
Miss Marple, *Murder at the Vicarage,* Totem Pole Playhouse, 1981.
Aunt Eller, *Oklahoma!,* Totem Pole Playhouse, 1981.
The Curious Savage, 1981.
Butterfly Days, 1981.
The Corn Is Green, 1982.
Wardrobe mistress, *Parade of Stars Playing the Palace,* Palace Theatre, New York City, 1983.
The Late Christopher Bean, Kennedy Center for the Performing Arts, Washington, DC, 1983.
Ernest in Love, 1983.

The Show-Off, Syracuse Stage, Syracuse, NY, 1983, then Paper Mill Playhouse, Millburn, NJ, 1984.
Old woman, *Candide,* Baltimore Opera Company, Baltimore, MD, 1984.
The Italian Lesson, Baltimore Opera Company, 1985.
Abby Brewster, *Arsenic and Old Lace,* 46th Street Theatre, 1986.
Julia Child, *Bon Appetit,* Terrace Theatre, Kennedy Center for the Performing Arts, 1989.
Elderly woman, *Mountain Language,* Classic Stage Company, CSC Theatre, New York City, 1989.
Meg, *The Birthday Party,* Classic Stage Company, CSC Theatre, 1989.
Philamente, *The Learned Ladies,* Classic Stage Company, New York City, 1991.
Romeo and Juliet, The Shakespeare Company, Washington, DC, 1994.
Night Seasons, Signature Theatre, New York City, 1994.
Stepmother, *Cinderella* (also known as *Rodgers and Hammerstein's Cinderella*), New York City Opera, Lincoln Center, New York City, 1995.
Madame Arcati, *Blithe Spirit,* South Coast Repertory Theatre, Costa Mesa, CA, 1995.
The Matchmaker, American Conservatory Theatre, Tucson and Phoenix, AZ, 1996.
Eleanor Roosevelt, *Eleanor: Her Secret Journey* (solo show), Westport Country Playhouse, Westport, CT, 1998.

Also appeared in *Sweeney Todd,* San Jose Civic Light Opera. Appeared at Peterborough Playhouse, Peterborough, NH, 1941; Chase Barn Playhouse, Whitefield, NH, 1947-48; and Pocono Playhouse, Mountainhome, PA, 1951-53.

Major Tours:

Myrtle Mae, *Harvey,* U.S. cities, 1948-49 and 1949-50.
Mrs. Coffman, *Come Back, Little Sheba,* U.S. cities, 1950-51.
Mrs. Ochs, *Rhinoceros,* U.S. cities, 1961.
Aary, *Morning's at Seven,* U.S. cities, 1976.
Title role, *Daisy Mayme,* U.S. cities, 1979-80.
The Show-Off, U.S. cities, 1983.
Clara's Play, U.S. cities, 1983.
Abby Brewster, *Arsenic and Old Lace,* U.S. cities, 1987.

Also appeared as Princess Puffer, *The Mystery of Edwin Drood,* U.S. cities.

Film Appearances:

(Film debut) Sister, *Damn Yankees* (also known as *What Lola Wants*), Warner Bros., 1958.
Sue, *Bells Are Ringing,* Metro-Goldwyn-Mayer, 1960.
Shirley Johnson, *Something Wild,* United Artists, 1961.
Sadie Finch, *Up the Down Staircase,* Warner Bros., 1967.
Mrs. Wrappler, *Cold Turkey,* United Artists, 1971.
Goldfarb's secretary, *Klute,* Warner Bros., 1971.
Mrs. Price, *The Buddy System,* Twentieth Century-Fox, 1984.
Waiting to Act, 1985.
Landlady, *The Trial,* Angelika Films, 1993.
Pansy Milbank, *Michael,* New Line Cinema/Turner Pictures, 1996.
This Is My Father, 1998.
Voice of Mrs. Jenkins, *Pocahontas II: Journey to a New World,* Walt Disney Home Video, 1998.
Birdie, *You've Got Mail,* Warner Bros., 1998.

Television Appearances; Series:

Gwen, *Woman with a Past,* CBS, 1954.
Edith Bunker, *All in the Family* (also known as *Justice for All*), CBS, 1971-79.
Jasmine Zweibel, *Bagdad Cafe* (also known as *Bagdad Gas and Oil*), CBS, 1990.
Title role, *Mrs. Piggle-Wiggle* (children's series), Showtime, 1994.
Voice of Edith Wilson, *The Great War* (also known as *The Great War and the Shaping of the Twentieth Century*), PBS, 1996.

Television Appearances; Pilots:

Edith Bunker, *Those Were the Days,* CBS, 1971.

Television Appearances; Movies:

Mrs. DeCamp, *Tail Gunner Joe,* NBC, 1977.
Isabel Cooper, *Isabel's Choice,* CBS, 1981.
Betty Eaton, *Angel Dusted,* NBC, 1981.
Title role, *Eleanor, First Lady of the World,* CBS, 1982.
Irene Wallin, *A Matter of Sex,* NBC, 1984.
Ariadne Oliver, *Agatha Christie's "Dead Man's Folly"* (also known as *Dead Man's Folly*), CBS, 1986.
Mother Goose, *Mother Goose Rock 'n' Rhyme,* The Disney Channel, 1990.
Henny Dutton, *Fire in the Dark* (also known as *Aging Parent*), CBS, 1991.
Leonora Tolliver, "The Habitation of Dragons," *TNT Screenworks,* TNT, 1992.
Mildred Mallory, *Ghost Mom* (also known as *Bury Me in Niagara* and *Bury Me in St. Louis, Louis*), Fox, 1993.
Mrs. Coons, *Lily Dale,* Showtime, 1996.
Mrs. Duncan, *Chance of a Lifetime,* CBS, 1998.

Television Appearances; Episodic:

"A Business Proposition," *Philco Television Playhouse,* NBC, 1955.
True Story, NBC, 1960.
"The End of the Beginning," *Robert Herridge Theater,* CBS, 1960.
"Bullets Cost Too Much," *Naked City,* ABC, 1961.
"The Patient," *Dr. Kildare,* NBC, 1961.
"Mr. Wilson's Housekeeper," *Dennis the Menace,* CBS, 1962.
"The Multiplicity of Herbert Konish," *Naked City,* ABC, 1962.
"The Barbara Bowers Story," *The Nurses,* CBS, 1962.
"The Hidden Jungle," *The Defenders,* CBS, 1962.
"Je t'Adore Muldoon," *Car 54, Where Are You?,* NBC, 1962.
"The Highest of Prizes," *Naked City,* ABC, 1963.
"The Bride Wore Pink," *Eleventh Hour,* NBC, 1963.
"Is Smiling," *Route 66,* CBS, 1963.
"The People's House," *My Three Sons,* ABC, 1964.
"The Raffle," *The Patty Duke Show,* ABC, 1965.
The Muppet Show, 1978.
Judith Klammerstadt, "A Girl Like Edith," *All in the Family* (also known as *Justice for All*), CBS, 1979.
Edith Bunker, *Archie Bunker's Place,* CBS, 1979.
Ogress, "Jack and the Beanstalk," *Faerie Tale Theatre,* Showtime, 1983.
Emily Farnsworth, *Scarecrow and Mrs. King,* CBS, 1983.
"The Legend of Das Gersterschloss (The Ghost Castle)," *Scarecrow and Mrs. King,* CBS, 1984.
"The Three Wishes of Emily," *Scarecrow and Mrs. King,* CBS, 1984.
Fairy Godmother, "Cinderella," *Faerie Tale Theatre,* Showtime, 1985.
Helen, "Grown Ups," *Broadway on Showtime,* Showtime, 1985, then *Great Performances,* PBS, 1986.
Widow, "Egypt," *The Love Boat,* ABC, 1986.
"Margaret Fuller," *An American Portrait,* CBS, 1986.
We the People (documentary), CBS, 1986.
Edna, "The Boss," *Trying Times,* PBS, 1989.
Helen, "Let Me Hear You Whisper," *American Playwrights Theatre: The One Acts,* Arts and Entertainment, 1990.
Narrator, "Elizabeth and Larry," *Shelly Duvall's Bedtime Stories,* Showtime, 1992.
"Fee Fie Foe Fum," *The Ray Bradbury Theatre,* 1992.
Emilie, "The Parallax Garden," *General Motors Playwrights Theater,* Arts and Entertainment, 1993.
Beakman's mom, *Beakman's World,* 1993.
Aunt Vivian, "The Road to Paris, Texas," *Grace under Fire,* ABC, 1994.
Aunt Mary Kosky, "Caroline and the Opera," *Caroline in the City,* NBC, 1995.
Nana Silverberg, *Murphy Brown,* 1996.
Mary, *Caroline and the City,* NBC, 1996.
Aunt Alda, *Everybody Loves Raymond,* CBS, 1996.
Gloria Utley, "Recipe for Disaster," *Style and Substance,* CBS, 1998.

Also appeared in *Armstrong Circle Theatre,* NBC; *Camera Three,* CBS; *The Carol Burnett Show,* CBS; *Danger,* CBS; *The Jackie Gleason Show,* CBS; *Laugh-In,* NBC; *The Mike Douglas Show,* ABC; *Omnibus,* CBS; *The Sonny and Cher Show,* CBS; *Studio One,* CBS; and *Today Is Ours,* NBC.

Television Appearances; Specials:

Marlo Thomas in Acts of Love—And Other Comedies, ABC, 1973.
Circus of the Stars, CBS, 1977.
Co-host, *CBS: On the Air,* CBS, 1978.
The Stars Salute Israel at Thirty, ABC, 1978.
Penny Sycamore, *You Can't Take It with You,* CBS, 1979.
Aunt Mary Dobkin, "Aunt Mary," *Hallmark Hall of Fame,* CBS, 1979.
Good Evening, Captain, CBS, 1981.
Miss Tweed, *Something's Afoot,* Showtime, 1982.
Parade of Stars, 1983.
Josephine, *Tender Places,* syndicated, 1987.
CBS Comedy Bloopers, CBS, 1990.
The 14th Annual Kennedy Center Honors: A Celebration of the Performing Arts, CBS, 1991.
All in the Family 20th Anniversary Special, CBS, 1991.
A Birthday Tribute to Julia Child—Compliments to the Chef!, PBS, 1993.
Fifty Years of Television: A Celebration of the Academy of Television Arts and Sciences Golden Anniversary, HBO, 1997.

Television Appearances; Awards Presentations:

The 6th Annual Television Academy Hall of Fame, Fox, 1990.
The 23rd Annual NAACP Image Awards, NBC, 1991.
The 48th Annual Tony Awards, CBS, 1994.
The 23rd Annual People's Choice Awards, 1997.

RECORDINGS

Albums:

(With others) Edith Bunker, *All in the Family,* Atlantic, c. 1972.

Videos:

A Simple Matter of Justice (documentary), Films, Inc., 1978.

Narrator, *A Place for the Spirit* (documentary), John F. Kennedy Center for the Performing Arts, 1985.

CD-ROM Discs:

Grandma Ollie's Morphabet Soup, 1996.

OTHER SOURCES

Periodicals:

TV Guide, June 11, 1994, p. 28.*

STEENBURGEN, Mary 1953-

PERSONAL

Surname is pronounced "*Steen*-ber-jen"; born February 8, 1953, in Newport, AR; daughter of Maurice (a freight-train conductor) and Nell (a school-board secretary) Steenburgen; married Malcolm MacDowell (an actor), 1980 (divorced, 1989); married Ted Danson (an actor), October 7, 1995; children: Lilly Amanda, Charlie (daughter). *Education:* Attended Hendrix College; studied acting with Sanford Meisner at the Neighborhood Playhouse, New York City, 1972.

Addresses: *Agent*—Ames Cushing, William Morris Agency, Inc., 151 South El Camino Dr., Beverly Hills, CA 90212-2775.

Career: Actress and producer. Former member of an improvisational comedy troupe. Also worked as a waitress.

Awards, Honors: Golden Globe Award nomination, best female acting debut in a motion picture, 1978, for *Goin' South;* Saturn Award, best actress, Academy of Science Fiction, Horror, and Fantasy Films, 1979, for *Time after Time;* New York Film Critics Award, Academy Award, and Golden Globe Award, all best supporting actress, Los Angeles Film Critics Association Award, and National Society of Film Critics Award, all 1980, for *Melvin and Howard;* Golden Globe Award nomination, best supporting actress in a motion picture, 1981, for *Ragtime;* Distinguished Service Award for the Performing Arts, Simon Wiesenthal Center, 1989, and Emmy Award nomination, best actress in a miniseries or special, both for "The Attic: The Hiding of Anne Frank," *General Foods Golden Showcase;* Screen Actors Guild Award nomination, best actress in a television movie or miniseries, 1998, for *About Sarah;* honorary doctorates from University of Arkansas at Little Rock and Hendrix College.

CREDITS

Stage Appearances:

Holiday, Old Vic Theatre, London, 1987.

Bargains, Arkansas Repertory Theatre, Little Rock, AR, 1990.

Candida, Broadway production, 1993.

Marvin's Room, Los Angeles production, 1994.

Film Appearances:

(Film debut) Julia Tate, *Goin' South,* Paramount, 1978.

Rabbit Test, Avco-Embassy, 1978.

Amy Robbins, *Time after Time,* Warner Bros., 1979.

Lynda Dummar, *Melvin and Howard,* Universal, 1980.

Mother, *Ragtime,* Paramount, 1981.

Adrian Hobbs, *A Midsummer Night's Sex Comedy,* Warner Bros., 1982.

Marjorie Kinnan Rawlings, *Cross Creek,* Universal, 1983.

Phoebe, *Romantic Comedy,* Metro-Goldwyn-Mayer/United Artists, 1983.

Ginny Grainger, *One Magic Christmas,* Buena Vista, 1985.

Katie McGovern, Julie Rose, and Evelyn, *Dead of Winter,* Metro-Goldwyn-Mayer/United Artists, 1987.

Young Sarah, *The Whales of August,* Island Alive, 1987.

Rose Pickett, *End of the Line,* Orion Classics, 1988.

Karen Buckman, *Parenthood,* Universal, 1989.

Elain Rutledge, *Miss Firecracker,* Corsair, 1989.

Clara Clayton, *Back to the Future Part III,* Universal, 1990.

Narrator, *The Long Walk Home,* Miramax, 1991.

Stella, *The Butcher's Wife,* Paramount, 1991.

Betty Carver, *What's Eating Gilbert Grape?,* Paramount, 1993.

Belinda Conine, *Philadelphia,* TriStar, 1993.

Sarah Davis, *Clifford,* Orion, 1994.

Mom, *It Runs in the Family* (also known as *My Summer Story*), Metro-Goldwyn-Mayer/United Artists, 1994.

Katherine Bellamy, *Pontiac Moon,* Paramount, 1994.

Jessie Caldwell, *Powder,* Buena Vista, 1995.

Sister Ida, *The Grass Harp,* Fine Line Features, 1995.

Gloria, *My Family* (also known as *East L.A., My Family, Cafe con Leche,* and *Mi Familia*), New Line Cinema, 1995.

Hannah Nixon, *Nixon,* Buena Vista, 1995.

Film Work:

Executive producer, *End of the Line,* Orion Classics, 1988.

Television Appearances; Series:

Voice of Clara, *Back to the Future* (also known as *Back to the Future: The Animated Series*), CBS, 1991.

Kate Montgomery, *Ink,* CBS, 1996-97.

Television Appearances; Miniseries:

Nicole Warren Diver, *Tender Is the Night,* Showtime, 1985.

Mary Gulliver, "Gulliver's Travels," *Hallmark Hall of Fame,* NBC, 1996.

Noah's wife, *Noah's Ark,* NBC, 1999.

Television Appearances; Episodic:

"Little Red Riding Hood," *Faerie Tale Theatre,* Showtime, 1983.

CBS This Morning, CBS, 1989.

Entertainment Tonight, syndicated, 1989.

Late Night with David Letterman, NBC, 1989.

The Pat Sajak Show, CBS, 1989.

Narrator, "Katy No-Pocket," *Shelley Duvall's Bedtime Stories* (animated), Showtime, 1992.

Catherine, "The Gift," *Directed By,* Showtime, 1994.

Herself, "Ellen: A Hollywood Tribute," *Ellen,* ABC, 1998.

Voice of Marjorie, "Retirement Is Murder," *Frasier,* NBC, 1998.

Television Appearances; Specials:

"Sanford Meisner: The Theatre's Best Kept Secret" (documentary), *American Masters,* PBS, 1990.

The Secrets of the Back to the Future Trilogy, 1990.

Earth and the American Dream, HBO, 1993.

The American Film Institute Salute to Jack Nicholson, CBS, 1994.

Voice of Christine Frederick, *A Century of Women* (also known as *A Family of Women*), TBS, 1994.

Earth Day at Walt Disney World, The Disney Channel, 1996.

Night of about 14 CBS Stars, Comedy Central, 1996.

Star Trek: 30 Years and Beyond, UPN, 1996.

Presenter, *The 1996 Emmy Awards,* ABC, 1996.

To Life! America Celebrates Israel's 50th, CBS, 1998.

Television Appearances; Movies:

Miep Gies, "The Attic: The Hiding of Anne Frank," *General Foods Golden Showcase,* CBS, 1988.

Title role, *About Sarah,* CBS, 1998.

Television Work; Series:

Executive producer, *Ink,* CBS, 1996-97.

OTHER SOURCES

Periodicals:

People Weekly, August 28, 1989, p. 77; November 21, 1994, pp. 69-72.*

STEVENS, William Christopher

See ALLEN, Steve

STEWART, Jane Ann

PERSONAL

Born in Texas; raised in Connecticut and Europe. *Education:* Studied art at University of California, Berkeley.

Career: Production designer.

CREDITS

Film Work; Production Designer, Except Where Indicated:

Art department associate, *The Lost Boys,* Warner Bros. 1987.

Art department associate, *Beetlejuice,* Warner Bros., 1988.

Art department associate, *The Accidental Tourist,* Warner Bros., 1988.

Rockula, Warner Home Video, 1989.

Candyman, TriStar, 1992.

Gas, Food, Lodging, IRS Releasing, 1992.

Inside Monkey Zetterland, IRS Releasing, 1993.

Art department associate, *Ed Wood,* Buena Vista, 1994.

Mi Vida Loca (also known as *My Crazy Life*), Sony Pictures Classics, 1994.

Erotique (also known as *Let's Talk About Sex*), Private Screenings, 1994.

Citizen Ruth (also known as *Meet Ruth Stoops*), Miramax, 1996.

Good Luck (also known as *Guys Like Us* and *The Ox and the Eye*), East West Film Partners, 1996.

The Souler Opposite, Curb Entertainment, 1997.

Election, Paramount, 1999.

Also worked as the production designer for the short films *Every Cake, Neil, Dizziness,* and *Driftwood.*

Television Work; Production Designer; Specials:
Rock the Vote, 1992.

Television Work; Movies; Production Designer, Except Where Indicated:
Love, Cheat & Steal, Showtime, 1993.
Invasion of Privacy, HBO, 1996.
Art direction, *If Looks Could Kill: From the Files of "America's Most Wanted,"* The WB, 1996.
Breast Men, HBO, 1997.
The Maker, HBO, 1997.

Other Television Work:
Collaborated with Alexander Payne, *Inside Out,* (cable series).*

STEWART, Patrick 1940-

PERSONAL

Born July 13, 1940, in Mirfield, England; son of Alfred (a professional soldier) and Gladys (a weaver; maiden name, Barraclough) Stewart; married Sheila Falconer (a choreographer), March 3, 1966 (divorced, 1990); married Wendy Neuss, 1998; children: Sophie Alexandra Falconer, Daniel Freedom. *Education:* Trained for the stage at Bristol Old Vic Theatre School. *Avocational interests:* Cinema, fell-walking.

Addresses: *Agent*—International Creative Management, 8942 Wilshire Blvd., Beverly Hills, CA 90211-1934. *Publicist*—Kelly Bush Public Relations, 7201 Melrose Ave., Los Angeles, CA 90046.

Career: Actor, writer, director, and producer. Appeared in repertory at Playhouse Theatre, Sheffield, England, 1959-61, Liverpool Playhouse, Liverpool, England, 1963-64, and with the Bristol Old Vic Theatre Company, Bristol, England 1965. Royal Shakespeare Company, associate artist, 1967—; Alliance for Creative Theatre, Education, and Research, joint artistic director of Shakespeare Company, associate director of company at University of California, Santa Barbara; acting teacher. Made television commercials for Pontiac, MasterCard, and RCA. Also worked as a journalist and furniture salesperson.

Member: British Association of Film and Television Arts.

Awards, Honors: Laurence Olivier Award, best supporting actor, Society of West End Theatre, 1979, for *Antony and Cleopatra;* Laurence Olivier Award nomination, best actor, 1979, for *The Merchant of Venice;* London Fringe Award, best actor, 1987, for *Who's Afraid of Virginia Woolf?;* Laurence Olivier Award and Drama Desk Award, best solo performance, New York Theatre Critics, both 1993, for *A Christmas Carol;* Screen Actors Guild Award nomination, best actor in a drama series, 1995, for *Star Trek: The Next Generation;* Blockbuster Award nomination, favorite science fiction actor, 1996, for *Star Trek: First Contact;* Grammy Award, best spoken word album for children, National Academy of Recording Arts and Sciences, 1996, for *Prokofiev: Peter and the Wolf;* received star on Hollywood Walk of Fame,1996; Blockbuster Award, favorite supporting actor in suspense category, 1997, for *Conspiracy Theory;* Emmy Award nomination and Golden Globe Award nomination, both best actor in a miniseries or television movie, 1998, for *Moby Dick;* named honorary associate artist, Royal Shakespeare Company.

CREDITS

Stage Appearances:
(Stage debut) Morgan, *Treasure Island,* Lincoln Repertory Company, Theatre Royal, Lincoln, England, 1959.
Title role, *Henry V,* Manchester Library Theatre, Manchester, England, 1963.
Aston, *The Caretaker,* Manchester Library Theatre, 1963.
(London debut) Second witness, *The Investigation,* Royal Shakespeare Company, Aldwych Theatre, London, 1966.
Sir Walter Blunt, *Henry IV, Part One,* Royal Shakespeare Company, Stratford-on-Avon, England, 1966.
Mowbray, *Henry IV, Part Two,* Royal Shakespeare Company, Stratford-on-Avon, 1966.
First player and player king, *Hamlet,* Royal Shakespeare Company, Stratford-on-Avon, 1966.
Second witness, *The Investigation,* Royal Shakespeare Company, Stratford-on-Avon, 1966.
Dauphin, *Henry V,* Royal Shakespeare Company, Stratford-on-Avon, 1966.
Hippolito, *The Revenger's Tragedy,* Royal Shakespeare Company, Stratford-on-Avon, 1966.
Duke Senior, *As You Like It,* Royal Shakespeare Company, Stratford-on-Avon, then Aldwych Theatre, both 1967.
Grumio, *The Taming of the Shrew,* Royal Shakespeare Company, Stratford-on-Avon, then Aldwych Theatre, both 1967.

Worthy, *The Relapse,* Royal Shakespeare Company, Stratford-on-Avon, then Aldwych Theatre, both 1967.

Borachio, *Much Ado about Nothing,* Royal Shakespeare Company, Stratford-on-Avon, then Aldwych Theatre, both 1968.

Cornwall, *King Lear,* Royal Shakespeare Company, Stratford-on-Avon, then Aldwych Theatre, both 1968.

Touchstone, *As You Like It,* Royal Shakespeare Company, Stratford-on-Avon, then Aldwych Theatre, both 1968.

Hector, *Troilus and Cressida,* Royal Shakespeare Company, Stratford-on-Avon, then Aldwych Theatre, both 1968.

Teddy Foran, *The Silver Tassie,* Royal Shakespeare Company, Aldwych Theatre, 1969.

Hippolito, *The Revenger's Tragedy,* Royal Shakespeare Company, Aldwych Theatre, 1969.

Hector, *Troilus and Cressida,* Royal Shakespeare Company, Aldwych Theatre, 1969.

Leatherhead, *Bartholomew Fayre,* Royal Shakespeare Company, Aldwych Theatre, 1969.

Edward IV, *Richard III,* Royal Shakespeare Company, Stratford-on-Avon, 1970.

Title role, *King John,* Royal Shakespeare Company, Stratford-on-Avon, 1970.

Stephano, *The Tempest,* Royal Shakespeare Company, Stratford-on-Avon, 1970.

Launce, *The Two Gentlemen of Verona,* Royal Shakespeare Company, Stratford-on-Avon, then Aldwych Theatre, both 1970.

(Broadway debut) Snout, *A Midsummer Night's Dream,* Billy Rose Theatre, 1971.

Snout, *A Midsummer Night's Dream,* Royal Shakespeare Company, AldwychTheatre, 1971.

Roger, *The Balcony,* Royal Shakespeare Company, Aldwych Theatre, 1971.

Mikhail Skrobotov, *Enemies,* Royal Shakespeare Company, Aldwych Theatre, 1971.

Kabac, *Occupations,* Royal Shakespeare Company, Palace Theatre, London, 1971.

Aufidius, *Coriolanus,* Royal Shakespeare Company, Stratford-on-Avon, 1972.

Bassianus, *Titus Andronicus,* Royal Shakespeare Company, Stratford-on-Avon, 1972.

Cassius, *Julius Caesar,* Royal Shakespeare Company, Stratford-on-Avon, 1972, then Aldwych Theatre, 1973.

Enobarbus, *Antony and Cleopatra,* Royal Shakespeare Company, Stratford-on-Avon, 1972, then Aldwych Theatre, 1973.

Aaron, *Titus Andronicus,* Royal Shakespeare Company, Aldwych Theatre, 1973.

Astrov, *Uncle Vanya,* Royal Shakespeare Company, Other Place Theatre, Stratford-on-Avon, 1974.

Eilert Lovborg, *Hedda Gabler,* Royal Shakespeare Company, Aldwych Theatre, 1975.

Larry Slade, *The Iceman Cometh,* Royal Shakespeare Company, Aldwych Theatre, 1976.

Oberon, *A Midsummer Night's Dream,* Royal Shakespeare Company, Royal Shakespeare Theatre, Stratford-on-Avon, then Aldwych Theatre, both 1977.

Doctor, *Every Good Boy Deserves Favour,* Royal Shakespeare Company, Royal Festival Hall, London, 1977.

Knatchbull, *That Good between Us,* Royal Shakespeare Company, Warehouse Theatre, London, 1977.

Shakespeare, *Bingo,* Royal Shakespeare Company, Warehouse Theatre, 1977.

Basho, *The Bundle,* Royal Shakespeare Company, Warehouse Theatre, 1977.

Enobarbus, *Antony and Cleopatra,* Royal Shakespeare Company, Royal Shakespeare Theatre, 1978, then Aldwych Theatre, 1979.

Shylock, *The Merchant of Venice,* Royal Shakespeare Company, Other Place Theatre, 1978, then Warehouse Theatre, 1979.

Theseus, *Hippolytus,* Royal Shakespeare Company, Other Place Theatre, 1978, then Warehouse Theatre, 1979.

Colonel Guieson, *The Biko Inquest,* Royal Shakespeare Company, Other Place Theatre, 1979.

Viktor Myshlaevksy, *The White Guard,* Royal Shakespeare Company, Aldwych Theatre, 1979.

Leontes, *The Winter's Tale,* Royal Shakespeare Company, Stratford-on-Avon, 1981, then London, 1982.

Title role, *Titus Andronicus,* Royal Shakespeare Company, Stratford-on-Avon, 1981, then London, 1982.

Sir Eglamour, *The Two Gentlemen of Verona,* Royal Shakespeare Company, Stratford-on-Avon, 1981, then London, 1982.

Title role, *Henry IV, Part One* [and] *Part Two,* Royal Shakespeare Company, Barbican Theatre, London, 1982-83.

Alexander Grant, *Body and Soul,* Palace Theatre, Watford, England, 1983.

King David, then title role, *Yonada,* National Theatre, London, 1985.

George, *Who's Afraid of Virginia Woolf?,* Young Vic Theatre, London, 1987.

A Christmas Carol (solo show), 1991-93, then Broadhurst Theatre, New York City, 1993, later Richard Rogers Theatre, New York City, 1994-95.

Gypsy of the Year, Virginia Theatre, New York City, 1995.

Prospero, *The Tempest,* New York Shakespeare Festival, Delacorte Theatre/Central Park, 1995, then Broadhurst Theatre, 1996.

Title role, *Othello,* Shakespeare Theatre, Washington, DC, 1997.

Lyman, *The Ride Down Mount Morgan,* Joseph Papp Public Theatre, New YorkCity, 1998.

Also appeared as Goldberg, *The Birthday Party,* title role, *Galileo,* and Shylock, *The Merchant of Venice;* appeared as Lyman Felt, *The Ride down Mt. Morgan,* an off-Broadway production.

Major Tours:

Duke de Gire, *Lady of the Camellias,* Old Vic Theatre Company, Australian, New Zealand, and South American cities, 1961-62.

Second officer, *Twelfth Night,* Old Vic Theatre Company, Australian, New Zealand, and South American cities, 1961-62.

Cafe customer, *Duel of Angels,* Old Vic Theatre Company, Australian, New Zealand, and South American cities, 1961-62.

Duke Senior, *As You Like It,* Royal Shakespeare Company, U.S. cities, 1967-68.

Grumio, *The Taming of the Shrew,* Royal Shakespeare Company, U.S. cities, 1967-68.

Worthy, *The Relapse,* Royal Shakespeare Company, U.S. cities, 1967-68.

Cornwall, *King Lear,* Royal Shakespeare Company, U.S. cities, 1968-69.

Touchstone, *As You Like It,* Royal Shakespeare Company, U.S. cities, 1968-69.

Borachio, *Much Ado about Nothing,* Royal Shakespeare Company, U.S. cities, 1968-69.

Hector, *Troilus and Cressida,* Royal Shakespeare Company, U.S. cities, 1968-69.

Eilert Lovborg, *Hedda Gabler,* Royal Shakespeare Company, U.S., Canadian, and Australian cities, 1975.

Stage Work:

Director, *Every Good Boy Deserves Favour,* 1993.

Film Appearances:

McCann, *Hennessy,* American International Pictures, 1975.

Eilert Lovborg, *Hedda,* Brut, 1975.

Leondegrance, *Excalibur,* Warner Bros., 1981.

Voice of Major, *The Plague Dogs* (animated), United International, 1982.

Exploring a Character, Films for the Humanities, 1983.

Mr. Duffner, *Uindii* (also known as *Races*), Toho-Toha, 1984.

Gurney Halek, *Dune,* Universal, 1984.

Dr. Armstrong, *Lifeforce,* TriStar, 1985.

Colonel Watson, *Code Name: Emerald* (also known as *Emerald*), Metro-Goldwyn-Mayer/United Artists, 1985.

Russian General, *Wild Geese II,* Allied Artists, 1985.

Dr. Mackie, *The Doctor and the Devils,* Twentieth Century-Fox, 1985.

Henry Grey, Duke of Suffolk, *Lady Jane,* Paramount, 1986.

Narrator, *Discovering Hamlet,* 1990.

Maitre d' at l'Idiot, *L.A. Story,* TriStar, 1991.

King Richard, *Robin Hood: Men in Tights,* Twentieth Century-Fox, 1993.

Narrator, *The Secret of Life on Earth,* 1993.

Narrator, *Liberation,* Samuel Goldwyn Company, 1994.

Loomis, *Gunmen,* IAC Film Sales/Dimension Pictures, 1994.

Captain Jean-Luc Picard, *Star Trek: Generations,* Paramount, 1994.

Voice of Adventure, *The Pagemaster* (animated), Twentieth Century-Fox, 1994.

Sterling, *Jeffrey,* Orion, 1995.

Captain Jean-Luc Picard, *Star Trek: First Contact,* Paramount, 1996.

Narrator, *Whales,* 1997.

Title role, *Dad Savage,* PolyGram Filmed Entertainment, 1997.

Dr. Jonas, *Conspiracy Theory,* Warner Bros., 1997.

Raif Bentley, *Masterminds,* Sony Pictures Entertainment, 1997.

Voice of Pharaoh Seti, *The Prince of Egypt* (animated), DreamWorks, 1998.

Captain Jean-Luc Picard, *Star Trek: Insurrection,* Paramount, 1998.

Title role, *Dad Savage,* PolyGram Video, 1998.

Film Work:

Associate producer, *Star Trek: Insurrection,* Paramount, 1998.

Television Appearances; Series:

The Inventor, *Eleventh Hour,* BBC, 1975.

Doctor Edward Roebuck, *Maybury,* BBC, 1980.

Captain Jean-Luc Picard, *Star Trek: The Next Generation* (also known as *Star Trek: TNG*), syndicated, 1987-94.

Host and narrator, *The Shape of the World,* PBS, 1991-92.

Television Appearances; Miniseries:

Serjanus, *I, Claudius,* BBC, 1976, then *Masterpiece Theatre,* PBS, 1977.

Karla, *Tinker, Tailor, Soldier, Spy,* BBC and PBS, both 1979.

Karla, *Smiley's People,* BBC, then syndicated, both 1982.

Playing Shakespeare, London Weekend Television, then PBS, 1983.

Television Appearances; Movies:

Clement Atlee, *The Gathering Storm,* 1974.

Wilkins, *Little Lord Fauntleroy,* CBS, 1980.

Party Secretary Gomulka, *Pope John Paul II,* CBS, 1984.

Captain Jean-Luc Picard, *Star Trek: The Next Generation—Encounter at Farpoint* (also known as *Encounter at Farpoint*), syndicated, 1987.

Malcolm Philpott, *Alistair MacLean's Death Train* (also known as *Death Train* and *Detonator*), USA Network, 1993.

Captain Jean-Luc Picard, *Star Trek: Deep Space Nine—Emissary* (also known as *Emissary*), syndicated, 1993.

Sergeant Mulvaney, *In Search of Dr. Seuss,* TNT, 1994.

Captain Jean-Luc Picard, *Star Trek: The Next Generation—All Good Things* (also known as *All Good Things*), syndicated, 1994.

John, *Let It Be Me,* Starz!, 1995.

Sir Simon de Canterville, *The Canterville Ghost,* ABC, 1996.

Mace Sowell, *Safe House,* Showtime, 1998.

Captain Ahab, *Moby Dick,* USA Network, 1998.

Television Appearances; Episodic:

Michael Williams, "The Defector," *Star Trek: The Next Generation,* syndicated, 1989.

Narrator, "Neptune's Cold Fury," *Nova,* PBS, 1990.

Narrator, "Mind of a Serial Killer," *Nova,* PBS, 1992.

"Gene Roddenberry: Star Trek and Beyond," *Biography,* Arts and Entertainment, 1994.

Host, *Saturday Night Live* (also known as *NBC's Saturday Night, Saturday Night,* and *SNL*), NBC, 1994.

Voice of Number One, "Homer the Great," *The Simpsons* (animated), Fox, 1995.

Narrator, *Sex and the Silver Screen,* Showtime, 1996.

Entertainment Tonight, 1998.

Appeared as narrator, "Great Plains Massacre" and "Reflections on a River," *Horizon,* BBC; narrator, "Henry VII," *Timewatch,* BBC; and narrator, *The Making of Modern London: London at War,* London Weekend Television; also appeared on *The Tonight Show with Jay Leno.*

Television Appearances; Specials:

Enobarbus, *Antony and Cleopatra,* ATV, 1973, then PBS, 1975.

Lenin, *Fall of Eagles,* BBC, 1973.

Anton, *The Artist's Story,* BBC, 1973.

Gurvich, *The Love Girl and the Innocent,* BBC, 1973.

Joseph Conrad, *Conrad,* BBC, 1974.

Father, *Joby,* Yorkshire Television, 1974.

Attlee, *A Walk with Destiny,* BBC, 1974.

Guthrum, *Alfred the Great,* BBC, 1974.

John Thorton, *North and South,* BBC, 1975.

Largo Caballero, *The Madness,* BBC, 1976.

Title role, *Oedipus,* BBC, 1976.

Jean, *Miss Julie,* BBC, 1977.

Milos, *When the Actors Come,* BBC, 1978.

Sergey Tolstoy, *Tolstoy: A Question of Faith,* BBC, 1979.

Doctor Knox, *The Anatomist,* BBC, 1980.

Claudius, *Hamlet* (also known as *Hamlet, Prince of Denmark* and *BBC Television Shakespeare: Hamlet, Prince of Denmark*), BBC and PBS, both 1980.

Signor Carini, *The Holy Experiment,* BBC, 1984.

Salieri, *The Mozart Inquest,* BBC, 1985.

Reverend Anthony Anderson, *The Devil's Disciple,* BBC, 1986.

Host and narrator, *MGM: When the Lion Roars,* TNT, 1992.

Out There II, Comedy Central, 1994.

Narrator, *Stargazers: One Hundred Years of Seeing at the Lowell Observatory* (also known as *Stargazers*), The Discovery Channel, 1994.

Voice, *500 Nations,* CBS, 1995.

Star Trek: 30 Years and Beyond, UPN, 1996.

Aliens Invade Hollywood, The Learning Channel, 1997.

Signature: George C. Wolfe, PBS, 1997.

Star Wars: The Magic and the Mystery, Fox, 1997.

Narrator, *Amazing Earth,* The Discovery Channel, 1998.

Thar She Blows! The Making of "Moby Dick," USA Network, 1998.

William Shatner, Arts and Entertainment, 1998.

Television Appearances; Awards Presentations:

The 45th Annual Primetime Emmy Awards, ABC, 1993.

Host, *The American Television Awards,* ABC, 1993.

Screen Actors Guild Awards, NBC, 1995.

Presenter, *The 49th Annual Tony Awards,* CBS, 1995.

The 38th Annual Grammy Awards, 1996.

Presenter, *The 2nd Annual Screen Actors Guild Awards,* 1996.
The 54th Annual Golden Globe Awards, 1997.
Presenter, *The 50th Emmy Awards,* 1998.

Television Work; Episodic:
Director, *Star Trek: The Next Generation* (also known as *Star Trek: TNG*), syndicated, between 1987 and 1994.

Television Work; Movies:
Co-producer, *The Canterville Ghost,* ABC, 1996.

RECORDINGS

Albums:
A Christmas Carol, Simon & Schuster Audioworks, 1991.
Prokofiev: Peter and the Wolf, Atlantic, 1996.

Video Games:
Voice of King Richard, *Lands of Lore: The Throne of Chaos,* Virgin Interactive, 1994.
Voice of Captain Jean-Luc Picard, *Star Trek: The Next Generation—A Final Unity,* Micropose, 1995.
Voice of Captain Jean-Luc Picard, *Star Trek: Generations,* Micropose, 1997.
Voice of Captain Jean-Luc Picard, *Star Trek: Insurrection,* Activision, 1999.
Voice of Captain Jean-Luc Picard, *Star Trek: Armada,* Activision, 1999.

WRITINGS

Stage:
Adapter (with Michael Glenny), *The Procurator* (based on *The Master and Margharita* by M. Bulgakov).

Radio:
Adapted *A Country Doctor's Notebook* and *A Christmas Carol.*

Other:
Author of "Shylock," *Players of Shakespeare,* Cambridge University Press; "Titus Andronicus," *Prefaces to Shakespeare,* BBC Publications; and *Wooing, Wedding and Repenting* (a Shakespeare anthology).

OTHER SOURCES

Periodicals:
American Theatre, February, 1998, p. 12.
People Weekly, March 16, 1998, p. 16.*

STILES, Julia 1981-

PERSONAL

Born March 28, 1981, in New York, NY.

Addresses: *Agent*—c/o Clare Ryu, United Talent Agency, 9560 Wilshire Blvd., Suite 500, Beverly Hills, CA 90212.

Career: Actress.

Awards, Honors: Karlovy Vary International Film Festival Award, best actress, 1998, for *Wicked.*

CREDITS

Film Appearances:
Young Nana's friend, *I Love You, I Love You Not,* Buena Vista, 1996.
Bridget O'Meara, *The Devil's Own,* Columbia, 1997.
Ellie Christianson, *Wicked,* Frankenstein Entertainment, 1998.
Neena Beal, *Wide Awake,* Miramax, 1998.
Katarina "Kat" Stratford, *10 Things I Hate about You,* Buena Vista, 1999.
Ophelia, *Hamlet,* Miramax, 1999.
Imogen, *Down to You,* Miramax, 1999.
Black and White, Screen Gems, 1999.
Desi, *O,* Dimension Films, 1999.

Television Appearances; Episodic:
Megan Walker, "The Secret," *Promised Land,* CBS, 1996.
Corey Sawicki, "Mother, May I?," *Chicago Hope,* CBS, 1997.

Television Appearances; Movies:
Phoebe Jackson, *Before Women Had Wings* (also known as *Oprah Winfrey Presents: Before Women Had Wings*), ABC, 1997.

Television Appearances; Specials:
Teen People's 21 Hottest Stars Under 21, ABC, 1999.

Television Appearances; Miniseries:
Katie Herlihy, *The 60's,* NBC, 1999.

OTHER SOURCES

Periodicals:
Time, April 12, 1999, p. 96.*

STONE, Oliver 1946-

PERSONAL

Full name, Oliver William Stone; born September 15, 1946, in New York, NY; son of Louis (a stockbroker) and Jacqueline (Goddet) Stone; married Najwa Sarkis (a political attache), May 22, 1971 (divorced, 1977); married Elizabeth Burkit Cox (a film production assistant), June 7, 1981 (divorced, 1993); companion of Chong Son Chong (an actress and model); children: (second marriage) Sean, Michael; (with Chong) Tara. *Education:* Attended Yale University, 1965; New York University, B.F.A. (film), 1971; studied under Martin Scorsese. *Religion:* Buddhist.

Addresses: *Office*—Ixtlan Productions, 201 Santa Monica Blvd., Suite 610, Santa Monica, CA 90401.

Career: Director, producer, and screenwriter. Free Pacific Institute, Cholon, Vietnam, teacher, 1965-66; taxi driver, New York City, 1971; Ixtlan Productions (film company), Santa Monica, CA, founder, 1977, partner, 1977—; founder of Illusion Entertainment Group. *Military service:* U.S. Merchant Marines, 1966. U.S. Army, 1967-68, served in the infantry, served in Vietnam; became specialist fourth class; received the Bronze Star with an oak leaf cluster and the Purple Heart.

Member: Directors Guild of America, Screen Writers Guild, Writers Guild of America, Academy of Motion Picture Arts and Sciences.

Awards, Honors: Academy Award, Golden Globe Award, and Writers Guild of America Award, best adapted screenplay, all 1979, for *Midnight Express;* Academy Award nomination, best original screenplay (with Richard Boyle), and Independent Spirit Award nomination (with Gerald Green), best feature, both 1987, for *Salvador;* Independent Spirit Award nomination, best director, 1989, for *Talk Radio;* Special Prize, Berlin International Film Festival, 1990; Special Award for meritorious achievement, ShoWest Convention, National Association of Theatre Owners, 1992; Special Jury Prize, Venice Film Festival, and Golden Globe Award nomination, best director—motion picture, 1995, both for *Natural Born Killers;* Academy Award nomination, best original screenplay (with Stephen J. Rivele andChristopher Wilkinson), 1995, for *Nixon;* Emmy Award (with Janet Yang, Abby Mann, and Diana Pokorny), outstanding movie made for television, 1995, for *Indictment: The McMartin Trial;* British Film and Television Arts Film Award nomination (with Alan Parker), best screenplay—adapted, 1997, for *Evita;* Hermosa Beach Film Festival Award, best documentary, 1998, for *The Last Days of Kennedy and King;* Crystal Iris, Brussels International Arts Festival, 1998.

Awards for *Platoon* include Directors Guild of America Award, outstanding directorial achievement in motion pictures, Independent Spirit Awards, best director and best screenplay, and Silver Berlin Bear, Berlin International Film Festival, best director, all 1986, Academy Award and Golden Globe Award, both best director, Bulgarian Cinematography Diploma Award, and Academy Award nomination and Golden Globe Award nomination (both with Richard Boyle), both best original screenplay, all 1987, and British Academy of Film and Television Arts Film Award, best director, 1988. Awards for *Born on the Fourth of July* include Academy Award and Golden Globe Awards, both best director, Golden Globe Award, best adapted screenplay (with Ron Kovic), Directors Guild of America Award, outstanding directorial achievement in motion pictures, Filmmaker of the Year Award from Motion Picture Bookers Club, Bulgarian Cinematography Diploma Award, and Academy Award nominations, best adapted screenplay (with Ron Kovic), and best picture (with A. Kitman Ho), all 1989, SANE Education Fund/Consider the Alternatives Peace Award, Consider the Alternative Productions, 1990, and British Film and Television Arts Film Award nomination (with Ron Kovic), best screenplay—adapted, 1991. Awards for *JFK* include Special Prize, Berlin International Film Festival, 1990, Golden Globe Award, best director, Academy Award nominations, best picture (with A. Kitman Ho) and best adapted screenplay (with Zachary Sklar), Golden Globe Award nomination, best screenplay (with Zachary Sklar), and Edgar Allan Poe Award nomination (with Zachary Sklar), best movie, all 1992, and British Film and Television Arts Film Award nomination (with Zachary Sklar), best screenplay—adapted, 1993.

CREDITS

Film Work:

Producer, *Sugar Cookies,* Troma Films, 1973.

Director and editor, *Seizure* (also known as *Queen of Evil*), American International Pictures, 1974.

Director, *Mad Man of Martinique* (short film), 1979.

Director and coeditor, *The Hand,* Warner Bros., 1981.

Producer (with Gerald Green) and director, *Salvador,* Hemdale, 1986.

Director, *Platoon,* Orion, 1986.
Director, *Wall Street,* Twentieth Century-Fox, 1987.
Director, *Talk Radio,* Universal, 1988.
Producer (with A. Kitman Ho) and director, *Born on the Fourth of July,* Universal, 1989.
Producer (with Edward R. Pressman and Michael Rauch), *Blue Steel,* Metro-Goldwyn-Mayer/ United Artists, 1990.
Producer (with Edward R. Pressman), *Reversal of Fortune,* Warner Bros., 1990.
Executive producer, *Iron Maze,* Academy Entertainment, 1991.
Director, *The Doors,* TriStar, 1991.
Producer (with A. Kitman Ho) and director, *JFK,* Warner Bros., 1991.
Executive producer, *Zebrahead,* Columbia, 1992.
Producer, *South Central,* Warner Bros., 1992.
Executive producer, *The Joy Luck Club,* Buena Vista, 1993.
Producer (with A. Kitman Ho) and director, *Heaven and Earth,* WarnerBros., 1993.
Producer (with A. Kitman Ho) and director, *Natural Born Killers,* Warner Bros., 1994.
Production assistant, *The New Age,* Wechsler Productions, 1994.
Executive producer, *Killer: A Journal of Murder* (also known as *The Killer*), Republic Pictures, 1995.
Producer and director, *Nixon,* Buena Vista, 1995.
Executive producer, *Freeway,* August Entertainment, 1996.
Producer, *The People vs. Larry Flynt,* Columbia, 1996.
Director, *U Turn* (also known as *Stray Dogs*), TriStar, 1996.
Executive producer, *The Last Days of Kennedy and King* (documentary), 1998.
Producer, *Savior,* Budua Productions, 1998.
Executive producer, *Chains* (also known as *Johnny Spain*), 1999.
Executive producer, *The Corrupter,* New Line Cinema, 1999.
Producer and director, *Any Given Sunday* (also known as *Gridiron, The League, Monday Night, On Any Given Sunday,* and *Playing Hurt*), Warner Bros., 1999.

Film Appearances:
Last Year in Vietnam, 1970.
Cliff, *The Battle of Love's Return,* Troma Films, 1971.
Bum, *The Hand,* Warner Bros., 1981.
(Uncredited) Army officer, *Platoon,* Orion, 1986.
Trader in office, *Wall Street,* Twentieth Century-Fox, 1987.
Newspaper reporter, *Born on the Fourth of July,* Universal, 1989.
(Uncredited) Film professor, *The Doors,* TriStar, 1991.
Himself, *Oliver Stone* (documentary), 1992.
Himself, *Dave,* Warner Bros., 1993.
Himself, *The Last Party* (documentary), Triton Pictures, 1993.
Voiceover during credits, *Nixon,* Buena Vista, 1995.

Television Work; Producer; Miniseries:
(With A. Kitman Ho, Michael Rauch, and Bruce Wagner) *Wild Palms,* ABC, 1993.

Television Appearances; Miniseries:
Himself, *Wild Palms,* ABC, 1993.

Television Work; Producer; Movies:
(With Janet Yang, Abby Mann, and Diana Pokorny) *Indictment: The McMartin Trial,* HBO, 1995.

Television Appearances; Specials:
The Story of Hollywood (also known as *Talking Pictures*), TNT, 1988.
Himself, *Oliver Stone: Inside Out,* Showtime, 1992.
The Kennedy Assassinations: Coincidence or Conspiracy (documentary), syndicated, 1992.
Beyond JFK: The Question of Conspiracy (documentary), 1992.
Our Hollywood Education (documentary), 1992.
Together for Our Children, syndicated, 1993.
1993: A Year at the Movies, CNBC, 1993.
The First 100 Years: A Celebration of American Movies, HBO, 1995.
Himself, *Frank Capra's American Dream* (documentary), 1997.
The Warner Bros. Story: No Guts, No Glory: 75 Years of Award Winners, TNT, 1998.
Himself, *AFI's 100 Years . . . 100 Movies* (documentary), 1998.
Himself, *Our Century,* The Learning Channel, 1999.

Television Appearances; Awards Presentations:
The ALMA Awards, 1998.

Also appeared in other award show presentations, including the Academy Awards, Golden Globe Awards, Independent Spirit Awards, and the MTV Video Music Awards.

Television Appearances; Episodic:
Naked Hollywood, Arts and Entertainment, 1991.
ABC News Nightline (also known as *Nightline*), ABC, 1991.
"Who Killed JFK? On the Trail of the Conspiracies," *Investigative Reports,* Arts and Entertainment, 1992.

American Cinema, PBS, 1995.

Narrator, "D. W. Griffiths," *Sex and the Silver Screen,* Showtime, 1996.

"The Naked and the Dead," *Great Books,* The Learning Channel, 1998.

"The Kennedys: Power, Seduction, and Hollywood," *The E! True Hollywood Story* (also known as *The Kennedys: Power, Seduction, and Hollywood: The E! True Hollywood Story*), E! Entertainment Television, 1998.

Other Television Appearances:

Welcome Home, HBO, 1987.

Firstworks, The Movie Channel, 1988.

The New Hollywood, NBC, 1990.

WRITINGS

Screenplays:

Seizure (also known as *Queen of Evil*), American International Pictures, 1974.

Midnight Express (based on Billy Hayes's autobiography of the same name), Columbia, 1978.

The Hand (adapted from Marc Brandel's novel *The Lizard's Tail*), Warner Bros., 1981.

(With John Milius) *Conan the Barbarian* (based on the works of Robert E. Howard), Universal, 1982.

Scarface (adapted from Howard Hawks's 1932 film of the same name), Universal, 1983.

(With David Lee Henry) *Eight Million Ways to Die* (based on the novel of the same name by Lawrence Block), TriStar, 1985.

(With Michael Cimino) *Year of the Dragon* (based on the novel of the same name by Robert Daley), Metro-Goldwyn-Mayer/United Artists, 1986.

(With Richard Boyle) *Salvador,* Hemdale, 1986, published in *Oliver Stone's Platoon and Salvador: The Screenplays,* Vintage (New York City), 1987.

(With Richard Boyle) *Platoon,* Orion, 1986, published in *Oliver Stone's Platoon and Salvador: The Screenplays,* Vintage, 1987.

(With Stanley Weiser) *Wall Street,* Twentieth Century-Fox, 1987.

(With Eric Bogosian) *Talk Radio* (based on Bogosian's stage play of the same name and Stephen Singular's book *Talked to Death: The Life and Murder of Alan Berg*), Universal, 1988.

(With Ron Kovic) *Born on the Fourth of July* (based on Kovic's autobiography of the same name), Universal, 1989.

(With J. Randall Johnson and Ralph Thomas) *The Doors* (based on John Densmore's book *Riders on the Storm*), TriStar, 1991.

(With Zachary Sklar) *JFK* (based on the books *On the Trail of the Assassins,* by Jim Garrison and *Crossfire: The Plot That Killed Kennedy,* by Jim Marrs), Warner Bros., 1991, published as *JFK: The Book of the Film; the Documented Screenplay,* Applause Theatre Books (New York City), 1992.

Heaven and Earth (based on Le Ly Hayslip's memoirs *When Heaven and Earth Changed Places: A Vietnamese Woman's Journey from War to Peace* and *Child of War, Woman of Peace*), Warner Bros., 1993.

(With Richard Rutowski and David Veloz) *Natural Born Killers* (based on a story by Quentin Tarantino), Warner Bros., 1994.

(With Stephen J. Rivele and Christopher Wilkinson) *Nixon,* Buena Vista, 1995, published as *Nixon: An Oliver Stone Film,* edited by Eric Hamburg, Hyperion (New York City), 1995.

(With Alan Parker) *Evita* (based on the musical of the same name by Andrew Lloyd Webber and Tim Rice), Buena Vista, 1996.

(Uncredited) *U Turn* (also known as *Stray Dogs*), TriStar, 1996.

Teleplays; Miniseries:

(With Bruce Wagner) *Wild Palms* (based on the comic strip by Bruce Wagner and Julian Allen), ABC, 1993.

Nonfiction:

(With Michael Singer) *Oliver Stone's Heaven and Earth: The Making of an Epic Motion Picture,* Tuttle (Rutland, VT), 1994.

Novels:

A Child's Night Dream, St. Martin's Press (New York City), 1997.

OTHER SOURCES

Periodicals:

Atlantic Monthly, July, 1997, pp. 96-100.

Cineaste, fall, 1996, pp. 33-37.

Esquire, December, 1997, pp. 38-41.

New Yorker, August 8, 1994, pp. 40-55.

New York Times, January 2, 1990, pp. C13, C20.

People Weekly, January 22, 1996, pp. 105-108.

Premiere, December, 1987, pp. 33-34, 37-38.

Time, October 6, 1997, p. 109; November 9, 1998, p. 94.

Vogue, December, 1987, pp. 166, 172.*

STRACHAN, Alan 1946-

PERSONAL

Full name, Alan Lockhart Thomson Strachan; born September 3, 1946, in Dundee, Scotland; son of Roualeyn Robert Scott and Ellen (Graham) Strachan; married Jennifer Piercey-Thompson. *Education:* Merton College, Oxford, B.Litt; University of St. Andrews, M.A. *Avocational interests:* Reading, music, tennis, travel.

Addresses: *Contact*—MLR, Ltd., 200 Fulham Rd., London SW10 9PN, England.

Career: Director and producer. Mermaid Theatre, London, England, associate director, 1971-75; Greenwich Theatre, London, England, artistic director, 1978-88; Theatre of Comedy, London, England, director, 1991-97; Churchill Theatre, Bromley, England, artistic director, 1995-97.

CREDITS

Stage Work; Director, Unless Otherwise Noted:

Assistant director, *The Tempest,* Mermaid Theatre, London, England, 1970.

OK for Sound, Mermaid Theatre, 1970.

The Watched Pot, Mermaid Theatre, 1970.

John Bull's Other Island, Mermaid Theatre, 1971.

The Old Boys, Mermaid Theatre, 1971.

Cowardy Custard (revue), Mermaid Theatre, 1972.

Misalliance, Mermaid Theatre, 1973.

(With others) *Cole* (revue), Mermaid Theatre, 1974.

Children, Mermaid Theatre, 1974.

A Family and a Fortune, Apollo Theatre, London, England, 1975.

Confusions, Apollo Theatre, 1976.

Yahoo, Queen's Theatre, London, England, 1976.

Just between Ourselves, Queen's Theatre, 1977.

The Immortal Hayden, Mermaid Theatre, 1977, then Greenwich Theatre, London, England, 1978.

An Audience Called Edouard, Greenwich Theatre, 1978.

Bedroom Farce, Amsterdam, the Netherlands, 1978.

Semi-Detached, Greenwich Theatre, 1979.

The Play's the Thing, Greenwich Theatre, 1979.

I Sent a Letter to My Love, Greenwich Theatre, 1979.

Private Lives, Greenwich Theatre, then Duchess Theatre, London, England, 1980.

Time and the Conways, Greenwich Theatre, 1980.

Present Laughter, Greenwich Theatre, then Vaudeville Theatre, London, England, 1981.

The Golden Age, Greenwich Theatre, 1981.

The Doctor's Dilemma, Greenwich Theatre, 1981.

Design for Living, Greenwich Theatre, then Globe Theatre, London, England, 1982.

The Paranormalist, Greenwich Theatre, 1982.

French without Tears, Greenwich Theatre, 1982.

The Dining Room, Greenwich Theatre, 1983.

An Inspector Calls, Greenwich Theatre, 1983.

A Streetcar Named Desire, Greenwich Theatre, then Mermaid Theatre, 1983.

Noel and Gertie, King's Head Theatre, London, England, 1983.

The Glass Menagerie, Greenwich Theatre, 1985.

Biography, Greenwich Theatre, 1985.

One of Us, Greenwich Theatre, 1986.

Relatively Speaking, Greenwich Theatre, 1986.

For King and Country, Greenwich Theatre, 1986.

The Viewing, Greenwich Theatre, 1987.

Women in Mind, Vaudeville Theatre, 1987.

The Perfect Party, Greenwich Theatre, 1987.

How the Other Half Loves, Greenwich Theatre, then Duke of York's Theatre, London, England, 1988.

The Deep Blue Sea, Haymarket Theatre Royal, London, England, 1988.

Noel and Gertie, Comedy Theatre, London, England, 1989.

Henceforward . . . , Vaudeville Theatre, 1989.

Toekomstmuziek, Amsterdam, the Netherlands, 1989.

Re: Joyce!, Fortune Theatre, London, England, 1989, then Vaudeville Theatre, 1989, later Long Wharf Theatre, New Haven, CT, 1989, then Vaudeville Theatre, 1991.

June Moon, Scarborough Theatre, London, England, 1989, then Hampstead Theatre Club, London, England, then Vaudeville Theatre, 1992.

Alphabetical Order, Scarborough Theatre, 1990.

Man of the Moment, Globe Theatre, 1990.

Other People's Money, Lyric Theatre, London, England, 1990.

Taking Steps, Circle in the Square Theatre, New York City, 1991.

And producer, *Hay Fever,* Albery Theatre, London, England, 1992.

London Assurance, Dublin, Ireland, 1993.

And producer, *The Prime of Miss Jean Brodie,* Strand Theatre, London, England, 1994.

Make Way for Lucia, Churchill Theatre, Bromley, England, 1995.

Switchback, Churchill Theatre, 1996.

Hoefeber, Copenhagen, Denmark, 1996.

Loot, West Yorkshire Playhouse, Leeds, Yorkshire, England, 1996.

All Things Considered, Scarborough Theatre, 1996, then Hampstead Theatre Club, 1997.

Live and Kidding, Duchess Theatre, 1997.
Hooikoorts, Amsterdam, the Netherlands, 1997.
Mrs. Warren's Profession, Guildford, England, 1997.
Troilus and Cressida, Open Air Theatre, Regent's Park, London, 1998.
The Merry Wives of Windsor, Open Air Theatre, Regent's Park, 1999.

Stage Work; Director; Major Tours:
Shakespeare's People, South African, U.S., British, and European cities, 1975-78.
Make Way for Lucia, 1995.
Switchback, 1996.
Mrs. Warren's Profession, 1997.

Also directed a touring production of *The Old Boys.*

Stage Work; Producer:
The Pocket Dream, Albery Theatre, London, England, 1992.
Six Degrees of Separation, Royal Court Theatre, London, England, then Comedy Theatre, both 1992.
Hysteria, Royal Court Theatre, 1993.
The Editing Process, Royal Court Theatre, 1994.
Under Their Hats (revue), King's Head Theatre, 1994.

Stage Work; Producer; Major Tours:
Out of Order, 1991.
Happy Families, 1993.

Stage Appearances:
Fabian, *Twelfth Night,* Hunter College Playhouse, New York City, 1970.

Television Work; Executive Producer:
Love on a Branch Limb, BBC, 1994.

WRITINGS

Writings for the Stage:
(With Gerald Frow and Wendy Toye) *Cowardy Custard* (revue), music and lyrics by Noel Coward, Mermaid Theatre, 1972.
(With Benny Green) *Cole* (revue), Mermaid Theatre, 1974.
Shakespeare's People, South African, U.S., British, and European cities, 1975-78.
Yahoo, Queen's Theatre, 1976.
Under Their Hats (revue), King's Head Theatre, 1994.

Other:
Contributor to periodicals.*

STRAUSS, Peter 1947-

PERSONAL

Born February 20, 1947, in Croton-on-Hudson, NY; married; wife's name, Nicole; children: Justin, Tristen. *Education:* Attended Northwestern University.

Addresses: *Agent*—The Gersh Agency, 232 North Canon Dr., Beverly Hills, CA 90210.

Career: Actor and producer.

Awards, Honors: Emmy Award nomination, outstanding lead actor in a limited series, 1976, for *Rich Man, Poor Man;* Emmy Award, outstanding performance by a leading actor in a special, 1979, for *The Jericho Mile;* Emmy Award nomination, outstanding actor in a limited series or special, and Golden Globe Award nomination, best performance by an actor in a miniseries or motion picture made for television, both 1981, for *Masada;* Golden Globe Award nominations, best performance by an actor in a miniseries or motion picture made for television, 1983, for *Heart of Steel,* 1985, for *Kane and Abel,* and 1993, for *Men Don't Tell.*

CREDITS

Television Appearances; Series:
Voice of Stoker, *Biker Mice from Mars* (animated), syndicated, 1993-94.
Dr. Nicholas Moloney, *Moloney,* CBS, 1996-97.

Television Appearances; Miniseries:
Luke's Kingdom, Yorkshire Television, 1976.
Rudy Jordache, *Rich Man, Poor Man* (also known as *Rich Man, Poor Man—Book I*), ABC, 1976.
Senator Rudy Jordache, *Rich Man, Poor Man, Book II,* ABC, 1976.
Eleazar Ben Yair, *Masada,* ABC, 1981.
Abel Rosnovski, *Kane and Abel,* CBS, 1985.
Dick Diver, *Tender Is the Night,* Showtime, 1985.
La Hire, *Joan of Arc,* CBS, 1999.

Television Appearances; Movies:
Arthur Danforth, *Man without a Country,* ABC, 1973.
Attack on Terror: The FBI vs. the Ku Klux Klan, CBS, 1975.
Joseph Kennedy, Jr., *Young Joe, the Forgotten Kennedy* (also known as *The Forgotten Kennedy*), ABC, 1977.

Larry "Rain" Murphy, *The Jericho Mile,* ABC, 1979.
Eddie Kagel, *Angel on My Shoulder,* ABC, 1980.
A Whale for the Killing, 1981.
Emory, *Heart of Steel,* ABC, 1983.
John Garry, *Under Siege,* NBC, 1986.
Judge Kenneth Hoffman, *Penalty Phase,* CBS, 1986.
Charley, Jr., *Proud Men,* 1987.
Romulus (some sources say Saul Grisman), *Brotherhood of the Rose,* NBC, 1989.
Title role, *Peter Gunn,* ABC, 1989.
Wayne Stracton, *83 Hours 'Til Dawn,* CBS, 1990.
Lieutenant Colonel Matt Ryan, *Flight of Black Angel,* Showtime, 1991.
Detective Lieutenant Max Cole, *Fugitive among Us,* CBS, 1992.
Warren Blackburn, *Trial: The Price of Passion,* NBC, 1992.
Ed MacAffrey, *Men Don't Tell,* CBS, 1993.
Larry McLinden, *Thicker Than Blood: The Larry McLinden Story,* CBS, 1994.
Ezra "Penny" Baxter, *The Yearling,* CBS, 1994.
Sam Yates, *Reunion,* CBS, 1994.
Thomas Cullen Davis, *Texas Justice,* ABC, 1995.
Spurensuche, [Austria], 1997.
Thomas Linthorne, *Seasons of Love* (also known as *Love on the Land*), CBS, 1998.
Dr. Sam Sheppard, *My Father's Shadow* (also known as *Mockery of Justice: The True Story of the Sheppard Murder Case* and *My Father's Shadow: The Sam Sheppard Story*), CBS, 1998.

Television Work; Movies:
Executive producer, *Seasons of Love* (also known as *Love on the Land*), CBS, 1998.

Television Appearances; Specials:
Narrator, "Journey to the Forgotten River," *National Geographic Specials,* PBS, 1990.
Segment host, *ABC's 40th Anniversary Special,* ABC, 1994.
Narrator, "Enchanted New Mexico," *Scenic Wonders of America,* The Disney Channel, 1995.
John Waylan, "In the Lake of the Woods," *Hallmark Entertainment Presents,* Fox, 1996.

Television Appearances; Awards Presentations:
The 15th Annual People's Choice Awards, 1989.
The 17th Annual People's Choice Awards, 1991.
Presenter, *The 1996 Emmy Awards,* ABC, 1996.

Television Appearances; Episodic:
"The Two Dollar Thing," *The Young Lawyers,* ABC, 1970.
Bobby Jepsen, "Timelock," *The Streets of San Francisco,* ABC, 1972.
Martin Novack, "For the Love of God," *The Streets of San Francisco,* ABC, 1973.
Stephen, "Angels in the Snow," *The Mary Tyler Moore Show,* CBS, 1973.
Tom Morgan, "Death with Father," *Hawaii Five-0,* CBS, 1974.
Reverend Will, "The Cure That Kills," *Cannon,* CBS, 1974.
Dave Nordorff, "A Killing in the Family," *Cannon,* CBS, 1974.
Lou Kovic, Jr., "Letters from the Grave," *The Streets of San Francisco,* ABC, 1975.
Narrator, "Pig Amok," *Duckman* (animated), USA Network, 1996.
Voice of Walter Langowski, "Man to Man, Beast to Beast," *The Incredible Hulk and Friends* (also known as *The Incredible Hulk;* animated), UPN, 1996.
Intimate Portrait: Heather Locklear, Lifetime, 1998.

Provided the voices of Dr. Steven Carlyle/Plant-Man, *Batman: The Animated Series,* Fox.

Film Appearances:
Hail Hero!, National General, 1969.
Honus Gent, *Soldier Blue,* Avco Embassy, 1970.
Man of Legend, 1971.
Il sergente Klems, 1971.
Thomas Lewis, *The Trial of the Catonsville Nine,* Cinema 5, 1972.
Wylie, *The Last Tycoon,* Paramount, 1977.
Voice of Justin, *The Secret of NIMH* (also known as *Mrs. Brisby and the Rats of NIMH;* animated), Metro-Goldwyn-Mayer, 1982.
Wolff, *Space Hunter: Adventures in the Forbidden Zone* (also known as *Adventures in the Creep Zone* and *Road Gangs*), Columbia, 1983.
Narrator, *Majdanek 1944,* 1987.
Brendan Grant, *Nick of Time,* Paramount, 1995.
Chip Carlson, *Keys to Tulsa,* Gramercy Pictures, 1997.

Stage Appearances:
Bill Allenson, *Einstein and the Polar Bear,* Cort Theatre, New York City, 1981.

Appeared in *Dance Next Door* and *The Dirty Man,* both at the Mark Taper Forum, Los Angeles, CA.

WRITINGS

Stories for Teleplays; Series:
Moloney, CBS, 1996-97.*

SUTHERLAND, Donald 1934(?)-

PERSONAL

Full name, Donald McNichol Sutherland; born July 17, 1934 (some sources say 1935), in St. John, New Brunswick, Canada; son of Frederick McLae (in sales) and Dorothy Isobel (McNichol) Sutherland; married Lois May Hardwick, 1959 (divorced); married Shirley Jean Douglas (an actress), 1966 (divorced); married Francine Racette (an actress); children: (second marriage) Kiefer (an actor), Rachel; (third marriage) Roeg, Rossif, Angus. *Education:* University of Toronto, B.A., 1956 (some sources say 1958); trained for the stage at the Academy of Music and Dramatic Arts, London, England.

Addresses: *Contact*—760 North La Cienega Blvd., Los Angeles, CA 90069. *Publicist*—Katherine Olin, PMK, 955 Carrillo Dr., Los Angeles, CA 90048-5400.

Career: Actor and producer. McNichol Pictures, Inc., founder, 1981, president, 1981—. Appeared with repertory companies in Perth, Scotland, and in Nottingham, Chesterfield, Bromley, and Sheffield, England. Provided voiceovers for and appeared in commercials; worked as a radio announcer and disc jockey in Canada. Also worked as a mine worker in Finland.

Awards, Honors: Golden Globe Award nomination, best motion picture actor in a musical or comedy, 1970, for *M*A*S*H;* Earl Grey Award, Academy of Canadian Cinema and Television, best acting performance in television in a leading role, 1978; Golden Globe Award nomination, best motion picture actor in a drama, 1980, for *Ordinary People;* Genie Award, Academy of Canadian Cinema and Television, best actor, 1983, for *Threshold;* Emmy Award, outstanding supporting actor in a miniseries or special, and Golden Globe Award, best supporting actor in a television series, miniseries, or motion picture, both 1995, for *Citizen X;* Golden Globe Award nomination, best supporting actor in a motion picture, 1998, for *Without Limits;* officer, Order of Canada; officier, l'Ordre des Artes et des Lettres of France; honorary Ph.D., St. Mary's University.

CREDITS

Film Appearances:

Soldier and old hag, *Il castello dei morti vivi* (also known as *Castle of the Living Dead* and *Crypt of Horror*), Malasky, 1964.

Nevney, *The Bedford Incident,* Columbia, 1965.

Joseph, *Fanatic* (also known as *Die! Die! My Darling*), Columbia, 1965.

Bob Carroll, *Dr. Terror's House of Horrors* (also known as *The Blood Suckers*), Regal, 1965.

Pussycat Alley (also known as *The World Ten Times Over*), Goldstone, 1965.

Francis, *Promise Her Anything,* Paramount, 1966.

Vernon Pinckley, *The Dirty Dozen,* Metro-Goldwyn-Mayer, 1967.

Scientist at computer, *Billion Dollar Brain,* United Artists, 1967.

Lawrence, *Interlude,* Columbia, 1968.

Lord Peter Sanderson, *Joanna,* Twentieth Century-Fox, 1968.

Chorus leader, *Oedipus the King,* Universal, 1968.

Dave Negli, *The Split,* Metro-Goldwyn-Mayer, 1968.

Ackerman, *Sebastian* (also known as *Mr. Sebastian*), Paramount, 1968.

Father Michael Ferrier, *Act of the Heart* (also known as *Acte du coeur*), Universal, 1970.

Charles/Pierre, *Start the Revolution without Me* (also known as *Two Times Two*), Warner Bros., 1970.

Captain Benjamin Franklin "Hawkeye" Pierce, *M*A*S*H,* Twentieth Century-Fox, 1970.

Title role, *Alex in Wonderland,* Metro-Goldwyn-Mayer, 1970.

Oddball, *Kelly's Heroes* (also known as *The Warriors*), Metro-Goldwyn-Mayer, 1970.

Christ figure, *Johnny Got His Gun,* Cinemation, 1971.

John Klute, *Klute,* Warner Bros., 1971.

Minister, *Little Murders,* Twentieth Century-Fox, 1971.

Himself, *F.T.A.* (also known as *The FTA Show, Foxtrot Tango Alpha,* and *Free the Army*), American International Pictures, 1972.

John Baxter, *Don't Look Now* (also known as *A Venezia . . . un dicembre rosso shocking*), Buena Vista, 1973.

Andy Hammond, *Lady Ice,* National General, 1973.

Veldini, *Steelyard Blues* (also known as *The Final Crash*), Warner Bros., 1973.

Dan Candy, *Alien Thunder* (also known as *Dan Candy's Law*), Cinerama, 1973.

Brulard, *S*P*Y*S,* Twentieth Century-Fox, 1974.

Corpse, *Murder on the Bridge* (also known as *End of the Game, Getting Away with Murder, Assassinio sul ponte,* and *Der Richter und sein Henker*), Twentieth Century-Fox, 1975.

Homer Simpson, *The Day of the Locust,* Twentieth Century-Fox, 1975.

Voice of Edward S. Curtis, *The Shadow Catcher,* 1975.

Bertolucci secondo il cinema (also known as *The Cinema according to Bertolucci* and *The Making of "1900";* documentary), Bauer International, 1975.

Attila, *1900* (also known as *Nineteen Hundred* and *Novecento*), Paramount, 1976.

Giacomo Casanova, *Casanova* (also known as *Fellini's Casanova* and *Il Casanova di Fellini*), Universal, 1976.

Liam Devlin, *The Eagle Has Landed,* Columbia, 1976.

Clumsy waiter, *Kentucky Fried Movie,* United Film Distribution, 1977.

Inspector Steve Carella, *Blood Relatives* (also known as *Les liens du sang*), SNS, 1977.

Jay Mallory, *The Disappearance,* World Northal, 1977.

Professor Dave Jennings, *National Lampoon's Animal House* (also known as *Animal House*), Universal, 1978.

Matthew Bennel, *Invasion of the Body Snatchers,* United Artists, 1978.

Agar, *The Great Train Robbery* (also known as *The First Great Train Robbery*), United Artists, 1979.

Robert Lees, *Murder by Decree* (also known as *Sherlock Holmes: Murder by Decree*), United Artists, 1979.

Narrator, *North China Commune* (documentary), National Film Board of Canada, 1979.

Reese Halperin, *A Very Big Withdrawal* (also known as *A Man, a Woman, and a Bank*), Avco-Embassy, 1979.

Calvin Jarrett, *Ordinary People,* Paramount, 1980.

Professor Roger Kelly, *Nothing Personal,* American International Pictures, 1980.

Frank Lansing, *Bear Island* (also known as *Alistair MacLean's Bear Island*), Columbia, 1980.

Narrator, *North China Commune,* National Film Board of Canada, 1980.

Nick the Noz, *Gas,* Paramount, 1981.

Henry Faber, *Eye of the Needle,* United Artists, 1981.

Jay Mallory, *The Disappearance,* World Northal, 1981.

Brian Costello, *Max Dugan Returns,* Twentieth Century-Fox, 1982.

Narrator of the diary, *A War Story* (documentary), National Film Board of Canada, 1982.

Dr. Thomas Vrain, *Threshold,* Twentieth Century-Fox, 1983.

Dr. Arthur Calgary, *Ordeal by Innocence,* Metro-Goldwyn-Mayer/United Artists, 1984.

Westlake, *Crackers,* Universal, 1984.

Sergeant-Major Peasy, *Revolution,* Warner Bros., 1985.

Brother Thaddeus, *Heaven Help Us* (also known as *Catholic Boys*), TriStar, 1985.

Father Bob Koesler, *The Rosary Murders,* Samuel Goldwyn Company, 1987.

Appleton Porter, *The Trouble with Spies,* De Laurentiis Entertainment Group, 1987.

Paul Gauguin, *Oviri* (also known as *The Wolf at the Door*), Manson, 1987.

John Reese, *Apprentice to Murder,* New World Pictures, 1988.

Ben du Doit, *A Dry White Season,* Metro-Goldwyn-Mayer, 1989.

Dr. Charles Loftis, *Lost Angels* (also known as *The Road Home*), Orion, 1989.

Warden Drumgoole, *Lock Up,* TriStar, 1989.

Ivan, *Cerro Torre: Schrei aus Stein* (also known as *Cerro Torre Scream of Stone, Scream of Stone,* and *Cerro Torre, le cri de la roche;* documentary), Alliance, 1990.

O'Connor, *Buster's Bedroom,* Les Productions du Verseau/NEF 2, 1990.

Ronald Bartel, *Backdraft,* Universal, 1991.

Jozef Burski, *Eminent Domain,* Triumph Releasing, 1991.

Colonel X, *JFK,* Warner Bros., 1991.

Henderson, *Shadow of the Wolf* (also known as *Agaguk*), Transfilm/Vision International/Le Studio Canal, 1992.

Merrick, *Buffy the Vampire Slayer,* Twentieth Century-Fox, 1992.

Rakuyo, 1992.

Jonathan Younger, *Younger and Younger* (also known as *Father and Son*), Academy Entertainment, 1993.

Frank, *Benefit of the Doubt* (also known as *Daddy's Home* and *Im Bann des Zweifels*), Miramax, 1993.

Flan Kittredge, *Six Degrees of Separation,* Metro-Goldwyn-Mayer, 1993.

Narrator, *People of the Forest: The Chimps of Gombe* (documentary), 1993.

Kirov, *Red Hot,* SC Entertainment International, 1993.

Bob Garvin, *Disclosure,* Warner Bros., 1994.

Andrew Nivens, *The Puppet Masters* (also known as *Robert A. Heinlein's Puppet Masters*), Buena Vista, 1994.

Punch, Journal Films, 1994.

A Century of Cinema (documentary), 1994.

General Donald McClintock, *Outbreak,* Warner Bros., 1995.

Lucien Wilbanks, *A Time to Kill,* Warner Bros., 1996.

Jack Shaw/Henry Fields, *The Assignment* (also known as *Jackal*), Sony Pictures Entertainment, 1997.

Conrad, *Shadow Conspiracy* (also known as *The Shadow Program*), Buena Vista, 1997.

Lieutenant Stanton, *Fallen,* Warner Bros., 1998.

Bill Bowerman, *Without Limits* (also known as *Pre*), Warner Bros., 1998.

Judge Rolf Rausenberg, *Free Money,* Malofilm, 1998.

Toscano, 1999.

The Setting Sun, 1999.
Captain Robert Everton, *Virus,* Universal, 1999.
Dr. Ben Hillard, *Instinct* (also known as *Ishmael*), Buena Vista, 1999.
Panic, Mad Chance/The Vault, 1999.

Film Work:
Producer (with others), *F.T.A.* (also known as *The FTA Show, Foxtrot Tango Alpha,* and *Free the Army*), American International Pictures, 1972.
Executive producer, *Steelyard Blues* (also known as *The Final Crash*), Warner Bros., 1973.

Television Appearances; Series:
Narrator, *The Prize: The Epic Quest for Oil, Money, and Power,* PBS, 1993.
Narrator, *Great Books,* The Learning Channel, 1996—.

Television Appearances; Miniseries:
Captain William Marsden, *The Oldest Living Confederate Widow Tells All,* CBS, 1994.

Television Appearances; Movies:
Fortinbras (prince of Norway), *Hamlet* (also known as *Hamlet at Elsinore*), BBC, 1964.
Benedeck, *The Sunshine Patriot,* NBC, 1968.
Ethan Hawley, *The Winter of Our Discontent* (also known as *John Steinbeck's The Winter of Our Discontent*), CBS, 1983.
Dr. Norman Bethune, *Dr. Bethune* (also known as *Bethune: The Making of a Hero*), [Canada], 1989.
(Uncredited) *Long Road Home,* 1991.
Roger Hawthorne, *The Railway Station Man,* TNT, 1992.
Doc Murdoch, *Quicksand: No Escape,* USA Network, 1992.
Dr. "Mac" Maclean, *The Lifeforce Experiment* (also known as *The Breakthrough*), syndicated, 1994.
Citizen Fetisov, *Citizen X,* HBO, 1995.
Garrett Lawton, *Hollow Point* (also known as *Rysk Roulette*), HBO, 1995.
Ted, *Natural Enemy,* HBO, 1997.
Dr. Bob Shushan, *Behind the Mask,* CBS, 1999.
General Beauregard, *C.S.S. Hunley,* TNT, 1999.

Television Appearances; Specials:
The Death of Bessie Smith, [Great Britain], 1965.
The Diahann Carroll Show, NBC, 1971.
The American Film Institute Salute to Frank Capra, CBS, 1982.
Voice of Paul Gauguin, *Paul Gauguin: The Savage Dream,* PBS, 1989.
Narrator, *Bhutan, the Last Shangri-La,* PBS, 1998.

Also appeared in *Hallmark Hall of Fame* and *Give Me Your Answer True;* appeared on British television in *Marching to the Sea* and *The Rose Tattoo.*

Television Appearances; Awards Presentations:
The 61st Annual Academy Awards Presentation, ABC, 1989.
The 49th Annual Golden Globe Awards, TBS, 1992.
Presenter, *The 66th Annual Academy Awards Presentation,* ABC, 1994.
Presenter, *The 47th Annual Primetime Emmy Awards,* Fox, 1995.

Television Appearances; Episodic:
"Flight into Danger," *Studio 4,* BBC, 1962.
"The Happy Suicide," *The Saint,* Associated Television, 1965.
Philip, "Millionaire's Daughter," *Gideon's Way,* Incorporated Television Company, 1965.
"All Is a Dream to Me," *Court Martial,* ABC, 1966.
"Lee Oswald—Assassin," *Play of the Month,* BBC, 1966.
"Escape Route," *The Saint,* Associated Television, 1967.
Jessel, "The Superlative Seven," *The Avengers,* Associated British Picture Corporation, 1967.
"Which Way Did He Go, McGill?," *Man in a Suitcase,* Incorporated Television Company, 1967.
"Day of Execution," *Man in a Suitcase,* Incorporated Television Company, 1968.
"Shadow of the Panther," *The Champions,* Incorporated Television Company, 1968.
"The Suntan Mob," *The Name of the Game,* NBC, 1969.
Voice of Hollis Hurlbut, "Lisa the Iconoclast," *The Simpsons* (animated), Fox, 1996.

Other Television Appearances:
Appeared in the Kate Bush music video "Cloud Busting."

Stage Appearances:
Wally, *The Male Animal,* Hart House Theatre, Toronto, Ontario, Canada, 1952.
Humbert Humbert, *Lolita,* Brooks Atkinson Theatre, New York City, 1981.

Appeared in *August for the People,* Royal Court Theatre, London, England; *The Tempest,* Hart House Theatre; and *Gimmick,* London, England; also appeared in *On a Clear Day You Can See Canterbury, The Shewing Up of Blanco Posnet,* and *Spoon River Anthology.*

WRITINGS

Screenplays:

(With others) *F.T.A.* (also known as *The FTA Show, Foxtrot Tango Alpha,* and *Free the Army*), American International Pictures, 1972.*

SWEENEY, Birdie
See SWEENEY, Birdy

SWEENEY, Birdy 1931-1999
(Birdie Sweeney)

PERSONAL

Born June 14, 1931, in Dungannon, County Tyrone, Northern Ireland; died, May 11, 1999, in Dublin, Ireland; wife, Alice; children: eight.

Career: Actor, comic, and bird impersonator. Also credited as Birdie Sweeney.

CREDITS

Film Appearances:

Blakes Barman, *Every Picture Tells a Story,* Falmingo/Every, 1984.
Instant Photo, *Reefer and the Model,* 1987.
(As Birdie Sweeney) Tommy, *The Crying Game,* Miramax, 1992.
(As Birdie Sweeney) Loner, *The Snapper,* Miramax, 1993.
Doctor of Sorts, *Moll Flanders,* Twentieth Century-Fox, 1996.
Matt, *The Fifth Province,* 1997.
Pat, *Downtime,* Manuel Salvador/Ima Films, 1997.
Man in Well, *The Butcher Boy,* Warner Bros., 1997.
Mr. Zesty, *Star Truckers* (also known as *Space Truckers*), Pachyderm Productions, 1997.
Lift Attendant, *Divorcing Jack,* Ariane Distribution, 1998.
Old Codger, *The Nephew,* SND, 1998.

Television Appearances; Series:

(As Birdie Sweeney) Eamonn Byrne, *Ballykissangel,* BBC-1, 1996.
Give My Head Peace, BBC Northern Ireland, 1999.

Television Appearances; Miniseries:

(As Birdie Sweeney) Uncle James, *Scarlett,* CBS, 1994.
Crossing Sweeper, *The Old Curiosity Shop,* The Disney Channel, 1995.
Patrick Dolan, *The Hanging Gale,* BBC, 1995, then Bravo, 1999.

Television Appearances; Movies:

Ancient Crofter, *Kidnapped,* The Family Channel, 1995.
Elderly Cutter, *The Tale of Sweeney Todd,* Showtime, 1998.

OTHER SOURCES

Electronic:

http://news.bbc.co.uk/hi/english/entertainment/newsid.*

T

TAYLOR, Gilbert 1914-

PERSONAL

Born April 12, 1914, in Bushey Heath, Hertfordshire, England.

Career: Cinematographer, camera operator, and director. Also known as Gil Taylor.

Awards, Honors: British Society of Cinematographers Award, best cinematography, 1976, for *The Omen;* British Academy of Film and Television Arts Award nomination, best British cinematography (black-and-white), 1965, for *Repulsion;* British Academy of Film and Television Arts Award nomination, best British cinematography (black-and-white), 1966, for *Cul-de-sac.*

CREDITS

Film Work; Cinematographer, Unless Otherwise Noted:

Camera operator, *Fame Is the Spur,* 1946.
Camera operator, *Brighton Rock* (also known as *Young Scarface*), 1947.
The Guinea Pig (also known as *The Outsider*), 1948.
Seven Days to Noon, 1950.
The Yellow Balloon, 1953.
The Weak and the Wicked, Allied Artists, 1953.
Sailor of the King (also known as *Brown on Resolution* and *Single Handed*), Twentieth Century-Fox, 1953.
Front Page Story, British Lion, 1954.
Crest of the Wave (also known as *Seagulls over Sorrento*), Metro-Goldwyn-Mayer, 1954.
As Long as They're Happy, 1955.
It's Great to be Young, 1956.
Woman in a Dressing Gown, 1957.
The Good Companions, Associated British Pathe Limited, 1957.
Ice-Cold in Alex (also known as *Desert Attack*), British International, 1958.
Tommy the Toreador, 1959.
Bottoms Up, 1960.
The Rebel (also known as *Call Me Genius*), 1961.
Petticoat Pirates, 1961.
The Full Treatment (also known as *Stop Me Before I Kill* and *The Treatment*), 1961.
A Prize of Arms, 1962.
Dr. Strangelove or: How I Learned to Stop Worrying and Love the Bomb (also known as *Dr. Strangelove*), Columbia, 1964.
A Hard Day's Night, Universal, 1964.
The Bedford Incident, Columbia, 1965.
Repulsion, Criterion Pictures, 1965.
Cul-de-sac, Nightmare Video, 1966.
Work Is a 4-Letter Word (also known as *Work Is a Four Letter Word*), Universal, 1967.
Theatre of Death (also known as *Blood Fiend* and *The Female Fiend*), Hemisphere Pictures, 1967.
Before Winter Comes, Columbia, 1969.
(As Gil Taylor) *Quackser Fortune has a Cousin in the Bronx* (also known as *Fun Loving*), JEF Films, 1970.
A Day at the Beach, 1970.
Macbeth, 1971.
Frenzy, Universal, 1972.
Undercovers Hero (also known as *Soft Beds and Hard Battles; Soft Beds, Hard Battles*), 1973.
The Omen (also known as *The Antichrist, Birthmark, Omen I, Omen I: The Antichrist* and *Omen I: The Birthmark*), Twentieth Century-Fox, 1976.
Star Wars (also known as *Star Wars: Episode IV: A New Hope*), Twentieth Century-Fox, 1977.
(As Gil Taylor) *Damien: Omen II* (also known as *Omen II* and *Omen II: Damien*), Twentieth Century-Fox, 1978.
Meetings with Remarkable Men, 1979.

Alan Conti, *Calendar Girl Murders* (also known as *Insatiable and Victimized*), ABC, 1984.
Steve Carr, *Perry Mason: The Case of the Shooting Star,* NBC, 1986.
Doctor Jonas Carson, *Not Quite Human,* ABC, 1987.
D.A. Vaughan, *Hitting Home,* 1987.
The Gift of Time, NBC, 1988.
Mr. Forndexter, *Fourteen Going on Thirty,* ABC, 1988.
Jack Lefcourt, *Dance 'Til Dawn* (also known as *Senior Prom*), NBC, 1988.
Dr. Jonas Carson, *Not Quite Human II,* Disney Channel, 1989.
Phil Beckman, *Jury Duty: The Comedy* (also known as *The Great American Sex Scandal*), ABC, 1990.
Dr. Jonas Carson/Bonus, *Still Not Quite Human,* The Disney Channel, 1992.
Raymond Holliman, *Rubdown,* USA Network, 1993.
Joplin Hardy, *Jack Higgins' The Windsor Protocol,* TMC, 1996.
Joplin Hardy, *Jack Higgins' Thunder Point,* 1996.
Magazine publisher, *The Secret She Carried* (also known as *Cradle Song*), NBC, 1996.
August Danforth, *Any Place But Home,* USA Network, 1997.

Television Appearances; Specials:

Host, *Miss Hollywood, 1986,* ABC, 1986.
The ABC Fall Preview Special, ABC, 1986.
Diabetes: Update '86, Lifetime, 1986.
The Eleventh Annual Circus of the Stars, CBS, 1986.
The Wildest West Show of the Stars, ABC, 1986.
Host, *The Calgary Olympic Holiday Special,* ABC, 1987.
The Crystal Light National Aerobic Championships, syndicated, 1987.
Host, *Walt Disney World's Very Merry Christmas Parade,* ABC, 1987.
Host, *Our Kids and the Best of Everything,* ABC, 1987.
Happy Birthday Hollywood, ABC, 1987.
Walt Disney World's Happy Easter Parade, ABC, 1987, then 1988.
Host, *1988 Miss Universe Pageant,* CBS, 1988.
Host, *1988 Miss USA Pageant,* ABC, 1988.
Comic Relief III, 1989.
The 15th Annual People's Choice Awards, 1989.
Host, *Walt Disney World's Very Merry Christmas Parade,* 1989.
Host, *Walt Disney World's Happy Easter Parade,* 1989.
Host, *ABC Fall Preview,* ABC, 1989.
The Television Academy Hall of Fame (also known as *The 6th Annual Television Academy Hall of Fame*), Fox, 1990.
Night of 100 Stars III, NBC, 1990.
The American Red Cross Emergency Test, ABC, 1990.
The 4th Annual American Comedy Awards, 1990.
The 16th Annual People's Choice Awards, 1990.
Host, *Walt Disney World Merry Christmas Parade,* 1990.
Host, *The Walt Disney World Happy Easter Parade,* 1990.
Host, *Twin Peaks & Cop Rock: Behind the Scenes,* ABC, 1990.
Host, *The Tube Test,* ABC, 1990.
Host, *Disorder in the Court: 60th Anniversary Tribute to the Stooges,* syndicated, 1990.
Welcome Home, America!-A USO Salute to America's Sons and Daughters, ABC, 1991.
Voices that Care, Fox, 1991.
The 43rd Annual Primetime Emmy Awards Presentation, 1991.
Host, *The Walt Disney World Happy Easter Parade,* ABC, 1991.
Host, *The Tube Test Two,* ABC, 1991.
Ringmaster, *The All New Circus of the Stars & Side Show XVII* (also known as *The 17th Annual All New Circus of the Stars and Side Show*), CBS, 1992.
Host, *Miss 1992 World America,* ABC, 1992.
Together for Our Children-M.U.S.I.C., syndicated, 1993.
Mo' Funny: Black Comedy in America, HBO, 1993.
The Defense Rests: A Tribute to Raymond Burr, NBC, 1993.
Lamb Chop in the Haunted House (also known as *Lamb Chop's Spooky Stuff*), PBS, 1994.
Phineas T. Wolf, *The Trial of Red Riding Hood,* Disney Channel, 1994.
Host, *TV's Funniest Families* (also known as *A Tribute to TV's Funniest Families*), NBC, 1994.
Lamb Chop's Special Chanukah, PBS, 1995.
Bob Hope's Young Comedians: A New Generation of Laughs, NBC, 1995.
Host, *The World's Greatest Magic II* (also known as *The 2nd Annual World's Greatest Magic*), NBC, 1995.
Co-host, *TV's Funniest Families 2: The Kids,* NBC, 1995.
Life and Death of Sam Kinison: The E! True Hollywood Story, E! Entertainment Television, 1996.
Host, *Salute to the Stooges,* Family Channel, 1996.
Shari's Passover Surprise, PBS, 1997.

Television Producer, Except Where Indicated; Series:

The Wizard of Odds, NBC, 1973.
Fernwood 2-Night, syndicated, 1977.

America 2-Night, syndicated, 1978.
Executive producer, *Thicke of the Night,* syndicated, 1983.
Creative consultant and co-executive producer, *Pictionary,* syndicated, 1997—.

Television Executive Producer; Movies:
(With others) *The Secret She Carried* (also known as *Cradle Song*), NBC, 1996.

Television Producer, Except Where Indicated; Specials:
Play It Again, Uncle Sam, PBS, 1975.
Anne Murray's Ladies Night, syndicated, 1979.
Olivia Newton-John's Hollywood Nights, ABC, 1980.
Executive producer, *Celebrations,* CBS, 1992.

WRITINGS

Television Series:
The Bobby Darin Amusement Company, NBC, 1972-73.
Fernwood 2-Night, syndicated, 1977.
The Richard Pryor Show, NBC, 1977.
America 2-Night, syndicated, 1978.
Thicke of the Night, syndicated, 1983-84.

Television Specials:
The Sandy Duncan Show, CBS, 1974.
The Flip Wilson Special, NBC, 1974, then 1975.
The Bobby Vinton Show, syndicated, 1975.
The Paul Lynde Comedy Hour, ABC, 1975.
Play It Again, Uncle Sam, PBS, 1975.
Lola, ABC, 1975, then 1976.
Mac Davis Christmas Special . . . When I Grow Up, NBC, 1976.
The Olivia Newton-John Show, ABC, 1976.
The Barry Manilow Special, ABC, 1977.
The Richard Pryor Special, NBC, 1977.
Olivia, ABC, 1978.
Anne Murray's Ladies Night, syndicated, 1979.
Olivia Newton-John's Hollywood Nights, ABC, 1980.
A Special Anne Murray Christmas, CBS, 1981.
The Richard Pryor Special, NBC, 1982.
Anne Murray's Caribbean Cruise, CBS, 1983.
Anne Murray's Winter Carnival . . . From Quebec, CBS, 1984.
Anne Murray: The Sounds of London, CBS, 1985.

Also wrote for Glen Campbell, Kenny Rogers and Bill Cosby.

Television Theme Composer; Series:
Celebrity Sweepstakes, NBC, 1974.
The Diamond Head Game, syndicated, 1975.
The Wheel of Fortune, 1975-83.
Stumpers, NBC, 1976.
Diff'rent Strokes (also known as *45 Minutes from Harlem),* NBC, 1978-85.
Joe's World, NBC, 1979.
Whew!, CBS, 1979.
The Facts of Life, NBC, 1979-88.

Television Movies:
Wrote *When Love Grows Old.*

Screenplays:
Wrote *The Noone Hour.*

Other:
Thicke writes a syndicated humor column for periodicals.

OTHER SOURCES

Periodicals:
People Weekly, September 25, 1995, p. 115.
Saturday Night, February, 1996, p. 42.*

THOMSON, Alex 1929-

PERSONAL

Born January 12, 1929, in London, England.

Career: Cinematographer, camera operator, and photographer.

Awards, Honors: Academy Award nomination, best cinematography, 1981, for *Excalibur;* British Society of Cinematographers Award, best cinematography, 1985, for *Legend;* British Society of Cinematographers Award, best cinematography, 1996, for *Hamlet.*

CREDITS

Film Work; Camera Operator, Unless Otherwise Noted:
Assistant camera operator, *Scent of Mystery* (also known as *Holiday in Spain*), 1960.
(Second unit) *Lawrence of Arabia,* Columbia, 1962.
Information Received, 1962.
Dr. Crippen, 1962.
Band of Thieves, R.F.D. Productions, 1962.
Just for Fun, Columbia, 1963.

Table Bay (also known as *Code 7, Victim 5* and *Victim Five*), Columbia, 1964.
The Masque of the Red Death, American International Pictures, 1964.
The Guest (also known as *The Caretaker*), 1964.
Nothing but the Best, 1964.
Seaside Swingers (also known as *The Adventures of Tim* and *Every Day's a Holiday*), 1965.
(Uncredited) *Doctor Zhivago,* Metro-Goldwyn-Mayer, 1965.
The Girl-Getters (also known as *The System*), 1966.
A Funny Thing Happened on the Way to the Forum, United Artists, 1966.
Judith (also known as *Conflict*), Paramount, 1966.
Fahrenheit 451, Universal, 1966.
Casino Royale (also known as *Charles K. Feldman's Casino Royale*), Columbia, 1967.
(Second unit), *The Man Who Would Be King* (also known as *Rudyard Kipling's The Man Who Would Be King*), Columbia, 1975.
(Second unit) *The Seven-Per-Cent Solution,* Universal, 1976.
Additional photography, *Superman,* Warner Bros., 1978.
Year of the Dragon, Metro-Goldwyn-Mayer/United Artists, 1985.
Date with an Angel, 1987.
The Sicilian, Twentieth Century-Fox, 1987.
Mr. Destiny, Buena Vista, 1990.
The Krays, Miramax, 1990.
Cliffhanger, TriStar, 1993.
Additional photography, *The Saint,* Paramount, 1997.

Film Work; Cinematographer:
Here We Go 'Round the Mulberry Bush, United Artists, 1968.
A Strange Affair, Paramount, 1968.
The Best House in London, Metro-Goldwyn-Mayer, 1968.
Alfred the Great, Metro-Goldwyn-Mayer, 1969.
I Start Counting, United Artists, 1970.
The Rise and Rise of Michael Rimmer, Seven Arts/Warner Bros., 1970.
The Night Digger (also known as *The Road Builder*), Metro-Goldwyn-Mayer, 1971.
Doctor Phibes Rises Again, Orion, 1972.
Fear is the Key, Paramount, 1973.
Deathline (also known as *Raw Meat*), American International Pictures, 1972.
(Second unit), *The Man Who Would Be King* (also known as *Rudyard Kipling's The Man Who Would Be King*), Columbia, 1975.
Rosie Dixon-Night Nurse, 1978.
The Class of Miss MacMichael, 1978.
A Game for Vultures, New Line Cinema, 1979.
The Cat and the Canary, Columbia, 1979.
Excalibur, Warner Bros., 1981.
Bullshot, 1983.
Eureka, United Artists, 1983.
The Keep, Paramount, 1983.
Electric Dreams, Metro-Goldwyn-Mayer/United Artists, 1984.
Legend, Universal, 1985.
Year of the Dragon, Metro-Goldwyn-Mayer/United Artists, 1985.
Duet for One, Cannon, 1986.
Raw Deal (also known as *Triple Identity*), DEG, 1986.
Labyrinth, TriStar, 1986.
Date with an Angel, 1987.
The Sicilian, Fox, 1987.
Track 29, Island, 1988.
High Spirits, TriStar, 1988.
Wings of Fame, 1989.
The Rachel Papers, United Artists, 1989.
Leviathan, Metro-Goldwyn-Mayer/United Artists, 1989.
Mr. Destiny, Buena Vista, 1990.
The Krays, Miramax, 1990.
Alien 3, Twentieth Century-Fox, 1992.
Cliffhanger, TriStar, 1993.
Demolition Man, Warner Bros., 1993.
Black Beauty, Warner Bros., 1994.
The Scarlet Letter, Buena Vista, 1995.
Executive Decision (also known as *Critical Decision*), Warner Bros., 1996.
Hamlet (also known as *William Shakespeare's Hamlet*), Columbia, 1996.
The Man Who Couldn't Open Doors, 1998.

Television Work; Cinematographer; Movies:
Skokie (also known as *Once They Marched Through a Thousand Towns*), CBS, 1981.*

TORRY, Guy

PERSONAL

From St. Louis, MO; brother of Joe Torry (an actor/comedian).

Addresses: *Agent*—Stacy Martin, William Morris Agency, 151 El Camino Drive, Beverly Hills, CA 90212.

Career: Actor, writer, and comedian. Creator of *Phat Comedy Tuesdays* at the Comedy Store.

CREDITS

Film Appearances:

Boo Men, *Sunset Park,* TriStar, 1996.

Doo Rag's Father, *Don't Be a Menace to South Central While Drinking YourJuice in the Hood* (also known as *Don't Be a Menace*), Miramax, 1996.

Little Train, *Back in Business* (also known as *Heart of Stone*), Columbia TriStar Home Video, 1997.

187 (also known as *One Eight Seven*), Warner Bros., 1997.

Lamont, *American History X,* New Line Cinema, 1998.

Indigo, *Ride,* Miramax, 1998.

Radio, *Life,* Universal, 1999.

Fish, *Trippin',* October Films, 1999.

Television Appearances; Series:

Little T, *The Good News* (also known as *Good News*), UPN, 1997.

Television Appearances; Episodic:

Martin Look-a-Like, *Martin,* Fox, 1994.

Television Appearances; Movies:

Little John, *Back in Business,* HBO, 1997.

Television Work; Series:

Production staff, *Martin,* Fox, 1993.

Also appeared on *Russell Simmon's Def Comedy Jam,* HBO.

WRITINGS

Television Episodes:

Martin, Fox, 1994.

Also writer for *Minor Adjustments,* NBC/UPN, and *Moesha,* UPN.*

TRESE, Adam 1969-

PERSONAL

Born January 4, 1969.

Addresses: *Agent*—Jill Littman, Bymel O'Neil, 8912 Burton Way, Beverly Hills, CA 90211.

Career: Actor. Member of The State University of New York Purchase Mafia, a group of working actors, directors, and producers (with Stanley Tucci, Wesley Snipes, Oarker Posey, Hal Hartley, and others).

CREDITS

Film Appearances:

Jon, *Laws of Gravity,* RKO Radio Pictures, 1992.

John, *The Saint of Fort Washington,* Warner Bros., 1993.

David Chambers, *The Underneath,* United International Pictures, 1995.

Gabriel, *Illtown,* The Shooting Gallery, 1996.

Jerry, *Palookaville,* Samuel Goldwyn, 1996.

Russell Schuster, *Polish Wedding,* Fox Searchlight, 1998.

Jimmy, *Camera Obscura,* 2000.

Television Appearances; Series:

Victor Yates, *Push,* ABC, 1998.

Television Appearances; Episodic:

Craig McGraw, "Manhood," *Law & Order,* NBC, 1993.

Chad Macinoy, *Murder, She Wrote,* CBS, 1993.

Gavin Robb, "Fire: Part 2," *Homicide: Life on the Street,* NBC, 1995.

Doug Russell, "One Big Happy Family," *NYPD Blue,* ABC, 1995.

Doug, "These Old Bones," *NYPD Blue,* ABC, 1996.

Sandrelli, *New York Undercover,* Fox, 1998.

Television Appearances; Specials:

John Kennedy Falletta, *Philly Heat,* ABC, 1995.

Agent Nick Ferro, *The Bureau,* ABC, 1996.

Television Appearances; Movies:

The Good Fight, Lifetime, 1992.

Stage Appearances:

Othello, New York Shakespeare Festival, Delacorte Theatre, Public Theatre, New York City, 1991.

"Program: The Stain," *In This Room* (double-bill), William Redfield Theatre, New York City, 1992.

Hobie, *Somewhere in the Pacific,* Playwrights Horizon Theatre, New York City, 1995.

Marco, *A View from the Bridge,* Roundabout Theater's Stage Right, New York City, 1997.

Stu, *Mercy,* Vineyard Theatre, New York City, 1998.

Cornelius Hackl, *The Matchmaker,* Williamstown Theatre Festival, Adams Memorial Theatre, Main Stage, Williamstown, MA, 1998.*

TURNER, Ted 1938-

PERSONAL

Full name, Robert Edward Turner III; born November 19, 1938, in Cincinnati, OH; son of Robert Edward (a billboard advertising magnate) and Florence (Rooney) Turner; married Judy Nye Hallisey (divorced); married Jane Shirley Smith (a flight attendant), 1964 (divorced, 1988); married Jane Fonda (an actress and fitness promoter), December 21, 1991; children: (first marriage) Robert Edward IV, Laura Lee; (second marriage) Beauregard, Rhett, Jennie. *Education:* Graduated from Brown University with a degree in the classics. *Avocational Interests:* Sailing, fishing.

Addresses: *Office*—c/o Turner Broadcasting System, 1050 Techwood Drive, N.W., Atlanta, GA, 30318.

Career: Broadcasting and sports executive, and environmentalist. President and chair of the board, WTBS (independent television station), Atlanta, GA, 1970-96, broadcast nationally by satellite, 1976-96; president and chair of the board, Turner Broadcasting System, Atlanta, 1979-96, with services including Cable News Network, 1980—, Turner Network Television, 1988—, CNN2, CNN Radio, and Cable Music Channel; Time Warner, Inc., vice chairman, 1996—; owner of some 3,600 films originally made for Metro-Goldwyn-Mayer, 1987—. Account executive, Turner Outdoor Advertising, Atlanta, GA, 1961-63, president and COO, 1963-70; owner and president, Atlanta Braves (baseball team), 1976—; part-owner and chair of the board, Atlanta Hawks (basketball team), 1977—. Martin Luther King Center, Atlanta, member of theboard of directors; Better World Society (an organization to promote socially conscious television programming), founder and executive, 1985-91; Turner Family Foundation (an organization which donates money), founder, 1991.

Member: National Cable Television Association, National Association for the Advancement of Colored People (board of directors, Atlanta chapter), National Audubon Society, Cousteau Society, Bay Area Cable Club.

Awards, Honors: Regional Employer of the Year Award, National Association for the Advancement of Colored People, 1976; Outstanding Entrepreneur of the Year, *Sales Marketing and Management Magazine,* 1979; President's Award, National Cable TV Association, 1979, 1989; Inductee, Hall of Fame, Promotions and Marketing Association, 1980; Salesman of the Year Award, Sales and Marketing Executives, 1980; Private Enterprise Exemplar medal, Freedoms Foundation at Valley Forge, 1980; Ace Special Recognition Award, National Cable TV Association, 1980; Communicator of the Year Award, Public Relations Society of America, 1981; Communicator of the Year Award, New York Broadcasters, 1981; International Communicator of the Year Award, Sales and Marketing Executives, 1981; National News Media Award, Veterans of Foreign Wars, 1981; Vanguard Award for Associates, National Cable Television Association, 1981; Distinguished Service in Telecommunications Award, Ohio University College of Communications, 1982; Carr Van Anda Award, Ohio School of Journalism, 1982; Edinburgh International TV Festival, Scotland, Special Award, 1982; Board of Governors Award, NATAS (Atlanta chapter), 1982; Drexel University, DSc in Commerce, 1982; Samford University, LLD, 1982.

Media Awareness Award, Vietnam Veterans Organization, 1983; Special Olympics Award, Special Olympics Committee, 1983; Dinner of Champions Award, Multiple Sclerosis Society (Georgia chapter), 1983; Praca Special Merit Award, New York Puerto Rican Association for Community Affairs, 1983; Inductee, Dubuque (Iowa) Business Hall of Fame, 1983; Central New England College of Technology, D. Entrepreneurial Science, 1983; World Telecommunications Pioneer Award, New York State Broadcasters Association, 1984; Golden Plate Award, American Academy Achievement, 1984; Boy Scouting Award, Boy Scout Council, Outstanding Supporter, 1984; Silver Satellite Award, American Women in Radio and TV, 1984; Lifetime Achievement Award, New York International Film and TV Festival, 1984; Atlanta University, LLD, 1984; D. Public Administration, 1984; Corporate Star of the Year Award, National Leukemia Society, 1985; Distinguished Achievement Award, University of Georgia, 1985; Tree of Life Award, Jewish National Fund, 1985; Business Executive of the Year Award, Georgia Security Dealers Association, 1985; Massachusetts Maritime Academy; University of Charleston, D. Business Administration, 1985; Lifetime Achievement Award, Popular Culture Association, 1986; George Washington Distinguished Patriot Award, S.R., 1986; Inductee, National Association for Sport and Physical Education Hall of Fame, 1986; Missouri Honor Medal, University of Missouri School of Journalism, 1987; Golden Ace Award, National Cable TV Academy, 1987; Lowell Thomas Award, International Platform Association, 1987; Sol Taishoff

Award for Excellence in Broadcast Journalism, National Press Foundation, 1988; Citizen Diplomat Award, Center for Soviet-American Dialogue, 1988; Chairman's Award, Cable Advertising Bureau, 1988; Directorate Award, NATAS, 1989; Paul White Award, Radio and TV News Directors Association, 1989; Business Marketer of the Year Award, American Marketing Association, 1989; Distinguished Service Award, Simon Wiesenthal Center, 1990; Glastnost Award, Vols. American and Soviet Life Magazine, 1990; Edward Weintal Prize for Diplomatic Reporting, Georgetown University's Institute for the Study of Diplomacy, 1990; Vanguard Award for Programmers, National Cable Television Association, 1990; Banff Television Festival Outstanding Achievement Award, 1991; named Man of the Year, *Time* Magazine, 1991; Named Yachtsman of the Year four times; winner of America's Cup as captain of the yacht *Courageous,* 1977.

CREDITS

Television Appearances; Specials:

Hope News Network (also known as *Bob Hope's News Network*), NBC, 1988.
CNN Special Report: A Conversation with Carl Sagan, CNN, 1989.
A Conversation with Castro, CNN, 1990.
The 11th Annual ACE Awards, 1990.
Ted Turner Talking with David Frost, PBS, 1991.
First Person with Maria Shriver, NBC, 1992.
MGM: When the Lion Roars (also known as *The MGM Story*), TNT, 1992.
November 22, 1963: Where Were You? A Larry King Special Live from Washington, TNT, 1993.
First Person with Maria Shriver, NBC, 1993.
Fourth Annual Environmental Media Awards, 1994.
The 10th Annual Television Academy Hall of Fame, 1994.
Naked News, Arts and Entertainment, 1995.
Barbara Walters Presents "The 10 Most Fascinating People of 1995," ABC, 1995.
Panelist, *An American Family and Television: A National Town Hall Meeting,* USA Network, Disney Channel, Bravo, Family Channel, Cartoon Channel, Nickelodeon, Animal Planet, STARZ!, Food Network, MSG Network, and Encore, 1997.
The Goodwill Games Opening Ceremonies, TBS, 1998.
American Film Institute's 100 Years ... 100 Movies, CBS, 1998.

Television Appearances; Episodic:

Arli$$, HBO, 1996.

Television Appearances; Miniseries:

(Cameo) Lieutenant Colonel W. T. Patton, *Gettysburg,* 1993.

Television Work:

Creator, *The Portrait of Great Britain,* TBS, 1990.
Creator, *Portrait of Japan,* TBS, 1992.
(As R.E. Turner) Creator, "The Cold War" (also known as "Cold War: A Television History"), *CNN Perspectives* (series), CNN, 1998.

Film Appearances:

Himself, *Southern Voices, American Dreams,* 1985.

Film Work:

Executive consultant, *Amazing Grace and Chuck,* TriStar, 1987.
Assistance, *Powaqqatsi,* 1988.

Sidelights: Ted Turner, founder and president of the Turner Broadcasting System, is one of the most visible entrepreneurs in the cable television industry. In the August 14, 1983 *New York Times,* Sandra Salmans observed: "If cable has a single pioneer, it is arguably brash, outspoken Ted Turner. The so-called 'Mouth of the South,' Mr. Turner has shaken up the television industry repeatedly since he entered it in 1970." She went on to note: "While he is still a controversial and perhaps unpopular figure in broadcasting, there are few who would quibble with his claim—widely publicized in his trade promotions—that 'I was cable before cable was cool.'" Indeed, Turner has turned a failing Atlanta UHF television station into WTBS, a cable channel estimated to reach more than half of all viewers nationwide; the "Superstation" specializes in Atlanta Braves baseball, vintage movies, and reruns of family-oriented situation comedies. Since December, 1976, WTBS hasbeen a regular feature of cable broadcasting, and since 1980 it has been joined by Turner's other successful venture, the Cable News Network, a twenty-four hour news-only station. A past winner of the America's Cup for yacht racing who admittedly loves the limelight, Turner told *American Film* (July, 1982) that he intends to keep "going after the networks" on both the business and entertainment fronts. "All they're doing now is reacting to me," he asserted. "I give them hell because they don't serve the public interest. They look at the viewer the same way a slaughterhouse looks at its pigs and cattle. They sell them by the pound to the advertiser—the same way they sell ham hocks and spare ribs."

Such flamboyant statements are characteristic of Turner, according to a June 16, 1980 *Newsweek* feature by Harry F. Waters. He wrote: "Robert Edward Turner III has so incensed, perplexed and dazzled his many adversaries that he has become something of a Southern folk hero." Describing him as "ever the Confederate rebel," the reporter cited Turner's public carousing with his baseball players and yachting crew and his reputation as a ladies' man among the sources of criticism and continued: "His elephantine ego sometimes repels even his friends; his 10,000-watt exuberance charms even his enemies. If Ted Turner were a television show, he would be 'That's Incredible!'" Turner's rise to prominence demonstrates his creative use of his energies. At the age of twenty-four he inherited the family billboard business, then six million dollars in debt; business pressures had driven his father to suicide. Against the advice of financial consultants, Turner canceled the sale of the business and then proceeded to restore it to success. Later he again ignored consultants' advice and bought a television station with annual losses of more than $500,000; within three years, Waters reported, it became one of the first independent stations in the country to show a substantial profit. As revenues increased, Turner purchased the Atlanta Braves baseball team and the Atlanta Hawks basketball team and began to show their games exclusively on his station. His other programming included situation comedies and reruns aimed at family viewers who might find certain network television programming offensive.

In 1976 Turner paid to have his station transmitted into other states by means of an RCA Satcom satellite that serviced cable television. Thereby he quadrupled his audience overnight without altering his programming and was able to dub the Atlanta Braves "America's team" because of the span of households in the WTBS audience. As cable found its way into more and more homes, so did Turner's station; it quickly became the nation's most profitable single television station. The Turner Broadcasting System—officially so named in 1979—has had an uneven track record on profits, however, because the founder continually experiments with new broadcasting services, including a heavy investment in such exclusive programming as Jacques Cousteau oceanographic specials and MGM-United Artists movies, and because subscription prices were cut in order to compete with rival cable stations. Cable industry analyst Paul Kagan told the *New York Times* (April 14, 1983) that Turner's habit "has been to keep putting his reach beyond his grasp. It's his style to go for the next brass ring." Turner even attempted takeovers of two of the three major networks, CBS and ABC, between 1984 and 1987; he was unsuccessful in both cases. Early in 1987, reacting to a 1986 operating loss in excess of $100 million, Turner sold shares in his company retaining for himself just fifty-one percent of the stock and conceding a voice in management decisions to the new investors. In turn, the board of directors announced plans to create a new cable network, Turner Network Television, that will air original shows, exclusive specials, and vintage films. At a press conference in October, 1987, Turner told the *New York Times* that he plans to spearhead "cable's premier network" with major awards ceremonies, sporting events, andfamily specials as well as regular offerings.

Turner shared his vision of his role in the media in the June 16, 1980 *Newsweek:* "I can do more today in communications than any conqueror ever could have done. I want to be the hero of my country. I want to get it back to the principles that made us good. Television has led us . . . down the path of destruction. I intend to turn it around before it is too late. And the hour *is* late." Turner has affirmed his vigilance in the promotion of moral values on television, seeing this as a service to future generations. Twice married and the father of five children, Turner divides his time between business in Atlanta and a second home on a 5,200-acre South Carolina plantation "dominated by a white-pillared mansion that evokes Tara in 'Gone with the Wind,"' according to Waters, who concluded that whatever Turner's detractors may say, the Atlanta businessman "has enlivened and enriched all the games he has entered. Though he may occasionally mistake himself for one of his military heroes, his sheer exuberance is always infectious." The reporter added: "More important, in an age of play-it-safe corporate bureaucracy, bold spirits like Turner have become precious commodities. . . . He is pushing television . . . to its farthest frontiers."

OTHER SOURCES

Periodicals:

Cosmopolitan, September, 1995, p. 262.
Current Biography, June, 1998, p. 52.
Harper's Magazine, December, 1997, p. 10.
Inc., April, 1997, p. 11.
People Weekly, December 25, 1995, p. 87.*

U-V

UNSWORTH, Geoffrey 1914-1978

PERSONAL

Born 1914, in London, England; died October 29, 1978, in Brittany, France; wife's name, Maggie.

Career: Cinematographer, actor, and camera operator.

Awards, Honors: British Society of Cinematographers Award, best cinematography, British Academy of Film and Television Arts Award, best British cinematography (color), and Academy Award nomination, best cinematography, all 1964, for *Becket;* British Academy of Film and Television Arts Award nomination, best British cinematography (color), 1964, for *Tamahine;* British Academy of Film and Television Arts Award, best cinematography, 1968, for *2001: A Space Odyssey;* British Society of Cinematographers Award, British Academy of Film and Television Arts Award, and Academy Award, best cinematography, all 1972, for *Cabaret;* British Academy of Film and Television Arts Award, best cinematography, 1972, for *Alice's Adventures in Wonderland;* British Academy of Film and Television Arts Award nomination, best cinematography, 1973, for *Zardoz;* British Academy of Film and Television Arts Award nomination, best cinematography, 1974, for *Murder on the Orient Express;* British Society of Cinematographers Award, and British Academy of Film and Television Arts Award, best cinematography, 1977, both for *A Bridge Too Far;* British Academy of Film and Television Arts Award nomination, best cinematography, 1978, for *Superman;* New York Film Critics Circle Award, Los Angeles Film Critics Association Award, British Academy of Film and Television Arts Award, and Academy Award, best cinematography, all 1979, for *Tess* (with Ghislain Cloquet).

CREDITS

Film Work; Cinematographer, Unless Otherwise Noted:

Camera operator, *The Life and Death of Colonel Blimp* (also known as *Colonel Blimp*), General Films Distributors/United Artists, 1943.

Camera operator, *A Matter of Life and Death* (also known as *Stairway to Heaven*), Universal, 1946.

The Laughing Lady, 1946.

The Man Within (also known as *The Smugglers*), 1947.

Jassy, 1947.

(Outdoors) *Blanche Fury,* General Films Distributors, 1947.

Scott of the Antarctic, Eagle Lion/General Films Distributors, 1948.

The Spider and the Fly, General Films Distributors, 1949.

Fools Rush In, General Films Distributors, 1949.

The Blue Lagoon, General Films Distributors, 1949.

Trio, General Films Distributors, 1950.

Double Confession, Associated British Films, 1950.

Where No Vultures Fly (also known as *Ivory Hunter*), Ealing, 1951.

The Clouded Yellow, Columbia, 1951.

Penny Princess, General Films Distributors, 1952.

Outpost in Malaya (also known as *The Planter's Wife, White Blood*), General Films Distributors, 1952.

Made in Heaven, 1952.

Turn the Key Softly, General Films Distributors, 1953.

The Sword and the Rose (also known as *When Knighthood was in Flower*), Walt Disney, 1953.

The Million Pound Note (also known as *Man with a Million*), United Artists, 1953.

The Seekers (also known as *Land of Fury*), Rank Organisation, 1954.

The Purple Plain, United Artists/Rank Organisation, 1954.

Value for Money, Rank Organisation, 1955.

Passage Home, General Films Distributors, 1955.
Simba (also known as *Simba-Mark of Mau Mau!*), Lippert, 1955.
Tiger in the Smoke, Rank Organisation, 1956.
Jacqueline, Rank Organisation, 1956.
A Town Like Alice (also known as *Rape of Malaya*), Rank Organisation, 1956.
Dangerous Exile, Rank Organisation, 1957.
Hell Drivers (also known as *Hard Drivers*), 1957.
Bachelor of Hearts, Rank Organisation, 1958.
A Night to Remember, Rank Organisation, 1958.
Northwest Frontier (also known as *Flame Over India*), Rank Organisation, 1959.
The World of Suzie Wong, Paramount, 1960.
Why Bother to Knock (also known as *Don't Bother to Knock*), 1961.
On the Double, 1961.
The Main Attraction, 1962.
The 300 Spartans (also known as *Lion of Sparta*), Twentieth Century-Fox, 1962.
Tamahine, 1964.
Becket, Paramount, 1964.
Othello, Warner Bros., 1965.
Genghis Khan (also known as *Dschingis Khan, Dzingis-Kan*), Columbia, 1965.
Half a Sixpence, Paramount, 1967.
Oh Dad, Poor Dad, Mama's Hung You in the Closet and I'm Feeling So Sad, Paramount, 1967.
The Dance of Death, Paramount, 1968.
The Bliss of Mrs. Blossom, Paramount, 1968.
2001: A Space Odyssey (also known as *Two Thousand and One: A Space Odyssey*), Metro-Goldwyn-Mayer, 1968.
The Reckoning (also known as *A Matter of Honour*), Columbia, 1969.
The Assassination Bureau, Paramount, 1969.
The Magic Christian, 1969.
Three Sisters, American Film Theatre/British Lion, 1970.
Cromwell, Columbia, 1970.
Goodbye Gemini, 1970.
Say Hello to Yesterday, 1971.
Unman, Wittering and Zigo, 1971.
Love and Pain and the Whole Damn Thing, Columbia, 1972.
Alice's Adventures in Wonderland, American National, 1972.
Cabaret, Allied Artists, 1972.
Zardoz, Twentieth Century-Fox, 1973.
Don Quixote, Walter Reed/Continental Distributing, 1973.
Baxter!, 1973.
The Return of the Pink Panther, United Artists, 1974.
The Internecine Project, Allied Artists, 1974.
The Abdication, Warner Bros., 1974.
Murder on the Orient Express, Paramount, 1974.
Lucky Lady, Twentieth Century-Fox, 1975.
Royal Flash, Twentieth Century-Fox, 1975.
A Matter of Time, 1976.
A Bridge Too Far, United Artists, 1977.
Superman (also known as *Superman: The Movie*), Warner Bros., 1978.
And actor, *The First Great Train Robbery* (also known as *The Great Train Robbery*), United Artists, 1979.
Tess, Columbia, 1979.
Superman II, Warner Bros., 1980.

Film Appearances:
The First Great Train Robbery (also known as *The Great Train Robbery*), United Artists, 1979.*

VANDER PYL, Jean 1919(?)-1999

PERSONAL

Full name, Jean Thurston Vander Pyl; born c. 1919, in Philadelphia, PA; died of lung cancer, April 13, 1999, in Dana Point, CA; daughter of John Howard and Kathleen (Hale) Vander Pyl; married Roger W. DeWitt, January 30, 1963; children: Roger Eugene; (previous marriage) Kathleen, Carroll Timothy, Michael John O'Meara; (stepchildren) Anthony, Peter. *Education:* Graduated from Beverly Hills High School and attended the University of California at Los Angeles, 1937-38.

Career: Actress. Radio actress, 1937-53; television actress, 1953-99; performed on the radio series *Calling All Cops;* played the mother on radio's *Father Knows Best* and many of Andy's girlfriends on radio's *Amos and Andy.*

Member: American Federation of Radio and Television Artists, Screen Actors Guild, Pi Beta Phi, Phi Beta.

CREDITS

Television Appearances; Series:
Voice of Wilma Flintstone, Pebbles Flintstone, and Mrs. Slate, *The Flintstones* (animated), ABC/NBC, 1960-66.
Voice of Rosie the Robot Maid, Mrs. Spacely, George Jetson's Mother-in-Law and secretary, and others, *The Jetsons* (animated), ABC/CBS/NBC/syndicated, 1962.

Voice of Maw Rugg, *The Atom Ant Show* (animated), NBC, 1965.

Voice of Ogee, *Magilla Gorilla* (animated), ABC/syndicated, 1966.

Ethel Carter, *Please Don't Eat the Daises,* NBC, 1966-67.

Voice of Maw Rugg, *The Atom Ant/Secret Squirrel Show* (animated), NBC, 1967.

Voice of Marge Huddles, *Where's Huddles?,* CBS, 1970.

Voice of Wilma Flintstone, *The Flintstones Comedy Hour* (animated; also known as *The Flintstones Show*), CBS, 1972-74.

Television Appearances; Episodic:

Voice of Goldie, *Top Cat* (animated; also known as *Boss Cat*), ABC, 1961.

Mrs. Woods, "Farewell To Penny," *Leave It To Beaver,* CBS/ABC, 1962.

Clara Miller, "Birthplace of a Future President," *Petticoat Junction,* CBS, 1968.

Gladys Tuttle, "The Valley Has a Baby," *Petticoat Junction,* CBS, 1968.

Misses Agnes Frisby, "Wings," *Petticoat Junction,* CBS, 1968.

Misses Agnes Frisby, "The Lady Doctor," *Petticoat Junction,* CBS, 1968.

Scooby-Doo, Where Are You? (animated), CBS/ABC, 1969.

The New Tom & Jerry Show (animated; also known as *The New Tom & Jerry /Grape Ape Show*), CBS/ABC, 1975.

Woman, *Blacke's Magic,* NBC, 1986.

Fan, "One Good Bid Deserves a Murder," *Murder, She Wrote,* CBS, 1986.

Voice of Wilma Flintstone, "Talent Show," *The Weird Al Show,* CBS, 1997.

Television Appearances; Movies:

Voice of Wilma Flintstone, *A Flintstone Christmas* (animated), 1977.

Voice of Wilma Flintstone and Rosie the Robot Maid, *The Jetsons Meet the Flintstones* (animated), syndicated, 1987.

Voice of Wilma Flintstone, *Hollyrock-a-Bye Baby* (animated), ABC, 1993.

Voice of Wilma Flintstone and Mrs. Slate, *I Yabba-Dabba Doo!* (animated), CBS, 1993.

Television Appearances; Specials:

Voice, *Hanna Barbera's 50th: A Yabba Dabba Doo Celebration,* TNT, 1989.

Voice of Winsome Witch, "Fender Bender 500," *Wake, Rattle & Roll,* syndicated, 1990.

Voice of Wilma Flintstone, *A Flintstone Family Christmas,* ABC, 1993.

Voice of Wilma Flintstone, *A Flintstones Christmas Carol,* syndicated, 1994.

Film Appearances:

Miss Zimmerman, *Deep In My Heart,* Metro-Goldwyn-Mayer, 1954.

Hey There, It's Yogi Bear (animated), Columbia, 1964.

Voice of Wilma Flintstone, *The Man Called Flintstone,* Columbia, 1966.

Mrs. Feldspar, *The Flintstones* (animated), Universal, 1994.

OTHER SOURCES

Electronic:

http://www.cnn.com/SHOWBIZ/TV/9904/13/wilma.voice.reut/.*

VIERNY, Sacha 1919-

PERSONAL

Born August 10, 1919, in Bois-le-Roi, France.

Career: Cinematographer and director.

Awards, Honors: Catalonian International Film Festival Award (Spanish film award), best cinematography, 1989, for *The Cook, the Thief, His Wife & Her Lover;* Catalonian International Film Festival Award, best cinematography, 1993, for *The Baby of Macon;* Catalonian International Film Festival Award, best cinematography, 1996, for *The Pillow Book.*

CREDITS

Film Work; Cinematographer, Unless Otherwise Noted:

Assistant director, *L'Ombre,* 1948.

Night and Fog (also known as *Nuit et brouillard;* documentary), 1955.

Letter From Siberia (also known as *Lettre de Siberie;* documentary), 1957.

Le Chant du Styrene (documentary), 1958.

Love Is When You Make It (also known as *Le Bel age*), 1959.

(With Michio Takahashi) *Hiroshima, Mon Amour,* Zenith, 1959.

The Season For Love (also known as *La Morte saison des amours*), 1960.
Merci Natercia!, 1960.
La Main chaude (also known as *La Mano calda* [Italy]), 1960.
Last Year at Marienbad (also known as *L' Annee derniere a Marienbad* and *L' Anno scorso a Marienbad* [Italy]), Astor, 1961.
Portrait Robot, 1962.
Climats, 1962.
Muriel (also known as *Muriel ou le temps d'un retour, Muriel, il tempo di un ritorno* [Italy] and *The Time of Return*), Lopert, 1963.
Do You Like Women? (also known as *Aimez-vous les femmes?*), 1964.
La Musica, 1966.
The Dance of the Heron (also known as *De Dans van de Reiger*), 1966.
The War Is Over (also known as *La Guerre est finie* and *Kriget ar slut* [Sweden]), 1966.
Caroline cherie (also known as *Caroline Cherie: Schon wie die Sunde*), 1967.
Belle de Jour (also known as *Bella di giorno* [Itlay]), Allied Artists, 1967.
Le Tatoue (also known as *Nemici. . .per la pelle*), 1968.
La Main (also known as *The Hand* and *La Mano* [Italy]), Warner Bros., 1970.
Bof! L'Anatomie d'un livreur, 1971.
Le Moine (also known as *Il Monaco* [Italy] and *The Monk*), Video Search of Miami, 1972.
La Sainte Famille, 1972.
Les Granges Brulees (also known as *The Investigator, La Mia legge* [Italy], and *Suspect of Murder*), 1973.
Stavisky (also known as *L' Empire d'Alexandre* and *Stavisky, il grande truffatore* [Italy]), Cinemation, 1974.
Baxter-Vera Baxter, 1976.
La Vocation suspendue (also known as *The Suspended Vocation*), 1977.
Le Diable dans la boite, 1977.
Le Rose et le blanc, 1978.
L' Hypothese du tableau vole (also known as *The Hypothesis of the Stolen Painting*), 1978.
La Bravade Legendaire, 1978.
Mon oncle d'Amerique (also known as *My American Uncle, My Uncle from America*, and *Les Somnambules*), New World, 1978.
Le Chemin Perdu, 1980.
Beau Pere (also known as *Stepfather*), 1981.
Las Tres coronas del marinero (also known as *Three Crowns of the Sailor* and *Les Trois couronnes du matelot* [France]), 1982.
Clash, 1984.
Flugel und Felleln (also known as *Flugel und Fesseln, L'Avenir d'Emile*, and *The Future of Emily*), 1984.
La Femme publique (also known as *The Public Woman*), 1984.
L'Amour a mort, 1984.
A Zed & Two Noughts (also known as *Zoo* and *A Zoo: A Zed & Two Noughts*), Skouras Pictures, 1985.
The Belly of an Architect (also known as *Il Ventre dell'architetto*), Hemdale, 1987.
Fear of Drowning, 1988.
Drowning By Numbers, 1988.
The Cook, the Thief, His Wife & Her Lover and *Le Cuisinier, le voleur, sa femme et son amant* [France]), Recorded, 1989.
And camera operator, *Prospero's Books* (also known as *L' Ultima tempesta* [Italy]), Miramax, 1991.
Rosa, 1992.
The Baby of Macon (also known as *Das Wunder von Macon* [Germany]), CineCompany, S.A., 1993.
The Pillow Book, Cine 360/Nuevo Mundo Vision, S.A., 1996.
Dormez, je le veux, Les Acacias, 1998.

Also directed three short films, c. 1948-51.*

von SYDOW, Max 1929-

PERSONAL

Original name, Carl Adolf von Sydow; born April 10, 1929, in Lund, Sweden; son of Carl Wilhelm (a professor of Scandinavian and Irish folklore) and Greta (Rappe) von Sydow; married Kerstin (some sources say Christina) Olin (an actress), August 1, 1951 (divorced, 1996); married Cathrine Brelet, April 30, 1997; children: (first marriage) Clas Wilhelm, Per Henrik. *Education:* Graduated from the Royal Dramatic Theatre Academy of Stockholm, 1951. *Avocational interests:* Gardening, traveling, nautical history.

Addresses: *Agent*—Paradigm, 25th Floor, 10100 Santa Monica Blvd., Los Angeles, CA, 90067.

Career: Actor and director. Cofounded a theatre group in Sweden, c. 1940s. *Military service:* Swedish Quartermaster Corps, 1947-48.

Awards, Honors: Royal Foundation of Culture Award, Sweden, 1954; Golden Globe Award nomination, best actor in a motion picture, 1967, for *Hawaii;*

Golden Globe Award nomination, best supporting actor in a motion picture, 1974, for *The Exorcist;* Guldbagge Award, Bodil Award, European Film Award, and Robert Award, all best actor, 1988, and Academy Award nomination, best actor, 1989, all for *Pelle erobreren;* Guldbagge Award, best direction, 1989, for *Ved vejen;* Best Actor Award, Tokyo International Film Festival, 1992, for *Dotkniecie reki;* Guldbagge Award and Bodil Award, both best actor, 1997, for *Hamsun.*

CREDITS

Film Appearances:

Nils, *Bara en mor* (also known as *Only a Mother*), Svensk Filmindustri, 1949.

Hand, *Froeken Julie* (also known as *Miss Julie*), Sandrews, 1951.

Olof, *Ingen mans kvinna,* Svensk Filmindustri, 1951.

Bergman, *Raetten att aelska,* Europa Film, 1956.

Knight, *Det sjunde inseglet* (also known as *The Seventh Seal*), Janus, 1956.

Henrik Aackerman, *Smultronstaellet* (also known as *Wild Strawberries*), Janus, 1957.

Gustaf Oemark (the minister of Uddarbo), *Praesten i Uddarbo* (also known as *The Minister of Uddarbo*), Nordisk Tonefilm, 1957.

Harry Andersson, *Naera livet* (also known as *Brink of Life* and *So Close to Life*), Nordisk Tonefilm, 1958.

Spion 503, Dansk Film Company, 1958.

Albert Emanuel Vogler, *Ansiktet* (also known as *The Face* and *The Magician*), Janus, 1958.

Toere, *Jungfrukaellan* (also known as *The Virgin Spring*), Svensk Filmindustry, 1959.

Anders Frost, *Broellopsdagen* (also known as *The Wedding Day* and *Ja!*), Nordisk Tonefilm, 1960.

Martin, *Saasom i en spegel* (also known as *Through a Glass Darkly*), Svensk Filmindustry, 1961.

The father, *Nils Holgerssons underbara resa* (also known as *Adventures of Nils Holgersson* and *The Wonderful Adventures of Nils*), Nordisk Tonefilm, 1962.

Married man, *Aelskarinnan* (also known as *The Mistress* and *The Swedish Mistress*), Svensk Filmindustry, 1962.

Jonas Persson, *Nattvardsgaesterna* (also known as *Winter Light*), Janus, 1963.

Jesus, *The Greatest Story Ever Told,* United Artists, 1965.

Kvist, "Uppehaall i myrlandet," *4 x 4* (also known as *Nordisk kvadrille*), Vaeinaen Filmi, 1965.

Scott Swanson, *The Reward,* Twentieth Century-Fox, 1965.

Oktober, *The Quiller Memorandum,* Twentieth Century-Fox, 1966.

Abner Hale, *Hawaii,* United Artists,, 1966.

Smaalands-Pelle, *Haer har du ditt liv* (also known as *Here's Your Life* and *This Is Your Life*), Svensk Filmindustri, 1966.

Johan Borg, *Vargtimmen* (also known as *The Hour of the Wolf*), Lopert, 1966.

Gustav Olofsson, *Svarta palmkronor* (also known as *Black Palm Trees*), Sandrews, 1968.

Jan Rosenberg, *Skammen* (also known as *Shame*), Lopert, 1969.

Magnus Rud, *Made in Sweden,* Svensk Filmindustri, 1969.

Andreas Winkelman, *En passion* (also known *A Passion* and *The Passion of Anna*), United Artists, 1970.

Colonel Vladimir Kosnov, *The Kremlin Letter,* Twentieth Century-Fox, 1970.

Salem, *The Night Visitor* (also known as *Salem Come to Supper*), UMC Pictures, 1971.

Gorenko, *Embassy* (also known as *Target: Embassy*), Hemdale, 1971.

Roy Lindberg, *Aeppelkriget,* Svensk Filmindustri, 1972.

Ingmar Bergman, 1972.

Karl-Oskar Nilsson, *Utvandrarna* (also known as *The Emigrants*), Warner Bros., 1972.

Karl-Oskar Nilsson, *Nybyggarna* (also known as *The New Land*), Warner Bros., 1973.

Father Merrin, *The Exorcist,* Warner Bros., 1973.

Harry Haller, *Steppenwolf,* 1974.

The baron, *The Ultimate Warrior,* Warner Bros., 1975.

Larsen, *Foxtrot* (also known as *The Far Side of Paradise* and *The Other Side of Paradise*), [France, Mexico, Norway, and Switzerland], 1975.

Professor Preobrazenskij, *Cuore di cane* (also known as *Heart of a Dog* and *Warum bellt, Herr Bobikow?*), [Italy and West Germany (now Germany)], 1975.

The father, *Aegget aer loest!,* Svensk Filmindustri, 1975.

Joubert, *Three Days of the Condor,* Paramount, 1975.

Matthew Lawrence, *Trompe l'oeuil,* 1975.

Captain Hortiz, *Il deserto dei tartari* (also known as *The Desert of the Tartars* and *Le desert des tartares*), Corona, 1976.

Chief magistrate Riches, *Cadaveri eccellenti* (also known as *The Context, Excellent Cadavers,* and *Illustrious Corpses*), United Artists, 1976.

Captain Gustav Schroeder, *Voyage of the Damned,* Avco-Embassy, 1977.

Himself, *A Look at Liv* (documentary), Win Kao Productions, 1977.

Lisa Carpi/police chief, *Gran bollito* (also known as *Black Journal* and *La signora degli orrori*), Italfrance Films, 1977.

Francois Marneau, *March or Die,* Columbia, 1977.

Father Merrin, *Exorcist II: The Heretic,* Warner Bros., 1977.

Shelley/Webber, *Brass Target,* Metro-Goldwyn-Mayer, 1978.

Dr. Bascomb, *Hurricane* (also known as *Forbidden Paradise*), 1979.

Gerald Mortenhoe, *La mort en direct* (also known as *Death in Full View, Deathwatch, Death Watch—Der gekaufte Tod,* and *Der gekaufte Tod*), Quartet Films, 1980.

Marcello, *Bugie bianche,* [Italy], 1980.

Emperor Ming the Merciless, *Flash Gordon,* Universal, 1980.

Major Karl von Steiner, *Victory,* Paramount, 1981.

Himself and the voice of Nijinsky, *She Dances Alone,* [United States and Austria], 1982.

King Osric, *Conan the Barbarian,* Universal, 1982.

Colonel O'Donnell, *Jugando con la muerte* (also known as *Target Eagle*), Esme International/Golden Sun, 1982.

S. A. Andree, *Ingenjoer Andrees luftfaerd* (also known as *The Flight of the Eagle*), Swedish Film Institute, 1982.

Brewmeister Smith, *Strange Brew* (also known as *The Adventures of Bob and Doug McKenzie*), Metro-Goldwyn-Mayer, 1983.

Ernst Stavaros Blofeld, *Never Say Never Again* (also known as *Warhead*), Warner Bros., 1983.

Carlo di Vilafratti, *Le cercle des passions* (also known as *Circulo de pasiones*), Cinema International Corporation, 1983.

Dr. Paul Novotny, *Dreamscape,* Twentieth Century-Fox, 1984.

Dr. Kynes, *Dune,* Universal, 1984.

Himself, *George Stevens: A Filmmaker's Journey* (documentary), Rosebud Communications, 1985.

Jurgen Brausch, *Code Name: Emerald* (also known as *Emerald*), Metro-Goldwyn-Mayer/United Artists, 1985.

Spinola, *Il pentito,* [Italy], 1985.

Dr. Louis Feldman, *Duet for One,* Cannon, 1986.

Frederick, *Hannah and Her Sisters,* Orion, 1986.

Dr. Huber, *The Second Victory* (also known as *Die Narbe* and *Der Zweite Sieg*), Films around the World, 1987.

August Strindberg, *Oviri* (also known as *The Wolf at the Door*), Manson, 1987.

Pappa Lasse, *Pelle erobreren* (also known as *Pelle the Conqueror* and *Pelle eroevraren*), Danish Film Institute/Swedish Film Institute/Kaerne, 1987.

Pope Clement VII, *Una vita scellerata* (also known as *A Violent Life* and *Cellini, una vita violenta*), [Italy, France, and Germany], 1990.

Dr. Peter Ingham, *Awakenings,* Columbia, 1990.

Von Schleheim, *Mio caro Dottor Graesler* (also known as *Dr. Graesler* and *The Bachelor*), Eidoscope International, 1990.

Thor Carlsson, *A Kiss before Dying,* Universal, 1991.

Henry Farber, *Bis ans Ende der Welt* (also known as *Until the End of the World* and *Jusqu'au bout du monde*), Warner Bros., 1991.

Joseph Meuller, *Father,* Northern Arts Entertainment, 1992.

Narrator, *Europa* (also known as *Zentropa*), Prestige Films, 1992.

The vicar, *Oxen* (also known as *The Ox*), First Run Features/Castle Hill Productions, 1992.

Henry Kesdi, *Dotkniecie reki* (also known as *The Silent Touch, The Touch,* and *Beroeringen*), Castle Hill Productions, 1992.

Johan Aakerblom (Anna's father), *Den goda viljan* (also known as *The Best Intentions, Con le migliori intenzioni, Den gode vilje,* and *Die besten absichten,* and *Les meilleures intentions*), Samuel Goldwyn Company, 1992.

Leland Gaunt, *Needful Things,* New Line Cinema, 1993.

Simon S. L. Fromm, *Morfars resa* (also known as *Grandfather's Journey* and *Grandpa's Journey*), Swedish Film Institute, 1993.

Joseph Kaufman, *Time Is Money,* 1994.

(Uncredited) Jacob Aakerblom *Lumiere et compagnie* (also known as *Lumiere and Company* and *Lumiere y compania;* documentary), Le Studio Canal/Alta Films,1995.

Judge Fargo, *Judge Dredd,* Buena Vista, 1995.

Narrator, *Atlanten* (also known as *The Atlantic*), Triangelfilm, 1995.

Truck Stop, 1996.

Knut Hamsun, *Hamsun,* Swedish Film Institute, 1996.

The vicar, *Jerusalem,* First Look Pictures, 1996.

Voice of August Andrie, *En frusen droem* (also known as *Their Frozen Dream;* documentary), Swedish Film Institute, 1997.

Voice characterization, *Hercules* (also known as *Hercules: From Zero to Hero;* animated), Buena Vista, 1997.

The tracker, *What Dreams May Come,* PolyGram Filmed Entertainment, 1998.

Snow Falling on Cedars, Universal, 1998.

Druids, 2000.

Also appeared in *Egg! Egg!*, *I Hausbandet,* and *Venetian Lies.*

Film Work; Director:

Ved vejen (also known as *Katinka* and *Vid vaegen*), Danish Film Institute, 1987.

Television Appearances; Miniseries:

King John of Portugal, *Christopher Columbus,* CBS, 1985.

Nansen, "The Last Place on Earth," *Masterpiece Theatre,* PBS, 1985.

Johan Aakerblom, *Den goda viljan,* [Sweden], 1991.

Baron Franz von Trotta und Cipolje, *Radetzkymarsch* (also known as *Radetzky March*), [Austria and Germany], 1994.

Jacob, *Enskilda samtal* (also known as *Private Confessions* and *Private Conversations*), SVT, 1996.

Television Appearances; Movies

The hunter, *Herr Sleeman kommer,* Sveriges, 1957.

Bo Stensson Svenningson, *Rabies,* Sveriges, 1958.

The Last Civilian, 1983.

Sidka, *Samson and Delilah,* ABC, 1984.

Peter Barak, *Kojak: The Belarus File* (also known as *The Belarus File*), CBS, 1985.

The apostle Peter, *Quo Vadis?,* USA Network, 1987.

Szaz, *Red King, White Knight,* HBO, 1989.

Brotherhood of the Rose, NBC, 1989.

The Wisdom and the Dream, 1989.

Father Siemes, *Hiroshima: Out of the Ashes,* NBC, 1990.

Dr. Aleksandr Bukhanovsky, *Citizen X,* HBO, 1995.

David, *Solomon,* RAI, 1997.

La principessa e il povero (also known as *Die Falsche Prinzessin*), [Germany and Italy], 1997.

Admiral Chernavin, *Hostile Waters* (also known as *Death of a Yankee* and *Peril en mer*), HBO, 1997.

Television Appearances; Specials:

Otto Frank, *The Diary of Anne Frank,* ABC, 1967.

"A Search for Strindberg," *N.E.T. Playhouse,* PBS, 1972.

The American Film Institute Salute to John Huston, 1983.

Voice only, "The Soldier's Tale," *Great Performances,* PBS, 1984.

Eugene O'Neill, *Och ge oss skuggorna,* [Sweden], 1993.

World of Film, 1993.

Professor Serebrejakov, *Onkel Vanja,* [Sweden], 1994.

Television Appearances; Awards Presentations:

The 15th Annual People's Choice Awards, CBS, 1989.

The 61st Annual Academy Awards Presentation, ABC, 1989.

Television Appearances; Episodic:

Dr. Sigmund Freud, "Vienna," *The Young Indiana Jones Chronicles,* ABC, 1993.

Stage Appearances:

August Strindberg, *The Night of the Tribades,* Helen Hayes Theatre, New York City, 1977.

Dr. Alfred Feldmann, *Duet for One,* Royale Theatre, New York City, 1981-82.

Prospero, *The Tempest,* London, England, 1988.

Appeared as the title role, *Peer Gynt;* and as Brick, *Cat on a Hot Tin Roof;* appeared in *Faust,* Paris, France, and Helsinki, Finland. Also appeared in *After the Fall, Ett dromspel, Henry IV, King John, La valse des toreadors, The Legend, Les sequestres d'Altona, The Misanthrope,* and *The Wild Duck.* Performed in Sweden with the Municipal Theatre of Norrkoeping-Linkoeping, 1951-53, the Municipal Theatre of Haelsingborg, 1953-55, the Municipal Theatre of Malmoe, 1955-60, and with the Royal Dramatic Theatre of Stockholm, 1960-74 and 1988; also performed in other Swedish productions.

RECORDINGS

Taped Readings:

(With others) *East of the Sun, West of the Moon,* Rabbit Ears, 1996.

OTHER SOURCES

Periodicals:

Booklist, November 15, 1996, p. 602.

New Republic, May 19, 1997, pp. 26-27.*

WALKER, Andrew Kevin 1964-
(Andrew Kelly, Andy Walker)

PERSONAL

Born in 1964.

Addresses: *Agent*—Gavin Palone, 9465 Wilshire Blvd., Suite 820, Beverly Hills, CA 90212.

Career: Writer and actor.

CREDITS

Film Appearances:
(As Andy Walker) Dead man, *Seven* (also known as *Se7en*), New Line Cinema, 1995.

WRITINGS

Screenplays:
Brainscan, Triumph Releasing, 1994.
Hideaway, TriStar, 1995.
Seven (also known as *Se7en*), New Line Cinema, 1995.
(Uncredited) *The Game,* PolyGram Filmed Entertainment, 1997.
8mm (also known as *8 Millimeter* and *Eight Millimeter*), Columbia, 1999.
Sleepy Hollow, Paramount, 1999.
Rendezvous With Rama, PolyGram Filmed Entertainment, 1999.
Planet of the Apes, Twentieth Century-Fox, forthcoming.

Television Episodes:
"Panic," *Perversions of Science,* HBO, 1997.

Television Specials:
Well-Cooked Hams, HBO, 1993.

OTHER SOURCES

Periodicals:
Entertainment Weekly, September 29, 1995, p. 37; August 8, 1997, p. 37.*

WALKER, Andy
See WALKER, Andrew Kevin

WALTERS, Barbara 1931-

PERSONAL

Full name, Barbara Ann Walters; born September 25, 1931, in Boston, MA; daughter of Lou (a nightclub operator and theatrical producer) and Dena (Selett) Walters; first marriage annulled; married Lee Guber (a theatrical producer), December 8, 1963 (divorced, 1976); married Merv Adelson (a television production executive), May 10, 1986 (divorced); children: (secondmarriage) Jacqueline Dena. *Education:* Sarah Lawrence College, B.A. (English), 1953.

Addresses: *Office—20/20,* 147 Columbus Ave., 10th Floor, New York, NY 10023; and Barbara Walters Specials, Barwall Productions, 825 Seventh Ave., 3rd Floor, New York, NY 10019-6014.

Career: Broadcast journalist and writer. Worked as a writer and producer for WNBC-TV, WPIX, and CBS-TV.

Member: National Association for Help for Mentally Retarded Children (honorary chairperson, 1970).

Awards, Honors: Named among One Hundred Women of Accomplishment, *Harper's Bazaar,* 1967 and 1971; named one of America's Seventy-Five Most Important Women, *Ladies' Home Journal,* 1970; Emmy Award nomination, best host or hostess of a talk, service, or variety series, 1974, for *Not for Women Only;* named Woman of the Year in Communications, 1974; named one of Two Hundred Leaders of the Future, *Time,* 1974; honorary L.H.D. degrees from Ohio State University and Marymount College, Tarrytown, NY, both 1975; Award of the Year, National Association of Television Program Executives, 1975; Emmy Award, best host or hostess of a talk, service, or variety series, 1975, for *The Today Show;* Mass Media Award, Institute for Human Relations, American Jewish Committee, 1975; Illinois Broadcasters Association established the Barbara Walters College Scholarship in Broadcast Journalism, 1975; named Woman of the Year, Theta Sigma Phi, and Broadcaster of the Year, International Radio and Television Society, 1975.

Gold Medal, National Institute of Social Sciences, 1976; Matrix Award, New York Women in Communications, 1977; Lowell Thomas Award, International Platform Association, 1977; Hubert H. Humphrey Freedom Prize, Anti-Defamation League, B'nai B'rith, 1978; named one of the Ten Women of the Decade, *Ladies' Home Journal,* 1979; named one of the Most Important Women of 1979, *Roper Report,* 1979; Emmy Award, best news program segment, and shared Emmy Award, best news and documentary programs and program segments, both 1980, for *ABC News Nightline;* Emmy Awards, best interviewer, 1982 and 1983, and Emmy Award nominations, best informational series, 1984, 1985, 1986, 1987 and 1988, all for *The Barbara Walters Special;* named one of the Women Most Admired by the American People, Gallup Poll, 1982, 1984; honorary L.H.D. degree, Wheaton College, 1983.

Named one of America's One Hundred Most Important Women, *Ladies' Home Journal,* 1983; Emmy Award, best interviewer, 1983, Emmy Award nomination, best interview segment, 1984, Emmy Award nomination, best background/analysis of a single current story, 1987, and Emmy Award, best interview segment, 1988, all for *20/20;* President's Award, Overseas Press Club of America, 1988; Lowell Thomas Award, Marist College, 1990; elected to Hall of Fame, Academy of Television Arts and Sciences, 1990; Lifetime Achievement Award, International Women's Media Foundation, 1992; Distinguished Service Award, National Association of Broadcasters, 1997.

CREDITS

Television Appearances; Series:

Regular correspondent, *The Today Show* (also known as *The Rise and Shine Review*), NBC, 1963-74.

Co-anchor, *The Today Show* (also known as *The Rise and Shine Review*), NBC, 1974-76.

Moderator, *Not for Women Only,* syndicated, 1974-76.

Co-anchor, *The ABC News with Harry Reasoner and Barbara Walters* (now *ABC World News Tonight*), ABC, 1976-78.

Correspondent, *20/20,* ABC, 1981-84.

Co-anchor, *20/20,* ABC, 1984—.

Substitute anchor, *ABC News Nightline* (also known as *Nightline*), ABC, 1991—.

Anchor, *Turning Point,* ABC, 1994.

Host, *The View,* ABC, 1997—.

Television Appearances; Specials:

The Barbara Walters Special, ABC, 1976, 1985-95.

All-Star Celebration Honoring Martin Luther King, Jr., NBC, 1986.

Host, *Liberty Weekend Preview,* ABC, 1986.

Host, *Life: Fifty Years* (also known as *The 50th Anniversary of Life Magazine*), ABC, 1986.

Commentator, *Liberty Weekend,* ABC, 1986.

Today at 35, NBC, 1987.

A Star-Spangled Celebration, ABC, 1987.

Sesame Street Special, PBS, 1988.

Host, *The 50th Barbara Walters Special,* ABC, 1988.

Anchor, *America's Kids: Why They Flunk* (also known as *Burning Questions*), ABC, 1988.

Fifty Years of Celebration: A Golden Celebration, CBS, 1989.

Reporter, *Presidential Inauguration,* ABC, 1989.

Anchor, *Survival Stories: Growing Up Down and Out* (also known as *Kids in Trouble: Fighting Back*), ABC, 1989.

America's Kids: Teaching Them to Think (also known as *Burning Questions*), ABC, 1989.

The 6th Annual Television Academy Hall of Fame, Fox, 1990.

Night of 100 Stars III, NBC, 1990.

Fifteen Years of MacNeil/Lehrer, PBS, 1990.

Presenter, *The 48th Alfred I. Dupont—Columbia University Awards,* PBS, 1990.

Anchor, *The Perfect Baby,* ABC, 1990.

The Best of Disney: 50 Years of Magic, ABC, 1991.

Host, *The Best of Barbara Walters: Legend—The New Generation,* ABC, 1992.

Donahue: The 25th Anniversary, NBC, 1992.

Host, *Twentysomething: What Happened to the American Dream?,* ABC, 1992.

Today at 40, NBC, 1992.
Legend to Legend Night, NBC, 1993.
Kathie Lee Gifford's Celebration of Motherhood, ABC, 1993.
The 12 Most Fascinating People of 1993, ABC, 1993.
Narrator, *In a New Light '93,* ABC, 1993.
Host, *What Is This Thing Called Love? The Barbara Walters Special,* ABC, 1993.
Host, *One on One: Classic Television Interviews,* CBS, 1993.
Host, *Great Television Moments: What We Watched,* ABC, 1993.
Host, *20/20 15th Anniversary Special,* ABC, 1993.
Segment host, "Watching History Happen," *ABC's 40th Anniversary Special,* ABC, 1994.
Presenter, *The Essence Awards,* Fox, 1994.
Host, "25/25," *Sesame Street's All-Star 25th Birthday: Stars and Street Forever!,* ABC, 1994.
Host, *In a New Light '94,* ABC, 1994.
Host, *The Barbara Walters Special: Happy Hour,* ABC, 1994.

Television Appearances; Episodic:
Correspondent, *World News Tonight,* ABC, 1978.
ABC News Nightline (also known as *Nightline*), ABC, 1980.
"Edward R. Murrow: This Reporter," *American Masters,* PBS, 1990.
Host, "Switched at Birth: Kimberly's Story," *Turning Point,* ABC, 1993.

Also appeared in episodes of *Issues and Answers,* ABC.

Television Work; Series:
Co-executive producer, *The View,* ABC, 1997—.

Television Work; Specials:
Executive producer, *The Barbara Walters Special,* ABC, 1992-93.

Stage Appearances:
Night of 100 Stars III, Radio City Music Hall, New York City, 1990.

Radio Appearances:
Moderator of the radio programs *Emphasis* and *Monitor.*

WRITINGS

Television Specials:
The Perfect Baby, ABC, 1990.
The Barbara Walters Special, ABC, 1990-94.
The Best of Barbara Walters: Legend—The New Generation, ABC, 1992.
What Is This Thing Called Love? The Barbara Walters Special, ABC, 1993.
20/20 15th Anniversary Special, ABC, 1993.
The Barbara Walters Special: Happy Hour, ABC, 1994.

Writer for *Issues and Answers,* ABC.

Television Series:
The Today Show (also known as *The Rise and Shine Review*), NBC, 1961-63.

Books:
How to Talk with Practically Anybody about Practically Anything, Doubleday (New York City), 1970.

Contributor to periodicals, including *Family Weekly, Good Housekeeping,* and *Reader's Digest.*

OTHER SOURCES

Periodicals:
Ladies' Home Journal, April, 1996, p. 128.
Life, November, 1997, p. 36.
Nation, December 15, 1997, p. 36.
Newsweek, May 6, 1974; May 3, 1976; October 11, 1976.
New York Times, May 2, 1976; August 23, 1992.
People Weekly, June 21, 1982; May 26, 1986.
Time, May 3, 1976; October 18, 1976.
Washington Star, April 23, 1976.*

WERNER, Tom 1950-

PERSONAL

Born in 1950, in New York City; married Jill (in business); children: Teddy, Carolyn, Amanda. *Education:* Harvard University, B.A., 1971.

Addresses: *Office*—Carsey-Werner Company, 4024 Radford Ave., Studio City, CA 91604.

Career: Television producer. ABC-TV, began as researcher, became programming executive, 1972-81; Carsey-Werner Company, Studio City, CA, partner and producer (both with Marcy Carsey), 1981—. Worked as a documentary filmmaker; member of the board of directors of the Old Globe Theatre. San Diego Padres baseball team, San Diego, CA, chair, 1991-94.

Member: Sharp Hospital (member of the board of directors).

Awards, Honors: Emmy Award (with Marcy Carsey and others), outstanding primetime comedy series, 1984, and Emmy Award nominations (with Marcy Carsey and others), outstanding primetime comedy series, 1985 and 1986, all for *The Cosby Show;* Image Award (with Marcy Carsey), National Association for the Advancement of Colored People, best episode in a comedy series or special, 1989, for an episode of *A Different World;* Wise Owl Award runner up (with Marcy Carsey, Jay Daniel, and Bruce Helford), Retirement Research Foundation, 1993, for *Roseanne;* inducted with Marcy Carsey into the Broadcasting and Cable Hall of Fame, 1996; Emmy Award nomination (with others), outstanding comedy series, 1998, for *3rd Rock from the Sun.*

CREDITS

Television Work; Executive Producer; With Marcy Carsey; Series:
Oh, Madeline, ABC, 1983-84.
The Cosby Show, NBC, 1984-92.
A Different World, NBC, 1987-93.
Roseanne, ABC, 1988-97.
Chicken Soup, ABC, 1989-90.
Grand, NBC, 1990.
Davis Rules, ABC, 1991, CBS, 1991-92.
You Bet Your Life, syndicated, 1992.
Frannie's Turn, CBS, 1992.
Grace under Fire (also known as *Grace under Pressure*), ABC, 1994-97.
Cybill, CBS, 1995-98.
Townies, ABC, 1996.
Men Behaving Badly, NBC, 1996-98.
3rd Rock from the Sun, NBC, 1996—.
Cosby, CBS, 1996—.
Damon, Fox, 1998-99.
That '70s Show (also known as *Feelin' All Right, The Kids Are Alright, Reeling in the Years,* and *Teenage Wasteland*), Fox, 1998—.

Television Work; Producer; With Others; Series:
She TV, ABC, 1994.

Television Work; Executive Producer; Movies:
(With Marcy Carsey and Michael O'Donoghue) *Single Bars, Single Women,* ABC, 1984.

Television Work; Executive Producer; With Marcy Carsey; Specials:
I Do, I Don't, 1983.
A Carol Burnett Special . . . Carol, Carl, Whoopi, and Robin, ABC, 1987.
Brett Butler: The Child Ain't Right, HBO, 1993.

OTHER SOURCES

Periodicals:
Broadcasting & Cable, November 18, 1996, pp. 28-30.
Time, September 23, 1996, pp. 68-70.*

WEST, Kevin

Addresses: *Agent*—The Artists Group, 10100 Santa Monica Blvd., Suite 2490, Century City, CA 90067. *Contact*—L.A. Talent, 8335 Sunset Blvd., Los Angeles, CA 90069.

Career: Actor. Has appeared in television commercials for Sprite (1987), Little Caesar's Pizza (1988), Rice Krispies (voice of Snap, 1990-96), Budweiser (1992), Claussen Pickles (1992), Bud Light (1993), Baskin-Robbins (1994), York Peppermint Patties (1996), Hallmark Cards (1997), Kodak (1997), AMD (1997), Reese's Peanut-Buttercups (1998), Frosted Cheerios (with Kathy Griffin, 1999), and Pop Tarts (1999).

Awards, Honors: Best Male Performance of the Year Award.

CREDITS

Film Appearances:
Stunts, *Cowboys Don't Cry,* 1988.
Second executive, *She's Out of Control,* Columbia, 1989.
Himself, *Moon of the Desperados,* 1990.
Bank teller, *Killer Tomatoes Strike Back,* Twentieth Century-Fox Video, 1990.
Concert MC, *Killer Tomatoes Eat France,* New World, 1991.
Egghead, *Killer Instinct* (also known as *Homicidal Impulse*), 1991.
First thug, *Delusion,* IRS Releasing, 1991.
Tour guide, *The Opposite Sex and How To Live With Them,* 1992.
Technician (with tigers), *Toys,* Twentieth Century-Fox, 1992.
Screenwriter, *Indecent Proposal,* Paramount, 1993.
Devo Controller, *Super Mario Bros.* (also known as *Super Mario Brothers*), Buena Vista, 1993.

Dorky man, *Last Resort* (also known as *National Lampoon's Last Resort* and *National Lampoon's Scuba School*), 1994.
Store clerk, *Clean Slate,* Metro-Goldwyn-Mayer, 1994.
Gay man, *Blankman,* Columbia, 1994.
Lyndon Executive, *Junior,* Universal, 1994.
Vincent Montgomery, *Houseguest,* Buena Vista, 1995.
T.C. Romulus, *Bio-Dome,* Metro-Goldwyn-Mayer, 1996.
(Uncredited) Pencilman, *Heaven's Prisoners,* New Line Cinema, 1996.
Dr. Flint, *Santa With Muscles,* Legacy Releasing/Santa Productions Inc., 1996.
Purple Lips, *L.A. Without a Map* (also known as *I Love L.A.* [France], *Los Angeles Without a Map,* and *Go! Go! L.A.* [Japan]), SND, 1998.
The Pharmacist, *Let the Devil Wear Black,* Trimark Pictures, 1999.
Bank manager, *Four Dogs Playing Poker,* 1999.
Vern, *Coyote Moon,* Paramount/Viacom, 1999.
Clyde, *Can't Stop Dancing,* 1999.

Television Appearances; Episodic:
Electrician, *All My Children,* ABC, 1970.
Crazy Delivery Man, *We Got It Made,* NBC/syndicated, 1988.
Juju, "Pilot," *Babes,* Fox, 1990.
Gene, "A Perfect Match," *Tequila and Bonetti,* CBS, 1992.
Mr. Stimpleman, "Back 2 School," *Boy Meets World,* ABC, 1994.
Stan Sells, "Long Arm of the Law," *Land's End,* syndicated, 1996.
Ahmed, "Pilot," *High Incident,* ABC, 1996. Ahmed, "Father Knows Best," *High Incident,* ABC, 1996.
Wally, "Janitor Dad," *Boy Meets World,* ABC, 1996.
Doctor, "Caroline and the Buyer," *Caroline in the City,* NBC, 1997.
Dave Stale, "He Got Job," *Kenan & Kel,* Nickelodeon Network, 1998.
Squid, "Wave Goodbye," *Black Scorpion,* 1998.
Beyond Belief: Fact or Fiction (also known as *Beyond Belief*), 1998.
Dr. Adam Toma, "The Bad Seed," *Team Knight Rider,* 1998.
Jeremy, "Bloodlines (1)," *The Pretender,* NBC, 1998.
Jeremy, "Bloodlines (2)," *The Pretender,* NBC, 1998.
Ziggy, "Cirque Du Skeeter," *Cousin Skeeter,* Nickelodeon Network, 1998.
Voice, *Disney's Hercules,* ABC, 1998.
Fred, *Sliders,* Fox, 1998.
Powder Man, "Wagon Train Pt. 1," *The Magnificent Seven,* CBS, 1999.

Television Appearances; Movies:
Toy store clerk, *Angel of Death,* CBS, 1990.

Television Appearances; Specials:
Origami man, *ABC's World's Funniest Commercials,* ABC, 1994.

Television Work:
Associate producer, *The Jon Stewart Show,* MTV, 1993.
Producer, *Steve Earle: To Hell and Back* (special), MTV, 1996.

Stage Appearances:
D'Oyly Carte Opera Company Gilbert & Sullivan, New York State Theater, New York City, 1978.*

WHALEY, Frank 1963-

PERSONAL

Born July 20, 1963, in Syracuse, NY. *Education:* Graduate of State University of New York at Albany.

Addresses: *Contact*—Shelter Entertainment, 9255 Sunset Blvd., Suite 1010, Los Angeles, CA 90069.

Career: Actor, musician, director, and writer. The Niagras (band), co-founder and drummer.

Awards, Honors: Grand Jury Prize nomination, Sundance Film Festival, 1999, for *Joe the King.*

CREDITS

Film Appearances:
Young Francis, *Ironweed,* TriStar, 1987.
Archie Graham, *Field of Dreams* (also known as *Shoeless Joe*), Universal, 1989.
Boy, *Little Monsters,* Metro-Goldwyn-Mayer, 1989.
Timmy, *Born on the Fourth of July,* Universal, 1989.
Steve Bushak, *The Freshman,* TriStar, 1990.
Michael Latchmer, *Cold Dog Soup,* 1990.
Robby Kreiger, *The Doors,* TriStar, 1991.
Jim Dodge, *Career Opportunities* (also known as *One Wild Night*), Universal, 1991.
Fake Oswald, *JFK,* 1991.
Archer Sloan, *Back in the U.S.S.R.,* Twentieth Century-Fox, 1992.
Father Paul Mundy, *A Midnight Clear,* InterStar Releasing, 1992.
Young Kid, *Hoffa,* Twentieth Century-Fox, 1992.

Arvid, *Swing Kids,* Buena Vista, 1993.
Brett, *Pulp Fiction,* Miramax, 1994.
Guy, *Swimming with Sharks* (also known as *The Boss* and *The Buddy Factor*), Trimark, 1994.
Frank, *I.Q.,* 1994.
Walter Cooper, *The Desperate Trail,* 1994.
Archie Landrum, *Homage,* Arrow Releasing, 1995.
Mickey Jelke, *Cafe Society,* Columbia/TriStar Home Video, 1995.
Joey, *The Winner,* Live Entertainment/Norstar Entertainment, 1996.
Himself, *Cannes Man,* Rocket Pictures Home Video, 1996.
Malcolm, *Bombshell,* Crystal Sky International/ Trimark, 1996.
Giles Prentice, *Broken Arrow,* Twentieth Century-Fox, 1996.
Brian, *Retroactive,* Orion Pictures Entertainment, 1997.
Frankie, *Glam,* Storm Entertainment, 1997.
Brett (in archival footage), *You're Still Not Fooling Anybody,* 1997.
Skee-ball Weasel, *Went to Coney Island on a Mission from God . . . Be Back by Five,* 1998.
Brett Conway, *Curtain Call* (also known as *Later Life*), 1998.
The Wall, 1998.

Film Work:
Director, *Joe the King* (also known as *Pleasant View Avenue*), 1999.

Television Appearances; Movies:
Arnie Woods, *Unconquered* (also known as *Invictus*), CBS, 1989.
Joey, *Flying Blind,* NBC, 1990.
James, "To Dance with the White Dog," *Hallmark Hall of Fame,* CBS, 1993.
Lee Harvey Oswald/Alik, *Fatal Deception: Mrs. Lee Harvey Oswald* (also known as *Marina's Story*), NBC, 1993.
Cole, "My Brother's Keeper," *Dead Man's Gun,* ABC, 1997.
Chamberlain, *When Trumpets Fade,* 1998.

Television Appearances; Specials:
Jeff Dillon, "Seasonal Differences," *ABC Afterschool Specials,* ABC, 1987.
Scott McNichol, "Soldier Boys," *CBS Schoolbreak Specials,* CBS, 1987.

Television Appearances; Series:
Bob Jones, *Buddy Faro,* CBS, 1998.

Television Appearances; Episodic:
Henry Marshall, "The Conversion," *The Outer Limits,* Showtime, 1995.

Other Television Appearances:
Sonny Day, *Life on the Flipside* (pilot; also known as *Homeward Bound* and *Pop Rock*), NBC, 1988.

Stage Appearances:
Cob, *Tigers Wild,* Playhouse 91, New York City, 1986.
The Years, Stage I, City Center Theatre, New York City, 1993.
Jimmy Bonaparte, *Veins and Thumbtacks,* Malaparte Theatre Company, Theatre Row Theatre, New York City, 1994.
Jacob, *Hesh,* Malaparte Theatre Company, Theatre Row Theatre, 1994.
Tom Casey, *The Great Unwashed,* Malaparte Theatre Company, Theatre Row Theatre, 1994.
Peter Hogancamp, *The Size of the World,* Circle Repertory Company, Circle in the Square Theatre, New York City, 1996.

Also appeared in a production of *Good Evening.*

WRITINGS

Screenplays:
Joe the King (also known as *Pleasant View Avenue*), 1999.

OTHER SOURCES

Periodicals:
Back Stage, April 5, 1996, p. 5.
Entertainment Weekly, April 25, 1997, p. 81.*

WILDER, Gene 1935-
(Jerry Silberman)

PERSONAL

Born Jerome Silberman, June 11, 1935, in Milwaukee, WI; son of William J. (an importer) and Jeanne (maiden name, Baer) Silberman; married Mary Joan Schutz, October 27, 1967 (divorced, 1974); married Gilda Radner (an actress and comedienne), 1982 (marriage ended with her death, May 20, 1989); married Karen Boyer, September 8, 1991; children: (first marriage) Katharine Anastasia. *Education:* University of Iowa, B.A., 1955; studied acting with Herman Gottlieb, 1946-51, at the Bristol Old Vic

Theatre School, 1955-56, at the Herbert Berghof Studio, 1957-59, and at the Actors Studio. *Avocational interests:* Tennis, fencing, and bridge.

Addresses: *Office*—Pal-Mel Productions, 1511 Sawtelle Blvd., Number 155, Los Angeles, CA 90025-3262. *Agent*—William Morris Agency, 151 El Camino Dr., Beverly Hills, CA 90212-2775.

Career: Actor, director, producer, and screenwriter. Worked variously as a chauffeur, toy salesman, and fencing instructor. Actors Studio, New York City, member, 1961—; Gilda Radner Ovarian Detection Center, Cedars-Sinai Medical Center, Los Angeles, CA, co-founder. *Military service:* U.S. Army, 1956-58.

Member: Actors' Equity Association, American Federation of Television and Radio Artists.

Awards, Honors: Clarence Derwent Award, 1962, for *The Complaisant Lover;* Academy Award nomination, best supporting actor, 1968, for *The Producers;* Golden Globe Award nomination, best motion picture actor—musical/comedy, 1972, for *Willy Wonka & the Chocolate Factory;* Academy Award nomination, best screenplay adapted from other material (with Mel Brooks), 1974, and Nebula Award, best dramatic presentation, 1975, both for *Young Frankenstein;* Golden Globe Award nomination, best motion picture actor—musical/comedy, 1977, for *Silver Streak.*

CREDITS

Film Appearances:

(Film debut) Eugene Grizzard, *Bonnie and Clyde,* Warner Bros., 1967.

Leo Bloom, *The Producers,* Embassy, 1967.

Quackser Fortune (title role), *Quackser Fortune Has a Cousin in the Bronx* (also known as *Fun Loving*), UMC, 1970.

Claude Coupe and Philippe DeSisi, *Start the Revolution without Me* (also known as *Two Times Two*), Warner Bros., 1970.

Willy Wonka (title role), *Willy Wonka and the Chocolate Factory,* Paramount, 1971.

Dr. Ross, *Everything You Always Wanted to Know about Sex* (*but were afraid to ask),* United Artists, 1972.

Jim, the Waco kid, *Blazing Saddles,* Warner Bros., 1974.

The Fox, *The Little Prince,* Paramount, 1974.

Stanley, *Rhinoceros,* American Film Theatre, 1974.

Dr. Frederick Frankenstein, *Young Frankenstein* (also known as *Frankenstein, Jr.*), Twentieth Century-Fox, 1974.

Sigerson Holmes, *The Adventures of Sherlock Holmes' Smarter Brother,* Twentieth Century-Fox, 1975.

George Caldwell, *Silver Streak,* Twentieth Century-Fox, 1976.

Rudy Valentine, *The World's Greatest Lover,* Twentieth Century-Fox, 1977.

Avram Belinsky, *The Frisco Kid* (also known as *No Knife*), Warner Bros., 1979.

Skip Donahue, *Stir Crazy,* Columbia, 1980.

Title role, "Skippy," *Sunday Lovers,* United Artists, 1980.

Michael Jordon, *Hanky Panky,* Columbia, 1982.

Theodore Pierce, *The Woman in Red,* Orion, 1984.

Larry Abbot, *Haunted Honeymoon,* Orion, 1986.

Hello Actors Studio (documentary), Actors Studio, 1987.

Dave, *See No Evil, Hear No Evil,* TriStar, 1989.

Duffy Bergman, *Funny about Love,* Paramount, 1990.

George/Abe Fielding, *Another You,* TriStar, 1991.

Voice of Snowbell, *Stuart Little,* Sony Pictures Entertainment, 1999.

Film Director, Except Where Indicated:

The Adventures of Sherlock Holmes' Smarter Brother, Twentieth Century-Fox, 1975.

And producer, *The World's Greatest Lover,* Twentieth Century-Fox, 1977.

Second unit director, *The Fish That Saved Pittsburgh,* 1979.

"Skippy," *Sunday Lovers,* United Artists, 1980.

The Woman in Red, Orion, 1984.

And producer, *Haunted Honeymoon,* Orion, 1986.

Television Appearances; Series:

Gene Bergman, *Something Wilder* (also known as *Young at Heart*), NBC, 1994.

Television Appearances; Episodic:

Happy Penny, "Wingless Victory," *Play of the Week,* WNTA, 1961.

Muller, "The Sound of Hunting," *Dupont Show of the Week,* NBC, 1962.

The Reporter, "Windfall," *Dupont Show of the Week,* NBC, 1962.

Wilson, "The Interrogators," *Dupont Show of the Week,* NBC, 1962.

German voice, *The Twentieth Century,* CBS, 1962.

Head waiter, "Reunion with Death," *The Defenders,* CBS, 1962.

Armstrong Circle Theatre, CBS, 1962.

Yonkel, "Home for Passover," *Eternal Light,* NBC, 1966.
"The Scarecrow," *Hollywood Television Theater,* PBS, 1972.
Inside the Actors Studio, 1995.
Himself, *The Frank Skinner Show,* 1997.

Television Appearances; Movies:
Lord Ravensbane/The Scarecrow, *The Scarecrow,* 1973.
Harry Evers, *Thursday's Game,* ABC, 1974.
Larry "Cash" Carter, *Murder in a Small Town,* PBS, 1999.
Mock Turtle, *Alice in Wonderland,* NBC, 1999.

Television Appearances; Specials:
Bernard, *Death of a Salesman,* CBS, 1966.
Ernie, "The Office Sharers," *The Trouble with People,* NBC, 1972.
Marlo Thomas in Acts of Love and Other Comedies, ABC, 1973.
Home for Passover, NBC, 1973.
Annie and the Hoods, ABC, 1974.
Baryshnikov in Hollywood, CBS, 1982.
Face to Face with Connie Chung, CBS, 1990.
A Party for Richard Pryor, CBS, 1991.
Laughing Matters (also known as *Funny Business*), Showtime, 1993.
Gilda Radner: In Her Own Words, Arts and Entertainment, 1993.
Countdown to Christmas (also known as *Santa's Journey*), NBC, 1994.
Gilda Radner: The E! True Hollywood Story, E! Entertainment Channel, 1997.

Stage Appearances:
(Stage debut) Balthazar, *Romeo and Juliet,* Milwaukee Playhouse, Milwaukee, WI, 1948.
Rosen, *The Late Christopher Bean,* Reginald Goode Theatre, Poughkeepsie, NY, 1949.
The Cat and the Canary, Reginald Goode Theatre, 1949.
Vernon, *Summer and Smoke,* Tower Ranch Tenthouse Theatre, Eagle River, WI, 1951.
The Drunkard, Tower Ranch Tenthouse Theatre, 1951.
Mansky, *The Play's the Thing,* Tower Ranch Tenthouse Theatre, 1951.
Mr. Weatherbee, *Arsenic and Old Lace,* Tower Ranch Tenthouse Theatre, 1951.
Howard, *Death of a Salesman,* Tower Ranch Tenthouse Theatre, 1952.
Ed, *Come Back, Little Sheba,* Tower Ranch Tenthouse Theatre, 1952.
The Principal, *The Happy Time,* Tower Ranch Tenthouse Theatre, 1952.
Twelfth Night, Cambridge Drama Festival, Cambridge, MA, 1959.
Macbeth, Cambridge Drama Festival, 1959.
(Off-Broadway debut) Frankie Bryant, *Roots,* Mayfair Theatre, 1961.
Andrew, *All the Way Home,* Playhouse-in-the-Park, Philadelphia, PA, 1961.
Hotel valet, *The Complaisant Lover,* Ethel Barrymore Theatre, New York City, 1961.
The Captain, *Mother Courage and Her Children,* Martin Beck Theatre, New York City, 1963.
Billie Bibbit, *One Flew over the Cuckoo's Nest,* Cort Theatre, New York City, 1963.
Smiley, *Dynamite Tonight,* York Theatre, New York City, 1964.
Various roles, *The White House,* Henry Miller's Theatre, New York City, 1964.
Harry Berlin, *Luv,* Royal Poinciana Playhouse, Palm Beach, FL, then Booth Theatre, New York City, both 1966.
Max Prince, *Laughter on the 23rd Floor,* Queens Theatre, London, England, 1996.

Major Tours:
Hotel valet, *The Complaisant Lover,* U.S. cities, 1962.
Julius Sagamore, *The Millionairess,* Theatre Guild, U.S. cities, 1963.
Various roles, *The White House,* U.S. cities, 1964.

Stage Work; Fencing Choreographer:
Twelfth Night, Cambridge Drama Festival, 1959.
Macbeth, Cambridge Drama Festival, 1959.

WRITINGS

Screenplays, Except Where Indicated:
(With Mel Brooks) *Young Frankenstein* (also known as *Frankenstein, Jr.*), Twentieth Century-Fox, 1974.
The Adventures of Sherlock Holmes' Smarter Brother, Twentieth Century-Fox, 1975.
The World's Greatest Lover, Twentieth Century-Fox, 1977.
"Skippy," *Sunday Lovers,* United Artists, 1980.
Also song writer, *The Woman in Red,* Orion, 1984.
(With Terence Marsh) *Haunted Honeymoon,* Orion, 1986.
(With Earl Barret, Arne Sultan, Eliot Wald, and Andrew Kurtzman) *See No Evil, Hear No Evil,* TriStar, 1989.

Television Writing; Movies:
Murder in a Small Town, PBS, 1999.

Books:
(With M. Steven Piver) *Gilda's Disease,* 1996.

OTHER SOURCES

Periodicals:
Us, May 29, 1989, pp. 30-37.*

WILLIAMS, Heathcote 1941-

PERSONAL

Born November 15, 1941, in Helsby, Cheshire, England; son of Heathcote Williams (a lawyer). *Education:* Studied law at Christ Church, Oxford.

Addresses: *Office*—c/o Curtis Brown, 168 Regent St., London W1R 5TB, England. *Agent*—Judy Daish Associates, 83 Eastbourne Mews, London W2 6LQ, England.

Career: Actor and writer. *Transatlantic Review,* London, England, associate editor, 1963-72; founding editor of the periodical *Fanatic* and (with Germaine Greer and others) of the Dutch periodical *Suck.* Member of theperforming group the Magic Circle; worked as a magician and fire eater. Also ran a squatting agency in Notting Hill, London, England.

Awards, Honors: *Evening Standard* Drama Award and Obie Award, *Village Voice,* both 1970, for *AC/DC;* George Devine Award, 1970; John Whiting Award, 1971.

CREDITS

Film Appearances:
Prospero, *The Tempest,* World Northal, 1980.
Dr. Holroyd, *Wish You Were Here* (also known as *Too Much*), Atlantic Releasing, 1987.
Peter Reed, *Stormy Monday,* Atlantic Releasing, 1988.
Dr. Haggage, *Little Dorrit* (also known as *Little Dorrit's Story* and *Nobody's Fault*), Cannon Screen Entertainment, 1988.
Man on the stairs, *Slipstream,* Atlantic Releasing, 1989.
Nick Greene and a publisher, *Orlando,* Adventure Pictures, 1993.
Jeremiah, *The Steal,* Poseidon Pictures, 1994.
Stephan Nuslauer, *In the Cold Light of Day* (also known as *The Cold Light of Day*), Meteor Film Productions, 1994.
Dr. Lake, *The Browning Version,* Paramount, 1994.
Shaper, *Blue Juice,* Skreba Films, 1995.
Looking for Richard, Twentieth Century-Fox, 1996.
Jeff, *Bring Me the Head of Mavis Davis,* Goldcrest Films, 1997.
Builder, *The Tango Lesson* (also known as *La lecon de tango*), Sony Pictures Classics, 1997.
Drosselmeier, *The IMAX Nutcracker,* IMAX Corporation/Sands Films, 1997.
Nucingen, *Cousin Bette,* Fox Searchlight Pictures, 1998.
La leggenda del pianista sull'oceano (also known as *A Pianist on the Ocean*), Fine Line Features, 1998.

Film Work; Director:
Wet Dreams, [the Netherlands and West Germany (now Germany)], 1974.

Television Appearances; Miniseries:
Laocoon, *The Odyssey* (also known as *Homer's Odyssey* and *Die Abenteuer des Odysseus*), NBC, 1997.

Television Appearances; Movies:
Marcello, *Alegria,* CTV, 1998.
Mr. Eaglet, *Alice in Wonderland,* NBC, 1999.

Television Appearances; Specials:
Josef Solokow, *Malatesta,* BBC, 1969.
W. S. H. (also known as *Weird S**t Happens*), BBC, 1994.

Television Appearances; Episodic:
Older guest, "The One with Ross's Wedding" (part two), *Friends,* NBC, 1998.

RECORDINGS

Taped Readings:
The Poetry Olympics, Volume 1, All Round Records, 1982.
(With others) *The New Testament: Selections from the Bible,* Naxos AudioBooks, 1997.

WRITINGS

Plays:
The Local Stigmatic, Traverse Theatre, Edinburgh, Scotland, then produced in London, England, 1966, later produced in Boston, MA, 1967, and Actors Playhouse, New York City, 1969, published in *Traverse Plays,* edited by Jim Haynes, Penguin (Harmondsworth, England), 1966, pub-

lished with *AC/DC* as *AC/DC and The Local Stigmatic: Two Plays,* Viking (New York City), 1973.

AC/DC, Royal Court Theatre, London, England, 1970, then Chelsea Theatre Center, Brooklyn Academy of Music, Brooklyn, New York City, 1971, later Goodman Theatre, Chicago, IL, 1975-76, published by Calder & Boyars (London, England), 1972, published with *The Local Stigmatic* as *AC/DC and The Local Stigmatic: Two Plays,* Viking, 1973.

(With W. Gaskill and M. Stafford-Clark) *The Speakers* (based on Williams's novel of the same name), produced in Birmingham, England, 1974, published with *Remember the Truth Dentist,* Calder & Boyars, 1980.

(With B. Flagg) *Remember the Truth Dentist,* produced in London, England, 1974, published with *The Speakers,* Calder & Boyars, 1980.

A Christmas Pantomine Play, produced in London, England, 1975.

(With T. Allen) *Very Tasty—A Pantomime,* produced in London, England, 1975.

An Invitation to the Official Lynching of Michael Abdul Malik, produced in Newcastle-upon-Tyne, England, 1975.

Anatomy of a Space Rat, produced in 1976.

Playpen, Royal Court Theatre, 1977.

The Immortalist, produced in London, England, 1977, published by J. Calder (London, England), 1978.

Hancock's Last Half-Hour, produced in London, England, 1977, then PAF Playhouse, Huntington Station, NY, 1978, edited by Ed Berman and published by Interaction, 1977.

Severe Joy, published by Calder & Boyars, 1979.

"At It," *Breach of the Peace,* Bush Theatre, London, England, 1982, then produced alone, Edinburgh, Scotland, and London, England, both 1983.

Whales, produced in Liverpool, England, and London, England, both 1986.

Screenplays:

(With Eddie Constantine and Vladimir Pucholt) *Crash,* 1980.

The Local Stigmatic, Chal Productions, 1986.

Also wrote *The Extraordinary Episodes of William Beckford.*

Teleplays; Specials:

(With Eddie Constantine and Vladimir Pucholt) *Malatesta,* BBC, 1969.

(With others) *What the Dickens!,* Channel Four, 1984.

Autogeddon, 1991.

Also wrote *The Caliph of Fonthill,* BBC.

Novels:

The Speakers, Hutchinson (London, England), 1964, Grove (New York City), 1967, adapted as a play with W. Gaskill and M. Stafford-Clark and produced in Birmingham, England, 1974, stage version published with *Remember the Truth Dentist,* Calder & Boyars, 1980.

Poetry:

Autogeddon, Zweitausendeins (Frankfurt am Main, Germany), 1985, Arcade (New York City), 1991.

Whale Nation, Harmony Books (New York City), 1988.

Falling for a Dolphin, Harmony Books, 1989.

Sacred Elephant, Harmony Books, 1989.

Comics:

Elephants, Knockabout Comics (London), 1981.

Nonfiction:

Manifestoes, Manifesten, Cold Turkey Press (Rotterdam, the Netherlands), 1975.

Contributor to periodicals, including the *Beast, Guardian, New Statesman* and the *Whole Earth Review.*

OTHER SOURCES

Books:

Findlater, Richard, editor, *At the Royal Court: Twenty-five Years of the English Stage Company,* Grove, 1981.

King, Kimball, *Twenty Modern British Playwrights, a Bibliography, 1956-1976,* Garland (New York City), 1977.

Taylor, John Russell, *The Second Wave: New British Drama for the Seventies,* Hill and Wang (New York City), 1971.*

WILLIAMS, Pat
See WILLIAMS, Patrick

WILLIAMS, Patrick 1939-
(Pat Williams)

PERSONAL

Full name, Patrick Moody Williams; born April 23, 1939, in Bonne Terre, MO; son of Wilson Moody and Jean (Murphy) Williams; married Catherine Greer, April 7, 1962; children: Elizabeth, Greer, Patrick. *Education:* Duke University, B.A., 1961. *Politics:* Democrat.

Addresses: *Office*—13245 Riverside Dr., Sherman Oaks, CA, 91423. *Agent*—Gorfaine/Schwartz Agency, 3301 Barham Blvd., Suite 201, Los Angeles, CA 90068.

Career: Composer. University of Utah, visiting professor, 1970-71; University of Colorado, visiting professor, 1975-77; Soundwings (recording company), owner, 1986—. *Military service:* U.S. Army.

Member: Academy of Motion Picture Arts and Sciences, Academy of Recording Arts and Sciences, Broadcast Music, Inc.

Awards, Honors: Grammy Award nomination (with Burt Bacharach), best arrangement accompanying a vocalist, 1971, for "Long Ago Tomorrow"; Grammy Award, best instrumental arrangement, and Grammy Award nomination, best jazz—big band arrangement, both 1974, for *Threshold;* Emmy Award nomination, outstanding achievement in music composition for a series, 1974, for *The Streets of San Francisco;* Pulitzer Prize nomination for music, 1977, for *AnAmerican Concerto;* Emmy Award nomination, outstanding achievement in music composition for a series, 1977, for *Columbo;* Emmy Award, outstanding achievement in music composition for a series, 1979, Emmy Award nominations, outstanding achievement in music composition for a series, 1978, 1980, 1981, all for *Lou Grant;* Academy Award nomination, best music, original song score and its adaptation, or best adapted score, 1980, for *Breaking Away;* Grammy Award nominations, best instrumental composition and best jazz fusion performance—vocal or instrumental, both 1980, for *An American Concerto;* Emmy Award, outstanding achievement in music composition for a limited series or special, 1981, for *The Princess and the Cabbie.*

Grammy Award nomination, best instrumental arrangement, 1983, for "Too Hip for the Room"; Emmy Award nomination, outstanding achievement in music composition for a series, 1983, for *Mr. Smith;* honorary doctorate, University of Colorado, 1983; Emmy Award nomination, outstanding achievement in music composition for a limited series or special, 1985, for *Seduced;* Grammy Award, best instrumental arrangement, 1986, for "Suite Memories"; Emmy Award nominations, outstanding achievement in music composition for a series, 1986 and 1987, both for *The Days and Nights of Molly Dodd;* Grammy Award nomination, best instrumental arrangement, 1987, for "Jive Samba"; Emmy Award nomination, outstanding achievement in music composition for a miniseries or a special, 1990, for *Decoration Day;* CableACE Award, 1994; Emmy Award nomination, outstanding individual achievement in music composition for a miniseries or a special, 1995, for *Kingfish: A Story of Huey P. Long;* Richard Kirk Award, Broadcast Music, Inc., 1998, for career achievement; another Emmy Award; other nominations for Emmy, Grammy, and CableAce Awards.

CREDITS

Film Work:

Orchestrator, *Shampoo,* Columbia, 1975.

Music director, *Just between Friends,* Orion, 1986.

Producer of music score, *Worth Winning,* Twentieth Century-Fox, 1989.

Film Appearances:

Performer of songs "Anything Goes," "Isn't It Romantic?," "Our Love Is Here to Stay," "That Old Feeling," "There Will Never Be Another You," "Where or When," "You Do Something to Me," "You Took Advantage of Me," *That Old Feeling,* Universal, 1997.

Television Appearances; Specials:

Sinatra Duets (documentary), CBS, 1994.

Stage Work:

Orchestrator (with Jack Andrews), *Golden Rainbow,* Sam S. Shubert Theatre, New York City, 1968.

RECORDINGS

Albums:

Threshold (includes "Threshold"), Capitol, 1974.

The Silent Spring, 1974.

Rhapsody, 1975.

An American Concerto, Keel One Music, 1977, Columbia, 1980.

Dreams and Themes (includes "Too Hip for the Room"), PCM, 1983.

Gulliver, Soundwings, 1985.

Romances, 1986.

An Overture to a Time, 1990.

Sinatraland, Capitol, 1998.

Other Recordings:

Theme for Earth Day, 1990.

Also recorded "New Orleans Knows" (with lyrics by Will Jennings).

Studio Work; Albums:

Arranger, musical director and conductor, Frank Sinatra, *Duets,* Capitol, 1993.

Arranger, musical director, and conductor, Frank Sinatra, *Duets II,* Capitol, 1994.

Also arranged albums for Gloria Estefan, Billy Joel, and Barbra Streisand.

Studio Work; Arranger; Songs:

(With Burt Bacharach) B. J. Thomas, "Long Ago Tomorrow," Scepter, 1971.

Bill Watrous, "Suite Memories," from the album *Someplace Else,* Soundwings, 1986.

"Jive Samba," from the album *10th Avenue,* Soundwings, 1987.

WRITINGS

Scores for Films; Unless Otherwise Noted:

(As Pat Williams) *How Sweet It Is!,* Buena Vista, 1968.

(As Pat Williams) *Don't Drink the Water,* Avco-Embassy, 1969.

(As Pat Williams) *A Nice Girl Like Me,* Avco-Embassy, 1969.

(As Pat Williams) *Pigeons* (also known as *The Sidelong Glances of a Pigeon Kicker*) Metro-Goldwyn-Mayer, 1970.

(As Pat Williams) *Macho Callahan,* Avco-Embassy, 1970.

(As Pat Williams) *Evel Knievel,* Fanfare, 1972.

(As Pat Williams) *Sssssss,* Universal, 1973.

Hex (also known as *The Shrieking*), Twentieth Century-Fox, 1973.

(As Pat Williams; with Billy Byers) *Moonchild,* American Filmmakers, 1974.

(As name Pat Williams) *Harrad Summer* (also known as *Student Union*), Cinerama, 1974.

(As name Pat Williams) *Framed,* Paramount, 1975.

I Wonder Who's Killing Her Now?, Cinema Arts, 1975.

Framed, Paramount, 1975.

And song "Just Let Me Go till I'm Gone," *Casey's Shadow,* Columbia, 1978.

The Cheap Detective (also known as *Snacka om deckare alltsaa!*), Columbia, 1978.

And title song, *The One and Only,* Paramount, 1978.

(As Pat Williams) *The Seniors* (also known as *The Senior*), Cinema Shares, 1978.

Breaking Away, Twentieth Century-Fox, 1979.

(As name Pat Williams) *Butch and Sundance: The Early Days,* Twentieth Century-Fox, 1979.

Cuba, United Artists, 1979.

And song "Keep It Loose," *Hot Stuff,* Columbia, 1979.

Hero at Large, Metro-Goldwyn-Mayer, 1980.

How to Beat the High Cost of Living (also known as *How to Beat the High Co$t of Living*), American International Pictures, 1980.

It's My Turn, Columbia, 1980.

And title song, *Used Cars,* Columbia, 1980.

Wholly Moses!, Columbia, 1980.

A Perfect Circle, 1980.

Charlie Chan and the Curse of the Dragon Queen, American Cinema, 1981.

Music and lyrics (with others) and background music, *The Best Little Whorehouse in Texas,* Universal, 1982.

And title song, *Some Kind of Hero,* Paramount, 1982.

The Toy, Columbia, 1982.

Marvin and Tige, Major, 1983.

Two of a Kind, Twentieth Century-Fox, 1983.

And arranger of songs "Out of Nowhere" and "Jesu, Word of God Incarnate," *All of Me,* Universal, 1984.

Best Defense, Paramount, 1984.

And song "Here's That Sunny Day" (with Will Jennings), *The Buddy System,* Twentieth Century-Fox, 1984.

Swing Shift, Warner Bros., 1984.

The Slugger's Wife (also known as *Neil Simon's The Slugger's Wife*), Columbia, 1985.

Just between Friends, Orion, 1986.

Violets Are Blue, Columbia, 1986.

(With others) *Broadcast News,* Twentieth Century-Fox, 1987.

(With David Foster) *Fresh Horses,* Columbia, 1988.

Worth Winning, Twentieth Century-Fox, 1989.

Cry Baby, Universal, 1990.

In the Spirit, Castle Hill Productions, 1990.

Big Girls Don't Cry . . . They Get Even (also known as *Stepkids*), New Line Cinema, 1991.

The Cutting Edge, Metro-Goldwyn-Mayer, 1992.

Stormchasers (documentary), Omnimax, 1995.

The Grass Harp, Fine Line Features, 1995.

The Reef, Hearst Entertainment, 1997.

That Old Feeling, Universal, 1997.

The Tears of Julian Po (also known as *Julian Po*), Fine Line Features, 1997.

Music for Television; Series:

Headmaster, CBS, 1970-71.

San Francisco International (also known as *San Francisco International Airport*), NBC, 1970-71.

The Mary Tyler Moore Show, CBS, 1970-77.
Funny Face, CBS, 1971.
Cannon, CBS, 1971-76.
Columbo, NBC, 1971-78.
The Sandy Duncan Show, CBS, 1972.
The Streets of San Francisco, ABC, 1972-77.
The Bob Newhart Show, CBS, 1972-78.
The Magician, NBC, 1973-74.
Friends and Lovers, CBS, 1974-75.
Doc, CBS, 1975-76.
Good Heavens, ABC, 1976.
Bert D'Angelo—Superstar, ABC, 1976.
Most Wanted, ABC, 1976-77.
The Tony Randall Show, ABC, 1976-77, CBS, 1977-78.
The Andros Targets, CBS, 1977.
Lou Grant, CBS, 1977-82.
A Man Called Sloane, NBC, 1979.
The Last Resort, CBS, 1979-80.
Maggie, ABC, 1981.
The Two of Us, CBS, 1981-82.
The Devlin Connection, NBC, 1982.
Mr. Smith, NBC, 1983.
*AfterM*A*S*H* (also known as *AfterMASH*), CBS, 1983-84.
Empire, CBS, 1984.
Suzanne Pleshette Is Maggie Briggs (also known as *Maggie Briggs*), CBS, 1984.
Fathers and Sons, NBC, 1986.
Heart of the City, ABC, 1986-87.
Barringtons, CBS, 1987.
The "Slap" Maxwell Story, ABC, 1987-88.
Theme music, *Mr. President,* Fox, 1987-88.
The Days and Nights of Molly Dodd, NBC, 1987-88, Lifetime, 1989-91.
Eisenhower and Lutz, CBS, 1988.
Theme song, *FM,* NBC, 1989-90.
The Simpsons, Fox, 1990—.
Cutters, CBS, 1993.
Black Tie Affair (also known as *Smoldering Lust*), NBC, 1993.
Extreme (also known as *Extreme Rescue*), ABC, 1995.

Music for Television; Miniseries:
Jewels (also known as *Danielle Steel's Jewels*), NBC, 1992.
Murder in the Heartland, ABC, 1993.
OP Center (also known as *Tom Clancy's OP Center*), NBC, 1995.
Ruby Ridge: An American Tragedy (also known as *Every Knee Shall Bow: The Siege at Ruby Ridge*), CBS, 1996.
Too Rich: The Secret Life of Doris Duke, CBS, 1999.

Music for Television; Movies:
The Failing of Raymond, ABC, 1971.
Lock, Stock and Barrel, NBC, 1971.
Terror in the Sky, CBS, 1971.
Hardcase, ABC, 1972.
Short Walk to Daylight, ABC, 1972.
Hitched, NBC, 1973.
Ordeal Inferno, ABC, 1973.
Ordeal, ABC, 1973.
Mrs. Sundance, ABC, 1974.
Murder or Mercy, ABC, 1974.
Stowaway to the Moon, CBS, 1975.
The Miracle of Kathy Miller, CBS, 1981.
The Princess and the Cabbie, CBS, 1981.
Young Lust, 1981.
Tomorrow's Child, ABC, 1982.
Moonlight, 1982.
The Fighter, CBS, 1983.
Seduced, CBS, 1985.
"Spot Marks the X," *The Disney Sunday Movie,* ABC, 1986.
Oceans of Fire, CBS, 1986.
The Rig, 1986.
Kojak: The Investigation, CBS, 1986.
Kojak: The Price of Justice, CBS, 1987.
Laguna Heat, HBO, 1987.
Double Standard, NBC, 1988.
Maybe Baby, NBC, 1988.
Columbo: The Juggler, ABC, 1989.
Columbo: Grand Deception, ABC, 1989.
Columbo: Murder, Smoke and Shadows, ABC, 1989.
Columbo: Sex and the Married Detective, ABC, 1989.
Columbo: Murder—A Self-Portrait, ABC, 1989.
Night Walk, CBS, 1989.
Good Night, Sweet Wife: A Murder in Boston, CBS, 1990.
Love and Lies (also known as *True Betrayal*), ABC, 1990.
Columbo: Murder in Malibu, ABC, 1990.
In Broad Daylight, NBC, 1991.
Keeping Secrets, ABC, 1991.
The Whereabouts of Jenny, ABC, 1991.
Back to the Streets of San Francisco, NBC, 1992.
Grave Secrets: The Legacy of Hilltop Drive (also known as *Grave Secrets*), CBS, 1992.
Legacy of Lies, USA Network, 1992.
Columbo: No Time to Die, ABC, 1992.
Blind Spot, CBS, 1993.
Geronimo, TNT, 1993.
Taking the Heat, Showtime, 1993.
Zelda, TNT, 1993.
Mercy Mission: The Rescue of Flight 771, 1993.
Accidental Meeting, USA Network, 1994.
Because Mommy Works, NBC, 1994.

French Silk, ABC, 1994.
Getting Gotti (also known as *The Diane Giacalone Story* and *Diane Giacalone: The John Gotti Story*), CBS, 1994.
Take Me Home Again (also known as *The Lies Boys Tell*), NBC, 1994.
The Corpse Had a Familiar Face, CBS, 1994.
The Gift of Love (also known as *Set for Life*), CBS, 1994.
Twilight Zone: Rod Serling's Lost Classics, CBS, 1994.
Betrayed: A Story of Three Women (also known as *Betrayed: The Story of Three Women*), ABC, 1995.
Deadline for Murder: From the Files of Edna Buchanan (also known as *Edna Buchanan: Miami Deadline*), CBS, 1995.
Her Hidden Truth (also known as *When Summer Comes*), NBC, 1995.
Kingfish: A Story of Huey P. Long, TNT, 1995.
Saved by the Light, Fox, 1995.
A Brother's Promise: The Dan Jansen Story (also known as *The Dan Jansen Story* and *Fall and Rise: The Dan Jansen Story*), CBS, 1996.
A Weekend in the Country (also known as *Moon Valley, Temecula,* and *Weekend in the Country*), USA Network, 1996.
After Jimmy, CBS, 1996.
My Very Best Friend, CBS, 1996.
Never Give Up: The Jimmy V Story (also known as *The Jim Valvano Story*), CBS, 1996.
A Walton Easter, CBS, 1997.
Childhood Sweetheart?, CBS, 1997.
Ed McBain's 87th Precinct: Heatwave (also known as *87th Precinct: Heatwave*), NBC, 1997.
Heart Full of Rain, CBS, 1997.
Home Invasion, NBC, 1997.
Mother Knows Best, ABC, 1997.
Sisters and Other Strangers (also known as *Suspicion of Innocence*), CBS, 1997.
A Change of Heart, 1998.
A Knight in Camelot, ABC, 1998.

Music for Television; Specials:
Topper Returns, 1973.
"Picnic," *Broadway on Showtime,* Showtime, 1986.
"American Nuclear," *CBS Summer Playhouse,* CBS, 1989.
Time Warner Presents the Earth Day Special (also known as *The Earth Day Special*), ABC, 1990.
Decoration Day, NBC, 1990.
Original music, *The Bob Newhart 20th 19th Anniversary Special,* CBS, 1991.
Great Television Moments: What We Watched, ABC, 1993.
Sinatra Duets (documentary), CBS, 1994.
"Journey," *Hallmark Hall of Fame,* CBS, 1995.
"The West Side Waltz," *CBS Playhouse 90s,* CBS, 1995.
More Secrets of the X-Files, Fox, 1996.

Music for Television; Pilots:
San Francisco International (also known as *San Francisco International Airport*), NBC, 1970.
Incident in San Francisco, ABC, 1971.
Travis Logan, D.A., CBS, 1971.
The Streets of San Francisco, ABC, 1972.
The Magician, NBC, 1973.
Topper Returns, NBC, 1973.
Friends and Lovers, CBS, 1974.
Crossfire, NBC, 1975.
The Lives of Jenny Dolan, NBC, 1975.
Ace, ABC, 1976.
Don't Call Us, CBS, 1976.
Most Wanted, ABC, 1976.
The Chopped Liver Brothers, ABC, 1977.
The Man with the Power, NBC, 1977.
The Andros Targets, CBS, 1977.
Stonestreet: Who Killed the Centerfold Model?, NBC, 1977.
Down Home, CBS, 1978.
Escapade, CBS, 1978.
The Many Loves of Arthur, NBC, 1978.
Mother and Me, M.D., NBC, 1979.
Stephanie, CBS, 1981.
Family in Blue, CBS, 1982.
In Security, CBS, 1982.
The James Boys, NBC, 1982.
Moonlight, CBS, 1982.
A Girl's Life, NBC, 1983.
*W*A*L*T*E*R,* CBS, 1984.
Fathers and Sons, NBC, 1985.
The Faculty, ABC, 1986.
Barringtons, CBS, 1987.
Old Dogs, ABC, 1987.
Reno and Yolanda, CBS, 1987.
Off Duty, CBS, 1988.
The Gregory Harrison Show, CBS, 1989.
Daughters of Privilege (also known as *Keys to the Kingdom*), NBC, 1991.

OTHER SOURCES

Periodicals:
Billboard, May 24, 1997, pp. 6-7.
Down Beat, June, 1998, p. 45.*

WILLIAMS, Vanessa
See WILLIAMS, Vanessa L.

WINSTON, Hattie 1945-

PERSONAL

Born March 3, 1945, in Greenville, MS. *Education:* Graduated from Howard University.

Addresses: *Contact*—Pakula King and Associates, 9229 Sunset, Suite 315, Los Angeles, CA 90069.

Career: Actress and vocalist.

Member: American Federation of Television and Radio Artists (national co-chair, Equal Employment Opportunities Committee), The Electric Company.

Awards, Honors: Obie Award, *Village Voice,* 1979, for *The Michigan;* Obie Award, *Village Voice,* 1980, for *Mother Courage and Her Children;* Hattie Winston Day, National Black Theatre Festival, Winston-Salem, NC, 1993 and 1997; Hattie Winston Collection, University of Louisville-Kentucky; Los Angeles Critics Dramalogue Awards, for *To Take Arms* and *Up the Mountain.*

CREDITS

Film Appearances:

Reporter, *Without a Trace,* Twentieth Century-Fox, 1983.

Mother, *Good to Go* (also known as *Short Fuse*), 1986.

Blanche Loudon, *Clara's Heart,* Warner Bros., 1988.

Foster, *A Show of Force,* Paramount, 1990.

Mrs. Todd, *Beverly Hills Cop III,* Paramount, 1994.

(Uncredited, scenes deleted) Robin's Mother, *Waiting to Exhale,* Twentieth Century-Fox, 1995.

Judge Meyer, *Sunset Park,* TriStar, 1996.

Simone, *Jackie Brown* (also known as *Rum Punch*), Miramax, 1997.

Hospital Nurse, *Living Out Loud* (also known as *The Kiss*), New Line Cinema, 1998.

Jo-Claire, *Meet the Deedles,* Buena Vista, 1998.

Mrs. Russel, *True Crime,* Warner Bors., 1999.

Stage Appearances:

Sister Fatima, *The Prodigal Son,* Greenwich Mews Theatre, New York City, 1965.

First Operator, *Day of Absence,* St. Mark's Playhouse, New York City, 1965-66.

Moses Gunn, *Song of the Lusitanian Bogey,* The Negro Ensemble Company, St. Mark's Playhouse, New York City, 1968.

Bubba Ryan, *Summer of the Seventeenth Doll,* The Negro Ensemble Company, St. Mark's Playhouse, New York City, 1968.

Praise Singer, *Kongi's Harvest,* The Negro Ensemble Company, St. Mark's Playhouse, New York City, 1968.

Standby, *Daddy Goodness,* The Negro Ensemble Company, St. Mark's Playhouse, New York City, 1968.

Second Extraordinary Spook, *God is a (Guess What?),* The Negro Ensemble Company, St. Mark's Playhouse, New York City, 1968-69.

Understudy for the role of Linda, *Does a Tiger Wear a Necktie?,* Belasco Theatre, New York City, 1969.

Petite Belle Lily, *Man Better Man,* The Negro Ensemble Company, St. Mark's Playhouse, New York City, 1969.

Bo Peep, *Sambo,* New York Shakespeare Festival, Public Theatre, New York City, 1969-70.

Dolores, *Billy Noname,* Truck & Warehouse Theatre, New York City, 1970.

Nell, *The Me Nobody Knows,* Orpheum Theatre, New York City, 1970; then Helen Hays Theatre, New York City, 1970-71.

The Black Experience Company, Washington Theatre Club, Washington D.C., 1970-71.

Understudy for the role of Silvia, *Two Gentlemen of Verona,* New York Shakespeare Festival, St. James Theatre, New York City, 1971-73.

Silvia, *Two Gentlemen of Verona,* New York Shakespeare Festival, St. James Theatre, New York City, 1971-73.

Leionah, *The Great MacDaddy,* The Negro Ensemble Company, St. Mark's Playhouse, New York City, 1974.

Cleo, *I Love My Wife,* Ethel Barrymore Theatre, New York City, 1977-79.

Pilar Murray, *The Michigan,* The Negro Ensemble Company, St. Mark's Playhouse, New York City, 1979.

Yvette, *Mother Courage and Her Children,* Public/Newman Theatre, New York City, 1980.

Also appeared in *Pins and Needles, Weary Blues, A Photo, Oklahoma!, The Tap Dance Kids, To Take Arms, Up the Mountain,* and *Scapino.*

Stage Work:

Vocalist, *Livin' Fat,* The Negro Ensemble Company, St. Mark's Playhouse, New York City, 1976.

Producer/director, *Black Nativity.*

Television Appearances; Series:

Sylvia, *The Electric Company,* PBS, 1971-76.

Gloria Davis, *Homefront,* ABC, 1991-92.
Alice Burgess, *Port Charles,* ABC, 1998.
Margaret Wyborn, *Becker,* CBS, 1998.

Television Appearances; Movies:
Ivy, *Hollow Image,* ABC, 1979.
Toni Gillette, *Nurse,* CBS, 1980.
One Woman's Courage, NBC, 1994.
Mrs. Peel, *The Cherokee Kid,* HBO, 1996.

Television Appearances; Specials:
Ed Sullivan's Broadway, NBC, 1973.
Officer Jessie Waters, *Ann in Blue,* ABC, 1974.
Lilah Reynolds, *Hope Division,* ABC, 1987.
Pauline Mackey, *Coming to America,* CBS, 1989.
Anna Mae, *Runaway,* PBS, 1989.
Narrator, *Satchmo: The Life of Louis Armstrong,* PBS, 1989.

Television Appearances; Miniseries:
Minnie Hershey, *The Dain Curse* (also known as *Dashiell Hammett's The Dain Curse*), CBS, 1978.
Daisy Voigt, *Common Ground,* CBS, 1990.

Television Appearances; Episodic:
Nurse Toni Gillette, *Nurse,* CBS, 1981.
Guest voice, "Coolio Runnings," *Duckman,* USA Network, 1994.
Saleslady, *Step By Step,* ABC, 1994.
Angela Williams, *High Incident,* ABC, 1996.
Mrs. Brooks, *Malcolm & Eddie,* UPN, 1996.
Irene, *Nick Freno: Licensed Teacher,* The WB, 1996.
Mom, *Arsenio,* ABC, 1997.
Felicia, *Smart Guy,* The WB, 1997.

OTHER SOURCES

Electronic:
http://marketing.cbs.com/primetime/becker/castbios/bio_hwinston.shtml.*

WLCEK, James 1964-
(Jimmy Wlcek)

PERSONAL

Born February 22, 1964, in New York, NY.

Addresses: *Contact*—United Artist Talent, 14011 Ventura Blvd., Suite 213, Sherman Oaks, CA 91423.

Career: Actor.

CREDITS

Film Appearances:
Marshall Marmillion, *Steel Magnolias,* TriStar, 1989.
(As Jimmy Wlcek) Eric, *Damien's Seed,* Mystique Films Inc., 1996.

Television Appearances; Series:
Ben Shelley, *Ryan's Hope,* ABC, 1987-89.
Jack Gibson, *One Life To Live,* ABC, 1989-90.
Linc Lafferty, *As the World Turns,* CBS, 1990-93.
Trent Malloy, *Walker, Texas Ranger,* CBS, 1997-99.
Trent Malloy, *Sons of Thunder,* CBS, 1999.

Television Appearances; Episodic:
(As Jimmy Wlcek) Brother John Mason, "Paradise Trail," *Walker, Texas Ranger,* CBS, 1998.*

WLCEK, Jimmy
See WLCEK, James

WONG, Kar-Wai 1958-
(Wang Jiawei, Kar Wai Wong)

PERSONAL

Born in 1958, in Shanghai, China; raised in Hong Kong.

Addresses: *Contact*—Hong Kong Film Liaison, 10940 Wilshire Blvd., Ste. 1220, Los Angeles, CA 90024.

Career: Writer, director, and producer.

Awards, Honors: Hong Kong Film Award nomination, best screenplay, 1988, for *The Final Test;* Hong Kong Film Award nomination, best director, 1989, for *As Tears Go By;* Hong Kong Film Award, best director, and Hong Kong Film Award nomination, best screenplay, 1991, for *Days of Being Wild;* Golden Leopard Award nomination, Locarno International Film Festival, and FIPRESCI Award, Stockholm Film Festival, both 1994, and Hong Film Award, best director, and Hong Kong Film Award nomination, best screenplay, both 1995, all for *Chungking Express;* Hong Kong Film Award nominations, best director and best screenplay, and Hong Kong Film Critics Society Awards, best director and best screenplay, all 1995, for *Ashes of Time;* Hong Kong Film Award nomination, best director, 1996, for *Fallen Angels;*

Independent Spirit Award nomination, best foreign film, 1997, for Chongqing senlin; Cannes Film Festival Award, best director, and Golden Palm nomination, Cannes Film Festival, and Golden Horse Award nomination, best director, all 1997, Independent Spirit Award nomination, best foreign film, and Hong Kong Film Award nominations, best director and best screenplay, all 1998, for *Happy Together.*

CREDITS

Film Director:

As Tears Go By (also known as *Wong gok ka moon, Carmen of the Streets, Mongkok Carmen, Rexie Naner, and Wang Jiao ka men*), 1989.

Days of Being Wild (also known as *A fei jing juen, Ah Fei's Story,* and *The True Story of Ah Fei*), In-Gear Film, 1991.

Ashes of Time (also known as *Dung che sai duk*), HKFM, 1994.

And executive producer, *Chungking Express* (also known as *Chongqing senlin*), Rolling Thunder, 1994.

And executive producer, *Fallen Angels* (also known as *Duoluo tianshi*), Kino International, 1995.

And producer, *Happy Together* (also known as *Cheun gwong tsa sit*), GoldenHarvest, 1997.

Beijing Summer, 1998.

Film Work; Other:

Executive producer, *The Eagle Shooting Heroes: Dong Cheng Xi Jiu* (also known as *Sediu Yinghung Tsun Tsi Dung Sing Sai Tsau*), 1994.

Producer, *First Love: A Litter on the Breeze* (also known as *Choh chin luen hau dik yi yan sai gaai*), 1997.

WRITINGS

Screenplays:

Intellectual Trio (also known as *Long feng zhi duo xing*), 1984.

The Last Victory, 1986.

The Final Test (also known as *Zui hou yi zhan*), 1987.

Flaming Brothers (also known as *Jiang hu long hu men* and *Dragon and Tiger Fight*), 1987.

The Haunted Cop Shop of Horrors (also known as *The Haunted Cop Shop* and *Meng gui cha guan*), 1987.

The Haunted Cop Shop of Horrors 2 (also known as *Meng gui xue tang*), 1988.

As Tears Go By (also known as *Wong gok ka moon, Carmen of the Streets, Mongkok Carmen, Rexie Naner,* and *Wang jiao ka men*), 1989.

Days of Being Wild (also known as *A Fei jing juen, A Fei zheng zhuan, Ah Fei's Story,* and *The True Story of Ah Fei*), In-Gear Film, 1991.

Gauyat Sandiu Haplui (also known as *Jiu yi shen diao xia lu, Saviour of Souls, Saviour of the Soul* and *Terrible Angel*), 1991.

Ashes of Time (also known *Dung che sai duk*), HKFM, 1994.

Chungking Express (also known as *Chongqing senlin*), Rolling Thunder, 1994.

Fallen Angels (also known as *Duoluo tianshi*), Kino International, 1995.

Happy Together (also known as *Cheun gwong tsa sit*), Golden Harvest, 1997.

Beijing Summer, 1998.

OTHER SOURCES

Periodicals:

Chicago Tribune, "Tempo," March 27, 1996, p. 7.

Interview, February, 1998, pp. 46-48.*

WOODARD, Charlain
See WOODARD, Charlayne

WOODARD, Charlaine
See WOODARD, Charlayne

WOODARD, Charlayne
(Charlain Woodard, Charlaine Woodard)

PERSONAL

Born in Albany, NY; married Alan Michael Harris, 1991. *Education:* Graduated from the Goodman School of Drama (now the DePaul University TheatreSchool) and the State University of New York.

Addresses: *Agent*—Agency for the Performing Arts, 9000 Sunset Blvd., 12th Floor, Los Angeles, CA, 90069.

Career: Film, television, and stage actress.

Member: Screen Actors Guild.

Awards, Honors: Antoinette Perry Award and Drama Desk Award nominations, best actress in a featured role (musical), both 1978, for *Ain't Misbehavin'*; Los Angeles Drama Critics Circle Awards, best play and playwright, 1993, for *Pretty Fire;* Drama Desk Award nomination, for *Hang on to the Good Times.*

CREDITS

Film Appearances:

"White Boys," *Hair,* United Artists, 1979.
Winona Margruder, *Hard Feelings* (also known as *Hang Tough*), Twentieth Century-Fox, 1982.
Jasmine, *Crackers,* Universal, 1984.
(As Charlaine Woodard) Lola, *Twister,* Warner Bros., 1988.
Singing secretary, *Me and Him,* Columbia, 1991.
Cindy, *He Said, She Said,* Paramount, 1991.
Cheryl Clark, *One Good Cop,* Buena Vista, 1991.
Janice Farrell, *The Meteor Man,* Metro-Goldwyn-Mayer, 1993.
Floor nurse, *Angie,* Caravan Pictures/Hollywood Pictures, 1994.
Eartha, *Babyfever,* Rainbow Releasing, 1994.
Angel Kosinsky, *Eye for an Eye,* Paramount, 1996.
Tituba, *The Crucible,* Twentieth Century-Fox, 1996.
Kate, *Around the Fire,* 1998.

Television Appearances; Series:

(As Charlaine Woodard) Vonda Greene, *Roseanne,* ABC, 1988-89.
Desiree McCall, *Days of Our Lives,* NBC, 1991-92.
Janice, *The Fresh Prince of Bel-Air,* NBC, 1991-93.
Gina Wilkes, *Chicago Hope,* CBS, 1996—.

Television Appearances; Miniseries:

Doosie, *Buffalo Girls,* CBS, 1995.
Rachel, *The Wedding* (also known as *Oprah Winfrey Presents: The Wedding*), ABC, 1998.

Television Appearances; Movies:

(As Charlaine Woodard) Title role, *Cindy,* ABC, 1978.
(As Charlain Woodard) Chandra, *God Bless the Child,* ABC, 1988.
Gail Devers, *Run for the Dream: The Gail Devers Story,* Showtime, 1996.
Adrienne Duvall, *Touched by Evil* (also known as *In the Shadow of Evil*), ABC, 1997.

Television Appearances; Episodic:

Nina Chambers, "Nina Loves Alex," *Taxi,* ABC and NBC, 1982.
Dorothy Marks, "Blood Money," *Spenser: For Hire,* ABC, 1985.
Paula Michelson, *Chicago Hope,* CBS, 1994.
Harriet Battle-Wilkins, *Sweet Justice,* NBC, 1994.
Arlene, "Flour Child," *Frasier,* NBC, 1994.
Charlene, *Bless This House,* CBS, 1995.

Stage Appearances:

Don't Bother Me, I Can't Cope, off-Broadway production, 1975.
Hair, Broadway production, 1977.
Ain't Misbehavin', Broadway productions, 1978-79 and 1988.
Pretty Fire, Odyssey Theatre, New York City, 1992, then Sylvia and Danny Kaye Playhouse, Manhattan Theatre Club, New York City, 1993-94.
Shen Te/Shui Ta, *The Good Person of Setzuan,* La Jolla Playhouse, San Diego, CA, 1994-95.
Neat, Manhattan Theatre Club, New York City, 1997.

Appeared in *A, My Name Is Alice, The Caucasian Chalk Circle, Dementos, Hang on to the Good Times, Paradise, Twelfth Night,* and *Under Fire;* performed at the New York Shakespeare Festival, New York City.

WRITINGS

Writings for the Stage:

Pretty Fire, Odyssey Theatre, 1992, then Sylvia and Danny Kaye Playhouse, Manhattan Theatre Club, 1993-94.
Neat, Manhattan Theatre Club, 1997.

OTHER SOURCES

Periodicals:

American Theatre, October, 1994, pp. 14-15.
Back Stage, January 24, 1997, p. 43.
Entertainment Weekly, January 24, 1997, p. EW3.
TCI, March, 1997, pp. 13-15.
Variety, January 13, 1997, p. 162.*

Y-Z

YARED, Gabriel 1949-

PERSONAL

Born October 7, 1949, in Beirut, Lebanon.

Addresses: *Office*—Gorfaine-Schwartz 13245 Riverside Drive, Suite 450, Sherman Oaks, CA 91423-2172.

Career: Composer, orchestrator, musician, and actor. Composer for Johnny Hallyday, Charles Aznavour, Michel Jonasz, Gilbert Becaud, Mireille Mathieu, Sylvie Vartan, Tania Maria, and Francoise Hardy.

Awards, Honors: Cesar Award nomination, best music written for a film, 1985, for *Betty Blue;* Cesar Award nomination, best music written for a film, 1987, for *Agent Trouble;* Cesar Award nomination, best music written for a film, 1988, for *Camille Claudel;* Cesar Award, best music written for a film, 1991, for *L'Amant;* Australian Film Institute Award nomination, 1993, for *Map of the Human Heart;* Golden Globe Award, best original score—motion picture, Academy Award, best music—original dramatic score, and Grammy Award, best instrumental composition written for a motion picture or for television, all 1996, for *The English Patient;* Grammy Award nomination, best instrumental composition written for a motion picture or for television, and Golden Satellite Award nomination, best motion picture score, 1998, both for *City of Angels*.

CREDITS

Film Work; Composer, Unless Otherwise Indicated:

Miss O'Gynie et les hommes fleurs (also known as *Miss O'Gynie and the Flower Man*), 1974.

Sauve qui peut (also known as *Every Man For Himself, Sauve qui peut la vie,* and *Slow Motion*), New Yorker Films, 1979.

Malevil (also known as *Malevil, Countdown der Neutronenbombe* [Germany]), 1981.

Invitation au Voyage, Triumph Releasing, 1982.

Sarah, 1983.

La Lune dans le caniveau (also known as *The Moon in the Gutter* and *Lo Specchio del desiderio* [Italy]), Triumph Releasing/Columbia, 1983.

Hannah K., Universal, 1983.

Interdit aux Moins de 13 Ans, 1983.

La Java des ombres, 1983.

La Scarlatine, 1983.

Le Telephone sonne toujours deux fois, 1984.

La Diagonale du fou (also known as *Dangerous Moves*), Spectrafilm, 1984.

Tir a Vue (also known as *Fire On Sight*), 1984.

Nemo (also known as *Dream One*), 1984.

Flagrant Desir (also known as *A Certain Desire* and *Flagrant Desire*), 1985.

Weda'an Bonapart (also known as *Adieu Bonaparte* [France]), 1985.

Scout Toujours, 1985.

And music conductor, *37.2 le matin* (also known as *37.2 Degrees in the Morning* and *Betty Blue*), Alive, 1986.

Desordre (also known as *Disorder*), 1986.

Beyond Therapy, New World, 1987.

Zone Rouge, 1986.

Agent Trouble, 1987.

L' Homme voile (also known as *The Veiled Man*), 1987.

Gandahar (also known as *Light Years*), Miramax, 1987.

Les Saisons du plaisir, 1987.

Clean and Sober, Warner Bros., 1988.

Le Testament d'un poete juif assassine, 1988.

Camille Claudel (also known as *Camille Claudel-Violence et passion*), 1988.

Une Nuit a l'assemblee nationale, 1988.
Tennessee Nights (also known as *Black Water*), Academy Video, 1989.
Romero, Four Seasons, 1989.
Marat, 1989.
Les 1001 nuits (also known as *Le Mille e una notte* [Italy] and *Sheherazade*), 1990.
Tatie Danielle, Prestige Films, 1990.
Vincent & Theo, Hemdale, 1990.
La Putain du roi (also known as *The King's Mistress* and *The King's Whore*), 1990.
L'Amant (also known as *The Lover*), Metro-Mayer-Goldwyn, 1991.
Map of the Human Heart (also known as *La carte du tendre*), Miramax, 1992.
L'Instinct de l'ange, 1992.
L'Arche et les deluges (also known as *The Ark and the Deluge*), 1992.
And musician, *IP5: Lile aux pachydermes* (also known as *IP5: The Island of Pachyderms*), 1992.
La Fille de l'Air (also known as *The Girl in the Air*), 1992.
Les Marmottes (also known as *The Groundhogs*), Cine Company, S.A., 1993.
Profil bas (also known as *Low Profile*), 1994.
Des feux mal eteints (also known as *Poorly Extinguished Fires*), 1994.
Noir comme le souvenir, 1995.
Wings of Courage (also known as *Guillaumet, les ailes du courage*), Sony Pictures Classics, 1995.
Arthur Rimbaud, 1996.
The English Patient, Miramax, 1996.
Tonka, Flach Pyramide International, 1997.
And orchestrator, *City of Angels,* Warner Bros., 1998.
And orchestrator, *Message in a Bottle,* Warner Bros., 1999.

Film Appearances:
Paul Jarry, *Sarah,* 1983.

Television Work; Composer, Unless Otherwise Indicated:
Fall From Grace (movie), 1994.
Jacques Yves-Cousteau: My First 85 Years (special), TBS, 1995.

RECORDINGS

Albums:
The Moon in the Gutter (soundtrack), DRG, 1983.
(Composer, conductor, producer, orchestration, and piano) *The Lover* (soundtrack), Varese Saraban, 1992.

Album Work:
(Keyboards, producer, and associate producer) *Map of the Human Heart* (soundtrack), PolyGram, 1993.
(Conductor) Mina, *Del Mio Meglio, Vol. 4,* EMI, 1993.
(Orchestration) *Wings of Courage* (soundtrack), Sony, 1995.
(Orchestration) Sacha Distel, *Very Best of Sacha Distel,* Arcade, 1998.
(Orchestration and arranger) *Arthouse Cafe, Vol. 2,* Silva, 1998.
(Orchestration and producer) *City of Angels* (soundtrack), Warner Bros., 1998.
(Orchestration and producer) *Message in a Bottle* (soundtrack), Atlantic, 1999.
(Composer) Michael Chertock, *Palace of the Winds: The Piano at the Movies,* Telarc, 1997.

OTHER SOURCES

Periodicals:
Entertainment Weekly, January 17, 1997, p. 62.
National Catholic Reporter, July 3, 1998, p. 20.*

ZIEGLER, Joseph

PERSONAL

Married Nancy Palk (an actress); children: three sons. *Education:* Studied at the National Theatre School in Montreal, Quebec and for several seasons at the Stratford and Shaw festivals.

Career: Actor. Soulpepper (a Toronto acting troupe), founder (with Albert Schultz, Susan Coyne, Martha Burns, and Ted Dykstra).

CREDITS

Film Appearances:
Vern Rawlins, *Oh, What a Night,* 1992.

Television Appearances; Series:
Dr. Jim Barker, *Side Effects,* CBC, 1994.
Len Hubbard, *Black Harbor,* CBC, 1996—.

Television Appearances; Movies:
Ray Sharp, *Dick Francis: In the Frame,* RTE, 1989.
Moffat, *Due South,* CBS, 1994.
Mr. Wilson, *Race To Freedom: The Underground Railroad,* The Family Channel, 1994.

Matt Eckhardt, *To Save the Children,* CBS, 1994.
Philip (the host), *Twists of Terror* (also known as *Primal Scream*), Showtime, 1996.

Television Appearances; Episodic:
"Hootch," *Hitchhiker,* HBO/USA Network, 1988.
Pat, "Dust To Dust," *War of the Worlds,* syndicated, 1989.
Dr. Hendricks, "In the Name of Science," *Alfred Hitchcock Presents,* NBC/USA Network, 1989.
Delehanty, "The Code," *Forever Knight,* CBS/syndicated, 1994.
Jack Burke, "Crime and Punishment," *E.N.G.,* 1994.
Inspector Moffat, "An Invitation To Romance," *Due South,* CBS, 1995.

Also appeared on the television series *Street Legal,* CBC, and *Empire Inc.*

Stage Appearances:
Spokesong, Manitoba Theatre Centre, Winnipeg, Canada, 1979-80.
Berowne, *Love's Labour's Lost,* Stratford Festival, Stratford, Ontario, Canada, 1984.
Hotspur, *Henry IV,* Stratford Festival, Stratford, Ontario, Canada, 1984.
George, Duke of Clarence, *The Tragedy of King Richard III,* New York Shakespeare Festival, Delacorte Theatre, New York City, 1990.

Appeared as the title role in *Hamlet,* Citadel Theatre, Edmonton, Alberta, Canada; member of Stratford Festival, Stratford, Ontario, Canada, 1985, 1987-88.

Stage Work; Director:
(Directorial debut) *The Two Mrs. Carrolls,* Shaw Festival, Niagara-on-the-Lake, Ontario, Canada, 1997.
The Shop At Sly Corner, Shaw Festival, Niagara-on-the-Lake, Ontario, Canada, 1998.

OTHER SOURCES

Periodicals:
Maclean's, August 29, 1994, p. 54; December 2, 1996, p. 88; June 9, 1997, p. 82; June 8, 1998, p. 51; August 3, 1998, p. 58.*

Cumulative Index

To provide continuity with *Who's Who in the Theatre,* this index interfiles references to *Who's Who in the Theatre,* 1st-17th Editions, and *Who Was Who in the Theatre* (Gale, 1978) with references to *Contemporary Theatre, Film and Television,* Volumes 1-25.

References in the index are identified as follows:

CTFT and volume number—*Contemporary Theatre, Film and Television,* Volumes 1-25
WWT and edition number—*Who's Who in the Theatre,* 1st-17th Editions
WWasWT—*Who Was Who in the Theatre*

Cumulative Index

Cumulative Index

C

Cumulative Index

Cumulative Index

D

E

F

G

Cumulative Index

H

Cumulative Index

I

J

K

Cumulative Index

L

M

Cumulative Index

Cumulative Index

Cumulative Index

P

Q

R

Cumulative Index

S

Cumulative Index

U

V

W

X

Y

Z